W9-AZT-285

Peterson's
MASTER THE
GED®
2013

PETERSON'S
Publishing

PUBLIC LIBRARY
APR   2012
SOUTH BEND, INDIANA

About Peterson's Publishing

Peterson's Publishing provides the accurate, dependable, high-quality education content and guidance you need to succeed. No matter where you are on your academic or professional path, you can rely on Peterson's print and digital publications for the most up-to-date education exploration data, expert test-prep tools, and top-notch career success resources—everything you need to achieve your goals.

Visit us online at **www.petersonspublishing.com** and let Peterson's help you achieve your goals.

For more information, contact Peterson's Publishing, 2000 Lenox Drive, Lawrenceville, NJ 08648; 800-338-3282 Ext. 54229.

© 2012 Peterson's, a Nelnet company

GED® and the GED Testing Service® are registered trademarks of the American Council on Education®, which was not involved in the production of, and does not endorse, this product.

HippoCampus™ content made available through The National Repository of Online Courses (NROC) and Monterey Institute for Technology and Education (MITE). © 2012. All Rights Reserved.

Facebook® and Facebook logos are registered trademarks of Facebook, Inc. Facebook, Inc. was not involved in the production of this book and make no endorsement of this product.

Previous editions © 1988, 1990, 1993, 1996, 1998, 2001, 2002, 2003, 2004, 2005, 2006, 2007, 2008, 2009, 2010, 2011

Bernadette Webster, Director of Publishing; Jill C. Schwartz, Editor; Ray Golaszewski, Manufacturing Manager; Linda M. Williams, Composition Manager; Carol Aickley, CD producer; Jeff Pagano, Jared Stein, CD Quality Assurance Analysts

ALL RIGHTS RESERVED. No part of this work covered by the copyright herein may be reproduced or used in any form or by any means—graphic, electronic, or mechanical, including photocopying, recording, taping, Web distribution, or information storage and retrieval systems—without the prior written permission of the publisher.

For permission to use material from this text or product, complete the Permission Request Form at http://www.petersons.com/permissions.

ISBN-13: 978-0-7689-3603-2 (Book only)
ISBN-10: 0-7689-3603-9 (Book only)
ISBN-13: 978-0-7689-3604-9 (Book with CD)
ISBN-10: 0-7689-3604-7 (Book with CD)

Printed in the United States of America

10 9 8 7 6 5 4 3 2 1   14 13 12

Twenty-seventh Edition

By printing this book on recycled paper (40% post-consumer waste), 735 trees were saved.

www.petersonspublishing.com/publishingupdates

Check out our Web site at www.petersonspublishing.com/publishingupdates to see if there is any new information regarding the test and any revisions or corrections to the content of this book. We've made sure the information in this book is accurate and up-to-date; however, the test format or content may have changed since the time of publication.

Certified Chain of Custody

60% Certified Fiber Sourcing and
40% Post-Consumer Recycled

www.sfiprogram.org

*This label applies to the text stock.

Sustainability—Its Importance to Peterson's Publishing

What does sustainability mean to Peterson's Publishing? As a leading publisher, we are aware that our business has a direct impact on vital resources—most especially the trees that are used to make our books. Peterson's Publishing is proud that its products are certified by the Sustainable Forestry Initiative (SFI) and that its books are printed on paper that is 40% post-consumer waste using vegetable-based ink.

Being a part of the Sustainable Forestry Initiative (SFI) means that all of our vendors—from paper suppliers to printers—have undergone rigorous audits to demonstrate that they are maintaining a sustainable environment.

Peterson's Publishing continuously strives to find new ways to incorporate sustainability throughout all aspects of its business.

OUR PROMISE
SCORE HIGHER. GUARANTEED.

Peterson's Publishing, a Nelnet company, focuses on providing individuals and schools with the best test-prep products—books and electronic components that are complete, accurate, and up-to-date. In fact, we're so sure this book will help you improve your score on this test that we're guaranteeing you'll get a higher score. If you feel your score hasn't improved as a result of using this book, we'll refund the price you paid.

Guarantee Details:

If you don't think this book helped you get a higher score, just return the book with your original sales receipt for a full refund of the purchase price (excluding taxes or shipping costs or any other charges). Please underline the book price and title on the sales receipt. Be sure to include your name and mailing address. This offer is restricted to U.S. residents and to purchases made in U.S. dollars. All requests for refunds must be received by Peterson's within 120 days of the purchase date. Refunds are restricted to one book per person and one book per address.

Send to:
Peterson's Publishing, a Nelnet company
Customer Service
2000 Lenox Drive
Lawrenceville, NJ 08648

This guarantee gives you the limited right to have your purchase price refunded only if you are not satisfied that this book has improved your ability to score higher on the applicable test. If you are not satisfied, your sole remedy is to return this book to us with your sales receipt (within 120 days) so that we may refund the amount you paid for the book. Your refund is limited to the manufacturer's suggested retail price listed on the back of the book. This offer is void where restricted or prohibited.

Contents

PART I: THE GED TESTS—THE BASICS

PART II: DETERMINING STRENGTHS AND WEAKNESSES

Contents

Contents

Credits

Passage about "Migrant Mother" excerpted from *No Caption Needed: Iconic Photographs, Public Culture, and Liberal Democracy*, "Migrant Mother," by Robert Hariman and John Louis Lucaites; University of Chicago Press Web site (http://www.press.uchicago.edu/Misc/Chicago/316062.html).

"Capitalism, a Love Story," by Josef Woodard; October 7, 2009; *Santa Barbara Independent* Web site (http://www.independent.com/news/2009/oct/07/emcapitalism-love-story,em/). Used with permission.

"Guatemala Avenue," by Andrew Kass; *Glimmer Train*, Issue 49 (Winter 2004), pp. 98–99. Used with permission.

"The Widower Garden," by Rikki Clark; *Glimmer Train*, Issue 72 (Fall 2009), p. 135. Used with permission.

"Scream," by Mary Morrissy; *Glimmer Train*, Issue 71 (Summer 2009), pp. 173–174. Used with permission.

Portions of ancient-world history review adapted from Wikimedia (http://en.wikibooks.org/wiki/World_History/). The work is released under CC-BY-SA (http://creativecommons.org/licenses/by-sa/3.0/).

"Bush 2000—No More Recounts…" Mike Thompson from the *Detroit Free Press*.

"Wonder How Long the Honeymoon Will Last?" by James Berryman. Marriage of Adolf Hitler and Joseph Stalin © CORBIS.

Paul Revere Engraving, Boston. Copyright © Library of Congress. British Cartoon, published 1780. Miriam and Ira D. Wallach Division of Art, Prints, and Photographs. The New York Public Library.

From Strong Government, Weak Government. "Cartoon of Grant in Carpet Bag." © Bettman/CORBIS.

"Bull in a China Shop." *San Francisco Chronicle*, February 27, 1919.

"Let's Throw Another Desert Storm." Mike Luckovich—*Atlanta Constitution,* Creators Syndicate.

"Poverty, Drugs, Ignorance." Dick Lochner/Tribune Media Services.

"Parole Board." Dick Lochner/Tribune Media Services.

"The North Atlantic Tea & Origami Society." John Danziger in *The Christian Science Monitor.* © 1994.

Le Pelley; reprinted by permission from *The Christian Science Monitor.* © 1970 *The Christian Science Monitor.* © 1970 The Christian Science Publishing Society. All Rights Reserved.

Before You Begin

You've decided to get your high school diploma by preparing to take the GED® high school equivalency diploma test. This is a great step! By now, you know that a high school diploma is a very important document to possess. With your diploma, you will be able to take advantage of training and educational opportunities beyond the high school level and increase your earning potential.

You want to do your best on this test, and that's why you purchased this book. Used correctly, this self-tutor will show you what to expect while giving you the most effective practice with subjects you can expect to see on the actual exam. Peterson's *Master the GED®* provides you with the necessary tools to make the most of the study time you have, including:

- **Top 10 GED® Test-taking Tips** lists the ten most important tips to help you score high on the GED®.

- **Part I** is essential reading if you are preparing to take the GED®. You'll find out about the overall structure of the GED®, what each section of the test covers, the scoring and passing requirements, scheduling and testing procedures, and what you need to do to get ready to take the exam.

- **Part II** allows you to dip your toes into the GED® waters by taking a Practice Diagnostic Test. Use the results of this Diagnostic Test to determine where you need to focus your GED® preparation.

- **Parts III–VII** review the subject matter for each test area of the GED®—Language Arts, Writing: Parts I and II; Social Studies; Science; Language Arts, Reading; and Mathematics—and offer you powerful strategies for attacking every question type you'll encounter in the actual exam.

- **Part VIII** consists of 2 full-length Practice Tests, with answer explanations for each question. Each test contains the same number and mix of question types you'll encounter on the actual exam. To accurately measure your performance on these Practice Tests, be sure to adhere strictly to the stated time limits for each section.

- **Word List** in the Appendix offers you a great tool to help boost your vocabulary for ALL of the GED® tests.

THE DIAGNOSTIC PRACTICE TEST AND PROCESS

The Diagnostic Practice Test does more than give you testing experience. It helps you recognize your strengths and pinpoint areas that need improvement. By understanding your "testing profile," you can immediately address your weak areas by working through the relevant review chapters, learning the pertinent test-taking tips, and studying the numerous examples and explanations provided.

The Review Sections

The Language Arts, Writing: Part I and the Social Studies sections include graphic illustrations in response to contemporary trends and current changes in curriculum, as well as the demands of the GED®. The Writing Test: Part I review covers sentence correction, revision, and construction; paragraph composition; and document organization.

The Social Studies review covers history, civics and government, economics, and geography. The review will help you sharpen your comprehension, analysis, evaluation, and application skills for the actual exam.

The Language Arts, Reading section provides an opportunity to improve your reading skills, which are necessary for good performance in reading and in all other academic areas. The selections consist of a wide range of reading matter, from poetry to a scene from a play to business memos and e-mails.

The Science section reviews those subjects that will appear on the actual GED® exam: life science (biology), earth science (geology and oceanography), space science (astronomy), and physical science (chemistry and physics). The review will help you with your ability to recall and understand information, draw inferences and conclusions, evaluate data, and apply concepts and ideas to other situations.

The Mathematics section provides user-friendly explanations of math processes in recognition of the particular difficulty that many students have in this area. The review, examples, and answer explanations will help you better comprehend the difficult concepts in the tested areas of numbers, number sense, and operations; data, statistics, and probability; algebra, functions, and patterns; and geometry, coordinate geometry, and measurement. In addition, there are clear, step-by-step directions on using the *Casio fx-260* calculator, which is what you will be given to use for Part I of the GED® Mathematics Test.

THE PRACTICE TESTS

When you have completed your reviews, take the Practice Tests under simulated test conditions to further sharpen your skills. Find a quiet place where you won't be distracted or interrupted, set a timer for the required time, and work through each test as though it were test day.

SPECIAL STUDY FEATURES

Overview

Each chapter begins with a bulleted overview listing the topics that will be covered in the chapter. You know immediately where to look for a topic that you need to work on.

Summing It Up

Each review chapter ends with a point-by-point summary that captures the most important items. The summaries are a convenient way to review the content of the chapters.

About the CD

If you have the CD edition of this book, you have additional GED® test preparation available to you. The CD links you to 3 online Practice Tests. We suggest that you begin by taking the Diagnostic Test. Once you have an idea of how you did and where to focus your preparation, review the material in the book. As the final part of your preparation, take the other tests in the book and online, via the CD.

LINKS TO HIPPOCAMPUS™

Need additional subject review in history, science, or math? Throughout *Master the GED*® 2013, you'll see links to HippoCampus.org, a great new way to get the extra subject help you need. From algebra to American government to biology, HippoCampus brings learning to life by providing multimedia lessons and course materials to students and teachers via the Web. Follow the links to the HippoCampus Web site, and you'll instantly have access to information on a wide variety of general education subjects.

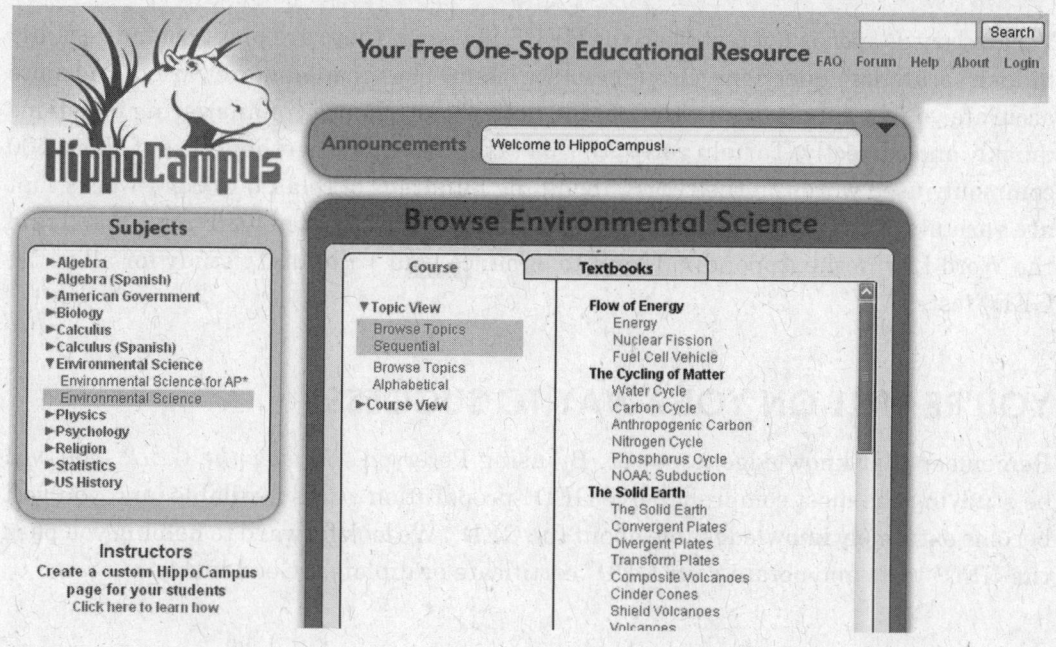

Throughout the Social Studies, Science, and Mathematics Review chapters, you'll see links that look like this:

http://bit.ly/hippo_bio2

Each link will take you to the specific subject you want to review. You can also use HippoCampus to take an actual refresher course. Either way, you'll not only have fun while learning, you'll also gain the extra knowledge and confidence you need to score high on your GED®.

A technical note: The HippoCampus Web site uses Adobe Flash. It's recommended that you have Adobe Flash Player 7.0 or higher installed on your system. In addition, some of the Environmental Science content require Apple QuickTime version 6 or higher. Be sure to have QuickTime set to enable embedded flash content (you will find this option in the QuickTime control panel under advanced settings). Finally, because HippoCampus contains multimedia instructional content, it is also recommended that you have a high-speed Internet connection, such as DSL or Cable Modem.

HippoCampus is a project of the Monterey Institute for Technology and Education (MITE). Its goal is to provide high-quality, multimedia content on general education subjects to high school and college students free of charge. HippoCampus is supported by The William and Flora Hewlett Foundation and was designed as part of Open Education Resources (OER). The continually growing content on HippoCampus has been created by colleges and universities worldwide.

Peterson's Publishing is proud to join forces with HippoCampus to offer students like you access to the finest—and most innovative—educational content and resources.

WORD LIST

Vocabulary *as such* is not tested on the GED®; however, there are plenty of indirect and hidden vocabulary questions throughout the exam. The broader, more varied, and more accurate your vocabulary knowledge, the better your chances of answering questions quickly and correctly. To help you with this task, we've put together a list of about 500 commonly used words on the GED®, including hundreds of related words—words that are variants of the primary words or words that share a common word root. You'll find the Word List in the Appendix. Use it to enhance your vocabulary study for all of the GED® tests.

YOU'RE WELL ON YOUR WAY TO SUCCESS

Remember that knowledge is power. By using Peterson's *Master the GED*®, you will be studying the most comprehensive GED®-preparation guide available, and you will become extremely knowledgeable about the GED®. We look forward to helping you pass the GED® tests and obtain your GED® certificate or diploma. Good luck!

GIVE US YOUR FEEDBACK

Peterson's publishes a full line of resources to help guide you. Peterson's publications can be found at high school guidance offices, college libraries and career centers, and your local bookstore or library. Peterson's books are now also available as eBooks.

We welcome any comments or suggestions you may have about this publication.

Peterson's Publishing
2000 Lenox Drive
Lawrenceville, New Jersey 08648
E-mail: custsvc@petersons.com

PART I

THE GED TESTS— THE BASICS

All About the GED®

Congratulations on taking the first step to advancing your academic career. Whether you are taking the GED® Tests to prepare for college entrance or looking for the career opportunities that become available after completing the GED® Tests, you are not alone. Since 1943, more than 17 million people have earned their GED® credential. It is estimated that in the United States today 1 out of every 7 high school students will complete their education by taking the GED® exams. In fact, in 2009, more than 470,000 individuals were awarded their high school credential.

This book was designed to assist you in successfully passing all five of the individual tests in the GED® battery. The lessons in this book will help you develop skills essential to passing each test, and the individual subject reviews will help you become comfortable with the knowledge areas covered on the tests. The GED®-style example questions provided throughout the lessons, along with the book's Diagnostic and Practice Tests, afford you plenty of practice with just the types of questions you will encounter on the real GED® Tests.

WHAT IS THE GED®

The **Tests of General Education Development,** or **GED® Tests,** are standardized tests that measure skills required of high school graduates in the United States and Canada. The ultimate goal in passing these exams is a certificate that is equivalent to a high school diploma. A GED® certificate can be useful for gaining admission to college, for obtaining certain vocational licenses, or for finding employment in the many types of jobs that require a high school diploma or its equivalent.

The battery of five GED® Tests are designed and administered by the GED® Testing Service® of the American Council on Education®. These tests were originally developed to help veterans returning from service in World War II regain academic skills and complete an education that had been interrupted by the war. Many returning veterans used this additional education to obtain civilian jobs. Since the 1940s, the emphasis of the GED® Tests has gradually shifted from knowledge required for industrial jobs to the kinds of knowledge and skills needed for today's information-driven world. In 2002, the test was revised to place more emphasis on adult-context information, in order to reflect changing demographics and vocational goals among the GED® Test-taking population. One thing has not changed, though: millions of motivated men and women like you have earned their high school credential by completing the GED® battery of tests.

THE FIVE GED® TESTS—AT A GLANCE

In order to pass the GED® Tests and earn a GED® certificate, for each subject area you must demonstrate a mastery of skills at least equal to the top two thirds of high school graduates. It is important to understand that, as the previous sentence suggests, each GED® Test is primarily a *skills* test rather than a knowledge test. Passing the GED® Tests does not require rote memorization or extensive knowledge of the subject areas they cover. Instead, each of the five tests is designed to gauge the same four broad skills:

- Comprehension (understanding and interpreting information)

- Analysis (drawing specific inferences and conclusions from information)

- Synthesis and evaluation (characterizing, generalizing from, and making judgments about information)

- Application (using information in ways other than those presented)

Of course, each of the five tests measures these skills in its own unique way. And to be successful on the GED® Tests, in addition to exercising this skill-set, you must apply your common knowledge and your common sense, both of which are acquired through everyday experiences and observations, as well as through rudimentary education.

The GED® Test Structure

The GED® Tests consist of five individual tests. Each test covers a different component of standard high school curriculum. The following table shows the various areas that each test covers, along with the number of questions available and the time limit for each test. Except for Part II of the Language Arts, Writing Test (the essay-writing exercise), each of the GED® Tests consists entirely of multiple-choice questions—*five* choices per question. So the basic question format is the same across all five tests.

TEST	CONTENT AREAS	NUMBER OF QUESTIONS	TIME LIMIT
Language Arts, Writing, Part I	Grammar and usage (30%) Sentence structure (30%) Writing mechanics (25%) Organization (15%)	50 multiple-choice	75 minutes[†]
Language Arts, Writing, Part II	Topic of general interest	1 essay (no word limit; at least 250 words suggested)	45 minutes[†]
Social Studies	U.S. history (25%) World history (15%) Civics and government (25%) Economics (15%) Geography (15%)	50 multiple-choice	70 minutes
Science	Life science (45%) Earth and space science (20%) Chemistry and physics (35%)	50 multiple-choice	80 minutes
Language Arts, Reading	Prose fiction (45%) Drama (15%) Poetry (15%) Nonfiction (25%)	40 multiple-choice	65 minutes
Mathematics	Arithmetic and numbers (20–30%) Data, statistics, and probability (20–30%) Algebra, functions, and patterns (20–30%) Geometry and measurement (20–30%)	50 questions (approximately 40 multiple-choice; approximately 10 grid-in) (Booklet 1—25 questions) (Booklet 2—25 questions)	90 minutes[††] (Booklet 1, calculator allowed—45 minutes) (Booklet 2, no calculator—45 minutes)

[†] During the Language Arts, Writing Test, if you complete Part I (the editing test) before the 75-minute time limit expires, you can begin work on Part II (the essay) immediately, at your option. But once you've turned to Part II, you will not be allowed to return to Part I.

[††] During the Mathematics Test, you will be given two separate test booklets. The first one will contain 25 questions, and you will be provided a calculator that you can use in answering these questions. After 45 minutes, you must stop work on Booklet 1, turn in your calculator, and proceed to Booklet 2, which also contains 25 questions.

The Language Arts, Writing Test

The Language Arts, Writing Test includes two parts. Part I consists of 50 multiple-choice questions and is essentially an *editing* test. What this means is that you will be examining brief selections of text in order to identify and fix problems in grammar, sentence structure, writing mechanics (use of commas and capitalization of proper nouns), and document organization. Part I also tests on the use of *homonyms* (words that sound alike but are spelled differently) but otherwise does not test on spelling, since writing and composition today are generally aided by computer spell-checkers.

During Part II of the Language Arts, Writing Test, you will plan and compose a hand-written essay. This part of the test is designed to measure your ability to communicate clearly and effectively. At least 2 trained readers will evaluate your essay based on content, organization, language (word choice and usage), and writing mechanics (grammar, sentence structure, etc.). The essay must respond to a specific topic involving a subject of general knowledge and interest. The topic will be provided; you won't be able to choose among topics. You will be asked to present your perspective on the topic and to support your ideas with reasons and examples from your reading, observations, and personal experiences.

The Social Studies Test

The Social Studies Test consists of 50 multiple-choice questions. Each question is based on a brief passage of text, a visual depiction, or both. As many as 20 of the questions may be accompanied by a visual (a diagram, table, graph, chart, cartoon, or other illustration). In some cases, the same visual applies to two or more questions.

The Social Studies Test is designed to measure your ability to understand, analyze, synthesize, evaluate, and apply a variety of social studies concepts. The content areas covered on the test are U.S. history, world history, civics and government, economics, and geography. (The version of the GED® administered in Canada covers Canadian history and government instead of U.S. history and government.) The Social Studies Test is *not* a knowledge test. Rather, it requires that you apply your critical-thinking skills in the context of social studies material, both written and visual. To succeed on the test, you need not memorize dates, names, events, geographical data, or other trivia. All the information you'll need to respond successfully to the questions will be provided.

The Science Test

The Science Test consists of 50 multiple-choice questions. Each question is based on a brief passage of text, a visual depiction, or both. Up to half the questions are accompanied by visuals (diagrams, tables, graphs, charts, and illustrations). In some cases, the same visual applies to two or more questions.

The Science Test is designed to gauge your ability to understand, analyze, synthesize, evaluate, and apply basic high school science concepts. The content areas covered on the test include life science (biology), earth and space science, and physical science (chemistry and physics). The Science Test is primarily a critical-thinking skills test rather than a knowledge test. Most of what you need to know to respond successfully to the questions will be provided. However, the test does presuppose the basic level of science knowledge that most people have acquired through their everyday observations and experiences.

The Language Arts, Reading Test

The Language Arts, Reading Test consists of 40 multiple-choice questions. The questions are presented in groups of four to eight questions—each group based on the same selection of text. The reading selections average about a half-page in length and are drawn from a wide variety of sources, including prose fiction, poetry, and drama as well as works of nonfiction ranging from informational articles and critical essays to biographies and workplace documents.

The Reading Test does *not* test your knowledge of literature or other factual information. Rather, the test is designed to gauge your ability to understand, analyze, and draw reasonable inferences from reading material, as well as to apply what you've read. So everything you will need to know in order to answer the questions correctly will be provided in the selections of text.

The Mathematics Test

The Mathematics Test consists of 50 questions altogether. Approximately 40 of these are standard multiple-choice questions. The other questions are "grid-in," which means that instead of selecting an answer among several choices, you will need to enter a numerical response or mark a point on a coordinate plane on a special grid.

Mathematics Test questions cover the basic math concepts and skills taught in high school, including operations on numbers; number forms, relationships, and patterns; elementary statistics and probability; algebra and functions; geometry (including coordinate geometry) and measurement; and basic trigonometry. Some questions are based on visuals such as geometry figures and data presented in graphical format (tables, charts, and graphs).

About half the questions require problem solving—in other words, working to a numerical solution. The remaining questions focus on concepts in a theoretical setting. Calculators are provided for the first part of the test (booklet 1, which contains 25 questions) but not for the second part (booklet 2, which also contains 25 questions). The first part places more emphasis on number operations and calculations, while the second part puts greater emphasis on math concepts, estimation, and "mental math." During each part, the difficulty level of questions increases, so that easier questions come before questions that test-takers generally find more challenging. Also, the questions in booklet 2 are generally more challenging than those in booklet 1. (Of the five GED® Tests, only the Mathematics Test arranges questions in order of difficulty.)

The procedural rules for the Mathematics Test can be a little confusing. Part I and Part II of the Math Test are not separate, 45-minute sections. In some states, after 45 minutes, the testing administrator collects the calculators that are used *only* for Part

I and then distributes the booklet for Part II (Part I booklets are not collected at this time). So, test-takers have no fewer than 45 minutes to complete Part II. However, test-takers completing Part I early (before 45 minutes have elapsed) can turn in their calculators and begin work on Part II immediately. Test-takers who complete Part II early (before the entire 90 minutes have elapsed) have the option of returning to Part I of the Math Test. But, it is important to note that test-takers returning to Part I will *not* have access to calculators during the remaining time.

GED® SCORING AND PASSING REQUIREMENTS

For each GED® Test, the more questions you answer correctly, the higher your score. No penalties are assessed for incorrect responses. Your GED® essay (Part II of the Language Arts, Writing Test) will be evaluated by 2 trained readers who score the essay on a scale of 0–6. Your score for Part II will be combined with your score for Part I (the multiple-choice portion) into a single Language Arts, Writing score.

To be eligible to receive your high school equivalency certificate, you must attain or exceed a minimum average score for all five tests *and* a minimum score for each test. Minimum passing scores vary somewhat from state to state.

Most states now use a "standard score" system, in which the number of correct answers on each GED® Test is converted to a 200–800 scale. Using a scaled scoring system accounts for the varying number of questions among the GED® Tests, as well as for possible variations in overall difficulty among different versions of a test. To illustrate how the GED® standard-score and pass-fail systems work, assume that your state requires an average score of at least 450 and a score of at least 410 for each test. With these minimum passing scores in mind, assume that 3 test-takers—Spencer, Austin, and Maria—earn the following scores for the five GED® Tests:

GED® TEST	SPENCER	AUSTIN	MARIA
Language Arts, Writing (Part 1)	455	440	430
Language Arts, Reading	430	525	510
Mathematics	415	405	460
Science	420	470	410
Social Studies	510	485	480
Average Score	446	465	458

Maria would have been the only test-taker among the 3 test-takers to have successfully passed the GED® requirements and earned her certificate. She attained at least a 410 score on each and every one of the five tests, and her average score for all five tests, 458, exceeded the average-score requirement of 450.

Spencer scored at least 410 on each of the five tests, but he failed to earn an average score of 450. In order to earn his GED® certificate, Spencer would need to repeat at least one of the five tests and better his previous score enough to boost his average score to at least 450. He should repeat at least one test—preferably test(s) he believes he can perform much better on his second time around.

Austin also exceeded the average-score requirement of 450. In fact, his average score, 465, was higher than Maria's. But Austin fell short of 410 on the Mathematics Test. In order for Austin to earn his GED® certificate, he would need to repeat that test and earn a score of at least 410 his second time around. But he would not need to retake any of the other four tests.

NOTE: GED® Test-takers also receive a *percentile rank* based on each of the scaled scores described above. Percentile ranks range from 0–99 percent and indicate the test-taker's performance compared to the entire GED®-testing population. For example, a percentile rank of 60 percent means that the test-taker scored higher than 60 percent of all other test-takers.

GED® AVAILABILITY, SCHEDULING, FEES, AND ONLINE TESTING

The GED® battery of tests is administered in every state of the United States, in every Canadian province, and in more than 100 international locations. The tests are offered in English, French, Spanish, large print, Braille, and even audiotape format. Special testing accommodations may be available for test-takers with a diagnosed learning disability, Attention Deficit/Hyperactivity Disorder, emotional/mental health conditions, physical/chronic health disabilities, or any other condition that may interfere with a test-taker's ability to fully demonstrate what he or she knows under standard testing conditions. For more information, visit www.acenet.edu and follow the links to the GED® Test and accommodations for disabilities.

Currently, there are more than 3,400 testing centers throughout the United States and Canada, as well as internationally. Testing centers are typically located at adult-education and community-education facilities. Some centers are located at military installations. Finding a convenient testing center should not be difficult if you live in a populous state. California, for example, boasts over 200 testing centers altogether, across every county in the state.

Local testing centers in the United States and Canada can be found by calling the toll-free hotline at 800-626-9433 (800-62-MY GED®). To find an international testing center, visit http://securereg3.prometric.com/.

GED® Testing is scheduled through the individual testing centers, not through the centralized Testing Service of a state or province. The five GED® Tests are typically administered over two or three consecutive days or during two consecutive weekends. (The total GED® Testing time is over 7 hours, not including breaks between tests—far too long for a single testing day.)

The number of times the GED® Tests are administered each year varies from one testing center to another. Each center establishes its own schedule. Centers in urban areas may offer testing every day, whereas centers in remote, rural areas may offer testing only once or twice a year. Each state sets its own GED® Testing fees, which average about $100 for the entire test battery but vary from one center to another.

It is important to note that the GED® Tests cannot be taken online. Test officials strongly warn of fraudulent online programs that offer high school equivalencies for a fee. As of this book's publication, the test is only offered in pencil/pen and paper format EXCEPT at certain official test sites. According to the GED® Testing Service, an electronic GED® exam is offered *only* at official test centers in Georgia, Florida, Texas, and California. Throughout the next years, the electronic exam should be introduced in other states. The goal is for the GED® to be a computer-based test by 2013.

A NEW GED®

In 2014, the GED® Testing Service will release a brand new GED® exam. The goal of this new assessment is to ensure that the GED® is a springboard for further education, training, and better paying jobs—and no longer just an endpoint in someone's studies. Four content areas—Literacy, Mathematics, Science, and Social Studies—will measure a foundational core of knowledge and skills, and an additional performance level will certify that adults are ready for college and careers.

RETAKING ALL OR PART OF THE GED®

Once you receive your GED® transcript (see "Score Transcripts and Your GED® Certificate"), you will be eligible to retake any or all of the individual GED® Tests for which you did not meet the minimum passing score for your state. Most testing centers charge an additional fee for retaking all or part of the GED®. You may retake the same test no more than twice during the same calendar year, and most states impose a waiting period before each retesting.

At the time of retesting, you will be given a different version of the exam, which means that you will not be tested on the same questions you worked with previously. Multiple scores for the same test (for example, the Mathematics Test) are *not* averaged. Only your highest score for each test is considered in determining whether you have attained the minimum passing score for that test.

SCORE TRANSCRIPTS AND YOUR GED® CERTIFICATE

Within six to eight weeks after testing, an official score report, or transcript, is mailed to test-takers who have met all the GED® requirements. If you fail to meet the requirements, you will receive an *unofficial* transcript instead. Official and unofficial transcripts provide scaled scores, but they do not provide the number of correct or incorrect answers for any of the five tests. The states' testing services do not accommodate requests to provide transcripts earlier than the six-to-eight-week period, and neither official nor unofficial GED® transcripts are made available over the Internet. Once you receive an official transcript, you may present it to a college-admissions office or as proof for employment purposes that you have met all GED® requirements.

The GED® certificate is a separate document issued by the state where you took the GED® Tests. (Some states refer to this document as a diploma.) GED® certificates are generally mailed together with official transcripts. However, most states require that you reach a minimum age before the certificate is issued to you. It is important to keep your certificate in a safe place because some states will issue only one to you.

Official duplicates of your transcript will generally be made available to you through your state, for a fee. Many states now refer requests for duplicate transcripts to Educational Testing Service (ETS), an outside organization that keeps the transcripts and handles test-takers' requests for duplicates.

GETTING READY FOR THE GED® TESTS

Be sure to give yourself plenty of time to prepare for all five of the GED® Tests. Many GED® candidates find that taking a course with an instructor gives them the needed structure to accomplish their goal. Others have the self-discipline to study on a regular basis without the structure of a class. Regardless of which method you use, GED® counselors often recommend spreading out GED® Testing—rather than taking all the GED® Tests in a short period of time—to allow plenty of time to prepare adequately for each test.

Setting and Sticking to a Study Schedule

If you're preparing for the GED® Tests on your own, set up a regular review and practice schedule, which ideally should begin several weeks before each exam. Use the Practice Tests in this book, along with the supplemental online practice questions, to apply the skills and knowledge you learn throughout the lessons in this book. If you have time, supplement this book with one or two other GED®-prep books, scheduling additional Practice Testing from those books. Try to stagger, or spread out, your Practice Testing evenly rather than waiting until the last few days—or even the last week—before the exam. This way, you will experience steady improvement over time, which will instill confidence that will motivate you and help boost your scores.

Getting ready for the GED® Tests is a bit like training for an athletic event. The more you practice under exam-like conditions, the better you'll perform during the actual exam. So be sure to take your Practice Tests under simulated testing conditions. Avoid interruptions and distractions, sit at a desk in a quiet spot, and adhere strictly to the time limit imposed during the actual test. Try to take each Practice Test from beginning to end in one sitting, just as you will during the actual test. Do not underestimate the role that endurance can play during the test. Be sure to thoroughly review each test after taking it, so you can identify your weaknesses and focus on them in further study.

Using Other Resources to Prepare for the Tests

To develop the skills you will need to pass the GED® Tests, start with this book and possibly one or two others that focus specifically on the GED® Tests. But if you have time, you should supplement these GED®-prep materials with relevant materials from a variety of other sources. Tap online and offline sources of local, national, and international news. Read articles from reputable magazines and Web sites focusing on current topics in science, economics, and politics. As you read, try to distinguish main ideas from supporting details, fact from opinion, and well-supported conclusions from poorly supported ones.

Examine charts, tables, and graphs provided in newspapers and magazines. Read a good daily newspaper and analyze its editorial cartoons (you'll see editorial cartoons on the GED® Social Studies Test). Ask yourself what ideas these various types of graphics are attempting to convey, what conclusions you can draw from them, and whether they are presenting information in an objective manner or from a certain slant or perspective.

Don't forget about textbooks and subject-review books, whether written for high school students or for a more general audience. At your library, you'll find basic introductory books on math, biology, physics, chemistry, earth science, astronomy, economics, history, civics, and geography. Multi-volume works such as the Time-Life book series contain easy-to-understand information relevant to the GED® Social Studies and Science Tests.

In short, spending time between now and test day to sharpen your reading and critical-thinking skills will serve you well during all of the GED® Tests.

The Day Before the Test and the Day of the Test

The day before your actual test, avoid studying or practicing for it. In fact, try to avoid even thinking about the test. Consider this day your day off to relax by seeing a movie or spending time with friends. Take some pressure off yourself, and your mind will be fresher on exam day. The night before the test, eat a good dinner and get a good night's rest. On the morning of the test, eat a good breakfast, and arrive at the testing center early so that you have time to unwind a bit before the exam. Chat with other test-takers about anything other than the test itself.

As you enter the testing room, try not to be nervous about taking the GED® Tests. Remind yourself that these tests are practical measures of knowledge that you have gained partially through study but mainly through your life experiences. In addition, find reassurance in the hard work and hours of preparation you have invested in this endeavor. As the testing clock starts to run, tackle your test with confidence and enthusiasm—knowing that you have done your best to prepare for it.

OBTAINING MORE INFORMATION ABOUT THE GED®

For locations and dates for GED® Testing in your area, contact your state's GED® Testing Service or a nearby GED® Testing Center. For general information about the GED® Tests, including information about future test changes, contact General Educational Development or consult the organization's official GED® Web site:

General Educational Development
GED® Testing Service
American Council on Education
One DuPont Circle, NW
Washington, D.C. 20036
800-626-9433 (toll-free)
www.acenet.edu

If you're interested in enrolling in a GED®-prep course, try contacting the adult-education or continuing-education department at your local community college or university. For additional self-study, you can utilize a variety of other GED®-prep books and GED® Web sites. You may also wish to purchase materials from Steck-Vaughn (www.gedpractice .com), the exclusive distributor of the actual GED® Tests administered throughout the United States and Canada. Keep in mind, however, that the materials available for purchase from Steck-Vaughn do *not* include any of the actual, previously administered GED® Tests or test questions.

TOP 10 GED® TEST-TAKING TIPS

Disclaimer; Please note that scoring, passing requirements, and testing procedures vary by state. Contact the testing service in your state for specific information.

The general strategies and tips provided here apply to all five of the GED® Tests (except for the essay portion of the Language Arts, Writing Test, which does not involve answering multiple-choice questions). Be sure to look over this Top-10 list again just before exam day—you'll be glad you did.

❶ Use your pencil to mark up the test booklet and scratch paper.
Using your pencil and paper can help you organize your thoughts, keep key ideas straight in your mind, and prevent careless errors. When reading a passage of text, remember to underline or circle words and phrases that are essential to understanding the passage's ideas. For lengthy or confusing text passages, jot down notes in the margins or make brief outlines on your scratch paper (which will be provided). During the portion of the Mathematics Test for which a calculator is not allowed, perform all but the simplest computations on your scratch paper. Use your pencil to cross out answer choices as you eliminate them and to earmark those you're unsure about and may want to re-visit if you have time.

❷ When answering a question based on visual information, size up the visual first.
Many questions on the Mathematics, Science, and Social Studies tests contain visual information (graphs, charts, illustrations, diagrams, and so forth). Inspect any such "visual" carefully. Try to understand what the visual involves and what its overall intent and meaning is. Be sure to read any title or caption, which may provide clues for answering the question at hand.

❸ Make sure you understand the question.
Read each question carefully so you know exactly what it is asking. Pay attention to key words such as *true, accurate, supports, probably,* and *most likely.* These words tell you the features to look for in the correct answer choice. Also look for words in capital letters such as NOT, LEAST, EXCEPT, and CANNOT. These capitalized words tell you that the question is being asked in the negative. (Note that these and other key words may also appear in **boldface.)** If a question is based on a passage

of text, read the question stem (the question itself, apart from the answer choices) before you read the passage so you have an idea of what to look for in the passage.

4 Attempt to answer the question in your own words before reading the answer choices.

If you can formulate your own answer to a question, by all means do so. Then you can simply look for the answer choice that best matches what you already know is correct. What's more, you'll waste less time trying to understand the other choices, which can often be confusing and even nonsensical.

5 Read all the answer choices carefully.

The first answer choice you read might appear to provide a good answer, but by reading further you may discover that there is a better choice. Never select a final answer before reading and carefully considering all five choices.

6 Select an answer choice that answers the question being asked.

This may seem obvious, but you should be careful not to choose an answer merely because it provides accurate information or a true statement, or because it is supported by information given in a passage of text or a visual. If the answer does not respond to the question, eliminate it.

7 Try to eliminate as many incorrect answer choices as possible.

Many questions will come with answer choices that are wrong because they provide the opposite of what the question asks for. For instance, a question that asks which statement is best supported by the text will probably come with at least two choices that are *contradicted* by the text. Some wrong-answer choices might be *off topic*, meaning that they convey ideas that are not relevant to the specific topic or the question. If you're paying attention, you can easily spot these sorts of answer choices and eliminate them to improve your odds of answering the questions correctly.

8 Apply common sense and common knowledge to your advantage.

Many questions may involve concepts and topics that are unfamiliar to you. You can use your real-life, practical knowledge and common sense to help you answer many such questions—or at least to narrow the answer choices. Don't be surprised how far common sense and common knowledge can take you on the GED®!

9 Answer every question, even if you need to guess.

Your score on each of the five tests is determined by the number of questions you answer correctly. You won't be penalized for incorrect answers, so you should never leave a question unanswered. If you don't know the answer, just guess—you have nothing to lose and everything to gain.

10 Pace yourself to leave enough time for reviewing your answers.

Don't be a constant clock-watcher, but do check the time every so often to make sure you are on pace to read and answer all questions within the time allowed. Try to maintain a pace that leaves you at least 5 minutes to return to those questions you were unsure about and reconsider them.

SUMMING IT UP

- The Tests of General Education Development, or GED® Tests, are standardized tests that measure skills required of high school graduates in the United States and Canada. The ultimate goal in passing these exams is a certificate that is equivalent to a high school diploma.

- The GED® Test cannot be taken online. You can take the GED® Tests almost anywhere in the United States and Canada and internationally at any of the 3,400 Official GED® Testing Centers, which are typically located at adult-education and community-education facilities. Some centers are located at military installations.

- The five GED® Tests are typically administered over two or three consecutive days or during two consecutive weekends.

- The tests that make up the GED® Test battery are Language Arts, Writing (Parts I and II); Social Studies; Science; Language Arts, Reading; and Mathematics. Except for Part II of the Language Arts, Writing Test, each of the GED® Tests consists entirely of multiple-choice questions—*five* choices per question.

- For each GED® Test, the more questions you answer correctly, the higher your score. No penalties are assessed for incorrect responses. The GED® essay (the Language Arts, Writing Test, Part II) is evaluated by 2 trained readers, and this score (on a scale of 0–6) is combined with your score for Part I (the multiple-choice portion) into a single Language Arts, Writing score.

- It's important to note that scoring, passing requirements, and testing procedures vary by state. You should contact the testing service in your state for specific information.

- In order to earn your GED®, you must attain or exceed a minimum average score for all five tests *and* a minimum score for each test. Again, note that minimum passing scores do vary somewhat from state to state.

- Getting ready for the GED® Tests is like training for an athletic event. The more you practice under exam-like conditions, the better you'll perform during the actual exam. Be sure to review each test after taking it, so you can identify your weaknesses and focus on them in further study.

- For general information about the GED® Tests, including information about future test changes, consult the official GED® Web site: www.acenet.edu.

PART II

DETERMINING STRENGTHS AND WEAKNESSES

CHAPTER 2   Practice Test 1: Diagnostic

Practice Test 1: Diagnostic

DIRECTIONS FOR TAKING THE DIAGNOSTIC TEST

Directions: The GED® Practice Test has five separate subtests: Language Arts, Writing (Parts I and II); Social Studies; Science; Language Arts, Reading; and Mathematics.

- Read and follow the directions at the start of each test.

- Stick to the time limits.

- Enter your answers on the tear-out Answer Sheets provided.

- When you have completed the entire test, compare your answers with the correct answers given in the Answer Key and Explanations at the end of this Practice Test.

- Remember to check the "Are You Ready to Take the GED®?" section to gauge how close you are to mastering the GED® exam.

diagnostic test

ANSWER SHEET PRACTICE TEST 1: DIAGNOSTIC TEST

Language Arts, Writing—Part I

1. ①②③④⑤   11. ①②③④⑤   21. ①②③④⑤   31. ①②③④⑤   41. ①②③④⑤
2. ①②③④⑤   12. ①②③④⑤   22. ①②③④⑤   32. ①②③④⑤   42. ①②③④⑤
3. ①②③④⑤   13. ①②③④⑤   23. ①②③④⑤   33. ①②③④⑤   43. ①②③④⑤
4. ①②③④⑤   14. ①②③④⑤   24. ①②③④⑤   34. ①②③④⑤   44. ①②③④⑤
5. ①②③④⑤   15. ①②③④⑤   25. ①②③④⑤   35. ①②③④⑤   45. ①②③④⑤
6. ①②③④⑤   16. ①②③④⑤   26. ①②③④⑤   36. ①②③④⑤   46. ①②③④⑤
7. ①②③④⑤   17. ①②③④⑤   27. ①②③④⑤   37. ①②③④⑤   47. ①②③④⑤
8. ①②③④⑤   18. ①②③④⑤   28. ①②③④⑤   38. ①②③④⑤   48. ①②③④⑤
9. ①②③④⑤   19. ①②③④⑤   29. ①②③④⑤   39. ①②③④⑤   49. ①②③④⑤
10. ①②③④⑤   20. ①②③④⑤   30. ①②③④⑤   40. ①②③④⑤   50. ①②③④⑤

Social Studies

1. ①②③④⑤   11. ①②③④⑤   21. ①②③④⑤   31. ①②③④⑤   41. ①②③④⑤
2. ①②③④⑤   12. ①②③④⑤   22. ①②③④⑤   32. ①②③④⑤   42. ①②③④⑤
3. ①②③④⑤   13. ①②③④⑤   23. ①②③④⑤   33. ①②③④⑤   43. ①②③④⑤
4. ①②③④⑤   14. ①②③④⑤   24. ①②③④⑤   34. ①②③④⑤   44. ①②③④⑤
5. ①②③④⑤   15. ①②③④⑤   25. ①②③④⑤   35. ①②③④⑤   45. ①②③④⑤
6. ①②③④⑤   16. ①②③④⑤   26. ①②③④⑤   36. ①②③④⑤   46. ①②③④⑤
7. ①②③④⑤   17. ①②③④⑤   27. ①②③④⑤   37. ①②③④⑤   47. ①②③④⑤
8. ①②③④⑤   18. ①②③④⑤   28. ①②③④⑤   38. ①②③④⑤   48. ①②③④⑤
9. ①②③④⑤   19. ①②③④⑤   29. ①②③④⑤   39. ①②③④⑤   49. ①②③④⑤
10. ①②③④⑤   20. ①②③④⑤   30. ①②③④⑤   40. ①②③④⑤   50. ①②③④⑤

Science

1. ①②③④⑤   11. ①②③④⑤   21. ①②③④⑤   31. ①②③④⑤   41. ①②③④⑤
2. ①②③④⑤   12. ①②③④⑤   22. ①②③④⑤   32. ①②③④⑤   42. ①②③④⑤
3. ①②③④⑤   13. ①②③④⑤   23. ①②③④⑤   33. ①②③④⑤   43. ①②③④⑤
4. ①②③④⑤   14. ①②③④⑤   24. ①②③④⑤   34. ①②③④⑤   44. ①②③④⑤
5. ①②③④⑤   15. ①②③④⑤   25. ①②③④⑤   35. ①②③④⑤   45. ①②③④⑤
6. ①②③④⑤   16. ①②③④⑤   26. ①②③④⑤   36. ①②③④⑤   46. ①②③④⑤
7. ①②③④⑤   17. ①②③④⑤   27. ①②③④⑤   37. ①②③④⑤   47. ①②③④⑤
8. ①②③④⑤   18. ①②③④⑤   28. ①②③④⑤   38. ①②③④⑤   48. ①②③④⑤
9. ①②③④⑤   19. ①②③④⑤   29. ①②③④⑤   39. ①②③④⑤   49. ①②③④⑤
10. ①②③④⑤   20. ①②③④⑤   30. ①②③④⑤   40. ①②③④⑤   50. ①②③④⑤

Language Arts, Reading

1. ①②③④⑤
2. ①②③④⑤
3. ①②③④⑤
4. ①②③④⑤
5. ①②③④⑤
6. ①②③④⑤
7. ①②③④⑤
8. ①②③④⑤
9. ①②③④⑤
10. ①②③④⑤

11. ①②③④⑤
12. ①②③④⑤
13. ①②③④⑤
14. ①②③④⑤
15. ①②③④⑤
16. ①②③④⑤
17. ①②③④⑤
18. ①②③④⑤
19. ①②③④⑤
20. ①②③④⑤

21. ①②③④⑤
22. ①②③④⑤
23. ①②③④⑤
24. ①②③④⑤
25. ①②③④⑤
26. ①②③④⑤
27. ①②③④⑤
28. ①②③④⑤
29. ①②③④⑤
30. ①②③④⑤

31. ①②③④⑤
32. ①②③④⑤
33. ①②③④⑤
34. ①②③④⑤
35. ①②③④⑤
36. ①②③④⑤
37. ①②③④⑤
38. ①②③④⑤
39. ①②③④⑤
40. ①②③④⑤

Mathematics—Part I

1. ①②③④⑤
2. ①②③④⑤
3. ①②③④⑤
4.

5. ①②③④⑤
6. ①②③④⑤
7. ①②③④⑤
8. ①②③④⑤
9. ①②③④⑤

10.

11. ①②③④⑤
12. ①②③④⑤
13. ①②③④⑤
14. ①②③④⑤
15. ①②③④⑤
16. ①②③④⑤
17. ①②③④⑤
18. ①②③④⑤

19.

20. ①②③④⑤
21. ①②③④⑤
22. ①②③④⑤
23. ①②③④⑤
24. ①②③④⑤
25.

answer sheet

Mathematics—Part II

26. ①②③④⑤
27. ①②③④⑤
28.
29. ①②③④⑤
30. ①②③④⑤
31. ①②③④⑤
32.
33. ①②③④⑤

34.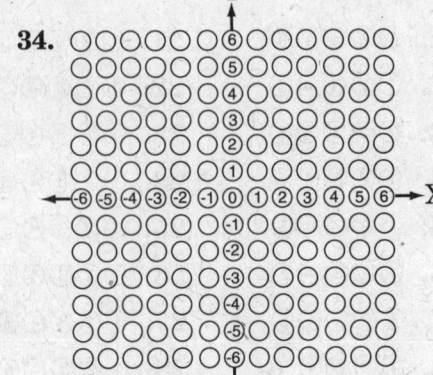

35. ①②③④⑤
36.
37. ①②③④⑤
38. ①②③④⑤
39. ①②③④⑤
40. ①②③④⑤
41. ①②③④⑤
42. ①②③④⑤

43. ①②③④⑤
44. ①②③④⑤
45. ①②③④⑤
46.
47. ①②③④⑤
48. ①②③④⑤
49.
50. ①②③④⑤

ANSWER SHEET PRACTICE TEST 1: DIAGNOSTIC TEST

Language Arts, Writing—Part II Essay Test

_____

_____

_____

_____

_____

_____

_____

_____

_____

_____

_____

_____

_____

_____

_____

_____

_____

_____

answer sheet

Language Arts, Writing—Part II Essay Test (continued)

_____

_____

_____

_____

_____

_____

_____

_____

_____

_____

_____

_____

_____

_____

_____

_____

_____

_____

_____

_____

LANGUAGE ARTS, WRITING

The Language Arts, Writing Test consists of two parts. Part I is a multiple-choice section, and Part II is an essay section. You must begin with Part I.

You will have 75 minutes to work on Part I. If you finish Part I early, you can proceed to Part II right away. The total time allowed for both parts of the test is 2 hours (120 minutes).

LANGUAGE ARTS, WRITING, PART I

75 Minutes • 50 Questions

Directions: This part of the Language Arts, Writing Test consists of 50 multiple-choice questions based on documents that contain numbered sentences. After reading a document, answer the multiple-choice questions that follow it.

Some of the numbered sentences contain errors in usage, sentence structure, or mechanics (spelling, punctuation, and capitalization). Other sentences are correctly written. The best answer to a question referring to a correctly written sentence is the one that leaves the sentence unchanged. The best version of a sentence will be consistent with the rest of the document in verb tense and point of view.

The time allowed to answer all 50 questions is 75 minutes. If you finish Part I early, you may proceed immediately to Part II (the essay section).

Record your answers on the answer sheet provided.

diagnostic test

QUESTIONS 1–9 REFER TO THE FOLLOWING E-MAIL MEMORANDUM.

Subject: Reduction in workforce

From: Jack Reingold <jack.reingold@titantechno.com>
To: All members of Omega sales team

(A)

(1) Clearly, today's challenging economic times are adversely effecting profits here at Titan Technologies, requiring that we pare internal expenses at every level within the organization. (2) As the entire Omega sales team knows, sales of Titan's patented medical devices were in steady decline over the past three years. (3) Last year they accounted for only 25 percent of our revenue, down from 40 percent five years ago. (4) To make matters worse, we're finding it difficult to raise enough capital to fund Titan's current research and development plans.

(B)

(5) Unavoidable is a reduction in our sales force, unfortunately. (6) I regret to inform you that the employment of all Omega sales team members will end Friday, October 18. (7) Be assured that each one of you will receive severance pay equal to your current base salary for a period of six months. (8) Also, your medical coverage will continue for one year or if you find other coverage, whichever occurs earlier.

(C)

(9) If you're planning to look for other employment, Titan management would like to aid you in your transition. (10) We have made arrangements with a consulting firm for this purpose. (11) They specialize in executive recruiting and are ready to assist you in this respect during the next six months. (12) Please contact Jenny Beazer in Human Resources (ext. 477) for details.

(D)

(13) The Omega team sales meeting scheduled for Monday, October 14, in light of these new developments, is canceled.

(E)

(14) I value greatly the contributions that each of you have made to this company, and I wish all of you the very best in your future endeavors.

In appreciation,

Jack Reingold
CEO, Titan Technologies

1. Sentence 1: **Clearly, today's challenging economic times are adversely effecting profits here at Titan Technologies, requiring that we pare internal expenses at every level within the organization.**

   Which correction should be made to sentence 1?

   (1) remove the comma after <u>Clearly</u>
   (2) replace <u>effecting</u> with <u>affecting</u>
   (3) replace <u>profits</u> with <u>prophets</u>
   (4) change <u>requiring</u> to <u>require</u>
   (5) replace <u>pare</u> with <u>pair</u>

2. Sentence 2: **As the entire Omega sales team knows, sales of Titan's patented medical devices <u>were in steady decline over</u> the past three years.**

   Which is the best way to write the underlined portion of sentence 2? If the original is the best way, select answer choice (1).

   (1) were in steady decline over
   (2) are steadily declining over
   (3) have been in steady decline for
   (4) were declining steadily during
   (5) has been declining steadily for

3. Sentence 5: **Unavoidable is a reduction in our sales force, unfortunately.**

   Which is the most effective way to write sentence 5? If the original way is best, select answer choice (1).

   (1) Unavoidable is a reduction in our sales force, unfortunately.
   (2) Unfortunately for our sales force, reductions can't be avoided.
   (3) Reducing our sales force was not to be avoided, unfortunately.
   (4) Unfortunately, reducing our sales force is unavoidable.
   (5) It is unfortunate that, for our sales force, a reduction is unavoidable.

4. Sentence 8: **Also, your medical coverage will continue for one year or if you find other coverage, whichever occurs earlier.**

   Which correction should be made to sentence 8?

   (1) remove the comma after <u>Also</u>
   (2) insert the word <u>either</u> after <u>for</u>
   (3) insert a comma after <u>year</u>
   (4) change <u>if</u> to <u>until</u>
   (5) change <u>whichever</u> to <u>whatever</u>

5. Sentence 9: **If you're planning to look for other employment, Titan management would like to aid you in your transition.**

   Which correction should be made to sentence 9?

   (1) remove the comma
   (2) change <u>would</u> to <u>will</u>
   (3) replace <u>aid</u> with <u>aide</u>
   (4) change <u>you</u> to <u>yourself</u>
   (5) no correction is necessary

6. Sentence 10 and Sentence 11: **We have made arrangements with a consulting firm for this purpose. They specialize in executive recruiting and are ready to assist you in this respect during the next six months.**

   The most effective combination of sentences 10 and 11 would include which group of words?

   (1) for this purpose, specializing in
   (2) consulting firm specializing in
   (3) for the next six months they are ready
   (4) To assist you in this respect, a consulting firm
   (5) arrangements to assist you in this respect

7. **Sentence 13: The Omega team sales meeting scheduled for Monday, October 14, in light of these new developments, is canceled.**

   The most effective revision of sentence 13 would begin with which group of words?

   (1) In light of these new developments

   (2) Canceling the scheduled meeting of

   (3) Scheduled for Monday, October 14

   (4) These new developments, which mean that

   (5) The Omega team sales meeting, due to

8. **Sentence 14: I value greatly the contributions <u>that each of you have made</u> to this company, and I wish all of you the very best in your future endeavors.**

   Which is the best way to write the underlined portion of sentence 14? If the original is the best way, select answer choice (1).

   (1) that each of you have made

   (2) made by all of you

   (3) that all you have made

   (4) that each of you has made

   (5) which were all made

9. Which revision would improve the effectiveness of the memorandum?

   (1) move sentence 1 to the beginning of paragraph B

   (2) move paragraph A to follow paragraph B

   (3) move paragraph C to follow paragraph D

   (4) join paragraphs C and D

   (5) move sentence 9 to follow sentence 13

QUESTIONS 10–17 REFER TO THE FOLLOWING PASSAGE OF TEXT.

(A)

(1) There's pressure put on many high-school students to take the most advanced placement classes and to score highest in their class on the SATs. (2) They're also pressured to participate in as many extracurricular activities as they can.

(B)

(3) For some the pressure may be fuel for success, for others it can be too much. (4) Try carrying a 4.6 grade-point average while being editor of the school newspaper and captain of the volleyball team is each quite an accomplishment in itself. (5) But to do them all at once might not be doing yourself any favors.

(C)

(6) You're only young once, as they say. (7) What about social life? (8) Overachieving students typically don't have time to date or hang out with friends. (9) For someone who was 18 years old and never took the time to truly enjoy his or her high-school years, it's too late.

(D)

(10) Some are pressured to take all the "correct" classes and join all the "correct" school clubs, ignoring the types of classes and activities they're best at. (11) It's far better to focus on what they're naturally good at and have a passion for, not on what other people tell you should be in an application to an Ivy League college.

(E)

(12) Trying to accomplish too many goals at once also means you might fail to achieve any of them by spreading yourself too thin. (13) Concentrate on what you like best, and forget the rest.

10. Sentence 1: **There's pressure put on many high-school students to take the most advanced placement classes and to score highest in their class on the SATs.**

The most effective revision of sentence 1 would begin with which group of words?

(1) The pressure put on many high-school students

(2) To take the most advanced placement classes

(3) Many high-school students are pressured to

(4) High-school students who take the most

(5) Putting pressure on many high-school students

11. Sentence 3: **For some the pressure may be fuel for success, for others it can be too much.**

Which correction should be made to sentence 3?

(1) remove the word the

(2) replace may be with maybe

(3) remove the comma after success

(4) insert the word but after the comma

(5) replace too with to

12. Sentence 4: **Try carrying a 4.6 grade-point average while being editor of the school newspaper and captain of the volleyball team is each quite an accomplishment in itself.**

Which is the best way to write the underlined portion of sentence 4? If the original is the best way, select answer choice (1).

(1) team is each quite an accomplishment in itself

(2) team. Any of them would be quite accomplished

(3) team itself. Each one is quite an accomplishment

(4) team, each one being quite an accomplishment

(5) team. Each is quite an accomplishment in itself

13. Sentence 5: **But to do them all at once might not be doing yourself any favors.**

Which correction should be made to sentence 5?

(1) replace to do with doing

(2) change might to may

(3) change doing to do

(4) change yourself to you

(5) no correction is necessary

14. Sentence 9: **For someone who was 18 years old and never took the time to truly enjoy his or her high-school years, it's too late.**

Which correction should be made to sentence 9?

(1) change who to whom

(2) change was to is

(3) remove the comma after years

(4) insert the word then after the comma

(5) replace it's with its

15. Which revision would improve the effectiveness of paragraph C?

(1) move sentence 9 to the beginning of paragraph C

(2) move sentence 6 to follow sentence 9

(3) remove sentence 6

(4) move sentence 7 to follow sentence 8

(5) move sentence 8 to follow sentence 9

16. Sentence 11: **It's far better to focus on what they're naturally good at and have a passion for, not on what other people tell you should be in an application to an Ivy League college.**

Which correction should be made to sentence 11?

(1) change they're to you're
(2) insert a comma after at
(3) remove the word on
(4) replace college with College
(5) no correction is necessary

17. Sentence 12: **Trying to accomplish too many goals at once also means you might fail to achieve any of them by spreading yourself too thin.**

If you rewrote sentence 12 beginning with

Also, spreading yourself too thin

the next words should be

(1) accomplishing too many goals
(2) by trying to accomplish too many
(3) to achieve any of your goals
(4) also means you are trying to accomplish
(5) by failing to achieve any of the goals

QUESTIONS 18–26 REFER TO THE FOLLOWING DOCUMENT.

(A)

(1) This page provides directions to the Central City Convention Center from the airport, train station, the 58 Freeway. (2) Be sure to print out this page and have it handy when reaching Central City.

From the Airport:

(B)

(3) If your arrival is by air you rent a car, follow the sign to Manning Road as you exit the airport. (4) Take Manning 1.5 miles south to Grant Avenue. (5) Look for the Marriott Hotel sign on the corner of Manning and Grant. (6) Turn left at Grant, then right on Dakota Street, about a half mile east on Grant. (7) The convention center is on your right, one block east on Dakota. (8) The address of the convention center is 33920 Dakota Street.

From Central Station:

(C)

(9) For those arriving by train, the convention center is within easy walking distance. (10) From Central Station, go west on 3rd Street two blocks, and then right on Dakota Street. You'll see the convention center on your left.

From the 58 Freeway:

(D)

(11) Traveling east on the 58 Freeway, take the Manning Road exit. (12) Turn left, go under the freeway, and continue on Manning 3 miles (about a mile passed Rodenberry Blvd.). (13) When you reach Lincoln Parkway, turn right and then make another right at Dakota Street (about half a mile east on Lincoln). (14) The convention center will be three blocks down Dakota, on your left.

(E)

(15) Traveling west on the 58 Freeway, take the East Lincoln Parkway exit. (15) After you take this exit you'll be on Lincoln. (16) Continue 2 miles northwest along Lincoln until you reach Dakota Street. (17) Turn left onto Dakota. (18) On Dakota, three blocks south of Lincoln, is the convention center.

18. Sentence 1: **This page provides directions to the Central City Convention Center from the airport, <u>train station, the 58 Freeway</u>.**

    Which is the best way to write the underlined portion of sentence 1? If the original is the best way, select answer choice (1).

    (1) train station, the 58 Freeway

    (2) the train station, and the 58 Freeway

    (3) from the train station, the 58 Freeway

    (4) and from the train station, the 58 Freeway

    (5) from the train station, and the 58 Freeway

19. Sentence 3: **If your arrival is by air you rent a car, follow the sign to Manning Road as you exit the airport.**

    Which correction should be made to sentence 3?

    (1) change <u>your arrival is</u> to <u>you arrive</u>

    (2) insert the word <u>and</u> after <u>air</u>

    (3) insert the word <u>than</u> after the comma

    (4) replace <u>sign</u> with <u>sine</u>

    (5) change <u>exit</u> to <u>have exited</u>

20. Sentence 6: **Turn left at Grant, then right on Dakota Street, about a half mile east on Grant.**

    Which is the most effective revision of sentence 6? If the original is the best version, select answer choice (1).

    (1) Turn left at Grant, then right on Dakota Street, about a half mile east on Grant.

    (2) After turning left at Grant, then right on Dakota Street, about a half mile east on Grant.

    (3) Turn left at Grant, about a half mile east on Grant. Then turn right on Dakota Street.

    (4) Turn right at Dakota Street about a half mile east of turning left at Grant.

    (5) Turn left at Grant. About a half mile east on Grant, turn right on Dakota Street.

21. Sentence 7: **The convention center is on your right, one block east along Dakota.**

    Which correction should be made to sentence 7?

    (1) replace <u>convention</u> with <u>Convention</u>

    (2) change <u>is</u> to <u>will be</u>

    (3) remove the comma after <u>right</u>

    (4) replace <u>one</u> with <u>won</u>

    (5) no correction is necessary

22. Which revision should be made to the placement of sentence 8?

    (1) move sentence 8 to the beginning of paragraph B

    (2) remove sentence 8

    (3) move sentence 8 to paragraph A

    (4) move sentence 8 to the end of paragraph C

    (5) no revision is necessary

23. Sentence 9: **For those arriving by train, the convention center is within easy walking distance.**

    Which correction should be made to sentence 9?

    (1) change <u>those</u> to <u>them</u>

    (2) insert <u>who is</u> after <u>those</u>

    (3) change <u>is</u> to <u>are</u>

    (4) remove the word <u>within</u>

    (5) no correction is necessary

24. Sentence 10: **From Central Station, go west on 3rd Street two blocks, and then right at Dakota Street.**

    Which correction should be made to sentence 10?

    (1) replace west with West
    (2) insert the word for after Street
    (3) change blocks to block
    (4) remove the word and after the comma
    (5) insert the word turn after then

25. Sentence 12: **Turn left, go under the freeway, and continue on Manning 3 miles (about a mile passed Rodenberry Blvd.).**

    Which correction should be made to sentence 12?

    (1) change go to and go
    (2) remove the word go
    (3) replace freeway with Freeway
    (4) remove the comma after freeway
    (5) replace passed with past

26. Sentence 18: **On Dakota, three blocks south of Lincoln, is the convention center.**

    The most effective revision of sentence 18 would begin with which group of words?

    (1) Three blocks, south of Lincoln
    (2) South on Lincoln three blocks
    (3) On Dakota is the convention
    (4) The convention center is
    (5) Three blocks south on Dakota

QUESTIONS 27–34 REFER TO THE FOLLOWING DOCUMENT.

Summary of GUAA Benefits

(A)

(1) All members of the Graystone University Alumni Association (GUAA) are entitled to the benefits listed in this summary.

(B)

(2) GUAA members receive the GUAA quarterly magazine *Graystone Heritage*. (3) Each issue highlights current alumni endeavors. (4) Each issue also features a message from the current president and lists recent accomplishments of Graystone university faculty.

(C)

(5) With many thousands of members, GUAA can offer affordable health and life-insurance coverage. (6) GUAA group coverage is underwritten by Americo Insurance Group. (7) Note that GUAA insurance benefits extend to qualifying members of members' family as well.

(D)

(8) Once a year in the third week of July, GUAA reserves Lake Burlwood Resort so members and their families can enjoy a retreat from their hectic daily lives and catch up with former classmates. (9) Activities for the entire family are available, ranging from swimming and canoeing to lectures, cooking classes, and art classes.

(E)

(10) GUAA members can contact former classmates and make new acquaintances by tapping an alumni network of over 300,000 members.

(F)

(11) Those joining GUAA are also entitled to the following four benefits:

- (12) A 10-percent discount on all items purchased at the campus store (excluding computer hardware)

- (13) Full access to the Faulding Library, including online access and including the library's Special Collections room

- (14) All resources at our career and job placement center (job listings, workshops, etc.)

- (15) Use of the Heritage House and Fleming Center facilities for receptions, conferences, and other private events (by reservation one year in advance)

(G)

(16) Graduating from Graystone University does not automatically enroll you in GUAA. (17) The easiest way to join GUAA is by enrolling online, at the GUAA Web site. (18) As a GUAA member, you can post your personal profile at our Web site so that other network members can easily connect with you.

27. Sentence 4: **Each issue also features a message from the current president and lists recent accomplishments of Graystone university faculty.**

Which correction should be made to sentence 4?

(1) change <u>features</u> to <u>feature</u>

(2) replace <u>president</u> with <u>President</u>

(3) insert a comma after <u>president</u>

(4) replace <u>university</u> with <u>University</u>

(5) no correction is necessary

28. Sentence 7: **Note that GUAA insurance benefits extend to qualifying <u>members of members' family</u> as well.**

Which is the best way to correct the underlined portion of sentence 7? If the original is the best way, select answer choice (1).

(1) members of members' family

(2) member's family

(3) family members

(4) families of a member

(5) members of a members'

29. Sentence 8: **Once a year in the third week of July, GUAA reserves Lake Burlwood Resort so members and their families can enjoy a retreat from their hectic daily lives and catch up with former classmates.**

Which correction should be made to sentence 8?

(1) insert a comma after <u>year</u>

(2) change <u>so</u> to <u>for</u>

(3) replace <u>can</u> with <u>to</u>

(4) replace <u>their</u> with <u>they're</u>

(5) insert a comma after <u>lives</u>

30. Sentence 9: **Activities for the entire family are available, ranging from swimming and canoeing to lectures, cooking classes, and art classes.**

The most effective revision of sentence 9 would begin with which group of words?

(1) Lectures, cooking classes

(2) Ranging from swimming

(3) Available are activities

(4) Swimming and canoeing

(5) Activities ranging from

31. Sentence 11: **<u>Those joining GUAA</u> are also entitled to the following four benefits.**

Which is the best way to revise the underlined portion of sentence 11? If the original is the best way, select answer choice (1).

(1) Those joining GUAA

(2) Joining GUAA, they

(3) By joining GUAA

(4) Members of GUAA

(5) Join GUAA. They

32. Sentence 13: **Full access to the Faulding Library, including online access <u>and including the library's</u> Special Collections room**

Which is the best way to revise the underlined portion of line 13? (Line 13 need **not** be a complete sentence.) If the original is the best way, select answer choice (1).

(1) and including the library's

(2) as well as to the library's

(3) as well as access to the library's

(4) of which includes library

(5) which includes the library's

33. Sentence 14: **All resources at our career and job placement center (job listings, workshops, etc.)**

The most effective revision of line 14 would begin with which group of words? (Line 14 need **not** be a complete sentence.)

(1) Any resource

(2) Use of all resources

(3) Accessing all

(4) Every resource

(5) All our resources

34. Which revision would improve the effectiveness of the document?

(1) move sentence 1 to the beginning of paragraph G

(2) move sentence 18 to follow sentence 10

(3) remove sentence 16

(4) move sentence 4 to follow sentence 2

(5) move sentence 7 to follow sentence 1

QUESTIONS 35–42 REFER TO THE FOLLOWING PASSAGE OF TEXT.

(A)

(1) Business failures aren't always caused by inefficiency or by poor relations between its management and lower-level workers. (2) A well-managed company failed because their leaders don't respond to an ever-changing world. (3) Leaders of a business might stumble into this trap by waiting too long to see what develops. (4) Other times they are simply so afraid to lose that they are incapable of the bold action required for success. (5) Regardless, if leaders operate with limited vision the company will suffer.

(B)

(6) What happened to the big auto company General Motors is a classic example. (7) As the latter half of the last century had began, GM was the world's preeminent auto company. (8) But Japan started producing cars that more people wanted because Japanese cars were more practical, efficient, and safer.

(C)

(9) GM ignored these developments and decided to continue its strategy of "planned obsolescence." (10) It tried to dictate what consumers would buy instead of responding to what consumers wanted. (11) While Japanese and European auto companies gained market share steadily throughout the 1990s and into the new century. (12) But GM stuck to its familiar ways.

(D)

(13) Eventually, GM did try to move forward with a new electric car, the Chevy Volt. (14) However, it was too late to save the company when that model went into development. (15) GM had been badly outmaneuvered and ended up bankrupt.

35. Sentence 1: **Business failures aren't always caused by inefficiency or by poor relations between its management and lower-level workers.**

    Which correction should be made to sentence 1?

    (1) change <u>Business</u> to <u>A business's</u>
    (2) change <u>failures</u> to <u>failure</u>
    (3) remove the word <u>by</u> after <u>or</u>
    (4) change <u>relations</u> to <u>relation</u>
    (5) remove the word <u>its</u>

36. Sentence 2: **A well-managed company <u>failed because their leaders don't</u> respond to an ever-changing world.**

    Which is the best way to write the underlined portion of sentence 2? If the original is the best way, select answer choice (1).

    (1) failed because their leaders don't
    (2) can fail if its leaders don't
    (3) could fail because their leaders didn't
    (4) might fail if their leaders didn't
    (5) fails when its leaders didn't

37. Sentence 4: **Other times they are simply so afraid to lose that they are incapable of the bold action required for success.**

    Which correction should be made to sentence 4?

    (1) remove the word <u>so</u>
    (2) replace <u>lose</u> with <u>loose</u>
    (3) insert a comma after <u>lose</u>
    (4) change <u>success</u> to <u>succeeding</u>
    (5) no correction is necessary

38. Sentence 7: **As the latter half of the last century had began, GM was the world's preeminent auto company.**

    Which correction should be made to sentence 7?

    (1) replace <u>latter</u> with <u>ladder</u>
    (2) replace <u>century</u> with <u>Century</u>
    (3) remove the word <u>had</u>
    (4) replace <u>world's</u> with <u>worlds'</u>
    (5) no correction is necessary

39. Sentence 8: **But Japan started producing cars that more people wanted because Japanese cars were more practical, efficient, and safer.**

    Which correction should be made to sentence 8?

    (1) insert the word <u>when</u> after <u>But</u>
    (2) change <u>Japan</u> to <u>Japanese</u>
    (3) change <u>that</u> to <u>which</u>
    (4) change <u>wanted</u> to <u>want</u>
    (5) insert the word <u>more</u> after the first comma

40. Sentence 9 and Sentence 10: **GM ignored these developments and decided to continue its strategy of <u>"planned obsolescence." It tried to dictate</u> what consumers would buy instead of responding to what consumers wanted.**

    Which is the best revision of the underlined portion of sentences 9 and 10?

    (1) "planned obsolescence" which was trying to dictate
    (2) "planned obsolescence" to try and to dictate
    (3) "planned obsolescence," trying to dictate
    (4) "planned obsolescence." Try to dictate
    (5) "planned obsolescence." They try to dictate

41. Sentence 11: **While Japanese and European auto companies gained market share steadily throughout the 1990s and into the new century.**

Which correction should be made to sentence 11?

(1) remove the word <u>While</u>

(2) replace <u>European</u> with <u>european</u>

(3) insert a comma after <u>share</u>

(4) replace <u>1990s</u> with <u>1990's</u>

(5) insert a comma after <u>1990s</u>

42. Sentence 14: **However, it was too late to save the company when that model went into development.**

The most effective revision of sentence 14 would include which group of words?

(1) It was too late, and saving the company

(2) too late, because to save the company

(3) development of that model to save

(4) into development too late to save

(5) Saving the company, however, was

QUESTIONS 43–50 REFER TO THE FOLLOWING DOCUMENT.

(A)

(1) All domestic and international flights of this airline are subject to the rules described in this notice.

(B)

(2) Up to three pieces of baggage altogether are allowed per each passenger. (3) Economy-class passengers are limited to one carry-on item. (4) Otherwise, up to two pieces of carry-on baggage are allowed, which includes items such as small suitcases and backpacks.

(C)

(5) In addition to carry-on baggage, one other personal item, such as an umbrella, purse, or laptop computer, will be allowed on board. (6) Briefcases and garment bags are considered carry-on, not personal items.

(D)

(7) The total weight of carry-on items cannot exceed 50 pounds. (8) The longest dimension of a carry-on item cannot exceed 22 inches. (9) All checked and carry-on baggage is subject to specific weight and size restrictions. (10) The total weight of checked baggage cannot exceed 70 pounds. (11) The longest dimension of the largest piece of checked baggage cannot exceed 62 inches.

(E)

(12) Federal regulations restrict certain sharp objects, sporting goods, tools, and firearms strictly to an aircraft's checked baggage areas. (13) Certain other types of items such as explosives and flammable liquids, can be neither checked nor carried on board.

(F)

(14) A non-flammable liquid (for example, shampoo or lotion) can be carried on board only if stored in a container not exceeding 3 ounces. (15) Liquids can expand, so to prevent a container from leaking or breaking, it is recommended that you fill it no more than three quarters of its full capacity (unless the container is new and unopened). (16) For a complete list of restricted items, you can either call the U.S. Transportation Security Agency or visit the TSA Web site (www.tsa.gov).

43. Sentence 2: **Up to three pieces of baggage altogether are allowed per each passenger.**

    Which correction should be made to sentence 2?

    (1) replace <u>altogether</u> with <u>all together</u>

    (2) change <u>are</u> to <u>is</u>

    (3) replace <u>allowed</u> with <u>aloud</u>

    (4) insert a comma after <u>allowed</u>

    (5) remove the word <u>each</u> after <u>per</u>

44. Sentence 4: **Otherwise, up to two pieces of carry-on baggage <u>are allowed, which includes</u> items such as small suitcases and backpacks.**

    Which is the best way to write the underlined portion of sentence 4? If the original is the best way, select answer choice (1).

    (1) are allowed, which includes

    (2) are allowed. Included is

    (3) is allowed, which includes

    (4) are allowed, including

    (5) are allowed. Included are

45. Sentence 5: **In addition to carry-on baggage, one other personal item, such as an umbrella, purse, or laptop <u>computer, will be</u> allowed on board.**

    Which is the best way to write the underlined portion of sentence 5? If the original is the best way, select answer choice (1).

    (1) computer, will be

    (2) computer, are

    (3) computers, will be

    (4) computer, is

    (5) computers, are

46. Sentence 6: **Briefcases and garment bags are considered <u>carry-on, not personal items</u>.**

    Which is the best way to write the underlined portion of sentence 6? If the original is the best way, select answer choice (1).

    (1) carry-on, not personal items

    (2) carry-on items, not personal items

    (3) as to be carry-on, not personal

    (4) carry-on items not personal

    (5) carry-on, which is not personal

47. Which revision would improve the effectiveness of paragraph D?

    (1) move sentence 10 to the beginning of paragraph D

    (2) remove sentence 8

    (3) move sentence 9 to the beginning of paragraph D

    (4) move sentence 8 to follow sentence 11

    (5) move sentence 10 to follow sentence 7

48. Sentence 13: **Certain other types of items such as explosives and flammable liquids, can neither be checked nor be carried on board.**

    Which correction should be made to sentence 13?

    (1) insert a comma after <u>items</u>

    (2) change <u>and</u> to <u>or</u>

    (3) remove the comma after <u>liquids</u>

    (4) change <u>nor</u> to <u>or</u>

    (5) change <u>carried</u> to <u>carrying</u>

49. Sentence 16: **For a complete list of restricted items, you can either call the U.S. Transportation Security Agency or visit the TSA Web site (www.tsa.gov).**

Which correction should be made to sentence 16?

(1) insert the word <u>these</u> after <u>of</u>

(2) remove the comma after <u>items</u>

(3) replace <u>Agency</u> with <u>agency</u>

(4) insert a comma after <u>agency</u>

(5) no correction is necessary

50. Which revision would improve the effectiveness of the document?

(1) join paragraphs B and C

(2) remove sentence 15

(3) move sentence 16 to follow sentence 1

(4) join paragraphs D and E

(5) move paragraph B to follow paragraph C

LANGUAGE ARTS, WRITING, PART II

45 Minutes • 1 Essay

Directions: This part of the Language Arts, Writing Test assesses your ability to write an essay on a familiar topic. In the essay, you will present your opinion or explain your views about the assigned topic. Your essay will be evaluated based on the overall quality of your writing, including content, organization, and the clarity and correctness of your writing. You must write only about the topic provided. If you write on a different topic, your essay will not be scored, and you will have to retake both parts of the Language Arts, Writing Test.

You will have 45 minutes to plan, write, and revise your essay. You may use scratch paper for notes, outlines, or a rough draft. Write your essay on the two pages of lined paper provided. The notes you make on scratch paper will not be read or scored. Write legibly using a ballpoint pen, so that your writing can easily be read by the evaluators.

ESSAY TOPIC

What kinds of character traits do you admire most in other people?

In your essay, identify specific admirable character traits and explain why you admire them. Use your personal observations, experience, and knowledge to support your essay.

Use this page for notes.

_____

_____

_____

_____

_____

_____

_____

_____

_____

_____

_____

_____

_____

_____

_____

_____

_____

_____

_____

_____

SOCIAL STUDIES

70 Minutes • 50 Questions

Directions: The Social Studies Test consists of multiple-choice questions involving general social studies concepts. The questions are based on brief passages of text and visual information (graphs, charts, maps, cartoons, and other figures). Some questions are based on both text and visual information. Study the information provided, and answer the question(s) that follow it, referring back to the information as needed. Record your answers on the Social Studies section of the answer sheet provided.

QUESTION 1 REFERS TO THE FOLLOWING INFORMATION.

UN peacekeeping forces are used when a neutral force is needed to ensure that a truce or peace agreement between two warring parties is enforced. The United Nations does not have any troops of its own and must rely on member countries to supply troops for its peacekeeping operations. As of March 2008, 113 countries were contributing a total of 88,862 military personnel to the UN. While the United States remains the largest financial contributor to the UN peacekeeping efforts, smaller, less wealthy nations supply the majority of the troops. The top five troop contributors to the United Nations are Bangladesh, Pakistan, India, Nigeria, and Ethiopia. As of February 2012, the UN had been involved in 63 peacekeeping operations, with 16 still in progress.

1. Which of the following statements identifies a similarity between UN forces and the military forces of individual countries?

   (1) UN forces try to maintain neutrality and engage only in peacekeeping missions.

   (2) The soldiers that form UN forces are from the military forces of other countries.

   (3) UN forces are paid for by contributions from many countries.

   (4) The soldiers of UN forces are never deployed in their own country.

   (5) UN forces are armed and sometimes engage in battle.

QUESTION 2 REFERS TO THE FOLLOWING INFORMATION.

The Eastern Woodland people of North America lived in what is now the northeastern part of the United States. The Mohawk, Oneida, Seneca, and other Native American groups there lived by hunting, farming corn and squash, fishing, and gathering berries. Native Americans of the Northwest, including Nootka, Tillamook, and Coos, survived by fishing for salmon, cod, herring, and halibut in the crowded streams and coastal waters and by using the trees of the huge forests of the area for many of their needs.

2. Based on information in the passage, which statement correctly compares the Native Americans of the Eastern Woodlands and the Northwest Coast?

    (1) Native Americans of both the Eastern Woodlands and the Northwest farmed.

    (2) Only the Native Americans of the Northwest fished,

    (3) The Eastern Woodlands peoples had a greater variety of food sources than the people of the Northwest Coast.

    (4) The Native Americans of the Northwest Coast were more advanced than those of the Eastern Woodlands.

    (5) The Native Americans of the Eastern Woodlands were more advanced than those of the Northwest Coast.

QUESTIONS 3 AND 4 ARE BASED ON THE FOLLOWING INFORMATION.

James Madison is sometimes known as the "father of the Constitution." He was a leading influence at the Constitutional Convention and wrote articles in support of the adoption of the Constitution. Here are some quotations from those articles:

"The accumulation of all powers—legislative, executive, and judiciary—in the same hands... is the very definition of tyranny."
   –James Madison, Federalist 47

"In order to lay a due foundation for that separate and distinct exercise of the different powers of government... it is evident that each [branch of government] should have a will of its own..."
   –James Madison, Federalist 51

3. Which statement best describes the argument Madison was making?

    (1) Instead of a president, executive power should be divided among several leaders.

    (2) The government's powers should be divided among Congress, the president, and the Supreme Court, and each of these institutions should operate independently.

    (3) A bill of rights should be added to the Constitution to prevent government from becoming tyrannical.

    (4) The president should carry out the will of Congress, which represents the people.

    (5) Supreme Court Justices should try to satisfy Congress rather than expressing their own independent views.

4. Based on the quotations from Madison, which one of the following values was most important to him?

    (1) the equality of all humans

    (2) democracy, or rule by the people

    (3) gaining power for himself

    (4) keeping the government from becoming oppressive

    (5) states' rights

QUESTION 5 IS BASED ON THE FOLLOWING INFORMATION.

During World War II, the United States fought together with Britain and the Soviet Union to defeat of Nazi Germany. The Soviet Union used the defeat of the Nazis as an opportunity to expand its territory, pushing its boundary much farther west and taking effective control of a number of Central European nations, including a section of Germany itself. The United States and Britain woke up to a new reality; they had stopped Germany from conquering Europe, but now most of Europe was in the hands of the Soviet Union. When the Soviet Union sought to take control of the sectors of Berlin still under the control of the United States and its allies, the U.S. decided to push back and try to stop the expansion of the Soviet Union. Thus began the Berlin Airlift to supply West Berlin, which had been blockaded by the Soviet forces. The Cold War had begun.

5. The author of the passage above infers that the cause of the Cold War was
   - (1) the defeat of the Nazis.
   - (2) the weakness of the United States and its allies after World War II.
   - (3) Soviet expansionism.
   - (4) the United States fighting with, rather than against, the Soviet Union in World War II.
   - (5) U.S. unwillingness to compromise.

QUESTIONS 6 AND 7 ARE BASED ON THE FOLLOWING CARTOON AND PASSAGE.

This cartoon was drawn in 1874 during the Reconstruction, an era of rebuilding after the U.S. Civil War.

6. To what does the motto "worse than slavery" above the head of the freed slaves refer?
   - (1) inhumane factory and farm labor conditions
   - (2) denying the children of freed slaves an education
   - (3) the Confederate South's cessation from the Union
   - (4) the development of white reactionary groups
   - (5) Southern lifestyles unfamiliar to former slaves

7. Which conclusion can best be drawn from this cartoon?
   - (1) Newly freed slaves had a difficult time adjusting to being treated as equals.
   - (2) Life for African Americans in the South improved as a result of the Civil War.
   - (3) True freedom for the African American would be a long struggle.
   - (4) The Ku Klux Klan was able and ready to help African Americans.
   - (5) Reconstruction succeeded in extending equality to the freed slaves.

QUESTION 8 IS BASED ON THE FOLLOWING INFORMATION.

The removal of the president from office is the ultimate check Congress has on the power of the president. The Constitution gives the House of Representatives the power, by a majority vote, to charge the president with "high crimes or misdemeanors"—an act referred to as impeachment. Then, the Senate conducts a trial of the president followed by a vote on whether or not to convict the president. A two-thirds majority is required to convict the president and remove him from office. Only 2 presidents have been impeached (charged) by the House of Representatives: Andrew Johnson in 1868 and William Clinton in 1998. In neither case did the Senate have the two-thirds majority necessary to convict the president and remove him from office. The removal of the president should be possible only in rare circumstances so that the separation of powers and the independence of the executive branch can be maintained.

8. Which statement expresses an opinion or a value judgment rather than a fact?

   (1) The removal of the president from office is the ultimate check Congress has on the power of the president.

   (2) The Senate conducts a trial of the president followed by a vote on whether or not to convict the president.

   (3) The removal of the president by Congress is difficult to accomplish due to the requirement of a two-thirds majority vote in the Senate.

   (4) Only rarely has a president been impeached, and never has Congress removed a president from office.

   (5) The removal of the president should be possible only in rare circumstances.

QUESTION 9 IS BASED ON THE FOLLOWING INFORMATION.

The introductory section, or "preamble," of the Declaration of Independence states in part: "When in the course of human events it becomes necessary for one people to dissolve the political bands which have connected them with another . . . a decent respect to the opinions of mankind requires that they should declare the causes which impel them to separation."

9. What does the Declaration of Independence set forth?

   (1) laws of a new nation

   (2) reasons for political separation

   (3) a list of constitutional guarantees

   (4) a new form of government

   (5) terms for establishing tariffs

QUESTIONS 10–12 REFER TO THE FOLLOWING GRAPH.
COST OF AN AVERAGE TRADITIONAL WEDDING

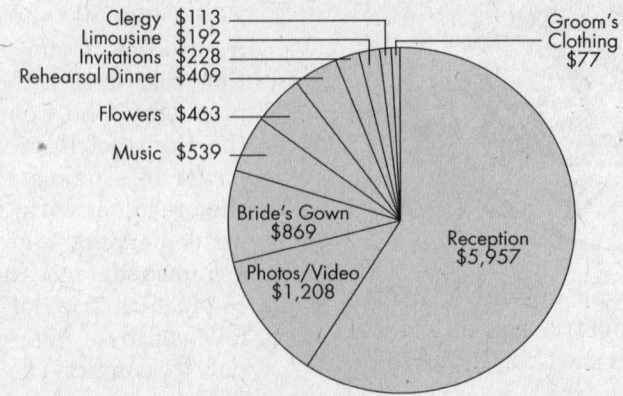

Clergy $113
Limousine $192
Invitations $228
Rehearsal Dinner $409
Flowers $463
Music $539
Bride's Gown $869
Photos/Video $1,208
Groom's Clothing $77
Reception $5,957

facebook.com/petersonspublishing

10. According to the graph, which two categories cost less than the limousine?
    - (1) invitations and clergy
    - (2) music and the flowers
    - (3) clergy and groom's clothing
    - (4) rehearsal dinner and invitations
    - (5) groom's and bride's clothing

11. A couple on a limited budget would save the most money by cutting back on which category?
    - (1) the reception
    - (2) the rehearsal dinner
    - (3) the invitations
    - (4) the photographs and video
    - (5) the music

12. The average traditional wedding shown in the graph costs slightly more than $10,000. About what portion of that amount is the cost of the reception?
    - (1) less than 10 percent
    - (2) about 90 percent
    - (3) about 30 percent
    - (4) a little less than half
    - (5) about 60 percent

QUESTIONS 13 AND 14 ARE BASED ON THE FOLLOWING INFORMATION.

A court of original jurisdiction has the authority to conduct the original trial of a case. This court is called the trial court. A court with appellate jurisdiction has the authority to hear an appeal of a case decided by a trial court. This court is called the appeals court. An appeals court does not conduct a new trial; instead if reviews the record of the trial and rules on whether or not the trial was conducted fairly and the law applied correctly.

U.S. FEDERAL COURT SYSTEM

COURT	ORIGINAL JURISDICTION	APPELLATE JURISDICTION
U.S. Supreme Court	Lawsuits between two state governments	Cases appealed from U.S. Court of Appeals and Cases appealed from state supreme courts
U.S. Courts of Appeals	None	Cases appealed from U.S. District Courts
U.S. District Courts	Cases involving federal law or the U.S. Constitution	None

13. What court would conduct the trial in a case in which the federal government charges a company of violating federal pollution regulations?
    - (1) a state trial court in the state in which the violation occurred
    - (2) the U.S. Supreme Court
    - (3) a state supreme court
    - (4) a U.S. District Court
    - (5) a U.S. Court of Appeals

14. Which court would conduct the trial in a case in which the state of Arizona is charging the state of California with violating an agreement between the two state governments on the usage of water from the Colorado River (which forms the boundary between the two states)?

   (1) U.S. Supreme Court

   (2) Arizona State Supreme Court

   (3) California State Supreme Court

   (4) U.S. District Court for Arizona

   (5) U.S. Court of Appeals for the Ninth District (which includes California and Arizona)

QUESTION 15 REFERS TO THE FOLLOWING INFORMATION.

MILITARY CAMPAIGNS—
U.S. REVOLUTIONARY WAR

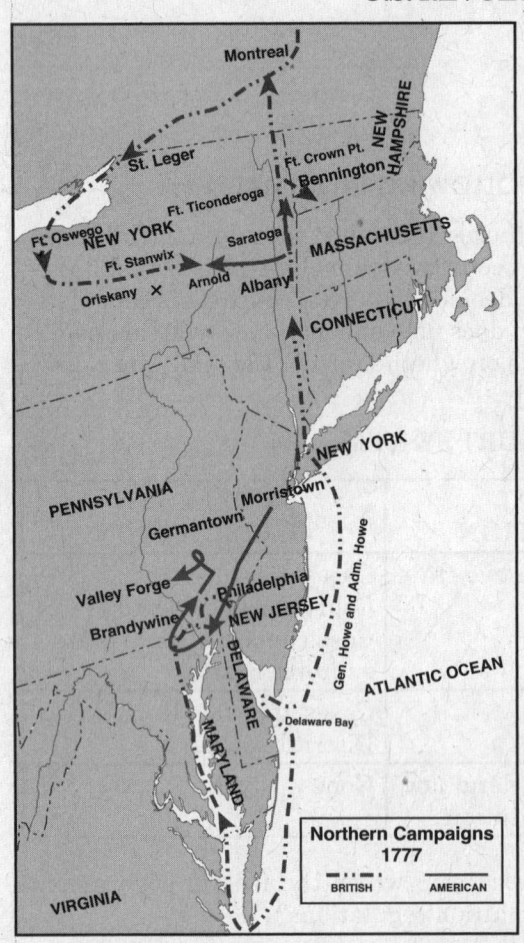

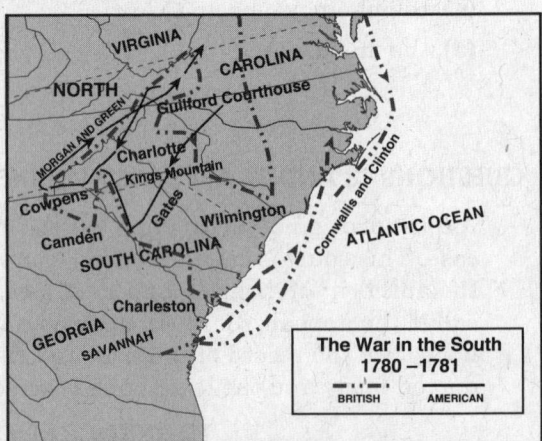

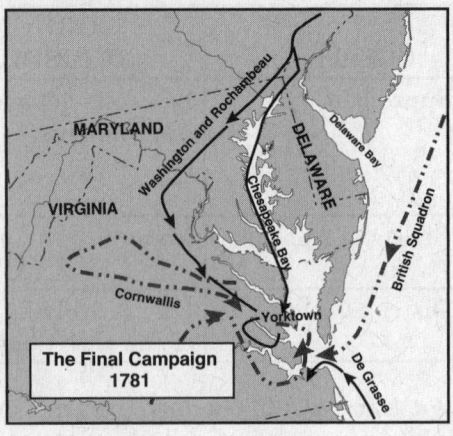

15. Which conclusion is best supported by the maps?

   (1) The Chesapeake Bay was of strategic importance to the British.

   (2) The final battle of the Revolutionary War took place in Pennsylvania.

   (3) General Howe's forces fought General Washington's forces.

   (4) The revolutionary army defeated the British by surrounding their forces.

   (5) The Revolutionary War began in the South and ended farther north.

President Franklin Roosevelt's New Deal (1933–1936) included a variety of programs designed to combat the Great Depression. The REA (now called Rural Utilities Service), TVA, and FDIC remain active today.

Works Progress Administration (WPA): Designed to reduce unemployment, the WPA employed 8 million people to build schools, airports, roads, bridges, national park lodges, and other public works.

Rural Electrification Administration (REA): The REA made loans available to rural electrification cooperatives organized by farmers in order to bring electrical power to rural areas.

Tennessee Valley Authority (TVA): Designed to spur the economic development of the Tennessee River Valley, the TVA built dams to generate electricity, control flooding, and allow river navigation.

Federal Deposit Insurance Corporation (FDIC): The FDIC set up a system to insure depositors in the case of a bank failure, thereby restoring trust in U.S. banks and ending runs on banks.

Civilian Conservation Corps (CCC): The CCC provided unskilled manual labor jobs for the unemployed in conservation projects on government-owned land.

16. One goal of the New Deal was to create jobs for the huge number of unemployed workers. Which one of the following New Deal programs would NOT do that?

    (1) Works Progress Administration

    (2) Rural Electrification Administration

    (3) Tennessee Valley Authority

    (4) Federal Deposit Insurance Corporation

    (5) Civilian Conservation Corps

17. Fiscal policy refers to government trying to influence the economy through its taxation and spending policies. Which statement best describes the economic beliefs underlying the fiscal policy of the New Deal?

    (1) Government should not try to fight a recession by creating government jobs; instead it should reduce regulation to encourage private enterprise to create jobs.

    (2) Government spending, especially to provide jobs for the unemployed, should be increased to stimulate the economy.

    (3) Government spending should be cut in order to balance the federal budget.

    (4) Since the government is taking in less money due to the depression, taxes should be raised to keep the government solvent.

    (5) Government should not spend tax dollars to improve the country's infrastructure.

18. Which New Deal program would most likely be of interest to an employed New York City worker who has some saved some money in a bank account?

    (1) Federal Deposit Insurance Corporation

    (2) Rural Electrification Administration

    (3) Tennessee Valley Authority

    (4) Works Progress Administration

    (5) Civilian Conservation Corps

QUESTIONS 19 AND 20 REFER TO THE FOLLOWING PASSAGE AND ILLUSTRATION.

The United States has seen steady, incremental monetary inflation going back to 1950. During a period of general monetary inflation, the price of goods and services increase (or "inflate") in terms of a specific currency (form of money), such as the U.S. dollar. At the same time, the value of that currency can decline relative to other currencies, depending on inflation rates in countries that use other currencies. The following illustration tells the story of the value of the U.S. dollar in selected years.

Purchasing Power of the Dollar

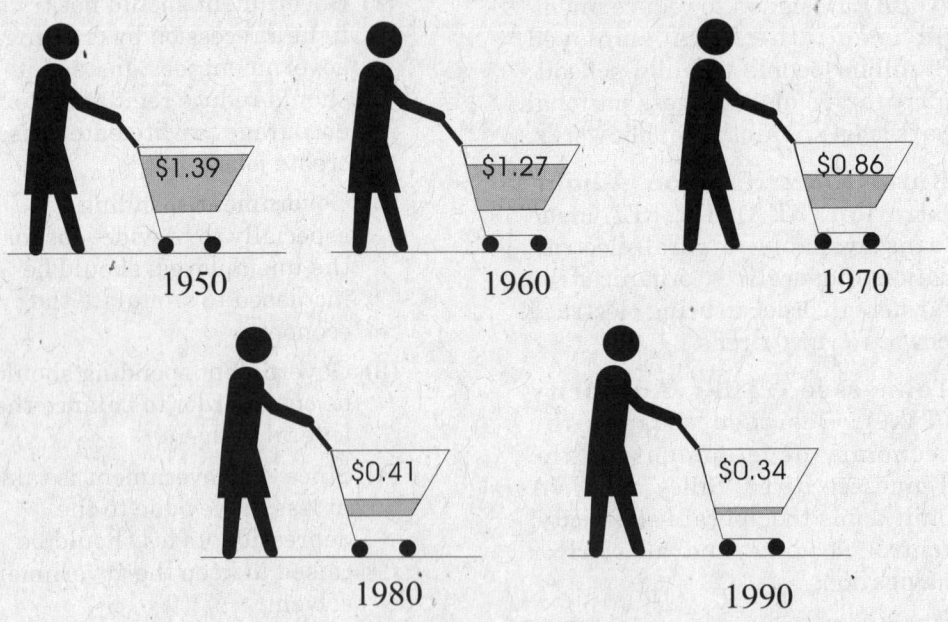

19. Referring to the illustration, which could be the base year, in which one dollar could buy one dollar's worth of goods?

    (1) 2001

    (2) 1976

    (3) 1967

    (4) 1983

    (5) 1900

20. During the first decade of this century, the Euro appreciated in value in relation to the U.S. dollar. How might a resident of a European country whose currency is the Euro be expected to respond to this relationship?

    (1) by taking vacations in the United States instead of Europe

    (2) by saving more money

    (3) by investing in European real estate

    (4) by exchanging their Euros for gold and silver

    (5) by spending more money on goods made in their own country

QUESTION 21 IS BASED ON THE FOLLOWING INFORMATION.

At the height of the Cold War struggle between the United States and the Soviet Union, President Kennedy stated in his inaugural address (January 20, 1961):

"In the long history of the world, only a few generations have been granted the role of defending freedom in its hour of maximum danger. I do not shrink from this responsibility—I welcome it. I do not believe that any of us would exchange places with any other people or any other generation. The energy, the faith, the devotion which we bring to this endeavor will light our country and all who serve it—and the glow from that fire can truly light the world. And so, my fellow Americans: ask not what your country can do for you but what you can do for your country."

21. What can we assume was President Kennedy's broad goal in making this speech?

    (1) encouraging people to accept higher taxes even if they don't get much in return

    (2) persuading Americans to join the Peace Corps

    (3) uniting Americans to support the struggle to contain the Soviet Union

    (4) getting more people to fight in the military

    (5) convincing Americans to join the civil rights movement

QUESTIONS 22–24 REFER TO THE FOLLOWING FIGURE AND INFORMATION.

LATITUDE AND LONGITUDE

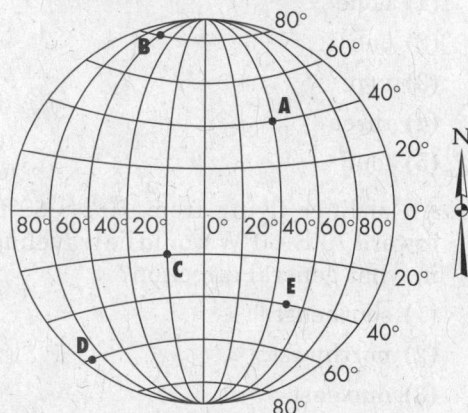

Mapmakers use meridians of longitude, which intersect at the two poles, and they use parallels of latitude to determine the exact locations of places on Earth. The meridian at 0° longitude is called the *prime meridian*. All other meridians of longitude are either east (E) or west (W) of the prime meridian. The equator, which separates the north latitudes (N) from the south latitudes (S), is at 0° latitude.

22. What would be the exact location of latitude 0° and longitude 0°?

    (1) anywhere along the equator

    (2) the point at which the prime meridian intersects the equator

    (3) the North Pole

    (4) the point at which the equator crosses latitude 0°

    (5) the point where the prime meridian intersects all other meridians

23. How many of the five points identified on the globe are located north of 60°S and between the prime meridian and 40°W?

    (1) none

    (2) one

    (3) two

    (4) three

    (5) four

24. An airliner flying from 30°N, 60°E toward 70°S, 60°W would be traveling in what general direction?

    (1) southeast

    (2) northwest

    (3) due east

    (4) southwest

    (5) northeast

QUESTION 25 IS BASED ON THE FOLLOWING INFORMATION.

Antarctica is the world's driest continent but paradoxically also contains most of the world's supply of fresh water. A desert is defined as a region that gets less than 10 inches of precipitation (rain, snow, sleet, etc.) a year. The coastal areas of Antarctica receive about 8 inches of annual precipitation, with the interior getting far less. The snow and ice that cover the continent and account for most of the fresh water on Earth have accumulated slowly over thousands of years. Ninety-eight percent of Antarctica is covered by ice, averaging one mile in depth.

25. Which of the following facts is most important in determining whether or not Antarctica is a desert?

    (1) Antarctica is the world's driest continent.

    (2) Antarctica is the coldest continent.

    (3) Antarctica has most of the world's fresh water supply.

    (4) Antarctica gets about 8 inches of precipitation along the coast, with much less precipitation in the interior.

    (5) Most precipitation in Antarctica is in the form of snowfall rather than rain.

QUESTION 26 IS BASED ON THE FOLLOWING INFORMATION.

The Vice President of the United States is given only one duty in the Constitution: to preside over the Senate. However, in practice, he seldom shows up to do this since this job is primarily a formality and doesn't give him any real power, except to break tie votes.

26. The vice president can be expected to be in the Senate chamber only when

    (1) a vote on an important bill or procedure is scheduled that is expected to be very close.

    (2) an important televised debate is taking place.

    (3) the Senate is conducting a trial of a president who has been impeached (charged with high crimes or misdemeanors) by the House.

    (4) the president requests the vice president speak for him in a Senate debate.

    (5) he wants to speak out on an issue.

QUESTION 27 REFERS TO THE FOLLOWING CARTOON.

27. What idea was the artist who drew the cartoon trying to convey?

    (1) The United States felt as though communism may spread chaos in Western Europe if Congress did not offer assistance to Western European nations.

    (2) The United States was in a race with the Soviet Union to help rebuild Western Europe.

    (3) Communists felt as though the U.S. Congress was being reckless with its foreign policy.

    (4) Western Europe needed assistance so badly that it would open its doors to democracy and communism as long as those nations received assistance.

    (5) The United States and the Soviets were racing to get out of Eastern Europe, and Western Europe was the only safe place to go.

QUESTIONS 28 AND 29 ARE BASED ON THE FOLLOWING PASSAGE.

The removal of Native Americans from land desired by white settlers began long before Americans crossed the Mississippi River. The Indian Removal Act of 1830 gave the U.S. government authority to relocate the native people of the South and Northwest to Indian Territory, an area set aside west of the Mississippi. There they would "cast off their savage habits and become an interesting, civilized, and Christian community," said President Jackson. During the forced migration, disease, severe weather, and hardships on the trail took their toll; thousands of Native Americans died. The Cherokee had a particularly hard time. Of about 20,000 removed from their homes, 4,000 died on the journey, which came to be known as the "Trail of Tears."

28. For what U.S. policy did the Indian Removal Act serve as a justification?

    (1) nonintervention

    (2) geographic expansion

    (3) civilizing Native Americans

    (4) Native American relocation

    (5) natural-resource conservation

29. What does the Cherokees' name for their journey, "Trail of Tears," suggest?

The name suggests that the Cherokees

(1) were forced to migrate against their will

(2) were not as civilized as other tribes

(3) planned to hurt the people responsible for their move

(4) wept constantly on the trail

(5) were frightened by the white settlers' guns

30. Retailers who operate only online have lower overhead costs than traditional print-catalog and brick-and-mortar retailers. In recent years, online retail sales have increased substantially, surpassing print-catalog sales. What is the best explanation for this development?

(1) People do not like being pressured by salespeople.

(2) People respond favorably to lower prices.

(3) Mail-order catalogs amount to wasted paper.

(4) You cannot test a product before you buy it online.

(5) Online ads are more persuasive than print ads.

QUESTIONS 31 AND 32 REFER TO THE FOLLOWING MAP.

TIME ZONES IN THE 48 CONTIGUOUS STATES

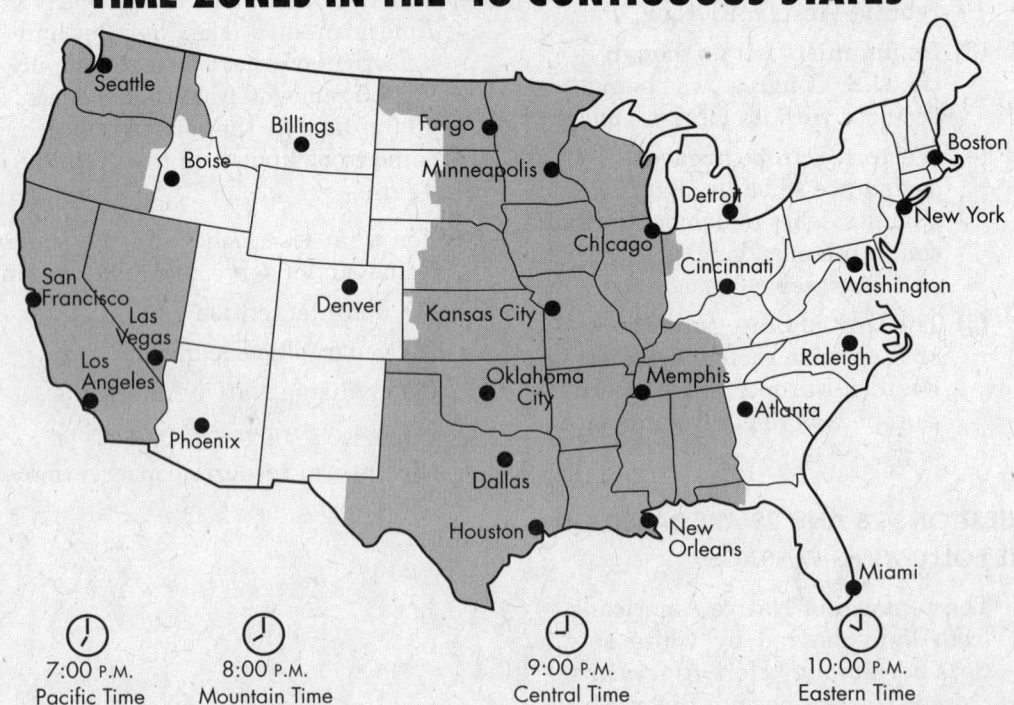

31. Which statement is supported by information on the map?

(1) Time zones are determined by scientists, not the government.

(2) Some states have more than one time zone.

(3) Excluding Alaska and Hawaii, there are only three time zones in the United States.

(4) People traveling from one time zone to another always lose an hour.

(5) The boundaries of time zones never change.

32. In which time zone in the United States would the coming of the new year first be celebrated?

(1) Eastern Time

(2) Central Time

(3) Mountain Time

(4) Pacific Time

(5) Alaska-Hawaii time

QUESTION 33 REFERS TO THE FOLLOWING INFORMATION.

From 1866 to 1915, around 25 million immigrants came to America, attracted to economic opportunities that the United States had to offer. Opportunistic labor-recruiting agents, steamship companies, and land-grant railroads all solicited labor overseas, advertising their abundant employment opportunities.

33. What was the main reason for the massive influx of immigrants to the United States from 1866 to 1915?

(1) expansion of overseas companies to the United States

(2) a desire for economic betterment

(3) political and religious persecution

(4) improved transportation technology

(5) fear that immigration would soon be prohibited

34. Although the number of members of the House of Representatives from a state varies according to state population, no state has fewer than one representative. After each census (every ten years), representation in the House is reconfigured.

What is a potential problem with the system outlined above?

(1) State lines can be redrawn to favor one political party.

(2) Small states are overrepresented in the House.

(3) Census figures often underestimate the U.S. population.

(4) Major shifts in population can occur very rapidly today.

(5) States with only one representative have no vote in Congress.

QUESTION 35 REFERS TO THE FOLLOWING INFORMATION.

In seventh-century Japan, land redistributions and higher taxes created a feudal system much like the one that characterized medieval Europe during the same period. Small farmers lost their land, leaving all the wealth and power in the hands of a few large landholders, who became feudal "lords" to the new tenant farmers. To defend their lands, these lords depended either on loyal family members or on "hired swords," who became known as samurai warriors. In the centuries that followed, Japan's emperors lost control over all but the capital city, and the samurai class gradually acquired the military and political power throughout much of rural Japan.

35. The rise of the samurai was facilitated by

   (1) the support by the samurai of the Japanese emperor.

   (2) land redistribution, which gave land to the samurai.

   (3) the desire of the Japanese to copy the feudal system of Europe.

   (4) the control of the capital city by the emperor.

   (5) the breakdown of central authority.

QUESTIONS 36 AND 37 ARE BASED ON THE FOLLOWING INFORMATION.

The distance of a region from the equator is only one of a number of factors that affect the climate of the region. Ocean currents have a big influence on climate; they can warm or cool shorelines as they pass. Altitude also has a strong influence, with climates getting colder as the altitude increases. Mountains not only tend to be colder but also wetter than other landforms. As air passing over mountains rises, it cools, and since cool air cannot hold as much moisture as warm air, rising air usually results in rainfall or snowfall. Prevailing winds also make a difference in climate; if prevailing winds bring polar air in winter and tropical air in summer, the climate will be characterized by extremes—very hot in the summer and very cold in the winter.

36. Which of the following would NOT have much influence on a region's climate?

   (1) distance from the equator

   (2) ocean currents

   (3) prevailing winds

   (4) altitude

   (5) population density

37. Murmansk is a Russian city on the Arctic Ocean far to the north of the Arctic Circle. Although it is one of Russia's farthest north ocean ports, it is one of the few that remains ice-free even in winter. What is the best explanation for this?

   (1) It must be closer to the equator.

   (2) Prevailing winds must be from the north.

   (3) There must be a warm ocean current.

   (4) There are no mountains nearby.

   (5) The altitude of the city must be lower than other Russian ocean port cities.

38. The system of checks and balances among branches of the federal government and between the two houses of Congress is also used in one way or another by every state. Forty-nine of the fifty states have bicameral, or two-house, legislatures. Nebraska is the only state with a unicameral, or one-house, legislature.

What is one possible disadvantage of the unicameral feature of Nebraska's legislative system?

   (1) Legislators might be too busy to vote on many important bills.

   (2) One interest group could dominate the entire legislature.

   (3) Voters would have fewer choices in elections.

   (4) Fewer people would have the opportunity to run for office.

   (5) The efficiency of state government could be compromised.

QUESTIONS 39 AND 40 REFER TO THE FOLLOWING INFORMATION.

WORLD WAR I—CHRONOLOGY OF KEY DATES AND EVENTS

1914   **June:** Austrian Archduke Franz Ferdinand and his wife are assassinated by Serbian students.

July: Blaming the Serbian government for the assassination, Austria declares war on Serbia; Russia, joined by France, mobilizes to support Austria.

August 1–3: Germany declares war on Russia and France and invades neutral Belgium. Britain demands that Germany withdraw from Belgium.

August 4: The Germans do not withdraw from Belgium, and the British declare war on Germany.

August: Russia marches on Prussia but is defeated by Germany at the Battle of Tannenberg.

August 13: Japan, through its formal alliance with Great Britain, declares war on Germany.

October 29: Turkey assists Germany in naval attack on Russia.

November 2: Russia declares war on Turkey.

November 5: Britain and France side with Russia to declare war on Turkey.

September–December: Germany initiates attacks on France and England (the attacks continue over the next two years).

1915   **May 25:** Italy enters the war on the side of Russia, Britain, and France.

1916   **February–November:** The Germans mount a continuing attack on France.

May 31–June 1: Germany and Britain engage in the war's only large-scale naval battle.

November 28: The Germans attack London for the first time, by air.

1917   **January–March:** In a German U-boat campaign, enemy and neutral ships, including some U.S. ships, are sunk on sight.

April 6: The United States declares war on Germany over the sinking of U.S. ships.

1918   **October:** The allies recover France and Belgium from German occupation.

October: The allies push Turkey back, forcing Turkey into an armistice treaty.

November: The allies push the Germans back beyond their critical line of defense.

November 9: Kaiser Wilhelm II of Germany abdicates his rule.

November 11: An Armistice is signed, bringing the war to an end.

39. Which of the following groups were allies in World War I?

    (1) Russia, Turkey, and Prussia

    (2) Russia, Britain, France, Italy, and the United States

    (3) Germany, Turkey, and Belgium

    (4) Japan, Germany, and Turkey

    (5) Britain, Belgium, Italy, and Turkey

40. Which statement best summarizes World War I?

    (1) A group of allies declares war on a small country, but the underdog ultimately wins.

    (2) A large bloc of aligned nations move to seize an entire region, but they are stopped by a superpower nation.

    (3) A flurry of unrelated wars among various countries eventually ends, but with no clear winners or losers.

    (4) One country invades another, and a group of nations opposed to the invasion rally to thwart the invader's plans.

    (5) A naval war between two small nations escalates into a ground and air war among several nations.

QUESTIONS 41 AND 42 REFER TO THE FOLLOWING INFORMATION.

The Constitution provides for changing times with a process for amendment, or change. Today, the Constitution includes 26 amendments. The first ten amendments, called the Bill of Rights, are outlined below.

BILL OF RIGHTS

First Amendment: Religious and political freedom

Second Amendment: The right to bear arms

Third Amendment: The right to refuse to house soldiers in peacetime

Fourth Amendment: Protection against unreasonable search and seizure

Fifth Amendment: The right of accused persons to due process of the law

Sixth Amendment: The right to a speedy and public trial

Seventh Amendment: The right to a jury trial in civil cases

Eighth Amendment: Protection against cruel and unusual punishment

Ninth Amendment: The rights of the people to powers that may not be spelled out in the Constitution

Tenth Amendment: The rights of the people and the states to powers not otherwise given to the federal government, states, or people

41. Which two amendments provide for changes over time in the circumstances and realities of American life?

    (1) the First and Second Amendments

    (2) the Fifth and Sixth Amendments

    (3) the Third and Fourth Amendments

    (4) the Ninth and Tenth Amendments

    (5) the Seventh and Eighth Amendments

42. A family that was forced by the U.S. Army to provide housing and food for a group of soldiers could appeal to the courts based on which amendment to the Constitution?

    (1) the Second Amendment

    (2) the Third Amendment

    (3) the Sixth Amendment

    (4) the Ninth Amendment

    (5) the Tenth Amendment

QUESTION 43 IS BASED ON THE FOLLOWING INFORMATION.

Although 476 A.D. is the year usually used to mark the fall of the Roman Empire in the west, its decline and fall was actually a gradual process that can't be given a single date. The "fall" of Rome in 476 A.D. was actually an internal revolt carried out by Germanic troops from within the Roman army. This event did not involve the defeat the Roman Army, which was already composed mainly of Germanic rather than Roman troops. Well before 476 A.D., the western Roman Empire had become increasingly populated and governed by Germanic peoples from the north. Historians are divided on when to date the end of the Roman Empire. Some use dates as early as the third century when the decline of Rome began, while others don't date the

end of the Roman Empire until the fall of Constantinople (present-day Istanbul, Turkey) in 1453.

43. Which general statement about the study of history is supported by information in the previous passage?

    (1) While historians sometimes disagree on the interpretation of history, they agree about the significance of particular events.

    (2) Historians tend to interpret history in the same way, although they disagree on the significance of particular events.

    (3) History is the study of dates and events, which is more scientific than the less exact study of gradual or underlying changes.

    (4) Major changes in history often happen gradually and resist attempts to assign a specific date to them.

    (5) Single earth-shaking events are more important in understanding history than gradual changes that are harder to date.

QUESTIONS 44 AND 45 REFER TO THE FOLLOWING PASSAGE.

When people make economic decisions, they must often give up something; for example, they give up taking a vacation in order to save for a car. The value of the thing given up is called *opportunity cost*. In another example, Maria is trying to decide whether to take a part-time night job that pays $200 per week or take courses for credit at the local community college. Her uncle will pay for her tuition and books if she decides to go to college. In addition, he will give her $100 per week.

44. What is Maria's opportunity cost of going to college?

   (1) $100 per week

   (2) college credits

   (3) the $200-per-week job

   (4) payment for tuition and books

   (5) working too slowly toward her degree

45. Why does Maria's decision involve opportunity cost?

   (1) She doesn't want her uncle to pay her college costs.

   (2) She wants both to work and to go to school.

   (3) Her resources (her uncle's money) are endless, so she can choose to take classes.

   (4) Her resources (time and money) are limited, so she must make a choice.

   (5) She would rather go to college than work at night.

46. Prior to the Pendleton Civil Service Reform Act of 1883, presidential and other federal government appointments were often made under an informal "spoils system," by which government jobs were given to loyal supporters rather than on the basis of merit.

Which of the following resulted from the demise of the spoils system?

   (1) civil liberties

   (2) political lobbying

   (3) civilian jury duty

   (4) term limits for elected officials

   (5) civil service exams

QUESTION 47 IS BASED ON THE FOLLOWING INFORMATION.

The Declaration of Independence contains the words "All people are created equal." Yet, at the time, half of the states had legalized slavery and only white, male landowners were permitted to vote in most states.

As the idea that all people really are equal has become more and more deeply embedded in American society, the right to vote has been extended. By the time of the Civil War, the property-owner requirement had been dropped, and states slowly expanded suffrage (the right to vote). After the Civil War, the Fifteenth Amendment (1870) granted African Americans the right to vote, and after World War I, the Nineteenth Amendment (1920) granted suffrage to women. The most recent extension of the right to vote was with the passage of the Twenty-sixth Amendment (1971) that lowered the voting age—which had been 21 in most states—to 18.

47. Which statement best summarizes this passage?

   (1) The right to vote has been extended several times since the nation was founded.

   (2) When the Declaration of Independence was written, most Americans didn't see the hypocrisy in stating "all men are created equal" because they had dehumanized slaves and thought women to be quite different from men.

   (3) As the idea of equality has taken deeper root in American democracy, the right to vote has gradually been extended to include those who are not wealthy, racial minorities, women, and young people.

   (4) Few Americans could actually vote when the Constitution was written.

   (5) Because voter turnout is so low in U.S. elections, the extension of the right to vote hasn't been something that has made much difference.

QUESTIONS 48 AND 49 REFER TO THE FOLLOWING TEXT AND GRAPH.

In 1991, U.S. economic growth stalled, and the country entered a recessionary period that lasted more than two years. During a recession, fewer people can afford to buy homes at prevailing prices and mortgage interest rates. The following graph shows new homes sales from August 1992 to July 1993.

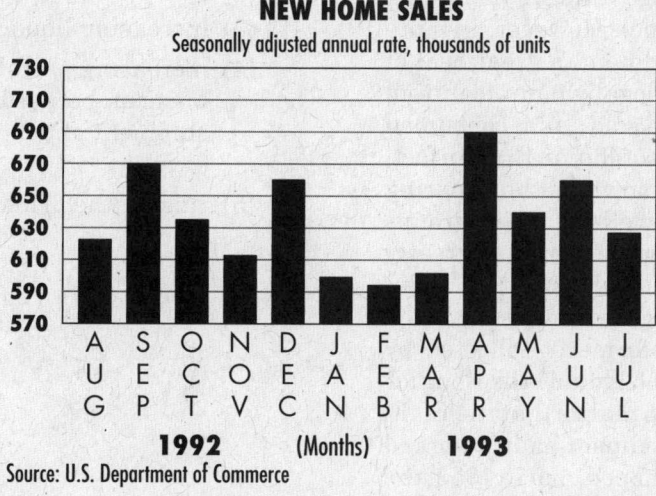

NEW HOME SALES
Seasonally adjusted annual rate, thousands of units

Source: U.S. Department of Commerce

48. Which statement does the graph best support?

   (1) Over the period shown, home prices declined but then increased.

   (2) The best time to buy a home was during the winter months.

   (3) Compared to 1991, the demand for housing in 1992 was weak.

   (4) The recession of the early 1990s ended by Spring of 1993.

   (5) Over the period shown, mortgage interest rates declined but then increased.

49. Around 2007, the United States entered another recession, and the demand for new homes fell again. However, mortgage interest rates were much lower than during the early 1990s.

Which is the best explanation for the decline in the demand for new homes, beginning in 2007?

   (1) Owners of pre-existing homes refused to sell their homes at a low price.

   (2) The population was declining, and so fewer people needed housing.

   (3) Home builders had shifted from residential construction to commercial projects.

   (4) The U.S. government had stepped up its loan assistance to first-time home buyers.

   (5) New homes were priced too high for prospective homeowners to afford.

QUESTION 50 REFERS TO THE FOLLOWING INFORMATION.

In 1919, the Eighteenth Amendment was passed making the manufacture, transport, and sale of alcoholic beverages illegal (including beer and wine). However, in spite of the amendment, a great deal of liquor was illegally manufactured, transported, sold, and consumed during the Prohibition Era. (In fact, that era is known as the "Roaring 20s.") Large well-organized groups of violent criminals profited greatly from this illegal activity. Meanwhile, the government lost the revenues it formerly collected by taxing alcohol. It didn't take long for Americans to realize that the Eighteenth Amendment hadn't worked as had been hoped, and in 1933, the Twenty-first Amendment repealed the Eighteenth Amendment.

50. Which proposal today can best be supported by citing the American experience with Prohibition?

(1) decriminalizing marijuana

(2) reducing access to legal abortion procedures

(3) increasing liquor taxes

(4) increasing patrols of the Mexican border to prevent the shipment of drugs into the country

(5) raising the drinking age

SCIENCE

80 Minutes • 50 Questions

Directions: The Science Test consists of multiple-choice questions designed to measure your knowledge of general science concepts. The questions are based on brief passages of text and visual information (charts, graphs, diagrams, and other figures). Some questions are based on both text and visual information. Study the information provided, and answer the question(s) that follow, referring back to the information as needed.

You will have 80 minutes to answer all 50 questions. Record your answers on the answer sheet provided.

QUESTION 1 REFERS TO THE FOLLOWING INFORMATION.

If one side of a stemmed plant receives more sunlight than the other side, the growth hormone auxin, which stimulates vertical growth of the elongated stem, will concentrate on the shady side of the stem in order to stimulate more growth there.

1. What will be the result of this phenomenon?

   The plant will

   (1) grow beyond its ability to nourish itself

   (2) increase in girth where auxin is concentrated

   (3) bend toward the light

   (4) wither where auxin is absent

   (5) bend toward the ground

QUESTION 2 REFERS TO THE FOLLOWING INFORMATION.

Carbon is the main element of all organic compounds and can be found in all forms of life. Carbon atoms bond easily with oxygen atoms, hydrogen atoms, and other abundant elements to form these compounds.

2. Based on the information, which statement do you know is accurate?

   (1) Carbon does not exist naturally in its pure form.

   (2) Carbon is an organic compound.

   (3) Carbon is used to make synthetic fuels.

   (4) Hydrogen cannot be separated from carbon.

   (5) All organic compounds contain carbon.

QUESTION 3 REFERS TO THE FOLLOWING DIAGRAM.

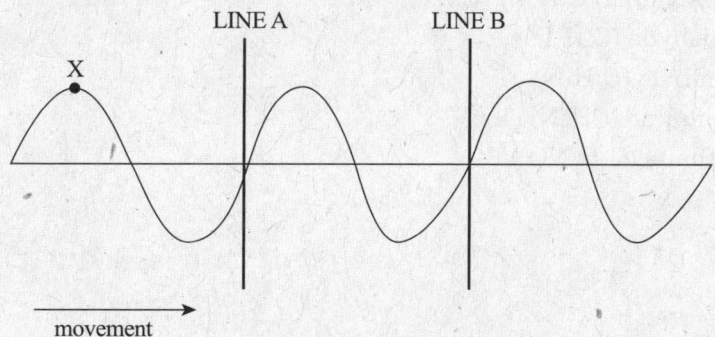

3. The wave crest shown as point X will reach line A in 3 seconds. In how many seconds will the same wave crest reach line B?

   (1) 7 seconds

   (2) 9 seconds

   (3) 10 seconds

   (4) 11 seconds

   (5) 14 seconds

QUESTION 4 REFERS TO THE FOLLOWING INFORMATION.

When you cut yourself and begin to bleed, the damaged tissues immediately release a chemical that initiates a chain reaction. Tiny disk-shaped platelets in your blood build up to form a plug at the injury site, and proteins in the blood plasma reinforce the clot by forming fibrous strands at the site. If a sample of blood is carefully removed from the blood vessel without allowing it to come in contact with the damaged tissue, and then the sample is placed on a smooth, plastic plate exposed to air, the blood will not clot. However, if a rough plastic plate or a glass plate is used instead, the blood will clot.

4. What helps cause blood to clot?

   (1) contact with a foreign object

   (2) low blood pressure due to loss of blood

   (3) constriction of the blood vessel

   (4) the accumulation of white blood cells

   (5) a response from damaged blood tissue

QUESTION 5 REFERS TO THE FOLLOWING CHART.

FIRST EIGHT ELEMENTS IN THE PERIODIC TABLE

periodic number	1	2	3	4	5	6	7	8
name and symbol	Hydrogen H	Helium He	Lithium Li	Beryllium Be	Boron B	Carbon C	Nitrogen N	Oxygen O
normal atomic mass*	1	4	7	9	11	12	14	16

* average mass in all of an element's forms, measured in *daltons*

5. Which compound has a normal atomic mass of 47?

   (1) dimethalymine (C_2H_7O)

   (2) acetaldehyde (C_2H_4O)

   (3) acrylonitrile (C_3H_3N)

   (4) methylamine (CH_5N)

   (5) nitroethane ($C_2H_5NO_2$)

QUESTION 6 IS BASED ON THE FOLLOWING INFORMATION.

The biosphere encompasses all life-sustaining regions of the Earth, its atmosphere, and its oceans. The most significant changes occurring in the biosphere today include:

- The deforestation of wilderness areas through the clear-cutting of trees to make wood products

- The pollution of rivers and oceans due to fertilizer and sewage runoff

- The depletion of the protective ozone layer of the Earth's atmosphere due to the overuse of certain air pollutants

- The desertification of grasslands due to livestock overgrazing, which reduces agricultural output and available habitats for native plant and animal species

6. Which is most clearly true of all four of the described changes in the biosphere?

   (1) They are caused by global climate change.
   (2) They are the result of human activity.
   (3) They are irreversible.
   (4) They affect the world's total food supply.
   (5) They provide more land for human habitation.

QUESTION 7 REFERS TO THE FOLLOWING DIAGRAM.

HIERARCHY OF MAJOR TAXONOMIC RANKS

(Classification of Modern Humans)

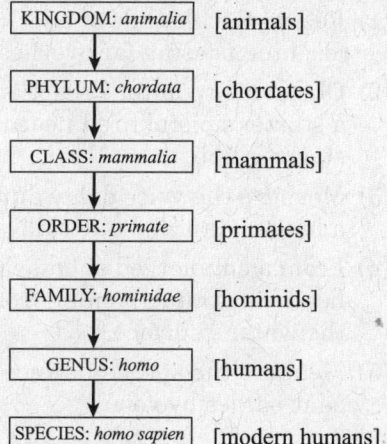

7. Panthers are members of the class *mammalia*, the order *carnivora* (meat eaters), the family *felidae* (cats), and the genus *panthera* (big cats). What can you infer from this information and from the diagram?

   (1) Panthers are the only members of the genus *panthera*.
   (2) Lions and panthers belong to the same species.
   (3) Panthers are primates but not *hominidae*.
   (4) Humans are members of the order *carnivora*.
   (5) Both panthers and humans are chordates.

8. Sound travels four times as fast through water as through air, about 1490 meters/second as compared to about 330 meters/second. Which of the following would be most useful in confirming either one or the other of these two speeds?

   (1) Record the altitude of a jet airplane passing far overhead.

   (2) Observe a sprinter's reaction to a starter's pistol fired near the starting line.

   (3) Measure the voice delay during a long-distance phone call.

   (4) From a submerged submarine, listen for sounds coming from the water's surface.

   (5) Measure the speed of a race car as it passes by you.

QUESTIONS 9 AND 10 REFER TO THE FOLLOWING INFORMATION.

Exposure to radiation or certain toxic substances sometimes triggers genetic alterations in certain types of cells. The altered genes then direct those cells to grow and reproduce abnormally. How this occurs starts with proteins within the cells. The protein cytoskeleton, the framework of protein strands that determines the cell's shape and size, can become disorganized and can shrink. The cell wall can become more permeable, resulting in the loss of cytoplasm (the gel-like substance that fills most of a cell) and protein. When proteins are altered or lost, cells can become unanchored from their proper tissues and are free to invade other nearby tissues. The altered genes can also direct the production of new blood vessels, which draw the oxygen needed to nourish these abnormal cells, which can then travel through the bloodstream to more remote parts of the body.

9. What is explained in the paragraph?

   (1) why some plants are poisonous to humans

   (2) how cancer develops and spreads

   (3) why some viruses cannot be treated

   (4) how asexual reproduction occurs

   (5) why our skeletons shrink as we age

10. If you use a microscope to examine a tissue sample containing the kind of cells described in the paragraph, which observation is LEAST likely?

    (1) Some cells are smaller than others.

    (2) Neighboring cells have grown apart.

    (3) Various cells differ in shape.

    (4) The cells are squeezed together.

    (5) The cells overlap in layers.

QUESTION 11 REFERS TO THE FOLLOWING ILLUSTRATION.

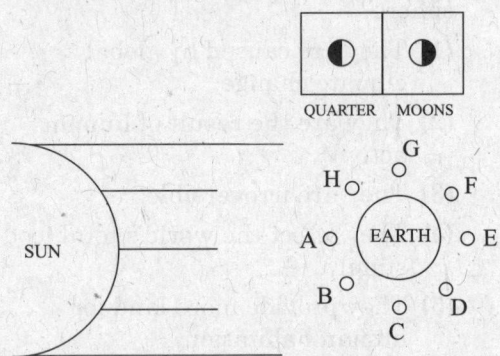

11. Referring to the illustration, at which moon positions would someone on Earth directly below the Moon see a quarter Moon in the sky?

    (1) positions A and E only

    (2) positions C and G only

    (3) positions B and H only

    (4) positions A, C, E, and G only

    (5) positions B, D, F, and H only

QUESTION 12 IS BASED ON THE FOLLOWING INFORMATION.

An atom with just one electron in its outer shell will seek to shed that electron so that its outer shell is complete. An atom whose outer shell is missing just one electron will seek to complete that shell by acquiring an electron from another atom.

12. An ion is an atom that has become either negatively or positively charged. How can an atom become a negative ion?

   (1) by acquiring an electron from another atom

   (2) by bonding with a positively charged atom

   (3) by transferring an election to another atom

   (4) by sharing an election with another atom

   (5) by transferring a proton to another atom

QUESTIONS 13 AND 14 REFER TO THE FOLLOWING DIAGRAM.

R= DOMINANT GENE FORM (ALLELE)
r= RECESSIVE GENE FORM (ALLELE)

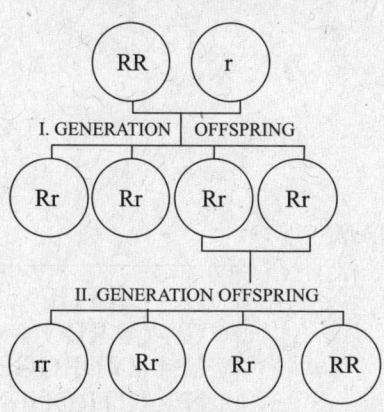

GENOTYPE	TRAIT FORM
RR	RED COLOR
Rr	RED COLOR
rr	WHITE COLOR

13. Among the first and second generations, how many offspring in total are red?

   (1) four

   (2) five

   (3) six

   (4) seven

   (5) eight

14. Below are four genotype pairs, each representing a set of parents. Without any more information than what the diagram presents, which of the four sets of parents might possibly produce a white child?

   A. rr rr

   B. RR rr

   C. Rr Rr

   D. rr Rr

   (1) B and D only

   (2) A and C only

   (3) C and D only

   (4) A, C, and D only

   (5) A, B, C, or D

QUESTION 15 REFERS TO THE FOLLOWING PASSAGE.

Plants consist of various types of cells that serve different functions. For example, epidermal cells, which form a plant's outer skin, often store food, while xylem cells, which are dead and hollow, transport water and nutrient salts to the other parts of the plant. Plant cells use structures called chloroplasts to make food for them by capturing the Sun's energy.

15. Why don't the epidermal cells that form the skin of an onion bulb contain chloroplasts?

    Onion bulbs

    (1) do not need water to survive
    (2) receive their energy from the Sun
    (3) grow underground
    (4) have no roots
    (5) contain only xylem cells

QUESTION 16 REFERS TO THE FOLLOWING ILLUSTRATION.

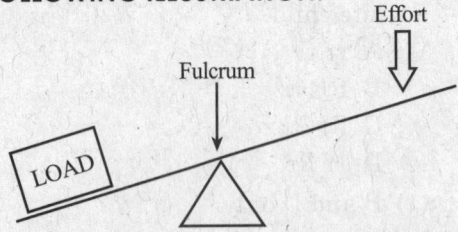

16. The mechanical advantage of using the type of machine shown above can be demonstrated by the use of which of the following tools?

    (1) a crowbar
    (2) a wedge
    (3) a wheelbarrow
    (4) pliers
    (5) a nutcracker

17. Storks, which have long bills, are found mainly around waters where small fish swim just below the surface. What does this characteristic of storks show?

    (1) Some storks travel great distances to find food.
    (2) Long-billed storks do not mate with short-billed storks.
    (3) Storks developed long bills through evolution.
    (4) Storks are not an endangered species.
    (5) Storks do not prey on land-dwelling animals.

QUESTION 18 REFERS TO THE FOLLOWING DIAGRAM.

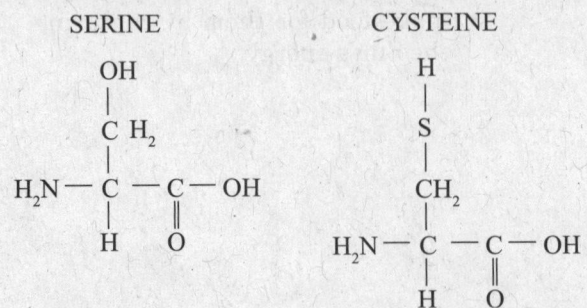

O – OXYGEN	
C – CARBON	
H – HYDROGEN	
N – NITROGEN	
S – SULFUR	
LEGEND	

18. How does a serine molecule differ from a cysteine molecule?

A serine molecule contains a different number of

(1) helium atoms

(2) oxygen atoms

(3) carbon atoms

(4) nitrogen atoms

(5) hydrogen atoms

QUESTION 19 REFERS TO THE FOLLOWING INFORMATION.

The DNA of every human includes two sex chromosomes, which determine gender and the traits associated with gender. Female sex chromosomes are both of type X, while a male has one X chromosome and one Y chromosome.

19. How is the gender of human offspring determined?

(1) solely by the male parent

(2) solely by the female parent

(3) equally by the male and female parents

(4) predominantly by the female parent

(5) predominantly by the male parent

QUESTION 20 REFERS TO THE FOLLOWING DIAGRAM.

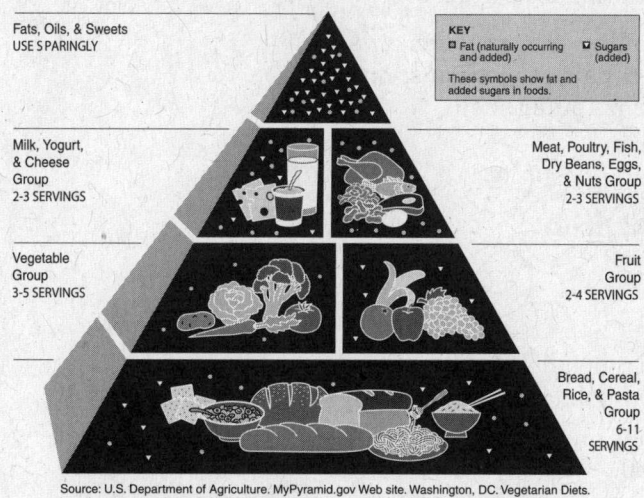

Food Guide Pyramid
A Guide to Daily Food Choices

Source: U.S. Department of Agriculture. MyPyramid.gov Web site. Washington, DC. Vegetarian Diets.
http://www.cnpp.usda.gov/FGPGraphicResources.htm. Accessed February 23, 2010.

20. What does the U.S. Department of Agriculture illustration suggest about a balanced diet?

(1) A balanced diet calls for at least three meals a day.

(2) People should consume less meat than they do.

(3) A balanced diet calls for fewer servings than unhealthful diets do.

(4) Overweight people should eat more vegetables and less pasta.

(5) Except for fruits, sweets should generally be avoided.

QUESTION 21 REFERS TO THE FOLLOWING INFORMATION.

Earth's magnetic North Pole is shifting at an accelerating rate from its earliest known position in northern Canada toward Russia. Scientists theorize that at the planet's center is liquid magma rapidly circulating around an iron core and that the core and magma are constantly moving.

21. What can you infer from the information?
    (1) The magnetic South Pole is not shifting.
    (2) Earth's geographic poles are at different locations than the magnetic poles.
    (3) Compasses are of little or no use anymore.
    (4) Earth's magnetic core is moving toward the planet's surface.
    (5) Magnets are generally globe-shaped and made of iron.

22. Covalent bonding occurs when two atoms share a pair of electrons, one from each atom's outer shell.

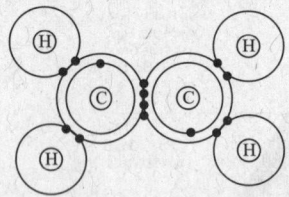

What can you conclude from the above information and diagram?
    (1) Carbon has one electron in its outer shell.
    (2) Hydrogen has one electron in its outer shell.
    (3) Carbon has eight electrons in its outer shell.
    (4) Hydrogen has two electrons in its outer shell.
    (5) Carbon has two electrons in its outer shell.

23. Although light waves can bend when passing through an extremely narrow opening or through a prism, generally speaking light travels in a straight line.

Which of the following observations does NOT provide support for the general assertion that light travels in a straight line?
    (1) At certain times of the month the Moon appears crescent-shaped.
    (2) During the daytime, you can estimate the time by looking at a tall building's shadow.
    (3) During target practice at a rifle range, you aim your gun at the bull's-eye.
    (4) The midday sun appears brighter than the late afternoon sun.
    (5) To see what is on the other side of a brick wall you must look over the wall.

QUESTION 24 REFERS TO THE FOLLOWING CHART.

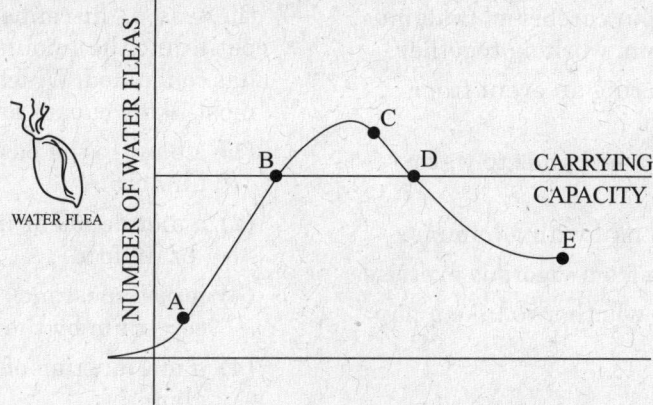

NOTE: When a population reaches carrying capacity, just enough resources are available to support the existing population.

24. Referring to the chart, what is occurring between points B and C?
    (1) The water flea population growth rate is slowing.
    (2) The carrying capacity is contracting.
    (3) The water flea population's death rate is declining.
    (4) The average life span of a water flea is decreasing.
    (5) The total water flea population is declining.

QUESTIONS 25 AND 26 REFER TO THE FOLLOWING INFORMATION.

<u>Forebrain</u>

- **Thalamus:** receives information from the sense organs and forwards it to the cerebrum

- **Cerebrum:** governs the body's activities and responses to sensory information

- **Hypothalamus:** receives information from internal organs and regulates vital biological processes (thirst, hunger, sleep, blood pressure, body temperature, etc.)

- **Pituitary gland:** portion of hypothalamus that secretes hormones to trigger appropriate biological responses to thirst, hunger, sleepiness, etc.

<u>Midbrain:</u> Controls information going to and from the brain and the central nervous system

<u>Hindbrain</u>

- **Pons:** delivers messages back and forth between the cerebrum or cerebellum and the spinal cord

- **Medulla oblongata:** maintains automatic functions and involuntary movements

- **Cerebellum:** coordinates intentional movement and other behavior

25. Which of the following is the best example of your cerebrum, thalamus, and cerebellum working together?

    (1) remembering an event from your past

    (2) rubbing your hands to warm them

    (3) hitting a nail with a hammer

    (4) sweating from vigorous exercise

    (5) deciding whether to take a nap

26. Eating disorders often result when there is a "disconnect" between appetite and the amount of food a person has consumed. Which of the following most likely causes eating disorders?

    (1) a blow to the base of the hindbrain

    (2) a diet deficient in iron and other "brain food"

    (3) mixed messages sent to the cerebrum by the pons

    (4) a malfunction of the pituitary gland

    (5) an injury to the brain's cerebral cortex

QUESTIONS 27 AND 28 REFER TO THE FOLLOWING INFORMATION.

The Hertzsprung-Russell Diagram plots stars according to luminosity (brightness), surface temperature, and spectral class (color). NOTE: Absolute magnitude is a measure of luminosity (brightness) that uses an inverted scale.

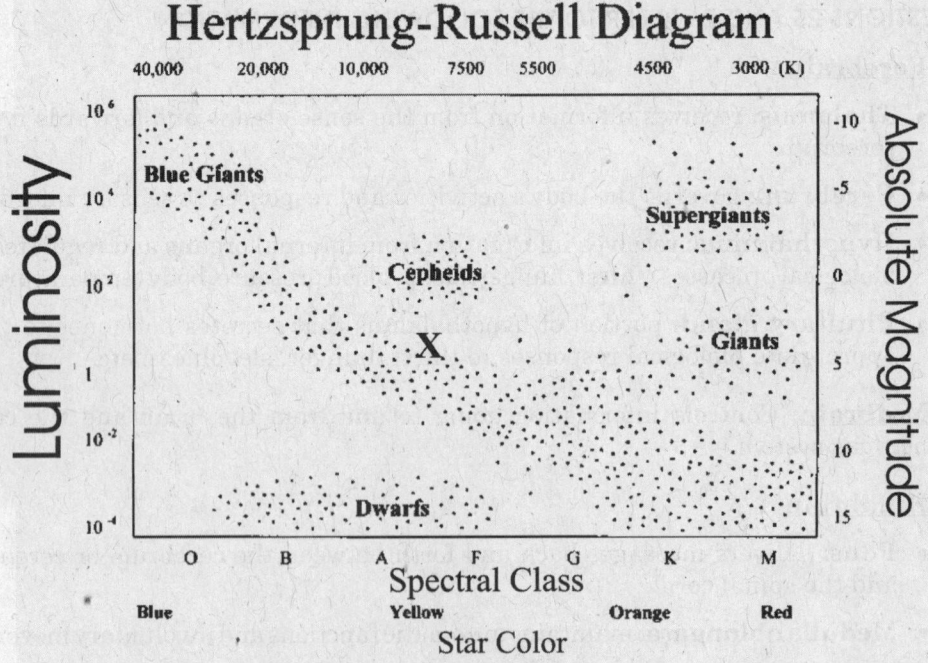

X = our solar system's Sun

27. Which statement does the Hertz-sprung-Russell Diagram best support?

  (1) Red stars are hotter than blue stars.

  (2) Supergiants are among the oldest stars.

  (3) Giants are among the coldest stars.

  (4) Dwarfs are more luminous than cepheids.

  (5) Orange stars are more luminous than red stars.

28. What conclusion can you draw from the Hertzsprung-Russell Diagram?

  (1) Our Sun is typical in terms of brightness and surface temperature.

  (2) Our Sun is old compared to most other stars.

  (3) The stars in the universe appear in broad bands and in clusters.

  (4) The number of stars in the universe is expanding.

  (5) Most stars in the universe can be seen through a telescope.

QUESTION 29 REFERS TO THE FOLLOWING ILLUSTRATION.

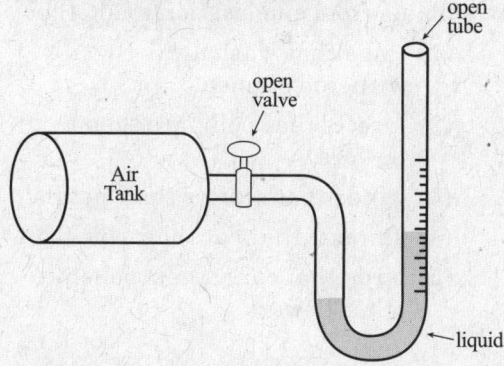

29. What is being measured by the simple instrument illustrated above?

  (1) the air pressure inside the tank

  (2) the atmospheric air pressure

  (3) the temperature of the liquid

  (4) the pressure against the outside of the tank

  (5) the atmospheric temperature

QUESTION 30 REFERS TO THE FOLLOWING ILLUSTRATION.

DEVELOPMENT OF A FRUIT-BEARING PLANT

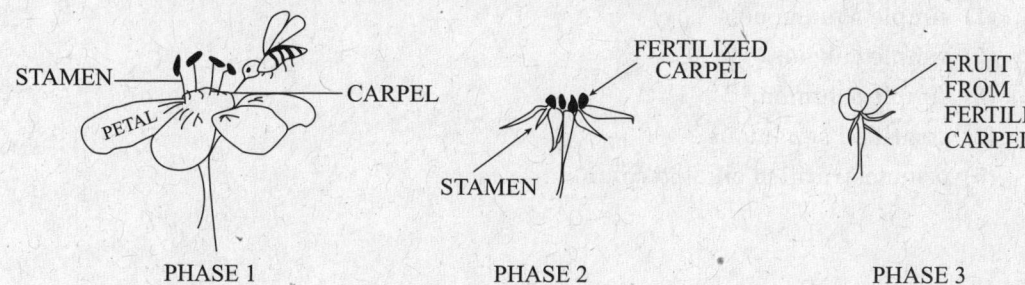

Phase 1: The flower attracts insects, which pollinate the carpel, resulting in fertilization. After fertilization occurs, the flower's petals wither.

Phase 2: A seed develops inside each carpel, an ovary wall encases each seed, and the ovary swells to form a pericap, while the flower's stamens wither.

Phase 3: The seed and pericap form a fruit, which attracts animals.

30. Among the following, which is probably responsible for spreading fruit-bearing plants from one location to another?

    (1) rains that wash away the withered stamens

    (2) insects that pollinate their flowers

    (3) winds that scatter their petals

    (4) animals that eat their ripe fruit

    (5) birds that carry their pollen to other flowers

QUESTION 31 REFERS TO THE FOLLOWING ILLUSTRATION AND INFORMATION.

TYPES OF EPITHELIAL TISSUE

| SIMPLE CUBOIDAL | SIMPLE SQUAMOUS | SIMPLE COLUMNAR | PSEUDOSTRATIFIED CILIATED COLUMNAR | STRATIFIED SQUAMOUS |

The illustrations show five types of tightly packed epithelial tissues, which form the thin membranes lining most internal and external surfaces of an animal's body. Thinner tissues allow for the exchange of particles through the membrane, whereas thicker tissues serve largely as a barrier.

31. Which type of epithelial tissue lines a lung's air sacs, which must freely pass oxygen to blood vessels in exchange for carbon dioxide?

    (1) simple squamous

    (2) simple cuboidal

    (3) simple columnar

    (4) stratified squamous

    (5) pseudostratified ciliated columnar

QUESTIONS 32 AND 33 REFER TO THE FOLLOWING INFORMATION.

In ecological communities, energy is transferred from producers (simple plant forms that obtain their energy through photosynthesis) up the food chain to primary, secondary, and tertiary consumers. Producers provide only about 1% of their energy, which they generate through photosynthesis, to primary producers. On average, consumers pass along about 10% of the energy they obtain from the trophic level below theirs to the next level up.

32. What portion of the energy that producers obtain through photosynthesis is passed up the food chain to secondary consumers?

    (1) 0.001 percent
    (2) 0.01 percent
    (3) 0.1 percent
    (4) 1.0 percent
    (5) 10 percent

33. Most ecological communities also include animal species that consume both plants and animals. They also include dentritivores (decomposers), which consume plants and animals that die without being eaten. Some dentritivores may also serve as prey for other animals. What would a diagram that accurately shows these relationships probably look like?

    The diagram would be

    (1) circular, or O-shaped
    (2) pyramid-shaped
    (3) separated into two or more chains
    (4) web-shaped
    (5) shaped like an inverted pyramid

QUESTIONS 34 AND 35 REFER TO THE FOLLOWING ILLUSTRATION.

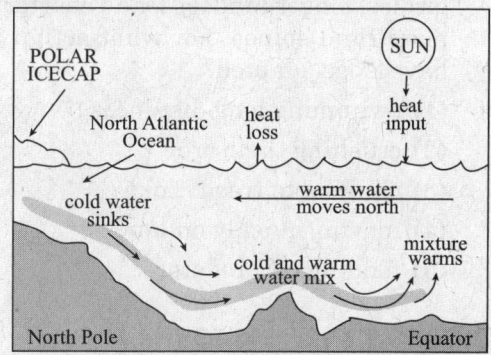

34. What overall idea does the diagram convey?

    (1) Ocean currents dictate the migratory patterns of ocean mammals.
    (2) The Atlantic Ocean's depth is greatest near the Equator.
    (3) Ocean water circulates between the equator and the North Atlantic Ocean.
    (4) Warm ocean water rises, while colder ocean water sinks.
    (5) Unusually warm air can disturb the normal currents of the Atlantic Ocean.

35. Which question does the diagram help answer?

    (1) Why does ocean water move northward from near the Equator?
    (2) Which is greater: heat loss from the ocean or heat input from the Sun?
    (3) Should scientists be concerned that the polar ice caps will melt away?
    (4) How fast do ocean currents of the North Atlantic move?
    (5) Which is more dense—cold water or warm water?

36. During their evolution, frogs have gradually developed stronger shoulder girdles, longer hind legs, and shorter, more rigid spines. For what activity have frogs adapted?

(1) swimming long distances

(2) crushing their prey

(3) clinging to tree trunks

(4) moving quickly on land

(5) fending off predators

QUESTION 37 REFERS TO THE FOLLOWING DIAGRAM.

10^{21}

10^{18} ← Gamma Rays

← X-rays

10^{15} ← Ultraviolet

← Visible spectrum (4×10^{14} through 8×10^{14})

10^{12} ← Infrared

← Radar

10^9 ← Television

10^6 ← Radio

Frequency (cycles/sec.)

37. All light waves travel at the same speed (rate of motion). Why can't we see gamma rays?

(1) They exist only in theory.

(2) Earth's atmosphere shields us from them.

(3) Their wave lengths are too short.

(4) They are too dark to see.

(5) Their wavelengths are too long.

QUESTION 38 REFERS TO THE FOLLOWING ILLUSTRATION AND INFORMATION.

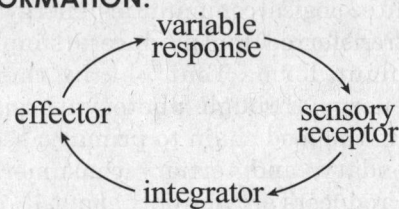

To maintain a stable internal state, or *homeostasis*, the body relies on receptors at or near the body's surface to sense destabilizing conditions. These receptors send messages to the body's integrator (the brain), which directs the appropriate effector to respond in a way that maintains homeostasis. Negative feedback occurs when the brain directs an effector to counteract, or negate, whatever is disrupting homeostasis. At times, however, the brain will provide positive feedback instead.

38. Which would be an example of positive feedback?

(1) Sweat glands emit water through pores to cool the skin.

(2) Muscle contractions intensify from the initial stage of labor until childbirth.

(3) Shivering becomes more intense as the weather grows colder.

(4) People normally stop eating once their hunger has been satisfied.

(5) The heart pumps harder as a person climbs a steep flight of stairs.

QUESTION 39 REFERS TO THE FOLLOWING GRAPH.

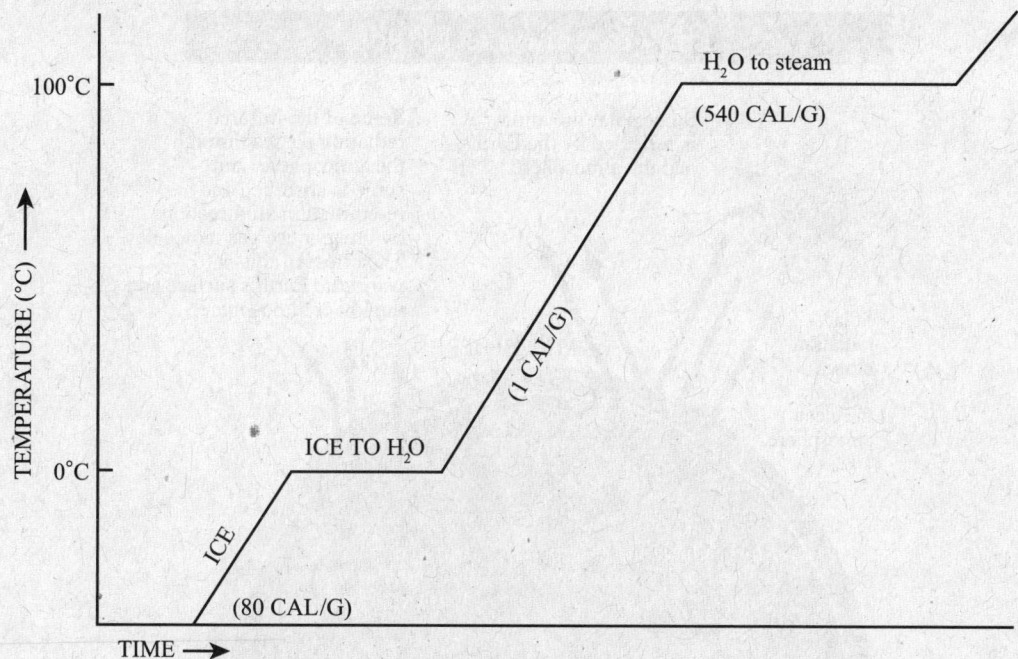

39. At a minimum, how much heat energy is required to change 1 gram of ice into steam?

    (1) 80 calories

    (2) 100 calories

    (3) 240 calories

    (4) 540 calories

    (5) 720 calories

QUESTION 40 REFERS TO THE FOLLOWING INFORMATION.

Like light matter, dark matter attracts all matter gravitationally, and so it sustains a gravitational field. As astronomers study a galaxy, they can infer the presence of dark matter if the galaxy's motion requires gravitational interactions greater than those that the galaxy's light matter should allow.

40. On what do scientists base their understanding of dark matter?

    (1) their knowledge about the color spectrum of light

    (2) a theoretical application of the principles of gravity

    (3) experiments they have performed in a laboratory

    (4) their direct observations of dark matter

    (5) observations made by astronauts from space

QUESTION 41 IS BASED ON THE FOLLOWING ILLUSTRATION.

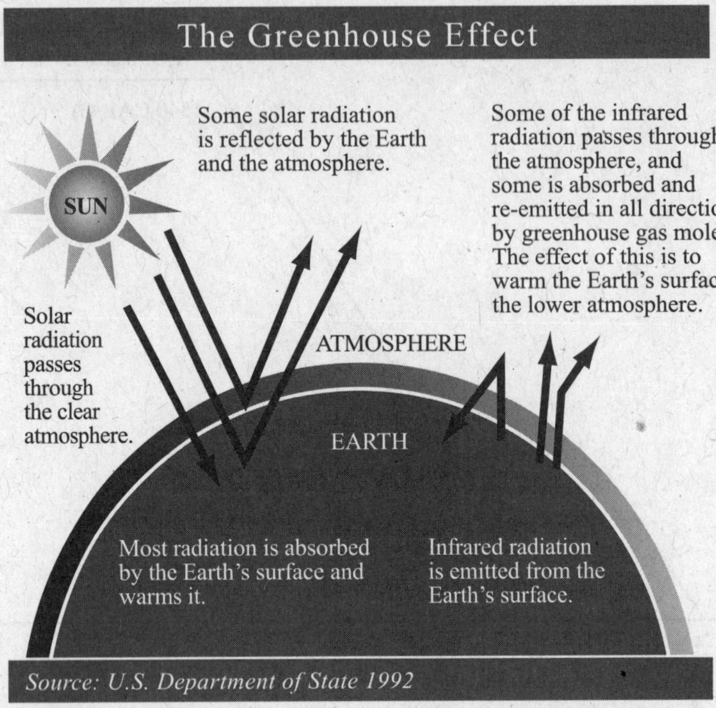

The Greenhouse Effect

Some solar radiation is reflected by the Earth and the atmosphere.

Some of the infrared radiation passes through the atmosphere, and some is absorbed and re-emitted in all directions by greenhouse gas molecules. The effect of this is to warm the Earth's surface and the lower atmosphere.

SUN

Solar radiation passes through the clear atmosphere.

ATMOSPHERE

EARTH

Most radiation is absorbed by the Earth's surface and warms it.

Infrared radiation is emitted from the Earth's surface.

Source: U.S. Department of State 1992

41. Which is an accurate statement about the greenhouse effect?

   (1) Solar radiation is prevented from passing through the atmosphere.

   (2) Much of the energy radiated from the Earth never leaves the atmosphere.

   (3) Most radiation reaching the Earth is reflected off its surface.

   (4) The Earth warms mainly due to atmospheric radiation.

   (5) Greenhouse plants are receiving less and less unfiltered light.

QUESTION 42 IS BASED ON THE FOLLOWING INFORMATION.

In a stable atom, the number of protons is the same as the number of neutrons. If the atom's nucleus gains or loses neutrons, it may spontaneously emit particles and energy—gamma rays, for example—through a process of radioactive decay, losing neutrons and possibly protons until its nucleus stabilizes. If the atom loses only neutrons, it becomes a different isotope of the same element. But if it loses protons, it becomes a different element.

42. What causes radioactive decay?

   (1) gamma rays

   (2) a loss of protons

   (3) unstable electrons

   (4) an unstable nucleus

   (5) a decaying proton

QUESTION 43 IS BASED ON THE FOLLOWING ILLUSTRATION.

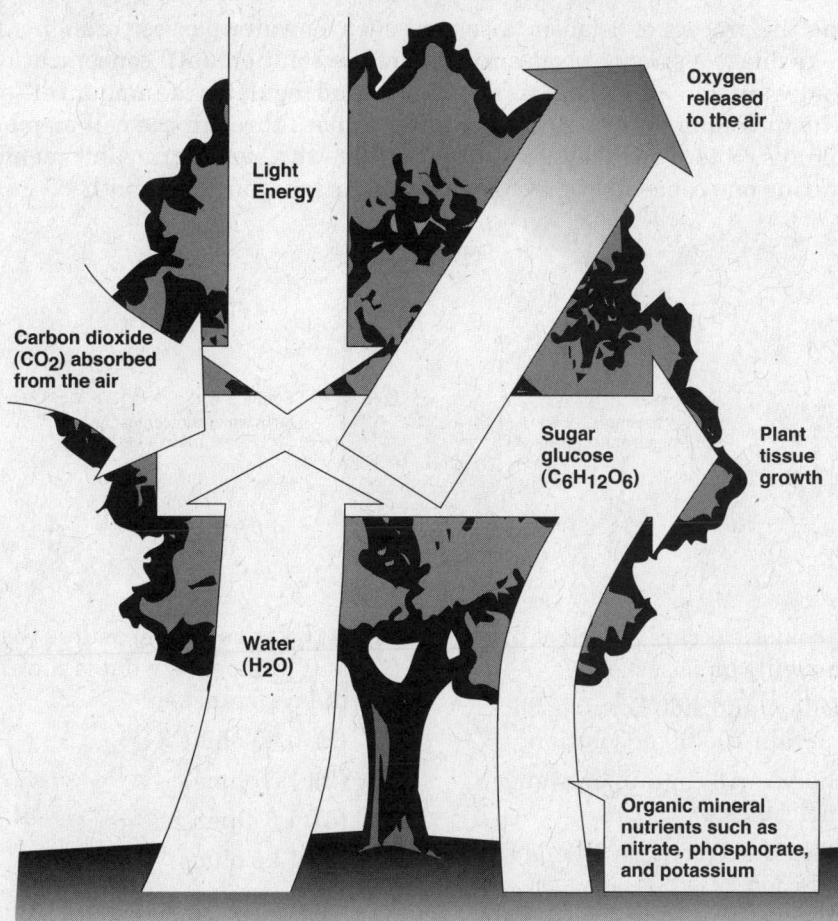

43. What is the best title for this illustration?

(1) "Anatomy of a Tree"

(2) "How Trees Survive"

(3) "The Life Cycle of a Tree"

(4) "Why We Need Trees"

(5) "Trees: From Seed to Maturity"

44. Which is LEAST likely to enhance the genetic diversity of a population?

(1) the random mating between the population's males and females

(2) the extinction of a species that the population had earlier consumed as prey

(3) migration of a foreign variety of the same species into the population

(4) a genetic mutation producing an extra toe in a mountain-dwelling mammal

(5) an abrupt, localized climate change affecting a small portion of the population

QUESTION 45 REFERS TO THE FOLLOWING INFORMATION AND ILLUSTRATION.

During the process of osmosis, a solvent such as water passes through a membrane to dilute a stronger concentration of the solution until concentrations on both sides are the same. Osmosis allows for—and regulates the amount of—water and the nutrients dissolved in that water to pass through the cell membranes of a plant's roots. The following illustration shows a semi-permeable membrane separating one concentration of a water-sugar solution from another.

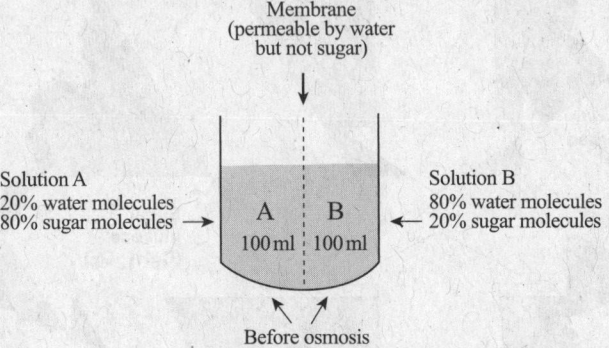

45. Once osmosis occurs, which of the following will you observe?

    (1) Side A and side B will each contain 100 ml of solution.

    (2) Side A will contain only sugar molecules.

    (3) Side B will contain 40 ml of solution.

    (4) Side A will contain 40 ml of solution.

    (5) Side B will contain only sugar molecules.

QUESTION 46 REFERS TO THE FOLLOWING INFORMATION.

A 4.5-volt battery sends an electrical current through a wire to a resistor. Resistance is measured in ohms (Ω). From the resistor, the current travels through another wire to an ammeter that measures the current in ampere units. The relationship among voltage (V), current (A), and resistance (Ω) is as follows:

$$\Omega = \frac{V}{A}$$

46. If the ammeter measures the current at 0.3 amperes, what is the amount of the resistance?

    (1) 0.45 ohms

    (2) 1.5 ohms

    (3) 4.5 ohms

    (4) 13.5 ohms

    (5) 15 ohms

47. A floating cork in the middle of the ocean bobs up and down with the waves but does not move laterally with the waves.

    Which of the following makes the most sense as the reason a cork would stay in the middle of the ocean rather than move toward the coastline?

    (1) Any wave's force is met with an equal opposing wave force.

    (2) Objects of low mass cannot move denser objects.

    (3) Waves transfer energy but not matter.

    (4) Earth's gravitational force is greater than the Moon's.

    (5) A wave's amplitude (height) is inversely proportionate to its length.

FORMATION OF AN ATOLL

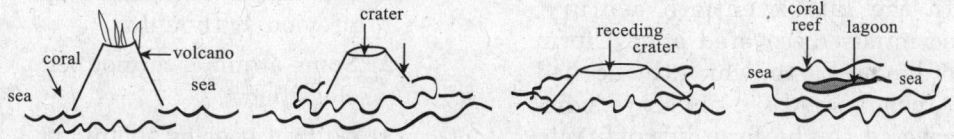

48. What does the sequence of illustrations show?
    (1) a rising sea level, which allows coral to grow in a volcanic island's lagoon
    (2) a lagoon forming when a volcanic lava flow erodes a coral reef
    (3) coral combining with volcanic ash to expand a volcanic island
    (4) a volcanic eruption filling a lagoon with lava, which cools to form a land mass
    (5) a lagoon forming as coral builds up around an eroding volcanic island

QUESTION 49 IS BASED ON THE FOLLOWING INFORMATION.

Charles' Law: Given a constant pressure, the volume of a gas varies directly with the absolute temperature (measured on the Kelvin scale).

Boyle's Law: Given a constant absolute temperature, the volume of a gas varies inversely with changes in pressure.

49. What does Charles' Law explain?
    (1) why you can soothe a bloated stomach by applying a hot water bottle
    (2) why sending a flame into a hot-air balloon takes you higher in the air
    (3) why you should not fill tires with air beyond the recommended maximum pressure
    (4) why you should fill your lungs with air before diving deep down into cold water
    (5) why pure oxygen can help revive a person who is lightheaded or has just fainted

QUESTION 50 IS BASED ON THE FOLLOWING INFORMATION.

In the late twentieth century, scientists discovered a new form of life on Earth, which they called Archaeans. At the time it was discovered, this life form did not fit into scientists' current classification scheme for biological life. It was generally believed that the vital cellular components of any living organism essentially break down at temperatures above 60° Centigrade. This thermal limit of cellular life, scientists thought, was fixed across all biological organisms. But in recent decades, Archaeans have repeatedly demonstrated that what had been thought to be the limit was too low. In fact, so-called "extremophilic" Archaeans have been discovered to thrive in temperatures as high as 160° Centigrade.

50. What conclusion does the discovery of Archaeans support?
   (1) The Earth is warmer than previously thought.
   (2) Some animals cannot be classified.
   (3) Mutant species abound in nature.
   (4) Scientific knowledge is ever-evolving.
   (5) The theory of evolution is flawed.

LANGUAGE ARTS, READING

65 Minutes • 40 Questions

Directions: The Language Arts, Reading Test consists of several passages of fiction and nonfiction reading material. Each passage is followed by several multiple-choice questions. After you read a passage, answer the questions that follow it, referring back to the passage as needed. Answer all questions based on what is stated and implied in the passage.

Immediately preceding each passage is a brief "purpose question" in bold type. These questions will help you focus your attention and to understand the purpose of each passage. You are not required to answer purpose questions.

Record your answers on the Language Arts, Reading section of the answer sheet provided.

QUESTIONS 1–6 REFER TO THE FOLLOWING PASSAGE.

WHO IS BETTER AT CARING FOR THE BABY?

Nanny sat at a low table giving Little B her supper after her bath. The baby had on a white flannel gown and a blue woolen jacket, and
5   her dark, fine hair was brushed up into a funny little peak. She looked up when she saw her mother and began to jump.

"Now, my lovey, eat it up like a
10   good girl," said Nanny, setting her lips in a way that Bertha knew, and that meant she had come into the nursery at another wrong moment.

The baby looked up at her again,
15   stared, and then smiled so charmingly that Bertha couldn't help crying: "Oh, Nanny, do let me finish giving her supper while you put the bath things away."

20   "Well, M'm, she oughtn't to be changed hands while she's eating," said Nanny, still whispering. "It unsettles her; it's very likely to upset her."

25   How absurd it was. Why have a baby if it has to be kept — not in a case like a rare, rare fiddle — but in another woman's arms? "Oh, I must!" said she.

30   Very offended, Nanny handed her over. "Now, don't excite her after her supper. You know you do, M'm. And I have such a time with her after!" Nanny went out of the
35   room with the bath towels.

"Thank heaven! Now I've got you to myself, my little precious," said Bertha, as the baby leaned against her. She ate delightfully, holding
40   up her lips for the spoon and then waving her hands. Sometimes she wouldn't let the spoon go; and sometimes, just as Bertha had filled it, she waved it away to the four winds.
45   When the soup was finished Bertha turned round to the fire. "You're nice — you're very nice!" said she, kissing her warm baby. "I'm fond of you. I like you."

50   And, indeed, she loved Little B so much — her neck as she bent forward, her exquisite toes as they shone transparent in the firelight — that all her feeling of bliss came
55   back again, and again she didn't know how to express it — what to do with it.

"You're wanted on the telephone," said Nanny, coming back
60   in triumph and seizing *her* Little B.

— from "Bliss,"
by Katherine Mansfield

1. What does Nanny's initial reaction to Bertha's arrival in the nursery suggest?

   (1) Nanny is relieved to have help with Little B.

   (2) Bertha's visit to the nursery is unwelcome.

   (3) Nanny is embarrassed by the untidy nursery.

   (4) Bertha's visit comes as a surprise to Nanny.

   (5) Nanny is upset with Little B for refusing to eat.

2. Which word best captures the central characteristic of Nanny?

   (1) generosity

   (2) disrespectfulness

   (3) immaturity

   (4) possessiveness

   (5) neglectfulness

3. By her thoughts, how does Bertha best reveal her relationship with Little B?

   (1) by comparing Little B to a rare musical instrument

   (2) by admiring Little B's neck and toes

   (3) by observing her own feeling of bliss

   (4) by admiring Little B's gown, jacket, and hair

   (5) by wondering whether Little B prefers Nanny

4. How would Nanny most likely describe Bertha?

   (1) as an affectionate but strict mother

   (2) as forgetful but well-meaning

   (3) as a gossip and a busybody

   (4) as an arrogant and demanding employer

   (5) as a thoughtless and inexperienced mother

5. If a close friend of hers were dying of an incurable illness, how would Bertha's character, as revealed in the passage, probably respond?

   Bertha would respond by

   (1) focusing on her own life and ignoring her friend

   (2) acting toward the friend as if the friend were in good health

   (3) arranging for a nurse to care for the friend

   (4) trying to take charge of her friend's financial affairs

   (5) grieving over the impending loss of the friend

6. What does the word "triumph" (line 60) suggest about Nanny?

   Nanny is

   (1) happy to have little B and the nursery to herself again

   (2) glad that Little B could spend time with Bertha

   (3) feeling justified in her total control over the nursery

   (4) a competitive person who enjoys beating others at games

   (5) relieved because the phone call was an excuse to take a break

QUESTIONS 7–11 REFER TO THE FOLLOWING PASSAGE, WHICH IS EXCERPTED FROM A SPEECH DELIVERED IN 1924.

CAN CHINA SURPASS OTHER NATIONS IN SCIENTIFIC INNOVATION?

Although we are behind the foreigners in scientific achievement, our native ability is adequate to the construction of a great material
5 civilization, which is proved by the concrete evidence of past achievements. We invented the compass, printing, porcelain, gunpowder, and the curing of tea and weaving of
10 silk. Foreigners have made good use of these inventions. Furthermore, many of the latest inventions in architecture in the West have been practiced in the East for thousands
15 of years. This genius of our race for material inventions seems now to be lost; and so our greatness has become but the history of bygone glories.
20 I believe that we have many things to learn from the West, and that we can learn. Many Westerners maintain that the hardest thing to learn is aerial science; already
25 many Chinese have become skillful aviators. If aeronautics can be learned, I believe everything can be learned by our people. But when

we learn from the West, we should
30 learn the latest invention instead
of repeating the various steps of
development. We may well learn,
for example, to adopt the centralized
plan of producing electricity, and
35 need not follow the old plan of
using coal to produce energy. In this
way we can easily within ten years
catch up with the West in material
achievement.

40 The time is critical. We have
no time to waste, and we ought to
take the latest and the best that
the West can offer. Our intelligence
is by no means inferior to that of
45 the Japanese. With our historical
background and our natural and
human resources, it should be
easier for us than it was for Japan
to rise to the place of a first-class
50 Power by a partial adaptation of
Western civilization. We ought to
be ten times stronger than Japan
because our country is more than
ten times bigger and richer than
55 Japan. China is potentially equal
to ten Powers.

7. What is the speaker's point in listing
past contributions of Chinese inven-
tors (lines 7–10)?

   (1) China deserves more credit for
past successes.

   (2) Most of the world's important
inventions are Chinese.

   (3) Chinese inventions have been
stolen by foreigners.

   (4) The Chinese have the ability to
create and achieve.

   (5) Life would be difficult without
scientific exploration.

8. What concerns the speaker about
learning from the West's scientific
achievements?

The speaker does not want China to

   (1) act aggressively or competitively
toward the West

   (2) repeat the West's mistakes

   (3) invest as many resources as the
West has

   (4) become too Western in outlook

   (5) repeat all stages of development

9. In pointing out that Chinese intelligence "is by no means inferior to that
of the Japanese" (lines 44–45), what
is the speaker trying to demonstrate?

   (1) that Chinese military defenses
are just as advanced as those of
the Japanese

   (2) that it was not easy for Japan to
become a Power

   (3) that China can become a Power
as easily as Japan did

   (4) that with little education,
the Chinese can surpass the
Japanese

   (5) that it will not be easy for China
to compete with Japan

10. As the word is used in the speech, what
is the meaning of *critical* (line 40)?

   (1) analytical

   (2) dangerous

   (3) momentous

   (4) immediate

   (5) approximate

11. Would the speaker approve of fast-food restaurants opening in China?

(1) probably, because he approves of Western innovations

(2) probably, if they were operated by the Chinese for Chinese profit

(3) no, because they are too representative of Western culture

(4) no, because they have nothing to do with material achievement

(5) no, because he wants China to maintain its distinct traditions

QUESTIONS 12–17 REFER TO THE FOLLOWING PASSAGE.

WHY DID MARTHY COME TO TOWN?

ANNA *(taking a package of Sweet Caporal cigarettes from the bag)*: Let you smoke in here, won't they?

MARTHY *(doubtfully)*: Sure. *(Then*
5 *with evident anxiety)* On'y trow it away if yuh hear someone comin'.

ANNA *(Lighting one and taking a deep inhale)*: Gee, they're fussy in this dump, ain't they? *(She puffs,*
10 *staring at the table top. MARTHY looks her over with a new penetrating interest, taking in every detail of her face. ANNA suddenly becomes conscious of this appraising*
15 *stare—resentfully)* Ain't nothing wrong with me, is there? You're looking hard enough.

MARTHY *(irritated by the other's tone—scornfully)*: Ain't got to look
20 much. I got your number the minute you stepped in the door.

ANNA *(her eyes narrowing)*: Ain't you smart! Well, I got yours, too, without no trouble. You're me forty
25 years from now. That's you! *(She gives a hard little laugh.)*

MARTHY *(angrily)*: Is that so? Well, I'll tell you straight, kiddo,

that Marthy Owen never— *(She*
30 *catches herself up short—with a grin.)* . . . Yuh said yuh was just outa the hospital?

ANNA: Two weeks ago. *(Leaning over to MARTHY confidentially)*
35 The joint I was in out in St. Paul got raided. That was the start. The judge give all us girls thirty days . . . . I got good and sick and they had to send me to the hospital. It
40 was nice there. I was sorry to leave it, honest!

MARTHY *(after a slight pause)*: Did yuh say yuh got to meet someone here?

45 ANNA: Yes. Oh, not what you mean. It's my Old Man I got to meet. Honest! It's funny, too. I ain't seen him since I was a kid — don't even know what he looks like — yust had
50 a letter every now and then. This was always the only address he give me to write him back. He's yanitor of some building here — used to be a sailor.

55 MARTHY *(astonished)*: Janitor!

ANNA: Sure. And I was thinking maybe, seeing he ain't never done a thing for me in my life, he might be willing to stake me to a room and
60 eats till I get rested up. *(Wearily)* Gee, I sure need that rest! I'm knocked out. *(Then resignedly)* But I ain't expecting much from him. Give you a kick when you're down,
65 that's what all men do. *(With sudden passion)* Men, I hate 'em — all of 'em! And I don't expect he'll turn out no better than the rest. *(Then with sudden interest)* Say, do you
70 hang out around this dump much?

—from *Anna Christie*,
by Eugene O'Neill

12. Based on the dialogue, how can Anna be characterized?

    Anna is
    (1) shy and withdrawn
    (2) distrustful of others
    (3) cruelly insensitive
    (4) quick with a comeback
    (5) easy to make fun of

13. Based on the scene, which takes place in a saloon, which of the following is most likely true?
    (1) Marthy is a regular patron of the saloon.
    (2) Anna and Marthy agreed to meet at the saloon.
    (3) Anna is surprised to see Marthy at the saloon.
    (4) Marthy works at the saloon.
    (5) Marthy is planning to meet a male friend at the saloon.

14. What is Marthy probably about to say when she "catches herself up short — with a grin" (lines 30–31)?

    Marthy was about to tell Anna that Marthy never
    (1) drank to the point of losing self-control
    (2) insulted other women about their age
    (3) made a living as a prostitute
    (4) showed disrespect for older people
    (5) traveled without the company of a man

15. Based on the dialogue, what is likely to happen next?
    (1) Marthy will offer Anna some food and a place to rest.
    (2) Anna will ask Marthy if she knows her Old Man.
    (3) Marthy will direct Anna to the building she is asking about.
    (4) Anna's Old Man will enter the saloon.
    (5) Marthy will tell Anna that her Old Man has died.

16. Later in the play, Anna meets her Old Man, and she responds to his paying her a compliment by saying, "Cut it! You talk same as they all do." In light of the dialogue between Anna and Marthy, what does this response suggest about Anna?
    (1) She is embarrassed by the compliment.
    (2) She is being sarcastic and actually enjoys the compliments.
    (3) She has known many insincere men in the past.
    (4) She is unsure how to behave around her Old Man.
    (5) She is tired and would rather eat and rest than talk.

17. The passage is from *Anna Christie*, written by Eugene O'Neill in the early twentieth century. Based on the passage, which of the following is LEAST likely an accurate characterization of the play?
    (1) an exploration of the harsh realities for many women of that era
    (2) a case study of westward expansion's impact on ordinary lives
    (3) a commentary on the power of love and forgiveness
    (4) a realistic examination of family conflict
    (5) a dramatization of the ups and downs of life

QUESTIONS 18–22 REFER TO THE
FOLLOWING PASSAGE.

IS A PICTURE OF A SOUP CAN TRULY ART?

For the Impressionists—Monet,
Renoir, Pissarro, and the others—
painting was a purely optic art:
light was the sole subject, the
object upon which it plays was
secondary. The people, places,
and things depicted told no story,
conveyed no special meaning; they
were, instead, merely patterns of
light to be captured on canvas. In
this regard, the Impressionists
were true precursors of twentieth-
century modernism. Taking their
cue from the Impressionists, mod-
ernists from the cubists to the pop
artists expanded the freedom of the
creator to make art from anything
and everything. Picasso, Braque,
and Juan Gris filled their still-life
works with various debris of the
modern city, even pasting discarded
printed labels and torn sheets of
newsprint into their pictures.

Six decades later, Andy Warhol
has carried the theme to its logical
conclusion with his *Campbell's
Soup Cans*, depicted with the
same grandiosity as the way kings
and saints were portrayed in a
neo-classical art. Though *Soup
Cans* was partly hand-painted
by Warhol rather than produced
entirely by silk-screening or some
other mechanical process, Warhol's
choice of subject matter reveals his
former vocation: commercial artist.
Predictably, the result is extremely
impersonal; for Warhol, any and
every subject is treated as a mere
commodity. Warhol's assorted
works carry a variety of messages
about consumerism, the crassness
of contemporary culture, and the
cult of celebrity. But above all else
Soup Cans daringly declares that if
art is purely an experiment in light
and color, then a soup can may rival

any king or saint in beauty and
importance. In this respect, Monet,
Renoir, and Pissarro would have
considered Warhol a true comrade.

18. What is the reviewer's main purpose
in the first paragraph?

The first paragraph is intended to
provide

(1) useful historical background

(2) an evaluation of the work under
review

(3) criticism of the Impressionists

(4) a useful definition of modern art

(5) a description of various painting
methods

19. Which statement does the passage
strongly support?

(1) Warhol created *Soup Cans*
spontaneously, without any
planning.

(2) *Soup Cans* was Warhol's first
attempt at impressionism.

(3) Warhol can be considered part
of the pop-art movement.

(4) Works such as *Soup Cans* make
sense only to the artist.

(5) Warhol did not like to paint by
hand.

20. Based on how the first word in each
pair is used in the passage, which
word-pair association is incorrect?

(1) precursor — forerunner (line 12)

(2) debris — images (line 20)

(3) vocation — job (line 36)

(4) daringly — boldly (line 45)

(5) comrade — brother (line 51)

21. What does the passage suggest that Andy Warhol shares with the Impressionists?

    (1) an irreverent approach to depicting religious themes in art

    (2) a desire to portray subjects in a realistic, photographic way

    (3) a keen interest in current political events and cultural trends

    (4) a fascination with the symbols of achievement and success

    (5) a disregard for the historical or political importance of a subject

22. Why does the reviewer think that the "extremely impersonal" nature of *Soup Cans* is predictable (lines 37–38)?

    (1) Warhol was biased against advertising.

    (2) The human subjects in Warhol's works show little personality.

    (3) Warhol himself never ate Campbell's soup.

    (4) Warhol's background was in commercial art.

    (5) It is easy to predict what the next work of art by Warhol will look like.

QUESTIONS 23–28 REFER TO THE FOLLOWING PASSAGE.

WILL THURM SUCCEED IN HIS PLAN TO OPEN A CASINO?

Just as the blessings were bestowed, about Christmas of '47, the Great Blizzard of the Century came roaring down from Canada,
5 dumping ten years worth of snow in three days. Sandy got stuck by Erma's folks, which was a merry enough situation by that point; but Thurm was socked in, alone, at the
10 Apricot.

Thurm had the whole Avenue pretty much to himself, with Pete off honeymooning with Ethel in Miami (which rankled Thurm somewhat),
15 and most of the Bayers gone home for the off season. Fiske and Jo tunneled over to the Apricot after the storm wore off, and reported finding Thurm at the bar in the
20 Mogambo Room, involved in a fifth of Dewars and a monumental case of cabin fever.

The monument in this case being the Mouton Rouge Casino. Thurm
25 probably meant *Moulin* Rouge, like Toulouse-Lautrec, as opposed to his version, the Red Lamb Casino.

But Thurm's imperfect French was as nothing compared to his
30 timing.

For when the air cleared and the snows settled into the late winter muck, and Thurm was still obsessed with a Red Lamb Casino that would
35 fill his hotel and Avenue all year round, he was faced with dissention within and suspicion without.

For one thing, having a red anything was bad form in those
40 days, and even pink was becoming unthinkable because of some very paranoid and well-placed nuts running around making everyone else paranoid about Communism
45 and secret codes. So Thurm, your classic free-market capitalist, was starting with a label that got some people weird.

When Thurm started floating
50 the idea to the City Chamber of Commerce and the Lake County Administrator's office, he was surprised by the repeated suggestion that this potential gold mine might
55 not be such a hot idea, for him particularly. The phrase "unsavory elements" got a lot of play. Thurm would retort that he'd dealt with unsavory characters a sight longer
60 than the Governor knew what a fart was, and had always come out smelling sweet. So they'd shrug, say, Okay, do what you want, but do it without us. And Thurm said,
65 All right (I'll show you), then they added, Well, you know you'll need

an act of the Legislature, and that was fine by Thurm, too.

— from "Guatemala Avenue," by
Andrew Kass

23. To what do "the blessings" (line 1) probably refer?

  (1) a Christmas celebration

  (2) a baptism

  (3) a wedding ceremony

  (4) the birth of a baby

  (5) Thanksgiving dinner

24. Approximately what time span do the events described in the passage cover?

  (1) about one day

  (2) at least a few days

  (3) about two weeks

  (4) at least a few months

  (5) more than six months

25. Which scenario might cause a problem similar to the one Thurm faced as a result of the name he chose for his planned Casino?

  (1) calling your Web site by a name already used for a similar site

  (2) changing your name to one that better suggests an air of sophistication

  (3) dating someone you mistakenly think is his or her identical twin

  (4) making a tactless joke about a deceased person at his or her funeral

  (5) ordering a meal from a menu printed in a language you don't understand

26. Which of the following common words does the narrator use in a metaphorical sense?

  (1) tunneled (line 17)

  (2) monument (line 23)

  (3) pink (line 40)

  (4) floating (line 49)

  (5) governor (line 60)

27. Why did city and county officials tell Thurm that his idea "might not be such a hot idea, for him particularly" (lines 54–55)?

  (1) The casino's overhead costs would exceed its revenues.

  (2) He might become involved with criminals, like it or not.

  (3) Few people had extra money to gamble in those days.

  (4) The proposed location was off the beaten track.

  (5) They planned to fine him for operating illegally.

28. Which word best describes Thurm, as his character is revealed in the passage?

  (1) pessimistic

  (2) manipulative

  (3) inexperienced

  (4) foolish

  (5) persistent

QUESTIONS 29–34 REFER TO THE FOLLOWING POEM.

IS THERE SUCH A THING AS A "JUST WAR"?

"Anthem for Doomed Youth"

What passing bells for these who die as cattle?

Only the monstrous anger of the guns.

Only the stuttering rifles' rapid rattle

Only patter out their hasty orisons.

5 No mockeries now for them; no prayers, no bells,

Nor any voice of mourning save the choirs,—

The shrill, demented choirs of wailing shells;

And bugles calling for them from sad shires,

What candles may be held to speed them all?

10 Not in the hands of boys, but in their eyes

Shall shine the holy glimmers of good-byes.

The pallor of girls' brows shall be their pall;

Their flowers the tenderness of patient minds,

And each slow dusk a drawing-down of blinds.

— *Wilfred Owen*

29. What is the purpose of using the specific words "rifles' rapid rattle" (line 3)?

(1) to suggest the nervousness felt by a soldier during battle

(2) to emphasize the anger of the people firing the rifles

(3) to stir the poem's reader into outrage against unjust wars

(4) to suggest the speed and ease with which rifle fire can kill

(5) to convey the rhythm and sound a rifle makes when it is fired

30. Which is the most likely setting for the observations described in lines 12–14 of the poem?

(1) a house of worship

(2) a military base

(3) a battlefield

(4) a soldier's home town

(5) an army hospital

31. In the context of the poem itself, what idea does the poem's title ("Anthem for Doomed Youth") convey?

(1) An entire generation of youth can be lost because of war.

(2) Being sent off to war makes a young person grow up quickly.

(3) War is futile because no side ever really wins.

(4) The national anthem can be interpreted as a call to war.

(5) War can cause young people to become disillusioned about life.

32. Which group of words from the poem best conveys its overall tone?

(1) monstrous anger (line 2)

(2) from sad shires (line 8)

(3) holy glimmers (line 11)

(4) patient minds (line 13)

(5) each slow dusk (line 14)

33. The poem draws a comparison between "choirs" (lines 6 and 7) and which of the following?

    (1) stuttering rifles

    (2) cannon shells

    (3) bugles

    (4) passing bells

    (5) prayers

34. Another poem written by Wilfred Owen around the same time as "Anthem for Doomed Youth" ends with a Latin phrase meaning "It is sweet and becoming to die for one's country." In light of "Anthem," what point was Owen probably trying to make by using this phrase?

    (1) Patriotism is an admirable virtue.

    (2) Death in battle should not be feared.

    (3) Dying for one's country is foolish at best.

    (4) To die in battle is to die with dignity.

    (5) Fallen soldiers should be honored as heroes.

QUESTIONS 35–40 REFER TO THE FOLLOWING PASSAGE.

WHAT DOES IT TAKE TO BE A SUCCESSFUL WRITER?

Anthony was late and the venerable philanthropist was awaiting him in a glass-walled sun parlor, where he was glancing through the morning
5 papers for the second time. They shook hands gravely. "I'm awfully glad to hear you're better," Anthony said.

The senior Patch, with an air of
10 having seen his grandson only last week, pulled out his watch.

"Train late?" he asked mildly.

It had irritated him to wait for Anthony. He was under the delusion
15 not only that in his youth he had handled his practical affairs with the utmost scrupulousness, even to keeping every engagement on the dot, but also that this was the direct
20 and primary cause of his success.

"It's been late a good deal this month," he remarked with a shade of meek accusation in his voice—and then after a long sigh, "Sit
25 down."

. . .

"Now that you're here you ought to *do* something," said his grandfather softly, "accomplish something."

Anthony waited for him to speak
30 of "leaving something done when you pass on." Then he made a suggestion:

"I thought—it seemed to me that perhaps I'm best qualified to
35 write—"

Adam Patch winced, visualizing a family poet with long hair and three mistresses.

"—history," finished Anthony.

40 "History? History of what? The Civil War? The Revolution?"

"Why—no, sir. A history of the Middle Ages." Simultaneously an idea was born for a history of the
45 Renaissance popes, written from some novel angle. Still, he was glad he had said "Middle Ages."

"Middle Ages? Why not your own country? Something you know
50 about?"

"Well, you see I've lived so much abroad—"

"Why you should write about the Middle Ages, I don't know. Dark
55 Ages, we used to call 'em. Nobody knows what happened, and nobody cares, except that they're over now." He continued for some minutes on the uselessness of such information,
60 touching, naturally, on the Spanish

Inquisition and the "corruption of the monasteries." Then:

"Do you think you'll be able to do any work in New York—or do you
65 really intend to work at all?" This last with soft, almost imperceptible, cynicism.

"Why, yes, I do, sir."

"When'll you be done?"

70 "Well, there'll be an outline, you see—and a lot of preliminary reading."

"I should think you'd have done enough of that already."

— from *The Beautiful and the Damned*, by F. Scott Fitzgerald

35. Based on the passage, what was most likely true of Patch during his youth?

(1) He took pride in his appearance.

(2) He was often late for his appointments.

(3) He enjoyed reading books about history.

(4) He enjoyed riding the trains.

(5) He lived in luxurious surroundings.

36. What does the phase "from some novel angle" (lines 45–46) mean?

(1) from the viewpoint of an angel or of God

(2) about a subject nobody has thought to write about

(3) in the form of a book written in prose fiction

(4) while reclining, as in bed or on a couch

(5) from a unique perspective on the subject

37. What does the passage reveal about Patch?

(1) He is Anthony's employer.

(2) He is a professional writer.

(3) He is gravely ill.

(4) He was a college professor.

(5) He was financially successful.

38. How would someone in Anthony's position most likely feel after the conversation with Patch?

(1) encouraged

(2) angry

(3) embarrassed

(4) flattered

(5) insulted

39. What does Patch seem to think of Anthony?

(1) He dislikes Anthony but feels obligated to him.

(2) He does not take Anthony very seriously.

(3) He expects Anthony to achieve great things.

(4) He finds Anthony to be rude and disrespectful.

(5) He suspects that Anthony wants something from him.

40. Later in the story, Anthony advises a friend who has found recent financial success as a writer, saying "Don't let the victor belong to the spoils." In light of the earlier conversation in the passage, what might the fact that Anthony was offering advice to a successful writer suggest about Anthony?

Anthony

(1) followed advice that Patch offered him

(2) is jealous of people who are successful

(3) considers himself to be a failure

(4) had been spoiled by Patch

(5) likes to give other people advice

MATHEMATICS

90 Minutes • 50 Questions

Directions: The Mathematics Test consists of 50 questions intended to measure your general mathematics skills, including your ability to solve math problems. The test consists of two parts:

- Part I: 25 questions
- Part II: 25 questions

Part I and Part II are **not** separately timed. If you finish Part I early, you may begin working on Part II right away.

The use of a calculator is allowed for Part I but **not** for Part II.

Disclaimer: The procedural rules for the Math test can be a little confusing. Part I and Part II of the Math test are not discrete, 45-minute sections. In some states, after 45 minutes the testing administrator collects the calculators for Part I and distributes the booklet for Part II (but Part I booklets are not collected at this time). So test-takers have no fewer than 45 minutes to complete Part II. However, test-takers completing Part I early (before 45 minutes have elapsed) can turn in their calculators and start work on Part II immediately. Test-takers who complete Part II early (before the entire 90 minutes have elapsed) will have the option to return to Part I of the test. But test-takers returning to Part I will not have access to calculators during this remaining time.

To answer some questions you will need to apply one or more mathematics formulas. The formulas provided on the next page will help you to answer those questions. Some questions refer to charts, graphs, and figures. Unless otherwise noted, charts, graphs, and figures are drawn to scale.

Answering Alternative-format Questions

To answer some questions, you will be required to write a number instead of selecting among five choices. You will record your answers to these questions using the following alternative-format grid:

To record an answer in this grid, write your answer in the top row. Enter only one character—a number digit, decimal point, or fraction bar—in a box. You may start in any column that will allow you to enter your entire answer. Fill in the corresponding bubble below each character you have written. (GED® answer sheets are machine-read, so only filled-in bubbles will be read.) Leave blank all columns you did not use to record your answer. No answer to an alternative-format question can be a negative number.

Do **not** enter a mixed number in the grid. Instead, enter a fraction or a decimal number. To represent the mixed number $2\frac{1}{2}$, for example, enter either the fraction **5/2** or the decimal number **2.5**. Grid only one answer, even if there is more than one correct answer.

Formulas

AREA	**Triangle:** $\frac{1}{2}$ × base × height **Rectangle:** length × width **Parallelogram:** length × height **Circle:** π × radius² **Right cylinder:** area of circular base × height **Trapezoid:** $\frac{1}{2}$(base₁ + base₂) × height
PERIMETER	**Triangle:** side₁ + side₂ + side₃ **Rectangle:** (2 × length) + (2 × width) **Parallelogram:** (2 × length) + (2 × height) **Circle (circumference):** 2π × radius *or* π × diameter ($\pi \approx 3.14$)
VOLUME	**Right cylinder:** area of base × height **Rectangular solid:** length × width × height **Cube:** (side)³ **Square pyramid:** $\frac{1}{3}$ × area base × height **Cone:** $\frac{1}{3}$ × π × radius² × height ($\pi \approx 3.14$)
COORDINATE GEOMETRY	**Distance between points** = $\sqrt{(x_2 - x_1)^2 + (y_2 - y_1)^2}$, where the two points are (x_1, y_1) and (x_2, y_2) **Slope of a line** = $\frac{y_2 - y_1}{x_2 - x_1}$, where (x_1, y_1) and (x_2, y_2) are any two points on the line
MEASURES OF CENTRAL TENDENCY	**Mean (simple average)** = $\frac{x_1 + x_2 + x_3 \ldots x_n}{n}$, where each x is the value of a different term and n is the total number of terms **Median** = the middle term in value if the number of terms is an *odd* number *or* $\frac{x + y}{2}$ (where x and y are the two middle terms in value) if the number of terms is an *even* number
OTHER FORMULAS	**Pythagorean Theorem:** (leg₁)² + (leg₂)² = (hypotenuse)² **Distance** = rate × time **Simple interest** = dollar amount × interest rate **Total cost** = cost per item × number of items

MATHEMATICS, PART I: QUESTIONS 1–25

THE USE OF A CALCULATOR IS ALLOWED FOR QUESTIONS 1–25.

1. The toll for driving on the Bay Parkway is $1.20 for the first mile and 55 cents for each additional mile. What is the toll for an 8-mile drive on the Bay Parkway?

   (1) $4.40

   (2) $5.05

   (3) $5.60

   (4) $6.90

   (5) $9.60

2. In an arithmetic sequence, each successive term is either greater than or less than the preceding term by the same amount. What is the tenth term of the arithmetic sequence 30, 27, 24, . . . ?

   (1) −30

   (2) −3

   (3) 0

   (4) 3

   (5) 10

3. If two sides of a triangle are 6.5 and 8.5 inches long, which of the following CANNOT be the length of the third side?

   (1) 5.5 inches

   (2) 6.5 inches

   (3) 9.5 inches

   (4) 12 inches

   (5) 15 inches

4. There are 78 sophomores at a school. Each is required to take at least one year of either Chemistry or Physics, but they may take both. 15 are enrolled in both Chemistry and Physics, and 47 are enrolled only in Chemistry. How many students are enrolled only in Physics?

   Mark your answer in the grid on your answer sheet.

5. The value of a new computer decreases 20% each year. Ryan originally purchased his computer for $1500.

   What is the value of Ryan's computer at the end of the second year he owns it?

   (1) $900

   (2) $950

   (3) $960

   (4) $1000

   (5) $1200

6. What is the value of $|7 - 2| - |2 - 7|$?

   (1) −14

   (2) −9

   (3) −5

   (4) 0

   (5) 10

7. Angelique has been in business for five years. In her first year, her profit was $7560. Her second year saw a profit of $5300. During her third and fourth years, she suffered a combined loss of $8450. Her fifth year saw a loss of $4220.

   Which describes Angelique's profit or loss for all five years combined?

   (1) a loss of $8640

   (2) a loss of $190

   (3) neither a profit nor a loss

   (4) a profit of $190

   (5) a profit of $8640

QUESTIONS 8 AND 9 ARE BASED ON THE FOLLOWING TABLE.

Shipping Rates for Express Parcel Service, Inc.

	Shipment Method		
	Ground	Air	Express
1 pound or less	$1.50	$2.25	$6.75
Each additional pound (or fraction) through 10 pounds	$0.40	$0.60	$1.15
Each additional pound (or fraction), 11 or more pounds	$0.25	$0.40	$0.75

8. How much would it cost to ship a 28-pound parcel by ground delivery?

   (1) $8.80
   (2) $9.60
   (3) $9.75
   (4) $10.40
   (5) $12.05

9. How much more would it cost to ship a parcel weighing 2.4 pounds by Express delivery than by Air delivery?

   (1) $2.80
   (2) $3.05
   (3) $3.60
   (4) $4.75
   (5) $5.60

QUESTION 10 IS BASED ON THE FOLLOWING DIAGRAM.

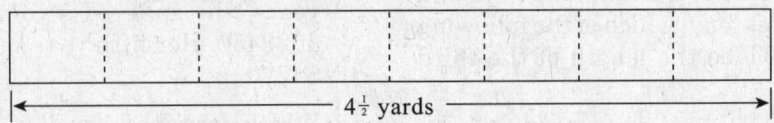

$4\frac{1}{2}$ yards

10. Brooke bought $4\frac{1}{2}$ running yards of cloth to make curtains. To create two panels for each of four windows, she cut the material into 8 panels of equal width, as shown by the dotted lines in the above figure.

    What is the width of each panel? Express your answer in inches.

    Mark your answer in the grid on your answer sheet.

11. To travel 1200 miles in their recreational vehicle, the Steiners paid a total of $450 for gas, at an average fuel cost of $3.00 per gallon.

    What was the vehicle's average mileage during the trip?

    (1) 8.0 miles per gallon
    (2) 10.4 miles per gallon
    (3) 12.0 miles per gallon
    (4) 14.5 miles per gallon
    (5) Not enough information is provided.

12. One-inch cubes must be packed into a rectangular packing box. Which of the following box sizes will accommodate the most cubes?

   (1) 12 inches × 10 inches × 12.5 inches
   (2) 10 inches × 15 inches × 10 inches
   (3) 20 inches × 7.5 inches × 10 inches
   (4) 12.5 inches × 15 inches × 8 inches
   (5) 6 inches × 12.5 inches × 20 inches

13. Adding $4\frac{1}{2}$ to $3\frac{3}{4}$ and then subtracting $2\frac{2}{5}$ from the sum results in which value?

   (1) $\frac{57}{10}$

   (2) $\frac{231}{40}$

   (3) $\frac{117}{20}$

   (4) $\frac{23}{4}$

   (5) $\frac{29}{5}$

14. Each interior angle of a regular polygon measures $\frac{180(s-2)}{s}$ degrees, where s represents the number of sides in the polygon. The below figure shows a regular polygon.

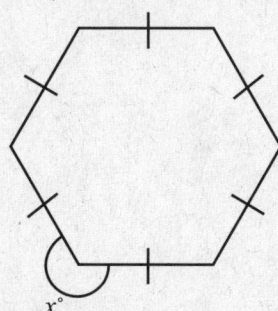

   What is the value of x ?
   (1) 120
   (2) 180
   (3) 220
   (4) 240
   (5) 260

QUESTIONS 15 AND 16 ARE BASED ON THE FOLLOWING GRAPH.

AREA OF WAREHOUSE UNITS A, B, C, AND D (AS PORTIONS OF TOTAL WAREHOUSE AREA)

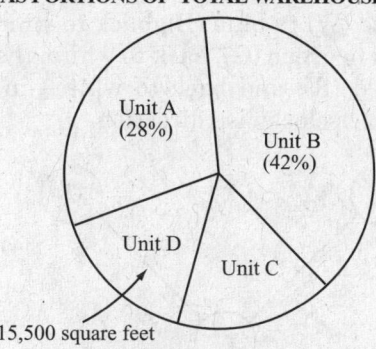

15,500 square feet

Total: 140,000 square feet

15. The graph shows the proportionate areas of 4 warehouse units: A, B, C, and D. Which of the following most closely approximates the square-foot area of Unit C?

   (1) 19,500
   (2) 23,000
   (3) 26,500
   (4) 37,500
   (5) 42,000

16. Rent for the unit is determined on a per-square-foot basis. The two largest units rent at one-half the monthly per-square-foot rate of either smaller unit. Which unit costs least to rent per month?

   (1) Unit A
   (2) Unit B
   (3) Unit C
   (4) Unit D
   (5) Not enough information is provided.

17. In the simple light show pictured below, a light starts at the center (white) at time zero and moves once every second in the following pattern: from white (W) to blue (B), back to white, then to green (G), back to white, then to red (R), and back to white—in a *counter*-clockwise direction.

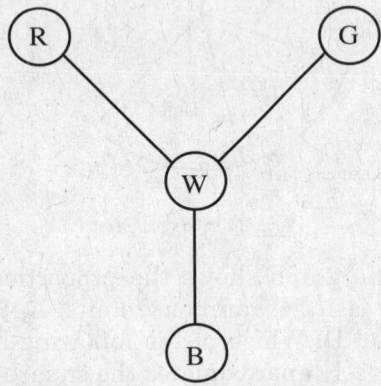

If the light continues to move in this way, what will be the color sequence from the 208th second to the 209th second?

(1) white to red

(2) white to blue

(3) white to green

(4) red to white

(5) green to white

18. Carlos is monitoring the temperature gauge in his sub-zero freezer every 15 minutes. The first hour, he observes a median temperature of 0°F (Fahrenheit) and a range in temperatures of 4.

Which of the following lists might provide the four temperatures that Carlos observed?

(1) −4.0°, −0.3°, 0.3°, 4.0°

(2) −1.2°, −3.3°, 0.7°, 1.1°

(3) −2.4°, 1.6°, 0.0°, 0.8°

(4) −2.6°, −1.2°, 1.4°, 1.2°

(5) 2.2°, 1.5°, −2.2°, −1.5°

19. A farmer wants to construct a fence to create a square horse corral with an area of 10,000 square feet. Fence posts along each side will be 10 feet apart at their center.

Including the four corner posts, how many posts are needed to construct the fence?

Mark your answer in the grid on your answer sheet.

QUESTIONS 20–22 ARE BASED ON THE FOLLOWING INFORMATION AND TABLE.

On a certain Monday, traffic monitors recorded vehicle speeds at two intersections—A and B—located a half mile from each other. The following table indicates the numbers of vehicles traveling at various speeds through each intersection during the noon hour that day (mph = miles per hour). The speed limit at intersection A is 30 mph, and the speed limit at intersection B is 35 mph.

	< 25 mph	25–26 mph	27–28 mph	29–30 mph	31–32 mph	33–34 mph	35–36 mph	37–38 mph	39–40 mph	> 40 mph
A	18	27	34	31	42	62	55	49	43	69
B	2	0	7	14	18	27	58	49	11	23

20. Approximately what portion of drivers obeyed the speed-limit law for intersection A?

   (1) 1 in every 4 drivers

   (2) 1 in every 3 drivers

   (3) 2 in every 5 drivers

   (4) 1 in every 2 drivers

   (5) 3 in every 5 drivers

21. Which graph best represents the distribution of speeds at intersection A as provided in the table?

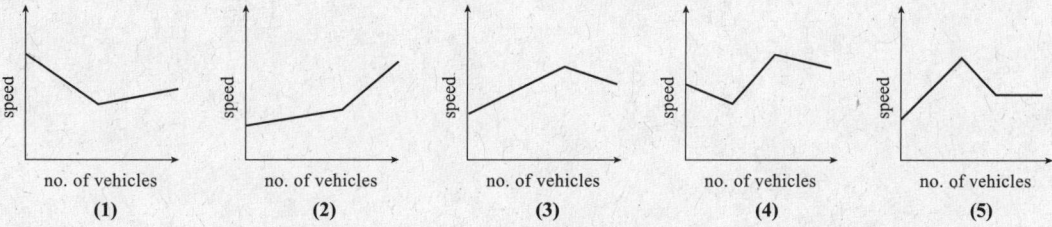

(1)	(2)	(3)	(4)	(5)

22. Which of the following, if true, best explains the distribution of speeds recorded at intersection A as compared with the distribution of speeds recorded at intersection B?

   (1) Weather conditions during the noon hour that Monday were poor.

   (2) Intersection A is located in a school zone.

   (3) The condition of the road surface through intersection A is poor.

   (4) No speed-limit signs are posted near either intersection.

   (5) Intersection B is closely monitored by law-enforcement officers.

23. Two ships leave the same island harbor at the same time, and after 4.5 hours they are 270 kilometers apart.

Which statement about the direction and average speed of the two ships could be true?

(1) They traveled in the same direction, one at 30 km/hr and the other at 50 km/hr.

(2) One traveled north at 25 km/hr, and the other traveled west at 30 km/hr.

(3) They traveled in the same direction, one at 10 km/hr and the other at 60 km/hr.

(4) They traveled in opposite directions, both at 35 km/hr.

(5) They traveled in opposite directions, one at 45 km/hr and the other at 15 km/hr.

24. If $f(x) = x^4$, for what value of a does $f(a) = 1296$?

(1) 4

(2) 6

(3) 648

(4) 2592

(5) Not enough information is provided.

25. A botanist observing the growth rate of a climbing vine records growth of 0.36 meters over one 24-day period. What was the vine's growth rate per day, expressed in centimeters?

[1 meter = 100 centimeters]

Mark your answer using the grid on your answer sheet.

MATHEMATICS, PART II: QUESTIONS 26–50

THE USE OF A CALCULATOR IS NOT ALLOWED FOR QUESTIONS 26–50.

26. If $\frac{a}{b} \cdot \frac{b}{c} \cdot \frac{c}{d} \cdot x = 1$, then which of the following represents the value of x?

(1) $\frac{a}{d}$

(2) $\frac{bd}{a}$

(3) d

(4) $\frac{d}{a}$

(5) $\frac{1}{a}$

27. The figure below shows two line segments connecting a circle's center to its circumference.

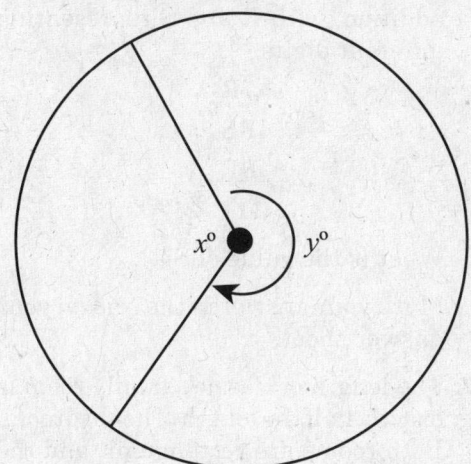

What is the value of y in terms of x?

(1) $\frac{360}{x}$

(2) $180 + x$

(3) $\frac{x}{180}$

(4) $360 - x$

(5) $\frac{x}{360}$

28. A certain clock runs 48 minutes slow every 12 hours. If the clock was set correctly at 1:00 p.m., then at 4:30 p.m. that day how many minutes behind the correct time is the clock running?

Mark your answer in the grid on your answer sheet.

29. In the figure below, line k is parallel to line m.

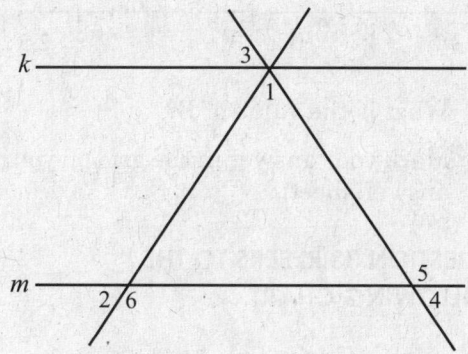

Which of the following equalities holds true in all cases?

(1) $m\angle 1 = m\angle 2$

(2) $m\angle 3 = m\angle 4$

(3) $m\angle 5 = m\angle 6$

(4) $m\angle 2 = m\angle 3$

(5) $m\angle 4 = m\angle 1$

30. If $x^2 + 4x = 0$, how many values of x are possible?

(1) none

(2) one

(3) two

(4) four

(5) infinitely many

31. If $x + y = a$, and if $x - y = b$, then which expression represents the value of x?

(1) $\frac{1}{2}(a + b)$

(2) $a + b$

(3) $a - b$

(4) $\frac{1}{2}ab$

(5) $\frac{1}{2}(a - b)$

32. In the number line shown below, the vertical marks are equally spaced.

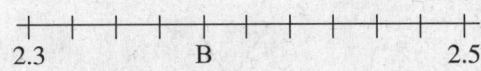

2.3   B   2.5

What is the value of B?

Mark your answer in the grid on your answer sheet.

QUESTION 33 REFERS TO THE FOLLOWING CHART.

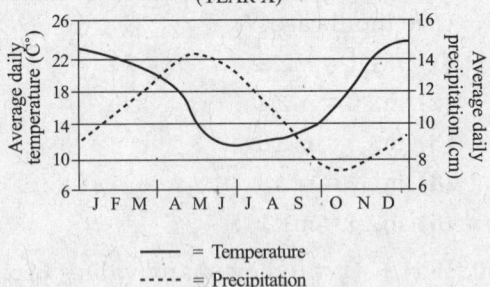

AMAZON RAINFOREST TEMPERATURE AND PRECIPITATION LEVELS (YEAR X)

— = Temperature
----- = Precipitation

33. What was the approximate amount of precipitation on the coldest day of year X?

(1) 11.5 cm

(2) 13.5 cm

(3) 16.0 cm

(4) 21.0 cm

(5) 24.5 cm

34. Quadrilateral $ABCD$ is a square. The coordinates of point A are (3,2), the coordinates of point B are (–3,2), and the coordinates of point C are (–3,–4).

Show the location of point D by marking the coordinate grid on your answer sheet.

35. How many different ways can you add four positive, odd integers together for a sum of 10? The integers may be used more than once, and the sequence of the integers should not be considered.

(1) one

(2) two

(3) three

(4) four

(5) five

36. Shown below is a correct problem in addition, with R and S representing different digits.

$$\begin{array}{r} 7R \\ RS \\ \underline{RR} \\ 117 \end{array}$$

What is the value of S?

Mark your answer in the grid on your answer sheet.

37. The length of Cassie's family room is exactly half the length of her bedroom. Both rooms are rectangular, and the area of the two rooms is the same. If Cassie's family room has a length of L and a width of W, which of the following represents the width of her bedroom?

(1) $2L$

(2) $L - \frac{1}{2}$

(3) $2W$

(4) W

(5) $\frac{W}{2}$

38. If $x = -1$, then what is the value of $x^{-2} + x^2$?

(1) -2

(2) -1

(3) 0

(4) 1

(5) 2

39. The number 40.5 is 500 times greater than which number?

(1) 0.00810

(2) 0.02025

(3) 0.0810

(4) 0.2025

(5) 0.810

40. If $m = n$ and $p < q$, then which of the following inequalities holds true in all cases?

(1) $m - p > n - q$

(2) $p - m > q - n$

(3) $m - p < n - q$

(4) $mp > nq$

(5) $m + q < n + p$

41. Twice the sum of 3 and a number N is 1 less than 3 times the number N.

Which equation can you use to find the value of N?

(1) $6 + N = 3N - 1$

(2) $2(3 + N) - 1 = 3N$

(3) $6 - 2N = 3N - 1$

(4) $2(3 + N) = 1 - 3N$

(5) $6 + 2N = 3N - 1$

QUESTION 42 REFERS TO THE FOLLOWING FIGURE.

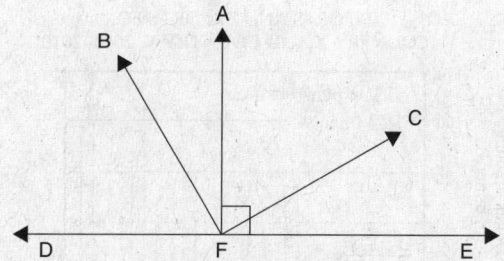

42. Referring to the above figure, you can find $\angle AFB$ if you know which of the following angle measures?

(1) $\angle AFC$

(2) $\angle BFD$

(3) $\angle CFE$

(4) $\angle BFC$

(5) $\angle DFC$

43. Which of the following expressions is equivalent to $(x + 2)(x - 2)$?

(1) $x^2 - 2$

(2) $x^2 - 4$

(3) $-2x^2$

(4) $4x^2$

(5) $2x - 4$

QUESTIONS 44 AND 45 REFER TO THE FOLLOWING GRAPH.

IMPORTS AND EXPORTS FOR
COUNTRY X AND COUNTRY Y, 2005–2010

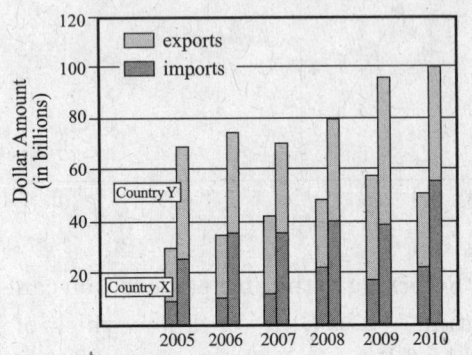

NOTE: For each year, the combined height of two bar segments shows total imports and exports of a country.

44. In which of the following years did Country Y's imports exceed Country X's imports by the smallest percentage?

    (1) 2005
    (2) 2006
    (3) 2007
    (4) 2008
    (5) 2010

45. Which of the following best describes Country Y's overall import and export trend over the six-year period shown?

    (1) The value of imports generally increased, but there was no clear export trend.
    (2) The value of imports generally increased, while the value of exports generally declined.
    (3) Neither the value of imports nor the value of exports exhibited a clear trend over the period.
    (4) The value of imports and exports both increased steadily in dollar value.
    (5) The value of imports increased but then declined, while the value of exports increased steadily.

46. At Hungry Boy restaurant, a complete meal comes with a choice of one appetizer and one vegetable from the following menu:

    Appetizers
    fruit
    soup
    salad

    Vegetables
    carrots
    squash
    peas

    What is the probability that a Hungry Boy patron will select salad and squash?

    Mark your answer in the grid on your answer sheet.

47. Water from a certain pond contains an average of 4.9 specimens of species Z per cubic centimeter. How many specimens of species Z are contained in 1 cubic millimeter of pond water?

    [1 cubic centimeter = 1000 cubic millimeters]

    (1) 4.9×10^{-3}
    (2) 4.9×10^{-2}
    (3) 4.9×10^{-1}
    (4) 4.9×10^{2}
    (5) 4.9×10^{3}

QUESTION 48 REFERS TO THE FOLLOWING FIGURE.

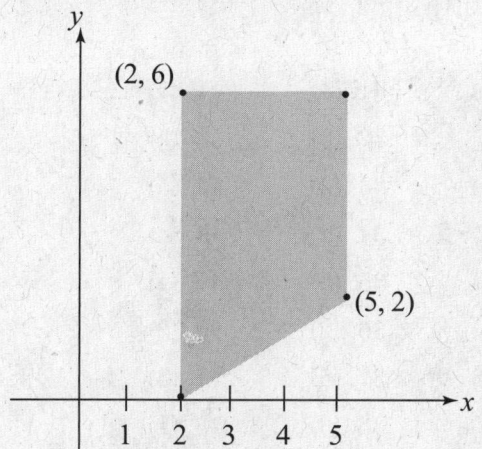

48. The shaded figure shown above is a trapezoid. What is its square-unit area?
    (1) 15
    (2) 16
    (3) 17
    (4) 18
    (5) 19

49. Machine X, Machine Y, and Machine Z each produce widgets. Machine Y's rate of production is one-third that of Machine X, and Machine Z's production rate is twice that of Machine Y.

    If Machine Y can produce 35 widgets per day, how many widgets can the three machines produce per day working simultaneously?

    Mark your answer in the grid on your answer sheet.

50. A group of travelers have assembled a tepee that has a circular base. As shown in the figure, the side of the tepee measures 3 meters from the ground to the tepee's peak, and the peak angle measures 50°.

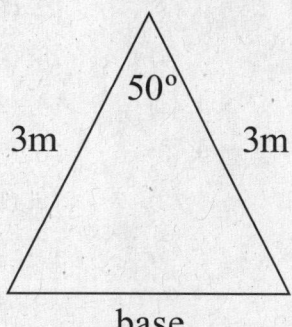

What is the diameter of the tepee's circular base?
    (1) 3cos32°
    (2) 3sin32°
    (3) 3sin16°
    (4) 6tan16°
    (5) 6sin25°

ANSWER KEY AND EXPLANATIONS

Language Arts Writing, Part I

1. (2)	11. (4)	21. (2)	31. (4)	41. (1)
2. (3)	12. (5)	22. (3)	32. (3)	42. (4)
3. (4)	13. (1)	23. (5)	33. (2)	43. (5)
4. (4)	14. (2)	24. (5)	34. (2)	44. (4)
5. (5)	15. (2)	25. (5)	35. (5)	45. (4)
6. (2)	16. (1)	26. (4)	36. (2)	46. (2)
7. (1)	17. (2)	27. (4)	37. (5)	47. (3)
8. (4)	18. (2)	28. (3)	38. (3)	48. (1)
9. (1)	19. (2)	29. (1)	39. (5)	49. (5)
10. (3)	20. (5)	30. (5)	40. (3)	50. (2)

1. **The correct answer is (2).** The word *effect* is a noun; the word *affect* is a verb. The latter word is correct in context.

2. **The correct answer is (3).** Sentence 2 refers to events occurring up to the present time. Accordingly, the present-perfect verb form *have been* should be used instead of the past-tense *were*.

3. **The correct answer is (4).** The structure of the original sentence is inverted. The word *unavoidable* and the phrase *a reduction in our sales force* should be switched. Choice (4) accomplishes just that, as well as changing *a reduction in* to the more concise *reducing*.

4. **The correct answer is (4).** The word *if* here suggests that medical coverage will continue when a former employee finds other coverage, which is just the opposite of the intended point. Replacing *if* with *until* fixes the problem.

5. **The correct answer is (5).** The sentence contains no errors, and implementing one of the proposed changes would either be unnecessary or result in a usage or mechanical error.

6. **The correct answer is (2).** In a combined sentence, the phrases *for this purpose* and *in this respect* are redundant. You can simply omit the former phrase, and then transform sentence 11 into a subordinate clause, as proposed in choice (2): *We have made arrangements with a consulting firm specializing in executive recruiting to assist you in this respect for the next six months.*

7. **The correct answer is (1).** The phrase *in light of these new developments* is awkwardly interjected between the subject (*meeting*) and the verb *is,* thereby obscuring the sentence's main idea: the meeting is canceled. The best solution is to either begin or conclude the sentence with this phrase. Choice (1) provides the former solution: *In light of these new developments, the Omega team sales meeting scheduled for Monday, October 14, is canceled.*

8. **The correct answer is (4).** The relative pronoun *each* is considered singular, hence it takes the singular verb *has,* not the plural form *have.* Choice (4) fixes the problem.

9. **The correct answer is (1).** Paragraph (A) mainly discusses recent developments at Titan, while paragraph (B) discusses actions to be taken in light of those developments. Sentence 1 belongs in paragraph (B). What's more, sentence 1 makes a good topic sentence for the paragraph, and so beginning the paragraph with this sentence improves the coherence of the memo.

10. **The correct answer is (3).** The most effective way to begin sentence 1 is with a phrase that is grammatically parallel to the phrase *They're also pressured to*, which is how sentence 2 begins. In essence, the first paragraph should read as follows: *[They] are pressured to . . . . They are also pressured to . . . .*

11. **The correct answer is (4).** The problem with sentence 3 is that it consists of two independent clauses spliced together with a comma. Inserting the word *but* after the comma corrects the problem and emphasizes the contrast between the sentence's two ideas.

12. **The correct answer is (5).** Sentence 4 is a run-on sentence and should be split into two separate sentences. Choice (5) provides an ideal way of doing so: *Try carrying a 4.6 grade-point average while being editor of the school newspaper and captain of the volleyball team. Each is quite an accomplishment in itself.*

13. **The correct answer is (1).** The two noun clauses *to do them . . .* and *doing yourself . . .* should be grammatically parallel, but they're not. Replacing *to do* with *doing* fixes the problem.

14. **The correct answer is (2).** The tense used at the beginning of the sentence should match the tense used at the end. The present tense makes the most sense in context: *For someone who is 18 years old . . . it's too late.*

15. **The correct answer is (2).** Sentence 6 provides a brief, pithy way of reiter-ating the idea expressed in sentence 9. Since sentence 6 flows naturally from sentence 9, it should follow that sentence.

16. **The correct answer is (1).** The second-person *you're* should be used because it matches the word *you* later in sentence 11 as well as in the next paragraph.

17. **The correct answer is (2).** Among the five alternatives, choice (2) provides the only continuation that makes for a clear and well-constructed sentence: *Also, spreading yourself too thin by trying to accomplish too many goals means you might fail to achieve any of them.*

18. **The correct answer is (2).** The three list items should be grammatically parallel, but they're not. Choice (2) is the only one that fixes the problem.

19. **The correct answer is (2).** As it stands, the first clause implies that anyone who arrives by air must rent a car, which makes little sense. Another problem with sentence 3 is that it consists of two independent clauses spliced together with nothing but a comma. Choice (2) provides a perfect way to correct both problems.

20. **The correct answer is (5).** The original sentence can be improved by listing action steps in their proper sequence: first turn left at Grant; then travel about a half mile east on Grant; then turn right at Dakota. Choice (5) articulates this sequence of steps clearly.

21. **The correct answer is (2).** The present-tense verb *is* implies that the reader is at the location while reading the sentence, which of course is not necessarily the case. The future tense is used for all other directions on the page, and so the future tense should be used in sentence 7 as well.

22. **The correct answer is (3).** The address information applies to all three

series of directions (from the airport, from the train station, and from the 58 Freeway), so it would be better positioned in the introductory paragraph A.

23. **The correct answer is (5).** The sentence contains no errors. Each of the four proposed changes would create a grammatical or sentence-logic error.

24. **The correct answer is (5).** The phrase *and then right* would be appropriate if the sentence had already mentioned a left turn (*turn left . . . and then right . . .*) But it is improper and confusing to say *go west . . . and then right*. Choice (5) corrects the problem.

25. **The correct answer is (5).** The word *past* (as in *he drove past Rodenberry Street*) should be used here instead of *passed* (as in *he passed Rodenberry Street).*

26. **The correct answer is (4).** The original sentence is awkwardly constructed. Choice (4) provides for the clearest and most graceful version of the sentence: *The convention center is on Dakota, three blocks south of Lincoln.*

27. **The correct answer is (4).** The sentence refers to a university by its name, and so the capitalized word *University* should be used.

28. **The correct answer is (3).** The underlined part modifies the singular *family* with the plural possessive *members'* (note the apostrophe after the *s*), implying that all GUAA members share a single family. Choice (3) fixes the problem with a concise alternative. Each of the other four choices creates a new problem.

29. **The correct answer is (1).** The phrase *in the third week of July* is a parenthetical idea, or appositive. Accordingly, the phrase should be set off by inserting a comma both before and after it.

30. **The correct answer is (5).** The phrase that begins with *ranging from* is intended to modify *Activities*. The sentence would be clearer if *Activities* came immediately before this phrase, as choice (5) provides: *Activities ranging from swimming and canoeing to lectures, cooking classes, and art classes are available for the entire family.* None of the other four choices provides for a revision that is as effective.

31. **The correct answer is (4).** The original version contains a vague pronoun reference. (To whom does *Those* refer?) Choice (4) fixes the problem by replacing the pronoun with its intended antecedent from sentence 10.

32. **The correct answer is (3).** The sentence intends to list two specific types of access to the library: online access and access to the Special Collections room. Choice (3) is the only one that provides for a grammatically parallel list and a sentence free of ambiguity or errors.

33. **The correct answer is (2).** Each of the other three list items (identified by bullets) has the same grammatical structure (*discount on . . .* , *access to . . .* , and *use of . . .*). The beginning of sentence 14 should be revised so it matches that structure. Choice (2) is the only one that provides an appropriate revision.

34. **The correct answer is (2).** Sentences 10 and 18 both focus on the benefits of accessing the GUAA member network. Positioning these two sentences together in the same paragraph makes sense and would improve the organization of ideas in the document.

35. **The correct answer is (5).** The pronoun *its* has no antecedent. A simple way to correct this error is to simply remove the word.

36. **The correct answer is (2).** If you read sentence 2 with sentence 1 in mind, it becomes clear that sentence 2 intends

to provide another reason that a business might fail or *can fail*, as choice (2) provides. Choices (1), (3), and (4) incorrectly use the plural *their* instead of *its*. Also, in choice (1), the tense shift from past to present is illogical, while in choice (5), the relative pronoun *when* is used together with the past-tense verb *didn't* in a way that confuses the sentence's time frame.

37. **The correct answer is (5).** Sentence 4 contains no errors. Each of the four proposed changes is unnecessary or would result in a usage or mechanical error.

38. **The correct answer is (3).** *Had began* is an improper conjugation of the verb *begin*. Removing the word *had* leaves the past-tense *began*, which is correct in this context.

39. **The correct answer is (5).** All three items in the list should be comparative, but they're not. The simplest ways to correct the error is to insert the word *more* immediately after the comma. The result is a grammatically parallel list: *more practical, more efficient, and safer*.

40. **The correct answer is (3).** Choice (3) provides a graceful and grammatically correct revision of the underlined portion. Choices (1) and (2) make no sense. Choice (4) provides for an imperative sentence (a command), which doesn't make sense in context. Choice (5) changes the pronoun *It* to the plural *They*, which is incorrect because the antecedent *GM* is singular; choice (5) also uses the present tense where the past tense is appropriate.

41. **The correct answer is (1).** Sentence 11 is actually a sentence fragment (an incomplete sentence). Removing the word *While* results in a complete, coherent sentence.

42. **The correct answer is (4).** Only choice (4) provides a group of words useful in forming an effective revision of the sentence: *However, that model*

went into development too late to save the company.

43. **The correct answer is (5).** The word *per* means "for each," hence the phrase *per each* is redundant. One way to fix the problem is to simply remove the word *each*.

44. **The correct answer is (4).** The problem with the original version is that the relative pronoun *which* does not refer clearly to its intended antecedent: *carry-on baggage*. Choice (4) provides an effective way to fix this pronoun-reference problem.

45. **The correct answer is (4).** In sentence 4, the tense shifts from the present to the future (*will be allowed*); however, the surrounding text provides no clues that this temporary tense shift is appropriate. Accordingly, the verb form *will be* should be replaced with *is*. (The sentence's singular subject, *item*, takes the singular verb form *is allowed*.)

46. **The correct answer is (2).** The two parts of the underlined portion should be grammatically parallel so that it is clear that both *carry-on* and *personal* refer to types of *items*. Choice (2) provides an effective solution.

47. **The correct answer is (3).** Sentence 9 makes a good topic sentence for paragraph D, so a more effective placement for this sentence would be at the beginning of the paragraph.

48. **The correct answer is (1).** A comma is needed before as well as after the appositive *such as explosives and flammable liquids*.

49. **The correct answer is (5).** Sentence 16 contains no usage errors or mechanical problems. Inserting the word *these* after *of*, choice (1), would illogically imply that the restrictions listed in the previous sentences constitute a complete list. The comma after *items*, choice (2), is appropriate to set off the initial modifying clause

from the main clause. The capitalized word *Agency,* choice (3), is correct here because it is part of the name of a specific government entity (as the acronym *TSA* makes clear). Inserting a comma, choice (4), between the two parts of the correlative pair *either . . . or* would amount to a confusing overuse of the comma.

50. **The correct answer is (2).** Sentence 1, which is the topic sentence of the document, tells us that the specific purpose of the document is to provide airline rules. Sentence 15 provides a mere suggestion, not a requirement, for packing liquids, and it is the only sentence that does not provide a rule. Since sentence 15 digresses from the topic at hand, removing it would serve to improve the overall unity of the notice.

Language Arts, Writing, Part II

Evaluating Your Practice Essay

Your actual GED® essay will be read and scored by 2 trained readers, who will evaluate it according to its *overall effectiveness,* considering how well you convey and support your main ideas, how well you organize those ideas, and how clearly and correctly you write throughout the essay.

It is difficult to be objective about one's own writing. So to help you evaluate your practice essay, you may wish to ask a mentor, teacher, or friend to read and evaluate it for you. In any case, use the following 4-point evaluation checklist. This list provides all of the elements of an effective, high-scoring GED® essay.

❶ Is the essay well-focused? (Does it clearly convey a central idea, and does it remain focused on that idea, as opposed to digressing from the topic or focusing too narrowly on certain minor points?)

❷ Does the essay develop its main ideas effectively, using persuasive reasons and relevant supporting examples?

❸ Is the essay well-organized? (Are the ideas presented in a logical sequence, so that the reader can easily follow them? Are transitions from one point to the next natural and logical? Does the essay have a clear ending, or did you appear to run out of time?)

❹ Does your essay demonstrate good control of grammar, sentence structure, word choice, punctuation, and spelling?

Each GED® reader will score your essay on a scale of 0–4 (the highest score is 4). If you can objectively answer "yes" to all four of the above questions, then your essay would earn a score of at least 3, and probably 4, from a trained GED® reader. Keep in mind, however, that the testing service will not award a separate score for the Writing Test, Part II (the essay). Instead, the service will combine your Part I and Part II scores according to its own formula, and then it will award a single overall Writing Test score.

Social Studies

1. (5)	11. (1)	21. (3)	31. (2)	41. (4)
2. (3)	12. (5)	22. (2)	32. (1)	42. (2)
3. (2)	13. (4)	23. (2)	33. (2)	43. (4)
4. (4)	14. (1)	24. (4)	34. (4)	44. (3)
5. (3)	15. (1)	25. (4)	35. (5)	45. (4)
6. (4)	16. (4)	26. (1)	36. (5)	46. (5)
7. (3)	17. (2)	27. (1)	37. (3)	47. (3)
8. (5)	18. (1)	28. (2)	38. (2)	48. (2)
9. (2)	19. (3)	29. (1)	39. (2)	49. (5)
10. (3)	20. (1)	30. (2)	40. (4)	50. (1)

1. **The correct answer is (5).** Both UN forces and the military forces of individual countries are usually armed and sometimes engage in battle. The other statements give facts about UN peacekeeping forces that are not generally true of the military forces of individual countries.

2. **The correct answer is (3).** While the diet of the Native Americans of the Northwest Coast relied heavily on fish, those of the Eastern Woodlands had a greater variety of food sources (farming, fishing, hunting, and gathering). Only the peoples of the Eastern Woodlands engaged in farming, so choice (1) is wrong. Since both groups fished, choice (2) incorrect. From the information given, it's impossible to tell which group of Native Americans was more advanced—a term that is very subjective and depends on how a person defines it—so choices (4) and (5) are incorrect.

3. **The correct answer is (2).** Madison argued that the government's powers should be divided among legislative, executive, and judicial branches of government and that each of these branches should "have a will of its own" or, in other words, be independent. He wanted to separate the branches, but not divide or separate leaders within those branches, choice (1). Since the two quotes do not mention a bill of rights, we don't know his position on a bill of rights, choice (3). Both statements in choices (4) and (5) contradict his belief that each branch of government should be independent and "have a will of its own."

4. **The correct answer is (4).** Madison's goal was to keep government from being oppressive, not to promote equality or democracy. Madison himself had slaves and supported limiting the right to vote to property owners, so neither equality, choice (1), nor democracy, choice (2), were values he held. Although Madison later became president, he's never been accused of trying to use the debate over the Constitution as a means of gaining power for himself, choice (3). Madison's position on states' rights, choice (5), is not addressed in these quotes, but he was a supporter of the Constitution and the strong central government it embodied.

5. **The correct answer is (3).** The author infers that the cause of the Cold War was Soviet expansionism. There's no indication in the passage that the author believes any of the other choices were causes of Cold War.

answers diagnostic test

6. **The correct answer is (4).** The cartoon illustrates the terrorizing of freed blacks by the Ku Klux Klan and other white reactionary groups.

7. **The correct answer is (3).** Nothing in the cartoon remotely suggests that freed slaves were being treated as equals, choices (1) and (5); or that their lives had improved, choice (2); or that the Klan helped them, choice (4). To the contrary, the cartoon suggests a continuing struggle for true equality.

8. **The correct answer is (5).** The use of the word "should" in the statement in choice (5) indicates it is not a fact, but rather a judgment or opinion. All the other answer choices are statements of facts broadly accepted as true.

9. **The correct answer is (2).** The preamble indicates that the reasons for political separation will be discussed in the document.

10. **The correct answer is (3).** According to the graph, the clergy costs $113 and the groom's clothing costs $77, which are both less than $192, the cost of the limousine.

11. **The correct answer is (1).** Since the reception is by far the greatest single expense, the greatest saving probably could be made there.

12. **The correct answer is (5).** If the wedding cost about $10,000 and the cost of the reception was just under $6,000, then a little more than half, or about 60 percent, of the total cost was for the reception.

13. **The correct answer is (4).** The U.S. District Courts (of which there are 89 districts) have original jurisdiction and conduct trials in cases involving federal laws and regulations. State supreme courts, choice (3), and U.S. Courts of Appeals, choice (5), do not have original jurisdiction and cannot conduct trials. The Supreme Court, choice (2), has original jurisdiction only in special cases. State trial courts, choice (1), generally take cases involving state laws, not federal laws.

14. **The correct answer is (1).** The U.S. Supreme Court is the trial court (court of original jurisdiction) in disputes between two state governments as specified in the Constitution. U.S. Courts of Appeals, choice (5), and state supreme courts, choices (2) and (3), do not have original jurisdiction and do not conduct trials. U.S. District Courts, choice (4), have original jurisdiction but not in cases involving two state governments.

15. **The correct answer is (1).** The left-hand map shows British forces traveling up the Chesapeake Bay in order to access certain areas north of the bay.

16. **The correct answer is (4).** Unlike most New Deal programs, the FDIC was not established to create jobs but to reform the financial system. The FDIC was designed to make banks less prone to failure and prevent runs on banks like those that occurred at the beginning of the Great Depression. All the other programs directly or indirectly created more jobs.

17. **The correct answer is (2).** The belief underlying the New Deal was that government should create jobs to stimulate the economy. The New Deal brought more, not less, government regulation of business, choice (1). Stimulating the economy by creating jobs was deemed more important than balancing the budget, choice (3). Raising taxes would have hurt the economy and was not part of most New Deal programs, choice (4). Many New Deal programs, including the WPA, REA, and TVA, used tax dollars to build or improve infrastructure, so choice (5) is incorrect.

18. **The correct answer is (1).** Since the person has a bank account, the establishment of the FDIC would guarantee that his or her money in

the bank would be safe. A resident of New York City would not be directly affected by the TVA, choice (3), or REA, choice (5). Since the person has a job, he or she would not be directly affected by the WPA, choice (4), or CCC, choice (5).

19. **The correct answer is (3).** As the passage notes, in terms of what a U.S. dollar can buy, its value has declined steadily since 1950 (or earlier). Although 1967 does not appear in the actual illustration, it is the only year listed among the choices that could be the base year used for comparison with the others.

20. **The correct answer is (1).** The growing buying power of the Euro compared to the U.S. dollar means that goods and services in the United States are relatively inexpensive to Europeans. It makes sense that they would take advantage of the weak U.S. dollar by spending their money here.

21. **The correct answer is (3).** President Kennedy was speaking in broad terms of the Cold War struggle against Soviet expansion. We can assume he wanted Americans to support this struggle in some way. Fighting in the military, choice (4), joining the Peace Corps, choice (2), and paying taxes, choice (1), would all be ways of supporting this struggle, but Kennedy wasn't just thinking of one of these things in particular, and the question specifically asks for the "broad" goal. Kennedy supported the civil rights movement, choice (5), but he was not talking about that in this part of his speech.

22. **The correct answer is (2).** Latitude 0° is the equator, and the prime meridian is longitude 0°, so the exact location would be where prime meridian intersects the equator, which happens to be a point in the Atlantic Ocean off the coast of Africa.

23. **The correct answer is (2).** Four of the points—A, B, C, and E—lie north of 60°S. Of those four points, only Point C lies west of the prime meridian but east of 40°W.

24. **The correct answer is (4).** The airliner would be moving in a south-westerly direction—from the area east of Point A toward the area a bit east of Point D.

25. **The correct answer is (4).** The passage defines a desert as a region having less than 10 inches of precipitation a year. Thus the only relevant fact in determining if Antarctica is a desert is the amount of precipitation it gets. The other answer choices all deal with other facts about Antarctica.

26. **The correct answer is (1).** The passage states the one real power of the vice president is to break tie votes, so he or she can be expected to be present when a Senate vote is scheduled that will be very close. Otherwise, serving as presiding officer is a formality that doesn't even allow the vice president to make speeches, choice (5), or take part in a debate, choices (2) and (4). Presiding over an impeachment trial, choice (3), would be largely a formality too; however, the Constitution actually gives this duty to the Chief Justice of the Supreme Court so there is no conflict of interest (the vice president would become president if the president were impeached).

27. **The correct answer is (1).** The United States wanted to help rebuild Western European nations so the United States, not the Soviets, would have influence over the Western European nations. The cartoon conveys this idea. None of the other choices are as well supported by the cartoon.

28. **The correct answer is (2).** The U.S. government pursued a policy of helping the settlers take the land from the native people—in other words, to expand the territory under their oc-

cupation and control. Native American relocation, choice (4), was the *means* of implementing the policy of geographic expansion, not the policy itself.

29. **The correct answer is (1).** The Cherokees viewed their forced migration with great bitterness and sorrow. There is no evidence in the passage that they actually wept, choices (4) and (5), or that they planned to hurt people, choice (3). The extent to which they were civilized, choice (2), was not related to their hardships.

30. **The correct answer is (2).** No evidence is provided to support choice (5). While choices (1), (3), and (4) might provide true statements, only choice (2) explains why online sales have eclipsed print-catalog sales. The fact that online retailers have lower overhead costs than print-catalog retailers suggests that online prices are lower overall and that consumers are responding favorably to those lower prices.

31. **The correct answer is (2).** The map shows that a number of states have more than one time zone within their boundaries. The boundaries of the time zones are not straight as they would be if determined by science, choice (1). There are four time zones, so choice (3) is wrong. People gain an hour traveling across a time zone boundary if they are going west but lose an hour if they are going east, making choice (4) incorrect. Since the boundaries are set by state or local governments, they can change, so choice (5) is wrong. Indianapolis for example, decided to move from Central Time to Eastern Time, but this decision remains controversial.

32. **The correct answer is (1).** Eastern time is earlier than all the other time zones in the United States.

33. **The correct answer is (2).** Immigrants were enticed by all the economic opportunities in the United States.

34. **The correct answer is (4).** One state might lose significant population to another over a period less than a decade. If so, then representation in Congress won't be balanced to reflect the population shift—at least not until after the next census.   35.
The correct answer is (5). The lack of central authority in Japan made the rise of the samurai possible. The samurai fought for and supported local nobles, not the emperor, choice (1). Land distribution gave land to local nobles, not the samurai, choice (2). The Japanese feudal system resembled that of Europe during the same time period, but these systems arose independently, choice (3); there is nothing in the passage to indicate that the Japanese wanted to copy Europe. The samurai rose to power in the countryside, not the capital city; the fact it was controlled by the emperor had little to do with the rise of the samurai, choice (4).

36. **The correct answer is (5).** Climate determines a region's population density more than population density determines the region's climate. This factor doesn't have much effect on a region's climate, although on a global scale, the world's increasing population density and use of carbon-producing fossil fuels is warming the planet. The other factors all have direct, determining influences on a region's climate.

37. **The correct answer is (3).** Murmansk is warmed by the Gulf Stream, which has a strong warming effect in winter on the climate of all northwestern Europe. The passage states it is farther to the north, which makes it farther from the equator, choice (1), than most Russian seaports. Prevailing winds from the north would make the city colder, not warmer, choice (2). Nearby mountains, choice (4), would

not have much effect in making a city's climate unusually warm for how far north it is. Seaports, by definition, all have pretty much the same altitude, which is near sea level, making choice (5) incorrect.

38. **The correct answer is (2).** The system of checks and balances, which prevents one group from gaining too much power, might not operate so well in Nebraska's one-house legislature as it does in two-house state legislatures.

39. **The correct answer is (2).** In World War I, Russia, Britain, France, Italy, and the United States were allied against Germany and Turkey.

40. **The correct answer is (4).** Though a simplistic account of the war, choice (4) is the most accurate among the five listed. After Austria declared war on Serbia (over an assassination), Russia and France mobilized to support Austria. In response to that support, Germany declared war on Russia and France and then invaded Belgium as well as attacked Russia, England, and France. In short, Russia, France, and their allies joined to wear down the initial invading country, Germany.

41. **The correct answer is (4).** The Ninth and Tenth Amendments give powers not otherwise described to the people and to the states.

42. **The correct answer is (2).** The Third Amendment protects citizens from having to house and feed troops during peacetime.

43. **The correct answer is (4).** This is an example of how many important developments in history happen gradually and can't easily be dated. Gradual changes are more the norm in history than single earth-shaking events, so choice (5) is wrong. Historians, who recognize their work is not scientific or exact, are generally more interested in gradual or underlying change than simple events and dates, so choice (3)

is incorrect. There is seldom complete agreement among historians about either general interpretations of history, choice (1), or the meaning of specific events, choice (2).

44. **The correct answer is (3).** By choosing to attend college, Maria gives up the opportunity of earning $200 per week.

45. **The correct answer is (4).** Maria's decision involves a choice between the part-time job and college classes. Because she can't be in two places at once or pay her college costs, choosing one means giving up the other.

46. **The correct answer is (5).** Appointing based on "merit" means that a position is given to the person most qualified to perform it. One way to determine which applicants are best qualified for a job is by administering an appropriate exam. (In fact, civil service exams were established by the Pendleton Civil Service Reform Act.)

47. **The correct answer is (3).** This statement brings together the concept of equality of the first paragraph and the information about the extension of the right to vote in the second paragraph and restates the main point of the entire passage. The statement in choice (1) summarizes only the second paragraph, not the entire passage. The statement in choice (2) expounds on the first paragraph with new analysis but doesn't summarize. The statement in choice (4) states one relevant fact but also does not summarize. The statement in choice (5) introduces an entirely new idea (that the extension of the right to vote hasn't made a difference) rather than summarizing the ideas and information presented in the passage.

48. **The correct answer is (2).** For the period shown, home-sales volume (number of units sold) reached its low during January, February, and into

answers diagnostic test

March. This fact suggests that demand for new homes was low during those months and that a prospective home buyer had more negotiating power during that time of the year.

49. The correct answer is (5). At a too-high price, demand for any product will decline—until prices are lowered enough to stimulate demand again. Since mortgage interest rates were low, the expense involved in paying interest on a mortgage loan was low (at least initially). So a reasonable

explanation for the decline in demand was that new-home prices were too high. If true, the statements in choices (1), (3), and (4) would serve to *increase* the demand for new homes. There is no evidence to support choice (2).

50. The correct answer is (1). The experience of Prohibition presented in this passage is most relevant to the debate over decriminalizing marijuana. The other proposed changes in policies are not as similar.

Science

1. (3)	11. (2)	21. (2)	31. (1)	41. (2)
2. (5)	12. (1)	22. (2)	32. (3)	42. (4)
3. (1)	13. (4)	23. (4)	33. (4)	43. (2)
4. (5)	14. (4)	24. (1)	34. (3)	44. (1)
5. (1)	15. (3)	25. (2)	35. (5)	45. (3)
6. (2)	16. (1)	26. (4)	36. (4)	46. (5)
7. (5)	17. (3)	27. (3)	37. (3)	47. (3)
8. (1)	18. (2)	28. (1)	38. (2)	48. (5)
9. (2)	19. (1)	29. (1)	39. (5)	49. (3)
10. (2)	20. (5)	30. (4)	40. (2)	50. (4)

1. The correct answer is (3). With added growth stimulation, the stem's shady side will grow vertically at a faster rate than the stem's sunny side. As a result, the stem will bend toward the light.

2. The correct answer is (5). Carbon is the main element in *all* organic compounds.

3. The correct answer is (1). The time it takes for crest X to reach line A is three-fourths the wave's period (the time it would take for crest X to reach the point of the next crest in the figure).

Hence the wave's period is 4 seconds. Line B is located one full wavelength plus three fourths of a second wavelength to the right of point X. Multiply that distance by the wave's period:

$$1\frac{3}{4} \times 4 = 7 \text{ seconds}$$

4. The correct answer is (5). The chemical response from the damaged tissue initiates the chain of responses that result in a blot clot that minimizes blood loss.

5. **The correct answer is (1).** Dimethalymine (C_2H_7O) contains two carbon atoms (mass of 24), seven hydrogen atoms (mass of 7), and one oxygen atom (mass of 16). The total atomic mass = 24 + 7 + 16 = 47.

6. **The correct answer is (2).** All four changes described in the passage are the result of human activity: clear-cutting forests, channeling fertilizer and sewage into rivers and oceans, overusing air pollutants, and allowing livestock to overgraze grasslands.

7. **The correct answer is (5).** The diagram shows that humans are members of the phylum *chordata* (chordates). The question provides that panthers belong to the class *mammalia,* which the diagram shows as a subcategory under the phylum *chordata.*

8. **The correct answer is (1).** If you know the altitude of the plane, along with the delay between the time the plane passes overhead and the time you hear the jet engines, you can determine the speed of sound by dividing the altitude by the time delay. Observing a sprinter's speed in reacting to a starter's pistol, choice (2) might be another way to measure the speed of sound. However, the pistol and sprinter might be too close to each other to create a measurable delay; what's more, the sprinter's reaction time will depend on other factors as well.

9. **The correct answer is (2).** The paragraph cites exposure to radiation or certain toxic substances as what can trigger the genetic changes causing cells to grow and multiply out of control. It is common knowledge that such exposures can result in various cancers. The paragraph also explains why the abnormal cells spread, as choice (2) indicates.

10. **The correct answer is (2).** When cells multiply with no normal controls, they crowd each other in the tissues where they reside. Thus they grow closer together, not farther apart. It is easy to visualize cells squeezed together, choice (4), or piling up choice (5). A disorganized or shrinking cytoskeleton would result in differentiation in shape, choice (3), or size, choice (1) among the observed cells.

11. **The correct answer is (2).** When the moon is at either position C or G, a person directly below the Moon would observe that half of the Moon's facing surface is lit by the Sun. Position A shows the new moon phase (none of the facing surface is lit). Position E shows the full Moon phase (unless a lunar eclipse is occurring). Positions B and H show crescent Moon phases (most of the facing surface is unlit). Positions D and F show autumn moon phases (most of the facing surface is lit).

12. **The correct answer is (1).** In the case of an atom whose outer shell is not complete, one or more electrons might acquire an electron from the outer shell of another atom. When this occurs, the acquiring atom becomes negatively charged (a negative ion), while the transferring atom becomes positively charged (a positive ion).

13. **The correct answer is (4).** Genotypes RR and Rr are expressed as red. All but one of the eight offspring shown in the diagram are red.

14. **The correct answer is (4).** The diagram shows that pairing Rr with Rr, the choice provided in C, produces one rr (white) child. Although the diagram does not show either pairing provided in A or D, we cannot rule out the possibility that either or both of these pairings would produce a white child.

15. **The correct answer is (3).** Onion bulbs grow underground, where chloroplasts would serve no function. It is the onion's vertical shoot that traps the Sun's energy and makes food.

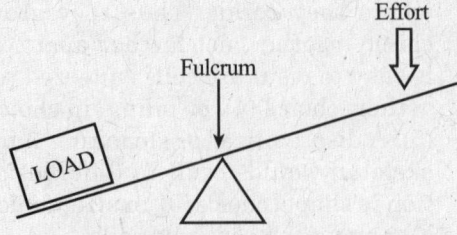

16. The correct answer is (1). By using a lever of the sort shown in the above illustration, you can increase the output force (moving the load) applying the same amount of, or possibly less, input force (effort).

17. The correct answer is (3). The stork's long bill helps it survive by allowing it to pluck its prey from just below the water's surface. This feature is a classic evolutionary adaptation.

18. The correct answer is (2). Serine contains 3 oxygen atoms, while cysteine contains only 2.

19. The correct answer is (1). The gender of human offspring is determined solely by the male parent. The female can only donate an X chromosome, while the male can donate either a Y or X chromosome. Thus, it is the male that determines the gender of the offspring.

20. The correct answer is (5). The higher a food group appears in the pyramid, the lower its proportion in a balance diet. The chart shows fats, oils, and sweets at the top of the pyramid and indicates that they should be used "sparingly."

21. The correct answer is (2). Since the magnetic North Pole is moving from Canada toward Russia, it is in a different location than the geographic North Pole. And since the magnetic North Pole is shifting, the magnetic South Pole must be shifting as well.

22. The correct answer is (2). The diagram shows each hydrogen atom bonded with one of the two carbon atoms. This can only occur because each hydrogen atom has one electron in its outer shell, which is paired with one electron in the outer shell of a carbon atom. Each carbon atom has four electrons altogether in its outer shell.

23. The correct answer is (4). The midday sun appears brightest because that light travels through less of the atmosphere than at other times of the day. The fact that we see shadows demonstrates that light does not bend around solid objects, choices (1) and (2). The fact that our line of vision is straight also demonstrates that light travels in a straight path, choices (3) and (5).

24. The correct answer is (1). After exceeding carrying capacity, the still-growing population lacks enough resources to support its current growth rate.

25. The correct answer is (2). Rubbing your hands together is a voluntary activity in response to sensing cold through your skin (a sense organ), which communicates that sensation to the thalamus. Your cerebrum receives that information from the thalamus and then dictates the appropriate voluntary response, which your cerebellum helps coordinate.

26. The correct answer is (4). The hypothalamus regulates vital biological functions such as appetite. Regulation of some such functions is accomplished through the pituitary gland, which secrets hormones stimulating appetite.

27. The correct answer is (3). The temperature scale is given across the top of the diagram. Temperatures *decrease* from left to right, so that stars with the lowest surface temperatures are plotted at the right end of the diagram. Giant stars are clustered near the diagram's right side, which means that they are among the coldest stars.

28. The correct answer is (1). Our solar system's Sun (denoted by the "X" on the diagram) is located near the center of the diagram. The other plotted points are distributed fairly equally above and below X, as well as to the left and to the right of X. This distribution tells you that the Sun is about average, or typical, in both its brightness (measured on the vertical scale) and its surface temperature (measured on the horizontal scale).

29. **The correct answer is (1).** If the tube were open at both ends, the level of the liquid would be the same on both sides of the "U" in the tube, since the atmospheric air would be exerting equal pressure on both ends. But the higher level on the right side of the "U" indicates that the pressure from the air tank is greater than the atmospheric pressure. (The various level marks up and down the tube provide a quantitative measure of that pressure.)

30. **The correct answer is (4).** Choice (4) is the only one that makes sense. In Phase 3 of development, the ripened pericap (fruit) attracts animals, and they, of course, eat the fruit. The droppings of these animals spread the fruit's seeds, from which new plants of the same type grow.

31. **The correct answer is (1).** An air sac within a lung functions by taking in oxygen, which it passes through its lining to blood vessels, which pass carbon dioxide back through the lining to be expelled into the air. To accomplish the exchange, the lining must be single layered, thin, and leaky (diffuse). The tissue shown as simple squamous best serves this purpose.

32. **The correct answer is (3).** One percent (1%) of the producer's energy is passed along to primary consumers. Then, 10% of that 1%, or 0.1% of the producer's energy, is passed along to secondary consumers.

33. **The correct answer is (4).** The presence of dentritivores as well as animals that consume both plants and animals implies a complex, interconnected system resembling a web.

34. **The correct answer is (3).** Following the arrows in the illustration shows that cold water in the North Atlantic Ocean (near the North Pole) sinks and then travels south toward the equator, warming and mixing with warmer water along the way. Once warmer, that water rises to the surface and moves northward to where it started in the North Atlantic.

35. **The correct answer is (5).** The diagram indicates that cold water in the North Atlantic sinks. The diagram also shows warmer water near the Equator rising to the surface. Together, these two pieces of information help show that cold water is denser than warm water.

36. **The correct answer is (4).** Longer hind legs enhance a frog's jumping ability, while a strong shoulder girdle and rigid spine help support the jump's landing. These abilities are useful only when moving about on land.

37. **The correct answer is (3).** Since all light waves travel at the same speed, higher frequency waves will have a shorter wavelength. The diagram shows gamma rays have the highest frequency of all types of light waves.

38. **The correct answer is (2).** The slight dilation of the cervix as the infant begins to push its way out of the womb triggers a receptor to send a message to the brain, which then directs the contraction of muscles to help the birth process along. These contractions increase dilation, which triggers additional, and more intense, contractions. This process is a good example of a positive feedback loop.

39. **The correct answer is (5).** Choice (1), 80 calories, represents what is needed to change the state from ice to water (the lower plateau); 100 calories, choice (2), are needed to raise the temperature from 0°C to 100°C; and

an additional 540 calories, choice (4), are needed to change the water into steam. The total amount of heat energy required is 720 calories.

40. The correct answer is (2). Scientists infer the existence of dark matter from how gravity operates on light matter. Thus their understanding of dark matter is theoretical.

41. The correct answer is (2). The illustration indicates that some of the infrared radiation emitted from the Earth's surface is absorbed by gas molecules in the atmosphere, which then re-emit that radiation. Some of this radiation returns to the Earth's surface again, and so a portion of the energy radiated from the Earth never escapes the atmosphere.

42. The correct answer is (4). A stable atom is one in which the number of protons matches the number of neutrons. Radioactive decay results from a change in the number of neutrons in the nucleus, which by definition creates instability.

43. The correct answer is (2). The illustration shows how a tree obtains what it needs to grow and survive. It receives energy from the Sun, it absorbs carbon dioxide from the air, and it draws water and minerals from the soil. The process by which a tree processes and uses light energy, carbon dioxide, and water is called *photosynthesis*. The title "How Trees Survive" encapsulates the concept. Choice (4) is incorrect because it focuses on just one aspect of photosynthesis: the emission of oxygen, which humans need, as waste into the air.

44. The correct answer is (1). Random mating, choice (1), does not in itself increase genetic diversity. Choice (4) describes one means by which genetic diversity increases—recombination within genes can create a new allele, thereby increasing genetic diversity. Each of the remaining choices

describes an event that might bring about an evolutionary adaptation, which serves to enhance the genetic diversity of the population.

45. The correct answer is (3). Sugar cannot pass through the membrane, so the amount of sugar on each side will not change. Water from side B, where the sugar concentration is weaker, will pass through the membrane to side A until concentrations are equalized. After 60 ml of water passes from side B to side A, you are left with 20 ml of water and 20 ml of sugar (a 50/50 concentration) on side B. Side A will have the same result: 80 ml of water and 80 ml of sugar (a 50/50 concentration).

46. The correct answer is (5). The equation is as follows:

$$\Omega = \frac{V}{A} = \frac{4.5}{0.3} = 15$$

47. The correct answer is (3). Choice (3) expresses a basic principle of wave energy. Even if you are unfamiliar with this principle, it provides the only reasonable explanation as to why a cork, which is a form of "matter," would not move laterally with waves in the middle of the ocean.

48. The correct answer is (5). The volcano loses height as its material erodes from the top down. Eventually, the top of the volcano is at sea level, while coral has built up just above that level. The volcano's cavity fills with water, forming a lagoon. (Coral also accumulates in the lagoon.)

49. The correct answer is (3). When you drive a car, road friction causes the car tires and the air in them to heat up, which in turn causes the volume of air in the tires to increase. By filling the tires beyond the recommended pressure, you risk a "blowout" while driving your car, especially at high speeds for a long period of time.

50. **The correct answer is (4).** The recent discovery of Archeaens, which changes scientists' assumptions about biological life, illustrates that our scientific knowledge is incomplete, and probably always will be.

Language Arts, Reading

1. (2)	11. (2)	21. (5)	31. (1)
2. (4)	12. (4)	22. (4)	32. (2)
3. (1)	13. (1)	23. (3)	33. (2)
4. (5)	14. (3)	24. (4)	34. (3)
5. (3)	15. (2)	25. (5)	35. (2)
6. (1)	16. (3)	26. (2)	36. (5)
7. (4)	17. (2)	27. (2)	37. (5)
8. (5)	18. (1)	28. (5)	38. (3)
9. (3)	19. (3)	29. (5)	39. (2)
10. (3)	20. (2)	30. (4)	40. (1)

1. **The correct answer is (2).** Upon seeing Bertha arrive at the nursery, Nanny "set her lips in a way that Bertha knew, and that meant she had come into the nursery at another wrong moment." The subsequent dialogue between Bertha and Nanny further suggests that Bertha's intrusion during feeding time is unwelcome.

2. **The correct answer is (4).** Nanny's possessive nature finds ample support in the passage—especially in the last sentence, where we are told that Nanny came back into the nursery and seized "her little B."

3. **The correct answer is (1).** In her thoughts, Bertha compares Little B to "a rare, rare, fiddle" that you take out of its case once in a while to admire. In this analogy, the "case" refers to Nanny's care. These thoughts reveal Bertha's recognition that Nanny is Little B's primary caregiver and that Bertha's role is merely that of occasional visitor.

4. **The correct answer is (5).** Nanny tells Bertha that Bertha unthinkingly excites the baby, conveniently leaving Nanny to deal with the consequences. From this statement, we can surmise that Nanny considers Bertha a thoughtless person. Nanny's repeated admonitions to Bertha about the baby's care suggest that Nanny thinks of Bertha as an inexperienced mother.

5. **The correct answer is (3).** Based on the passage, it appears that Bertha has relinquished care of her child to a full-time nanny. Accordingly, Bertha would probably arrange for someone else, such as a nurse, to provide full-time care for her dying friend.

6. **The correct answer is (1).** We can infer from the details provided by much of the passage that Nanny and Bertha continually compete for Little B and for how Little B's time is spent in the nursery. The narrator's use of the word "triumph" suggests that this round was in Nanny's favor, since Bertha had to not only relinquish the baby but leave the nursery as well.

7. **The correct answer is (4).** The point of the opening sentences is that China once had the genius to create and invent and that it can rekindle this "native ability."

8. **The correct answer is (5).** In the second paragraph, the speaker expresses his desire to borrow inventions from the West without repeating all the stages of development.

9. **The correct answer is (3).** The speaker's point is that since the Chinese are just as intelligent as the Japanese, China can do anything that Japan can do.

10. **The correct answer is (3).** The speaker's point is that China must act now or risk losing ground in becoming a Power. In this context, "momentous" (highly important as a moment in time or history) is the only choice that makes sense.

11. **The correct answer is (2).** The speaker approves of Western inventions, but here he appears to approve only if they can be adapted and used by the Chinese for "material achievement."

12. **The correct answer is (4).** Anna immediately responds to Marthy's cutting remark about sizing up Anna with the quick jab of her own: "You're me forty years from now."

13. **The correct answer is (1).** Marthy knows the saloon's policy about cigarette smoking, so she has undoubtedly patronized the saloon before.

14. **The correct answer is (3).** The dialogue that follows clearly suggests that Anna works as a prostitute. But Marthy had already sized her up. Based on Anna's appearance and demeanor, Marthy had guessed Anna's profession.

15. **The correct answer is (2).** Anna has come to meet her Old Man, but she doesn't know what he looks like. In asking Marthy whether she "hang[s] out around this dump much," Anna is clearly hoping that Marthy knows him and can direct Anna to him.

16. **The correct answer is (3).** Anna tells Marthy that she hates all men and that they all "kick you when you're down." Clearly, her experiences with other men have predisposed her to think unkindly of her Old Man.

17. **The correct answer is (2).** From the dialogue we can infer that the Old Man is Anna's father. Based on what she reveals of her attitude toward him, choices (3) and (4) seem quite plausible themes. Anna and Marthy both appear to live difficult, rough-and-tumble lives, and so choices (1) and (5) each provides a plausible theme as well. Choice (2) is the best answer—although the play might very well be set during the era of westward expansion in North America, nothing in the dialogue suggests that this expansion and how it impacted people's live is the play's focus.

18. **The correct answer is (1).** The first paragraph discusses the various artists and art movements that led up to and influenced Warhol's work. In other words, the paragraph serves mainly to provide historical background.

19. **The correct answer is (3).** Warhol borrowed from the cubists and pop artists who preceded him and then experimented with these art forms further.

20. The correct answer is (2). The sentence suggests that examples of debris might include discarded printed labels and torn sheets of newspaper, which are not "images" of a modern city. (The word *debris* means left-over material.) Each other answer choice provides a good synonym for the word as it is used in the passage.

21. The correct answer is (5). By choosing a soup can as a subject, Andy Warhol shows his disregard for the importance given to conventional subjects—as did the Impressionist who preferred to depict a lowly street scene as his subject, instead of the conventional, accepted subjects of his time.

22. The correct answer is (4). In the previous sentence, the reviewer notes that Warhol's choice of subject (a soup can) reveals his former vocation (job) as a commercial artist. Such artists are hired to produce art involving impersonal subjects such as consumer products.

23. The correct answer is (3). The narrator tells us that a great snowstorm arrived "Just as the blessings were bestowed, about Christmas of '47." The narrator then describes the whereabouts and activities of various characters just after the storm hit, noting that Pete and Ethel were honeymooning. So it is most likely that "the blessings" that "were bestowed" refers to their wedding.

24. The correct answer is (4). The events described in the passage began "about Christmas" (line 2). Later in the passage, the narrator describes what happened "when the air cleared and the snows settled into the late winter muck" (lines 31–33). So the passage's events span at least a few months—from Christmas to late winter.

25. The correct answer is (5). Thurm called his casino a name containing the French word for "red." He chose the name without understanding what it meant, like a restaurant patron ordering the wrong item because the menu is in an unfamiliar language.

26. The correct answer is (2). The narrator tells us that the "monument in this case" is "the Mouton Rouge Casino." The comparison between these two unlike things is a good example of a metaphor.

27. The correct answer is (2). City and county officials suggested to Thurm that the casino might attract "unsavory elements," which generally means criminals.

28. The correct answer is (5). The narrator tells us that Thurm was "obsessed" (line 33) with his casino plan. The narrator also tells us that city and county officials tried repeatedly to discourage him from his casino plans, but Thurm persisted, confident that he would overcome whatever obstacles he might encounter.

29. The correct answer is (5). The rhythm and, to a lesser extent, the sound of the words "rifles' rapid rattle" mimic the "rat-a-tat" you hear from a "stuttering" rifle. This sort of mimicry is a device often used by poets as a type of imagery.

30. The correct answer is (4). The girls described in the poem's final three lines are most likely the girlfriends, fiancés, and wives of soldiers missing in battle. The girls have been waiting for the soldiers to return home from the war.

31. The correct answer is (1). The words "die as cattle" in the poem's first line strongly suggest the idea of young soldiers dying *en masse*, like cattle led to a slaughterhouse. The words "them all" in the first line of the second stanza reiterate the idea of a mass death. Choice (1) is the only one that articulates this idea.

32. The correct answer is (2). The poet uses the idea of a funeral as the central metaphor throughout the poem, and words such as "mourning" (line 6) and "wailing" (line 7) strongly convey the sadness associated with the event, as does the word *sad* in the phrase "from sad shires." (The word *shire* refers literally to a county or district, but the word is used in the poem figuratively, probably in reference to the battlefield.)

33. The correct answer is (2). In lines 4–8, the noise of shells (shot from cannons) is used as a metaphor for the collective voice of a choir.

34. The correct answer is (3). Underlying Owen's words in "Anthem for Doomed Youth" is a critical attitude toward war. His specific focus is on all the lives cut short and the needless grief and suffering that inevitably result from war. Taken literally, the closing words of his other poem would suggest quite the opposite attitude. But he wrote both poems around the same time. Thus, it is likely that Owen cited that Latin phrase in the context of pointing out its absurdity—in other words, that it is not "becoming" but rather foolish to die for one's country.

35. The correct answer is (2). According to the passage, Patch is under the "delusion" (mistaken belief) that, as a young man, he was scrupulous (careful with details) to keep "every engagement on the dot." The fact that Patch is deluded means that, in fact, Patch was *not* scrupulous in being on time.

36. The correct answer is (5). In context, the word *novel* means "new and unique," and the word *angle* means "perspective or focus." Anthony's idea is to write about the Renaissance popes from a fresh, unique viewpoint—one that's different from the way others have written about the same subject.

37. The correct answer is (5). Early in the passage we learn that Patch is a *philanthropist* (a wealthy person who gives money to charitable causes) and that he attributes all his "success" to his scrupulous attention to practical affairs.

38. The correct answer is (3). It seems that Anthony had been making up a story about his writing plans and that Patch saw through him. Mild embarrassment is the only emotional reaction among the five choices that makes sense in this situation.

39. The correct answer is (2). Patch seems to suspect that Anthony is making excuses for being late. He also seems to suspect that Anthony has no serious plans for work or for writing anything while in New York. In other words, he does not seem to take what Anthony tells him seriously.

40. The correct answer is (1). Anthony's advice to his friend suggests that Anthony might have had similar successes, and thus is in a position to give him advice on how to handle that sort of success. In the passage conversation (which occurred earlier), Patch prods Anthony to get serious about work. So perhaps Anthony took Patch's advice.

Mathematics: Part I, Questions 1–25

1. (2)	6. (4)	11. (1)	16. (4)	21. (3)
2. (4)	7. (4)	12. (2)	17. (1)	22. (5)
3. (5)	8. (2)	13. (3)	18. (4)	23. (5)
4. 16	9. (5)	14. (4)	19. 40	24. (2)
5. (3)	10. 20.25 or 81/4	15. (3)	20. (1)	25. 1.5 or 3/2

1. **The correct answer is (2).** Here's how to calculate the toll:

   $1.20 + (7)($0.55) = $1.20 + $3.85 = $5.05

2. **The correct answer is (4).** Each successive term is 3 less than the preceding term. Here's the series of ten terms: {30, 27, 24, 21, 18, 15, 12, 9, 6, 3}. Including the first term (30), the tenth term in the series is 3.

3. **The correct answer is (5).** The sum of the lengths of any two sides of a triangle must be greater than the length of the third side. Thus, in the triangle at hand, the length of the longest side must be less than 15 inches.

4. **The correct answer is 16.** Let $C =$ the number of students enrolled in Chemistry only. Let $P =$ the number of students in Physics only. Let $B =$ the number of students in both Chemistry and Physics:

   $C + P + B = 78$, so $47 + P + 15 = 78$.

   $P = 16$

5. **The correct answer is (3).** Multiply $1500 by 20%. Subtract your answer from $1500. Multiply this answer by 20%, and subtract your answer again:
   $1500 × 0.20 = $300
   $1500 − $300 = $1200
   $1200 × 0.20 = $240
   $1200 − $240 = $960

6. **The correct answer is (4).**

   $$|7 − 2| − |2 − 7| = |5| − |−5|$$
   $$5 − 5 = 0$$

7. **The correct answer is (4).** Combine the numbers from the profitable years, and combine the numbers from the years Angelique suffered a loss:

   $7560 + $5300 = $12,860 (profit)

   $8450 + $4220 = $12,670 (loss)

   Subtract losses from profits:

   $12,860 − $12,670 = $190 (profit for all five years combined)

8. **The correct answer is (2).** To determine the cost of shipping a 28-pound parcel by ground, you need to apply three different per-pound rates: $1.50 for the first pound, $0.40 for pounds 2–10, and $0.25 for pounds 11–28. Here's the calculation:

   $1.50 + ($0.40)(9) + ($0.25)(18) = $9.60

9. **The correct answer is (5).** The cost of shipping a 2.4-pound parcel by Express delivery would be $6.75 + ($1.15)(2) = $9.05. The cost of shipping the same parcel by Air delivery would be $2.25 + ($0.60)(2) = $3.45. The difference between the two totals is $5.60.

10. **The correct answer is 20.25 or 81/4.** First, convert yards to inches:

    $$4\frac{1}{2} \text{ yards} = 4(36) \text{ inches} + 18 \text{ inches}$$
    $$= 162 \text{ inches}$$

    Then divide:

    $$162 ÷ 8 = 20\frac{1}{4} = 20.25 \text{ or } \frac{81}{4}$$

11. **The correct answer is (1).** The total number of gallons used during the trip was $\frac{450}{3.00} = 150$. The vehicle's mileage was $\frac{1200}{150} = 8$ mpg.

12. **The correct answer is (2).** All five boxes have the same volume: 1500 cubic inches. In the boxes described in each incorrect choice, however, space must be left empty along one of the faces of the box. On the other hand, the box with dimensions $10'' \times 15'' \times 10''$ can be packed full of one-inch cubes without leaving any empty space.

13. **The correct answer is (3).** Your first step is to convert mixed numbers to fractions:

$$\frac{9}{2} + \frac{15}{4} - \frac{12}{5}$$

The lowest common denominator is 20. Convert each fraction, then combine:

$$\frac{9}{2} + \frac{15}{4} - \frac{12}{5} = \frac{90 + 75 - 48}{20} = \frac{117}{20}$$

14. **The correct answer is (4).** Each interior angle measures

$$\frac{180(6-2)}{6} = 720 \times 6 = 120°$$

The angle whose measure is $x°$ combines with its vertical angle (interior to the hexagon) to total $360°$—the total number of degrees in a circle. Thus, $x = 360 - 120 = 240$.

15. **The correct answer is (3).** First, find the size of Unit D as a percentage of the total warehouse size. Unit D occupies 15,500 square feet—or approximately 11%—of the 140,000 total square feet in the warehouse. Thus, Unit C occupies about 19% of that total $(100 - 28 - 42 - 11 = 19)$. In terms of square feet, then, the size of Unit C is approximately $0.19 \times 140,000 = 26,600$ square feet. Of the five answer choices, 26,500 is the closest approximation to this number.

16. **The correct answer is (4).** Unit D is the smallest space, accounting for about 11% of the total $(15,000 \div 140,000)$. The size of Unit D is less than half the size of Unit A (the smaller of the two large units). Therefore, even at twice the per-square-foot rate of Unit A, Unit D still costs least to rent.

17. **The correct answer is (1).** Here's the sequence up to the 12th second:

0 W	4 W	8 W	11 R
1 B	5 R	9 G	12 W
2 W	6 W	10 W	
3 G	7 B		

Every time you reach a time divisible by 6, the sequence starts over with W and proceeds: W-B-W-G-W-R. 204 is divisible by 6; hence, starting at the 204th second, here are the light's movements through the 209th second:

204 W	206 W	208 W
205 B	207 G	209 R

As you can see, the movement from the 208th to the 209th second is from white (W) to red (R).

18. **The correct answer is (4).** The median is the arithmetic mean of the two middle numbers. Given a median of 0 (zero), the two numbers must have the same absolute value, although either both are zero (0) or one is negative while the other is positive (for example, -1 and 1). Choices (1), (4), and (5) satisfy this requirement. But only choice (4) provides a range of 4 (the difference on the number line between the lowest and highest recorded temperatures: -2.6 and 1.4).

19. **The correct answer is 40.** The corral is to be square, and so the length of any side equals $\sqrt{10,000} = 100$.

Constructing one complete side, including both end posts, requires 11 posts (not 10) spaced 10 feet apart. Constructing two of the other three sides requires only 10 posts, while the fourth side requires only 9 posts since its end posts are already in place. The total number of posts needed is 11 + (2)(10) + 9 = 40.

20. **The correct answer is (1).** For intersection A, 110 drivers (18 + 27 + 34 + 31) drove at 30 mph or slower. The *total* number of drivers at intersection A was 430. The ratio of 110 to 430 is about 1 to 4.

21. **The correct answer is (3).** At intersection A, the number of motorists at successive speed ranges climbed steadily through the 33–34 mph range, and then declined gradually through 39 mph. The decline at speeds exceeding 40 mph may or may not have been gradual. (No frequency distribution for that uppermost range is provided.)

22. **The correct answer is (5).** As a portion of the total number of vehicles at each intersection, far fewer motorists exceeded the 35-mph speed limit at intersection B than the 30-mph speed limit at intersection A. Choice (5) is the only one that provides a reasonable explanation for this distinction.

23. **The correct answer is (5).** Take each answer choice in turn. For each ship, you first apply the distance formula: Rate × 4.5 = Distance. If the ships move in the same direction, you then subtract the shorter distance from the longer one. If the ships move in opposite directions, you then combine the two distances by addition. Only under the scenario in choice (5) are the two ships 270 miles apart after 4.5 hours:

$$45(4.5) + 15(4.5) = 202.5 + 67.5 = 270$$

You can rule out the scenario in choice (2) without applying the Pythagorean Theorem because the combined distance traveled is less than 270 miles. (The combined length of any two sides of a triangle is always greater than the length of the third side.)

24. **The correct answer is (2).** $a^4 = 1296$. So $a = \sqrt[4]{1296} = 6$. (Apply the square-root operation twice.)

25. **The correct answer is 1.5 or 3/2.** In order to find the growth rate per day, first divide by 24 (the number of days):

0.36 meters ÷ 24 = 0.015 meters

To convert to centimeters, shift the decimal point to the right by two places:

0.015 m $= 1.5$ or $\dfrac{3}{2}$ cm

Mathematics: Part II, Questions 26–50

26. (4)	31. (1)	36. 3	41. (5)	46. 1/9
27. (4)	32. 2.38	37. (5)	42. (2)	47. (1)
28. 14	33. (2)	38. (5)	43. (2)	48. (1)
29. (2)	34. (3, –4)	39. (3)	44. (4)	49. 210
30. (3)	35. (3)	40. (1)	45. (1)	50. (5)

26. **The correct answer is (4).** In combining terms, you can cancel out b and c. This leaves $\frac{a}{d} \cdot x = 1$. To isolate x on one side of the equation, multiply both sides by $\frac{d}{a}$.

27. **The correct answer is (4).** The entire circle contains 360°, and so $y = 360 - x$.

28. **The correct answer is 14.** Divide the 12-hour period into 24-half hours periods. Every half-hour, the clock runs $48 \div 24 = 2$ minutes slow. After 3.5 hours, the clock is running $7 \times 2 = 14$ minutes slow.

29. **The correct answer is (2).** $\angle 3$ corresponds to $\angle 4$, both of which are formed by the same transversal of lines k and m. Thus, m$\angle 3$ = m$\angle 4$ in all cases.

30. **The correct answer is (3).** Factor out x on the left side of the equation: $x(x + 4) = 0$. There are two possible x-values, or roots: $x = 0$; $x = -4$.

31. **The correct answer is (1).** Add the two equations:

$$\begin{array}{r} x + y = a \\ \underline{x - y = b} \\ 2x = a + b \\ x = \frac{1}{2}(a + b) \end{array}$$

32. **The correct answer is 2.38.** The region of the number line from 2.3 to 2.5 has been divided into 10 congruent regions. The distance from 2.3 to 2.5 is 0.2. Thus, the vertical marks are spaced at intervals of 0.02. Accordingly, B = 2.38.

33. **The correct answer is (2).** The lowest average daily temperature (solid line) occurred near the end of June. Checking the dotted line (precipitation) corresponding to that time against the *right*-hand scale, the precipitation that day was approximately 13.5 cm.

34. **The correct answer is (3,–4).** When point A (3,2), and point B (–3,2) are connected, they form a horizontal line segment of length 6. Each side of the square must have a length of 6. The missing corner is 6 units below (3,2), which puts it at (3,–4).

35. **The correct answer is (3).** Determine the answer systematically, beginning with the largest possible integer:

$7 + 1 + 1 + 1 = 10$

$5 + 3 + 1 + 1 = 10$

$3 + 3 + 3 + 1 = 10$

As you can see, there are three different ways.

36. **The correct answer is 3.** First, notice that R must equal either 1 or 2; otherwise, the sum of the three "tens" digits would exceed 11. Assuming R = 1, the "ones" column tells us that the value of S would necessarily be 5. But the "tens" column would not add up correctly. Therefore, R must equal 2 and, accordingly, S must equal 3.

37. **The correct answer is (5).** The length of the bedroom (the longer room) is $2L$. Since the two areas both

equal $L \times W$, the width of the bedroom must be $\frac{W}{2}$.

38. **The correct answer is (5).** Any term raised to a negative power is the same as the reciprocal of the term—but raised to the *positive* power:

    $(-1)^{-2} + (-1)^2 = \frac{1}{(-1)^2} + 1 = \frac{1}{1} + 1 = 2$

39. **The correct answer is (3).** A quick way to divide by 500 is to first divide by 1000 and multiply the quotient by 2. In this problem, divide 40.5 by 1000 by shifting the decimal point 3 places to the left. Then, multiply the quotient by 2: $(0.0405)(2) = 0.0810$.

40. **The correct answer is (1).** In choice (1), unequal quantities are subtracted from equal quantities. The differences are unequal, but the inequality is reversed because unequal numbers are being subtracted from, rather than added to, the equal numbers.

41. **The correct answer is (5).** Twice the sum of 3 and the number N is written as $2(3 + N)$, or $6 + 2N$. The phrase "1 less than 3 times the number N" is written as $3N - 1$.

42. **The correct answer is (2).** The figure indicates that $\angle AFE$ is a right angle ($\angle AFE = 90°$). That angle and $\angle AFD$ are supplementary. (They combine to form a straight 180° line). Therefore, $\angle AFD = 90°$. If you know $\angle BFD$, you can find $\angle AFB$ by subtracting $\angle BFD$ from 90.

43. **The correct answer is (2).**

    $(x + 2)(x - 2) = x^2 + 2x - 2x - 4 = x^2 - 4$

    Note that $(x + 2)(x - 2)$ is the "difference of two squares": $(x^2 - y^2)$ in the factored form:

    $(x + y)(x - y)$, where $y = 2$

44. **The correct answer is (4).** For each year, compare the heights of the two dark bars. The year 2008 was the only one among the five choices for which

Country Y's imports (about \$39 billion) were less than twice Country X's imports (about \$21 billion).

45. **The correct answer is (1).** To answer this question, examine the right bar for each of the six years shown. The size of the dark portion (Country Y's imports) increases up to 2008 and then remains about the same from 2008 through 2009. It then increases again from 2009 to 2010. So the general trend over the six-year period was for the value of imports to increase. The size of the bar's light portion (Country Y's exports) decreases through 2007, then increases through 2009, and then decreases from 2009 to 2010. So there is no clear export trend for the six-year period as a whole.

46. **The correct answer is 1/9.** Each of the two groups contains three items. Thus, the probability of selecting any one item in a group is one in three, or $\frac{1}{3}$. To find the probability of selecting fruit and squash, multiply the two independent probabilities:

    $$\frac{1}{3} \times \frac{1}{3} = \frac{1}{9}$$

47. **The correct answer is (1).** Express 4.9 in scientific notation: 4.9×10^0. To convert this number from cubic centimeters to cubic millimeters, divide by 1000. To accomplish this in scientific notation, subtract 3 from the exponent: 4.9×10^{-3}

48. **The correct answer is (1).** Divide the shaded figure into a rectangle with vertices at (2,6), (5,6), (2,2), and (5,2) and a right triangle with vertices at (5,2), (2,2), and (2,0). The rectangle's height and width are 4 and 3, respectively, and so its area is $4 \times 3 = 12$. The triangle has legs of length 3 and 2, and so its area is $\frac{1}{2} \times 3 \times 2 = 3$. The sum of the two areas is $12 + 3 = 15$.

answers diagnostic test

49. The correct answer is 210. The key to handling this question is to convert ratios to fractional parts that add up to 1. The ratio of X's rate to Y's rate is 3 to 1, and the ratio of Y's rate to Z's rate is 1 to 2. You can express the ratio of all three as 3:1:2 (X:Y:Z). Accordingly, Y's production accounts for $\frac{1}{6}$ of the total widgets that all three machines can produce per day. Given that Y can produce 35 widgets per day, all three machines can produce $(35)(6) = 210$ widgets per day.

50. The correct answer is (5). As you can see from the figure below, letting

x = the radius of the base, $\sin 25° = \frac{x}{3}$;

$x = 3\sin 25°$; and the diameter of the entire base = $6\sin 25°$.

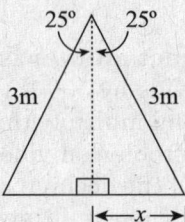

ARE YOU READY TO TAKE THE GED®?

When you have finished taking this Diagnostic Test, and you have checked your answers against those listed in the Answer Key and Explanations, it is time to compare the number of correct answers with the table below.

	All Set—Well-Prepared	Most Likely Ready	Possibly Ready	Need More Preparation
Language Arts, Writing, Part I	38–50	26–37	18–25	0–17
Language Arts, Writing, Part II	4	3	2	1
Social Studies	38–50	26–37	18–25	0–17
Science	38–50	26–37	18–25	0–17
Language Arts, Reading	30–40	21–29	14–20	0–13
Mathematics	38–50	26–37	18–25	0–17

Seeing where your Diagnostic Test scores fall will help you determine your best study plan. You should devote most of your study time to those subjects where your scores fell in the "Need More Preparation" or the "Possibly Ready" columns. A helpful review of each of these topics can be found in this book. Read through the text, and pay close attention to the numerous examples with full answer explanations. This should help you better understand and master the material for the actual GED® exam. If you have time, go over those subjects where your scores fell in the "Most Likely Ready" column. And, if you have a lot of time, read through your "All Set—Well-Prepared" areas for an extra boost of confidence. However, if time gets tight, just focus on your weakest areas.

Following your review and when you feel ready, take one of the Practice Tests, and see how much closer you are to being all set and totally ready to take the actual GED® exam.

PART III

THE LANGUAGE ARTS, WRITING TEST

Mastering the Language Arts, Writing Test, Part I

OVERVIEW

- All about the Language Arts, Writing Test, Part I
- Answering sentence correction questions
- Answering sentence revision questions
- Answering sentence construction questions
- Answering paragraph composition questions
- Answering document organization questions
- General test-taking strategies
- Summing it up

chapter 3

THE LANGUAGE ARTS, WRITING TEST, PART I—IN A NUTSHELL

Time allowed: 75 minutes (you can begin Part II if you finish Part I early)

Number of documents: Expect 6 to 8 (the number can vary)

Length of each document: 200–300 words, 12 to 22 numbered sentences

Total number of questions: 50 multiple-choice (5 choices per question)

Number of questions per document: Expect 6 to 10 (the number can vary)

ALL ABOUT THE LANGUAGE ARTS, WRITING TEST, PART I

Part I of the Language Arts, Writing Test is essentially an *editing* test designed to gauge your ability to review a document and spot grammatical errors and other writing problems that call for correction or revision. Part I consists of several documents. Each document is followed by several multiple-choice questions that are based on it. Expect six to eight documents altogether, and expect six to ten questions based on each document (fifty questions in total).

Some documents may be excerpts from informational texts such as newspaper or magazine articles. Others may be drawn from workplace and community documents, such as policy and mission statements, employee manuals, and business communications (memos, e-mails, and letters). Still others may be simple instructional texts that explain how to do such things as plan a vacation or buy or sell a car. Some documents may be accompanied by a title to help you understand what sort of document you're dealing with.

Each document will be 200–300 words in length and will contain twelve to twenty-two sentences. Here is an example of a GED®-style instructional, or "how-to," text. This one happens to come with a title. This document illustrates certain features that all documents on the Writing Test, Part I share in common:

- Sentences are numbered in sequence.

- Paragraphs are lettered in sequence.

- Some (but not all) of the sentences are flawed in some way.

HOW TO INTERVIEW FOR A JOB

(A)

(1) Although many people think that a job interview are stressful and difficult, a job interview can be an exciting event. (2) The key to making the job interview process less stressful is confidence. (3) The applicant, must accept the challenge, of convincing the prospective employer that he is the best candidate for the job. (4) Nice cologne is a plus. (5) A person applying for a job should approach the prospective employer with a positive, winning attitude. (6) The applicant should explain what he has to offer to the prospective employer. (7) The applicant should promote himself and tout his strengths.

(B)

(8) And during the interview, the applicant should firmly shake the hand of the person interviewing him. (9) The applicant should look the prospective employer in the eye and maintaining eye contact throughout the interview. (10) The applicant should concentrate about the questions and answer them confidently. (11) When answering questions, applicants should avoid fidgeting and stuttering. (12) At the conclusion of the interview, the applicant should tell the interviewer that he appreciates the opportunity and he looks forward to another conversation at a later date.

Regardless of what sort of text you're dealing with, the questions will all cover the same sorts of writing issues. Below is the breakdown of the broad areas covered by the Writing Test, Part I. As indicated by percentage numbers, some areas receive greater emphasis than others. Note that the test questions cover only certain topics within each area, as listed here. Don't worry if you are unfamiliar with some of the terms here; this book's grammar review explains all you need to know for the Writing Test, Part I.

- **Grammar and usage** (30 percent): Subject-verb agreement, verb tense, and pronoun reference

- **Sentence structure** (30 percent): Fragments, comma splices, and run-ons; parallelism; coordination and subordination; placement of modifiers

- **Writing mechanics** (25 percent): Spelling (homonyms, contractions, and possessives only); capitalization of proper nouns; use of commas for punctuation

- **Organization** (15 percent): Text divisions; paragraph organization; topic sentences; document unity and coherence

To cover these four areas, the test-makers use five basic question types, according to what sort of revision is called for:

❶ Sentence correction (identifying and correcting an error in a sentence)

❷ Sentence revision (revising the underlined part of a sentence)

❸ Sentence construction (reconstructing a sentence)

❹ Paragraph composition (rearranging or splitting a paragraph, or inserting a new sentence into a paragraph)

❺ Document organization (splitting, joining, moving, and removing paragraphs)

The first three question types are used mainly to test on grammar, usage, mechanics, and sentence structure. The last two types are used to gauge your ability to recognize and create logical transitions from one idea to another within a paragraph or from one paragraph to the next. Of all five question types, sentence correction is used most frequently.

Questions that focus just on one or two sentences from the document will restate those sentences. For example, look at a sentence correction question based on "How to Interview for a Job."

Sentence 1: **Although many people think that a job interview are stressful and difficult, a job interview can be an exciting event.**

Which of the following corrections should be made to sentence 1?

(1) change <u>Although</u> to <u>Because</u>

(2) change <u>are</u> to <u>is</u>

(3) delete the comma

(4) change <u>be</u> to <u>is</u>

(5) no correction is necessary

In sentence 1, the noun *interview* is singular and therefore should take a singular verb form *is* instead of the plural form *are*. **The correct answer is (2).**

In the pages ahead, you'll take a closer look at each question type on the Writing Test, Part I. For each type you'll examine different variations and learn useful strategies and tips. At the end of the lesson, you'll review some general strategies that apply to all types of documents and question types.

ANSWERING SENTENCE CORRECTION QUESTIONS

As previously noted, the **sentence correction** format is the most commonly used format on the Writing Test, Part I. In this format, a question restates one of the numbered sentences from the document and then asks what correction should be made to it. An answer choice might propose that you *remove* or *insert* a word or punctuation mark, *change* a certain word to another word, or *replace* a word or brief phrase with a different one. In some cases, choice (5) will propose that "no correction is necessary."

In some sentence correction questions, the answer choices will all focus on the same aspect of sentence writing—for example, mechanics (punctuation, capitalization, and spelling). More often, however, the five answer choices will cover at least two of the three aspects of writing sentences: usage, mechanics, and sentence structure.

Here are some useful strategies and tips for handling sentence correction questions:

- Always evaluate the five answer choices in order—from (1) to (5). Why? Because that's the order in which they'll appear in the sentence. Choice (1) appears first in the sentence, choice (2) appears next, and so on.

- If two answer choices provide different ways of correcting the same error, you've missed something, and you should read the sentence more carefully.

- Look out for answer choices that correct one error but create another. Remember that all parts of a sentence are interrelated. So when evaluating any answer choice, keep the entire sentence in mind.

- Don't assume that an answer choice is the best one just because it proposes a change that would result in an effective and grammatically correct sentence. If an answer choice proposes a change, that change must be truly necessary in order to fix the sentence. Otherwise, look for a better answer choice.

- Resist the urge to "hyper-correct." In some questions, choice (5) will state that "no correction is necessary." Always look for this option. If you see it, be especially wary of the proposed changes in choices (1)–(4). Each and every one of them might either be unnecessary or create an error where there was none. If so, you should select choice (5) as the correct answer.

The following GED®-style paragraph and five example questions illustrate the sentence correction format. The analysis that follows each question explains how to apply one or more of the strategies listed above.

(1) The main problem with a shopping bag made of paper is that they can rip too easily. (2) Plastic bags are stronger, easier to carry, and last longer. (3) However, there's two big drawbacks to using plastic bags. (4) First, most types of plastic are made with a form of oil, which we have used far too much of this finite resource. (5) Second, since plastic does not decompose, plastic products pollute our land and water unless they're reused.

Sentence 1: **The main problem with a shopping bag made of paper is that they can rip too easily.**

Which correction should be made to sentence 1?

(1) replace <u>main</u> with <u>mane</u>

(2) change <u>bag</u> to <u>bags</u>

(3) change <u>is</u> to <u>are</u>

(4) remove the word <u>that</u>

(5) change <u>they</u> to <u>it</u>

In sentence 1, the noun *bag* is singular, but the pronoun *they,* which clearly refers to *bag,* is plural. Here's the applicable rule of grammar: a pronoun must agree in number (either singular or plural) with the noun to which it refers (called the *antecedent*).

It might appear that either choice (2) or choice (5) corrects the pronoun-reference error in sentence 1. But does this mean that either choice is correct? No. Read the sentence again using *bags* in place of *bag,* and you'll "hear" the incorrect phrase *a paper shopping bags.* Removing the word *a* would fix the sentence, but choice (2) doesn't propose this change. So among the five proposals, the only one that corrects the error is to change *they* to *it*. **The correct answer is (5).**

Sentence 2: **Plastic bags are stronger, are easier to carry, and longer lasting.**

Which correction should be made to sentence 2?

(1) remove the word <u>are</u> after <u>stronger</u>

(2) change <u>easier</u> to <u>easy</u>

(3) replace <u>to</u> with <u>too</u>

(4) remove the comma after <u>carry</u>

(5) no correction is necessary

Notice that sentence 2 lists a series of three features. Here's the applicable rule of grammar: all items in a series should be grammatically parallel. Read sentence 2 with this rule in mind, and you'll notice what is called "faulty parallelism." The second feature (*are easier to carry*) is not parallel to the third feature (*longer lasting*). One starts with the verb *are,* while the other one does not. One way to fix the problem is to insert the word *are* immediately after *and*. However, this option is not listed among the five choices. Another way to fix the problem is to remove the word *are* after *stronger,* which is what choice (1) suggests. The result is a series of three parallel items: (1) *stronger,* (2) *easier to carry,* and (3) *longer lasting.* **The correct answer is (1).**

Sentence 3: **However, there's two drawbacks to using plastic bags.**

Which correction should be made to sentence 3?

(1) remove the comma after <u>However</u>

(2) change <u>there's</u> to <u>there are</u>

(3) remove the word <u>to</u>

(4) remove the word <u>using</u>

(5) insert the word <u>of</u> after <u>using</u>

In sentence 3, the phrase *to using plastic bags* might not be so concise and graceful as the same phrase without the word *using*. But the phrase is not grammatically incorrect, and its meaning is clear enough. So the change proposed in choice (4) is not necessary, and you should look for a better answer choice.

The word *there's* is a contraction of the two-word phrase *there is*. Read the sentence with the two-word phrase, and you'll notice that the singular verb form *is* does not agree with the plural subject *drawbacks*. As choice (2) proposes, *there's* should be replaced with *there are*. **The correct answer is (2).**

Sentence 4: **First, most types of plastic are made with a form of oil, which we have used far too much of this finite resource.**

Which correction should be made to sentence 4?

(1) change <u>are</u> to <u>have been</u>

(2) replace <u>made</u> with <u>maid</u>

(3) remove the word <u>which</u>

(4) change <u>which</u> to <u>and</u>

(5) replace <u>too</u> with <u>to</u>

In sentence 4, the time frame for the action in the first clause is the present (*types...are made*). Choice (1) proposes to use the present-perfect tense (*have been made*). Here's the applicable rule of grammar: The present-perfect tense should be used to indicate action occurring in the past and ending at the present time. The present-perfect tense is not incorrect here, and it makes sense, especially since the second clause is framed in the same tense. However, the present tense works just as well, if not better. So the tense change that choice (1) proposes is unnecessary, and you should look for a better answer choice.

Read sentence 4 straight through. The final words *this finite resource* should strike you as "tacked on" to the end. Indeed, sentence 4 is a run-on sentence. Changing *which* to *and* fixes the error by transforming the second clause into an independent clause, connected to the original main clause by the word *and*. **The correct answer is (4).**

> Sentence 5: **Second, since plastic does not decompose, plastic products pollute our land and water unless they're reused.**
>
> Which correction should be made to sentence 5?
>
> **(1)** remove the word <u>since</u>
>
> **(2)** remove the comma after <u>decompose</u>
>
> **(3)** change <u>pollute</u> to <u>pollutes</u>
>
> **(4)** replace <u>they're</u> with <u>their</u>
>
> **(5)** no correction is necessary

Sentence 5 is a long, complex sentence. In addition to a main clause (*plastic products pollute our land and water*), the sentence contains two subordinate clauses, an introductory element (*Second*), and no fewer than three commas. You might naturally assume that somewhere in this complex sentence lies an error. But choice (5) proposes the possibility that the sentence is error free. So don't look for errors that might not be there. Let's examine the four proposed changes:

Choice (1): The word *since* makes perfect sense in context, and, in fact, removing it would result in a grammatical error known as a *comma splice*—in which two independent clauses are connected together by only a comma.

Choice (2): The comma after *decompose* is needed to avoid confusion. Without the comma, the sentence would suggest (nonsensically) that plastic decomposes plastic products.

Choice (3): The singular verb form *pollute* agrees with its plural subject *products*. Changing *pollute* to *pollutes* would create a subject-verb agreement error.

Choice (4): The word *their* is a possessive form of *they* and would make no sense in context. The word *they're* is a contraction of the two-word phrase *they are*. The plural pronoun form *they* correctly refers to the plural noun *products*.

The sentence contains no errors, so choice (5) is the right option.
The correct answer is (5).

ANSWERING SENTENCE REVISION QUESTIONS

A **sentence revision** question restates one numbered sentence (or possibly two consecutive sentences) from the document. Part of the sentence will be underlined, and five alternative ways to write the underlined part will be presented.

Your task is to identify the best of the five alternatives. The first answer choice will leave the underlined part unchanged, so you should select choice (1) if you think the sentence is better with the original, underlined part than with any of the four revisions.

The answer choices might all focus on the same aspect of sentence writing—either sentence structure, usage, or mechanics. Usually, though, the five answer choices will cover at least two of those three aspects.

To handle sentence revision questions, follow these suggestions:

- Don't make your final selection until you've considered all five choices. More than one proposed revision might be better than the original version. Without examining all five choices you can't know for sure which is best.

- The underlined part might be flawed in more than one way. An answer choice might fix one flaw but not another. Again, always consider all five choices before making your final selection.

- Be sure to consider the entire sentence. Keep in mind that all parts of a sentence are interrelated. By examining just the underlined part, or even that part along with what immediately precedes or follows it, you can easily overlook a problem. The same applies to each proposed revision as well.

- Remember your task is to identify "the best way to write the underlined portion." What this means is that you should look not just for grammatical errors but also for other problems, such as awkwardness, misplaced modifiers, and problems in sentence sense or logic. Also, rule out any revision that distorts or alters the intended meaning of the sentence.

The following GED®-style paragraph and questions illustrate the sentence revision format. The analysis that follows each question explains how to apply one or more of the above suggestions.

(6) Whether you use paper, or plastic, fewer bags help conserve resources and protects our environment. (7) To avoid choosing a bag every time you go shopping, take your own reusable bag with you. (8) Also, try not to go shopping more often than necessary, because it will help you save gas by making fewer trips.

Sentence 6: **Whether <u>you use paper, or plastic, fewer bags help</u> conserve resources and protects our environment.**

Which is the best way to write the underlined portion of sentence 6? If the original is the best way, select answer choice (1).

(1) you use paper, or plastic, fewer bags help

(2) paper or plastic, fewer bags help

(3) you use paper, or plastic, few bags help

(4) you should use paper or plastic, fewer bags help

(5) you use paper or plastic, using fewer bags helps

In sentence 6, the object of the verb *use* is *paper or plastic*. Splitting this element with a comma makes for an awkward and confusing clause, and so the comma should be removed. If you were to focus only on this problem and select the first answer choice that fixes it, you would select choice (2).

But read the entire sentence carefully, and not just the underlined part. Notice that the main clause *fewer bags help conserve resources . . .* doesn't make sense. In themselves, "fewer bags" do not conserve resources; what conserves resources is "*using* fewer bags." The best answer choice must also fix this problem. Not until you reach choice (5) do you find a revision that fixes both problems. **The correct answer is (5).**

Sentence 7: **To avoid choosing a bag every time you go shopping, take your own reusable bag with you.**

Which is the best way to write the underlined portion of sentence 7? If the original is the best way, select answer choice (1).

(1) To avoid choosing

(2) Avoid choosing

(3) If you didn't choose

(4) Avoid the choice of

(5) To avoid to choose

If you focus on just the underlined part of sentence 7 and on the four alternatives to the underlined part, you won't be able to answer the question. In itself, choices (1) through (4) all look perfectly acceptable. (You can rule out choice (5) because it provides a very awkward-sounding phrase.) So to answer the question, you'll need to consider other parts of sentence 7 as well.

You can rule out choices (2) and (4). Each results in a *comma splice* (two independent clauses connected by only a comma), which is a clear grammatical error. Choice (3) introduces the past-tense verb form *didn't*. But does the past tense make sense in the context of the sentence as a whole? No. The sentence clearly intends to establish a present-to-future time frame. By mixing tenses, choice (3) confuses the time frame of the sentence's action.

Each of the proposed revisions either results in a grammatical error, choices (2) and (4), or makes the sentence confusing or awkward, choices (3) and (5). The original, underlined version is the best one. **The correct answer is (1).**

> Sentence 8: **Also, try not to go shopping more often than necessary, because it will help you save gas by making fewer trips.**
>
> Which is the best way to write the underlined portion of sentence 8? If the original is the best way, choose option (1).
>
> **(1)** because it will help you save gas by making fewer trips
>
> **(2)** and you will save gas by making fewer trips
>
> **(3)** because the fewer the trips will help you save gas
>
> **(4)** since making fewer tips will help you save gas
>
> **(5)** because doing so will mean fewer trips and less gas

As in the two previous examples (sentences 6 and 7), examining just the underlined part and the four alternatives doesn't help much here. You'll need to consider the five choices in the context they would appear in the sentence as a whole.

The problem with the underlined part of sentence 8 is with the pronoun *it*. Here's the applicable rule: Every pronoun should have a clear *antecedent*—a noun to which the pronoun refers. Reading the entire sentence should tell you that by the word *it,* the writer intended to refer to the noun clause *making fewer trips*. But the reference is unclear, isn't it? One way to clear up the confusion is to eliminate the pronoun, possibly replacing it with its intended antecedent. This is exactly what choices (2) and (5) do, but each creates a new problem. Choice (2) replaces *because* with *and,* thereby losing the logical connection between the sentence's two ideas. Choice (5) is awkward and confusing. The clause *because the fewer the trips the less gas you use* would be far better, but this option is not among the choices.

So even though choices (2) and (3) fix the pronoun-reference problem, you should keep looking for a better choice. Choice (4) also clears up the pronoun-reference by eliminating the pronoun *it,* without creating a new problem. **The correct answer is (4).**

ANSWERING SENTENCE CONSTRUCTION QUESTIONS

A **sentence construction** question restates a numbered sentence from the document and then presents five alternative versions of all or part of the sentence. Your task is to determine which alternative is the most effective.

In some cases, the first answer choice will leave the sentence unchanged, in which case you should select choice (1) if you think the original sentence is more effective than any of the four proposed revisions. In other cases, all five choices will revise the sentence in some way. Most sentence construction questions focus on the same aspect of sentence writing: sentence structure. However, some might cover usage and/or mechanics as well. Not all sentence construction questions use exactly the same format. Before looking at each variation, read the following GED®-style paragraph:

(9) We should use paper bags and not plastic bags because the damage by us that way is less to the environment. (10) Reducing plastic bag use would happen by charging store customers for them. (11) Recycled paper bags, because they are stronger than bags made from virgin wood, can be used more often. (12) Ideally, we should take our own reusable bags with us when we shop. (13) We should not rely on stores to provide us with bags.

Finding the Best Choice to Continue the Sentence

In one variation on the sentence construction format, the question proposes a way to rewrite the beginning of the sentence, and then it asks you what the next words should be. You'll be given five alternatives. Although there may be several effective ways to continue the sentence, your choices are limited to five. To analyze the answer choices, expect to do some brainstorming and experimenting. In your mind, you should run through many variations of the sentence. Try to formulate a revised version of the entire sentence (not just part of it) using each of the five groups of words, one at a time. A good sentence must incorporate all of the original sentence's ideas in a graceful, logical manner, without splitting parts of the sentence that naturally belong together. If you can't accomplish this in one sentence, look for a better answer choice. Here's an example:

Sentence 9: **We should use paper bags and not plastic bags because the damage by us that way is less to the environment.**

If you rewrote sentence 9 beginning with

The damage

the next words should be

(1) in using plastic bags

(2) we do to the environment

(3) by us using paper bags

(4) is less to the environment

(5) that paper bags do

In sentence 9, the passively voiced phrase *damage by us* is awkward. To make matters worse, the word *damage* is separated from what it refers to: *the environment*. A good revised sentence must correct both problems. The actively voiced phrase *damage we do to* is clearer and more graceful. Choice (2) provides this phrase and makes it clear that the writer is referring to environmental damage. Try formulating a sentence beginning with *The damage we do to the environment*. Is it possible to incorporate all of the sentence's ideas in a single, clear sentence? Yes, it is. Here's one good version: *The damage we do to the environment when we use paper bags is less than when we use plastic bags*. Try using each of the four other phrases to formulate an effective, concise sentence that incorporates all of the ideas in the original sentence, including the idea that we should use paper bags. You'll find that you can't. **The correct answer is (2).**

Five Alternatives to the Beginning of the Sentence

A second variation of the sentence construction format provides five alternatives to the beginning of a numbered sentence from the document. Your task is to determine which way works best for rewriting the sentence. Here's what you should know in order to handle this question type:

- Try to revise the original sentence before reading the answer choices. If you have trouble doing so, try building a sentence using each of the five phrases, one at a time.

- Expect to do some brainstorming and experimenting. Trial-and-error is the best way to eliminate poor choices and to zero in on the best one.

- For each answer choice, try to formulate a revised version of the *entire sentence*. The most effective revision will incorporate all of the original sentence's ideas in a graceful, logical manner, without splitting parts of the sentence that naturally belong together. If you can't accomplish this in one sentence, look for a better answer choice.

- Keep in mind that there may be more than one good way to begin the sentence at hand, but your options are limited to the five that are listed.

Let's apply these strategies to an example question:

> **Sentence 10: Reducing plastic bag use would happen by charging store customers for them.**
>
> The most effective revision of sentence 10 would begin with which group of words?
>
> **(1)** How to reduce the use of plastic bags
>
> **(2)** What would happen when customers
>
> **(3)** By stores reducing the use of
>
> **(4)** If store customers were charged
>
> **(5)** Plastic bags charged by stores

Sentence 10 is awkward and confusing—no doubt about it. But what is the best way to reconstruct it without complicating it further? Try reversing the order of the two ideas in the sentence. Start with the proposal that stores charge their customers for plastic bags. You'll find that the other idea in the sentence flows naturally as a conclusion. Here's a good version of the complete sentence: *If store customers were charged for plastic bags, fewer plastic bags would be used.* Experiment with the other answer choices, and you'll find that only choice (4) provides the opening words of a revision that incorporates all of the sentence's ideas into a clear, well-constructed sentence. **The correct answer is (4).**

Words That Can Appear Anywhere in the Sentence

A third variation on the sentence construction format is similar to the one described above, except that in the third one the group of words can appear *anywhere* in the sentence. This feature can make for a more challenging question. Here's how to handle this difficult question type:

- Don't bother trying to revise the original sentence before reading the answer choices. Start by examining each choice, in turn.

- Try to "build" an effective revision around each group of words. Start with what makes sense leading up to the group of words, and then try to complete the sentence in a way that makes sense.

- The most effective revision will incorporate all of the original sentence's ideas in a graceful, logical manner, without splitting parts of the sentence that naturally belong together. Don't worry: only one answer choice will clearly fit the bill.

Let's apply this advice to an example question.

> Sentence 11: **Recycled paper bags, because they are stronger than bags made from virgin wood, can be used more often.**
>
> The most effective revision of sentence 11 would include which group of words?
>
> **(1)** can be used more often, and are stronger
>
> **(2)** More often, recycled paper bags can be
>
> **(3)** from virgin wood, recycled paper bags
>
> **(4)** paper bags, stronger than bags made of
>
> **(5)** because paper bags, which are used more

Notice that the clause set off by commas interrupts the flow of ideas. As an experiment, before examining the answer choices let's try reconstructing the sentence from scratch, so that the ideas flow more naturally. Here are some possibilities for the framework of the revised sentence:

> *Recycled bags are stronger than . . . , so they can be used more often.*
>
> *Recycled bags can be used more often than . . . because they are stronger.*
>
> *Compared to bags made from virgin wood, recycled bags are stronger, and so . . . .*

Might all this effort help you identify the best answer choice? Perhaps. But the effort is probably not worth the time spent. Instead, simply examine each answer choice in turn, and see if you can build an effective revision of sentence 11 around it. Start with choice (1). Ask yourself what could precede this group of words *and* make sense there? There's only one possibility. From the beginning:

> *Recycled bags can be used more often, and are stronger . . . .*

Now, ask yourself what should come next. You're left with only one option that makes any sense. Again, from the beginning:

Recycled bags can be used more often, and are stronger than bags made from virgin wood . . . .

You should already see that this revision is not effective. The point of the original sentence is being lost. So eliminate choice (1). Next, consider choice (2). Notice that this group of words begins with the capitalized word *More,* which means that the sentence must begin with the group of words. Ask yourself what must come next. There's only one possibility. From the beginning:

More often, recycled paper bags can be used. . . .

Now, can you complete this sentence in a logical and clear manner, incorporating all of the sentence's ideas? No, you can't. Eliminate choice (2). Perform a similar analysis for choices (3), (4), and (5), and you'll discover that only choice (3) provides a group of words that you can incorporate into a complete and effective revision of sentence 11. The complete sentence would look similar to this one:

Because they are stronger than bags made from virgin wood, recycled paper bags can be used more often.

The correct answer is (3).

When the Question Involves Two Consecutive Numbered Sentences

A sentence construction question might involve two consecutive numbered sentences (rather than just one sentence). These questions usually ask how best to combine the two sentences into one. Ask yourself what the logical connection is between the ideas in the two sentences. You'll find that with just the right linking word or brief phrase, you can convey the logical connection between ideas quite effectively.

Sentence 12 and Sentence 13: **Ideally, we should take our own reusable bags with us when we shop. We should not rely on stores to provide us with bags.**

The most effective combination of sentences 12 and 13 would include which group of words?

(1) when we shop, rather than relying

(2) relying on stores, we should take

(3) we go shopping, and stores should not

(4) to the store, we should not rely

(5) reusable bags, instead we should take

The two sentences are closely related. But how are their ideas connected? Clearly, the writer is trying to convey the idea that we should take our own bags to the store *instead of* using fresh bags supplied by the store. Of the five groups of words, only the group in choice (1) links the two ideas in a way that conveys this message. (The phrase *rather than* is an alternative to *instead of.)* Choice (5) is tempting because it contains the appropriate linking word *instead*. However, constructing a meaningful sentence around *reusable bags, instead we should take* is difficult, if not impossible. **The correct answer is (1).**

ANSWERING PARAGRAPH COMPOSITION QUESTIONS

A Writing Test, Part I question might ask you to reconstruct a paragraph by one of the following two ways:

1 *Rearranging* the paragraph's sentences

2 *Inserting* a new sentence, usually at the beginning of a paragraph

Rearranging the Paragraph's Sentences

The type of question tests your ability to recognize and create logical transitions from one idea to another within a paragraph. The question might focus on the position of one particular sentence, or it might involve as many as all of the paragraph's sentences. An answer choice might propose *moving* a particular sentence, or it might propose *removing* it. To handle the question, read the entire paragraph, paying close attention to how its ideas flow from one to the next. Each sentence should lead naturally and logically to the next one. Wherever you lose the paragraph's "train of thought" is where the sentence sequence should be changed.

Here's what else you should keep in mind when tackling these questions:

- One sentence might express a general idea, while the other sentences provide examples, reasons, or other details that explain or support that idea. A general idea should usually be expressed first, as the paragraph's topic sentence. A sentence that does not fit within the paragraph's general topic should be removed from the paragraph.

- The overall theme of the paragraph might help you determine the best sentence sequence. For instance, a paragraph's sentences might discuss past events that occurred in a chronological order, or they might list steps to be followed in chronological order. If so, it probably makes sense to sequence the sentences in that order.

- A key word or brief phrase, especially at the beginning of a sentence, can provide an additional clue as to where the sentence should be positioned. Words and phrases such as *however, nevertheless,* and *on the other hand* suggest contrast or opposition to an idea expressed in the preceding sentences. And words such as *therefore, thus,* and *so* suggest that the sentence provides a conclusion, which should follow the sentences that contain evidence upon which the conclusion is based.

Let's apply some of these ideas to a GED®-style question. In the following paragraph, though the sentences themselves may be flawed, you should focus strictly on paragraph structure to answer the question.

(1) The main problem with a shopping bag made of paper is that they can rip too easily. (2) However, there's two big drawbacks to using plastic bags. (3) Most types of plastic are made with a form of oil, which we have

used far too much of this finite resource. (4) Also, since plastic does not decompose, plastic products pollute our land and water unless they're reused. (5) Plastic bags are stronger, easier to carry, and longer lasting.

Which revision would improve the effectiveness of this paragraph?

(1) remove sentence 2

(2) move sentence 3 to the beginning of the paragraph

(3) move sentence 5 to follow sentence 1

(4) move sentence 4 to follow sentence 2

(5) remove sentence 5

Start by reading sentences 1 and 2. Ask yourself whether sentence 1 flows naturally and logically into sentence 2. Notice the word *However,* which anticipates an idea that opposes the preceding one. Something needed to complete the logical connection between the two sentences seems to be missing. Make a mental note of this, and then read on.

Notice that sentence 2 practically tells you what should follow it: a list of two reasons *not* to use plastic bags. Indeed, sentence 3 provides one such reason, and sentence 4 provides a second such reason. (Sentence 4's introductory word *Also* is a good clue as to what to expect from the sentence.) So, sentences 2, 3, and 4 are probably best left together, in their current order. Read on.

The final sentence (5) unexpectedly switches to the opposing argument, stating an *advantage* to using plastic bags. Clearly, sentence 5 does not belong where it is. The answer choices supply two options for sentence 5: either move it or remove it. Choice (3) suggests repositioning sentence 5 between sentences 1 and 2. This revision is exactly what's needed to link the idea in sentence 1 to the idea in sentence 2. **The correct answer is (3).**

Inserting a New Sentence

A second type of paragraph composition question suggests inserting a new sentence—usually at the beginning of a paragraph. Your task is to decide which of the five sentences would be most effective if inserted in that position. These questions usually test your ability to identify appropriate topic sentences for paragraphs.

To handle this type of question, you need to understand the paragraph's scope—what it covers and what it doesn't cover. Assuming the new sentence is to be inserted at the beginning of the paragraph, the correct answer will most likely provide a good topic sentence for the paragraph—a general statement that covers all the paragraph's ideas, but only those ideas. Here's a good example, based on the following (flawed) paragraph.

(6) The main reason not to use plastic bags is they cause considerable damage to our environment. (7) Most types of plastic are made with a form of oil, which we have used far too much of this finite resource. (8) Also, since plastic does not decompose, plastic products pollute our land and water unless their reused. (9) On the other hand, shopping bag

made of paper they can rip too easily. (10) Plastic bags are stronger, easier to carry, and last longer.

Which sentence would be most effective if inserted at the beginning of this paragraph?

(1) Paper bags should be used instead of plastic bags whenever possible.

(2) Paper bags and plastic bags each have their distinct advantages and drawbacks.

(3) Our natural environment is damaged greatly by our use of plastic bags.

(4) One advantage of plastic bags is that no wood products are used to make them.

(5) For the sake of our natural environment, we should all stop using plastic bags.

Before you can answer this question, you need to understand the flow of the paragraph's ideas, from start to finish. Notice that sentences 6–8 make a case against plastic bags, while sentences 9 and 10 make a case against paper bags (and for plastic bags). With this recap in mind, it becomes clear that choice (2) provides an appropriate topic sentence for the paragraph. **The correct answer is (2).**

ANSWERING DOCUMENT ORGANIZATION QUESTIONS

Some Writing Test, Part I questions will focus not on individual sentences or the arrangement of sentences but rather on the "bigger picture"—how a document is organized into paragraphs. A question of this type will propose the following sorts of revisions:

- Splitting a paragraph into two separate paragraphs

- Combining two paragraphs by removing a paragraph break

- Moving an entire paragraph to a new position

- Removing an entire paragraph

To handle these questions, keep in mind that each paragraph should cover its own distinct topic. The overall theme of the document (for instance, "point and example," "pros and cons" or "step-by-step instructions") might help you determine where paragraph breaks belong. Breaks should occur wherever the flow of ideas changes course, such as:

- Between different examples or reasons given in support of a main point

- Between an argument for a certain proposal and an argument against it

- Between distinctly different steps in a process

To determine whether a paragraph should be split into two separate paragraphs, look for where the flow of ideas changes course. This is where a paragraph break should go. Here's an example based on the following paragraph (some of the sentences themselves contain flaws, but for this question type you should focus strictly on the paragraph as a whole).

(6) Plastic bags are more harmful to the environment than paper bags. (7) Therefore, we should all make a special effort to use fewer plastic bags. (8) The best way to discourage people from using plastic bags is to charge store customers for them. (9) Educating people about how much damage these bags can do would also help. (10) Whether you use paper or plastic, by using fewer bags, you help conserve resources and protect our environment. (11) So minimize the number of bags you need when you shop. (12) Take your own reusable bag with you. (13) You can help the environment even more by using bags made from recycled paper and cloth. (14) Recycled paper bags are stronger and so can be used more often than bags made from virgin wood.

Which revision would improve the effectiveness of this document?

Begin a new paragraph with

(1) sentence 8

(2) sentence 9

(3) sentence 10

(4) sentence 11

(5) sentence 12

As it stands, this paragraph covers two related, yet distinguishable, topics. Sentences 6–9 focus on plastic bags. Beginning with sentence 10, however, the focus widens to embrace paper bags as well. Inserting a paragraph break between sentences 9 and 10 would help the reader follow the shifting course of the discussion. (Inserting a paragraph break between sentences 12 and 13 might also be helpful, but this revision is not listed among the five answer choices.) **The correct answer is (3).**

Now read the following GED®-style document from start to finish. (Once again, some of the sentences themselves contain flaws; but for document organization questions, you should focus strictly on the document's structure.) Then, attempt the question that follows the document. Notice that each proposed revision involves either *joining* two paragraphs, *moving* a paragraph, or *removing* a paragraph.

(A)

(1) At the grocery store we are always asked whether we want paper or plastic. (2) The main problem with a shopping bag made of paper is that they can rip too easily. (3) Often, the bottom of the bag rips open. (4) If the bag has paper handles, the handles tear off the bag very easily. (5) Plastic bags are stronger and therefore last longer, and they are easier to carry.

(B)

(6) Of course, plastic bags have drawbacks of there own. (7) First, most types of plastic are made with a form of oil, we have used up far too much of this finite resource. (8) Second, since plastic does not decompose, plastic products pollute our land and water unless they are reused. (9) The damage done to the environment by paper bags is much less.

(C)

(10) Whether you use paper or plastic, using fewer bags help conserve resources and protect our environment. (11) One good way to reduce the use of shopping bags would be to charge store customers for them upon checkout. (12) Otherwise, to avoid using a new bag every time you go shopping, get in the habit of taking your own reusable bag with you to the store. (13) Also, try not to go shopping more often than necessary, because you'll probably use fewer bags this way.

(D)

(14) If you use paper bags, try to use recycled bags. (15) We will help the environment even more if paper bags are made from recycled paper and cloth. (16) The reason for this is recycled bags are stronger than bags made from virgin wood, so they last longer.

(E)

(17) Deciding between paper and plastic bags is not an easy decision to make. (18) Ultimately, however, the best response to the question is to say that you don't need either.

Which revision would improve the effectiveness of the document?

(1) join paragraphs A and B

(2) move paragraph B to follow paragraph C

(3) join paragraphs C and D

(4) remove paragraph D

(5) move paragraph E to the beginning of the document

To answer this question, there's no shortcut to reading the entire document. (You should read through an entire document in any event, *before* you try to answer any of the questions.) Try to identify the general topic of each paragraph, paying special attention to how the paragraphs relate to one another:

Paragraph (A) discusses drawbacks of paper bags (the opening sentence introduces the general topic: the "paper vs. plastic" decision).

Paragraph (B) discusses drawbacks of plastic bags.

Paragraph (C) lists ways to reduce our use of paper *and* plastic bags.

Paragraph (D) discusses advantages of recycled paper bags over new paper bags.

Paragraph (E) recaps the ideas presented in paragraphs (A), (B), and (C).

Having looked at the document as a whole, you can now see that paragraph (D) does not fit into the document's theme: paper, plastic, or neither. The overall unity and cohesiveness of the document would be improved by removing this paragraph, which is choice (4). **The correct answer is (4).**

GENERAL TEST-TAKING STRATEGIES

Here are some general strategies for tackling the GED® Writing Test, Part I. Most apply to all types of documents and questions. Put these strategies to work on the Practice Tests in this book, and then review them again just before exam day.

- **Read a document straight through before answering any questions based on it.** Read the document quickly from beginning to end. Don't bother to take notes, and don't pay too much attention to specific grammatical errors (you'll find plenty of them!). Instead, pay attention mainly to the following:

  o The basic *sequence of ideas* from one paragraph to the next—a confusing or illogical sequence means that one of the questions will probably cover it.

  o The *time frame* (past, present, and future) used in the document—an illogical or confusing shift in time frame means that one of the questions will probably cover it.

This strategy will help you to focus and to anticipate at least some of the questions. The documents are short (200 to 300 words), so 30 seconds should be ample time for this task.

- **"Listen" to sentences for anything that doesn't sound right.** In answering questions about particular sentences, listen to them—as if you were reading aloud—for anything that sounds awkward, confusing, or just plain weird. If you hear something wrong, trust you ear and your instinct.

- **Apply the four basic principles for error-spotting in GED® sentences.** If you're not sure what the problem with a particular sentence is, follow these four steps to uncover it:

  1 Find the verb, then its subject. Check for subject-verb agreement, correct tense, and proper verb formation.

  2 Examine all pronouns. Make sure each has a clear antecedent with which it agrees in person and number.

  3 Examine sentence structure. Make sure modifiers are attached to what they modify, parallel ideas are grammatically parallel, and comparisons are clear and logical.

  4 Listen for awkwardness or "gobbledygook" (anything that simply makes no sense).

- **Try to formulate an answer *before* reading the choices.** In tackling a question about a particular sentence, think about how you would write the sentence. Do this before looking at any of the answer choices. Try rephrasing a faulty sentence part, figuring out what word or punctuation mark you'd eliminate, change, move, or add. You'll zero in on the correct choice more quickly this way, and you're less likely to become confused and tempted by wrong answer choices. Keep in mind that this strategy works for most, but not all, question types on the Writing Test, Part I. Exceptions to the rule are noted in the grammar review, which follows this lesson.

- **Pace yourself properly.** The Writing Test, Part I consists of several distinct question sets, each set based on a different document. The number of questions per set can vary from five to ten (the average number is eight). Plan to spend a bit more time on long question sets than on shorter ones. Your time limit for answering all fifty questions is 75 minutes. Try to answer ten questions every 15 minutes, on average. If you're falling behind, try to pick up your pace.

SUMMING IT UP

- Part I of the Language Arts, Writing Test is basically an *editing* test that is designed to measure your ability to review a document and spot grammatical errors and other writing problems that need to be corrected or revised. Expect six to eight documents altogether and six to ten questions based on each document (fifty questions in total). Each document will be 200–300 words in length and will contain twelve to twenty-two sentences.

- The Writing Test, Part I questions cover grammar and usage, sentence structure, writing mechanics, and organization. The five basic question types are: sentence correction, sentence revision, sentence construction, paragraph composition, and document organization. Of all five question types, sentence correction is used most frequently.

- All documents on the Writing Test, Part I share the following things in common: the sentences are numbered in sequence, the paragraphs are lettered in sequence, and some (but not all) of the sentences are flawed in some way.

- For sentence correction questions, always evaluate the five order choices in order, from (1) to (5); look out for answer choices that fix one error but create another; and avoid correcting a sentence that doesn't need to be corrected.

- For sentence revision questions, remember that you need to identify "the best way to write the underlined portion." Aside from grammatical errors, look for other problems, such as awkwardness, misplaced modifiers, and problems in sentence sense or logic. Also, rule out any revision that distorts or alters the intended meaning of the sentence.

- Most sentence construction questions focus on sentence structure. However, some might cover usage and/or mechanics as well. Sentence construction questions vary in format; make sure you become familiar with these different types of questions.

- Paragraph reconstruction questions ask you to recreate a paragraph by either *rearranging* the paragraph's sentences or *inserting* a new sentence, usually at the beginning of a paragraph.

- Document organization questions propose the following types of revisions: splitting a paragraph into two, combining two paragraphs, moving a paragraph to a new position, and removing an entire paragraph. Keep in mind that each paragraph should cover its own distinct topic.

Writing Review

OVERVIEW

- **Sentence structure**
- **Usage**
- **Writing mechanics**
- **Summing it up**

SENTENCE STRUCTURE

Sentence structure refers to how a sentence's parts fit together as a whole. Sentence structure problems account for about 35 percent of the GED® Language Arts, Writing Test, Part I. In this section, you'll learn to spot these problems and how to correct or revise GED® sentences to fix them.

Structural Errors

A GED® sentence might be structured in a way that results in one of the following grammatical errors:

- Sentence fragments

- Run-ons and comma splices

- Faulty parallelism involving series

- Faulty parallelism involving correlatives

Don't worry if some of the terms listed above are unfamiliar to you. You'll learn what they mean in the pages ahead.

Sentence Fragments

A complete sentence must include both a subject and a predicate. The **subject** of a sentence is the word or phrase that describes what the sentence is about. A complete subject is a noun or pronoun plus any of the words directly related to that noun or pronoun. The **predicate** is the part of the sentence that says something about the subject. The predicate, or complete verb, includes all the words that, together, say something about the subject. Look at this sentence:

Aaron tried to start his car but couldn't.

In this sentence, the word *Aaron* is the complete subject. The rest of the sentence, which says something about Aaron, is the predicate, or complete verb. The word *tried* is the verb that establishes the predicate.

chapter 4

An incomplete sentence is called a **sentence fragment.** On the GED®, you probably won't have any trouble recognizing and fixing a short sentence fragment like the next one, which lacks a predicate. In the complete sentence, notice that the verb *are* establishes a predicate.

> **fragment (incorrect):** Expensive private colleges, which for most families are out of financial reach.

> **complete sentence (correct):** Expensive private colleges are out of financial reach for most families.

A longer fragment is more likely to escape your detection, especially if you're not paying close attention:

> **fragment (incorrect):** As most of the engineers and other experts have agreed, their responsibility for building safe bridges, as well as for maintaining them.

> **complete sentence (correct):** As most of the engineers and other experts have agreed, they are responsible not only for building safe bridges but for maintaining them as well.

In the complete sentence, the subject is *they,* and the predicate is the verb *are* and the words that follow that verb.

If you're not sure whether a sentence is complete, ask yourself two questions: What's the subject? Where's the verb that establishes a predicate?

Run-ons and Comma Splices

An **independent clause** is a sentence part that can stand alone as a complete sentence. There's nothing wrong with combining two such clauses into one sentence, as long as you connect them properly.

Connecting two independent clauses without using a punctuation mark or any words to make the connection results in a grammatical error called a **run-on** sentence. One way to correct the error is to split the sentence in two using a period. Another solution is to add a comma, followed by an appropriate connecting word:

> **run-on (incorrect):** Dan ran out of luck Mike continued to win.

> **correct:** Dan ran out of luck. Mike continued to win.

> **correct:** Dan ran out of luck, but Mike continued to win.

Connecting two independent clauses with only a comma results in an error known as a **comma splice.** One way to correct the error is to insert an appropriate connecting word after the comma:

> **comma splice (incorrect):** Dan ran out of luck, Mike continued to win.

> **correct:** Dan ran out of luck, though Mike continued to win.

It can be easy to overlook a longer run-on or comma splice unless you're reading carefully. Here's an example of a longer comma splice:

comma splice: The Aleutian Islands of Alaska include many islands near the populated mainland, the majority of them are uninhabited by humans.

In reading this sentence, it isn't until you reach the word *are* that the comma splice becomes apparent. One way to correct the error is to remove the word *are*. Another way to correct the error is to transform the second independent clause into a *dependent* clause by changing the word *them* to *which*.

Faulty Parallelism Involving Series

Sentence elements that are grammatically equal should be constructed similarly; otherwise, the result will be what is referred to as **faulty parallelism.** For instance, whenever you see a list, or series, of items in a sentence, look for inconsistent or mixed use of:

- Prepositions (such as *in, with,* or *on*)
- Gerunds (verbs with an *-ing* added to the end)
- Infinitives (plural verb preceded by *to*)
- Articles (such as *a* and *the*)

In the following sentence, the preposition *to* is not applied consistently to every item in the series:

faulty: Flight 82 travels first to Boise, then to Denver, then Salt Lake City.

(The word *to* precedes only the first two of the three cities in this list.)

parallel: Flight 82 travels first to Boise, then Denver, then Salt Lake City.

parallel: Flight 82 travel first to Boise, then to Denver, and then to Salt Lake City.

In the next sentence, the gerund *being* is not applied consistently:

faulty: Being understaffed, lack of funding, and being outpaced by competitors soon resulted in the fledgling company's going out of business.

(Only two of the three listed items begin with the gerund *being*.)

parallel: Understaffed, underfunded, and outpaced by competitors, the fledgling company soon went out of business.

parallel: As a result of understaffing, insufficient funding, and outpacing on the part of its competitors, the fledgling company soon went out of business.

In the next sentence, the article *the* is not applied consistently:

faulty: Among *the* mountains, *the* sea, and desert, we humans have yet to fully explore only the sea.

parallel: Among *the* mountains, sea, and desert, we humans have yet to fully explore only the sea.

parallel: Among *the* mountains, *the* sea, and *the* desert, we humans have yet to fully explore only the sea.

Faulty Parallelism Involving Correlatives

The preceding section described how a list of items in a series can suffer from faulty parallelism. A similar problem can occur in sentences that contain **correlatives.** Here are the most common ones:

either . . . or . . .

neither . . . nor . . .

both . . . and . . .

not only . . . but also . . .

When a correlative is used in a sentence, the element immediately following the first correlative term must be grammatically parallel to the element following the second term.

faulty: Students wishing to participate in the study group should *either* contact me by telephone *or* should e-mail me.

parallel: Students wishing to participate in the study group should *either* contact me by telephone *or* e-mail me.

faulty: Students wishing to participate in the study group *either* should contact me by telephone *or* e-mail.

parallel: Students wishing to participate in the study group should contact me by *either* telephone *or* e-mail.

Awkward and Confusing Sentence Structures

A GED® sentence that is free of errors might nevertheless be structured in a way that makes the sentence's ideas confusing, vague, ambiguous, or even nonsensical. These sorts of structural problems include the following:

- Improper coordination or subordination
- Mixing of two structures together in one sentence
- Omission of a key word needed for sentence logic
- Improper placement of modifiers
- Dangling modifiers
- Improper splitting of a grammatical unit
- Stringing together too many subordinate clauses

Don't worry if some of the terms listed above are unfamiliar to you. You'll learn what they mean in the pages ahead.

Improper Coordination or Subordination

A GED® sentence that is free of grammatical errors may nevertheless be structured in a way that overemphasizes certain ideas, so that the reader misses the sentence's main point. If a sentence conveys two equally important ideas, they should be separated as two distinct clauses of similar length—to suggest equal importance.

mixed and unbalanced: Julie and Sandy, *who* are twins, are both volunteers.

separated but unbalanced: Julie and Sandy were the first two volunteers for the fund-raising drive, *and* they are twins.

separated and balanced: Julie and Sandy are twins, *and* they are both volunteers.

On the other hand, if a sentence involves only one main idea, that idea should receive greater emphasis, as a main clause, than the other ideas in the sentence.

balanced: Julie and Sandy, *who* are twins, were the first two volunteers for the fund-raising drive.

In the preceding sentence, notice that the less important idea (that Julie and Sandy are twins) is contained in a brief, modifying clause that describes Julie and Sandy. This is an effective way to deemphasize an idea that is not the main idea of the sentence.

To suggest similarity in ideas, a **coordinating conjunctive** such as *and* should be used. To suggest dissimilarity, or contrast, in ideas, a **subordinating conjunctive** such as *but, though, although,* or *whereas* should be used.

similar ideas: Julie and Sandy were identical twins, *and* they both liked to travel.

similar ideas: Julie and Sandy were identical twins, *and* so were Tracy and Judy.

dissimilar ideas: Julie and Sandy were identical twins, *but* they had completely different ambitions.

dissimilar ideas: Julie and Sandy were identical twins, *whereas* Tracy and Judy were merely fraternal twins.

Mixing Sentence Structures

If two or more clauses in the same sentence express parallel ideas, they should be grammatically parallel to each other. Otherwise, the reader might find the sentence awkward and confusing.

This problem often occurs when a sentence mixes the **active voice** with the **passive voice.** In a sentence expressed in the active voice, the subject *acts upon* an object. Conversely, in a sentence expressed in the passive voice, the subject *is acted upon by* an object. Here are two sets of examples:

mixed: Although the house was built by Gary, Kevin built the garage.

parallel (passive): Although the house was built by Gary, the garage was built by Kevin.

parallel (active): Although Gary built the house, Kevin built the garage.

mixed: All hardback books are to be sorted today, but wait until tomorrow to sort paperbacks.

parallel (passive): All hardback books are to be sorted today, but paperbacks are not to be sorted until tomorrow.

parallel (active): Sort all hardback books today, but wait until tomorrow to sort paperbacks.

Omitting Words Needed for Sentence Logic

If a sentence excludes a necessary word, the omission can obscure or confuse the meaning of the sentence. The unintentional omission of "little" words—prepositions, pronouns, conjunctives, and especially the word *that*—can make a big difference.

omission: The newscaster announced the voting results were incorrect.

(What did the newscaster announce: the results or the fact that the results were incorrect?)

clearer: The newscaster announced *that* the voting results were incorrect.

Look out especially for an omission that results in an illogical comparison, as in the following sentences. It can easily slip past you if you're not paying close attention.

illogical: The color of the blouse is different from the skirt.

logical: The color of the blouse is different from *that* of the skirt.

illogical: China's population is greater than any country in the world.

(This sentence draws an illogical comparison between a population and a country and illogically suggests that China is not a country.)

logical: China's population is greater than *that of* any *other* country in the world.

In many cases, the word *that* is optional. For example, here's a sentence that makes sense either with or without it:

Some evolutionary theorists believe [that] humans began to walk in an upright posture mainly because they needed to reach tree branches to obtain food.

Improper Placement of Modifiers

A **modifier** is a word or phrase that describes, restricts, or qualifies another word or phrase. Modifying phrases are typically set off with commas, and many such phrases begin with a relative pronoun (*which, who, that, whose, whom*).

Modifiers should generally be placed as close as possible to the word(s) they modify. Positioning a modifier in the wrong place can result in a confusing or even nonsensical sentence.

misplaced: His death shocked the entire family, which occurred quite suddenly.

better: His death, which occurred quite suddenly, shocked the entire family.

misplaced: *Nearly dead,* the police finally found the victim.

better: The police finally found *the victim, who was nearly dead.*

unclear: Bill punched Carl while wearing a mouth protector.

clear: While wearing a mouth protector, Bill punched Carl.

Modifiers such as *almost, nearly, hardly, just,* and *only* should immediately precede the word(s) they modify, even if the sentence sounds correct with the parts separated. For example:

misplaced: Their 1-year-old child *almost* weighs *40 pounds.*

better: Their 1-year-old child weighs *almost 40 pounds.*

Note the position of *only* in the following sentences:

unclear: The assistant was *only* able to detect obvious errors.

clear: *Only the assistant* was able to detect obvious errors.

unclear: The assistant was able to *only* detect *obvious errors.*

clear: The assistant was able to detect *only obvious errors.*

The general rule about placing modifiers near the words they modify applies most of the time. In some cases, however, trying to place a modifier near the words it modifies actually confuses the meaning of the sentence, as with the modifier *without his glasses* in the following sentences.

unclear: Nathan can read the newspaper and shave *without his glasses.*

(It is unclear whether *without his glasses* refers only to *shave* or to both *shave* and *read the newspaper.*)

unclear: *Without his glasses, Nathan* can read the newspaper and can shave.

(This sentence implies that these are the only two tasks Nathan can perform without his glasses.)

clear: *Even without his glasses,* Nathan can read the newspaper and shave.

So don't apply the rule without checking to see whether the sentence as a whole makes sense.

Dangling Modifiers

A *dangling modifier* is a modifier that doesn't refer to any particular word(s) in the sentence. The best way to correct a dangling-modifier problem is to reconstruct the modifying phrase or the entire sentence.

> **dangling:** *Set by an arsonist,* firefighters were unable to save the burning building.

> (What was set by an arsonist?)

> **better:** Firefighters were unable to save the burning building from *the fire set by an arsonist.*

> **dangling:** *By imposing price restrictions on oil suppliers,* these suppliers will be forced to lower production costs.

> (Who imposed the price restrictions?)

> **better:** *If price restrictions are imposed on oil suppliers,* these suppliers will be forced to lower production costs.

Despite the rule against dangling modifiers, a dangling modifier may be acceptable if it is an **idiom,** which means it is considered correct because it has been in common use over a long period of time.

> **acceptable:** *Judging* from the number of violent crimes committed every year, our nation is doomed.

> (This sentence makes no reference to whomever is judging; but it is acceptable anyway.)

> **acceptable:** *Considering* that star's great distance from the Earth, its brightness is amazing.

> (This sentence makes no reference to whomever is considering; but it is acceptable anyway.)

Splitting a Grammatical Unit

Splitting clauses or phrases apart by inserting other words between them often results in an awkward and confusing sentence.

> **split:** The value of the dollar *is not,* relative to other currencies, *rising* universally.

> **better:** The value of the dollar *is not rising* universally relative to other currencies.

> **split:** The government's goal this year *is to provide* for its poorest residents *an economic safety net.*

> **split:** *The government's goal* is to provide an economic safety net *this year* for its poorest residents.

> **better:** The government's goal this year is to provide an economic safety net for its poorest residents.

Sentences should not split their infinitives. An **infinitive** is the plural form of an "action" verb, preceded by the word *to*. If *to* is separated from its corresponding verb, then you're dealing with a **split infinitive** and a sentence that is grammatically incorrect.

> **improper (split):** The executive was compelled *to,* by greed and ambition, *work* more and more hours each day.

> **correct:** The executive was compelled by greed and ambition *to work* more and more hours each day.

> **improper (split):** Meteorologists have been known *to* inaccurately *predict* snowstorms.

> **correct:** Meteorologists have been known *to predict* snowstorms inaccurately.

Strings of Subordinate Clauses

A *subordinate clause* is one that does not stand on its own as a complete sentence. Stringing together two or more subordinate clauses can result in an awkward and confusing sentence. If possible, these sentences should be restructured to simplify them.

> **awkward:** Barbara's academic major is history, *which* is a very popular course of study among liberal arts students, *with whom* political science is the most popular major.

> **better:** Barbara's academic major is history, which is second only to political science as the most popular major among liberal arts students.

USAGE

About 50 percent of the GED® Language Arts, Writing Test, Part I involves verb and pronoun *usage*—that is, whether these types of words are used correctly in sentences. The test covers only the following areas of usage:

- Subject-verb agreement

- Verb tense (verb forms and tense shifting and mixing)

- Pronoun case, reference, and agreement

In this section you'll review the rules for these aspects of usage.

Subject-Verb Agreement

A verb should always "agree" in number—either singular or plural—with its subject. A singular subject takes a singular verb, while a plural subject takes a plural verb:

> **incorrect (singular):** The *parade were* spectacular.

> **correct (singular):** The *parade was* spectacular.

> **incorrect (plural):** The parades *was* spectacular.

> **correct (plural):** The parades *were* spectacular.

In the preceding examples, it's easy to tell whether the subject is singular or plural. But in other cases, it's not so easy, as you'll learn in the following sections.

Interrupting Phrases

Don't be fooled by any words or phrases that might separate the verb from its subject. In each sentence below, the singular verb *was* agrees with its subject, the singular noun *parade:*

> **incorrect:** The *parade* of cars *are* spectacular.

> **correct:** The *parade* of cars *is* spectacular.

> **incorrect:** The *parade* of cars and horses *are* spectacular.

> **correct:** The *parade* of cars and horses *is* spectacular.

An intervening clause set off by commas can serve as an especially effective "smokescreen" for a subject-verb agreement error. Pay careful attention to what comes immediately before and after the intervening clause. Reading the sentence without the clause often reveals a subject-verb agreement error.

> **incorrect:** John, as well as his sister, *were* absent from school yesterday.

> **correct:** *John,* as well as his sister, *was* absent from school yesterday.

Pronoun Subjects

Determining whether a sentence's subject is singular or plural isn't always as simple as you might think. You can easily determine whether a personal pronoun such as *he, they,* and *its* is singular or plural. But other pronouns are not so easily identified as either singular or plural. Here are two lists, along with some sample sentences, to help you keep these pronouns straight in your mind:

SINGULAR PRONOUNS

anyone, anything, anybody	nobody, no one, nothing
each	what, whatever
either, neither	who, whom, whoever, whomever
every, everyone, everything, everybody	

> **correct:** *Every* possible cause *has* been investigated.

> **correct:** *Each* one of the children here *speaks* fluent French.

> **correct:** *Neither* of the pens *has* any ink remaining in *it.*

> **correct:** *Whatever* he's doing *is* very effective.

> **correct:** *Everything* she touches *turns* to gold.

Even when they refer to a compound subject joined by *and*, the pronouns listed above remain *singular*.

> **correct:** *Each adult and child* here *speaks* fluent French.

> **correct:** *Every* possible *cause and suspect was* investigated.

PLURAL PRONOUNS

both	others
few	several
many	some

> **correct:** *Few* would *argue* with that line of reasoning.

> **correct:** *Many claim* to have encountered alien beings.

> **correct:** *Some thrive* on commotion, while *others need* quiet.

Compound and Other Types of Subjects

It's especially easy to overlook a subject-verb agreement problem in a sentence involving a compound subject (multiple subjects joined by connectors such as the word *and* or the word *or*). If joined by *and*, a compound subject is usually plural (and takes a plural verb). But if joined by *or*, *either . . . or*, or *neither . . . nor*, compound subjects are usually singular.

> **plural:** The chorus *and* the introduction *need* improvement.

> **singular:** *Either* the chorus *or* the introduction *needs* improvement.

> **singular:** *Neither* the chorus *nor* the introduction *needs* improvement.

In some cases, you can't tell whether a subject is singular or plural without looking at how it's used in the sentence. This is true of so-called *collective* nouns and nouns of *quantity*. These special situations might call for either a singular verb or a plural verb, depending on whether the noun is used in a singular or plural sense.

> **correct:** Four years *is* too long to wait. (*four years* used in singular sense)

> **correct:** Four years can *pass* by quickly. (*four years* used in plural sense)

Noun clauses are considered singular. A **noun clause** is one that starts with either a **gerund** (a noun ending in *-ing*) or an **infinitive** (a verb preceded by the word *to*). In each of the next two sentences, the italicized noun clause is accompanied by a singular verb (in bold):

> **correct:** *Mastering several musical instruments* **requires** many years of practice.

> **correct:** Among my least favorite chores **is** *to pick up after my husband.*

Verb Tense

Verb **tense** refers to how a verb's form indicates the *time frame* (past, present, or future) of a sentence's action. In this section, you'll focus specifically on:

- Choosing a verb tense
- Verb forms used for each tense
- Improper shifting and mixing of tenses (including conditional perfect tenses)

The first two topics listed above provide a foundation for the third topic, which is the main verb-tense issue that the GED® tests on.

Verb Tenses and Verb Forms

There are six regular verb tenses in total. A sentence should use one of three *simple* tenses—either *present, past,* or *future*—to "simply" indicate one of the three time frames.

> **simple present:** They *have* enough money to buy a car.
>
> **simple past:** They *had* enough money to buy a car.
>
> **simple future:** They *will have* enough money to buy a car.

> **simple present:** I *am losing* my mind.
>
> **simple past:** I *was losing* my mind.
>
> **simple future:** I *will lose* my mind.

The present-perfect tense is used for actions that began in the past and continued up until the present:

> **present perfect:** He *has eaten* enough food (but *has* continued to eat anyway).
>
> **present perfect:** She *has been trying* to lose weight (for the past year).

The past-perfect tense is used for actions that began in the past and continued up until a more recent time in the past:

> **past perfect:** He *had eaten* enough food (but *had* kept eating anyway).
>
> **past perfect:** She *had been trying* to lose weight (until recently).

The future-perfect tense is used for actions beginning in the future and continuing up until a more distant point in the future:

> **future perfect:** He *will have eaten* enough food (once he *has* finished eating dessert).
>
> **future perfect:** By year's end, she *will have been trying* to lose weight (for nearly six months).

With many verbs, the same form is used for all tenses, except that *-ed* is added for the past tenses—as in *walk, walked*. However, other verbs take distinct forms for different tenses. Notice how forms of the following three verbs (in bold) vary, depending on the tense.

Tense	To Have	To Be	To See
present	has (have)	is (are)	see
past	had (have)	was (were)	saw
future	will have	will be	will see
present perfect	have had	has been (have been)	have seen
past perfect	had had	had been	had seen
future perfect	will have had	will have been	will have seen

Determining the correct verb form for any tense is a matter of practice and experience with the English language. If a verb form "sounds" incorrect, your ear is probably telling you that it is. Test your ear by listening to the following incorrect sentences as you read them.

> **incorrect:** We *be* too far along to quit now; we *have went* past the point of no return.

> **correct:** We *are* too far along to quit now; we *have gone* past the point of no return.

> **incorrect:** The pilot *seen* the mountain but *flied* too low to avoid a collision.

> **correct (present tense):** The pilot *sees* the mountain but *is flying* too low to avoid a collision.

> **correct (past tense):** The pilot *saw* the mountain but *flew* too low to avoid a collision.

> **correct (past-perfect tense):** The pilot *had seen* the mountain but *had flown* too low to avoid a collision.

> **incorrect:** After we *gone* to the training session, we *begun* to work on the job assignment.

> **correct (present tense):** After we *go* to the training session, we *will begin* to work on the job assignment.

> **correct (past tense):** After we *went* to the training session, we *began* to work on the job assignment.

> **correct (future-perfect tense):** Even before we *go* to the training session, we *will have begun* to work on the job assignment.

If you have trouble hearing incorrect verb forms, consult an English usage book that contains lists of verbs and their conjugations (the word *conjugations* refers to verb forms for different tenses).

Shifting or Mixing Verb Tenses

A sentence should not needlessly *mix* tenses or *shift* tense from one time frame to another in a confusing manner.

> **incorrect:** If it rains tomorrow, we cancel our plans.

> **correct:** If it rains tomorrow, we will cancel our plans.

> **incorrect:** When Bill arrived, Sal still did not begin to unload the truck.

> **correct:** When Bill arrived, Sal still *had not begun* to unload the truck.

The problem with mixing and shifting tenses also applies to sentences like these:

> **incorrect:** *To go* to war is *to have traveled* to hell.

> **correct:** *To go* to war is *to go* to hell.

> **correct:** *To have gone* to war is *to have traveled* to hell.

> **incorrect:** *Seeing* the obstacle *would have allowed* him to alter his course.

> **correct:** *Having seen* the obstacle *would have allowed* him to alter his course.

> **correct:** *Seeing* the obstacle *would allow* him to alter his course.

Conditional Perfect Tense

To indicate that something would be completed at some point in time (past, present, or future) *if* a certain condition were met, a sentence should use the *conditional perfect tense*. The GED® test-makers are reluctant to test on this tense because it can be tricky. But you should be ready for it anyway, just in case.

To employ the conditional perfect tense properly, a sentence will use words such as *would, should,* or *could,* as well as words such as *if, had,* or *were.* Here are three pairs of examples (all sentences are correct):

> *Should* the college lower its tuition, I *would* probably enroll.

> *If* the college *were* to lower its tuition, I *would* probably enroll.

> *Had* he driven slower, he *would* have noticed the new building.

> *If* he *had* driven slower, he *would* have noticed the new building.

> They *could have* reached home in time for dinner *were* it not for the sudden storm.

> *Had* it not rained suddenly, they *could have* reached home in time for dinner.

If a sentence mixes a regular verb tense (either simple or perfect) with the conditional perfect tense, then it is grammatically incorrect. For example, look at these incorrect versions of the preceding examples:

incorrect: If the college *lowers* its tuition, I *would* probably enroll.

(The first clause uses the present tense, but the second clause implies the conditional perfect tense.)

incorrect: *Had* he driven slower, he *will* notice the new building.

(The first clause implies the conditional perfect tense, but the second clause uses the future tense.)

incorrect: They *will have* reached home in time for dinner *were* it not for the sudden storm.

(The first clause uses the future-perfect tense, but the second clause implies the conditional perfect tense.)

Pronoun Case, Reference, and Agreement

Pronouns include **personal pronouns** and **relative pronouns.** Personal pronouns (words such as *they, me,* and *his*) refer to specific people, places, and things and indicate whether they are singular or plural. Relative pronouns (words such as *which* and *who*) are not specific in their reference.

Which personal or relative pronoun you should use in a sentence depends mainly on: (1) where the pronoun appears in the sentence, and (2) what noun, if any, the pronoun refers to.

Personal Pronoun Case

Personal pronouns take different forms, called *cases,* depending on how they're used in a sentence. You'll find all the various cases in the following table.

	Subjective case:	Possessive case:	Objective case:	Objective case— reflexive:
first-person singular	I	my, mine	me	myself
first-person plural	we	our, ours	us	ourselves
second-person singular	you	your, yours	you	yourself
second-person plural	you	your, yours	you	yourselves
third-person singular	he, she, it	his, her, hers, its	him, her, it	himself, herself, itself
third-person plural	they	their, theirs	them	themselves

You can generally trust your ear when it comes to detecting personal-pronoun errors. In some cases, however, your ear can betray you, so make sure you are "tuned in" to the following uses of pronouns.

incorrect: Either him or Trevor *would be* the best spokesman for our group.

correct: Either Trevor or *he would be* the best spokesperson for our group.

incorrect: The best spokesperson for our group *would be* either him or Trevor.

correct: The best spokesperson for our group *would be* either *he* or Trevor.

(Any form of the verb *to be* is followed by a subject pronoun, such as *he*.)

incorrect: One can't help admiring *them* cooperating with one another.

correct: One can't help admiring *their cooperating* with one another.

(The *possessive* form is used when the pronoun is part of a "noun clause," such as *their cooperating*.)

incorrect: In striving to understand others, we also learn more about *us*.

correct: In striving to understand others, *we* also learn more about *ourselves*.

(A *reflexive* pronoun is used to refer to the sentence's subject.)

Choice of Relative Pronoun

The English language includes only the following handful of *relative* pronouns: *which, who, that, whose, whichever, whoever,* and *whomever.* Don't worry about what the term "relative pronoun" means. Instead, just remember the following rules about when to use each one.

Use *which* to refer to things. Use either *who* or *that* to refer to people.

incorrect: Amanda, *which* was the third performer, was the best of the group.

correct: Amanda, *who* was the third performer, was the best of the group.

correct: The first employee *that* fails to meet his or her sales quota will be fired.

correct: The first employee *who* fails to meet his or her sales quota will be fired.

Whether you should use *which* or *that* depends on what the sentence is supposed to mean.

one meaning: The third page, *which* had been earmarked, contained several typographical errors.

different meaning: The third page *that* had been earmarked contained several typographical errors.

Notice that the first sentence above merely describes the third page as earmarked, while the second sentence also suggests that the page containing the errors was the third earmarked page. So the two sentences carry two different meanings.

Whether you should use *who* (*whoever*) or *whom* (*whomever*) depends on the grammatical function of the person (or people) being referred to. This is a tricky area of English grammar, and the GED® test-makers are reluctant to test on it. But you should ready for it anyway, so here are two good examples.

> **incorrect:** It was the chairman *whom* initiated the bill.

> **correct:** It was the chairman *who* initiated the bill.

(When referring to the sentence's subject, the subjective pronoun *who* should be used.)

> **incorrect:** The team members from East High, *who* the judges were highly impressed with, won the debate.

> **correct:** The team members from East High, with *whom* the judges were highly impressed, won the debate.

(When referring to the sentence's object, the objective pronoun *whom* should be used.)

Agreement with Antecedent

An *antecedent* is simply the noun to which a pronoun refers. In GED® sentences, make sure that pronouns agree in number (singular or plural) with their antecedents.

> **singular:** Studying other artists actually helps a young *painter* develop *his* or *her* own style.

> **plural:** Studying other artists actually helps young *painters* develop *their* own style.

Singular pronouns are generally used in referring to antecedents such as *each, either, neither,* and *one.*

> **correct:** *Neither* of the two countries imposes an income tax on *its* citizens.

> **correct:** *One* cannot be too kind to *oneself.*

If a pronoun and its antecedent are far apart, it can be especially easy to overlook an agreement problem, as in this example:

> **incorrect:** *Neither a* brilliant movie *script nor* a generous *budget* can garner critical acclaim without a good director to make the most of *them.*

In the above sentence, the antecedent of *them* (a plural pronoun) is *script* or *budget* (singular). One way to remedy the disagreement is to replace *them* with *it.* Since the antecedent and pronoun are so far apart, another solution is to replace the pronoun with its antecedent—for example, with *that script or budget.*

Ambiguous and Vague Pronoun References

Pronouns provide a handy, shorthand way of referring to identifiable nouns. But unless the identity of the pronoun's antecedent (the noun to which it refers) is clear, using a pronoun will leave the reader guessing what its intended antecedent is. In other words, *every pronoun in a sentence should have a clearly identifiable antecedent.*

Here's a sentence in which the pronoun could refer to either one of two nouns:

> **ambiguous:** Minutes before Kevin's meeting with Paul, *his* wife called with the bad news.

According to the sentence, whose wife called? Kevin's or Paul's? The answer is not clear. To correct this sort of ambiguous pronoun reference, either replace the pronoun with its antecedent or reconstruct the sentence to clarify the reference.

> **clear:** Minutes before Kevin's meeting with Paul, *Kevin's* wife called with the bad news.

> **clear:** *Kevin's* wife called with the bad news minutes before *his* meeting with Paul.

Another sort of ambiguous pronoun reference occurs when a sentence shifts from one pronoun to another in a way that leaves the reader confused. Here's an example:

> **ambiguous:** When *one* dives in without looking ahead, *you* never know what will happen.

In this sentence, *you* might refer either to the diver (*one*), to someone observing the diver, or to anyone in general. Here are two alternative ways of clearing up the ambiguity:

> **clear:** *One* never knows what will happen when *one* dives in without looking ahead.

> **clear:** When *you* dive in without looking ahead, *you* never know what will happen.

If a pronoun has no identifiable antecedent at all, the sentence should be reworked to eliminate the pronoun. Here's a sentence that makes this sort of vague pronoun reference, followed by a version that fixes the problem:

> **vague:** When the planets are out of alignment, *it* can be disastrous. (*It* does not refer to any noun.)

> **clear:** Disaster can occur when the planets are out of alignment.

WRITING MECHANICS

About 25 percent of the Language Arts, Writing Test, Part I involves writing mechanics. The test covers only the following mechanics issues:

- Use of the comma for punctuation
- Use of the apostrophe for possessives and contractions
- Homonyms (words that sound alike but are spelled differently)
- Capitalization (distinguishing between proper and common nouns)

In this section you'll review the rules for these aspects of writing mechanics.

Note that the GED® does not test on any punctuation marks besides the comma and the apostrophe, and it does not test on the spelling of any words besides homonyms.

Proper and Improper Uses of Commas

A comma indicates a pause that should correspond to a pause in the logic of the sentence. The commas make it clear to the reader that the logic of the sentence is being (temporarily) interrupted. The GED® tests four different uses (and misuses) of the comma. Pay particular attention to the last one listed below, which the GED® covers more frequently than the others.

- Overuse of the comma, resulting in the splitting of a grammatical unit
- Too few commas, resulting in a confusing sentence
- Commas in a series (a list of three or more items)
- Commas used in pairs to set appositives (parenthetical phrases)

Commas that Split a Grammatical Unit

Commas should not needlessly separate parts of the sentence that "want" to be together, such as the subject and verb:

> **incorrect:** Former secretary of state Henry Kissinger, is the author of several books on the history of diplomacy.

In the above sentence, the verb *is* should not be separated by a comma from its subject *Henry Kissinger* (unless a parenthetical phrase intervenes between them—not the case here).

Similarly, no comma should come between the verb and a subject complement that may follow it:

> **incorrect:** The nineteenth-century explorers Lewis and Clark may be, two of America's most-admired historical figures.

In the same way, a preposition should not be separated from its object by a comma:

> **incorrect:** As the storm continued, pieces of driftwood as well as, large quantities of sand were blown up onto the front porch.

In the above sentence, the preposition *as well as* needs to remain connected to its object, the phrase *large quantities of sand*.

When commas are overused on the GED®, it will usually be in sentences like these examples, where the commas jarringly separate parts of the sentence that seem to "want" to be together. These abuses are generally pretty easy to spot.

Commas for Sentence Sense

A tougher task is deciding whether a sentence uses too *few* commas, a problem that can easily confuse the reader. Here's the guideline: A sentence should use the minimum number of commas needed for a reader to understand the intended meaning of the sentence.

too few commas: Chandra is learning Spanish although acquiring this new skill is not one of her job duties.

better: Chandra is learning Spanish, although acquiring this new skill is not one of her job duties.

The first sentence above is a run-on sentence, which connects two or more independent clauses with a conjunction (such as *but, and,* or *although*) but no comma. Some run-on sentences, such as the previous example, can be fixed by inserting a comma immediately before the conjunction. Others, like the next example, are better split into two sentences:

too few commas: Chandra is learning Spanish but acquiring this new skill is not one of her job duties and she should not be paid for the time she devotes to this activity.

better: Chandra is learning Spanish, but acquiring this new skill is not one of her job duties. Therefore, she should not be paid for the time she devotes to this activity.

Commas in a Series

When three or more words, phrases, or clauses are presented in sequence, or series, they should be separated by commas. Here are examples of each:

commas separating a list of words: The Galapagos Islands boast some of the world's most unusual plants, birds, mammals, reptiles, and fish.

commas separating a list of phrases: We looked for the missing gloves under the sofa, in the closet, and behind the dresser, but we never found them.

commas separating a list of clauses: The plot of the movie was a familiar one: boy meets girl, boy loses girl, mutant from outer space devours both.

Notice two things about how these lists are crafted. First, you normally insert the word *and* before the final item in the series (*plants, birds, mammals, reptiles, and fish*). Second, the last comma (the one after *reptiles* in this example) is optional. Sometimes called the serial comma, it may be included or omitted according to taste. (The GED® test-makers have no special preference, and there's no "right" or "wrong" about it on the exam.) The other commas, however, are not optional; they must be used.

Commas for Setting off Introductory Elements

Common introductory phrases such as *for example* and *first of all* should be followed by a comma; otherwise, the sentence won't make grammatical sense. For example, removing the comma from either of the next two sentences would confuse its meaning:

> To begin with, the new ordinance does nothing to protect tenants.

> However, we decided to drive west instead of east.

A longer introductory element, which is usually a dependent clause, can be more difficult to detect. Introductory, dependent clauses typically begin with words and phrases such as the following:

Although	Whenever	Regarding	Since
Though	If	As for	As a result of
Unless	With respect to		

Regardless of the specific word or phrase used to begin the introductory clause, a "pause" (comma) will probably be helpful, and may be needed, at the end of the clause in order for the reader to follow the flow of ideas in the sentence. Here are two examples:

> Aside from the fact that his feet were blistered and swollen, there was no reason Jim should not have finished the race.

> Without first setting up a PayPal account, you won't be able to purchase that item from the Web site.

Commas for Setting Off Appositives (Parenthetical Phrases)

An **appositive** is a phrase that names or describes a noun. Appositives should be set off by commas; otherwise, the sentence won't make grammatical sense. In the following example, the phrase *the great left-handed Dodger pitcher* is an appositive that describes Sandy Koufax. Notice that without *both* commas the sentence is rather confusing.

> **confusing:** Sandy Koufax the great left-handed Dodger pitcher was the guest of honor at this year's sports club banquet.

> **still confusing:** Sandy Koufax, the great left-handed Dodger pitcher was the guest of honor at this year's sports club banquet.

> **clear:** Sandy Koufax, the great left-handed Dodger pitcher, was the guest of honor at this year's sports club banquet.

An appositive can be as brief as a few words. Or it can be quite lengthy, as in this example:

> I was surprised to learn that Paula, my cousin Frank's former girlfriend and a well-known local artist, had decided to move to Santa Fe.

To determine the correct use of commas in sentences like the preceding ones, try this test: Read the sentence without the phrase. If it still makes grammatical sense and the meaning is basically the same, then the phrase is parenthetical and should be set off by commas. Both of the preceding examples pass the test:

Sandy Koufax ... was the guest of honor at this year's sports club banquet.

I was surprised to learn that Paula ... had decided to move to Santa Fe.

The Apostrophe (for Possessives and Contractions)

The apostrophe is used for two purposes: possessives and contractions. Both are frequently tested on the GED® Language Arts, Writing Test, Part I. A **possessive** is used to indicate ownership or some other close connection between a noun or pronoun and what follows it. Form the possessive as follows:

- For a singular noun, add *'s* (apostrophe followed by the letter *s*):

    the company's employees

    the cat's meow

- For a plural noun ending in *s*, just add an apostrophe:

    the Jacksons' first home

    the wolves' pack leader

- For a plural noun that does not end in *s*, add *'s* (apostrophe followed by the letter *s*):

    the school alumni's favorite reunion spot

    the cattle's hooves

The possessive pronouns *his, hers, its, ours, yours,* and *theirs* contain no apostrophes.

Be especially careful about positioning the apostrophe in plural nouns such as the following three, which the GED® tests on quite frequently:

men's (not *mens'*)

women's (not *womens'*)

children's (not *childrens'*)

The other use of an apostrophe is in a **contraction,** which is a word made up of at least two words from which letters have been omitted for easier pronunciation.

The apostrophe is usually (but not always!) inserted in place of the letters omitted. If in doubt, mentally "expand" the contraction to determine which letters have been left out; this is often a useful guide to determine where the apostrophe belongs. For example:

We've got to go. = *We have* got to go.

She *won't* mind. = She *will not* mind.

The following is a list of common contractions, grouped according to the contraction's second word (in bold). Any of these contractions might be used on the GED® to test you on word *usage*. Notice that some of these contractions are homonyms (they sound just like one or more other words). The GED® tests on these words quite often.

not

can't = cannot (one word)

couldn't = could not

didn't = did not

hadn't = had not

hasn't = has not

haven't = have not

isn't = is not

wasn't = was not

weren't = were not

won't = will not

wouldn't = would not

have

I've = I have

they've = they have

we've = we have

who've = who have

could've = could have

would've = would have

had (would)

I'd = I had (I would)

he'd = she had (she would)

she'd = he had (he would)

they'd = they had (they would)

we'd = we had (we would)

where'd = where had (where would)

who'd = who had (who would)

is

it's = it is (do not confuse with *its*)

he's = he is

she's = she is

what's = what is

whatever's = whatever is

that's = that is

there's = there is

where's = where is

who's = who is (do not confuse with *whose*)

are

they're = they are (do not confuse with *their* and *there*)

we're = we are

you're = you are (do not confuse with *your*)

am

I'm = I am

will

I'll = I will

he'll = he will

she'll = she will

they'll = they will

it'll = it will

Homonyms (Words that Sound Alike)

A **homonym** is a word that sounds just like another word but is spelled differently. Here are two examples (the GED® often tests on these homonyms):

than

Gary was taller *than* Joshua but shorter *than* Michael.

then

First you should change your clothes, *then* you should eat dinner.

affect

> The blinking lights won't *affect* you if close your eyes.

effect

> The blinking lights had a slightly hypnotic *effect*.

On the GED® Writing Test, Part I, expect several "correction" questions testing on homonyms. To prepare for these questions, study the following lists. They contain many of the homonyms you should know for the GED®.

Contractions and Their Homonyms

Be sure not to confuse certain contractions with their homonyms. These tricky words appear frequently on the GED®.

it's (it is)

> There no secret to scoring high; *it's* all a matter of practice.

its

> The groundhog saw *its* shadow, and so we can expect more cold weather ahead.

there's

> In case *there's* any doubt on your part, I've brought a letter of reference with me.

theirs

> Victory was once ours, but now it is *theirs*.

they're (they are)

> Once *they're* gone, we can finally have peace and quiet.

their

> The two employees set *their* differences aside and finished the project.

there

> In order to go *there* you'll need to take the ferry.

who's (who is)

> Find out *who's* to blame for starting the fire.

whose

> Find out *whose* car this is, and warn them that it might be towed.

Common Two-word Phrases and Their Homonyms

Be on the lookout for the following two-word phrases and their one-word homonym counterparts.

all ready

If the four of you are *all ready* to leave, then we can take the same bus.

already

Sherry has left *already*, so I need to find someone else to drive me home.

all together

Are we *all together*, then, in opposing the proposed law?

altogether

He counted six raccoons *altogether*, four gray and three red.

all ways

In *all ways*, the newly engaged couple seemed incompatible.

always

The problem with dessert is that it's *always* served last, when I'm already full.

any one

I'm sure *any one* of you can jump higher than I can.

anyone

Does *anyone* here know how to jumpstart a car?

every day

Tiffany runs 3 miles *every day* before work.

everyday

Gang violence is an *everyday* occurrence in this part of town.

every one

Each and *every one* of you must keep quiet, or else they'll hear us.

everyone

If *everyone* talks at once we'll never accomplish anything.

there for

I will always be *there for* you.

therefore

I think, *therefore* I am.

Some Challenging Homonyms You Might Find on the GED®

You're probably familiar with most, if not all, of the following words. Nevertheless, it's remarkably easy to confuse any of these words with their respective homonyms. Be sure you know the difference in spelling and meaning between the words in each pair.

accept

Please *accept* this gift as a token of my appreciation.

except

Every staff member *except* Bruce attended the office party.

capital

The nation's *capital* is Washington, D.C.

Through its stock offering, the company was able to raise more *capital*.

capitol

The dome of the *capitol* building shone brightly in the afternoon sun.

cast

Jim was in a skiing accident, and his leg will be in a *cast* for two months.

The fisherman *cast* his rod toward the river, hoping to catch his dinner.

The movie's *cast* included Daniel Day-Lewis and Penelope Cruz.

caste

People born into a *caste* social system find it impossible to improve their standard of living.

complement

The brick driveway is a perfect *complement* to the house's metal trim.

compliment

She paid him a *compliment* by telling him that he had good fashion sense.

council

The head of the community *council* made the final decision.

counsel

A married couple wanting to divorce should seek separate legal *counsel*.

dual

Immigrants with *dual* citizenship can easily land a job in this country.

duel

The final tennis match turned out to be a long, drawn-out *duel*.

principal

Gwen's incompetence was the *principal* reason she was fired from her job.

The elementary school *principal* knew every student's name.

principle

My guiding *principle* is to treat others how I would like to be treated.

stationary

Riding a *stationary* bike is good exercise, but I prefer riding a real bike.

stationery

Since e-mail has become popular, few people buy *stationery* for writing letters.

Other Common GED® Homonyms

Here's a list of many of the other homonyms you might encounter on the GED® Language Arts, Writing Test, Part I. They're all common, everyday words, and so you probably know what they mean. Nevertheless, you can easily confuse any of these words with its homonym if you're not paying careful attention.

aisle, isle	dear, deer	plain, plane
ate, eight	earn, urn	profit, prophet
bare, bear	for, fore, four	read, red
based, baste	know, no	right, write
beat, beet	ladder, latter	seas, sees, seize
blew, blue	lead, led	steal, steel
boar, bore	meat, meet	to, too, two
brake, break	might, mite	waist, waste
cell, sell	miner, minor	ware, wear
clause, claws	pair, pare	weather, whether
coarse, course	peace, piece	would, wood

Capitalization of Proper Nouns

Of course, the first word in each new sentence is capitalized. But there are many instances where a word that falls somewhere within the sentence should be capitalized as well, and these are the words that the GED® covers. Here's the general rule for capitalizing words:

Capitalize all **proper nouns** and words derived from them, such as adjectives. Do not capitalize **common nouns**. A proper noun is the name of a specific person, place, or thing. All other nouns are common nouns.

This section covers the types of proper nouns you're most likely to encounter on the GED®.

People

Any particular person's name is capitalized. Any title accompanying a person's name is also capitalized. Study and compare the italicized words in these sentences:

Send copies of the letter to *Mr. and Mrs. Stefanski* and to *Dr. Reed.*

While in the U.S. Army, *Corporal Yates* served directly under an ambitious *captain* who later became *General* Eisenhower and, eventually, *President* Eisenhower.

Peter Innis was *president* of the company the year that *Chairman Stanton* resigned as board *chairman.*

Titles for named relatives are capitalized. Otherwise, a word that identifies a family relationship is considered a common word. Study and compare the italicized words in these sentences:

We went to the art museum with *Father* and *Aunt Janice.*

Yesterday my *father* took my sister and me to the art museum. I think any *father* should take his child to an art museum at least once.

Institutions, Organizations, and Groups

Names of schools, businesses, and other organizations are capitalized. Specifically named offices, branches, and agencies are also capitalized. Study and compare the italicized words in these sentences:

Prior to Dr. Kingston's tenure as head of the *Office of Transportation,* he served as head of the *School of Architecture* at *Drysdale College.*

The chief financial officer of *Unicost Corporation* attended this state's most prestigious *university,* where she majored in *sociology.*

After graduating *Franklin High School,* he went to work for the U.S. *government,* at the *Bureau of Printing and Engraving.*

If you join the *Army,* the U.S. government will pay for your college tuition. Even so, I refuse to join an *army* that invades other countries.

Names that identify groups of people by nationality, ethnicity, religion, tribe, or other such category are capitalized.

Sioux City, which is Iowa's capital city, is named for the *Sioux* tribe of *American Indians.*

You'll find *Danes* to be most hospitable, although the *Danish* pastries alone are worth the trip.

Artistic and Other Creative Works

Titles of literary works (books, poems, short stories, treaties, etc.), as well as magazines, movies, songs, visual art works, and other similar works are capitalized.

> The new issue of *Time* includes an interesting article entitled "Movie Rags to Movie Riches."

> Apparently, *The Wizard of Oz* did not make a profit until a decade after the movie was released.

Depending on the type, a named artistic work is also italicized (or underlined) or enclosed in quotation marks. The GED® does not cover these rules.

Specifically named artifacts (documents, treasures, etc.) are also capitalized.

> Every grade-school student in the United States learns to recite the *Pledge of Allegiance*. But very few students ever memorize the *Bill of Rights* or the *Gettysburg Address*.

> The *Dead Sea Scrolls* and the *Shroud of Turin* are subjects of great controversy among scholars.

Time Periods and Events

Days of the week, months of the year, and specific holidays are capitalized (even when preceded by the word *a*). But the words *week, month,* and *year* themselves are not.

> This year, *Thanksgiving* will fall on a *Thursday,* and *Christmas* will fall on a *Monday.* But next year they'll both fall on the last *Thursday* of the month.

> It rained every Sunday during the *month of April*.

Seasons of the year are capitalized only if personified (named as though a person).

> I look forward to *Autumn* and the brisk weather it will bring.

> The temperature has risen into the eighties nearly every day this *summer*.

Only specifically named historical events, periods, and eras are capitalized.

> The South's surrender to the North marked the end of the *Civil War*.

> The nation's bloodiest *civil war* claimed more than a half-million lives.

> During the *Great Depression,* unemployment among working-age men reached 25 percent.

> The current recession might end up as bad as the *depression* of the 1930s.

Times of the day, such as *dawn, noon,* and *midnight,* and the word *o'clock* are common nouns (not capitalized).

Geographic Regions

Words involving compass direction (north, south, east, west, northeast, etc.) are capitalized when they refer to specific geographical section or region (or, for example, when they are part of a street name).

> The *Southeast* is more humid than the *Southwest*.

> The *East* coast of *North America* receives more annual rainfall than the continent's *West* coast.

> This restaurant is widely acclaimed for its delicious *Southern* cuisine.

But these words are not capitalized when used to merely indicate direction.

> Hike up the *eastern* flank of the mountain, and you'll be treated to a spectacular view of the valley.

> Turn *north* when you reach the stop sign, then look for City Hall on the *east* side of *West* 75th Street.

Specifically named municipalities (cities, townships, and counties), states, regions, and countries are capitalized. Otherwise, words such as *city, county,* and *state* are not capitalized. Study and compare the italicized words in these sentences:

> When driving along *Thompson County's* main highway, expect to encounter numerous speed traps, especially within *Hilltown's city* limits.

> Our entire *Scandinavian* excursion was a worthwhile experience. The fiords along the *Norway* coast were magnificent.

Streets, Landmarks, and Geographic Features

Only specifically named streets, roads, highways, freeways, and others are capitalized.

> If you're driving south on *Skyline Parkway*, merge onto the *freeway,* and then look for the *Lake Street* exit.

> We live near *Roosevelt Avenue,* which parallels *Park Lane.* You can take either *street* to get to our house.

Buildings and other landmarks, parks and monuments, mountains and valleys, and bodies of water (rivers, lakes, seas, and oceans) are capitalized. Study and compare the italicized words in these sentences:

> No trip to Washington, D.C., is complete without a visit to the *Capitol* and the *Lincoln Memorial.* After seeing the *memorial,* be sure to take a stroll along the *Potomac River.*

> The *Great Lakes* are the world's largest bodies of fresh water. Among the five *lakes, Superior* is the largest.

As they approached Earth, the shuttle crew could clearly observe the *Great Wall of China* and even the *Three Gorges Dam*.

Celestial Bodies

Specifically named celestial bodies (planets, moons, stars, etc.) are also capitalized. Study and compare the italicized words in these sentences:

In a solar eclipse, *the Moon* travels directly between *Earth* and *the Sun*. During this type of eclipse the Moon blocks out almost all *sunlight*.

Ganymede is the largest *moon* orbiting the planet *Jupiter*.

We could not dig any deeper because just beneath the *earth* we hit an impervious layer of hardpan.

SUMMING IT UP

- Sentence structure refers to how a sentence's parts fit together as a whole. Sentence structure problems account for about 35 percent of the GED® Language Arts, Writing Test, Part I.

- Among the kind of grammatical errors in structure, GED® sentence structure problems might show sentence fragments, run-ons and comma splices, faulty parallelism involving series, or faulty parallelism involving correlatives.

- About 50 percent of the GED® Language Arts, Writing Test, Part I involves verb and pronoun *usage*—that is, whether these types of words are used correctly in sentences. The test covers subject-verb agreement, verb tense (verb forms and tense shifting and mixing), and pronoun case, reference, and agreement.

- About 25 percent of the Language Arts, Writing Test, Part I involves writing mechanics. The test covers only the following mechanics issues: use of the comma for punctuation, use of the apostrophe for possessives and contractions, homonyms (words that sound alike but are spelled differently), and capitalization (distinguishing between proper and common nouns).

- The GED® does not test on any punctuation marks besides the comma and the apostrophe, and it does not test on the spelling of any words besides homonyms (a word that sounds just like another word but is spelled differently).

Mastering the Language Arts, Writing Test, Part II

chapter 5

OVERVIEW

- All about the Language Arts, Writing Test, Part II
- How GED® essays are evaluated
- What's not tested
- How GED® essays are scored
- The essay topic
- Writing your essay: from brainstorm to final product
- Developing and connecting your paragraphs
- Writing style
- Sample persuasive essays
- Sample expository essay
- Suggestions for writing and evaluating your practice essays
- General test-taking strategies
- Summing it up

THE LANGUAGE ARTS, WRITING TEST, PART II—IN A NUTSHELL

Time allowed: 45 minutes (but you'll have additional time if you finish Part I early)

Total number of questions: 1 essay topic (the topic will be provided)

ALL ABOUT THE LANGUAGE ARTS, WRITING TEST, PART II

Part II of the Language Arts, Writing Test assesses your ability to communicate your ideas and thoughts in writing. You will be asked to present your opinion or explain your views about a specific topic. You will not be given a choice of topics to write on, and you *must* write only about the topic provided. If you write on a different topic, your essay will not be scored, and you will have to retake *both* parts of the Language Arts, Writing Test.

Here are the basic rules and procedures for the Writing Test, Part II:

- The allotted time altogether to plan, write, and revise your essay is 45 minutes. However, if you finish Part I (the editing test) early, you can start work on Part II right away. So you may have more than 45 minutes for your essay, depending on your pace during Part I. Note that when you complete Part II, you <u>cannot</u> go back to Part I.

189

- Scratch paper will be provided for jotting down notes, making an outline, and sketching out a rough draft. The notes you make on scratch paper will not be read or scored.

- You must write your essay on the *two* pages of lined paper provided for this purpose. This two-page answer sheet provides ample space to write a well-developed essay on the assigned topic. (To get an idea of the space provided, look at the Writing Test, Part II answer sheet in this book's Practice Tests.)

- To help ensure that your writing can easily be read by evaluators, you will use a ballpoint pen (not a pencil) to write your essay. This means that you will not be able to erase anything you write on the answer sheet. Nor will you be allowed to use any liquid paper correction fluid or white tape to cover over what you've written. So if you need to correct a mistake or rewrite a sentence, you'll strike through (cross out) your mistake.

HOW GED® ESSAYS ARE EVALUATED

Your GED® essay will be read and scored by 2 trained readers hired by the testing service for this purpose. The readers will evaluate your essay according to its *overall effectiveness*, considering how well you convey and support your main ideas, how well you organize those ideas, and how clearly and correctly you write throughout the essay. More specifically, GED® essay readers are instructed to evaluate and score GED® essays according to these four criteria:

❶ Your ability to maintain proper focus. Your essay should respond directly to the assigned prompt. It should clearly convey a central idea and should remain focused on that idea, without digressing from the topic or focusing too narrowly on certain minor or tangential points.

❷ Your ability to develop and support ideas effectively. You should support the main points of your essay with reasons and examples that are relevant and persuasive.

❸ Your ability to present ideas in a well-organized manner. In order for the readers to understand your ideas and to follow your train of thought, you should present the points of your essay in a logical and natural sequence, using transitions that help connect the ideas together.

❹ Your ability to write correctly and clearly. Your essay should demonstrate good control of grammar, sentence structure, punctuation, and spelling. By your choice of words and by the way you use them, your essay should also show good control of the English language.

In applying these four criteria and awarding scores, GED® readers will use what is called a "holistic" approach. What this means is that the readers will evaluate the *overall effectiveness* of your essay, but they will not use any strict formula for applying the criteria. This approach allows readers more scoring flexibility.

Also, keep in mind that the readers will evaluate your essay based on the *quality*, and not the quantity, of your writing. So a brief essay that is fully developed, well-organized, and well-written will, in all likelihood, earn a higher score than a much longer essay that is poorly developed, organized, and written.

Finally, notice that criteria 3 and 4 cover the same knowledge areas as those covered by the Writing Test, Part I (the editing test). So knowing the rules and guidelines for grammar, usage, sentence structure, paragraph and document structure, and writing mechanics will serve double duty: it will help you edit GED® documents (Part I) *and* write your GED® essay (Part II).

WHAT'S NOT TESTED

In evaluating and scoring your essay, GED® readers focus only on the evaluation criteria you just read about. Many test-takers will make the mistake of trying to impress the readers in ways that the readers really don't care about. Other test-takers will be too concerned about saying the "right thing" and not concerned enough about how they say it. To avoid these mistakes, here's what you need to keep in mind:

- **There is no "correct" answer.** First and foremost, remember that there is no "best" response or "correct" answer to any GED® essay question. What's important is how effectively you present and support your ideas. Also, there is no "correct" structure or number of paragraphs for a GED® essay. (However, in this lesson you will learn some useful guidelines for structuring your essay.)

- **Special knowledge about the topic at hand won't matter.** The GED® Writing Test Part II is a *skills* test. So, you don't need any special knowledge of the topic presented in order to produce a high-scoring essay. Besides, the Writing Test topics are not technical in nature. So, though you'll need to know something about the subject, common everyday knowledge will be enough.

- **The Writing Test, Part II is not a vocabulary exercise.** You won't score points with the readers by using obscure or so-called "big" words—the kinds of words that high school students preparing for the SAT might learn just for that test. When it comes to vocabulary, all that matters to the readers is that the words you use make sense in context.

- **The Writing Test, Part II is not a creative writing exercise.** Some test-takers will make the mistake of using an imaginative writing style or essay structure in order to impress the readers with their originality. Simply put, this is a bad idea. The GED® is not the place to experiment with imagery, to display wit or humor, or to prove to the reader that you have "Hemingway potential." Impress the reader with strong organization and communication skills—not with your astounding creativity.

- **Occasional, minor mechanical errors will not hurt your score.** In evaluating your essay, the readers will focus mainly on the big picture: your ideas, how you've organized them, and the overall quality of your writing. They'll overlook the occasional punctuation error, awkward sentence, or even misspelled word. But don't get the wrong idea. Frequent problems, even the little ones, can add up to leaving a negative impression overall, which might hurt your score. So don't ignore these details altogether.

HOW GED® ESSAYS ARE SCORED

Applying the four evaluation criteria listed earlier, each of your 2 GED® readers will score your essay on a scale of 0–4 (the highest score is 4). Neither reader will be aware of the other reader's evaluation or score. The two individual scores are then averaged into a combined, or final, essay score. For example:

Reader A awards a score of **4**

Reader B awards a score of **3**

The combined score is **3.5**

If the scores of the 2 readers differ by at least *two* points on the 0–4 scale, then a third, very experienced reader will read your essay and determine the final score. This procedure helps safeguard against any GED® reader who might assign an unrealistically high or low score to an essay, for whatever reason. Here are two examples:

Reader A awards a score of **3**

Reader B awards a score of **1**

(The two scores differ by two points, and so Reader C reads the essay and determines that Reader A's score was too high and Reader B's score was too low.)

Reader C awards a final score of **3.**

Reader A awards a score of **4**

Reader B awards a score of **2**

(The two scores differ by two points, and so Reader C reads the essay and determines that Reader A's score was much too high and that Reader B's score was more appropriate but a bit low.)

Reader C awards a final score of **2.5**.

Keep in mind that you will not be awarded a separate score for the GED® Writing Test, Part II (the essay). Instead, your Part I and Part II scores will be combined according to the testing service's own formula, and then you will be awarded a single overall Writing Test score. Therefore, in order to receive credit for the Language Arts, Writing Test, you must successfully complete both parts of the test.

THE ESSAY TOPIC

As noted earlier, the topic for your GED® essay will be provided, and you must write only on that topic. You will not know the topic ahead of time, but this fact should not worry you. The topic will be one that is familiar to you or to any other GED® test-taker—one that you *will* have something to say about based on your own experiences, observations, and knowledge. Rest assured that the GED® test-makers will not try to stump or confuse you by asking you to write on an obscure topic that you might know nothing about. After all, the Writing Test, Part II is designed to measure your ability to write, not to recall facts about obscure subjects.

Specific GED® essay topics, or prompts, can vary widely. (The word "prompt" refers to the entire stated topic and question, which *prompt* you as to what to write about.) Regardless of the topic, your prompt will be designed for you to respond with either a persuasive essay or an expository essay.

Persuasive Essays

A **persuasive** essay adopts a viewpoint or an opinion on an issue and then attempts to convince, or *persuade*, the reader to agree with that viewpoint or opinion. Each of the following two GED®-style prompts calls for a persuasive essay.

Essay Topic 1

Some people think that the best way to assess a student's academic performance is through a letter-grade system, but others think a pass/fail system is fairer.

Write an essay expressing your viewpoint on this issue. Support your viewpoint with relevant reasons and examples.

Essay Topic 2

In your opinion, should people always be required to pay for music and videos they download from the Internet?

Write an essay expressing your viewpoint on this issue. Support your viewpoint with relevant reasons and examples.

Notice that prompts 1 and 2 raise commonly debated issues, and then ask you to express a viewpoint on them, defending your viewpoint with supporting reasons and examples. To develop an essay on topic 1, you might discuss key advantages and disadvantages of each grading system, and then take sides based on your own experiences or observations. To develop an essay on topic 2, you might provide arguments both for and against free access to music and videos, and then decide which is more important: ensuring artists are paid for the work or ensuring the widest possible distribution. Of course, these are just a few of the many ways you might develop essays on these two topics.

Expository Essays

An **expository** essay is, as the word suggests, an essay that *explains* something. It asserts a point and then helps the reader understand that point by explaining it in greater depth, perhaps by providing relevant examples, reasons, or other details. Each of the following two GED®-style prompts calls for an expository essay. Notice that both prompts focus on personal experiences, values, and preferences, which is typical of these kinds of prompts.

Essay Topic 3

Who has been the most influential person in your life?

In your essay, identify that person and explain why and in what ways he or she has influenced you so much. Use your personal observations, experience, and knowledge to support your essay.

Essay Topic 4

What characteristics do you look for in a true friend?

In your essay, identify those characteristics and explain why a true friend is someone who possesses them. Use your personal observations, experience, and knowledge to support your essay.

Notice that prompts 3 and 4 ask you to express an opinion or view, and then explain it. To develop an essay on topic 3, you might recount key experiences with the person and discuss how those experiences shaped your thinking, outlook, or goals. To develop an essay on topic 4, you might focus on character traits such as honesty and loyalty, describing two or three examples where a friend's honesty or loyalty meant a lot to you.

Here's a diverse list of questions that represent the sorts of topics that appear on the GED®. Keep in mind that, as in the four preceding examples, any of these questions would be part of a longer prompt asking you to explain your answer or develop your viewpoint.

10 Topics for Persuasive Essays

1. Which is more important: teamwork or individual initiative?
2. Should high school students hold part-time jobs?
3. What should colleges focus on: teaching job skills or providing a general education?
4. Is computerized instruction a good substitute for live instructors?
5. Which is more essential to individual success: innate talent or perseverance and effort?
6. Does television do more harm than good, or vice versa?
7. Should students be required to wear uniforms or conform to a dress code?
8. Are digital books better than printed books?
9. Should the voting age be lowered from 18 to 16?
10. On balance, do high-tech gadgets save us time or rob us of time?

10 Topics for Expository Essays

1. What does it mean to live a successful life?
2. What three personal possessions to you cherish the most?

③ What three books have influenced your life the most?

④ What is the most serious problem facing the town or city where you live?

⑤ What personality traits do you find most appealing in other people?

⑥ What is one goal that you hope to achieve within the next five years?

⑦ What methods do you use to manage your time?

⑧ What personal attributes are most critical for achieving success in life?

⑨ What two animals best symbolize key aspects of human nature?

⑩ What three far-away places do you most hope to visit during your lifetime?

As you can see from these two lists, you're bound to be familiar enough with whatever topic you encounter on the test to write a brief essay on it. So you don't need to worry that you might draw a complete "blank"—you won't.

WRITING YOUR ESSAY: FROM BRAINSTORM TO FINAL PRODUCT

Writing is probably something you do every day without giving it much thought. Whether you write letters, e-mails, or memos, you know that writing is simply putting your thoughts into written form. Some people get intimidated when they are required to write a formal essay that will be read and graded by someone. You shouldn't be intimidated at all, though. For the GED®, you just need to follow certain steps to ensure you've performed the tasks you need to do so that the GED® readers will reward you.

In writing their GED® essay, many test-takers make the mistake of diving in head first. They immediately start writing on their answer sheets (in pen), without planning their essays ahead of time. While a few test-takers may be able to compose a good essay this way, the vast majority won't. Essays written "on the fly" usually turn out poorly organized and written. Rather than expressing and developing a central idea in a clear, well-organized manner, these essays tend to lose focus and ramble, without a clear train of thought, and sometimes without a clear beginning or end.

Instead of simply scribbling like mad on your answer sheets, you should spend some time up front thinking about what you should write and how you should organize your ideas. And you should save some time at the end to proofread your essay. Below is a 7-step plan to help you budget your time and produce a solid essay within your 45-minute time limit.

7-Step Plan for Writing a GED® Essay

Plan your essay (5 minutes):

① Brainstorm ideas and make notes.

② Review your notes and decide on a central idea or viewpoint.

③ Organize your ideas into an outline.

Write your essay (35 minutes):

④ Write a brief introductory paragraph.

⑤ Write the body paragraphs of your essay.

⑥ Write a brief summary or concluding paragraph.

Review your essay (5 minutes):

⑦ Proofread to find errors you can easily fix.

The suggested time limits for each step are merely guidelines, not hard-and-fast rules. As you practice composing your own essays under timed conditions, start with these guidelines, and then adjust to a pace that works best for you personally.

In the following pages, you'll walk through each step in turn, applying the following GED®-style prompt:

> **Essay Topic 5**
>
> In your opinion, should high schools be responsible not only for teaching academic subjects and skills but also for teaching ethical and social values?
>
> Write an essay in which you take a position on this issue. Support your position with reasons and examples.

Step 1: Brainstorm Ideas and Make Notes

Your first step in developing a GED® essay is to brainstorm ideas that are relevant to the topic. For topic 5, try to think of some reasons and examples supporting not just one but *both* sides of the issue.

> **One side of the issue:** Schools should teach *only* academic subjects and skills.
>
> **The other side of the issue:** Schools should also teach ethical and social values.

To conjure up ideas for your essay, you can draw on any of the following:

- Your own experiences
- Classroom discussions
- Books, articles, and other writings
- Stories people have told you
- Current events

As you think of ideas, don't commit to a viewpoint *yet*, and don't try to filter out what you think might be unconvincing reasons or weak examples. Just let all your ideas flow onto your scratch paper, in no particular order. (You can sort through them during steps 2 and 3.) Here's what a test-taker's notes on essay topic 5 might look like after a few minutes of brainstorming:

whose values?

- Amish

- suburbanites

- yuppies

- Jewish or Christian

student body too diverse?

schools need to focus on basics

what areas?

- sex education

- classroom cooperation vs. competition

- drugs and violence

teacher can teach values by setting example

Notice that some notes are grouped together to reflect one train of thought (If schools were to teach ethical values, whose values would they teach? What kinds of behavior should schools address in teaching values?). Other notes reflect assorted, random ideas. The notes aren't well organized, but that's okay. The point of brainstorming is just to generate a bunch of ideas—the raw material for your essay. Let your ideas flow freely, and you'll have plenty of material for your essay.

Step 2: Review Your Notes and Decide on a Central Idea or Viewpoint

Decide on the basic view or opinion that you intend to support in your essay. Your notes from step 1 should help you decide. Review the ideas you jotted down, and then ask yourself for what viewpoint you can make a strong case. It's perfectly acceptable to take clear sides on an issue. But it's also okay to take a "middle-ground" position in which you agree partly with more than one viewpoint. For example, here are three different viewpoints on Essay Topic 5:

One side of the issue: Schools should teach *only* academic subjects and skills.

The other side of the issue: It is just as important for schools to teach values as it is to teach academics.

A middle-ground position: Schools should focus on academic subjects, but they should also take *some* time to stress certain values that everyone should share.

Pick the three or four ideas from your notes that best support your view. These should be ideas that you think make sense and that you know enough about to write at least a few sentences on. Put a checkmark next to those ideas, to signify that these are the ones you're certain you want to use in your essay. If there aren't enough ideas, take one or two of the ideas you like and elaborate on them. Think of related ideas, add details or examples, and use these to fill out your list.

Step 3: Organize Your Ideas into an Outline

Next, decide on a sequence for the ideas. They should flow naturally and logically from one to another. Once you've decided on a sequence for your ideas, number them accordingly in your notes. At this point, you might want to create a separate outline, or you might be able to transform your notes from step 1 into an outline. Here's an example of how a test-taker might transform the notes based on Essay Topic 5 into a simple outline by numbering the notes according to the order the essay will present them:

---

(2) whose values?

- Amish

- suburbanites

- yuppies

- Jewish or Christian

(1) student body too diverse?

(3) schools need to focus on basics

(4) what areas?

- sex education

- classroom cooperation vs. competition

- drugs and violence

(3) teacher can teach values by setting example

(5) U.S. schools lag in teaching basics

Notice that this test-taker has decided to adopt the view that schools should teach academics only, and not ethical and social values. The first three points in his notes all fit nicely into an essay that supports this viewpoint. Notice that he plans to combine two related ideas [both earmarked with the number (3)] into the same basic point. He also thought of an additional idea that might make a good final point—that U.S. schools lag most other countries in academic standards. So he made a note of that idea (5).

He decided to start with the idea that the United States is diverse (1), which means that many different cultures and value systems are represented. From this idea, it makes sense to ask whose values would be taught in schools, and to use the examples listed in (2). This leads nicely to the point about focusing on academics (3), while allowing for some time to discuss certain behaviors (4). And, finally, he plans to end with the point that U.S. students lag behind others (5).

As already mentioned, you might prefer to create a separate outline based on your notes. Doing so shouldn't take much time, and it will give you another chance to think about your ideas and how you should organize them into paragraphs. Here's what an outline based on this test-taker's initial notes might look like.

```
(1) student body too diverse
   whose values would be taught?
   - Amish
   - suburbanites
   - yuppies
   - Jewish or Christian
(2) schools need to focus on basics
   - teacher can teach basic values by setting example
(3) admit some areas too important not to teach in
   school
   - sex education
   - classroom cooperation vs. competition
   - drugs and violence
(4) biggest problem: U.S. schools lag in teaching basics
```

Notice that the test-taker has combined a few points, jotted down the ideas in sequence, and filled out the notes a bit. Notice that point (3) recognizes certain exceptions to the view that schools should teach only academics.

Following this outline, it appears that the test-taker plans to compose four body paragraphs, one for each numbered point. (The *body* of an essay includes all paragraphs except for an introductory and a concluding paragraph.) There is no "correct" or "best" number of body paragraphs for a GED® essay. Three or four body paragraphs is a manageable number for a 45-minute essay. The prompt itself may help you decide on how many body paragraphs to include—for example, if a prompt asks you to identify three people who have influenced your life. But no matter which prompt you get, be sure to include *at least two* body paragraphs.

Step 4: Write a Brief Introductory Paragraph

Once you've spent about 5 minutes planning your essay, it's time to write it. You'll begin with a brief introductory paragraph. In your initial paragraph, try to accomplish the following:

- Show that you understand the topic.
- Show that you have a clear view or opinion on the topic.
- Provide a glimpse of how you will support your ideas in your essay.

You can probably accomplish all three goals in two to three sentences. Don't go into details yet by listing specific reasons or examples that support our view. This is what your essay's body paragraphs are for. Also, don't begin your introductory paragraph by repeating the essay prompt word-for-word. Instead, show the reader from the very first sentence that you're thinking for yourself. Here's a good introductory paragraph for Essay Topic 5:

Introductory paragraph (Essay Topic 5)

All young people should learn academic skills and ethics. In my view, however, any high school in a country as diverse as the U.S. should limit what it teaches to academic subjects. Teaching ethical and social values should be left to parents and churches.

The opening paragraph makes an important first impression on the reader, so take great care in writing it. To help ensure that it's as good as it can be, consider writing a rough draft of the paragraph on your scratch paper first.

Step 5: Write the Body Paragraphs of Your Essay

During step 5, your task is to get your supporting points from your brain and your scratch paper onto your answer sheets. Here's what you need to keep in mind as you write:

- Be sure the first sentence of each paragraph begins a distinct train of thought and clearly conveys to the reader the essence of the paragraph.

- Arrange your paragraphs so your essay flows logically and persuasively from one point to the next. Try to stick to your outline, but be flexible.

- Try to devote at least two, but no more than three or four, sentences to each main point in your outline.

- Don't stray from the topic at hand, or even from the points you seek to make. Be sure to stay well focused on both.

Below are the body paragraphs of a response to Essay Topic 5. These paragraphs are based on our notes from step 3, but there are a few differences.

Body paragraphs (Essay Topic 5)

The biggest problem with teaching ethical and social values is deciding what values schools should teach. Not all ethical values are the same. For example, the Amish way of life placed a high value on simplicity, and they might be offended by being taught the values of others. Or what about children from Jewish and Christian households? In our diverse society, these children often attend school together. Parents of one group might be very upset if the school's teachers taught only the other group's values.

To avoid these kinds of conflicts, teachers must focus strictly on academic subjects. We send children to school to learn math, English, history, and science. How would you feel if your child came home ignorant about geometry but knowing all about someone else's religious or ethical ideas? I would be very upset as a parent. Besides, teachers can always teach values like respect and common courtesy by setting an example for their students.

But why can't schools just teach about the values of all different religious and cultural groups? This sounds like a good idea. But high school students in the U.S. lag students in many other countries in academic achievement. So it would be foolish for high schools to take time away from teaching academic subject to teach ethics and values. Young people need a solid academic background, or they won't be able to compete for the best jobs after they finish school.

Notice that the test-taker tried to stick to his outline while at the same time remaining flexible. He left suburbanites and yuppies out of the essay altogether, possibly because they seemed unnecessary. He also left out point 4 of his outline, perhaps because he didn't want to risk running out of time. Since point 4 supports the opposing viewpoint, it's not as crucial as the other points.

During step 5, consider using your scratch paper to sketch out a *rough draft* of at least your first body paragraph. Doing so should take less than 5 minutes, and it can help ensure that you're setting out in the right direction, presenting your ideas clearly in an appropriate tone and writing style.

Step 6: Write a Brief Summary or Concluding Paragraph

Unless your essay has a clear end, the reader might think you didn't finish in time. That's not the impression you want to make. So be sure to reserve time to wrap up your essay. Convey your central idea (your view or opinion) and main supporting ideas in a clear, concise, and forceful way. Two or three sentences should be enough for this purpose. If an especially insightful concluding point occurs to you, the final sentence of your essay is a good place for it.

Here's a brief but effective concluding paragraph for the response to Essay Topic 5. It assures the reader that the test-taker has organized his time well and finished the writing task. Also, notice that this brief summary does not introduce any new reasons or examples. Instead, it simply provides a quick recap, which is all you need to accomplish with your final paragraph.

Final paragraph (Essay Topic 5)

In conclusion, the most responsible way for schools to educate students is to make sure they learn what they need for college and their careers. Schools should stick to teaching academics, and let families and churches teach morality in their own way and on their own time.

From beginning to end (including the introductory, body, and concluding paragraphs), the preceding sample essay runs just over 300 words in length. So it's not especially lengthy. Nor is it a literary masterpiece. Nevertheless, it expresses a clear viewpoint, supports a viewpoint with relevant reasons and examples, is well organized, and is written in a clear and effective manner. In short, it contains all the elements of a high-scoring GED® essay.

Step 7: Proofread to Find Errors You Can Easily Fix

Save the last few minutes to proofread your essay from start to finish for mechanical problems that you can quickly and easily fix, such as errors in spelling, punctuation, and word choice. Since you're required to write your GED® essay in pen, you can't erase what you write, and you won't be permitted to use any correction liquid or tape. But you can strike-through (cross out) words and phrases and replace them by writing just above or below your strike-through, or in the margin. Just make sure your corrections are clear and legible.

Avoid making major revisions or rewriting significant portions of your essay. By striking and replacing entire sentences or paragraphs, you'll leave the reader with the impression that you have difficulty organizing and expressing your ideas. What's more, your essay will look sloppy, which can leave a negative impression on the reader.

DEVELOPING AND CONNECTING YOUR PARAGRAPHS

An effective GED® essay will contain much more than just a series of general statements. Ideally, you will have only a few general statements, and the majority of your writing will be dedicated to creating purposeful, specific details—facts, comparisons, reasons, and examples to illustrate the point you are trying to make.

Topic Sentences

Each body paragraph in your essay should help explain and support your essay's central idea, of course. But each body paragraph should have its own central idea as well, which you should express in a **topic sentence.** The topic sentence of each paragraph should be a major point in support of the central idea. The paragraph's other sentences should all relate directly to the topic sentence, providing information that explains or supports the topic sentence's idea.

Look again at the first body paragraph from the essay on Essay Topic 5. This time, the topic sentence is in bold. Notice that all other sentences serve to explain the idea conveyed in the topic sentence.

> **The biggest problem with teaching ethical and social values is deciding what values schools should teach.** Not all ethical values are the same. For example, the Amish way of life placed a high value on simplicity, and they might be offended by being taught the values of others. Or what about children from Jewish and Christian households? These children often attend school together. Parents of one group might be very upset if the school's teachers taught only the other group's values.

The sentences that make up a paragraph should be presented in a logical order. An essay that flows logically from one paragraph to another so that its ideas are easily understood is said to be *coherent*. The reader expects your body paragraphs to flow from and support your central idea, as well as to flow logically from one to the next. As you introduce new ideas, keep your reader grounded by using a consistent structure from one paragraph to the next. Repeating key words or phrases, or using variations of the same phrases, can be especially helpful, allowing the reader to "connect the dots." Here are two examples:

First body paragraph:

One way that spending too much time on the Internet can be harmful . . . .

Second body paragraph:

A second problem with spending too much time on the Internet is . . . .

Third body paragraph:

A final problem with Internet overuse is . . . .

First body paragraph:

I admire my dog for his courage. . . .

Second body paragraph:

I also admire my dog for his loyalty. . . .

Third body paragraph:

Most of all, however, I admire my dog for his ability to love unconditionally. . . .

Try to develop your own arsenal of words and phrases that connect ideas together so the reader can understand how they flow from one to another. Certain words and phrases lead the reader forward and imply the building of an idea or thought. Certain other words and phrases prompt the reader to compare ideas or draw conclusions from the preceding thoughts. Following are several lists of words and phrases that writers often use as bridges between ideas.

Words and phrases that help connect ideas of equal weight:

first, second, . . .	finally	next
additionally	further	what's more
also	furthermore	
equally important	in addition	

Words and phrases that signal *comparison* and *contrast*:

although	conversely	to the contrary
but	however	whereas
by comparison	in contrast	while
by the same token	more importantly	
compared to	on the other hand	

Words and phrases used to *qualify* or point out an *exception* to an assertion of fact:

depending on	in some circumstances	sometimes
despite	in spite of	yet
infrequently	nevertheless	
in rare instances		

Words and phrases that signal *sequence* (chronological, logical, or rhetorical):

first, second(ly),	concurrently	previously
third(ly), . . .	consequently	simultaneously
after	finally	subsequently
beforehand	next	then

Words and phrases that signal the use of a supporting *example*:

as an illustration	in this case	take the case of
consider	in this situation	to demonstrate
for example	on this occasion	to illustrate
for instance	one possible scenario	
in another case		

Words and phrases that signal a *conclusion*:

accordingly	hence	therefore
as a result	it follows that	thus

Use these phrases for your concluding or summary paragraph:

all things considered	in essence	on balance
in a nutshell	in short	on the whole
in brief	in sum	summing up
in conclusion	in the final analysis	to recapitulate

It takes practice to develop a knack for writing paragraphs that use connecting words effectively. After taking the Writing Test, Part II Practice Tests in this book, if you need to improve your writing further, you can use the list of expository and persuasive essay topics found earlier in this chapter as prompts for writing additional practice essays.

WRITING STYLE

Your writing style refers to the words and phrases you choose to use and how you use them, how you structure your sentences, and the overall voice and tone you use in your writing. To ensure yourself a high score on your GED® essay, strive for writing that is

- appropriate in tone and "voice" for academic writing.

- clear and concise (easy to understand, and direct rather than wordy or verbose).

- varied in sentence length and structure (to add interest and variety as well as to demonstrate maturity in writing style).

- correct and appropriate in word choice and usage.

All of this is easier said than done, of course. Don't worry if you're not a natural when it comes to writing the kind of prose that's appropriate for the GED®. You *can* improve your writing for your exam, even if your time is short. Start by reading the suggestions and guidelines below. But, keep in mind: improvement in writing comes mainly with practice. So you'll also need to apply what you learn here to the Practice Tests in this book and to the supplementary writing prompts provided at the end of this lesson.

Overall Tone and Voice

In general, you should try to maintain a somewhat *formal* tone throughout your essay. An essay that comes across as casual or conversational—like a personal e-mail or blog entry—is probably a bit too informal for the GED®. Here are some specific guidelines:

- The overall tone should be analytical, which means that it should appeal to the reader's intellect. Don't overstate your view or opinion by using extreme or harsh language that appeals to emotions instead.

- When it comes to your main points, a very direct, even forceful voice is perfectly acceptable. Just don't overdo it.

- It is perfectly acceptable, though optional, to refer to yourself from time to time in your essay. Just be consistent. For example, be sure not to mix phrases such as *I disagree with* or *In my view* with phrases such as *We cannot assume that*.

- Avoid puns, double-meanings, play on words, and other forms of humor. Sarcasm is also entirely inappropriate for your GED® essay. Besides, the reader might not realize that you're trying to be humorous being sarcastic, in which case your remark might confuse the reader, who might award your essay a low score as a result.

Clear and Concise Writing

With enough words, anyone can make a point; but it requires skill and effort to make a point with concise phrases. Before you commit to paper any sentence you have in mind, ask yourself whether it seems a bit clumsy or too long, and whether you can express the same idea more concisely and clearly. Use your scratch paper to write a rough draft of the sentence or sentences you're not sure how to write.

Although punctuation is probably the least important aspect of your GED® essay, be sure to use just enough commas to make sure the reader understands your point. Too few commas might confuse the reader, while too many can interrupt the sentence's flow.

Sentence Length and Variety

Sentences that vary in length make for a more interesting and persuasive essay. Your sentences should be varied in style and length. Abrupt, short sentences might be appropriate for making crucial points, but an entire paragraph written in short, choppy sentences is distracting and suggests a certain immaturity. Compare the following two passages:

Ineffective:

Some television shows have too much violence. This is not good for young children. They may learn to be violent themselves. They see too much fighting and shooting on television.

More effective:

The television shows that have too much violence may not be good for young children. The fighting and shooting on these shows may teach children to be violent themselves.

Here's another illustrative pair of passages:

Ineffective:

Many books are interesting. I especially enjoy science fiction. I like it because it deals with the future sometimes. One of my favorite authors is Jules Verne. He wrote about some things that came true.

More effective:

Although I enjoy a variety of books, my favorite type is science fiction. One of my favorite authors is Jules Verne. Verne wrote many of his stories about the future, and much of what he wrote about has actually come true.

Effective Use of Language

To score high with your essay, you'll need to convince the readers that you can use the English language correctly and clearly. By all means, show the reader that you possess a strong vocabulary and know how to use it. But don't resort to obscure, SAT-style vocabulary just to impress the reader. The impression you're more likely to make is that you're trying to mask poor content with window dressing. Also avoid **colloquialisms** (slang and vernacular). Otherwise, instead of nailing your essay, it'll turn out lousy, and you'll be totally out of luck and end up on the skids, big time. (Did you catch the *four* colloquialisms in the preceding sentence?)

In evaluating your GED® essay, the readers also take into account your **diction**—your choice of words as well as the manner in which a word is used. When you commit an error in diction, you might be confusing one word with another because the two words look or sound similar. Or you might be using a word that isn't the best one to convey the idea you have in mind. Although it is impossible in these pages to provide an adequate diction review, here are some guidelines:

- If you're the least bit unsure about the meaning of a word you're thinking of using in your essay, don't use it. Why risk committing a diction error just to impress the reader with your vocabulary?

- If a phrase sounds wrong to your ear, change it until it sounds correct to you.

- The fewer words you use, the less likely you'll commit an error in diction. So when in doubt, go with a relatively brief phrase that you still think conveys your point.

Persuasive Writing

As noted at the beginning of this lesson, the GED® Writing Test, Part II will prompt you to express your view or opinion on a specific topic. In order for your essay to be effective, it must be persuasive. The best way to persuade the reader, of course, is to provide good ideas supported by sound reasons and relevant examples, all presented in a logical sequence. But you can also persuade the reader through your writing style. The art of persuasive writing (or speaking) is referred to as **rhetoric.** Effective rhetorical writing makes its points clearly and forcefully by placing appropriate emphasis on different ideas.

The main way to make a rhetorical point effectively is to use appropriate connecting words between ideas. In the first example that follows, notice that it is difficult to determine the writer's point because of a structure that gives both ideas equal weight. The second and third examples clarify the point by using appropriate connecting words (in italics), as well as by a few other revisions.

Equal weight on both ideas (ineffective):

Many people try in futility to plan out every detail of their lives. They often end up changing their plans due to events they did not foresee.

Greater emphasis on one idea (effective):

It is futile to try planning out every detail of our lives, *since* we often end up changing our plans due to events we did not foresee.

Greater emphasis on the other idea (effective):

People often change their plans due to events they did not foresee. *Nevertheless*, most people continue trying, often in vain, to plan out every detail of their lives.

The second and third examples carry far more persuasive "punch" than the first, don't they? Each one is a good example of effective rhetorical writing: it makes a clear point, and in a forceful way.

Another way to emphasize a point is by using an abrupt, short sentence. Good topic sentences for paragraphs are often written in this style. Just be sure that the sentences supporting that point are longer; otherwise, the emphasis will be lost on the reader. You should not have any trouble identifying the short, punchy topic sentence in either of the following two paragraphs.

Rhetorical emphasis on the last sentence:

While the richest people in our country find ways to add to their own wealth, thousands of people die on the streets in our nation each day, and thousands more go hungry or suffer from nearly intolerable living conditions. Millions have inadequate health insurance, and millions more have no health insurance at all. In short, we have an empathy crisis.

Rhetorical emphasis on the first sentence:

Corporations are not evil. The people who run them simply try to maximize profits for the corporation's owners. So when you hear complaints about a CEO cutting employee benefits or outsourcing jobs, remember that the CEO is only doing <u>his</u> job, which is what the company's owners want.

You can also use punctuation for rhetorical emphasis. To emphasize a particular idea, you can end a sentence with an exclamation mark instead of a period. Also, you can emphasize a particular word by underlining it, as in the second example above. (In handwriting, underlining serves as a substitute for italics.) But use these two rhetorical devices *very* sparingly; one of each in your essay is plenty! (Notice the use of both devices in the preceding sentence.)

Sentences that pose questions can also provide rhetorical emphasis. Like short, abrupt sentences, **rhetorical questions** can help persuade the reader—or at least help to make your point. They can be quite effective. They also add interest and variety. Yet how many GED® test-takers think to incorporate them into their essays? Not many.

(By the way, the previous two sentences pose and answer a rhetorical question.) Just don't overdo it: one rhetorical question is plenty for one essay. And be sure to provide an answer to your question.

Finally, you can emphasize a point using rhetorical words and phrases such as *undeniably, absolutely, clearly, without a doubt, the fact is,* and *anyone would agree that.* By themselves these words and phrases mean very little; to be truly effective, they must be backed up by sound ideas and convincing reasons and examples. But they can help add rhetorical flair to your essay. Just don't overuse them.

SAMPLE PERSUASIVE ESSAYS

A good way to review the principles of effective essay writing is to see how they are put into practice. First, take a look at a GED®-style essay prompt that calls for a *persuasive* type of essay:

Essay Topic 6

In your opinion, should high schools allow students to choose their own courses during their senior year?

Write an essay in which you take a position on this issue. Support your position with reasons and examples.

Following are two essays responding to Essay Topic 6. After each essay is a commentary that evaluates it holistically in terms of the evaluation criteria you examined earlier in this lesson. Each essay runs about 300 words—brief enough for any GED® test-taker to organize and write in 45 minutes but long enough to present and fully develop a viewpoint. And both essays are good examples of what top-scoring GED® essays might look like.

As you study these two essays, notice that they differ significantly in perspective, or viewpoint. Don't worry if your viewpoint would have differed from the ones expressed in these samples, or if you would have used different supporting reasons or examples. Remember, there is no "correct" or "best" view or opinion when it comes to the GED® essay.

Also notice that the two essays differ significantly in their organization, or structure. The first essay provides three main supporting reasons, using three body paragraphs. In contrast, the second essay examines arguments for two opposing positions, using only two body paragraphs altogether. Neither structure is better than the other; they both work well.

Keep in mind that these essays, though not perfect models, are more polished than what most GED® test-takers would produce in 45 minutes. Also, while they're intended to provide ideas for organizing and expressing ideas effectively, avoid using them as fixed models for copying.

Essay 1

There are valid arguments for and against allowing high school seniors to choose their own courses. In my opinion, however, they are better prepared for life if they have the freedom to choose their classes. This opinion is based mainly on three reasons.

First, if seniors are not free to select the kinds of courses that interest them the most, they probably won't be very motivated in school. When students aren't motivated to learn and study, their grades suffer, and their options in life will be limited. Poor academic performance can also result in low self-esteem.

Second, every person has different strengths and weaknesses. Some are naturally better at math and science. Others are more talented in art or music. By age 16, most young people already have a good idea what they're good at. This is the time to start focusing on your strengths. If you take the same classes as everyone else, you'll have trouble later on competing with others who share your strengths but develop them to the fullest.

Third, if seniors are not allowed to make their own decisions about what classes they take, they won't learn to take responsibility for the consequences of their own decisions. This is part of growing up and becoming prepared for life, which in my opinion is part of what students should learn in high school. So if a student wants to take only easy classes that don't involve much homework, let him. He'll probably learn a valuable lesson from it.

In sum, requiring all seniors to take the same classes would result in many students not attaining their full potential and not learning to take responsibility for their own decisions. Therefore, they should have this freedom.

Commentary on Essay 1

Organization:

This essay is well-organized. It provides a brief introduction that expresses a clear view, three supporting points (one in each of the next three paragraphs), and a final paragraph that provides a clear ending to the essay. The sequence of ideas is logical, and transitions from one paragraph to the next are adequate.

Development of ideas:

The essay makes clear the writer's viewpoint on the issue, and the three reasons given in support of that viewpoint are logically convincing. The third supporting point (about students learning to be responsible) is especially insightful and would help distinguish this essay from lower-scoring ones. However, both this point and the first one (about motivation and self esteem) are underdeveloped. This problem is especially apparent at the end of the second paragraph, where the writer asserts that poor academic performance lowers self-esteem but does not explain how this point supports the central idea. Another problem with the essay is that, except in the fourth paragraph where the writer recognizes that students might abuse the freedom to choose their own classes, the essay really does not discuss arguments for the contrary viewpoint. The essay would be improved by doing so, perhaps in a separate paragraph. The essay's concluding remarks sum up the essay's central idea and major supporting points nicely, but the final sentence is weak.

Writing ability and use of language:

The language in the essay is easy to understand and free of word choice or usage errors. The essay contains very few problems in sentence structure or sense, although there are a few places where sentences could be improved or combined for better rhetorical impact. Also, the third paragraph of the essay needlessly shifts case from third-person to second-person. But these are all minor problems, and since they do not interfere with the reader's understanding of the essay, they would probably not adversely affect the essay's score. Except for the use of the phrase "in my opinion" in both the first and fourth paragraphs, which is perfectly acceptable, the writer successfully avoids repeating words and ideas from either the essay itself or the prompt.

Overall evaluation:

This essay's strong organization, clear and consistent position, sound reasoning, rhetorical balance, and solid use of language would earn it a top score of 4.

Essay 2

I'm sure a lot of school officials and parents disagree about the amount of freedom seniors should have to choose their own courses. Persuasive arguments can be made for either viewpoint. Personally, I think that the best system is one that requires certain "core" classes but allows students to choose other classes according to their interests and natural abilities.

The world of work is unpredictable and continually evolving. Occupational fields that are booming one year might wither the next. Workers trained in specific occupations that are then outsourced to other countries can find themselves without a broad enough background to find new jobs. Therefore, it is crucial today that students keep as many career options open as possible. Requiring students to taking a broad core courses that cover all general academic areas helps ensure that they are prepared for whatever might lie ahead in life.

Those with an opposing viewpoint might argue that a student with a keen interest or special talent in one particular area might never blossom if they spend all their time taking classes in other areas. For example, one of my best friends is a very gifted musician and loves nothing more than composing and playing music. It's students like my friend that should be free to spend more school time in music classes. However, students like my friend are the exception. Besides, there's no reason that they cannot pursue their particular passion during their free time. And I see no reason why any high school can't allow at least a few elective courses in addition to a core senior year curriculum to accommodate students like these.

In the end, most high school seniors won't realize their full potential, or even realize what their full potential might be, if they're left to steer their own ship. Therefore, required core classes for all high school seniors is a good idea.

Commentary on Essay 2

Organization:

This essay demonstrates solid organization skills. It provides a brief introduction that states a central idea, followed by a major supporting point (second paragraph), a paragraph addressing an opposing viewpoint, and a final, concluding paragraph. The sequence of ideas in the body of the essay is logical and rhetorically effective.

Development of ideas:

The essay's central idea—that the best system is essentially a compromise, or hybrid, involving the two opposing viewpoints—shows that the writer understands the complexity of the issue and can adopt an independent viewpoint. The reasons given in support of both viewpoints are sound and persuasive, and the supporting examples are relevant and helpful. The writer successfully manages to develop arguments for both viewpoints in a reasonably brief essay. Therein, however, lies the essay's chief weakness. It fails to develop its thesis that a hybrid system providing a core curriculum but with built-in flexibility would be best. The central idea is only partially developed in the final paragraph, where the writer recommends a hybrid system almost as an afterthought. What's more, in that paragraph the writer ultimately adopts one of the two stated viewpoints rather than the one that the central idea recommends. For overall coherence and thematic unity, the writer should have either revised the central idea or developed it more fully.

Writing ability and use of language:

The essay shows strong language skills. Variety in sentence length and structure lends interest to the essay and shows maturity in writing style. Sentences flow logically and smoothly from one to the next. There are no problems in syntax, grammar, or usage. The writer successfully avoids repeating the wording used in the prompt. In the essay's concluding remarks, the writer avoids simply repeating main points from earlier in the essay, and instead provides an original and interesting metaphor. The final sentence, however, falls a bit flat, leaving the reader with the impression that the writer ran out of time for a more thoughtful ending to the essay.

Overall evaluation:

Due to its clear structure, its well-developed arguments for both viewpoints, and its mature writing style, this essay would earn a top score of 4, despite the problem involving thematic development.

SAMPLE EXPOSITORY ESSAY

Next, take a look at a GED®-style essay prompt that calls for an *expository* type of essay:

Essay Topic 7

In what three ways does computer technology benefit you most in your everyday life?

In your essay, identify those three ways and explain their significance to you. Use your personal observations, experience, and knowledge to support your essay.

Following is an essay that responds to this prompt. As you read it, you'll no doubt notice that the writer discusses his or her personal life, which is a perfectly appropriate response to this particular prompt. Of course, you might have identified three entirely different sorts of benefits than this writer did.

Like the previous two sample essays, this one runs about 300 words and is a good example of what a top-scoring GED® essay might look like. It is not intended as a perfect model, but it is a bit more polished than what most GED® test-takers would produce in 45 minutes. Following the essay is a commentary that evaluates it in terms of the same criteria used to evaluate any GED® essay.

Essay 3

It is difficult to narrow down the long list of ways that computer technology benefits me to just three. Thanks to computers, I can communicate with more people from different walks of life, learn about the world from my netbook, and on and on. But if I had to select the three most significant benefits, they would probably have to do with my efficiency, my artistic creativity, and my health.

I use computer technology every day to be more efficient in my work and in my play. At work, we use productivity software to plan and coordinate projects. Our computer network makes collaborating on projects quicker, which helps keep projects moving. At home, computers help me order take-out and access movies and music more efficiently.

Another significant way computer technology helps me personally is by providing tools for musical creativity. I write and record music as a hobby, and I use different kinds of software that let me use whatever sounds I want to "lay down tracks" on my Mac. I've created some pretty complex music that I never could have without computer technology.

But the biggest way that computer technology benefits me personally involves a health problem that I've had for a while. At first, I didn't know what was wrong with me. I didn't have health insurance, so I couldn't afford expensive doctors and lab tests. But I found an online forum where people with similar symptoms helped diagnose me. I have a type of auto-immune disease that I had never heard of. There's no cure for it, but thanks to the forum I learned about treatments that help alleviate some of my symptoms.

In short, thanks to computer technology, I'm more efficient, I write better songs, and I hurt a little less during each day. Maybe these benefits wouldn't mean much to someone else, but they mean the world to me.

Commentary on Essay 3

Organization:

Like the previous two essays, this essay is well-organized. It provides a brief intro-duction that identifies the "three ways," thereby helping the reader anticipate what will follow—and in what sequence. Each of the three body paragraphs focuses on precisely what is expected, and the final paragraph provides a tidy recap of the essay.

Development of ideas:

In addition to identifying the "three ways" as requested in the prompt, the introductory paragraph lets the reader know that the writer has given the topic some thought. This is a clever way to begin the essay, and one that would help make a positive first impression. In the first body paragraph, the writer adequately develops the idea of efficiency at work but neglects to develop the idea of efficiency at home. Notice that the writer does not explain why the efficiencies she mentions are significant to her, as requested in the prompt. At least one explanatory sentence here would have been helpful. Of the three body paragraphs, the third is the most fully developed. Relating a personal story to the reader is a perfectly appropriate way to respond to this sort of prompt, and the writer succeeds in telling a story that shows what a significant benefit the Internet has proven to be for her personally. Like the opening paragraph, the final paragraph is distinctive and clever, summing up the writer's thoughts in a way that would leave a positive impression on any reader.

Writing ability and use of language:

As in the previous two essays, the language in the essay is easy to understand and free of word choice or usage errors. The overall writing style and voice may seem just a bit informal, but the style is appropriate considering the personal nature of the topic under discussion. In the second body paragraph, enclosing the phrase "lay down tracks" is a good idea because it tells the reader that the writer is using slang or vernacular quite intentionally here. The structures and rhythms of the final paragraph's sentences demonstrate a mature writing style and a real flair for writing.

Overall evaluation:

This essay shows good organization skills, good command of language, and a flair for expository writing that engages the reader. Despite the fact that the third major sup-porting idea is not well developed, this essay would earn a top score of 4.

SUGGESTIONS FOR WRITING AND EVALUATING YOUR PRACTICE ESSAYS

To improve your writing, there is no substitute for practice. Start by using the essay prompts in this book's Practice Tests. For additional practice, you can write on any of the sample topics listed earlier in this chapter.

Always practice under exam-like conditions. Limit your time to 45 minutes. Use scratch paper for notes, outlines, and rough drafts, but write your final draft in *pen* using two pages of lined paper. Experiment in allocating your time among your various tasks:

- Brainstorming (note-taking)
- Organizing your ideas (outlining)
- Writing rough drafts
- Writing the final draft
- Proofreading and fixing problems

Keep practicing until you've learned to allocate your time in a way that works best for you.

Be sure to evaluate each practice essay you write. Be critical. Try to identify your weaknesses, so that you can focus on eliminating them. A good way to improve on weaknesses is to *rewrite* an entire practice essay. Spend no more than 25 minutes to write your revised version; focus mainly on correcting the most glaring problems with your earlier draft.

You may find it difficult to judge your own writing objectively, so consider asking a friend, family member, coworker, or teacher to read and evaluate your essays as well. You might be surprised how useful their feedback can be. In any case, use the following 4-point checklist to evaluate your practice essays. This list provides all of the elements of an effective, high-scoring GED® essay.

1. Is the essay well-focused? (Does it clearly convey a central idea, and does it remain focused on that idea, as opposed to digressing from the topic or focusing too narrowly on certain minor points?)

2. Does the essay develop its main ideas effectively, using persuasive reasons and relevant supporting examples?

3. Is the essay well-organized? (Are the ideas presented in a logical sequence, so that the reader can easily follow them? Are transitions from one point to the next natural and logical? Does the essay have a clear ending, or did you appear to run out of time?)

4. Does your essay demonstrate good control of grammar, sentence structure, word choice, punctuation, and spelling?

Your GED® essay will be scored on a scale of 0–4 (the highest score is 4). In evaluating a practice essay, if you can objectively answer "yes" to all four of the previous questions, then the essay would earn a score of at least 3, and probably 4, from a trained GED® reader.

GENERAL TEST-TAKING STRATEGIES

Here are some general strategies for writing GED® essays. Most reiterate key points of advice made earlier in this lesson. Apply these strategies to the Practice Tests and to the sample prompts listed earlier in this lesson, and then review this list again just before exam day.

Organize your thoughts before you write.

Use your scratch paper to make notes and to construct an outline of your major points and supporting reasons and examples. Before you start writing your final essay, write a rough draft of at least the introductory and first body paragraphs. Just be sure to leave enough time to write your final essay.

Express a clear view or opinion on the topic.

If the prompt asks you to express a view or opinion on an issue, it's perfectly acceptable to take clear sides with one position. It's also perfectly okay to take a "middle ground" position in which you agree *partly* with each of two opposing viewpoints. Remember: in writing your essay, there is no "correct" or "best" answer.

Develop each major point of your outline with reasons and/or examples.

You won't persuade the reader—or earn a high score—by merely asserting your views and opinions without explaining or justifying them. Develop your central idea and each major supporting point with sound reasons and relevant examples. In fact, the prompt will instruct you to do precisely that.

Stay well-focused on the topic at hand.

Don't digress from the specific topic that is presented. Your central idea must address the topic directly, and each body paragraph should relate directly to your central idea. Don't distract the reader by addressing him or her personally. In particular, do not boast about or apologize for your essay; doing either may very well lower your score.

Appeal to reason, not emotion.

The GED® essay is an *intellectual* exercise. It's perfectly appropriate to criticize particular behaviors or viewpoints. But do not use the essay as a forum to "preach" to the reader by appealing to his or her emotions. Avoid extremes in tone and attitude. In particular, do not provide even a hint of prejudice or jingoism (excessive patriotism).

Don't dwell on one point; but don't try to cover everything, either.

Avoid harping on one particular supporting point, even if you think it's your strongest one. Instead, try to cover as many points from your outline as you have time for, devoting no more than one paragraph to each one. You might not have time to cover everything you want to, but the readers understand your time constraints. Stick to your outline, ration your time, and you'll do fine.

Keep it simple; the reader will reward you for it.

Don't make the GED® essay task more difficult than it needs to be for you to attain a solid score. Keep you sentences clear and simple. Use a simple, straightforward structure for your essay. Avoid using "fancy" words just to impress the reader. Don't waste time trying to come across as ultra-brilliant, mega-insightful, or super-eloquent.

Look organized and in control of the task.

Show the reader that you know how to present your thoughts in an organized manner. Present your main points in a logical, easy-to-follow sequence, using logical paragraph breaks between major supporting points. Use a consistent voice and tone throughout your essay. Your introductory and concluding paragraphs are especially key to looking organized and in control. Be sure to include both, and make sure that both reveal your central idea.

It's quality, not quantity, that counts.

The only limitations on essay length are the time limit and the amount of space provided (two lined pages). Whether the readers prefer a briefer or longer essay depends on the essay's quality, not on its length. GED® readers don't count words. Be sure to incorporate into your essay all the elements recommended in this lesson, and the length of your essay will take care of itself.

Don't lose sight of your primary objectives.

During the time you have to produce your essay, your four main objectives are to:

- Maintain focus on the topic and on your central idea.

- Develop your ideas using sound reasons and relevant examples.

- Present you ideas in a logical, well-organized manner.

- Express your ideas through simple, clear writing that is correct in grammar, diction, spelling, and punctuation.

Never lose sight of these four objectives. Accomplish them all, and you can be assured that you've produced a solid, high-scoring GED® essay.

SUMMING IT UP

- Part II of the Language Arts, Writing Test assesses your ability to communicate your thoughts and ideas in writing. You will be asked to present your opinion or explain your views about a specific topic. You will not be given a choice of topics to write on, and you must write *only* about the topic provided. An essay on a different topic essay will not be scored, and you will have to retake *both* parts of the Language Arts, Writing Test.

- You will have 45 minutes to plan, write, and revise your essay. If you finish Part I of the Writing Test early, you can immediately begin Part II. However, when you complete the essay, you are not permitted to go back to Part I. Scratch paper will be provided, but you must write your essay in pen on the two lined sheets of paper.

- There is no correct answer or best response, and there is no correct structure or number of paragraphs for a GED® essay. You don't need to be an expert about the topic at hand; common everyday knowledge is enough. You may make a few minor errors and still achieve a very good score.

- Two trained GED® readers will score your essay on a scale of 0–4 (the highest score is 4). Neither reader is aware of the other's evaluation or score. The two scores are then averaged into a final essay score. Readers are looking for essays that are fully developed, well-organized, and well-written.

- The essay prompt is designed for you to respond with either a persuasive essay or an expository essay. A **persuasive** essay adopts a viewpoint or an opinion on an issue and then tries to convince, or persuade, the reader to agree with that viewpoint or opinion. An **expository** essay asserts a point and then helps the reader understand that point by explaining it in greater depth, with relevant examples, reasons, or other details.

- When practicing essay writing—and during the real test—be sure to remember the following important steps: brainstorming (note-taking), organizing your ideas (outlining), writing the rough draft, writing the final draft, and proofreading and fixing problems.

PART IV
THE SOCIAL STUDIES TEST

Mastering the
Social Studies Test

chapter 6

OVERVIEW

- All about the Social Studies Test
- What's tested—and what's *not* tested
- Formats used for GED® Social Studies questions
- Subject areas for GED® Social Studies questions
- Source material for GED® Social Studies questions
- Question types based on the four skill areas
- Questions based on visual depictions
- General test-taking strategies
- Summing it up

THE SOCIAL STUDIES TEST—
IN A NUTSHELL

Time allowed: 70 minutes

Total number of questions: 50 multiple choice (5 choices per question)

Format: Each question is based on a text passage and/or visual depiction

Length of text passages: Up to 150 words

Number of questions per passage or visual: Expect 1 to 5 (1 or 2 is most common)

ALL ABOUT THE SOCIAL STUDIES TEST

The broad academic field of **social studies** includes a wide variety of subjects, all involving human activity and relations. These subjects include history, political science (civics and government), economics, sociology, anthropology, psychology, and geography (as well as some others). The GED® Social Studies Test is designed to measure a variety of abilities within the context of just four of these subject areas: history, political science (civics and government), economics, and geography.

The test consists of 50 multiple-choice questions. Here's the breakdown in terms of the subject areas that the test covers (percentages and numbers may vary slightly):

25% (12 or 13 questions)	U.S. history (or Canadian* history)
15% (7 or 8 questions)	World history

25% (12 or 13 questions)	Civics and government
20% (10 questions)	Economics
15% (7 or 8 questions)	Geography

The test questions are *not* grouped by content area. Instead, questions from all areas listed above are mixed together.

*Note that the version of the GED® administered in the United States includes questions about U.S. history, while the Canadian version of the GED® contains questions about Canadian history instead.

WHAT'S TESTED—AND WHAT'S *NOT* TESTED

Perhaps the most fundamental point to keep in mind about the GED® Social Studies Test is that it is *not* a knowledge test. Regardless of content area—history, civics and government, economics, or geography—all the information you'll need to answer a question will be provided. In this respect, the GED® Social Studies Test is a lot like GED® Language Arts, Reading Test. Rather than demonstrating subject knowledge, your task will be to demonstrate the following set of skills:

- Comprehension (recalling and understanding)

- Analysis (drawing inferences and conclusions)

- Evaluation (synthesizing)

- Application (applying concepts and ideas to other situations)

Though the Social Studies test is designed to measure skills rather than knowledge, keep in mind that with some prior knowledge of the four content areas listed above, you can expect to handle the questions with greater ease and confidence. The review materials later in this part of the book are designed to help you in this respect.

FORMATS USED FOR GED® SOCIAL STUDIES QUESTIONS

The GED® Social Studies Test contains fifty multiple-choice questions. Each question will list five choices. Most questions will be based on brief passages of text, which may vary in length from a few sentences to as many as 150 words (about one fourth of a page). A question involving a passage of text might refer to it either as a "passage" or as "information" or "text." The remaining questions will be based on maps, charts, cartoons, diagrams, and other visual depictions. Some (but not all) visual depictions will be accompanied by a brief passage of text. Finally, many of the questions will be presented in groups of two to five, all questions in a group based on the same passage and/or visual depiction.

SUBJECT AREAS FOR GED® SOCIAL STUDIES QUESTIONS

As outlined earlier, the subject areas you'll encounter on the Social Studies Test are limited to history, civics and government, economics, and geography. Though you can review each area in depth later in this part of the book, here's an initial survey of each one.

History

History can be defined as the record of past events or as the subject matter that makes up those records. On the GED®, you'll review historical facts and records and glean information from them by applying reading-comprehension and analytical skills. Remember: the questions will not require you to recall random historical facts such as names, dates, or other trivial information, so you need only be able to work within a historical context to succeed in answering history questions. However, if you have a good background in history, particularly in U.S. (or Canadian) history, you will have an advantage when dealing with these questions.

History questions account for about 40 percent of the test—about twenty questions. Of these questions, expect twelve or thirteen to involve U.S. history (or Canadian history if you are taking the test in Canada). If you're taking the U.S. version of the GED®, expect at least one question involving each of the following broad eras of U.S. history:

- Settling the New World, and the colonial period

- The struggle for independence, and early U.S. government

- Westward expansion

- The Civil War and Reconstruction

- Industrialization, big business, and the Gilded Age

- Twentieth-century turbulence and the U.S. rise to superpower status

- The late-twentieth century and contemporary events

The remaining seven or eight history questions will deal with world history and international affairs. A world history question might focus on virtually any of the world's regions and any era of human history, including the following:

- Human beginnings and early civilizations (through 1000 BC)

- Classical traditions, empires, and religions (1000 BC–300 BC)

- Growing trade, hemispheric interactions, and the first global age (300 BC–AD 1770)

- The age of revolutions (1750–1914)

- The modern world (1900–present): urbanization; world wars; global depression; advances in science and technology; new democracies of Africa, Asia, and South America; the Cold War; and "Global Culture"

Also, note that **anthropology** concepts, which involve the cultural history of humankind, are sometimes incorporated into GED® world history questions.

Civics and Government

Questions about **civics and government,** both of which are aspects of political science, account for about 25 percent of the test (twelve to thirteen questions). On the U.S. version of the GED®, you might encounter questions dealing with any of the following aspects of civics and government:

- Political systems of the world

- Theories and forms of government

- Foundations of the U.S. system of government

- The Federal system (federal powers and state sovereignty)

- Checks and balances (the three branches of government)

- Political parties and the U.S. political system

- The U.S. legal and court system (and the legal rights of U.S. citizens)

On the U.S. version of the GED®, many civics and government questions will be based on the concepts embodied in the following important documents:

- The U.S. Declaration of Independence

- The original (un-amended) U.S. Constitution

- Amendments to the U.S. Constitution

- The Federalist Papers

- Landmark U.S. Supreme Court opinions

A question involving one of these documents might quote the document, or it might paraphrase or summarize the document.

Economics

Economics questions, or those dealing with the study of how humans use resources to meet their material needs, will account for about 20 percent of the test (ten questions or so). Here are the broad aspects of economics you can expect these questions to involve:

- Economic systems of the world

- Monetary policy and financial institutions

- Supply and demand

- Factors of production

- Government and the economy

- Labor relations

- Foreign trade

An economics question might be framed in an historical context (such as the Great Depression of the 1930s), or it might present a hypothetical scenario instead. Expect some economics questions to refer to tables, charts, and graphs. Finally, note that some economics questions might incorporate certain psychology concepts—especially those relating to advertising or consumer behavior.

Geography

Expect about 15 percent of the Social Studies questions (seven to eight questions) to focus on **geography**, which is the study of Earth's physical features and the way humans adapt to those features. Among possible topics for a GED® geography question are the following:

- Globes and maps
- Latitude, longitude, and time zones
- Topography and climate
- Population and demography
- Environmental issues

On the GED®, though you'll probably encounter a few geography questions based solely on textual information, most geography questions will involve a visual depiction—a map, globe, graph, chart, or table—in addition to, or instead of, text.

SOURCE MATERIAL FOR GED® SOCIAL STUDIES QUESTIONS

The source material for the GED® Social Studies Test includes primary as well as secondary sources. **Primary sources** are those that are original and contemporary to whatever event or development the source documents. Examples of primary sources include historical documents, laws, speeches, newspaper articles, political cartoons, and maps. **Secondary sources** are those that are based on primary sources or other secondary sources. A textbook is a good example of a secondary source.

GED® Social Studies questions are based on a variety of primary and secondary sources. As noted earlier, a question may be from a textual source, a visual source, or a combination of textual and visual sources. Regardless of the source, remember that you will *not* need to recognize or identify any document or the source of any information. Rather, your task will be to understand, evaluate, analyze, or apply the source information you are given.

QUESTION TYPES BASED ON THE FOUR SKILL AREAS

To succeed on the GED® Social Studies Test, you will need to demonstrate proficiency in four critical-thinking skill areas: comprehension, application, analysis, and evaluation. You will use all four skills throughout the test. In the next few pages, you'll examine each skill more closely. Note that the GED®-style example questions here are all based on passages of text, rather than on visuals. In the next section, you'll learn how to handle questions involving visuals.

Comprehension Questions

Comprehension questions require that you read and recall information contained in a passage. In most cases, they also require that you *understand* and *interpret* that information—in other words, to grasp or comprehend—the ideas and concepts that the passage's words convey. Some comprehension questions will require you to understand the main idea of a passage—much like a main-idea question in the Language Arts, Reading Test. To handle this sort of question, look for an answer choice that sums up the passage. Other comprehension questions focus instead on the passage's details.

Though the correct answer choice might restate a phrase from the passage word-for-word, more likely it will either paraphrase or provide an interpretation of passage information. In other words, comprehension questions typically focus on a passage's *ideas* rather than on exactly how those ideas are expressed. Incorrect answer choices will often contradict passage information or provide assertions that are unsupported by the passage or that do not respond to the specific question that is asked.

To understand how a comprehension question might require that you interpret—rather than merely recall—what you've read in a passage, study the following two examples.

QUESTION 1 REFERS TO THE FOLLOWING INFORMATION.

During the 1700s, Europeans reaped many benefits of the agricultural revolution. New methods of farming increased food production and variety on many farms. New foods added much-needed variety to the diets of many Europeans. Larger and more balanced diets bolstered the immune systems of many Europeans and helped them become stronger and healthier.

1. Which development occurred in eighteenth-century Europe?

    (1) Over-farming left the soil unfertile for subsequent generations.

    (2) Advances in farming technology enhanced the health of the population.

    (3) Severe droughts resulted in famine throughout farming and other rural areas.

    (4) Industrialization left Europe with relatively few farmers.

    (5) Farmers imported more and more of their food from other regions of the world.

Notice that choice (2), which is the correct choice, does not simply repeat a particular part of the passage, word-for-word. Instead, it combines and paraphrases two closely related ideas: first that new farming methods increased food variety, and, second, that greater food variety led to better health among many Europeans. The passage does not include the word "technology," nor does it refer to the "population." Nevertheless, choice

(2) provides a good interpretation of these two closely related ideas from the passage. None of the other four statements is supported by the passage. In fact, choices (1), (2), and (4) run contrary to the passage's ideas. **The correct answer is (2).**

QUESTION 2 REFERS TO THE FOLLOWING INFORMATION.

International trade occurs when goods manufactured in a country are sent elsewhere, or *exported*, for sale, while goods manufactured elsewhere are brought into the country, or *imported*, for sale in the country. Often, governments can raise money by imposing taxes (tariffs) on goods they import from other countries. Although tariffs are paid for by the manufacturers of the goods, the cost of the tax is usually built into the product itself, which means that the tax is passed on to the consumer. A manufacturer is often able to realize a profit by producing an excess of goods and then exporting the surplus. When the manufacturer can do this, often the cost of production is lowered on each unit produced, so the final selling price is reduced for the products sold in the country of production.

2. How are the lowest prices on manufactured goods often realized?

When a manufacturer can

(1) impose a tariff on imported goods

(2) import materials it needs to make its products

(3) pass along a tariff to consumers

(4) export a surplus of goods

(5) sell all its products in other countries

Choice (4) essentially provides the point of the final two sentences of the passage: by producing more units, a manufacturer often can reduce its per-unit cost and then pass the savings on to domestic consumers while charging more for surplus sales in foreign countries. Though the passage does not explicitly state that this is how the lowest price on manufactured goods is realized, you can interpret the information in this way.

Choice (1) contradicts the passage: it is a government, nor a manufacturer, that imposes tariffs. Choice (2) is unsupported by the passage—whether a manufacturer can save money by imported materials depends on the cost of those materials. Choice (3) indicates an activity that manufacturers can do, according to the passage. But choice (3) is incorrect because passing along a tax is not how the lowest price is realized. So choice (3) does not answer the question. Choice (5) contradicts the passage: it is when a manufacturer sells only its surplus goods, while retaining the rest of its goods for domestic sales, that the lowest price is realized—on domestic sales. If a manufacturer can produce more goods, the cost of production per item is often reduced. The surplus of manufactured goods can be exported, and the manufacturer can pass the production savings on to customers in the country where the product was produced. **The correct answer is (4).**

As the second of the above two examples illustrates, when handling comprehension questions involving lengthier passages, be sure to focus on the part of the passage that the question asks about. Some of the incorrect answer choices will probably involve other parts of the passage—parts that are not relevant to the question at hand.

Analysis Questions

Analysis questions go beyond understanding the information in a passage or visual. Analysis involves organizing the information; explaining how ideas, facts, or data connect together; identifying patterns; and recognizing inferences, conclusions, and meanings beyond what is stated. Some analysis questions may require you to *infer* historical or economic causes or effects. (To infer is to draw a reasonable conclusion based on certain information.) Other analysis questions might require you to point out similarities and differences between two events, eras, systems, or other phenomena. Still other analysis questions may require you to distinguish fact from opinion. These are just some of the many possibilities for analysis questions.

QUESTION 3 REFERS TO THE FOLLOWING INFORMATION.

Industrialized countries need uninterrupted supplies of oil in order for their economies to function. The Organization of Petroleum Exporting Countries (OPEC) has made major inroads in helping certain less-industrialized countries become more self-sustaining. Because these countries have a virtual monopoly on the export of oil, they have been able to raise oil prices substantially.

3. Why do some industrialized nations oppose OPEC?

   (1) They don't want competition in the production of oil.

   (2) Higher oil prices can raise the cost of running an economy.

   (3) Some non-industrialized nations have little or no oil reserves.

   (4) OPEC is not a member of the United Nations.

   (5) They fear that non-industrialized countries will run out of oil.

The passage does answer this question explicitly. To answer the question, you must infer an effect, or consequence, of what OPEC has achieved. Because oil is a valuable commodity in almost every area of an industrialized nation's economy, the cost of running such an economy would rise proportionately to the cost of oil, hurting the nation's economy (which is obviously a result that no nation would want for itself). **The correct answer is (2).**

QUESTION 4 REFERS TO THE FOLLOWING INFORMATION.

Communism is both a political and an economic system in which the major means of production and distribution of goods and products are shared in common by all the people. In its purest form, communism would mean even the sharing of all property. The term is generally used to describe the economic systems in Soviet Russia and China. *Socialism* is an economic system in which the majority of productive resources, both human-made and natural, are owned and controlled by the state or its agencies. Because production is divided amongst the population, under socialism production is assumed to be more equitable (fairer) and more efficient than under Western-style capitalism.

4. What do Communism and Socialism have in common?

    (1) a preference for private ownership of resources

    (2) a preference for competition over cooperation

    (3) the fact that both are political as well as economic systems

    (4) the division of production amongst all the people

    (5) the idea that capitalism is fairer to consumers

To answer this question, you must note the similarities and differences between the two systems.

Neither Communism nor Socialism promotes private ownership of resources, choice (1), nor does either promote competition in business, choice (2). Only Communism is considered both a political as well as an economic system, choice (3). Both systems, however, believe in the division of production amongst all the people, choice (4). How the division is made may differ, but both support the theory that division of production is good. As for choice (5), the passage does not compare capitalism to either Communism or Socialism—in fact, it never even mentions capitalism. **The correct answer is (4).**

QUESTION 5 REFERS TO THE FOLLOWING INFORMATION.

After the Great War, later referred to as World War I, the United States, Great Britain, and France joined forces and drew up terms for the defeated Germany. The terms, known as the Treaty of Versailles, reflected the allies' position that Germany was to blame for the war. Consequently, the treaty provided that Germany was forbidden to have a military air force, and that the German army and navy were to be strictly limited in size. In addition, under the treaty Germany was required to pay 132-billion gold marks in reparations to nations it had harmed during the war. Germany had no choice but to abide by all these terms.

5. Which of the following is an opinion, rather than a fact, about the conclusion and immediate aftermath of World War I?

(1) Germany had little or no say when it came to the terms of the treaty.

(2) Germany's punishment was unfair since other nations had harmed Germany as well.

(3) After the Great War, Germany was left without an air force to defend itself.

(4) France was one of the nations that participated in the Great War.

(5) Germany disbanded its army and navy after the Great War.

Based on the passage information, choices (3), (4), and (5) are clearly accurate, and so you can eliminate them. Choice (1) is not a fact provided in the passage. So does this mean that the statement in choice (1) is merely an opinion? No. The passage makes it clear that the treaty was drawn up by the countries that had opposed Germany, and that Germany "had no choice but to abide by" the terms of the treaty. So you can infer that Germany had little or no say in the treaty negations. In contrast, choice (2) is merely on opinion. Whether the treaty terms were fair may very well depend on one's perspective on the war. **The correct answer is (2).**

Evaluation Questions

Evaluation involves drawing on your comprehension and analytical skills in order to make an assessment, judgment, or critique or to draw a conclusion. An evaluation question might ask you to characterize an event, era, or system described or outlined in a passage. Or it might ask you to recognize a potential benefit or drawback of an economic or political policy, or with a particular statute (law). An evaluation question might present a point of view, along with numbered statements that either reflect or oppose that point of view. Evaluation questions often involve quotations and historical documents.

In handling these questions, what's just as important as recognizing a fair assessment of the information is recognizing unfair assessments and judgments. Be on the lookout for wrong-answer choices that speculate too much—that jump to conclusions or judgments that are unreasonable based solely on the information provided.

QUESTION 6 REFERS TO THE FOLLOWING INFORMATION.

"The ostensible cause of the war was the issue of slavery. However, slavery was just one of many issues that drove a wedge between the two sides. One of the main points of contention between the two sides was the issue of states' rights. Another issue was the favoritism shown in Congress toward the North. The final straw, though, was the election of Abraham Lincoln, a candidate who did not receive a true mandate of the people based on the number of votes he received."

6. The war to which the person who wrote the quoted words was the U.S. Civil War. Which of the following is most likely true about the author of the quoted words?

The author

(1) sympathized with the South

(2) was opposed to slavery

(3) saw many causes of the war

(4) participated in the war

(5) was opposed to the war

The question asks you to make an assessment or draw a conclusion about the author based on what he or she wrote. So you need to understand the quotation's specific points as well as the author's broader point. Because the author identifies several possible contributing factors leading to the Civil War, it is fair to conclude that the author, in fact, recognized that the war had many causes. Though some of the points that the author makes might be the same ones that a Southern sympathizer might have pointed out, it is unfair to conclude based solely on the passage that the author sympathized with the South, choice (1). **The correct answer is (3).**

QUESTION 7 REFERS TO THE FOLLOWING INFORMATION.

The Fourteenth Amendment to the U.S. Constitution provides in part: ". . . (3) No person shall be a Senator or Representative in Congress, or elector of President and Vice President, or hold any office, civil or military, under the United States, or under any State, who, having previously taken an oath, as a member of Congress, or as an officer of the United States, or as a member of any State legislature, or as an executive or judicial officer of any State, to support the Constitution of the United States, shall have engaged in insurrection or rebellion against the same, or given aid or comfort to the enemies thereof. But Congress may by a vote of two thirds of each House, remove such disability. . . ."

7. What is the intent of this portion of the Fourteenth Amendment?

(1) to encourage criminal prosecution of elected officials

(2) to ensure party loyalty at all levels of government

(3) to enhance the security of the nation and its states

(4) to encourage patriotic citizens to run for Congress

(5) to make an exception to state sovereignty

The question requires you to evaluate and characterize the quoted portion of the Fourteenth Amendment. The portion lists a number of government offices, and then forbids any person who poses a threat to the government from holding any of the listed public offices. Choice (3) provides a good characterization of what this provision was intended to accomplish. Notice that choices (1) and (4) go too far. The purpose of the quoted part of the Fourteenth Amendment is more limited than either choice (1) or choice (4) suggests. Choice (2) is incorrect because the provision is concerned with loyalty to the state and federal governments, not to any political party. **The correct answer is (3).**

Application Questions

Application questions require you to use information from a passage (or visual) in a way that is different from the way it is presented to you. In other words, your task is to apply the ideas to new situations and contexts. Use your understanding of the concept described in the passage, along with common sense, to identify the correct answer.

QUESTION 8 REFERS TO THE FOLLOWING INFORMATION.

During a period of economic recession, the nation's gross national product (GDP) is in decline, which means that the economy as a whole is producing fewer goods and providing fewer services than previously.

8. How is a small business LEAST likely to behave during an economic recession?

    (1) by putting its products on sale

    (2) by giving loyal employees a pay raise

    (3) by limiting the kinds of products it sells

    (4) by depleting its inventory of goods

    (5) by using its profits to pay down debts

This question requires you not just to understand the definition of a recession, but also to apply the concept to a situation not specifically described in the passage. When fewer goods and services are produced, everyone makes less money and, in turn, everyone has less money to spend. The behaviors described in choices (1), (3), and (4) make perfect sense in this situation. (Eliminate those choices.) Since a business is unlikely to expand during a recession, it is more likely to use profits to pay down debt, choice (5), than to reinvest in the business—for example, by rewarding loyal employees with a pay raise, choice (2). **The correct answer is (2).**

QUESTION 9 REFERS TO THE FOLLOWING INFORMATION.

A *lobbyist* is a person who represents a group of people and whose job it is to work for the special interests of that group. A lobbyist will contact members of Congress in order to make sure that money is allocated for the group's work, by trying to persuade them that the interests he or she represents are more worthy than others to receive a share of available financial resources.

9. Which activity would be most closely associated with lobbying?

(1) explaining to a legislator why he or she should run for reelection

(2) petitioning the city council to pass a law outlawing smoking in public places

(3) convincing the boss to throw an office party that will improve worker morale

(4) staging a labor-union strike in protest of unfairly low wages

(5) running for mayor against a popular and well-funded opponent

Choice (3) is the only one that describes an interest held in common by a group of people (employees), and where someone representing the group attempts to obtain a benefit (a party) for the group from someone in a position to give it to them (the boss) by persuading that person of the benefits of doing so (improvement in worker morale). **The correct answer is (3).**

QUESTIONS BASED ON VISUAL DEPICTIONS

Approximately 40 percent of the questions on the Social Studies Test are based on a visual depiction of some sort or on a brief passage of text accompanied by a visual depiction. The "visual" may be a chart, graph, or table; or it might be a political cartoon, photo, or other illustration; or it might be a map, diagram, or timeline.

Questions based on visuals are designed to gauge your ability to interpret the meaning of the visual (as well as the accompanying text, if any). Even if you do not recognize the visual or don't understand it initially, you can still figure out the best answer by looking for clues or for things you do recognize.

In the following pages, you examine the types of visuals appearing most frequently on the test. You'll see some examples of each type, and you'll learn how to handle them.

Editorial Cartoons

The kinds of cartoons on the GED® Social Studies Test are not the sort you'll find in the comics section of your newspaper. Instead, they're the type that appear in a newspaper's editorial section, which contains articles, essays, and cartoons expressing opinions about current events. These **editorial cartoons** are sometimes referred to as *political cartoons*, even though they often deal with a much wider range of issues—from political and economic to social and cultural.

Editorial cartoonists are not concerned with providing information. Instead, through their cartoons they express their opinions and perspectives (their "slant") on current events and issues of the day. Their cartoons carry messages that are usually critical of prevailing ideas, well-established institutions, and influential individuals—especially political figures in the public eye at the moment. Editorial cartoonists often employ humor, sarcasm, and irony to convey their messages.

As for how these cartoonists convey their messages, their cartoons often show human-like characters, which the artist typically uses to depict a specific, well-known public figure—for example, a president or presidential candidate, a dictator or leader from another country, a high-ranking government official, or even an influential commentator from the media. The editorial cartoonist will usually portray the specific person as a **caricature,** which exaggerates the person's prominent physical features.

Of course, when a cartoon shows a caricature of a specific, well-known person, you know that the message of the cartoon has to do with that person. But editorial cartoonists often use human-like characters, animals, and even objects to represent, or *symbolize* something else, such as the following:

- A group of specific individuals—for example, the Supreme Court or a legislative body (such as the U.S. Senate)

- A geographically defined entity—for example, a particular state or nation, the North or the South (as during the U.S. Civil War), or the European Union

- An organization or alliance—for example, a political party, the United Nations, an oil cartel such as OPEC, political lobbyists, big business, or the so-called "tea baggers"

- An abstract idea, an ideology, or a cause—for example, free-market capitalism, white supremacy, religious fundamentalism, social welfare, environmentalism, the so-called "war on terror," or gun control

Here are just a few of the symbols often used in editorial cartoons:

- An eagle, to represent democracy or freedom

- A hammer-and-sickle, to represent Communism

- A donkey, to represent the Democratic political party

- An elephant, to represent the Republican political party

- A soldier, to represent one of the countries involved in a war

- A judge, to represent the concept of justice

- A beggar, to represent social welfare

- A pile of money, to represent greed or capitalism

Sometimes, specific individuals become so closely associated with an ideology, cause, or concept that a cartoonist will use a caricature of that person as a symbol—especially if the readership is sophisticated enough to understand the symbolism. For example:

- Lenin has come to represent Soviet-style Communism.

- Theodore Roosevelt has come to represent opposition to monopolies and big business.

- Adolf Hitler has come to represent persecution and is even seen as the embodiment of evil.

- Franklin D. Roosevelt has come to represent New Deal–style, or so-called "big" government.

- Richard Nixon has come to represent political scandal, secrecy, and dirty politics.

As you examine the characters and objects in an editorial cartoon, look for clues as to what they represent. The cartoonist may write a word or brief phrase directly on the characters (especially their clothing) as well as on other pictured objects to help the audience understand the symbolism. Look carefully for any such clues, as they typically appear in small print. Remember: if the cartoonist went to the trouble of writing words anywhere in the visual, those words will no doubt be useful in understanding the idea that the cartoonist was trying to convey.

Also pay close attention to how the characters appear and what they are doing or saying. A character might be drawn to appear noble and victorious or aggressive and evil; or a character might be drawn to appear defeated, injured, or victimized. Two characters may appear to be fighting or angry with each other, or they might appear friendly toward one another. Body postures, facial expressions, modes of dress, objects carried or held, and other visual clues can be useful in understanding a cartoon's message. In addition, spoken words—usually written in bubbles above the characters—are even more crucial to that message.

Finally, editorial cartoons sometimes come with **captions**—words appearing below the illustration. A caption might indicate what a character is saying, or it might provide a clue as to how to interpret or evaluate the cartoon. If the cartoon includes a caption, you can be certain that it is crucial in understanding the message of a cartoon.

QUESTION 10 REFERS TO THE FOLLOWING POLITICAL CARTOON.

10. In the cartoon, what does the artist imply about President George H. Bush?

   (1) He believes that a parade may lead to a military victory in Operation Desert Storm.

   (2) He is more interested in helping big business than in promoting education and urban development.

   (3) He would rather celebrate a military victory than face pressing social problems.

   (4) He is the cause of all education, economic, racial, and urban problems in the United States.

   (5) He believes that a parade will help people feel better about U.S. lives lost in the war.

If you happen to know about the U.S. war in Iraq during the early 1990s and the presidency of George H. Bush (1988–92), this knowledge could help you understand the cartoon's message. But remember: the questions on the Social Studies Test will provide everything you need in order to analyze and answer them. Even if you did not recognize the person in the cartoon as President George H. Bush, you could determine that it is Bush because the question stem refers to him by that name.

Examine the elements of the illustration. Think about what Bush is saying as he sits amidst the four simple downward-pointing charts. He has just had the idea of a military victory parade. At the same time, the four charts all have to do with domestic problems. What point do you think the cartoonist was trying to convey? Perhaps that Bush is trying to ignore or distract himself from these four problems.

Now examine each answer choice, in turn. You can eliminate choice (1) based on what Bush is saying in the cartoon. He is suggesting another victory parade, which means that the victory has probably already occurred. Besides, it is unlikely that a parade in itself would lead to victory. Choice (2) is only partially supported by the cartoon. Indeed, Bush appears uninterested in solving education and urban problems (represented by three of the charts). However, nothing in the cartoon suggests that he is more interested in helping big business. Moving on to choice (3), it provides a good statement of our interpretation. But let's examine the remaining two choices anyway. Choice (4) is partially supported by the cartoon, since the domestic problems are occurring while Bush is president. But choice (4) says nothing about what Bush is saying. Remember: if a cartoonist puts words in a character's mouth, you can be sure those words are important in understanding the cartoon. Choice (5) might make sense absent the four charts. But remember: written words in the cartoon are always important in understanding the cartoonist's intended message. **The correct answer is (3).**

QUESTION 11 REFERS TO THE FOLLOWING CARTOON.

WONDER HOW LONG THE HONEYMOON WILL LAST?

11. What idea is the artist who created the cartoon trying to convey?

Hitler and Stalin

(1) should be partners because they have a lot in common

(2) were on unfriendly terms before forming a partnership

(3) have formed an alliance that they hope to keep secret from their mutual enemies

(4) have formed a partnership whose prospects are uncertain

(5) have common enemies who were surprised at their alliance

As with the previous question, your knowledge of twentieth-century history may be useful in interpreting the cartoon, yet it isn't needed to answer the question at hand. You may not have recognized Stalin in the cartoon. But notice the hammer-and-sickle symbol, together with the swastika, on the wedding cake. These symbols provide a clue as to the identity of both characters. In any event, the question provides this information.

In this question, the caption is crucial to understanding the message. Posing the question "Wonder how long the honeymoon will last?" suggests that a new marriage, though happy at first, might turn sour over time. The cartoon implies that the relationship is good at the onset, but the future of the relationship is uncertain, choice (4). Choice (1) is incorrect because the cartoon shows Hitler and Stalin already partners. Choices (2) and (3) may or may not provide accurate historical information, but since the cartoon provides no clue as to the past relationship between Hitler and Stalin, choice (2), or about whether their alliance was secret, choice (3), you can rule out both choices. Choice (5) is in fact an historically accurate statement, and, if you relied on your outside knowledge, you might have found it tempting. However, it ignores the caption, whereas choice (4) does not. Remember again: if a cartoon provides a caption, you can be sure that it is crucial to understanding the cartoonist's intended meaning. **The correct answer is (4).**

Maps

During the Social Studies Test, you'll encounter at least one or two geography and/or history questions based on maps. Don't expect to find the kinds of maps you use in your everyday life to help you find your way across town or from one city to another. Instead, what you're likely to see are any of the following kinds of maps, depending on the sort of information the map is intended to provide:

Political map: This is the most familiar type of map to most people. It shows political boundaries of cities, states, and countries as well as capitals and other major cities. On the GED®, a map of this type might cover a multi-state region, an entire country, a multi-country region, or an entire continent (and possibly the seas and oceans around it).

Topographical map: This type of map shows the locations of natural features such as rivers, lakes, seas, mountain ranges, and deserts. It may also focus on the locations of natural resources such as minerals, timber (forests) and other forms of vegetation or crops, and even animal life. A topographical map may also provide elevations (altitude) at various locations.

Historical map: This type of map provides a timeline of key historical events according to where they took place. Historical maps often provide *callouts*, which list events and/or dates and point to the places on the map showing where the events occurred.

The three categories listed above are not mutually exclusive. For example, a map may provide political boundaries as well as geographical features. Historical maps typically show politically defined regions such as colonies, provinces, nations, territories, kingdoms, and even empires.

Regardless of which type of map a test question involves, you should start by reading the title of the map. The title will provide clues as to what information the map conveys. Next, locate the map key, or **legend** (if any). The legend is often located off to the side or at the bottom of the map. It will explain the symbols used on the map as well as any colors or shading used on the map. The legend may also contain a map **scale** that indicates distances on the map. Here's an example of a typical map legend:

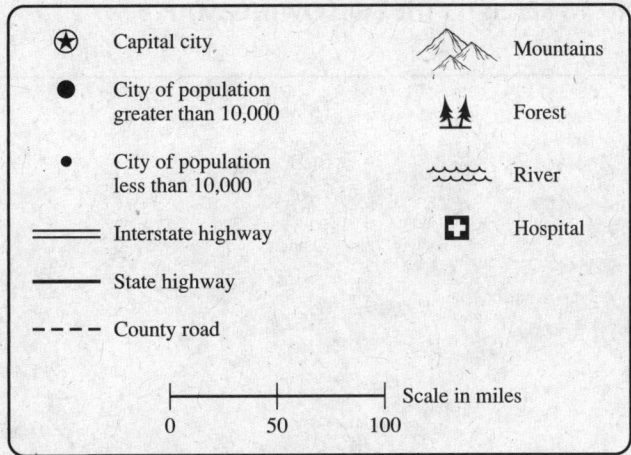

The specific types of maps you might encounter on the test are not defined solely by the three broad categories listed above. Here are some specialized map types that appear frequently on the GED® Social Studies Test:

Weather map: shows weather patterns throughout a region (temperatures, precipitation, highs and lows, etc.)

Population map: illustrates population density, population patterns, or the populations of cities, counties, states, regions, or countries

Time zone map: shows the different time zones across a region

Navigational map: shows lines of meridian (longitudinal lines) and latitude lines, along with their degree measures in relation to the equator (for latitude lines) and to the first meridian (for meridian lines). This type of map is most commonly used for sea navigation and is how GPS devices are programmed to identify specific locations on Earth.

Since maps can be used to display any sort of geographically specific information, a myriad of specialized map types are possible. The following two maps, each of which is accompanied by two GED®-style questions, illustrate two such types.

QUESTIONS 12 AND 13 REFER TO THE FOLLOWING MAP.

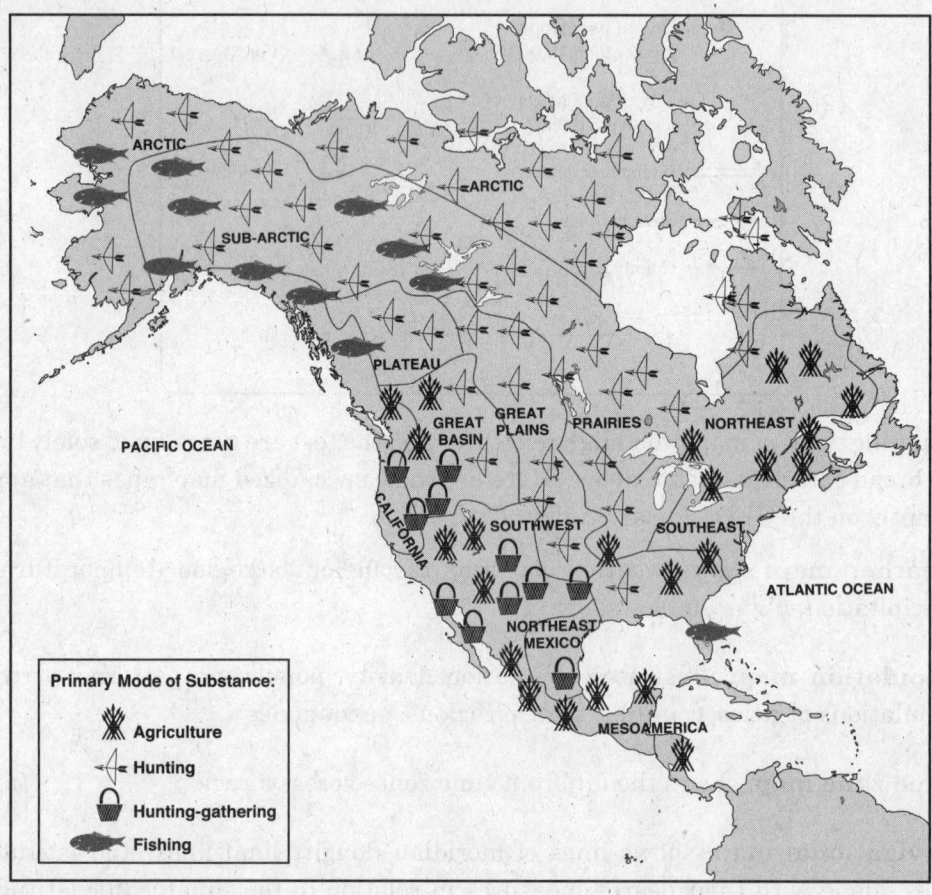

12. The majority of early Native Americans who fished for their sustenance were located primarily in what region of North America?

    (1) the Northeast

    (2) the West

    (3) the Northwest

    (4) the North

    (5) the South

Referring to the map's legend, you can see that fishing, represented by the fish symbol, took place mainly in the northwestern part of the continent. An elementary knowledge of geography and directions is enough here to identify the northwestern part of North America. **The correct answer is (3).**

13. What means of sustenance were available to the early Native Americans of the Great Basin?

(1) primarily fishing

(2) primarily hunting

(3) hunting and gathering

(4) hunting, fishing, and gathering

(5) hunting, gathering, and agriculture

To answer this question, you need to locate the Great Basin area on the map (in the map's left-central region). In that area you'll find the symbols for agriculture, hunting, and hunting-gathering. **The correct answer is (5).**

QUESTIONS 14 AND 15 REFER TO THE FOLLOWING MAP.

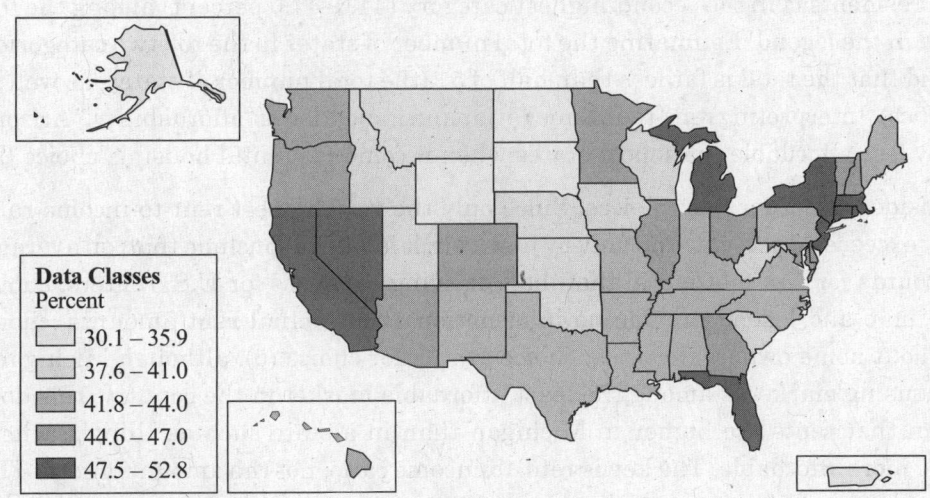

Percent of Renter-occupied Units Spending 30 Percent or More of Household Income on Rent and Utilities (2008)

Data Classes
Percent
30.1 – 35.9
37.6 – 41.0
41.8 – 44.0
44.6 – 47.0
47.5 – 52.8

United States: Estimate: 45.9 Percent, Margin of Error: +/-0.1 Percent
Source: U.S. Census Bureau, 2006-2008 American Community Survey

14. In how many states, including Alaska and Hawaii, is the percentage of households who rent their residence rather than own it 30.1 to 41.0 percent?

(1) 4

(2) 11

(3) 15

(4) 46

(5) Not enough information is provided.

This question illustrates the importance of reading the title of a map. According to this map's title, the map provides only the rent-to-income ratio in each state, which is entirely different from the renter-to-owner ratio. Not enough information is provided to answer this question. **The correct answer is (5).**

---

15. Which conclusion do the data presented in the map best support?

(1) On average, U.S. renters pay more for rent than for all other living expenses combined.

(2) Arizona rental housing is less affordable than rental housing in most other states.

(3) The average rent in Georgia is greater than in most other states.

(4) States with the highest rent-to-income ratio have the highest home ownership rates.

(5) Average rent in the Midwest is greater than in the Southeast but less than in the Southwest.

This is a relatively difficult question. Focusing on choice (2), the rent-to-income ratio for Arizona residents is in the second-highest category (44.6–47.0 percent) among the five provided in the legend. Estimating the total number of states in the top two categories, you'll find that the total is far less than half of 51 (the total number of states, as well as Puerto Rico). Interpreting rent-to-income ratio as an indication of "affordability," Arizona is clearly less affordable than most states when it comes to rental housing, choice (2).

Now consider the other four choices. Since only the very highest rent-to-income ratio category exceeds 50 percent, and only by just a bit, it is safe to conclude that, on average, rent accounts for *less* (not more) than half of living expenses for U.S. rehters, choice (1). The map and legend provide no information about actual rent amounts, choice (3), or about home ownership rates, choice (4). As for choice (5), although Michigan's rental housing market is among the least affordable market in the country, this does not mean that rents are higher in Michigan than in a state such as Illinois, where rents are more affordable. The key is rent-to-income ratio, not the amount of rent. **The correct answer is (2).**

Graphical Data Displays

Several questions on the Social Studies Test will be based on data presented in graphical format. A question of this type might be based on a table, bar graph, line chart, picture graph, or circle graph (pie chart). These displays are usually used for test questions involving geography and economics. This book's Mathematics lesson explains how to read, interpret, and analyze data presented in each of these formats. Be sure to review those materials when preparing for the GED® Social Studies Test. Keep in mind, however, that on the Social Studies Test, the emphasis is not on number-crunching but rather on the following skills:

- Understanding what the graphical display is intended to show

- Reading and interpreting the data

- Understanding the significance of the data

- Drawing general conclusions from the data

Though you may need to perform simple arithmetic tasks such as counting or adding, you won't need to calculate precise percents, ratios, or averages. (These skills are measured on the Mathematics Test instead.)

The next two GED®-style questions are based on the same picture graph and illustrate that the focus of data-display questions on the Social Studies Test is far more on understanding and interpreting graphs in a Social Studies context than on applying math.

QUESTIONS 16 AND 17 REFER TO THE FOLLOWING GRAPHS.

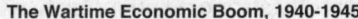

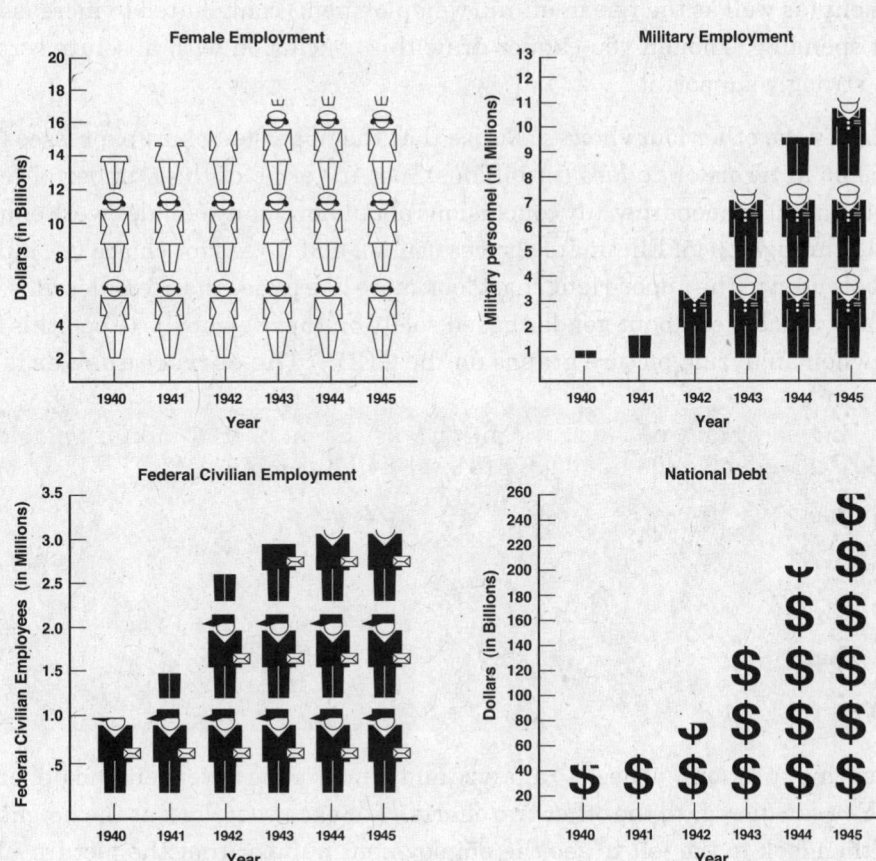

16. What conclusion can you draw from the information presented in the charts?

From 1940 through 1945

(1) the employment rate among males was greater than among females

(2) all of the U.S. military personnel were males

(3) a rise in federal civilian employment contributed to increased government spending

(4) the greatest increase in employment was among females

(5) the national debt increased mainly due to the number of women who went to work

Focusing on choice (3), the upper-right and lower-left charts show that military employment and federal civilian employment both rose over the course of the war. The lower-right chart shows that government *debt* rose over the course of the war. Together, the three charts strongly support the inference that the rise in federal civilian employment (as well as the rise in military employment) contributed to increased government spending. Though you cannot draw this conclusion with absolute certainty, the data strongly support it.

Now consider the other four choices. Notice that the upper-left chart expresses female employment in terms of *dollars* (in billions), not in terms of the number of females employed. So you cannot draw any conclusions about how many females were employed from 1940 through 1945. Eliminate choices (1), (4), and (5). As for choice (2), although the symbols used in the upper-right chart look more like males than females, it is unfair to draw any conclusion about gender based solely on these symbols. (Keep this lesson in mind when analyzing picture graphs on the GED®.) **The correct answer is (3).**

17. During how many of the years shown was the number of military employees more than double the number of federal civilian employees?

(1) one

(2) two

(3) three

(4) four

(5) five

To answer this question you need to analyze and compare the lower-left and upper-right charts. (You can disregard the other two charts.) For each year, look at the height of the picture, then look to the left to see the employment number that the picture's height represents. Start with the year 1940. Notice that federal civilian employees (lower-left chart) and the number of military employees (upper-right chart) both numbered about 1.0 million. The second number is *not* more than twice the first number. Perform a similar analysis for each subsequent year (notice that approximating the numbers will suffice, and that very little math is involved):

1941: 2.0 million (military employment) is *not* more than twice 1.5 million (federal civilian employment).

1942: 3.5 million (military employment) is *not* more than twice 2.6 million (federal civilian employment).

1943: 8.0 million (military employment) is more than twice 3.0 million (federal civilian employment).

1944: 10.5 million (military employment) is more than twice 3.2 million (federal civilian employment).

1945: 12.0 million (military employment) is more than twice 3.3 million (federal civilian employment).

As you can see, during three of the six years, military employment was more than double federal civilian employment. **The correct answer is (3).**

GENERAL TEST-TAKING STRATEGIES

Here are some general strategies for tackling the GED® Social Studies Test. These points of advice generally apply to all types of questions. Put these strategies to work on the Practice Tests in this book, and then review them again just before exam day.

First, read the question(s) based on a passage of text or visual depiction.

Before you look at a visual or read even a brief passage, read the question stem (the question itself, but not the answer choices). If the passage or visual comes with more than one question, read all the question stems first. This task should only take 10 to 15 seconds. The question(s) may provide clues as to what you should focus on and think about as you read the text or analyze the visual.

Read a passage of text straight through before answering any questions based on it.

If a question or group of questions refers to a passage of text, read the passage from beginning to end without interruption. Pay careful attention to how the ideas connect together. Think about what the overall message, or main idea, of the text is. Also think about whether the ideas lead naturally to any conclusion or inference. If they do, the chances are good that the question(s) will focus on this feature.

Use your pencil as you read a longer passage.

Passages can run up to 150 words in length (about one fourth of a page)—long enough to merit taking pencil to paper and marking up the passages. Underline key words and phrases, and jot down notes in the margins. As with the Language Arts, Reading Test, using your pencil while you read helps you to think actively about what you're reading. It also helps you find information in the passage you need as you answer the question(s).

When reading charts, graphs, maps, and timelines, don't get bogged down in every detail.

Some visual depictions will contain more information than you'll need to answer the question(s) based on them. In fact, one of the skills you're being tested on is your ability to sort through that information to determine what is relevant (and what is not relevant) to the question at hand. So don't waste time analyzing every detail in a visual. Instead, focus your attention on what the question asks about.

Read any title or caption accompanying a map, chart, graph, or cartoon.

Many times, the title or caption will give you a clue about the true meaning of the visual. You can then use this clue to help clarify the question and eliminate incorrect answers.

Apply common sense.

Many questions, especially about economics and geography, may be unfamiliar to you at first glance. However, remember that you use and make decisions concerning economics and geography every day. Use your real-life, practical economics and geography skills to help you on the test.

If possible, formulate your own answer to a question before reading the answer choices.

For each question, try to formulate your own response to it, and *then* scan the choices for something resembling your home-grown answer. This technique will keep you from becoming confused and distracted by wrong answer choices.

Pace yourself properly.

You're allowed 70 minutes to answer all fifty questions. GED® Social Studies questions are not presented in any set order of difficulty. So after 30 minutes, you should have answered at least twenty-two or twenty-three questions, and after 60 minutes you should have answered at least forty-four or forty-five of the questions. If you're falling behind, pick up the pace. In any event, try to answer all fifty questions with at least 5 minutes to spare, so you can go back and reconsider any responses you were unsure about.

SUMMING IT UP

- GED® Social Studies Test questions test your knowledge of important principles, concepts, events, and relationships.

- The Social Studies Test contains fifty multiple-choice questions, and each question lists five choices. Most questions are based on brief passages of text, which vary in length from a few sentences to as many as 150 words (about a quarter of a page). A question involving a passage of text might refer to it either as a "passage" or as "information" or "text." Other questions are based on maps, charts, cartoons, diagrams, and other visual depictions. Some visual depictions are also accompanied by a brief passage of text.

- The questions cover U.S. (or Canadian*) history, world history, civics and government, economics, and geography. (*The Canadian version of the GED® contains questions about Canadian history instead of U.S. history.)

- The GED® Social Studies Test is not a knowledge test—all the information you will need to answer a question will be provided. You will need to demonstrate that you can comprehend the material, draw inferences and conclusions, evaluate the information, and apply concepts and ideas to other situations.

- The best way to do well on this test is to read the front section of a major newspaper everyday, watch the news on TV, listen to serious discussions of current events on public radio, and think about current issues. It may also be helpful to go to your local library and look at the atlases, maps, and news magazines.

Social Studies Review

OVERVIEW

- **History**
- **Civics and government**
- **Economics**
- **Geography**
- **Historical documents on the GED® Social Studies Test**
- **Canadian History**
- **Summing it up**

The GED® Social Studies Test is designed to measure critical-thinking skills rather than knowledge. Nevertheless, with some prior familiarity with the four content areas covered on the test (history, civics and government, economics, and geography) you can expect to handle the questions with greater ease and confidence. The review materials in this part of the book are designed to help you in this respect. Keep in mind that this review is intended only to highlight the four content areas listed above. It is by no means intended to be a comprehensive examination of these areas.

Review questions are provided throughout this Social Studies review. As you answer them, keep in mind that the passages of text on which they are based are longer than those on the actual GED® Social Studies Test. To assist readers preparing for the GED® in Canada, sections focusing on Canadian history and government are included later in this review. Also later in the review are summaries of key U.S. historical documents covered on the Social Studies Test.

HISTORY

This history review begins at the very beginning of civilization. It then traces the development of Western civilization from its roots in the ancient empires of Europe through the European Middle Ages and Renaissance Era, and to the Age of Exploration that ultimately led to the founding of the thirteen British colonies. The review then focuses mainly on U.S. history, although some of that history is presented in the context of the world affairs and relations between the United States and other nations.

QUESTIONS 1 AND 2 ARE BASED ON THE FOLLOWING INFORMATION.

Beginnings and Early Civilizations

It is generally believed that at the start of the most recent Ice Age, which lasted from about 20,000 years ago until about 12,000 years ago, the world's entire human population numbered less than 1 million. Their existence revolved around hunting and gathering rather than growing plants or raising animals for food. Hunter-gatherer families belonged to larger groups of tribes. Though the cold temperatures of the Ice Age killed off some tribes, others moved toward the equator, seeking warmer temperatures. Yet, at the end of the Ice Age humans were finding life even more difficult. As temperatures and sea levels rose, Earth's plant and animal life dwindled. To survive, humans learned to control the development of various plant and animal species. By cultivating small plots of land through what is called *horticulture,* human families could accumulate surplus food, and by breeding animals according to traits they found desirable, they could cultivate a predictable source of meat and other animal products.

Around 4500 BCE, *agriculture* began making rapid inroads in five areas worldwide. These five areas are sometimes called cultural hearths because of their role in establishing both culture and civilization in their regions of the world. Four of these areas came into existence in river valleys. One area was Egypt, in which the Nile River became a garden country quite early. The second region was Mesopotamia, located in the Tigris and Euphrates river valley. The third area was the Indus River valley in India, and the fourth area was in China. The fifth region was Mesoamerica, or what is now southern Mexico and Central America. This area followed a substantially different pattern from the other four. It had no vast river systems in which to build elaborate agricultural systems. Here, agriculture grew out of horticulture, as the gardens needed to sustain the local populations that became larger and larger.

Known as the ancient Near East, the areas of Egypt and Mesopotamia are considered to be the cradle of Western civilization. The people of the Near East were the first to practice intensive year-round agriculture. They produced the first writing system, invented the potter's wheel and then the vehicular and mill wheels, and created the first centralized governments, law codes, and empires. The people of the Near East also introduced social stratification, slavery, and organized warfare, and they laid the foundation for the fields of astronomy and mathematics.

Between 5000 BCE and 500 BCE, the Near East was home to successive waves of cultures, borrowing from and cooperating with one another for resources, ideas, and culture as well as competing with one another militarily for land and prestige. The Near East is where the first cities appeared. Near the confluence of the Tigris and Euphrates Rivers, several city-states competed for land, power, and prestige while fending off barbarians. These city-states became the ancient Greece of the region, providing written language, architecture, religion, and cultural norms to the societies that followed. Babylon, located not far from modern-day Baghdad, was the first city-state to assemble a true kingdom around itself in Mesopotamia. The Babylonians used the waterways for communication and to control their wide empire that spread across the river valleys.

In the area of Greece, from around 3000 to 1100 BCE, the Minoan civilization inhabited the Aegean island of Crete, and, from around 1600 to 1100 BCE, the Mycenaean culture dominated the mainland. Mycenaean civilization began with the arrival of many tribes, which by around 1600 BCE had established themselves as political units. The Mycenaeans quite possibly lived under Minoan dominance until around 1400 BCE, when they conquered Crete. Sometime around 1100 BCE, the Dorian tribe from the north invaded and destroyed the Mycenaean civilization. Greece was subsequently thrown into a Dark Age, from which it took several centuries to recover. It was during the Dark Ages that the city-state began to develop.

Around the Nile River, even by 6000 BCE, advanced agricultural practices had developed, as did large-scale building construction. By about 3000 BCE, Egypt had become united as a kingdom under a single monarch, ushering in a thousand-year period of great order and stability. Protected from outside forces by impassible desert, and immune to change because of the orderly, predictable nature of life, Egypt thrived and advanced in all aspects of culture—from religion and art to language, customs, and overall quality of life. It was during this time that the Egyptian dynasties erected the pyramids as monuments to their god-kings. By around 1500 BCE, Egypt had risen to become an international power, solidifying its power on a regional scale.

1. Which was a direct consequence of the last Ice Age, which ended around 12,000 years ago?

   (1) an age of barbarism, without order or rule of law

   (2) the domestication of animals

   (3) movement of human populations to colder climates

   (4) the formation of the great rivers of the Near East

   (5) the development of the city-state

The warming trend that followed the Ice Age destroyed much of the plant and animal life that the hunter-gatherer humans had relied on for food. To survive, humans developed ways to ensure their food supply. It was during this period that humans first began cultivating plants and breeding animals. **The correct answer is (2).**

2. Which did NOT contribute to the development of civilization in Mesopotamia and ancient Egypt?

   (1) the location of great rivers

   (2) political control by dynastic monarchies

   (3) geographic barriers against enemy invasions

   (4) the rise of the democratic state

   (5) innovations in agriculture

These ancient civilizations developed around great rivers because the rivers provided water needed for large-scale agriculture, answer choices (1) and (5). In Egypt, a stable monarchy and a vast desert to protect against invaders helped the culture thrive and advance, answer choices (2) and (3). The rise of the democratic state did not occur until later, in Greece. **The correct answer is (4).**

QUESTIONS 3 AND 4 ARE BASED ON THE FOLLOWING INFORMATION.

Classical Traditions, Empires, and Religions

The classical civilizations (roughly the first millennium BCE) differed from earlier civilizations in that their basic need for water and food was met. Freed from a preoccupation with mere survival, civilizations of this period could devote more attention to the arts, architecture, religion, and philosophy and to developing systems of law and government that divided decision-making power. They could also turn their attention outward—toward overseas trade and toward expanding their territories by military force.

The Rise of Rome

By the beginning of the ninth century BCE, the seven hills that rose from the marshy land along the Tiber River's eastern shore were occupied by people in village communities who kept farms in the low-lying areas and retreated to their hilltops for defense. Once the seven villages united, they constructed a wall around their territory and began charging a toll for the use of a ford (and later the bridge) across the marshy lowland. This toll was to prove an early source of Rome's wealth. The city of Rome itself was founded sometime between 850 and 700 BCE. It remained a minor town for a hundred years or so, until the Etruscans—a confederation of towns to the north—took over the city relatively peacefully around 640 BCE. A series of kings governed the town for more than a century thereafter. In 509 BCE, the Romans expelled their king and established a Republic that ruled Rome for the next four centuries. The Republic was in essence a broad oligarchy, with the city's aristocrats dominating politics, economics and social life. The Romans developed effective military and foreign policies, which enabled them to conquer Italy, and then, between 394 and 290 BCE, to engage in three wars with another early superpower, Carthage, for control of the western Mediterranean Sea.

The Emergence of Classical Greece from its Dark Ages

Little is known with certainty about ancient Greece during its Dark Age, since the Dorian tribes, who had destroyed and replaced the Mycenaean civilization, had no written language. They were a warring people, who devoted themselves instead to developing tools for battle. (They replaced bronze with the lighter material iron for weaponry and armor, thereby ushering in the Iron Age.) During the Dark Age, the region was a collection of warring city-states called *poleis* (singular: *polis*). Two of the more important poleis were Athens and Sparta, which spoke different dialects of Greek and had different cultural bases and histories. Ultimately, these differences expressed themselves in distinct forms of government. (Athens is credited with creating democracy: equal rule by all citizens.)

Despite their warring ways and the mountains that separated them, the various independent poleis of ancient Greece developed commonalities in culture, language, religion, and government. It was during this time period that Greeks began to identify themselves and each other as *Hellenes*. In spite of their rivalries, they became culturally united. Contributing to this sense of loose unity were the Olympic Games, which began in 776 BCE and featured athletes from the various poleis who competed against one another as a religious ritual. Eventually, around 600 BCE, Greece's Dark Age came to an end, and what followed was an explosive surge of Greek culture.

Classical Greek culture held a distinct set of ideals concerning beauty, life, and the world in general. During the classical era, Greek playwrights and poets came to express the harsh realities of the human condition through various gods and goddesses. The Greek ideals found physical expression in architecture and art that emphasized simplicity and realism. Greek scholars established a study of history emphasizing a communal identity among humankind. And philosophers laid the groundwork for modern ideas of government, law, and justice, which emphasized reason, intellectual inquiry, and the pursuit of wisdom over superstition and religion.

While flourishing culturally, the Greek poleis lost interest in maintaining a strong and unified military. The Greek independent city-states and loose confederations were no match against Philip of Macedon or his son Alexander the Great. They also were inferior against the rising power of Rome, which, under its generals, would eventually come to conquer Greece. But the Romans would come to adapt the classical Greek culture, keeping it alive.

The Decline and Fall of Egypt

Drought, famine, and the rise of an aristocracy helped bring about the end of the Old Kingdom of dynastic rule in Egypt and usher in a period of new prosperity, in which nobles and ordinary citizens began to share in Egypt's wealth. The appearance of foreign invaders, the Hyksos, also changed and renewed Egyptian culture. The resurgence of Egyptian power after the pharaohs of the Sixteenth Dynasty drove out the Hyksos and led to Egyptian imperialism and major building programs that proclaimed the might of the pharaohs and the gods who watched over them.

However, new ideas in religion and political changes in the wider world tended to limit Egyptian power in unexpected ways. Successive waves of invasion made Egypt a land of outward-looking leadership and inward-looking commoners, and it widened the divide between governors and those governed. Egypt became the breadbasket of two successive empires, but the very nature of its wealth—in agriculture and critical products—made it a tempting target to Persian and Islamized Arab alike. At the same time, lacking in other material resources it needed (particularly iron and straight timber), Egypt had no choice but to import these items, thereby depleting its wealth and losing control of the Africa-Asia trade routes. Regular conflicts with other states sapped Egypt's military resources. Eventually, in the 6th century BCE, Egypt fell to the Second Babylonian Empire. The Persians added Egypt to their empire in the fifth century BCE, Alexander the Great conquered Egypt in the third century BCE, and then Julius Caesar and Octavian Augustus Caesar annexed Egypt for the Roman Empire in the first century BCE Egypt would not achieve independence from outside forces until the seventh century CE.

3. The origins of the Roman Empire can be traced to which of the following?

  (1) the Dorian conquest of a small village in Italy

  (2) the distinctive geography of the city of Rome

  (3) an invasion by an Egyptian pharaoh

  (4) a great volcanic eruption

  (5) Rome's control of the world's gold supply

Rome's village communities could keep farms in the low-lying areas along the Tiber River's eastern shore while retreating to their hilltops for defense. Moreover, once they united and constructed a bridge across the marshy lowland, they began to amass wealth by charging a toll for accessing the mountains from the river. **The correct answer is (2).**

4. A student of classical Greek literature would most likely read which of the following sorts of works?

  (1) a poem about the fall of the Roman Empire

  (2) a battle tale written by a Dorian warrior

  (3) a philosophical essay about the meaning of life

  (4) a ballad once sung by traveling troubadours throughout Europe

  (5) a diary of a sea captain recounting his voyage to the New World

Classical Greek literature includes philosophical works by Plato, Socrates, Aristotle, and their contemporaries about life's larger questions. **The correct answer is (3).**

QUESTIONS 5 AND 6 REFER TO THE FOLLOWING INFORMATION.

The Middle Ages, Growing Trade, The Renaissance, and The First Global Age

After the fall of the Roman Empire, Europe entered what is commonly called the Middle Ages (or medieval period), a transition period between the classical age and the Renaissance—from roughly AD 500–1450. In Northern Europe, this was a relatively "uncivilized" period. At the same time, however, globalization in the form of international trade was taking hold. Africa's trans-Sahara route, the Indian Ocean, and the Silk Route connecting Western Europe with China were the most significant trade routes of the Middle Ages. Later, trade expanded to the New World, after European explorers sought a new route to India but found America instead.

The Roman Empire

The early centuries of the Roman republic heralded its rise to prominence in the Italian peninsula. The tiny city-state was blessed with adept leadership and had little trouble conquering or allying with all the southern Italian city-states. The empire then expanded east. It conquered Greece and united the political structures, religions, and intellectual and technological achievements of the two civilizations.

As the Empire grew even farther, it became difficult to govern, despite its excellent road systems. Barbarian invasions were only the catalyst that brought the gradual end of the empire. Over the centuries, the costs of maintaining a large military grew greatly. Extravagances at home depressed the economy, while various epidemics and a series of poor harvests across the empire weakened the Empire further. The fall of the Roman Empire was a gradual one; some regions considered themselves a part of the empire up to the early eighth century. In fact, the Byzantium or Eastern Roman Empire survived to the mid-fifteenth century.

The Dark Ages and the Rise of the Germanic Kingdoms

The period between the fall of the Roman Empire and AD 1100, commonly known as the European Dark Ages, was a relatively obscure period characterized by barbarism and political fragmentation. As this age was marked by the inhibition of learning and intellectual development, its people typically came to understand life's events and the natural world in simplistic terms—as either the work of God or the devil.

During the Dark Ages, the Germanic tribes supplanted the Roman Empire as the dominate force in Europe. The most significant of these forces was the Frankish Empire. Charlemagne, the greatest of the Frankish kings, expanded the Frankish Empire to northern Italy and Spain as well as to parts of Germany. Charlemagne's empire did not last long after his death, however. His son lost land to Muslims in the south, Slavs to the east, and the Vikings in the north.

The Vikings, or Norse, were Germanic Scandinavian seafarers who raided and settled many regions of Northern Europe during the ninth, tenth, and eleventh centuries. Denmark and Scandinavia had existed well outside the borders of the Roman Empire. By the end of the eighth century, the region contained many small tribal kingdoms. Farming and fishing accounted for most of the economy. Growing populations and limited fertile land were probably the reason for the Norse movement to find new homes across the sea. Norse settlers founded communities and maintained important trade routes from Greenland east to the heart of Russia, and they developed a fearsome reputation as warriors and plunderers. Their descendants played crucial roles in the later history of France, England, Ireland, and the Russian principalities, and they were the first Europeans to visit and settle in North America.

The High Middle Ages and the Feudal System

The High Middle Ages generally refers to the period between the Dark Ages and the Renaissance, from about AD 1100–1450. The dominant politico-economic system of this period was the feudal system. Under feudalism, the nobility (the lords) held lands from the Crown in exchange for military support, while members of the peasantry were allowed to live on their lord's land in exchange for labor or a share of their produce.

Religion was the most important force in Europe during both the Dark Ages and the High Middle Ages. This period saw the rise of monasticism, whereby men who became monks isolated themselves from the world and provided service to the church by copying manuscripts, creating art, educating people, and working as missionaries; and women who became nuns or sisters could receive an education and escape unwanted marriage. The two largest orders of monks were the Franciscans, founded by Francis of Assisi and known for their charitable work, and the Dominicans, founded by St. Dominic, who focused on teaching, preaching, and suppressing heresy. The Pope, through the church, was as powerful as any nation—perhaps more powerful than most. The ultimate display of power by the medieval papacy was the Crusades, a series of military expeditions to recover the Holy Land (Jerusalem) from the Saracen Muslims. Though no fewer than twelve Crusades took place altogether, from 1096 to 1272, they were largely unsuccessful, having been poorly organized and carried out. In the end, the Holy Land was left to the Muslims.

The European Renaissance

During the mid-fourteenth century, a renewed interest in Greek and Roman ideas from the classical period grew into what is called the Renaissance era. This movement started in the Italian city-states, which had amassed great wealth from trade with the East and had superior access to the ancient documents and artifacts of Greece and Rome. The wealthy Italians who fueled the Renaissance, such as the Medici family, considered the medieval period an unfortunate break in a tradition that they sought to renew in all aspects of life, whether politics, the sciences, or the arts.

Whereas the focus of medieval life had been on community and religion, mainly for the sake of comfort and survival during that harsh period, the Renaissance saw the rise of individualism and a focus on human nature rather than God. This significant shift manifested itself in every aspect of thought and expression.

The Renaissance soon spread to Northern Europe, where it took a distinctly different turn. There, religious scholars sympathetic to the Greek ideas of individualism began to question the empty rituals, piety, and morality of the Roman Catholic Church. These Christian humanists advocated a simpler religion that was more accessible to individuals on a personal level. The eventual result was the Protestant Reformation, marking a permanent schism within the Church.

Exploration of the New World

Beginning in the late fourteenth century, European explorers embarked on a series of expeditions of discovery and conquest. Their goals were to amass great wealth by conquering indigenous peoples, to bring fame to their monarchs and themselves for their daring exploits, and to bring Christianity to the regions that they explored and exploited. The first explorers were motivated by fabulous tales from the Orient brought back by Marco Polo and other Italian traders, and especially by the valuable products they brought with them, such as spices, silk, gold, and silver. Portugal's Prince Henry sought a sea route to India around Africa, so Portuguese traders could bypass the Italian middlemen who had monopolized the Oriental luxury trade. Under his direction, Portuguese explorers explored much of the African coast and established profitable trading posts in the Niger delta and farther south in Angola. Eventually, Portuguese explorers reached Southern India's trading cities. Within a mere fifty years, Portugal essentially controlled the Indian Ocean, with strategically located trading posts and naval military might.

While Portugal set its sights on dominating the Indian Ocean, Spain also began to explore and seek colonies. **Christopher Columbus,** an enterprising Italian merchant with sailing experience on Portuguese trade vessels in the Indian Ocean, attempted to voyage across the Atlantic to India and break the Portuguese trade monopoly. Columbus landed in the Bahamas, and not in India, though he thought he had reached India.

http://bit.ly/hippo_his96

By the end of the fifteenth century, Spain and Portugal dominated trade and territories in Asia and the Americas. Portugal controlled most of the Indian Ocean trade, as well as the spice plantations in Indonesia, while Spain controlled extensive parts of Central and South America. Fearing a war between the two rivals, the Pope helped negotiate the Treaty of Tordesillas, which essentially divided the world in half, with both countries receiving exclusive rights in their respective hemispheres. England, France, and the Netherlands refused to comply with the Treaty of Tordesillas and began to explore and establish their own colonies in the Americas.

http://bit.ly/hippo_his2

France founded colonies in much of eastern North America, on a number of Caribbean islands, and in South America, primarily as trading posts for exporting products such as fish, sugar, and furs. Through the explorers Cartier and Champlain, France established a fur trading post in 1608 that would grow into the city of Quebec. Extending their reach, the French claimed a large territory in Canada and the Great Lakes region. Then "New France" grew west of the Great Lakes into Wisconsin and south to the Gulf of Mexico. In 1682, the entire Mississippi River watershed was claimed for France. Named Lousiane, it gave France control of the Mississippi Valley and the Great Plains in addition to its holdings in the Great Lakes and Canada.

http://bit.ly/hippo_his1

5. Which of the following did NOT characterize European medieval times?

   (1) invasions by the Norse

   (2) artistic freedom

   (3) plagues and famines

   (4) monasticism

   (5) strict obedience to the Church

Artistic expression flourished during the European Renaissance, which followed the medieval period. This renewal of free thought and expression was fostered by wealthy art patrons who sought to make up for previous centuries, during which artistic expression had been suppressed as well as neglected in the interest of mere survival. **The correct answer is (2).**

6. The European explorers of the fourteenth and fifteenth centuries were motivated by all of the following with the possible exception of which one?

(1) converting native peoples to their religion

(2) acquiring new land for their countries

(3) the possibility of personal fame

(4) Papal proclamations to go forth and explore

(5) the possibility of personal fortune

European explorers were enlisted and supported in their explorations by their monarchs. They were not following any directives from the Pope. **The correct answer is (4).**

QUESTIONS 7 AND 8 REFER TO THE FOLLOWING INFORMATION.

The New World

By 1700, the Portuguese, Spanish, French, and British had all established colonies in the New World. In 1607, Jamestown, Virginia, became the first permanent British settlement in the New World. Jamestown and other settlements and colonies were created as joint-stock companies. Joint-stock companies were business ventures in which a large number of people invested small amounts of money. This allowed the investors to avoid the risk of losing huge sums of money. A total of thirteen British colonies appeared on the eastern coast of North America over the next 125 years, each with its own identity. The British sponsored the colonies and the journeys of the colonists because the British hoped to make vast amounts of trade revenue from trade with the colonies. The colonists

from England who sailed to the New World sought freedom of worship, a voice in their government, and a fresh start with land of their own. Some colonists, many of those in Georgia, for example, sought refuge from the law in the New World. By 1763, after an armed conflict with the French (known in the Americas as the French and Indian War and known in Europe as the Seven Years War), the British controlled a large portion of the North American continent. Unfortunately for those Native Americans who occupied the lands of North America before the arrival of the Europeans, colonization meant the end of many Native American cultures. Partly because of armed conflict and partly because of the introduction of European diseases into North America, the Europeans caused the death of many, many Native Americans.

Between the time of their arrival in the New World and the years prior to the War for American independence, the colonists developed their own ideas about the way the colonies should be governed. Consequently, many of the colonists disagreed with the way the British governed the colonies. Among these points of contention was the problem of taxation without representation. In other words, the colonists did not like the fact that they were being forced to pay increasing British taxes, but they were never allowed much, if any, say in the way the British governed the colonies. Many of the colonists also resented the presence of British troops throughout the colonies. These disagreements, among others, caused tension between the colonies and the British government and led to one of the most monumental events in history, the War for American Independence (also known as the American Revolution or Revolutionary War).

7. Why did the British sponsor expeditions and colonists in the New World?

   (1) The British population explosion forced the British to seek relief from high population density by sending some of its population elsewhere.

   (2) The British encouraged the expeditions and colonists so that the colonists could escape the widespread famine facing the British Isles.

   (3) The British wanted to establish colonies and find new goods to bolster the British economy.

   (4) The British government wanted to give the colonists an opportunity to experiment with new religions.

   (5) The British government sent people to the New World who posed a threat to the stability of the British government.

The British saw the economic benefits of establishing colonies and supporting exploring expeditions based on the examples of the Spanish and Portuguese. **The correct answer is (3).**

8. What was the colonists' main point of contention with the British government?

   (1) taxation without being allowed a fair voice in the government of the colonies

   (2) the brutality of the British soldiers against the Native Americans

   (3) the high taxes on tea

   (4) the slow communications between the British government and the colonies

   (5) the lack of a constitutional government in the colonies

The colonists thought it was unfair that they paid taxes to the British government yet had no say in the way they were governed by the British. **The correct answer is (1).**

QUESTIONS 9 AND 10 ARE BASED ON THE FOLLOWING INFORMATION.

The Struggle for American Independence

Between 1765 and 1776, the British imposed a number of taxes on the colonies that the colonists viewed as unfair. Some of the items taxed by the British included sugar, playing cards, newspapers, and tea. In many cases, the colonists displayed their displeasure and anger by burning officials in effigy, tarring and feathering officials, and even throwing massive amounts of tea into harbors. In response, the British government tried to limit and control the trade of the

 http://bit.ly/hippo_his8

 http://bit.ly/hippo_his6

 http://bit.ly/hippo_his8

 http://bit.ly/hippo_his11

 http://bit.ly/hippo_his12

 http://bit.ly/hippo_his13

 http://bit.ly/hippo_his14

 http://bit.ly/hippo_his15

American colonies. In further attempts to keep the colonies from straying too far from British rule, the British attempted to reduce the power of the American lawmaking assemblies. To even further discourage protest, the British legislature would pass special bills targeting specific troublesome colonists for imprisonment and to strip them of their wealth, which was then given to the Crown.

After much debate within the colonies, the colonial leaders, with the support of many of the colonists, decided to cut ties with Great Britain and declare the independence of the colonies from British rule. Some of the colonists known as loyalists, however, did not want to break away from the mother country; they still felt a sense of duty and loyalty toward England. In 1776, the colonial leaders signed the **Declaration of Independence,** which officially declared that the colonies were no longer under British rule. The British refused to recognize the independence of the colonies. As a result, war broke out in the colonies between the American colonists and the British soldiers.

The colonists mustered an army made up of many militiamen, or citizen soldiers, and very few professional soldiers. The British, on the other hand, fielded an army of professionally trained soldiers along with a formidable navy. Although the revolutionary army was outnumbered and perhaps outclassed, they had a few advantages. The revolutionists had great leadership, they were fighting from a defensive position, and they passionately believed in the cause for which they fought. With the aid of the French, Dutch, and Spanish—all of whom were enemies of the British—the Americans won an improbable victory over the British and gained their independence. Interestingly, by the end of the war, the colonies were only a minor concern for the British as they were also in the midst of a global conflict, fighting against the nations of France, Holland, and Spain. Tired of war, American and British diplomats met in Paris and signed the **Treaty of Paris of 1783** in which Britain recognized the independence of the colonies. After the dust settled, the thirteen colonies stood loosely united as the United States of America.

---

9. From the Declaration of Independence: "The history of the present King of Great Britain is a history of repeated injuries and usurpations, all having in direct object the establishment of an absolute Tyranny over these States."

All of the following are "injuries and usurpations" to which the Declaration of Independence refers, EXCEPT which one?

(1) unfair taxation

(2) controlling trade

(3) limiting lawmaking authority

(4) imprisoning protesters

(5) prohibiting public assembly

The British engaged in the activities described in choices (1) through (4). However, they did not prohibit public assembly. **The correct answer is (5).**

10. Which of the following conclusions can be drawn concerning the War for American Independence?

  (1) The Americans might not have won the war without the aid of foreign countries.

  (2) The British would have lost the colonies in America even if the French and Spanish had not declared war on the British.

  (3) The emotional attachment the Americans had to their homes played little or no role in the defeat of the British.

  (4) Every colonist wanted independence from British rule.

  (5) Almost no colonists wanted independence from British rule.

If France, Spain, and Holland had not supplied money and supplies, and if these countries had not declared war on the British, the colonies might have lost the war and remained under British control. **The correct answer is (1).**

QUESTIONS 11 AND 12 REFER TO THE FOLLOWING INFORMATION.

The Early U.S. Government

Over the next several years, the states worked hard to settle their differences and agree on a system of government that best suited all of the states. Since 1781, the colonies had operated under the **Articles of Confederation,** the first constitution of the United States. Under the Articles, the colonies were united as a loose union of states, the Congress held the majority of the political power, and there was no executive branch of the government. The entire national government was weak. In 1787, leaders from each of the states met at the Constitutional Convention and outlined a plan for a new government. Some argued for a weak central government that was unlike the British government, while others argued for a very strong central government. Eventually the states compromised. The resulting plan was the **U.S. Constitution.** Eventually, all of the states ratified, or approved, the Constitution, or plan of government; it became the official plan of government in 1789. In 1791, the United States adopted ten amendments, or changes, to the Constitution. These changes, known as the **Bill of Rights,** protected the rights of individuals.

About the same time, the nation's first political parties were forming as a result of disagreements over the proper political and financial policies for the new nation. The two parties that emerged were the **Federalists** and the **Republicans.** The Federalists, who were led by the wealthy and educated, sought a strong central government steered by the elite. The Republicans, on the other hand, believed in the ability of the common people to govern themselves. Republican leaders like James Madison and Thomas Jefferson wanted to limit the powers of the federal government and protect states' rights. The two parties also differed in the area of foreign policy. The Republicans supported the French Revolution while the Federalists thought that the French Revolution was a terrifying act against an established government. Disputes between the Federalists and the Republicans reached new heights in the election of 1800. The Republican candidate Thomas

 http://bit.ly/hippo_his16

 http://bit.ly/hippo_his17

http://bit.ly/hippo_his18

http://bit.ly/hippo_his20

 http://bit.ly/hippo_his22

Jefferson was elected President. This election showed that the American people believed in the power of the people to determine the course the country would take. The Federalists never won another presidential election.

11. Those opposed to a strong central government in the early days of the United States were concerned most about which of the following?

    (1) the possibility of the government becoming oppressive the way that King George had been to the colonists

    (2) the possibility that no good candidates could be found to run such a government

    (3) the possibility that the states could not agree on a leader for such a government

    (4) the idea that the states had to be a part of a single nation instead of each forming its own country

    (5) the idea of forming a country independent of British rule

Anti-Federalists did not want a government with the potential to oppress its constituents the way the king had done this to the colonists. **The correct answer is (1).**

12. Disagreement over the correct path for the new government to take resulted in which of the following?

    (1) the U.S. Civil War

    (2) the creation of the first two American political parties

    (3) the Bill of Rights

    (4) the French Revolution

    (5) the Articles of Confederation

There were two predominant ideas about the direction that the new government should go. The politicians chose sides, and those two sides became the Federalists and the Republicans. **The correct answer is (2).**

QUESTIONS 13 AND 14 REFER TO THE FOLLOWING INFORMATION.

U.S. Expansion and Growing Pains

One of the most important decisions Jefferson made as president was to expand westward. Jefferson acquired a huge amount of land known as the **Louisiana Purchase.** For a bargain price, Jefferson bought all the land between the Mississippi River in the east and the Rocky Mountains in the west, from the Gulf of Mexico in the south to the Canadian border in the north. For only $15 million, the United States doubled the size of its territory. Eventually, the United States would create fourteen more states in the land of the Louisiana Purchase. The

 http://bit.ly/hippo_his23

growing size of the United States helped earn international respect. The westward expansion of the United States was a difficult task. Settlers faced uncharted land, harsh climates, and Native Americans who did not welcome those who might drive them out of their homeland. Nevertheless, the Americans pressed onward and gradually adapted to life on the frontiers.

As the new nation continued to grow and become more self-sufficient, it struggled with policies concerning international trade. The United States passed legislation that hurt trade between the United States and Great Britain and France. The British took exception to this and responded with animosity. The British navy made it a common practice to stop American ships on the open seas, claiming that it was searching for deserters, those who had illegally left the British navy. Often the British captured Americans on these ships and forced them into the British navy. They also confiscated American ships and goods. These actions, along with reports of British aid to hostile Native Americans, moved Congress to declare war on the British. Known as the **War of 1812,** this conflict did not settle any of the issues that started it, but the United States emerged victorious.  The war brought the nation together and earned the United States respect in the eyes of many European countries. The period of time that followed the war was marked by further expansion, with the addition of Florida, and an increased American role in international diplomacy and politics. President Monroe issued  the **Monroe Doctrine** and declared that the United States would not allow any further European colonization or expansion in the Western Hemisphere. As the United States earned a reputation as an up-and-coming nation, it was able to increase its trade with other nations. This helped stimulate the country's  economy and that of each of the states. The northern states concentrated on manufacturing and production while the southern states focused on agriculture, or farming. The northern states, most of whose population was urban (in cities), became a society centered on industry and big business. The southern states,  most of whose population was rural (in the countryside), became a society centered on plantations and the production of crops such as cotton and sugar. Large plantations grew throughout the South and became the economic backbone of the southern economy. Although all the states maintained loyalty to the nation, the two regions were often very competitive. The two sections of the country competed for political power within the Congress and for the presidency. As a result of this competition, along with other major issues such as slavery, tensions between the North and the South grew.

In the West, the United States continued to expand by annexing Texas and Oregon.  The **annexation** of these two regions stirred great emotion. Adding Texas to the Union meant the addition of a slave territory. This possibility angered many in the North until the situation with Oregon developed. If the United States added Oregon, a non-slave territory, it could add Texas, a slave territory, and maintain equilibrium between the slave states and non-slave states. By 1846, both territories were added to the United States. However, Mexico went to war  with the United States over Texas. Eventually, the United States negotiated a treaty with Mexico that added California, New Mexico, and part of Arizona to U.S. holdings in exchange for $15 million. The issue of **slavery** moved front  and center again as both the North and the South argued over whether or not the new territories should allow slavery. In an attempt to divert or delay major problems between the North and the South, politicians passed legislation such as the **Compromise of 1850,** which made sure the number of free states and  slave states remained equal as new states were added to the nation. After 1850,

http://bit.ly/hippo_his35

some of the new territory prohibited slavery, while other territories permitted the settlement of slave owners and non-slave owners alike. The United States then passed fugitive slave laws that required runaway slaves to be returned to their owners. Then the Supreme Court issued the **Dred Scott decision,** which opened all new territories to slavery. The South felt that the North was trying to abolish slavery, an act the southern states saw as a violation of their state rights.

13. By what means was the majority of new territory added to the United States?

    (1) warfare

    (2) conspiracies

    (3) diplomacy

    (4) purchases

    (5) trade

Although some U.S. territory came after war, most land was purchased from other countries. The Louisiana Purchase is a good example of such a purchase. **The correct answer is (4).**

14. Which of the following was perhaps the MOST controversial issue surrounding new territories that were added to the United States?

Whether the new territory would

    (1) be rural or urban

    (2) be Federalist or Republican

    (3) be industrial or agricultural

    (4) be hostile or friendly to Native Americans

    (5) allow slavery or prohibit slavery

Slave states wanted all the new territory to be open to slavery, while non-slave states wanted slavery prohibited in the new territories. **The correct answer is (5).**

QUESTIONS 15 AND 16 REFER TO THE FOLLOWING INFORMATION.

The U.S. Civil War and Reconstruction

http://bit.ly/hippo_his36

In the presidential **election of 1860,** the issue of slavery came to a head. The southern Democrats split into two factions, or groups, and put forth two different candidates, each with different yet pro-slavery beliefs. The Republicans nominated Abraham Lincoln, a candidate who did not support the idea of slavery in the new territories. A fourth party put forth yet another candidate. With American votes scattered among the four candidates, Lincoln won the controversial election with less than 40 percent of the popular vote. After Lincoln won, South Carolina seceded, or withdrew, from the Union. Shortly thereafter, ten more southern states followed South Carolina and created the **Confederate States of America.** In order to save the Union, the North went to war in 1861 against the southern states that seceded.

 http://bit.ly/hippo_his37

Lincoln made it clear that he had no intention of allowing any state to secede from the Union. He called up troops from the remaining loyal states and went to war to preserve the Union. The South was at a disadvantage in the **Civil War** because it lacked the manufacturing power and transportation that the North had. In addition, most of the fighting was done in the South. After four years of bloody fighting, in what was often known as the War Between the States, the South surrendered. Slavery ended, and the United States survived. Although America suffered heavy casualties in both the North and the South, the war resolved two important issues. First, the authority of the nation took precedence over the states. Second, slavery was abolished throughout the United States.

 http://bit.ly/hippo_his38

 http://bit.ly/hippo_his39

Lincoln, thankful that the Union was still intact, intended to allow the southern states back into the Union with relatively easy terms. However, he was assassinated before he could put his plan into action. After Lincoln's death, a vindictive Congress initiated a period known as Reconstruction, during which time the South lived under very oppressive conditions. The Union had been saved, but the South harbored great resentment against the North for the harsh treatment it endured after the war. Many Southerners were especially resentful of having to allow African Americans to vote and hold public office. These feelings endured in the southern states for several generations after the war.

15. Which of the following statements is true?

(1) The South seceded from the Union because Southerners feared Reconstruction.

(2) The South seceded from the Union because of the issue of slavery.

(3) The South seceded from the Union because of the issue of slavery, its concern about states' rights, and other issues.

(4) The South seceded from the Union because the North threatened to take all political power away from the South.

(5) The South seceded from the Union because Southerners did not want Texas annexed.

The issues of slavery, states' rights, the threat of new free territories upsetting the equilibrium, and other issues all played a part in the South's secession. **The correct answer is (3).**

16. President Lincoln decided to go to war with the South for which of the following reasons?

   (1) to end slavery

   (2) to punish the South for having slaves

   (3) to confiscate its wealth

   (4) to preserve the Union

   (5) to win the election of 1860

Lincoln refused to allow the nation to be dissolved over any issue, so he sent troops into the South to prevent them from leaving the Union. **The correct answer is (4).**

QUESTIONS 17 AND 18 REFER TO THE FOLLOWING INFORMATION.

Industrialization

 http://bit.ly/hippo_his26

In the late 1800s, the United States followed the lead of Europe and began moving toward **industrialization.** The number of factories and manufacturing plants across the country increased, and big business became a way of life for many Americans. Inventions made life easier and businesses more efficient. The cities grew as rural people flocked to the cities to find work in the factories. American citizens were not the only people who benefited from the industrialization of America. People rushed to the United States from all over the world in search of the jobs offered by the factories. Others left their homes abroad and rushed to the United States to receive free land that the government was giving away in the West. The concept of **Manifest Destiny** inspired Americans to expand westward all the way to the Pacific Ocean, and Americans did just that.

 http://bit.ly/hippo_his30

 http://bit.ly/hippo_his43

Railroads sprawled across the country and provided better transportation for goods and people. The construction of railroads was given special attention by the U.S. government. The government granted huge tracts of land to railroad companies and offered special loans to the railroad companies. The economy boomed, and businesses grew into corporations. Some corporations grew so large that they became monopolies; in other words, some companies were so large that they had no competition. Even though the government passed laws against monopolies, the laws were hardly enforced. Because business was so good, this era became known as the Gilded Age. However, scandal and **corruption** marked this era, too. The influence of big business and the incredible amounts of money that big business had at its disposal led many politicians to make secret arrangements with companies and individuals or to overlook certain violations. President Grant's administration was hit especially hard by scandal.

 http://bit.ly/hippo_his44

 http://bit.ly/hippo_his45

In the years that followed the Civil War, the government took a laissez-faire approach toward business and industry; in other words, the government let business and industry go along with little or no regulation. It seemed toward the end of the 1800s that the government was allowing many situations and problems to go untended. Eventually, the government began monitoring labor conditions and regulating big business. As scandals were discovered, Americans called for reform, or change. Reformers known as Progressives sparked sweeping reforms at the local, state, and national levels in the areas of business and labor.

During the late 1800s, labor issues and disputes between workers and employers prompted workers to form **labor unions.** The labor unions began in the first years after the Civil War, and by the end of the century, membership numbered nearly 1 million workers. The unions used their power to strike and bargain for better wages, better working conditions, and better benefits for their members. Unfortunately, some of the strikes were marked by violence.

 http://bit.ly/hippo_his46

Just before the turn of the century, the United States became involved in the **Spanish-American War** partly over issue of the liberation of Cuba and partly in retaliation for the sinking of an American ship in Cuba. Prompted by Yellow Journalism, or sensational exaggerated journalism, America went to war with Spain after an American ship was sunk in a Havana harbor. The United States won the war in a very short amount of time. As a result of victory in the war, the United States gained control over several foreign lands, including Guam, the Philippines, Puerto Rico, and Cuba. By gaining control of lands outside of North America, the United States had become an imperialist nation. American imperialism brought criticism from countries around the world and from politicians in the United States.

 http://bit.ly/hippo_his47

17. Manifest Destiny can be summed up in which of the following statements?

(1) The United States is destined to stretch from the Atlantic to the Pacific.

(2) The United States is destined to be covered in railroads.

(3) The United States is destined to open its doors to immigrants from other countries.

(4) The United States is destined to remove Native Americans from all land that it desires.

(5) The United States is destined to be the greatest industrial power in the world.

The idea of Manifest Destiny arose in the nineteenth century and suggested that the United States expand all the way to the Pacific Ocean in the West. **The correct answer is (1).**

18. Westward expansion benefited the most from which of the following?

(1) government-appointed labor

(2) government loans and grants of land

(3) clear maps provided by explorers

(4) slavery in the new U.S. territories

(5) reconstruction politics

The government provided land to railroad companies for laying track, and it also provided loans to finance the construction of the railroads. **The correct is answer is (2).**

QUESTIONS 19 AND 20 REFER TO THE FOLLOWING INFORMATION.

Twentieth-Century Turbulence and the Rise of the United States to Superpower Status

The beginning of the twentieth century saw more reform in many areas of life in the United States. Trusts, or combinations of companies that reduced competition, came under government scrutiny. Conditions in factories drew much attention, and the government responded by cleaning up unsanitary conditions. This made working conditions better for the factory and food-packing plant workers and made the products safer for consumers. The government set aside many acres of land for national parks and wildlife preserves. The United States also began construction of the **Panama Canal** to join the Atlantic and Pacific Oceans; this would allow ships to pass through the canal instead of rounding the entire South American continent.

During the early twentieth century, the United States devoted much time and energy to international diplomacy. The American policy of "Speak softly and carry a big stick" meant that the United States let its policies and intentions be known through diplomacy, and it backed that up with military action when needed. When World War I, or the Great War as it was known then, erupted in Europe, the United States faced a dilemma. President Wilson wanted to maintain **neutrality** in the war. However, after German **submarines** sank the *Lusitania*, a British passenger ship that contained 128 U.S. passengers, the United States entered the war on the side of the Triple Entente (Great Britain, France, and Russia). The United States tipped the scales in favor of the Triple Entente, and U.S. troops returned home victorious. At the conclusion of World War I, the United States led a failed attempt to establish the **League of Nations** as an international peacekeeping organization; the U.S. Congress refused to allow the United States to join, so the League proved ineffective.

In the years following the war, the United States enjoyed a period of terrific prosperity. Business and industry grew and expanded. Individuals invested heavily and spent large sums of money on things like sporting events, parties, movies, nightclubs, and other forms of entertainment. Politically, the United States implemented many new tariffs on imports to protect U.S. interests at home. The government began regulating public utilities and the rates they charged both businesses and consumers. The government used a Constitutional amendment to ban the production and sale of alcoholic beverages; this period was known as **Prohibition.** Another Constitutional amendment gave women the right to vote for the first time in the United States. Millions of immigrants flocked to the United States from war-torn Europe seeking new financial opportunities.

During this era of prosperity, many individuals purchased stocks by putting up a small percentage of the stock purchase price and borrowing the rest of the purchase price from the investor. This was a very risky investment strategy. Stock prices continued to rise and investors continued to borrow money to buy stocks. Then in 1929, the Stock Market crashed, and banks failed in the United States and in Europe. In other words, panicked investors began selling off their high-priced stocks at a feverish pace. The feeling of panic struck not only the United States

http://bit.ly/hippo_his48

http://bit.ly/hippo_his49
http://bit.ly/hippo_his50

http://bit.ly/hippo_his51

http://bit.ly/hippo_his52

http://bit.ly/hippo_his53

but also the rest of the world. By 1932, many banks had failed, factories closed, workers found themselves unemployed, and mortgages were foreclosed. Facing record unemployment and economic hardships, Americans elected **Franklin D. Roosevelt** as president in 1932. He instituted reforms and economic recovery programs in his **New Deal.** Roosevelt's New Deal programs included relief for businesses and individuals through new government agencies that put people to work doing public works projects. These measures, along with the onset of World War II, eventually led the United States out of the Great Depression.

On December 7, 1941, the Japanese attacked the U.S. military base at Pearl Harbor in Hawaii. Almost immediately, the United States entered **World War II** on the side of the Allies (Great Britain and the Union of Soviet Socialist Republics, or USSR) against the Axis Powers (Germany, Italy, and Japan). The massive war effort stimulated the economy and created millions of jobs for Americans. In 1945, after four years of fierce fighting against the Axis Powers in Europe and in the Pacific, President Harry Truman dropped two **atomic bombs** on Japan. Shortly thereafter the war ended, and the United States stood victorious alongside the other Allied Powers. The United States emerged from World War II not just as a legitimate world power but as a superpower. After the war, with the influence and leadership of the United States, world leaders divided Germany into different zones of influence, established the United Nations, and launched efforts to help rebuild war-torn nations. The United States joined the International Court of Justice, launched the National Security Council, and established the CIA or Central Intelligence Agency.

In the years that followed World War II, the United States found itself in an ideological disagreement with the **Soviet Union** and the Eastern Bloc, or eastern European nations under the influence of communism in the Soviet Union. The United States committed itself to stop the spread of communist ideas and eventually became the enemy of the Soviet Union and its allies. For years, the United States remained deadlocked in a Cold War, or a war of rhetoric and ill will, with the Soviet Union. The fear of nuclear holocaust and communism marked the next twenty-five years.

American troops did not stay home long after they returned from World War II. Only five years after World War II, American troops were deployed to South Korea to fight against the communist threat posed by the North Koreans in an undeclared war (**Korean War**) that ended with no real winner. Then in the 1960s, the United States deployed more troops to **Vietnam** in another controversial, undeclared war. The American troops were eventually brought home, and Vietnam fell to the communists. Each time the troops returned home from fighting in Korea and Vietnam, they had a difficult time readjusting to civilian life. The troops were not received as heroes the way World War II troops were, and many of the soldiers faced emotional problems as a result of their experiences abroad.

19. Why was the League of Nation formed after World War I?

It was formed to

(1) promote trade among nations

(2) prevent another world war

(3) pressure Germany into surrendering to the allied forces

(4) prevent the spread of Communism

(5) spread democracy throughout Europe

At the close of World War I, U.S. President Truman insisted that all countries signing the Treaty of Versailles agree to form the League of Nations for the purpose of keeping world peace through deterrence, so that another world war would not happen again. (The U.S. Congress, which under the Constitution must ratify all treaties that a U.S. President enters, refused to agree to U.S. membership in the League.) **The correct answer is (2).**

20. The Great Depression followed an era of which of the following?

(1) careful financial planning by individuals but not by businesses

(2) widespread corruption with the Savings and Loan corporations

(3) carefree lifestyles, risky investing, and poor financial management on the part of brokers

(4) world war

(5) industrialization

It was an era of carefree lifestyles, risky investing, and poor financial management on the part of brokers. Investors speculated wildly, and brokers unwisely issued credit to individuals who wanted to purchase large amounts of stocks. **The correct answer is (3).**

QUESTIONS 21 AND 22 REFER TO THE FOLLOWING INFORMATION.

The Late Twentieth Century and Contemporary Events

The 1950s were a tumultuous decade in the United States as many Americans reacted to the struggle for civil rights. In 1954, the Supreme Court desegregated schools in the landmark decision *Brown* v. *Board of Education of Topeka*. The civil rights movement built on that momentum. As people like Rosa Parks and Martin Luther King Jr. led the **civil rights movement** in a dignified and peaceful manner, groups like the Ku Klux Klan promoted violence against African Americans and those who fought for the rights of African Americans, and individuals like Arkansas Governor Faubus inhibited progress toward equal rights for American citizens. In 1957, Congress created the Civil Rights Commission, which investigated civil rights violations. As a result of the Commission's

http://bit.ly/hippo_his63

http://bit.ly/hippo_his64

investigations, the government appointed officials to safeguard the voting rights of African Americans.

The 1960s saw heightened tensions between the United States and the Soviet Union reach a boiling point during the **Cuban Missile Crisis.** The two world powers moved dangerously close to nuclear war as President Kennedy forced the Soviets to remove missiles from Cuba. Then, in 1963, to the horror of the nation, President Kennedy was assassinated. The rest of the decade was marked by domestic problems concerning the deployment of troops to Vietnam to fight communism. Many Americans disagreed with American involvement there, and they took to the streets in protest. The civil rights situation improved during the 1960s with the passage of the 24th Amendment, which eliminated the poll tax, and the **Voting Rights Act of 1965** that aided African Americans in the voting process. The 1960s ended with a cultural phenomenon known as Woodstock, a massive free concert in New York, where thousands of young Americans spent days reveling in drugs, sex, and rock and roll to forget about the problems that faced the nation.

 http://bit.ly/hippo_his97

 http://bit.ly/hippo_his66

 http://bit.ly/hippo_his65

Many Americans grew wary of the government as corrupt officials and oil shortages marked the 1970s. **President Nixon** resigned following a scandal in which several people were arrested for breaking into the Democratic National Headquarters. Nixon and his advisers knew about the break-in and about illegal wiretaps. In 1973, Vice President Spiro Agnew was indicted for tax evasion and bribery, further damaging citizens' trust in the government. The tension between the United States and the USSR declined in the 1970s in what became known as détente. Economically, the end of the 1970s brought further recession, an unfavorable balance of trade, high unemployment, and a very high rate of inflation.

 http://bit.ly/hippo_his67

 http://bit.ly/hippo_his68

In the 1980s, conservative Republican leadership under **President Ronald Reagan** pushed for less government and more military spending. The economy recovered, but the government's deficit spending caused national debt to spiral. U.S. relations with the Soviets grew tense again as the United States unveiled its "Star Wars" program, a missile defense system. At the end of the decade, U.S. and Soviet leaders agreed to reduce and end existing stockpiles of weapons.

 http://bit.ly/hippo_his69

During the 1990s, the United States enjoyed the end of the Cold War and celebrated the collapse of the Soviet Union. However, the 1990s also saw the liberal use of U.S. military power in many places around the world including Panama, Iraq, Bosnia, and Somalia. Eventually, the government cut military spending, along with some social programs, in an attempt to reduce the national debt. **President Bill Clinton**'s administration was marked by scandals as the millennium drew to a close.

 http://bit.ly/hippo_his70

The new millennium brought with it a presidential election unlike any that the United States had ever previously seen. By a very controversial margin of just a very few votes, **George W. Bush** defeated Al Gore. Less than a year later came the terrorist attacks on the Pentagon, the World Trade Center, and in Pennsylvania. In the immediate aftermath of the "9/11" event, the United States sent forces to Afghanistan to flush out Osama Bin Laden and his terrorist group. Shortly thereafter, the Bush administration convinced the U.S. Congress that in order to prevent further terrorist attacks on U.S. soil and to stem the development of nuclear weapons by dictator enemies, the United States should invade Iraq and topple Saddam Hussein's regime. In April 2003, the United States invaded Iraq, and in December of that year Hussein was finally captured.

 http://bit.ly/hippo_his71

The U.S. occupation of Iraq grew controversial over the next few years. Widely publicized abuses of Iraqi soldiers captured by U.S. forces and generous "no-bid" contracts given to U.S. companies loyal to the Bush administration brought the occupation under increasing scrutiny and criticism. In the meantime, Osama bin Laden, the apparent mastermind of the 9/11 terrorist attacks, remained at large, and loose networks of terrorist organizations were proliferating throughout the Middle East, especially in Afghanistan. In November of 2008, Barack Obama was elected President, and by the close of the decade, the United States had begun to take affirmative steps to extricate the country from Iraq and return to a policy of diplomacy rather than unilateral military action against would-be enemy states—while at the same time increasing U.S. presence in Afghanistan for the purpose of defeating terrorist organizations that pose a threat to U.S. security.

On the economic front, the first decade of the new millennium saw federal economic policies that were decidedly favorable to big business. The Federal Reserve Bank lowered interest rates to historically low levels in order to bring the nation out of the recession that followed the "dot-com" era collapse and the events of September 2001. Low interest rates encouraged spending and borrowing, which stimulated economic growth. Nevertheless, real economic growth remained stagnant throughout the decade. The only growth to speak of occurred in the health-care, financial, and real-estate sectors. At the same time, true production declined. Traditional manufacturing jobs continued to move overseas, leaving middle-class Americans worse off economically at the end of the decade than when it began.

http://bit.ly/hippo_his72

At the same time, federally chartered banks were permitted to engage for the first time in high-risk, high-return leveraged investing. A combination of lax lending standards for home loans (mortgages), upon which many of the banks' investments hinged, and low interest rates created a debt "bubble" in which consumers and large businesses alike would ultimately be unable to repay their debts. By the end of 2008, the U.S. economy was on the verge of collapse—a collapse that was prevented only by a massive infusion of credit from the federal government to save the large commercial banks. As the decade came to a close, a home-foreclosure crisis and an escalating unemployment rate had left **President Barack Obama**'s administration little choice but to engage in a massive spending, or stimulus, campaign to create new jobs, bolster the manufacturing sector, help struggling homeowners, and reign in the imprudent investments and lending practices of previous years.

21. The 24th Amendment, which was ratified in 1964, outlawed the use of a tax as a precondition to voting in any federal election. Given the historical context in which the 24th Amendment became law, whose rights were advocates of the amendment most concerned with promoting?

(1) tax evaders

(2) unwed mothers

(3) convicted felons

(4) African Americans

(5) recent immigrants

It was during the 1960s that the struggle for civil rights on the part of African Americans came to a head, led by individuals such as Martin Luther King Jr. Poll taxes levied by certain Southern states had the effect of disenfranchising poor people, and in the South, that meant that a disproportionate number of African Americans were effectively denied the right to vote. **The correct answer is (4).**

22. What was responsible for the collapse of the Soviet Union in the late 1980s and early 1990s?

(1) an economic depression that resulted in a popular uprising

(2) civil war among its states

(3) overthrow of the central government by an Eastern European alliance

(4) the Soviet leader's decision that a democratic government would work better

(5) economic and military burdens that weakened the Soviet Union internally

By the mid-1980s, the centralized, or command, economy of the Soviet Union was becoming too burdensome and expensive to manage. At the same time, the Soviets were draining their resources fighting a losing war in Afghanistan. Ultimately, the Soviet Union collapsed under the weight of these burdens it had put on itself. **The correct answer is (5).**

CIVICS AND GOVERNMENT

Simply put, political science is the study of government, the methods of governing, and those who lead governments. As long as people have been organized into states, people have needed a government to maintain order. The form of government each society has used throughout history has depended on a number of factors including the size of the state and the traditions of the state. Many of the forms of government used throughout history, though, have been determined, directly affected, or influenced by the means the leader used to assume the leadership of a government. Although there are many different types of government, there are a few basic political systems in which all governments may be classified.

QUESTIONS 23 AND 24 REFER TO THE FOLLOWING INFORMATION.

Political Systems

One very old political system is **democracy.** Democracy means "rule by the people." In a democracy, the people make decisions in matters of government. Democracy dates back to ancient Greece and has changed only slightly since its birth so many years ago. There are two types of democracies that exist: a true democracy and a representative democracy. In a **true democracy,** also called a direct democracy or pure democracy, the people make all the decisions. A true democracy is only possible within a small geographic area, such as a small country or a small town, because a large area makes the exchange of information slow and inefficient. In a **representative democracy,** the people elect representatives to make decisions for them. A republic is a representative democracy. The United States is a good example of a representative democracy.

Another very old political system, even older than democracy, is a **monarchy.** Monarchy means "rule by monarch," which can be either a king or queen. In a monarchy, the right to rule is hereditary, meaning that the right is passed down through a king's or queen's family from generation to generation. There are a few types of monarchies that exist. An **absolute monarchy** is one in which the monarch controls every aspect of life within his or her kingdom. The absolute monarch controls every facet of economics, politics, diplomacy, and often religion and culture. Louis XIV of France was the epitome of an absolute monarch. A **constitutional monarchy,** such as Great Britain, is a monarchical government in which the power of the monarch is limited by a constitution or written laws.

Dictatorship is a third form of government. The ruler of a dictatorship, a dictator, has complete rule over his state. Often the dictator assumes control of the state after a military takeover of a government and then maintains control through military force. A dictator usually rules strictly and controls most aspects of the government, often to the point of being oppressive. Cuba under Fidel Castro and Iraq under Saddam Hussein are good examples of dictatorships.

A fourth political system is an **oligarchy.** Oligarchy means "rule by a few." The "few" often is a group of people who lead in the style of a dictator. This group is not a group that is elected. Rather, the group usually takes control in much the same way as a dictator, after a military takeover. Also like a dictator, an oligarchy maintains control with the military. If the group takes control after a revolution, the group is referred to as a junta. Ancient Sparta, a very militaristic society, maintained an oligarchy.

A form of government rarely seen anymore is an **aristocracy.** An aristocracy, ruled by aristocrats, is a system in which the best suited to rule have the power to rule. The best suited to rule, according to the aristocrats, are those who are of privileged birth and who are well educated. Usually aristocrats have great wealth and vast amounts of land. The American South before the Civil War could be considered an aristocracy.

23. The most efficient form of government in a time of crisis would most likely be which of the following?

    (1) dictatorship

    (2) oligarchy

    (3) democracy

    (4) aristocracy

    (5) monarchy

Because one person with total control of a government can make decisions much more quickly than any other kind of government, a dictatorship is the most efficient, especially in a time of war or other emergency. **The correct answer is (1).**

> **24.** Which of the following political systems allows citizens the most opportunities to participate in the political process?
>
> **(1)** dictatorship
>
> **(2)** oligarchy
>
> **(3)** democracy
>
> **(4)** aristocracy
>
> **(5)** monarchy

Democracy is the correct answer because this political system is built on the idea that the people should control the government. **The correct answer is (3).**

QUESTIONS 25 AND 26 REFER TO THE FOLLOWING INFORMATION.

THE U.S. GOVERNMENT

The U.S. government can be classified as a **republic,** an indirect democracy. The men who created the foundations of the U.S. government believed the government should be carefully laid out in a written plan, or constitution. According to the U.S. Constitution, the U.S. government is a **federal government.** In other words, the power and authority of the government is divided between the national government, state governments, and local governments. Each level of government has certain authority and responsibilities. Also, according to the Constitution, each level of government is split into three branches, each with separate duties. The three branches include the legislative branch, the executive branch, and the judicial branch. This is known as **separation of powers.** The founders of the United States deliberately divided all the power between the different levels and the different branches of government so that no one person or part of the government could assume too much power. In addition, the founders made sure that each branch of government had the authority to limit the power of the other two branches. This, too, was a preventive measure against any one branch becoming too powerful.

The Three Branches of Government

As you have already learned, the U.S. Constitution divides the government into three branches, each with its own responsibilities and duties. The **legislative branch** makes the laws, the **executive branch** enforces the laws, and the **judicial branch** interprets the laws. Let's examine each of the three branches more closely.

The Legislative Branch

According to Article I of the Constitution, the power to make laws belongs to the legislative branch of government. The word legislative means "law making," so

http://bit.ly/hippo_his73

the legislative branch of government is the one that makes laws. The legislature, or the law-making body, is the U.S. Congress. The U.S. Congress is known as a bicameral legislature. In other words, the Congress has two parts, or houses. These are the House of Representatives and the Senate. Although their powers are practically the same, the House of Representatives, sometimes referred to as the House, is the lower house, while the Senate is the upper house of the legislature. The legislators, or lawmakers, in the **House of Representatives** total 435. The representatives represent each of the fifty states, and the number of representatives from each state is based on a state's population. Each state is guaranteed at least one representative regardless of population. The representatives each represent a district within his or her home state. Representatives serve two-year terms of office, and all of the representatives are elected in their states every two years. In order to run for the office of U.S. Congressional Representative, a person must meet three criteria or qualifications. The candidate must

- be at least 25 years old.
- have been a U.S. citizen for at least seven years.
- live in the state he or she intends to represent.

There are no limits on the number of terms that a representative may serve.

http://bit.ly/hippo_his74

The **Senate** is slightly different from the House of Representatives. There are 100 senators in the Senate, 2 from every state regardless of how large or small a state's population. Senators serve six-year terms, and one third of the senators are elected every two years. In order to be a U.S. Senator, a candidate must meet some stricter requirements than those for a candidate for the House. A candidate for the U.S. Senate must

- be at least 30 years old.
- have been a citizen of the United States for at least nine years.
- be a resident of the state he or she intends to represent.

Currently there is no limit on the number of terms a senator may serve.

http://bit.ly/hippo_his75

As you just learned, the legislative branch of government makes laws. Let's look at exactly how the legislature creates a law. First, a legislator must present an idea for a potential law in the form of a **bill.** After the legislator—senator or representative—writes the bill, the bill goes to either the clerk of the House or the clerk of the Senate, where the bill receives a name and a number. From here, the bill travels to a committee. A committee is a small group of members of congress who specialize in a particular area of legislation. For example, the Armed Service Committee deals specifically with legislation concerning the U.S. armed forces. If the committee does not like the bill, it may "pigeonhole" it or "table" it by setting it aside and not dealing with it again. If this happens, the bill is said to have died in committee. If the committee likes the bill, it sends the bill to the House and Senate where the members of Congress debate the bill, make any changes they feel are necessary, and then vote on the bill. If either house votes against the bill, or defeats the bill, the bill dies. If majorities of both houses approve the bill, the bill goes before the entire Congress for a vote. If a majority of Congress approves the bill, it goes before the President for his approval. The President may sign the bill and make it law, or he can veto, or kill, the bill. However, another majority vote in Congress can override the veto and make the bill law. This process may seem slow and inefficient, but this slow process prevents the government from making any hasty decisions.

The Constitution grants Congress a number of powers that are clearly defined in the text of the Constitution. These powers are known as enumerated powers, expressed powers, or delegated powers. Some of these powers include the authority to tax and collect taxes from the American people, coin or print money, declare war on another country, borrow money, and maintain a proper national defense with an army and a navy. Some powers of Congress are limited to only one house or the other. For example, only the House can impeach, or bring formal charges against, the president, but only the Senate can hold a trial for the president. In addition, only the Senate can approve treaties with other countries. The Constitution granted Congress other unnamed powers through the elastic clause. The elastic clause allows Congress some amount of flexibility to deal with new issues that the founders could not foresee.

25. Which of the following may indicate that the Senate is the upper house of the U.S. legislature?

   (1) Senators must have graduate degrees.

   (2) Candidates must be lawyers before they can be elected to the Senate.

   (3) Requirements for senatorial candidates are a little more exclusive than requirements for those seeking a seat in the House.

   (4) There are fewer senators than there are representatives.

   (5) The Senate is located at a higher elevation than the House of Representatives.

The fact that senatorial candidates must meet more strict qualifications indicates that the founders of the United States wanted senators to be more qualified than representatives. This indicates that the Senate must have been held in higher regard at one point in history. **The correct answer is (3).**

26. Which of the following is a reason why California may have more influence than Alaska in the House of Representatives?

   (1) California covers a larger geographical region than Alaska.

   (2) California is located within the continental United States and Alaska is not.

   (3) Alaska has not been a part of the United States as long as California.

   (4) California has more experienced representatives than Alaska.

   (5) California has a larger population than Alaska.

Seats in the House are appropriated to states according to population. If a state has more representatives than another state, it likely also has more influence than that state. **The correct answer is (5).**

QUESTIONS 27 AND 28 REFER TO THE FOLLOWING INFORMATION.

The Executive Branch

Article II of the Constitution lays forth the powers of the executive branch of government. It is the responsibility of the executive branch to see that the laws of the land are carried out or enforced. The head of the executive branch is the President. Underneath the President are the Vice President and all the departments and agencies necessary to make sure that the country's laws are enforced and administered properly.

According to Article II, a candidate for president must meet only three qualifications or requirements. The presidential candidate must be

http://bit.ly/hippo_his76

- a native-born (not naturalized) citizen.
- at least 35 years of age.
- a resident of the United States for at least fourteen years.

Presidential elections are held every four years. Although the American people cast their votes for the President (and Vice President), the Electoral College actually elects the President. The Electoral College consists of electors from each state who cast their votes for presidential candidates one month after the popular election. Originally, no law set a limit on the number of terms, although George Washington suggested that no president serve more than two terms so as not to build and maintain too much power. The Twenty-second Amendment, ratified in 1951, set the term limit at two terms.

http://bit.ly/hippo_his77

The President serves in three major roles during his term in office. First, the President serves as the **Chief Executive.** As the Chief Executive, the President is responsible for making sure that all the laws of the land are carried out properly. Obviously, one man cannot carry out all the laws by himself. Therefore, the President must appoint officials to head executive agencies and departments to carry out and enforce the laws. The heads of the executive departments are members of the President's cabinet. The cabinet is the group of the President's closest advisers who offer advice to the President about issues within his or her department. Also, as Chief Executive, the President can issue executive orders. An executive order is a directive or command that has the weight of law but does not require approval of either the Congress or the Supreme Court. Most often, executive orders are issued during times of war, crisis, or emergency. Second, the President serves as the **Chief Diplomat.** As the Chief Diplomat, the President has the responsibility of appointing ambassadors, meeting and greeting foreign dignitaries, and making treaties. The Senate must approve any appointments or treaties, though. The third major role of the President is that of **Commander in Chief** of the military. Although the President cannot declare war, the President can deploy troops to foreign lands or activate troops here in the United States to help in times of emergency. Additionally, during war the President is the highest commander of all the U.S. armed forces.

In addition to these major responsibilities, the President also plays many smaller roles. As the legislative leader, the President often introduces legislation into Congress, influences the direction of legislation, and vetoes, or rejects, proposed legislation. As the party leader, the President promotes his political party, appoints leadership positions within the party, and endorses party candidates who are seeking election. As the judicial leader, the President appoints justices to the Supreme Court and other federal courts. Furthermore, the President may grant a pardon to someone convicted of a crime. Finally, as Chief of State, the President serves as a symbol of the American people. For example, the President may visit another country on behalf of the United States or issue a public statement on behalf of the United States.

The immediate assistant to the President is the **Vice President.** The Vice President is the only other member of the executive branch mentioned in Article II of the Constitution. If for some reason the President dies, leaves office, or becomes unable to carry out the Presidential duties, the Vice President becomes the new President. In 1947, Congress decided to lay out a plan for exactly who is next in line for the Presidency in the case of some emergency. After the Vice President, the Speaker of the House is next in line, followed by the President Pro Tempore of the Senate, the Secretary of State, Secretary of the Treasury, Secretary of Defense, the Attorney General, and the other cabinet members.

As you learned earlier, the President's closest advisers are the members of his **cabinet.** The cabinet members are the heads of the executive departments. Some of the departments include the following: Department of State, which carries out the nation's foreign policy; Department of the Treasury, which collects taxes and prints money; Department of Defense, which controls the U.S. armed forces; Department of Justice, which heads national law enforcement; and Department of Education, which guides and provides funding for the nation's schools. In all, there are fourteen cabinet positions. The cabinet members receive appointments from the President. Then, the cabinet members choose other worthy candidates to fill positions within the executive departments that they oversee.

 http://bit.ly/hippo_his78

The last part of the executive branch is the collection of agencies known as the executive agencies. Within each Executive Department, many smaller agencies exist. Some of these agencies, known as executive agencies, include the Central Intelligence Agency (CIA), the National Aeronautics and Space Administration (NASA), and the Environmental Protection Agency (EPA). Some of these agencies, including the Federal Reserve System and the National Labor Relations Board, are called regulatory commissions. Some agencies, such as the U.S. Postal Service, are government corporations.

27. Powers of the President include all EXCEPT which of the following?

   (1) the power to introduce legislation

   (2) the power to veto legislation

   (3) the power to send troops into a country

   (4) the power to declare war

   (5) the power to grant amnesty to a criminal

Only Congress can declare war on another country. **The correct answer is (4).**

28. Which of the following would be the responsibility of a cabinet member?

   (1) overriding an executive order

   (2) heading a department within the executive branch of government

   (3) declaring war

   (4) approving or rejecting a presidential appointment

   (5) making laws in his or her area of expertise

Each member of the cabinet heads one of the executive departments within the executive branch. **The correct answer is (2).**

QUESTIONS 29 AND 30 REFER TO THE FOLLOWING INFORMATION.

The Judicial Branch

 http://bit.ly/hippo_his81

 http://bit.ly/hippo_his79

 http://bit.ly/hippo_his80

The third branch of the U.S. government, outlined in Article III of the Constitution, is the judicial branch. The Constitution establishes the **Supreme Court** as the head of the judicial branch. The Supreme Court's main responsibility is to hear appealed cases from lower courts. However, the Supreme Court's other responsibility is to determine the constitutionality of the laws and actions of other branches of government and lower courts. This is the power of judicial review. The Supreme Court has 8 justices, or judges, who were appointed by the President, and a Chief Justice, also appointed by the President. Although the President can appoint anyone to be a Supreme Court justice, the Senate has the power to reject a President's nomination. The justices maintain their seats on the Supreme Court for life.

The Supreme Court has the authority to hear, or has jurisdiction over, both criminal and civil cases that have been appealed to the high court. Criminal cases are those dealing with crimes, while civil cases are those that deal with disputes between two or more parties. The Supreme Court has original jurisdiction over cases in which a foreign diplomat is involved or in which a state is involved. In other words, these two kinds of cases may originate with the Supreme Court instead of only being appealed to the Supreme Court. The Supreme Court is the highest court in the United States, but the lowest federal courts in the United States are known as Federal District courts. The District courts are the courts in which the trials and lawsuits begin, or originate. Federal District courts hear both criminal and civil cases. If one of the parties involved in a case at the district-court level believes that an error occurred during the trial, the case can be appealed to a Federal Court of Appeals. If one of the parties involved in the appealed case still believes that the case needs to be heard by a higher court, the party can appeal the case to the Supreme Court. Both the Federal Appeals courts and the Supreme Court can decide to hear a case or dismiss a case and leave it as is.

29. Which of the following is true of the Supreme Court?

The Supreme Court

(1) hears only civil cases

(2) hears only criminal cases

(3) is the highest court in the United States

(4) can be overruled by a presidential veto

(5) advises the President on legislation that should be introduced into Congress

Once a case has been decided by the Supreme Court, there are no more courts to which the case may be appealed. **The correct answer is (3).**

30. What is the main responsibility of the Supreme Court?

(1) to hear and decide appealed cases

(2) to hear and decide cases between foreign countries

(3) to represent the United States in international court

(4) to resolve disputes between individuals and businesses

(5) to declare presidential acts unconstitutional

The Supreme Court's greatest responsibility is to hear and decide cases that have been appealed from the lower courts. **The correct answer is (1).**

QUESTIONS 31 AND 32 REFER TO THE FOLLOWING INFORMATION.

Checks and Balances

As you learned earlier, the writers of the Constitution divided the U.S. government into three branches—the legislative, executive, and judicial—so that no one part of the government would develop too much power. The writers of the Constitution also included in the plan of government another system of safeguards against one branch dominating any other branch. This is known as the **system of checks and balances.** Each branch of government has the ability to check the power of the other two branches and that helps balance the powers of the branches.

Let's look at a few examples of some of the checks each branch has on the others. The executive branch can check the power of the legislative branch by vetoing legislation and can check the power of the judicial branch by appointing judges. The legislative branch can check the power of the executive branch by overriding vetoes, by rejecting presidential appointments or nominations, and by impeaching the President. The legislative branch can check the power of the judicial branch by impeaching judges and by rejecting judicial appointments. The judicial branch can check the power of the executive branch by declaring acts of the President unconstitutional. The judicial branch can check the power of the legislative branch by declaring laws unconstitutional. This system may seem like it could cause inefficiency in the government, but it helps maintain a healthy balance of power between the three branches.

The U.S. Federal System

When the thirteen colonies first came together under the Articles of Confederation, they still governed themselves. Once they permanently united as the United States of America, the states retained many rights to continue governing themselves. The government of the country became the shared responsibility of the national government and the state governments. Things such as marriage laws, educational standards, and election laws were left to the discretion of the states. In addition, some powers were set aside even for local governments. This division of government on different levels is known as **federalism.**

 http://bit.ly/hippo_his82

State and Local Governments

 http://bit.ly/hippo_his83

The powers set aside specifically for the states are known as reserved powers and are provided for in the **Tenth Amendment.** To avoid any conflict between state and federal law, the writers of the Constitution made sure to include in Article VI a provision that states that the Constitution and the laws created by Congress take priority over any state or local laws. This clause in Article VI is known as the Supremacy Clause.

The United States requires that each state have a republican form of government. In other words, each state must operate as a republic. There are no other requirements for state governments than that. Most states, however, used the U.S. Constitution as the model for their state constitutions. Therefore, most state governments are very similar to that of the U.S. government, even though they do not have to be. All states have a governor who serves as the head of the executive branch in his or her state. All states, with the exception of Nebraska, have two legislative houses in their legislative branch. Each state has its own court system, although there are many variations of court system structures.

The Constitution requires that the state governments and the federal government work together. For example, a state law enforcement agency may work with a federal law enforcement agency on a special case. The Constitution also facilitates cooperation among states. The "full faith and credit clause" of the Constitution requires that states accept each other's legal decisions and documents. It is the "full faith and credit clause" that makes one state recognize the marriage licenses or drivers licenses from another state. States also cooperate through the process of extradition. Extradition is when a state sends a suspected criminal back to the state in which the suspect is accused of committing a crime.

Although state governments tend to be very similar to the federal government, local governments vary greatly. Some local governments are headed by a mayor, or a chief executive officer elected by the people of the city or town. In these municipalities, a city council often aids the mayor in the administration of the local government. In other municipalities, a council is elected, and then a city manager is hired to handle the business operations. Still other municipalities are run by elected commissioners; each commissioner is responsible for a certain area of operation, such as water or public safety.

31. Which of the following did the writers of the Constitution provide in their plan of government to ensure that no branch of government grew too powerful?

   (1) government monitors who watch for corruption

   (2) Supreme Court elections

   (3) three separate divisions of government, each with different responsibilities

   (4) two houses in the legislature

   (5) nine Supreme Court justices

With the political power divided three ways, no part of the government has the ability to dominate politically. **The correct answer is (3).**

32. According to the Constitution, state governments must do which of the following?

   (1) establish a pure democracy

   (2) establish a republican form of government

   (3) establish a federal system at the state level

   (4) require municipalities to have a republican form of government

   (5) prohibit all forms of government except for democracy within the state

The only requirement a state government must meet according to the Constitution is that it have a republican form of government. **The correct answer is (2).**

QUESTIONS 33 AND 34 REFER TO THE FOLLOWING INFORMATION.

The U.S. Political System

Since the earliest days of the United States, Americans have had differing opinions on the way the country should be governed. These differences in opinions in the formative years of the nation led to the development of the first two political parties, the Federalists and the Republicans. A political party is a group of people who hold similar values and have similar ideas about the proper leadership of the government. Often people form or join political parties based on beliefs about how weak or strong the central government should be, how much or how little the government should tax or spend, or how federal money is spent. Both political parties and members of political parties can be classified based on their ideas about government. On the one hand, liberals, who are often referred to as being on the left, generally advocate political change and social progress. Conservatives, on the other hand, generally advocate very slow change, if any, to the existing political and social order. Those individuals who fall somewhere in between liberal and conservative are often referred to as moderates.

The basic goal of a political party is to get its candidate elected to a public office. By doing so, the political party can influence public policy in a way that is in line with the political ideology of the party. The political parties also have another important function in the U.S. political system. In addition to influencing the policies of the government, political parties further strengthen the system of checks and balances. The parties keep a close eye on the actions of the other parties in power and help ensure that there is no abuse within the system. Furthermore, political parties give citizens a sense of belonging in the political arena and give citizens a voice in all levels of politics.

As you just learned, political parties want their candidates elected to office. In order to elect a candidate, the political party and the candidate must go through a long process. In many elections, candidates must first win a preliminary election called a primary. Each party holds a primary election in which voters choose a candidate to represent their party in the main election. For example, in a Republican primary, Republican voters choose from a list of potential Republican candidates. The winner of the Republican primary will run against candidates from other parties in the main election. Some primary elections, known as open primaries, are open to all voters. Closed primaries are primary elections in which voters must declare a party and choose from that party's candidates. One of the ways candidates get elected is by promoting their platforms. A platform is a list of beliefs, values, or ideas that a particular candidate or political party holds as their own. Voters usually use candidates' platforms to evaluate and choose the candidate they want to be in office.

Individuals who are not content with simply participating in a political party often form or join pressure groups. Pressure groups are those with a particular agenda or list of needs and wants. These pressure groups work diligently to persuade legislators in the lawmaking process. This active persuasion of legislators is known as lobbying. Lobbyists often try to meet with legislators to sway the legislators one way or the other during the lawmaking process. For example, an environmental lobbyist would try to persuade legislators to pass legislation that seeks to improve the environment.

33. People may join a political party for any of the following reasons EXCEPT which one?

(1) to voice an opinion collectively instead of individually

(2) to discover ideas of governing different from their own

(3) to promote a particular candidate in an election

(4) to vote in a closed primary

(5) to associate with people who share similar political ideas

People do not join political parties to find new and different ideas.
The correct answer is (2).

34. Which of the following would most likely hire a lobbyist to persuade legislators to pass a new law?

    (1) the Boy Scouts of America

    (2) a church in Georgia

    (3) a tobacco company in North Carolina

    (4) a single parent on welfare

    (5) a person convicted of a felony

A tobacco company would want certain laws passed or certain laws changed, and they could afford to hire lobbyists to try to accomplish that goal. **The correct answer is (3).**

QUESTIONS 35 AND 36 REFER TO THE FOLLOWING INFORMATION.

CANADIAN GOVERNMENT

The Canadian Constitution establishes the responsibilities of the federal government, or a government in which responsibilities are divided between national, provincial, and municipal governments. In addition to those duties enumerated, or named, in the Constitution, the federal government also controls all issues not specifically charged to the provincial or territorial governments. Like the government of the United States, powers are divided among three separate branches of government.

Governor General

As a constitutional monarchy, Canada is governed by a monarch whose powers are defined by the Constitution. The monarch, or Head of State, is Queen Elizabeth II. The Queen, on the advice of Canada's Prime Minister, appoints a Governor General. The Governor General is traditionally appointed to a five-year term. The Governor General then fulfills all of the duties of the Head of State on behalf of the Queen.

The duties of the Governor General include executing orders-in-council and other state documents, appointing all superior court judges, and giving "royal assent" to bills passed by the House of Commons and the Senate before they can become law. The Governor General also summons, prorogues (ends a session), and dissolves Parliament.

Prime Minister

The Prime Minister is the leader of the party with the most seats in the House of Commons. In addition to controlling the House of Commons, the Prime Minister advises the Queen on her appointment of the Governor General and thus enjoys quite a bit of power. The Prime Minister also oversees the Cabinet. Members of the Cabinet include the heads of the Ministries, the Prime Minister's Office, and the Privy Council Office. Canada has eighteen Ministries that cover all areas of government. Some of the Ministries are Finance, Canadian Heritage, Health, Justice, and Veteran Affairs. The Prime Minister's Office handles things related to the Prime Minister's role as Party Leader. For example, the Prime Minister's Office handles public relations and decides which matters need the Prime Minister's attention and which do not. The Privy Council Office has a number of responsibilities that range from advising the Prime Minister on national security matters to working as a liaison between the Prime Minister and the Cabinet.

Parliament

Canada has a bicameral legislature, or a legislature with two houses. The two houses include the House of Commons and the Senate. The House of Commons, also called the Green Chamber, is made up of 301 members who are elected in general elections at least every five years. The number of members is based on population. At any given time, several different political parties may be represented in the House of Commons. However, the party with a majority of seats in the House of Commons is asked to form the government of Canada. If no party holds a majority, then the parties are asked to form a partnership to form a minority government.

The Senate, or Red Chamber, was created to protect regional, provincial, and minority interests. Unlike the House of Commons, senators are appointed by the Governor General on the basis of "equal representation" and are not elected based on population. There are 105 seats in the senate. To be appointed as a Senator, one must be at least 30 years old, be a Canadian citizen by birth or naturalization, have a net estate worth at least $4000, own property in the province for which they are appointed worth $4000, and be a resident of the province he or she is appointed to represent.

The Judiciary

The Supreme Court consists of a Chief Justice and 8 justices. Each is appointed and holds office until the age of 75. A justice may be removed from office for incapacity or misconduct by the Governor General (on address of the Senate and House of Commons). The Supreme Court issues judgments and advises on questions concerning constitutional interpretation, the constitutionality of legislation, and the powers of Parliament and the Provinces. Another important branch of the Judiciary is the Tax Court. Created in 1983, the Tax Court is the first level of appeals for taxpayers.

Below the Supreme Court and the Tax Court is the Federal Court. A superior court of record with both civil and criminal jurisdiction, the Federal Court of Canada is divided into the Federal Court of Appeal and the Federal Court, Trial Division. The trial division hears lawsuits and applications to review government actions. The Court of Appeal hears appeals from the Trial Division and supervises the decisions of government tribunals. Appeals from the Court of Appeal are made to the Supreme Court.

The Provincial and Territorial Government

Each of the ten provinces and the three territories has its own capital in which its government is centered. Each province is headed by a Lieutenant Governor, and a Commissioner heads each territory. Generally speaking, provinces and territories differ in a few ways. All land in a province is controlled by the province itself while land in a territory is controlled by the federal government. Also, provinces are included in the Constitutional amendment process while territories are not. The governments of both provinces and territories are responsible for the education and welfare of their inhabitants, the administration of justice, and the protection of natural resources within the boundaries.

The Municipal Government

Below the provincial and territorial governments are the municipal governments. Within each province and territory there exist many municipalities in the form of regions, counties, and districts called "Upper Tier" municipalities. "Lower Tier" municipalities are cities and townships. The provincial and territorial governments have the power to create and modify the municipal, or local, governments. Also, the provincial and territorial governments have the power to assign certain responsibilities to the townships. These may include things such as animal control, water and sewage management, and economic development.

35. Which of the following statements concerning the Canadian federal government is true?

    (1) The Canadian government has loose ties with Great Britain, most notably its association with the Sovereign.

    (2) The Judiciary clearly has more power than the other two branches of Canadian government.

    (3) Because of the structure of the Canadian government, it would be relatively easy for one person or one party to abuse powers and take control of the government.

    (4) The municipal governments have nearly the same amount of authority as the provincial and territorial governments.

    (5) The government of Canada stands in stark contrast to the government of the United States.

The Sovereign is still the highest position in the order of precedence in Canada, so it would be correct to state that the Canadian government has loose ties with Great Britain, most notably its association with the Sovereign. **The correct answer is (1).**

36. Which of the following government positions indicates the importance of political parties in the Canadian government?

    (1) Mayor

    (2) Governor General

    (3) Queen

    (4) Prime Minister

    (5) Chief Justice

The Prime Minister is the leader of the party that has the most seats in the House of Commons. **The correct answer is (4).**

ECONOMICS

The study of economics is the study of the way society uses limited resources to meet its material needs. To be more specific, economics deals with the production, distribution, and consumption of goods. The field of economics can generally be divided into two major areas: microeconomics and macroeconomics. Microeconomics, also known as price theory, examines how supply, demand, and competition cause differences in prices, profits, wages, and other aspects of economics. In the area of microeconomics, economists assume that proprietors or entrepreneurs seek to make the most profit possible and that consumers spend their money to seek the most pleasure possible. Macroeconomics looks at the larger picture of economics and examines such things as employment and national income. Macroeconomics developed after the publication of a book called *The General Theory of Employment, Interest, and Money* in 1935 by a British economist named John Maynard Keynes.

Although economics has been a vital part of the life of every state in history, the academic field of economics did not take on a life of its own until a brilliant Scottish moral philosopher, Adam Smith, wrote *Inquiry into the Nature and Causes of the Wealth of Nations* in 1776. Smith's landmark work is still used today by economists and students of economics. Paramount to Smith's economic theory was the idea of the "invisible hand." Smith believed that the government should be directly involved in the economy as little as possible. He argued that if consumers were left alone to act in their own interests and on their own behalf, a natural force, an invisible hand, so to speak, would point the national economy in a direction that would benefit the greatest number of people. As a result, Smith was a critic of the economic policy of mercantilism. Mercantilism, a popular government practice during the time, was a system in which all national economic policy was directed by the goal of national self-sufficiency. In other words, a mercantilist nation sought to make its economy better by becoming less and less reliant on other nations' goods. Mercantilist nations sought to stockpile gold and silver, to keep wages as low as possible, and to keep the population growing. Smith disagreed with this policy of government manipulation of the economy.

A group of French economists, known as physiocrats, reacted to the mercantilists by advocating free trade and a laissez-faire approach to the economy. *Laissez faire* is a term that means the government takes a "hands off" approach to economic policy. Free trade means that the government allows both imports and exports to come and go freely. The physiocrats believed in a single tax to raise money for the state instead of the manipulation of the economy; Smith agreed with their ideas.

Other notable economists include Thomas Malthus, David Ricardo, and John Stuart Mill. Although these economists had some philosophical differences, they all basically agreed on some major principles. They all believed in a free market economy, the right to own private property, and the ability of competition to drive an economy. Another economist was Karl Marx. Marx took a different approach to economic theory, though. Marx, a socialist, believed that those who owned the means of production historically had exploited the working class. Therefore, Marx advocated the elimination of private property and the collective ownership of both property and industry. Marx outlined his economic theories in the historic Communist Manifesto, co-authored by Frederick Engels.

QUESTIONS 37 AND 38 REFER TO THE FOLLOWING INFORMATION.

Economic Systems

The study of economics is the study of the way society uses limited resources to meet its material needs. Because material needs are often unlimited and because material resources, or capital, are limited, governments must make decisions about the manner in which the resources will be used or distributed throughout the society. The manner in which a government distributes capital is a factor that determines which economic system a government will use. Other determining factors are the values held by the government and the freedoms the government extends to the society it governs. The most common economic systems are capitalism, socialism, and communism.

Capitalism

Capitalism is an economic system in which private ownership of material resources, or capital, is not only allowed but also encouraged. In fact, a key characteristic of a capitalist system is the fact that both land and capital is privately owned. Also key is the belief that there is practically no limit to the wealth that can be created through a capitalist system. Another key characteristic of a capitalist system is that consumers in free markets drive economic activity. Individuals make their own financial decisions without interference by the government. Individuals are free to save, invest, and spend as they will. In addition, all parties involved are free to use their income to seek maximum pleasure and are free to seek maximum profits in business ventures. In the business sector, businesses also compete in a free market. In other words, prices, production, and distribution are determined by the competition within the market instead of by the government. Government intervention occurs in a capitalist economy only when the best interest of the public is at stake. For example, the government may intervene in the market in cases of monopolies or price gouging. Another vital role of government in a capitalist system is to protect the nation from foreign attacks or intervention. The United States is a good example of a capitalist economy, also referred to as a market economy.

Socialism

In the economic system known as socialism, the government is in charge of the redistribution of wealth, and the major industries are either owned publicly or cooperatively. The major industries controlled by the government include health care, transportation, heavy industry (steel production, manufacturing, etc.), and banking. In addition, natural resources, public utilities, and finance corporations are nationalized. Competition is reduced to a minimum in these industries with the goal of creating an egalitarian, or equal opportunity, economic environment. Although there is some limited private ownership of capital, individuals work with the government to determine goods and services that should be produced and the manner in which they are distributed. Only smaller interests are left to individuals. The goal of a socialist economic system is the formation of a classless society. A key characteristic of a socialist economy is a very high tax rate. The high taxes provide revenue to fund things such as free public education and health care. Sweden is a great example of a socialist economy. Although socialism and communism were once thought of as very similar, modern socialists would be quick to point out that communism now often denotes an oppressive, authoritarian regime.

Communism

In a communist economic system, the government does not permit private ownership of either capital or the means of production. A communist government owns the property within the state and determines the way the goods and services should be distributed. The goal of a communist government is to distribute goods and services in a manner that serves the common good, or in a manner that benefits everyone the most, so that private interests are sacrificed for the welfare of the majority. Theoretically, a communist society is a classless society in which everyone in it works according to his or her ability and is provided for according to his or her need. Also theoretically, a communist society eventually will need no official state government. Critics of communism will point out that pure communism is practically impossible, though. The former Soviet Union is the most striking example of a modern communist economy, also referred to as a command economy. However, communism under leaders like Lenin and Stalin did not even remotely resemble the communism as described by Marx and Engels.

Mixed Economies

Economists are quick to point out that there is no economic system that is purely capitalist, socialist, or communist. In every economic system, there are some elements of other economic systems present. In most cases, the term *mixed economy* is used to describe an economy that has elements of multiple economic systems. The United States, although generally capitalistic, is a good example of a mixed economy. For example, there is some government operation or subsidy of industries, such as health care and transportation, and the New Deal economic recovery program under President Franklin Roosevelt contained many elements of socialism, as did the social reform of President Lyndon Johnson.

37. Which of the following is a characteristic of communism?

    (1) less government intervention in the economy than in socialism

    (2) less government intervention than in capitalism

    (3) free market economy

    (4) more government intervention than in capitalism

    (5) more prosperous economy than capitalism

In communism, the government controls every facet of the economy. **The correct answer is (4).**

38. An individual investor would be most free to manage his money in which of the following economic systems?

(1) a capitalist economy

(2) a socialist economy

(3) a communist economy

(4) an economy with socialist and communist elements

(5) an economy with capitalist and communist elements

Capitalism encourages investments and allows more economic freedom than other economic systems. **The correct answer is (1).**

QUESTIONS 39 AND 40 REFER TO THE FOLLOWING INFORMATION.

Factors of Production

When economists talk about production within an economic system, they must consider the three factors of production. These factors are natural resources, capital, and labor. Usually the factors of production cannot fully meet the demands of the consumers, or people who use the goods produced. **Natural resources** are the raw materials necessary for the production of goods. For example, trees are necessary for the production of houses, paper, and wooden furniture.

Capital can be any equipment, factories, or property necessary for the conversion of raw materials into finished goods. This type of capital is referred to as fixed capital. Capital can also refer to money that is invested to support the production of goods. This type of capital, called circulating capital, can be wages paid to laborers or raw materials used in production. Any capital that can be sold for cash is considered liquid capital, while capital that cannot be easily converted to cash is known as frozen capital.

In economics, the term **labor** is used to describe the work it takes to convert raw materials into goods and services. Labor may refer to the people who actually do the work manufacturing the raw materials and producing the goods. Laborers may be factory assembly line workers, truck drivers, sales agents, or other people involved in the production and distribution of goods. Labor may even refer to people in a service industry, such as doctors or teachers that provide services for others.

When considering productivity, economists also consider the **law of diminishing returns.** The factors of production, when used together in the correct proportions, will produce an end result sufficient for a society. However, according to the law of diminishing returns, at a certain point, any additional resources (raw materials, labor, or capital) fail to produce any additional product. In fact, according to the law, at a certain point, additional resources may even result in less production than before the additional resources were added.

39. The natural resources required to build a log home include which of the following?

    (1) trees, land, and construction workers

    (2) land and construction workers

    (3) trees

    (4) trees and land

    (5) land

The answer choice "trees" is correct because land is considered capital and construction workers are considered laborers. **The correct answer is (3).**

40. The law of diminishing returns could be applied to which of the following situations?

    (1) salaries of factory workers are raised

    (2) new raw materials are supplied to a factory to produce a brand-new product

    (3) the number of assembly line workers in an efficient factory is cut in half to reduce company spending

    (4) the number of assembly line workers in an efficient factory is doubled while the amount of raw materials remains the same

    (5) a human-operated assembly line is replaced by a new, computerized assembly line to run more efficiently

With twice as many workers in an already efficient factory, the workers will probably get in each other's way and reduce efficiency and production. **The correct answer is (4).**

QUESTIONS 41 AND 42 REFER TO THE FOLLOWING INFORMATION.

Supply and Demand

The primary force and one of the basic principles of economics is that of **supply and demand.** Supply can be defined as all the goods available regardless of price. Demand can be defined as the desire of the consumers to purchase goods. Producers supply goods with the hope that consumers will demand goods. Producers must set prices on the goods high enough that they still make a profit after paying for all the costs of production. Consumers seek to pay the lowest price possible for goods. Producers must set the amount of production based on the demand for goods. The price and the availability of goods determine the demand. These factors working together make up the principle of supply and demand.

If a given item, a car for example, has a high profit yield, a great number of producers will be interested in production of the good. The producers of the cars will compete for a share of the market. If the market is flooded with cars, or if there are too many cars on the market, and the supply of cars is greater than the demand, buyers either cannot or will not buy all of the supply of cars. If this happens, there will be a surplus that will then cause car prices to fall. This may increase the demand for the cars. If an item, such as a car, has a price that is low enough to make consumers want the item, it will be in demand. If the price of the car falls too much, there may be such a demand that producers cannot supply the item fast enough to meet the demand. If the demand exceeds the supply, the prices will rise.

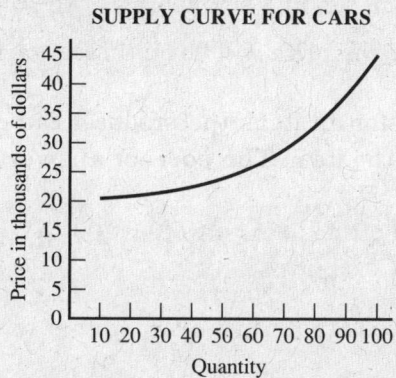

SUPPLY CURVE FOR CARS

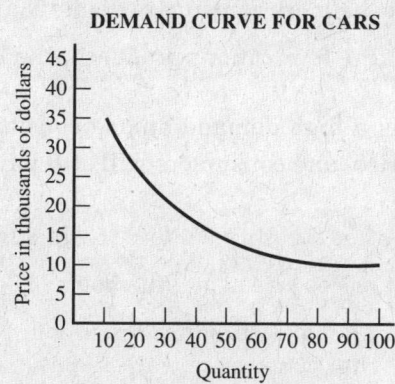

DEMAND CURVE FOR CARS

To make a market stable, producers must exactly determine the amount of goods that consumers will demand and the price that the consumers will pay for those goods. When this point is reached, it is called **equilibrium.** On the following chart, the point of equilibrium is the point at which the two curves intersect. When the price for goods rises above equilibrium, there is a decreased demand and, therefore, more goods than consumers want. This creates a surplus. If the opposite happens, that is, if the price falls below equilibrium, the demand increases, and there is a shortage. These are the laws of supply and demand.

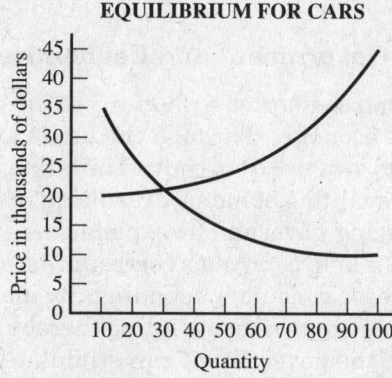

EQUILIBRIUM FOR CARS

It should be noted that the laws of supply and demand are only valid in an economic system in which the markets are relatively undisturbed by the government. Because supply and demand depend on market conditions, an economy in which the government controls the market would not follow the laws of supply and demand. For example, during times of war in the United States or at any given time in the former USSR, the markets were somewhat manipulated by the government. That invalidated the mechanisms of supply and demand in those places.

41. What conclusion can be drawn from the principles of supply and demand?

(1) the lower the profit an item generates, the more producers will be interested in producing that item

(2) the higher the price of an item, the higher the demand will be for that item.

(3) the more consumers demand an item, the lower the prices will go

(4) the more consumers demand an item, the higher the prices will go

(5) the fewer items produced, the lower the price will be on those items

If there is a high demand among consumers for an item, the producer can charge a higher price, and consumers will still pay for the item. **The correct answer is (4).**

42. Market stability will occur when which of the following occurs?

(1) prices rise above the point of equilibrium

(2) producers produce the amount of goods that consumers want at the price that consumers want to pay

(3) a surplus is created

(4) a shortage is created

(5) prices fall below the point of equilibrium

Stability occurs when producers produce the amount of goods the consumers want at a price that consumers feel is fair. **The correct answer is (2).**

QUESTIONS 43 AND 44 REFER TO THE FOLLOWING INFORMATION.

Government and Economics

The United States has a free market economy, yet the government still plays a vital role in steering the economy. Through the use of taxation, the government can create revenue for its own use or to control inflation. Inflation can be defined as a rise in prices or a devaluing of money, resulting in decreased buying power for consumers. By reducing government expenditures or by adjusting the tax rate, the government can help control or correct inflation. Taxation can also be used to increase or decrease consumer spending. By increasing the tax rate, the government can discourage consumer spending thereby slowing the economy. By decreasing the tax rate, the government can stimulate or encourage consumer spending, investing, and business transactions because people have more money to spend and invest. It should be noted that not all inflation is bad, though. Slow and gradual inflation is normal and even good for an economy. Inflation of 10 percent annually coupled with high price increases would cause concern for economists. The government also controls social programs like welfare, unemployment benefits, Medicare, and Social Security. The government manages the funds used to operate these programs and distributes the funds to citizens who need assistance. All of these practices are part of the government monetary policy known as the fiscal policy. The practice of increasing taxation or restricting public spending is called the contractionary fiscal policy. The practice of reducing taxation and stimulating public spending is known as the expansionary fiscal policy.

Money, Monetary Policy, and Financial Institutions

The use of money is the method of exchange employed in economic systems in lieu of bartering. Whatever currency an economic system uses is its money. The money supply of a nation is mostly coins and paper money, or bills, along with deposits made to banks. The use of money in an economic system is controlled through monetary policy. In the United States, the Federal Reserve Board controls the monetary policy. The Federal Reserve Board, currently chaired by Ben Bernanke, directs the monetary policy by regulating the money and credit available for use in the country. It does this by setting the reserve ratio and setting the discount rate. The reserve ratio is the amount of money that lending institutions can lend and the amount of money they must hold in reserve. By setting the reserve ratio, the Federal Reserve Board controls the supply of money that is available for banks and savings and loan associations to lend to consumers. The Federal Reserve Board tightens the supply of money by raising the reserve ratio. On the other hand, the Federal Reserve Board loosens the supply of money by dropping the reserve ratio. The discount rate is the interest rate that the Federal Reserve Board charges to member banks to borrow money. Banks then charge consumers a higher interest rate on loans than they pay to the Federal Reserve. The more money that banks want to borrow, the more it costs to borrow the money. The hike in the cost discourages banks from borrowing more and reduces bank demand for extra reserve money. The Federal Reserve Board also sets the margin requirement that determines the amount of cash a purchaser must pay up front when buying stocks; this helps deter speculation, as in the kind that led to the Great Depression.

Labor Relations

As you learned earlier, when speaking within the realm of economics, labor refers to the people who actually do the work manufacturing the raw materials and producing goods, or the people who provide services for others. All dealings between labor and management over labor issues are called labor relations. Many years ago, laborers constantly fought for better wages and working conditions, often with little or no success. One reason for the lack of success during pre-industrial America was because employers dealt directly with individual employees. As industrialization took over, though, employers faced many employees instead of just a few individuals. Government regulations eventually set limits on the number of hours workers had to work and the minimum wages workers could receive. These regulations helped curb dangerous working conditions. Labor, however, remained largely unorganized.

In the 1930s, the Wagner Act allowed laborers to organize and negotiate with management concerning disputes. The labor organizations became known as unions, and these negotiations became known as **collective bargaining.** Collective bargaining occurs when leaders of the labor unions meet with employers and management to negotiate wages, hours, conditions, benefits, or other issues. Collective bargaining is often successful. Many times independent arbitrators handle the negotiations between the two sides. However, when collective bargaining does not work, laborers may go on strike. When workers strike, or stop working, the government may intervene and end the strike, or the government may help facilitate successful negotiations. The threat of a strike is most successful during negotiations when the unemployment rate is relatively low. If there are plenty of unemployed workers who are willing to replace the strikers, the strike loses its effectiveness.

43. Government can control aspects of the economy by controlling which of the following?

(1) unemployment

(2) checking and savings accounts

(3) the value of money

(4) salary caps

(5) taxation

Taxation is the correct choice because a higher tax rate slows the economy, while a lower tax rate stimulates the economy. **The correct answer is (5).**

44. The Federal Reserve Board is vital to the economy because of its policies concerning which of the following?

(1) labor disputes

(2) Social Security

(3) interest rates

(4) minting of new coins and bills

(5) unemployment

The Federal Reserve Board's policies on the reserve ratio and discount rate directly affect the nation's interest rates. **The correct answer is (3).**

QUESTIONS 45 AND 46 REFER TO THE FOLLOWING INFORMATION.

Foreign Trade

A major part of any economic system is foreign trade. Few nations are completely self-sufficient and isolated from the rest of the world. Therefore, countries must trade with other countries for the raw materials, goods, and services they need. Often countries specialize in goods that create a high demand in other parts of the world. Specialization in a particular good may occur because of a country's expertise in that area or because a country can produce that good cheaply or efficiently. Adam Smith recognized that economic specialization led to an increase in output, and he encouraged foreign trade in specialized goods. Smith went even further and said that a country should specialize in goods that it could produce more cheaply and efficiently than its trade partners. David Ricardo modified this theory when he advocated specialization in goods, not just when a country could produce goods more cheaply than competitors, but also when a country can sell those goods for a better price abroad than at home.

Goods that are shipped out of a country to another country are known as **exports;** goods brought into a country from another country are called **imports.** To maintain a healthy economy, the goal of a country is to export more goods than it imports. Economists call this occurrence a favorable balance of trade. In order to protect domestic goods, countries often add a special tax, called a **tariff**, to imports so that domestic goods are more competitively priced. If the tariffs are too high, the country whose imports are being taxed will retaliate with tariffs on goods of their own. Another way that countries protect their interests is through the use of import quotas. Import quotas limit the number of particular foreign goods that may enter a country. Quotas are often very successful in reversing trade imbalances. On occasion, government health or safety standards prevent foreign goods from entering the domestic market. Government support of domestic industries provides additional advantages for domestic industries and puts foreign competitors at a disadvantage. It is very important that governments carefully manage their overseas trade; many workers in each country depend on producing goods for overseas trade.

45. Which of the following might occur if a country's tariffs were set too high?

(1) the country would become very rich

(2) the country's trade partners would retaliate with high tariffs of their own

(3) the country would go bankrupt

(4) the prices of domestic goods would plummet

(5) the prices of domestic goods would skyrocket

Many nations have become involved in tariff wars when one country raises tariffs only to have its trade partner do the same. **The correct answer is (2).**

46. Which of the following makes most sense as a foreign-trade goal for a country?

(1) to produce and sell more goods domestically than internationally

(2) to import more goods than it exports

(3) to export more goods than it imports

(4) to charge wealthy countries higher prices than third-world countries

(5) to export as few goods and services as possible

This favorable balance of trade allows a country to make more income than it spends on importing goods. **The correct answer is (3).**

GEOGRAPHY

Geography is more than states and capitals or latitude and longitude. Geography is the study of the Earth's physical features and the way people have adapted to these physical features. Geography is concerned not only with physical geographic features but also with cultural geographic features. Physical geographic features include things such as land, water, mountains, and plains. Cultural geographic features include things such as human architecture or man-made changes to the Earth's physical features. The science of geography can be divided into two branches: systematic and regional. Systematic geography deals with individual elements of the Earth's physical and cultural features. Regional geography, on the other hand, deals with the physical and cultural features within a particular region, or area, of the Earth's surface.

Systematic geography includes a number of different fields within the realm of physical geography. Part of physical geography is cartography, or mapmaking. Another important part of physical geography is oceanography, or the study of the Earth's oceans; climatology examines the Earth's weather patterns; and geomorphology looks at the way the surface of the Earth has changed. Other areas of physical geography include biogeography, or the study of the distribution of plants and animals, and soil geography, or the study of the distribution of soil and soil conservation. Systematic geography also includes a number of fields within the realm of cultural geography, or the study of how human social and cultural life affects geography. Economic geography, for example, examines how business and industry have affected the geographic environment. Political geography looks at nations, states, cities, and other man-made areas and examines how geography influences these political units; political geography often involves some political science, too. Military geography is the study of how the geography of a particular area may affect military operations. Military geography is especially important today in light of the events in the Middle East.

Regional geography deals with similarities and differences between various regions of the Earth. Regional geographers look closely at the unique combinations of features that make regions similar or different. Sometimes regional geography includes the study of places as small as cities. This special type of regional geography is called microgeography. Other times, regional geography includes the study of entire areas like the Arctic Circle or the Pacific Rim. These large areas are called macrodivisions and are part of macrogeography. Within macrodivisions, geographers may study smaller regions that make up the larger division of land based on such features as language, climate, or religion.

QUESTIONS 47 AND 48 REFER TO THE FOLLOWING INFORMATION.

The Role of Geographers

The role of geographers, or those who study the Earth's physical and cultural features, is twofold. First, a geographer studies geography. A geographer may use any number of sources to study a particular area of geography. A geographer may use maps, pictures, satellite information, or surveys to collect information.

A geographer may also go to the area he or she is studying to get information directly from the source. The second role of a geographer is to describe the Earth's physical features. A geographer may help create maps or analyze data for businesses or the government. The use of computers has aided geographers in their work in the last twenty years. Each year, geographers continue to find more practical applications for their work.

Themes of Geography

Vital to the study of geography is a working knowledge of the themes of geography, the ability to use maps and globes, an understanding of topography and climate, and an understanding of environmental issues. The National Council for Geographic Education developed five themes of geography. Those who study geography, called geographers, study the Earth's surface within the context of these five themes: location, place, environment, movement, and region.

The first theme is **location.** In geography, location means an exact and precise position on the Earth's surface. Any place on Earth can be marked as an exact position on a globe. This exact position is known to geographers as an absolute location. Because of the imaginary grid of horizontal and vertical lines that is placed over the globe, any position on Earth can be marked with pinpoint accuracy. These lines are known as latitude and longitude. Relative location is described by landmarks, direction from or distance from another location, or by associating one location with another location.

Geographers refer to the second theme of geography as **place.** Place has a special meaning within the context of geography, and it not only means where a location is but also what a location is like. In other words, place deals with the physical features that make a particular location similar to or different from another location. These features can be natural features such as climate, terrain, or wildlife; man-made features such as buildings or dams; or human characteristics such as economics or culture.

The third theme of geography is **environment.** The environment of an area includes the area's natural surroundings. Geographers study not only an area's environment but also the way that humans interact with it. For example, humans have reacted to mountainous environments by building roads over the mountains or tunnels through them. In addition, geographers study not only the way humans adapt to and modify the environment but also the extent to which humans depend on it.

Through the theme of **movement,** geographers study the relationship between places. Movement is concerned with the ways humans interact with other humans in other places. It can deal with the trade of imports and exports, travel, or even communication between humans. For geographers, movement pertains to the movement of humans, goods, or ideas.

The final theme of geography is known as **region.** A region is any area, regardless of size, that contains common characteristics. To a geographer, a region may be as small as a city block or as large as a continent. Common characteristics, not size, determine region. The characteristics that determine region can be natural physical features such as climate or landscape or man-made features such as religion, culture, or political boundaries. In the field of geography, there are three different kinds of regions. First, *formal regions* are those defined by some type of governmental or political boundaries. Second, *functional regions* are those defined by a service of some type. For example, a television service area is an example of a functional region. Once a service is ended, the functional region no longer exists. Finally, *vernacular regions* are those that are loosely defined by people's ideas about the region. An example of a vernacular region would be the Midwest or the Middle East.

47. Which theme of geography would be of concern to a geographer who is studying a winding desert highway?

    (1) location

    (2) place

    (3) environment

    (4) movement

    (5) region

The geographer is studying a desert highway. In the "environment" theme, choice (3), geographers study an area's environment and natural surroundings as well as the way humans interact with it. **The correct answer is (3).**

48. The "region" theme of geography would most likely apply to which of the following?

    (1) an area 200 miles square

    (2) an area that averages a daily temperature of 37 degrees Fahrenheit during the winter months

    (3) an area marked by a diverse population

    (4) an area that is home to a diverse collection of wildlife species

    (5) an area that used to be a wetland but was partially drained and converted to farmland

The "region" theme would apply to an area with a similar characteristic, such as winter climate, throughout the entire area. **The correct answer is (2).**

QUESTIONS 49 AND 50 REFER TO THE FOLLOWING INFORMATION.

Globes and Maps

Vital to the study of geography are the geographer's tools, the globe and the map. A globe is a spherical representation of a map of the Earth. Because the Earth is round, a flat representation of the Earth is inaccurate; therefore, a globe is the most accurate way to study the Earth's surface. However, a globe is not the most efficient or convenient vehicle for geographical information. Therefore, geographers most often rely on the flat representations of the Earth's surface known as maps.

Maps come in all shapes and sizes and convey a wide variety of information. There are as many different kinds of maps as there are kinds of information that a map can illustrate. For example, a political map shows political borders or boundaries between countries, states, counties, etc. A topographical map illustrates physical features such as mountains, hills, valleys, rivers, or prairies. A contour map illustrates the elevation of physical features. A population map illustrates population density or how many people live in a particular area. A weather map, or climate map, illustrates the forecasted or current weather for an area.

So that geographers can understand the information on a map, mapmakers, or cartographers, usually include a legend somewhere on the map. A legend is like a key that contains the meanings of the symbols used on the map. A legend may also contain a scale that shows distance relative to the map. By using the legend and the scale, geographers can use a map for the purpose it was intended. The following illustration is an example of a map legend.

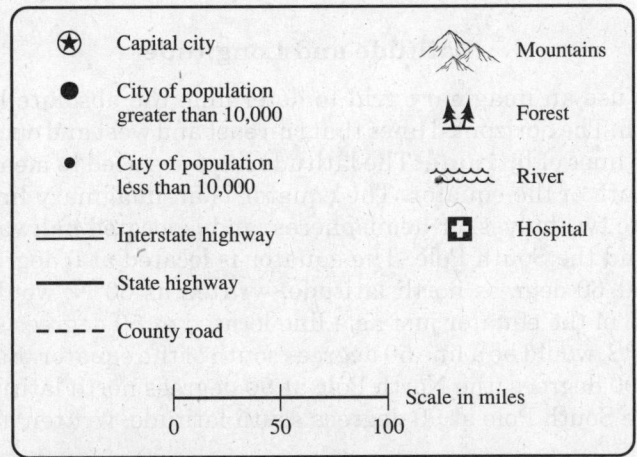

49. Which of the following would be the most likely use of a globe?

    (1) to determine the elevation of a plateau in Asia

    (2) to study the climate of Antarctica

    (3) to find all the cities in Texas with a population over 100,000

    (4) to use as a guide while traveling through Canada

    (5) to get an accurate picture of the land around the North and South Poles

Because a flat map cannot accurately illustrate a round surface, a globe is the most accurate representation of the Earth's surface, especially around the poles. **The correct answer is (5).**

50. Which of the following maps would be the best choice to discover the capital of Albania?

(1) a political map

(2) a topographical map

(3) a contour map

(4) a population map

(5) a weather or climate map

A political map illustrates political boundaries, city populations, capital cities, and more. **The correct answer is (1).**

QUESTIONS 51–53 REFER TO THE FOLLOWING INFORMATION.

Latitude and Longitude

Geographers use an imaginary grid to determine the absolute location of any place on Earth. The horizontal lines that run east and west and encircle the Earth are known as lines of **latitude.** The latitude lines are used to measure distances north and south of the equator. The equator is an imaginary line that divides the Earth into two halves, or hemispheres, and is located halfway between the North Pole and the South Pole. The equator is located at 0 degrees latitude. A line located at 60 degrees north latitude, written as 60°N, would be a line 60 degrees north of the equator just as a line located at 50 degrees south latitude, written as 50°S, would be a line 50 degrees south of the equator. Each of the poles is located at 90 degrees, the North Pole at 90 degrees north latitude, written as 90°N, and the South Pole at 90 degrees south latitude, written as 90°S.

LONGITUDE AND LATITUDE

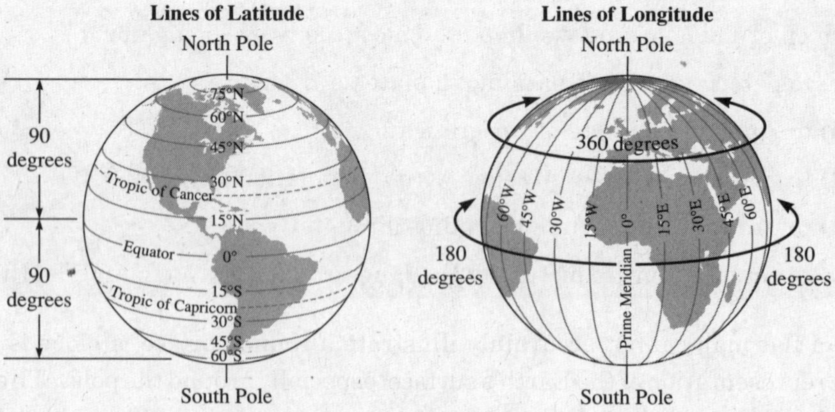

Lines of Latitude

Lines of Longitude

The vertical lines that run north and south around the Earth are known as lines of **longitude.** Longitude measures distances east and west of the Prime Meridian, which is the vertical line located at 0 degrees longitude that runs from pole to pole through the city of Greenwich, England. On the opposite side of the world is the International Date Line, which is located at 180 degrees longitude. A line located 120 degrees west of the Prime Meridian would be written as 120°W, while a line located at 70 degrees east of the Prime Meridian would be written as 70°E.

The lines of latitude and longitude cross over each other and form an imaginary grid on the Earth's surface. The point at which a line of latitude and a line of longitude intersect is known as a **coordinate.** A coordinate is the way a geographer notes an absolute location. For example, the map below shows the intersection of the 45 degrees north latitude line and 100 degrees west longitude line in the state of South Dakota. The coordinate for that intersection would be written as 45°N 100°W.

QUESTIONS 51–53 ARE BASED ON THE FOLLOWING MAP.

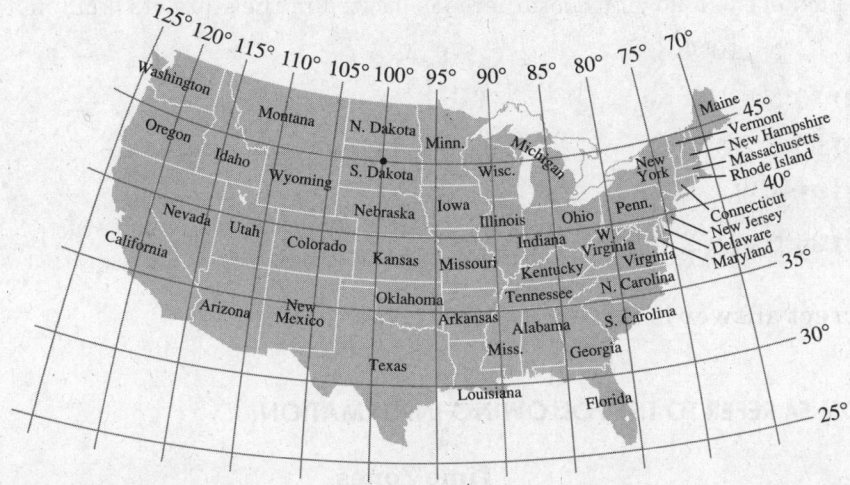

51. Which of the following lines is located closest to the equator?

   (1) 45°N

   (2) 125°W

   (3) 70°W

   (4) 25°N

   (5) 95°W

Of those listed, the line noted in answer choice (4) is only 25° away from the equator; therefore, it is closer to the equator than the other latitude lines on the map. **The correct answer is (4).**

52. In which state would you be standing if you were standing at 35°N 120°W?

(1) Tennessee

(2) California

(3) Arizona

(4) Florida

(5) Nevada

At 35°N 120°W, you would be standing in California. **The correct answer is (2).**

53. Which of the following coordinates is located in the state of Oklahoma?

(1) 35°N 110°W

(2) 35°N 98°W

(3) 93°N 35°W

(4) 25°N 98°W

(5) 35°N 98°W

The correct answer is (5).

QUESTION 54 REFER TO THE FOLLOWING INFORMATION.

Time Zones

Another important set of imaginary vertical lines divides the Earth into twenty-four geographic regions. These regions are known as time zones. Each time zone represents one hour of the day and measures a distance of approximately 15 degrees across. All clocks within the same time zone should be set to the same time and generally are 1 hour later than those of the time zone to the immediate west. The 0 degrees longitude line, known as the **Prime Meridian,** runs north and south through the Royal Greenwich Observatory in Greenwich, England. Each of the twelve time zones to the west of the Prime Meridian decrease in time by 1 hour, while each of the time zones to the east of the Prime Meridian increase in time by 1 hour. **The International Date Line** lies on the opposite side of the world from the Prime Meridian and is located at 180 degrees longitude. The time zones on each side of the Date Line are actually in different days. If a person crosses the International Date Line heading west, he will lose a day; if a person crosses the International Date Line heading east, he will gain a day.

TIME ZONES ACROSS THE UNITED STATES

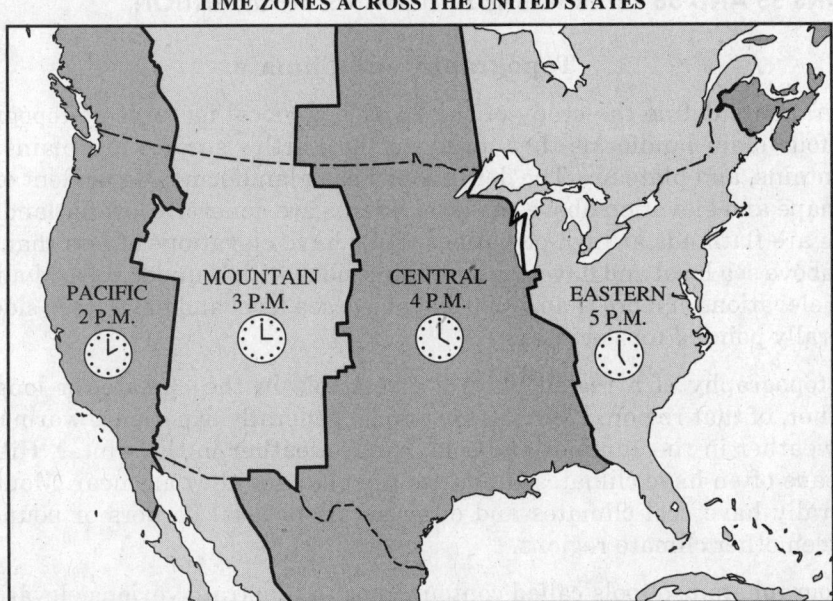

Travel and weather forecasting during the 1800s made standard time zones necessary as scheduling conflicts arose. After railroad systems in North America adopted the four time zones assigned to North America, the British helped gain support for time zone usage around the world. The continental United States and Canada are within four time zones: Eastern, Central, Mountain, and Pacific. While most time zones remain standard, there are a few exceptions. China, for example, spans about 50 degrees of longitude and several time zones. However, China operates under a single time zone, that of the eastern part of the country. Also, the International Date Line bends at the Bering Strait, between Russia and Alaska, so that all of Russia falls within the same day's time.

54. Based on the information in the previous map, the sun would rise first in which of the following time zones?

(1) Pacific

(2) Mountain

(3) Central

(4) Eastern

(5) none of the above

The Sun rises in the east; therefore, the Eastern time zone would see the Sun first. **The correct answer is (4).**

QUESTIONS 55 AND 56 REFER TO THE FOLLOWING INFORMATION.

Topography and Climate

Geographers define the study of the Earth's physical features as topography. The four main landforms that make up the Earth's surface are plains, hills, mountains, and plateaus. The definition of each landform is dependent on both its shape and elevation above sea level. Plains are generally low flatlands. Plateaus are flatlands at high elevations. Hills have elevations of less than 1,000 feet above sea level and have gently sloping sides with rounded tops. Mountains have elevations of more than 1,000 feet above sea level and have steep sides and generally pointed tops or peaks.

The topography of a region plays a direct role in the climate, or long-term weather, of that region. Plains, for example, generally experience warm or hot, dry weather in the summer and cold, windy weather in the winter. Hills and plateaus often have climates similar to the plateaus they are near. Mountains generally have cool climates and often act as natural borders or boundaries between other climate regions.

Cartographers use tools called contour lines to illustrate various elevations of landforms on maps. The higher an elevation is, the closer together on the map are the contour lines. Conversely, the lower an elevation, the farther apart the contour lines. Cartographers often create entire maps that illustrate elevation. These maps are called contour maps.

55. Which of the following would a topographer be LEAST interested in studying?

(1) a skyscraper in Paris

(2) a valley in California

(3) a mountain range in South America

(4) a plateau in Mexico

(5) the hills of central Texas

Topography is concerned with the Earth's physical features, and a skyscraper is man-made. **The correct answer is (1).**

56. One might expect to find the coolest summer climate in which of the following areas?

(1) a large prairie

(2) a plateau west of a hilly region

(3) a mountain range

(4) a hilly region

(5) a valley between two mountains

Because a mountain range has a high elevation, it is reasonable to expect that it would have a cool climate, even in the summer months. **The correct answer is (3).**

QUESTIONS 57 AND 58 REFER TO THE FOLLOWING INFORMATION.

Environmental Issues

As humans interact with the physical features of the Earth's surface, they often make changes to those features. Many times, those changes have an impact on the environment. The impact of human interaction on the environment often has far-reaching and lasting effects. These effects raise a number of environmental issues and concerns. One of the most pressing environmental concerns is the rate at which the tropical rain forests are disappearing. Every minute between 30 and 50 acres of rain forest are cut down. This is a serious concern because the rain forests help supply oxygen for the Earth, and they help supply great amounts of the world's medicines.

Another serious concern is the **water supply** in southwest Asia and North Africa. Industrialization, irrigation demands, and population explosion are placing a heavy strain on the water supply there. There is speculation that in less than fifteen years there will not be enough water to meet the needs in those regions.

In many parts of Africa, the process known as **desertification** is claiming many acres of land. Desertification can be defined as the process of creating deserts. A lack of soil conservation due to uncontrolled use of trees and shrubs for firewood allows desert winds to blow away valuable topsoil. The trees and shrubs are important because their roots hold the soil in place.

A problem that faces many places around the world is **habitat loss.** Because of the draining of wetlands, the cutting of forests, and the plowing of grasslands, natural habitats are being lost at an alarming rate. Habitat loss leaves countless animal species homeless. Many of these homeless species are forced to then interact with humans. Interaction of this nature often leads to injury, death, or extinction for many such species.

57. The most serious threat to the rain forests is which of the following?

   (1) parasites

   (2) flooding

   (3) erosion and desertification

   (4) human adaptation of the Earth's physical features

   (5) warfare

Humans are cutting down the rain forests every day—therefore, humans are the greatest threat to the future of the rain forests. **The correct answer is (4).**

58. Desertification could possibly be prevented if African governments took what action?

    (1) irrigation of land after it has become desert

    (2) replacement of lost topsoil after it has blown away

    (3) replanting of trees and grasses to prevent valuable topsoil from eroding

    (4) prohibition of the use of trees and shrubs for firewood, or prohibit fires altogether

    (5) passage of laws restricting topsoil use

Without trees, shrubs, and other vegetation to hold the soil in place, the topsoil will blow away. Therefore, if vegetation were replaced before the erosion occurred, desertification might be prevented. **The correct answer is (3).**

HISTORICAL DOCUMENTS ON THE GED® SOCIAL STUDIES TEST

The Social Studies Test will contain an excerpt from at least one of the following historical documents: the Declaration of Independence, the U.S. Constitution, the Federalist Papers, or landmark Supreme Court cases. To help you become more familiar with each of these documents, we will examine them closely here. Before you take the Social Studies Test, take time to read some of each of these documents just to familiarize yourself with the language and the style of each one.

 http://bit.ly/hippo_his84

The Declaration of Independence

On July 4, 1776, the members of the Philadelphia Congress adopted a motion that "The united colonies are, and of right ought to be, free and independent states…" Thomas Jefferson led a committee appointed to write a statement declaring the thirteen colonies officially free of British reign. The resulting document was the Declaration of Independence. Jefferson's task was not an easy one, however. He needed to clarify the colonies' purpose in fighting Britain. He succeeded, and by doing so, he appealed to other colonies to declare their independence and encouraged other nations to support the colonies against Britain.

Jefferson begins the Declaration of Independence by asserting that all people have rights to which they are entitled by nature. He states that governments are established to protect those rights, and when a government fails to do so, people should abolish it and create a new government that will protect their rights.

The Declaration of Independence then takes on a more personal tone, stating that the King of Great Britain, George III, has misused his power in a number of specific ways. Basically, half of the Declaration is devoted to listing the ways in which King George abused his power. Pointing out that their previous attempts to compel the king to respect human rights had failed, Jefferson asserts that logically the Americans did the only thing they could do to preserve the rights of all people—they declared independence from Great Britain. The Declaration, a moving document, had the desired effect and enticed great support for the war against Britain.

The U.S. Constitution

The Preamble

"We, the People of the United States, in Order to form a more perfect Union, establish Justice, insure domestic Tranquility, provide for the common defense, promote the general Welfare, and secure the Blessings of Liberty to ourselves and our Posterity, do ordain and establish this Constitution for the United States of America."

A preamble is a statement of purpose. The Preamble to the Constitution paraphrases the purpose of the Constitution. It answers the question of why the Constitution was created.

Articles of the Constitution

The Articles of the Constitution outline the plan for the government under which we currently live. As discussed earlier, three branches of government, the executive, legislative, and judicial, divide the power and keep any one part of the government from dominating another. Each branch keeps a check on the others, thus the terms "separation of powers" and "checks and balances." To balance the power of the three branches of government, each has a "check" to limit the powers of the other two. For example, although Congress may pass a bill, the president has the power to veto it. Congress may, however, override a presidential veto by a two-thirds majority vote. Finally, the Supreme Court may declare a law unconstitutional. These powers are named, or enumerated, in Articles I, II, and III of the Constitution. Let's look more closely at each of these Articles.

Article I. Legislative Department

The legislative branch is outlined in Article I of the Constitution. The U.S. legislature, called Congress, is made up of two houses—the House of Representatives and the Senate. Both houses are made up of representatives elected from the states. The House representation is based on state population, while the Senate consists of two senators from each state. The representatives are elected to two-year terms, while the senators are elected to six-year terms. The legislative branch "creates" the law under which we are governed.

Article II. Executive Department

Article II of the Constitution details the executive branch of government. The executive branch consists of the president, vice president, and various agencies and departments that administer and enforce the laws.

The president serves a four-year term and cannot serve more than two terms. The president and the vice president are elected by a vote of the people. However, there is a process known as the Electoral College, through which the results of the popular election must be certified. A president can, although it is rare, receive a majority of the popular vote and still lose the election because of the Electoral College vote. The executive branch "enforces" the laws under which we live.

Article III. Judicial Department

http://bit.ly/hippo_his85

Article III of the Constitution provides that the "judicial power belongs to the federal courts." It is in this Article that the Supreme Court and inferior, or lower level, courts are created. As you've already learned, the Supreme Court "checks" the other two branches of government by declaring certain laws unconstitutional. The Supreme Court has the power to rule on cases involving a state and a citizen of another state, disputes between states, between citizens of different states, between a state and its citizens, or between a foreign state and U.S. citizens. It also may consider conflicts arising at sea or regarding patents and copyrights. Most of the time, the Supreme Court hears "appeals" of decisions made by "inferior" courts. However, the Court does have "original" jurisdiction, or the right to hear an original case and not an appealed case, in some instances. These include cases involving ambassadors or other public ministers, consuls, and those cases in which a state is a party.

Although originally created with a Chief Justice and five associate judges, the Supreme Court is now composed of nine justices, each appointed for life by the president with approval from the Senate. The Court acts by issuing opinions that explain why the Court makes particular rulings. A majority of the Court must agree before the ruling becomes law. The judiciary "interprets" the law.

Article IV. Relations of the States to One Another

The goal of this article is to promote respect between the states, also known as "full faith and credit." It requires that the citizens of different states be treated similarly. It also requires states to honor the legal decisions and legal documents of other states.

Article V. The Process of Amendment

This article explains the manner in which the Constitution may be amended or changed.

Article VI. General Provisions

Article VI notes that the United States took on debts of the Confederacy, confirms that the Constitution, federal laws, and treaties "are the supreme law of the land," and requires federal and state officers to take an oath to support the Constitution.

Article VII. Ratification of the Constitution

The authors of the Constitution wrote this article with an eye toward putting the Constitution into action. Article VII provides that the Constitution becomes effective when ratified by the conventions of nine states.

The Amendments

In the years following the ratification, or approval, of the Constitution, many leaders wanted to make sure that the rights of individuals were protected. The Constitution did not specifically list those protected rights, so the states' leaders decided to add amendments, or changes and additions, to the Constitution. The

http://bit.ly/hippo_his87

first ten amendments are known collectively as the Bill of Rights. The other amendments were added periodically as the need arose throughout the course of American history. Let's look at each one of those amendments.

The Bill of Rights

The first ten amendments to the Constitution are known as the Bill of Rights. Many states ratified the Constitution only because they believed it would be amended to include the rights implemented in the Bill of Rights.

First Amendment—Religious and Political Freedom: The First Amendment prevents Congress from interfering with the freedom of religion, speech, and the press. It also incorporates the right to assemble and to petition the government.

Second Amendment—Right to Bear Arms: This amendment gives citizens a limited right to arm themselves, or keep weapons. There is some debate over whether this right is intended to be the right of the states or the right of individuals.

Third Amendment—Quartering of Troops: The purpose of the Third Amendment was to stop soldiers from taking over homes for their own use without the consent of the owner. The amendment provides that such "quartering," or "room and board," may occur "in a manner to be prescribed by law."

Fourth Amendment—Searches and Seizures: The Fourth Amendment forbids "unreasonable searches" and the issuance of warrants without "probable cause," or good reason.

Fifth Amendment—Right to Life, Liberty, and Property: The Fifth Amendment guarantees a citizen's rights while on trial as well as the rights to life, liberty, and property. When someone refuses to testify at trial and "takes the Fifth," they are said to be invoking their rights as established in the Fifth Amendment. It is also called a right against self-incrimination. The Fifth Amendment also provides that an individual must not be held for committing a crime without being "indicted." In addition, the Fifth Amendment protects against "double jeopardy," or the risk of being tried twice for the same offense. The Fifth Amendment also ensures individuals' "due process" rights, or the right to be moved through the criminal justice system in a proper fashion.

Sixth Amendment—Protection in Criminal Trials: Citizens are guaranteed a right to a speedy trial, an impartial jury, and the right to an attorney in the Sixth Amendment. The accused also has a right to "confront witnesses" against him or her at trial.

Seventh Amendment—Suits at Common Law: If there is a dispute over something valued at $20 or more, then the Seventh Amendment provides that citizens have a right to a jury trial in federal court. However, this type of case is not normally heard in federal court now.

Eighth Amendment—Bail and Punishment: The Eighth Amendment prohibits fines and punishments that, in essence, "don't fit the crime." It is said to be "cruel and unusual" to sentence someone unfairly, and the Eighth Amendment prohibits this.

Ninth Amendment—Considering Rights Not Enumerated: Fearing that the enumeration of certain rights would lead to the exclusion, or omission, of other rights, the authors of the Bill of Rights included the Ninth Amendment

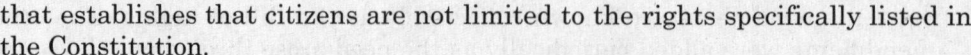

that establishes that citizens are not limited to the rights specifically listed in the Constitution.

Tenth Amendment—Powers Reserved to States and to People: Similar to the rationale behind the Ninth Amendment, the Tenth Amendment was created to reassure the states that they would retain power in those areas not specifically granted to the Federal Government.

The Other Amendments

Eleventh Amendment—Suits against a State: The Eleventh Amendment clarifies the original jurisdiction of the Supreme Court concerning a suit brought against a state by a citizen of another state.

Twelfth Amendment—Election of the President and Vice President: The Twelfth Amendment explains how the Electoral College chooses the president and vice president. It also states that the two should work together, and that the vice president should become president if the president can no longer stay in office.

Thirteenth Amendment—Slavery Prohibited: Slavery was abolished in the United States by the addition of the Thirteenth Amendment.

Fourteenth Amendment—Civil Rights for Ex-Slaves and Others: The Fourteenth Amendment ensures that all citizens of all states enjoy rights on the state level as well as the federal level. It has also been interpreted as providing for "due process" at the state level.

Fifteenth Amendment—Suffrage for Blacks: This amendment prohibits the use of race as a requirement or disqualification for voting.

Sixteenth Amendment—Income Taxes: The Sixteenth Amendment authorizes the collection of income taxes.

Seventeenth Amendment—Direct Election of Senators: Prior to the Seventeenth Amendment, senators were selected by the legislatures of the various states. Now, they could be elected by the vote of the citizens.

Eighteenth Amendment—National Prohibition: This amendment prohibits the sale or manufacture of alcohol in the United States. It was later repealed by the Twenty-First Amendment.

Nineteenth Amendment—Woman Suffrage: Just as the Fifteenth Amendment prohibits the use of race as criteria for voting, the Nineteenth Amendment prohibits the use of gender as a requirement or disqualification for voting.

Twentieth Amendment—Presidential and Congressional Terms: The Twentieth Amendment sets new start dates for congressional terms and also addresses what to do if a president dies before he is sworn into office.

Twenty-First Amendment—Prohibition Repealed: The Twenty-First Amendment repealed the Eighteenth Amendment, which had prohibited the sale or manufacture of alcohol in the United States.

Twenty-Second Amendment—Anti-Third Term Amendment: This amendment limits a president to two 4-year terms in office. There is an exception for a vice president who takes over because the president is unable to continue. In that case, the limit is a total of ten years as president.

Twenty-Third Amendment—District of Columbia Vote: This amendment gave Washington, D.C., representation in the Electoral College.

Twenty-Fourth Amendment—Poll Tax: The Twenty-Fourth Amendment prohibits charging a tax for placing a vote in a federal election.

Twenty-Fifth Amendment—Presidential Succession and Disability: This amendment states the order of succession should the president be unable to continue holding office.

Twenty-Sixth Amendment—Lowering Voting Age: Citizens who were 18 years old could vote after the passage of this amendment.

http://bit.ly/hippo_his89

Twenty-Seventh Amendment—Congressional Pay Increases: The Twenty-Seventh Amendment requires that any law that increases the pay of legislators may not take effect until after the next election.

The Federalist Papers

The Federalist Papers are a collection of eighty-five essays written by John Jay, James Madison, and Alexander Hamilton. They are considered one of the most important contributions made to American political thought. The papers were intended to influence states, particularly New York, to adopt the Constitution.

The delegates who signed the Constitution stipulated that it would take effect only after approval by ratifying conventions in nine of thirteen states. Because New York and Virginia were big and powerful, a vote against ratification from either of them would have been disastrous. The New York governor, George Clinton, clearly was opposed to the Constitution.

Hoping to persuade the New York convention to ratify the Constitution, Jay, Madison, and Hamilton wrote a series of letters defending the Constitution to New York papers under the pseudonym Publius. These letters are known collectively as The Federalist Papers. Clinton Rossitor said, "The message of The Federalist reads: no happiness without liberty, no liberty without self-government, no self-government without constitutionalism, no constitutionalism without morality—and none of these great goods without stability and order."

Landmark Supreme Court Cases

http://bit.ly/hippo_his90

The Supreme Court has issued many cases of historical significance that have directly affected our rights as individuals. Let's look at a summary of some of those "landmark" cases that definitely changed rights in America.

Marbury v. *Madison—1803*

Prior to his death, President John Adams attempted to fill a number of judicial vacancies. Some of the commissions were not delivered to the appointees prior to Adams's death. One of the appointees who did not receive his commission, William Marbury, sued Secretary of State James Madison to get his commission as Justice of the Peace.

This issue came before the Court on its "original jurisdiction" (i.e., it was not on appeal from an inferior court), and it placed the Court in a difficult position. If the Court were to issue a writ of mandamus, or order, forcing Madison to turn over the commission, and he refused, the power of the Court would be weakened.

On the other hand, to refuse to issue the writ of mandamus could be perceived as weakness or fear of the executive branch.

Ultimately, the Court's decision declared that Madison should have delivered the commission to Marbury but held that it did not have the power to issue a writ of mandamus. The Court declared that such power exceeded the Court's authority as granted in Article III of the Constitution. The writ of mandamus authority had been given to the Court by the Judiciary Act of 1789, a congressional act. Thus, the Court held an act of Congress unconstitutional. Ironically, by declaring that it did not have the power to order Madison to turn over the commission, the Court effectively strengthened its power over the other two branches of government.

http://bit.ly/hippo_his91

This case exemplifies the Court's power as the "last word" on the meaning of the Constitution. It established the judicial branch as an equal power in the three branches of government. The power to declare acts of Congress unconstitutional is one that the Court has used sparingly over the years. The legislature is, however, always aware that the Court could declare a law unconstitutional. This awareness alone helps maintain the constitutionality of newly created laws.

Dred Scott v. Sandford—1857

Dred Scott was a black slave who lived on free (non-slavery) land with his owner for several years. He tried, unsuccessfully, to sue in state court for his freedom. He then filed suit in federal court. The basis of his claim to establish his freedom was that he had lived on free soil for more than five years in an area of the country where the Missouri Compromise of 1820 forbade slavery.

http://bit.ly/hippo_his92

The Supreme Court ruled that Scott was a slave and not a citizen and therefore did not have the right to sue in federal court. The right to file suit is a right limited to citizens in Article III of the Constitution. A majority of the Court held that, because a slave was the private property of his master, the Missouri Compromise unconstitutionally took the slave owner's property without due process of law. Thus, a slave could be taken into any territory and held there. The reason? The Fifth Amendment clearly forbids Congress from depriving people of their property without due process. To allow Scott his freedom would be to deprive his owner of his "property." The Court found the Missouri Compromise unconstitutional, and Dred Scott remained a slave.

Plessy v. Ferguson—1896

Homer Adolph Plessy was a resident of Louisiana and a citizen of the United States. He was of partial African descent. He paid for a first-class ticket on the East Louisiana Railway, a passenger train that ran through Louisiana. When he boarded the train, Plessy found a seat in a car that was filled with white people and was designated for white passengers. The train conductor informed Plessy that he would have to find a seat in a car not designated for white people or he would be forced to leave the train. Plessy refused and was arrested.

Plessy was found guilty of violating a state statute that required passenger trains to provide "separate, but equal" accommodations for white and black people. The statute also imposed criminal punishment on those passengers who refused to comply. Plessy brought suit challenging the Louisiana statute as an unconstitutional violation of his due process rights under the Fourteenth Amendment. The Supreme Court held that the statute requiring "separate but equal" facilities was constitutional, rationalizing that separate facilities for blacks and whites satisfied the Fourteenth Amendment as long as they were equal. In other words, the Court found that segregation does not in itself constitute unlawful discrimination.

Brown v. *Board of Education of Topeka, Kansas—1955*

http://bit.ly/hippo_his93

Linda Brown, a black third-grade student, walked a mile everyday to get to her "black" school, even though a school designated for white children was much closer to her home. Linda's father tried to enroll her in the "white" school, but the school refused to accept Linda as a student. The Browns got help from the National Association for the Advancement of Colored People (NAACP) and sued the school board. The Supreme Court, hearing the case on appeal, ordered oral arguments in the case twice before reaching a decision. The question before the court: "Does segregation of children in public schools solely on the basis of race, even though the physical facilities and other 'tangible' factors may be equal, deprive the children of the minority group of equal educational opportunities?"

Thus, the question of "separate but equal" was once again before the court. The Court's decision in *Plessy* v. *Ferguson,* a finding that separate facilities are not unconstitutional as long as they are equal, seemed to hold the answer in this case as well. However, fifty-nine years had passed, and this time, the Court's ruling was quite different. Significantly, the opinion of the Court was unanimous. The decision: "We conclude that in the field of public education, the doctrine of 'separate but equal' has no place. Separate educational facilities are inherently unequal."

The *Brown* decision did not abolish segregation in any areas other than public schools, but it was a start toward integrating the races in many areas of life. The Court did not overrule *Plessy* v. *Ferguson,* because it limited the decision in Brown to public schools. The ruling did, however, have a significant impact on the segregation of the races in many public facilities. Slowly, integration began. That was fifty-five years ago. We can only imagine how different integration might have been if the Court's decision in *Plessy* over 100 years ago had held separate facilities to be "inherently unequal."

http://bit.ly/hippo_his94

Miranda v. *Arizona—1966*

Ernesto Miranda was arrested for raping an 18-year-old girl. The police arrived at Miranda's home at night and asked him to go with them to the police station. Miranda, claiming he did not realize he had a choice, went with the police. After 2 hours of interrogation, Miranda confessed to the crime.

On appeal to the Supreme Court, Miranda argued that he would not have confessed to the crime if he had been advised of his right to remain silent and to have an attorney. In a 5-4 decision, the Court determined that a suspect must be warned prior to custodial interrogation of his right to remain silent, that any statement he does make may be used against him, and that he has a right to an attorney. Specifically, the Court stated: "He must be warned prior to any questioning that he has the right to remain silent, that anything he says can be used against him in a court of law, that he has the right to the presence of an attorney, and that if he cannot afford an attorney one will be appointed for him prior to any questioning if he so desires." Thus, the infamous "Miranda" warnings.

http://bit.ly/hippo_his95

Roe v. Wade—1973

Roe was a single, pregnant woman who brought suit to challenge the constitutionality of the Texas laws that made getting an abortion or performing an abortion illegal. The laws did except those abortions performed on medical advice to save the mother's life.

The Court held that the law violated the due process clause of the Fourteenth Amendment, which protects the right to privacy against state action. This right, the Court found, includes a woman's qualified right to terminate her pregnancy. The Court acknowledged that the state has a legitimate interest in protecting both the pregnant woman's health and the potentiality of human life, and placed those rights on a scale that tips further to the state's interests as the pregnancy progresses.

During the first trimester, the Court stated, the decision should be left to the attending physician. After that, the state could regulate the abortion procedure in ways "reasonably related" to the mother's health. Subsequent to "viability," or the ability of the child to live outside of the womb, the Court held that the state could regulate abortion and even prohibit it except where necessary to save the life of the mother. Many abortion cases have followed *Roe,* but this was the first to hold a woman's right to privacy, outweighing the state's interest in protecting her health and the unborn child.

Nixon v. United States—1974

During the presidential election of 1972, burglars broke into the Democratic National Committee's headquarters in Watergate. A federal grand jury indicted the Attorney General and others, alleging conspiracy and obstruction of justice. The grand jury named President Richard Nixon as a co-conspirator.

Investigations revealed that Nixon taped many conversations that took place in the oval office. The tapes were subpoenaed, and Nixon released edited transcripts but refused to release anything more, claiming "executive privilege." Executive privilege protects the president from being compelled by the judicial branch to turn over confidential executive branch material.

The question before the Court: Does the president have the right under executive privilege to refuse to surrender material to federal court? In a unanimous (8-0, Justice Rehnquist did not participate) decision, the Court held that Nixon had to turn over the tapes. The Court stated: "[N]either the doctrine of Separation of Powers, nor the need for confidentiality of high-level communications, without more, can sustain an absolute, unqualified Presidential privilege of immunity from judicial process under all circumstances. The President's need of complete candor and objectivity from advisors calls for great deference from the courts. However, when the privilege depends solely on the broad, undifferentiated claim of public interest in the confidentiality of such conversations, a confrontation with other values arises. Absent a claim of need to protect military, diplomatic, or sensitive national security secrets, we find it difficult to accept the argument that even the very important interest in confidentiality of Presidential communications is significantly diminished by production of such material for in camera inspection with all the protection that a district court will be obliged to provide." With this decision, the Court limited the president's use of "executive privilege" to the need to protect military secrets, diplomatic secrets, or national security.

The rationale is based on the idea that the courts will protect the information and treat it as confidential.

Hustler Magazine, Inc. v. *Falwell—1988*

Reverend Jerry Falwell filed suit against *Hustler* magazine because the magazine published a cartoon that portrayed Falwell as engaging in an incestuous relationship with his mother in an outhouse.

The Supreme Court held that, in order to protect the free flow of ideas and opinions, the First and Fourteenth Amendments prohibit public figures and public officials from recovering for "intentional infliction of emotional distress" when the speech that causes the distress could not reasonably be taken as implying the truth. In essence, because the cartoon was obviously a joke, and because Falwell was a "public figure," *Hustler* had the right to print the cartoon under the First Amendment to the Constitution. If an individual places himself in a position to be known by the public, then he takes on the risk of being the topic of jokes.

Boy Scouts of America v. *Dale—2000*

The Boy Scouts revoked Dale's position as assistant scoutmaster in a New Jersey troop after learning that he was homosexual. Dale sued, claiming violation of a state statute prohibiting discrimination on the basis of sexual orientation. The Supreme Court held that the Boy Scouts could not be required to include Dale in its organization. The Court stated that to require mandatory inclusion of unwanted individuals into the organization would violate the Boy Scouts' First Amendment right of "expressive association." Forced membership, the Court found, is unconstitutional if it affects the group's ability to advocate its collective viewpoints. Because the Boy Scouts believed that a homosexual lifestyle conflicted with its philosophies, the inclusion of Dale would have hindered the Boy Scouts' ability to teach its views. Thus, to protect the Boy Scouts' First Amendment rights, it could not be forced to include Dale in its membership.

CANADIAN HISTORY

QUESTIONS 1 AND 2 REFER TO THE FOLLOWING INFORMATION.

The Earliest Canadians

The earliest inhabitants of Canada most likely traveled from Asia to North America across a land bridge that spanned the Bering Strait. The nomadic hunters probably followed large game into North America at least 10,000 years ago. Once in North America, they scattered across the continent and formed their own communities, each with its own distinct language. A new wave of nomads probably migrated to North America about 4,000 years ago. Although the earliest Canadians settled across North America, the greatest concentrations of people were located along the Pacific Coast and in what is now Ontario. Over the centuries, the inhabitants of Canada developed a number of languages and cultures unique to Canada, including the Algonquian and the Athapaskan language groups. These groups, and others, interacted only with each other until AD 985.

The Arrival of Europeans

In approximately 985, the first Europeans, the Vikings, landed on, explored, and settled Greenland. They also explored the northeastern coast of Canada. About fifteen years later, the famous Viking Leif Ericson sailed from Greenland to a place he called Vinland, which was probably modern-day Newfoundland. Although exploration and trade continued along the northeast coast of Canada, the Viking colonies did not last long, and by the early fifteenth century, Europeans no longer maintained contact with North America.

Toward the end of the fifteenth century, European explorers began exploring North America's eastern coast again. John Cabot unsuccessfully searched the coast for the Northwest Passage, a sea route that Europeans believed would lead to the wealthy Asian trade empires. In the sixteenth century, France sponsored Jacques Cartier to continue the search for the Northwest Passage. Cartier was also unsuccessful in locating a sea route to Asia and was later unsuccessful at establishing a colony in North America.

Later attempts at colonization also met with little success. However, the Europeans discovered the vast wealth of fish and whales available to commercial fishermen off the coast of Labrador, in the Gulf of St. Lawrence, and in the Grand Banks. Fishermen from Spain, France, England, and Portugal took advantage of the bountiful catch found here. Eventually the English explorer Sir Humphrey Gilbert claimed Newfoundland for England. After the Spanish and Portuguese left the area, the English settled the northern part of Newfoundland, and the French settled the southern part. These settlers entered into a trade relationship with the natives. The bulk of the trading was done with furs, especially beaver furs. The European demand for beaver products, particularly hats, launched an industry in Canada that remained a vital part of its economy for many years to follow.

The indigenous, or native, peoples of Canada traded with the European settlers and formed many alliances with the Europeans. Because of the large amount of Canadian territory and the relatively small number of Europeans in Canada, few conflicts emerged between Europeans and the indigenous nations they encountered in Canada. The Europeans made some attempts to Christianize the natives, but they found little success. The greatest negative effect of the trade relationship was the transmission of European diseases to the indigenous people of Canada. Diseases in epidemic proportions spread quickly and decimated vast numbers of natives wherever the Europeans went. The indigenous population of Canada continued to decline even into the twentieth century.

1. Which of the following is most likely true of the first inhabitants of Canada?

   (1) The first inhabitants of Canada were probably civilized.

   (2) The first inhabitants of Canada were probably of Asian descent.

   (3) The first inhabitants of Canada settled in permanent shelters as soon as they arrived in Canada.

   (4) The first Canadians were indigenous to North America.

   (5) The first Canadians probably were great farmers.

The first people in Canada likely crossed the land bridge between Asia and modern-day Alaska. **The correct answer is (2).**

2. Which of the following best describes the relationship between the Europeans who explored North America and the natives of Canada?

   (1) The two groups were involved in nearly incessant warfare.

   (2) The two groups formed a military alliance.

   (3) The two groups had a relationship based on trade.

   (4) The two groups freely exchanged information about cultures and farming techniques.

   (5) The two groups never had contact with one another.

The Europeans and the natives exchanged many goods and generally maintained a good relationship. **The correct answer is (3).**

QUESTIONS 3 AND 4 REFER TO THE FOLLOWING INFORMATION.

Early Canadian Colonies

As France began to see the huge dividends paid by the fur trade in Canada (which was known as New France), it officially claimed and began defending the area. England, a perennial enemy of France, disputed the claim. France realized that new, permanent settlements needed to be built if the claim to New France was going to be legitimate. Therefore, France used the fur trade to finance the construction of new forts and settlements. France settled at Quebec, an inland site well protected from foreign aggression. France then employed an economic policy known as mercantilism. Under mercantilism, a trade company was given control over New France. In exchange, the company agreed to ship all exports to France and to purchase all of its raw materials and supplies from France. The French also created strong alliances with the Huron and the Algonquian, two local nations of indigenous peoples. With the help of these two peoples, the French colony grew and prospered. The French also created many maps of the area, and in the 1630s and 1640s, they established colonies at Trois-Rivières and Montreal. The colonies remained dependent upon the fur trade and their relationship with the natives. This presented a problem in the mid-1600s, though, when the French aided the Huron in a losing effort against the Iroquois. The devastation of the Huron nearly cost France the colonies.

Conflict with the British

In the second half of the seventeenth century, the French increased their defenses and population in New France. Also during the late seventeenth century, the French sponsored significant exploration of North America, both westward across Canada and southward along the Mississippi River in the Louisiana territory. The English re-entered the picture during this same time period when the Hudson Bay Company, an English trade company, began competing with the French for the fur trade. The French responded by building more forts in French territory and along the frontier.

In the 1680s, the French found themselves in conflict with the British in several parts of the world, including North America. In King William's War during the 1690s, the French and British troops in North America exchanged guerrilla raids and attacks for nearly a decade before signing a treaty that returned North America to the way it was before the war. In 1702, Queen Anne's War erupted between the two powers and later ended with France giving up some of its territory. The next half-century or so was a period of high tensions but no war. France continued to expand its fur trade and its relationship with the indigenous peoples in and around New France.

However, in 1754, the French and Indian War broke out between the French and the British. Many natives fought on both sides of the conflict. The French held their ground well against the British, who greatly outnumbered the French. However, at the war's end in 1763, France ceded its territory to Great Britain. Quebec, Nova Scotia, Newfoundland, and Rupert's Land were now under British control. Great Britain immediately sought to ease tensions between the British and the natives in Canada by signing treaties with them.

3. The French and the English competed most for which of the following in Canada?

   (1) the fur trade

   (2) Indian alliances

   (3) the western territories

   (4) influence over the colonial government

   (5) access to the Mississippi River

Both nations wanted control of the lucrative fur trade, which brought about fierce competition between the two rivals. **The correct answer is (1).**

4. Which of the following is true about the situation after the end of the French and Indian War?

   (1) No indigenous peoples had become involved in the conflict between France and Great Britain.

   (2) The French territories remained unchanged from the beginning of the war.

   (3) The French added to their territories much land formerly under British rule.

   (4) The French and the British signed a treaty that allied the two powers against the indigenous peoples of Canada.

   (5) France lost much land to Britain.

Rupert's Island, Quebec, Nova Scotia, and Newfoundland all went to Great Britain after the war. **The correct answer is (5).**

QUESTIONS 5 AND 6 REFER TO THE FOLLOWING INFORMATION.

Early British Rule

At first, Britain hoped to institute British customs and British-style government in its new territory. However, that plan did not work because of the resistance of the Canadian people, most of whom were originally French. With the Quebec Act of 1774, Great Britain allowed French law, French customs, and even Catholicism to continue in Canada. This went a long way toward reconciliation between the French Canadians and the British government. The Quebec Act also returned some land to Quebec and saved Montreal's fur trade, the backbone of its economy. The Canadian colonies grew, but they remained only loosely linked to each other.

With relative peace and security in Canada, the bulk of British forces left Canada. This opened the door for trouble with the thirteen British colonies to the South. In 1775 and 1776, the thirteen British colonies along the Atlantic coast (now known as the United States) decided to break away from British control. During the time the colonies fought the British, they also invaded Quebec and Montreal. The British eventually drove the Americans out of Canada, but they failed to prevent the colonies from winning their independence. During and after the war, many loyalists—those Americans still loyal to Great Britain—fled the colonies and sought refuge in Canada. The British government rewarded these refugees for their loyalty by granting them land and other financial benefits.

The loyalists who settled in Canada expected they would be living in a British land, but what they found was an unfamiliar and uncomfortable French-style society. By 1791, these loyalists had voiced their displeasure with the situation on many occasions. The British government responded by dividing Quebec into two separate colonies called Upper Canada and Lower Canada. Each colony received a new constitution. The predominantly French Lower Canada retained its French culture and laws while the mostly British Upper Canada received new English laws that favored both the English nobility and the Protestant religion.

When the United States declared war on Great Britain in 1812, the United States thought it might be able to take advantage of the perceived vulnerability of Canada. U.S. troops invaded Upper Canada but were soundly defeated by British forces and natives allied with the British. This act of aggression created an anti-American sentiment throughout much of Canada, particularly in Upper Canada.

5. For which of the following reasons might the Canadian people have been resistant to British rule?

(1) Most of the people in Canada liked the government that they had already established there.

(2) Most of the people in Canada did not like people who spoke English.

(3) Most Canadians at the time were of French descent, and the French and British generally have never gotten along very well.

(4) The British refused to allow French customs and traditions to be practiced in Canada.

(5) The British established a cruel, oppressive government in Canada.

The French and British had a long history of disputes. **The correct answer is (3).**

6. What steps did the British take to give aid to refugees from the thirteen colonies during the War for American Independence?

(1) The government gave them safe passage back to Great Britain.

(2) The government granted them tracts of land in Canada.

(3) The government refused to give them any aid and encouraged them to return to America.

(4) The government took land and wealth away from the natives and gave it to the refugees.

(5) The government forced them to enlist in the British army to fight against the rebels in the colonies.

The British government wanted to reward the loyalists for their loyalty to Great Britain. **The correct answer is (2).**

QUESTIONS 7 AND 8 REFER TO THE FOLLOWING INFORMATION.

Westward Expansion and Immigration

In the late eighteenth and early nineteenth centuries, two companies battled for control of the fur trade and sparked westward expansion in Canada. The Hudson Bay Company had been granted a monopoly on the fur trade, but a company founded by French-Canadian fur traders defied the monopoly. The North West Company explored, mapped, and tapped the natural resources of Canada all the way to the Pacific Coast. Both companies struggled for influence throughout the western territories. Friction between the two companies often resulted in outbreaks of violence in frontier towns. Finally, in 1821, the two companies merged and the Hudson Bay Company assumed control of the Canadian fur trade. However, by the end of the nineteenth century, the timber industry replaced the fur trade as the leading industry in Canada.

During the nineteenth century, millions of Europeans migrated to North America to seek new opportunities. Perhaps 1 to 2 million of these people, most from England, Ireland, and Scotland, migrated to Canadian territories. They were willing to take the risk of moving to the frontier because of the promise of free farmland. Upper Canada grew faster than any other part of the Canadian territory. Relatively few immigrants, on the other hand, moved to the far north or the far west. Not until the gold rush in the second half of the nineteenth century did a significant number of settlers move to the Pacific region. As the immigration continued, the native peoples of British North America gradually became the minority of the population.

7. Which of the following statements could be made concerning the competition between the two trade companies in Canada?

   (1) The competition between the two companies nearly caused a civil war.

   (2) The indigenous people were caught in the middle of the war between the two trade companies.

   (3) The two trade companies encouraged good, healthy competition in the marketplace.

   (4) The competition between the two companies ultimately led to the mapping and exploration of some of the western parts of Canada.

   (5) The revenue produced by the two trade companies provided a major boost for the French, British, and Canadian economies.

In order to find more resources and stay competitive with the Hudson Bay Company, the North West Company moved westward, exploring and mapping as it went. **The correct answer is (4).**

8. Which of the following was the primary reason for the massive immigration to Canada during the early 1800s?

   (1) The government offered land grants to anyone who wanted to settle on the frontier.

   (2) World War in Europe drove millions from their homes.

   (3) The prospects of finding a job in the factories of Canada prompted many Europeans to immigrate.

   (4) The gold rush made many people seek their fortunes.

   (5) Oppressive governments in the United States and Great Britain created a large number of political refugees who sought safety in Canada.

Immigrants to Canada received large tracts of land on which they could settle and build homes. **The correct answer is (1).**

QUESTIONS 9 AND 10 REFER TO THE FOLLOWING INFORMATION.

Radicals, Reformers, the Act of Union, and Confederation

Because most of the non-indigenous inhabitants of Canada during the early 1800s were hardworking farmers and fishermen, the traditional British aristocratic system of government did not please many of the Canadians. In the early 1800s, two groups called for a change in the government. The moderate group of people who sought change was known as reformers. The reformers liked the British system of government, but they wanted a parliamentary system with an elected legislature instead of one that was appointed. The radicals, the more liberal of the two groups, sought publicly elected officials within a republic modeled after the governments of France and the United States. Many in Canada, especially in Lower Canada, pointed to Britain as the root of many of the social, political, and economic problems that Canada faced. These feelings erupted in an armed rebellion in 1837 that eventually ended in victory for the British. The political climate in Lower and Upper Canada convinced Great Britain that something needed to be done in order to maintain peace.

In 1841, the British passed the Act of Union, which created the province of Canada. This province had two sections, Canada East and Canada West (formerly Lower Canada and Upper Canada, respectively). The act gave Canada West the same representation as the larger Canada East, and it made English the official language. Eventually, the government, which the Act of Union created, was dissolved. The Canadian provinces won the right to local self-government, and Britain retained the right to manage foreign affairs, defense, and the appointment of provincial governors.

During this time, a two-party system emerged in Canadian politics. Also during this time, industry began to grow in Canada. Trade restrictions and tariffs were eased, and North American trade flourished. Railroads were built across Canada that carried both passengers and cargo. Telegraph lines connected many parts of Canada and North America. Shipbuilding reached an all-time high in British North America. For some parts of Canada, this period was a golden age.

During the 1850s, talk of unifying the Canadian provinces was a topic of great debate. In the 1860s, when the Southern states of the United States tried to secede from the United States, talk of Canadian unification intensified. Canada, Nova Scotia, New Brunswick, Prince Edward Island, and Newfoundland met to discuss unification, or Confederation, as it came to be known. The legislative leaders approved the Seventy-two Resolutions, which was a draft of a constitution.

Under the Confederation, the governmental responsibilities would be split between a national government and provincial governments. The Confederation was not a move toward independence, though. Leaders wanted to maintain ties with Britain to prevent aggression from the United States. After ratification of the Seventy-two Resolutions, the Dominion of Canada was created in 1867. The new Canada had four provinces: Quebec, Ontario, New Brunswick, and Nova Scotia. Ottawa was chosen as the national capital. Great Britain did not repeal the Confederation, so in 1871, the last British troops left Canada.

The new nation moved immediately to expand westward. In 1869, Canada added the Northwest Territories, land that Canada purchased from the Hudson Bay Company. In 1871, British Columbia joined Canada, followed by Prince Edward Island two years later. Canada later added the Arctic Archipelago, Newfoundland,

and Labrador. Two other important steps taken by the new Canada were the creation of the Royal Mounted Police and the beginning of the transcontinental railroad.

9. One of the major concerns about the Act of Union was which of the following?

(1) It did not preserve the heritage and culture of Quebec.

(2) It gave two areas the same vote even though the populations of the two areas were not the same.

(3) It allowed for no more than two parties in the Canadian political system.

(4) It officially blamed Great Britain for all the problems in Canada.

(5) It united all of Canada under a new government and not under the British monarch.

Upper and Lower Canada received equal representation, but the populations of the two were not equal, thus making the representation unfair. **The correct answer is (2).**

10. Which of the following statements best defines *confederation*?

(1) Confederation meant that Canada would no longer have ties with Britain.

(2) Confederation meant that Britain and Canada would become united as one nation under God.

(3) Confederation meant that the Canadian provinces would be loosely united but still under the monarch.

(4) Confederation meant that some of the Canadian provinces would secede from the British Empire the way the Southern states did in the United States.

(5) Confederation meant that Canada would form an alliance with the United States.

Confederation meant that the provinces would be united, but they would remain under the control of the British monarch. **The correct answer is (3).**

QUESTIONS 11 AND 12 REFER TO THE FOLLOWING INFORMATION.

Industrialization and Immigration

The late 1800s proved to be a time of industrial growth for many parts of Canada. Many cities located along the railroad benefited by having their goods shipped by rail. The main areas of industrial growth were in Montreal and Ontario. The populations in those two cities grew as people flocked to the cities in search of work. Many people made the transition from rural workers to urban wage laborers.

This brought with it organized labor in the form of unions. The Atlantic cities, however, suffered during this time because their wooden ships were becoming obsolete due to the new steel ships. The government also implemented tariffs during this time to help boost the Canadian economy. Another economic boost to the Canadian economy was the discovery of gold in the Yukon Territory just before the turn of the century. People rushed by the thousands to the Yukon Territory to seek their fortunes. Further economic boosts came with the development of Canada's natural mineral and hydroelectric resources in central Canada.

As the economy boomed in Canada at the turn of the twentieth century, immigrants flocked to Canada. Many of these immigrants moved to Canada from Britain and the United States. However, for the first time many immigrants moved to Canada from other European nations, particularly from Eastern Europe. The Canadian government granted many tracts of land in the far west to the immigrants, and the immigrants began to develop the frontier. Many Canadians distrusted the immigrants who did not come from Britain, though. This fear and distrust caused backlash against the immigrants several times in the late 1800s and the early 1900s.

Canada, the British Empire, and Problems in Quebec

In the 1890s, a new Prime Minister adopted the popular Conservative political view that Canada should stand by the British Empire no matter what, even in matters of imperialism, or expansion into other lands. This policy was popular with most of the Canadians of British descent, but many of the French-speaking Canadians strongly opposed the policy. When Great Britain entered the Boer War in South Africa, many Canadians were ready to fight alongside the British. However, the French-speaking population opposed the popular policy because they were not willing to fight in Britain's wars on other continents. Furthermore, the French-speaking Canadians, most of whom were in Quebec, believed that the rest of Canada did not respect them, which caused a deep rift between Quebec and the other provinces.

The Canadian government felt pressure from both French and British Canadians over the extent to which Canada should help the British Empire. In 1910, Britain expected Canada to contribute to its navy. Instead of contributing, Canada built a small fleet of its own to sail alongside the British navy. Popular opinion turned to outrage again when Canada ratified a treaty with the United States that reduced tariffs and duties, a treaty that U.S. officials saw as a step toward the annexation of Canada. The people of Canada expressed their displeasure, which led to the Conservative Party winning the election of 1911.

In 1914, the British declared war on Germany. This meant that all British holdings, including Canada, were at war, too. Canada responded quickly to Britain's call and sent tens of thousand of Canadians to help with the war effort. The war had a huge impact on Canada. The government imposed Canada's first income tax in 1917. Also, women replaced men in the factories and consequently earned the right to vote. Another result of the war was the increased tension between Quebec and the rest of Canada. One of the biggest points of contention was the conscription, or draft, that began in 1918. This draft practically split the country because it proved to Quebec that English-speaking Canada would ignore French-speaking Canada in matters of national importance.

After the war, Canadians felt a deeper sense of nationalism than they ever had before due mostly to the large number of Canadian casualties in the war. Canada began to act as an independent, sovereign nation during treaty negotiations. In 1926, the British government acknowledged Canada's equality with Great Britain. Then, in 1931, Canada was declared a sovereign state; however, it remained under the British monarch.

11. Which of the following was a result of industrialization in Canada?

    (1) People moved from urban areas to rural areas in search of jobs.

    (2) People moved from rural areas to urban areas in search of jobs.

    (3) Railroads were built after Canada completed all of its factories.

    (4) Millions of people lost their jobs because machines replaced humans at work.

    (5) The western territories became the financial center of Canada.

People moved from the country into cities to find work in factories. **The correct answer is (2).**

12. Which of the following was a major concern of Quebec during the late eighteenth and early nineteenth centuries?

    (1) Quebec feared that the United States would annex its territory.

    (2) Quebec feared that the rest of Canada did not respect its heritage and culture and, therefore, did not respect Quebec in important matters.

    (3) Quebec feared that French would be outlawed within its own borders.

    (4) Quebec feared that all its inhabitants would be drafted for World War I.

    (5) Quebec feared that the rest of Canada would not allow Quebec to participate in the government.

English-speaking Canada often ignored the needs and wants of French-speaking Quebec. **The correct answer is (2).**

QUESTIONS 13 AND 14 REFER TO THE FOLLOWING INFORMATION.

The Twentieth Century after World War I

Canada faced many problems after the First World War. Returning soldiers had a difficult time returning to a normal life in Canada. The economy did not boom during the 1920s in Canada as it did in the United States. Industry had difficulty making the transition from wartime production to peacetime production. Unemployment was high, and labor unrest loomed large, especially in the Atlantic regions. To make matters worse, Canada felt the effects of the Great Depression immediately. Many of Canada's trade partners closed their doors to Canadian goods, and foreign investors no longer had money to invest in Canada.

Even though the economic decline slowed in the 1930s, the economy did not fully recover until World War II. Canada was initially hesitant to become involved in the war, but the government felt it had no other choice. As the war progressed, the government put the issue of conscription to a vote by the people. All of Canada, with the exception of Quebec, favored the draft. Canada launched a major war effort, and the economy bounced back and did well during the war years.

After the war, the Canadian government moved more and more toward governmental control of the economic and financial aspects of the country. Government spending increased to compensate for the lack of business investments in Canada. A number of major social programs, including medical insurance and health care, were launched in the twenty years after the war. The economy boomed because Canada suddenly found itself with a seemingly endless number of markets for Canadian goods in Europe. Both industry and the population increased greatly after the soldiers returned from the war. Also after the war, Canada joined the North Atlantic Treaty Organization (NATO) and played an increased role in international politics.

Problems in Quebec refused to go away, even after World War II. Many in Quebec wanted to break away from English-speaking Canada. Quebec wanted self-government and reduced Canadian control over affairs within Quebec. The situation in Quebec came to a head in the early 1970s when terrorism, kidnappings, and mass arrests occurred as a result of the Quebec dispute. Other provinces and indigenous peoples followed the lead of Quebec and demanded more provincial control and less national control over provincial affairs.

In 1982, Canada cut its final formal legislative ties with Britain by earning the right to amend its constitution. In 1987, the subject of Quebec came up again. Quebec asked for special legislation that would protect its special culture and heritage. The accord, however, did not survive. Again in 1992, Canada had an opportunity to recognize Quebec as a "distinct society," yet, that, too, failed to succeed. Throughout the 1990s, Quebec talked of secession, but the highest court in the land declared secession unconstitutional.

Indigenous peoples did reap one reward in the late 1990s as a new province, Nunavut, was added. In addition, Canada established a Healing Fund to help apologize to the indigenous peoples for the many years of injustice. Even today, the subjects of indigenous peoples' rights and an independent Quebec are at the forefront of Canadian issues.

13. Which of the following can be said of Canada after World War I?

(1) Canada strengthened its ties to Great Britain.

(2) Canada moved to cut all ties with Great Britain.

(3) Canada cut some of the last ties with Great Britain.

(4) Canada had the strongest military in the Western Hemisphere.

(5) Canada gave women the right to vote long after most modern nations.

Although Canada did cut some ties, it remained under the British monarch after World War I and remains so even today. **The correct answer is (3).**

14. Which of the following is true of Canada immediately after World War II?

(1) The Canadian economy declined tremendously because of the Canadian war efforts.

(2) The Canadian economy boomed because of an increase in foreign markets for Canadian goods.

(3) Canada's role in international politics dwindled until Canada no longer had any input in the international political arena.

(4) Canada's population doubled because of Eastern European immigration.

(5) Canada's indigenous peoples were granted an apology from the government along with their own province.

Following World War II, Canada shipped many of its goods to the war-torn countries of Europe. **The correct answer is (2).**

SUMMING IT UP

- The GED® Social Studies Test is designed to measure critical-thinking skills rather than knowledge. However, reviewing the four content areas covered on the test—history, civics and government, economics, and geography—will help you handle the questions with greater ease and confidence.

- This history review begins at the very beginning of civilization. It then traces the development of Western civilization from its roots in the ancient empires of Europe through the European Middle Ages and Renaissance Era, to the Age of Exploration that ultimately led to the founding of the thirteen British colonies. The review then focuses mainly on U.S. history, although some of that history is presented in the context of the world affairs and relations between the United States and other nations.

- The Social Studies Test will contain an excerpt from at least one of the following historical documents: the Declaration of Independence, the U.S. Constitution, the Federalist Papers, or landmark Supreme Court cases. Before you take the Social Studies Test, read through parts (if not all) of each of these documents to familiarize yourself with their language and style.

- A review of Canadian government, civics, and history is also provided here for those students preparing to take the GED® exam in Canada.

PART V

THE SCIENCE TEST

Mastering the Science Test

chapter 8

OVERVIEW

- All about the science test
- What's tested—and what's *not* tested
- Formats used for GED® science questions
- Subject areas for GED® science questions
- Question types based on the four skill areas
- Application questions
- Questions based on visual depictions
- General test-taking strategies
- Summing it up

THE SCIENCE TEST—IN A NUTSHELL

Total time allowed: 80 minutes

Total number of questions: 50 multiple-choice (5 choices per question)

Format: Each question is based on a text passage and/or visual depiction

Length of text passages: Up to 250 words (but most are 2 to 4 sentences)

Number of questions per passage or visual: 1 to 4 (1 or 2 is most common)

ALL ABOUT THE SCIENCE TEST

The broad academic field of science includes a wide variety of subjects, all involving the **natural sciences** (as opposed to the social sciences, which are covered on the Social Studies Test). These subjects include life science (biology), earth science (geology and oceanography), space science (astronomy), and physical science (chemistry and physics). The GED® Science Test is designed to measure a variety of abilities within the context of all of these subject areas. The test consists of fifty multiple-choice questions. Here's the breakdown in terms of the subject areas that the test covers (percentages and numbers may vary slightly):

45% (22 or 23 questions)	Life science (biology)
20% (10 questions)	Earth science and astronomy
35% (17 or 18 questions)	Physical science (chemistry and physics)

The test questions are *not* grouped by content area. Instead, questions from all areas listed above are mixed together.

WHAT'S TESTED—AND WHAT'S *NOT* TESTED

The most important point to keep in mind about the GED® Science Test is that it is *not* primarily a knowledge test. Regardless of content area—life science, earth or space science, or physical science—all but the most basic information you'll need to answer a question will be provided. That said, the test assumes, or presupposes, a certain level of common knowledge about the physical world around us. For example:

- That all animals require food, which they convert to energy, in order to grow and survive

- That gravity works to keep us grounded, and that Earth has an atmosphere of air, which becomes thinner with altitude

- That the Moon revolves around the Earth, which revolves around the Sun in 365 days

- That water freezes (or melts) and vaporizes (boils) at different temperatures

- That pushing an object up a steep incline requires more total force than pushing it across flat ground

But beyond these sorts of everyday facts, which most people know from observation and experience, no specific knowledge of science is required to perform well on the test. (In this respect, the GED® Science Test is a lot like the GED® Social Studies and Language Arts, Reading tests.) Rather than demonstrating subject knowledge, your primary task during the Science Test will be to apply the following skills:

- Comprehension (recalling and understanding)

- Analysis (drawing inferences and conclusions)

- Evaluation (synthesizing)

- Application (applying concepts and ideas to other situations)

Though the Science Test is designed to measure skills rather than knowledge, keep in mind that with some prior knowledge of the subject areas covered on the test, you can expect to handle the questions with greater ease and confidence.

FORMATS USED FOR GED® SCIENCE QUESTIONS

The GED® Science Test consists of fifty multiple-choice questions. Each question lists five choices. Most questions are based on brief passages of text, which vary in length from a few sentences to as many as 250 words (about one third of a page). A question involving a passage of text might refer to it either as a "passage" or as "information" or "text." The remaining questions will be based on graphs, charts, tables, diagrams, illustrations, and other visual depictions. Some visual depictions will be accompanied by a brief passage of text. Finally, some of the questions will be presented in groups of two to four (two is most common); all questions in a group are based on the same passage and/or visual depiction.

SUBJECT AREAS FOR GED® SCIENCE QUESTIONS

As outlined earlier, the subject areas you'll encounter on the Science Test include life science (biology), earth and space science, and physical science (chemistry and physics). Here you can take a brief survey of each area.

Don't be intimidated by the scope of any one of these subject areas, or by the technical terminology and complex concepts they often involve. Rest assured: The GED® covers only the most basic concepts taught in basic high school science classes. And as noted earlier, all technical definitions and other information you'll need to answer the questions will be provided. Remember: the GED® Science Test is not a trivia or science knowledge quiz; rather, its main purpose is to measure your reading and critical-thinking skills within the context of science subject matter.

Life Science Biology

Biology can be defined as the scientific study of living organisms, including plants and animals. Biology is a broad and deep field, which is why a greater portion of GED® science questions involve biology than any of the other fields. One way to break down this vast field of study is into its three major branches:

Zoology: the scientific study of *animals*, including their structural characteristics, physiology (vital functions for growth, sustenance, and development), reproduction, and pathology (diseases)

Botany: the scientific study of *plants*, including their structural characteristics, physiology (vital functions for growth, sustenance, and development), reproduction, and pathology (diseases)

Ecology: the scientific study of how plants and animals interact with their environment

Another way to break down the field of biology is by scale:

Cellular biology involves the cell as the basic structural unit of living matter

Molecular biology involves the structure and actions of proteins and nucleic enzymes as well as heredity and how organisms process the energy needed to sustain life

Organism biology explores the individual forms of life (for example, an oak tree or a human being)

Population biology studies the organism as a member of a community and as part of an environment, or ecosystem

Biology questions account for approximately 45 percent of the Science Test—about twenty-two or twenty-three questions. Among these questions, there is no set number from each branch listed above, although you can expect a fairly even distribution.

Earth and Space Science

Earth science is the study of origins, composition, and physical features of the Earth. Like life science (biology), earth science can be broken down into various branches:

Geology: the scientific study of the Earth's rocks, minerals, land forms, and the processes that have directed them since the Earth's origins

Oceanography: the scientific study of the oceans' physical characteristics and composition, the movement of their waters, and the topography of ocean floors; oceanography also includes the study of ocean life (in this respect, oceanography and biology overlap)

Meteorology: the scientific study of the Earth's atmosphere and of atmospheric conditions (weather and climate)

Mineralogy: a branch of geology that involves the study of minerals—their composition and properties, as well as where they are found

Space science refers to the following two related fields:

Astronomy: the scientific study of the universe and of the size, composition, motion, and evolution of celestial bodies (stars, planets, galaxies, and nebula)

Astrophysics: a branch of astronomy that deals with the physical and chemical processes that occur in the universe and in interstellar space, including the structure, evolution, and interactions of stars and systems of stars

On the GED®, questions about earth and space science account for about 20 percent of the test (ten questions). Expect to encounter more questions dealing with earth science than with space science, although there is no fixed proportion.

Physical Science (Chemistry and Physics)

Physical Science includes the fields of chemistry and physics. **Chemistry** is the scientific study of the composition, properties, and interactions (or reactions) of elements and compounds (combinations of elements) and of the changes that elements and compounds undergo.

Physics is the scientific study of matter, energy, space, and time—and how they are interrelated. Physics is closely related to all other fields of science, since its laws are universal. The living systems of biology are made of matter particles that follow the laws of physics. Chemistry explores how atoms, small units of matter, interact to form molecules according to the laws of physics. And, to a great extent, the study of geology and astronomy deals with the physics of the Earth and celestial bodies, respectively.

Chemistry and physics questions account for about 35 percent of the test (seventeen or eighteen questions). Expect about the same number of questions from each of these two fields.

QUESTION TYPES BASED ON THE FOUR SKILL AREAS

To succeed on the GED® Science Test, you will need to demonstrate proficiency in four critical-thinking skill areas: comprehension, application, analysis, and evaluation. You will use all four skills throughout the test. In the next few pages, you'll examine each skill more closely. Note that the GED®-style example questions here are all based on passages of text, rather than on visual depictions. In the next section, you'll learn how to handle questions involving visuals.

Comprehension Questions

Comprehension questions require that you read and recall information contained in a passage. And in most cases, they also require that you *understand* and *interpret* that information—in other words, to grasp or comprehend—the ideas and concepts that the passage's words convey. Some comprehension questions will require you to understand the main idea of a passage, much like a main-idea question in the Language Arts, Reading Test. To handle this sort of question, look for an answer choice that sums up the passage. However, most comprehension questions on the Science Test focus instead on the passage's details.

Comprehension questions usually involve passages of text that are longer than average—at least four or five sentences and sometimes more than one paragraph. You may discover that you need to read the passage more than once to answer these questions. That's perfectly okay, since the total time allowed for taking the test, 80 minutes, should provide enough time for you to read the passages more than once.

Though the correct answer choice might restate a phrase from the passage word-for-word, more likely it will either paraphrase or provide an interpretation of passage information. In other words, comprehension questions typically focus on a passage's *ideas* rather than on exactly how those ideas are expressed. Incorrect answer choices will often contradict passage information or provide assertions that are unsupported by the passage or that do not respond to the specific question that is asked.

Don't make comprehension questions more difficult than the test-makers intend them to be. These questions are not meant to trick you, to test your ability to find underlying, "hidden" meanings within the language of the text, or to find out which test-takers already possess in-depth knowledge of the complexities of the science topic at hand. To understand how comprehension questions require merely that you understand and interpret what you've read in a passage, study the following two example questions. Both questions are based on a brief passage involving physics.

QUESTIONS 1 AND 2 REFER TO THE FOLLOWING INFORMATION.

Light travels in waves consisting of vibrating electric and magnetic fields. Stronger vibrations cause an increase in brightness. The frequencies of the waves can also be different. Blue light, for example, has a higher frequency than red light, and the distance between its vibrations, or wavelength, is shorter than the wavelength of red light. Black is the absence of light, and white light is the mixture of all colors. When white light passes through a prism, it is split into a band of colors called the spectrum.

1. Which statement is best supported by the information?

    (1) Short waves have a stronger magnetic field than longer waves do.

    (2) Light waves vibrate more strongly and at a higher frequency than sound waves do.

    (3) People are more attracted to high-frequency waves than to lower-frequency ones.

    (4) White light, which lacks any color, has no measurable wavelength or wave frequency.

    (5) Short waves have higher frequencies than longer waves do.

This question focuses on the idea that frequencies among different colors of light waves vary. To illustrate this idea, the passage points out that a blue light wave has a higher frequency and a shorter length than a red wave does. Choice (5) provides a more general way of making this point. In other words, it captures the idea conveyed in the third and fourth sentences.

Let's briefly examine the other four answer choices. The passage makes no connection between magnetism and wave frequency, choice (1); it never mentions sound waves, choice (2); and it provides no information about what property in a light wave attracts people, choice (3). As for choice (4), it contradicts the passage, which tells us that white light is a mixture of all colors—not that it lacks color. Besides, the passage does not state, nor does it suggest, that the frequency or length of a white light wave cannot be measured. **The correct answer is (5).**

2. Which of the following explains why a rainbow occurs when drops of water act as a prism?

    (1) The light waves are traveling fast enough to create color.

    (2) A rainbow is made up of white light.

    (3) There are a number of frequencies involved.

    (4) White light from the sun is dispersed through the drops.

    (5) The electric and magnetic fields have strong vibrations.

Answering this question requires that you read and understand the last sentence of the passage. Don't let the fact that the question involves a rainbow, which is not mentioned in the passage, confuse you. The question simply requires that you interpret a rainbow as one way to see the color spectrum—the band of colors mentioned in the paragraph's last sentence. The drops of water act as a prism when the white light from the sun is dispersed through the water; the drops split the light into bands of color. Of course, to answer this question you need to know what a rainbow looks like. But this is just the sort of common, everyday knowledge that the GED® Science Test presumes you have. Choice (4) appears to provide a good explanation.

Let's examine the four other answer choices. Choice (1) is incorrect because the passage neither states nor implies that a certain speed is needed to create color. Choice (2) is incorrect because we all know that a rainbow contains many colors. Choice (3) provides an accurate statement in that different color bands of the spectrum have different frequencies. But choice (3) does not explain why this occurs—in other words, it does not respond to the question. Choice (5) is incorrect because the passage makes no connection between a magnetic field (mentioned only in the first sentence) and a prism. **The correct answer is (4).**

The preceding two questions demonstrate the sort of wrong-answer choices to look for in comprehension questions. Be on the lookout for any answer choice that contradicts the passage information, goes off the passage's topic, or provides true information that nevertheless does not answer the specific question asked.

Analysis Questions

Analysis questions go beyond understanding the information in a passage or visual. Analysis involves organizing the information, explaining how ideas, facts, or data connect together, identifying patterns, and drawing inferences and conclusions from the information given. Many analysis questions will require you to *infer* cause or effect in terms of a biological, chemical, or physical process. (To infer is to draw a reasonable conclusion based on certain information.) Other analysis questions will require you to point out similarities and differences between two or more types of organisms, processes, or other scientific phenomena. These are just some of many possibilities for analysis questions.

The next question is based on a passage involving botany (a branch of biology). To analyze the question, you need to first understand different facts and then connect those facts together in order to draw a logical conclusion from them.

QUESTION 3 REFERS TO THE FOLLOWING INFORMATION.

All of the Earth's energy is produced through photosynthesis, which is the process by which green plants, algae, and some bacteria take light from the sun and convert it to chemical energy. Only organisms that contain chlorophyll can undergo photosynthesis. Chlorophyll is the pigment that makes plants green. The process of photosynthesis usually occurs in the leaves of plants.

3. What can you conclude from the information?

(1) If a plant does not have leaves, it cannot produce energy.

(2) If a plant is not green, it cannot produce energy.

(3) On cloudy days, photosynthesis does not occur.

(4) Photosynthesis does not occur in the winter.

(5) All living things undergo photosynthesis.

The paragraph does not answer this question explicitly. To answer the question, you must draw an inference, or conclusion, from the information provided. According to the paragraph, only organisms with chlorophyll can undergo photosynthesis—the process by which plants produce energy—and it is chlorophyll that gives plants their green color. Thus, you can conclude that only green plants produce energy. Stated differently, this process cannot occur in anything other than a green plant, choice (2).

Compared to choice (2), the other answer choices provide unreasonable, poorly supported conclusions based on the information provided. Choice (1) goes too far, by assuming that chlorophyll exists only in the *leaves* of plants. But the paragraph does not say this is so, and our everyday observations suggest otherwise. For example, most of us have observed the green color in pine needles, which are not leaves. In order for choice (3) or choice (4) to be correct, you must assume that absolutely no light is available for photosynthesis on cloudy days, choice (3), or during the winter, choice (4). These are not reasonable assumptions, as they violate common sense as well as our everyday experience. As for choice (5), it provides a far-too sweeping conclusion: animals are living things, but they do not contain chlorophyll. **The correct answer is (2).**

The next question is based on a passage involving astronomy. To analyze the question, you first need to understand and organize various facts about two different things. Then you need to analyze the differences between those two things.

QUESTION 4 IS BASED ON THE FOLLOWING INFORMATION.

Like Earth, Mercury—the smallest planet—revolves around the Sun. It takes nearly 88 days to make one revolution around the Sun. Earth takes 365 days to complete one revolution around the Sun. Earth completes one revolution on its own axis in 24 hours, or one day. Mercury, on the other hand, takes 58.5 Earth days to slowly make one turn on its axis.

4. Based on the information, which is an accurate distinction between Mercury and Earth?

(1) Any spot on Mercury is sunlit longer than any spot on Earth.

(2) Earth passes Mercury as they both revolve around the Sun.

(3) Mercury's orbit around the Sun is circular, whereas Earth's orbit is elliptical.

(4) Mercury orbits the Sun at a slower speed than Earth does.

(5) Mercury's year is longer than Earth's year.

Any spot on the surface of Mercury is exposed to the Sun for longer periods of time because it takes Mercury 58.5 Earth days to make one turn on its axis. (Any spot on Mercury faces the Sun for approximately 29 hours at a time, whereas on Earth the maximum is approximately 12 hours.) So answer choice (1) is a good answer.

Let's examine the other four choices. Choices (2) and (5) all contradict the information in the passage. Choice (3) is completely unsupported by the passage, which tells us nothing about the shape of either orbit. Choice (4) is more difficult to assess than the others. We know from the paragraph that Mercury orbits the Sun in fewer days than Earth does. But does this mean that Mercury is moving at a faster or slower speed than Earth? We don't know, at least not from the information provided. The answer depends not only on the time of one orbit around the Sun but also on the distance traveled during one such orbit. The passage does not give enough information to compare the speed of the two planets. **The correct answer is (1).**

The preceding questions demonstrate the sort of answer choices to be wary of when handling analysis questions:

- A choice that contradicts the passage information

- A choice that relies on crucial facts that the passage does not provide

- A choice that violates common sense or simple logic

- A choice that is inconsistent with your everyday observations and experiences

Synthesis and Evaluation Questions

Synthesis and evaluation questions involve drawing general assessments and conclusions from specific information. To "synthesize" science information is to understand what various pieces of information mean when you consider them all together, as a whole. In the context of the Science Test, a synthesis question might ask you to characterize a phenomena, process, or system described in a passage. An evaluation question might ask you to recognize a potential benefit or drawback with a new science technology, or with the way that technology is applied. Or it might ask you to recognize a flaw in a scientific claim or hypothesis, possibly related to a certain experiment.

In handling these questions, what's just as important as recognizing a reasonable assessment or conclusion is recognizing unfair assessments and conclusions. Be on the lookout for wrong-answer choices that speculate too much—answer choices that jump to conclusions that are unwarranted based solely on the information provided.

Here is a synthesis question based on a passage involving mineralogy, one of the earth sciences.

QUESTION 5 REFERS TO THE FOLLOWING INFORMATION.

There are three types of rocks on the Earth's surface: igneous, metamorphic, and sedimentary. Igneous rocks have been formed by the cooling of molten magma where temperatures are extremely high. Metamorphic rocks have been formed by the compression of older rocks. They are formed below the surface of the Earth where both the temperature and pressure are high. Sedimentary rocks are formed by weathering or the remains of living organisms. These are formed on the surface of the Earth under low pressures.

5. Based on the information, which of the following is most probably true about the three types of rock?

The three types of rocks

(1) can be found only on Earth

(2) look very much the same

(3) are found in different places

(4) are all approximately the same age

(5) all disintegrate with age

This question doesn't focus on just one part of the passage. To answer it, you instead need to read and understand all the details, and then synthesize them to form a broader perspective. The passage tells us that some rocks are formed below the surface of the Earth, that some come from volcanoes, and that some are the result of weathering or the remains of living organisms that have been found in different locations. Because the three types of rocks are all formed differently under different conditions, they cannot all be found in the same location. Choice (3) is a good answer.

Let's examine the other answer choices. The passage mentions nothing about whether these types of rocks are found on other celestial bodies, choice (1); about what the three types look like, choice (2); or their relative ages, choice (4). As for choice (5), sedimentary rocks are often the result of weathering, and so they do tend to "disintegrate" with age. However, the passage suggests just the opposite about metamorphic rocks, which are formed by compression. So choice (5) is only partially correct. **The correct answer is (3).**

Next, look at an evaluation question based on a passage involving meteorology, another one of the earth sciences.

QUESTION 6 REFERS TO THE FOLLOWING INFORMATION.

Water moves through a natural cycle of evaporation, cloud formation, rainfall, collection, and evaporation. In this cycle, water is self-purifying. Thus, smoke from industrial sites that is brought to earth by rainfall is not a problem because the water purifies itself of the pollutants.

6. Which of the following, if true, would weaken the claim that water purifies itself through the cycle described above?

(1) Rainfall can cause flooding, which can upset the ecological balance.

(2) The polluters creating the industrial smoke are unwilling to reduce the amount of their pollution.

(3) When the pollutants enter the clouds, much of them stay there.

(4) Many of the pollutants evaporate with ground water into the air.

(5) Water vapor containing industrial pollutants can travel great distances through the air.

This question asks you to assess, or critique, the assertion made in the brief passage. Your task is to recognize additional evidence that would weaken the conclusion that the smoke is not a problem because the water purifies itself. The passage describes a self-purifying cycle. But if smoke from industrial sites is brought back to the Earth by rainfall and then evaporates with the water, it will return to the clouds where it becomes part of the cycle. In this event, the water would not purify itself properly. So choice (4) provides information that, if true, would weaken the conclusion in the passage.

Let's examine the other answer choices. Choice (1) is incorrect because flooding is not related to the cycle described in the passage. Choice (2) is incorrect because the fact the industrial pollution carries on does nothing to disprove the claim that water rids itself of that pollution. The statement in choice (3), if true, would actually make the purification cycle easier, since the pollutants would not cycle around with the water. Choice (5) is incorrect because the distance that the pollutants travel before falling to the Earth in rain has nothing to do with the process of evaporation—water can evaporate anywhere. **The correct answer is (4).**

APPLICATION QUESTIONS

Application questions require you to use information in a passage (or visual) in a way that is different from the way it is presented to you. For example, a question might ask about the effect of a particular biological or chemical process or a law of physics under specific conditions. Or, a question might ask you to identify an example or a practical use of a concept, principle, or process. These are just some of the possibilities. Use your understanding of the information in the passage, along with your everyday experience and common sense, to identify the correct answer.

Here are two application questions involving physics.

QUESTION 7 REFERS TO THE FOLLOWING INFORMATION.

A fluid can exert a buoyant force, helping an object to float, but it can also exert a downward force because of the weight of the fluid above it. The suit of a deep-sea diver must contain a jacket of compressed air whose pressure counteracts the external water pressure.

7. Why do deep-sea divers wear jackets of compressed air?

   (1) They allow a diver to expand his chest in order to breathe.

   (2) They make a diver more buoyant in the water.

   (3) They allow a diver to go to defy gravity.

   (4) They keep a diver from drowning in case there is a leak in his suit.

   (5) They provide an extra source of air for the diver to breathe.

The compressed air in the diver's jacket protects the diver by forming a bubble of air around him, which acts as a cushion against the pressure of the water, allowing him to breathe and expand his chest. The explanation provided by choice (1) makes sense.

Let's examine the other four answer choices. The jacket might make the diver more buoyant, choice (2), which means that it would help the diver to float. But deep-sea divers want to go deep into the water rather than float, and so it makes no sense that a compressed-air jacket would be used mainly for buoyancy. You can eliminate choice (3) for essentially the same reason. Choices (4) and (5) assert essentially the same reason: the air in the jacket can be used for breathing. But this function has nothing to do with external water pressure, which the passage indicates is the effect of this type of jacket. **The correct answer is (1).**

QUESTION 8 REFERS TO THE FOLLOWING INFORMATION.

Newton's First Law: An object will remain in motion or in a state of rest unless something influences it and changes its course. (This property is referred to as inertia.)

Newton's Second Law: The change of motion is proportional to the force of change. (The greater the applied force, the greater the acceleration.)

Newton's Third Law: For every action (or applied force) there is an equal and opposite reaction.

8. Which is an example of Newton's Second Law?

    (1) two shopping carts colliding in a grocery store

    (2) the whiplash you would experience in a car by suddenly applying the brake

    (3) a mother pushing a baby carriage

    (4) allowing air to escape from a balloon

    (5) a child falling off a bike

The force the mother uses to push the carriage is proportional to how fast the carriage moves, so choice (3) seems an apt illustration of Newton' Second Law.

Let's examine the other answer choices. Choices (1) and (5) are examples of the first law, while choices (2) and (4) are examples of the third law. **The correct answer is (3).**

QUESTIONS BASED ON VISUAL DEPICTIONS

The GED® Science Test is more visually oriented than any of the other tests in the GED® battery. Nearly half of the questions on the Science Test will be based on a visual depiction of some sort. Some of these questions will also be accompanied by a brief passage of text. The "visual" might be a chart, graph, or table displaying quantitative information (data); it might be a flow chart showing a biological or chemical system or process; it might be a diagram or table that organizes information into classes, categories, or characteristics; it might provide a sequence of illustrations showing multiple steps, phases, or stages in a biological, geological, or chemical process. Or it may be a drawing, photo, or even a cartoon showing science as it applies to our everyday lives.

Questions based on visuals are designed to gauge your ability to understand what these visuals depict and what they mean, to analyze the information they contain, and to apply them to real-world situations. Even if you do not recognize a visual or don't understand it initially, you can still figure out the best answer to the question at hand by looking for clues in the visual, the accompanying text (if any), and the question itself.

In the following pages, you'll examine some of the types of visuals appearing frequently on the test. You'll see some examples of each type and learn how to handle them.

Illustrations that Include Arrow Symbols

The arrow symbol is used extensively in the Science Test. Arrows are used in physics questions to show the direction of physical flow or travel, as from a light or sound source, and to show the direction of pressure or other force on an object. Arrows are used in astronomy questions to show direction of travel, rotation, and orbit. Arrows are used in earth science and biology questions to indicate flow and circulation in oceans, the atmosphere, organ systems, and ecosystems. Arrows are even used in chemistry questions to indicate chemical reactions.

Pay careful attention to any arrows in an illustration, as you can be sure that they will be crucial to answer the question at hand. Note whether an arrow is pointing:

- Upward (against gravity) or downward (pulled by gravity)

- Toward or away from an object (possibly suggesting *magnetism* or a difference in *mass*)

- In a straight line versus a bent line (which might suggest *reflection, deflection,* or *refraction*)

- Through an opening versus a membrane or wall (which might suggest *permeability*)

- In a one-way circular pattern (possibly suggesting *rotation* or a continuous *cycle*)

- In each of two opposite directions (possibly suggesting an *exchange* of energy, gases, liquids, etc.)

- In a single, continuous line versus a line that splits in different directions (which might suggest a *dispersion* pattern for light or sound waves, or the dispersion of atoms or molecules)

QUESTIONS 9 AND 10 REFER TO THE FOLLOWING ILLUSTRATION AND BRIEF PASSAGE OF TEXT.

The following diagram illustrates three types of levers. All three are dependent on the effort (E), load (L), and fulcrum (F). Any lever in which the load and effort balance each other is said to be in equilibrium.

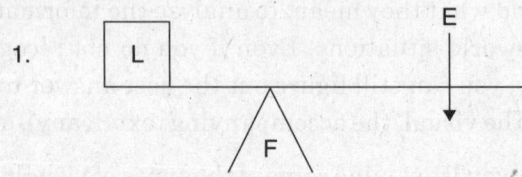

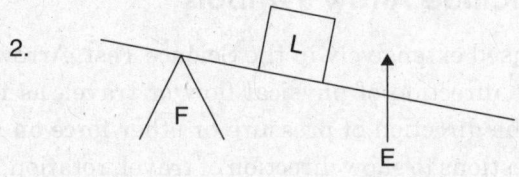

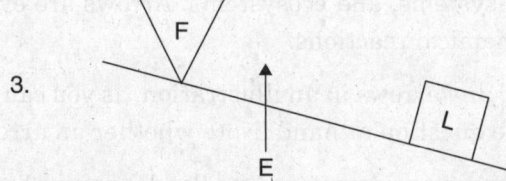

9. Which general principle do all three illustrations help demonstrate?

(1) The function of a fulcrum is to balance effort and load.

(2) Effort and load are equal physical forces.

(3) Effort increases load through the application of air pressure.

(4) A load is pulled down toward the Earth by effort and gravity.

(5) Effort and load are opposing physical forces.

To answer this question, you need to compare the pictures and note their similarities and differences. In all three pictures, the fulcrum provides a fixed point of rotation for the plank and the load. Apply your common sense and everyday experience to visualize what is happening in each picture. Pictures 2 and 3 show the effort pushing *up* to counteract the weight of the load. Picture 1 shows a *downward* effort that serves to push the load *up*, as in a seesaw. So in all three pictures, the effort and load are opposing physical forces. Choice (5) is a good answer, but let's examine the other four answer choices. Only in Picture 1 does the fulcrum balance the effort and the load, and so choice (1) is an incorrect general principle. None of the three pictures assumes that the effort and load are equal in force, and so choice (2) provides an unfair generalization.

Choice (3) provides a confusing, nonsensical statement that you can easily eliminate. Choice (4) is only partially correct. It is true that the gravity works to push the load downward; however, all three pictures show the effort working to lift the load upward. **The correct answer is (5).**

> **10.** Which of the following provides one example of each of the three types of levers shown in the three pictures, in the order they are shown?
>
> **(1)** pliers; diving board; crane
>
> **(2)** hammer; wedge; seesaw
>
> **(3)** crowbar; wheelbarrow; baseball bat
>
> **(4)** scissors; ramp; pulley
>
> **(5)** saw; forklift; bottle opener

To answer this question, you need to interpret what is happening in each of the three pictures by applying your sense of how physical forces operate in the real world. Notice that Picture 1 shows a seesaw type of lever: you apply downward effort at one end of the rigid object, and move the load on the other side of the fulcrum upward. A crowbar works in the same way. Picture 2 resembles a wheelbarrow, where the fulcrum is the wheel. Lifting from the far right, where the handles are located, reduces the effort needed to lift the load up from the ground. Focusing on Picture 3, imagine yourself applying effort near the pivoting fulcrum thereby magnifying the force with which the other end of the rigid object moves in the same direction as your effort. You are imagining how tools such as a hammer and a baseball bat work. As your grip on the hammer or bat moves farther up toward the load (the nail or ball), the magnifying effect of your effort diminishes. **The correct answer is (3).**

Graphical Data Displays

Several questions on the Science Test are based on data presented in graphical format. A question of this type might be based on a table, bar graph, line chart, or circle graph (pie chart). These displays may be used for any of the subject areas covered by the test.

This book's Mathematics lesson explains how to read, interpret, and analyze data presented in each of these formats. Be sure to review those materials when preparing for the GED® Science Test. Keep in mind, however, that on the Science Test the emphasis is not on number-crunching but rather on the following skills:

- Understanding what the graphical display is intended to show

- Reading and interpreting the data

- Understanding the significance of the data

- Drawing general conclusions from the data

- Applying the ideas conveyed by the display to specific scenarios

Though you may need to perform simple arithmetic tasks such as counting or adding, you won't need to calculate precise percents, ratios, or averages. (These skills are measured on the Mathematics Test instead.)

The next two GED®-style chemistry questions are based on the same table. Both illustrate that the focus of data-display questions on the Science Test is far more on understanding and interpreting scientific data than on performing math on the data.

QUESTIONS 11 AND 12 REFER TO THE FOLLOWING TABLE.

Substance	pH	
Gastric juice	1.0	ACID
Tomato juice	4.1	
Milk	6.6	
Pure water	7.0	NEUTRAL
Toothpaste	9.9	
Milk of magnesia	10.5	ALKALINE

The pH of a substance is the measurement of the hydrogen-ion concentration in a water-based solution. Acids are distinguished by a sour taste, while bases taste bitter. When there is a combination of acids and a base, the substance is neutralized.

11. If a person were suffering from acid indigestion, which of the following would most likely alleviate the problem?

(1) brushing his or her teeth

(2) drinking a mixture of milk of magnesia and pure water

(3) drinking pure water

(4) drinking a mixture of water and milk

(5) drinking a mixture of milk of magnesia and tomato juice

To answer the question, you need to examine the table to see that the pH levels are presented from lowest pH (relatively acidic) to the higher pH levels (relatively alkaline). A mixture of the milk of magnesia and water would best neutralize the acid, creating a more balanced pH. (Drinking pure milk of magnesia might be even more effective, but this option is not listed among the choices.) **The correct answer is 2.**

12. How would a solution with a pH level of 2.9 probably taste?

The solution would have

(1) a tomato-like taste

(2) a slightly bitter taste

(3) no taste at all

(4) a slightly sour taste

(5) a neutral taste

To answer this question you need the information in both the passage and the table. According to the passage, acidic substances taste sour, while alkaline substances (bases) taste bitter. Common sense should tell you that the lower the pH level, the more sour an acid and, similarly, the higher the pH level the more bitter the base. A solution with a pH level of 2.9 would taste sour because of its acid content. (Whether the sour taste is subtle or strong is not important in distinguishing the correct answer choice from the incorrect choices.)

Choice (1) is incorrect because the liquids listed in the table's left-hand column are merely examples. To assume that the table provides a complete list of acidic and alkaline liquids defies common sense and everyday experience. **The correct answer is (4).**

Illustrations that Show Spatial Relationships

Some questions on the Science Test focus on how the physical world around us (as well as inside us) arranges itself spatially. Showing where different distinct objects or other masses are located in relation to one another is usually best accomplished with a visual depiction, which might show, for example:

- Locations and distances involving celestial bodies

- Layers of the Earth's atmosphere

- Stratification (layering) of rocks, minerals, and sediments that form the Earth

- Configurations of chemical compounds, in which molecules link together in specific ways

- Separation of gases, liquids, or solids either naturally or in a laboratory experiment

- Layers of cells and tissues in a plant or animal

The possibilities listed above are just some of many. The next GED®-style question involves the earth sciences as well as physics. As with most questions based on both textual and visual information, you'll need both to help you answer the question.

QUESTION 13 REFERS TO THE FOLLOWING DIAGRAM AND INFORMATION.

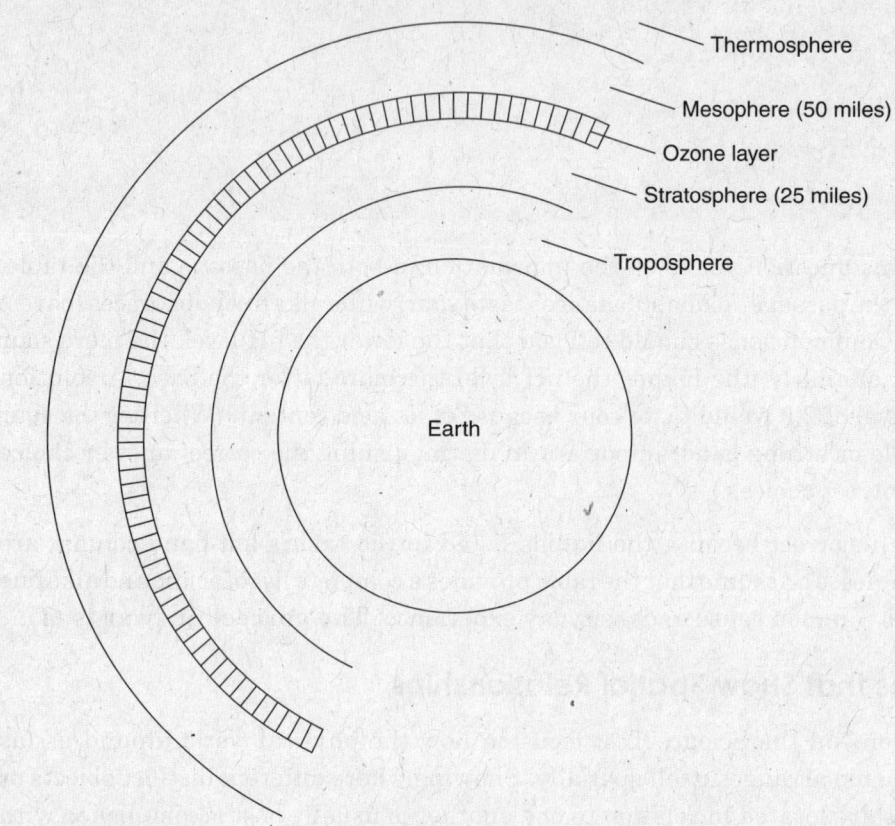

Temperature levels fall from ground level to the top of the troposphere, but then they rise with altitude in the stratosphere.

13. Which of the following statements, assuming it is true, would best account for the rise in temperature?

   (1) High-altitude air contains more gases than low-altitude air.

   (2) The troposphere blocks the Sun's rays.

   (3) The surface of the Earth is warming gradually.

   (4) Air is thinner at higher altitudes than at lower ones.

   (5) The ozone layer traps heat as the heat rises.

The illustration shows that the stratosphere is closer to the ozone layer than the troposphere is. If the ozone layer traps rising heat, as choice (5) suggests, the effect would be to raise air temperatures as you approach the ozone layer from the stratosphere. So choice (5) is a good answer.

Let's examine the other answer choices. Choices (1) and (4) are both incorrect for essentially the same reason: neither one explains why air temperatures would initially change in one direction as altitude increases but then change course as altitude increases. It doesn't matter whether either statement is accurate or not—neither one responds to the question. Choice (2) is incorrect because the troposphere is below the stratosphere (as the figure shows) and hence cannot interfere with the amount of sunlight reaching the stratosphere. Choice (3) is incorrect because global warming makes sense as a *result* rather than a cause of the ozone layer's trapping air. **The correct answer is (5).**

The next GED®-style question involves astronomy and is based solely on visual information. Don't be concerned that it contains very few words to help you interpret it. Rest assured: all you'll need to answer the question, aside from your common sense and everyday experience, is provided in the picture.

QUESTION 14 REFERS TO THE FOLLOWING ILLUSTRATION.

Solar Eclipse

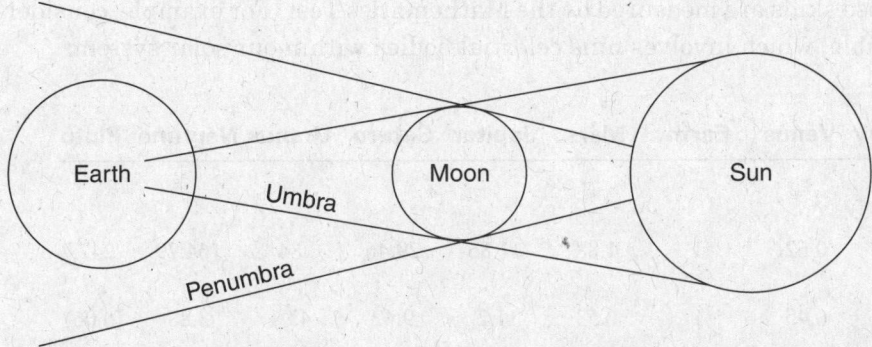

14. Referring to the illustration, what is true during a solar eclipse?

   (1) The Moon appears brightest from within the boundaries of the penumbra.

   (2) From Earth, the Moon appears to move faster than the Sun.

   (3) The side of the Moon not seen from Earth is cast in darkness.

   (4) Sunlight is dimmest within the field referred to as the umbra.

   (5) The shadow cast by the Earth hides the Moon from our view.

If you are unfamiliar with solar eclipses, use your everyday experience to figure out what is happening in the illustration. You know that when any object is lit from one direction, it casts a shadow in the opposite direction. Use this common knowledge along with the illustration to figure out what happens during a solar eclipse. The Moon is positioned between the Earth and Sun, thereby casting a shadow on the Earth. It makes sense that the area at the center of the shadow (identified in the illustration as the umbra) will be darkest, while the shadow around its periphery (the penumbra) will be somewhat lighter. Choice (4) is a good answer.

Let's examine the other answer choices. Choice (1) contradicts what the illustration shows: the Moon is casting a shadow within the boundaries of the field labeled as the penumbra. Choice (2) is incorrect because the illustration provides no information, or even clue, about the motion of the Earth, Moon, or Sun. Choice (3) contradicts what the illustration shows: the side of the Moon facing away from the Earth is bathed in direct sunlight. Choice (5) is incorrect because the illustration shows the Moon's shadow cast on the Earth, not the other way around. **The correct answer is (4).**

In the preceding example, did you notice that the illustration was accompanied by a title? Remember: some (but not all) illustrations on the Science Test will come with a title or descriptive caption that may help you understand and interpret the illustration.

Math and the GED® Science Test

As noted earlier, though some Science Test questions will involve numbers, you won't be asked to calculate precise ratios, percents, or averages or to do any number-crunching to speak of. Those skills are measured by the Mathematics Test. For example, consider the following table, which involves nine celestial bodies within our solar system:

	Mercury	Venus	Earth	Mars	Jupiter	Saturn	Uranus	Neptune	Pluto
Years to revolve around Sun	0.24	0.62	1	1.88	11.86	29.46	84	164.79	247.7
Radius (Earth = 1)	0.38	0.45	1	0.53	11.2	9.42	4.01	3.88	(0.06)

A Mathematics Test question based on the data in this table might ask you to calculate a ratio of one radius to another, or it might ask you to calculate a time difference (measured perhaps in Earth days) between one planet's year and another planet's year. But the Science Test would not pose these sorts of questions. Instead, a Science Test question might ask you how many of the celestial bodies other than Earth have a greater radius than that of Earth—or a longer year than Earth's year. Or the question might ask you what kinds of conclusions you can, or cannot, draw from the data. (For instance, the table provides no information about rotation, distance between planets, or distance from the Sun.)

But this does not mean that math plays absolutely no part on the Science Test. For at least a few questions, expect to perform some arithmetic such as counting or adding numbers. For example, a chemistry question might ask for the total mass of a chemical compound, in which case you would add up the atomic masses of the elements that make up the compound, accounting for the number of molecules per element. (Don't worry: the question would provide all the information you would need.)

A physics question might ask you to apply the definition of a unit of measurement to a specific situation. Here's a GED®-style example involving *hertz*, which is the unit of measurement used for sound-wave frequency. As you can see, all the information about sound waves you need to answer the question is provided.

QUESTION 15 REFERS TO THE FOLLOWING INFORMATION.

The frequency of a sound wave is measured in units referred to as the *hertz*. One hertz is equal to one wave per second, and 1 kilohertz is equal to 1000 hertz. If you tune your radio dial to 89.0, that number would signify the frequency of the radio station, in kilohertz.

15. What is the frequency of sound waves received at 98.6 on the radio dial?

(1) 1000 waves per second

(2) 9800 waves per second

(3) 98,600 waves per second

(4) 98.6 hertz

(5) 98,600 hertz

If the radio dial is tuned to 98.6, this would mean that the waves are traveling at 98,600 waves per second because 1 kilohertz is equal to 1000 waves per second: $1000 \times 98.6 = 98,600$. **The correct answer is (3).**

Or, a Science Test question might ask you to apply one of the simple formulas that express the basic laws of physics. Here are just some of those formulas:

$v = \dfrac{d}{t}$ velocity = distance ÷ time

$a = \dfrac{32 \text{ ft}}{s^2}$ acceleration during freefall = 32 feet / (number of seconds)^2

$F = m \cdot a$ force = mass × acceleration

$w = F \cdot d$ work = force × displacement

$v = l \cdot f$ velocity = wavelength × frequency

$V = I \cdot r$ voltage = current (amp) × resistance (ohms)

Don't worry: you won't need to memorize any formulas for the test. If a question requires you to apply a formula, it will provide that formula, along with the numbers you need to answer the question.

QUESTION 16 REFERS TO THE FOLLOWING INFORMATION.

In an electrical circuit, the amount of voltage is equal to the electric current (measured in amperes) multiplied by total resistance, measured in ohms (Ω). A certain battery generates 8 volts of electricity, which is sent through a wire circuit to a small electric motor. Three resistors, each of which provides 6 ohms (Ω) of resistance, have been placed in the circuit.

16. What is the maximum current that will return to the battery via the circuit?

   (1) less than 0.1 amperes

   (2) between 0.1 and 0.5 amperes

   (3) between 0.5 and 1.0 amperes

   (4) between 1.0 and 2.0 amperes

   (5) more than 2.0 amperes

The *maximum* current would return to the battery if the electric motor were shut off so that it does not use any electricity. The question provides the formula you need to answer it: voltage = current (amp) × resistance (ohms). In this case, voltage = 8 and total resistance = 6 × 3 = 18. To find the strength of the current after it passes through, plug these numbers into the general equation (in physics, the symbol I is used to indicate ampere units):

$$8 = I \times 18$$
$$\frac{8}{18} = I$$
$$\frac{4}{9} = I$$

As you can see, the algebra and math are very simple, and no precise calculations are required. The fraction $\frac{4}{9}$ is just under 0.5 (one half). **The correct answer is (2).**

In short, during the Science Test you might need to do some counting and some simple addition, and you might need to solve a simple equation or two. But otherwise, don't expect the Science Test to gauge your math skills.

GENERAL TEST-TAKING STRATEGIES

Here are some general strategies for tackling the Science Test. Put these strategies to work on the Practice Tests in this book, and then review them again just before exam day.

First read the question(s) based on a passage of text or visual depiction.

Before you look at a visual or read even a brief passage, read the question stem (the question itself, but not the answer choices). If the passage or visual comes with more than one question, read all the question stems first. This task should only take 10 seconds or so. The question(s) may provide clues as to what you should focus on and think about as you read the text or analyze the visual.

Read a passage of text straight through before answering any questions based on it.

If a question or group of questions refers to a passage of text, read the passage from beginning to end without interruption. Pay careful attention to definitions. If more than one term is defined, pay special attention to any differences between the two concepts, processes, or features defined. Think about whether the information in the passage leads logically to a particular conclusion or inference. If it does, the chances are good that you'll be asked about this feature.

Use your pencil as you read longer passages.

Though most Science Test passages are brief (two to four sentences is most common), a few might run as long as 250 words (about a third of a page)—long enough to merit taking pencil to paper. For these passages, underline key words and phrases, and jot down notes in the margins. As with the Language Arts, Reading Test and the Social Studies Test, using your pencil while you read helps you to think actively about what you're reading. It also helps you find information in the passage you need as you answer the question(s).

When examining visuals that provide quantitative information, don't get bogged down in the data.

A Science Test question may refer to a table, chart, or graph that presents quantitative information. The visual may very well contain more data than you'll need to answer the question(s) based on it. In fact, one of the skills you're being tested on is your ability to sort through that data to determine what is relevant (and what is not relevant) to the question at hand. So don't waste time analyzing every piece of data in a visual. Instead, focus your attention on what the question asks about.

Mine diagrams and illustrations for helpful clues for answering the questions.

Many visuals will include arrows showing cause-and-effect, sequence of events in a process, or direction of motion, energy, or force. Pay special attention to these arrows, as they are often crucial to analyzing the question at hand. Also pay attention to labels used for various objects shown in an illustration. Finally, some visual depictions will come with a descriptive title or caption, which you should use to help you interpret the visual, understand the question, and eliminate incorrect answers.

Make realistic assumptions when interpreting illustrations.

Some questions will involve illustrations depicting aspects of the physical world, but in a simplified manner. Make common-sense assumptions when interpreting these figures. For example, you can assume that lines that appear straight are intended to depict straight lines, that the natural forces of gravity, motion, and energy operate normally, and so forth. In other words, don't try to outsmart the test-makers by splitting hairs; you'll only defeat yourself.

Apply your common sense and real-world experience—up to a limit.

Many questions on the Science Test—whether they involve physics, earth sciences, ecology, biology, chemistry, and even astronomy—deal with phenomena that most of us have observed or experienced in our own lives. Use your life experiences, along with your common sense, to help you answer these questions. But don't use your outside knowledge as a *substitute* for reading and trying to understand the text and/or the visual depiction provided. Rather, use that knowledge to safeguard against selecting answer choices that are contrary to common sense and real-life experience—in other words, that simply don't make sense.

Take care when handling questions stated in the negative.

Some questions may be stated in the negative rather than the affirmative. These questions are likely to use capitalized words in phrases such as "NOT accurate," "EXCEPT which one," or "LEAST likely." These questions are not intended to trick you, but they can be confusing. Take great care not to turn these questions around in your head when answering them.

Pace yourself properly.

You're allowed 80 minutes to answer all fifty questions. GED® Science Test questions are not presented in any set order of difficulty. So after 30 minutes you should have answered at least twenty questions (more than a third of all fifty questions), and after 60 minutes you should have answered at least forty questions (more than two thirds of all fifty questions). If you're falling behind, pick up the pace. In any event, try to answer all fifty questions with at least 5 minutes to spare, so you can go back and reconsider any responses you were unsure about.

SUMMING IT UP

- The GED® Science Test consists of fifty multiple-choice questions. The subject areas covered include life science (biology), earth science and astronomy, and physical science (chemistry and physics).

- GED® science questions require that you read passages and comprehend or analyze the material presented in the passages, along with the charts, diagrams, graphs, illustrations, tables, and other visual depictions.

- The GED® Science Test is more visually oriented than any of the other tests in the GED® battery. Pay careful attention to any arrows in an illustration; you can be sure that they will be crucial to answer the question at hand.

- Synthesis and evaluation questions involve drawing general assessments and conclusions from specific information. You will need to be able to recognize unfair assessments and conclusions—wrong-answer choices that jump to conclusions that are unwarranted given the information provided.

- You won't need to memorize any formulas for the GED® Science Test. If a question requires you to apply a formula, it will provide that formula, along with the numbers you need to answer the question.

- Some GED® Science Test questions will involve numbers, but you won't be asked to calculate precise ratios, percents, or averages or to do any serious number-crunching.

- Many questions on the Science Test deal with phenomena that you have observed or experienced in your everyday life. Use your experiences, along with your common sense, to help you answer these questions.

Science Review

chapter 9

OVERVIEW

- What you'll find in this review
- Science and the scientific method
- Life science: biology
- Earth and space science
- Chemistry
- Physics
- Summing it up

WHAT YOU'LL FIND IN THIS REVIEW

The GED® Science Test is designed primarily to measure critical-thinking skills rather than knowledge. Nevertheless, with some prior familiarity with the three content areas covered on the test (life sciences, earth and space science, and physical science) you can expect to handle the questions with greater ease and confidence. The review materials in this part of the book are designed to help you in this respect. Keep in mind that this review is intended only to highlight the content areas listed above. It is by no means intended to be a comprehensive examination of these areas.

Review questions are provided throughout this review. As you answer them, keep in mind that the sections of text on which they are based are longer than selections of text on the actual GED® Science Test.

SCIENCE AND THE SCIENTIFIC METHOD

Since the dawn of humankind, people have searched for explanations as to why the physical world around them is the way it is. Early explanations were most often based on religious and superstitious ideas. **Science** attempts to provide explanations for natural phenomena through investigation—more specifically, through observation and experimentation, as well as through theoretical explanation.

In order to sort out unreasonable explanations from plausible ones, scientists apply logic and common sense by means of a process called the **scientific method.** This method involves four fundamental steps:

❶ **Observation:** During this first step, the scientist carefully observes a particular natural phenomenon, either directly (by using the five senses) or with the aid of any number of tools, such as telescopes, microscopes, temperature and pressure gauges, and other recording and measuring devices.

2 **Hypothesis:** During this second step, the scientist thinks about the set of facts obtained through observation, and he or she formulates a statement (the *hypothesis*) or series of statements that appear to logically explain the set of facts in a unified way. A good hypothesis is a simple statement intended to apply to a general set of circumstances.

3 **Experiment:** During the third step, the scientist designs and conducts experiments to determine whether the hypothesis is acceptable or whether it should be rejected or modified—in other words, to test the hypothesis.

4 **Conclusion:** During the fourth step, the scientist analyzes the results of the experiment(s) conducted during the third step. The results might support the hypothesis, or they might suggest that the hypothesis should be rejected or modified.

 http://bit.ly/hippo_bio1

The proper conclusion (the final step described above) depends on whether the experimental results are consistent with the hypothesis. If the hypothesis is rejected or needs to be modified to fit the experimental results, new experiments are then designed and conducted to test a modified or new hypothesis in light of the experimental results. It is through a continuous cycle of new observations, new hypotheses, and further experimentation that scientists arrive at the best answers to their questions about the natural world.

Most people, including non-scientists, apply the scientific method in their everyday lives, often without realizing it. For example, assume that you are experiencing a stinging sensation in your stomach (an *observation*). You would probably want to know its cause so that you can remedy the problem. You might *hypothesize* that drinking coffee is the cause. In order to test your hypothesis, you might *experiment* by discontinuing coffee consumption for a period of days and monitoring the results. You would then reach a *conclusion* based on the results.

Reliable scientific conclusions depend on properly designed and conducted experiments. In the preceding experiment, for example, suppose you had discontinued coffee *and* alcohol consumption and observed that your stomach discomfort disappeared after a week. You could not reliably conclude that it was the coffee—rather than the alcohol or a combination of coffee and alcohol—that caused your stomach discomfort. A good test of your hypothesis would require that all possible factors other than coffee consumption remain unchanged, or constant, during the experiment. Researchers refer to such factors as **controls,** and they refer to factors that are changed to test the hypothesis as **variables.**

QUESTION 1 REFERS TO THE FOLLOWING INFORMATION.

A researcher combines equal amounts of three different clear liquids—X, Y, and Z—in a beaker, and she observes that the mixture turns blue in color. The researcher hypothesizes that liquid X turns blue when combined with any other liquid.

1. Which is the best way to test the hypothesis?

    (1) Repeat the experiment, but change the proportions of the three liquids.

    (2) Combine liquid X with a liquid other than Y or Z.

    (3) Perform the same experiment again.

    (4) Heat liquid X by itself, and observe its color response.

    (5) Combine liquids Y and Z with a liquid other than X.

Liquid X is the control, and the other liquids are the variables. Change the variable to test the hypothesis. **The correct answer is (2).**

LIFE SCIENCE: BIOLOGY

http://bit.ly/hippo_bio2

Biology is the scientific study of living organisms, including plants and animals. This field consists of three major branches: *zoology* (the study of animals), *botany* (the study of plants), and *ecology* (the study of how plants and animals interact with their environment).

In this review, you will explore the field of biology by *scale*. The review begins by examining biological life at the cellular and molecular level. Then it moves up in scale, to examine the biological organism in terms of its organ systems and as an individual. The review will conclude by examining individual organisms as members of a community and as part of an ecosystem.

Cellular Biology

http://bit.ly/hippo_bio3

The **cell** is the basic unit of structure and function for most living things. Cells arise from pre-existing cells by independent, self-reproduction. All living organisms are composed of one or more cells. Cells vary in size, shape, and function. A bacterial cell, for instance, is invisible to the naked eye. Bacteria only become visible when they appear as colonies of millions of cells. At the other extreme, a single muscle cell can reach 9 inches in length (about a million times larger than a bacterial cell). It is estimated that the human body is composed of some 100 trillion cells.

Cell Structure

Cells are the basis of life, heredity, structure, and function of every organism. Each cell contains a variety of different structures called **organelles** ("little organs"). The **nucleus** of a cell is one of the most important organelles. The nucleus is the control center for all cellular activity. Within the *nucleoplasm* of a nucleus are long, thin fibers called *chromatin* on which are found *genes,* which contains all the genetic information for each cell. (This topic is examined in greater detail later in this review.)

Every cell has a **membrane** that encloses the cell and is selectively permeable to what enters and exits the cell. Inside the membrane, organelles are embedded in a gelatinous substance called **cytoplasm,** which fills the cell. The cytoplasm is the cell's manufacturing area and contains small *vacuoles,* which are storage areas; *mitochondria,* which release energy for cell operations; and *ribosomes,* which combine amino acids into proteins.

http://bit.ly/hippo_bio3

Cells are classified as **prokaryotic** (before a nucleus) and **eukaryotic** (possessing a true nucleus). Prokaryotic cells lack a nuclear membrane and membrane-bound organelles. They are unicellular, mainly microscopic organisms, such as bacteria and cyanobacteria. It is estimated that prokaryotes appeared some 3.5 billion years ago, and many scientists hypothesize that prokaryotic organisms evolved into eukaryotic cells. Eukaryotes include all cells in animals and plants, as well as in *protists,* unicellular organisms that can be plant-like or animal-like in unique ways. Eukaryote cells are characterized by a true nucleus that is bound by a membrane and membrane-bounded subcellular organelles. Eukaryotes can be unicellular, as in the case of the amoeba, or multicellular, as seen in humans. Eukaryotic cells possess many organelles to carry out cellular processes such as energy production, waste disposal, cellular transport, and product production.

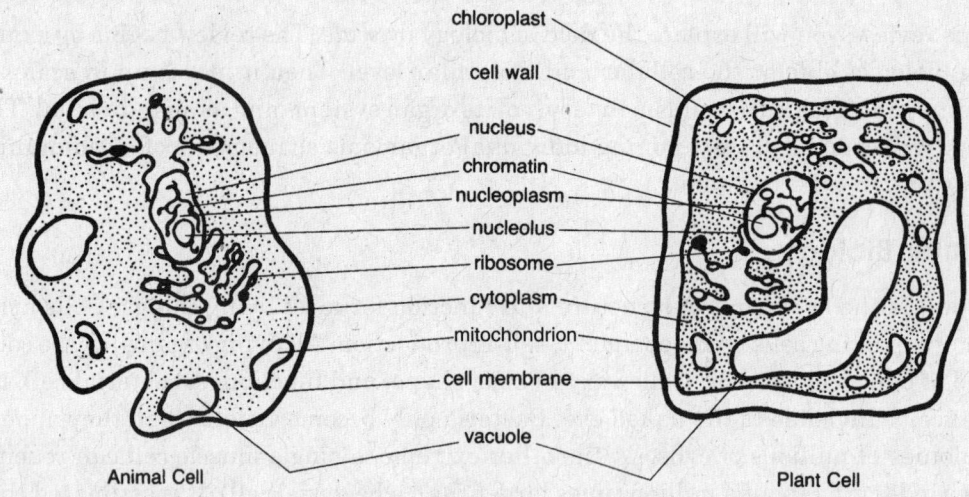

Although all eukaryotic cells are similar in structure, plant cells differ from animal cells in three important respects:

- Plant cells have a firm outer boundary called the *cell wall.* This wall supports and protects the plant cell.

- Vacuoles (storage areas) in the plant cell are much larger than those in the animal cell.

- Within the cytoplasm, many plant cells contain small green structures called *chloroplasts.* These chloroplasts contain *chlorophyll,* which enables the plant cell to make food.

http://bit.ly/hippo_bio5

CELL MEMBRANE AND TRANSPORT

As noted earlier, cell membranes control the movement of materials into and out of the cell. The cell membrane is semi-permeable and allows only certain materials to enter and leave the cell. A cell membrane is a fluid-like sheet that is embedded with proteins and carbohydrate chains. This sheet creates an effective barrier against lipids (fats), while the sheet's proteins and carbohydrates act as receptors or identifiers for the movement of molecules from external sources.

While many factors are necessary for cell survival, **cellular transport**—the movement of particles into and out of the cell—is one of the most important. Cellular transport can be either passive or active. Movement by **passive transport** is accomplished through **diffusion,** by which particles move from an area of high concentration to an area of lower concentration until equilibrium is reached. Water is the largest component of the cell protoplasm. The diffusion of water through a semi-permeable membrane is known more specifically as **osmosis.** Diffusion is a "passive" form of transport because it requires no energy. In contrast, **active transport** is used when a cell needs to move a substance from an area of lower concentration to an area of higher concentration; to do this, a cell must use energy.

CELLULAR FUNCTIONS—METABOLISM AND ENERGY PATHWAYS

All cells require a constant source of energy. Gathering, storing, and using this energy is referred to as a cell's **metabolism.** We consume nutrients to provide our bodies with the building blocks necessary to synthesize new materials needed by our cells. Unlike plants and some microscopic organisms, humans and other animals can't simply absorb energy through our skin. Instead, animal cells have to break food down in order to release the energy stored in the food.

Both plant and animal cells rely on metabolic pathways to convert substances into forms of energy that can be used by each cell. These conversions are controlled through **enzymes,** which are proteins that act as a biological catalyst. What this means is that enzymes speed up the rate of a reaction by lowering the amount of activation energy needed. Without enzymes it would take weeks, even months, for foods to break down completely.

Enzymes are also necessary in order for the vital cellular reactions of *photosynthesis* and *cellular respiration* to occur, as described next.

CELLULAR FUNCTIONS—PHOTOSYNTHESIS AND CELLULAR RESPIRATION

http://bit.ly/hippo_bio6

Photosynthesis is the food-manufacturing process by which green plants convert carbon dioxide (CO_2) from the air and water (H_2O) from the soil into glucose ($C_6H_{12}O_6$), which is a simple sugar, and oxygen (O_2). The sugars that the plant produces through photosynthesis can be used to make other compounds needed for the plant to sustain itself and grow. The green pigment in plants, called **chlorophyll,** captures the Sun's light energy, which fuels this manufacturing process. Oxygen is a byproduct of this reaction and is released into the atmosphere or used in cellular respiration (see below). Here's the chemical equation for photosynthesis:

$$6\,CO_2 + 6\,H_2O \rightarrow C_6H_{12}O_6 + 6\,O_2$$

Note that one molecule of glucose (sugar) combined with six molecules of oxygen to form six molecules of carbon dioxide and six molecules of water. The energy produced by this reaction is used by the cell.

Cellular respiration is used to free chemical energy from molecules of glucose for biological work. There are many types of respiration, but the most familiar is *aerobic* respiration, which converts carbohydrates (glucose) into carbon dioxide, water, and high-energy molecules of **ATP,** which is the source of energy for many metabolic processes. Here's the chemical equation for aerobic respiration:

$$C_6H_{12}O_6 + 6\,O_2 \rightarrow 6\,CO_2 + 6\,H_2O + ATP$$

Respiration begins in the cytoplasm of the cell in a process known as **glycolysis** (sugar-breaking). The products of glycolysis then move to the mitochondria, where they are converted into energy-rich ATP molecules. Catabolic reactions such as respiration produce energy by the breakdown of larger molecules.

QUESTIONS 2 AND 3 REFER TO THE FOLLOWING DIAGRAM AND INFORMATION.

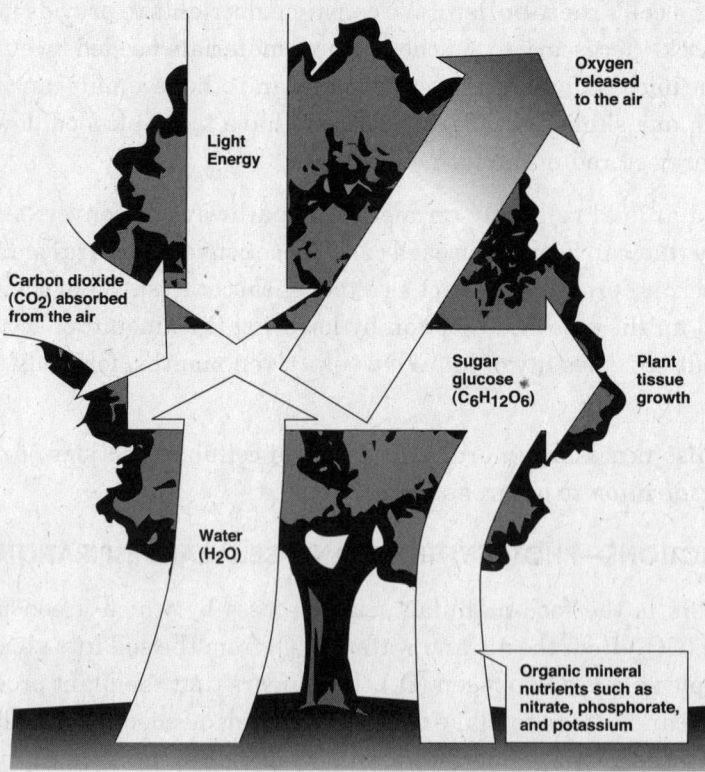

The oxygen produced by photosynthesis is necessary for cellular respiration, and the carbon dioxide produced by respiration is necessary for photosynthesis. In short, photosynthesis and cellular respiration are the Yin and Yang of energy: they are two complementary parts of a cycle of energy that is necessary for life to exist.

2. Which of the following exhibits passive cellular transport in a plant?

    (1) The plant's chloroplasts absorb light energy from the Sun.

    (2) The plant's leaves emit oxygen into the air as a waste product.

    (3) The plant's mitochondria send glucose throughout the plant.

    (4) The plant's roots absorb water from nearby soil.

    (5) The plant's stem delivers ATP molecules to the plant's leaves.

Passive transport involves a natural diffusion process, by which water moves from an area of higher concentration to one of lower concentration until equilibrium is reached. When you water a plant, the roots absorb it through osmosis, a form of diffusion, as needed to deliver that water to drier parts of the plant. **The correct answer is (4).**

3. Which is NOT required in order for a plant to carry out photosynthesis?

    (1) carbon dioxide

    (2) light from the Sun

    (3) glucose

    (4) water

    (5) chlorophyll

Glucose is a product of photosynthesis. Carbon dioxide, sunlight, water, and chlorophyll are all essential for the process of photosynthesis. **The correct answer is (3).**

The Molecular Basis of Life—DNA and Protein Synthesis

 http://bit.ly/hippo_bio7

The structure and composition of living organisms varies greatly, from single-celled bacteria to complex multicellular organisms with differentiated cell types and inter-connected organ systems. Regardless of the complexity, every living entity contains a blueprint for its construction in the form of a chain of molecules called deoxyribonucleic acid (**DNA**).

In all living organisms, this DNA is housed inside the cell—the membrane-enclosed unit that contains the machinery and supplies for the life functions or metabolic processes of the cell. Prokaryotes (meaning before nucleus) house their DNA in a loosely defined region of the cell called a **nucleoid.** Eukaryotes (meaning possessing a true nucleus) sequester their DNA inside a **nucleus**—a separate, membrane-bound compartment.

DNA is an amazingly simple chemical structure, yet it contains an entire library of information on how to make, maintain, and reproduce an organism; it also keeps a record of clues to the organism's evolutionary history. The entire sequence of DNA in an organism is called its **genome.** The genetic blueprint so carefully preserved in a genome is stored in the DNA's linear sequence of molecules, referred to as **bases.** A DNA chain is constructed with four different bases: *adenine* (A), *guanine* (G), *cytosine* (C), and *thymine* (T). Two strands of *nucleotides* lain side by side are connected by chemical pairings of complementary (matching) bases: adenine (A) pairs with thymine (T), and guanine (G) pairs with cytosine (C). The bonds between these molecules impose a twisting force (torsion) on the structure and cause it to wind slightly, much like a spiral staircase. This creates the familiar *double helix* shape of a DNA molecule.

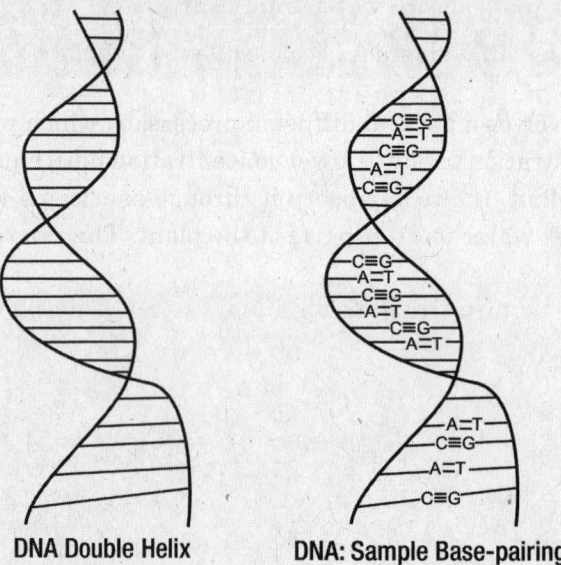

DNA Double Helix   **DNA: Sample Base-pairing**

DNA is needed for all **protein synthesis** (the making of proteins) that occurs in cells. **Proteins** are complex chemical compounds that provide the foundations for the structural and functional components of every cell in an organism. All proteins consist of long chains of **amino acids** that link together in different three-dimension structures that define different proteins. There are twenty different amino acids that can link in myriad different ways. The precise structure of each protein is determined by a "language," or *code,* which DNA deciphers and translates. DNA then directs the construction of each protein (a "word" in the language) according to this code's specific instructions for the linking, or *sequencing,* of amino acids.

4. What is the function of DNA?

   (1) to create amino acids

   (2) to bind proteins together

   (3) to regulate cell division

   (4) to direct protein synthesis

   (5) to encase a eukaryote's nucleus

DNA provides the instructions, or blueprint, for how different amino acids are to be linked together to form proteins. **The correct answer is (4).**

Cellular Replication and Reproduction—Mitosis and Meiosis

Duplication of a cell's DNA is required both for cellular replication—to replenish dying cells—and for reproduction. In unicellular organisms, these two processes are the same. DNA is duplicated before the cell divides to produce two separate organisms, each with the original amount of DNA. This asexual method of reproduction is known as **binary fission.**

In multicellular organisms, a similar process called **mitosis** is used to replenish lost cells. However, reproduction is more complex and begins with specialized cells called **gametes** (eggs and sperm in animals), each of which provide only half of the DNA contained in other cells.

MITOSIS

http://bit.ly/hippo_bio8

All cells must have a mechanism for perpetuation, growth, maintenance, and repair. If you've ever had a bad haircut or painful sunburn, in time your hair grew back and your skin peeled to reveal new skin. You can thank cellular division for this.

This process begins first with nuclear division—before the remainder of the cell divides. In cells of eukaryotic (multicellular) organisms, the nucleus normally carries two sets of genetic information. In this case the cell is said to be **diploid.** If a cell carries only one set of genetic information, it is said to be **haploid.** To begin cell division, unorganized DNA exits the nucleus in the strand-like form called *chromatin*. Once a cell is ready to divide, this chromatin coils and condenses into structures called **chromosomes,** which carry units of inheritance called *genes*. A chromosome in a non-dividing cell exists in a duplicated state where two copies—sister *chromatids*—are attached together at a central point. A nonreproductive human cell contains 46 chromosomes altogether—23 pairs of chromatids.

The process of mitosis consists of four sequential stages:

❶ Prophase: The nuclear envelope dissolves; chromatin organizes into chromosomes; a fibrous spindle forms to connect opposite ends of the cell.

❷ Metaphase: Duplicated chromosomes align at the equatorial plane of cell, along the spindles.

❸ Anaphase: The two chromatids of a duplicated chromosome separate and move toward opposite ends of the cell.

❹ Telophase: A nuclear envelope develops around a "daughter" cell; the chromosomes uncoil and revert back to chromatin; and the entire cell divides into two. (This division of the entire cell is called **cytokinesis.**)

Between cell divisions is a period referred to as **interphase,** during which the cell increases in volume, makes proteins and other crucial components, and replicates its DNA in preparation to divide again. The following illustration shows what the different phases of mitosis, including interphase, actually look like.

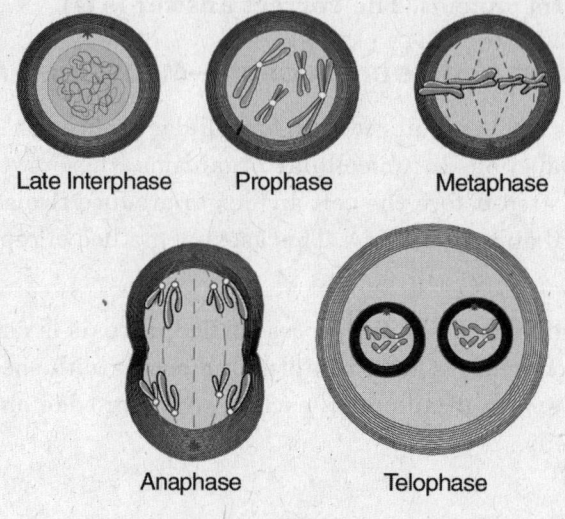

Late Interphase   Prophase   Metaphase

Anaphase   Telophase

Mitosis

Animal cell division is similar to plant cell division, but there are a few differences. In animal cells, cytokinesis results in a *cleavage furrow* (shown below), which divides the cytoplasm. In plant cells, a *cell plate* forms in the center and progresses to the cell membrane. The result is a cell wall separating the two cells.

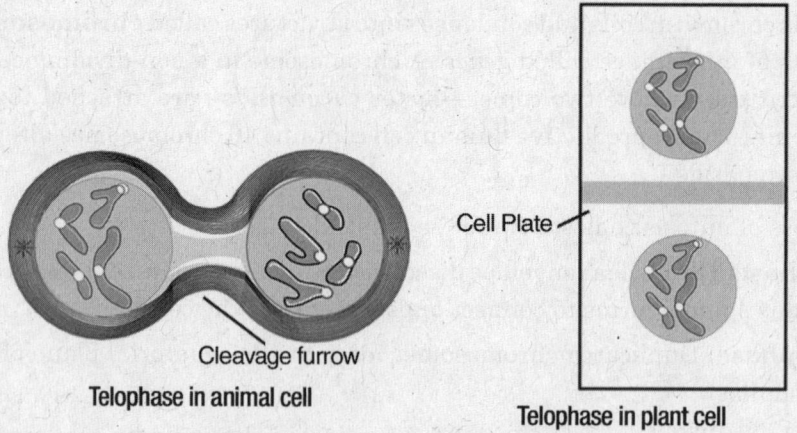

Cleavage furrow

Cell Plate

Telophase in animal cell

Telophase in plant cell

In animal cells, after mitosis is complete, a cell has replicated the same genetic information initially donated by the egg and sperm cells. Except for random mutations, all of an organism's cells produced by mitosis have the same genes. The earliest cells created by mitosis are referred to as **stem cells.** Cells then differentiate into specialized cells by activating certain genes while repressing others. For example, muscle cells produce contractile proteins while thyroid cells produce hormones that control metabolism. Each of these types of cells has a specific function, but it cannot perform the function of the other. The differentiating process is crucial—it explains why hair cells replace hair cells while skin cells replace skin cells.

MEIOSIS

http://bit.ly/hippo_bio9

The process of cell division known as **meiosis** occurs only in specialized reproductive cells of eukaryotic (multicellular) plants and animals. In animals, organs called **gonads** produce these reproductive cells, which are called **gametes.** In humans, the testes produce sperm and the ovaries produce ova (eggs).

Human *non*-reproductive cells contain 23 pairs of chromosomes, as noted earlier. Of these 23 pairs, 22 are non-sex-related, or *autosomal,* while the 23rd pair is exclusively responsible for determining sex (male or female) and sex-related traits. A reproductive cell (sperm or ovum), however, does not carry a duplicate of any of the 23 chromosomes. Instead, it contains a total of only 22 *single* chromosomes and one *single* sex chromosome—23 chromosomes altogether. (The genetic complement is later restored once an egg is fertilized by a sperm cell.)

Meiosis, like mitosis, is a multiphase process. However, meiosis involves two divisions— *meiosis I* and *meiosis II*—rather than just one, and the *four* resulting daughter cells are each genetically different from the parent cell. This important distinction ultimately explains why you are uniquely different from each of your two parents.

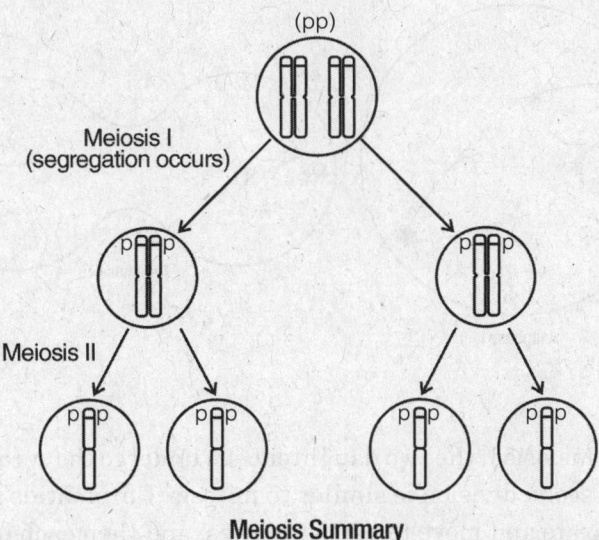

Meiosis Summary

 http://bit.ly/hippo_bio10

The first step in meiosis I is **Interphase,** during which DNA is replicated in preparation for division. The chromatin organizes into chromosomes—each of 46 chromosomes consisting of two identical chromatids (diploids), just as in cells about to undergo mitosis. Then comes **Prophase I,** during which the nuclear envelope dissolves and *homologous* chromosomes (which have genes for the same trait) pair up and exchange genetic material in a process called "crossing over." This process does not occur during mitosis. Next comes **Metaphase I,** during which the chromosomes line up as a unit along an equatorial line.

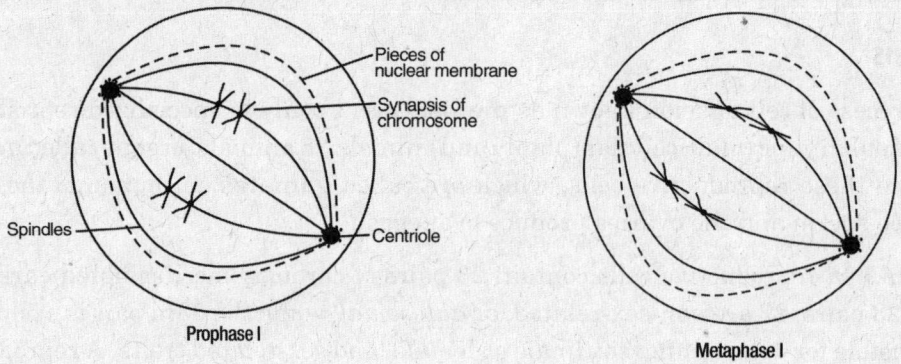

In the next phase, **Anaphase I,** each chromosome pair separates, its two sister chromatids moving toward opposite poles of the cell. Thus, 23 chromosomes end up at one end of the cell, and 23 end up at the other end. During the final phase, **Telophase I,** a nuclear envelope reforms around each new daughter nucleus, and the cell itself divides. Each of the two daughter cells has one set of 23 chromosomes. However, every chromosome still consists of two chromatids at this point. In other words, each of the two daughter cells is diploid.

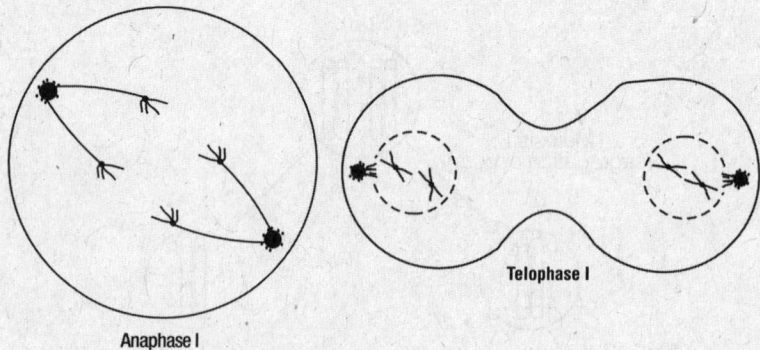

Immediately after meiosis I, the two daughter cells undergo the second meiotic division (Meiosis II). This second division is similar to mitosis. Chromatids from each of the 23 chromosomes separate and move to opposite poles, and then each of the two daughter cells divides. The 23 chromatids in each of the four new cells form the chromosomes of those cells. At this point each daughter cell is haploid.

 http://bit.ly/hippo_bio11

The four new cells become gametes (reproductive cells), each with 23 chromosomes that vary genetically from the original parent cell. In a human female, just one of these new reproductive cells can become a functional gamete (an egg). In the human male, however, all four new cells become viable sperm cells. The union of the egg and one of the sperm restores the full complement of 46 chromosomes in the fertilized human cell, or *zygote*.

5. In what respect is reproduction in unicellular organisms different from reproduction in multicellular organisms?

(1) Unicellular organisms reproduce simply by replacing dying cells.

(2) Unicellular organisms divide before their DNA is duplicated.

(3) Unicellular organisms depend on egg fertilization for reproduction.

(4) Unicellular organisms duplicate their DNA before they divide into separate organisms.

(5) The reproductive process is the same in both types of organisms.

Before dividing into two separate organisms, a unicellular organism duplicates its DNA. In contrast, multicellular organisms do not simply duplicate their DNA but rather combine one half and another half of DNA from two different gametes, such as a sperm cell and an egg cell. **The correct answer is (4).**

6. In terms of cell reproduction, which of the following helps explain the genetic differences between a child and its parents?

(1) Chromosomes' pairs exchange genes before the first meiotic cell division occurs.

(2) Reproductive cells create new chromosomes, which are unique to the child.

(3) After the initial meiotic cell division, the nucleus of each daughter cell dissolves.

(4) After the initial meiotic cell division, all chromosomes break apart and reconfigure in a random manner.

(5) During the second meiotic division, each pair of chromosomes fuses together to become one.

In meiosis, the "crossing over" process that occurs just before the first meiotic cell division results in an exchange of genes between each of the 23 pairs of chromosomes. It is this exchange that all but ensures that daughter cells will differ genetically from their "mother" cell. **The correct answer is (1).**

Genetic Inheritance

Genetics is the study of the principles of heredity and the variation of inherited traits among related organisms. These principles, upon which the field of modern genetics is based, were established in the nineteenth century by Austrian monk Gregor Mendel. In 1866, Mendel performed a number of simple but ingenious breeding experiments with garden pea plants and observed consistent, predictable patterns in terms of what traits are passed down from generation to generation. Mendel understood that some sort of hereditary factor was involved.

 http://bit.ly/hippo_bio12

Mendelian Inheritance

We now know that the traits (or **phenotypes**) Mendel discovered are controlled by **genes.** Genes exist as heritable units on a **chromosome.** A chromosome may possess thousands of genes. Since each human is a product of the combination of both maternal and paternal chromosomes—23 from the egg and 23 from the sperm—we carry genes from both parents. Genes determine our physical and mental development and dictate all of our individual characteristics or traits, everything from eye and hair color to blood type to the ability to roll your tongue. Genes come in alternative forms called **alleles.** We receive one allele from each parent. These alleles determine how each specific phenotype (such as eye color) is expressed. For example, the gene governing eye color can take the form of an allele for brown eyes or an allele for blue eyes.

Mendel proposed that a gene can be either a **dominant** allele for a certain trait or a **recessive** allele for that trait. The distinction between them is key to understanding heredity. Dominant alleles are *expressed*, which means they are actually shown as a trait. What's more, dominant alleles can "mask" the expression of recessive alleles. Recessive alleles can only be expressed when they are in the **homozygous** state, which means that alleles from both parents are the same. (A **heterozygous** state exists when the alleles are different.)

These principles, set forth by Mendel based on his observations of pea plants, are referred to today as Mendel's Laws of Inheritance (the first two listed below were introduced in the previous section):

The Law of Segregation: Each allele possessed by a parent will be passed into separate gametes (for example, egg and sperm cells in animals) during meiosis.

The Law of Independent Assortment: In each gamete, alleles of one gene separate independently of all other genes, allowing for new combinations of alleles through recombination.

The Law of Dominance: Each gene has two alleles, one inherited from each parent. Alleles are either **dominant** or **recessive** in their expression; dominant alleles "mask" the expression of recessive alleles.

http://bit.ly/hippo_bio13

Statistical Predictions of Individual Inheritance

Based on the patterns of inheritance that Mendel observed, it is possible to make predictions about the probability of a particular allele being passed on to an offspring and to make predictions about the phenotypic expression of an allele in the next generation.

All the genes that dictate the expression of a person's phenotypes are referred to collectively as the person's **genotype.** When certain genotypes of the parents are known for a specific trait, a simple diagram called a **Punnett square** can be used to predict the probability that the trait will be expressed in their offspring. Consider, for example, a genetic *cross* between the genes of two parents involving a single trait: the ability to roll the sides of one's tongue to form a "U" shape. We will designate **R** as the dominant allele, representing tongue-rolling ability, and **r** as the recessive allele representing a lack of tongue-rolling ability. Assume, for example, that the genotype of one parent is **RR** and the genotype of the other parent is **rr.** To construct a Punnett square for a cross such as this, the genes for one parent are placed along the side of the square and the genes for the other parent are placed along the top:

(Parents)   **RR** × **rr**

The Punnett square for this cross:

	R	R
r	**Rr**	**Rr**
r	**Rr**	**Rr**

All the resulting offspring of this cross are heterozygous dominant (Rr)—this is their genotype. As a result, all offspring will be tongue rollers—this is the expression of their phenotype. Now, members of this first generation can be crossed to assess the probability that their offspring will be tongue-rollers:

(Parents)   **Rr** × **Rr**

The Punnett square for this cross:

	R	r
R	**RR**	**Rr**
r	**Rr**	**rr**

Notice in this cross that three of the four squares are dominant—either RR or Rr. This means that there is a 75 percent probability that any member of this generation will be a tongue-roller. This is a phenotypic probability, of course, since it involves the actual expression of the trait.

You can also determine genotypic probabilities by examining the square:

- Homozygous dominant (RR)—25 percent probability
- Heterozygous dominant (Rr)—50 percent probability
- Homozygous recessive (rr)—25 percent probability

In genetics, phenotypic and genotypic probabilities are often expressed as ratios. Referring to the preceding Punnett square, the phenotypic ratio for tongue-rolling is 3:1, while the genotypic ratio for tongue-rolling is 1:2:1.

A Punnett square can also be used for crosses involving two traits that are independent of each other. The possible combinations are greater, yet the method is the same. Consider, for example, the texture and color of pea plants. Suppose that a yellow wrinkled pea will be crossed with a green smooth pea. The yellow color (Y) is dominant to green (y), and the smooth texture (S) is dominant to wrinkled (s). A cross between a purebred green, smooth pea plant and a yellow, wrinkled pea plant yields the following results:

(Parents)   **SSYY × ssyy**

The Punnett square for this cross:

	SY	SY	SY	SY
sy	SsYy	SsYy	SsYy	SsYy
sy	SsYy	SsYy	SsYy	SsYy
sy	SsYy	SsYy	SsYy	SsYy
sy	SsYy	SsYy	SsYy	SsYy

All the offspring from this cross will be green and smooth (these are their phenotypes). Genotypically, they will all be heterozygous dominant for both traits (Ss and Yy). If we cross two heterozygous peas to one another, though, the offspring will not all look alike. In the following cross, notice all the different genotypes produced:

SsYy × SsYy

	SY	Sy	sY	sy
SY	SSYY	SSYy	SsYY	SsYy
Sy	SSYy	SSyy	SsYy	Ssyy
sY	SsYY	SsYy	ssYY	ssYy
sy	SsYy	Ssyy	ssYy	ssyy

Tallying up each different phenotype, you will find four different specific types, in a 9:3:3:1 ratio:

- 9 squares show dominance for both traits (SYYY, SSYy, SsYY, or SsYy)

- 3 squares show dominance for one trait and recessive for the other (SSyy or Ssyy)

- 3 other squares show dominance for one trait and recessive for the other (ssYY or ssYy)

- 1 square shows recessive for both traits (ssyy)

Deviations from Classic Mendelian Patterns

 http://bit.ly/hippo_bio14

Since Mendel's discoveries, other patterns of gene expression have been identified that deviate from the "classic" Mendelian dominant/recessive patterns. Noteworthy among these are the following three:

Co-dominance: In this deviation, neither of the two different alleles governing the same trait is dominant over the other, and *both* are expressed. For example, three alleles—A, B, and O—determine human blood type. The A and B alleles are co-dominant, and the O allele is recessive. Individuals with the AB genotype are phenotypically distinct (type AB blood) from individuals with the AA or AO (type A), BB or BO (type B), and OO (type O) genotype.

Incomplete dominance: In this deviation, neither of the two different alleles governing the same trait is dominant over the other, and the heterozygote is an intermediate between the two homozygous phenotypes—for example, a mix or hybrid of two colors. A snapdragon homozygous for a red allele (RR) has a red flower, and one that is homozygous for a white allele (WW) has a white flower. But a heterozygous (RW) cross results in a *pink* flower.

Sex linkage: One of our 23 pairs of chromosomes determines our sex—either male (**X**) or female (**Y**). The combination XX results in a female, while XY results in a male. These sex chromosomes carry the genes that govern the development of sex organs as well as secondary sex characteristics—body shape, body hair, and so forth. The X chromosome is much larger than the Y chromosome. As a result, a variety of recessive alleles on an X chromosome have no dominant alleles on the Y chromosome to mask them. This explains why only males experience color blindness or male pattern baldness: these alleles are recessive but will always be expressed because they cannot be masked by dominant *non*-color-blindness or *non*-balding alleles from the female.

7. When neither of two different alleles governing the same trait is dominant over the other, what could be the result (each choice considered individually)?

    A. Both alleles will be distinctly expressed.

    B. The alleles will be expressed as a hybrid.

    C. A genetic mutation will express itself in a unique way

    D. Neither allele will be expressed.

    (1) A only

    (2) A and B only

    (3) B and C only

    (4) C and D only

    (5) A, B, C, and D

The alleles might be co-dominant, in which case both will be distinctly expressed, as noted in statement A. Or they might be incomplete dominance, in which case a mix or hybrid will result, as noted in statement B. **The correct answer is (2).**

8. Assume that two parents are both heterozygous for a certain physical trait, which can either be present or absent in its expression. What is the expected genotypic ratio among their offspring?

    (1) 1:1

    (2) 2:1

    (3) 1:2:1

    (4) 3:1

    (5) no ratio (all offspring will express the trait phenotypically)

Since both parents are heterozygous, the cross would be Tt × Tt (where T = dominant and t = recessive). Constructing a Punnett square would reveal the following: **TT** (one possibility), **Tt** (two possibilities), and **tt** (one possibility). The ratio is 1:2:1. **The correct answer is (3).**

Bacteria and Viruses

Beginning in this section, this review enlarges the scale on which it examines biological life from the molecular level to that of the individual organism. At this level, a good starting point is with two of the smallest such forms—bacteria and viruses. **Bacteria,** also known as *microbes* or *germs*, are microscopic organisms that reproduce primarily asexually. Most other organisms, including humans, are covered inside and out with what is referred to as a normal *flora* of bacterial populations. **Viruses** differ from bacteria in their simplified body structure and composition, their mode of replication, and in that they depend on a living host cell for replication.

 http://bit.ly/hippo_bio15

Types of Bacteria

Bacteria are neither animals nor plants—they occupy their own pigeonhole in the modern classification system for biological life. (The system is outlined later in this review.) Bacteria can be either **autotrophic** (they synthesize food by converting light to chemical energy) or **heterotrophic** (they require other organisms to serve as a food source). They can also be divided into three main groups based on characteristics such as shape, motility (ability to move about on their own), metabolism, and mode of reproduction:

- **Eubacteria** (true bacteria) come in three shapes: coccus (spherical), bacillus (rod-shaped), and spirillum (spiral-shaped). One example of eubacteria is *Escherichia coli*, or *E. coli*, a bacterium that grows in small numbers as a part of the natural flora of human skin, intestinal tract, and genital tract. Under a compromised immune system, however, overgrowth of this bacterium can result in illness or even death.

- **Cyanobacteria** perform photosynthesis to convert light energy into chemical energy for food. The green gooey stuff you sometimes see in standing pools of water (also known as pond scum) is an example of cyanobacteria.

- **Archaeobacteria** is a recently discovered group of bacteria. These microbes are typically found in extreme environments, such as on glaciers and in underwater volcanic vents.

Bacteria have simple structures. Since they are prokaryotes, they lack a membrane-bound nucleus and membrane-bound organelles. The following picture shows the basic body plan for a typical bacterium. A bacterium cell contains strands of DNA, a plasma membrane, a cell wall, and a capsule. This simple structure allows for the rapid division of the bacterium, usually by way of binary fission—a form of asexual reproduction.

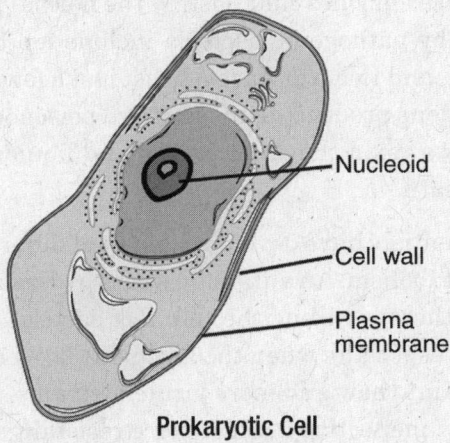

Prokaryotic Cell

Bacteria's Relationships with Plants and Animals

When most people think of bacteria, they think of disease-causing organisms. But many bacteria actually serve beneficial and even necessary functions vis-à-vis humans and the environment. Some microbes, for example, recycle dead materials and sewage into smaller molecules that can be returned to the environment. The pharmaceutical industry uses bacteria in the manufacture of antibiotics and vitamins. Many of the foods we eat, such as yogurt and cheese, are the product of bacterial metabolism. Alcohol, acids, and many other chemicals are products of bacterial cultures.

Bacteria provide an ideal illustration of **symbiosis** in action. Two different types of organisms are said to have a *symbiotic* relationship when there is an ongoing, close association between them. A symbiotic relationship can be either **mutualistic** or **parasitic.** In a mutualistic relationship, each organism obtains a benefit from its association with the other. In a parasitic relationship, one organism obtains a benefit while the other organism is harmed by the relationship. (In a third type of symbiosis, called *commensalism,* one organism benefits while the other is neither benefited nor harmed.)

Bacteria maintain many sorts of mutualistic relationships with many different types of plants. For example, the roots of bean plants form a mutualistic relationship with bacteria that are capable of converting atmospheric nitrogen into a useable form, which not only benefits the plant but also the soil surrounding the plants. This process is known as **nitrogen fixation.** The cycling of nitrogen is achieved exclusively by bacteria.

Bacteria maintain mutualistic relationships with animals as well—including humans. For example, the digestive system in humans relies on intestinal bacteria to aid in digestion and to produce antibiotics that prevent the growth of pathogenic bacteria (see below). Another example involves herbivores such as cows, which lack the enzyme needed to digest cellulose and thus depend on certain bacterial microbes to convert their food into simple sugars. In turn, the methane gas (CH_4) produced as a byproduct of these microbes is used as a fuel source by humans in some parts of the world.

Of course, bacteria can also be parasitic. These forms are called **pathogens,** meaning that they are disease-causing. Pathogenic bacteria invade healthy tissues. Their metabolic processes release enzymes that destroy the normal physiology of this tissue. Human diseases caused by pathogenic bacteria include leprosy, syphilis, gonorrhea, tuberculosis, strep throat, and Lyme disease—to list just a few. Through their bacterial metabolism, other pathogens produce toxins that are poisonous to humans. Botulism, for example, is caused by a toxin that infects food and liquids. When ingested, it can cause illness and even death.

To combat pathogens, scientists have developed a host of different kinds of **antibiotics** that disrupt bacterial metabolism. An antibiotic works by weakening and rupturing the cell wall of a bacterium, thereby killing the cell. But bacteria often develop immunity to a particular antibiotic, especially when the antibiotic is overused. As bacteria divide rapidly, they can develop into new and more virulent strains. For example, antibiotics such as penicillin are now ineffective against more resistant strains of some bacteria. Researchers are continually developing new and stronger antibiotics to combat the ability of bacteria to develop immunity to existing antibiotics.

Viruses

Viruses cannot reproduce on their own accord or perform basic cellular tasks such as protein synthesis, and so most scientists do not consider them to be independent living organisms. A **virus** is simply a strand of genetic material, either DNA or RNA, encapsulated in an outer protein shell. Viruses act as intracellular parasites in all types of organisms. They can only reproduce inside a living cell. Once inside the host cell, viruses take over the replication machinery of the host cell. They transfer their genome into the cell of the host organism, integrate their DNA sequence into the host DNA, and let the host cell replicate, transcribe, and translate the virus's genes. Viral genomes contain genes for directing the replication and packaging of complete copies of the virus, so that eventually the host cell bursts open and releases new viruses to infect other cells.

The living host upon which viruses absolutely depend for replication can be of plant, bacterial, or animal origin. Viruses are host-specific in that they invade only one type of cell, which provides necessary *receptor sites* for the virus to attach itself. For example, the virus that causes polio attaches to neurons, the virus responsible for mumps attaches to salivary glands, and the virus that causes chicken pox attaches to skin cells. Though they are the smallest infectious agents known to humans, what they lack in size they more than make up for in destructive power. They are responsible for a wide variety of devastating human diseases, such as HIV/AIDS, hepatitis B, and herpes.

To treat viral infections, prevention is the key. Early investigations into the spread of disease, in particular smallpox, prompted the development of **vaccines.** In 1796, Dr. Edward Jenner discovered that milkmaids who contracted cowpox from cows showed a natural immunity against the more virulent smallpox. From this discovery, a new form of disease prevention was born. Vaccines are developed by using nonpathogenic strains of viruses or killed viral strains. The vaccine is introduced into an organism, and then the organism's immune system produces antibodies to fight the inactive virus. Later, if the organism encounters these particles again, it has already developed a defense, or immunity, to them.

Through genetic engineering in recent decades, scientists have devised ways for organisms other than the infected one to independently produce inactive components of a virus. For example, plants such as bananas can be engineered to become "edible vaccines" by splicing genes from a bacterium or virus with a bacterium that naturally occurs in the soil in which the banana plant grows. The bacterium in the soil then infects the growing plant, transferring the foreign gene along with it. Scientists hope that in this way, large quantities of vaccines can be produced inexpensively and distributed to areas of the world that lack conventional health care. Through this and other innovative approaches, researchers hope to eventually win the ongoing battle against these unseen and potentially deadly invaders.

http://bit.ly/hippo_bio16

9. Bacteria reproduce at a higher rate than any other organism. What allows bacteria to replicate so rapidly?

(1) They receive their energy from inorganic substances.

(2) Their cell structure is very simple.

(3) They feed on host organisms without providing any benefit in return.

(4) Vaccines are generally ineffective in killing bacteria.

(5) They can reproduce in nearly any environment, no matter how hostile.

The simple cell structure of bacteria is the key to their ability to replicate so rapidly. **The correct answer is (2).**

10. How does a vaccine work to prevent a viral infection?

It works by

(1) boosting the immune system with viral-fighting vitamins

(2) introducing a bacterium that encounters and kills the virus

(3) replacing the organism's natural DNA with the anti-DNA

(4) stimulating the production of antibodies to fight the virus

(5) strengthening cell walls so that the virus cannot enter the cells

A vaccine introduces an inactive strain of the virus. The body's immune system then produces antibodies to fight the inactive virus. If the body is later exposed to a pathogenic strain of the virus, the appropriate antibodies are already there to fight it off. **The correct answer is (4).**

Modern Taxonomy and the Five Kingdoms

 http://bit.ly/hippo_bio17

Attempts to categorize or classify all life forms date back to ancient times. Our current classification system is based on the one developed by Carolus Linnaeus, who in the 1700s made a major step in bringing order to the natural world. He laid the foundation for modern **taxonomy,** our system of classification and nomenclature (naming). Linnaeus used Latin to name organisms, so that everyone involved in the field of science could use a universal language for the names of organisms. He then created a system of *binomial nomenclature*, which uses a two-part name that illustrates the special characteristics of each organism. The binomial later evolved into the *genus* and *species* of modern taxonomic classification (see below).

Our modern classification scheme starts with five major groups, called **kingdoms.** This is the largest grouping category. As classification continues, it becomes increasingly specific. The seven main hierarchical levels in this classification system are as follows (note that in plants the term *division* is used instead of *phylum*):

Modern Taxonomy

Kingdom
Phylum
Class
Order
Family
Genus
Species

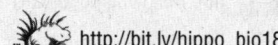

The following is a brief overview of the five kingdoms: Prokaryotae (also called Monera), Protista, Mycetae, Plantae (plants), and Animalia (animals).

Kingdom Prokaryotae (Monera)

Prokaryotae (also called Monera) are simple, single-celled, microscopic organisms and are the most primitive and ancient of all life forms. They lack a distinct cell nucleus, and their DNA is not organized into chromosomes. Prokaryotae play a variety of roles in the biological world:

- Some are pathogenic (disease-causing).

- Some serve to break down gaseous nitrogen into inorganic compounds that are biologically usable (through a process called **nitrogen fixation**).

- Some serve to decompose organic matter, so that it can enrich the soil and nourish plant life.

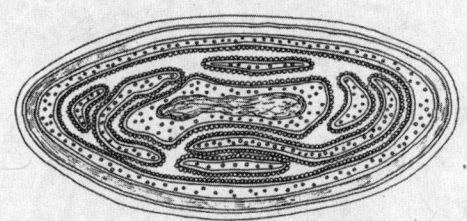

Typical Prokaryotic Cell

Members of this Kingdom Prokaryotae include **bacteria** and **cyanobacteria** (a special form of bacteria). There are more than 4,800 known kinds of bacteria. Most need oxygen to live, but other bacteria do not. Within the latter group, some can withstand small amounts of oxygen, while others find oxygen poisonous and will die if subjected to large amounts. (Bacteria are examined in more detail elsewhere in this review.)

Cyanobacteria are a special type of bacteria that are autotrophic and photosynthetic, which means that they manufacture their own food by harnessing the Sun's light and absorbing inorganic substances such as carbon dioxide and ammonia. The most common cyanobacteria are blue-green algae (though they belong to a different kingdom than other types of algae). If a body of water contains appropriate and abundant nutrients, a growth explosion of blue-green algae can occur, creating a "floating carpet," or algal bloom. Much—perhaps even most—of the Earth's oxygen is attributable to the photosynthetic activity of these great masses of Cyanobacteria, which come in nearly 8,000 known species.

 http://bit.ly/hippo_bio19

Kingdom Protista

Many members of this kingdom are single-celled and move about freely as individual organisms. Others, however, form colonies with other organisms of their type. The latter are *eukaryotic* cells—they have a distinct nucleus as well as other structures found in more advanced cells.

 http://bit.ly/hippo_bio2-0

PROTOZOA

Protozoa are distinguished from other protists in their locomotive ability and by how they obtain food. Two common protozoa are the amoeba and the paramecium. An **amoeba** is a formless cell that uses *pseudopods* to move and to obtain food by simply engulfing it. A **paramecium** moves about by using hairlike *cilia*, which is also used by the paramecium to direct a current of water containing food into the organism's gullet (like a mouth and stomach all in one).

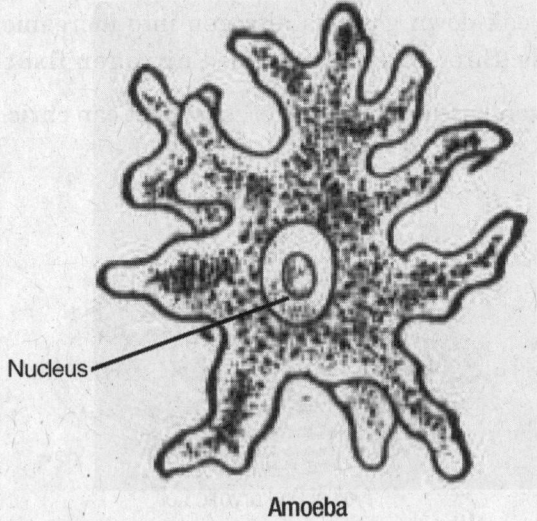

Nucleus

Amoeba

Some protozoa are pathogenic. Different types of protozoa are responsible for serious diseases such as amoebic dysentery, malaria, and African sleeping sickness (a debilitating, wasting disease).

 http://bit.ly/hippo_bio21

ALGAE (PLANT-LIKE AUTOTROPHS)

Algae are classified in the Kingdom Protista, but algae are quite different from amoebas and paramecia. Algae are *autotrophic*—they contain chloroplasts with pigment for photosynthesis—and include green, brown, red, and golden algae, as well as diatoms, euglena, and dinoflagellates. Most seaweed is a collection of algal cells. Due to seaweed's high nutritional value, it accounts for a major portion of the human diet in many parts of the world, especially near the coasts in Asia.

- *Diatoms* are widely used commercially for the reflective and abrasive nature of their shells. Paints used for marking highway lanes often contain *diatomaceous* earth, and many types of toothpaste contain diatom shells because of their abrasive quality.

- *Euglena* are perhaps the most curious of the various forms of algae. Euglena are normally *autotrophic*—they contain chloroplasts with pigment for photosynthesis. However, under low light or the absence of light, they can switch to a *heterotrophic* mode, meaning they can obtain their energy by consuming other organisms. They move by flagella, which is more characteristic of protozoa.

- *Dinoflagellates* are one of the main components of plankton. Some species can undergo explosive population growth, creating seas of red or brown referred to as "red tide" and producing great amounts of neurotoxins that kill both marine and human life.

SLIME MOLDS (FUNGUS-LIKE HETEROTROPHS)

http://bit.ly/hippo_bio22

You may have seen slime molds when camping or hiking. These amoeba-like cells dwell in dark, warm, moist areas—on damp soil or in decaying plant matter such as rotting leaves and logs—and move about, often in slug-like colonies, when food becomes scarce. During a portion of its lifecycle, one type of slime mold develops into a multicellular structure that produces and releases spores. In this form, a slime mold resembles a fungus, which is discussed next.

Kingdom Mycetae

http://bit.ly/hippo_bio23

The common name for any member of the Kingdom Mycetae is **fungus.** These are mainly non-motile, non-photosynthetic heterotrophic organisms. What this means is that they have no independent means of mobility, and they obtain the energy they need by consuming other organisms. Most fungi, including molds and mushrooms, are multicellular. However, this kingdom does include a few unicellular types as well, such as yeast. Fungi survive and spread by producing and releasing spores, which are made sexually or asexually. When released, the spores are carried by wind or water and can travel hundreds of miles from their point of origin.

Fungi can be either *saprophytic* or *symbiotic*. Saprophytes absorb nutrients from dead organisms. Symbiotic fungi are either parasitic (causing, for example, athlete's foot and ringworm) or mutualistic. Lichens are a form of mutualistic fungus; they afford protection to algae and cyanobacteria in exchange for the food energy that algae and cyanobacteria provide.

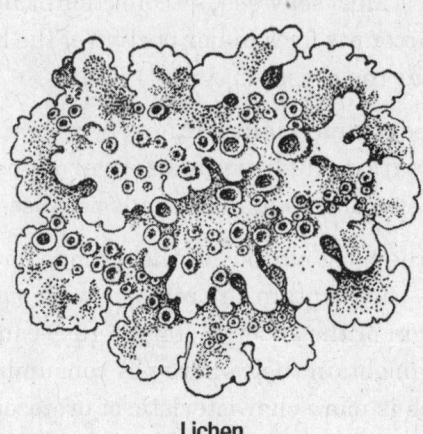

Lichen

A variety of commercial foods—mushrooms, blue cheese, beer, and soy sauce, to name a few—are fungi products.

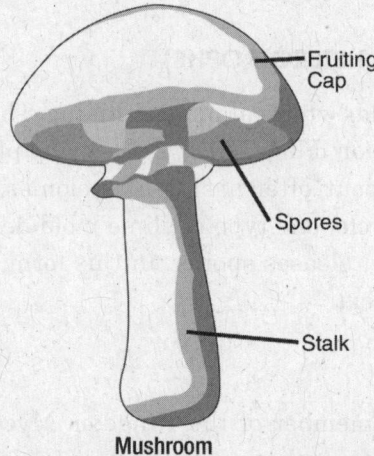

Mushroom

11. Which of the following is the most specific category in the modern taxonomic classification system?

    (1) class

    (2) family

    (3) phylum

    (4) order

    (5) kingdom

Of the five categories listed, the most specific is *family*. **The correct answer is (2).**

12. What do all protists share in common?

(1) They are a food source for humans living near the ocean.

(2) They can move about freely in water.

(3) They must consume organic matter to survive.

(4) They can reproduce either asexually or sexually.

(5) They dwell in water or in watery tissues of organisms.

Protozoa and algae are water dwellers, and slime molds dwell in the moist tissues of rotting leaves or logs. Choices (1), (2), (3), and (4) each describe some, but not all, protists. **The correct answer is (5).**

Kingdom Plantae (Plants)

http://bit.ly/hippo_bio24-1

Organisms in the three kingdoms previously discussed are very simple compared to the organisms in Kingdom Plantae (plants). All plants are multicellular, and they all are autotrophic, which means that they generate their own food. Nearly all plants do so by using their photosynthetic pigment **chlorophyll** found in organelles called **chloroplasts.**

NONVASCULAR PLANTS AND VASCULAR PLANTS

http://bit.ly/hippo_bio24

Plants have adapted to live in practically every type of environment. They evolved in form, activity, and function over millions of years. The multitude of plants within this kingdom is staggering. But they all fall into two major groups of plants: nonvascular and vascular. By far, the simpler of the two forms is **nonvascular** (division *Bryophyta*). Nonvascular plants have no true roots, stems, or leaves. Lacking these structures, they are limited in two ways. First, they cannot grow very high—only a few inches in height, on average. Second, they can dwell only in a consistently moist environment. Nonvascular plants include mosses, liverworts, and hornworts. Among these forms, only mosses contain specialized tissues for transporting water or other nutrients from one part of the plant to another, and only to a limited extent.

A **vascular** plant is one that contains specialized tissues for carrying water, dissolved nutrients, and food from one part of the plant to another. Vascular plants represent the vast majority of plants. Their complex vascular tissues show that they have successfully adapted to living on land. They are mainly diploid throughout their lifecycle, which means that they reproduce sexually—one pair of chromosomes from each parent are inherited by offspring.

Vascular plants generally have roots, stems, and leaves. **Roots** anchor a plant into soil, from which the plant draws water and nutrients through osmosis. Humans eat a variety of roots, including carrots and radishes, to name just a few. **Stems** support leaves and transport raw materials from roots to leaves and synthesized food from leaves to roots and other parts of the plant. Humans eat the stems of a variety of plants, including celery, sugar cane, and several others.

 http://bit.ly/hippo_bio25

Leaves are the major photosynthetic portion of a plant. Their *chlorophyll*—the pigment that gives plants their green appearance—receives sunlight, while the underside of the leaf takes in carbon dioxide through tiny openings called **stomata.** The plant then combines the carbon dioxide with water to produce energy in the form of glucose. As a waste product of the process, oxygen is then released through the leaf's pores. (The process by which a leaf exchanges gases in this way is called **transpiration.**)

The major parts of a typical leaf are as follows:

- *Epidermis:* Outer layer of stomata and hair cells, as well as a waxy cuticle that prevents water loss

- *Guard cells:* Epidermal cells that change shape according to water amounts in leaf; create tiny openings called stomata, which close or open to control the rate of water loss and gas exchange

- *Palisade layer:* Contains chloroplasts, arranged vertically for maximum photosynthesis

- *Spongy layer:* Loosely arranged chloroplasts that allow for water, oxygen, and carbon dioxide circulation

- *Vascular bundles:* Xylem and phloem tissues in bundles

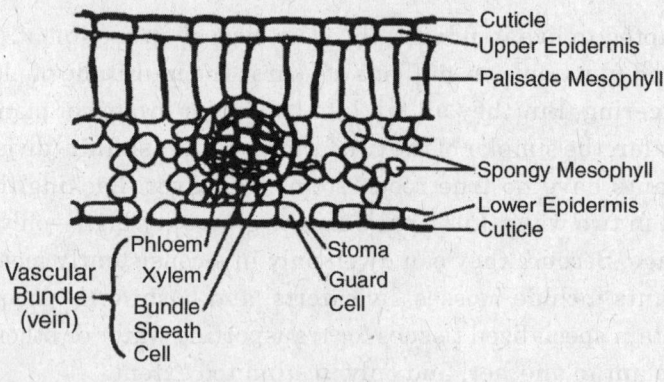

Cross section of a typical leaf

Vascular bundles of xylem and phloem are present in most other parts of a vascular plant as well. A plant's **xylem** consists of hollow cells that form tubes for carrying water from soil into roots and for transporting water to above-ground portions of the plant. A plant's **phloem** consists of thickened sieve-like cells that transport organic molecules produced in one part of the plant to storage regions in another part (for example, the sugars produced by photosynthesis in the leaf move to the root for storage).

SEEDLESS AND SEED-BEARING VASCULAR PLANTS

 http://bit.ly/hippo_bio26

Some vascular plants are seedless. These plants propagate by producing and disseminating spores. Examples include club mosses, horsetails, and ferns. Other vascular plants are seed-producing. A **seed** is actually a reproductive organ—a specialized structure that contains an embryo enclosed in an outer, protective seed coat. Under the right conditions and with water, the seed can germinate and grow into an adult plant.

Seed-producing vascular plants include gymnosperms and angiosperms. Literally translated as "naked seed," **gymnosperms** produce seeds on the surfaces of woody, leaf-like structures called cones. The pine tree is one well-known example of a gymnosperm. Gymnosperm cones are reproductive structures: male cones produce pollen, and female cones produce ovules on the same tree. During the process of pollination, pollen is transferred by wind, insects, or rain from a male cone to the eggs of the female cone.

Angiosperms produce fruits, which attract animals that eat the fruit and then disperse its seeds. This group of plants is considered the highest order of evolution in the plant kingdom. Unlike gymnosperms, angiosperms produce coated seeds that are enclosed by tissues of an ovary, which is part of the plant's flower. The ovary and other tissues develop into the mature structure that is the fruit. When you eat a piece of fruit, you are actually consuming a plant's mature ovary.

There are 300,000 varieties of plants that produce flowers, fruits, and seeds. All flowering plants are considered angiosperms. The two major categories of angiosperms are **monocots** and **dicots.** The distinction between the two involves a structure called a **cotyledon.** The cotyledon contains the embryo and stores nutrients for germination of the embryo. A monocot's seed contains only one cotyledon. Examples include orchids as well as grasses such as rye, corn, wheat, and rice. A dicot's seed contains two cotyledons. Dicots account for the majority of angiosperms—about 180,000 varieties—including most herbaceous (non-woody) plants, flowering shrubs, and trees. Examples of dicots include legumes (beans), apples, and oak trees.

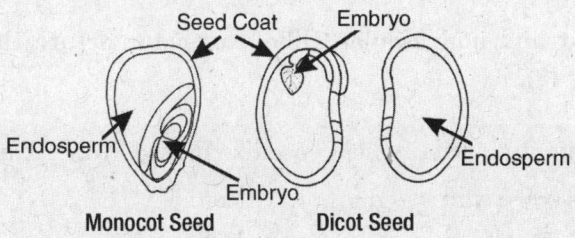

Flowers are the specialized reproductive organs for flowering plants. They contain both the male and female portions of the plant, as shown and described in the following diagram:

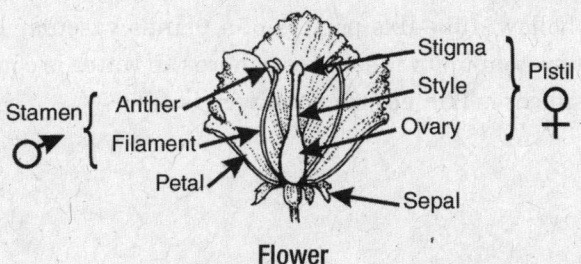

- **Petals:** The floral portions of the plant, usually ornate to attract pollinators
- **Pistil:** The female reproductive parts (stigma, style, ovary)
  - *Stigma*—the portion on which pollen lands
  - *Style*—the slender tube-like portion between the stigma and ovary
  - *Ovary*—contains the egg and site of fertilization; the ovary matures into the fruit with seeds
- **Stamen:** The male reproductive parts (anther, filament)
  - *Anther*—produces pollen
  - *Filament*—the stalk on which the anther sits
- **Sepals:** The protective portion of the unopened flower

In an angiosperm, pollination occurs when pollen is transferred from the anther to the stigma. Some angiosperms can self-pollinate, while others rely on insects, birds, or wind to carry pollen from the anther of one plant to the stigma of another.

13. All of the following characteristics most clearly distinguish vascular plants from nonvascular plants EXCEPT for which one?

Vascular plants can

(1) grow in a vertical direction

(2) obtain water and nutrients from beneath the earth

(3) manufacture their own food

(4) transport food from one part of the plant to another

(5) survive for a time without moisture in their immediate environment

All plants, vascular and nonvascular alike, can manufacture their own food. **The correct answer is (3).**

14. Which statement about a typical vascular plant is LEAST accurate?

(1) The roots store water and other nutrients.

(2) The chloroplasts capture energy from the Sun.

(3) The leaves exchange carbon dioxide for oxygen.

(4) The phloem regulates the plant's water intake.

(5) The xylem transports glucose from leaves to roots.

The phloem is the hollow, tube-like portion of a plant's vascular bundle that carries water from the root system up to the leaves, where the water is combined with carbon dioxide to produce glucose. **The correct answer is (4).**

Kingdom Animalia (Animals)

Animals have adapted to live in practically every environment on Earth. From habitat to size and from form to color, animals show amazing variety. There are at least 4 million known species of animals. But all are multicellular; and all are heterotrophic, meaning they must obtain food by consuming other organisms. All members of the animal kingdom share the following characteristics:

- They are *motile*, which means they can move from place to place during all stages of their life; they can also move one part of their body in respect to the other parts.

- They are not photosynthetic (they do not produce their own energy but rather obtain that energy by consuming other organisms).

- They reproduce sexually (although some may reproduce asexually as well).

- They consist of multiple cells (they are *multicellular*), many of which organize into tissues and then into complex organ systems.

Within the animal kingdom are different phyla (the next level down in the taxonomic classification system). Following are the main features and representative members of each phylum. Note that the phyla listed here begin with the more basic forms and advance to more complex forms. The phylum *chordata*, the last one listed here, is examined in greater detail than the others.

PHYLUM PORIFERA (SPONGES)

- **Features:** Stationary (sessile) organisms as adult; contain pores for circulation of water and food

- **Members:** Marine and freshwater sponges

PHYLUM CNIDARIA (CNIDARIANS)

- **Features:** Secrete a hard, surrounding covering for protection; have a two-form lifecycle (a stationary, or sessile, *polyp* produces a free-floating *medusae*); radial symmetry (body forms symmetrical around a center); stinging tentacles surround a mouth used for both ingesting food and eliminating waste.

- **Representative members:** Hydra, jellyfish, corals, sea anemone

PHYLUM PLATYHELMINTHES (FLATWORMS)

- **Features:** Free-living, nonsegmented carnivores with a sac-type digestive system

- **Representative members:** Planarian, tapeworm, fluke (tapeworms are segmented parasites that live in the digestive tract of vertebrates and have no digestive system; flukes are both external and internal parasites with flattened bodies that live off of fluids from their host)

PHYLUM ASCHELMINTHES (ROUNDWORMS)

- **Features:** Cylindrical bodies and a complete digestive tract; not segmented; can be free-living or parasitic; especially useful for recycling in soil habitats

- **Representative members:** Nematode, pinworm

PHYLUM ANNELIDA (SEGMENTED WORMS)

- **Features:** Occupy marine environments (exception: earthworms); segmented bodies; can be parasitic (example: blood-sucking leech); have developed organ systems, including circulatory, muscular, digestive, and nervous system.

- **Representative members:** Earthworm, leech, polychaetes

PHYLUM ARTHROPODA (ARTHROPODS)

- **Features:** Some possess a head thorax and abdomen (insects, spiders); have appendages such as jointed legs, antennae, mouthparts, and wings; have external exoskeleton armor; metamorphose from egg, larva, and pupa to adult; most are terrestrial, but some are marine dwellers (Class *Crustacea*)

- **Members:** Class *Insecta* (insects), Class *Arachnida* (spiders), Class *Diploda* (millipedes), Class *Chilopoda* (centipedes), Class *Crustacea* (crustaceans)

PHYLUM MOLLUSCA (MOLLUSKS)

- **Features:** Soft bodies (some are protected by shells); some have a ventral, muscular foot (example: bivalves, in which two shells are hinged together); have well-developed circulatory and nervous systems

- **Representative Members:** Bivalves (clam, mussel), squid, snail, octopus

 http://bit.ly/hippo_bio30

PHYLUM ECHINODERMATA (ECHINODERMS)

- **Features:** Marine dwelling; possess tubular feet and a water-circulating system; lattice-like internal skeleton and usually a hard, spiny outer covering; adults exhibit radial body symmetry (a five-pointed body form)

- **Representative members:** Starfish, sand dollar, sea cucumber, sea urchin

 http://bit.ly/hippo_31

PHYLUM CHORDATA VERTEBRATA (VERTEBRATES)

This is the most advanced phylum in terms of evolutionary development. Three evolutionary developments make the *chordata* phylum so advanced:

- A *notochord*—a flexible rod that provides structural support

- A *dorsal nerve chord* on the back or upper surface, which in some animals differentiates into a brain and spinal cord

- One or more *pharyngeal gill slits* for carbon dioxide/oxygen exchange (in higher animals, these slits can appear as passages leading from the nose and mouth to the esophagus)

The phylum *chordata* includes several different classes—the taxonomic system's next level down—as listed and briefly described below. Animals in the first four classes are *cold-blooded,* which means that their internal body temperature varies directly with external temperature. Animals in the remaining two classes are *warm-blooded,* meaning they normally maintain a constant internal body temperature. (Note that only two of several classes of fish are listed here.)

- **Class Chondrichthyes (cartilaginous fish)**
  - **Features:** Cold-blooded; cartilage skeleton and fins
  - **Members:** Sharks and rays

 http://bit.ly/hippo_bio32

- **Class Osteichthyes (bony fish)**
  - **Features:** Cold-blooded; bony skeleton, fins, and scales; use gills to process oxygen from water; mainly external fertilization
  - **Members:** trout, bass, carp

 http://bit.ly/hippo_bio33

- **Class Amphibia (amphibians)**
  - **Features:** Cold-blooded; moist skin with no scales; external fertilization; undergo *metamorphosis* (dramatic change from fishlike form to four-legged, air-breathing terrestrial form) during development after birth or hatching; three-chambered heart
  - **Members:** Frog, salamander, toad

- **Class Reptilia (reptiles)**
  - **Features:** Cold-blooded; body covering of scales and horns; internal egg fertilization
  - **Members:** Snake, turtle, crocodile, lizard

 http://bit.ly/hippo_bio34

- **Class Aves (birds)**
  - **Features:** Warm-blooded; wings and forelimbs; hard bill that covers the jaw; covering of feathers; internal fertilization; eggs enclosed in calcium-enriched shell; four-chambered heart
  - **Members:** Chicken, crow, eagle

 http://bit.ly/hippo_bio35

- **Class Mammalia (mammals)**
  - **Features:** Warm-blooded; hair covers body, feed young with mammary glands; internal fertilization; four-chambered heart
  - **Members:**

 http://bit.ly/hippo_bio36

    - *Monotremes* (primitive egg-laying)—duck-bill platypus
    - *Marsupials* (mother carries young in body pouch)—kangaroo
    - *Rodents* (incisor teeth that grow continually)—rat, squirrel, mouse
    - *Cetaceans* (marine; forelimbs modified to flippers)—dolphin, porpoise, whale
    - *Carnivores* (meat-eaters)—dog, wolf, cat
    - *Primates* (large brain; stand erect; ability to grasp and hold objects)—human, ape, monkey, lemur

15. Animals belonging to which of the following phyla have body forms that exhibit radial symmetry?

   A. cniderians
   B. roundworms
   C. arthropods
   D. echinoderms

 (1) A only

 (2) A and B only

 (3) A and D only

 (4) B and C only

 (5) B, C, and D only

All cniderians and echinoderms have body forms that exhibit radial symmetry. In this shape, the body extends symmetrically outward from a central mouth or other opening. **The correct answer is (3).**

16. Which *chordata* class could be characterized as a "hybrid," exhibiting a combination of characteristics from two other such classes?

   (1) cartilaginous fish

   (2) amphibians

   (3) reptiles

   (4) birds

   (5) mammals

Amphibians undergo a metamorphosis after birth or hatching, beginning as water-breathing, fishlike animals and then transforming into terrestrial, air-breathing animals with four legs. In this respect, they are a hybrid of fish and reptiles, both of which are also cold-blooded. **The correct answer is (2).**

Homeostasis and the Body's Organ Systems

 http://bit.ly/hippo_bio37

The body is a remarkable complex of various organ systems that function together in unison—like the components of a properly calibrated and well-oiled machine. For example, the organ systems naturally work together to ensure that the body's internal conditions remain stable, and if conditions deviate from their normal ranges, to return them to normal. Appropriate organ responses to internal changes help ensure steady body temperature, blood pressure, and the chemical composition of body fluids. The body's tendency to maintain the stability of these and other internal conditions is referred to as **homeostasis.**

The body's organ system works together in many other ways as well. The best way to understand these connections is to examine each of the organ systems, in turn. This section briefly describes the structure, components, and functions of the body's various organ systems, as well as how they function together with one or more of the other systems.

The Integumentary System

The integumentary system includes skin, sweat glands, oil glands, hair, and nails. It is the largest organ in the body. Our skin is a barrier between our bodies and the external environment. It prevents water loss, mechanical and chemical damage, and microbial invasion. Skin is composed of two distinct regions: the **epidermis** and the **dermis.** These two regions are further divided into several functional layers. The third region just beneath the skin is the **hypodermis.** It is not considered a part of the skin, but it serves a protective function similar to skin.

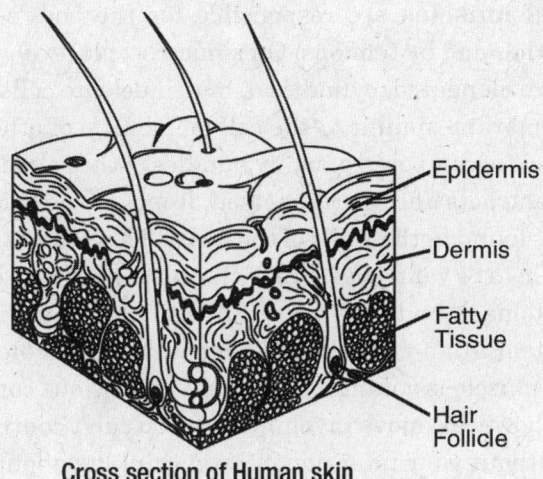

— Epidermis

— Dermis

— Fatty Tissue

— Hair Follicle

Cross section of Human skin

The Skeletal System

The skeletal system supports the body and acts as a lever system for the muscles, creating movement at joints. This system contains **bones,** of course, which provide for movement and support. But bones also serve as a mineral depository. What's more, the marrow at the center of our bones is where our new blood cells are formed. The 206 bones in the normal human body can be divided into two major groups: the *axial* skeleton (80 bones that run the axis of the skeleton) and the *appendicular* skeleton (126 bones that include the limbs and the pectoral and pelvic girdles).

Bones articulate, or meet, with one another at joints. **Cartilage** lines the joints to prevent bones from rubbing against each other. Depending on the type of movement at a joint, the cartilage can provide either a smooth articulating surface or a strong adhesion between bones. To help stabilize movable joints, such joints utilize a band-like type of connective tissue known as a **ligament.** Finally, **tendons** attach muscles to bone at joints.

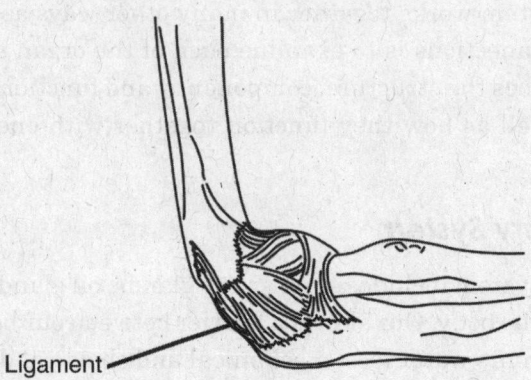

Ligament

The Muscular System

The more than 600 muscles in the human body come in three types: skeletal, cardiac, and smooth. **Skeletal muscles** are responsible for the body's movement and are attached to bone at either end by tendons. On a microscopic level, the fibers that make up skeletal muscles are elongated, cylindrical, multinucleate cells that are encased by a **sarcolemma:** a membrane similar to the cell membrane of other cells containing a single nucleus. A muscle is composed of many bundles of these fibers working together. Each time a muscle contracts and shortens itself, it moves the body part it is attached to. **Cardiac muscle** is found in the walls of the heart. This muscle allows for the strong pumping action of the heart's ventricles. **Smooth muscle** is found in the walls of hollow organs, such as the stomach and intestines. Cardiac and smooth muscles coordinate with the nervous system in an entirely different way than skeletal muscles do. The movement of skeletal muscle is voluntary—you have conscious control over it. Cardiac and smooth muscles, however, move involuntary—you can't control them consciously. Instead, they work without your intention or even thinking about it.

The Nervous System

The nervous system, along with the endocrine system (you will read about this next), is responsible for coordinating all of the physiological processes in the body. The nervous system responds rapidly to external stimuli and to messages from the brain. It regulates a myriad of actions from breathing and digestion to the blink of an eye and the beating of the heart.

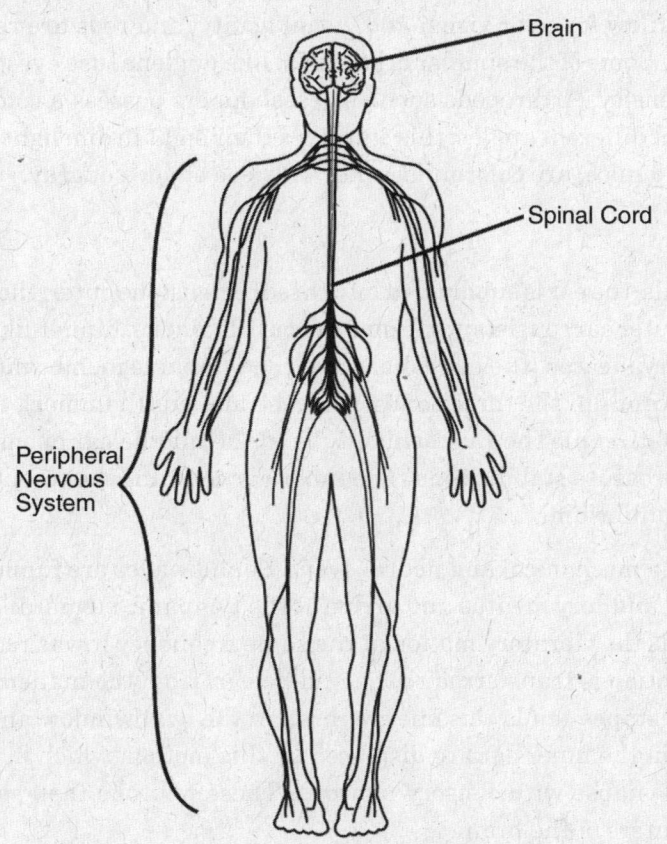

Peripheral Nervous System

The **peripheral nervous system** extends away from the spine and into the limbs. It carries impulses from sensory neurons to the **central nervous system,** which consists of the brain and spinal cord. The brain processes incoming sensory information and translates it into instructions. It then sends those instructions to the appropriate organs of the body, so the body can respond to the initial sensory information. The **neuron** is the functional unit of nervous tissue that is used by the central and peripheral nervous systems.

Taste, vision, hearing, balance, and smell are integral parts of the nervous system. They allow us to interact with and interpret external stimuli as well as monitor internal changes of a chemical or physical nature. Different animals utilize these senses to different degrees. Also, some nonhuman animals possess senses that humans lack altogether. For instance, some species of birds detect the magnetic field of the Earth; honeybees see ultraviolet light; and rattlesnakes sense infrared radiation from objects at a distance.

THE EYE

Visual perception in humans is like a camera lens. Light enters through an adjustable lens that, like film, focuses the image on a receptor called the **retina.** Within the retina are specialized photoreceptors called **rods** and **cones** that detect different properties of light. Cones allow for color vision and visual acuity, and rods are responsive in low light conditions. Some of the simpler organisms, like euglena, use eyespots that merely detect light intensity. Arthropods such as grasshoppers possess a compound eye that lets light enter at different angles; this enhances their sight in dim light. Other animals, such as deer and mice, are colorblind—they only see shades of gray.

THE EAR

In higher animals, the ear is subdivided into three regions: the outer, the middle, and the inner ear. The outer ear consists of the pinna (a cartilaginous, funnel-like structure), the external auditory meatus (the ear canal), and the tympanic membrane (the eardrum). The middle ear contains the three ear ossicles: the malleus (hammer), the incus (anvil), and the stapes (stirrup). The Eustachian tube in the middle ear opens into the throat and allows for pressure stabilization. The inner ear contains the receptors for hearing, balance, and equilibrium.

Hearing is both a mechanical and neural event. Sound waves are funneled into the ear via the external auditory meatus and arrive at the tympanic membrane. The tympanic membrane sends the vibratory motion at the same frequency it was received to the ear ossicles. The motion is transferred to the middle ear, from the malleus to the incus to the stapes. The stapes sends this energy through the oval window and into the inner ear. The fluids in the inner ear are displaced by this motion, which in turn stimulates hair cells that synapse with sensory neurons. These neurons then send messages to the auditory centers of the brain.

The Endocrine System

The **endocrine system** is composed of specialized organs called **glands,** which secrete chemical messengers called hormones. These hormones are carried throughout the body by the circulatory system, but they have only site-specific responses and can only attach to recognized receptor molecules of certain cells. The response time of hormones varies according to the outcome that is needed. For instance, epinephrine and norepinephrine (released from the adrenal medulla gland) can cause a rapid behavioral response known as the "flight or fight" response. This causes the heart rate, blood pressure, and breathing rate to increase as well as to direct blood to skeletal muscle. The following table lists each major gland, the major hormones it releases, and its function.

Major Endocrine Glands and Functions

Endocrine Gland	Hormones Released	Functions
*Pituitary (both anterior and posterior)	1. Growth hormone 2. Anti-diuretic hormone	1. Regulator of muscle, bone, and connective tissue growth 2. Increases re-uptake of water into blood from renal tubules; increases blood pressure
Thyroid	1. Thyroxin 2. Calcitonin	1. Regulates cellular metabolism 2. Decreases calcium ions in blood
Parathyroid	Parathyroid hormone	Increases calcium ions in blood
Pancreas	1. Insulin 2. Glucagon	1. Lowers blood-sugar levels; increases rate of metabolism of stored sugar 2. Increases blood-sugar levels by converting glycogen to glucose; synthesizes glucose; and releases glucose to blood from liver cells
Adrenal glands	1. Corticosteroid 2. Epinephrine	1. Decreases sodium ion excretion; influences cellular metabolism and provides resistance stressors; contributes to secondary sexual characteristics during puberty 2. Increases blood-sugar levels, heart rate, blood pressure, and respiratory rate; shunts blood to skeletal muscle; mobilizes the sympathetic nervous system for short-term stressors or emergencies
Testes	Testosterone	Starts the maturation of male reproductive organs, secondary sexual characteristics at puberty, and sex drive
Ovaries	1. Estrogen 2. Progesterone	1. Initiates maturation of female reproductive organs and secondary sexual characteristics at puberty 2. Promotes breast development and menstrual cycle

*The pituitary gland has an effect on all of the major glands. The few listed in this table do not represent the total number of hormones released from the pituitary.

17. Which of the following helps provide for homeostasis in the human body?

    (1) cardiac muscles, which pump more blood to skeletal muscles when you sense danger

    (2) retinal cones, which allow you to see the difference between red and green traffic lights

    (3) sweat glands, which help cool your body on a hot summer day

    (4) sensory neurons, which send a message to your brain to remove your hand from a hot iron

    (5) inner ear receptors, which help you keep your balance during a tennis match

Through the process of homeostasis, your body seeks to maintain optimal states, including an optimal internal body temperature. When your body heats up too much, the integumentary system goes to work to secrete sweat, which helps reduce body temperature. **The correct answer is (3).**

18. Which of the following is the best analogy to the nervous system?

    (1) a motor

    (2) a radio broadcast

    (3) a nuclear reactor

    (4) a computer

    (5) a bee hive

A computer receives input, which is transmitted to a central processor, which then provides instructions as to the proper response to that input. The nervous system functions in a similar way. **The correct answer is (4).**

The Cardiovascular System

Many multicellular organisms, such as humans, consist of trillions of cells that need a rapid and efficient way to meet their physiological needs. During cellular metabolism, cells take in nutrients, create waste, and store, make, and use molecules—all of which need to be transported to other parts of the body. The cardiovascular system provides transportation by using several integrated parts. The heart pumps blood into **arteries,** which distribute the blood to the organs. Blood is pumped into successively smaller arteries until it enters thin-walled vessels called **capillaries.** Blood is diffused through capillary beds so material can be exchanged between the blood and organ tissues. Blood then percolates through the capillary beds and into **veins,** which gradually merge with larger veins until the blood returns to the heart.

CARDIAC PHYSIOLOGY

The right side of the heart, the **right ventricle,** pumps blood to the lungs, which are near the heart. The larger **left ventricle** sends blood to the **aorta,** the main artery which delivers blood to the rest of the body. The left ventricle must contract with greater force, and this force creates a higher pressure in the arteries. Each contraction of the heart is reflected in the heartbeat. (When you take your pulse, you are actually measuring your heartbeat rate.)

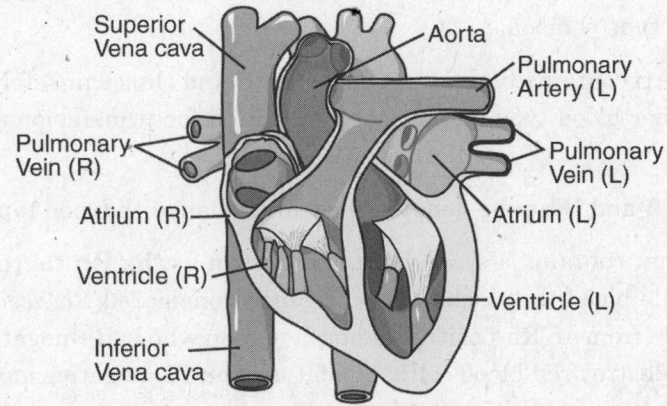

Heart and Associated Vessels

Blood pressure is measured through the heartbeat. There are two phases to a heartbeat. The first is referred to as **systolic pressure** and is the result of the strong contraction of the ventricles as blood is pumped into the aorta. The second phase is **diastolic pressure,** which is the result of ventricular relaxation.

BLOOD

The largest component of blood is a fluid matrix called **plasma.** Blood plasma, which is mostly water, transports a host of materials, including wastes, nutrients, hormones, electrolytes, and proteins, cells, and heat from one body region to another. Most notably, within the plasma are erythrocytes (red blood cells), leukocytes (white blood cells), and thrombocytes (platelets), each of which performs a unique function:

- **Red blood cells** consist mainly of **hemoglobin,** which are the molecules that transport oxygen throughout the bloodstream.

- **White blood cells** serve as a defense mechanism against disease, tumors, parasites, toxins, and bacteria; they move from blood to tissues, and they produce antibodies for long-term protection.

- **Platelets** are tiny disk-shaped cells that seal small ruptures in blood vessels and assist in blood clotting.

Human blood is categorized by four types—A, B, AB, and O—according to which type of antigens are present on the surface of a person's red blood cells. (Letters A and B represent different types of antigens.) An **antigen** is a substance that stimulates the production of an **antibody** when introduced into the body. Antibodies circulating throughout a person's bloodstream normally recognize the antigens in that same person's blood and do not react with them. However, if one type of blood is transfused with another type of blood, antibodies in the new blood can react with the foreign antigens by binding to them, resulting in clumping of the blood. Thus, a safe **blood transfusion** requires that the antigens of the donor's blood match those of the donee's blood:

- Blood type O contains no antigens and thus can safely be used for any blood transfusions, regardless of the blood type of the person receiving the transfusion. On the other hand, individuals with blood type O can receive transfusions only from donors with type O blood.

- Blood type AB contains both antigens A and B and thus can safely be transfused with any other blood type but cannot be donated for transfusions with any other blood type.

- Blood types A and B can be donated for transfusion with blood type AB.

Human blood that contains a special antigen known as the **Rh factor** is considered *Rh positive*, while blood that lacks this antigen is considered *Rh negative*. If given a blood transfusion from an Rh-positive donor, a person who is Rh-negative can produce antibodies that destroy red blood cells. The fetus of an Rh-negative mother can nevertheless be Rh positive, in which case the mother's blood will produce these antibodies, thus threatening the life of the fetus. Under this circumstance, a transfusion of blood from an Rh-positive donor can save the life of the fetus.

The Respiratory System

The cyclic exchange of respiratory gases within an organism is known as **respiration.** Most vertebrates use lungs for gas exchange, although animals such as frogs use both a lung and moist skin to exchange gases.

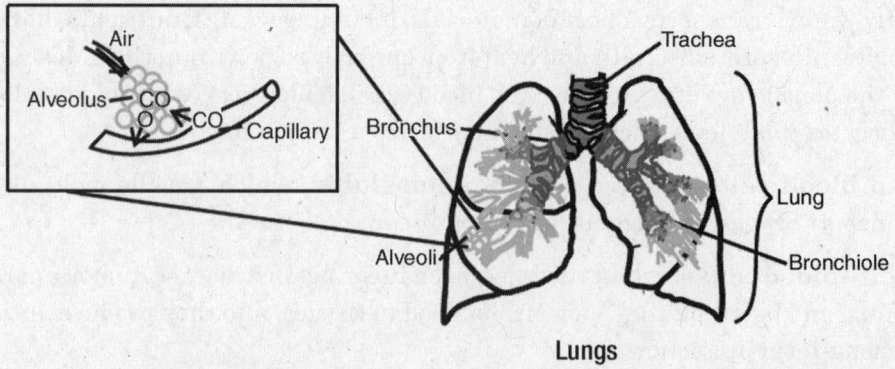

Lungs

Mammals have the most complex respiratory systems of all animals, with successively smaller branching tubes that open into vascularized sacs. Oxygen enters the lungs through the **bronchi**—two large tubes that branch off the trachea—which phase into smaller **bronchioles,** which then terminate in **alveolar sacs.** These sacs are covered with capillaries to facilitate gas exchange across the thin walls of the **alveoli.**

The Digestive System

Cells need a constant supply of nutrients for energy and as building blocks to assemble macromolecules. The **digestive system** allocates and processes these nutrients. The human digestive system, in all its complex functions, is nothing more than a long muscular tube extending from the mouth to the anus. Along this pathway are several modified pouches and segments to perform specific tasks, including nutrient intake, mechanical and chemical processes of digestion, nutrient uptake, and the elimination of undigested material.

When food reaches the stomach, both mechanical and chemical functions go to work on it. The muscles in the walls of the stomach churn, mixing the food with gastric juice and **pepsin,** which digests proteins. The majority of chemical digestion and nutrient absorption occurs in the **small intestine.** To assist with this process, the **pancreas** delivers several **enzymes:** *trypsin,* which breaks large polypeptides into amino acids; *amylase,* which changes polysaccharides to simpler forms; and *lipase,* which breaks fat down into glycerol and fatty acids. The **liver** assists by producing **bile,** which physically emulsifies fats to improve digestion. Virtually all nutrient absorption occurs in the small intestine, where the nutrients pass through the walls into the blood vessels. The blood then moves into capillaries, and the nutrient-laden blood is taken to the liver and then to the body tissue.

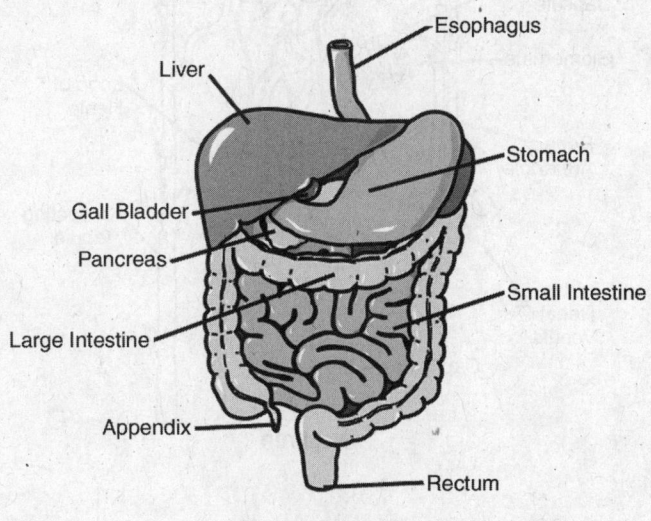

Digestive System

Not all food is digested, of course. Some moves into the **large intestine** to be processed. Any water and available minerals from the food are absorbed into the blood vessels of the walls of the large intestine and are returned to circulation. Bacterial action produces vitamin K, which is also absorbed into blood vessels and returned to circulation. The remainder of bacteria and undigested food form the main component of feces, which are passed as waste from the body.

The Renal System

Cellular metabolism of every organism produces fluid waste products, such as urea and nitrogenous wastes, which need to be separated from useful products, such as water, and then disposed of. Simple organisms perform this task by diffusing waste directly into their surrounding environment. More complex organisms, on the other hand, use a tube system, or **renal system,** to excrete fluid wastes.

Vertebrates have one of the most complex renal systems of all organisms. It centers around the **kidney,** which is responsible for several functions:

- Blood filtration (the kidneys separate the filtrate from cellular components within blood)
- Monitoring of waste concentrations in blood
- Reabsorption from filtrate
- Return of reusable components back to blood
- Secretion for eventual removal of filtrate

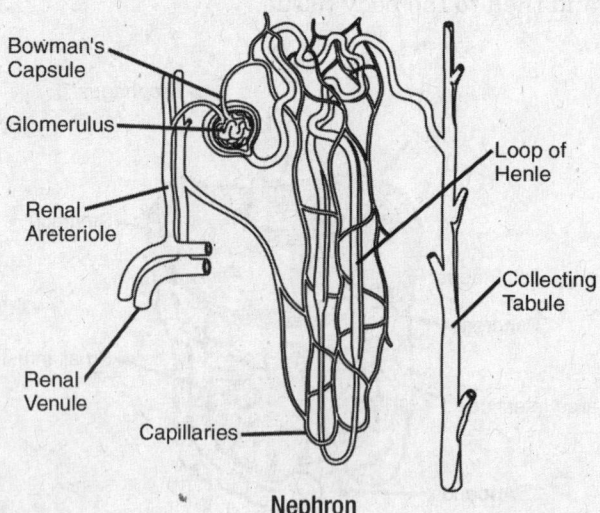

Nephron

Each kidney is composed of more than 2 million specialized units called **nephrons,** which play a large role in maintaining homeostasis by retaining useful substances and getting rid of waste products. Any useable molecules, including water, are reabsorbed and returned to circulation. Whatever is still left after this reabsorption process is waste, which is moved through the ureter to the bladder, where it waits to be passed from the body.

The Reproductive System

The primary goal of the reproductive system is the continuation of a species. There are many forms of reproduction, yet the degree of an organism's complexity is a good indicator of how it reproduces. **Asexual reproduction** does not require any of the complex structures used by eukaryotic cells. **Binary fission** is a type of asexual reproduction that is used by prokaryotic cells like bacteria. These cells merely replicate a simple loop of DNA and then undergo cytokinesis. **Fragmentation,** as seen in phylum *Porifera* (sponges), is another asexual form of reproduction. In this form, a piece of the body breaks away and matures into a larger form.

Vertebrates reproduce sexually by producing **gametes** (eggs and sperm) through their reproductive organs, called **gonads.** Females produce ova, or eggs, within their main reproductive structures, the ovaries. A hormone released by the pituitary gland stimulates egg production. An embryo develops from the initial **zygote,** a fertilized egg. If fertilization does not occur, the egg and its newly created uterine lining are sloughed off the walls of the uterus and moved out of the body. Males manufacture sperm within their major reproductive organ, the **testes.** The hormone **testosterone** signals and maintains sperm production. As with the female reproductive system, a pituitary hormone stimulates the production of sperm cells.

19. Which of the following is responsible for oxygen transport throughout the body?

    (1) nephrons in the kidneys

    (2) capillaries and veins

    (3) alveolar sacs in the lungs

    (4) enzymes produced by the pancreas

    (5) hemoglobin in red blood cells

Red blood cells consist mainly of hemoglobin molecules, which are responsible for transporting oxygen throughout the body through the bloodstream. Choice (2) is incorrect because veins return oxygen-depleted blood back to the lungs. **The correct answer is (5).**

20. Where does most nutrient absorption occur in the body?

    (1) the small intestine

    (2) the stomach

    (3) the liver

    (4) the large intestine

    (5) the lungs

It is through the lining in the long, serpentine small intestine that the nutrients from the food we eat are absorbed into the bloodstream and transported to cells throughout the body. **The correct answer is (1).**

Evolution, Natural Selection, and Speciation

Evolution is the process by which species of plants and animals arise from earlier life forms and undergo change over time. Our understanding of evolution is rooted largely in the theories of twentieth-century scientist Charles Darwin. Based on his observations of different traits among certain animal species, Darwin theorized that species evolve as a result of **natural selection**—a process by which the strongest, or "fittest," among offspring survive to reproduce, passing the particular traits that helped them survive on the next generation. Over many, many generations, genetic traits that help a species adapt to its environment become increasingly common among individuals, while less useful traits wither.

Darwin's theories of evolution and natural selection have since been refined to accommodate the theories of punctuated equilibrium, sexual selection, and genetic drift.

- **Punctuated equilibrium:** Darwin proposed that species evolution is a gradual, nearly constant process. Recent investigations involving fossil evidence suggest, however, that evolution occurs in spurts (*punctuations*), between which are long time periods of stability (*equilibrium*) when no change in the species occurs. Environmental events such as sudden and dramatic climate changes, which we know have occurred many times both globally and regionally throughout our planet's history, lend support to this idea: it is when a species confronts a sudden environmental change that it is forced to adapt to that change by evolving.

- **Sexual selection:** This type of selection occurs when individuals in a population compete not for resources and survival but rather for mates. For example, males with characteristics such as aggressiveness, great size, or strength or colorful feathers might be more successful in attracting mates, and thus their genetic traits will ultimately survive over many generations.

- **Genetic drift:** Studying isolated and relatively small populations, researchers have shown that certain genetic traits sometimes survive or wither over time by random chance. Like rolling genetic dice and getting the same trait many times in a row, against the statistical odds, a species can evolve in an aimless, or drifting, manner that has nothing to do with survival of the fittest.

Given that populations continually evolve, at what point does a population evolve into a new species? The generally accepted definition of the biological species concept is a population of organisms that is reproductively isolated from all other populations. This definition is generally accepted for vertebrate species, although other legitimate alternative definitions exist that take into account the diversity of reproductive biology (sexual, asexual, budding, etc.), and natural histories and life cycles.

Speciation occurs in three stages:

❶ A population becomes isolated. Speciation begins when a group of individuals separates into an isolated population that no longer exchanges individuals with the parent population. Physical or geographical barriers to migration can occur from changes in the environment, such as a new stream resulting from a storm, creating allopatric (living separately) species. Isolation can also be due to a change in a trait, such as behavior or coloration that prevents individuals from interbreeding with dissimilar individuals in the population, even if they are living together in the same geographical area.

 http://bit.ly/hippo_bio41

❷ The isolated population evolves independently. Once isolated, individuals will naturally accumulate random mutations, but they will also be subjected to a different set of selective pressures and/or evolutionary processes from that of the original population, and thus evolve differently from the parent population.

 http://bit.ly/hippo_bio42

❸ Reproductive isolating mechanisms evolve. Eventually the separated populations will evolve to a point where they can no longer interbreed because of reproductive isolating mechanisms. These are grouped into two categories: *Pre-zygotic mechanisms* prevent reproduction, and include physical mechanisms that prevent successful copulation or fertilization; behavioral mechanisms that prevent successful solicitation of a mate; or temporal mechanisms in which mating seasons or fertility patterns are no longer synchronized. *Post-zygotic mechanisms* result in offspring with gene combinations that are fatal, cause sterility, or otherwise prevent reproduction.

 http://bit.ly/hippo_bio43

21. Which of the following is LEAST likely to contribute to the development of a new species?

   (1) volcanic activity that reforms a region's landscape

   (2) a shift in a population's sexual selection criteria

   (3) an adaptive response to the appearance of a new predator

   (4) genetic drift within an isolated population

   (5) a local climate change that alters a population's breeding season

Choice (3) simply describes natural selection, whereby the traits of a species' fittest and most adaptable individuals are the ones that are passed on to subsequent generations. In itself, natural selection does not cause speciation. **The correct answer is (3).**

Ecology

 http://bit.ly/hippo_bio44

Ecology is the scientific study of the interactions among organisms and between communities of organisms and the environment. All of these interactions determine where organisms are found, in what numbers they are found, and why they are found where they are. In this section, we will briefly explore the main concepts in this field of study.

The Biosphere

The term **biosphere** refers to the entire part of the Earth that supports life. The biosphere consists of the surface of the Earth, of course, but it also encompasses the lithosphere (the rocky crust of the Earth), atmosphere (the air we breath, which consists mainly of nitrogen and oxygen), and the hydrosphere (all of the water on Earth). This section examines the part of the biosphere appearing on the Earth's surface. The lithosphere, atmosphere, and hydrosphere are examined in the Earth Science review.

Environments, Ecosystems, and Biomes

 http://bit.ly/hippo_bio45

Ecologists define an **environment** as any external factor that can influence an organism during its lifetime. These environmental influences can be divided into two categories:

- *Biotic factors:* living things that affect an organism

- *Abiotic factors:* nonliving things, such as water, air, geology, and the Sun, that can affect an organism

Biotic and abiotic factors are interrelated. For example, plants rely on many abiotic factors, including rainfall and temperature, for proper growth. If either should change dramatically in a particular region, plant growth will decline, which in turn will reduce food sources and habitats for animals.

The term **ecosystem** refers to an entire community of organisms, their physical environment, and how the interactions among that community and between the community and that environment. Similar ecosystems are often grouped together to form larger ecosystems called **biomes.** While more extensive in size and complexity than an ecosystem, a biome is still a biotic community subjected to abiotic environmental factors. Different biomes support different organisms—both plant and animal—due to their differences in geography, climate, and resources. Following is a descriptive list of the world's major biomes, beginning with the coldest in the north and progressing south toward the equator. (Although aquatic biomes are not listed here, understand that biomes include swamps and marshes, lakes and rivers, estuaries, the inter-tidal zone, and the ocean.)

http://bit.ly/hippo_bio46
http://bit.ly/hippo_bio47
http://bit.ly/hippo_bio48

TUNDRA

Region: Northernmost biome, to the north of coniferous forest

Climate: Bitter cold with thin soil covering a permanent layer of frost

Vegetation: Consists of lichens, mosses, grasses, and small shrubs

Animals: Vary according to the season: lemmings, arctic fox, arctic hare, lynx, grizzly bear, caribou, reindeer, musk ox

 http://bit.ly/hippo_bio49

CONIFEROUS FOREST

Region: Northern portions of North America, Europe, and Asia

Climate: Cold, but not so cold as the tundra; the winters are long

Vegetation: Consists of coniferous trees (pine, fir, spruce) and small amounts of deciduous trees

Animals: Large and small herbivores such as moose, elk, mice, and hares and some predators like the lynx, foxes, bears, and wolverines

TEMPERATE FOREST

Region: West and central Europe, eastern Asia, and eastern North America

Climate: Seasonal, temperatures are below freezing in the winter and summers are warm and humid

Vegetation: Deciduous (leaf-shedding) and coniferous trees, ferns, lichens, moss

Animals: Great variety of mammals, such as squirrels, porcupines, raccoons, black bears, coyotes

TROPICAL RAIN FOREST

Region: Central America, northern South America, some parts of Africa and Asia

Climate: No seasonal variation, high temperatures averaging 82°F, acidic soil, heavy and frequent rainfall

Vegetation: Dense canopy created by tall trees, many symbiotic plant/tree relationships

Animals: Extreme diversity in animals, many exotic types of insects, large numbers of birds, amphibians, and reptiles; a few large predators such as tigers

The world's atmospheric oxygen comes mainly from its rain forests, even though this biome accounts for less than 7 percent of the planet's land mass. Rain forest trees and other plants continually recycle carbon dioxide into oxygen, thereby providing the air we breathe and regulating the Earth's climate. About half of the world's plant and animal species reside only in rain forests. About half of this biome has been stripped of its trees for their timber and for grazing. It is estimated that as many as 130 different plant and animal species grow extinct every day as a result. Moreover, with fewer trees to absorb carbon dioxide, these molecules are accumulating in the atmosphere and reflecting more and more of the Sun's heat back to the Earth, thereby contributing to global warming.

GRASSLAND

Region: Central Russia, Siberia, southern India, northern Australia, some portions of Africa and South America

Climate: Seasonal, hot and dry in summers, heavy rainfall in wet season; frequent brush fires, thick, rich soils

Vegetation: Variety of grass species and bushes, few woodlands

Animals: Mainly large grazing species such as bison, rhinos, zebras, giraffes; predators include wolves, hyenas, lions, leopards; some burrowing animals such as prairie dogs

http://bit.ly/hippo_bio53

DESERT

Region: Northern and southwestern Africa, southwestern United States, northern Mexico, Australia, and parts of Asia and Middle East

Climate: Hot, dry climate by day and cold nights, very little rainfall, thin soil

Vegetation: Drought-adapted plants such as cacti, shrubs, and bushes with shallow roots or long tap roots

Animals: Mainly reptiles and some rodents, owls, vultures, hawks, and many insects

Once suitable for agriculture, a significant portion of the Earth's grassland biome is currently in the process of **desertification**—in other words, it is becoming part of the planet's desert biome. The current desertification trend is due partly to overgrazing and partly to global warming exacerbated by deforestation.

22. Which of the following does NOT help to explain the differences between the Earth's biomes?

   (1) precipitation levels

   (2) human activity

   (3) soil type

   (4) latitude

   (5) proximity to oceans

Human activity such as overgrazing and deforestation can slowly transform a region from one biome type to another. However, these activities do not distinguish the various biomes from one another. **The correct answer is (2).**

Food Chains and Food Webs

http://bit.ly/hippo_bio54

Biotic communities within an ecosystem are structured according to each organism's main source of food. **Producers** are *autotrophic*—they manufacture their own food from inorganic substances. Autotrophs include green plants and photosynthetic bacteria, both of which use solar energy to convert nutrients into glucose. (Autotrophs include other types of bacteria as well.) **Consumers** are *heterotrophic,* which means that they rely on other organisms as their food source. There are three sub-types of consumers:

- **Primary consumers** (herbivores), which feed directly on producers
- **Secondary consumers** (carnivores), which feed only on primary consumers
- **Tertiary consumers** (carnivores), which feed on secondary consumers

Decomposers are heterotrophic but feed on waste or dead material: dead plants of all kinds, fecal waste, and dead animals; they recycle raw materials to the ecosystem. A simple feeding pathway among organisms in an ecosystem can be shown in a **food chain.** Here is an example of a simple food chain:

Humans (secondary consumer) → fish (primary consumer) → plankton (producer)

Food chains represent a transfer of energy from one organism to another. All organisms need a source of food to survive, so all organisms participate in food chains. Energy (food) moves through a series of levels—from producer to herbivore to carnivore. These levels are called **trophic levels** (the word *trophic* means "feeding"). The following diagram shows the hierarchy of the feeding levels:

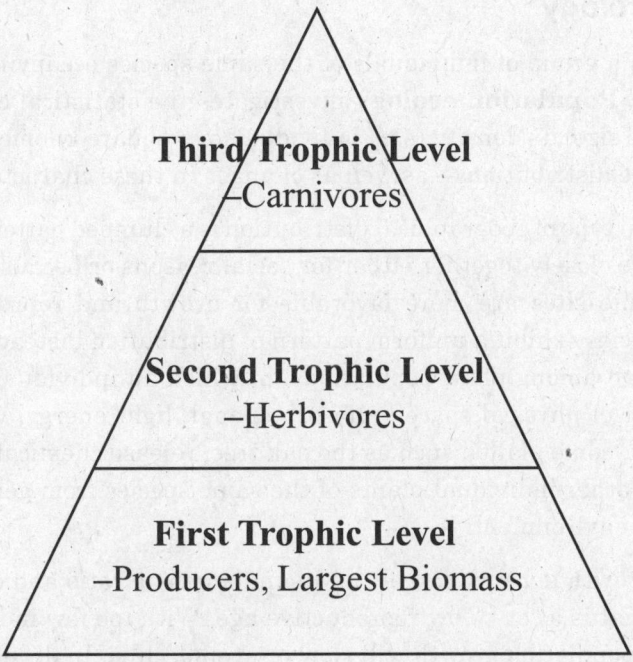

Third Trophic Level
–Carnivores

Second Trophic Level
–Herbivores

First Trophic Level
–Producers, Largest Biomass

Producers account for the main portion of the **biomass**—the total amount of food available for consumption in the ecosystem. On average, producers pass only about 1 percent of their biomass to primary consumers, which in turn pass about 10 percent of their biomass to secondary consumers. At each higher level, again, about 10 percent of biomass is passed up to the next trophic level. The great majority of biomass is not consumed but rather is converted to energy used for growth and survival.

Of course, humans don't only eat fish, herbivore populations don't only eat one kind of plant, and carnivore populations don't consume only one type of herbivore. Thus the simple food chain is an oversimplification for most ecosystems. A more complete model is a **food web,** which links many food chains together into a matrix that represents complex feeding relationships.

Habitats and Niches

http://bit.ly/hippo_bio55

Feeding relationships dominate the structure of an ecosystem. However, an ecosystem isn't just one giant free-for-all characterized by severe interspecies competition for food. Each population of animals occupies a particular **habitat**—a particular locale such as a forest community or an arid, grassy plain in which a species is best suited to live according to its biological adaptations. Different species can even become "specialists" within their habitats by occupying a **niche.** A niche refers to all specific biotic and abiotic elements an organism incorporates for its survival, such as feeding location, food source, feeding schedule, source of shelter, and nesting location. For example, many birds may occupy a forest habitat, but some eat seeds and others eat worms and insects; some birds eat high up in a tree and others closer to the ground. In other words, various types of birds in the same habitat occupy different niches.

Population Ecology

A **population** is a group of individuals of the same species occupying the same geographical region. **Population ecology** investigates the statistical characteristics of a population—its size, its density (e.g., individuals per square kilometer), and its geographical and age distributions—as well as changes in these characteristics.

The most common type of geographical distribution is a clumped pattern, where groups of individuals live closely together either for social reasons or because environmental conditions at some sites are more favorable for growth and reproduction than at others. Some species exhibit a uniform pattern of distribution instead. This pattern is especially common among plant populations, in which an individual typically needs a certain amount of physical space to absorb enough light energy, water, and other nutrients. In fact, some plants, such as the oak tree, release chemicals into the soil in order to prevent other individual plants of the same species from germinating in the same immediate environment.

A population's growth depends largely on its male-female ratio and on the portion of the population that is at or below reproductive age. With too few individuals capable of reproduction, population growth will slow or even decline. In developing countries, human populations are more evenly distributed among all age groups than in developed countries, where a greater portion of the population is older than reproductive age. This distinction is shown on the following two **population diagrams:**

POPULATION AGE STRUCTURE – SPECIES X

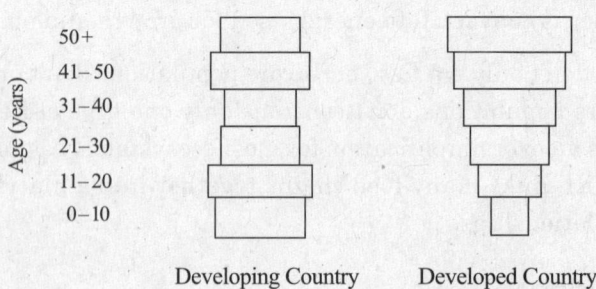

The maximum growth rate of a population under ideal environmental conditions is referred to as its **biotic potential,** expressed as a rate of population increase per individual. (For example, if an overall insect population can triple in one 24-hour period, then its biotic potential is 3 per individual per day.) Due to factors such as disease, limited food resources, and predation, populations rarely meet their biotic potential;

yet this rate is useful as a baseline with which to compare actual reproductive rates and monitor changes. Every species has a maximum biotic potential; bacteria have the highest rate of all living organisms.

Just as the growth rate of any population is limited, so is its size. A given environment has only so many resources to support a population. The maximum population of a particular organism that a given environment can support is referred to as **carrying capacity.** The most significant limiting factors in carrying capacity are food resources and physical space. A population may exceed its carrying capacity temporarily if the birth rate is extremely great, though eventually the population will decline to reflect the scarcity of food resources and/or space.

23. Which of the following best helps to explain why feeding structures in most biotic communities are better described as food "webs" rather than food "chains"?

  (1) Many different types of plants can exist in the same community.

  (2) Without a sufficient food source, animals will move to another community.

  (3) Some types of plants are not consumed by any other organisms.

  (4) If animal life disappears, then so does plant life.

  (5) Many animals consume plants as well as other types of animals.

The simple model of linear food "chain" does not account for the fact that the same animal might be a primary consumer (plant-eater) in one chain *and* a secondary consumer (meat-eater) in other chain. A "web" in which various chains are interconnected better represents a community's complete feeding structure. **The correct answer is (5).**

24. A colony of termites feeds off the wood frame of an old house for several years, but then it disappears. Assuming that the termites were not exterminated by humans, what most likely happened?

  Eventually, the termite population

  (1) exceeded its biotic potential

  (2) was consumed by secondary consumers

  (3) exhausted all of its available biomass

  (4) exceeded its carrying capacity

  (5) encountered competition for the same food source

The termites' environment (the house's wood frame) contained a limited amount of food resources to support the growing termite population. Once this *carrying capacity* was exceeded, in all likelihood the termites died off. **The correct answer is (4).**

EARTH AND SPACE SCIENCE

The study of our planet and outer space encompasses several fields of science. Geology deals with the composition of the Earth and past and present events (both interior and exterior) that have shaped it. Oceanography involves physics, biology, chemistry, and geology as they pertain to ocean-related processes. Meteorology is the study of the Earth's atmosphere, weather, and climate. Astronomy is the study of the universe and the objects in it, including stars, planets, nebula (dust particles), and so forth.

 http://bit.ly/hippo_env1

The Earth's Formation, History, and Composition

Among physicists, the prevailing theory today about the formation of the Earth is that our solar system was born out of a rotating cloud of dust gas, a *nebula*, that flattened into a disk, rotated clockwise, and then contracted under the influence of gravity. This theory would explain how the planets' orbits came to lie in nearly the same plane as they move around the Sun. Scientists think it took more than 1 billion years for gravity to cause the Earth's building blocks to settle and contract. Once this occurred, a sorting process called **differentiation** took place in which materials making up the forming proto-planets were sorted by densities. Materials with heavier densities sank to become the core material, and the lighter materials rose to the surface. The outer surface cooled and became the crust.

Earth's History

Based on radiometric evidence, the Earth is estimated to be 4.5 billion years old. Earth's history has been divided into eras. You may be familiar with some of these eras. Here are the four major geologic eras of Earth's history:

Precambrian: Approximately 4 billion years ago; no life on land; life flourished in the ocean, first with bacteria, then sponges, corals, jellyfish, and worms

Paleozoic: From 545 to 245 million years ago; defined by the advent, evolution, and extinction of many life forms; life began moving from water to land as land emerged and formed; the first plants and amphibians emerged

Mesozoic: From 245 to 66 million years ago (180 million years in duration); spans the Triassic, Jurassic, and Cretaceous periods; each period has unique characteristics, but one unifying element is the presence of dinosaurs, which first appeared in the Triassic period but experienced mass extinction by the end of the Cretaceous period

Cenozoic: From 66 million years ago to the present; characterized by extensive evolution and natural selection; many distinct species began to form; hominids (a branch of animals that includes modern humans) first began to develop

Radiocarbon Dating

Much of what we know about past life forms and eras has been gathered from fossil evidence. **Fossils** represent the remains of living things preserved in layers of ancient rock, or *strata*. Fossils can be petrified when deposited minerals replace the original organism; petrified wood is one example. Other fossils are created when impressions form through compression, leaving a carbonaceous film of an organism. Sometimes an entire plant or organism is preserved, such as when a piece of amber (petrified tree sap) traps an insect.

Fossils provide proof that different life forms have existed at different times throughout Earth's history. Geologists can use the mineral and biological samples in various strata to determine the age of rock layers through a method referred to as **absolute dating** or **radiocarbon dating.** In general terms, this dating method involves the element carbon, which is found in all biological life. Carbon 12, the normal form of the element, contains 6 protons and 6 neutrons. However, the isotope carbon 14 contains 8 neutrons and hence is unstable. It decays radioactively into other elements at a certain rate. The time required for 50 percent of a pure sample of a radioactive isotope, such as carbon 14, to decay is referred to as the isotope's **half-life.** Through radiocarbon dating, the amount of a particular radioactive isotope in a sample can be measured and used to determine the age of the sample.

Composition of the Earth

The Earth consists of several layers. The Earth's **lithosphere,** or outer shell, is made of the crust and upper mantle. The **crust** is the outermost, thinnest layer, and shows the greatest degree of variation; the average thickness of the crust is 3 to 25 miles. It is composed of rocks enriched with silicon, potassium, and sodium. The oceanic crust is denser than the continental crust.

The **mantle** is a middle layer that extends halfway to the Earth's center at a depth of 1,800 miles. It is composed of silicate enriched with magnesium and iron and is slightly denser than the crust. Due to high temperatures and pressure, the rocks in the mantle tend to be fluid.

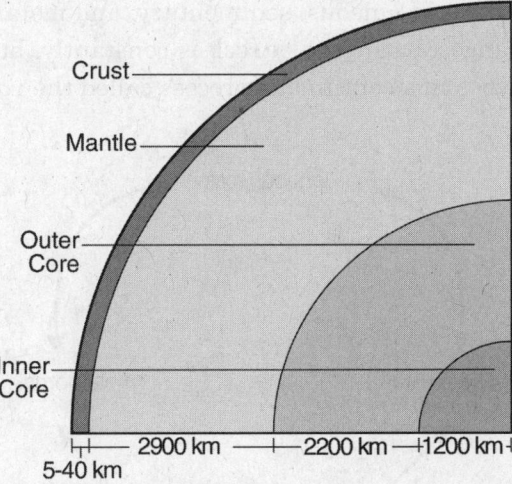

The **core,** which is the innermost layer, consists of an outer and an inner core. The **outer core** is mainly molten and consists of nickel, iron, and sulfur. It is 1,400 miles thick. The **inner core** is solid and is composed of iron and nickel. The core is much denser than either the mantle or the crust.

25. Which of the following is a possible objective of radiocarbon dating?

    (1) to determine the composition of layers deep beneath the Earth's surface

    (2) to compare the length of one geologic era to another

    (3) to determine the age of extinct species of animals

    (4) to identify and distinguish among radioactive metals

    (5) to determine the age of the Earth

Fossils are remains of living organisms and contain carbon that decays over time. By determining the extent of the decay through radiocarbon dating, it is possible to calculate how long ago the organism lived. **The correct answer is (3).**

26. Which of the following statements about the Earth's composition is true?

    (1) The outer crust is uniform in its thickness.

    (2) The Earth's core is a fiery, gaseous ball.

    (3) Deeper layers are colder because they receive less warmth from the Sun.

    (4) The core is made primarily of lead, which stabilizes the Earth as it rotates.

    (5) Deeper layers are denser than layers nearer the surface.

The Earth's core is denser than the mantle (the middle layer), which is denser than the crust. **The correct answer is (5).**

Rocks, Soil, and Changes to the Land

Rocks are composed of combinations of different minerals. As described next, there are three basic categories of rock: igneous, sedimentary, and metamorphic. As the Earth undergoes gradual changes, each type of rock is constantly, but slowly, transformed into one of the other types in a continuous process called the **rock cycle.**

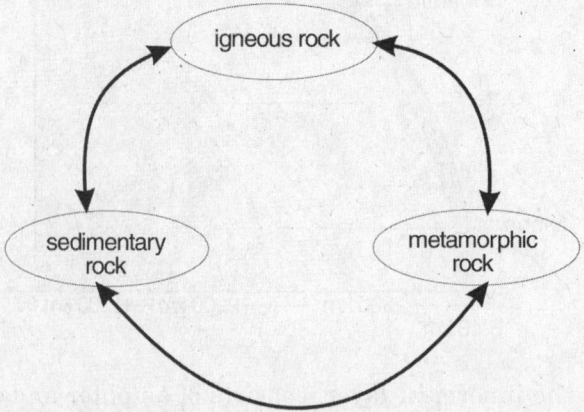

Igneous rock forms from the cooling and solidifying of molten rock, or magma, which becomes lava once it reaches the Earth's surface. *Intrusive* igneous rock, such as granite, forms from magma cooling slowly below the Earth's surface. This allows for a larger crystal size. *Extrusive* igneous rock forms when magma cools quickly on the Earth's surface, resulting in a finer texture. Volcanic rock in the form of basalt is an example of extrusive igneous rock.

Sedimentary rock appears as small rock fragments formed from the deposition of sediment due to erosion or weathering, or by chemical processes. These small fragments can be carried into bodies of water (by wind or rain), where they sink to the bottom and deposit in layers. Sedimentary rock can be classified further into the following three types:

- *Clastic* rocks are formed by bits of previously existing rock. The pieces can be small and sand-like or larger pebbles. Sandstone is one example of clastic rock.

- *Organic* rocks are formed from previously living life forms.

- *Chemical* rocks are formed from dissolved minerals left from evaporated water. Limestone and chalk are examples of chemical rocks.

Metamorphic rock, like the other types, forms from preexisting rock. The unique feature of metamorphic rock is that it is formed when rocks are subjected to high temperatures and pressure, which chemically change the original rock into something different. Metamorphic rock can be igneous, sedimentary, or metamorphic. Marble is one example of a metamorphic rock.

Weathering

Aiding in the rock cycle described above is the process of **weathering,** which encompasses a variety of mechanical and chemical events that slowly disintegrate and decompose rocks. **Mechanical events** such as the freezing and thawing of water within the cracks of rocks can cause the rocks to expand and crack. Rocks can be mechanically worn away by the movement of wind as well. Fine sand particles act as an abrasive and wear rock away over time. Water that flows continuously over rocks can also result in mechanical weathering. Rock particles scrape against each other in the flow of water in a lake or river, smoothing one another.

Rocks can also weather as a result of **chemical events** that act to dissolve rocks. One example of such an event involves **acid rain,** which occurs when human-made pollutants in the atmosphere combine with rainwater and become acidic. The acid compounds that are formed, including sulfuric acid, can be strong enough to weather rocks.

Soil

Soil is created from weathered rocks. There are two main types of soil. **Residual soil** is found on top of the rock from which it formed. **Transported soil** has moved from its rock of origin, so it may not resemble the underlying rock. Another type of soil, **humus,** is created from dead organisms such as animals—especially worms, insects,

 http://bit.ly/hippo_env2

 http://bit.ly/hippo_env3

http://bit.ly/hippo_env4

bacteria, and fungi—and decayed plant matter. This form of soil is very important for plant growth. So soil is actually a mixture of weathered rock and organic material, and hence varies depending on the type of rock from which it formed and the biota of the soil.

Forces of Erosion and Deposition

http://bit.ly/hippo_env5

Erosion is a major force that is responsible for the gradually changing landscape of the Earth. Erosion occurs when rocks and soil are moved from one place and are ultimately deposited in another place. Erosion can be caused by a variety of forces, including water, wind, gravity, and glaciers.

WATER

Running water produced as run-off by rain flows downhill, carrying particles with it as it moves. When the water moves onto land, it can erode the land and create gullies. Arid regions that do not have much vegetation to hold down the soil (by roots) or to absorb the water experience even more erosion. The gullies can become deep enough to form streams that cause further erosion by the abrasion of moving sediments against rocks. Rapidly moving water can carry a huge amount of sediment, and over time it can completely change a landscape. Hillsides that lack any vegetation show the most pronounced effects of water erosion. The Grand Canyon was formed over the course of many millennia in exactly this way.

The term **alluvium** refers to the silt, clay, sand, gravel, and other sedimentary material deposited by flowing water. Alluvium can be deposited in riverbeds or into bodies of standing water to form *deltas*. It can also be spread out across a plain in a fan-shaped way that's referred to as an **alluvial fan.**

WIND

Wind carries sediments many miles, and the abrasive effects of the sediments can create new sediments. The effect of wind erosion is more dramatic in some places than others.

GRAVITY

The force of gravity is a constant on Earth—and it plays a role in erosion. Just as we are pulled by gravity, so, too, are land masses. Gravity pulls on rocks and soil, sending them down slopes in an action called **mass wasting.** Rapid mass wasting occurs in the forms of landslides and mudslides. Landslides result when earthquakes loosen soil or when rain water pushes rocks down a slope. Mudslides occur after heavy rains or when volcanic eruptions cause snow to melt off the top of mountains.

GLACIERS

The size of glaciers makes it easy to understand how they can cause erosion. Glaciers are like huge ice slugs slowly moving across a landscape and pushing large rocks on a layer of ice and mud. This results in heavy glacial abrasion. Glaciers also leave large boulders or foreign particles from different regions behind as they melt and move. An example of glacial abrasion is Yosemite Valley in California.

27. Which would NOT be considered a cause of rock weathering?

    (1) pollutants in the air combined with rain

    (2) compression at high temperatures

    (3) the freezing of water in cracks between rocks

    (4) fine windblown sand particles

    (5) rapidly flowing water, as in a river

The force of compression does not aid in the disintegration of rocks. To the contrary, at high temperatures compression forms metamorphic rocks such as marble. All choices other than choice (2) are causes of rock weathering. **The correct answer is (2).**

28. How was the Grand Canyon formed?

    (1) by soil erosion

    (2) by the natural rock cycle

    (3) by glacial abrasion

    (4) by water erosion

    (5) by wind currents

The Grand Canyon was formed by the continuous downhill water flow that carried away rock sediments, resulting in gullies that grew deeper and deeper over time. **The correct answer is (4).**

Global Change—Plate Tectonics and Land Forms

 http://bit.ly/hippo_env6

Approximately 225 million years ago, all of the continents were joined together as one major continent called Pangea. This land mass eventually broke up into several smaller land masses that drifted apart until they became today's seven continents. On a map or globe, they look as though they could fit together, like pieces of a jigsaw puzzle. This and other evidence gave birth to the **continental drift theory.** Scientists are convinced that the continents are continuing to shift, driven by the interactions between tectonic plates. According to **plate tectonics theory,** the thin crust of the Earth (both the bottom of the oceans and the continents) is a bit like a bowl of soup with crackers floating on top. The soup is rock that flows under heat and pressure in the upper mantle, just beneath the crust. The crackers are the crust. The crust and upper mantle constantly shift against one another. There are about seven major plates and two dozen minor plates that make up the Earth's crust. This theory explains earthquakes, volcanic action, how mountain ranges are formed, and the locations of the continents.

As noted earlier, the Earth's lithosphere, or outer shell, is made of the crust and upper mantle. Within the upper mantle, differences in temperature cause currents to form. Magma heated by the core rises toward the crust, while magma close to the crust cools off and sinks. The result of this cycle is the formation of **convection currents,** which apply compression and tension on the lithosphere, pulling apart or compressing the plates. The consequences of this phenomenon can be dramatic and devastating where plates meet at **faults.** There are four basic types of movement that can occur between adjacent plates:

- Convection currents can move magma to the surface, **splitting** apart the surface and creating a gap that is filled with solidified molten material. Mid-ocean ridges were created in this manner.

- Plates can gradually slide past one another in a process called **shearing.** This movement can cause earthquakes. The San Andres Fault in California is a prime example of shearing.

- One plate (the more dense of the two) slides under the plate that is less dense in a process called **subduction.** As the plate that is sliding under is forced down through the crust, it melts, and periodically it will erupt to the surface. Mount Saint Helens, a volcano that erupted in 1980 in Washington State, was induced when one plate off the Pacific Coast slid under the continental plate.

- Two plates can **collide** with one another at faults. This may produce earthquakes, but its more gradual effect is the formation of mountains. The compression forces cause the plates to lift up and form mountains. The Himalaya Mountains in Central Asia provide the Earth's most conspicuous demonstration of plate collision.

Let's look closer at how the forces of plate tectonics transform the Earth's surface.

Mountains

Folded mountains develop by the slow compression of sedimentary and/or volcanic rock layers. This process results in mountains that are wavelike—they look like a carpet that has been pushed together. Examples of this type of mountain range include the Appalachians, Alps, and Northern Rockies. **Fault mountains** develop when tensile force is exerted along a crack in the crust. Over time, a mountain is formed, with one side bounded by a normal fault of a medium to high angle. The spreading of the crust segments by tensile force causes cracking, and the crust is lifted up. An example of this sort of mountain formation is the Sierra-Nevada range in California.

 http://bit.ly/hippo_env7

Volcanoes

Volcanoes are formed by igneous activity—the cooling and hardening of magma—below the lithosphere. When the hot magma beneath the lithosphere is under great pressure and high temperatures, it erupts to the surface and forms a volcano. When the magma reaches the surface of the lithosphere, it is called lava. Not all volcanic activity is the same. Some eruptions are violent, while others are calm. Most major volcanic eruptions, as well as major earthquakes, occur in three major zones of the world where most of the Earth's plates meet.

Earthquakes

Pressures built up within the Earth can also result in **earthquakes.** When the crust shifts and moves, vibrations of varying degree—earthquakes—are created. As noted earlier, tectonic plates move along boundaries, or faults. Plates can push together, pull apart, or slide along each other. These movements reduce the tension and compression forces created by convection currents within the upper mantle. The released tension is the earthquake.

The strength of earthquakes are measured and compared based on the amplitude of the waves they create, called **seismic waves.** These waves are divided into three types:

- **Primary waves** (P, or longitudinal, waves) are compressed waves that travel very fast, especially through denser materials of a solid, liquid, or gaseous nature. The damage they cause is moderate.

- **Secondary waves** (S, or transverse, waves) are side-to-side waves that travel at speeds slower than P waves. S waves only travel through solids and cause more damage than P waves. We know that the Earth's outer core is molten because these waves are lost in seismograph analysis.

- **Surface waves** (L, or Love and Rayleigh, waves) cause a shifting and shaking in the Earth's crust, both up and down and side to side. L waves are the slowest waves, but they cause the most extensive damage.

An earthquake or volcanic eruption occurring on the ocean floor can cause massive waves called **tsunamis.**

29. Plate tectonics theory explains all of the following phenomena EXCEPT which one?

(1) the direction of ocean currents

(2) earthquake activity

(3) volcanic eruptions

(4) the formation of mountain ranges

(5) the locations of the continents

Ocean currents have nothing to do with plate tectonics. On the other hand, the shifting of the plates that make up the Earth's crust are what causes the earth to quake, volcanoes to erupt, mountain ranges to form, and continents to move. **The correct answer is (1).**

30. Which force is at work both in earthquakes and volcanic eruptions?

(1) subduction

(2) gravity

(3) pressure

(4) cooling

(5) shearing

Convection currents are created when magma nearer the core heats up and rises while magma closer to the crust cools and sinks. These currents create compression (pressure), as well as tension (pulling) on the plates, resulting in earthquakes. When magma beneath the lithosphere becomes hot enough, sufficient pressure to cause a volcanic eruption can build up. **The correct answer is (3).**

Natural Resources

http://bit.ly/hippo_env8

A **natural resource** is anything we obtain from the natural environment to meet our energy needs. Renewable resources, such as air and water, are replenished in the environment through natural cycles. Many natural resources are finite or nonrenewable—when the supply is depleted, they are gone forever. Nonrenewable resources include copper, iron, oil, coal, and natural gas.

Renewable Energy

Renewable energy sources can be replenished in a short period of time. The five types of renewable sources used most often are biomass, solar, hydropower (water), wind, and geothermal.

http://bit.ly/hippo_env9

Biomass: Biomass is organic material that has stored sunlight in the form of chemical energy. It includes wood, straw, and manure.

Solar: Solar energy is the sun's solar radiation that reaches the Earth. It can be converted directly or indirectly into other forms of energy, such as heat and electricity.

Hydropower: Hydropower is created when moving water, such as a river or a waterfall, is directed, harnessed, or channeled. Water flows through a pipe and then turns the blades in a turbine to spin a generator that produces electricity.

Wind: Humans have used the wind as an energy source for thousands of years. For example, sails capture wind to propel boats, and windmills use wind to generate electricity.

Geothermal: When steam and hot water have been naturally trapped in the Earth's crust, engineers drill into the crust and allow the heat to escape, either as steam or very hot water. The steam then turns a turbine that generates electricity. This is known as geothermal energy.

Nonrenewable Energy

Nonrenewable energy sources are extracted from the earth as liquids, gases, and solids. Oil, coal, and natural gas are called **fossil fuels** because they are created from the carbon in the buried remains of plants and animals that lived millions of years ago.

 http://bit.ly/hippo_env10

Oil: Oil is formed from the remains of marine animals and plants that have been covered by layers of mud. Heat and pressure from these layers turn the remains into crude oil. After the oil is removed from the ground, it is sent to a refinery, where the different parts of the crude oil are separated into useable products ranging from motor gasoline and propane to ink, bubble gum, and dishwashing liquid.

Coal: Coal beds are found near the ground's surface. Power plants burn coal to make steam; the steam then turns turbines to generate electricity. Separated ingredients of coal (such as methanol and ethylene) are used to make plastics, tar, and fertilizers. Coal also plays an integral role in the steel-making process.

Natural Gas: Like oil and coal, natural gas is formed when plant and animal remains decay and are covered by mud and soil. Pressure and heat change this organic material to natural gas. The main ingredient in natural gas is methane. It is used to heat homes and is an essential material for products such as paints, fertilizer, and antifreeze.

Uranium ore is a solid metal that is mined and converted to a fuel. Uranium is not a fossil fuel. **Nuclear power** plants produce energy through the fission or splitting of uranium atoms, which creates heat. That heat boils water to make the steam that turns a turbine-generator. The part of the plant where the heat is produced is called the reactor core.

 http://bit.ly/hippo_env11

31. Which of the following is involved in the process of converting renewable as well as nonrenewable natural resources to energy?

   (1) steam

   (2) carbon

   (3) wind

   (4) the Sun

   (5) fossils

Geothermal energy is produced when steam (a renewable resource) is released from the Earth's crust; energy is produced from coal (a nonrenewable resource) by burning the coal to make steam; and energy is produced by nuclear fission when the heat from fission boils water to make steam. In all three processes, steam is used to drive turbines that generate electric power. **The correct answer is (1).**

Oceanography

Oceans cover just over 70 percent of the Earth's surface and account for about 97 percent of the planet's total water. Globally, the composition of ocean water includes a variety of ions, including chloride, sodium, sulfate, magnesium, calcium, potassium, and bicarbonate. The average salinity (salt concentration) of ocean water worldwide is 3.5 percent.

Oceans produce **currents** that have predictable patterns worldwide (see map below). These currents, which develop from global wind patterns and water-temperature differences, help control temperatures within the oceans as well as in the atmosphere.

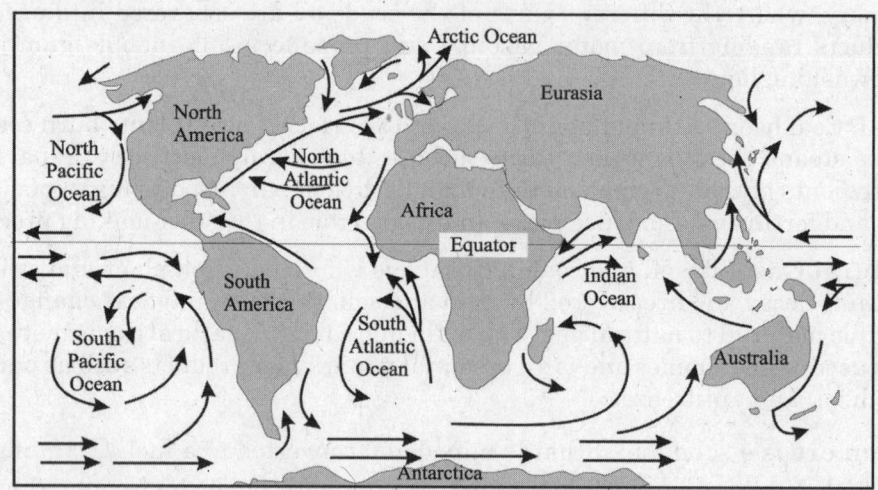

Continental margins are areas where the continents meet the oceans. Continental margins are made of continental shelves, which are submerged extensions of the continental crust beneath the oceans. The **continental shelf** projects outward from the coast to a depth of about 100 meters (325 feet). It is thought that the continental shelf may have been dry land at one time when oceans were smaller than their present sizes. The continental shelf gives way to the **continental slope,** which drops steeply to the ocean's bottom. The continental shelf then becomes the **abyssal plain** of the deep ocean floor. The abyssal plain is about 4,000–5,000 meters below sea level. This distance beneath the surface does not make it a hot spot for sea life. In fact, the abyssal plain is like a barren desert. Most sea life and vegetation are clustered closer to shallow shore waters where sunlight is more abundant.

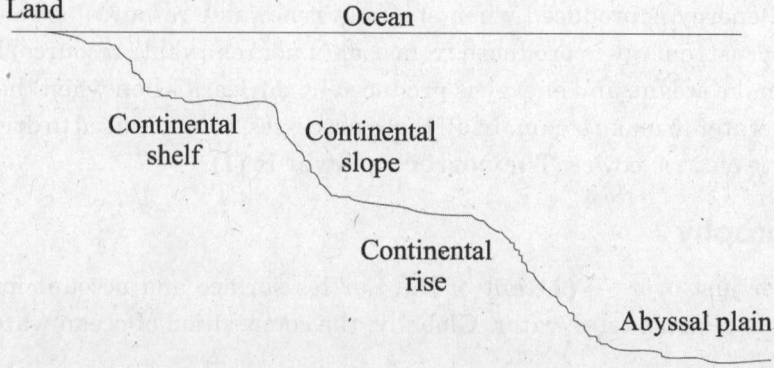

Notable topographical features of sea floor include the following:

- **Seamounts:** Submarine volcanic peaks, which above sea level form islands (Hawaii is an example of a seamount)

- **Mid-ocean ridges:** Long linear walls that can rise about 1.5 miles above the surrounding ocean floor and are formed by pronounced seismic and volcanic activity (when the ocean floor spreads apart and new ocean crust is created)

- **Trenches:** Narrow, curved depressions in the ocean floor that can reach depths of more than 7 miles

 http://bit.ly/hippo_env12

QUESTION 32 REFERS TO THE FOLLOWING MAP.

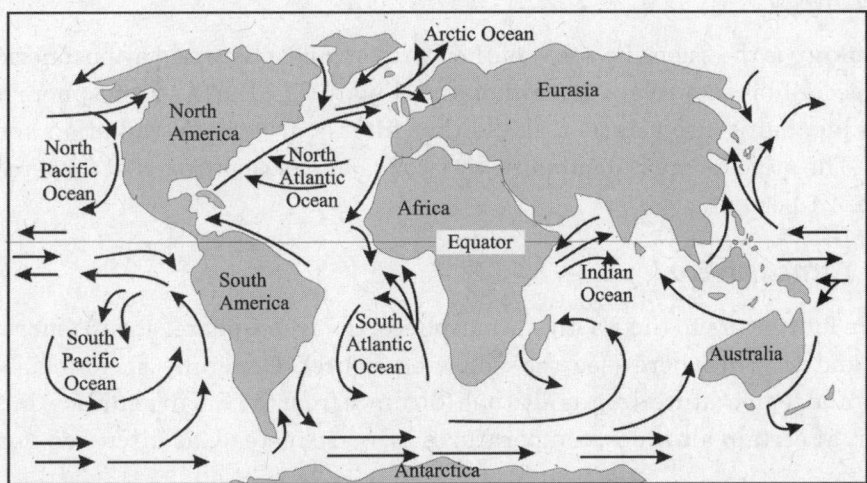

32. Which of the following makes the most sense as a reason for the ocean-current patterns shown on the above map?

(1) The magnetic poles attract the ocean water's hydrogen ions.

(2) Rainfall is heaviest near the Equator and lightest near the poles.

(3) Global winds generally blow from north to south.

(4) The narrow ocean straits between some continents act as water funnels.

(5) Cold water tends to sink, while warm water tends to rise.

Cold water is denser than warm water, and so water near the poles sinks while warmer water near the Equator rises. This simultaneous sinking and rising facilitates a circulation pattern that is then directed by prevailing winds, which vary from region to region. **The correct answer is (5).**

33. What is the main reason that sea life cannot thrive near the deep ocean floor?
(1) The water is too cold.
(2) There is not enough sunlight.
(3) The ocean current is too strong.
(4) The pressure of overhead water is too great.
(5) There is not enough food.

The ocean depths receive practically no sunlight. Green plants need sunlight to produce their own food through photosynthesis, and animal life in the sea rely on those plants for food. Thus, life cannot thrive near deep ocean floors. **The correct answer is (2).**

Meteorology

Meteorology is the scientific study of the Earth's atmosphere and atmospheric conditions, especially as they relate to weather and climate. The Earth's atmosphere not only sustains life, but it also acts as a shield that filters out harmful radiation and small meteors. The atmosphere is dominated by two major gases, nitrogen at 78 percent and oxygen at 21 percent.

 http://bit.ly/hippo_env13

Earth's Atmosphere

There are four layers to the Earth's atmosphere: the troposphere, stratosphere, mesosphere, and thermosphere (see the following figure). Generally speaking, both air pressure and temperature drop as altitude (distance from the Earth's surface) increases. However, at certain altitudes, temperatures increase instead, as discussed next.

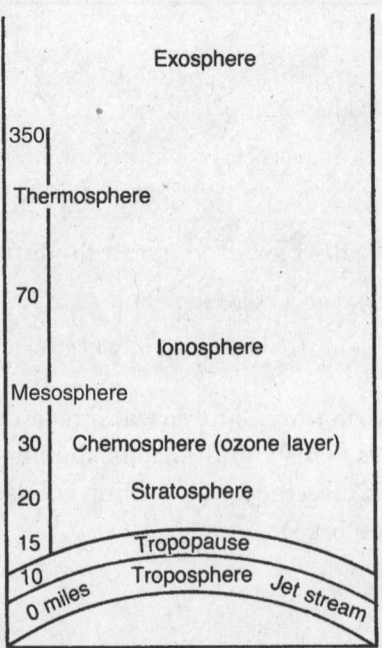

THE TROPOSPHERE

The **troposphere** is the lowest layer and accounts for about 80 percent of the Earth's atmosphere. From ground level, it extends to an altitude that varies from 4 to 10 kilometers. The troposphere is the main layer of atmospheric circulation. The lowest portion of the troposphere (the "jet stream" in the figure) is where most of Earth's weather occurs.

THE STRATOSPHERE

The **stratosphere** is above the troposphere. Though air temperature generally drops with altitude, in the stratosphere it remains constant and actually increases up to the mesosphere. The reason for the increase is that 90 percent of all atmospheric ozone, which traps warming carbon dioxide and other greenhouse gases (discussed in more detail under "Greenhouse Gases, Global Warming, and Ozone Depletion"), are contained in the upper part of the stratosphere.

THE MESOPHERE

The **mesosphere** lies above the stratosphere and is the layer where meteors first start to burn upon entering the atmosphere. The boundary between the mesosphere and stratosphere marks the outer limit of the high ozone concentration, and so it is at this boundary where temperature once again begins to drop as altitude increases.

THE IONOSPHERE (OR THERMOSPHERE)

Above the mesosphere, at about 62 miles, are the **ionosphere** and **thermosphere.** These two terms are often used interchangeably to describe the same layer. The air at this level is thin and highly reactive to incoming solar radiation. Within this layer, temperatures rise again as the air molecules absorb short-wave radiation produced by **solar wind.** Solar wind is a stream of ionized gases blown from the Sun at supersonic velocities. During periods of peak velocity, the temperature in the thermosphere can reach as high as 1225°C (2237°F), while during periods of low solar wind activity temperatures can fall to as low as 225°C (437°F). These temperature fluctuations are due to the thin nature of air at this altitude—there are few molecules present to absorb and distribute heat. (The term *therm*osphere alludes to this layer's high temperatures, while the term *ion*osphere alludes to its electrically charged nature.)

GREENHOUSE GASES, GLOBAL WARMING, AND OZONE DEPLETION

 http://bit.ly/hippo_env14

In addition to nitrogen and oxygen, Earth's atmosphere contains trace amounts of other gases as well. One of these trace gases is carbon dioxide (CO_2). What this gas lacks in abundance—only about 0.035 percent of the total atmosphere—it makes up for in impact. Carbon dioxide, along with water vapor and methane, make up what are known as **greenhouse gases,** which are also naturally occurring in Earth's atmosphere. As radiant light from the Sun enters our atmosphere, it is changed to heat energy or infrared waves. This infrared heat cannot pass out of the atmosphere because greenhouse gases trap it. The resulting global warmth, called the **greenhouse effect,** plays a vital role in maintaining Earth's hospitable climate and its fragile ecosystems. In fact, without these gases, the Earth would be quite a bit colder, rendering it an ice-cold planet unsuitable for many forms of life.

Since the early twentieth century, and especially in recent decades, polluting emissions from cars, factories, and homes have increased the amount of carbon dioxide in the atmosphere. Because carbon dioxide traps heat, many scientists believe that there is a direct cause-and-effect relationship between increased carbon dioxide and increased temperatures around the world. This phenomenon is called **global warming.** Current trends indicate that the atmospheric temperatures are on the rise. At the same time that humans have been producing more and more greenhouse gases through industrialization, they have been stripping the world's forests. Trees and other plants absorb CO_2 during photosynthesis, and then emit the oxygen we breathe as a waste product. But fewer forests means more carbon dioxide accumulation in the atmosphere, which contributes further to global warming.

Along with global warming is another human-induced atmospheric problem referred to as **ozone depletion.** The Earth's ozone layer acts as a natural filter in the stratosphere, protecting life on Earth from overexposure to the Sun's harmful ultraviolet radiation. However, the stratosphere's ozone layer has become compromised by human use of harmful chemicals, especially a group of chemicals called **chlorofluorocarbons (CFCs),** which are used in refrigerants, foam, solvents, and propellants. The overuse of CFCs has actually caused "holes" to appear in the ozone layer. The problem has recently reached an alarming level, and most of the world's developed nations have agreed by treaty to drastically limit their use and production of CFCs.

34. What accounts for increasing temperatures in the thermosphere?
  (1) friction from incoming meteors
  (2) variations in air pressure
  (3) exposure to short-wave solar radiation
  (4) the absence of air molecules at this atmospheric layer
  (5) a high concentration of ozone

As the atmosphere's outermost layer, the thermosphere absorbs the Sun's short-wave radiation (solar wind), which can increase temperatures dramatically there. **The correct answer is (3).**

35. Which is an accurate statement about greenhouse gases?
  (1) They protect us from the Sun's harmful radiation.
  (2) They are toxic to most humans and therefore pose a threat to our species.
  (3) They provide some of the air that humans breathe.
  (4) They keep the Earth warm enough to sustain life.
  (5) They are harmful to many plants that humans depend on for food.

http://bit.ly/hippo_env15

Greenhouse gases trap some of the Sun's radiation after it reflects off the Earth's surface, thereby helping to keep the Earth warm enough to sustain life as we know it. **The correct answer is (4).**

Weather and Climate

Although the Sun hits the Earth everywhere, solar energy is strongest at the equator, where light rays are received most directly, and weakest at the poles, where the Sun's light waves hit the surface at an angle, or slant. The air in the Earth's atmosphere circulates in an attempt to equalize temperatures. It is this circulation that initiates what we call **weather**—the many atmospheric conditions at any one place in a given time frame.

ATMOSPHERIC (AIR) PRESSURE

The Earth's atmosphere has a mass of 5 thousand million tons. Most of this lies in the troposphere, within 18 kilometers (11 miles) of the planet's surface. Gravity maintains this mass in an envelope surrounding the Earth. The mass of the atmosphere applies downward pressure, called **atmospheric pressure,** on the Earth.

The greater the air density, the greater the atmospheric pressure. Atmospheric pressure decreases with altitude for two reasons. First, at higher altitudes there are fewer air particles to exert downward pressure. Second, the higher the altitude, the shorter the column of air overhead. Temperature and humidity affect air pressure as well. Colder temperatures produce denser air and greater air pressure; moist (humid) air has a lower density and pressure than dry air.

AIR MASSES

Air masses are large bodies of air distinguished by their temperature and humidity. Air masses develop due to local conditions in their place of origin. For instance, if an air mass develops over the tropics, it is going to be warm. If an air mass develops over the poles, it will be cold.

When two air masses of different characteristics collide and mix, fluctuating weather conditions result. This meeting of two air masses is called a **front.** A **cold front** develops when cold, dry air pushes under warmer, moister air, forcing the warmer air up. A **warm front** develops when warm, moist air pushes over colder, dryer air. In either case, the warm air, being lighter than cold air, rises and cools, then condenses along the boundary, resulting in precipitation such as rain or snow. Thunderstorms are often associated with cold fronts. Other front types include a **stationary front** (when air masses move parallel to one another without mixing) and the **occluded front** (when a fast-moving cold front overtakes a warm front).

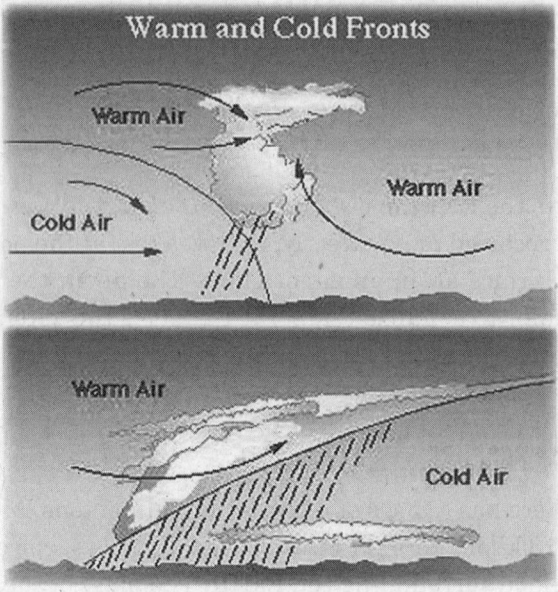

HUMIDITY

Humidity forms when the Sun's energy warms up a body of water, and then the water evaporates into the air as vapor. At any given temperature, the air can hold only a limited amount of moisture. If the saturation point is surpassed, water vapor condenses and returns back to the Earth as precipitation (rain or snow).

Relative humidity refers to the ratio between the amount of water vapor in the air and the maximum amount of water vapor the air can hold without condensing, at a given temperature. The ratio is expressed as a percentage. As relative humidity reaches 100 percent, precipitation is likely because the air cannot hold any additional water vapor. Warm air can hold more water vapor than cold air, which explains why humidity is usually associated with warm temperatures, especially near large bodies of water.

The temperature at which water vapor condenses and turns to liquid is called **dew point.** At dew point, large droplets of water may appear on surfaces as **dew,** while smaller droplets may remain suspended in the air as **fog.** As just suggested, humid air, which is usually warm, has a higher dew point than dry air. This explains why dew and fog tend to form when the air temperature is relatively cold.

http://bit.ly/hippo_env16

THE WATER CYCLE

The process that begins when the Sun's energy warms a body of water to the point of evaporation and ends when the vapor condenses and returns to the body of water is referred to as the **water cycle.** Water moves to the atmosphere by evaporation in the form of water vapor. If the air is warmer, it rises through the atmosphere, where it is cooled. Condensation occurs when this cooled air becomes saturated and the water vapor condenses into water droplets or ice particles, which then return to the Earth's surface as precipitation.

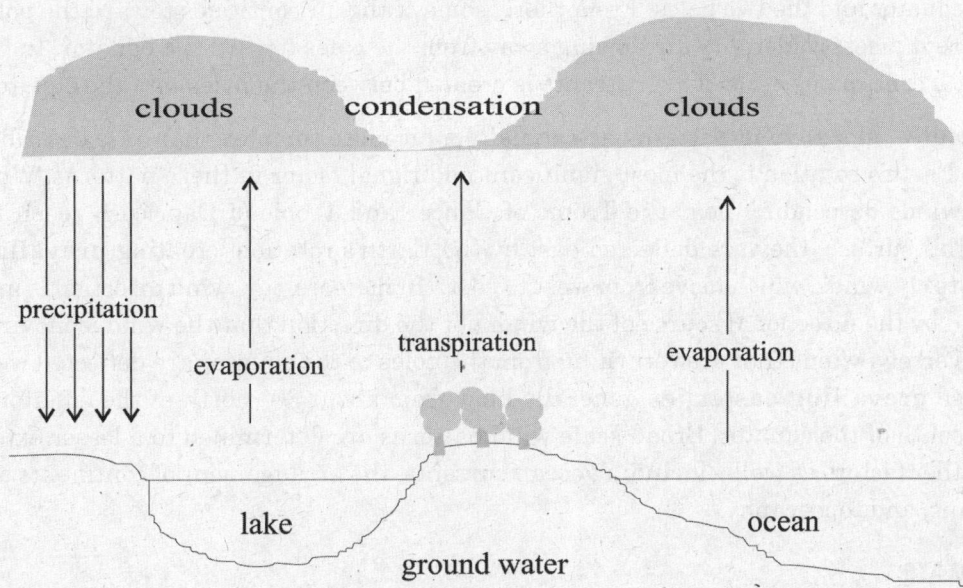

Alongside this component of the water cycle is a second component involving plants. Ground water is absorbed by plant roots, which make use of the nutrients contained in the water. Then, through the process of **transpiration,** the plant gives off vapor containing water as well as waste products. The water vapor rises, cools, and condenses, resulting in precipitation that returns the water to the ground, and the cycle repeats.

CLOUD FORMATION

Clouds form when warm air rises and then cools below the dew point, forming fine water droplets or ice particles suspended in the atmosphere. Clouds almost always form along weather fronts, where cold and warm air masses collide. **Cumulus clouds,** which appear puffy, are the type most often associated with the unstable weather conditions of weather fronts. By observing the movement of cumulus clouds, it is possible to assess the movement of fronts. (The word suffix –*nimbus* signifies a certain type of storm cloud. For instance, *cumulonimbus* clouds are cumulous clouds that are likely to produce violent thunderstorms.)

Of course, there are other types of clouds as well. The two most common types are **cirrus** and **stratus.** Cirrus clouds are wispy and are composed mainly of ice crystals. Stratus clouds are relatively flat and occur in moist, stable air; these clouds are composed of water droplets.

WIND

Wind is created when air moves from an area of high atmospheric pressure to one of lower atmospheric pressure. Large-scale wind patterns on Earth are mainly the result of uneven heating of the Earth's surface by the Sun. More solar radiation is received near the equator than at the poles. As the warm air at the equator rises, it creates a zone of low pressure that draws air up toward it. After the warm air rises, it moves toward the poles, cooling along the way until it is dense enough to descend, about midway between the equator and the two poles. From there, some of the air continues toward the poles, where it meets colder, dry air flowing away from the poles toward the equator. In this way, a continuous cycle of air currents is created between the poles and the equator.

Of course, global wind patterns are actually a bit more complex than just described. The Earth's rotation is the most significant additional factor in these patterns. When the winds descending near the Tropic of Cancer and Tropic of Capricorn reach the Earth's surface, they are deflected east by the Earth's rotation, creating **prevailing westerly** winds, which move from west to east. (In meteorology, wind direction is indicated by the directional source of the wind, not the direction that the wind is moving.) Conversely, winds that are returning from the poles to the equator are deflected west. These **prevailing easterlies** generally blow from about 30° north of the equator to 30° south of the equator. Broad-scale wind patterns are determined to a lesser extent by other factors as well—including ocean currents, the arrangement of continents and oceans, and topography.

CLIMATE

Climate refers to a region's general weather conditions, such as temperature, winds, and rainfall. A region's climate is affected mainly by **latitude** (distance from the equator). In general, regions located at or near the equator experience continuous warming and high rainfall and are virtually seasonless. Regions farther above and below the equator become more seasonal, with warm-to-hot summers and cool-to-cold winters. Near the poles, winters become increasingly longer.

Latitude is not the only determining factor in a region's climate. Broad-scale wind patterns play a significant role as well, as do temperature differences between land and sea. Warm ocean currents affect the climate of regions near the ocean. In general, coastal regions experience more moderate temperatures than inland regions. The warm water near these regions warms the air above the water, which in turn raises temperatures of the air above the nearby land.

A region's topography also plays a role in determining its climate. Elevation is especially significant. It is not uncommon to see snow-capped mountains in regions near the equator. The higher the elevation, the more likely a region is subjected to thin air, which does not hold heat well.

36. Warm, moist air is generally associated with which of the following?

(1) low air pressure

(2) easterly winds

(3) cirrus clouds

(4) high elevation

(5) a stationary front

Warm air is less dense than colder air, and moist air is less dense than dry air. Air density is related directly to air pressure: the higher the density, the heavier the air and the more downward pressure it exerts. **The correct answer is (1).**

---

37. Which of the following does NOT contribute to the Earth's broad-scale wind patterns?

(1) air temperatures

(2) the presence or absence of clouds

(3) the angles at which the Sun's rays strike the Earth's surface

(4) atmospheric pressure

(5) the Earth's rotation on its axis

The presence or absence of clouds, choice (2), is partly the result rather than the cause of wind patterns. Each of the other answer choices provides a contributing factor in the Earth's broad-scale wind patterns. **The correct answer is (2).**

Astronomy

Astronomy is the scientific study of the universe and of the size, composition, motion, and evolution of celestial bodies: stars, planets, galaxies, and nebula (fine gas and dust particles). **Astrophysics,** a branch of astronomy, deals with the physical and chemical processes that occur in the universe and in interstellar space, including the structure, evolution, and interactions of stars and systems of stars.

Our accumulated knowledge of our universe comes from direct observation with the naked eye and, more recently, from observations made with powerful telescopes and from other technologies used for detection and measurement. Based on knowledge gained by observation and measurement, along with principles of mathematics, astrophysicists develop theoretical models to explain star formation and interaction, the nature of matter throughout the universe, and the evolution of the universe. These theories are not "knowledge" in the true scientific sense, of course, since a theory can ultimately be proven or disproved by subsequent observations.

A Brief History of Astronomy

Through centuries of scientific investigation, humans have tried to understand how our universe came to be, whether there is order or structure to the universe and, if so, what universal laws and principles govern that order. The early Greeks observed that celestial objects, which they called *planets* (the Greek word for "wanderer"), appeared to move across the sky in relation to stars such as Polaris (North Star), which seemed to be fixed. They concluded that the Earth remained stationary while the heavens rotated around it. This **geocentric (Earth-centered) theory** went largely unchallenged until the sixteenth century, when Polish astronomer Nicolaus Copernicus theorized that all planets, including Earth, traveled in regular, circular paths, called *orbits,* around the Sun. This theory became known as the Copernican or **heliocentric (Sun-centered)**

theory. Later, German astronomer Johannes Kepler modified this theory by asserting that planets moved in oval-shaped elliptical orbits.

Then, in the early seventeenth century, Italian scientist Galileo Galilei made several significant discoveries with a telescope. He discovered four of Jupiter's moons and observed that they orbited around that planet, thereby demonstrating *empirically* (through observation rather than theory) for the first time that not all celestial bodies revolve around Earth. Galileo also observed the changing illuminations, or phases, of Venus—an observation that was consistent with the heliocentric theory. Galileo's work was denounced by the Catholic Church because his observations ran contrary to the Church's dogma that man was at the center of the universe. As we know, however, Galileo was correct, and his work provided the scientific foundation upon which modern astronomy has since developed.

Earth's Orbit, Rotation, and Tilt

Earth exhibits two kinds of movement: **rotation** and **revolution.** Rotation is the spinning action of Earth on its **axis,** an imaginary line extending from pole to pole through the Earth's center. The Earth rotates once every 24-hour period. This produces daily cycles of daylight and night. Day and night exist because only half the planet can face the Sun at any one time. **Revolution** is the movement of Earth around the Sun. It takes Earth about 365 days to complete one revolution around the Sun at a distance of 93 million miles. This orbit is in an oval, or *elliptical,* pattern. Planets closer to the Sun take less time to orbit the Sun than planets farther away. For example, Mercury's complete orbit takes only eighty-eight "Earth days," whereas Jupiter's complete orbit takes about twelve "Earth years." The Sun's gravitational pull keeps the planets within their orbital paths.

Term	Definition	Diagram
rotation	the spinning of a body on its axis, like a top	axis
revolution	the movement of a body around another body	Earth / Sun

The seasonal variations experienced between the equator and each of the two poles is mainly due to rotational **tilt** of the Earth. The Earth's axis is not perpendicular to the elliptical plane that defines its orbit around the Sun. The Earth's axis is inclined at a tilt of about 23° from perpendicular. This tilt causes some parts of Earth to receive more sunlight and other parts to receive less, accounting for the different seasons.

The Moon

Except for Mercury and Venus, all of the planets in our solar system have satellites, or **moons.** Earth's moon (referred to simply as "the Moon") is about 238,000 miles from Earth and orbits Earth once every twenty-eight days in a slightly elliptical orbit. The Moon's rate of rotation as it orbits Earth is such that from Earth we see only the same half of the Moon. The so-called "dark side" of the Moon always faces away from Earth.

The Moon does not emit its own light; rather, it reflects light from the Sun. As the Moon orbits the Earth, it appears to cycle through a series of **phases** as the Sun lights it at different angles in relation to the Earth's position. On nights when we do not see any of the sunlit portion of the Moon, the side of the Moon facing the planet is completely dark. This is called a **new Moon.** As the Moon continues its 28-day orbit of Earth, more and more of it becomes visible to us. When half of the Moon's circular face is visible, it is known as a **quarter Moon.** When the entire circular face of the Moon is visible, it is known as a **full Moon.** During the second half of each month, we see less and less of the Moon's face, until at the end of a 28-day cycle the sunlit portion of the Moon is entirely out of our view, and the cycle renews with the new Moon.

The gravity on the Moon is about one-sixth that of Earth. It is the gravitational attraction of the Moon and, to a lesser extent, the Sun that cause **tides** here on Earth. The highest high tides occur when the Moon and Sun are in the same direction from Earth, so that their gravitational pulls reinforce each other. The lowest high tides occur when the Moon and Sun are at right angles in relation to the Earth, so that their gravitational forces counteract each other.

Solar and Lunar Eclipses

The Sun and Moon appear to be approximately the same size in our sky. This is because the Sun happens to be about 400 times wider than the Moon *and* about 400 times farther than the Moon from Earth. When the Moon is positioned directly between the Sun and the Earth, the Moon blocks our view of the Sun. This infrequent alignment of the Sun, Moon, and Earth is referred to as a **solar eclipse.** During this type of eclipse, the Moon casts a shadow on the Earth. At the center of the shadow, where the Sun is entirely hidden from view, the shadow is darkest. (This area is referred to as the **umbra.**) Farther away from the shadow's center, where only part of the Sun is hidden from view, the shadow is lighter. (This area is referred to as the **penumbra.**) A solar eclipse is the only event during which stars are clearly visible in the daytime sky. Since the Moon and the Earth both travel in elliptical orbits, the Moon is closer to the Earth during some solar eclipses than during others. The duration of a solar eclipse is longer when the Moon is closer to the Earth. The maximum duration of a total solar eclipse is between 7 and 8 minutes. A **lunar eclipse** occurs when the Earth is positioned directly between the Sun and the Moon so that the Earth's shadow is cast upon the Moon.

The Solar System

Our **solar system** includes all celestial bodies that orbit around the Sun. The planets in our solar system can be divided into two categories based on physical characteristics. The **terrestrial planets** include Mercury, Venus, Earth, and Mars. They are composed of the same basic rock materials—hence the name "terrestrial." The **Jovian** (Jupiter-like) planets are Jupiter, Saturn, Uranus, and Neptune. They are made mostly of gases such as hydrogen, helium, and methane. Due to its position on the edge of our universe, its small size, and what scientists now know about its composition, Pluto is no longer considered a planet.

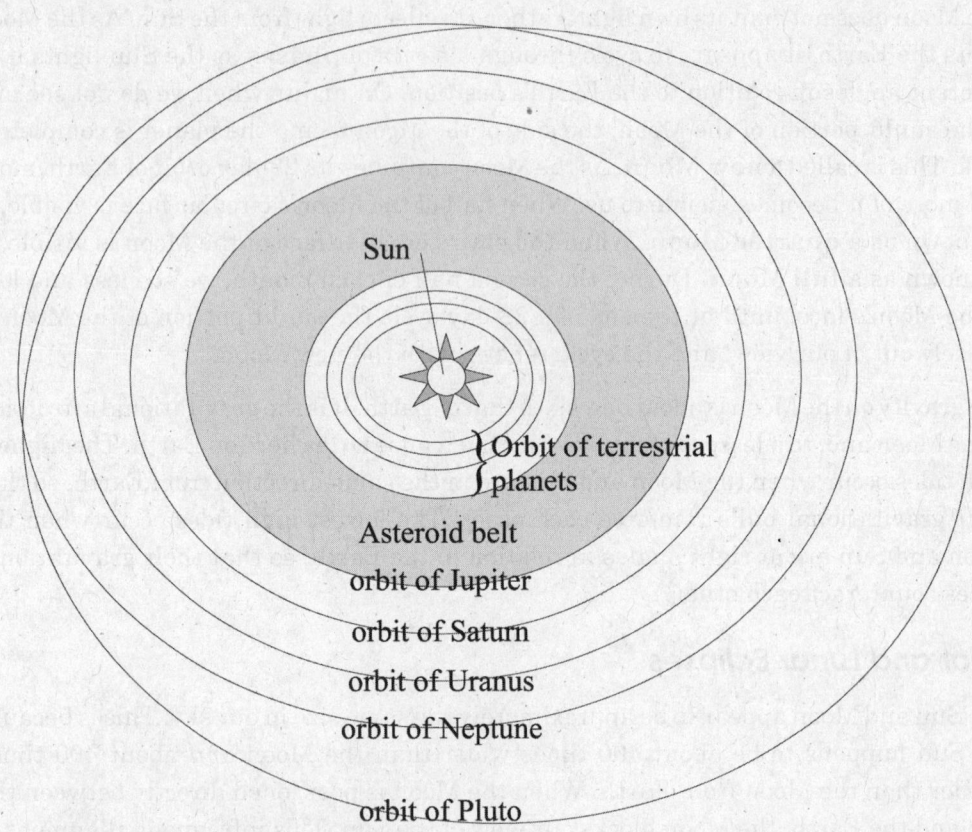

Mainly due to differences in size and distance from the Sun, the two type of planets—terrestrial and Jovian—differ in their basic characteristics. Because the terrestrial planets are much smaller than the Jovian planets, they have weaker gravitational fields, which account for their lighter atmospheres. Terrestrial planets have high densities and consist mainly of a solid mineral crust with metals, along with some gases and ice. The Jovian planets are characterized by lower densities because they consist mainly of gaseous emission and varying degrees of ice.

Between Mars and Jupiter is a great **asteroid belt,** as shown in the preceding illustration. The largest of these rocky, irregularly shaped bodies is about 620 miles in diameter. The total number of asteroids in this belt may be as high as a million, but their total mass is believed to be less than 3 percent of the Moon's mass. It is generally thought that during the formation of our solar system, a plethora of smaller planets were drawn outward by Jupiter's gravitation pull. Through frequent collisions with one another, they fragmented into smaller bodies, and then established their own belt of orbit about the Sun, just inside Jupiter's orbit.

38. Which of the following is a result of the tilt of Earth's axis in relation to Earth's elliptical orbit around the Sun?

    (1) the ebb and flow of tides along ocean and sea shores

    (2) the difference in temperatures between Equatorial regions and polar regions

    (3) differences in total glacial accumulations between the two polar ice caps

    (4) the fact that the Moon's orbit around Earth is elliptical rather than circular

    (5) clear seasonal weather patterns midway between the Equator and each pole

As a result of Earth's tilt, each hemisphere—the Northern and Southern—receives the most direct sunlight during its summer months, and the least during its winter months. **The correct answer is (5).**

39. Lunar eclipses occur far more frequently than solar eclipses. Which of the following best explains this fact?

    (1) The Moon is much smaller in diameter than the Sun.

    (2) The Moon's orbit is elliptical, whereas the Sun's orbit is circular.

    (3) The Moon and the Sun appear approximately the same size in the sky.

    (4) The Moon orbits Earth on a different elliptical plane than the one on which Earth orbits the Sun.

    (5) The Moon is much closer to Earth than the Sun is.

If the Moon's orbit around Earth were on the same plane as Earth's orbit around the Sun, lunar and solar eclipses would occur with equal frequency. It is the fact that the planes are distinct that explains the difference in frequency between a lunar eclipse and a solar eclipse. **The correct answer is (4).**

Our Sun and Other Stars

The glowing orb that we see during the day and call **the Sun** is composed of about 90 percent hydrogen and 10 percent helium, with trace amounts of metals. It is the result of a fusion of gases burning at temperatures reaching 27,000,000°F at the Sun's core. (The Sun's surface temperature is about 11,000°F). The energy the Sun generates is produced by **nuclear fusion,** a reaction that converts four hydrogen nuclei into one helium nucleus. The staggering amount of energy the Sun generates through this process provides all the heat and light to sustain life on Earth.

The Sun is about 93 million miles away, and its mass is about 330,000 times that of the Earth. Compared to other stars, the Sun is actually medium-sized. It appears so much larger to us only because it is so much closer than any other star. The next closest star is light-years away. (One light-year is defined as the distance light travels in one Earth year.)

SOLAR ACTIVITY

The surface of the Sun is characterized by turbulent phenomena that are loosely analogous to weather storms on Earth. **Sunspots** are magnetic fields that appear dark to us because they are cooler than other areas of the Sun's surface. Sunspots form a vortex akin to tornadoes on Earth and can last from a few days to several weeks. Heightened sunspot activity is usually associated with the appearance of **solar flares,** eruptions of hydrogen gas having temperatures as high as 100 million°F. Solar flares emit tremendous amounts of energy, mainly in the form of X-rays, and can last from a few hours to several days.

Sunspot and solar-flare activity on the Sun can affect the Earth's atmosphere. Charged particles from the solar wind whipped up by solar flares are channeled through the Earth's magnetic field around its magnetic poles. These particles collide with atoms in the upper atmosphere, ionizing them and making them glow in a brilliant display of colored lights called **auroras**—as seen in the skies near the Earth's two magnetic poles. Heightened solar-wind activity is also deemed responsible for disruptions in telecommunications signals that pass through regions of the upper atmosphere that have been electrically charged by these winds.

CHARACTERISTICS AND LIFE CYCLES OF STARS

Scientists are now able to measure and analyze stars to distinguish among star types according to various characteristics. Following is one version of the **Hertzsprung-Russell (H-R) diagram** (named for its creators). The H-R diagram organizes and presents key characteristics of stars in graphical form. The diagram plots stars according to luminosity (brightness), surface temperature, and spectral class (color). Absolute magnitude and luminosity measure the same phenomenon, except that absolute magnitude is measured on an inverted scale. (Notice that the numbers at the right side decrease as you move up the scale.) The temperature scale is given across the top of the diagram. Notice that temperatures *decrease* from left to right, so that stars with the highest surface temperatures are plotted at the *left* end of the diagram.

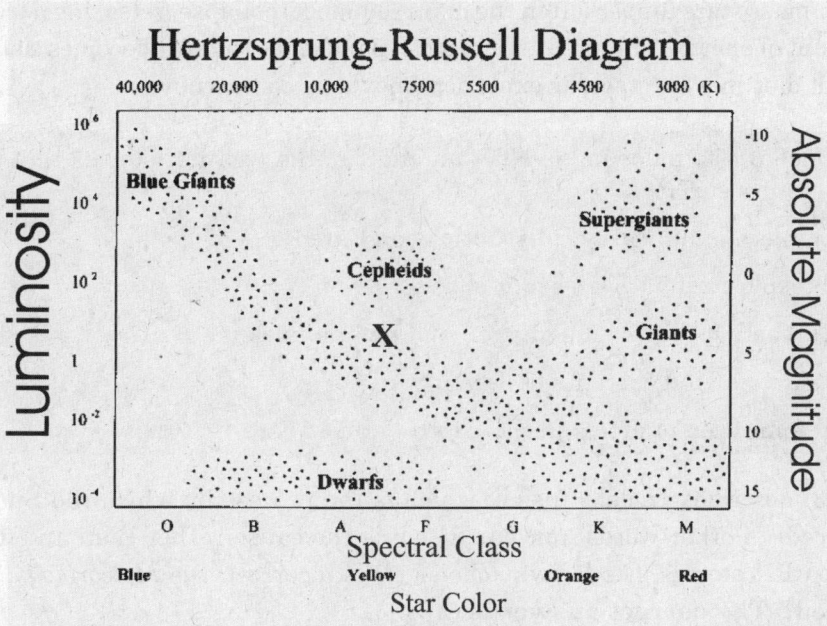

The Hertzsprung-Russell diagram shows most stars plotted in a large cluster that sweeps from the diagram's upper left to its lower right. This swath of stars is referred to as the **main sequence.** This swath suggests that brighter stars are generally hotter and, conversely, that darker stars are cooler. The Sun—marked by an X on the diagram—is classified as a yellow main-sequence star. Notice that the Sun is a fairly average star in terms of its temperature and brightness. Relative to the main sequence, stars classified as **Giants** and **Supergiants** are relatively bright in comparison to their temperature. Conversely, stars classified as **Dwarfs** are relatively dark in comparison to their temperature.

The life of a star is sustained by the thermonuclear reactions in its core. The energy produced by these reactions prevents gravitational collapse of the core onto its own center. Referring to the H-R diagram, main-sequence stars are believed to be in the middle phase of their development, when a star's nuclear reactions are stable and its fluctuations in temperature and luminosity are minor.

As a star increases in age, the nuclear fuel of its core runs low and eventually exhausts itself. At this point, it is thought, the star moves off the main sequence and may become either a white dwarf, a giant, or a supergiant—depending on the star's mass:

- Low-mass stars (lower right in the main sequence) continue to burn until all fuel is used, and then collapse into white dwarfs.

- Medium-mass stars (middle of the main sequence) temporarily expand into red giants as their gravitational energy is converted to heat. Once the red giant has exhausted its remaining energy, it will also shrink into a white dwarf. In some cases, the gas released as a red giant collapses and creates a glowing sphere of gas called a planetary nebula.

• High-mass stars (upper left in the main sequence) collapse, releasing a tremendous amount of energy. This creates a rapid expansion as the star becomes a supergiant, and it dies in a spectacular explosion known as a supernova.

40. Which of the following is NOT an effect of the weather storms that occur on the Sun's surface?

(1) telecommunications disruptions on Earth

(2) explosive hydrogen eruptions

(3) reactions between hydrogen and helium nuclei

(4) global wind currents on Earth

(5) ionization of atoms in the Earth's atmosphere

Choice (3) describes nuclear fusion, which is the process by which the Sun's energy is produced. In other words, nuclear fusion is the cause rather than an effect of the Sun's weather storms. (As for why choice (4) is incorrect, see *Meteorology,* earlier in this review.) **The correct answer is (3).**

QUESTION 41 REFERS TO THE FOLLOWING DIAGRAM.

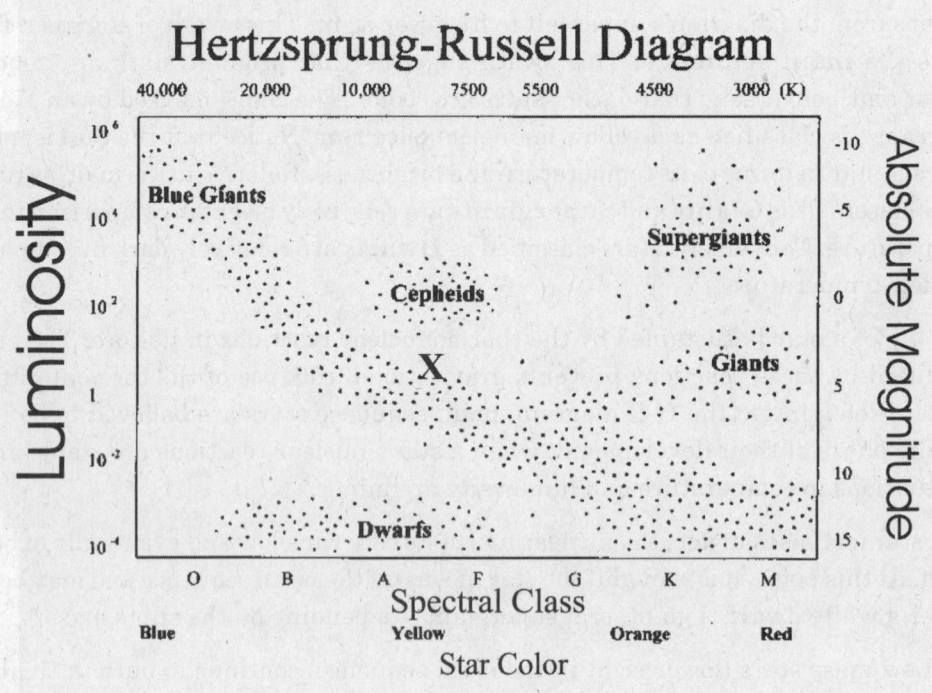

41. In reference to the Hertzsprung-Russell diagram above, how can main-sequence stars be characterized?

Main-sequence stars

(1) are similar to one another in temperature

(2) are relatively bright compared to their age

(3) are medium-sized for their age

(4) are stable in temperature and luminosity

(5) usually die an explosive death

Main-sequence stars are believed to be in the middle phase of their development, when a star's nuclear reactions are stable and its fluctuations in temperature and luminosity are minor. **The correct answer is (4).**

CHEMISTRY

Chemistry is the study of the composition, interactions, properties, and structure of matter and the changes that matter undergoes. It involves looking at ways to take substances apart and put the parts together again in new ways. For example, scientists are able to create substances as varied as metal alloys, paint, plastics, medicine, and perfumes by manipulating elements and compounds.

Properties and Physical States of Matter

Matter describes anything that occupies space and has mass (defined below). It is found in everything, but not all matter is the same. For instance, compare the matter found in concrete to the matter in a cheese steak. Both are considered matter, yet each has properties that make it uniquely different. In fact, there are only four basic properties that are shared by all matter (although these are physics concepts, they are essential in chemistry as well):

- **Mass** is a measure of the amount of matter that constitutes an object. The mass of an object is what gives it gravity—the force that attracts other objects—but mass is not affected by gravity. In physics, mass is defined and measured in terms of *inertia,* which is an object's resistance to any kind of change in motion. In a sense, then, mass measures inertia in terms of numbers. The most widely used unit of measure for mass is the *kilogram* (kg).

- **Weight**, unlike mass, fluctuates according to location in the universe. It is a measure of gravitational force of attraction that Earth exerts on an object.

- **Volume** is the measure of space something can occupy. An empty glass can potentially hold a specific amount of fluid, and when empty, it can hold air. When the space of the glass is occupied by either the fluid or air, it represents the volume.

- **Density** is a ratio of mass per unit volume. It represents the relationship between how much mass per unit volume an object has. This relationship can be expressed or calculated by the following formula: $D = \dfrac{mass}{volume}$

There are four possible physical states of matter:

- **Gas:** Matter in the gaseous state relies on its container for both shape and volume. (Example: steam)

- **Liquid:** Matter in the liquid state takes on the shape of whatever container it is put in. However, a liquid has a definite volume that does not depend on the container it is put in. (Example: water)

- **Solid:** Matter in the solid state has a definite shape and volume regardless of the container. (Example: ice)

- **Plasma:** A unique state of matter that only appears to be solid. In reality, it is an ionized gas. (To *ionize* an atom or collection of atoms is to give it an electrical charge either by adding or removing one or more electrons.)

Matter can change both physically and chemically. A physical change is a change in a substance's shape, size, or state. No chemical reaction is involved with a physical change. The particles that make up the substance remain essentially the same. So a diamond that is pulverized into diamond powder or a potato that gets mashed are both examples of a physical change. In each instance, the diamond and potato take on a different appearance, but they are still made of the same particles.

A chemical change is a bit different. When matter experiences a chemical change, it actually changes into a new substance with different properties from its former self. For example, when you crack an egg shell, the egg comes out translucent and fluid. However, when you scramble the egg in a pan and start cooking it, the egg turns yellow and becomes solid. It has changed chemically and cannot return to its former composition.

42. Which of the following illustrate chemical rather than physical changes to matter?
    A. a car chassis rusting from overexposure to water
    B. butter melting in a pan
    C. gasoline burning and becoming vapor
    D. water vapor condensing and turning to rain

(1) A and B only

(2) A and C only

(3) B and D only

(4) B, C, and D

(5) A, B, C, and D

Melted butter can be cooled to return it to its former solid state. Rain water can be boiled to return it to its former gaseous state (water vapor.) On the other hand, water reacts chemically with the iron in a car chassis to disintegrate it, and as gasoline burns, it becomes oxygen and carbon dioxide, which cannot be recombined to form gasoline. **The correct answer is (2).**

---

43. Assume that you poured two liquids—one green and one yellow—in a glass. Then, no matter how much you stir the mixture, the green liquid settles to the bottom, and the yellow liquid rises to the top. What can you reliably conclude from this observation?

(1) The two liquids are incapable of reacting chemically with each other.

(2) The green liquid is denser than the yellow liquid.

(3) The green liquid has more weight than the yellow liquid.

(4) The green liquid contains solid matter, whereas the yellow liquid does not.

(5) You cannot draw any reliable conclusions.

Denser substances sink in relation to substances that are less dense. Choice (1) is incorrect because although the two liquids clearly did not undergo a chemical change, they might at some other temperature or pressure. Choice (3) is incorrect because we do not know how much liquid of either type was poured into the glass. **The correct answer is (2).**

The Universe of the Atom

 http://bit.ly/hippo_phys1

All matter is made up of atoms. The **atom** is the smallest particle of matter. (The word atom is derived from the Greek *atomos,* meaning "not cuttable.") Though theories about atoms date back to ideas proposed by ancient Greek philosophers, it would be another 2,000 years before researchers would develop a provable atomic theory. In the eighteenth century, building upon the work of his contemporaries, John Dalton proposed that the essential difference between atoms is their mass. Dalton proposed the Law of Conservation of Mass and constructed the first table of relative atomic weights and postulated the Law of Multiple Proportions. During the nineteenth century, Russian scientist Dmitri Mendeleev correctly ordered atoms by mass. In the early twentieth century, Ernest Rutherford discovered the "empty" nature of atoms, meaning that the mass of an atom concentrated at a positively charged central core, which he named the *nucleus*. And in 1913, Danish scientist Niels Bohr proposed that energy levels of an atom were like the orbits of planets—a proposal that led to the "solar system" model of the atom. While some of these scientists' proposals and theories have since been disproved, by providing the fundamentals upon which their successors could build, they were invaluable in advancing modern atomic theory.

Atomic Structure

All matter is made up of atoms, and all atoms are made up of subatomic particles: **electrons, protons,** and **neutrons.** While all three particles have mass, there are three major differences:

- Electrons have a negative charge (–).

- Protons have a positive charge (+).

- Neutrons have no charge.

Electrons and protons can repel and attract each other without physically touching. Opposite charges attract (electron to proton), and like charges repel (proton to proton or electron to electron).

Each atom has a specific arrangement for its subatomic particles. The nucleus of an atom, or central core, contains protons and neutrons. The electrons occupy several energy levels around the nucleus. In the past, scientists thought these energy levels orbited the nucleus like the planets orbit the sun. More recently, however, electron placement has been described as an "electron cloud" because the electrons move so rapidly, like blades of a fan. Today, scientists know that an electron occupies a certain region of space. Each region contains electrons that move at about the same speed, which enables us to determine where an electron is at a certain time. The path an electron takes to go from point to point, however, is unpredictable. (This proposition is known as the *Heisenberg's uncertainty principle*.)

Electron Configuration

The term **electron configuration** refers to the distribution of electrons among available levels of an atom. Electrons reside in energy levels called **atomic orbitals.** The number and location of electrons in any atom determine the type of chemical reactions in which the atom may participate with other types of atoms. Different types of atoms vary in their number of energy levels. The outermost energy level is also called the **outer valence.** An atom will seek to complete its outer valence by reacting to or bonding with other atoms:

- The first energy level (level 1) is completed when it holds 2 electrons.

- The second energy level (level 2) is completed when it holds 8 electrons.

- The third energy level (level 3) is completed when it holds 18 electrons.

The next figure shows electron configurations for four types of atoms that have relatively simple structures (the inner circle represents the nucleus, where protons and neutrons reside):

P = proton
N = neutron
e⁻ = electron

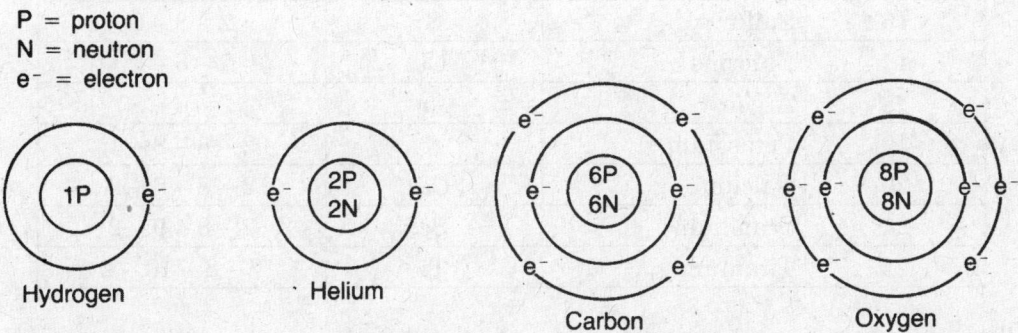

Hydrogen   Helium   Carbon   Oxygen

Notice that hydrogen and helium atoms have only one energy level, whereas carbon and oxygen have two energy levels. Also notice that of the four types of atoms, only helium has a completed outer valence. The other three types—hydrogen, carbon, and oxygen—will seek to complete their outer valances by reacting to or bonding with other atoms.

Protons, Neutrons, Atomic Weight, and Isotopes

The number of protons in an atom defines the atom as a specific **element.** For example, the nucleus of a carbon atom *always* contains six protons, and this number of protons is exclusive and unique to carbon. The number of protons can be used as an identifying marker for an element. This marker is referred to as an element's **atomic number.** The following table ranks the first twenty-two elements by their atomic number—that is, by the number of protons. For each element, the table also shows the element's symbol and electron distribution among orbitals.

ATOMIC NUMBER	ELEMENT	SYMBOL	ELECTRON DISTRIBUTION
1	Hydrogen	H	1
2	Helium	He	2
3	Lithium	Li	2 – 1
4	Beryllium	Be	2 – 2
5	Boron	B	2 – 3
6	Carbon	C	2 – 4
7	Nitrogen	N	2 – 5
8	Oxygen	O	2 – 6
9	Fluorine	F	2 – 7
10	Neon	Ne	2 – 8
11	Sodium	Na	2 – 8 – 1
12	Magnesium	Mg	2 – 8 – 2
13	Aluminum	Al	2 – 8 – 3
14	Silicon	Si	2 – 8 – 4

ATOMIC NUMBER	ELEMENT	SYMBOL	ELECTRON DISTRIBUTION
15	Phosphorus	P	2 – 8 – 5
16	Sulfur	S	2 – 8 – 6
17	Chlorine	Cl	2 – 8 – 7
18	Argon	Ar	2 – 8 – 8
19	Potassium	K	2 – 8 – 8 – 1
20	Calcium	Ca	2 – 8 – 8 – 2
21	Scandium	Sc	2 – 8 – 9 – 2
22	Titanium	Ti	2 – 8 – 10 – 2

All neutral atoms of an element have the same number of protons (which are positively charged) and electrons (which are negatively charged). However, they don't necessarily have the same number of neutrons. An **isotope** occurs when atoms of the same element differ in the number of neutrons in the nuclei. For example, here are three isotopes of the element hydrogen:

Hydrogen's neutral form (*Hydrogen*): 1 proton, no neutrons

One hydrogen isotope (*Deuterium*): 1 proton, 1 neutron

Another hydrogen isotope (*Tritium*): 1 proton, 2 neutrons

Neutrons have no charge, but they have the same mass as protons. The **atomic weight,** or **mass number,** of an atom is the number of protons plus the number of neutrons (the unit of measurement is called the *Dalton*). For example, hydrogen has an atomic weight of 1, whereas deuterium and tritium have atomic weights of 2 and 3, respectively.

44. If atom X has an atomic weight of 19, which of the following is a possible combination of particles within that atom?

(1) 19 electrons, 19 protons, and 19 neutrons

(2) 19 electrons, 19 protons, and 8 neutrons

(3) 9 electrons, 9 protons, and 18 neutrons

(4) 10 electrons, 9 protons, and 9 neutrons

(5) 9 electrons, 9 protons, and 10 neutrons

The atomic weight is the sum of the number of protons and neutrons. Only in choice (5) do those two numbers total 19. **The correct answer is (5).**

45. What is the distinguishing feature of each different element?

    (1) the number of protons it contains

    (2) the number of neutrons it contains

    (3) the number of electrons it contains

    (4) the number of atoms it contains

    (5) the total number of protons and neutrons it contains

The number of protons is what distinguishes each element from all the others. **The correct answer is (1).**

Elements and Compounds

An **element** is a substance that cannot be broken down into simpler substances. Atoms (or ions) of different elements join by chemical bonds in certain proportions to form a **compound.**

Elements

More than 115 different elements are currently known; 92 of these elements are known to occur in nature. Elements include such substances as hydrogen, carbon, potassium, and lead. Each element has been assigned a one-letter or two-letter symbol. Most of these symbols include the first letter of the element's name, though some do not. For example, the symbol for carbon is **C,** and the symbol for iron is **Fe.** Each element is composed of atoms having the same **atomic number,** which means that each atom contains the same number of protons as all other atoms of that element. Atoms of each element also share the same electron configurations.

The modern **Periodic Table of Elements** ranks all of the elements according to the atomic number and organizes them into *families* based on similar chemical and physical properties. Each horizontal row in the Periodic Table is called a *period.* Moving from left to right in a row, the elements in a period transition from metals to nonmetals, and atomic numbers and mass increase. The elements in each column are together called a *group.* Groups contain elements that have the same number of electrons in their outermost energy level (outer valance).

The following figure shows a left-hand and a right-hand portion of the Periodic Table. Notice that hydrogen (H), lithium (Li), sodium (Na), and potassium (K) are in the far left column (group) because they each have just one outer-valence electron. Also notice that the gases in the right-hand group have completed outer valances. These gases are called **noble gases** and are completely inert, meaning that they will not react or bond with other types of atoms. Finally, notice that each element has its own "calling card" on the periodic table, showing its symbol, electron distribution, atomic weight, and atomic number.

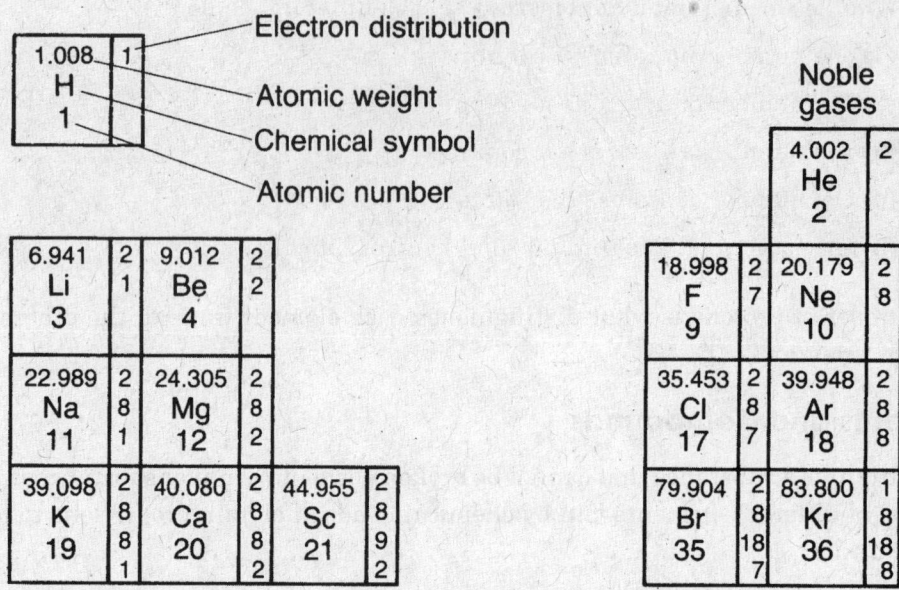

Elements fall into three categories: metals, nonmetals, and metalloids.

- **Metals** conduct electricity, are malleable, and can be drawn into wires or flattened into sheets. Metals can also be polished for shine and have high melting points (although mercury turns liquid at room temperature). Elements such as copper, silver, and iron are just a few examples of metals.

- **Nonmetals** are unsuitable for conducting electricity, and they are non-shiny. Also, some solid nonmetals are not very malleable and can shatter on impact. Finally, nonmetals have lower melting points than metals. (Nonmetals occupy the upper right-hand corner of the periodic table.)

- **Metalloids** are elements such as silicon and boron that have properties that are similar to both metals and nonmetals.

Compounds and Bonds

There are two major types of "friendships" that atoms like to form: **ionic bonds** and **covalent bonds.** In this section, you'll learn what each term means, and you'll learn the laws related to these relationships.

IONS: FORMATION AND COMPOUNDS

Electrical forces of attraction hold matter together. As noted earlier, however, an element's atoms are electrically neutral. So how can different atoms attract each other if they are neutral? Though atoms can't attract, combinations of atoms can transfer electrons or share electrons to form **compounds.** When atoms reorganize their electrons in this way, they are "reacting" to other atoms and are no longer called "atoms." At this point, they become **ions.** An ion is an atom with a charge, either positive or negative. The neutral state is altered because the atom has either gained or lost one or more electrons. In the nomenclature of chemistry, an ion with a positive charge keeps the same name as the atoms from which it was made, while a negatively charged ion is renamed to end with *-ide.*

Ions of opposite charges attract one another strongly. When they get together, they form **ionic compounds.** Consider table salt, for example. Normally, the parent elements, sodium (Na) and chlorine (Cl), can't be brought together. However, certain changes in their electron configurations can take place, creating the ionic compound NaCl, which we know as table salt.

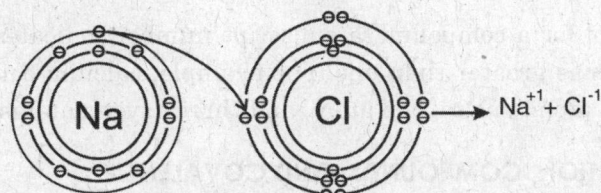

Formation of Ions

As the previous illustration shows, the single electron in the outermost energy level in the sodium ion (Na) is transferred to the outer valance of the chlorine ion (Cl). The outer valance of the chloride ion gains an electron from the sodium ion. This forms a stable ionic bond with an *octet* formation (four pairs of two electrons in the outer valance). Atoms and ions whose outer valance contains eight electrons enjoy more stability than those that lack eight electrons at this level.

Because like charges repel, all the new sodium ions move away from one another. The same is true for all the chloride ions. But the chloride and sodium ions attract each other, thereby becoming a stable compound we know as sodium chloride, or table salt. The net force of attraction between the oppositely charged ions is called the **ionic bond.**

REDOX REACTIONS AND IONIC COMPOUNDS

The simple reaction that drives the formation of ionic compounds is a **redox reaction.** This reaction draws its name from two important chemical events that occur during electron transfer:

- *Reduction:* The gaining of electrons
- *Oxidation:* The losing of electrons

In a redox reaction, one substance is the **oxidizer**—it causes the oxidation of the other substance by accepting electrons from it. The other substance is the **reducer**—it reduces a substance by giving it electrons. In table salt, sodium is the reducer because it gives electrons to the chlorine atom, which makes the chloride ion. Chlorine is the oxidizer; by accepting electrons from sodium, it oxidizes sodium atoms to ions. The oxidizing agent is the one that is always reduced. Look at another example:

$$Mg \quad + \quad O_2 \quad \rightarrow \quad MgO$$

electron configuration   electron configuration   Magnesium Oxide

2 8 ②   2 ⑥

In this example, magnesium (Mg) is the reducing agent. It reduces oxygen and loses two electrons, becoming Mg^{2+}, magnesium ion. Oxygen is the oxidizing agent. It oxidizes magnesium and gains two electrons, becoming O^{2-}, oxide ion. Here are some additional examples of ionic compounds:

Sodium fluoride (NaF)—prevents cavities

Silver chloride (AgCl)—photographic film

Magnesium sulfate ($MgSO_4$)—laxative

Calcium carbonate ($CaCO_3$)—antacid

NOTE: In the symbol for a compound, a subscript number indicates the number of atoms if that number is greater than one. For example, calcium carbonate ($CaCO_3$) contains one calcium atom, one carbon atom, and three oxygen atoms.

MOLECULES: FORMATION, COMPOUNDS, AND COVALENCE

There are some nonmetals whose atoms cannot become ions by the transfer of electrons (as described in the previous section). So some other form of bonding must occur. Compounds that are composed only of nonmetals consist of **molecules** instead of ions. Molecules are small particles of neutral charge, consist of at least two atoms, and have enough electrons to make the system neutral (no net charge). A compound consisting of molecules is called a **molecular compound.**

Note, however, that some elements exist with two atoms to each molecule—in other words, they react with themselves. These are called **diatomic molecules** and contain atoms of only one element. Notable examples include the following (the right-hand column shows how the molecule is illustrated):

Cl_2 Cl—Cl

O_2 O—O

N_2 N—N

I_2 I—I

Br_2 Br—Br

F_2 F—F

H_2 H—H

Covalent bonds are formed by the sharing pairs of electrons between atoms. One outer-valance electron from each atom can be shared between their atomic nuclei. The following diagrams show two ways covalent bonds can be depicted in the phosphorous trichloride (PCl_3) molecule:

$$\ddot{:}\ddot{C}l\ddot{:}\ddot{P}\ddot{:}\ddot{C}l\ddot{:} \qquad \ddot{:}\ddot{C}l—\ddot{P}—\ddot{C}l\ddot{:}$$
$$\ddot{:}\ddot{C}l\ddot{:} \qquad\qquad\qquad \ddot{:}\ddot{C}l\ddot{:}$$

The left-hand diagram shows an electron-dot configuration where only outer electrons are shown. The right-hand diagram shows the bond-line structure. If you count the shared pair for each atom in the PCl_3 molecule, you notice that each has eight electrons in the outermost energy level (the outer valance). Atoms whose outer valance contains eight electrons are most stable.

The diagram of a PCl_3 molecule shows one pair of electrons shared between atoms. However, in other cases two or even three pairs of electrons can be shared in forming certain covalent bonds. Atoms of nonmetal elements differ in their ability to share electrons. Oxygen can form two bonds, nitrogen can form three bonds, and carbon can form four bonds. The term **covalence** refers to the number of outer-valence electrons an atom of one element must share with another atom so that the outer valence will contain eight electrons altogether and hence become stable. For example, a hydrogen atom only needs one more electron to satisfy the octet rule, so its covalence is 1. Here are four different element families and the covalence number of each:

Carbon family: 8 − 4 = 4 covalence

Nitrogen family: 8 − 5 = 3 covalence

Oxygen family: 8 − 6 = 2 covalence

Halogen family: 8 − 7 = 1 covalence

46. What is the difference between an atom and an ion?

   (1) An atom is positively charged, but an ion is negatively charged.

   (2) An atom has an even number of electrons in its outer valence, whereas an ion has an odd number.

   (3) An atom is neutral, but an ion has an electrical charge.

   (4) An atom has an electrical charge, but an ion does not.

   (5) An atom is negatively charged, but an ion is positively charged.

An atom has the same number of protons as electrons, and so it has no net charge (it is neutral). When an atom gains or loses an electron to a different atom, it becomes an ion—with either a positive or negative charge. **The correct answer is (3).**

47. Which of the following best explains why carbon atoms form covalent bonds with atoms of many other elements?

  (1) Carbon is the only element that has enough electrons to bond with more than four other atoms.

  (2) Carbon's covalence of 4 leads to several possible ways to complete its outer valence.

  (3) Carbon atoms cannot bond with other carbon atoms, except in a controlled laboratory environment.

  (4) Carbon is present in every kind of living organism on Earth.

  (5) A carbon atom contains the same number of protons as outer-valence electrons.

Carbon has a covalence of 4, which means it will seek to add four more additional electrons for its outer valence. Several combinations are possible—for example: 4, 3 + 1, 2 + 2, or 1 + 1 + 1 + 1. Thus atoms with a covalence of 1, 2, 3, or 4 are all candidates for covalent bonding with carbon. **The correct answer is (2).**

Mixtures, Solutions, and Solubility

Mixtures come in three basic types: solutions, suspensions, and colloids.

- A **solution** is a uniform mixture of two or more substances that have reacted chemically. Salt water is a good example of a solution. This solution consists of NaCl (table salt) and water. Once they have reacted chemically, the two are indistinguishable. Nevertheless, you could physically separate them by evaporating the water, leaving the salt behind.

- A **suspension** is a mixture in which small particles are distributed throughout a liquid or gas but have not reacted chemically with it, and, if left undisturbed, the particles will settle to the bottom. Muddy water is a good example of a suspension.

- A **colloid** is a mixture containing tiny particles that are distributed uniformly throughout a liquid or gas, have *not* reacted chemically with it, and do *not* settle to the bottom. Fog is a good example of a colloid. Particles in a colloid are smaller than those in a suspension but larger than those in a solution.

Solubility

The **solute** of a solution is the substance that dissolves. A solute can be a liquid or a solid. The **solvent** is the medium in which the solute dissolves. In chemistry, water is referred to as the "universal solvent," which means that the properties of water give it the ability to dissolve many substances. In the case of salt water, salt is the solute that dissolves in water, the solvent.

Solubility refers to the ability of a solute to dissolve in a solvent under certain conditions, such as a given temperature or pressure. If additional solute can be dissolved in a fixed volume of solvent, then the solution has not yet reached its **saturation** level. In saturated solutions, a point has been reached in which no more solute can be dissolved in the solvent. In chemistry, the uniform measure used for solubility is the number of **moles** per 1 liter of solvent. A mole is a universally used unit measure for mass (1 mole = 58.5 grams).

In some cases, creating a solution can result in a net temperature change. For example, calcium chloride releases heat upon dissolving. On the other hand, ammonium nitrate decreases in temperature, becoming cooler upon dissolving. Chemical reactions that release heat (increase temperature) are referred to as **exothermic reactions,** and those that absorb heat (decrease temperature) are referred to as **endothermic reactions.** This is the chemistry behind the hot and cold packs that are used to ease swelling tissue and soothe pulled muscles.

Temperature and pressure can affect solubility—the amount of the solute that can be dissolved in a given amount of solvent. For most solid solutes, an increase in temperature will lead to an increase in solubility. For gases, the effect of temperature is opposite: gases become less soluble at higher temperatures. This is why carbonated drinks are served with ice to keep them cool longer; the cooler temperature decreases the formation of carbon dioxide bubbles. Changes in pressure have a very small effect on the solubility of a liquid or a solid, but for gases an increase in pressure increases solubility.

Equilibrium

If excess, undissolved solute is present, a saturated solution sets up a system of **dynamic equilibrium.** If you add more solute to an already saturated solution, some dissolves while some reforms as the original solute. These two opposing activities result in no net change. For example, assume that NaCl crystals are added to an already saturated solution of NaCl and water. Some of those crystals will dissolve as ions and become part of the solution, yet some of those dissolved ions will attach to an undissolved crystal surface and reform crystals, which "fall out" of solution. Eventually, the rates at which ions dissolve and reform as crystals become equal, so that there is no net change in the solution's concentration or in the mass of undissolved solute. Factors such as temperature, concentration, and pressure can upset equilibrium and shift it. The shift can be in favor of a forward reaction, producing more products, or backward, in favor of the solute.

48. Milk is an example of a colloid. What does this fact suggest about milk?

(1) Milk boils at a lower temperature than water.

(2) Milk becomes transparent if you don't shake it occasionally.

(3) If left undisturbed, the cream in milk will rise to the top.

(4) Whole milk is heavier than skim milk.

(5) Milk appears uniformly cloudy, even if left unshaken.

The fact that milk is a colloid means that it contains tiny particles that are uniformly distributed in water and will not settle to the bottom, even if left undisturbed. (Do not confuse those particles with cream, which contains fat and therefore rises to the top.) **The correct answer is (5).**

49. A powdery substance is added to pure hot water and seems to disappear. The mixture remains clear but now has a distinct odor. What conclusion can be drawn from this observation?

(1) The water has not yet reached boiling point.

(2) The water is not beyond full saturation with the powder.

(3) Any additional powder will settle to the bottom of the water.

(4) The mixture has absorbed heat and is now cooler.

(5) The odor is caused by heat created when the powder reacted with the water.

The fact that the powder disappears, leaving clear water, strongly suggests that it has dissolved in the water. Thus, the mixture is a solution (not a colloid or suspension) that has not surpassed its saturation point at the current water temperature. **The correct answer is (2).**

Acids, Bases, and the pH Scale

Acids and bases are two different yet closely related classes of compounds. **Acids** form hydrogen ions when dissolved in water. The more acidic the substance, the greater the concentration of hydrogen ions. You're probably familiar with a variety of acids, such as vinegar, lemon juice, and of course the gastric juice of your stomach, which helps break down food. Acids usually have a sour taste. In contrast to acids, **bases** form few hydrogen ions when dissolved in water. The fewer hydrogen ions formed, the more basic, or *alkaline,* the substance. You're probably familiar with various bases as well, such as household ammonia, lye, bleach, milk of magnesia, and bicarbonate of soda. Bases are usually bitter to the taste.

The **pH scale** was developed to measure the relative acidity or alkalinity of a substance. The term **pH** or **pH level** is used to refer to the concentration of hydrogen ions in a solution. The higher the concentration of hydrogen ions, the more acidic the compound, and the *lower* the level on the pH scale. The scale for pH ranges from 0 to 14. A pH of 7 is the baseline that represents a neutral solution. Pure water has a neutral pH of 7. In acidic solutions the pH is less than 7, and in basic (alkaline) solutions the pH is greater than 7. The following chart shows a pH scale with some common pH values:

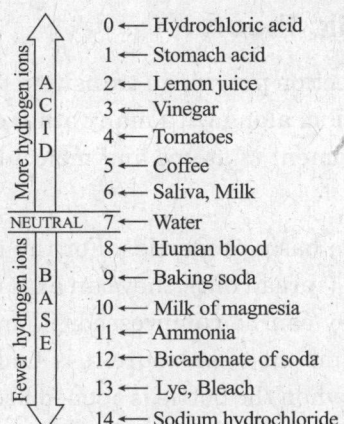

In an aqueous (water) solution, acids and bases react to neutralize each other, yielding water and one form or another of salt (after boiling the solution, what is left are salts):

Acid + Base → Water + Salt

HCl + NaOH → H_2O (water) + NaCl (sodium chloride, a form of salt)

HNO_3 + KOH → H_2O (water) + KNO_3 (potassium nitrate, a form of salt)

The result is a pH level between that of either substance—closer to 7 on the pH scale. Thus milk of magnesia helps neutralize the acidity of your stomach's gastric juice. Similarly, since milk is slightly alkaline while coffee is acidic, adding milk to coffee helps neutralize the beverage. Keep in mind that the pH scale is logarithmic, not linear. So combining a substance with a pH of 6 with a substance having a pH of 8 will not yield a neutral pH of 7—but it will reduce the overall pH by just a bit.

One way to test the pH level of a solution is to dip **litmus paper** in it. Litmus is an organic powder derived from lichens (a fungus). Litmus paper is coated with the powder. Acids turn blue litmus paper red, while bases turn red litmus paper blue.

50. A person is admitted to the hospital with a blood pH of 7.10. The normal range for the pH of blood is 7.35–7.45. Which of the following should be administered to restore the patient's blood pH level to normal?

(1) water

(2) hydrochloric acid

(3) pH-normal blood from a donor

(4) sodium bicarbonate

(5) pure hydrogen ions

Sodium bicarbonate is more alkaline than blood and therefore would help boost the pH level of the patient's blood to the normal range. **The correct answer is (4).**

http://bit.ly/hippo_phys2

Gas Laws and the Kinetic Theory

This final chemistry review section provides a transition to the review of physics, which deals with the concept of motion, along with many other concepts. The motion of gases can be explained by the movement of atoms and molecules, and so this topic involves chemistry as well.

Gases generally share certain basic properties. For the most part, they can mix with one another, they can diffuse (spread out), they can expand to fill containers, and they are elastic, which means they can be compressed. Compressed gas causes a spring-like action due to the high amount of pressure it is under. For example, a cork in a champagne bottle shoots out when the bottle is opened because the volume is increased and the pressure is released (decreased). Rapidly expanding gas usually cools, which is the key principle behind a CO_2 fire extinguisher. When compressed quickly, gases usually heat up. Try touching your bicycle pump as you rapidly fill your tire with air. The pump gets hot, and so does the tire.

Pressure is defined as the force per unit area: $P = \dfrac{F}{A}$. The SI (standard international) unit of measurement for pressure is the *Pascal* (pa), though other units are used as well for this purpose.

The gas properties previously described are expressed in a series of gas laws involving three variables:

- Pressure (*P*)
- Temperature (*T*)
- Volume (*V*)

Boyle's Law (Pressure-Volume Law)

In 1661, Robert Boyle discovered that gas pressure is inversely related to volume at a constant temperature. The mathematical representation of Boyle's Law is as follows:

$$P_1 V_1 = P_2 V_2$$

Another way of expressing this law is that pressure (*P*) × volume (*V*) is constant, as long as temperature and the number of gas molecules remain constant. As the pressure increases, the volume decreases, and as pressure decreases, volume increases. Look at the container in the following diagram. In illustration (a), the container is filled with air and sealed with a lid that you can raise and lower. At the present height of the lid, the gas molecules are spread out. The nature of gas particles is such that they want to fill every possible space. So as gas particles move to occupy space, they collide into the sides of the container. This exerts a force onto the sides of the container. This is the pressure created by the gas inside the container.

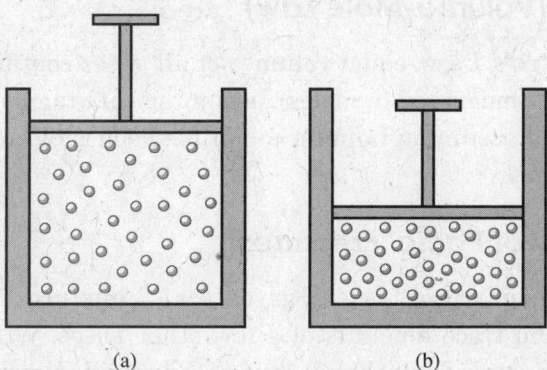

(a)   (b)

Now look at illustration (b). As the lid is lowered, the gas particles are closely packed together. They are still moving and undergoing collisions at the same rate, but now they don't have far to travel before colliding with the sides of the container. So the shorter distance has increased the rate of collisions. The increase in collision enhances the internal pressure, which is inverse to the volume change (volume decreases as the lid moves down).

Charles's Law (Temperature-Volume Law)

In 1787, Jacques Charles discovered that the volume of a fixed amount of gas at constant pressure is directly proportional to temperature. The mathematical representation of **Charles's Law** is as follows:

$$\frac{V_1}{T_1} = \frac{V_2}{T_2}$$

This law goes into action when a hot air balloon rises. Balloonists heat the air inside the balloon. The heated air expands and becomes less dense than the surrounding air, allowing the balloon to lift and float.

Gay-Lussac's Law (Pressure-Temperature Law)

Gay-Lussac's Law states that the pressure of gas is directly proportional to temperature:

$$\frac{P_1}{T_1} = \frac{P_2}{T_2}$$

The warnings you see on aerosol cans provide an example of this law. Aerosol cans are sealed, and even when the product is used up, residual gas remains inside the can. These gases are used as propellants, and most are under a high pressure and are flammable. So you may see a warning on the can concerning the temperature range at which the product can be stored, as well as a warning not to place the cans in an incinerator. The high heat in the incinerator will raise the temperature in the can, which in turn increases the pressure. Inevitably, the can will burst.

Avogadro's Law (Volume-Mole Law)

According to **Avogadro's Law,** equal volumes of all gases contain the same number of molecules (generally measured in moles), assuming that temperature and pressure are equal as well, and assuming no interaction between molecules. In other words, they have the same mass.

Dalton's Law (Law of Partial Pressures)

Many gas samples are a mixture of several gases. Air is a mixture of 79 percent nitrogen, 21 percent oxygen, and trace amounts of a few other gases. With altitude changes, the volume-to-volume ratios don't change, but each individual pressure of oxygen and nitrogen does change. **Dalton's Law** states that the total pressure exerted by a mixture of gases is equal to the sum of the individual partial pressures.

http://bit.ly/hippo_phys3

The Kinetic Theory of Gases

The **kinetic theory of gases** explains the gas properties you've just reviewed in terms of the motion of atoms and molecules. Under the kinetic theory, properties such as pressure and temperature are seen as statistical outcomes of the overall behavior of large numbers of gas particles. More specifically, the theory goes that gas particles are in a state of random, straight-line motion in all directions and are moving too fast and are too far apart to establish any force of attraction or repulsion. When they collide, they bounce off one another with the same amount of kinetic energy they had prior to the collision, so no energy is lost—that is, the temperature of the gas remains constant absent a change in pressure or volume. Pressure exerted on an object by a gas is the net result of the collisions of all the gas molecules against the object.

> **51.** Which statement explains why a balloon filled with helium rises in the air?
>
> **(1)** Helium is a gas that is lighter than air.
>
> **(2)** Helium maintains a higher temperature than air.
>
> **(3)** Helium molecules move faster than air molecules.
>
> **(4)** At a given temperature, helium expands more quickly than air.
>
> **(5)** Helium atoms collide with balloon walls, forcing the balloon upward.

Helium is lighter (less dense) than air. Do not confuse this phenomenon with a hot-air balloon, in which increasing the temperature of air in the balloon causes the air to expand and become lighter than the surrounding air. **The correct answer is (1).**

52. Which of the following best illustrates Boyle's Law?

(1) the pressure people feel in their ears during high-altitude flight

(2) a physician's recommendation to apply heat to a boil on the skin

(3) the blast of cool air you feel when you open a door to an air-conditioned building on a hot day

(4) the recommendation on aerosol cans to store them at room temperature

(5) the recommended maximum air pressure printed on automobile tires

At a given temperature, gas pressure is inversely related to volume. Like removing a cork from a bottle, opening a door to a room of air under compression releases the pressure. Choice (5) better illustrates Charles's Law: When a car tire heats up while moving quickly across the ground, the volume of air in the tire expands. **The correct answer is (3).**

PHYSICS

Physics is the scientific study of matter, energy, space, and time—and how they are interrelated. Physics is closely related to all other fields of science, since its laws are universal. The living systems of biology are made of matter particles that follow the laws of physics. Chemistry explores how atoms, small units of matter, interact to form molecules according to the laws of physics. And the study of geology and astronomy deal to a great extent with the physics of the Earth and of celestial bodies.

Motion: Velocity, Mass, and Momentum

 http://bit.ly/hippo_phys4

Our universe is filled with objects in motion. **Motion** is described in terms of speed, velocity, and acceleration. **Speed** refers to rate of motion and can be either instantaneous—as recorded by the speedometer of a car, for instance—or an average rate over a period of time. Speed can be expressed in many ways—for example, as kilometers per hour (km/h) or centimeters per second (cm/sec). **Velocity** refers to speed *in a given direction:* for example, 50 miles per hour *east*. Velocity can change if either speed or direction changes. So a body in motion along a curved path is undergoing a continuous change in velocity, whether or not the speed is changing. **Acceleration** is the rate at which velocity changes. Acceleration is determined by dividing the change in velocity by the change in time:

$$a = \frac{V_2 - V_1}{T}$$

An increase in velocity over a period of time is referred to as **positive acceleration,** while a decrease in velocity over time is referred to as **negative acceleration.** Referring to the preceding formula, if the initial velocity (V_1) is greater than the subsequent velocity (V_2), then the acceleration over time T is negative. Since acceleration is expressed in terms of velocity, any change in direction is also a change in acceleration. A body in motion along a curved path is undergoing a continuous change in acceleration, whether or not the speed is changing.

Mass and Momentum

The term **mass** is not the same as weight. Mass refers to the amount of matter contained in a particular object or body. Mass is often expressed as **density mass,** typically as mass per volume. For example, a bowling ball has a greater mass density than a Nerf ball. The bowling ball contains far more matter per volume than the Nerf ball.

Momentum is defined as mass multiplied by velocity (*mass × velocity*) and remains constant unless an outside force—such as friction—acts upon it. In other words, to change the momentum of an object, a force is required. For example, in a vacuum (a "closed system"), a 10-pound object moving in a straight path at 50 meters per second has the same momentum as a 25-pound object moving in the same straight direction path at a speed of 20 meters per second.

Objects in motion under the influence of gravity are in **free-fall.** Objects released from rest, thrown upward, or thrown downward, are in free-fall once released. All objects in a near-vacuum, regardless of their mass, fall at the same rate of 9.8 m/sec^2.

Energy and Work

If all motion occurred in a vacuum, no change in velocity, or in momentum, would ever occur—as no energy would be needed to set objects in motion or keep them in motion. But motion rarely occurs in a vacuum. It not only changes over time, but it also requires energy, or the ability to do work. There are two major types of energy. **Potential energy** is energy that results from the position or condition of an object rather than from its motion. A coiled spring, a charged battery, or a weight held above the ground are all examples of this potential energy. In contrast, **kinetic energy** refers to the energy an object (or wave) possesses due to its motion. The amount of the kinetic energy depends on the object's velocity and mass—or, in the case of waves, the wave's velocity, frequency, and amplitude.

In physics, the word **work** refers to the transfer of energy from one object to another. Potential energy can be transferred to kinetic energy. In most instances, work is performed in order to move the other object over a distance. To accomplish work, the application of **force** is required. Pushing a lawn mower across the lawn, lifting a bucket of water, and pulling open a refrigerator door are all examples of work. In each case, you transfer your potential energy to another object by applying force upon it. Of course, applying a force upon an object does not always result in work done on that object. For example, pushing on a stationary wall results in no work because the wall doesn't move.

Work is equal to the amount of force multiplied by the distance over which it is applied:

Work = Force × Distance

Work and energy are generally measured in a unit called the *joule* (j), although other units are used as well depending on the forms of energy involved—for example, light, heat, chemical, mechanical, or electrical.

> **53.** Which is most likely to occur if a loose bundle of feathers and a golf ball, each having a mass of 1 kilogram, are thrown straight up with equal but slight force from the Moon's surface?
>
> **(1)** The golf ball will fall to the Moon's surface before the feathers.
>
> **(2)** The feathers will fall to the Moon's surface before the golf ball.
>
> **(3)** Neither object will return to the Moon's surface.
>
> **(4)** They will fall to the Moon's surface at the same time.
>
> **(5)** Both objects will accelerate indefinitely.

The two objects have the same mass and velocity, and so they have the same constant momentum. Without atmospheric air friction to alter the momentum of either one, both will maintain the same velocity regardless of their form or shape. Eventually, however, both will fall to the Moon's surface—and at the same time—but only because of the Moon's gravitational pull. **The correct answer is (4).**

QUESTION 54 REFERS TO THE FOLLOWING GRAPH.

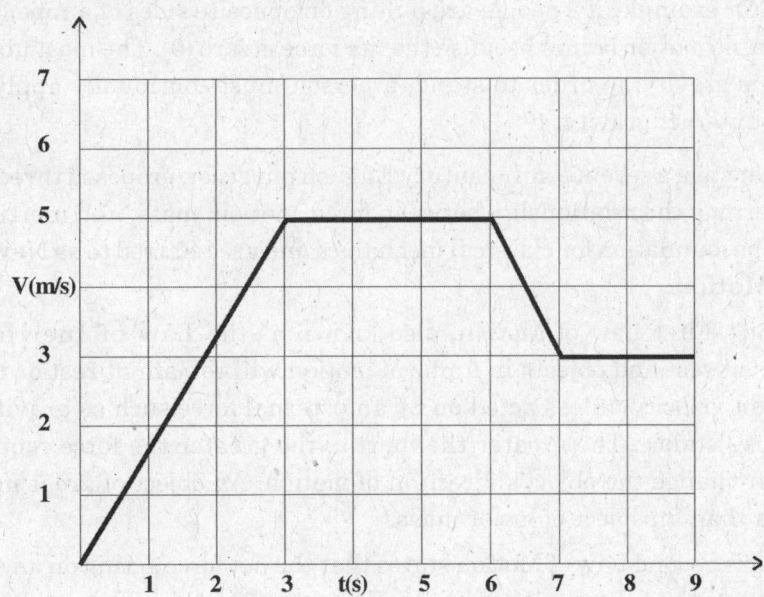

54. The graph shows a track athlete running a race along a straight track. Velocity as a function of time is shown for the first 9 seconds of the race. What is occurring from 3 to 6 seconds into the race?

(1) negative acceleration

(2) positive acceleration

(3) constant velocity

(4) a change in speed

(5) a change in direction

Up to second 3, the runner is accelerating (velocity is increasing). From second 3 through second 5, velocity is constant at 5 meters per second. During second 6, negative acceleration is occurring, and during seconds 7 through 9, velocity is once again constant. **The correct answer is (3).**

Inertia, Force, and the Laws of Motion

Force refers to any of a variety of factors that cause an object to change speed or direction. It can be a push or pull that starts, stops, or changes the direction in which an object may be traveling. Force occurs when you lift a can of soda to your mouth or when you slam a door shut. Motion or a change in direction only occurs when there is a *net* force. For example, if 2 people are pulling on opposite sides of a rope, both applying equal force, no motion occurs because the net force is zero (0). The most ubiquitous force in nature is gravity; in order to stand, a person must continually apply an opposing force to counteract gravity.

Sir Isaac Newton, a seventeenth-century English physicist, proposed three fundamental laws concerning the relationship between force, motion, mass, and inertia. These laws provided the foundation for classical mechanics and are referred to as **Newton's Three Laws of Motion:**

http://bit.ly/hippo_phys7

❶ Newton's First Law of Motion, also known as the **Law of Inertia**, states that objects at rest and objects in uniform motion will remain at rest or in motion at a constant velocity unless acted on by an external force such as gravity, friction, or other resistance. The greater the inertia, the greater the force required to start, stop, or change the object's direction of motion. An object of great mass has more inertia than an object of lower mass.

http://bit.ly/hippo_phys8

❷ Newton's Second Law of Motion states that the net force acting on an object is equal to its mass times its acceleration, or $F = m \times a$. This law is also called the **Law of Force.** The unit of force is known as a *Newton*. In this formula, m is the mass of the object, measured in kilograms, and a is the acceleration in meters per second per second m/s^2. Thus, a force of 1 Newton = 1 kg m/s^2.

http://bit.ly/hippo_phys11

❸ Newton's Third Law of Motion states that for every action there is an equal and opposite reaction. In other words, when one object exerts a force on a second object, the second object exerts an equal force on the first in an opposing direction. This law is also called the **Law of Action and Reaction.** For example, when you hit a tennis ball with a racket, the racket exerts a forward force on the ball while the ball exerts an equal backward force on the racket.

Friction is a force on objects that are in contact with each other. The force of friction resists motion of the objects relative to each other. Friction always works in the opposite direction of motion. For example, a traveling automobile has a certain amount of inertia based on its momentum. But the contact between the tires and the road creates a frictional force that acts upon the automobile to decrease its rate of motion.

 http://bit.ly/hippo_phys12

55. What force must a baseball bat exert on a baseball of a mass 0.2 kg to give it an acceleration of 8500 m/sec2 ?

   (1) 42.5 Newtons

   (2) 170 Newtons

   (3) 425 Newtons

   (4) 1700 Newtons

   (5) Not enough information is given.

Apply the equation $F = m \times a$:

$F = 0.2 \times 8500 = 1700$ Newtons. **The correct answer is (4).**

56. Which of the following demonstrate(s) Newton's First Law of Motion?

    A. the thrust of a rocket engine during liftoff

    B. the exertion of a weightlifter pressing a barbell overhead

    C. the lean of a motorcyclist in the direction of a turn

    D. the effort needed to stop yourself after stepping off a moving bus

   (1) A only

   (2) C only

   (3) D only

   (4) A and D only

   (5) C and D only

A moving motorcycle and a moving bus passenger both have inertia—they tend to remain in motion in the same direction and at the same velocity. Force is required to change a motorcycle's direction or to stop forward movement after jumping off a moving bus. Statement A demonstrates Newton's Third Law, and statement B demonstrates Newton's Second Law. **The correct answer is (5).**

http://bit.ly/hippo_phys13

Heat and Thermodynamics

Heat refers to the energy that flows from a body of higher temperature to one of lower temperature. The physical tendency is for energy to continue to flow in this direction until **thermal equilibrium** is reached—in other words, until the temperatures of the two systems are equal. For example, if you mixed two glasses of water of unequal temperatures together, the warmer portion becomes cooler until the entire mixture is equal in temperature.

Heat energy is produced by the vibrations of molecules—the greater the vibrations, the greater the heat. The standard unit of heat is the *calorie,* defined as the amount of heat required to increase the temperature of 1 gram of water by 1° Celsius. (Another type of calorie, the food calorie, is defined as 1000 calories.) The standard unit of measurement of heat is the joule (J): one calorie equals 4.186 J.

http://bit.ly/hippo_phys14

Transfer of Heat

The scientific study of heat transfer is called **thermodynamics.** Among the four laws of thermodynamics, the first two are the most fundamental. The first law states that the amount of energy added to a system is equal to the sum of its increase in heat energy and the work done to the system. The second law states that heat energy cannot be transferred from a body at a lower temperature to a body at a higher temperature without additional energy.

Heat can be transferred in three ways:

http://bit.ly/hippo_phys15

- **Conduction** is the transfer of heat through a solid material. In conduction, kinetic energy is transferred from faster molecules to slower molecules by direct contact. But the positions of the molecules change very little, if any, so the solid material (the conductor) maintains its structure. Conduction explains how the handle of a cooking pan or the portion of a teaspoon sticking out of a hot cup of tea heats up, even though the handle or spoon is not in direct contact with the heat source. Different solid materials vary greatly in their ability to conduct heat. Poor conductors absorb more heat than they transfer and hence make good heat insulators.

http://bit.ly/hippo_phys16

- **Convection** refers to the transfer of heat through a fluid (either a liquid or gas). The liquid or gas near the heat source heats up, and then expands outward from the source, resulting in currents. The heated (less dense) liquid or gas rises, and cooler (denser) liquid or gas moves inward toward the heat source, where it is then heated. It is this circulatory process that is at work in convection ovens and many ocean currents.

http://bit.ly/hippo_phys17

- **Radiation** is the transfer of heat by electromagnetic waves. The molecules of a substance receiving these waves of energy absorb that energy, thereby increasing their own kinetic energy and thus the temperature of the substance. Radiant energy is widely used in everyday life. For example, microwaves provide the energy for heating food in a microwave oven, and ultraviolet waves provide the energy that can tan and burn your skin.

Specific Heat and Latent Heat

Not all substances absorb heat to the same extent. In other words, substances differ widely in their **heat capacity (or thermal capacity),** defined as the ratio of the heat energy absorbed by a substance to its increase in temperature. A measure referred to as **specific heat** is used to express heat capacity. Specific heat is defined as the amount of heat required to raise the temperature of 1 gram of a substance by 1°C. The specific heat of water is 1 calorie per gram. The specific heat of iron is 0.11, which means that 1 gram of iron would require 0.11 calories to increase in temperature by 1°C. The specific heat of water is higher than that of iron, so if the same amount of heat is applied to equal quantities of water and iron, the iron will feel hotter.

 http://bit.ly/hippo_phys18

Substances often undergo changes of state—solid to liquid (or vice versa) or liquid to gas (or vice versa). During the brief phase that a change of state occurs, a substance either absorbs or releases heat while the temperature actually remains constant. This type of heat is called **latent heat.** The latent heat absorbed by the air when water condenses is what is behind the power of thunderstorms and hurricanes.

 http://bit.ly/hippo_phys19

57. Which of the following statements is NOT accurate?

  (1) Heat can flow only from a body of higher temperature to one of lower temperature.

  (2) Heat energy is produced by the vibrations of molecules.

  (3) Kinetic energy in a solid substance is transferred from faster molecules to slower molecules by direct contact.

  (4) Electromagnetic wave energy can increase the temperature of a substance by increasing the kinetic energy of its molecules.

  (5) Thermal equilibrium occurs when a cold gas or liquid increases in temperature until it equals that of its surrounding atmosphere.

The statements in choices (1), (2), (3), and (4) are accurate statements. The statement in choice (5), however, contradicts the first law of thermodynamics. **The correct answer is (5).**

58. A steel spoon and a silver spoon are put into a cup of hot coffee at the same time. The silver spoon rapidly approaches the temperature of the coffee, while the steel spoon increases in temperature only slightly. What explains the difference?

  (1) The steel spoon has a lower specific heat.

  (2) The silver spoon has a lower specific heat.

  (3) The steel spoon retains more latent heat than the silver spoon.

  (4) The silver spoon retains more latent heat than the steel spoon.

  (5) The silver spoon radiates heat at a faster rate than the steel spoon.

The steel spoon has a lower thermal capacity, as measured by specific heat. **The correct answer is (2).**

Waves

The concept of a **wave** is one of the most important in physics. A wave can be an oscillation or vibration that creates a disturbance in a medium, such as water or air, as in the case of sound waves. Or a wave can be a series of quantitative values moving through space, as in the case of electromagnetic waves.

Scientists measure waves in various ways, and these measurements are used to identify such phenomena as the visibility and color of light, the pitch and loudness of a sound, and the strength of an electromagnetic wave. These measurements are based on the various features of any wave, as shown in the next diagram.

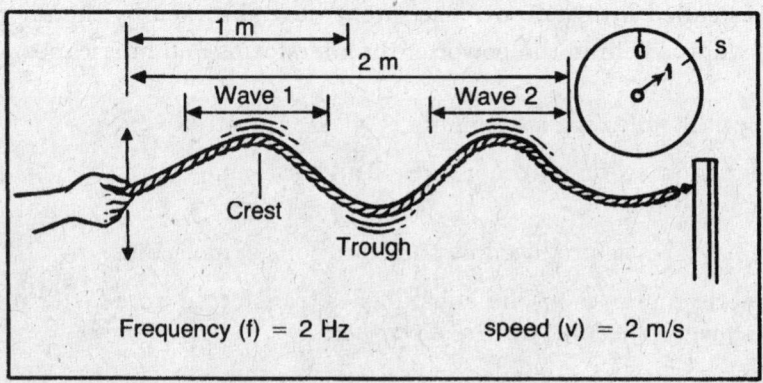

As you can see in this diagram, the **crest** of a wave is its top, and the **trough** of the wave is its bottom. A wave's **amplitude** is *half* the vertical distance from peak to trough and is used to measure the strength, or magnitude, of a wave. The **wavelength** is the distance between consecutive troughs or consecutive crests. Referring to the diagram, assume that the wavelength is 1 meter. Visualize the waves moving from left to right at 2 meters per second, which is the wave's velocity. The number of crests passing a certain point (a "cycle") per unit time is the **frequency** of a wave. At a given wave velocity, the shorter the wavelength the higher the frequency. Each of the following two equations expresses a wave's frequency:

$$\text{frequency} = \frac{\text{velocity}}{\text{wavelength}}$$

$$\text{frequency} = \frac{\text{wave cycles}}{\text{unit of time}}$$

Wavelength is generally measured in meters, while frequency is measured in *hertz*. (1 hertz = 1 cycle per second.) Electromagnetic waves vary in wavelength and frequency, but in a vacuum they all travel at the speed of light, which is 3×10^8 m/sec.

Light Waves

Light travels in waves. The variations of colors we see are a result of different frequency ranges of light. The light spectrum ranges from long radio waves to short gamma rays. Humans can see color only within a particular range called the **visible spectrum.** The visible spectrum for humans ranges from low-frequency, red waves to high-frequency, violet waves.

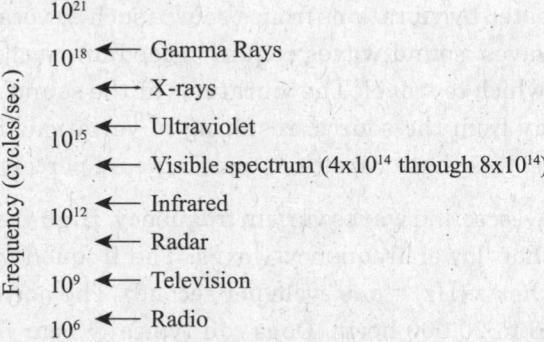

Frequency (cycles/sec.)

10^{21}

10^{18} ← Gamma Rays

← X-rays

10^{15} ← Ultraviolet

← Visible spectrum (4×10^{14} through 8×10^{14})

10^{12} ← Infrared

← Radar

10^{9} ← Television

10^{6} ← Radio

As shown above, the invisible spectrum is composed of many different rays, each one marked by a distinct frequency range. Infrared rays are detectable through heat; X-rays travel through matter and are used to view structures beneath the skin; ultraviolet rays from the sun can damage skin; and gamma rays—the shortest rays—originate from radioactive substances.

Light normally moves along a straight line called a **ray.** When a ray of light hits a surface such as a mirror, the light is reflected back. The light ray moving toward the mirror is the **incident ray.** The ray of light bouncing back is the **reflected ray.** As the next figure shows, the angle of the incident ray and the angle of the reflected ray are equal.

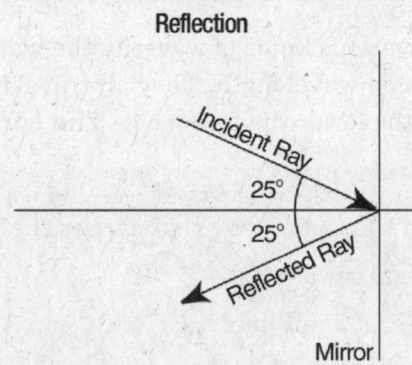

Reflection

Incident Ray

25°

25°

Reflected Ray

Mirror

When light rays pass through different mediums, such as air and water, the rays can bend. The bending of light rays is called **refraction.** You may have noticed that objects immersed in water or some other liquid seem bent or broken at the point where they enter the liquid.

A **rainbow** is the result of both refraction and reflection. Rays of light entering a water droplet suspended in air bend, then reflect off the back surface of the droplet, and then refract again when exiting the droplet. In this way, the droplet serves as a **prism,** dispersing various light waves entering each droplet into different frequencies of the color spectrum, depending on the angle at which they reflect off the back of the round water droplet.

Sound Waves

 http://bit.ly/hippo_phys22

Sound waves are created by vibrations from a source such as vocal chords or a speaker cones. Unlike light waves, sound waves require a medium such as air, water, or an elastic solid through which to travel. The vibrations at the sound's source push the air or other medium away from the source, resulting in variations in pressure, density, and even temperature. It is these variations that our ears perceive as distinct sounds.

Like other types of waves, sound waves vary in frequency. High-frequency sound waves are higher in pitch than lower frequency waves. The frequency of a sound wave is measured in hertz (1 hertz (Hz) = one cycle per second). The normal range for human hearing is between 20 to 20,000 hertz. Dogs can typically hear frequencies of 50,000 Hz. Ultrasound technology uses a very high frequency of 106 Hz. Sound waves also vary in amplitude. The greater the amplitude of the wave, the "louder" the sound, as measured in *decibels*.

59. Ultraviolet waves and X-rays differ from each other in which respect?

    (1) wavelength

    (2) amplitude

    (3) velocity

    (4) angle of reflection

    (5) visibility

The key distinction among various kinds of waves in the light spectrum involves their frequencies, which depends on wavelength. They all travel at the same speed, and so the longer the wavelength the lower the frequency. **The correct answer is (1).**

60. A certain AM radio station broadcasts at a frequency of 550 kHz. What does this mean in terms of the radio wave that carries the station's broadcast?

    (1) The wavelength is 0.55 meters.

    (2) The wavelength is 0.55 millimeters.

    (3) The wave's frequency is within the audible range for humans.

    (4) The wave is received by radios at a rate of 550 cycles per second.

    (5) The wave is received by radios at a rate of 550,000 cycles per second.

One kilohertz = 1000 hertz. (550 × 1000 = 550,000) So the wave frequency is 550,000 cycles per second. **The correct answer is (5).**

Magnetism

Individual atoms can form magnetic fields when closed loops called *lines of force* come together densely to form north and south poles. If the magnetic fields of all of the atoms in a substance are aligned, the entire substance acts as a single **magnet** with a north pole and a south pole and a surrounding magnetic field of closed loops. To show the magnetic field of a magnet, iron filings can be sprinkled on a piece of paper under which the magnet has been placed. The filings will align themselves along the loops in the magnetic field.

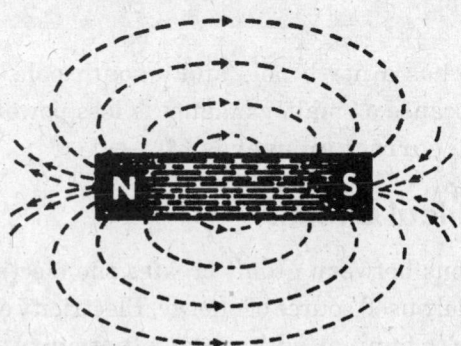

Iron and iron-based metals are most readily magnetized and are attracted to magnets. The north pole of one magnet attracts the south pole of another, but two north poles and two south poles repel one another.

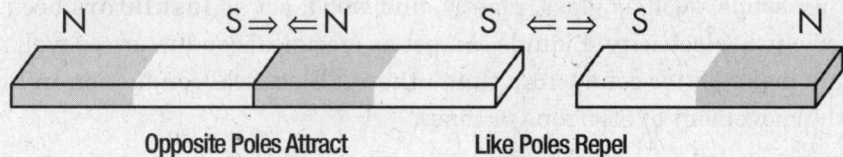

Opposite Poles Attract   **Like Poles Repel**

Once magnetized, some iron-based metals can become **permanent magnets.** These are the kinds of magnets you find on refrigerator doors. Others can act as magnets only in the presence of an electric current. When a wire coil is wrapped around an iron core and an electric current is run through the wire, the entire apparatus becomes an **electromagnet.** "Turning off" the magnet simply requires discontinuing the electric current. You have probably seen large electromagnets used at scrap yards to lift and move junked metal objects.

61. If a permanent magnet is cut in two, each piece becomes a separate magnet. Which of the following will be true as a result?

(1) One piece will carry a positive charge, and the other piece will carry a negative charge.

(2) The two pieces will attract each other.

(3) The two pieces will repel each other.

(4) Each piece will have a north and south magnetic pole.

(5) The magnetic force of each piece will be the same as that of the magnet before it was cut.

By definition, a magnet has a north pole and a south pole, with opposing charges. Choice (5) is incorrect because a smaller magnet is less powerful than a larger one of the same substance. **The correct answer is (4).**

Electricity and Electrical Circuits

http://bit.ly/hippo_phys23

The movement of electrons between atoms creates the electric currents we know as electricity—the most widely used source of energy. Electricity exists in two forms: static and electric current. You're familiar with **static electricity,** especially if you've ever shuffled across a carpet in your socks and then touched something. This form of electricity is called "static" because it is an electric charge resting on an object. In contrast, an **electric current** occurs through the movement of electrons. Electrons can move through all three states of matter (solids, liquids, and gases). Some solids, especially metals, can act as good **electrical conductors** because they allow electrons to flow easily. Other solids, such as glass, plastic, and wood, act as **insulators** because they conduct very little electricity. Liquids can act as electrical conductors as well and, like solids, some make better conductors than others. (Electrical conduction in liquid can occur by the movement of electrons or ions.)

The strength of an electric current is measured in units called *amperes* (amps). Amperes measure the flow of electric charge past a certain point in one second (coulomb/sec). **Resistance** is the opposition to a current and is measured in *ohms* (Ω). Voltage is the energy that moves an electrical current through the conductor. Voltage is measured in Joules per coulomb (J/coulomb).

An **electrical circuit** is a closed path for electrons to flow along. Circuits provide usable electricity to power everything from light bulbs to televisions. A typical electrical circuit consists of the following components:

- A power source, such as a battery

- A conductor, usually a wire, for electrons to flow through

- Resistors—devices, such as a light bulb or television, that use the energy

- A switch that opens and closes the path around which the current flows

An electrical current can be measured and expressed in amperes by applying **Ohms Law:**

$$\text{current} = \frac{\text{voltage}}{\text{resistance } (\Omega)}$$

There are two basic types of electrical circuits. A **series circuit** is one in which the current must pass through every resistor in order to return to the battery or other power source. If a resistor anywhere in the circuit "goes out," the circuit breaks. In the next illustration, for example, if one light bulb goes out, all of the other bulbs will also go out.

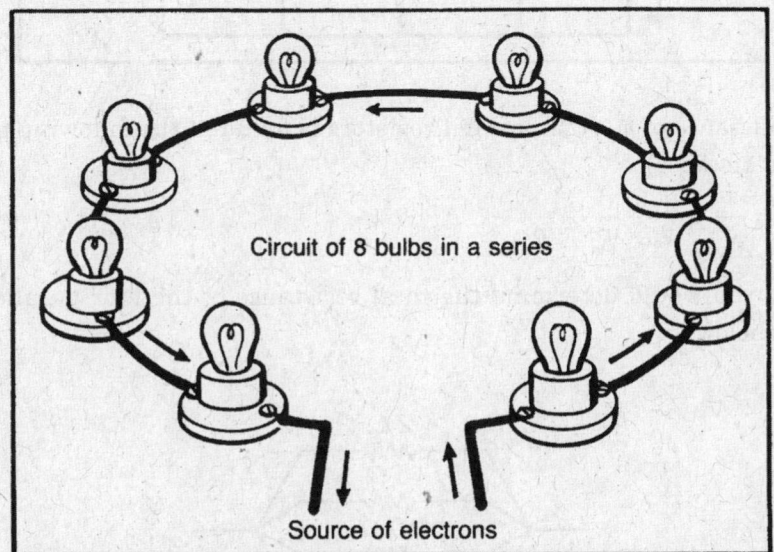

Circuit of 8 bulbs in a series

Source of electrons

When more than one resistor is in a series circuit, the value of all resistors are added together to determine the total resistance. For example, in the following schematic of a series circuit, the total resistance = 12Ω. (The squiggly line represents a resistor.)

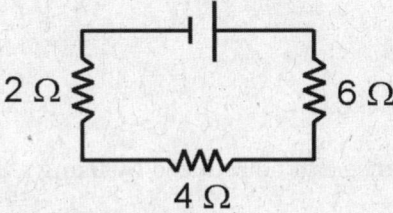

A **parallel circuit** is one in which the main current is divided into individual pathways; if there is a block or break in any part of one path, the electrons are still permitted to flow through via the other pathway. The circuit illustrated next provides a different pathway for each of four appliances. If one appliance is turned off, the others can still operate.

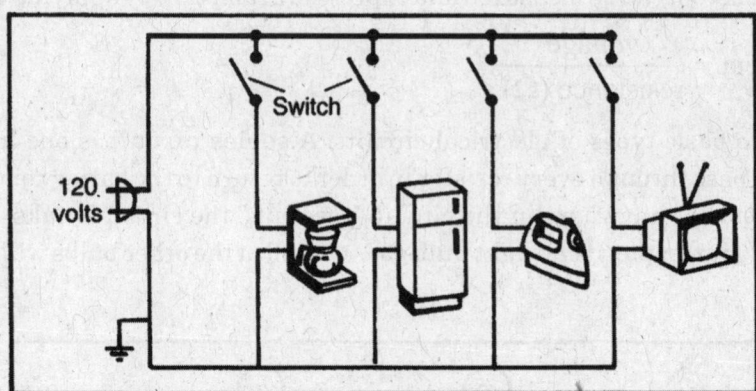

The total resistance of a set of parallel resistors is found in the following manner (R_T is the total resistance):

$$\frac{1}{R_T} = \frac{1}{R_1} + \frac{1}{R_2} + \frac{1}{R_3} + \frac{1}{R_4} + \ldots$$

Here is how you would determine the total resistance of the four parallel resistors represented below:

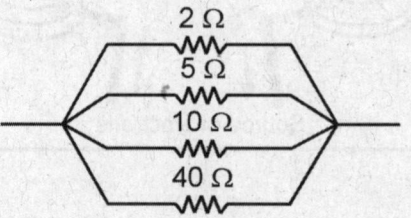

$$\frac{1}{R_T} = \frac{1}{2\Omega} + \frac{1}{5\Omega} + \frac{1}{10\Omega} + \frac{1}{40\Omega}$$

$$\frac{1}{R_T} = .825\Omega$$

$$R_T \approx 1.21\Omega$$

As you can see, total resistance can be reduced by using a parallel circuit instead of a series circuit.

62. How much current flows through a device that has a resistance of 60Ω when a 12-volt charge is supplied?

(1) 0.2 amps

(2) 0.72 amps

(3) 2.0 amps

(4) 7.2 amps

(5) 20 amps

Apply Ohm's law:

$\text{current} = \dfrac{12\text{V}}{60\Omega} = 0.2 \text{ amps}$. **The correct answer is (1).**

QUESTION 63 REFERS TO THE FOLLOWING DIAGRAM.

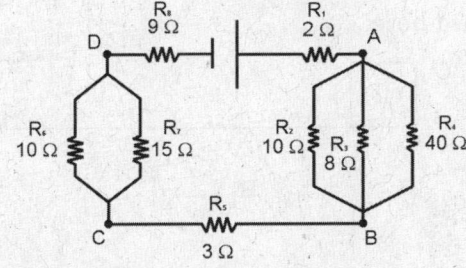

63. The electrical circuit represented above incorporates both series and parallel circuitry. What is the total resistance from point B to the end of the circuit?

(1) 6Ω

(2) 10Ω

(3) 18Ω

(4) 22Ω

(5) 28Ω

First find the total resistance of the parallel circuitry between points C and D:

$$\frac{1}{R_T} = \frac{1}{10\Omega} + \frac{1}{15\Omega}$$

$$\frac{1}{R_T} = \frac{3}{30\Omega} + \frac{2}{30\Omega}$$

$$\frac{1}{R_T} = \frac{5}{30\Omega} = \frac{1}{6\Omega}$$

$$R_T = 6\Omega$$

Then add this resistance to the series resistors 3Ω and 9Ω. The total resistance is 18Ω. **The correct answer is (3).**

Simple Machines

The mechanical devices that allow us to perform everyday tasks are called machines. Everyday devices such as door knobs, zippers, and scissors are all based on certain basic mechanical principles. Most mechanical devices are composed of variations on the six **simple machines** described next. These machines provide a **mechanical advantage,** which means that by using them properly, the force required to move an object over a given distance is reduced. (In other words, they make work easier.)

The Lever

A **lever** consists of a rod or pole that rests on an object at a fixed point called a **fulcrum.** The object to be lifted is referred to as the **load** and may be placed at various positions with respect to the fulcrum. There are three types of levers based on fulcrum placement, as illustrated and described here:

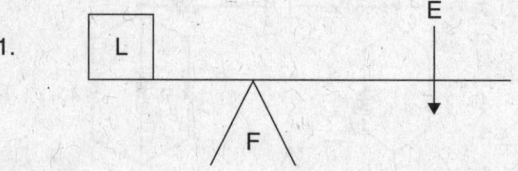

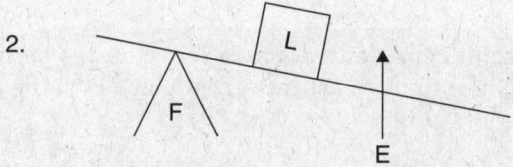

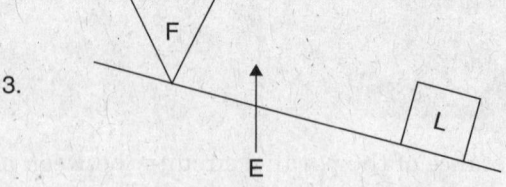

1. **First-class levers** have a fulcrum that is positioned centrally, between the load (what is being lifted) and the **force** (the exertion applied to do the lifting). Examples of this class of lever include a seesaw, scissors, pliers, and a crowbar.
2. **Second-class levers** have a fulcrum at one end, the force at other end, and the load in the middle. A wheelbarrow is a good example of this type of lever.
3. **Third-class levers** have a fulcrum and force at one end and the load at the other. Examples of this type of lever include tongs and the hammer.

The Pulley

 http://bit.ly/hippo_phys24

A **pulley** alters the direction in which a force moves a load so the load moves upward as the force is applied downward. The basic pulley consists of a single wheel over which a belt, chain, or rope is run to change the direction of the pull on the load.

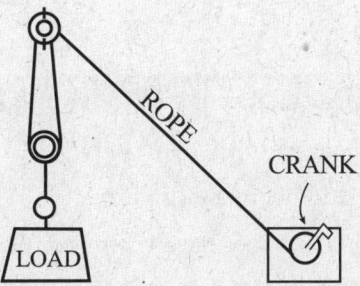

As shown above, a pulley system that consists of two or more wheels further reduces the force needed to lift a load by distributing the work over a longer length of belt, rope, or chain. The total amount of work that must be done to lift the load a given distance is the same as with a single-wheel pulley. However, the work is distributed over a greater distance, and so less force (exertion) is required.

The Incline Plane, the Screw, and the Wedge

 http://bit.ly/hippo_phys25

An **incline plane** (shown below) is simply a ramp. Heavy objects can be moved to a higher position more easily by pushing or pulling them up a ramp rather than lifting them vertically. The more gradual the incline, the less force is required to move the load but the more distance the load must be moved to reach the top. In any case, the total work required is the same. A sloping driveway and a staircase are two examples of inclined planes.

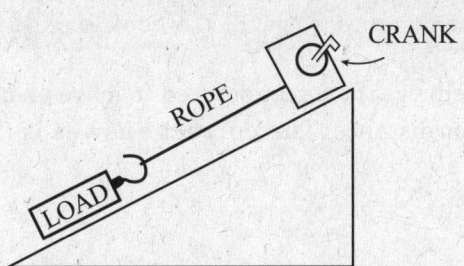

A **screw** is an incline plane in a spiral rather than a straight-path configuration. Drilling into a piece of wood at the gradual angle of the screw's threads requires less force (exertion) than hammering a nail straight down into the wood. A **wedge** is another specialized incline plane. When you use a wedge, you apply force to the plane to move it under the load, thereby lifting the load up onto the plane (the wedge). Examples of a wedge include a letter opener and an axe.

The Wheel and Axle

The mechanical advantage of a **wheel-and-axle** machine is provided by the large diameter of the wheel compared to that of the axle. The wheel's circular path is greater, but less force is required to rotate it than to rotate the smaller axle. Examples of a simple wheel-and-axle machine include a door knob, bicycle pedals, a steering wheel, and a screwdriver.

64. How might you enhance the mechanical advantage of a first-class lever?

(1) Move the fulcrum closer to the load to be lifted.

(2) Increase the load and decrease the force.

(3) Move the fulcrum closer to where the force is to be applied.

(4) Shorten the bar that rests on the fulcrum.

(5) Reverse the direction of the force.

Moving the fulcrum closer to the load (and farther from where the force is applied) increases the leverage—less force is required to lift the load. **The correct answer is (1).**

65. What do a double-wheel pulley, an incline plane, a screw, a wedge, and a wheel-and-axle device share in common?

Each type of machine provides a mechanical advantage by

(1) applying force more directly on an object to be moved

(2) distributing the same work over a greater distance

(3) reducing resistance of an object by circular motion instead of straight-line motion

(4) creating a store of energy in an object to be moved

(5) decreasing the distance over which an object must be moved

Each type of machine reduces the force required to move an object by distributing the total work over a greater distance. **The correct answer is (2).**

SUMMING IT UP

- The GED® Science Test measures critical-thinking skills rather than knowledge. However, a review of the three content areas—life sciences, earth and space science, and physical science—will help you to handle the test questions with greater ease and confidence.

- Science attempts to provide explanations for natural phenomena through investigation. In order to sort out unreasonable explanations from plausible ones, scientists apply logic and common sense by means of the scientific method, which involves four fundamental steps: observation, hypothesis, experiment, and conclusion.

- Biology is the scientific study of living organisms, including plants and animals, and consists of three major branches: zoology, botany, and ecology. This review began by examining biological life at the cellular and molecular level; then, biological organisms were examined in terms of organ systems and as individuals. The review concluded by examining individual organisms as members of a community and as part of an ecosystem.

- Geology deals with the composition of the Earth and past and present events (both interior and exterior) that have shaped it. Oceanography involves physics, biology, chemistry, and geology as they pertain to ocean-related processes. Meteorology is the study of the Earth's atmosphere, weather, and climate. Astronomy is the study of the universe and the objects in it.

- Chemistry is the study of the composition, interactions, properties, and structure of matter and the changes that matter undergoes. It involves looking at ways to take substances apart and put the parts together again in new ways.

- Physics is the scientific study of matter, energy, space, and time—and how they are interrelated. Physics is closely related to all other fields of science, since its laws are universal. The living systems of biology are made of matter particles that follow the laws of physics. Chemistry explores how atoms, small units of matter, interact to form molecules according to the laws of physics. The study of geology and astronomy deal to a great extent with the physics of the Earth and of celestial bodies.

PART VI

THE LANGUAGE ARTS, READING TEST

Mastering the Language Arts, Reading Test

chapter 10

OVERVIEW

- **Taking the Language Arts, Reading Test**
- **Understanding fiction**
- **Understanding nonfiction**
- **General test-taking strategies**
- **Summing it up**

THE LANGUAGE ARTS, READING TEST— IN A NUTSHELL

Time allowed: 65 minutes

Number of passages: Expect 6 to 8 (the number can vary)

Length of each passage: 200–400 words (10 to 25 lines for poetry)

Total number of questions: 40 multiple-choice (5 choices per question)

Number of questions per passage: Expect 4 to 8 (the number can vary)

TAKING THE LANGUAGE ARTS, READING TEST

The Language Arts, Reading Test gauges your ability to understand, interpret, evaluate, synthesize, and apply information contained in fiction as well as nonfiction texts. The test consists of several reading passages, each one followed by several multiple-choice questions. Reading Test passages are drawn from a wide variety of sources. Here's the breakdown of what you can expect during the Reading Test:

- **Fiction (75 percent):** 30 questions, based on passages from the following categories:
  - **Prose fiction** (three passages, eighteen questions)
  - **Drama** (one passage, six questions)
  - **Poetry** (one poem, six questions)

- **Nonfiction (25 percent):** 10 questions, based on passages from any *two* of the following categories:
  - **Informational and opinion texts** (articles, editorials, speeches, and position papers)

- Literary nonfiction (biographies, autobiographies, diaries, journals, letters, essays, and oral history)
- Critical reviews of the visual and performing arts (painting, sculpture, mixed media, film, stage productions, and musical recordings and productions)
- Workplace and community documents (policy and mission statements, employee handbooks and training manuals, employee benefits statements, business communications, and legal documents)

Regardless of what sort of passage you're dealing with, the questions will all cover the same basic reading skills. Here is the breakdown of the broad skill areas covered by Reading Test questions. As indicated by the percentage numbers, some areas receive greater emphasis than others.

- **Comprehension (20 percent):** Understanding and recalling specific information from the passage

- **Analysis and Interpretation (30–35 percent):** Understanding what is suggested or implied in the passage and drawing reasonable inferences and conclusions from passage information

- **Evaluation and Synthesis (30–35 percent):** Understanding the passage's central idea and concern; inferring the author's intent or purpose; recognizing the purpose of and relationships among various parts of the passage; characterizing the passage as a whole

- **Application (15 percent):** Applying what is stated and implied in the passage to other contexts; applying the author's reasoning to other situations

During the Reading Test, expect a total of six to eight passages and four to eight questions per passage—forty questions in total. Each passage of prose will be 200 to 400 words in length (about a half page, on average), and the poem will be ten to twenty-five lines in length. Here are two additional features common to all passages:

- Every fifth line of each passage will be numbered. Some questions might refer to portions of the passage by line number.

- Immediately preceding each passage is a brief **purpose question** in bold face. Purpose questions are designed to help you focus your attention and anticipate what each passage is about. You will not be required to answer purpose questions.

In the pages ahead, you'll learn how to read and understand the various types of fiction and nonfiction passages you'll encounter on the test. For each type, you'll read sample passages and attempt GED®-style questions based on them. At the end of the lesson, you'll review some general strategies—ones that apply to every kind of reading passage.

UNDERSTANDING FICTION

A work of **fiction** is one that is made up; in other words, it involves imaginary people and events. Works of fiction can take a variety of different forms, but the three main forms are *prose fiction*, *drama*, and *poetry*. On the GED® Reading Test, you can expect at least five reading passages involving fiction. A prose or drama passage will be 200–400 words in length (about a half page, on average). A passage of poetry will be eight to twenty-five lines in length. Here's a breakdown of what you can probably expect (keep in mind that the number of passages and questions may very slightly):

- Prose fiction (three passages, eighteen questions in total)

- Drama (one passage, six questions)

- Poetry (one passage, six questions)

A passage may provide an entire work of fiction if the work is brief, as in the case of many poems. Generally, however, passages are excerpted from longer works of fiction—novels, short stories, and plays.

In the following sections, you'll learn more about all three types of fiction, and you'll learn how best to read fiction in order to understand it in ways that will help you most on the GED®. For each type, you'll also read a variety of sample passages and answer GED®-style questions based on them.

The Elements of Fiction

Most passages on the GED® Reading Test are passages of fiction. As was just noted, a fictional work is a work based on someone's imagination. In other words, the story, characters, and other elements of a fictional work are made up by the author. Even stories based on real people or real situations can be fiction. A work of fiction can be in the form of a short story, a novel, a poem, or a drama. The term **prose fiction** is generally used in reference to short stories and novels, as opposed to plays or poems. (The word *prose* refers to the ordinary form of writing or speaking.)

The **plot** in fiction is the story line—the story's events strung together in a particular sequence or order. A story's events can flow chronologically (in the order they occur in time) or they can be revealed out of order or sequence. Works of fiction usually begin with the first event and trace subsequent events chronologically. However, the author may choose a different sequence instead. For instance, the author may begin the story with the final event and then unravel the plot by going back to the first event in order to explain what led up to the event.

A story's **narrator** is the "voice" that tells the story—the storyteller. The narrator relates the story's events as he sees them unfold, from his *point of view*. Usually a story is told from either a first-person or a third-person point of view. A work written in **first person** is told from the narrator's own perspective. Throughout the story, the narrator speaks in terms of *I* or *me*, so the reader follows the story as seen through the narrator's eyes. When reading fiction that is written in first person, the reader is limited by the narrator's limited knowledge. The reader knows only what the narrator sees and thinks, and must interpret the actions and thoughts of the other characters through the narrator's eyes, responding to events and other characters through the narrator's subjective perspective. In contrast, a work of fiction written in **third person** is told from the perspective of a narrator who knows and reveals *everything* to the reader. From this point of view, the narrator does not speak in terms of *I* but rather in terms of *he*, *she*, and *they*. The third-person point of view allows the reader glimpses of all the characters' actions and feelings through an all-knowing, or omniscient, narrator.

The figures involved in the plot are known as **characters.** The main characters are those around whom the plot revolves. Minor characters are incidental characters who become involved in the plot to a lesser extent. A story's characters are revealed to the reader in several different ways. Usually, the narrator describes what the characters look like and tells the reader about their personalities. Characters are also revealed by how they act and what they say. For instance, a character might behave in a consistently shy manner, or continually talk about herself, or use poor grammar in his or her speech. Finally, characters are understood by what the others in the story say or think about them. A character's spoken words to another character are referred to as **dialogue.**

The **tone** of a story is the attitude of the narrator or the author toward the subject or event. The reader's impression of the subject or event may be colored by how the narrator or author feels about it. The **mood** is an overall atmosphere the author creates by carefully selecting certain words and details. The **setting** of a story is the author's description of the time and place in which the story occurs. Not only does the setting make the story more real for the reader, it also helps to create the mood of the story. An event that occurs at midnight on a rainy night creates more of a mood of fear than the same event occurring on a sunny day.

Authors of fiction use a variety of **literary devices** to help convey ideas, emphasize certain points, incite the reader's imagination, and provide a more interesting and enjoyable reading experience. To help describe a story's setting or to describe how the story's characters experience certain events, fiction authors often employ **imagery**— the use of language to convey a sense experience (sight, sound, smell, taste, or touch). To help convey ideas and enhance interest, fiction authors often use **figurative language**—the use of language in ways that give words and phrases a meaning other than their common, or *literal*, meaning. A particular instance of figurative language is commonly referred to as a **figure of speech.**

Figurative language can be used to make an abstract idea concrete or to vitalize an idea. Often a figure of speech will compare two seemingly different things to reveal their similarities. For instance, when someone says they are *on pins and needles* waiting for something to happen, that person is using a figure of speech. Obviously, the person is not literally on pins and needles. The expression, however, does convey the person's excitement about whatever might happen.

An author's use of figurative language might apply to larger elements of a story as well, perhaps even to the entire story. For example, an entire narrative might serve as a *metaphor* or as a *symbol*, by which the story's events are intended either to substitute for or represent some other story. Or a narrative might be intended as an *allegory*, which can either be understood literally or taken to mean something more, or deeper, as well.

Literary devices, especially figurative language, are used most often in poetry. Later in this lesson you'll learn how to read and understand poetry. There you'll take a closer look at the various literary devices that poets and prose fiction writers use.

Prose Fiction

Your GED® Reading Test will probably contain three prose fiction passages that are drawn from short stories and novels. Each passage will be 200–400 words in length (a half page, more or less). Even a 400-word passage is a very manageable piece of text; you should have little difficulty reading 400 words and remembering the information within the passage.

One prose-fiction passage will be from a pre-1920 work, another will be from a work written from 1920–1960, and a third will be from a post-1960 work. So you can expect to encounter a variety of writing styles, characters, cultural settings, and historical references. A passage might contain only narrative, but more likely it will contain dialogue as well. A passage's style might be formal and heavy-handed, or it might be casual or even conversational. In short, expect anything. Keep in mind, though, that the GED® will *not* test you on your knowledge of literature, literary traditions, or specific authors. To answer the test questions, all you'll need to know will be expressed or implied in the passages and in the questions themselves.

Regardless of when or by whom a work of prose fiction was written or what style of writing the author uses, the guidelines for reading and understanding prose fiction are essentially the same. As you read a passage of prose fiction, ask yourself the following questions that focus on the very same reading skills that the GED® covers:

- **Who is the narrator?** Is the story told in the first person—from the narrator's perspective? Or is it told in the third person—from the perspective of an all-knowing observer outside the story itself?

- **What is the setting and mood of the passage?** Through the narrator or the characters, the reader might infer when and where certain events are taking place. Are they occurring during a particular era, decade, year, or season? During wartime, a time of prosperity and optimism, or a time of strife and despair? In a big city, in a rural village, or on a remote island? In a modest apartment, a large mansion, or a restaurant? What are the weather and other environmental conditions? Is the overall mood somber, joyous, upbeat, or tense? Understanding the setting and mood can help you interpret the passage's events and the characters' actions.

- **What is the author's main concern in the passage?** Think about the passage as a whole. Ask yourself what the author's intent is, as revealed through the narrator. Here are just a few examples of what an author might be trying to accomplish:

  - Describing a predicament or difficult situation
  - Inferring causes and consequences by recounting a series of events
  - Revealing the relationship between characters through their conversation
  - Revealing a character through his or her thoughts, actions, and reactions

- **What overall tone does the narrator set?** Pay attention to words and phrases that suggest the narrator's tone or attitude concerning the story's events and characters. Do the narrator's descriptions of the events suggest they are positive and welcome or that they are dreaded and portend bad things ahead? Do the narrator's descriptions of a character suggest approval, admiration, or sympathy, or does the narrator use language that seems to mock, deride, or make fun of the character?

- **What does the passage reveal about the story's characters?** A character's specific actions, spoken words, and thoughts can reveal a lot about his or her personality, motives, attitudes, and mood. They can also reveal how the character sees and relates to the story's other characters. They can reveal, too, how the character might behave in other situations. Pay careful attention to these details.

- **Beyond their literal meaning, what do the passage's words and ideas infer or suggest?** As noted earlier, fiction authors use a variety of literary devices to convey ideas. For example, be on the lookout for an author's use of the following devices:
  - *Irony* (a discrepancy between an actual situation and what one would normally expect under the circumstances)
  - *Paradox* (a situation that seems contradictory yet in fact is not)
  - *Metaphor* (naming one thing as a substitute for something else, as if the two are one and the same)

- **What events might have led to or might follow the ones described in the passage?** More specifically, ask yourself questions such as the following:
  - How might the situation described in the passage have come about?
  - Are the characters behaving in a way that certain prior events might help explain?
  - Do the characters' thoughts and their dialogue suggest what they might do later in the story?
  - Given the circumstances, what would naturally and logically occur next in time?

Inferring context from the passage can help you interpret the passage's events and the characters' actions.

Rest assured that GED® prose-fiction questions will not ask you to uncover obscure, hidden meanings behind the passage. Rather, the questions will focus on what we've just covered—the passage's main concern, setting, mood, tone, sequence of events, and character development—all as stated or implied in the passage.

In the following brief passage, which is about half the length of an average GED® passage, imagery and figurative language are used effectively to establish setting, mood, and tone, all of which serve to make a point in a powerful way. Read the passage, and then answer the three questions that follow it.

QUESTIONS 1–3 REFER TO THE FOLLOWING PASSAGE.

Dark spruce forest frowned on either side the frozen waterway. The trees had been stripped by a recent wind of their white covering of frost, and they seemed to lean towards each other, black and ominous, in the fading light. A vast silence reigned over the land. The land itself was a desolation, lifeless, without movement, so
5 lone and cold that the spirit of it was not even that of sadness. There was a hint in it of laughter, but of a laughter more terrible than any sadness—a laughter that was mirthless as the smile of the Sphinx, a laughter cold as the frost and partaking of the grimness of infallibility. It was the masterful and incommunicable wisdom of eternity laughing at the futility of life and the effort of life. It
10 was the Wild, the savage, frozen-hearted Northland Wild.

— from *White Fang*, by Jack London

1. Which word best describes the atmosphere of the setting?

   (1) desolation

   (2) mysteriousness

   (3) sadness

   (4) danger

   (5) tranquility

The narrator suggests desolation (meaning solitariness, loneliness, or isolation) from such imagery as the forest frowning, the trees being black and ominous, the fading light, and the land being lifeless. It would be natural to sense isolation and solitariness when all life is fading around you. **The correct answer is (1).**

2. What does "a laughter that was mirthless as the smile of the Sphinx" (line 7) imply?

   (1) a joyful smile

   (2) warmth and happiness

   (3) a sarcastic smile

   (4) a smile without warmth

   (5) a wise smile

The author is using figurative language here to convey an idea. Notice that he is drawing a comparison between two very different things: a land's laughter and a Sphinx's smile. (In fact, each of these two things is a figure of speech in itself, not to be read literally.) The fact that the Sphinx is made of stone and that the narrator describes the scene as cold and lonely both indicate that the smile of the Sphinx is one without warmth. **The correct answer is (4).**

3. Which statement best captures the essential idea of the passage?

   (1) The North is wild beyond compare.

   (2) In the North, life is short and brutal.

   (3) In the North, time endures all life.

   (4) Winter in the North can be deadly.

   (5) Silence and stillness are precious.

This deceptively difficult question essentially asks what the author's main point is in the passage. To answer it, you need to synthesize the passage's ideas and evaluate the passage as a whole. The narrator does refer to the "savage. . . Northland Wild"—choice (1), the futility of life—choice (2), the "lifeless" land—choice (4), and the "vast silence" and land "without movement"—choice (5). However, none of these observations captures the essence of the paragraph. The passage's main thrust is best expressed by the second-to-last sentence: "It was the masterful and incommunicable wisdom of eternity laughing at the futility of life and the effort of life" (lines 8–9). In other words, the passing of time ultimately defeats all life in the North. **The correct answer is (3).**

The next passage, also about half the length of an average GED® passage, was written by the same author as in the previous example. But here the focus is on character rather than setting and mood.

QUESTIONS 4–6 REFER TO THE FOLLOWING PASSAGE.

In the midst of roughness and brutality, Genevieve had shunned all that was rough and brutal. She saw but what she chose to see, and she chose always to see the best, avoiding coarseness and uncouthness without effort, as a matter of instinct. To begin with, she had been peculiarly unexposed. An only child, with an
5 invalid mother upon whom she attended, she had not joined in the street games and frolics of the children of the neighborhood. Her father, a mild-tempered, narrow-chested, anaemic little clerk, domestic because of his inherent disability to mix with men, had done his full share toward giving the home an atmosphere of sweetness and tenderness.

— from *The Game*, by Jack London

4. Which of the following does NOT account for Genevieve's character?

   (1) the fact she was an only child

   (2) the neighborhood children

   (3) her mother's invalidity

   (4) her father's domestic nature

   (5) her instincts

All choices except for choice (2) list factors that influenced Genevieve's character. The children in the neighborhood did not influence her because she had little contact with them. **The correct answer is (2).**

---

5. Which word best describes Genevieve?

    (1) anemic

    (2) predictable

    (3) timid

    (4) naive

    (5) sweet

Genevieve had clearly lived a sheltered life ("she had been peculiarly unexposed"). She intentionally avoided exposure to anything "rough and brutal" and to the "coarseness and uncouthness" of the real world. She preferred to keep to herself rather than joining in street games with other children. As a result, she was probably a bit innocent in the ways of the world, or *naive*. **The correct answer is (4).**

---

6. Which job would Genevieve's father probably be most suited for?

    (1) building inspector

    (2) school teacher

    (3) business manager

    (4) car salesman

    (5) gentleman's butler

The father is described as "domestic because of his inherent disability to mix with men." What this probably means is that he lacked an ability to get along in the working world, where he would have to compete and deal with other men. Because he was accustomed to the domestic life, and in fact had provided a very nice home atmosphere, he would probably make an excellent gentleman's butler. **The correct answer is (5).**

Unlike either of the previous passages, the next passage consists mainly of dialogue. (Its word length would be about average for a GED® reading passage, although it might appear longer due to its many paragraph breaks.) As you read the passage, ask yourself who the narrator is and how the 3 characters are related to one another. Also pay close attention to what their behavior suggests about each of them individually and about their relationship with one another. To follow the events as they unfold in the passage, try to visualize the scene. As is typical of GED® prose-fiction passages, the passage's concluding sentences leave you asking questions that are likely to be the focus of at least one or two *test* questions.

QUESTIONS 7–12 REFER TO THE FOLLOWING PASSAGE.

On the 24th of May, 1863, my uncle, Professor Liedenbrock, rushed into his little house, No. 19 Konigstrasse, one of the oldest streets in the oldest portion of the city of Hamburg. Martha must have concluded that she was very much behindhand, for the dinner had only just been put into the oven.

5 "Well, now," said I to myself, "if that most impatient of men is hungry, what a disturbance he will make!"

"Mr. Liedenbrock so soon!" cried poor Martha in great alarm, half opening the dining-room door.

"Yes, Martha; but very likely the dinner is not half cooked, for it is not two 10 yet. Saint Michael's clock has only just struck half-past one."

"Then why has the master come home so soon?"

"Perhaps he will tell us that himself."

"Here he is, Monsieur Axel; I will run and hide myself while you argue with him."

15 And Martha retreated in safety into her own dominions. I was left alone. But how was it possible for a man of my undecided turn of mind to argue successfully with so irascible a person as the Professor? With this persuasion I was hurrying away to my own little retreat upstairs, when the street door creaked upon its hinges; heavy feet made the whole flight of stairs to shake; and the 20 master of the house, passing rapidly through the dining room, threw himself in haste into his own sanctum.

But on his rapid way he had found time to fling his hazel stick into a corner, his rough broadbrim upon the table, and these few emphatic words at his nephew: "Axel, follow me!"

25 I had scarcely had time to move when the Professor was again shouting after me: "What! not come yet?" And I rushed into my redoubtable master's study.

Otto Liedenbrock had no mischief in him, I willingly allow that; but unless he very considerably changes as he grows older, at the end he will be a most original character.

— from *Journey to the Center of the Earth*, by Jules Verne

7. From whose point of view are the events in the passage described?

The events are described from the point of view of

(1) Martha

(2) the author

(3) Monsieur Axel

(4) an outside observer

(5) Otto Liedenbrock

The narration is in first person—from the point of view of Monsieur Axel, who is Professor Liedenbrock's nephew. The narrator's identity is not clear until Martha says "Here he is, Monsieur Axel; I will run and hide myself while you argue with him," after which the narrator comments, "I was left alone." **The correct answer is (3).**

8. Which description best characterizes the Professor, as he is revealed in the passage?

   (1) absent-minded

   (2) generous

   (3) mischievous

   (4) decisive

   (5) demanding

In the passage the narrator (Axel) uses the words "impatient" (line 5) and "irascible" (line 17) to describe Professor Liedenbrock. (The word *irascible* means "disagreeable.") However, none of the five answer choices matches these two descriptive words. To answer the question, you must infer some other trait from the Professor's behavior, as seen through Axel's eyes. Notice that Martha is worried that she might be in trouble with the Professor because dinner was late. Notice also that the Professor shouts to his nephew, "Axel, follow me!" These portions of the narrative both strongly suggest that the Professor is a *demanding* person. **The correct answer is (5).**

9. What does the passage suggest about Martha?

   (1) She is often late cooking dinner.

   (2) She looks to Axel for support.

   (3) She is afraid of losing her job.

   (4) She is Otto Liedenbrock's niece.

   (5) She often feels sorry for herself.

When dinner is not ready for the Professor, Martha asks Axel to intercept the Professor while she hides in her quarters. Based on this narrative, we can infer that Martha looks to Axel to help her out in difficult situations. **The correct answer is (2).**

10. The narrator remarks that unless Otto Liedenbrock changes as he grows older, "at the end he will be a most original character" (lines 28–29).

   The narrator's point about Otto Liedenbrock is that as he grows older,

   (1) he will be known for his originality

   (2) his students will no longer enjoy his teaching methods

   (3) he will act like a character from a play

   (4) people will find him very difficult to be around

   (5) he will begin imagining things due to old age

To interpret the meaning of the quoted words, look at their context. In the first part of the same sentence, Axel says, "Otto Liedenbrock had no mischief in him, I willingly allow that; but unless he changes. . . ." Axel seems to imply here that Liedenbrock might develop traits like mischievousness as he gets older, in which case other people may find him very difficult to put up with. **The correct answer is (4).**

11. Based on how the first word in each pair is used in the passage, which word-pair association is incorrect?

    (1) behindhand — late (line 4)

    (2) dominions — apartment (line 15)

    (3) sanctum — bedroom (line 21)

    (4) broadbrim — hat (line 23)

    (5) emphatic — urgent (line 23)

To answer this vocabulary-in-context question, you need to follow the passage's sequence of events. The narrator tells us that the Professor hurried into his "sanctum" and from there summoned Axel (the narrator) to join him. Axel (the narrator) then tells us that he joined the Professor "in his study." So the word *sanctum* is used here to refer to a study (den or library), not a bedroom. Each other answer choice provides a good synonym for a word as it is used in the passage. **The correct answer is (3).**

12. Which of the following events is most likely to occur next?

    (1) The Professor will realize that dinner is late and will become angry.

    (2) The Professor will have a serious conversation with Axel.

    (3) The Professor will leave the house to go teach a class.

    (4) Martha will apologize to the Professor for the half-cooked dinner.

    (5) Axel will sit down to eat with Martha but without the Professor.

Martha, who is probably the Professor's live-in cook, has hidden herself in her quarters. Meanwhile, the Professor has called his nephew Axel into his study. Since the Professor is nowhere near the dining area, he is not likely to suddenly realize that dinner is late, choice (1). He has obviously just come home for dinner, and so he is unlikely to leave immediately, choice (3). Nothing in the passage indicates that Martha will be rushing to the Professor's study with an apology, choice (4). Martha is most likely the hired help and probably won't be eating with the Professor's family, choice (5). Only choice (2) provides a plausible continuation of the story. **The correct answer is (2).**

Drama

One of your GED® Reading Test passages will be an excerpt from a **drama,** which is a **play** for acting on stage or for broadcasting. The author of a play is referred to as the

playwright. A GED® drama excerpt may be taken from any literary era. For example, an excerpt might be drawn from the work of a late-nineteenth century or early twentieth-century playwright such as Henrik Ibsen or Oscar Wilde. Or, it might be drawn from a modern work by a playwright such as Eugene O'Neill, Tennessee Williams, or Neil Simon. In any case, GED® drama passages are comparable in word length to prose passages, although they might appear longer due to frequent paragraph breaks.

Although drama is written for actors to perform, many people read drama for pleasure just as they would read prose fiction or poetry. In fact, drama and prose fiction have a lot in common. Both rely on setting, plot, and character development to tell a story. However, drama is distinct in a number of ways. First, a drama or play is divided into **acts** and **scenes** instead of parts and chapters. At the beginning of each act or scene, the playwright usually describes its **setting:** time, place, and possibly a description of the interior or exterior where the action occurs. Although this description is intended for the director and actors, it also helps readers to understand the play's action. Setting descriptions are often italicized to help the reader identify them.

Second, the text of a drama or play is presented almost entirely in the form of **dialogue,** which refers to the words spoken by the actors. The lines of dialogue will follow the name of the character who speaks the lines. Rather than using quotation marks to indicate dialogue, the name of the character is written, and then the words the character speaks are written. The challenge of a playwright is to write the character's dialogue in such a way that the dialogue tells the audience (or reader) exactly what the character is thinking and feeling.

Third, if a character needs to perform a certain action on stage, the playwright will write **stage directions** either before or after (or sometimes in the middle of) the character's lines of dialogue. Stage directions are enclosed by parentheses; they may also be italicized. Playwrights also use stage directions to suggest how the actors should deliver their lines—for example, with surprise or anger. Stage directions can even help direct the actors' motivation, postures, and facial expressions.

Most of the guidelines for reading and understanding drama are the same as those for understanding prose fiction. However, reading a play can be more difficult than reading a novel or short story since the author is not speaking directly to the reader. There is no narrator to set the mood of a play, interpret the characters' statements, or describe their thoughts, feelings, and motives. Instead, the reader must rely entirely on the setting, dialogue, and stage directions. Of these three elements, dialogue is the most important, since drama consists almost entirely of dialogue. Think carefully about what the characters suggest or infer by their statements, and what the scene's dialogue suggests about the relationships among the characters.

GED® questions involving drama will focus largely on inferences based on dialogue. But some questions might require you to summarize a scene, identify the setting, place the scene in a greater context, or draw other conclusions from the passage. The questions will not require you to have knowledge of other parts of the drama, but you may be required to predict the future actions or infer previous actions of the characters based on the passage.

In the following example, notice that the setting (place and situation) is important to understanding the scene's action, but the stage directions are not.

QUESTIONS 13–16 REFER TO THE FOLLOWING DRAMATIC PASSAGE.

Covent Garden at 11:15 p.m. Torrents of heavy summer rain. Cab whistles blowing frantically in all directions. Pedestrians running for shelter into the market and under the portico of St. Paul's Church, where there are already several people, among them a lady and her daughter in evening dress. They are all peering out gloomily at the rain, except one man with his back turned to the rest, who seems wholly preoccupied with a notebook in which he is writing busily. The church clock strikes the first quarter.

THE DAUGHTER. *(in the space between the central pillars, close to the one on her left)* I'm getting chilled to the bone. What can Freddy be doing all this time? He's been gone twenty minutes.

THE MOTHER. *(On her daughter's right)* Not so long. But he ought to have got us a cab by this.

A BYSTANDER. *(On the lady's right)* He won't get no cab not until half-past eleven, missus, when they come back after dropping off their theatre fares.

THE MOTHER. But we must have a cab. We can't stand here until half-past eleven. It's too bad.

THE BYSTANDER. Well, it ain't my fault, missus.

THE DAUGHTER. If Freddy had a bit of gumption, he would have got one at the theatre door.

THE MOTHER. What could he have done, poor boy?

THE DAUGHTER. Other people got cabs, Why couldn't he? *(Freddy rushes in out of the rain from the Southampton Street side, and comes between them closing a dripping umbrella. He is a young man of twenty, in evening dress, very wet around the ankles.)*

THE DAUGHTER. Well, haven't you got a cab?

FREDDY. There's not one to be had for love or money.

THE MOTHER. Oh, Freddy, there must be one. You can't have tried.

THE DAUGHTER. It's too tiresome. Do you expect us to go and get one ourselves?

FREDDY. I tell you they're all engaged. The rain was so sudden: nobody was prepared; and everybody had to take a cab. I've been to Charing Cross one way and nearly to Ludgate Circus the other; and they were all engaged.

THE MOTHER. Did you try Trafalgar Square?

FREDDY. There wasn't one at Trafalgar Square.

THE DAUGHTER. Did you try?

FREDDY. I tried as far as Charing Cross Station. Did you expect me to walk to Hammersmith?

THE DAUGHTER. You haven't tried at all.

THE MOTHER. You really are very helpless, Freddy. Go again; and don't come back until you have found a cab.

FREDDY. I shall simply get soaked for nothing.

THE DAUGHTER. And what about us? Are we to stay here all night in this draught, with next to nothing on? You selfish pig.

— from *Pygmalion*, by George Bernard Shaw

13. Why are the characters standing around outside?

    (1) they've been out shopping

    (2) they've just left the theatre

    (3) they've forgotten their umbrellas

    (4) they refuse to take a bus

    (5) they've been visiting friends

The stage directions at the beginning of the passage indicate that the characters are wearing evening dress, and the bystander comments that there will be no more cabs until they come back after dropping off their theatre fares. **The correct answer is (2).**

14. Which of the following phrases best describes the daughter?

    (1) a down to earth girl

    (2) a girl in love with Freddy

    (3) a reasonable girl

    (4) a pleasant person

    (5) an unreasonable person

The daughter is unreasonable and refuses to accept Freddy's explanation for why he couldn't get a cab. She insists that Freddy didn't really try. **The correct answer is (5).**

15. As revealed in the passage, which of the following statements about the mother is probably most accurate?

    (1) She tries to look out for Freddy's best interests.

    (2) She wants what is best for her daughter.

    (3) She doesn't care about other people.

    (4) She is a loving person.

    (5) She is concerned about those around her.

The mother's telling Freddy that he is helpless and insisting that he go back out into the rain reveals that she cares little about his welfare. **The correct answer is (3).**

16. What will the daughter most likely think about Freddy in the future?

    (1) He isn't good enough for her.

    (2) He truly loves her.

    (3) He is sensible.

    (4) He has her best interests at heart.

    (5) He is amusing to her.

Because she is so demanding, the daughter is difficult to please. She feels that Freddy is not really trying his hardest to make her happy. **The correct answer is (1).**

Pay Attention to Stage Directions

The next passage is from another drama by the same playwright. Notice that these stage directions are more important in understanding the interaction between characters than the stage directions were in the previous passage.

QUESTIONS 17–19 REFER TO THE FOLLOWING PASSAGE.

Stephen comes in. He is a gravely correct young man under twenty-five, taking himself very seriously.

STEPHEN. What's the matter?

LADY BRITOMART. Presently, Stephen.

(Stephen submissively walks to the settee and sits down. He takes up The Speaker.*)*

LADY BRITOMART. Don't begin to read, Stephen. I shall require all your attention.

STEPHEN. It was only while I was waiting—

LADY BRITOMART. Don't make excuses, Stephen. *(He puts down* The Speaker.*)* Now! *(She finishes her writing; rises; and comes to the settee.)* I have not kept you waiting very long, I think.

STEPHEN. Not at all, Mother.

LADY BRITOMART. Bring me my cushion. *(He takes the cushion from the chair at the desk and arranges it for her as she sits down on the settee.)* Sit down. *(He sits down and fingers his tie nervously.)* Don't fiddle with your tie, Stephen: there is nothing the matter with it.

STEPHEN. I beg your pardon. *(He fiddles with his watch chain instead.)*

LADY BRITOMART. Now are you attending to me, Stephen?

STEPHEN. Of course, Mother.

LADY BRITOMART. No: it's not of course. I want something much more than your everyday matter-of-course attention. I am going to speak to you very seriously, Stephen. I wish you would let that chain alone.

STEPHEN. *(hastily relinquishing the chain)* Have I done anything to annoy you, Mother? If so, it was quite unintentional.

LADY BRITOMART. *(astonished)* Nonsense! *(With some remorse)* My poor boy, did you think I was angry with you?

STEPHEN. What is it, then, Mother. You are making me very uneasy.

— from *Major Barbara*, by George Bernard Shaw

17. Why does Stephen probably fidget around his mother?

    (1) because he doesn't like her

    (2) because he is in a hurry to go somewhere

    (3) because he doesn't care much about her

    (4) because she makes him insecure

    (5) because he just wants to get away from her

The dialogue and stage directions reveal that Lady Britomart is in the habit of telling her son Stephen what to do and say, and that her son Stephen tries to accommodate her. From this we can infer that Stephen's mother is overbearing and that, as a result, she probably makes Stephen feel insecure. **The correct answer is (4).**

18. Most likely who or what is *The Speaker*?

    (1) the play's narrator

    (2) a phonograph record

    (3) a newspaper or book

    (4) the title of the story Lady Britomart is writing

    (5) Lady Britomart

Stephen picks up *The Speaker*, and then his mother tells him not to read, immediately after which he puts down *The Speaker*. We can infer from this action that *The Speaker* is reading material, probably a book. **The correct answer is (3).**

19. As revealed in the passage, how does Lady Britomart generally treat her son?

    (1) with common respect

    (2) as if he were a child

    (3) with strict discipline

    (4) she spoils him

    (5) she is abusive towards him

We're told that Stephen is 25 years old and a serious young man. Yet Lady Britomart treats him as if he were a child. Based on her behavior in this scene, she is probably in the habit of watching over him and telling him how to act. But the passage does not strongly suggest that she disciplines (punishes) or abuses her son, choices (3) and (5). **The correct answer is (2).**

Poetry

A **poem** is a composition in words that is concerned largely with feeling or imaginative description. Poems are presented in **verse,** meaning that their lines are constructed according to a meter which takes into account not only the ideas and words used in each line but also their rhythms and sounds, much like music. Poets often use rhyming techniques to reinforce the rhythm and ideas of their poems. Poems are generally briefer and contain fewer details than works of prose fiction. Their emphasis lies more in the arrangement of details than on the details themselves.

Though a poem might be written strictly to evoke images and feelings, poems are generally written to communicate thoughts and ideas as well—for example, that war is futile, that love is bittersweet, or that nature is mysterious. Some poems are written to recount past events—in other words, to tell a story. In any case, at the heart of any good poem are the imaginative ways in which its ideas are expressed and arranged.

Connotation and Imagery

Regardless of the poem's intent, poets use a number of literary tools to express their ideas. Instead of using words only in their literal sense, poets often make use of **connotations**—broad overtones in meaning—that a word might carry beyond its dictionary definition. A word's connotations will vary depending on the context in which it is used and on whatever associations the reader makes when reading it in context. Here are two examples:

> *the fragrant sight of her spun-gold hair*
>
> *a sponge sky, whose warmth I knew not*

The word *fragrant* literally means a pleasant, perfume-like smell. Yet in this instance it is being used to connote, or suggest, a pleasing sight. The word *sponge* is ordinarily used as a noun to refer to something that soaks up or absorbs. Here, however, it is being used as an adjective to describe a sky. The connation here is probably that the sky is completely cloudy, hence it is soaking up or absorbing the warmth of sunlight.

Another powerful literary tool used extensively in poetry is **imagery,** which refers to the use of language to convey a sense experience. For example, a poet who refers to a storm that *snows a blanket* or *rains sheets* is using sight imagery. Although we associate the word *image* with our sense of sight, imagery can involve any of the senses: sight, sound, smell, taste, or tactile experiences (either touch or internal body sensations). For instance, a poet who refers to a *drum's galloping cadence* or a *violin's tender aural caress* is using sound imagery.

Figurative Language

Rather than rely on everyday language to create poems, poets often use **figurative** language to lend deeper meaning and greater intensity to their poetry. To use figurative language is to say something that actually means something else. In other words, what is being said is not to be taken literally. By using figurative language to enhance the emotional intensity and imaginative appeal of a poem, the poet can convey so much more than through literal language alone.

Probably the most commonly used types of figurative language are the *simile* and *metaphor*. Both are used to compare unlike things. The difference has to do with whether the comparison is expressed or implied. A **simile** is an expressed comparison using words such as *like* or *as*. We all use similes every day without thinking about it—for example, when we refer to being *tired as a dog* or to *sleeping like a baby*. Here are a few additional, more poetic examples:

> *that dreary moment somber as a funeral*
>
> *this onerous hour that seems forever*

In the first line, a certain moment is being compared to a funeral. In the second line, an hour of time is being compared to an eternity. A **metaphor** implies a comparison by substituting one thing for another, as though they were one and the same. The metaphor might name both things, or it might not. Consider these two related statements:

> *She was a tall drink of water.*
>
> *The tall drink of water thirsted for more.*

In the first sentence, *a tall drink of water* is used as a metaphor for *She*, and both the figurative and the literal term are named. In the second sentence, however, only the figurative term is named.

Closely related to a metaphor are *symbolism* and *allegory*. A **symbol** is one thing used to represent something more than that thing. For a poet, a single death can be symbolic of the fleeting nature of all life, and a stroll in the woods can by symbolic of life's journey. An **allegory** is a narrative or description that has both a surface meaning and a second, underlying meaning. For example, a poem about what someone sees when looking in the mirror (the surface meaning) might also be understood in terms of what that person sees inside them when they reflect on their own thoughts (the underlying meaning).

Other types of figurative language often used in poetry include personification, paradox, and irony. **Personification** involves attributing human qualities to an animal, an object, or even a concept. Here are a few examples:

> *The setting sun sang its lullaby.*
>
> *The barn gate jeered and complained to the sudden gust.*

A **paradox** is a description, statement, or situation that seems contradictory but when fully understood actually makes sense. It might be described in just a few descriptive words—for example, *thunderous silence* or *noble theft*—or in a statement such as *the* *best offense is a good defense.* Or, it might characterize a situation, as when a rich but unfulfilled man gives away his fortune in order to realize true wealth.

Irony refers to a situation that is surprisingly unlike what one might expect given the circumstances. For example, dying of thirst while disabled within sight of a river would be considered ironical. A mighty warrior dying by his own sword would also be considered ironical. Irony is a powerful tool because it allows the poet to convey an idea without asserting it directly; the poet leaves the irony of a situation to the reader to discover.

Sound and Rhythm

The poet's toolkit is by no means limited to connotation and figurative language. Poets often make use of the *sounds* and *rhythms* of words and phrases to help convey mood, emotion, and even ideas. One specific technique that poets often use is **alliteration:** the use of several words beginning with the same sound. Alliteration gives a line of poetry an almost musical quality. Here are a few examples:

The unknown is a taunt, a terrifying tease.

I float and frolic and fiddle all the day long.

Notice that in both examples the alliteration adds a rhythmic dimension to the line. Also, notice in the second example that the alliteration reinforces the idea of repeating the same activity "all the day long." In this way, the device is being used to convey meaning as well.

Another device poets use to convey sound and rhythm is **onomatopoeia,** which refers to the use of a particular word or phrase in order to mimic a sound. Many words are inherently onomatopoeic. In other words, they sound like what they describe—for example, *boom* or *swish*. (You could probably lists dozens more off the top of your head.) To mimic repeated sounds, a poet might use a series of onomatopoeic words, which might be alliterative as well. Here are a few examples:

The rain dripped, dropped, then dripped.

Clang and clatter goes the clutter of my mind.

Handling Poetry on the GED®

The GED® Reading Test will contain one poem, which will be eight to twenty-five lines in length. There is really no limit as to the type of poem that you might encounter. It might be a poem by a contemporary poet, or it might be a poem by a classical poet, written long ago. Rest assured: the GED® will *not* test you on your knowledge of specific poetic forms, nor will the GED® test you on your knowledge of particular poets.

Regardless of the type of poem or when or by whom it was written, the guidelines for reading and understanding any poem are essentially the same. As you read a poem, ask yourself three key questions:

❶ *Who is the speaker?* (The poet? Some other narrator? A thing or concept, which that poet is personifying?)

❷ *Who is the speaker addressing?* (Himself or herself? A friend or lover? The reader? A group of people, a nation, or the world? An idea or concept, using personification?)

❸ *What is the speaker's main concern or intent?* (To express praise, love, or admiration toward someone or something? To express indignation or outrage over something? To express a certain outlook on life? To reflect on the poet's own foibles and faults?)

In reading poetry, also follow these additional suggestions:

- As you read, pay close attention to the poet's use of connotation, imagery, figurative language, sound, and rhythm. This attention will help you interpret the poem and understand the poet's intent.

- Allow the poem's lines to flow from one to next. Except at punctuation marks, line breaks in poems are not intended to interrupt or complete a thought.

- Try not to get bogged down in analyzing every line or in figuring out what unfamiliar words might mean. You won't be tested on everything in the poem, so you don't want to waste your time.

- After reading the poem, think about it as a whole and how the title (if it is provided) relates to it.

The following example is in the form of a *sonnet*, which is a fourteen-line poem that conforms to certain rules for meter and rhyme. As you read it, ask yourself who the speaker is, who the speaker is addressing, and what the speaker's intent is. As you'll see, the questions based on the poem focus largely on these questions.

QUESTIONS 20–23 REFER TO THE FOLLOWING POEM.

> **Sonnet to Liberty**
> Not that I love thy children, whose dull eyes
> See nothing save their own unlovely woe,
> Whose minds know nothing, nothing care to know,—
> But that the roar of thy Democracies,
> 5 Thy reigns of Terror, thy great Anarchies,
> Mirror my wildest passions like the sea
> And give my rage a brother—! Liberty!
> For this sake only do thy dissonant cries
> Delight my discreet soul, else might all kings
> 10 By bloody knout or treacherous cannonades
> Rob nations of their rights inviolate
> And I remain unmoved—and yet, and yet,
> These Christs that die upon the barricades,
> God knows it I am with them, in some things.
>
> —Oscar Wilde

20. What word best captures the dominant feeling expressed in lines 1–7?

   (1) enthusiasm

   (2) despair

   (3) optimism

   (4) uncertainty

   (5) outrage

From the language used, the reader should sense the poet's excitement and spiritedness. The strong, declarative exclamations in line 7 provide perhaps the strongest clue as to what the poet is feeling. **The correct answer is (1).**

21. Who or what is the poet speaking to in line 5 ("Thy reigns of Terror, thy great Anarchies")?

   (1) himself

   (2) God

   (3) the reader

   (4) liberty

   (5) his country

Notice also that line 1 refers to "thy children." So the correct answer should name something or someone that make sense as having children, reigns of terror, and great anarchies—perhaps in the figurative rather than literal sense. The title provides an additional clue: the poet is addressing the concept of Liberty (notice that this concept is capitalized in line 7). **The correct answer is (4).**

22. To whom or what does "These Christs" (line 13) refer?

   (1) the poet's children

   (2) the poet's brother

   (3) democracies of the world

   (4) soldiers who died for liberty

   (5) mighty kings

The context makes clear that "These Christs" are the soldiers who "die upon the barricades" in order to save liberty. **The correct answer is (4).**

23. What is the poet's likely intent in writing the sonnet?

The poet is mainly concerned with expressing his

(1) rage at democracies that wage senseless wars

(2) kinship with the spirit of liberty

(3) sense of loss over his dead child

(4) right as a citizen to speak out

(5) sorrow over lives lost due to war

Answering this question requires that you synthesize the sonnet's ideas. In the first three lines, the poet admits that he does not love Liberty's children. But then, in lines 4–7, the poet continues by expressing his empathy, or kinship, with Liberty (he says that Liberty mirrors his own passions and rage). In lines 8–10, the poet expresses his appreciation for liberty in view of the alternative (monarchy). Finally, in lines 12–14, the poet qualifies his identification with Liberty by acknowledging his sorrow over soldiers who die defending Liberty. In sum, lines 1–7 express the poet's overall intent, while lines 8–11 provide some additional reflections about his emotional identification, or kinship, with the idea of Liberty. **The correct answer is (2).**

Figurative Language

In answering GED® poetry questions, you might need to know the names of specific literary devices, such as personification or alliteration. More likely, however, your task will be to understand how a poet uses those devices. The next poem makes extensive use of figurative language. As you read the poem, try to identify which forms of figurative speech are being used and what feelings and ideas the figurative language helps to convey. These insights will help you answer the questions that follow the poem.

QUESTIONS 24–28 REFER TO THE FOLLOWING POEM.

Down dropped the breeze, the sails dropped down,
'Twas sad as sad could be;
And we did speak only to break
The silence of the sea!
5 All in a hot and copper sky,
The bloody Sun, at noon,
Right up above the mist did stand,
No bigger than the Moon.
Day after day, day after day,
10 We stuck, nor breath nor motion;
As idle as a painted ship
Upon a painted ocean.
Water, water, everywhere,
And all the boards did shrink;
15 Water, water, everywhere,
Nor any drop to drink.

   —from "Rime of the Ancient Mariner," by Samuel Taylor Coleridge

24. What situation is this passage most likely describing?

  (1) travelers stranded in the desert

  (2) a ship's crew caught in a fierce storm

  (3) soldiers resting after a battle

  (4) a leisurely riverboat excursion

  (5) sailors lost at sea

This poem excerpt mentions sails, the sea, a ship, the ocean, and water everywhere. Nowhere in the excerpt does the poet mention a storm, choice (2); to the contrary, the poem refers to the "silence of the sea" (line 4) and to the "idle" ship and sea (lines 11–12). In all likelihood, the poet is referring to the despair of sailors whose ship is lost at sea. **The correct answer is (5).**

25. What technique does the poet use to convey the narrator's state of mind?

  (1) repeating certain phrases and lines

  (2) using words that sound like what they describe

  (3) describing physical sensations through the use of imagery

  (4) using words in a confusing and nonsensical way

  (5) incorporating the narrator's spoken words into the poem

Repetition is used in lines 1 and 9, as well as in lines 13 and 15 when considered separately and together. The use of repetition emphasizes the narrator's boredom and fatigue from experiencing nothing new as the hours (and perhaps days) go by. **The correct answer is (1).**

26. The poet draws all of the following comparisons EXCEPT which one?

  (1) the ocean and a painting

  (2) the Sun and the Moon

  (3) a ship and a painting

  (4) the sky and the sea

  (5) the breeze and the sails

The narrator observes that the Sun and Moon stand above the mist (lines 5–7) but does *not* compare the sky to the sea, choice (4). Line 1 implies a similarity between the breeze and the sails, choice (5). Lines 11–12 compare the ship and the ocean to a painting, choices (1) and (3). Line 8 compares the size of the Moon to that of the Sun, choice (2). **The correct answer is (4).**

27. Which of the following groups of words from the passage illustrates the same type of figurative language as "The bloody Sun, at noon" (line 6)?

 (1) "The silence of the sea!" (line 4)

 (2) "All in a hot and copper sky" (line 5)

 (3) "No bigger than the Moon" (line 8)

 (4) "All the boards did shrink" (line 14)

 (5) "Water, water, everywhere" (line 15)

The use of *bloody* to describe the Sun at noon is an example of personification as well as the use of imagery. Of the five other lines provided, only line 5—choice (2)—illustrates either of these two types of figurative language. The phrase "a hot and copper sky" is an example of the use of imagery. Though the other four lines also describe sense experiences, the descriptions in these lines are more literal than figurative. **The correct answer is (2).**

28. Which situation is most similar to the one described by lines 15 and 16 ("Water, water, everywhere, / Nor any drop to drink")?

 (1) a well that goes dry due to evaporation

 (2) a grape that shrinks into a raisin in the sun

 (3) an astronaut who runs out of food rations

 (4) a steakhouse restaurant that serves seafood as well

 (5) a nutrition expert who dies young of heart disease

Lines 15 and 16 express an ironical situation: the sailors are surrounded by water, yet ironically they have no water that is fit to drink. The situation of a nutrition expert who dies young of heart disease would also be considered ironical, since such an expert would not be expected to have serious nutrition-related health problems. **The correct answer is (5).**

A Poet's Use of Imagery

The next poem is probably more difficult to understand and interpret than either of the previous two. As you read this poem, avoid getting bogged down or "stuck" by trying to interpret every word and phrase. For example, you may not understand part of the first line, but don't worry about it. Instead, try to capture the poem's overall concern and sentiment, paying attention to the poet's use of imagery and figurative language.

QUESTIONS 29–32 REFER TO THE FOLLOWING POEM.

The Death of Autumn

When reeds are dead and a straw to thatch the marshes,
And feathered pampas-grass rides into the wind
Like aged warriors westward, tragic, thinned
Of half their tribe, and over the flattened rushes,
5 Stripped of its secret, open, stark and bleak,
Blackens afar the half-forgotten creek, —
Then leans on me the weight of the year, and crushes
My heart. I know that Beauty must ail and die,
And will be born again, —but ah, to see
10 Beauty stiffened, staring up at the sky!
Oh, Autumn! Autumn! —What is the Spring to me?

                          —Edna St. Vincent Millay

29. According to the poem, what is true of pampas-grass?

During the Autumn months, pampas-grass

(1) completely disappears

(2) is flattened by the wind

(3) blows toward the west

(4) invades other areas, like warriors

(5) sheds its feather blossoms

This is a simple comprehension question. In lines 2 and 3, the poet observes that "feathered pampas-grass rides into the wind / Like aged warriors westward." Choice (1) is incorrect because the pampas-grass is "thinned / Of half their tribe" only (lines 3 and 4). **The correct answer is (3).**

30. Which word best describes the mood of the poem?

(1) joy

(2) loneliness

(3) hostility

(4) despondency

(5) resentment

The mood of the poem is one of *despondency*, which means "losing heart or having low spirits." The poet refers to the weight of another year passing as crushing her heart. Although she looks forward to another spring, she is depressed and despondent, about the coming winter. Even if you don't know what *despondency* means, you can easily eliminate the other answer choices since none finds any support in the poem. **The correct answer is (4).**

31. An *aphorism* is a brief, often-used maxim or statement of principle. Which of the following aphorisms illustrates the same poetic device as the words "I know that Beauty must ail and die" in line 8 of the poem?

   (1) All humans have a date with Destiny.

   (2) Dead men tell no lies.

   (3) Beauty is in the beholder's eye.

   (4) Death waits for no man.

   (5) The meek shall inherit the Earth.

In line 8, the poet attributes the human qualities of sickness and death to the concept of beauty. Similarly, the idea of "a date with Destiny" personifies the concept of destiny. **The correct answer is (1).**

32. What does the poet mean by the question "What is the Spring to me?" at the end of the poem?

   By this question, the poet might be inferring that she

   (1) expects a brief winter season this year

   (2) expects to die during the coming winter

   (3) wouldn't care if Spring never came

   (4) hopes to see different plant life next Spring

   (5) wonders why she longs for Spring

Read as a whole, the poem tells you that the speaker (who is probably the poet herself) does not welcome the bleak winter months, and line 11 suggests that during Autumn she is already looking forward to Spring. Posing the question seems to be the poet's way of expressing her wonder about what it is about Spring that she longs for so much. Although this is just one reasonable interpretation, the other answer choices are not supported by the poem. **The correct answer is (5).**

UNDERSTANDING NONFICTION

A written work of **nonfiction** is one that involves real people and events, either past or present. Nonfiction can take a variety of different forms, from a brief article or diary entry to a book or even a multivolume work. On the GED® Reading Test, you can expect at least two reading passages involving nonfiction. Each passage will be 200 to 400 words in length (about a half page, on average). The passage may provide an entire work if it is brief. More often, however, passages are excerpted from longer works. GED® nonfiction passages are drawn from the following broad categories:

- Informational and opinion texts (articles, papers, editorials, speeches, and the like)

- Works of literary nonfiction (biographies and autobiographies, diaries, journals, letters, essays, and oral history)

- Critical reviews of the visual and performing arts (painting and sculpture, film and television, plays and other stage productions, and the like)

- Workplace and community documents (policy and mission statements, employee handbooks and manuals, business communications, and the like)

In the following sections, you'll learn more about all of these types of nonfiction, and you'll learn how best to read nonfiction in order to understand it in ways that will help you most on the GED®. For each category, you'll also read a variety of sample passages and answer GED®-style questions based on them.

Informational and Opinion Texts

On the Reading Test, one of the nonfiction passages of text might present a combination of factual information and opinion, or perspective, on that information. The text might have originally appeared in an essay, an article, an editorial, a position paper, a work of cultural commentary, or some other opinion piece. The text might be drawn from a magazine, newspaper, Web site, or public speech, or it might be excerpted from a book-length work. The text might be contemporary, or it might have been written (or spoken) during an earlier century. The specific source of the text may or may not be provided.

Any topic is fair game for an informational or opinion text. The text might involve current events and human affairs, sociological or cultural trends, science or technology, business or economics, popular psychology, or education, to name just some broad areas. Don't worry: you won't need any special knowledge of the topic to answer the questions based on the text. Everything you'll need to know will be stated or implied in the text itself.

Like any GED® nonfiction text, an informational or opinion text will present a **main idea,** or **central point.** You might find that the main idea is neatly expressed in either the opening or closing sentences. Or, you might need to synthesize all of the information in the text to determine the main idea. The main idea will be broad enough to encompass the entire text without going beyond or off the topic.

Related to the text's main idea (central point) is its **central concern** or focus. To determine a text's central concern, ask yourself what issue, problem, events, or developments the text mainly addresses. The central concern will embrace the text's main idea and all supporting information, without departing from the topic at hand. In other words, a text's central concern is one that is neither too broad nor too narrow in focus.

Also related to the text's main idea is the author's **primary purpose** or **objective,** as revealed in the text. In the case of a purely informational text, the primary purpose might be to:

- Inform of facts
- Summarize events
- Relate observations
- Provide alternative explanations

But if the text also expresses an opinion or point of view, then its author is clearly interested in accomplishing more than simply presenting facts. The author is also trying to convince or persuade the reader (or listener) in some way. In this case, the primary purpose might be to:

- Argue for or defend a certain position on an issue
- Advocate for a cause or a course of action
- Promote an ideology or a value system
- Recommend a particular solution to a problem
- Forecast, predict, or warn of future events

After reading the passage for the first time, think about what the author wrote. Ask yourself what the overall topic is and why the author might have written the text. Formulate a sentence or two that expresses the main idea. You may even wish to jot it down in your test booklet.

Understanding the main idea, central concern, and primary purpose of a passage will help you handle many different types of test questions—not just ones that ask "What is the main idea of the passage?" or "What is the central concern of the text?" For example, understanding the "big picture" will help you apply the author's viewpoint to new situations as well as to determine what else the author would agree and disagree with.

QUESTONS 33–35 REFER TO THE FOLLOWING PASSAGE.

The residential real-estate boom and bust of the early 2000s, characterized by overbuilding in areas where land was cheap, was really nothing new. In the 1970s, the idea of building so-called "New Towns" to absorb growth was considered a potential cure-all for urban problems in the United States. It
5 was assumed that by diverting residents from existing centers, current urban problems would at least get no worse. It was also assumed that, since European New Towns had been financially and socially successful, the same could be expected in the United States.

In the end, these ill-considered projects actually weakened U.S. cities further
10 by drawing away high-income residents. While industry and commerce sought in turn to escape, the lower-income groups left behind were unable to provide the necessary tax base to support the cities. As it turns out, the promoters of New Towns were the developers, builders, and financial institutions motivated only by personal financial gain. Not surprisingly, development occurred in
15 areas where land was cheap and construction profitable rather than where New Towns were genuinely needed. What's more, the failure on the part of planners and federal legislators to consider social needs resulted not in the

sort of successful New Towns seen in Britain but rather in nothing more than sprawling suburbs.

20   Thirty years later, our situation may be even worse. Our new sprawling "exurbs," which are located farther away from urban centers than the suburbs of the '70s, are at risk of becoming ghettos for squatters and low-income renters. In many areas, the new exurbs are turning into virtual wastelands. I fear that we are just beginning to incur the social and economic costs of our failure to
25   reign in large-scale home construction in areas where it is not needed.

33. What is the author's primary concern in the passage?

  (1) to explain why building new homes in the United States is a bad idea

  (2) to explain how the New Town concept was developed in the United States

  (3) to compare British New Towns with U.S. New Towns

  (4) to point out problems of sprawling real-estate development

  (5) to analyze the impact of New Towns on U.S. urban centers

In the passage, the author explains how and why New Towns in the U.S. failed to solve urban problems and to provide the sort of social environment hoped for. But the opening sentence and closing paragraph tell us that the author has a broader concern in mind. In discussing New Towns, the author is citing one cautionary example of how out-of-control real-estate development motivated by greed can result in serious social problems. Choice (4) provides a good way of expressing this broader concern. **The correct answer is (4).**

34. Based on the passage, with which statement would the author most likely agree?

  (1) Businesses located in urban centers are likely to fail.

  (2) Suburbs provide a thriving social center for their residents.

  (3) Air pollution is largely attributable to suburban commuters.

  (4) City life is preferable to living in outlying suburbs.

  (5) New Towns provided a poor model for social planning.

There might be an element of truth in choices (1), (3), and (4), but each one is incorrect. Choice (1) goes too far by making the sweeping claim that *any* business located in an urban core will probably fail. Choice (3) is incorrect because the passage mentions nothing about air pollution. Choice (4) is wrong because the passage does not try to weigh city life against suburban life. The best way to avoid being tempted by these wrong-answer choices is to formulate the passage's main idea before you read them. Notice that choice (5) states the passage's main idea with which, of course, the author would agree. **The correct answer is (5).**

35. What is a good analogy to the New Towns established in the United States?

   (1) a business that fails due to lack of demand for its products

   (2) a computer program designed to fix one problem but that creates another

   (3) a scientific theory that lacks supporting evidence

   (4) a new drug that, due to its side effects, is not approved for legal use

   (5) a new game that attracts little interest because its rules are unfair

This question requires that you apply the passage's ideas to a new situation. As long as you understand the main idea and its supporting points, you shouldn't have any trouble answering the question. New Towns were designed to absorb population growth, but in attempting to achieve this goal the cities were left with new problems. Thus, like a computer program that attempts to fix one problem but creates another, New Towns were a new innovation that tried to solve one problem but created another along the way. **The correct answer is (2).**

Supporting Points, Attitude, and Tone

It's not enough for an author of an informational or opinion text to simply assert a main idea as fact and expect the reader to accept it as such. The author should also develop that idea through **supporting reasons and examples.** As you read the text, try to follow the author's line of reasoning, from main idea to the evidence used to support it.

You might find it helpful to jot down supporting points, so you can answer questions about them without reading the passage again. But don't try to jot down or remember every small detail from the passage. Instead, note where different kinds of details are located in the passage, so you can find them quickly if you need them for answering certain questions.

As you read the passage, also pay attention to the author's **attitude** toward the subject being discussed. In an informational text, the main concern might be to examine two different sides of an issue or two different proposed solutions to a problem, without clearly taking sides. Or the main concern might be to investigate and evaluate possible causes of a current situation or to predict future events based on currently available information. In these cases, the author is likely to approach the subject with an attitude of curiosity, neutrality, and possibly indecisiveness. In contrast, in an opinion text such as an editorial, speech, or essay, the author's attitude may be highly critical or judgmental; or it may be supportive, admiring, or even praising.

Closely related to the author's attitude is the overall **tone** used in the text. In texts that are mainly informational, the tone is generally detached and objective. But in opinion texts, which are often intended to persuade others or spur the reader (or listener) to action, the tone can be emotional, harsh, urgent, or even accusatory.

Sensing the author's attitude and tone can help you understand the purpose of the overall text and of each supporting point. The author's attitude and tone can also provide clues as to how the author would respond to various situations, what kinds of assertions the author would agree or disagree with, and even the author's occupation and the type of source from which the text is drawn.

QUESTIONS 36–38 REFER TO THE FOLLOWING PASSAGE.

The steady growth of the world's population has clearly created a food production and distribution crisis. The time has come for government development
agencies and agronomists to admit that all of their grandiose projects that are
supposed to help feed the world's poorest nations are not actually serving this
5   purpose.
Their vast irrigation systems, power dams, new industrial establishments,
and massive loans for "economic growth" and for food imports to poor nations
serve mainly the interests of powerful agribusiness. All the loan dollars from
our banks to fund these large-scale projects accomplish very little to feed a
10   hungry world. Instead, they leave poor nations in perpetual, and ever-increasing,
indebtedness—and their poorest citizens no better off. The multinational corporations who set up manufacturing facilities in Third World countries lure
the poor from the land to the city slums, paying them subsistence wages. And
what the facilities produce are consumer products that only affluent people,
15   mainly people in developed nations, can afford.
It is past time for all of us to speak truth to power in order to end this system
of dependence and poverty, by which the people of the poorest nations serve
as wage slaves to the rich, or in refusing to do so, starve. First, we must turn
to simpler approaches that help promote self-sufficiency and that embrace the
20   environmentalists' credo that smaller is better. Exporting simple agricultural
technology, by way of services as well as implements, would be a good start.
But this step alone is not enough. Underdeveloped societies must also help
themselves by implementing reforms that result in a fairer distribution of land
and access to water. Ultimately, however, means must be found to make it
25   contrary to anyone's interest to keep others poor. Unfortunately, movement in
this direction seems unlikely, unless and until the world's wealthiest nations
muster the political will to change things.

36. How does the author develop the passage's central idea?

   (1) by arguing that the world hunger crisis cannot be solved

   (2) by attacking the motives of bankers and big business

   (3) by explaining why there is no world hunger crisis

   (4) by providing statistics involving famine in the Third World

   (5) by listing examples of successful hunger-relief programs

The passage's central idea is that current approaches to the world hunger crisis are ineffective and should be replaced with better approaches. To support the central idea, the author explains how large-scale loans and projects that are supposed to help feed the hungry are actually designed by bankers and big business to serve their own interests, choice (2). To further support the central idea, the author lists alternative approaches that would be more effective. But choice (5) is incorrect because the author does not cite any specific programs that have already proven successful. **The correct answer is (2).**

37. Which form of aid to a poor nation would the author be most likely to recommend?

(1) the building of a large irrigation system

(2) the provision of credit for purchasing consumer goods

(3) the development of a hydroelectric plant

(4) the provision of agricultural tools

(5) the construction of an automobile factory

This question delves into the details of the author's supporting points. Choices (1), (2), (3), and (5) provide examples of the massive development projects that the author rejects as ineffective. You may not have remembered all of the projects listed at the beginning of the second paragraph, and jotting them all down would take too much time. But finding the list and checking it against the answer choices is a quick and easy task. As for the correct answer, choice (4), in the third paragraph the author strongly recommends programs that provide "simple agricultural technology," including "implements," which means agricultural tools. This is a major supporting point that you should have remembered or jotted down. **The correct answer is (4).**

38. Which word best characterizes the overall tone of the text?

(1) optimism

(2) regret

(3) urgency

(4) apathy

(5) despair

The text is clearly a call to action. Notice the author's use of the word "crisis" and the phrases "The time has come" and "It is past time," which convey a sense of *urgency*. On the other hand, nothing in the text suggests that the author feels particularly *optimistic* or *regretful*, choices (1) and (2). The word *apathetic*, choice (4), conveys just the opposite tone of the one conveyed in the text. As for choice (5), although the third paragraph suggests that unless certain measures are taken the world hunger crisis might never be solved, the reader does not sense that the author is pleading or feels hopeless, and so the word *despair* does not characterize of the overall tone as well as the word *urgency*. **The correct answer is (3).**

Literary Nonfiction

One of the passages on the GED® Reading Test might be excerpted from a work of **literary nonfiction.** Like other types of nonfiction, literary nonfiction involves real-world events and people (as opposed to fiction, which involves imaginary events and people). What sets *literary nonfiction* apart from other nonfiction is that its value and integrity lies largely in the beauty of the language used and in the work's emotional effect. In other words, how ideas are expressed can contribute as much to the work as the ideas themselves. In this sense, literary nonfiction has quite a bit in common with prose fiction. In fact, many of the greatest works of literary nonfiction were written by authors who also wrote great works of fiction.

Works of literary nonfiction can take a variety of forms, any of which might appear on the GED® Reading Test. One form is the **biography,** which is a work about the life of a real-life person other than the author, also referred to as the **biographer.** The subject of a biography might be either living or deceased at the time the biography is written. A biography can be written about *any* person, not just someone who is well-known. Biographies are generally book-length works, similar in length to a novel rather than a short story. But a biography can be briefer, more like a short story. Short biographies that cover only one facet of the subject's life are commonly referred to as **biographical sketches.**

Since a biography is about someone else, its author will generally use the third-person narrative, referring to the subject as "he" or "she." Of course, the author might include self-references as well, especially if the author is (or was) personally acquainted with the subject (for example, "When *I* first met the President, *he* was a member of Congress"). Also, many biographies contain first-person accounts from the subject's point of view—for example, excerpts from letters or diaries written by the subject, or from his or her conversations with others.

As you read a biography or an excerpt from one, ask yourself the following questions (these questions are just the sort that the GED® might ask):

- *What specific events surrounding the subject's life does the passage reveal?* The passage may involve a series of events over either a short or long span of time. Or it may involve essentially one moment in time: a particular conversation, incident, or "day in the life of" the subject.

- *What is it about the subject that the author seeks to reveal to the reader?* A biography might focus on a person's public achievements, successes, and failures. Or it might focus on the subject's "inner life": his or her motivations, core values, psychological profile, or private persona.

- *What is the author's overall impression of the subject?* Ask yourself whether that overall impression is positive, negative, or neutral. A neutral approach, in which the author recounts the subject's life and times as a detached observer, is quite common in biographical literature. But the biographer might show clear admiration or a bit of sympathy for the subject. Or just the opposite might be the case, as when the subject is an infamous scoundrel. Pay attention to the author's tone and language, which provide clues as to the biographer's own viewpoint on the subject, if any. Keep in mind that a biographer's own perspective need not be consistent with popular opinion. In fact, many biographies are written in order to dispel commonly held opinions about well-known people, or at least show their "other side"—the side hidden from public view.

- *If the biographer knew the subject personally, what was the nature of their relationship?* Biographies are often written by family members, casual acquaintances, professional colleagues, and childhood friends. Perhaps the two were once on friendly terms but had a "falling out," as is the case with many so-called "tell-all" books. In any event, try to determine whether their relationship was close or distant, friendly or unfriendly.

- *Does the passage reveal what other people thought of the subject?* Almost any biography will discuss people who either knew the subject personally or for some other reason have something informative or insightful to say about the subject. Be sure not to mistake the perspectives or insights of other people with those of the biographer.

QUESTIONS 39–42 REFER TO THE FOLLOWING PASSAGE.

[The following excerpt is from a biography about Sojourner Truth, a crusader for the rights of African Americans and women, who was born into slavery and named Isabella.]

After emancipation had been decreed by the State, some years before the time fixed for its consummation, Isabella's master told her if she would do well, and be faithful, he would give her "free papers," one year before she was legally free by statute. In the year 1826, she had a badly diseased hand, which
5 greatly diminished her usefulness; but on the arrival of July 4, 1827, the time specified for her receiving her "free papers," she claimed the fulfillment of her master's promise; but he refused granting it, on account (as he alleged) of the loss he had sustained by her hand. She plead that she had worked all the time, and done many things she was not wholly able to do, although she knew she
10 had been less useful than formerly; but her master remained inflexible. Her very faithfulness probably operated against her now, and he found it less easy than he thought to give up the profits of his faithful Bell, who had so long done him efficient service.

But Isabella inwardly determined that she would remain quietly with him
15 only until she had spun his wool—about one hundred pounds—and then she would leave him, taking the rest of the time to herself. "Ah!" she says, with emphasis that cannot be written, "the slaveholders are TERRIBLE for promising to give you this or that, or such and such a privilege, if you will do thus and so; and when the time of fulfillment comes, and one claims the promise,
20 they, forsooth, recollect nothing of the kind; and you are, like as not, taunted with being a LIAR; or, at best, the slave is accused of not having performed his part or condition of the contract." "Oh!" said she, "I have felt as if I could not live through the operation sometimes. Just think of us! so eager for our pleasures, and just foolish enough to keep feeding and feeding ourselves up
25 with the idea that we should get what had been thus fairly promised; and when we think it is almost in our hands, find ourselves flatly denied! Just think! how could we bear it?"

39. What does the narrative of Isabella imply about slaveholders?

The slaveholders' cruelty toward their slaves was based on

(1) twisted emotions

(2) desire for profit

(3) fear of confrontation

(4) racism

(5) misunderstanding

The idea that slaveholders' cruelty was based on their desire for profit is implied in lines 7–8 ("the loss he had sustained by her hand") and in line 12 ("to give up the profits of his faithful Bell . . ."). **The correct answer is (2).**

40. What is it about Truth's slaveholder that she mainly objects to?

(1) his harassment

(2) his brutality

(3) his unfairness

(4) his bigotry

(5) his hypocrisy

In the passage, the author clearly depicts Isabella's slaveholder as unfair: he breaks his promises despite Isabella's faithfulness. On the other hand, nowhere in the passage does the author suggest that her slaveholder harassed or brutalized her, choices (1) and (2). And though he may have been a bigot or a hypocrite, choices (4) and (5), the passage does not indicate that Isabella noted either trait or objected to it. **The correct answer is (3).**

41. Which word best describes Isabella's state of mind during the time recounted in the second paragraph?

(1) resigned

(2) calculating

(3) desperate

(4) embittered

(5) hopeful

The author suggests that earlier (during the time period recounted in the first paragraph), Isabella was somewhat hopeful but that later (during the time recounted in the second paragraph), Isabella's state of mind was essentially that of an aggrieved and bitter victim of all the various sins described in that paragraph. **The correct answer is (4).**

> **42.** The passage is excerpted from an 1850 biography about Sojourner Truth, who was born into slavery in 1797 and named Isabella. In view of these facts, which method was LEAST likely used by the biographer to reveal Truth's character, thoughts, and feelings?
>
> **(1)** recounting what people she knew said of her
>
> **(2)** paraphrasing letters that Truth wrote
>
> **(3)** recalling conversations with Truth
>
> **(4)** dramatizing Truth's life experiences
>
> **(5)** quoting entries from Truth's diary

Based on the dates provided in the question, the biographer probably lived during the same time as Truth, and may have survived her. So it makes sense that in gathering material for the biography, the author would have consulted Truth's letters and diaries, if any existed. The author would probably have sought out people who knew Truth personally, or knew of her, for their insights. And of course, if the author knew Truth personally, Truth's conversations with the author would have provided an important source of material. On the other hand, nothing in the passage suggests that the author was attempting to dramatize Truth's life. **The correct answer is (4).**

Autobiographies and Autobiographical Sketches

During the Reading Test you might encounter an excerpt from a work in which the author has written mainly about his or her own life experiences, rather than someone else's. This sort of writing may take any one of various forms. An **autobiography** is a personal account of one's life and is usually a book-length work. An **autobiographical sketch,** akin to a short story as opposed to a novel, is a briefer account of a select few of one's experiences. Closely related to the autobiographical sketch are the **diary,** a daily record of events or thoughts; the **journal,** a regular record of observed events; and the **personal letter,** in which the writer shares his or her experiences and thoughts with someone else.

In using these forms, writers generally go further than merely relating personal experiences. They also record their reflections, opinions, and feelings involving those experiences—more specifically, how they affect the writer's outlook and perceptions of life, other people, and the world around them. With the possible exception of the journal, all of these forms are highly personal and can reveal a lot about the writer's emotional inner life: his or her true motives and values as well as his or her hopes, fears, and other feelings. All of these sorts of revelations are just what you can expect GED® questions to focus on.

QUESTIONS 43–47 REFER TO THE FOLLOWING PASSAGE.

I never met my first love. She must have been a sweet and sad child. Her photographs inspire my imagination to reconstruct the outlines of her soul, simple and austere as a primitive church, extensive as a castle, stately as a tower, deep as a well . . . all of her, aglow with innocence and a certain gravity

5 in which are mixed the delights of childhood and the reverie of first youth. Her photographs invite one to try to imagine the timbre and rhythm of her voice, the ring of her laughter, the depth of her silences, the cadence of her movements, the direction and intensity of her glances. Her arms must have moved like the wings of a musical and tranquil bird; her figure must have yielded with the

10 gentleness of a lily in an April garden. How many times her translucent hands must have trimmed the lamps of the vigilant virgins who know not the day or the hour; in what moments of rapture did her mouth and eyes accentuate their sadness? When did they emphasize her sweet smile?

No, I never met her. And yet, even her pictures were with me for a long time

15 after she died. Long before then, my life was filled with her presence, fashioned of unreal images, devoid of all sensation; perhaps more faithful, certainly more vivid, than these almost faded photographs. Hers was a presence without volume, line or color; an elusive phantom, which epitomized the beauty of all faces without limiting itself to any one, and embodied the delicacy of the best

20 and loftiest spirits, indefinitely.

I now believe that an obscure feeling, a fear of reality, was the cause of my refusal to exchange the formless images for a direct knowledge of her who inspired them. How many times, just when the senses might have put a limit to fancy did I avoid meeting her; and how many others did Fate intervene!

25 On one of the many occasions that I watched the house in which my phantom lived, I decided to knock; but the family was out.

—from "Alda," by Agustín Yáñez

43. What does the author mean when he says "I never met my first love" (line 1)?

(1) He loved unconditionally.

(2) His first love died young.

(3) He fell in love with someone he never really knew.

(4) He never fell in love.

(5) His first love was not a human being.

This is a completely literal statement, typical of an autobiography. As the rest of the passage makes clear, the author never really knew Alda. **The correct answer is (3).**

44. How does the description in the first paragraph flow?

    (1) from sound to sight

    (2) from smell to sight to sound

    (3) from sight to touch

    (4) from touch to sound to sight

    (5) from sight to sound to movement

To answer this question, you need to look back at the paragraph and trace its structure. The author describes what Alda looked like, speculates on what she sounded like, and guesses how she moved, in that order. **The correct answer is (5).**

45. What does the author mean by saying that he is "devoid of all sensation" (line 16)?

    (1) He has no sense of who Alda might be

    (2) He does not see, hear, or touch Alda.

    (3) He cannot be sensible where Alda is concerned.

    (4) He has little judgment.

    (5) He feels nothing for Alda.

Reread the surrounding text to remind yourself of the author's main point. Alda's presence has no sensation for him because he has not really met her. **The correct answer is (2).**

46. What does the third paragraph accomplish that neither of the previous paragraphs does?

The third paragraph

    (1) suggests an explanation for the author's behavior

    (2) describes the author's photographs of Alda

    (3) mentions the elusive qualities of Alda

    (4) compares Alda to someone the author loved later

    (5) expresses regret for losing Alda's love

In the first sentence of paragraph 3, the author suggests that his fear of reality was the reason he failed to meet Alda. This is the first time he has made such a suggestion. Paragraph 3 might also be said to support choice (3), but so do paragraphs 1 and 2. Choices (4) and (5) are not supported anywhere in the passage. **The correct answer is (1).**

47. What would be a good title for this excerpt, as a chapter in an autobiography?

   (1) A Tragic Love Affair

   (2) First and Only Love

   (3) My Dead Sweetheart

   (4) Love and Photography

   (5) Remembrance of a Phantom Love

When you are asked to choose a title, you are really being asked to summarize the passage. In this case, choice (1) does not work—we don't know that this is tragic. Choice (2) does not work because we have no hint that this was the narrator's only love, choice (3) is incorrect because the two were never sweethearts, and choice (4) is clearly irrelevant. Choice (5) accurately reflects the scope and tone of the excerpt. **The correct answer is (5).**

Literary Essays

Another form of literary nonfiction you might find on the Reading Test is the **literary essay.** Unlike a journal or diary, which records its writer's experiences, a literary essay presents a writer's ideas or observations involving a particular subject. The essay might present the writer's thoughts on abstract concepts such as love, life, or justice; it might provide social, cultural, or political commentary; or it might record the writer's observations and reflections on nature and the physical world. In short, any subject is possible.

Literary essays are generally subjective, presenting their writers' own viewpoints and insights on particular topics. A typical essay is intended to convey a main idea or central point, which the writer develops with supporting details (examples and reasons). The reader might find the main idea nicely expressed either near the beginning or end of the essay. Or, the reader might be left to determine the main idea by synthesizing the essay as a whole. An essay on nature and the physical world may provide broad assertions about divinity or beauty, supported by vivid descriptions and colorful imagery—much like poetry. An essay on concepts such as love, justice, or human suffering may draw conclusions about human nature or the meaning of life, supported by specific observations of societal or human behavior.

As you read an essay (or an excerpt from an essay), try to identify the main idea and how the details support that idea. A critical essay may contain arguments from logic, in which case you should try to follow the author's line reasoning—from the writer's observations to the conclusions that the writer draws from those observations. Also pay attention to the essay's tone: the language used to help convey the attitude or viewpoint of the writer.

QUESTIONS 48–51 REFER TO THE FOLLOWING PASSAGE.

In the North, for every one thousand workers over sixteen years of age there are eighty-three workers under sixteen; while in the South, for every one thousand workers in the mills over sixteen years of age there are three hundred and fifty-three under sixteen. Some of these are eight and nine years
5   old, and some are only five and six. For a day or a night at a stretch these little children do some one monotonous thing—abusing their eyes in watching the rushing threads; dwarfing their muscles in an eternity of petty movements; befouling their lungs by breathing flecks of flying cotton; bestowing ceaseless, anxious attention for hours, where science says that "a twenty-minute strain
10 is long enough for a growing mind." And these are not the children of recent immigrants, hardened by the effete conditions of foreign servitude. Nor are they Negro children who have shifted their shackles from field to mill. They are white children of old and pure colonial stock. Think of it! Here is a people that has outlived the bondage of England, that has seen the rise and fall of slavery
15 —a people that must now fling their children into the clutches of capital, into the maw of the blind machine . . .

Fifty thousand children. mostly girls, are in the textile mills of the South. Six times as many children are working now as were working twenty years ago. Unless the conscience of the nation can be awakened, it will not be long
20 before one hundred thousand children will be hobbling in hopeless lockstep to these Bastilles of labor.

—Edwin Markham

48. Why does the author use the words "abusing," "dwarfing," and "befouling" (lines 6–8)?

The author uses these words to show

(1) the diverse jobs available for children

(2) the quality of the work performed in the mills

(3) how little respect for life mill workers have

(4) how adults fare no better than children

(5) health hazards for children who work in mills

The words appear in a list of children's tasks and clearly describe the harm those tasks do. **The correct answer is (5).**

49. By quoting "science" (line 9), what point is the author supporting?

(1) Young muscles are built by hard labor.

(2) Mill work helps develop the mind.

(3) Children should not work long hours.

(4) Mill work is physically strenuous.

(5) All children should attend school.

Read in context, the point is that it may harm a growing mind (of a child) to spend too long a time on any single task, and twenty minutes should be the limit. **The correct answer is (3).**

---

50. What does the author mean by "shifted their shackles from field to mill" (line 12)?

    (1) taken their slaves from country to city

    (2) changed from field slaves to slaves of the mills

    (3) shifted the investments from farms to factories

    (4) went from job to job without finding stable work

    (5) left a life of servitude for a better life

Do not read more into these words than is there. The author merely speaks of a simple shift in "shackles," or servitude, not an improvement in status. **The correct answer is (2).**

---

51. The passage is from an essay by Edwin Markham, one of the "muckrakers" of the early 1900s who tried to reveal inhumane working conditions in factories. In view of these facts, what comparison was Markham drawing by using the phrase "maw of the blind machine" (line 16)?

The author is comparing mill work to a

    (1) senseless device

    (2) matriarchic society

    (3) cruel, unfeeling mother

    (4) monstrous ogre

    (5) tool that blinds workers

The word *maw* means "jaws," particularly of a meat-eating variety. Even if you did not know this, the underlying theme of a faceless monster seeking to destroy young children is strongly implied by Markham's descriptive language. **The correct answer is (4).**

Oral History

Yet another form of writing that is considered literary nonfiction is **oral history,** which is an interpretation of historical information, based on the personal experiences and opinions of the speaker. Oral history may be based on first-hand accounts of events or on stories passed down over the years by word of mouth. Folklore, myths, and legends are also considered oral history, even though they are mainly fictional. Once written down, oral histories can read very much like short stories, complete with characters, dialogue, and plot that tell a chronology of past events. You should apply the same tools for understanding oral history as you would for understanding prose fiction.

A distinctive feature of oral history is that these works are often intended to teach a moral or lesson by presenting a simple story that serves as a guide for listeners (or readers) for conducting their own lives.

QUESTIONS 52–55 REFER TO THE FOLLOWING PASSAGE.

In the old days it was not unusual to find several generations living together in one home. Usually, everyone lived in peace and harmony, but this situation caused problems for one man whose household included, besides his wife and small son, his elderly father.

5 It so happened that the daughter-in-law took a dislike to the old man. He was always in the way, she said, and she insisted he be removed to a small room apart from the house.

Because the old man was out of sight, he was often neglected. Sometimes he even went hungry. They took poor care of him, and in winter the old man often
10 suffered from the cold. One day the little grandson visited his grandfather.

"My little one," the grandfather said, "go and find a blanket and cover me. It is cold and I am freezing."

The small boy ran to the barn to look for a blanket, and there he found a rug. "Father, please cut this rug in half," he asked his father.

15 "Why? What are you going to do with it?"

"I'm going to take it to my grandfather because he is cold."

"Well, take the entire rug," replied the father.

"No," his son answered, "I cannot take it all. I want you to cut it in half so I can save the other half for you when you are as old as my grandfather. Then
20 I will have it for you so you will not be cold."

His son's response was enough to make the man realize how poorly he had treated his own father. The man then brought his father back into his home and ordered that a warm room be prepared. From that time on he took care of his father's needs and visited him frequently every day.

52. What does the narrator mean by the phrase "several generations" (line 1)?

(1) many years

(2) separate lifetimes

(3) children, parents, and grandparents

(4) several breeding periods

(5) more than one beginning

Only choice (3) makes sense in the context of many generations living under one roof. **The correct answer is (3).**

53. Why was the elderly man removed from the house?

    (1) There wasn't enough space in the house.

    (2) His son disliked being around him.

    (3) There wasn't enough food to feed him.

    (4) His son's wife insisted on it.

    (5) The house was not heated.

The narrator tells us that the daughter-in-law insisted on having him removed from the house because she disliked him and considered him to be in the way. But this does not necessarily mean that the house was not large enough for him, choice (1). **The correct answer is (4).**

54. What is a good analogy to the grandchild's actions?

    (1) rationing fresh water among people in a lifeboat

    (2) teaching an old dog a new trick

    (3) sharing a candy bar with a friend

    (4) saving money for your own retirement

    (5) donating money to an overseas charity

The grandson's actions are selfless: he simply wants to help both his grandfather *and* his father. To help both, he wants to cut the rug in half, like someone in a lifeboat who divides up available fresh water to help ensure that everyone survives. **The correct answer is (1).**

55. The passage is a modern translation of a tale from the Hispanic Southwest. In the tale, what did the elderly man's son probably learn?

    (1) Letting others go hungry is morally wrong.

    (2) Respecting your elders can benefit you.

    (3) Children cannot be trusted to do what is right.

    (4) Each of us must ultimately provide for ourselves.

    (5) Elderly people need the company of others.

Though not necessarily the tale's primary lesson, the man sees now that his kindness will be rewarded when he himself becomes old. In other words, his kindness will benefit him someday. **The correct answer is (2).**

Critical Reviews of the Visual and Performing Arts

The GED® Reading Test might include a passage of text that provides a **critical review** (a commentary or critique) involving the visual or performing arts. The **visual arts** include such arts as painting and drawing, sculpture, photography, film, and television. The **performing arts** include such arts as music (recordings and performances), dance, plays, and other stage productions. The passage might provide a critical review of a particular work or production. Or it might comment on various works of a particular artist, or even on an entire genre or movement—for example, bebop jazz music or the Impressionist school of painting. Don't worry if your knowledge of the review's subject is limited; the passage will provide all you'll need to know in order to answer the questions based on it.

The review will likely contain some description of the work. It might also indicate when and where the work was created, as well as the materials and processes used to create it. And if the review concerns a specific visual work, such as a painting, the review will probably be accompanied by a visual depiction of the work. The visual depiction may help you understand the review and answer the questions based on it. But be sure you answer the questions based on the text, and not on the visual depiction. Otherwise, you may be lured by a wrong-answer choice that accurately describes the work but does not answer the question.

Of course, the review will go beyond simply describing and providing background information. In a critical review, the author's main purpose is to *evaluate*, and so the review will express a subjective viewpoint, based on the author's own opinion, which should not be mistaken for fact.

Art critics and commentators rarely state explicitly that they love or detest the work under review. Instead, they often leave it up to the reader to infer what they think, based on how they've characterized or described their subjects. One way to identify a reviewer's opinions is to pay close attention to the reviewer's attitude toward the subject, as shown through the overall tone of writing. The reviewer's tone provides clues as to whether—and how much—the reviewer approves or disapproves of the subject. Art critics tend to be negative in their reviews, but a review or commentary of the arts can be entirely positive as well.

QUESTIONS 56–58 REFER TO THE FOLLOWING PHOTOGRAPH AND PASSAGE.

[The following is a commentary on a photograph entitled "Migrant Mother" (above) by noted photographer Dorothea Lange, who took the photograph in 1936 during the height of the Great Depression.]

It is not difficult to see how the photograph captures simultaneously a sense of individual worth and class victimage. The close portraiture creates a moment of personal anxiety as this specific woman, without name, silently harbors her fears for her children, while the dirty, ragged clothes and bleak
5   setting signify the hard work and limited prospects of the laboring classes. The disposition of her body — and above all, the involuntary gesture of her right arm reaching up to touch her chin — communicates related tensions. We see both physical strength and palpable worry: a hand capable of productive labor and an absent-minded motion that implies the futility of any action in such
10   impoverished circumstances. The remainder of the composition communicates both a reflexive defensiveness, as the bodies of the two standing children are turned inward and away from the photographer (as if from an impending blow), and a sense of inescapable vulnerability, for her body and head are tilted slightly forward to allow each of the three children the comfort they need, her
15   shirt is unbuttoned, and the sleeping baby is in a partially exposed position.

These features of the photograph are cues for emotional responses that the composition manages with great economy. At its most obvious, "Migrant Mother" communicates the pervasive and paralyzing fear that was widely acknowledged to be a defining characteristic of the depression and experienced
20   by many Americans irrespective of income. Thus, the photograph embodies a limit condition for democracy identified by Franklin Delano Roosevelt in his first inaugural address: "The only thing we have to fear is fear itself. . . ."

56. Which of the following characterizations of "Migrant Mother" would the reviewer probably agree is most accurate?

   (1) a study in contrast

   (2) a contrived portrait

   (3) an unfair social commentary

   (4) a frightening image

   (5) an appeal to charity

The reviewer observes in the photograph no fewer than three contrasts: "a sense of individual worth and class victimage" (lines 1–2); "both physical strength and palpable worry" (line 8); "both a reflexive defensiveness . . . and a sense of inescapable vulnerability" (lines 11–13). Choice (4) is incorrect because the reviewer does not suggest that the image itself is frightening but rather that it communicates the fear experienced by people during the Great Depression. Choice (5) is incorrect because nowhere in the text does the reviewer suggest that the photograph was taken in order to encourage people to be more charitable. **The correct answer is (1).**

57. Which element of the photograph does the reviewer seem to admire the most?

   (1) the photographer's use of light and shadow on the face of the mother

   (2) the mother's reaction to seeing her children's pictures being taken

   (3) the sense of hope that is evident on the mother's face

   (4) the positioning of the subjects within the photograph's frame

   (5) the maternal love shown by the way the mother holds her baby

Notice that the photograph itself provides little guidance for answering the question. To respond to the question, you need to understand the ideas contained in the text. In the first paragraph, the reviewer observes how effectively the positions and postures of the photographer's subjects convey their emotional, psychological, and social condition, choice (4). Nowhere in the text does the reviewer mention the use of light and shadow, choice (1), nor does the reviewer mention the mother's reaction to either her or her children being photographed, choice (2). According to the reviewer, the mother displays fear, anxiety, and worry, but the reviewer never mentions that she shows hope, choice (3). As for choice (5), the only mention of the baby is that its partial exposure suggests vulnerability. **The correct answer is (4).**

> **58.** The reviewer writes that certain features of the photograph "are cues for emotional responses that the composition manages with great economy" (lines 16–17). What does this remark suggest about the photographer?
>
> The photographer was skilled at
>
> **(1)** capturing the best possible image in a single shot
>
> **(2)** connecting emotionally with her subjects
>
> **(3)** producing striking images with inexpensive equipment
>
> **(4)** prompting her subjects to show their emotions for the camera
>
> **(5)** creating photographs that carry an emotional impact

The features that the reviewer refers to are the subject's postures and positions described in the previous paragraph. In saying that these feature are "cues for emotional responses," the reviewer probably means they cause the viewer to react emotionally to the photograph. (The phrase "with great economy" probably means that the photographer achieved this impact through sparing but effective use of certain compositional techniques.) **The correct answer is (5).**

Additional Information in Critical Reviews

Of course, a review or commentary need not be entirely positive or negative. It might provide a positive evaluation of one aspect of a work (for example, a painting's composition) yet a negative evaluation of another aspect of it (for example, the artist's use of color).

Also keep in mind that critical reviews often provide background information about the work and artist under review, such as the following:

- How the work compares to works previously created by the same artist

- How the work compares to similar works by other artists

- How the artist or work might have been influenced by previous artists and their works

Pay close attention to any such information; you'll probably be tested on it.

QUESTIONS 59–62 REFER TO THE FOLLOWING PASSAGE.

In the past decade, it has seemed as if Michael Moore has had his finger on the pulse of issues concerning us. We had his take on post-Columbine gun control, conspiracy notions surrounding 9/11, the American health-care mess, and now a broadside attack on the c-word itself, *Capitalism: A Love Story*, hot
5 on the heels of America's financial tsunami.
From another perspective, of course, Moore can also be seen as a shrewd Great American entrepreneur, like an ambulance chaser who seizes on subjects, rattling the public's interests and feeding them entertaining mock-exposés full of flimsy reasoning, genuinely funny showboating, and wanton disregard for
10 basic journalistic integrity. The film's clever title may ultimately be less ironic

than intended by the most successful hyper-capitalist in the history of documentary filmmaking. Of course, Moore's films become infinitely more enjoyable once you yank away the standards by which docs are conventionally judged.

15   This time out, Moore seizes the economically frazzled moment to take a look at the fissures leading to our current crisis, pinpointing the beginning of the morass in Reaganomics. He pretends to examine the complex and sinister forces leading to the economic meltdown, but winds up throwing up his hands trying to define "derivatives." To dig up fresh material in the larger story, he heads down subplot paths—for instance, a corrupt children's detention facility

20   in Pennsylvania, the morbid "Dead Peasants" insurance policy secretly taken out by companies on their workers. He revisits his first, and best, film, *Roger & Me*, from 20 years ago, and is still trying, vainly, to interview important people, who generally refuse to talk to him.

    Like the other films in the Moore oeuvre, *Capitalism* has much to offer,

25   including a spur to communal conversation on a topic all too close to home. At the same time, he's up to his old questionable tricks, as a provocateur with an entertainer's soul. He comes off as a well-meaning, bulbous, bullhorn-bearing buffoon, entertaining millions, raking millions of dollars into his ever fatter, happy, capitalist bank account, and delivering repeated blows to the presumed

30   integrity of the documentary genre.

59. In writing that the film's title "may ultimately be less ironic than intended" (line 10–11) by Moore, what does the reviewer mean?

    (1) The film's subjects generally dislike Moore.

    (2) The film is actually about what its title implies.

    (3) The film does not contain any love scenes.

    (4) Moore loves making money.

    (5) Moore thoroughly enjoyed making the film.

In the previous sentence, the reviewer describes Moore as a "shrewd Great American entrepreneur," suggesting that he has a cunning business sense in the tradition of other Americans who started their own hugely successful businesses. So the title (*Capitalism: a Love Story*) is *un*-ironic in the sense that Moore himself—much like the film's subjects whom he is criticizing—has a passion or love for producing money-making, box-office hits. **The correct answer is (4).**

60. What is the reviewer's main concern in the third paragraph (lines 14–23)?

    (1) to provide the reader a sense of the film's content

    (2) to show that *Roger & Me* was a better film than *Capitalism*

    (3) to show that the film devotes too much time to its subplots

    (4) to give examples of Moore's filmmaking techniques

    (5) to show that Moore does not understand high finance

The third paragraph is essentially a synopsis of the film. Although the reviewer implies that it is not so good as *Roger & Me*, choice (1), this is not the reviewer's main point in the paragraph. **The correct answer is (1).**

61. What does the reviewer's opinion of Moore as a filmmaker seem to be?

The reviewer probably thinks that Moore

(1) is out of touch with the cultural mainstream

(2) sets a high standard for documentary films

(3) has a flair for entertaining

(4) pays little attention to details

(5) is a skilled director and film editor

In the second paragraph, the reviewer writes that *Capitalism* displays Moore's "genuinely funny showboating." Later, the reviewer writes that Moore has "an entertainer's soul" and that in his film he is "entertaining millions." The clear suggestion is that Moore has a talent for entertaining others through his work. Though the reviewer mentions the film's many factual inaccuracies, the reviewer does not say that they were unintentional on Moore's part, choice (4). Though the reviewer clearly thinks Moore is skilled as a producer-director and as a "star" of his own films, Moore's editing skills, choice (5), are not discussed in the review. **The correct answer is (3).**

62. Which is an accurate characterization of the review as a whole?

(1) scathing

(2) even-handed

(3) flattering

(4) unfairly critical

(5) superficial

The review evaluates the film positively in some respects and negatively in others. Since the review notes both the good and the bad, choices (1), (3), and (4) are incorrect. As for choice (5), the review is detailed and insightful, quite the opposite of superficial. **The correct answer is (2).**

Workplace and Community Documents

A final genre of nonfiction texts you might see on the Reading Test is what the test-makers call **workplace and community documents.** The text might be a statement of policy, a mission statement, guidelines or rules for workplace behavior, an excerpt from an employee handbook or training manual, a statement of employee benefits, a communication (e-mail, written memorandum, or letter), or even a legal document, such as an employment contract. Also, depending on the document type, the text might contain headings or numbered lists.

These documents are a lot like the workplace and community documents on the Reading Test. What's different is that, instead of looking for errors within the document, your task is to apply your comprehension, analysis, synthesis, and application skills to it. As you read a workplace or community document, try to answer the following questions for yourself:

- Who is the intended *audience*? (A specific individual? All or only certain employees? A general community?)

- What is the overall *scope* of the document? (Does it address only specific policies, procedures, or problems? Or is it broader in scope?)

- What *goal* or *objective* of the institution is the document intended to further? (For example, the document's purpose might be to enhance workplace efficiency, thwart employee misconduct, increase profits or revenues, obtain funding, or attract new clients or customers.)

- What is the writer's *point of view*? (Does the document express an opinion about any specific issue, or does it simply provide information?)

- What is the overall *tone* of the document? (The overall tone might be objective; but if a document serves as a warning—to employees, for example—the tone might be somewhat sharp or even accusatory.)

Also, if the document has a title, ask yourself what it suggests about the document's audience, scope, and purpose.

If you encounter a statement of policy or a mission statement on the test, expect at least one question asking what the broad policy or mission is. (A **policy** is a general principle or broad course of action adopted by an institution as a guide for conducting its affairs.)

To understand the policy or mission, you may need to synthesize information from various parts of the document. Also, policy and mission statements typically provide details explaining how the institution implements its policy or mission. So expect test questions about those supporting details as well.

QUESTIONS 63 AND 64 REFER TO THE FOLLOWING PASSAGE.

The Women's Service Association is an organization of over 500 women in the community committed to promoting volunteerism, developing the potential of women, and improving our community through effective action and leadership of trained volunteers. During its 75-year history, the Women's Service Association
5 has initiated hundreds of community improvement projects through partnerships with local agencies, churches, and educational institutions. The Women's Service Association's commitment to the quality of life in Washington County is demonstrated by our educational and community outreach projects. Each is designed to improve the physical, intellectual, and emotional development
10 of children and adolescents.

[The document continues by discussing some of the association's recent activities in more detail, and by announcing an upcoming fund-raising event.]

63. Which best expresses the mission of the Women's Service Association?

    (1) helping unemployed community residents find work

    (2) promoting economic growth in the community

    (3) promoting the rights of women and children

    (4) helping to improve quality of life in the community

    (5) aiding in education of children in the community

The paragraph does not state the association's broad objective, or mission, in a single, concise sentence. To identify the best answer choice, you need to read the whole paragraph, noting that the association is involved in promoting various community causes through its initiatives and activities. Choice (4) best expresses what all of these causes have in common. **The correct answer is (4).**

64. Which of the following activities is most likely to be attributable to the Women's Service Organization?

    (1) construction of a gazebo at a retirement home

    (2) fund-raising for a political candidate

    (3) construction of an inner-city children's library

    (4) sponsorship of a men-only educational seminar

    (5) sponsorship of a soup kitchen for the unemployed

This question focuses on specific activities that support the mission statement. While any of the answer choices might be a worthy service project, an inner-city children's library is the only project that is an example of a sort of cause that the association is involved in (see the last sentence). **The correct answer is (3).**

Policy Statements

Akin to a mission statement, a policy statement typically provides details about how to implement the policy at hand. But unlike a mission, a policy is typically implemented through specific rules, regulations, and guidelines. When reading a policy statement, try to:

- Distinguish between a general policy and a specific policy, which is a rule or guideline that supports a general policy.

- Distinguish between *rules*, which require or prohibit certain behavior, and *guidelines*, which are merely suggestions as to how to further a policy.

- Pay attention to any consequences (discipline or punishment) for violating a rule or regulation. If consequences are discussed, pay attention to whether they vary, depending on the specific violation.

A policy statement that provides rules and regulations may contain so-called "legalese," which refers to words and phrases used in legal documents. If you run across legalese, don't be surprised if one of the test questions focuses on it. Don't worry: you should be able to figure out what the legalese means from its context. In fact, this skill is exactly what you're being tested on.

The following excerpt could be part of a policy statement, an employee handbook or training manual, or even an employment agreement. All of these types of documents can contain statements of policy as well as specific rules, regulations, or guidelines.

QUESTIONS 65–67 REFER TO THE FOLLOWING DOCUMENT EXCERPT.

[The document begins with Section 1, and then continues with Section 2, as follows.]

Section 2

2.1. Metacorp has a no-tolerance policy with respect to employee pilfering. As used in this section, "pilfering" means the taking of any company property, regardless of its monetary value, for personal rather than company use, whether temporarily or permanently.

2.2. Any employee who is determined to have pilfered company property will be subject to disciplinary action in accordance with the guidelines set forth herein concerning warnings and subsequent termination of employment, and with applicable state and federal laws.

2.3. If an employee submits a false report of a violation under this section, that employee will be subject to immediate disciplinary action, which may include termination of employment without warning. For purposes of this provision, a "false report" is any report that the reporting employee knew or should have known was untrue or inaccurate, either in whole or in part.

65. Why did the company include Section 2 in the document?

 (1) to catch employees suspected of pilfering

 (2) to discourage employees from pilfering

 (3) to make it easier for the company to fire its employees

 (4) to encourage employees to report pilfering incidents

 (5) to attract employees who are trustworthy

The first sentence of paragraph 2.1 expresses the company's general policy that it will not tolerate pilfering, while the rules that follow warn employees of harsh consequences should they violate the policy. Clearly, the main purpose of the section is to discourage employees from pilfering. Choices (1), (3), and (5) all provide advantages of having this type of policy, but none expresses the *purpose* of the policy. Choice (4) is incorrect because paragraph 2.3 actually *discourages* the reporting of pilfering. **The correct answer is (2).**

66. What would happen to a Metacorp employee who borrows a coffee carafe from work but forgets to return it?

Under Section 2, the employee would probably

(1) be required to replace the company's carafe with a new one

(2) be fired by Metacorp because the company has a no-tolerance policy

(3) not be subject to discipline, because the employee intended to return the item

(4) not be subject to discipline, because the item is inexpensive

(5) receive a warning if this was the employee's first violation of Section 2

To answer this question, you need to distinguish between consequences for pilfering (Section 2.2) and those for falsely reporting pilfering (Section 2.3). The applicable section is 2.2, which mentions "warnings" as a pre-termination procedure. Assuming this was a first offense, the pilfering employee's only discipline would probably be a warning. **The correct answer is (5).**

67. For which behavior would a Metacorp employee most likely be disciplined?

(1) taking home a company desk that was just thrown away

(2) reporting a pilfering incident that was never actually observed

(3) throwing away paper that could have been reused by the company

(4) using a company telephone to make long-distance, personal calls

(5) driving a company vehicle to a business-related conference

To answer this question correctly, you need to understand the definition of "false report." Its definition, provided in paragraph 2.3, contains some legalese. Choice (2) describes what might be considered submitting a false report, depending on the circumstances. If the reporting employee had absolutely no reason to suspect a coworker of pilfering, then it is possible that the employee knew or *should have known* that the report was false *in whole or in part*. **The correct answer is (2).**

Communication Documents

Another type of workplace or community document you might encounter is a communication such as an e-mail, memo, or letter. The communication might be to a particular person, or it might be to a group. In its ideas and its tone, a communication is more likely than other workplace and community documents to be *subjective*—that is, to communicate a distinct point of view and attitude toward the topic at hand, and possibly toward the recipient of the communication as well.

Here are some suggestions for reading and understanding a communication document:

- Try to identify its main idea, and note the details provided in support of that idea.

- Ask yourself: Why did the author compose this e-mail, memo, or letter? What was the author trying to accomplish by doing so?

- As with other workplace and community documents, look for policy statements, and distinguish between supporting rules and supporting guidelines.

- If the communication begins by identifying the sender, recipient, and/or the subject, pay attention to those lines. They can provide clues about the communication's topic and point of view.

QUESTIONS 68–70 REFER TO THE FOLLOWING MEMO.

From: Jason Renaldi <jason.renaldi@theberwyngroup.com>

To: All Berwyn Corporation employees

Subject: Employee dress code and lunchtime policy

Beginning on Wednesday, January 17, our company dress code requiring all men and women to wear business suits will not apply on Wednesdays. All employees will be permitted to dress casually each Wednesday, at their option. Jeans will be considered appropriate attire, but T-shirts and/or shorts will be considered inappropriate. Women may wear open-toed shoes, but men may not. Management encourages you to enjoy the freedom of "casual Wednesdays" while still dressing in good taste.

Also beginning on January 17, you may take up to one-and-a-half hours for lunch, between 11:30 to 2:00. To make up the half-hour of work lost due to a longer lunch, you must either arrive up to 30 minutes earlier to start your Wednesday workday or leave 30 minutes later to end your workday. If you prefer a relatively late Wednesday lunch, management has arranged for the mobile food vendor Cuisine on Wheels to serve lunch in our parking lot from 12:45 to 1:45 every Wednesday—again, starting on January 17. For those of you leaving the premises for Wednesday lunch, as always we encourage you to carpool and to dine with your coworkers.

I'm confident that a more leisurely lunch and casual attire will leave us all that much more excited about whatever challenges lie ahead during the rest of the work week. As always, I welcome your continuing feedback on these and other working conditions.

Jason Renaldi
Human Resources Director
Berwyn Corporation

68. Which is the most likely purpose of the e-mail?

    (1) to announce policies designed to improve employee morale

    (2) to inform workers of recent company developments

    (3) to introduce incentives for job performance

    (4) to forewarn employees of unwelcome policy changes

    (5) to defend the company's dress code and lunch-hour policy

The closing paragraph reveals the purpose of the new policies: to help workers face the second half of the work week with a positive outlook—in other words, to improve their morale. **The correct answer is (1).**

69. Which of the following best describes the tone of the e-mail?

    (1) complimentary

    (2) constructively critical

    (3) friendly

    (4) defensive

    (5) casual

Although "friendly" might not be the first word you'd think of to describe the tone of the e-mail, it's an apt word. Choice (5) might seem appropriate, but the "casual Wednesday" policy itself should not be confused with the somewhat formal tone in which that policy is communicated. Choice (1) is incorrect for the same reason: the new policy might be interpreted as a compliment to employees, but the policy itself is something entirely different from the tone of the communication. **The correct answer is (3).**

70. What will be required of Berwyn Corporation employees in the future?

    On Wednesdays, employees of Berwyn Corporation must

    (1) dress in good taste

    (2) eat lunch off the Berwyn premises

    (3) carpool to lunch

    (4) wear jeans to work

    (5) work as long as on other work days

The author implies that workers must compensate for a longer lunch by either starting the workday earlier or ending it later. All other details mentioned in the e-mail are guidelines, or suggestions, rather than rules or requirements. **The correct answer is (5).**

GENERAL TEST-TAKING STRATEGIES

Here are some general strategies for tackling the Language Art, Reading Test. These points of advice generally apply to all types of passages and questions. Put these strategies to work on the Practice Tests in this book, and then review them again just before exam day.

Read the questions based on a passage before you read the passage itself.

Each passage of text on the Reading Test will be followed by four to eight questions that refer to it. Before you read the passage, read the question stems (the questions themselves, but not the answer choices). This task should only take you 20 seconds or so. Some of the questions will provide clues as to what you should look for and think about as you read.

Read the "purpose question" and the passage's title (if any) before reading the passage.

Immediately preceding each passage is a brief "purpose question" in **bold** face. Purpose questions are designed to help you anticipate what each passage is about. They will not appear as actual test questions. By all means, read the purpose question, but don't take any more than a few seconds to think about it. Also note the passage's title, if one is supplied. The title may help you anticipate the scope of the topic, the passage's main idea, or the author's intent and attitude.

Read each passage straight through before answering any questions based on it.

Read the passage from beginning to end. Focus mainly on the flow of ideas from one to another. Maintaining this mind-set will help you understand the passage's main ideas and tone, as well as the author's overall concern and purpose in mentioning various details—all of which in turn will help you answer the questions.

Use your pencil as you read each passage.

Don't be afraid to mark up your test booklet. Underline key words and phrases in the passage, and jot down notes in the margins. Using your pencil while you read helps you to think actively about what you're reading. It also helps you find information in the passage you need as you answer the questions.

Don't get bogged down in details as you read a passage.

Some GED® reading passages will be loaded with details: examples, descriptions, dates, and so forth. If you try to absorb all of the details as you read, you'll not only lose sight of the ideas behind the details, you'll also lose reading speed. Don't get bogged down in the details, especially those you don't fully understand. Instead, gloss over them. Note where examples, lists, and other details are located. Then, if you're asked a question involving those details, you can quickly and easily locate them and read them more carefully.

Sum up a passage after you read it.

After reading an entire passage, take a few seconds to recap it. If the passage is non-fiction, ask yourself what the author's main point and major supporting points are. If the passage is from a fictional story, recap events in your mind. Remind yourself about the flow of the discussion or events, without thinking about all the details. Seeing the "big picture" may be enough to answer as many as half the questions.

If possible, formulate your own answer to a question before reading the answer choices.

For each question, try to formulate your own response to it, and *then* scan the choices for something resembling your home-grown answer. This technique will keep you from becoming confused and distracted by wrong-answer choices.

To answer a question that quotes the passage, expect to "read around" the quoted text.

A particular question might quote a word, line, or entire sentence from the passage. If so, be sure you understand the *context* of the quote before answering the question. Re-read the sentences preceding and following the quote. Chances are, you'll need to understand what precedes and follows the quote to recognize the best answer choice.

To avoid skipping around the passage, answer the questions in sequence.

The sequence of questions generally corresponds to where the passage addresses each one. For example, a question about the first paragraph will probably appear earlier than a question about the second paragraph. Answering the questions in sequence helps you "go with the flow" of ideas as the passage presents them. So avoid "shopping around" for easy questions, unless you're running out of time. Keep in mind, however, that some questions *might* appear out of sequence and that questions involving the entire passage can appear anywhere in the sequence.

Pace yourself properly.

Expect the Reading Test to include six to eight question sets (seven sets is most common), and four to eight questions per set (five to six questions is most common)—forty (40) questions in total. You're allowed 65 minutes to answer all forty questions. So after 30 minutes, you should have answered at least twenty questions. If you haven't, pick up your pace. In any event, try to answer all forty questions with a few minutes to spare, so you can go back and reconsider any responses you were unsure about.

SUMMING IT UP

- The Language Arts, Reading Test gauges your ability to understand, interpret, evaluate, synthesize, and apply information contained in fiction as well as nonfiction texts. The test consists of several reading passages, each one followed by several multiple-choice questions.

- Reading Test passages are drawn from a wide variety of sources, including fiction (prose, drama, and poetry), nonfiction (informational and opinion texts, literary nonfiction, and critical reviews of the visual and performing arts), and workplace and community documents.

- The broad reading skill areas tested in the Reading Test include comprehension, analysis and interpretation, evaluation and synthesis, and application.

- The Language Arts, Reading tests lasts 65 minutes. You should expect a total of six to eight passages and four to eight questions per passage—forty questions in total. Each passage of prose will be 200 to 400 words in length (about a half page), and the poem will be ten to twenty-five lines in length. Purpose questions appear before each passage and are designed to help you focus your attention and anticipate what each passage is about. You are not required to answer purpose questions.

PART VII
THE MATHEMATICS TEST

Mastering the
Mathematics Test

chapter 11

THE MATHEMATICS TEST—IN A NUTSHELL

Time allowed: 90 minutes

Total number of questions: 50

Part I: 45 minutes, 25 questions (calculator allowed)

Part II: 45 minutes, 25 questions (calculator NOT allowed)

ALL ABOUT THE MATHEMATICS TEST

The GED® Mathematics Test is designed to measure a variety of skills, including:

- Understanding and applying mathematical concepts and formulas

- Quantitative reasoning and problem solving

- Translating verbal language into mathematical terms

- Computing, estimating, and rounding numbers

- Analyzing and interpreting graphical data (charts, graphs, tables)

To measure these skills, the test covers four broad knowledge areas, each one accounting for 20–30 percent of the test:

- **Numbers, number sense, and operations** (20–30 percent)

543

- Basic operation with numbers
- Integers, divisibility, factoring, and multiples
- Number signs, absolute value, the real number line, and ordering
- Decimals, place value, and scientific notation
- Percents and fractions
- Exponents (powers) and roots
- Ratio and proportion

- **Data, statistics, and probability** (20–30 percent)
  - Measures of central tendency (mean, median, range)
  - Frequency distribution
  - Comparing data sets
  - Probability

- **Algebra, functions, and patterns** (20–30 percent)
  - Setting up and evaluating algebraic expressions
  - Linear equations and equation systems
  - Algebra word problems
  - Algebraic inequalities
  - Factorable quadratic expressions
  - Functional relationships, including series and patterns

- **Geometry, coordinate geometry, and measurement** (20–30 percent)
  - Parallel lines, transversals, and perpendicular lines
  - Properties of triangles, quadrilaterals, and other polygons
  - Properties of circles (area, circumference, interior degree measures)
  - The Pythagorean theorem
  - Right triangle trigonometry
  - Three-dimensional figures (rectangular solids, right cylinders, square pyramids, cones)
  - Coordinate geometry
  - Systems of measurement for length, area, volume, weight, mass

Keep in mind that many of questions will involve more than one of the four broad areas listed above. For example, solving a geometry problem might also require algebra.

FORMAT AND FEATURES OF THE MATHEMATICS TEST

The GED® Mathematics Test actually consists of two parts—Part I and Part II—contained in separate booklets. Each part consists of twenty-five questions, and you will have 45 minutes for each part.

During Part I (questions 1–25), you are permitted to use a calculator. The calculator you will use is the *Casio fx-260* solar calculator, and it will be provided to you at the testing center. (You'll examine that calculator's functions a few pages ahead.) During Part II (questions 26–50), the use of a calculator is *not* allowed. As you might expect, answering Part I questions will involve more computations than answering Part II questions, which emphasize concepts, estimating, and so-called "mental math." Nevertheless, expect to perform some calculations during Part II as well.

All but about ten of the fifty questions on the Mathematics Test are multiple-choice (five choices) questions. The remaining ten questions or so will require you to provide your own answer using an answer grid or a coordinate plane provided on your answer sheet. (You'll look at these alternative question formats just ahead as well.)

Here are some additional features of the Mathematics Test:

- Many of the questions are presented in "real-world" settings involving practical, everyday situations.

- Expect at least a third of the questions to refer to charts, graphs, tables, and geometry figures. These figures are drawn to scale unless otherwise noted.

- For some multiple-choice questions, answer choice (5) will state: "Not enough information is provided." A question that includes this answer choice may or may not provide sufficient information for you to answer the question posed.

As with every other part of the GED®, you will be provided scratch paper for both parts of the Mathematics Test. You will also be provided the same list of formulas as the one that appears before each of the Mathematics Practice Tests. You may or may not need all of these formulas during the test.

Finally, during each part of the Mathematics Test, easier questions generally appear before more challenging questions. This is only a general rule; you may find some earlier questions to be more difficult for you than some of the subsequent questions.

MEASUREMENTS AND THE MATHEMATICS TEST

During the Mathematics Test, you will be solving problems involving measurement of currency (money), time, length, weight, volume, and possibly mass. Some of these questions will require you to convert one unit of measurement to another. You will be expected to know the most commonly used conversion rates—the ones that people in the United States use in their everyday lives and that are listed next.

NOTE: An asterisk (*) signifies that the test question might provide the conversion rate.

    Currency (money) conversions:

100 cents	= 1 dollar
10 dimes	= 1 dollar
20 nickels	= 1 dollar
4 quarters	= 1 dollar

Time conversions:

60 seconds (sec)	= 1 minute (min)
60 minutes	= 1 hour (hr)
24 hours	= 1 day
7 days	= 1 week (wk)
12 months (mo)	= 1 year (yr)
365 days	= 1 year

Length conversions:

12 inches (in)	= 1 foot (ft)
3 feet	= 1 yard (yd)

Weight conversions:

16 ounces (oz)	= 1 pound (lb)
* 2000 pounds	= 1 ton (T)

Liquid measure conversions:

* 8 ounces (oz)	= 1 cup
* 2 cups	= 1 pint (pt)
* 2 pints	= 1 quart (qt)
* 4 quarts	= 1 gallon (gal)

Answering a test question may require you to convert numbers from one *system* of measurement to another—especially to and from the metric system. You will not be expected to know these sorts of conversion rates. The question at hand will provide the rate you should use.

USING THE CASIO FX-260 CALCULATOR FOR PART I

When you take the GED® Mathematics Test, you will be allowed to use a calculator only for questions 1–25 (Part I of the test), and NOT for questions 26–50 (Part II of the test). Though you are not *required* to use a calculator for Part I, to avoid careless computational errors, you should use a calculator for all but the simplest calculations.

You are not permitted to bring and use your own calculator. Instead, you will be provided with a *Casio fx-260* calculator at the testing center. This calculator is solar powered, so you don't need to plug it in or worry about battery charge. Although you will be given instructions on how to use the calculator, it is recommended that you purchase (or borrow) the *Casio fx-260* calculator and practice using it before the day of the exam.

Casio fx-260 Calculator

To turn on the calculator, press the **ON** key in the upper right-hand corner. You should see "**DEG**" in the center of the display and the number **0** (zero) at the right side of the display. This indicates that the calculator is on and working properly.

Basic Operations

To add or subtract numbers, enter the numbers and **+** and **–** keys. For example, to perform the operation **54 – 26 + 13,** press the following keys in order:

5 **4** **–** **2** **6** **+** **1** **3** **=**

The answer on the display should be **41.**

To multiply and divide , use the **×** and **÷** keys. For example, to perform the operation **48 × 23,** press the following keys in order:

4 **8** **×** **2** **3** **=**

The answer on the display should be **1104.** Similarly, to perform the operation **465 ÷ 2.5,** press the following keys in order:

4 **6** **5** **÷** **2** **.** **5** **=**

The answer on the display should be **186.**

To solve a problem that involves parentheses, press the keys as you see the problem written. For example, to calculate **10(42 + 6),** press the following keys in order:

1 **0** **(** **4** **2** **+** **6** **)** **=**

The answer on the display should be **480.**

To enter a negative number, press the `+/-` key, which is directly above the `7` key. For example, one way to perform the operation **−12 + 6** is to press the following keys in order:

`1` `2` `+/-` `+` `6` `=`

The answer on the display should be **−6.**

To find the square of a number, use the `x²` key located in the top row of keys. For example, to find **11²** (which is equivalent to 11 × 11)**,** press the following keys in order:

`1` `1` `x²` `=`

The answer on the display should be **121.**

Using the SHIFT Key

If you look at the keys on the *Casio fx-260* calculator, you will notice yellow symbols and functions above the keys. To use these functions, you must press the **SHIFT** key in the upper-left corner, then the key below the function you want to use. **Do NOT press both keys at the same time.** The two functions involving the **SHIFT** key that you will most likely use are *percent* and *square root*.

The percent symbol (%) is just above the `=` key. To express a number as a *percent*, enter the number and then press the **SHIFT** key. For example, one way to find **30% of 1850** is to press the following keys in order:

`1` `8` `5` `0` `×` `3` `0` `SHIFT` `=`

The answer on the display should be **555.**

To find a square root, use the `SHIFT` key with the `x²` key (located in the top row of keys). For example, to find $\sqrt{1369}$ press the following keys in order:

`1` `3` `6` `9` `SHIFT` `x²` `=`

The answer on the display should be **37.**

Clearing the Memory

To perform a new calculation, you need to clear the calculator's memory by pressing either the red `AC` key or the `ON` key. This will clear all of your previous entries.

RECORDING YOUR ANSWERS TO ALTERNATIVE FORMAT QUESTIONS

Approximately ten of the fifty questions on the Mathematics Test are called **alternate format** questions. To answer these questions, you provide your own answer instead of selecting an answer from a list of five choices.

An alternative-format question is inherently more difficult than the same question accompanied by multiple choices because you cannot use process of elimination or scan the answer choices for clues as to how to solve the problem. What's more, the alternative format practically eliminates the possibility of lucky guesswork. Nevertheless, just as with multiple-choice questions, the difficulty level of alternative-format questions runs the gamut—from easy to challenging.

To answer all but one or two alternative-format questions, you will record your response on an answer grid that looks like this:

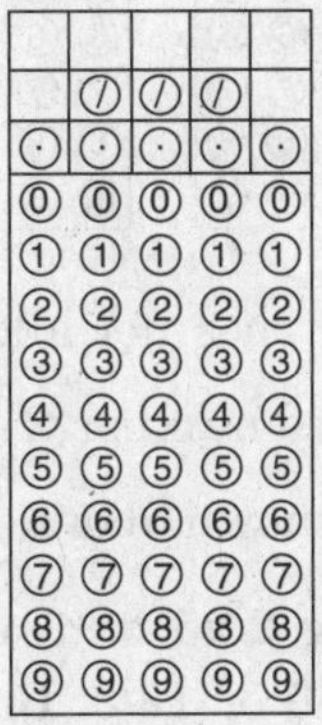

To record an answer on this grid, write your answer in the top row. Enter only one character in a box. You may start in any column that will allow you to enter your entire answer. Then, fill in the corresponding bubble below each character you have written. Leave blank all columns you did not use to record your answer.

For example, to enter the number **361,** you can fill in the grid in any of these three ways (any one would be read as the integer 361):

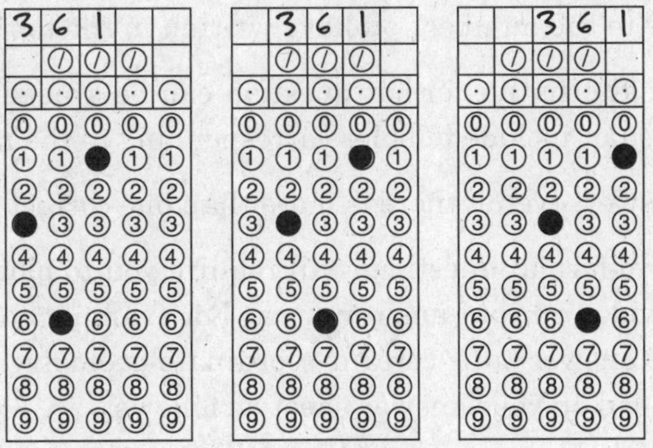

To enter a non-integer answer, you can provide your response as either a fraction or a decimal number. Fill in either a decimal-point bubble or a fraction-bar bubble on the answer grid. For example, the decimal number 2.25 is equivalent to the fraction $\frac{9}{4}$. To enter this value as your response to a question, you can choose either form, as shown next:

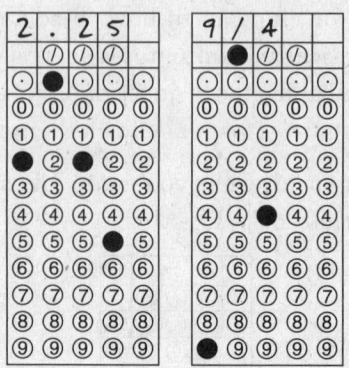

The alternative-format answer grid does not allow for the entry of mixed numbers, such as $2\frac{1}{4}$. So to represent the mixed number $2\frac{1}{4}$, you must enter either the decimal number **2.25** or the fraction **9/4,** as shown above.

In the previous example, assuming **2.25** or **9/4** is the correct answer, you would also receive credit for entering **2.250** or **18/8.** But these responses require filling in additional bubbles, which wastes time. So you should leave unneeded rows blank, and you should reduce fractions to their simplest form.

In using this alternative-format answer grid, also keep in mind:

- GED® answer sheets are machine-read, which means that the machine that scans answer sheets recognizes only filled-in bubbles. The numbers you write in the top row of your grid will not be read. So, be very careful to fill in the bubbles that correspond correctly to the number you have written in the top row.

- No answer to an alternative-format question can be a negative number. (Notice that the grid does not include bubbles corresponding to the minus sign.)

- Grid only one answer, even if there is more than one correct answer.

One or two alternative-format questions will require you to plot a point on the (x, y) coordinate plane provided on your answer sheet. For example, to mark the coordinate point $(2, -3)$ as your answer to a certain coordinate-geometry question, fill in the coordinate grid provided on your answer sheet as follows:

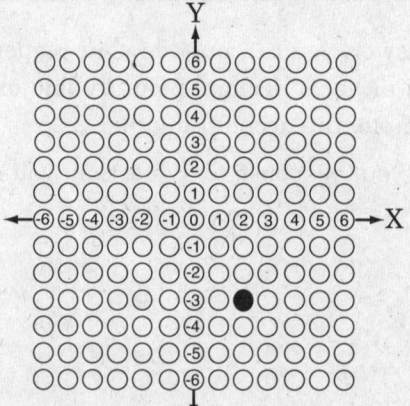

In this example, the first number in the coordinate is **2,** so the filled-in bubble is two places to the right of the *y*-axis (the vertical line with arrows). The second number is **–3,** so the filled-in bubble is three places below the *x*-axis (the horizontal line with arrows).

STRATEGIES FOR SOLVING MATH PROBLEMS

About 50 percent of the questions on the Mathematics Test will involve problem solving—in other words, working to a solution expressed as either a number or an expression containing variables (such as *x* and *y*). In this section, you'll learn specific strategies for solving problems. Most of these strategies apply only to multiple-choice questions, which account for 80 percent of all questions on the test.

The examples you'll see here run the gamut in terms of the concepts covered. If you don't fully understand a certain concept illustrated here, you can review it later in this part of the book.

Scan the Answer Choices for Clues

Scan the answer choices to see what all or most of them have in common—such as radical signs, exponents, factorable expressions, or fractions. Then try to formulate a solution that looks like the answer choices.

EXAMPLE 1 (EASIER):

If $a \neq 0$ or 2, then the expression $\dfrac{\frac{1}{a}}{2-a}$ is equivalent to which of the following?

   (1) $\dfrac{1}{2a - a^2}$

   (2) $\dfrac{2}{a - 2}$

   (3) $\dfrac{1}{2a}$

   (4) $\dfrac{1}{a^2}$

   (5) $\dfrac{2}{2a - 1}$

Notice what all the answer choices have in common: Each one is a fraction in which the denominator contains the variable *a*, but the numerator doesn't. And, there are no fractions in either the numerator or the denominator. That's a clue that your job is to manipulate the expression given in the question so that the result includes these features. Multiplying the numerator fraction by the reciprocal of the denominator will give you a result that has these features:

$$\frac{\frac{1}{a}}{2-a} = \frac{1}{a} \times \frac{1}{2-a} = \frac{1}{2a - a^2}$$

The correct answer is (1).

EXAMPLE 2 (MORE CHALLENGING):

A team of archeologists and engineers plan to build a pyramid using ancient construction materials and methods. As shown below, the base of the pyramid is to be square, and each of the four angles at the apex of the pyramid is to measure 90°.

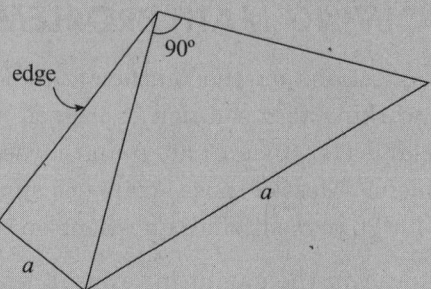

If the pyramid's base measures a meters on each side, which of the following represents the length of any of the four edges that extend from the pyramid's base to its apex?

(1) $\dfrac{a}{3}\sqrt{2}$

(2) $\dfrac{a}{3}\sqrt{3}$

(3) $\dfrac{a}{2}\sqrt{2}$

(4) $\dfrac{3}{4}a$

(5) $\dfrac{12}{13}a$

Notice that $\sqrt{2}$ and $\sqrt{3}$ appear in three of the five expressions listed among the answer choices. With sufficient knowledge of the Pythagorean theorem, you will recognize each of these two values as the hypotenuse of a certain right-triangle shape. With this clue in mind, bisect any triangular face of the pyramid into two smaller right triangles, as shown below.

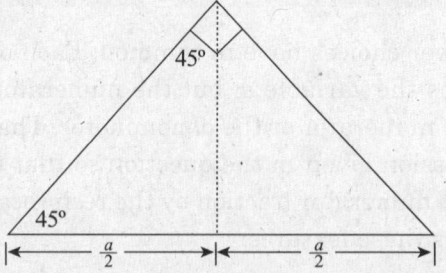

The length of each leg of a smaller triangle is $\dfrac{a}{2}$. From the Pythagorean theorem, you know that the length of the hypotenuse of any 90°-45°-45° triangle is the product of $\sqrt{2}$ and the length of either leg. So, in this case, the hypotenuse, or "edge" of the pyramid, measures $\frac{a}{2}\sqrt{2}$ meters. **The correct answer is (3).**

Don't Be Lured by Obvious Answer Choices

Expect to be tempted by wrong-answer choices that are the result of common errors in reasoning, in calculations, and in setting up and solving equations. Never assume that your solution is correct just because you see it among the answer choices.

EXAMPLE 3 (EASIER):

What is the value of $(8 + 8)^2 - (7 + 7)^2$?

   (1) 30

   (2) 60

   (3) 256

   (4) 452

   (5) 1695

Each wrong answer choice is the result of a common error:

If you make the mistake of distributing the power to each term in parentheses, you might select choice (1): $8^2 + 8^2 - 7^2 - 7^2 = 64 + 64 - 49 - 49 = 30$.

If you make the mistake of distributing the subtraction sign to both "7"s before squaring, you might select choice (3): $(8 + 8)^2 - (7 - 7)^2 = 16^2 - 0 = 256$.

If you make the mistake of adding instead of subtracting, you might select choice (4): $(8 + 8)^2 + (7 + 7)^2 = 16^2 + 14^2 = 256 + 196 = 452$.

If you make the mistake of multiplying instead of adding, you might select choice (5): $(8 \times 8)^2 - (7 \times 7)^2 = 64^2 - 49^2 = 4{,}096 - 2401 = 1695$.

Here is the correct calculation: $16^2 - 14^2 = 256 - 196 = 60$, choice (2).

The correct answer is (2).

EXAMPLE 4 (MORE CHALLENGING):

The average of six numbers is 19. When one of those numbers is taken away, the average of the remaining five numbers is 21. What number was taken away?

   (1) 2

   (2) 6.5

   (3) 9

   (4) 11.5

   (5) 20

In this example, two of the wrong answer choices are especially enticing. Choice (1) would be the correct answer to the question: "What is the difference between 19 and 21?" But this question asks something entirely different. Choice (5) is the other too-obvious choice. 20 is simply 19 + 21 divided by 2. If this solution strikes you as too simple, you've got good instincts. You can solve this problem quickly by simply comparing the two *sums*. Before the sixth number is taken away, the sum of the numbers is 114 (6 × 19). After taking away the sixth number, the sum of the remaining numbers is 105 (5 × 21). The difference between the two sums is 9, which must be the value of the number taken away. **The correct answer is (3).**

Size up the Question to Narrow Your Choices

If a multiple-choice question asks for a number value, you can probably narrow down the answer choices by estimating the size and type of number you're looking for. When handling word problems, use your common sense and real-world experience to formulate "ballpark" estimates.

Also, keep in mind that if the answer choices are all numbers, they'll be listed in order—from least in value to greatest in value. This feature can help you zero-in on viable choices.

EXAMPLE 5 (EASIER):

Stephanie deposited $1000 in an account that earns 5% **simple** interest. If she made no additional deposits, what was Stephanie's account balance after two years?

(1) $1050

(2) $1100

(3) $1102.50

(4) $1125.75

(5) $1152.25

If you understand that simple interest is an *annual* rate, and if you know that 5% of $1000 is $50, then you can narrow your choices. The account earned $50 in interest the first year, but *slightly more* than $50 the second year because it earned interest on the first year's interest. So the correct answer must be a bit greater than $1100. You can eliminate choices (1) and (2). All that's left is to perform the calculation:

5% of $1050 = 0.05 × $1050 = $52.50.

Add this amount of interest to the $50 earned during the first year:

$1000 (initial deposit) + $50 (year 1 interest) + $52.50 (year 2 interest) = $1102.50.

The correct answer is (3).

EXAMPLE 6 (MORE CHALLENGING):

A container holds 10 liters of a solution which is 20% acid. If 6 liters of pure acid are added to the container, what percent of the resulting mixture is acid?

(1) 8

(2) 20

(3) $33\frac{1}{3}$

(4) 40

(5) 50

Common sense should tell you that when you add more acid to the solution, the percent of the solution that is acid will increase. So you're looking for an answer that is a percent greater than 20. Only choices (3), (4), or (5) fit the bill. If you need to guess at this point, your odds are one in three of answering the question correctly. Here's how to solve the problem:

The original amount of acid is (10)(20%) = 2 liters. After adding 6 liters of pure acid, the amount of acid increases to 8 liters, while the amount of total solution increases from 10 to 16 liters. The new solution is $\frac{8}{16}$, or 50%, acid, choice (5). By the way, did you notice the too-obvious answer—choice (1)? That's because 8 liters is the *amount* of acid in the resulting mixture. **The correct answer is (5).**

Know When to Plug in Numbers for Variables

If the answer choices contain variables such as x and y, the question might be a good candidate for the "plug-in" strategy. Pick simple numbers (so the math is easy), and substitute them for the variables. You'll need your pencil and scratch paper for this strategy.

EXAMPLE 7 (EASIER):

If one dollar can buy m pieces of paper, how many dollars are needed to buy p reams of paper? [1 ream = 500 pieces of paper]

(1) $\dfrac{500}{p+m}$

(2) $\dfrac{m}{500p}$

(3) $\dfrac{500p}{m}$

(4) $\dfrac{p}{500m}$

(5) $500m(p-m)$

You can solve this problem conventionally or by using the plug-in strategy.

The conventional way: The question is essentially asking: "1 is to m as what is to p?" Set up a proportion (equate two ratios, or fractions). Then convert either pieces of paper to reams (divide m by 500) or reams to pieces (multiply p by 500). The second conversion method is used below. Cross-multiply to solve for x:

$$\frac{1}{m} = \frac{x}{500p}$$
$$mx = 500p$$
$$x = \frac{500p}{m}$$

The plug-in strategy: Pick easy-to-use values for m and p. Let's try $m = 500$ and $p = 1$. At \$1 for 500 sheets, it obviously takes exactly \$1 to buy one ream of paper. Start plugging these values into each of the five expressions in turn. The correct choice will provide a value of 1. Choice (1) doesn't work, and neither does choice (2). But choice (3) works:

$$\frac{500p}{m} = \frac{500(1)}{500} = 1$$

There's no need to test choices (4) and (5). **The correct answer is (3).**

EXAMPLE 8 (MORE CHALLENGING):

If a train travels $r + 2$ miles in h hours, which of the following represents the number of miles the train travels in 1 hour and 30 minutes?

- **(1)** $\dfrac{3r + 6}{2h}$
- **(2)** $\dfrac{3r}{h + 2}$
- **(3)** $\dfrac{r + 2}{h + 3}$
- **(4)** $\dfrac{r}{h + 6}$
- **(5)** $\dfrac{3}{2}(r + 2)$

This is an algebraic word problem involving rate of motion (speed). As in the previous problem, you can solve this problem either conventionally or by using the plug-in strategy.

The conventional way: Notice that all of the answer choices contain fractions. This is a clue that you should try to create a fraction as you solve the problem. Given that the train travels $r + 2$ miles in h hours, you can express its rate in miles per hour as $\frac{r + 2}{h}$. In $\frac{3}{2}$ hours, the train would travel $\left(\frac{3}{2}\right)\left(\frac{r + 2}{h}\right) = \frac{3r + 6}{2h}$ miles.

The plug-in strategy: Pick easy-to-use values for r and h. Let's try $r = 8$ and $h = 1$. Given these values, the train travels 10 miles ($8 + 2$) in 1 hour. So obviously, in $1\frac{1}{2}$ hours the train will travel 15 miles. Start plugging these r and h values into the answer choices. For this question, you won't need to go any further than choice (1):

$$\frac{3r + 6}{2h} = \frac{3(8) + 6}{2(1)} = \frac{30}{2} \text{ , or } 15$$

The correct answer is (1).

By the way, even if you had no clue how to handle this question, you could at least quickly eliminate choice (5). It omits h! Common sense should tell you that the correct answer must include both r and h.

The plug-in strategy can be very useful when you don't know how to set up the algebraic expression or equation that the problem requires. But keep in mind that this strategy can be time-consuming if the correct answer is far down in the list of choices. So use it only if you don't know how to set up the correct algebraic expression or equation.

Know When—and When Not—to Work Backward

If a multiple-choice question asks for a number value, and if you draw a blank as far as how to set up and solve the problem, don't panic. You might be able to work backward by testing the answer choices, each one in turn.

On the GED® Mathematics Test, numerical answer choices are always listed in order of value, from least to greatest. So when working backward from the answer choices, the best place to start is with choice (3), which provides the middle value. If choice (3) provides a number that is too great, then the correct answer must be either choice (1) or choice (2). Conversely, if choice (3) provides a number that is too small, then the correct answer must be either choice (4) or choice (5).

EXAMPLE 9 (EASIER):

A ball is dropped from 192 inches above level ground. After the second bounce, it rises to a height of 48 inches. If the height to which the ball rises after each bounce is always the same fraction of the height reached on its previous bounce, what is this fraction?

(1) $\frac{1}{8}$

(2) $\frac{1}{4}$

(3) $\frac{1}{3}$

(4) $\frac{1}{2}$

(5) $\frac{2}{3}$

The fastest route to a solution is to plug in an answer. Try choice (3), and see what happens. If the ball bounces up $\frac{1}{3}$ as high as it started, as choice (3) provides, then after the first bounce it will rise up $\frac{1}{3}$ as high as 192 inches, or 64 inches. After a second bounce, it will rise $\frac{1}{3}$ as high, or about 21 inches. But, the problem states that the ball rises to 24 inches after the second bounce. So, choice (3) cannot be the correct answer. We can see that the ball must be bouncing higher than one third of the way; so the correct answer must be a larger fraction, meaning either choice (4) or choice

(5). You've already narrowed your odds to 50 percent. Try plugging in choice (4), and you'll see that it works: $\frac{1}{2}$ of 192 is 96, and $\frac{1}{2}$ of 96 is 48. **The correct answer is (4).**

In the previous example, although it would be possible to develop a formula to answer the question, doing so would be senseless, considering how quickly and easily you can work backward from the answer choices.

Working backward from numerical answer choices works well when the numbers are easy, and when few calculations are required, as in the preceding question. In other cases, applying algebra might be a better way.

EXAMPLE 10 (MORE CHALLENGING):

How many pounds of nuts selling for 70 cents per pound must be mixed with 30 pounds of nuts selling at 90 cents per pound to make a mixture that sells for 85 cents per pound?

   (1) 8.5

   (2) 10

   (3) 15

   (4) 16.5

   (5) 20

Is the easier route to the solution to test the answer choices? Let's see. First of all, calculate the total cost of 30 pounds of nuts at 90 cents per pound: $30 \times 0.90 = \$27$. Now, start with choice (3). 15 pounds of nuts at 70 cents per pound costs $10.50. The total cost of this mixture is $37.50, and the total weight is 45 pounds. Now you'll need to perform some long division. The average weight of the mixture turns out to be between 83 and 84 cents—too low for the 85 cent average given in the question. So you can at least eliminate choice (3).

You should realize by now that testing the answer choices might not be the most efficient way to tackle this question. Besides, there are ample opportunities for calculation errors. Instead, try solving this problem algebraically by writing and solving a system of equations. Here's how to do it. The cost (in cents) of the nuts selling for 70 cents per pound can be expressed as $70x$, letting x equal the number that you're asked to determine. You then add this cost to the cost of the more expensive nuts ($30 \times 90 = 2700$) to obtain the total cost of the mixture, which you can express as $85(x + 30)$. You can state this algebraically and solve for x as follows:

$$70x + 2700 = 85(x + 30)$$
$$70x + 2700 = 85x + 2550$$
$$150 = 15x$$
$$10 = x$$

At 70-cents per pound, 10 pounds of nuts must be added in order to make a mixture that sells for 85 cents per pound. **The correct answer is (2).**

Look for the Simplest Route to the Answer

For many GED® math questions, there's a long way and a short way to get to the correct answer. When it looks like you're facing a long series of calculations or a complex system of equations, always ask yourself if there's an easier, more intuitive way of answering the question.

EXAMPLE 11 (EASIER):

What is the value of $\frac{150}{450} \times \frac{750}{300} \times \frac{450}{1500}$?

Mark your answer in the grid on the answer sheet.

Whether or not you use a calculator for this question, multiplying and dividing these large numbers is needlessly time-consuming. What's more, the more calculations you make, the more likely you'll commit a computation error. Look carefully at the numbers involved. Notice that you can factor all of these numbers across fractions. After factoring, the three fractions that remain can be easily combined. Here's one possibility:

$$\frac{150}{450} \times \frac{750}{300} \times \frac{450}{1500} = \frac{1}{1} \times \frac{1}{2} \times \frac{1}{2} = \frac{1}{4}$$

The correct answer is 1/4 or .25. To receive credit for a correct answer, you would enter either **1/4** or **.25** in the grid on your answer sheet.

EXAMPLE 12 (MORE CHALLENGING):

What is the difference between the sum of all positive **even** integers less than 32 and the sum of all positive **odd** integers less than 32?

    (1) 0

    (2) 1

    (3) 15

    (4) 16

    (5) 32

To answer this question, should you add up two long series of numbers on your scratch paper or with the calculator? No. In this case, it is a waste of time, and you risk committing calculation errors along the way. A smart test-taker will notice a pattern and use it as a shortcut. Compare the initial terms of each sequence:

even integers: 2, 4, 6, . . . , 30

odd integers: 1, 3, 5, . . . , 29, 31

Notice that for each successive term the odd integer is one less than the corresponding even integer. There are a total of 15 corresponding integers, so the difference between the sums of all these corresponding integers is 15. But the odd-integer sequence includes one additional integer: 31. So the difference is $31 - 15 = 16$. **The correct answer is (4).**

Keep in mind: GED® math questions are not designed to gauge your ability to make lengthy, repetitive calculations on your scratch paper or with the calculator. Combining three or four numbers using basic operations will probably be the limit of what is expected of you. So again, if you're facing a long series of computations, especially with large numbers, look for a quicker, easier way to answer the question.

Solve Problems by Starting with What You Know

It's easy to get lost in a complex math problem requiring several steps to solve. If you're at a loss as to how to begin, start with the information you know. Then ask yourself what you can deduce from that information. This approach will very likely lead you, step-by-step, to the solution.

EXAMPLE 13 (EASIER):

Cassie can assemble 4 computers in one hour, and Hillary can assemble 12 computers in one hour. Working at the same time, Cassie, Hillary, and a third worker, Jodie, can assemble 192 computers during an 8-hour shift. How many computers can Jodie assemble in one hour?

Mark your answer in the grid on the answer sheet.

Two of the numbers are given as an hourly rate of work, and the other number is given as a rate of work per 8-hour shift. A good place to start is to convert one rate to the other. Let's try converting the total per-shift work rate to an hourly rate: $192 \div 8 = 24$. So you know that Hillary, Jodie, and Cassie can assemble 24 computers in an hour. Now ask yourself what else you know. You know that Cassie's hourly rate of work is 4 and that Hillary's hourly rate of work is 12. Now ask yourself what you deduce from this information. If you subtract those two numbers from 24, you'll find Jodie's hour rate of work, which is the answer to the question:

$$24 - 4 - 12 = 8$$

The correct answer is 8. To receive credit for a correct answer, you would enter **8** in the grid on your answer sheet.

EXAMPLE 14 (MORE CHALLENGING):

In a group of 20 singers and 40 dancers, 20 percent of the singers are under 25 years in age, and 40 percent of the entire group is under 25 years in age. What portion of the dancers is under 25 years in age?

(1) 20 percent

(2) 24 percent

(3) 40 percent

(4) 50 percent

(5) 60 percent

To answer this question, you need to know the total number of dancers as well as the *number* of dancers under 25 years in age. The question provides the first number: 40. To find the second number, start with what the question provides, and figure out what else you know. Keep going, and eventually you'll arrive at your destination. Of the whole group of 60, 24 are under 25 years in age (40% of 60 is 24). 20 percent of the 20 singers, or 4 singers, are under 25 years in age. Hence, the remaining 20 people under 25 must be dancers. That's the second number you needed to answer the question. 20 is *50%* of 40. **The correct answer is (4).**

Search Geometry Figures for Clues

Some GED® geometry questions will be accompanied by figures. They are there for a reason: the pieces of information a figure provides can lead you, step-by-step, to the answer.

EXAMPLE 15 (EASIER):

In the coordinate plane shown below, $\overline{PM}$ is congruent to $\overline{MQ}$.

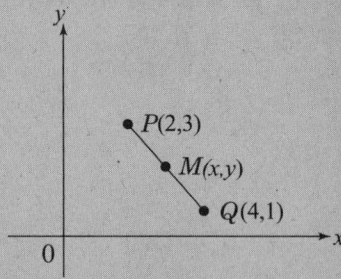

M is the midpoint of $\overline{PQ}$

What are the (x,y) coordinates of point M?

(1) $(3\frac{1}{2}, 1\frac{1}{2})$

(2) $(3,2)$

(3) $(2\frac{1}{2}, 3\frac{1}{2})$

(4) $(2, 3)$

(5) $(3\frac{1}{3}, 2\frac{1}{3})$

To answer the question, you need to examine the specific coordinates provided in the figure. Given that $\overline{PM}$ is congruent, or equal in length, to $\overline{MQ}$, the x-coordinate of point M is half the horizontal distance from 2 to 4 (P to Q), at 3. Similarly, the y-coordinate of point M is half the vertical distance from 3 to 1 (P to Q), at 2. The (x,y) coordinates of point M are (3,2). **The correct answer is (2).**

EXAMPLE 16 (MORE CHALLENGING):

Point O lies at the center of the circle shown in the below figure.

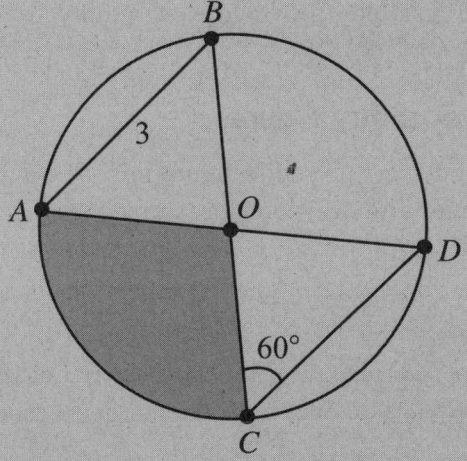

What is the area of the circle's shaded region, expressed in square units?

(1) $\frac{3}{2}\pi$

(2) 2π

(3) $\frac{5}{2}\pi$

(4) $\frac{8}{3}\pi$

(5) 3π

This question asks for the area of a portion of the circle defined by a central angle. To answer the question, you'll need to determine the area of the entire circle as well as what portion (fraction or percent) of that area is shaded. Search the figure for a piece of information that might provide a starting point. If you look at the 60° angle in the figure, you should recognize that both triangles are equilateral (all angles are 60°) and, extended out to their arcs, form two segments, each $\frac{1}{6}$ the size of the entire circle. What's left are the two largest segments, each of which is twice the size of a small segment. So the shaded area must account for $\frac{1}{3}$ the circle's area.

Now you've reduced the problem to the simple mechanics of calculating the circle's area, then dividing it by 3. In an equilateral triangle, all sides are congruent. Examining the figure once again, notice length 3, which is also the circle's radius (the distance from its center to its circumference). The area of any circle is πr^2, where r is the circle's radius. Thus, the area of the circle is 9π. The shaded portion accounts for $\frac{1}{3}$ the circle's area, or 3π. **The correct answer is (5).**

As the preceding examples show, GED® geometry figures are intended to provide information helpful in solving the problem. But they're not intended to *provide* the answer through visual measurement. Make sure you solve the problem by working with the numbers and variables provided, not simply by looking at the figure's proportions.

Sketch Your Own Geometry Figure

A geometry problem that doesn't provide a figure might be more easily solved if it had one. Use your scratch paper and draw one for yourself. It will be easier than trying to visualize it in your mind.

EXAMPLE 17 (EASIER):

Line A is perpendicular to line B, and the intersection of line B and line C forms a 35° angle. Which statement about the relationship between line A and line C is correct?

(1) Line A is parallel to line C.

(2) Line A is perpendicular to line C.

(3) The intersection of line A and line C forms a 35° angle.

(4) The intersection of line A and line C forms a 125° angle.

(5) The intersection of line A and line C forms a 145° angle.

It's difficult to visualize all the lines and angles in your head in order to answer this question. So first draw perpendicular lines A and B. Then draw line C through line A at an acute angle of approximately 35° (a rough approximation will suffice), and mark that angle measure. You can now see a *right* triangle with interior angles 90°, 35°, and 55°. (The interior angles of any triangle total 180° in measure.)

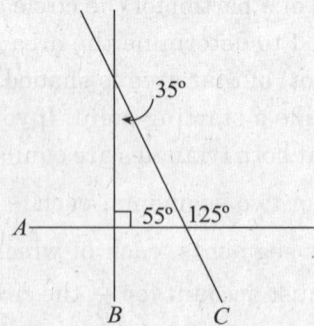

Since 55° is not among the answer choices, you need to determine the measure of either adjacent angle, which is *supplementary* to the 55° angle. (This means that the two angles combine to form a straight, 180° line.) Either of the two exterior angles adjacent to the 55° angle must measure 125° (180° − 55°). **The correct answer is (4).**

EXAMPLE 18 (MORE CHALLENGING):

On the xy-coordinate plane, points $R(7,-3)$ and $S(7,7)$ are the endpoints of the longest possible chord of a certain circle. What is the area of the circle?

    (1) 7π

    (2) 16π

    (3) 20π

    (4) 25π

    (5) 49π

There are lots of "7"s in this question, which might throw you off track without at least a rough picture. To keep your thinking straight, scratch out your own rough xy-grid and plot the two points. You'll see that R is located directly below S, so chord $\overline{RS}$ is vertical.

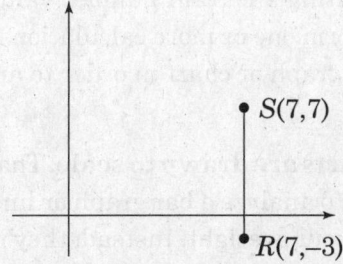

Accordingly, the length of $\overline{RS}$ is simply the vertical distance from -3 to 7, which is 10. By definition, the longest possible chord of a circle is equal in length to the circle's diameter. In this case, the circle's diameter is 10, and thus its radius is 5. The circle's area is $\pi(5)^2 = 25\pi$. **The correct answer is (4).**

ANALYZING GRAPHICAL DATA (GRAPHS, CHARTS, AND TABLES)

At least ten of the fifty questions on the Mathematics Test involve analyzing data presented in graphical form. GED® data-analysis questions are most often based on the following types of data displays:

- Bar graphs

- Line charts

- Picture graphs

- Circle graphs (pie charts)

- Tables

GED® data-analysis questions are designed to gauge your ability to read, compare, and interpret charts, graphs, and tables, as well as to calculate numbers such as percentages, ratios, fractions, and averages based on data presented in a graphical format. Here are some features of GED® data-analysis questions you should know about:

- **The number of displays per question and questions per display can vary.** The questions usually come in sets of 2–3, each question in a set referring to the same graphical data. Some questions or sets may involve just *one* chart, graph, or table; other questions or sets may involve *two or more* charts, graphs, or tables.

- **Important additional information may be provided.** Any additional information that you might need to know to interpret the graphical display will be indicated above, below, or to the side of it. Be sure to read this information!

- **Some questions might ask for an approximation.** This is because the test-makers are trying to gauge your ability to interpret graphical data, not your ability to crunch numbers to the "*n*th" decimal place.

- **Answering a question often involves multiple steps.** Though an easier question might simply involve locating a certain number value on a chart or graph, most questions ask you to perform one or more calculations as well. Also, you may need to refer to more than one graph or chart in order to answer a question, which will involve additional steps.

- **Bar graphs and line charts are drawn to scale.** That's because visual *estimation* is part of what's required to analyze a bar graph or line chart's graphical data. But they aren't drawn to test your eyesight. Instead, they're designed for a comfortable margin for error in visual acuity. Just don't round up or down too far.

- **For picture graphs, pie charts, and tables, visual scale is not important.** You'll interpret these displays based strictly on the numbers provided.

Bar Graphs

A **bar graph** looks like what the name implies: it consists of a series of vertical or horizontal bars representing number values. The higher (or longer) the bar, the greater the number value.

A bar graph includes a **vertical axis** and a **horizontal axis.** Each scale shows a different measure or other variable. Examine the following graph. The vertical scale indicates a number expressed in *thousands*. The numbers on this vertical scale range from 0 to 22,000. The horizontal scale indicates ages ranging from 25 to 65+ (which means 65 and older). Notice that the ages are given in five-year intervals; ages falling between these intervals are not represented.

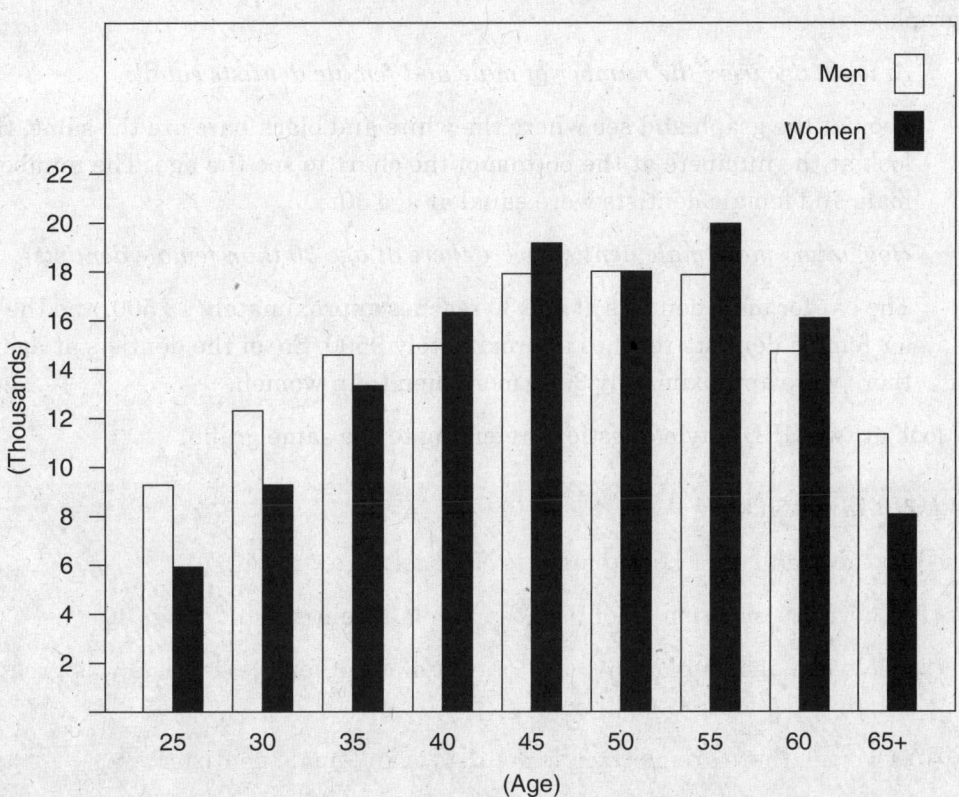

Dentists in Kansas by Age and Sex, 2003

But what do the "thousands" (vertical scale) and the ages (horizontal scale) involve? Examine the information above the illustration. This is the label, or title, for the graph. It tells you that the vertical scale indicates the number of *dentists* (in thousands), while the horizontal scale indicates *age* categories for dentists. It also tells you that these numbers involve one state during one year only: Kansas in 2003.

Finally, what is the distinction between a white bar and a black bar? Examine the **legend** in the upper-right corner. It tells you that for each age interval, the white bar represents the number of dentists who are men, and the black bar represents the number of dentists who are women.

So by examining the height of a white (or black) bar in each age category, you can "see" the approximate number of men (or women) dentists at each age interval. For example, in Kansas during 2003:

- Approximately 15,000 dentists were 40-year-old men

- Approximately 20,000 dentists were 55-year-old women

- Just over 8000 dentists were women 65 years of age or older

Notice that these numbers are approximations, or estimates. Remember: in analyzing GED® bar graphs you won't need to provide precise values for numbers appearing on scales such as the vertical scale in this example.

Now answer a few questions involving a bit more than identifying a single value on the graph:

At what age were the number of male and female dentists equal?

Look at the graph and see where the white and black bars are the same, then look at the numbers at the bottom of the chart to see the age. The number of male and female dentists were equal at age 50.

How many more male dentists were there at age 30 than female dentists?

The bar for male dentists at age 30 reaches approximately 12,500, and the bar for female dentists reaches approximately 9500. So, of the dentists at age 30, there were approximately 3000 more men than women.

Now look at two GED®-style questions referring to the same graph.

EXAMPLE 19 (EASIER):

Based on the graph, which statement is NOT accurate?

  (1) There are more male dentists than female dentists under age 40.

  (2) Between ages 40 and 60, the total number of female dentists was greater than male dentists.

  (3) Overall, there are more male dentists than female dentists.

  (4) The number of female dentists decreased between ages 60 and 65+.

  (5) The only time the number of male dentists is greater than female dentists is prior to age 40.

All of the statements are true according to the graph except choice (5). When examining the graph carefully, the number of male dentists is also greater than female dentists in the 65+ age group. **The correct answer is (5).**

EXAMPLE 20 (MORE CHALLENGING):

At which age did the number of male dentists increase the LEAST over the number of female dentists?

  (1) age 25

  (2) age 30

  (3) age 35

  (4) age 45

  (5) age 65+

First, notice that in the age 45 group, choice (4), there were more female dentists than male dentists. Therefore, you can eliminate choice (4) on this basis alone. No calculations are necessary when comparing choices (1), (2), (3), and (5). For each of these age groups (25, 30, 35, and 65+), examine the height difference between the two bars. The question asks for the *least* increase. At ages 25, 30, and 65+, the differences in the heights of the bars is clearly greater than at age 35. Therefore, choices (1), (2), and (5) can be eliminated. The only remaining group is age 35, where the difference between the number of male and female dentists is small. **The correct answer is (3).**

Line Charts

A **line chart** consists of one or more lines running from left to right. Line charts are constructed by first plotting points at regular intervals, then connecting those points with **trend lines** (lines that suggest increases and decreases from one interval to the next). But the only data you know for sure are those indicated by the points themselves, and not by the lines. The higher the point on a line, the greater the number value the point represents.

Like bar graphs, line charts include a vertical axis and a horizontal axis, each showing a different measure or other variable. Examine the following line chart. The vertical scale indicates a number expressed in *thousands*. The numbers on this vertical scale range from 0 to 45,000. The horizontal scale indicates months of the years; all twelve months are represented.

Number of Coffee and Tea Drinkers over 12 months

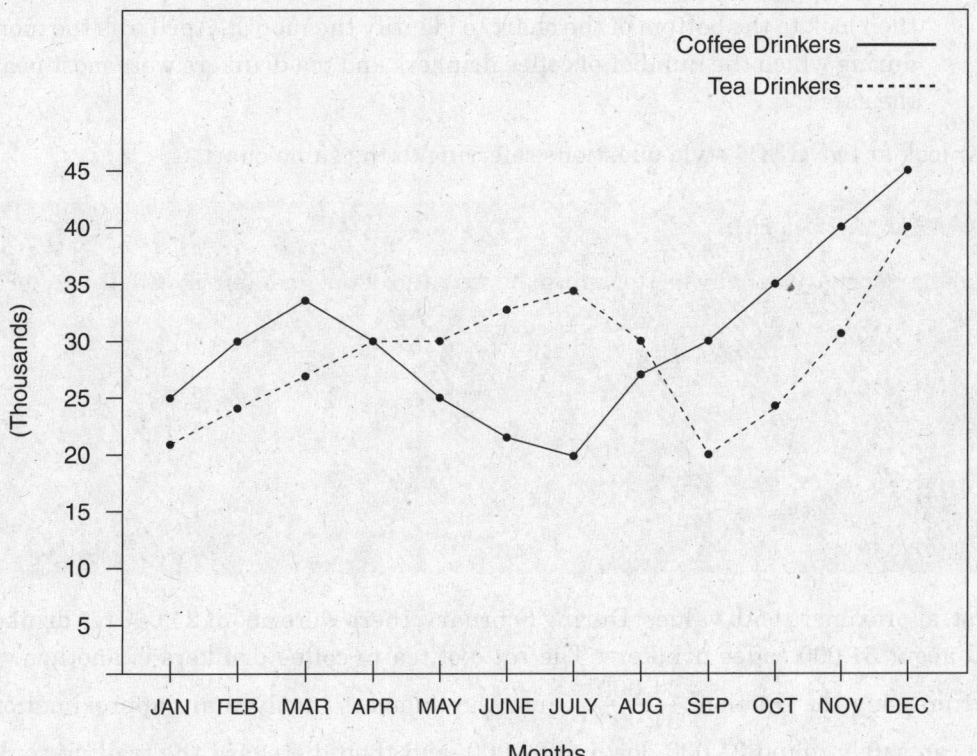

The chart's label, or title, above the illustration tells you that the vertical scale indicates the number of *coffee and tea drinkers* in thousands. The legend in the upper-right corner tells you that the solid line represents coffee drinkers, while the dotted line represents tea drinkers. By examining the height of the solid (or dotted) line at each point, you can "see" the approximate number of coffee (or tea) drinkers for that month. For example:

- The number of coffee drinkers in May was approximately 25,000.

- The number of tea drinkers in November was approximately 32,000.

These numbers are approximations, or estimates. As with bar graphs, analyzing GED® line charts won't require identifying precise values for numbers appearing on scales such as the vertical scale in this example.

Now answer a few questions involving a bit more than identifying a single number value on the chart:

> *During what month was the number of coffee drinkers greatest?*

> Look at the solid line and follow it to the highest point (dot) on the chart. Then look to the bottom of the chart to see the month. December saw the greatest number of coffee drinkers.

> *During what month were the number of coffee drinkers and tea drinkers most nearly the same?*

> Look at the chart to see at what point the solid and dotted lines intersect, and then look to the bottom of the chart to identify the month. April was the month during which the number of coffee drinkers and tea drinkers were most nearly the same.

Now look at two GED®-style questions referring to the same chart.

EXAMPLE 21 (EASIER):

During February, what was the approximate ratio of tea drinkers to coffee drinkers?

- **(1)** 2 to 5
- **(2)** 2 to 3
- **(3)** 4 to 5
- **(4)** 5 to 3
- **(5)** 5 to 2

First, approximate both values: During February, there were about 24,000 tea drinkers and about 31,000 coffee drinkers. The *ratio* of tea to coffee drinkers is another way of expressing the fraction $\frac{24,000}{31,000}$. Since the numbers involved are approximations, you can safely round 31,000 down to 30,000, and then disregard the trailing zeroes. Factoring 24 and 30 leaves the simple fraction $\frac{4}{5}$, or a ratio of 4 to 5. **The correct answer is (3).**

EXAMPLE 22 (MORE CHALLENGING):

During which month was the total number of coffee drinkers and tea drinkers the lowest?

  (1) January

  (2) May

  (3) August

  (4) September

  (5) December

Your task here is to add together the number of coffee drinkers and tea drinkers. But there's no need to perform calculations for each of the months listed. Instead, focus on the months when the number of both coffee and tea drinkers were both low—in other words, where both points are low on the chart. January is a viable choice, and so is September. Combine *approximate* numbers for each of these two months:

January: 21,000 (tea) + 25,000 (coffee) = 46,000

September: 20,000 (tea) + 30,000 (coffee) = 50,000

Thus, January saw the lowest combined consumption. **The correct answer is (1).**

Picture Graphs

A **picture graph** uses appropriate symbols to represent information. Counting the number of pictures or *partial* pictures gives you the information needed. Look at the picture graph below.

Amount Spent on Textbooks at College Level, 2007

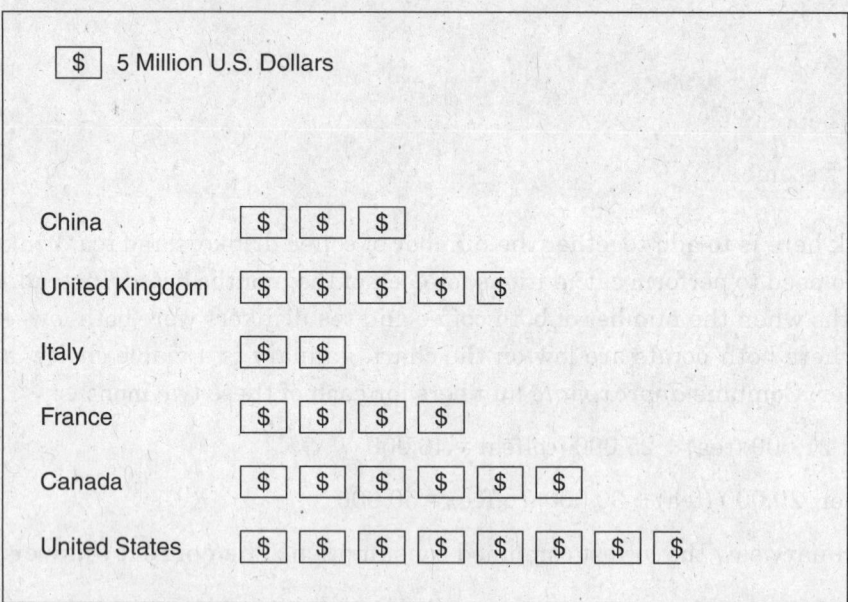

The legend in the upper-left corner tells you that each symbol—a dollar bill in this case—represents $5 million. The label, or title, above the graph tells you that the dollar amounts are for money spent on college-level textbooks in 2007. Looking at the left side of the graph, you can see that dollar amounts are provided for six specific countries.

Now answer a few simple questions involving the graph:

Which country spent the least amount on college textbooks?

Italy has only two symbols, so that country spent the least amount.

How many U.S. dollars were spent on college textbooks in China?

By counting the symbols and multiplying by 5 (each symbol represents $5 million), you can see that China spent 3 × 5 = $15 million on college textbooks.

Now look at two GED®-style questions referring to the same graph.

EXAMPLE 23 (EASIER):

If $1.00 (U.S.) has the same value as $1.10 denominated in Canadian dollars, how many *Canadian* dollars did Canada spend on college-level textbooks?

(1) $20.7 million

(2) $27.0 million

(3) $29.7 million

(4) $30.3 million

(5) $33.0 million

Solving this problem requires two steps. Nevertheless, it's relatively easy. First, determine how many U.S. dollars Canada spent: $6 \times 5 = \$30$ million. Second, convert to Canadian dollars: 30 million $\times 1.1 = \$33$ million. **The correct answer is (5).**

EXAMPLE 24 (MORE CHALLENGING):

Among the countries represented, what was the median U.S. dollar amount spent by a country on college-level textbooks?

(1) $18,275,000

(2) $21,125,000

(3) $22,500,000

(4) $25,000,000

(5) $37,500,000

The number of countries is 6, which is an even number. The *median* of an even number of values is the average of the two middle values. (This definition is included on the "formula sheet" provided during the test.) In this example, the two middle values are for France ($4 \times 5 = \$22$ million) and the United Kingdom ($4.5 \times 5 = \$22.5$ million). The average of these two dollar amounts is $21.125 million, or $21,125,000. **The correct answer is (2).**

Circle Graphs

Circle graphs are sometimes referred to as **pie charts.** They show the parts, or segments, of a whole. Most often, the parts are expressed as percents of the whole. The parts of the whole add up to 100 percent. Reading circle graphs should not involve visual estimation. Rely only on the numbers provided, and not on the visual size of any segment in relation to the whole. Here's an example of a circle graph:

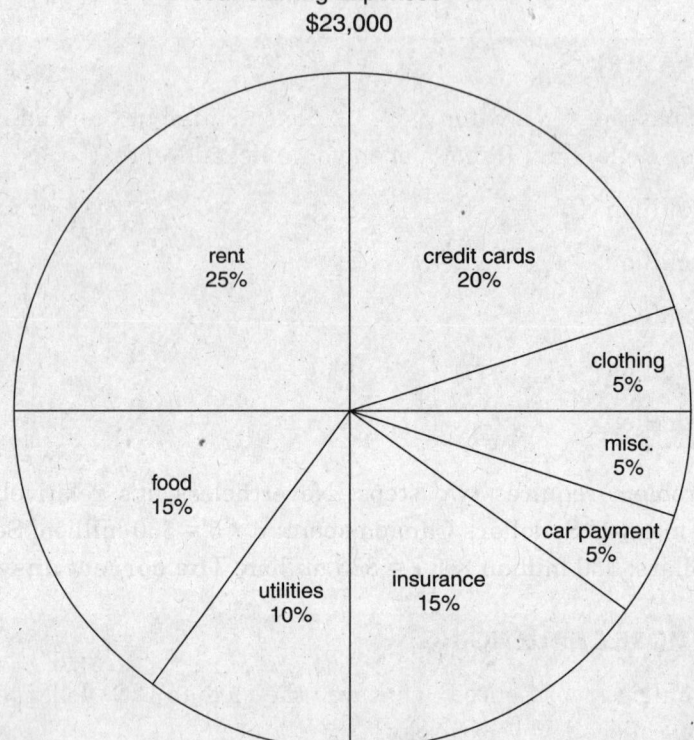

Joan's Living Expenses 2009
$23,000

The label, or title, above the graph tells you that each segment on the graph represents a percent of Joan's total living expenses ($23,000) for 2009. To determine her expenditures for each category, you would multiply the percent by her total salary.

Now answer a few simple questions involving the data in this graph:

How much did Joan spend for insurance?

Insurance accounted for 15% of Joan's living expenses. Convert 15% to a decimal number, then multiply: Joan spent $23,000 × 0.15 = $3450 on insurance.

How much did Joan spend on rent and utilities combined?

You can add the two percentages first: 25% (rent) + 10% (utilities) = 35%. Calculate the combined dollar amount: Joan spent $23,000 × 0.35 = $8050 on rent and utilities.

Now look at two GED®-style questions referring to the same chart.

EXAMPLE 25 (EASIER):

How much more did Joan spend on food than on clothing?

- **(1)** $560
- **(2)** $1150
- **(3)** $2300
- **(4)** $3450
- **(5)** Not enough information is provided.

First, subtract 5% from 15%. Joan spent 10% more of her total expenses on food than on clothing. Then express 10% as a dollar amount: $23,000 × 0.10 = $2300. **The correct answer is (3).**

EXAMPLE 26 (MORE CHALLENGING):

Assume that Joan's total living expenses increase by 10 percent every year and that her credit card expenses increase by 5 percent every year. Approximately what portion of Joan's total 2010 living expenses went toward credit cards?

- **(1)** 18%
- **(2)** 19%
- **(3)** 20%
- **(4)** 21%
- **(5)** 22%

This question requires multiple steps, leaving ample opportunity for calculation errors. However, you can easily increase your odds by narrowing the choices. If Joan's *total* living expenses increase every year at a greater rate than her credit card expenses, the initial 20% that constitutes just the credit card portion will *decrease* with each passing year. So the correct answer must be less than 20%. Eliminate choices (3), (4), and (5). To decide between choices (1) and (2), calculate Joan's 2010 credit card expenses and her 2010 total living expenses. This question would probably appear on Part I of the test, so you could use the calculator for the following computations.

2010 credit card expenses:
$4600 + (0.05)($4600) = $4830

2010 total living expenses:
$23,000 + (0.10)($23,000) = $25,300

To determine Joan's 2010 credit card expenses as a percentage of her total living expenses, divide. The question asks for an approximate percent, so you can round off your answer a bit:

$$\frac{4830}{25,300} \approx 0.19, \text{ or } 19\%.$$

The correct answer is (2).

Tables

A **table** consists of rows and columns of data. Beside each row and above each column is a heading that tells you what the numbers in the row or column signify. Most of us read tables every day: television, bus, and work schedules; menus; and even calendars are all everyday examples of tables. So you should have little trouble reading GED® tables. Nevertheless, the tables on the test will be unfamiliar to you, and some of the questions can be a bit more challenging than you might expect. Look at the following table.

Resort	Snowfall (2009)	Snowfall (2010)	No. of Visitors (2009)	No. of Visitors (2010)
Blue Mountain	14.8 ft.	18.6 ft.	28,300	31,350
High Top	12.8 ft.	19.0 ft.	12,720	11,830
Crystal Hill	20.6 ft.	15.3 ft.	22,440	25,100
Snow Ridge	21.2 ft.	16.4 ft.	9580	12,360

Notice that for each of the four resorts, two pieces of data are provided for each of the two years: 2009 and 2010. This table does not come with a title or other explanatory information. But you don't need any to understand the table. Now answer a few simple questions involving the tabular data:

Which resort saw the least snowfall in 2009?

High Top saw only 12.8 feet of snowfall in 2009. All three other resorts saw more than that.

How much more snow fell in High Top than in Crystal Ridge in 2010?

Subtract the amount at Crystal Ridge (15.3) from the amount at High Top (19.0). The difference is 3.7 feet.

How many more visitors came to Crystal Hill in 2010 than in 2009?

Subtract the number in 2009 (22,440) from the number in 2010 (25,100). The difference is 2660.

Now look at two GED®-style questions referring to the same table.

EXAMPLE 27 (EASIER):

Which resort experienced the greatest *percent* change in number of visitors from 2009 to 2010?

    (1) Blue Mountain

    (2) High Top

    (3) Crystal Hill

    (4) Snow Ridge

    (5) Not enough information is provided.

To answer the question, you don't need to calculate precise percent changes. Instead, compare changes among the resorts by rough estimation. Notice that for each of three resorts—Blue Mountain, Crystal Hill, and Snow Ridge—the change was roughly 3000. (For High Top, the change was far less, so you can rule out choice (2).) Also notice that the actual numbers are lowest for Snow Ridge, which means that the *percent* change at Snow Ridge was the highest. **The correct answer is (4).**

EXAMPLE 28 (MORE CHALLENGING):

Based on the 2009 and 2010 data, what can be inferred about the four resorts?

    (1) The higher a resort's elevation, the greater the snowfall at that resort.

    (2) The four resorts received more visitors altogether in 2009 than in 2010.

    (3) The numbers of visitors were not consistently related to snowfall amounts.

    (4) The four resorts received more snowfall altogether in 2010 than in 2009.

    (5) The lower the temperature at a resort, the more people visited the resort

The data in the table contradict statements (2) and (4), and the table contains no data about either elevation or temperature, choices (1) and (5). In contrast, the data strongly support choice (3). Only at Blue Mountain did the number of visitors vary directly with the amount of snowfall. (Both increased from 2009 to 2010.) At each of the other three resorts, the two variables varied *inversely*. At High Top, snowfall increased from 2009 to 2010, but the number of visitors decreased from one year to the next. At Crystal Hill and Snow Ridge, snowfall decreased from 2009 to 2010, but the number of visitors increased from one year to the next. **The correct answer is (3).**

ROUNDING, SIMPLIFYING, AND CHECKING YOUR CALCULATIONS

No GED® test-taker is immune to committing number-crunching errors—with or without a calculator. In this section, you'll learn how to approximate and round off numbers to help you solve problems quickly. You'll also learn how to simplify certain kinds of operations to make calculating numbers easier. Finally, you'll learn when it's best to use the calculator during Part I, as well as how best to check your calculations.

Approximations and Rounding

One of the skills measured on the GED® Mathematics Test is your ability to *approximate* number values. Some multiple-choice questions will clearly indicate that an approximate value will suffice. For example, a question might ask which choice is "most nearly equal to" a given expression. Or it might ask for "the approximate area" of a certain geometric figure. Read the question carefully for phrases such as these. If you see this sort of phrase, it tells you that you can *round off* some of your calculations yet work to a solution that is closest to the value provided as the correct answer.

How to Round off a Number

When you round off a number, you eliminate one or more of the digits from the right end of the number. But this doesn't mean that you ignore those digits. Consider the number **4834.826.** If you simply ignore all digits to the right of the decimal point, you're left with 4834. But you have not rounded off the number to the nearest unit, because "**.826**" is closer to 1 than to 0. In this case, rounding off this number to the nearest unit requires increasing the "ones" digit from 4 to 5, so that the entire rounded number would be **4835.** For the record, here's the same number rounded off to all possible places:

4834.826 rounded to:	equals:	what we've done:
the nearest hundredth	4834.83	round .826 up to .830
the nearest tenth	4834.8	round .82 down to .80
the nearest unit	4835	round 4.8 up to 5.0
the nearest ten	4830	round 34 down to 30
the nearest hundred	4800	round 834 down to 800
the nearest thousand	5000	round 4834 up to 5000
the nearest ten thousand	0	round 4834 down to 0

But what about rounding the number 5, which lies midway between 0 and 10. Do you round it up or down? It doesn't matter. Don't worry: the correct response to a GED® math question will *not* depend solely on whether you round the number 5 up or round it down. For example, if the solution to a problem is 4.5, you won't be asked to choose between 4 and 5 as the closest approximation.

Numbers with Non-repeating Decimal Places

Many numbers, especially square roots, include an infinite number of non-repeating decimal places. $\sqrt{2}$, $\sqrt{3}$, and π are three examples that appear frequently on the GED® because they are essential to certain geometry formulas. So how should you handle them? On the GED®, answer choices often express such numbers "as is" rather than as their decimal or fractional equivalents, so that you won't have to deal with their values at all. But if a question should require you to estimate the values of such numbers, rounding them to the nearest tenth will usually suffice, unless the question tells you the approximate value you should use in your calculation. Here's a simple example involving the value of π.

EXAMPLE 29:

Which of the following most closely approximates the area of a circle whose radius is 3 centimeters?

    (1) 18 cm²

    (2) 27 cm²

    (3) 28 cm²

    (4) 30 cm²

    (5) 36 cm²

The phrase "most closely approximates" tells you that you can round off some numbers and still narrow the choices to the correct answer. Notice that the answer choices are integers—a further clue that you can probably round off your calculation and work to the correct solution. The area of a circle is equal to πr^2, where r represents the circle's radius. To the nearest tenth, $\pi = 3.1$. Substituting 3.1 for π:

$$\text{Area} = 3.1 \times 3^2 = (3.1)(9) = 27.9$$

If you're uncomfortable with rounding π to just one decimal place, use a slightly more precise value for π. To the nearest hundredth, $\pi = 3.14$. (The "formulas page" you'll be given during the test will provide this approximate value for π.) Substitute 3.14 for π in the same equation:

$$\text{Area} = 3.14 \times 3^2 = (3.14)(9) = 28.26$$

As you can see, either rounded value (3.1 or 3.14) leads you to the closest approximation among the five choices. **The correct answer is (3).**

In the preceding example, what if the two closest values among the answer choices were 28 and 28.5? Using 3.1 as an approximate value of π would have resulted in the wrong answer. 27.9 is closer to 28 than to 28.5, while 28.26 is closer to 28.5 than to 28. Don't worry; you won't be required to slice the numbers this finely on the GED®.

Rounding off Numerators and Denominators

Nowhere is rounding more valuable than in dealing with fractions. Assume, for example, that a certain question on Part II (calculator not allowed) requires you to divide 47 by 62. The quotient can be expressed as the fraction $\frac{47}{62}$. Since 47 is a prime number, you can't simplify the fraction or the division. And if you apply long division, you'll find it time consuming to find the precise quotient:

$$62\overline{)47} = 0.7580645$$

But this is not the sort of number that you'll be required to compute on the GED®—with or without a calculator. If you face an operation such as this one, an approximation will almost always suffice to answer the question. If you're on Part II (calculator not allowed), decide whether to round the numbers up or down, and by how far. But be sure to round both numbers *in the same direction* (either up or down), in order to minimize the change to the value of the overall fraction.

For example, in performing the operation 47 ÷ 62, you can round 47 *down* to 45 and 62 *down* to 60, or you can round 47 *up* to 50 and 62 *up* to 65. Either method will result in a close enough approximation of the quotient 0.7580645:

$$\frac{47}{62} \approx \frac{45}{60} = \frac{3}{4}, \text{ or } 0.75$$

$$\frac{47}{62} \approx \frac{50}{65} = \frac{10}{13}, \text{ or approximately } 0.77$$

Whether you should round up or down depends on how easy it is to divide the revised numerator by the denominator. In the operation 47 ÷ 62, rounding *up* is easier because you can simplify the resulting fraction. To underscore this idea, consider the fraction $\frac{42}{83.8}$. You can round both numbers *up*, and then simplify:

$$\frac{42}{83.8} \approx \frac{45}{85} = \frac{9}{17}$$

Better still, though, you can round both numbers *down*:

$$\frac{42}{83.8} \approx \frac{40}{80} = \frac{1}{2}$$

The second result is an easier fraction to work with and might suffice if the answer choices are expressed only to the nearest half unit.

Techniques for Combining Numbers

Here you'll learn some grouping techniques that can help you add, subtract, and multiply numbers efficiently. You'll also learn how to simplify multiplication and division of numbers that contain "trailing zeros." These techniques can be especially helpful during Part II of the test (calculator not allowed). But you can also apply them to Part I (calculator allowed) in order to check your calculator work.

Cancel Numbers if Possible (Addition and Subtraction)

When combining a series of numbers by addition and/or subtraction, look for number pairs or larger groups that "cancel out"—in other words, that add up to 0 (zero). Consider this series of numbers:

$$17 + 10 - 14 - 3$$

The conventional method is to add each term to the next one, from left to right. But since $-14 - 3 = -17$, those two terms "cancel out" the number 17. In other words, the three numbers add up to 0 (zero). So you know that all four numbers must add up to 10.

Combine Similarly Signed Numbers First (Addition and Subtraction)

Another technique for combining by addition and subtraction is to add positive and negative numbers separately, and then subtract the second sum from the first. Consider this series of numbers:

$$23 - 12 - 14 + 7 - 8$$

The conventional method is to subtract 12 from 23, then subtract 14, then add 7, then subtract 8—in other words, to move from left to right. If pressed for time, it's remarkably easy to overlook minus signs and to add when you should be subtracting. So instead (or to check the work you performed the conventional way), combine the positive numbers and the negative numbers separately, then subtract the sums as follows:

$23 + 7 = 30$ (sum of positive terms)

$12 + 14 + 8 = 34$ (sum of negative terms)

$30 - 34 = -4$ (total sum)

Round One Number Up and Another Down (Addition and Subtraction)

Yet another method of combining by addition or subtraction is to round one number up and another one down by the same amount. For example, 89 is 11 *less* than 100, while 111 is 11 *greater* than 100. So 89 + 111 is the same as 100 + 100 = 200. Here's an example with four terms instead of just two:

$$251 + 423 + 749 + 77$$

Notice that $251 + 749$ is the same as $250 + 750 = 1000$. Also notice that $423 + 77$ is the same as $425 + 75 = 500$. So the calculation boils down to $1000 + 500 = 1500$, which can be performed quickly yet accurately.

Multiply Numbers in the Easiest Sequence

You can multiply three or more numbers together most efficiently by looking for number pairs that combine easily. Consider the following expression:

$$25 \times 3\frac{1}{2} \times 16$$

To combine all three numbers, you can start with any pair. But the operation 25×16 is the easiest one to start with: $100 \times 16 = 1600$, and so 25×16 must equal one fourth of 1600, or 400. Now perform the second operation:

$$400 \times 3\frac{1}{2} = (400 \times 3) + (400 \times \frac{1}{2}) = 1400$$

Strip Away Trailing Zeros When Multiplying or Dividing

When facing multiplication involving large numbers ending in zeros, called "trailing zeros," many test-takers will include the zeros in their calculation (whether using the calculator or pencil and paper). But this method can easily result in a calculation error. Instead, strip away the trailing zeros before doing the math.

Consider the operation 4200×6000. Follow these three steps to make sure you handle the zeros correctly:

1. Ignore all the trailing (consecutive) zeros at the end of the numbers.

2. Multiply whatever numbers are left: $42 \times 6 = 252$.

3. Add back the zeros to the end of your product. In this example, we ignored 5 zeros, so the answer is 252 with 5 zeros to the right: 25,200,000.

Now consider the same two numbers, except that the operation is division: $4200 \div 6000$. Follow these three steps to make sure you handle the zeros correctly:

1. Ignore the zeros, and divide what's left: $42 \div 6 = 7$.

2. Cancel (cross out) every trailing zero in the numerator for which there is also a trailing zero in the denominator. In this example, all zeros cancel out except for one zero in the denominator.

3. For every extra zero in the denominator, move the decimal point in your quotient to the *left* one place. In this case, take the quotient, 7, and move the decimal point one place to the left. The answer is 0.7.

or

4. For each extra zero in the numerator, move the decimal point to the right one place. (This step doesn't apply to this particular example, but see below.)

Let's try this method again, this time reversing the numerator and the denominator ($6000 \div 4200$):

1. Ignore the zeros, and divide what's left: $\frac{6}{42} = \frac{1}{7}$, or about 0.14.

2. Cancel trailing zeros in the numerator and denominator.

3. You're left with one extra zero in the numerator, so move the decimal point to the right *one* place. The answer is about 1.4. (To express the answer as a fraction, you would add the extra zero to the numerator: $\frac{10}{7}$.)

Remember: you can ignore trailing zeros, but only temporarily. You'll have to tag them back onto your final number. And you can't ignore zeros between non-zero numbers (like 308).

Using the Calculator to Your Advantage

The use of a calculator is permitted only during Part I of the Mathematics Test. As noted earlier, a *Casio fx-260* calculator will be provided, and you should make sure you are thoroughly familiar with this calculator before taking the test.

For many questions on Part I, the calculator may be helpful. For some of these questions, however, using the calculator may be unnecessary or may actually slow you down. In any event, remember that a calculator is only a tool to avoid computing mistakes; it cannot take the place of understanding how to set up and solve a mathematical problem.

Here's a question for which a calculator might be helpful:

The price of one dozen roses is $10.80. At this rate, what is the price of 53 roses?

The simplest way to approach this question is to divide $10.80 by 12, which gives you the price of one rose, then multiply that price by 53:

$10.80 \div 12 = $0.90

$0.90 \times 53 = $47.70

Although the arithmetic is fairly simple, using a calculator might improve your speed and accuracy. But in some questions involving numbers, using the calculator might actually slow you down because the question is set up to be solved in a quicker, more intuitive manner. Here's an example:

If $x = \frac{1}{2} \times \frac{1}{3} \times \frac{3}{2} \times \frac{4}{81}$, what is the value of $\sqrt{x}$?

To answer this question, you could use a calculator to perform all the steps:

5. Multiply the numerators.

6. Multiply the denominators.

7. Divide the product of the numerators by the product of the denominators.

8. Compute the square root.

But using a calculator is far more trouble than it's worth here. The problem is set up so that all numbers but 81 cancel out, so it's more quickly and easily solved this way (without a calculator):

$$\cancel{7} \times \frac{1}{\cancel{3}} \times \frac{\cancel{3}}{\cancel{2}} \times \frac{\cancel{4}}{81} = \frac{1}{81} \; ; \; \sqrt{\frac{1}{81}} = \frac{1}{9}$$

Checking Your Calculations

Computation errors are the leading cause of incorrect answers on the GED® Mathematics Test. Take this fact as your cue to check your work on every question before proceeding to the next one. If answering a question involved only one simple calculation, then by all means perform that calculation again; it should only take a few seconds of your time.

For questions involving multiple calculations, checking your work does not necessarily mean going through all the steps in the same sequence a second time. You're less likely to repeat the same mistake if you use some other approach. Try reversing the computational process. If you've added two numbers together, check your work by subtracting one of the numbers from the sum:

$$56 + 233 = 289$$

$$289 - 233 = 56 \text{ (check)}$$

If you've subtracted one number from another, check your work by adding the result to the number you subtracted:

$$28.34 - 3.8 = 24.54$$

$$24.54 + 3.8 = 28.34 \text{ (check)}$$

If you've multiplied two numbers, check your work by dividing the product by one of the numbers:

$$11.3 \times 6.65 = 75.145$$

$$75.145 \div 11.3 = 6.65 \text{ (check)}$$

If you've divided one number by another, check your work by multiplying the quotient by the second number:

$$789 \div 3 = 263$$

$$263 \times 3 = 789 \text{ (check)}$$

And if you simply don't have time to recalculate, whether forward or in reverse, you may still have time to recalculate the *smallest digit* (the one farthest to the right) to make sure it's correct. This check is quick and easy since you don't have to think about carried numbers. For example:

$$289 - 233 + 4722 \text{ (the last digit should be 8)}$$

$$11.3 \times 6.65 \text{ (the last digit should be 5)}$$

GENERAL TEST-TAKING STRATEGIES

Here are some general strategies for tackling the GED® Mathematics Test. Some of the points of advice encapsulate specific strategies you learned in the preceding pages. Apply all the strategies from this lesson to the Practice Tests in this book, and then review them again just before exam day.

Size up each question to devise a plan for handling it.

After reading a question, scan the answer choices (if any) and devise a plan of action for answering the question. Decide what operations or other steps are required to solve the problem. After some brief thought, if you still don't know where to start, try making a reasoned guess, and then move on to the next question. (Remember: you won't be penalized for incorrect answers.)

Be certain you know what the question is asking.

On the Mathematics Test, careless reading is a leading cause of wrong answers. So be doubly sure you answer the precise question being asked. For example, does the question ask for the mean or the median? Circumference or area? A sum or a difference? A perimeter or a length of one side only? A total or an average? Feet or inches? Gallons or liters? Multiple-choice questions often bait you with incorrect answer choices that provide the *right* answer but to the *wrong* question. Don't fall for this ploy: know what the question is asking.

Look around for clues as to how to answer each question.

Be sure to read *all* information pertaining to the question. This includes not just the question itself, but also the answer choices and all information above, below, and beside a chart, graph, table, or geometry figure. Though you may not need every bit of information provided in order to answer the question at hand, reviewing it all helps ensure that you don't overlook what you need.

Don't hesitate to use your scratch paper.

You will be provided with scratch paper, and by all means use it! Draw diagrams for geometry problems that don't supply them. Drawing a diagram often helps you visualize not only the problem but also the solution. Jot down any formulas or other equations needed to answer the question at hand. Remember also that during Part II you will not be allowed to use the calculator. So use scratch paper during this part for all but the simplest calculations. (Immediately after the test, the test administrator will collect and then discard all scratch paper. So nothing you write on scratch paper will affect your score or be read by anyone.)

Save time by estimating and rounding.

If a question asks for an approximate value, you can safely round off your calculations. Just be sure not to round too far or in the wrong direction. Either the question itself or the answer choices should tell you how far you can round. Even if the question doesn't ask for an approximate value, you might be able to use estimation and rounding to zero-in on the correct answer—or at least eliminate choices that are too far off the mark.

Take the easiest route to the correct answer.

For some multiple-choice questions, it may be easier to work backward from the answer choices. For some algebra word problems, it might be easier to plug in numbers for variables instead of setting up and solving equations. When facing a long series of calculations, try to think of a shortcut. Avoid precise calculations when rough estimates will suffice. In short, be flexible in your approach: use whatever method reveals the answer.

Check your work before leaving any question.

The most common mistakes on math tests result not from lack of knowledge but from carelessness, and the GED® Mathematics Test is no exception. So before recording any response on your answer sheet:

- Do a reality check. Ask yourself whether your solution makes sense for what the question asks. (This check is especially appropriate for word problems.)

- Make sure you used the same numbers as were provided in the question and that you didn't inadvertently switch numbers or other expressions.

- For questions where you solve algebraic equations, plug your solution into the equation(s) to make sure it works.

- Confirm *all* your calculations. It's amazingly easy to commit errors in even the simplest calculations, especially under GED® exam pressure. Using scratch paper the first time around makes this task easier.

Pace yourself properly.

You won't be penalized for incorrect answers, so don't spend too much time on any one question. Use your time to answer all the questions that are not difficult for you, and then go back and work on the tougher ones if there's time. You'll have 90 minutes to answer 50 questions altogether. Part I and Part II are equal in length—25 questions each. Neither part is inherently more difficult or time-consuming than the other. So try to complete Part I within 40 minutes, reserving 5 minutes to return to questions you had trouble answering confidently. Follow the same approach for Part II.

SUMMING IT UP

- You will have 90 minutes to take Part I and Part II of the Mathematics Test. There are 25 questions in Part I and 25 questions in Part II. You may use a calculator *only* during Part I of the Mathematics Test.

- The calculator you will use during this test is the *Casio fx-260* solar calculator. You will be given one to use at the testing center, but it is highly recommended that you purchase or borrow one and become familiar with it *before* taking the test.

- The Mathematics Test measures understanding and applying mathematical concepts and formulas, quantitative reasoning and problem solving, translating verbal language into mathematical terms, analyzing and interpreting graphical data, and computing, estimating, and rounding numbers.

- Four broad knowledge areas are covered on the Mathematics Test: numbers, number sense, and operations (20–30 percent); data, statistics, and probability (20–30 percent); algebra, functions, and patterns (20–30 percent); and geometry, coordinate geometry, and measurement (20–30 percent).

- You will be given scratch paper for both parts of the Mathematics Test; however, it will be collected at the end of the test, and your handwritten calculations will not have any effect on your score. You will also receive a list of formulas that you may or may not need to refer to during the test.

- Forty of the fifty questions on this test are multiple-choice questions. The remaining ten questions require you to provide your own answer using the answer grid or coordinate plane provided on your answer sheet.

- For the alternative-format answer grid, remember that GED® answer sheets are machine-read, which means that only the filled-in bubbles will be scanned. The numbers you write in the top row of the grid will not be read. No answer to an alternative-format question can be a negative number. You must grid only one answer, even if there is more than one correct answer.

Math Review: Numbers

chapter 12

OVERVIEW

- What you'll find in this review
- Order and laws of operations
- Number signs and the four basic operations
- Integers and the four basic operations
- Factors, multiples, and divisibility
- Decimal numbers, fractions, and percentages
- Ratio and proportion
- Ratios involving more than two quantities
- Exponents (powers) and scientific notation
- Square roots (and other roots)
- Summing it up

WHAT YOU'LL FIND IN THIS REVIEW

In this review, you'll focus on:

- *Properties* of numbers (signs, integers, absolute value, and divisibility)

- *Forms* of numbers (fractions, mixed numbers, decimal numbers, percentages, ratios, exponential numbers, and radical expressions)

- *Operations* on numbers (the four basic operations and operations on exponential numbers and radical expressions)

Although this review is more basic than the next two in this part of the book, don't skip over it. The knowledge areas covered here are basic building blocks for all types of GED® math questions.

The GED®-style questions throughout this review are multiple-choice questions. The actual exam also includes questions in an alternative format, in which you supply the numerical answer to the question.

ORDER AND LAWS OF OPERATIONS

The following rules apply to all operations on numbers as well as on variables (such as x and y).

Order of operations

❶ operations inside parentheses

❷ operations with square roots and exponents

http://bit.ly/hippo-alg15

③ multiplication and division

④ addition and subtraction

Examples:

$(2 + 4) \times (7 - 2) = 6 \times 5$ (operate inside parentheses before multiplying)

$3 \times 4^2 = 3 \times 16$ (apply exponent before multiplying)

$5 + 7 \times 3 - 2 = 5 + 21 - 2$ (multiply before adding or subtracting)

$6 - 8 \div 2 + 3 = 6 - 4 + 3$ (divide before adding or subtracting)

The Commutative Law (addition and multiplication *only*)

$a + b = b + a$

$a \times b = b \times a$

Examples:

$3 + 4 = 4 + 3$

$3 \times 4 = 4 \times 3$

The Associative Law (addition and multiplication *only*)

$(a + b) + c = a + (b + c)$

$(ab)c = a(bc)$

Examples:

$(6 + 2) + 5 = 8 + 5 = 13$

$6 + (2 + 5) = 6 + 7 = 13$

$(3 \times 2) \times 4 = 6 \times 4 = 24$

$3 \times (2 \times 4) = 3 \times 8 = 24$

The Distributive Law

$a(b + c) = ab + ac$

$a(b - c) = ab - ac$

Examples:

$2(3 + 4) = 2 \times 7 = 14$

$(2)(3) + (2)(4) = 6 + 8 = 14$

$9(4 - 2) = 9 \times 2 = 18$

$(9)(4) - (9)(2) = 36 - 18 = 18$

http://bit.ly/hippo_alg16

NUMBER SIGNS AND THE FOUR BASIC OPERATIONS

A **positive number** is any number *greater than zero*, and a **negative number** is any

number *less than zero*. The **sign** of a number indicates whether it is positive (+) or

negative (–).

Be sure you know the sign—either positive or negative—of a non-zero number that

results from combining numbers using the four basic operations (addition, subtraction,

multiplication, and division). Here's a table that includes all the possibilities. A

number's sign is indicated in parentheses. A question mark (?) indicates that the sign

depends on which number is greater.

Addition:

(+) + (+) = +

(−) + (−) = −

(+) + (−) = ?

(−) + (+) = ?

Examples:

$5 + 3 = 8$

$−5 + (−3) = −8$

$5 + (−3) = 2$ but $3 + (−5) = −2$

$−5 + 3 = −2$ but $−3 + 5 = 2$

Subtraction:

(+) − (−) = (+)

(−) − (+) = (−)

(+) − (+) = ?

(−) − (−) = ?

Examples:

$6 − (−1) = 7$

$−6 − 1 = −7$

$6 − 1 = 5$ but $1 − 6 = −5$

$−6 − (−1) = −5$ but $−1 − 6 = 5$

Multiplication:

(+) × (+) = +

(+) × (−) = −

(−) × (−) = +

Examples:

$7 × 2 = 14$

$7 × (−2) = −14$

$(−7) × (−2) = 14$

Division:

(+) ÷ (+) = +

(+) ÷ (−) = −

(−) ÷ (+) = −

(−) ÷ (−) = +

Examples:

$8 ÷ 4 = 2$

$8 ÷ (−4) = −2$

$−8 ÷ 4 = −2$

$−8 ÷ (−4) = 2$

Multiplying and Dividing Negative Terms

Multiplication or division involving any *even* number of negative terms gives you a positive number. On the other hand, multiplication or division involving any *odd* number of negative terms gives you a negative number.

> **Examples (*even* number of negative terms):**
> $(5) × (−4) × (2) × (−2) = +80$ (two negative terms)
> $(−4) × (−3) × (−2) × (−1) = +24$ (four negative terms)

> **Examples (*odd* number of negative terms):**
> $(3) × (−3) × (2) = −18$ (one negative terms)
> $(−4) × (−4) × (2) × (−2) = −64$ (three negative terms)

http://bit.ly/hippo_alg24

Absolute Value

A number's **absolute value** refers to its distance from zero (the origin) on the real-number line. The absolute value of x is indicated as $|x|$. The absolute value of any number other than zero is always a positive number. The concept of absolute value boils down to these two statements:

If $x \geq 0$, then $|x| = x$
Example: $|3| = 3$
Example: $|0| = 0$

If $x < 0$, then $|x| = -x$
Example: $|-2| = -(-2) = 2$

GED® questions that involve combining signed numbers often focus on the concept of absolute value.

EXAMPLE 1 (EASIER):

What is the value of $|-2 - 3| - |2 - 3|$?

    (1) -2

    (2) -1

    (3) 0

    (4) 1

    (5) 4

$|-2 - 3| = |-5| = 5$, and $|2 - 3| = |-1| = 1$. Performing subtraction: $5 - 1 = 4$. **The correct answer is (5).**

EXAMPLE 2 (MORE CHALLENGING):

The number M is the product of seven negative numbers. The number N is the product of six negative numbers and one positive number.

Which of the following holds true for all possible values of M and N ?

    (1) $M - N > 0$

    (2) $M \times N < 0$

    (3) $N + M < 0$

    (4) $N \times M = 0$

    (5) $N - M < 0$

The product of seven negative numbers is always negative (M is a negative number). The product of six negative numbers is always a positive number, and the product of two positive numbers is always a positive number (N is a positive number). Thus, the product of M and N must be a negative number. Choices (1) and (3) may or may not hold true, depending on the specific values of *M* and *N*. Choices (4) and (5) cannot hold true. **The correct answer is (2).**

INTEGERS AND THE FOUR BASIC OPERATIONS

http://bit.ly/hippo_alg25

An **integer** is any non-fraction number on the number line: {. . . −3, −2, −1, 0, 1, 2, 3, . . .}. Except for the number zero (0), every integer is either positive or negative and either even or odd. When you combine integers using a basic operation, whether the result is an odd integer, an even integer, or a non-integer depends on the numbers you combined. Here are the possibilities:

Addition and Subtraction:
integer ± integer = integer
even integer ± even integer = even integer (or possibly zero)
even integer ± odd integer = odd integer
odd integer ± odd integer = even integer (or possibly zero)

Multiplication and Division:
integer × integer = integer
integer ÷ non-zero integer = integer, but only if the numerator is divisible by
    the denominator (if the result is a quotient with no remainder)
odd integer × odd integer = odd integer
even integer × non-zero integer = even integer
even integer ÷ 2 = integer
odd integer ÷ 2 = non-integer

GED® questions that test you on the preceding rules sometimes look like algebra problems, but they're really not. Just apply the appropriate rule. If you're not sure of the rule, plug in simple numbers to zero-in on the correct answer.

EXAMPLE 3 (EASIER):

M < *N* < 0. If *M* and *N* are both integers, which of the following holds true for all possible values of *M* and *N* ?

    (1) *M* − *N* is a positive integer.

    (2) *N* − *M* is a positive non-integer integer.

    (3) *N* + *M* is a negative integer less than *N*.

    (4) *M* × *N* is a negative integer less than *M*.

    (5) *N* − *M* is a non-integer greater than *N*.

Combining two integers by addition, subtraction, or multiplication always results in an integer, so you can eliminate choices (2) and (5). Since both numbers are negative, adding them together results in an even smaller number. **The correct answer is (3).**

EXAMPLE 4 (MORE CHALLENGING):

If P is an odd integer, and if Q is an even integer, which of the following expressions CANNOT represent an even integer?

(1) $3P - Q$

(2) $3P \times Q$

(3) $2Q \times P$

(4) $3Q - 2P$

(5) $3P - 2Q$

Since 3 and P are both odd integers, their product ($3P$) must also be an odd integer. Subtracting an even integer (Q) from an odd integer results in an odd integer in all cases except where $3Q = P$, in which case the result is 0 (zero). **The correct answer is (1).**

FACTORS, MULTIPLES, AND DIVISIBILITY

A **factor** (of an integer n) is any integer that you can multiply by another integer for a product of n. The factors of any integer n include 1 as well as n itself. Figuring out whether one number (f) is a factor of another (n) is simple: Just divide n by f. If the quotient is an integer, then f is a factor of n (and n is **divisible** by f). If the quotient is not an integer, then f is not a factor of n, and you'll end up with a **remainder** after dividing.

For example, 2 is a factor of 8 because $8 \div 2 = 4$, which is an integer. On the other hand, 3 is not a factor of 8 because $8 \div 3 = \frac{8}{3}$, or $2\frac{2}{3}$, which is a non-integer. (The remainder is $\frac{2}{3}$.) Keep in mind these basic rules about factors, which are based on its definition:

RULE 1: Any integer is a factor of itself.

RULE 2: 1 and −1 are factors of all integers (except 0).

RULE 3: The integer zero (0) has no factors and is not a factor of any integer.

RULE 4: A positive integer's largest factor (other than itself) will never be greater than one half the value of the integer.

On the "flip side" of factors are **multiples**. If f is a factor of n, then n is a multiple of f. For example, 8 is a multiple of 2 for the same reason that 2 is a factor of 8: because $8 \div 2 = 4$, which is an integer.

A **prime number** is a positive integer that is divisible by (a multiple of) only two positive integers: itself and 1. Zero (0) and 1 are not considered prime numbers; 2 is the first prime number. Here are all the prime numbers less than 50:

2 3 5 7

11 13 17 19

23 29

31 37

41 43 47

As you can see, factors, multiples, and divisibility are simply different aspects of the same concept. So, a GED® question about factoring or prime numbers is also about multiples and divisibility.

EXAMPLE 5 (EASIER):

The number 24 is divisible by how many different positive integers other than 1 and 24?

    (1) two

    (2) three

    (3) four

    (4) five

    (5) six

The question asks for the number of different factors of 24 (other than 1 and 24). A good way to answer the question is to begin with 2 and work your way up to the largest possible factor, 12, which is half the value of 24:

$2 \times 12 = 24$

$3 \times 8 = 24$

$4 \times 6 = 24$

If you continue in this manner, you'll see that you've already accounted for all factors of 24, which include 2, 3, 4, 6, 8, and 12. **The correct answer is (5).**

EXAMPLE 6 (MORE CHALLENGING):

If $n > 6$, and if n is a multiple of 6, which of the following is always a factor of n?

    (1) $n - 6$

    (2) $n + 6$

    (3) $\frac{n}{3}$

    (4) $\frac{n}{2} + 3$

    (5) $\frac{n}{2} + 6$

Since 3 is a factor of 6, 3 is also a factor of any positive-number multiple of 6. Thus, if you divide any multiple of 6 by 3, the quotient will be an integer. In other words, 3 will be a factor of that number (n). Choice (1) is incorrect because $n - 6$ is a factor of n only if $n = 12$. Choice (2) is wrong because $n + 6$ can never be a factor of n because $n + 6$ is greater than n. Choice (4) is incorrect because you always end up with a remainder of 3. Finally, you can eliminate choices (4) and (5) because the largest factor of any positive number (other than the number itself) is half the number, which in this case is $\frac{n}{2}$. **The correct answer is (3).**

DECIMAL NUMBERS, FRACTIONS, AND PERCENTAGES

Any number can be expressed in the form of a decimal number, a fraction, or a percent. You use **decimal numbers** in your daily life every time you make a purchase at a store. Most of us are familiar with decimals in terms of money. When you have $5.87, you have 5 whole dollars, 8 dimes (or 8 tenths of a dollar), and 7 cents (or 7 hundredths of a dollar). When a number is written in decimal form, everything to the left of the decimal point is a whole number, and everything to the right of the decimal point represents a part of the whole (a tenth, hundredth, thousandth, and so on). Adding zeros to the *end* of a decimal number does not change its value. For example, the decimal number 0.5 is the same as 0.50 or 0.5000. But adding a zero to the *front* (the left) of the number *will* change the number's value. For example, 0.5 means "five tenths," but 0.05 means "five hundredths."

A **fraction** is a part of a whole. There are 10 dimes in each dollar, so one dime is one tenth of a dollar—one of ten equal parts. The fraction to represent one tenth is written $\frac{1}{10}$. The top number of a fraction is called the **numerator,** and the bottom number is called the **denominator. A proper fraction** is one in which the numerator is less than the denominator. An **improper fraction** is one in which the numerator is the same as or greater than the denominator. $\frac{1}{10}$ is a proper fraction, but $\frac{12}{10}$ is an improper fraction. Sometimes you will see a whole number and a fraction together. This is called a **mixed number.** $4\frac{3}{5}$ is an example of a mixed number.

A **percent (%)** is a fraction or decimal number written in a different form. 25% written as a decimal number is 0.25. A percent expressed as a fraction is the number divided by 100. For example, 25% written as a fraction is $\frac{25}{100}$. The number before the percent sign is the numerator of the fraction.

Converting One Number Form to Another

GED® math questions involving fractions, decimal numbers, or percents often require you to convert one form to another as part of solving the problem at hand. You should know how to convert quickly and confidently. For percent-to-decimal conversions, move the decimal point two places to the *left* (and drop the percent sign). For decimal-to-percent conversions, move the decimal point two places to the *right* (and add the percent sign). Percents greater than 100 convert to numbers greater than 1.

Examples (converting percents to decimal numbers)

9.5% = 0.095

.95% = 0.95

950% = 9.5

Examples (converting decimal numbers to percents)

0.004 = 0.4%

0.04 = 4%

0.4 = 40%

4.0 = 400%

For percent-to-fraction conversions, *divide* by 100 (and drop the percent sign). For fraction-to-percent conversions, *multiply* by 100 (and add the percent sign). Percents greater than 100 convert to numbers greater than 1.

Examples (converting percents to fractions)

$$8.1\% = \frac{8.1}{100}, \text{ or } \frac{81}{1000}$$

$$81\% = \frac{81}{100}$$

$$810\% = \frac{810}{100} = \frac{81}{10}, \text{ or } 8\frac{1}{10}$$

Example (converting fractions to percents)

$$\frac{3}{8} = \frac{300}{8}\% = \frac{75}{2}\%, \text{ or } 37\frac{1}{2}\%$$

To convert a fraction to a decimal number, divide the numerator by the denominator, using long division or your calculator. Keep in mind that the result might be a precise value, or it might be an approximation with a never-ending string of decimal places. Compare these three examples:

$\frac{5}{8} = 0.625$ The equivalent decimal number is precise after three decimal places.

$\frac{5}{9} \approx 0.555$ The equivalent decimal number can only be approximated (the digit 5 repeats indefinitely).

$\frac{5}{7} \approx 0.714$ The equivalent decimal number can only be approximated; there is no repeating pattern by carrying the calculation to additional decimal places.

EXAMPLE 7 (EASIER):

What is the sum of $\frac{3}{4}$, 0.7, and 80% ?

(1) 0.425

(2) 1.59

(3) 1.62

(4) 2.04

(5) 2.25

Since the answer choices are expressed in decimal terms, express all terms to decimals: $\frac{3}{4} = 0.75$ and 80% = 0.8.

Then add: 0.75 + 0.7 + 0.8 = 2.25. **The correct answer is (5).**

EXAMPLE 8 (MORE CHALLENGING):

What is 150% of the product of $\frac{1}{8}$ and 0.4 ?

(1) 0.025

(2) 0.075

(3) 0.25

(4) 0.75

(5) 2.5

One way to solve the problem is to first express $\frac{1}{8}$ as its decimal equivalent 0.125.

Next multiply: 0.125 × 0.4 = 0.05. Then, express 150% as the decimal number 1.5, and calculate the product: 1.5 × 0.05 = 0.075. **The correct answer is (2).**

Fraction-Decimal-Percent Equivalents

Certain fraction-decimal-percent equivalents appear on the GED® more often than others. The numbers in the following tables are especially common. You should memorize this table, so that you can convert these numbers quickly during the test.

Percent	Decimal	Fraction
50%	0.5	$\frac{1}{2}$
25%	0.25	$\frac{1}{4}$
75%	0.75	$\frac{3}{4}$
10%	0.1	$\frac{1}{10}$
30%	0.3	$\frac{3}{10}$
70%	0.7	$\frac{7}{10}$
90%	0.9	$\frac{9}{10}$
$33\frac{1}{3}\%$	$0.33\frac{1}{3}$	$\frac{1}{3}$
$66\frac{2}{3}\%$	$0.66\frac{2}{3}$	$\frac{2}{3}$

Percent	Decimal	Fraction
$16\frac{2}{3}\%$	$0.16\frac{2}{3}$	$\frac{1}{6}$
$83\frac{1}{3}\%$	$0.83\frac{1}{3}$	$\frac{5}{6}$
20%	0.2	$\frac{1}{5}$
40%	0.4	$\frac{2}{5}$
60%	0.6	$\frac{3}{5}$
80%	0.8	$\frac{4}{5}$
$12\frac{1}{2}\%$	0.125	$\frac{1}{8}$
$37\frac{1}{2}\%$	0.375	$\frac{3}{8}$
$62\frac{1}{2}\%$	0.625	$\frac{5}{8}$
$87\frac{1}{2}\%$	0.875	$\frac{7}{8}$

Decimal Numbers and Place Value

Place value refers to the specific value of a digit in a decimal number. For example, in the decimal number 682.793:

> The digit 6 is in the "hundreds" place.
> The digit 8 is in the "tens" place.
> The digit 2 is in the "ones" place.
> The digit 7 is in the "tenths" place.
> The digit 9 is in the "hundredths" place.
> The digit 3 is in the "thousandths" place.

So, you can express 682.793 as follows: $600 + 80 + 2 + \frac{7}{10} + \frac{9}{100} + \frac{3}{1000}$.

EXAMPLE 9 (EASIER):

The number 40.5 is 1000 times larger than which of the following numbers?

    (1) 0.405

    (2) 0.0405

    (3) 0.0450

    (4) 0.00405

    (5) 0.000405

To find the solution, divide 40.5 by 1000 by moving the decimal point 3 places to the left. **The correct answer is (2).**

EXAMPLE 10 (MORE CHALLENGING):

The letter M represents a digit in the decimal number 0.0M, and the letter N represents a digit in the decimal number 0.0N. Which expression is equivalent to 0.0M × 0.0N?

    (1) $\frac{1}{10,000} \times M \times N$

    (2) 0.000MN

    (3) $\frac{1}{1000} \times M \times N$

    (4) 0.00MN

    (5) $\frac{1}{100} \times M \times N$

Suppose digits M and N are both 1. To find the product of 0.01 and 0.01, you multiply 1 by 1 (N × M), then add together the decimal places in the two numbers. There are four places altogether, so the product would be 0.0001, which is equivalent to $\frac{1}{10,000}$.

Thus, whatever the values of N and M, 0.0M × 0.0N = $\frac{1}{10,000} \times (M \times N)$.

The correct answer is (1).

Simplifying Fractions

A fraction can be simplified to its *lowest terms* if its numerator number and denominator number share a common factor. Here are a few simple examples:

$$\frac{6}{9} = \frac{(3)(2)}{(3)(3)} = \frac{2}{3} \quad \text{(you can "cancel" or "factor out" the common factor 3)}$$

$$\frac{21}{35} = \frac{(7)(3)}{(7)(5)} = \frac{3}{5} \quad \text{(you can "cancel" or "factor out" the common factor 7)}$$

Before you perform any operation with a fraction, always check to see if you can simplify it first. By reducing a fraction to its lowest terms, you'll simplify whatever operation you perform on it.

Adding and Subtracting Fractions

To combine fractions by addition or subtraction, you combine numerators over a **common denominator.** If the fractions already have the same denominator, simply add (or subtract) numerators:

$\frac{3}{4} + \frac{2}{4} = \frac{3+2}{4} = \frac{5}{4}$ (the two fractions share the common denominator 4)

$\frac{1}{7} - \frac{3}{7} = \frac{1-3}{7} = \frac{-2}{7}$, or $-\frac{2}{7}$ (the two fractions share the common denominator 7)

If the fractions don't already have a common denominator, you'll need to find one. You can always multiply all of the denominators together to find a common denominator, but it might be a large number that's clumsy to work with. So instead, try to find the **least (or lowest) common denominator (LCD)** by working your way up in multiples of the largest of the denominators given. For denominators of 6, 3, and 5, for instance, try out successive multiples of 6 (12, 18, 24 . . .), and you'll hit the LCD when you get to 30.

When combining fractions by either addition or subtraction, pay close attention to the + and − signs. Also, don't let common numerators fool you into thinking you can add or subtract without a common denominator.

EXAMPLE 11 (EASIER):

$\frac{5}{3} - \frac{5}{6} + \frac{5}{2}$ is equal to which fraction?

  (1) $\frac{15}{11}$

  (2) $\frac{5}{2}$

  (3) $\frac{15}{6}$

  (4) $\frac{10}{3}$

  (5) $\frac{15}{3}$

To find the LCD, try out successive multiples of 6 until you come across one that is also a multiple of both 3 and 2. The LCD is 6 itself. Multiply each numerator by the same number by which you would multiply the fraction's denominator to give you the LCD of 6. Place the three products over this common denominator. Then, combine the numbers in the numerator. (Pay close attention to the subtraction sign.) Finally, simplify to lowest terms.

$$\frac{5}{3} - \frac{5}{6} + \frac{5}{2} = \frac{5(2) - 5 + 5(3)}{6} = \frac{10 - 5 + 15}{6} = \frac{20}{6}, \text{ or } \frac{10}{3}, \text{ which is choice (4).}$$

The correct answer is (4).

EXAMPLE 12 (MORE CHALLENGING):

If $\frac{x}{3}$, $\frac{x}{7}$, and $\frac{x}{9}$ are all positive integers, what is the *least* possible value of x?

    (1) 36

    (2) 42

    (3) 54

    (4) 63

    (5) 72

The answer to the question is the least value of x that is a multiple of all three denominators. In other words, the question asks for the least common denominator. Working your way up in multiples of the largest denominator, 9, you'll find that 63 is the lowest multiple that is also a multiple of both 7 and 3. Thus, $x = 63$.

The correct answer is (4).

Multiplying and Dividing Fractions

To combine fractions by multiplication, multiply the numerators, and multiply the denominators. The denominators need not be the same.

$$\frac{1}{2} \times \frac{5}{3} \times \frac{1}{7} = \frac{(1)(5)(1)}{(2)(3)(7)} = \frac{5}{42}$$

To divide one fraction by another, first invert the divisor (the number after the division sign) by switching its numerator and denominator. (This new fraction is called the **reciprocal** of the original one.) Then combine by multiplying.

$$\frac{\frac{2}{5}}{\frac{3}{4}} = \frac{2}{5} \times \frac{4}{3} = \frac{(2)(4)}{(5)(3)} = \frac{8}{15}$$

To simplify the multiplication or division, cancel factors common to a numerator and a denominator before combining fractions. You can cancel across fractions. Take, for instance, the operation $\frac{3}{4} \times \frac{4}{9} \times \frac{3}{2}$. Looking just at the first two fractions, you can factor out 4 and 3, so the operation simplifies to $\frac{{}^1\cancel{3}}{{}^1\cancel{4}} \times \frac{{}^1\cancel{4}}{{}^3\cancel{9}} \times \frac{3}{2}$. Now, looking just at the second and third fractions, you can factor out 3, and the operation becomes even simpler: $\frac{1}{1} \times \frac{1}{{}^1\cancel{3}} \times \frac{{}^1\cancel{3}}{2} = \frac{1}{2}$.

Apply the same rules in the same way to variables (letters) as to numbers.

EXAMPLE 13 (EASIER):

Which expression is equal to $\frac{2}{a} \times \frac{b}{4} \times \frac{a}{5} \times \frac{8}{c}$?

    (1) $\frac{ab}{4c}$

    (2) $\frac{10b}{9c}$

    (3) $\frac{8}{5}$

    (4) $\frac{16b}{5ac}$

    (5) $\frac{4b}{5c}$

Since you're dealing only with multiplication, look for factors and variables (letters) in any numerator that match those in any denominator. Canceling common factors leaves $\frac{2}{1} \times \frac{b}{1} \times \frac{1}{5} \times \frac{2}{c}$.

Combining numerators and combining denominators gives you the answer $\frac{4b}{5c}$.
The correct answer is (5).

EXAMPLE 14 (MORE CHALLENGING):

Which is a simplified form of the complex fraction $\dfrac{\frac{3}{5} + \frac{3}{4}}{\frac{3}{4} - \frac{3}{5}}$?

    (1) $-\frac{57}{20}$

    (2) $\frac{27}{10}$

    (3) 5

    (4) $\frac{27}{4}$

    (5) 9

Convert all four fractions to fractions with the least common denominator, 20. Then, add together the two numerator fractions and the two denominator fractions.

$$\frac{\frac{3}{5} + \frac{3}{4}}{\frac{3}{4} - \frac{3}{5}} = \frac{\frac{12}{20} + \frac{15}{20}}{\frac{15}{20} - \frac{12}{20}} = \frac{\frac{27}{20}}{\frac{3}{20}}$$

Then, multiply the resulting numerator fraction by the reciprocal of the resulting denominator fraction:

$$\frac{\frac{27}{20}}{\frac{3}{20}} = \left(\frac{27}{20}\right)\left(\frac{20}{3}\right) = \frac{27}{3} = 9$$

The correct answer is (5).

Mixed Numbers

As noted earlier, a *mixed number* consists of a whole number along with a simple fraction. The number $4\frac{2}{3}$ is an example of a mixed number. Before combining fractions, you might need to convert mixed numbers to simple fractions. To do so, follow these three steps:

1 Multiply the denominator of the fraction by the whole number.

2 Add the product to the numerator of the fraction.

3 Place the sum over the denominator of the fraction.

For example, here's how to convert the mixed number $4\frac{2}{3}$ to a fraction:

$$4\frac{2}{3} = \frac{(3)(4) + 2}{3} = \frac{14}{3}$$

To add or subtract mixed numbers, you can convert each one to a fraction, then find their LCD and combine them. Or, you can add together the whole numbers, and add together the fractions separately. To perform multiple operations, always perform multiplication and division before you perform addition and subtraction.

EXAMPLE 15 (EASIER):

What is the sum of $2\frac{1}{6}$, $3\frac{1}{5}$, and $5\frac{1}{15}$?

    (1) $9\frac{11}{15}$

    (2) $10\frac{13}{30}$

    (3) $10\frac{4}{5}$

    (4) $11\frac{3}{10}$

    (5) $12\frac{17}{20}$

One way to combine these mixed numbers is to first convert the mixed numbers to fractions:

$$2\frac{1}{6} + 3\frac{1}{5} + 5\frac{1}{15} = \frac{13}{6} + \frac{16}{5} + \frac{31}{15}$$

But as you can see, to combine numerators over a LCD, you'll be dealing with large numbers. An easier method is to add together the whole numbers, and add together the fractions separately:

$$(2 + 3 + 5) + \frac{1}{6} + \frac{1}{5} + \frac{1}{15} = 10 + \frac{5 + 6 + 2}{30} = 10\frac{13}{30}$$

The correct answer is (2).

EXAMPLE 16 (MORE CHALLENGING):

If you subtract $3\frac{2}{3}$ from $\dfrac{4\frac{1}{2}}{1\frac{1}{8}}$, what is the resulting fraction?

(1) $\frac{1}{4}$

(2) $\frac{1}{3}$

(3) $\frac{11}{6}$

(4) $\frac{17}{6}$

(5) $\frac{11}{2}$

First, convert all mixed numbers to fractions. Then, eliminate the complex fraction by multiplying the numerator fraction by the reciprocal of the denominator fraction (cancel across fractions before multiplying):

$$\dfrac{\frac{9}{2}}{\frac{9}{8}} - \frac{11}{3} = \left(\frac{9}{2}\right)\left(\frac{8}{9}\right) - \frac{11}{3} = \left(\frac{1}{1}\right)\left(\frac{4}{1}\right) - \frac{11}{3} = \frac{4}{1} - \frac{11}{3}$$

Then, express each fraction using the common denominator 6. Finally, subtract:

$$\frac{4}{1} - \frac{11}{3} = \frac{12 - 11}{3} = \frac{1}{3}$$

The correct answer is (2).

Problems Involving Percent

A GED® question involving percent might involve one of these three tasks:

- Finding the percent of a number

- Finding a number when a percent is given

- Finding what percent one number is of another

Regardless of the task, four distinct numbers are involved: the part, the whole, the percent, and 100. The problem will give you three of the numbers, and your job is to find the fourth. An easy way to deal with percent problems is to set up a grid to decide which number is missing, and then solve for that missing number. Arrange the grid as follows:

part	percent
whole	100

The left column is actually a fraction that is equal to the right-column fraction. (Think of the middle horizontal line as a fraction bar.) The two fractions have the same value. Once you set up the problem in this way, you can solve it by these steps:

❶ Simplify the known fraction, if possible.

❷ Multiply the diagonally situated numbers that you know.

❸ Divide the product by the third number you know.

To see how this is done, study the following three examples.

Finding the Percent

30 is what percent of 50?

In this question, 50 is the whole, and 30 is the part. Your task is to find the missing percent:

30	?
50	100

First, simplify the left-hand fraction $\frac{30}{50}$ to $\frac{3}{5}$. Then, multiply the two diagonally situated numbers you know: $3 \times 100 = 300$. Finally, divide by the third number you know: $300 \div 5 = 60$. This is the answer to the question. *30 is 60% of 50.*

Finding the Part

What number is 25% of 80?

In this question, 80 is the whole, and 25 is the percent. Your task is to find the part:

?	25
80	100

First, simplify the right-hand fraction $\frac{25}{100}$ to $\frac{1}{4}$.

?	1
80	4

Then multiply the two diagonally situated numbers you know: $1 \times 80 = 80$. Finally, divide by the third number you know: $80 \div 4 = 20$. This is the answer to the question. *25% of 80 is 20.*

Finding the Whole

75% of what number is 150?

In this question, 150 is the part, and 75 is the percent. Your task is to find the whole:

150	75
?	100

First, simplify the right-hand fraction $\frac{75}{100}$ to $\frac{3}{4}$.

150	3
?	4

Then multiply the two diagonally situated numbers you know: $150 \times 4 = 600$. Finally, divide by the third number you know: $600 \div 3 = 200$. This is the answer to the question. *75% of 200 is 150.*

Percent Increase and Decrease

The concept of percent change is familiar to everyone. For example, investment interest, sales tax, and discount pricing all involve percent change. Here's the key to answering GED® questions involving this concept: percent change always relates to the value *before* the change. Here are two simple examples:

10 increased by what percent is 12?

❶ The amount of the increase is 2.

❷ Compare the change (2) to the original number (10).

❸ The change in percent is $\frac{2}{10}$, or 20%.

12 decreased by what percent is 10?

❶ The amount of the decrease is 2.

❷ Compare the change (2) to the original number (12).

❸ The change is $\frac{2}{12}$, or $\frac{1}{6}$ (or $16\frac{2}{3}\%$).

Notice that the percent increase from 10 to 12 (20%) is *not* the same as the percent decrease from 12 to 10 ($16\frac{2}{3}\%$). That's because the original number (before the change) is different in the two questions.

GED® percent-change problems typically involve tax, interest, profit, discount, or weight. In handling these problems, you might need to calculate more than one percent change.

EXAMPLE 17 (EASIER):

A computer originally priced at $500 is discounted by 10%, then by another 10%. What is the price of the computer after the second discount, to the nearest dollar?

(1) $400

(2) $405

(3) $425

(4) $445

(5) $450

After the first 10% discount, the price was $450 ($500 minus 10% of $500). After the second discount, which is calculated based on the $450 price, the price of the computer is $405 ($450 minus 10% of $450). **The correct answer is (2).**

EXAMPLE 18 (MORE CHALLENGING):

A merchant discounts an item priced at $80 by 25%. Later, the merchant discounts the item again, this time to $48. What *percent* was the second discount?

(1) 18

(2) 20

(3) 25

(4) 27.5

(5) 30

After the first discount, the price was $60 (the difference between $80 and 25% of $80 ($80 − $20). The second discount was $12 (the difference between $60 and $48). Calculate the discount rate using the price *before* the *second* discount: $\frac{12}{60} = \frac{1}{5}$, or 20%. **The correct answer is (2).**

RATIO AND PROPORTION

A **ratio** expresses proportion or comparative size—the size of one quantity *relative to* the size of another. Write a ratio by placing a colon (:) between the two numbers. Read the colon as the word "to." For example, read the ratio 3:5 as "3 to 5." As with fractions, you can reduce ratios to lowest terms by canceling common factors. For example, given a menagerie of 28 pets that includes 12 cats and 16 dogs:

- The ratio of cats to dogs is 12:16, or 3:4 ("3 to 4").

- The ratio of dogs to cats is 16:12, or 4:3 ("4 to 3").

- The ratio of cats to the total number of pets is 12:28, or 3:7 ("3 to 7").

- The ratio of dogs to the total number of pets is 16:28, or 4:7 ("4 to 7").

Another way of saying that two ratios (or fractions) are equivalent is to say that they are *proportionate*. For example, the ratio 12:16 is proportionate to the ratio 3:4. Similarly, the fraction $\frac{12}{16}$ is proportionate to the fraction $\frac{3}{4}$.

Determining Quantities from a Ratio

You can think of a ratio as parts adding up to a whole. In the ratio 5:6, for example, 5 parts + 6 parts = 11 parts (the whole). If the actual total quantity were 22, you'd multiply each element by 2: 10 parts + 12 parts = 22 parts (the whole). Notice that the ratios are the same. In other words, 5:6 is the same ratio as 10:12.

Another way to think about a ratio is as a fraction. Since you can express any ratio as a fraction, you can set two equivalent, or proportionate, ratios equal to each other, as fractions. So the ratio 16:28 is proportionate to the ratio 4:7 because $\frac{16}{28} = \frac{4}{7}$. If one of the four terms is missing from the equation (the proportion), you can solve for the missing term using the same method that you learned for solving percent problems:

❶ Simplify the known fraction, if possible.

❷ Multiply the diagonally situated numbers you know.

❸ Divide the product by the third number you know.

For example, if the ratio 10:15 is proportionate to 14:?, you can find the missing number (?) by first setting up the following grid (which expresses an equation with two fractions):

10	14
15	?

Reading the ratio 10:15 as a fraction, simplify it to $\frac{2}{3}$.

2	14
3	?

Then, multiply the two diagonally situated numbers you know: 3 × 14 = 42. Finally, divide by the third number you know: 42 ÷ 2 = 21. The ratio 10:15 is equivalent to the ratio 14:21.

In a GED® ratio question, even if the quantities initially appear difficult to work with, it's a good bet that doing the math will be easier than it might seem.

EXAMPLE 19 (EASIER):

A class of students contains only freshmen and sophomores. 18 of the students are sophomores. If the ratio between the number of freshmen and the number of sophomores in the class is 5:3, how many students altogether are in the class?

    (1) 30

    (2) 36

    (3) 40

    (4) 48

    (5) 56

Let's apply a part-to-whole analysis to answer this question. Look first at the ratio and the sum of its parts: 5 (freshman) + 3 (sophomores) = 8 (total students). These aren't the actual quantities, but they're *proportionate* to those quantities. Given 18 sophomores altogether, sophomores account for 3 parts—each part containing 6 students. Accordingly, the total number of students must be 6 × 8 = 48. **The correct answer is (4).**

EXAMPLE 20 (MORE CHALLENGING):

If 3 miles is equivalent to 4.83 kilometers, then 11.27 kilometers are equivalent to how many miles?

    (1) 16.1

    (2) 8.4

    (3) 7.0

    (4) 5.9

    (5) 1.76

The decimal numbers may appear daunting, but they simplify nicely. This feature is typical for the GED® Mathematics Test. The question essentially asks: "a ratio of 3 to 4.83 is equivalent to a ratio of *what* to 11.27?" Set up a proportion grid (which expresses an equation with two fractions):

3	?
4.83	11.27

You might notice that the ratio (or fraction) $\frac{3}{4.83}$ simplifies to $\frac{1}{1.61}$. Using this simplified ratio might help you multiply and divide the numbers, especially during Part II (calculator not allowed). Otherwise, first multiply the diagonally situated numbers you know: $3 \times 11.27 = 33.81$. Then, divide by the third number you know: $33.81 \div 4.83 = 7$. A ratio of 3 to 4.83 is equivalent to a ratio of 7 to 11.27. **The correct answer is (3).**

RATIOS INVOLVING MORE THAN TWO QUANTITIES

A more complex GED® ratio problem might involve a ratio among three (or possibly more) quantities. The best way to handle these problems is with a part-to-whole approach, where the "whole" consists of more than two "parts."

EXAMPLE 21 (EASIER):

Machine X, Machine Y, and Machine Z each produce widgets. Machine Y's rate of production is one third that of Machine X, and Machine Z's production rate is twice that of Machine Y. If Machine Y can produce 35 widgets per day, how many widgets can the three machines produce per day working simultaneously?

(1) 105

(2) 164

(3) 180

(4) 210

(5) 224

The key to handling this question is to convert ratios to fractional parts that add up to 1. The ratio of X's rate to Y's rate is 3 to 1, and the ratio of Y's rate to Z's rate is 1 to 2. You can express the ratio among all three as 3:1:2 (X:Y:Z). Accordingly, Y's production accounts for $\frac{1}{6}$ of the total widgets that all three machines can produce per day. Given that Y can produce 35 widgets per day, all three machines can produce $(35)(6) = 210$ widgets per day. **The correct answer is (4).**

EXAMPLE 22 (MORE CHALLENGING):

Three lottery winners—Alan, Brenda, and Carl—are sharing a lottery jackpot. Alan's share is one fifth of Brenda's share and one seventh of Carl's share. If the total jackpot is $195,000, what is the dollar amount of Carl's share?

(1) $15,000

(2) $35,000

(3) $75,000

(4) $105,000

(5) $115,000

At first glance, this problem doesn't appear to involve ratios. (Where's the colon?) But it does. The ratio of Alan's share to Brenda's share is 1:5, and the ratio of Alan's share to Carl's share is 1:7. So you can set up the triple ratio: A:B:C = 1:5:7

Alan's winnings account for 1 of 13 equal parts (1 + 5 + 7) of the total jackpot. $\frac{1}{13}$ of $195,000 is $15,000. Accordingly, Brenda's share is 5 times that amount, or $75,000, and Carl's share is 7 times that amount, or $105,000. **The correct answer is (4).**

Proportion Problems Requiring Unit Conversions

GED® ratio or proportion problems often involve units of measurement, such as inches, ounces, or gallons. These problems sometimes require that you convert one unit to another—for example, feet to inches, pounds to ounces, or quarts to gallons. The problem will provide the conversion rate if it is not commonly known.

The problem might ask for nothing more than a conversion. To solve this sort of problem, set up a proportion and then cross-multiply and divide. Here are two examples for review:

4.8 ounces is equivalent to how many pounds? [1 pound = 16 ounces]

Set up the proportion $\frac{9}{2} + \frac{15}{4} - \frac{12}{5}$. Cross-multiply (diagonally) what you know: 4.8 × 1 = 4.8. Then divide by the third number: 4.8 ÷ 16 = 0.3. (4 ounces is equivalent to 0.3 pounds.)

If Trevor hiked 13.6 kilometers, how many miles did he hike?
[1 mile = 1.6 kilometers]

Set up the proportion $\frac{1}{1.6} = \frac{?}{13.6}$. Cross-multiply (diagonally) what you know: 13.6 × 1 = 13.6. Then divide by the third number: 13.6 ÷ 1.6 = 8.5. (Trevor hiked 8.5 miles.)

Not all GED® conversion-rate questions are so simple as the two preceding examples. A question might require *two* conversions, or it might use *letters* instead of numbers—in order to focus on the process rather than the result. Though these problems may seem intimidating, they are actually not very difficult. You can easily solve them by applying the same method you would use to solve simpler conversion-rate problems.

EXAMPLE 23 (EASIER):

The distance from City 1 to City 2 is 840 kilometers. On an accurate map showing both cities, 1 centimeter represents 75 kilometers. On the map, how many millimeters separate City 1 and City 2? [1 centimeter = 10 millimeters]

(1) 11

(2) 45

(3) 63

(4) 89

(5) 112

First, set up the proportion $\frac{1 \text{ cm}}{75 \text{ km}} = \frac{?}{840}$. Then cross-multiply (diagonally) what you know: $840 \times 1 = 840$. Then divide by the third number: $840 \div 75 = 11.2$. On the map, the distance from City 1 to City B = $840 \div 75 = 11.2$ centimeters. But 11.2 is *not* the answer to the question. Your final step is to convert centimeters to millimeters. The problem provides the conversion rate: $11.2 \times 10 = 112$. **The correct answer is (5).**

EXAMPLE 24 (MORE CHALLENGING):

A candy store sells candy only in half-pound boxes. At c cents per box, which of the following is the cost of a ounces of candy? [1 pound = 16 ounces]

(1) $\frac{ac}{8}$

(2) $\frac{a}{16c}$

(3) ac

(4) $\frac{c}{a}$

(5) $\frac{8c}{a}$

This question is asking: "c cents is to one box as *how many cents* are to a ounces?" Set up a proportion, letting "?" represent the cost of a ounces. Because the question asks for the cost of *ounces*, convert 1 box to 8 ounces (a half pound). $\frac{c}{8} = \frac{?}{a}$. Next, cross-multiply (diagonally) two terms that are provided (in this case, they are variables rather than numbers): $c \times a = ca$. Then divide by the third term that is provided: $\frac{ca}{8}$. (The expression ca, which signifies $c \times a$, is equal to ac, which signifies $a \times c$.) **The correct answer is (1).**

EXPONENTS (POWERS) AND SCIENTIFIC NOTATION

 http://bit.ly/hippo_alg17

An **exponent** refers to the number of times that a number (referred to as the **base number**) is multiplied by itself, *plus 1*. In the exponential number 2^4, the base number is 2 and the exponent is 4. To calculate the value of 2^4, you multiply 2 by itself *three* times: $2^4 = 2 \times 2 \times 2 \times 2 = 16$. An exponent is also referred to as a **power**. So you can express the exponential number 2^4 as "2 to the 4th power."

On the GED®, questions involving exponents usually require you to combine two or more exponential numbers using one of the four basic operations. To do so, you need to know certain rules. Can you combine base numbers *before* applying exponents to the numbers? The answer depends on which operation you're performing.

Combining Exponents by Addition or Subtraction

The rules for combining exponential numbers by addition or subtraction are very restrictive. You *can* combine exponential numbers *if* the base numbers and powers (exponents) are all the same. Here is the general rule, along with a simple example showing two ways to combine the numbers:

$$a^x + a^x + a^x = 3(a^x)$$

$$3^2 + 3^2 + 3^2 = (3)(3^2) = 3 \times 9 = 27$$

$$3^2 + 3^2 + 3^2 = 9 + 9 + 9 = 27$$

Otherwise, you cannot combine either base numbers or exponents. It's as simple as that. Here's the rule in symbolic form as it applies to different base numbers:

$$a^x + b^x \neq (a + b)^x$$

$$a^x - b^x \neq (a - b)^x$$

Substituting some simple numbers for a, b, and x illustrates the rule. In the following two examples, notice that you get a different result depending on which you do first: combine base numbers or apply each exponent to its base number.

Combining by addition:

$$(4 + 2)^2 = 6^2 = 36$$

$$4^2 + 2^2 = 16 + 4 = 20$$

Combining by subtraction:

$$(4 - 2)^2 = 2^2 = 4$$

$$4^2 - 2^2 = 16 - 4 = 12$$

EXAMPLE 25 (EASIER):

$a^7 + a^7 + a^7$ is equivalent to which of the following?

    (1) a^{21}

    (2) $3^7 \times a^7$

    (3) $7 \times a^3$

    (4) $3 \times a^7$

    (5) $21a$

You can combine terms here because base numbers and exponents are all the same. Adding together 3 of any quantity is the same as 3 *times* that quantity. **The correct answer is (4).**

EXAMPLE 26 (MORE CHALLENGING):

If $x = -2$, what is the value of $x^5 - x^2 - x$?

    (1) -70

    (2) -58

    (3) -34

    (4) 4

    (5) 26

You cannot combine exponents here, even though the base number is the same in all three terms. Instead, you need to apply each exponent, in turn, to the base number, then subtract:

$$x^5 - x^2 - x = (-2)^5 - (-2)^2 - (-2) = -32 - 4 + 2 = -34$$

The correct answer is (3).

Combining Exponents by Multiplication or Division

http://bit.ly/hippo_alg18

Follow two basic rules for combining exponential numbers by multiplication and division.

RULE 1: You can combine base numbers first, but only if the exponents are the same. Here's the rule in symbolic form:

$$a^x \times b^x = (ab)^x$$

$$a^x \div b^x = (a \div b)^x \text{ or } \frac{a^x}{b^x} = \left(\frac{a}{b}\right)^x$$

Substituting some simple numbers for a, b, and x illustrates Rule 1. In the following two examples, notice that you get the same result whether or not you combine base numbers first.

http://bit.ly/hippo_alg19

    Combining by multiplication:

    $(4 \times 2)^2 = 8^2 = 64$

    $4^2 \times 2^2 = 16 \times 4 = 64$

    Combining by division:

    $(10 \div 2)^2 = 5^2 = 25$

    $10^2 \div 2^2 = 100 \div 4 = 25$

RULE 2: You can combine exponents first, but only if the base numbers are the same. When multiplying these terms, add the exponents. When dividing them, subtract the denominator exponent from the numerator exponent:

$$a^x \times a^y = a^{(x+y)}$$

$$a^x \div a^y = a^{(x-y)} \text{ or } \frac{a^x}{a^y} = a^{(x-y)}$$

Substituting some simple numbers for a, b, and x illustrates Rule 2. In the following two examples, notice that you get the same result whether or not you combine exponents first.

Combining by multiplication:

$2^3 \times 2^2 = 8 \times 4 = 32$

$2^{(3+2)} = 2^5 = 2 \times 2 \times 2 \times 2 \times 2 = 32$

Combining by division:

$2^5 \div 2^2 = 32 \div 4 = 8$

$2^{(5-2)} = 2^3 = 2 \times 2 \times 2 = 8$

When the same base number appears in a division problem, or in both numerator and denominator of a fraction, you can factor out (cancel) the number of powers common to both. To illustrate, consider the operation $9^6 \div 9^4$, or its equivalent fraction $\dfrac{9^6}{9^4}$. To find the quotient, you can either combine exponents, applying Rule 2, or you can factor out (cancel) 9^4 from each term:

Combining exponents first:

$\dfrac{9^6}{9^4} = 9^{(6-4)} = 9^2 = 81$

Canceling common factors first:

$\dfrac{9^6}{9^4} = \dfrac{9^4 \times 9^2}{9^4} = \dfrac{9^2}{1} = 81$

EXAMPLE 27 (EASIER):

When you divide $\dfrac{a^2b}{b^2c}$ by $\dfrac{a^2c}{bc^2}$, what is the result?

(1) $\dfrac{1}{a}$

(2) $\dfrac{1}{b}$

(3) 1

(4) $\dfrac{b}{a}$

(5) $\dfrac{c}{b}$

First, cancel common factors in each term. Then you'll see that the numerator and denominator are the same, which means that the quotient must equal 1:

$\dfrac{a^2b}{b^2c} \div \dfrac{a^2c}{bc^2} = \dfrac{a^2}{bc} \div \dfrac{a^2}{bc} = 1$

The correct answer is (3).

EXAMPLE 28 (MORE CHALLENGING):

What is the value of $\dfrac{x^3 - y^4}{x^3 y^4}$, where $x = 2$ and $y = -2$?

    (1) $-\dfrac{3}{32}$

    (2) $-\dfrac{1}{16}$

    (3) $\dfrac{1}{32}$

    (4) $\dfrac{1}{16}$

    (5) 1

One way to answer this question is to simplify the fraction by distributing the denominator to each term in the numerator, then cancel common factors. But an easier way to solve the problem is to plug in the x and y values that are provided, and do the math:

$$\frac{x^3 - y^4}{x^3 y^4} = \frac{2^3 - (-2)^4}{2^3 \times (-2^4)} = \frac{8 - 16}{8 \times 16} = \frac{-8}{128} = -\frac{1}{16}$$

The correct answer is (2).

Additional Rules for Exponents

http://bit.ly/hippo_alg20

For the GED®, you should also keep in mind these three additional rules for exponents.

❶ When raising an exponential number to a power, multiply exponents:

    Rule: $\left(a^x\right)^y = a^{xy}$

    Example: $\left(2^2\right)^3 = 2^{(2)(3)} = 2^6 = 64$

❷ Any number other than zero (0) raised to the power of 0 (zero) equals 1:

    Rule: $a^0 = 1\ [a \neq 0]$

    Example: $13\ = 1$

❸ Raising a base number to a negative exponent is equivalent to 1 divided by the base number raised to the exponent's absolute value:

    Rule: $a^{-x} = \dfrac{1}{a^x}$

    Example: $4^{-2} = \dfrac{1}{4^2} = \dfrac{1}{16}$

These three rules are all fair game for the GED®. In fact, a GED® question might require you to apply more than one of these rules.

EXAMPLE 29 (EASIER):

What is the value of $5^{-2} \times 5^{-1} \times 5^0$?

    (1) -125

    (2) $-\dfrac{1}{25}$

    (3) 0

    (4) $\dfrac{1}{125}$

    (5) $\dfrac{1}{5}$

Rewrite each of the first two terms under the numerator 1, but with a positive exponent. Then multiply:

$$\frac{1}{5^2} \times \frac{1}{5} \times 1 = \frac{1}{25} \times \frac{1}{5} \times 1 = \frac{1}{125}$$

The correct answer is (4).

EXAMPLE 30 (MORE CHALLENGING):

What is the value of $\left(2^3\right)^2 \times 4^{-3}$?

    (1) -64

    (2) $-\dfrac{1}{8}$

    (3) 1

    (4) $\dfrac{3}{2}$

    (5) 16

Multiply exponents in the first term. Rewrite the second term under the numerator 1, but with a positive exponent: $\left(2^3\right)^2 \times 4^{-3} = 2^{(2)(3)} \times \dfrac{1}{4^3} = \dfrac{2^6}{4^3} = \dfrac{2^6}{2^6} = 1$.

The correct answer is (3).

Exponents and the Real Number Line

Raising numbers to powers can have surprising effects on the size and/or sign (negative versus positive) of the number. You need to consider four separate regions of the real-number line.

For numbers greater than 1 (right of 1 on the number line):

Raising the number to a power greater than 1 gives a higher value. The greater the power, the greater the value. For example:

    $9^2 < 9^3 < 9^4$ (and so on)

For numbers less than –1 (left of –1 on the number line):

If the number is raised to an **even** power (such as 2, 4, or 6), the result is a number greater than 1. The greater the power, the greater the value. For example:

$$-3 < -3^2 < -3^4 < -3^6 \text{ (and so on)}$$

If the number is raised to an **odd** power (such as 3, 5, or 7), the result is a number less than –1. The greater the power, the smaller the value (the farther *left* on the number line). For example:

$$-2 > -2^3 > -2^5 > -2^7 \text{ (and so on)}$$

For fractional numbers between 0 and 1:

Raising the number to a power greater than 1 gives a *smaller positive* value. The greater the power, the smaller the value. For example:

$$\frac{2}{3} > \left(\frac{2}{3}\right)^2 > \left(\frac{2}{3}\right)^3 > \left(\frac{2}{3}\right)^4 \ldots > 0$$

For fractional numbers between –1 and 0:

Raising the fractional number to an **odd** power greater than 1 gives a *greater negative* value. The greater the power, the greater the value (approaching zero). For example:

$$-\frac{2}{3} > -\left(\frac{2}{3}\right)^3 > -\left(\frac{2}{3}\right)^5 \ldots < 0$$

Raising the fractional number to an **even** power greater than 1 gives a *positive fractional value* between 0 and 1. The greater the power, the lower the positive value (approaching zero). For example:

$$-\frac{2}{3} > -\left(\frac{2}{3}\right)^2 > -\left(\frac{2}{3}\right)^4 \ldots > 0$$

GED® questions involving exponents and the number line can be confusing. Nevertheless, they can be quite manageable if you keep in mind the four different regions of the number line.

EXAMPLE 31 (EASIER):

If $-1 < x < 0$, which of the following must be true?

    (1) $x^4 < -1$

    (2) $x^4 > 1$

    (3) $0 < x^4 < 1$

    (4) $x^4 = 1$

    (5) Not enough information is provided.

This question tests you on the rule that a negative fractional value raised to an even power (in this case 4) results in a fractional positive number, between 0 and 1.
The correct answer is (3).

EXAMPLE 32 (MORE CHALLENGING):

If $x^2 > 1 > y^2$, which of the following must be true?

(1) $x^3 > y^3$

(2) $x > y$

(3) $x^3 < y^3$

(4) $x < y$

(5) Not enough information is provided.

Given $x^2 > 1$, x (as well as x^3) could be either greater than 1 or less than −1. Given $y^2 < 1$, y (as well as x^3) must be greater than −1 but less than 1.

The correct answer is (5).

Exponents You Should Know

For the GED®, memorize the exponential values in the following table. These are the ones you're most likely to see on the exam.

Power and Corresponding Value

Base	2	3	4	5	6	7	8
2	4	8	16	32	64	128	256
3	9	27	81	243			
4	16	64	256				
5	25	125	625				
6	36	216					

 http://bit.ly/hippo_alg21

Scientific Notation

Scientific notation is a system for writing extremely large numbers. In scientific notation, an integer or decimal number between 1 and 10 is written to the power of 10. For example, the number 380,000,000 can be written as 3.8×10^8. The number between 1 and 10 that you are working with is 3.8. When you count the number of zeros plus the number to the right of the decimal point, you can see that there are 8 digits. That means that the exponent is 8. A negative exponent signifies a fractional number.

To illustrate further, here's a list of related decimal numbers and their equivalents in scientific notation:

837,000 = 8.37×10^5 (decimal point shifts 5 places to the left)

8370 = 8.37×10^3 (decimal point shifts 3 places to the left)

837 = 8.37×10^1 (decimal point shifts 1 place to the left)

8.37	$= 8.37 \times 10^0$ (decimal point unchanged in position)
0.837	$= 8.37 \times 10^{-1}$ (decimal point shifts 1 place to the right)
0.0837	$= 8.37 \times 10^{-2}$ (decimal point shifts 2 places to the right)
0.000837	$= 8.37 \times 10^{-4}$ (decimal point shifts 4 places to the right)

A GED® question might ask you to simply convert a number to scientific notation form, or the other way around.

EXAMPLE 33 (EASIER):

A computer can process data at the rate of 3.9×10^8 bits per second. How many bits can the computer process in 0.02 seconds?

    (1) 7.8×10^4

    (2) 7.8×10^6

    (3) 1.95×10^7

    (4) 7.8×10^8

    (5) 1.95×10^9

To answer the question, first multiply the rate by the number of seconds: $(0.02)(3.9 \times 10^8) = 0.078 \times 10^8$. Since the answer choices are in proper scientific notation, shift the decimal point to the right two places and lower the power accordingly: 7.8×10^6. **The correct answer is (2).**

EXAMPLE 34 (MORE CHALLENGING):

A particle travels at the rate of 52,500 meters per second. Expressed in millimeters, how far will the particle travel in 7×10^{-7} seconds?
[1 meter = 1000 millimeters]

    (1) 0.3675

    (2) 3.675

    (3) 7.5

    (4) 36.75

    (5) 75

Express 52,500 in scientific notation: 5.25×10^4. To convert this number from meters to millimeters, multiply by 1000 or 10^3:

$$(5.25 \times 10^4)(10^3) = 5.25 \times 10^7.$$

To answer the question, apply the following formula: distance = rate × time.

$$D = (5.25 \times 10^7)(7.0 \times 10^{-7})$$
$$= (5.25)(7) \times 10^{(7-7)}$$
$$= 36.75 \times 10^0$$
$$= 36.75 \times 1$$
$$= 36.75$$

The correct answer is (4).

SQUARE ROOTS (AND OTHER ROOTS)

The **square root** of a number n is a number that you "square" (multiply it by itself, or raise to the power of 2), to obtain n. The **radical sign** signifies square root and looks like this: $\sqrt{}$. Here's a simple example of a square root:

$$2 = \sqrt{4} \text{ (the square root of 4) because } 2 \times 2 \text{ (or } 2^2) = 4$$

The **cube root** of a number n is a number that you raise to the power of 3 (multiply by itself twice) to obtain n. You determine higher roots (for example, the "fourth root") in the same way. Except for square roots, the radical sign will indicate the root to be taken. For example:

$$2 = \sqrt[3]{8} \text{ (the cube root of 8) because } 2 \times 2 \times 2 \text{ (or } 2^3) = 8$$

$$2 = \sqrt[4]{16} \text{ (the fourth root of 16) because } 2 \times 2 \times 2 \times 2 \text{ (or } 2^4) = 16$$

For the GED®, you should know the rules for simplifying and for combining radical expressions.

Simplifying and Combining Radical Expressions

On the GED®, look for the possibility of simplifying radicals by moving what's under the radical sign to the outside of the sign. Check inside square-root radicals for **perfect squares**: factors that are squares of nice tidy numbers or other terms. The same advice applies to perfect cubes, and so on. Study the following three examples:

$$\sqrt{4a^2} = 2a$$

4 and a^2 are both perfect squares. So you can remove them from under the radical sign, and change each one to its square root.

$$\sqrt[3]{27a^6} = 3a^2$$

27 and a^6 are both perfect cubes. So you can remove them from under the radical sign, and change each one to its cube root.

$$\sqrt{8a^3} = \sqrt{(4)(2)a^3} = 2a\sqrt{2a}$$

8 and a^3 both contain perfect-square factors; remove the perfect squares from under the radical sign, and change each one to its square root.

The rules for combining terms that include radicals are quite similar to those for exponents. Keep the following two rules in mind; one applies to addition and subtraction, while the other applies to multiplication and division.

RULE 1 (addition and subtraction): If a term under a radical is being added to or subtracted from a term under a different radical, you cannot combine the two terms under the same radical.

$$\sqrt{x} + \sqrt{y} \neq \sqrt{x + y}$$
$$\sqrt{x} - \sqrt{y} \neq \sqrt{x - y}$$
$$\sqrt{x} + \sqrt{x} = 2\sqrt{x} \text{ , not } \sqrt{2x}$$

RULE 2 (multiplication and division): Terms under different radicals can be combined under a common radical if one term is multiplied or divided by the other, but only if the radical is the same.

$$\sqrt{x}\sqrt{x} = \left(\sqrt{x}\right)^2 \text{ , or } x$$
$$\sqrt{x}\sqrt{y} = \sqrt{xy}$$
$$\frac{\sqrt{x}}{\sqrt{y}} = \sqrt{\frac{x}{y}}$$
$$\sqrt[3]{x}\sqrt{x} = ? \text{ (you cannot combine)}$$

EXAMPLE 35 (EASIER):

$\left(2\sqrt{2a}\right)^2$ is equivalent to which of the following expressions?

 (1) $4a$

 (2) $4a^2$

 (3) $8a$

 (4) $8a^2$

 (5) $16a$

Square each of the two terms, 2 and $\sqrt{2a}$, separately. Then combine their squares by multiplication: $\left(2\sqrt{2a}\right)^2 = 2^2 \times \left(\sqrt{2a}\right)^2 = 4 \times 2a = 8a$. **The correct answer is (3).**

EXAMPLE 36 (MORE CHALLENGING):

$\sqrt{24} - \sqrt{16} - \sqrt{6}$ simplifies to which of the following expressions?

 (1) $\sqrt{6} - 4$

 (2) $4 - 2\sqrt{2}$

 (3) 2

 (4) $\sqrt{6}$

 (5) $2\sqrt{2}$

Although the numbers under the three radicals combine to equal 2, you cannot combine terms this way. Instead, simplify the first two terms, then combine the first and third terms:

$$\sqrt{24} - \sqrt{16} - \sqrt{6} = 2\sqrt{6} - 4 - \sqrt{6} = \sqrt{6} - 4.$$

The correct answer is (1).

Roots You Should Know

Below is a list of common roots, for your reference. You don't need to memorize these roots for the GED®. However, for Part II of the test (calculator not allowed) it may be useful to commit to memory the first three roots in each column. Notice that the cube root of a positive number is positive, and the cube root of a negative number is negative.

Square roots of "perfect square" integers:	Cube roots of "perfect cube" positive integers:	Cube roots of "perfect cube" negative integers:	Other roots you should know:
$\sqrt{121} = 11$	$\sqrt[3]{8} = 2$	$\sqrt[3]{-8} = -2$	$\sqrt[4]{16} = 2$
$\sqrt{144} = 12$	$\sqrt[3]{27} = 3$	$\sqrt[3]{-27} = -3$	$\sqrt[4]{81} = 3$
$\sqrt{169} = 13$	$\sqrt[3]{64} = 4$	$\sqrt[3]{-64} = -4$	$\sqrt[5]{32} = 2$
$\sqrt{196} = 14$	$\sqrt[3]{125} = 5$	$\sqrt[3]{-125} = -5$	
$\sqrt{225} = 15$	$\sqrt[3]{216} = 6$	$\sqrt[3]{-216} = -6$	
$\sqrt{256} = 16$	$\sqrt[3]{343} = 7$	$\sqrt[3]{-343} = -7$	
$\sqrt{625} = 25$	$\sqrt[3]{512} = 8$	$\sqrt[3]{-512} = -8$	
	$\sqrt[3]{729} = 9$	$\sqrt[3]{-729} = -9$	
	$\sqrt[3]{1000} = 10$	$\sqrt[3]{-1000} = -10$	

SUMMING IT UP

- For the Mathematics Test, it is important to review *properties* (signs, integers, absolute value, and divisibility), *forms* (fractions, mixed numbers, decimal numbers, percentages, ratios, exponential numbers, and radical expressions), and *operations* (the four basic operations and operations on exponential numbers and radical expressions). The knowledge areas that are covered here are basic building blocks for all types of GED® math questions

- GED® math questions involving fractions, decimal numbers, or percents often require you to convert one form to another as part of solving the problem at hand. Do your best to learn how to convert quickly and confidently.

- Certain fraction-decimal-percent equivalents appear on the GED® more often than others. The numbers in the tables in this chapter are especially common. Try to memorize them so that you can convert these numbers quickly during the test.

- A GED® question involving percent might involve one of the following tasks: finding the percent of a number, finding a number when a percent is given, or finding what percent one number is of another.

- GED® ratio or proportion problems often involve units of measurement, such as inches, ounces, or gallons. These problems sometimes require that you convert one unit to another.

- An **exponent** refers to the number of times that a number (referred to as the **base number**) is multiplied by itself, *plus 1*. On the GED®, questions involving exponents usually require you to combine two or more exponential numbers using one of the four basic operations.

- Remember these three rules for exponents: When raising an exponential number to a power, multiply exponents; any number other than zero (0) raised to the power of 0 (zero) equals 1; and raising a base number to a negative exponent is equivalent to 1 divided by the base number raised to the exponent's absolute value.

- For the GED®, memorize the exponential values in the table that appears in this chapter. These are the ones you're most likely to see on the exam.

- On the GED®, look for the possibility of simplifying radicals by moving what's under the radical sign to the outside of the sign. Check inside square-root radicals for **perfect squares:** factors that are squares of nice tidy numbers or other terms. The same advice applies to perfect cubes, and so on.

Math Review: Algebra and Descriptive Statistics

chapter 13

OVERVIEW

- **What you'll find in this review**
- **Linear equations in one variable**
- **Linear equations in two variables**
- **Linear equations that can't be solved**
- **Solving algebraic inequalities**
- **Factorable quadratic expressions (one variable)**
- **Factorable quadratic expressions (two variables)**
- **Functions**
- **Measures of central tendency (mean, median, and range)**
- **Arithmetic series**
- **Probability**
- **Word problems involving formulas**
- **Summing it up**

WHAT YOU'LL FIND IN THIS REVIEW

This review focuses on algebra and descriptive statistics. First you'll review the following algebra skills:

- Solving a linear equation in one variable

- Solving a system of two equations in two variables by substitution and addition-subtraction

- Recognizing unsolvable equations

- Handling algebraic inequalities

- Factoring quadratic expressions

- Finding the roots of quadratic equations by factoring

- Handling functions

- Solving formula word problems (weighted average, simple interest, and rate)

Later, you'll examine the concepts of mean, median, range, arithmetic series, and probability.

The GED®-style questions throughout this review are multiple-choice questions. The actual exam also includes questions in an alternative format, in which you supply the numerical answer to the question.

http://bit.ly/hippo_alg1

LINEAR EQUATIONS IN ONE VARIABLE

Algebraic expressions are usually used to form **equations,** which set two expressions equal to each other. Equations contain at least one **variable:** a letter such as x or y that represents a number that can *vary.* Most equations you'll see on the GED® are **linear equations,** in which the variables don't come with exponents.

To find the value of a linear equation's variable (such as x) is to **solve the equation.** To solve any linear equation containing only one variable, your goal is always the same: isolate the variable on one side of the equation. To accomplish this, you may need to perform one or more of the following operations on both sides, depending on the equation:

❶ Add or subtract the same term on both sides.

❷ Multiply or divide both sides by the same term.

❸ Clear fractions by cross-multiplication.

❹ Clear radicals by raising both sides to the same power (exponent).

Whatever operation you perform on one side of an equation you must also perform on the other side; otherwise, the two sides won't be equal. Performing any of these operations on *both* sides does not change the equality; it merely restates the equation in a different form.

Solving an Equation Using the Four Basic Operations

http://bit.ly/hippo_alg2

To find the value of the variable (to solve for x), you may need to either add a term to both sides of the equation or subtract a term from both sides. Here are two examples:

Adding the same number to both sides:
$$x - 2 = 5$$
$$x - 2 + 2 = 5 + 2$$
$$x = 7$$

Subtracting the same number from both sides:
$$\frac{3}{2} - x = 12$$
$$\frac{3}{2} - x - \frac{3}{2} = 12 - \frac{3}{2}$$
$$x = 10\frac{1}{2}$$

The first system isolates x by adding 2 to both sides. The second system isolates x by subtracting $\frac{3}{2}$ from both sides. In some cases, solving for x requires that you either multiply or divide both sides of the equation by the same term. Here are two examples:

Multiplying both sides by the same number:
$$\frac{x}{2} = 14$$
$$2 \times \frac{x}{2} = 14 \times 2$$
$$x = 28$$

Dividing both sides by the same number:

$$3x = 18$$

$$\frac{3x}{3} = \frac{18}{3}$$

$$x = 6$$

The first system isolates x by multiplying both sides by 2. The second system isolates x by dividing both sides by 3. If the variable appears on both sides of the equation, first perform whatever operation is required to position the variable on just one side—either the left or the right. The next system positions both x-terms on the left side by subtracting $2x$ from both sides:

$$16 - x = 9 + 2x$$

$$16 - x - 2x = 9 + 2x - 2x$$

$$16 - 3x = 9$$

Now that x appears on just one side, the next step is to isolate it by subtracting 16 from both sides, and then dividing both sides by -3:

$$16 - 3x = 9$$

$$16 - 3x - 16 = 9 - 16$$

$$-3x = -7$$

$$\frac{-3x}{-3} = \frac{-7}{-3}$$

$$x = \frac{7}{3}$$

EXAMPLE 1 (EASIER):

For what value of x does $2x - 6$ equal $x - 9$?

   (1) -9

   (2) -6

   (3) -3

   (4) 2

   (5) 6

First, write the verbal description as the equation $2x - 6 = x - 9$. Then position both x-terms on the same side. To place them both on the left side, subtract x from both sides. Then combine x-terms:

$$2x - 6 - x = x - 9 - x$$

$$x - 6 = -9$$

Finally, isolate x by adding 6 to both sides:

$$x - 6 + 6 = -9 + 6$$

$$x = -3$$

The correct answer is (3).

EXAMPLE 2 (MORE CHALLENGING):

If $12 = \dfrac{11}{x} - \dfrac{3}{x}$, then what is the value of x ?

   (1) $\dfrac{3}{11}$

   (2) $\dfrac{1}{2}$

   (3) $\dfrac{2}{3}$

   (4) $\dfrac{11}{12}$

   (5) $\dfrac{11}{3}$

First, combine the x-terms: $12 = \dfrac{11 - 3}{x}$. Next, clear the fraction by multiplying both sides by x:

$$12x = 11 - 3$$
$$12x = 8$$

Finally, isolate x by dividing both sides by 12:

$x = \dfrac{8}{12}$, or $\dfrac{2}{3}$

The correct answer is (3).

 http://bit.ly/hippo_alg3

Cross-multiplying and Clearing Radicals to Solve an Equation

If an equation equates two fractions, use **cross-multiplication** to eliminate the fractions. Combine each numerator with the denominator on the other side by multiplying diagonally across the equation. Then set one product equal to the other. (In effect, cross-multiplication is a shortcut method of multiplying both sides of the equation by both denominators.) Here's a simple example:

$$\frac{x}{3} = \frac{12}{2}$$
$$(2)(x) = (3)(12)$$
$$2x = 36$$
$$x = \frac{36}{2}, \text{ or } 18$$

If the variable appears under the square-root radical sign $\sqrt{\ }$, eliminate ("clear") the radical sign by squaring both sides of the equation. Use the same method to clear cube roots and other roots—as in the right-hand example below:

$$\sqrt{4x} = 3 \qquad\qquad \sqrt[3]{2x} = 4$$
$$\left(\sqrt{4x}\right)^2 = 3^2 \qquad\qquad \left(\sqrt[3]{2x}\right)^3 = 4^3$$
$$4x = 9 \qquad\qquad 2^3 x^3 = 64$$
$$x = \frac{9}{4} \qquad\qquad x^3 = \frac{64}{8}, \text{ or } 8$$

Be careful when you square both sides of an equation. In some instances, doing so will produce a variable such as x^2, in which case the equation is *quadratic* rather than linear. This means that it might have more than one solution. You'll examine quadratic equations later in this review.

EXAMPLE 3 (EASIER):

If $3\sqrt{2x} = 2$, then what is the value of x?

(1) $\frac{1}{18}$

(2) $\frac{2}{9}$

(3) $\frac{1}{3}$

(4) $\frac{5}{4}$

(5) 3

First, clear the radical sign by squaring all terms:

$$\left(3^2\right)\left(\sqrt{2x}\right)^2 = 2^2$$
$$(9)(2x) = 4$$
$$18x = 4$$

Next, isolate x by dividing both sides by 18:

$x = \frac{4}{18}$, or $\frac{2}{9}$

The correct answer is (2).

EXAMPLE 4 (MORE CHALLENGING):

For what value of a does $\frac{7a}{8}$ equal $\frac{a+1}{3}$?

(1) $\frac{8}{13}$

(2) $\frac{7}{8}$

(3) 2

(4) $\frac{7}{3}$

(5) 15

First, cross-multiply (multiply diagonally across the equation) and equate the two products:

$$(3)(7a) = (8)(a + 1)$$

Next, combine terms (distribute 8 to both a and 1):

$21a = 8a + 8$

Next, isolate a-terms on one side by subtracting $8a$ from both sides; then combine the a-terms:

$21a - 8a = 8a + 8 - 8a$
$\qquad 13a = 8$

Finally, isolate a by dividing both sides by 13:

$$\frac{13a}{13} = \frac{8}{13}$$
$$a = \frac{8}{13}$$

The correct answer is (1).

http://bit.ly/hippo_alg4

LINEAR EQUATIONS IN TWO VARIABLES

In the preceding section, you examined linear equations in one variable only, and you saw that you can find the value of the variable by isolating it on one side of the equation. This is not so, however, for a linear equation in two (or more) different variables. Consider the following equation, which contains two variables:

$x + 3 = y + 1$

What is the value of x? It depends on the value of y, doesn't it? Similarly, the value of y depends on the value of x. Without more information about either x or y, you simply cannot find one of the other value. However, you *can* express x in terms of y, and you can express y in terms of x:

$x = y - 2$
$y = x + 2$

The two above equations are really the same. You can't solve it because it contains two variables. Look at a more complex example: $4x - 9 = \frac{3}{2}y$.

Solve for x in terms of y:

$$4x = \frac{3}{2}y + 9$$
$$x = \frac{3}{8}y + \frac{9}{4}$$

Solve for y in terms of x:

$$\frac{4x - 9}{\frac{3}{2}} = y$$
$$\frac{2}{3}(4x - 9) = y$$
$$\frac{8}{3}(x - 6) = y$$

To determine numerical values of x and y, you need a system of two linear equations with the same two variables. Given this system, there are two different methods for finding the values of the two variables: the substitution method and the addition-subtraction method.

The Substitution Method

 http://bit.ly/hippo_alg5

To solve a system of two equations using the **substitution method,** follow these steps (we'll use x and y here):

1 In *either* equation isolate one variable (x) on one side.

2 Substitute the expression that equals x in place of x in the other equation.

3 Solve that equation for y.

4 Now that you know the value of y, plug it into *either* equation to find the value of x.

Consider these two equations:

Equation A: $x = 4y$
Equation B: $x - y = 1$

In equation B, substitute $4y$ for x, and then solve for y:

$$4y - y = 1$$
$$3y = 1$$
$$y = \frac{1}{3}$$

To find x, substitute $\frac{1}{3}$ for y into either equation. The value of x will be the same in either equation.

Equation A: $x = 4\left(\frac{1}{3}\right) = \frac{4}{3}$

Equation B: $x - \frac{1}{3} = 1$; $x = \frac{4}{3}$

The Addition-Subtraction Method

 http://bit.ly/hippo_alg6

Another way to solve for two variables in a system of two equations is with the **addition-subtraction** method. Here are the steps:

1 "Line up" the two equations by listing the same variables and other terms in the same order. Place one equation above the other.

2 Make the coefficient of *either* variable the same in both equations (you can disregard the sign) by multiplying every term in one of the equations. (A **coefficient** is a variable's number. For example, in the term $7x$, the coefficient of x is 7.)

3 Add the two equations (work down to a sum for each term), or subtract one equation from the other, to eliminate one variable.

Consider these two equations:

Equation A: $x = 2 + 3y$
Equation B: $2x + y = 4$

In equation A, subtract $3y$ from both sides, so that all terms in the two equations "line up":

> Equation A: $x - 3y = 2$
> Equation B: $2x + y = 4$

To solve for y, multiply each term in Equation A by 2, so that the x-coefficient is the same in both equations:

> Equation A: $2x - 6y = 6$
> Equation B: $2x + y = 4$

Subtract Equation B from Equation A, thereby eliminating x, and then isolate y on one side of the equation:

$$2x - 6y = 6$$
$$\underline{2x + y = 4}$$
$$0x - 7y = 2$$
$$-7y = 2$$
$$y = -\frac{2}{7}$$

 http://bit.ly/hippo_alg7

Which Method Should You Use?

Which method, substitution or addition-subtraction, you should use depends on what the equations look like to begin with. To understand this point, look at this system of two equations:

$$\frac{2}{5}p + q = 3q - 10$$
$$q = 10 - p$$

Notice that the second equation is already set up nicely for the substitution method. But you could use addition-subtraction instead; you'd just have to rearrange the terms in both the equations first:

$$p - 2q = -10$$
$$p + q = 10$$

Now, look at the following system:

$$3x + 4y = -8$$
$$x - 2y = \frac{1}{2}$$

Notice that the x-term and y-term already line up nicely here. Also notice that it's easy to match the coefficients of either x or y: multiply both sides of the second equation by either 3 or 2. This system is an ideal candidate for addition-subtraction. To appreciate this point, try using substitution instead. You'll discover that it takes far more number crunching.

In short, to solve a system of two linear equations in two variables, use addition-subtraction if you can quickly and easily eliminate one of the variables. Otherwise, use substitution.

EXAMPLE 5 (EASIER):

If $q = \frac{p}{10}$ and $q = 4.4 - p$, what is the value of $\frac{p}{q}$?

(1) −4.4

(2) 1.1

(3) 2.2

(4) 10

(5) Not enough information is provided.

Since the question asks for $\frac{p}{q}$ (rather than either p or q), you can answer it by applying just the first of the two equations:

$$q = \frac{p}{10}$$
$$10q = p$$
$$10 = \frac{p}{q}$$

The correct answer is (4).

EXAMPLE 6 (MORE CHALLENGING):

If $3x + 4y = -8$, and if $x - 2y = \frac{1}{2}$, what is the value of x ?

(1) −12

(2) $-\frac{7}{5}$

(3) $\frac{1}{3}$

(4) $\frac{14}{5}$

(5) 9

To solve for x, you want to eliminate y. You can multiply each term in the second equation by 2, and then add the equations:

$$
\begin{aligned}
3x + 4y &= -8 \\
\underline{2x - 4y} &= \underline{1} \\
5x + 0y &= -7 \\
x &= -\frac{7}{5}
\end{aligned}
$$

The correct answer is (2).

LINEAR EQUATIONS THAT CAN'T BE SOLVED

Never assume that one linear equation with one variable is solvable. If you can reduce the equation to $0 = 0$, then you can't solve it. In other words, the value of the variable could be any real number. Here's a simple example:

$$3x - 4 = 5x - 4 - 2x$$
$$3x - 4 = 3x - 4$$
$$0 = 0$$

In some cases, what appears to be a system of two equations in two variables might actually be the same equation expressed in two different ways. In other words, what you're really dealing with are two equivalent equations, which you cannot solve. Consider these two equations:

Equation A: $x + 4y = 16$
Equation B: $y = 4 - \dfrac{x}{4}$

If you multiply each term in Equation B by 4, you'll see that Equations A and B are the same:

Equation A: $x + 4y = 16$
Equation B: $4y = 16 - x$

On the GED®, whenever you encounter a question that calls for solving one or more linear equations, and answer choice (5) provides something other than a numerical answer, size up the equation to see whether it's one of these two types of unsolvable problems. If so, the correct answer choice will be (5).

EXAMPLE 7 (EASIER):

If $-1 < x < 1$, and if $3x - 3 - 4x = x - 7 - 2x + 4$, then how many real numbers does the solution set for x contain?

(1) 0

(2) 1

(3) 2

(4) 3

(5) infinitely many

All terms on both sides cancel out:

$$3x - 3 - 4x = x - 7 - 2x + 4$$
$$-x - 3 = -x = 3$$
$$0 = 0$$

Thus, x could equal any real number between -1 and 1 (not just the integer 0).
The correct answer is (5).

EXAMPLE 8 (MORE CHALLENGING):

$2b = 60 - 2a$, and $a + b = 30$. What is the value of a ?

   (1) −10

   (2) −2

   (3) 10

   (4) 12

   (5) No solution is possible.

An unwary test-taker might assume that the values of both a and b can be determined with both equations together, because they appear at first glance to provide a system of two linear equations with two unknowns. But they don't. You can rewrite the first equation so that it is identical to the second:

$$2b = 60 - 2a$$
$$2b = 2(30 - a)$$
$$b = 30 - a$$
$$a + b = 30$$

As you can see, the equation $2b = 60 - 2a$ is identical to the equation $a + b = 30$. Thus, a and b could each be any real number. You can't solve one equation in two variables. **The correct answer is (5).**

SOLVING ALGEBRAIC INEQUALITIES

 http://bit.ly/hippo_alg8

You solve algebraic inequalities in the same manner as equations. Isolate the variable on one side of the equation, factoring and canceling wherever possible. However, one important rule distinguishes inequalities from equations:

RULE: Whenever you multiply or divide by a negative number, you must *reverse* the inequality symbol. Expressed in symbolic form: if $a > b$, then $-a < -b$.

The following simple example demonstrates this important rule:

      $12 - 4x < 8$ (original inequality)

        $-4x < -4$ (subtract 12 from both sides; inequality unchanged)

          $x > 1$ (both sides divided by − 4; inequality reversed)

Here are some additional rules for dealing with algebraic inequalities.

❶ Adding or subtracting unequal quantities to (or from) equal quantities:

     If $a > b$, then $c + a > c + b$

     If $a > b$, then $c - a < c - b$

❷ Adding unequal quantities to unequal quantities:

If $a > b$, and if $c > d$, then $a + c > b + d$

❸ Comparing three unequal quantities:

If $a > b$, and if $b > c$, then $a > c$

❹ Combining the same *positive* quantity with unequal quantities by multiplication or division:

If $a > b$, and if $x > 0$, then $xa > xb$

If $a > b$, and if $x > 0$, then $\dfrac{a}{x} > \dfrac{b}{x}$

If $a > b$, and if $x > 0$, then $\dfrac{x}{a} < \dfrac{x}{b}$

❺ Combining the same *negative* quantity with unequal quantities by multiplication or division:

If $a > b$, and if $x < 0$, then $xa < xb$

If $a > b$, and if $x < 0$, then $\dfrac{a}{x} < \dfrac{b}{x}$

If $a > b$, and if $x < 0$, then $\dfrac{x}{a} > \dfrac{x}{b}$

EXAMPLE 9 (EASIER):

If $-2x > -5$, then which of the inequalities holds true?

(1) $x > \dfrac{5}{2}$

(2) $x < \dfrac{5}{2}$

(3) $x > -\dfrac{2}{5}$

(4) $x < \dfrac{2}{5}$

(5) $x > -\dfrac{5}{2}$

Divide both sides of the equation by -2, and reverse the inequality:

$-2x > -5$

$\dfrac{-2x}{-2} < \dfrac{-5}{-2}$

$x < \dfrac{5}{2}$

The correct answer is (2).

EXAMPLE 10 (MORE CHALLENGING):

If $a > b$, and if $c > d$, then which of the following inequalities holds true in all cases?

(1) $a - b > c - d$

(2) $a - c > b - d$

(3) $c + d < a - b$

(4) $a - c < b + d$

(5) $b + d < a + c$

To handle this question, you need to remember that if unequal quantities (c and d) are added to unequal quantities of the same order (a and b), the result is an inequality in the same order. This rule is essentially what answer choice (5) says. **The correct answer is (5).**

FACTORABLE QUADRATIC EXPRESSIONS (ONE VARIABLE)

 http://bit.ly/hippo_alg9

A **quadratic expression** includes a "squared" variable, such as x^2. An equation is quadratic if you can express it in this general form: $ax^2 + bx + c = 0$, where:

x is the variable

a, b, and c are integers

$a \neq 0$

b can equal 0

c can equal 0

Here are four examples (notice that the b-term and c-term are not essential; in other words, either b or c, or both, can equal zero):

Equation: $2w^2 = 16$
General quadratic form: $2w^2 - 16 = 0$ (no b-term)

Equation: $x^2 = 3x$
General quadratic form: $x^2 - 3x = 0$ (no c-term)

Equation: $3y = 4 - y^2$
General quadratic form: $y^2 + 3y - 4 = 0$

Equation: $7z = 2z^2 - 15$
General quadratic form: $2z^2 - 7z - 15 = 0$

Every quadratic equation has exactly two solutions, called **roots.** (But the two roots might be the same.) On the GED®, you will probably be able to find the two roots by **factoring.** To solve any factorable quadratic equation, follow these three steps:

① Put the equation into the standard form: $ax^2 + bx + c = 0$.

② Factor the terms on the left side of the equation into two linear expressions (with no exponents).

③ Set each linear expression (root) equal to zero and solve for the variable in each one.

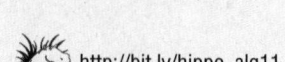 http://bit.ly/hippo-alg10 Some quadratic expressions are easier to factor than others. If either of the two constants b or c is zero, factoring is very simple. In fact, in some cases, no factoring is needed at all—as in the second equation below:

A factorable quadratic equation with no c-term:

$$2x^2 = x$$
$$2x^2 - x = 0$$
$$x(2x - 1) = 0$$
$$x = 0, \quad 2x - 1 = 0$$
$$x = 0, \frac{1}{2}$$

A factorable quadratic equation with no b-term:

$$2x^2 - 4 = 0$$
$$2(x^2 - 2) = 0$$
$$x^2 - 2 = 0$$
$$x^2 = 2$$
$$x = \sqrt{2}, -\sqrt{2}$$

In sum, when dealing with a quadratic equation, your first step is usually to put it into the general form $ax^2 + bx + c = 0$. But keep in mind: The only essential term is ax^2.

 http://bit.ly/hippo_alg11 A **binomial** is an algebraic expression that contains *two* terms. You can rewrite the product of two binomials by multiplying each term in one binomial by each term in the other, adding together all four terms. To organize this task, apply the **FOIL** method:

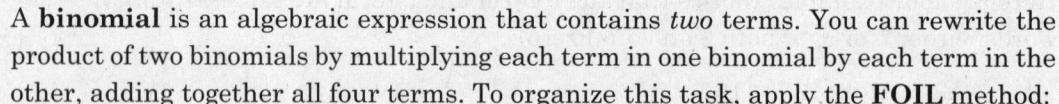 http://bit.ly/hippo_alg12
(F) the product of the **first** terms of the two binomials

(O) the product of the **outer** terms of the two binomials

(I) the product of the **inner** terms of the two binomials

(L) the product of the **last** (second) terms of the two binomials

Here are two simple demonstrations of the **FOIL** method:

$$(x + 2)(x + 3) = x^2 \text{ (F)} + 3x \text{ (O)} + 2x \text{ (I)} + 6 \text{ (L)} = x^2 + 5x + 6$$

$$(2x - 1)(x + 1) = 2x^2 \text{ (F)} + 2x \text{ (O)} - x \text{ (I)} - 1 \text{ (L)} = 2x^2 + x - 1$$

In both examples, notice that the two middle terms, **(O)** and **(I)**, can be combined. The simplified result is a **trinomial,** which is an algebraic expression that contains *three* terms. On the GED®, quadratic trinomials are generally *factorable* into two binomials.

Factoring trinomials often involves a bit of trial and error. You need to apply the **FOIL** method *in reverse*. To accomplish this task, keep in mind the following relationships between the general quadratic form $ax^2 + bx + c$ and the **FOIL** method:

http://bit.ly/hippo_alg13

> **(F)** is the first term (ax^2) of the quadratic expression
>
> **(O + I)** is the second term (bx) of the quadratic expression
>
> **(L)** is the third term (c) of the quadratic expression

To factor the quadratic expression $x^2 + 3x + 2$, for example, first identify its components:

> **(F)** $= x^2$
>
> **(O + I)** $= 3x$
>
> **(L)** $= 2$

http://bit.ly/hippo_alg14

Then create a binomial "shell" to fill in numbers as you determine them. Remember: in the general quadratic form, a, b, and c are all *integers*, and so all coefficients and other numbers in both binomial must be integers. In this example, since **(F)** is x^2, the first term in each binomial must be x:

> $(x + ?)(x + ?)$

Since **(L)** is 2, the product of the two last terms (signified by "?") must be 2. The only possibilities are 2 and 1 or −2 and −1. Try them both:

> $(x + 2)(x + 1) = x^2 + 2x + x + 2$
>
> $(x − 2)(x − 1) = x^2 − 2x − x + 2$

As you can see, the first option is the one that simplifies to $x^2 + 3x + 2$.

Remember that on the GED®, quadratic trinomials will probably be factorable into two binomials, so that you can apply the FOIL method to determine them.

EXAMPLE 11 (EASIER):

Which of the following is a factor of $x^2 − x − 6$?

   (1) $(x + 6)$

   (2) $(x + 1)$

   (3) $(x − 3)$

   (4) $(x − 2)$

   (5) $(x + 3)$

Notice that x^2 has no coefficient. This makes the process of factoring into two binomials easier. Set up two binomial shells: $(x + ?)(x + ?)$. The product of the two missing second terms (the "L" term under the FOIL method) is −6. The possible integral pairs that result in this product are (1,−6), (−1,6), (2,−3,), and (−2,3). Notice that the second term in the trinomial is $-x$. This means that the sum of the two integers whose product is -6 must be -1. The pair $(2,-3)$ fits the bill. Thus, the trinomial is equivalent to the product of the two binomials $(x + 2)$ and $(x - 3)$. To check your work, multiply the two binomials, using the FOIL method:

$$(x + 2)(x - 3) = x^2 - 3x + 2x - 6$$
$$= x^2 - x + 6$$

The correct answer is (3).

EXAMPLE 12 (MORE CHALLENGING):

How many different values of x does the solution set for the equation $4x^2 = 4x - 1$ contain?

    (1) none

    (2) one

    (3) two

    (4) four

    (5) infinitely many

First, express the equation in standard form: $4x^2 - 4x + 1 = 0$. Notice that the c-term is 1. The only two integral pairs that result in this product are $(1,1)$ and $(-1,-1)$. Since the b-term $(-4x)$ is negative, the integral pair whose product is 1 must be $(-1,-1)$. Set up a binomial shell:

$$(? - 1)(? - 1)$$

Notice that the a-term contains the coefficient 4. The possible integral pairs that result in this product are $(1,4)$, $(2,2)$, $(-1,-4)$, and $(-2,-2)$. A bit of trial-and-error reveals that only the pair $(2,2)$ works. Thus, in factored form, the equation becomes $(2x - 1)(2x - 1) = 0$.

To check your work, multiply the two binomials, using the FOIL method:

$$(2x - 1)(2x - 1) = 4x^2 - 2x - 2x + 1$$
$$= 4x^2 - 4x + 1$$

Since the two binomial factors are the same, the two roots of the equation are the same. In other words, x has only one possible value. **The correct answer is (2).**

(Although you don't need to find the value of x in order to answer the question, solve for x in the equation $2x - 1 = 0$; $x = \dfrac{1}{2}$.)

FACTORABLE QUADRATIC EXPRESSIONS (TWO VARIABLES)

In the world of math, solving nonlinear equations in two or more variables can be *very* complicated. But for the GED®, all you need to remember are these three general forms:

Sum of two variables, squared:

$(x + y)^2 = x^2 + 2xy + y^2$

Difference of two variables, squared:

$(x - y)^2 = x^2 - 2xy + y^2$

Difference of two squares:

$x^2 - y^2 = (x + y)(x - y)$

You can verify these equations using the FOIL method:

$(x + y)^2$ $\qquad\qquad$ $(x - y)^2$ $\qquad\qquad$ $(x + y)(x - y)$
$= (x + y)(x + y)$ $\qquad$ $= (x - y)(x - y)$ $\qquad$ $= x^2 + xy - xy - y^2$
$= x^2 + xy + xy + y^2$ $\quad$ $= x^2 - xy - xy + y^2$ $\quad$ $= x^2 - y^2$
$= x^2 + 2xy + y^2$ $\qquad$ $= x^2 - 2xy + y^2$

For the GED®, memorize the three equation forms listed here. When you see one of these forms on the exam, you will probably need to convert it to another form.

EXAMPLE 13 (EASIER):

If $x^2 - y^2 = 100$, and if $x + y = 2$, then what is the value of $x - y$?

(1) –2

(2) 10

(3) 20

(4) 50

(5) 200

If you recognize the *difference of two squares* when you see the form, you can handle this question with ease. Use the third equation you just learned, substituting 2 for $(x + y)$, then solving for $(x - y)$:

$x^2 - y^2 = (x + y)(x - y)$
$\quad 100 = (x + y)(x - y)$
$\quad 100 = (2)(x - y)$
$\quad\ \ 50 = (x - y)$

The correct answer is (4).

EXAMPLE 14 (MORE CHALLENGING):

If $\dfrac{x+y}{x-y} = \dfrac{x+y}{x}$, which of the following expresses the value of x in terms of y ?

(1) $-y$

(2) y^2

(3) $\dfrac{y}{2}$

(4) $y - 1$

(5) $2y$

Apply the cross-product method to eliminate fractions. Rewrite the equation in its unfactored form. (If you recognize the difference of two squares, you'll rewrite more quickly.) Simplify, and then solve for x:

$$x(x + y) = (x - y)(x + y)$$
$$x^2 + xy = x^2 - y^2$$
$$xy = -y^2$$
$$x = -y$$

The correct answer is (1).

FUNCTIONS

In a **function** or **functional relationship,** the value of one variable depends upon the value of, or is "a function of," another variable. In mathematics, the relationship is expressed in the form $y = f(x)$—where y is a function of x.

To find the value of the function for any value x, simply substitute the x-value for x wherever it appears in the function. In the following function, for example, the function of 2 is 14, and the function of −3 is 4.

$$f(x) = x^2 + 3x + 4$$
$$f(2) = 2^2 + 3(2) + 4 = 4 + 6 + 4 = 14$$
$$f(-3) = -3^2 + 3(-3) + 4 = 9 - 9 + 4 = 4$$

Determine the function of a variable expression the same way—just substitute the expression for x throughout the function. In the above function, here is how you would find $f(2 + a)$:

$$f(2 + a) = (2 + a)\ + 3(2 + a) - 4$$
$$= 4 + 4a + a\ + 6 + 3a - 4$$
$$= a\ + 7a + 6$$

On the GED®, a challenging function question might ask to apply the same function twice.

EXAMPLE 15 (EASIER):

If $f(a) = 9$, then for which function does $a = 6$?

(1) $f(a) = 9a$

(2) $f(a) = 3$

(3) $f(a) = \frac{2}{3}a$

(4) $f(a) = a + 3$

(5) Not enough information is provided.

In each answer choice, substitute 9 for $f(a)$, and substitute 6 for a. Of the four functions listed, only the one in choice (4) holds true: $9 = 6 + 3$. **The correct answer is (4).**

EXAMPLE 16 (MORE CHALLENGING):

If $f(x) = 2x$, then $\frac{1}{f(x)} \times f\left(\frac{2}{x}\right)$ is equal to which of the following expressions?

(1) $\frac{1}{x}$

(2) 1

(3) $\frac{x^2}{2}$

(4) x

(5) $\frac{2}{x^2}$

To rewrite the first term, simply substitute $2x$ for $f(x)$. To rewrite the second term, substitute $\frac{2}{x}$ for x in the function $f(x) = 2x$. Then combine the terms by multiplication:

$$\frac{1}{f(x)} \times f\left(\frac{2}{x}\right) = \left(\frac{1}{2x}\right)\left(2 \times \frac{2}{x}\right) = \frac{4}{2x^2} = \frac{2}{x^2}$$

The correct answer is (5).

MEASURES OF CENTRAL TENDENCY (MEAN, MEDIAN, AND RANGE)

Arithmetic mean (simple average), median, and range refer to different ways of describing a set of numbers with just one number. Each measures the *central tendency* of a set of numbers. Here's the definition of each one:

> **Arithmetic mean (simple average):** In a set of n terms, the sum of the terms divided by n.

Median: The middle term in value, or the average (mean) of the two middle terms if the number of terms is even.

Range: The difference in value between the greatest and the least term in a set.

For example, given a set of six numbers {8, –4, 8, 3, 2, and 7}:

$$\text{mean} = 4 \left(\frac{8 - 4 + 8 + 3 + 2 + 7}{6} = \frac{24}{6} = 4 \right)$$

median = 5 (the average of 3 and 7, which are the two middle terms in value: {–4, 2, 3, 7, 8, 8}

range = 12 (the difference on the number line between 8 and –4)

The mean and median might be the same, or they might differ from each other (as in the previous example).

GED® questions involving mean (simple average) usually involve calculating the mean by adding terms together $(a + b + c + \ldots)$ and dividing the sum by the number of terms (n):

$$\text{mean} = \frac{(a + b + c + \ldots)}{n}$$

But a question might instead require you to find a missing term when the mean (average) of all the terms is known. To solve this type of problem, plug what you know into the arithmetic-mean formula. Then, use algebra to find the missing number. For example, if the average of 2 and another number (N) is 5, here's how you would find the value of N:

$$5 = \frac{2 + N}{2}$$
$$10 = 2 + N$$
$$8 = N$$

Approach arithmetic-mean problems that involve *variables* (such as a and b) the same way as those involving only numbers.

EXAMPLE 17 (EASIER):

What is the mean (simple average) of $\frac{1}{5}$, 25%, and 0.09 ?

(1) 0.18

(2) 20%

(3) $\frac{1}{4}$

(4) 0.32

(5) $\frac{1}{3}$

Since the answer choices are not all expressed in the same form, first convert numbers into whichever form you think would be easiest to work with when you add the numbers together. In this case, the easiest form to work with is probably the decimal-number form. So, convert the first two numbers into decimal form, and then find the sum of the three numbers:

$$0.20 + 0.25 + 0.09 = 0.54$$

Finally, divide by 3 to find the average:

$$0.54 \div 3 = 0.18$$

The correct answer is (1).

EXAMPLE 18 (MORE CHALLENGING):

If A is the average of P, Q, and another number, which of the following represents the missing number?

(1) $\frac{1}{3}(A + P + Q)$

(2) $3A - P + Q$

(3) $A - P + Q$

(4) $3A - P - Q$

(5) $3A - P + Q$

Let x = the missing number. Solve for x by the arithmetic-mean formula:

$$A = \frac{P + Q + x}{3}$$
$$3A = P + Q + x$$
$$3A - P - Q = x$$

The correct answer is (4).

ARITHMETIC SERIES

In an **arithmetic series** of numbers, there is a constant (unchanging) difference between successive numbers in the series. In other words, all numbers in an arithmetic series are evenly spaced on the number line. All of the following are examples of arithmetic series:

- Successive integers
- Successive even integers
- Successive odd integers
- Successive multiples of the same number
- Successive integers ending in the same digit

On the GED®, an arithmetic-series question might ask for the *mean* (average) of a series, or it might ask for the *sum*. Since the numbers are evenly spaced, the mean and median of the series are the same. To find the mean, instead of adding all the terms and then dividing, you can find the median or, even easier, compute the average of the least number and the greatest numbers (the endpoints of the series). Faced with calculating the average of a series of evenly-spaced integers, you can shortcut the addition. Study the following examples:

The mean (and median) of all *even* integers 20 through 40 is $\dfrac{20 + 40}{2} = \dfrac{60}{2} = 30$.

The mean (and median) of all integers −11 through 20 is $\dfrac{-11 + 20}{2} = \dfrac{9}{2} = 4\dfrac{1}{2}$.

The mean (and median) of all positive two-digit numbers ending in the digit 5 is $\dfrac{15 + 95}{2} = \dfrac{110}{2} = 55$.

The mean (and median) of all integers greater than −100 but less than 100 is $\dfrac{-99 + 99}{2} = 0$. (The set's negative and positive numbers all cancel out.)

Finding the *sum* of an arithmetic (evenly spaced) series of numbers requires only one additional step: multiplying the average (which is also the median) by the number of terms in the series. When calculating the sum, be careful to count the number of terms in the series correctly. For instance, the number of positive *odd* integers less than 50 is 25, but the number of positive *even* integers less than 50 is only 24.

EXAMPLE 19 (EASIER):

What is the average of the first 20 positive integers?

- **(1)** $7\dfrac{1}{2}$
- **(2)** 10
- **(3)** $10\dfrac{1}{2}$
- **(4)** 15
- **(5)** 20

Since the terms are evenly spaced (an arithmetic series), take the average of the first term (1) and the last term (20):

$$\dfrac{1 + 20}{2} = \dfrac{21}{2}, \text{ or } 10\dfrac{1}{2}$$

The correct answer is (3).

EXAMPLE 20 (MORE CHALLENGING):

What is the sum of all odd integers *between* 10 and 40?

    (1) 250

    (2) 325

    (3) 375

    (4) 400

    (5) 450

The average of the described numbers is $\frac{11 + 39}{2} = \frac{50}{2}$, or 25. The number of terms in the series is 15. (The first term is 11, and the last term is 39.) The sum of the described series of integers $= 25 \times 15 = 375$. **The correct answer is (3).**

PROBABILITY

Probability refers to the statistical chances, or "odds," of an event occurring (or not occurring). By definition, probability ranges from 0 to 1. Probability is never negative, and it's never greater than 1. Here's the basic formula for determining probability:

$$\text{Probability} = \frac{\text{number of ways the event can occur}}{\text{total number of possible occurrences}}$$

Probability can be expressed as a fraction, a percent, or a decimal number. The greater the probability, the greater the fraction, percent, or decimal number.

Determining Probability (Single Event)

Probability plays an integral role in games of chance, including many casino games. In the throw of a single die, for example, the probability of rolling a 5 is "one in six," or $\frac{1}{6}$, or $16\frac{2}{3}\%$. Of course, the probability of rolling a certain other number is the same. A standard deck of 52 playing cards contains 12 face cards. The probability of selecting a face card from a full deck is $\frac{12}{52}$, or $\frac{3}{13}$. The probability of selecting a queen from a full deck is $\frac{4}{52}$, or $\frac{1}{13}$.

To calculate the probability of an event NOT occurring, just *subtract* the probability of the event occurring *from 1*.

EXAMPLE 21 (EASIER):

If you randomly select one candy from a jar containing two cherry candies, two licorice candies, and one peppermint candy, what is the probability of selecting a cherry candy?

(1) $\frac{1}{6}$

(2) $\frac{1}{5}$

(3) $\frac{1}{3}$

(4) $\frac{2}{5}$

(5) $\frac{3}{5}$

There are two ways among five possible occurrences that a cherry candy will be selected. Thus, the probability of selecting a cherry candy is $\frac{2}{5}$. **The correct answer is (4).**

EXAMPLE 22 (MORE CHALLENGING):

A bag of marbles contains twice as many red marbles as blue marbles, and twice as many blue marbles as green marbles. If these are the only colors of marbles in the bag, what is the probability of randomly picking from the bag a marble that is NOT blue?

(1) $\frac{1}{6}$

(2) $\frac{2}{9}$

(3) $\frac{2}{5}$

(4) $\frac{2}{7}$

(5) $\frac{5}{7}$

Regardless of the number of marbles in the bag, the red-blue-green marble ratio is 4:2:1. As you can see, blue marbles account for $\frac{2}{7}$ of the total number of marbles. Thus, the probability of picking a marble that is NOT blue is $1 - \frac{2}{7} = \frac{5}{7}$.
The correct answer is (5).

Determining Probability (Two Events)

To determine probability involving two or more events, it is important to distinguish probabilities involving **independent** events from an event that is **dependent** on another one.

Two events are *independent* if neither event affects the probability that the other will occur. The events may involve the random selection of one object from *each of two or more groups*. Or they may involve the random selection of one object from a group, then *replacing* it and selecting again (as in a "second round" or "another turn" of a game).

In either scenario, to find the probability of two events BOTH occurring, MULTIPLY together their individual probabilities:

probability of event 1 occurring

$$\times$$

probability of event 2 occurring

$$=$$

probability of both events occurring

For example, assume that you randomly select one letter from each of two sets: {A, B} and {C, D, E}. The probability of selecting A and C $= \frac{1}{2} \times \frac{1}{3} = \frac{1}{6}$.

To calculate the probability that two events will *not both* occur, subtract the probability of both events occurring from 1.

Now let's look at *dependent* probability. Two distinct events might be related in that one event affects the probability of the other one occurring—for example, randomly selecting one object from a group, then selecting a second object from the same group *without replacing* the first selection. Removing one object from the group *increases the odds* of selecting any particular object from those that remain.

For example, assume that you randomly select one letter from the set {A, B, C, D}. Then, from the remaining three letters, you select another letter. What is the probability of selecting both A and B? To answer this question, you need to consider each of the two selections separately.

In the first selection, the probability of selecting either A or B is $\frac{2}{4}$. But the probability of selecting the second of the two is $\frac{1}{3}$. Why? Because after the first selection, only *three* letters remain from which to select. Since the question asks for the odds of selecting both A and B (as opposed to either one), multiply the two individual probabilities: $\frac{2}{4} \times \frac{1}{3} = \frac{2}{12}$, or $\frac{1}{6}$.

EXAMPLE 23 (EASIER):

A gaming die is a cube with numbers 1–6 on its faces, each number on a different face. In a roll of two dice, what is the probability that the two numbers facing up will total 12?

(1) $\frac{1}{64}$

(2) $\frac{1}{36}$

(3) $\frac{1}{12}$

(4) $\frac{1}{9}$

(5) $\frac{1}{6}$

The only two-number combination on the dice that can total 12 is 6 + 6. The probability of rolling 6 on each die is $\frac{1}{6}$. Accordingly, the probability of rolling 6 on both die is $\frac{1}{6} \times \frac{1}{6} = \frac{1}{36}$. **The correct answer is (2).**

EXAMPLE 24 (MORE CHALLENGING):

Two pairs of socks are randomly removed from a drawer containing five pairs: two black, two white, and one blue. What is the probability of first removing a black pair and then, without replacement, removing a white pair from the drawer?

(1) $\frac{1}{10}$

(2) $\frac{1}{5}$

(3) $\frac{1}{4}$

(4) $\frac{1}{3}$

(5) $\frac{2}{5}$

When removing the first pair, the probability that the pair removed will be black is $\frac{2}{5}$. Four pairs of socks remain, two of which are white. The probability of removing a white pair of socks from among those four is $\frac{2}{4}$. Combine the two probabilities by multiplying:

$\frac{2}{5} \times \frac{2}{4} = \frac{4}{20}$, or $\frac{1}{5}$

The correct answer is (2).

WORD PROBLEMS INVOLVING FORMULAS

Certain types of GED® word problems call for you to apply a formula. Here are the three types of formulas you can expect to apply during the GED®:

- Weighted average (based on the formula for arithmetic mean)

- Simple interest (on a monetary investment)

- Rate

The formulas for simple interest and rate will be on the formulas sheet provided during the test.

In the next few pages, you'll learn how to handle these three types of word problems. Remember: for any type of word problem, including these three, you might be able to work backwards from the answer choices as well. Even if not, you can often narrow down your choices by estimating the size of the answer.

Weighted Average Problems

You solve *weighted average* problems using the arithmetic-mean (simple average) formula, except you give the set's terms different weights. For example, if a final exam score of 90 receives *twice* the weight of each of two mid-term exam scores 75 and 85, think of the final-exam score as *two* scores of 90—and the total number of scores as 4 rather than 3:

$$WA = \frac{75 + 85 + (2)(90)}{4} = \frac{340}{4} = 85$$

Similarly, when some numbers among terms might appear more often than others, you must give them the appropriate "weight" before computing an average. A weighted-average problem might ask you to find the average, or it might provide the weighted average and ask for one of the terms. These questions sometimes require conversion from one unit of measurement to another.

EXAMPLE 25 (EASIER):

During an 8-hour trip, Brigitte drove 3 hours at 55 miles per hour and 5 hours at 65 miles per hour. What was her average rate, in miles per hour, for the entire trip?

    (1) 58.5

    (2) 60

    (3) 61.25

    (4) 62.5

    (5) 66.25

Determine the total miles driven: (3)(55) + (5)(65) = 490. To determine the average over the entire trip, divide this total by 8, which is the number of total hours: 490 ÷ 8 = 61.25. **The correct answer is (3).**

EXAMPLE 26 (MORE CHALLENGING):

A certain olive orchard produces 315 gallons of oil annually, on average, during four consecutive years. How many gallons of oil must the orchard produce annually, on average, during the next six years, if oil production for the entire ten-year period is to meet a goal of 378 gallons per year?

(1) 240

(2) 285

(3) 396

(4) 420

(5) 468

In the weighted-average formula, 315 annual gallons receives a weight of 4, while the average annual number of gallons for the next six years (x) receives a weight of 6:

$$378 = \frac{1260 + 6x}{10}$$
$$3780 = 1260 + 6x$$
$$3780 - 1260 = 6x$$
$$420 = x$$

This solution (420) is the average number of gallons needed per year, on average, during the next six years. **The correct answer is (4).**

Investment Problems

GED® *investment* problems involve interest earned (at a certain percentage rate) on money over a certain time period (usually a year). To calculate interest earned, multiply the original amount of money by the interest rate:

amount of money × interest rate = amount of interest on money

For example, if you deposit $1000 in a savings account that earns 5% interest annually, the total amount in the account after one year will be $1000 + 0.05($1000) = $1000 + $50 = $1050.

A GED® investment question might involve more than simply calculating interest earned on a given principal amount at a given rate. It might call for you to set up and solve an algebraic equation. When handling this sort of problem, it's best to eliminate percent signs.

EXAMPLE 27 (EASIER):

Gary wishes to have $2970 in a savings account at the end of the year. How much must Gary deposit in his account at the start of the year if the account pays him 8% interest per year?

- **(1)** $2575
- **(2)** $2680
- **(3)** $2732
- **(4)** $2750
- **(5)** $3208

Letting x equal the original amount deposited, set up the following equation: $x + 0.08x = 2970$. Combining terms on the left side of the equation: $1.08x = 2970$. Solve for x:

$$x = \frac{2970}{1.08} = 2750$$

Thus, Gary must invest $2750 at the start of the year to end with $2970. **The correct answer is (4).**

EXAMPLE 28 (MORE CHALLENGING):

Fiona deposits D dollars in a savings account that earns 10% interest per year. At the end of one year, she then deposits the total amount in another savings account, which earns 5% per year.

Which of the following represents the total amount in the account after the two-year period, in dollars?

- **(1)** $0.95D$
- **(2)** $1.05D$
- **(3)** $1.105D$
- **(4)** $1.10D$
- **(5)** $1.5D$

The total dollar amount after the first year is $D + 0.10D$, or $1.1D$. Fiona deposits $1.1D$ in an account earning 5%. After one year, her total is $1.1D + 0.05(1.10)D$, which equals $1.10D + 1.005)D$, or $1.105D$. **The correct answer is (3).**

Problems Involving Rate

A *rate* is a fraction that expresses a quantity per unit of time. For example, the rate of travel is expressed this way:

$$\text{rate of travel} = \frac{\text{distance}}{\text{time}}$$

Similarly, the rate at which a machine produces a certain product is expressed this way:

$$\text{rate of production} = \frac{\text{number of units produced}}{\text{time}}$$

A GED® rate question will usually provide two of the three terms, and then it will ask you for the value of the third term. A rate question might also require you to convert a number from one unit of measurement to another.

EXAMPLE 29 (EASIER):

If a printer can print pages at a rate of 15 pages per minute, how many pages can it print in $2\frac{1}{2}$ hours?

(1) 1375

(2) 1500

(3) 1750

(4) 2250

(5) 2500

Apply the following formula: $\text{rate} = \frac{\text{\# of pages}}{\text{time}}$. The rate is given in terms of minutes, so convert $2\frac{1}{2}$ hours to 150 minutes. Determine the number of pages by applying the formula to these numbers:

$$15 = \frac{\text{\# of pages}}{150}$$
$$(15)(150) = \text{\# of pages}$$
$$2250 = \text{\# of pages}$$

The correct answer is (4).

EXAMPLE 30 (MORE CHALLENGING):

A passenger train and a freight train leave from the same station at the same time. Over 3 hours, the passenger train travels 45 miles per hour faster, on average, than the freight train.

Which of the following expresses the combined distance the two trains have traveled after 3 hours, where x represents the number of miles the freight train traveled per hour, on average?

  (1) $3x + 45$

  (2) $6x + 45$

  (3) $3x + 120$

  (4) $3x + 135$

  (5) $6x + 135$

Since x equals the rate (speed) of the freight train, you can express the rate of the passenger train as $x + 45$. Substitute these values for time and rate into the formula for each train:

Formula: rate × time = distance
Passenger: $(x + 45)(3) = 3x + 135$
Freight: $(x)(3) = 3x$

The combined distance that the two trains covered is $3x + (3x + 135) = 6x + 135$.

The correct answer is (5).

SUMMING IT UP

- For the Mathematics Test, be sure to review the following algebra skills: solving a linear equation in one variable, solving a system of two equations in two variables by the substitution method and the addition-subtraction method, recognizing unsolvable equations, handling algebraic inequalities, factoring quadratic expressions, finding the roots of quadratic equations by factoring, handling functions, and solving formula word problems (weighted average, simple interest, and rate).

- Most algebraic equations you'll see on the GED® Math Test are linear. Remember the operations for isolating the unknown on one side of the equation. Solving algebraic inequalities is similar to solving equations: Isolate the variable on one side of the inequality symbol first.

- Weighted-average problems and currency problems can be solved in a similar manner by using the arithmetic mean (simple average) formula.

- Mixture and investment problems on the Mathematics Test can be solved using what you've learned about proportion and percentage questions. Rates of production and travel questions can be solved using the strategies you've learned about fraction problems. GED® *investment* problems involve interest earned (at a certain percentage rate) on money over a certain time period (usually a year).

- A GED® rate question (*rate* is a fraction that expresses a quantity per unit of time) will usually provide two of the three terms, and then it will ask you for the value of the third term. A rate question might also require you to convert a number from one unit of measurement to another.

Math Review: Geometry

chapter 14

OVERVIEW

- **What you'll find in this review**
- **Congruency and similarity**
- **Angles**
- **Triangles**
- **Quadrilaterals**
- **Polygons**
- **Circles**
- **Three-dimensional (3-D) geometric figures**
- **Right-triangle trigonometry**
- **Coordinate geometry**
- **Summing it up**

WHAT YOU'LL FIND IN THIS REVIEW

In this review, you'll examine the areas of geometry covered on the Mathematics Test. They include the following:

- Congruency and similarity

- Angles, parallel and perpendicular lines, and transversals

- Two-dimensional figures (triangles, quadrilaterals, polygons, and circles)

- Three-dimensional figures (cubes and other rectangular solids, cylinders, cones, and square pyramids)

- Basic right-triangle trigonometry

- Coordinate geometry (points, lines, and other figures on the *xy*-coordinate plane)

The GED®-style questions throughout this review are multiple-choice questions. The actual exam also includes questions in an alternative format, in which you supply the numerical answer to the question.

CONGRUENCY AND SIMILARITY

Two geometric figures that have the same size and shape are said to be **congruent.** The symbol for congruency is ≅. Two angles are congruent if their degree measure (size) is the same. Two line segments are congruent if they are equal in length. Two triangles are congruent if the angle measures and sides are all identical in size. (The same applies to figures with more than three sides.)

If a two-dimensional geometric figure, such as a triangle or rectangle, has exactly the same shape as another one, then the two figures are **similar.** Similar figures share the same angle measures, and their sides are proportionate (though not the same length). Look at the figure below.

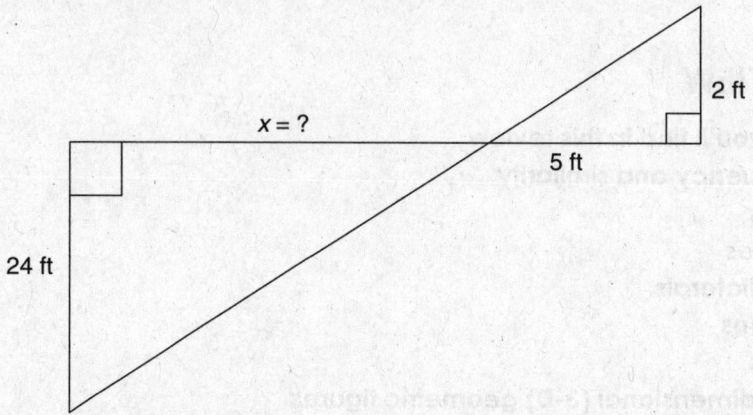

In order to find the length of the corresponding side of the larger triangle, you must set up a proportion. The triangles are similar, and so their sides are in proportion. To solve the proportion, cross multiply: $2x = 120$. Then, to find x, divide 120 by 2: $120 \div 2 = 60$. The unknown side is 60 feet in length. (You'll examine triangles in greater detail later in this review.)

ANGLES

Angles are indicated by the angle symbol ($\angle$). They are measured in degrees (°). The letter "m" is used to indicate the measure of an angle. The line that extends in only one direction from a point is called a **ray.** Lines, rays, or line segments meet at a point called the **vertex.** Angles are usually named by letters, as in the below figure.

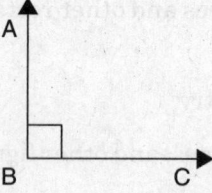

The name of the above angle is m$\angle ABC$. This angle is called a **right angle** because m$\angle ABC = 90°$. The small square drawn in the angle indicates that it is a right angle. When two lines meet to form a right angle, they are said to be **perpendicular** to each other, as indicated by the symbol $\perp$. In the above figure, $\overline{BA} \perp \overline{BC}$.

An angle that measures less than 90° is called an **acute** angle. $\angle VWX$ in the following figure is an acute angle. An angle that measures more than 90° is called an **obtuse** angle. $\angle EFG$ in the following figure is an obtuse angle.

A **straight angle** measures 180°. ∠XYZ below is a straight angle. Two or more angles whose measures add up to 180° are called **supplementary.** In the next figure, ∠DEG forms a straight line and therefore measures 180°. ∠DEF and ∠FEG are supplementary angles; their measures add up to 180°.

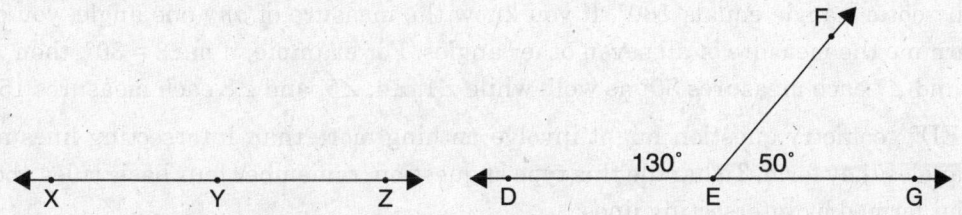

Two angles are called **complementary** angles when their measurements add up to 90° (a right angle). In the next figure, m∠ABC = 90°. ∠ABE and ∠CBE are complementary because their measurements add up to 90°. You also know that m∠ABD = 90° because ∠ABD and ∠ABC combine to form a straight line, which measures 180°.

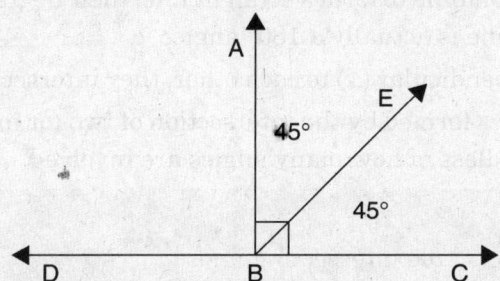

In geometry, the set of points that makes up a flat surface is referred to as a **plane.** When two lines in the same plane never meet, no matter how far they are extended, they are called **parallel lines** and are indicated by the symbol ‖. If two parallel lines are intersected by a third line, eight angles are formed. The line that intersects two parallel lines is called the **transversal.** If a transversal intersects two parallel lines perpendicularly (at a 90° angle), all eight angles that are formed are right angles (90°). Otherwise, some angles are acute, while others are obtuse. Look at the next figure.

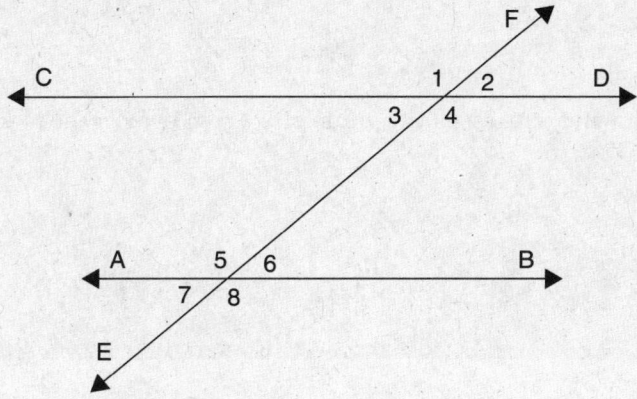

As noted earlier, angles that are equal in degree measure are called *congruent* angles (the symbol ≅ indicates congruency). In the previous figure, you can see that eight angles have been formed. The four acute angles (∠2, ∠3, ∠6, and ∠7) are congruent, and the four obtuse angles (∠1, ∠4, ∠5, and ∠8) are also congruent. Each pair of angles that are opposite each other in relation to a vertex (for example, ∠2 and ∠3) are called **vertical angles.** Vertical angles are always congruent.

Four angles formed by two intersecting lines add up to 360° in measure. In the preceding figure, m∠1 + m∠2 + m∠3 + m∠4 = 360°. (The same holds true for angles 5, 6, 7, and 8.) In the figure, the measure of any one of the four acute angles plus the measure of any obtuse angle equals 180°. If you know the measure of *any* one angle, you can determine the measure of all seven other angles. For example, if m∠2 = 30°, then ∠3, ∠6, and ∠7 each measures 30° as well, while ∠1, ∠4, ∠5, and ∠8 each measures 150°.

A GED® geometry question might involve nothing more than intersecting lines and the angles they form. To handle this type of question, remember four basic rules about angles formed by intersecting lines:

❶ Vertical angles (angles across the vertex from each other and formed by the same two lines) are equal in degree measure, or congruent (≅). In other words, they're the same size.

❷ If adjacent angles combine to form a straight line, their degree measures total 180. In fact, a straight line is actually a 180° angle.

❸ If two lines are perpendicular (⊥) to each other, they intersect at right (90°) angles.

❹ The sum of all angles formed by the intersection of two (or more) lines at the same point is 360°, regardless of how many angles are involved.

EXAMPLE 1 (EASIER):

The figure below shows three intersecting lines.

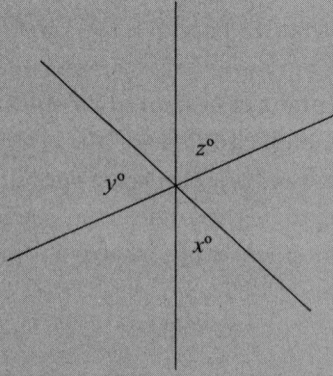

Which of the following expresses the value of $x + y$ in every case?

   (1) $2z$

   (2) $180 - z$

   (3) z

   (4) $360 - z$

   (5) $z + 90$

The angle vertical to the one whose measure is given as $z°$ must also measure $z°$. That angle and the angles whose measures are $x°$ and $y°$ combine to form a straight (180°) line. In other words, $x + y + z = 180$. Accordingly, $x + y = 180 - z$. **The correct answer is (2).**

EXAMPLE 2 (MORE CHALLENGING):

Line R intersects line P and line Q at a 45° angle. Which statement must be true?

   (1) Line P is parallel to line Q.

   (2) Line P intersects line Q at a 45° angle.

   (3) Line P is perpendicular to line Q.

   (4) Line Q intersects line R at a 135° angle.

   (5) Line R is perpendicular to line P.

Lines P and Q may or may not be parallel. But any two lines intersecting at a 45° angle also form a 135° at the vertex because adjacent angles combine to form a straight, 180° line. **The correct answer is (4).**

TRIANGLES

The **triangle** is a 3-sided shape. All triangles, regardless of shape or size, share the following four properties:

❶ **Length of the sides.** Each side is shorter than the sum of the lengths of the other two sides. (Otherwise, the triangle would collapse into a line.)

❷ **Angle measures.** The measures of the three interior angles total 180°.

❸ **Angles and opposite sides.** Comparative angle sizes correspond to the comparative lengths of the sides opposite those angles. For example, a triangle's largest angle is opposite its longest side. (The sides opposite two congruent angles are also congruent.)

❹ **Area.** The area of any triangle is equal to one-half the product of its base and its height (or "altitude"): Area = $\frac{1}{2}$ × base × height. You can use any side as the base to calculate area.

The area formula is included on the Formula Sheet provided during the test.

The next figure shows three particular types of triangles. GED® test questions often involve these three types.

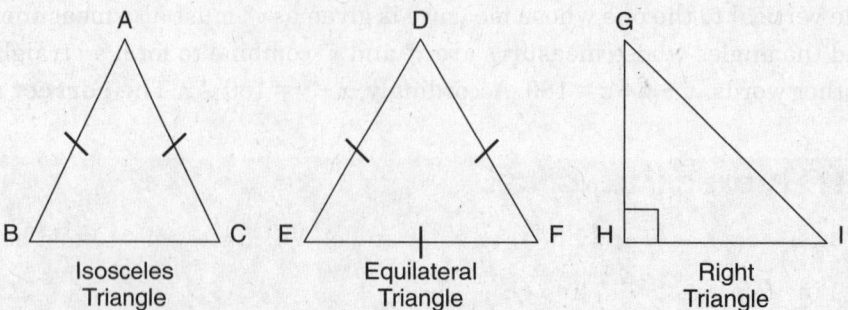

Isosceles Triangle   Equilateral Triangle   Right Triangle

An **isosceles triangle** is one in which two sides (and two angles) are congruent. In the above figure, $\angle$B and $\angle$C are congruent, and the sides opposite those two angles, $\overline{AB}$ and $\overline{AC}$, are congruent. In an **equilateral triangle,** all three angles are congruent, and all three sides are congruent. In a **right triangle,** one angle is a right angle, and the other two angles are acute angles. The longest side of a right triangle (in this case, $\overline{GI}$) is called the **hypotenuse.** In the pages ahead, you'll examine each of these three types of triangles in greater detail.

EXAMPLE 3 (EASIER):

The length of one side of a certain triangular floor space is 12 feet. Which of the following CANNOT be the lengths of the other two sides?

    (1) 1 foot and 12 feet

    (2) 8 feet and 4 feet

    (3) 12 feet and 13 feet

    (4) 16 feet and 14 feet

    (5) 24 feet and 24 feet

The length of any two sides combined must be greater than the length of the third side. **The correct answer is (2).**

EXAMPLE 4 (MORE CHALLENGING):

In triangle T, the degree measure of one interior angle is three times that of *each* of the other two interior angles. What is the measure of triangle T's largest interior angle?

    (1) 72°

    (2) 90°

    (3) 108°

    (4) 120°

    (5) 180°

The ratio among the three angles is 3:1:1. Letting $x =$ the length of either short side:

$$x + x + 3x = 180$$
$$5x = 180$$
$$x = 36$$

The largest angle measures $3 \times 36 = 108°$. **The correct answer is (3).**

Right Triangles and the Pythagorean Theorem

In a right triangle, one angle measures 90° and, of course, each of the other two angles measures less than 90°. The **Pythagorean theorem** involves the relationship among the sides of any right triangle and can be expressed by the equation $a^2 + b^2 = c^2$. As shown in the next figure, the letters a and b represent the lengths of the two **legs** (the two shortest sides) that form the right angle, and c is the length of the hypotenuse (the longest side, opposite the right angle).

Pythagorean theorem: $a^2 + b^2 = c^2$

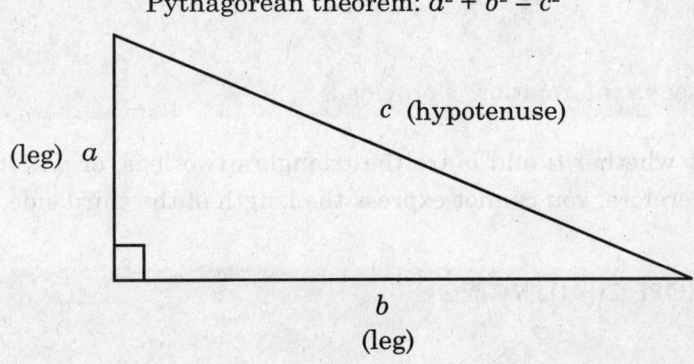

The Pythagorean theorem is included on the Formula Sheet provided during the test.

For any right triangle, if you know the length of two sides, you can determine the length of the third side by applying the Pythagorean theorem. Study the following two examples:

If the two shortest sides (the legs) of a right triangle are 2 and 3 inches in length, then the length of the triangle's third side (the hypotenuse) is $\sqrt{13}$ inches:

$$a^2 + b^2 = c^2$$
$$2^2 + 3^2 = c^2$$
$$4 + 9 = c^2$$
$$13 = c^2$$
$$\sqrt{13} = c$$

If a right triangle's longest side (hypotenuse) is 4 inches in length, and if another side (one of the legs) is 2 inches in length, then the length of the third side (the other leg) is $\sqrt{12}$ inches:

$$a^2 + b^2 = c^2$$
$$a^2 + 2^2 = 4^2$$
$$a^2 + 4 = 16$$
$$a^2 = 12$$
$$a = \sqrt{12}$$

EXAMPLE 5 (EASIER):

In a right triangle, one angle measures 90°. If two sides of a certain right triangle have lengths a and b, what is the length of the third side in terms of a and b?

(1) $a + b$

(2) $\sqrt{a^2 + b^2}$

(3) $\dfrac{a + b}{2}$

(4) $\sqrt{a \times b}$

(5) Not enough information is provided.

You don't know whether a and b are the triangle's two legs, or whether one is the hypotenuse. Therefore, you cannot express the length of the third side. **The correct answer is (5).**

EXAMPLE 6 (MORE CHALLENGING):

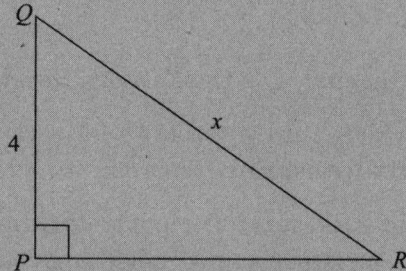

Which of the following expresses the unit length of $\overline{PR}$ in the above figure?

(1) $\sqrt{x^2 - 4}$

(2) $x + 4$

(3) $\sqrt{x + 16}$

(4) $x - 4$

(5) $\sqrt{x^2 - 16}$

The question asks for the length of leg $\overline{PR}$ in terms of the other two sides. Apply the Pythagorean theorem (let y = the length of $\overline{PR}$):

$$4^2 + y^2 = x^2$$
$$16 + y^2 = x^2$$
$$y^2 = x^2 - 16$$
$$y = \sqrt{x^2 - 16}$$

The correct answer is (5).

Pythagorean Side Triplets

A Pythagorean side triplet is a specific side ratio that satisfies the Pythagorean theorem. In each of the following triplets, the first two numbers represent the ratio between the lengths of the two legs (a and b), and the third, and largest, number represents the length of the hypotenuse (c) in relation to the two legs:

Side ratio	Pythagorean theorem
$(a : b : c)$	$(a^2 + b^2 = c^2)$
$1 : 1 : \sqrt{2}$	$1^2 + 1^2 = (\sqrt{2})^2$
$1 : \sqrt{3} : 2$	$1^2 + (\sqrt{3})^2 = 2^2$
$3 : 4 : 5$	$3^2 + 4^2 = 5^2$
$5 : 12 : 13$	$5^2 + 12^2 = 13^2$
$8 : 15 : 17$	$8^2 + 15^2 = 17^2$
$7 : 24 : 25$	$7^2 + 24^2 = 25^2$

Each triplet above is expressed as a *ratio* because it represents a proportion among the triangle's sides. All right triangles with sides having the same proportion, or ratio, have the same shape. For example, a right triangle with sides of 5, 12, and 13 is smaller but exactly the same shape (proportion) as a triangle with sides of 15, 36, and 39.

To save valuable time on GED® right-triangle problems, learn to recognize numbers (lengths of triangle sides) that are multiples of Pythagorean side triplets.

EXAMPLE 7 (EASIER):

Which of the following does NOT describe a right triangle?

A triangle with sides

   (1) 3 inches, 4 inches, and 5 inches

   (2) 6 inches, 8 inches, and 10 inches

   (3) 5 inches, 12 inches, and 13 inches

   (4) 10 inches, 24 inches, and 26 inches

   (5) 6 inches, 10 inches, and 20 inches

Choices (1) and (2) describe 3:4:5 triangles. Choices (3) and (4) describe 5:12:13 triangles. Choice (5) does not describe a right triangle ($6^2 + 10^2 \neq 20^2$). In fact, since the sum of the two sides (6 inches + 10 inches) is not greater in length than the third side (20 inches), this isn't even a triangle at all. **The correct answer is (5).**

EXAMPLE 8 (MORE CHALLENGING):

Two boats leave the same dock at the same time, one traveling due west at 30 miles per hour and the other due north at 40 miles per hour. If they maintain those speeds, how far apart are the boats after three hours?

(1) 60 miles

(2) 90 miles

(3) 120 miles

(4) 150 miles

(5) 210 miles

The distance between the two boats after three hours forms the hypotenuse of a triangle in which the legs are the two boats' respective paths. The ratio of one leg to the other is 30:40, or 3:4. So you know you're dealing with a 3:4:5 triangle. The slower boat traveled 90 miles (30 mph × 3 hours). 90 corresponds to the number 3 in the 3:4:5 ratio, so the multiple is 30 (3 × 30 = 90). 3:4:5 = 90:120:150. **The correct answer is (4).**

Pythagorean Angle Triplets

In two (and only two) of the unique triangles identified in the preceding section as Pythagorean side triplets, all degree measures are *integers*:

The angles of a $1 : 1 : \sqrt{2}$ triangle are 45°, 45°, and 90°.

The angles of a $1 : \sqrt{3} : 2$ triangle are 30°, 60°, and 90°.

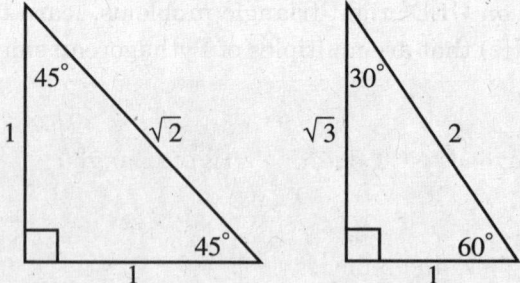

If one acute angle of a right triangle is given as 45°, and you know the length of one side, then you can find the lengths of the other sides. For example:

If one leg is 5, then the other leg must also be 5, while the hypotenuse must be $5\sqrt{2}$.

If the hypotenuse is 10, then each leg must be $\dfrac{10}{\sqrt{2}} = \dfrac{10}{\sqrt{2}} \times \dfrac{\sqrt{2}}{\sqrt{2}} = 5\sqrt{2}$ (divide hypotenuse by $\sqrt{2}$ and clear the radical from the denominator).

Similarly, if you know that one acute angle of a right triangle is either 30° or 60°, then given the length of any side you can find the lengths of the other sides. For example:

If the shortest leg (opposite the 30° angle) is 3, then the other leg (opposite the 60° angle) must be $3\sqrt{3}$, and the hypotenuse must be 6 units long (3 × 2).

If the hypotenuse is 10, then the shorter leg (opposite the 30° angle) must be 5, and the longer leg (opposite the 60° angle) must be $5\sqrt{3}$ (the length of the shorter leg multiplied by $\sqrt{3}$).

To save time on GED® right-triangle problems, be on the lookout for either of the two Pythagorean angle triplets.

EXAMPLE 9 (EASIER):

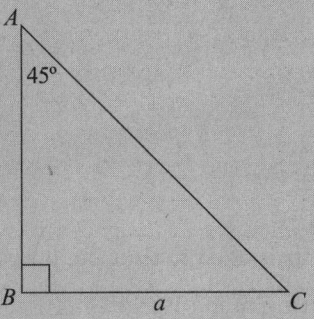

Which of the following expresses the length of $\overline{AC}$ in the above figure?

(1) $2a$

(2) $a\sqrt{2}$

(3) $a\sqrt{3}$

(4) $2\sqrt{a}$

(5) a^2

The 45° angle tells you that $\overline{AB}$ and $\overline{BC}$ are congruent (equal in length). So the ratio of the three sides is $1:1:\sqrt{2}$. Given that each leg has a length of a, the ratio is $a:a:a\sqrt{2}$. **The correct answer is (2).**

EXAMPLE 10 (MORE CHALLENGING):

As shown in the figure below, $\overline{AC}$ is 5 units in length, m∠ABD = 45°, and m∠DAC = 60°.

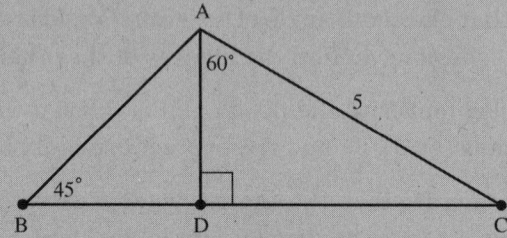

What is the unit length of $\overline{BD}$?

   (1) $\dfrac{7}{3}$

   (2) $2\sqrt{2}$

   (3) $\dfrac{5}{2}$

   (4) $\dfrac{7}{2}$

   (5) Not enough information is provided.

To find the length of $\overline{BD}$, you first need to find the length of $\overline{AD}$. Notice that ∆ADC is a 30°-60°- 90° triangle. The ratio among its sides is 1:$\sqrt{3}$:2. Given that $\overline{AC}$ is 5, $\overline{AD}$ must be $\dfrac{5}{2}$. (The ratio 1:2 is equivalent to a ratio of $\dfrac{5}{2}$ to 5.) Next, notice that ∆ABD is a 45°-45°-90° triangle. The ratio among its sides is 1:1:$\sqrt{2}$. You know that $\overline{AD}$ is $\dfrac{5}{2}$ units in length. Thus, $\overline{BD}$ must also be $\dfrac{5}{2}$ units in length. **The correct answer is (3).**

Isosceles and Equilateral Triangles

An *isosceles* triangle has the following special properties:

1 Two of the sides are congruent (equal in length).

2 The two angles opposite the two congruent sides are congruent (equal in size or degree measure).

If you know any *two* angle measures of a triangle, you can determine whether the triangle is isosceles. Subtract the two angle measures you know from 180. If the result equals one of the other two measures, then the triangle is isosceles. For example:

> If two of the angles are 55° and 70°, then the third angle must be 55° (180 − 55 − 70 = 55). The triangle is isosceles, and the two sides opposite the two 55° angles are congruent.

If two of the angles are 80° and 20°, then the third angle must be 80° (180 − 80 − 20 = 80). The triangle is isosceles, and the two sides opposite the two 80° angles are congruent.

In any isosceles triangle, lines bisecting the triangle's three angles each bisect its opposite side. The line bisecting the angle connecting the two congruent angles divides the triangle into two congruent right triangles.

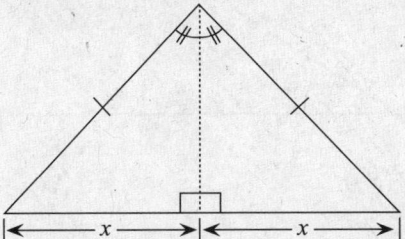

So, if you know the lengths of all three sides of an isosceles triangle, you can determine the area of the triangle by applying the Pythagorean theorem.

All **equilateral triangles** share the following three properties:

1 All three sides are congruent (equal in length).

2 The measure of each angle is 60°.

3 Area = $\dfrac{s^2\sqrt{3}}{4}$ (s = any side)

For the GED®, you won't need to know the area formula for an equilateral triangle, and the formula will NOT appear on the Formula Sheet provided during the exam. If you need to find an equilateral triangle's area but don't recall the formula, you can bisect the triangle and combine the two smaller areas. As shown below, any line bisecting one of the 60° angles divides an equilateral triangle into two right triangles with angle measures of 30°, 60°, and 90° (one of the two Pythagorean angle triplets). Accordingly, the side ratio for each smaller triangle is 1: $\sqrt{3}$:2. The area of this equilateral triangle is $\dfrac{1}{2}(2)\sqrt{3}$, or $\sqrt{3}$.

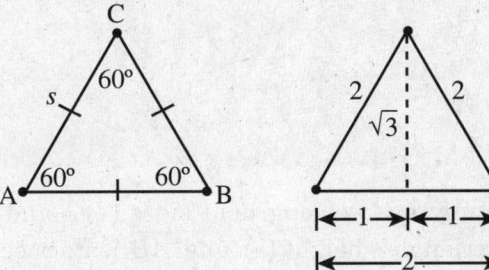

On the GED®, equilateral triangles often appear in problems involving *circles*, which you'll examine later in this review.

EXAMPLE 11 (EASIER):

As shown in the figure, $\overline{BC}$ is 6 units in length, $m\angle A = 70°$, and $m\angle B = 40°$.

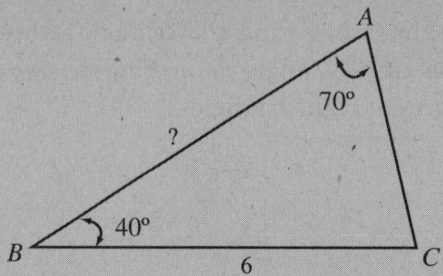

What is the unit length of $\overline{AB}$?

(1) 5

(2) 6

(3) 7

(4) $5\sqrt{2}$

(5) Not enough information is provided.

Since $m\angle A$ and $m\angle B$ add up to 110°, $m\angle C = 70°$ (70 + 110 = 180), and you know the triangle is isosceles. Since $m\angle A = m\angle C$, $\overline{AB} \cong \overline{BC}$. Given that $\overline{BC}$ is 6 units in length, $\overline{AB}$ must also be 6 units in length. **The correct answer is (2).**

EXAMPLE 12 (MORE CHALLENGING):

Two sides of a triangle are each 8 units in length, and the third side is 6 units in length. What is the area of the triangle, expressed in square units?

(1) 14

(2) $12\sqrt{3}$

(3) 18

(4) 22

(5) $3\sqrt{55}$

Bisect the angle connecting the two congruent sides ($\overline{BC}$ and $\overline{AC}$ in $\triangle ABC$ below). The bisecting line is the triangle's height (h), and $\overline{AB}$ is its base, which is 6 units long.

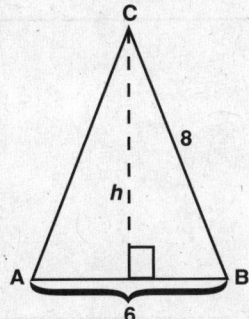

You can determine the triangle's height (h) by applying the Pythagorean theorem:

$$3^2 + h^2 = 8^2$$
$$h^2 = 64 - 9$$
$$h^2 = 55$$
$$h = \sqrt{55}$$

A triangle's area is half the product of its base and height. Thus, the area of $\triangle ABC = \frac{1}{2}(6)\sqrt{55} = 3\sqrt{55}$. **The correct answer is (5).**

QUADRILATERALS

A **quadrilateral** is any four-sided figure. The GED® emphasizes four specific types of quadrilaterals: the square, the rectangle, the parallelogram, and the trapezoid.

Rectangles, Squares, and Parallelograms

A **parallelogram** is a quadrilateral in which opposite sides are parallel. A **rectangle** is a special type of parallelogram in which all four angles are right angles (90°). A **square** is a special type of rectangle in which all four sides are congruent (equal in length). Certain characteristics apply to all rectangles, squares, and parallelograms:

- The sum of the measures of all four interior angles is 360°.

- Opposite sides are parallel.

- Opposite sides are congruent (equal in length).

- Opposite angles are congruent (the same size, or equal in degree measure).

- Adjacent angles are supplementary (their measures total 180°).

For the GED®, you should know how to determine the perimeter and area of each of these three types of quadrilaterals.

The Square

To find the perimeter of a square, multiply any side by 4. To find area, simply square any side.

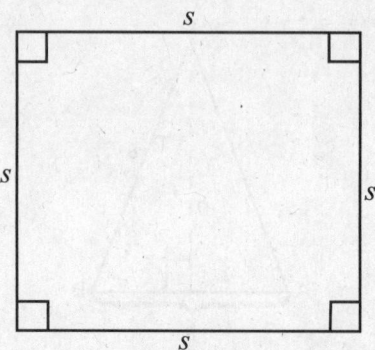

Perimeter = $4s$ [s = side]

Area = s^2

Both formulas are included on the Formula Sheet provided during the test.

GED® questions involving squares come in many varieties. For example, you might need to determine an area based on a perimeter, or you might need to do just the opposite—find a perimeter based on a given area. For example:

The area of a square with a perimeter of 8 is 4.

$s = 8 \div 4 = 2; s^2 = 4$

The perimeter of a square with area 8 is $8\sqrt{2}$.

$s = \sqrt{8} = 2\sqrt{2} ; 4s = 4 \times 2\sqrt{2}$

Or, you might need to determine a change in area resulting from a change in perimeter (or vice versa). These are just some of the possibilities.

EXAMPLE 13 (EASIER):

Nine square tiles, each with an area of 25 square centimeters, have been arranged to form a larger square. What is the perimeter of the large square?

(1) 60 centimeters

(2) 100 centimeters

(3) 150 centimeters

(4) 225 centimeters

(5) 625 centimeters

The side of each square = $\sqrt{25}$ or 5 sq. cm. Aligned to form a large square, the tiles form three rows and three columns, each column and row with side $5 \times 3 = 15$. The perimeter = $15 \times 4 = 60$. **The correct answer is (1).**

EXAMPLE 14 (MORE CHALLENGING):

If a square's sides are each increased by 50%, by what percent does the square's area increase?

(1) 75%

(2) 100%

(3) 125%

(4) 150%

(5) 200%

The easiest way to answer this question is to plug in simple numbers. Assume that the square's original side length is 1. Its area is also 1. Increase the side length to 1.5, and then square it to find the new area: $1.5 \times 1.5 = 2.25$. Comparing 1 to 2.25, the percent increase is 125%. You can also solve the problem conventionally. Letting s = the length of each side before the increase, area = s^2. Let $\frac{3}{2}s$ = the length of each side after the increase, the new area = $\left(\frac{3}{2}s\right)^2 = \frac{9}{4}s^2$. The increase from s^2 to $\frac{9}{4}s^2$ is $\frac{5}{4}$, or 125%.
The correct answer is (3).

The Rectangle

To find the perimeter of a rectangle, multiply width by 2, and multiply length by 2, and then add the two products. To find area, multiply length by width.

Perimeter = $2l + 2w$

Area = $l \times w$

Both formulas are included on the Formula Sheet provided during the test.

GED® questions involving non-square rectangles also come in many possible varieties. For example, a question might ask you to determine area based on perimeter, or vice versa. Or, a question might require you to determine a combined perimeter or area of adjoining rectangles.

EXAMPLE 15 (EASIER):

In the figure below, all intersecting line segments are perpendicular.

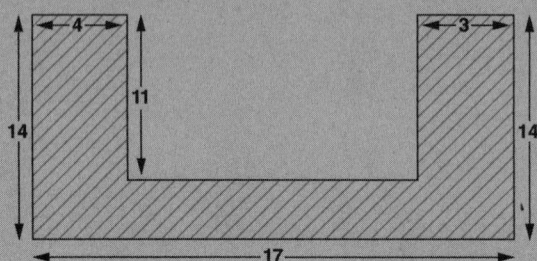

What is the area of the shaded region, in square units?

(1) 84

(2) 118

(3) 128

(4) 139

(5) 238

The figure provides the perimeters you need to calculate the area. One way to find the area of the shaded region is to consider it as what remains when a rectangular shape is cut out of a larger rectangle. The area of the entire figure without the "cut-out" is $14 \times 17 = 238$. The "cut-out" rectangle has a length of 11, and its width is equal to $17 - 4 - 3 = 10$. Thus, the area of the cut-out is $11 \times 10 = 110$. Accordingly, the area of the shaded region is $238 - 110 = 128$. **The correct answer is (3).**

Another way to solve the problem is to partition the shaded region into three smaller rectangles, as shown in the next figure, and summing up the area of each.

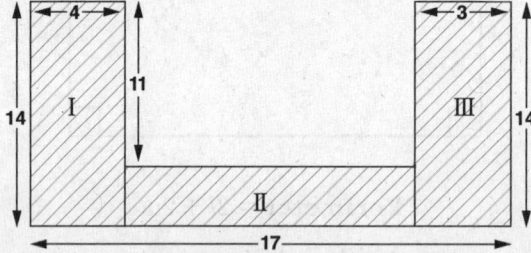

EXAMPLE 16 (MORE CHALLENGING):

The length of a rectangular closet with area 12 square meters is three times the closet's width. What is the perimeter of the closet?

(1) 10 meters

(2) 12 meters

(3) 14 meters

(4) 16 meters

(5) Not enough information is provided.

The ratio of length to width is 3:1. The ratio 6:2 is equivalent, and $6 \times 2 = 12$ (the area). Thus, the perimeter = $(2)(6) + (2)(2) = 16$. **The correct answer is (4).**

The Parallelogram

To find the perimeter of a parallelogram, multiply the width by 2, multiply the length by 2, and then add the two products. To find area, multiply the base by the **altitude,** which is the parallelogram's *height*, not the length of any side.

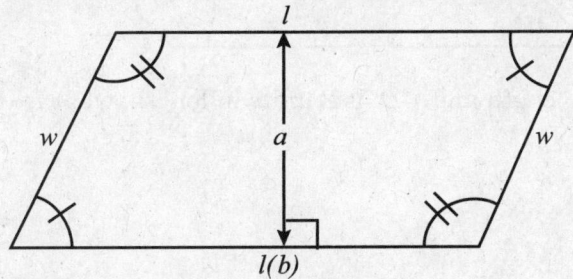

Perimeter = $2l + 2w$

Area = base $(b) \times$ altitude (a)

Of these two formulas, *only* the area formula is included on the Formula Sheet provided during the test.

A GED® question about a non-rectangular parallelogram might focus on angle measures. These questions are easy to answer. In any parallelogram, opposite angles are congruent, and adjacent angles are supplementary. (Their measures total 180°.) So, if one of a parallelogram's angles measures 65°, then the opposite angle must also measure 65°, while the two other angles each measure 115°.

A more difficult question about a non-rectangular parallelogram might focus on area. To determine the parallelogram's altitude, you might need to apply the Pythagorean theorem (or one of the side or angle triplets).

EXAMPLE 17 (EASIER):

If one of a parallelogram's interior angles measures $a°$, which of the following expresses the combined measures of its two adjacent angles?

  (1) $2a$
  (2) $2a + 90$
  (3) $180 - a$
  (4) $180 + a$
  (5) $360 - 2a$

$\angle a$ is supplementary to both its adjacent angles. Thus, the degree measure of each adjacent angle = $180 - a$. Express their sum by adding: $(180 - a) + (180 - a) = 360 - 2a$. **The correct answer is (5).**

EXAMPLE 18 (MORE CHALLENGING):

In the figure below, $\overline{AB} \parallel \overline{CD}$, $\overline{AD} \parallel \overline{BC}$, and m$\angle B = 45°$.

If $\overline{BC}$ is 4 units in length and $\overline{CD}$ is 2 units in length, what is the area of quadrilateral $ABCD$?

(1) 4

(2) $4\sqrt{2}$

(3) 6

(4) 8

(5) $6\sqrt{2}$

Since $ABCD$ is a parallelogram, its area = base (4) × altitude. To determine altitude (a), draw a vertical line segment connecting point A to $\overline{BC}$, which creates a 45°-45°-90° triangle.

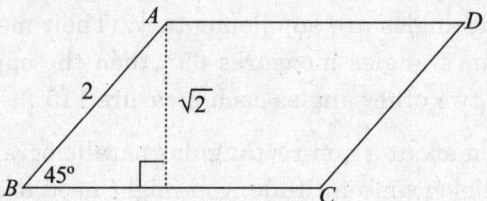

The ratio of the triangle's hypotenuse to each leg is $\sqrt{2}$:1. The hypotenuse $\overline{AB} = 2$. Thus, the altitude (a) of $ABCD$ is $\frac{2}{\sqrt{2}}$, or $\sqrt{2}$. Accordingly, the area of $ABCD = 4 \times \sqrt{2}$, or $4\sqrt{2}$. **The correct answer is (2).**

Trapezoids

A **trapezoid** is a quadrilateral with only one pair of parallel sides. All trapezoids share these four properties:

❶ Only one pair of opposite sides is parallel.

❷ The sum of all four angles is 360°.

❸ Perimeter = the sum of the four sides.

❹ Area = half the sum of the two parallel sides, multiplied by the altitude (a).

The next figure shows a trapezoid in which $\overline{BC} \parallel \overline{AD}$.

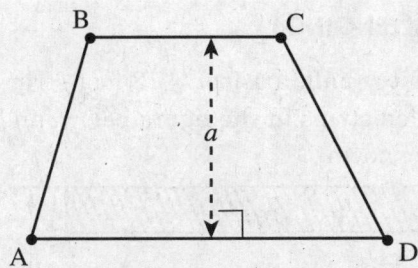

$$\text{Perimeter} = \overline{AB} + \overline{BC} + \overline{CD} + \overline{AD}$$

$$\text{Area} = \frac{\overline{BC} + \overline{AD}}{2} \times a$$

The area formula for a trapezoid is included on the Formula Sheet provided during the test.

GED® trapezoid problems generally provide all but one of the values in the area formula, and then ask for the missing value.

EXAMPLE 19 (EASIER):

A metal sheet the shape of a trapezoid is to be assembled from a square piece and a triangular piece, as shown below.

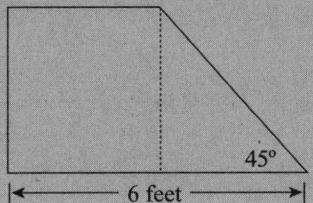

What is the area of the assembled product?

   (1) 12 square feet

   (2) $13\frac{1}{2}$ square feet

   (3) 15 square feet

   (4) $17\frac{1}{2}$ square feet

   (5) 21 square feet

To answer this question, you don't need to apply the area formula. The 45° angle tells you that the triangle's two legs are the same length, which is also the height of the square. Since the two pieces together run 6 feet in length, each piece is half that length. Thus the altitude (dotted line) is 3. The area of the square $= 3^2 = 9$. The area of the triangle $= \frac{1}{2} \times 3^2 = \frac{9}{2}$. The combined area is $13\frac{1}{2}$ square feet. **The correct answer is (2).**

EXAMPLE 20 (MORE CHALLENGING):

To cover the floor of an entry hall, a 1-foot × 12-foot strip of carpet is cut into two pieces, shown as the shaded strips in the figure below, and each piece is connected to a third carpet piece, as shown.

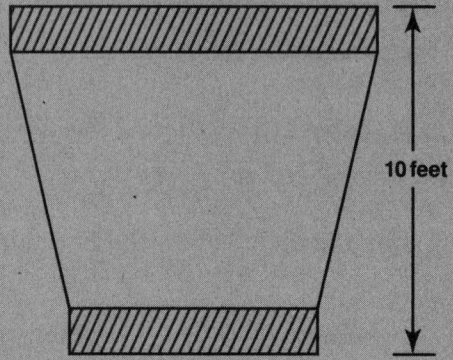

If the 1-foot strips run parallel to each other, what is the total area of the carpeted floor?

- **(1)** 46 square feet
- **(2)** 48 square feet
- **(3)** 52.5 square feet
- **(4)** 56 square feet
- **(5)** 60 square feet

The altitude of the trapezoidal piece is 8. The sum of the two parallel sides of this piece is 12' (the length of the 1' × 12' strip before it was cut). You can apply the trapezoid formula to determine the area of this piece:

$$A = 8 \times \frac{12}{2} = 48$$

The total area of the two shaded strips is 12 square feet, so the total area of the floor is 60 square feet. **The correct answer is (5).**

POLYGONS

Polygons include all two-dimensional figures formed only by line segments. For the GED®, the two most important points about polygons to remember are these two reciprocal rules:

❶ If all angles of a polygon are congruent (equal in degree measure), then all sides are congruent (equal in length).

❷ If all sides of a polygon are congruent (equal in length), then all angles are congruent (equal in degree measure).

A polygon in which all sides are congruent and all angles are congruent is called a **regular polygon.**

You can use the following formula to determine the sum of all interior angles of *any* polygon whose angles each measure less than 180° (n = number of sides):

$(n - 2)(180°)$ = sum of interior angles

This formula is NOT included on the Formula Sheet provided during the test. The test question will provide the formula if needed.

For *regular* polygons, the average angle size is also the size of every angle. But for *any* polygon (except for those with an angle exceeding 180°), you can find the average angle size by dividing the sum of the angles by the number of sides. One way to shortcut the math is to memorize the angle sums and averages for polygons with three to eight sides:

3 sides: $(3 - 2)(180°) = 180° \div 3 = 60°$

4 sides: $(4 - 2)(180°) = 360° \div 4 = 90°$

5 sides: $(5 - 2)(180°) = 540° \div 5 = 108°$

6 sides: $(6 - 2)(180°) = 720° \div 6 = 120°$

7 sides: $(7 - 2)(180°) = 900° \div 7 \approx 129°$

8 sides: $(8 - 2)(180°) = 1080° \div 8 = 135°$

You can add up known angle measures to find unknown angle measures.

EXAMPLE 21 (EASIER):

The measures of a polygon's interior angles total $(n - 2)(180°)$, where n = number of sides. If four of the interior angles of a five-sided polygon measure 100° each, what is the measure of the fifth interior angle?

(1) 40°

(2) 60°

(3) 90°

(4) 140°

(5) Not enough information is provided.

The total number of degrees in the polygon = $(5 - 2)(180°) = 540°$. The four known angles total 400°, and so the fifth angle must be 140°. **The correct answer is (4).**

EXAMPLE 22 (MORE CHALLENGING):

The regular octagon pictured below is 12 inches on each side and has been divided into 9 smaller pieces.

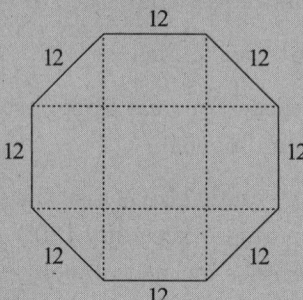

Which of the following most nearly approximates the area of the octagon?

(1) 670 square inches

(2) 790 square inches

(3) 860 square inches

(4) 1000 square inches

(5) 1150 square inches

The center segment, a square, is 12 inches on each side and thus has an area of 144 square inches. Each of the four triangles is an isosceles right triangle, with the hypotenuse given as 12 inches. The ratio of the hypotenuse's length to the length of each leg is $\sqrt{2}$:1. To determine the length of each base, divide 12 by $\sqrt{2}$. Using 1.4 as an approximate value for $\sqrt{2}$, the length of each base is approximately 8 inches. The approximate area of each triangle = $\frac{1}{2}(8)(8) = 32$ square inches. The approximate area of each of the four non-square rectangles is $8 \times 12 = 96$. Combine the approximate areas of the octagon's nine pieces:

$144 + (4)32 + 4(96) = 144 + 128 + 396$

$= 668$ square inches

Since the question asks for the closest approximation, the correct answer would then be choice (1), 670 square inches. **The correct answer is (1).**

CIRCLES

For the GED®, you should be familiar with the following basic terminology involving circles:

- **circumference:** the distance around the circle (its "perimeter")

- **radius:** the distance from a circle's center to any point along the circle's circumference

- **diameter:** the greatest distance from one point to another on the circle's circumference (twice the length of the radius)

- **chord:** a line segment connecting two points on the circle's circumference (a circle's longest possible chord is its diameter, passing through the circle's center)

As noted above, a circle's diameter is twice the length of its radius. The next figure shows a circle with radius 6 and diameter 12.

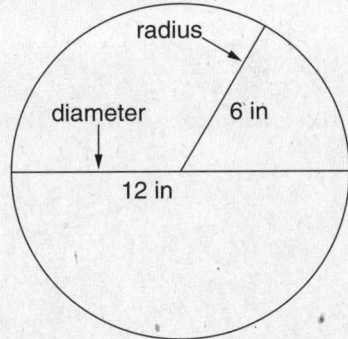

During the GED®, you'll apply one, or possibly both, of two basic formulas involving circles (r = radius, d = diameter):

> **Circumference** = $2\pi r$, or πd
>
> **Area** = πr^2

Both formulas are included on the Formula Sheet provided during the test. The value of π is approximately 3.14. The Formula Sheet will indicate this approximate value. A close fractional approximation of π is $\frac{22}{7}$.

With the circumference and area formulas, all you need is one value—area, circumference, diameter, or radius—and you can determine all the others. Referring to the circle shown above:

> Given a circle with a diameter of 12:
>> radius = 6
>>
>> circumference = 12π
>>
>> area = $\pi(6)^2 = 36\pi$

For the GED®, you won't need to work with a value of π any more precise than 3.14 or $\frac{22}{7}$. In fact, you might be able to answer a circle question using the symbol π itself, without approximating its value.

EXAMPLE 23 (EASIER):

If a circle with radius r has an area of 4 square feet, what is the area of a circle whose radius is $3r$?

    (1) 6π square feet

    (2) 36 square feet

    (3) 12π square feet

    (4) 48 square feet

    (5) 72 square feet

The area of a circle with radius $r = \pi r^2$, which is given as 4. The area of a circle with radius $3r = \pi(3r)^2 = 9\pi r^2$. Since $\pi r^2 = 4$, the area of a circle with radius $3r = (9)(4) = 36$. **The correct answer is (2).**

EXAMPLE 24 (MORE CHALLENGING):

If a circle's circumference is 10 centimeters, what is the area of the circle?

(1) $\dfrac{25}{\pi}$ cm^2

(2) 5π cm^2

(3) 22.5 cm^2

(4) 25 cm^2

(5) 10π cm^2

First, determine the circle's radius. Applying the circumference formula $C = 2\pi r$, solve for r:

$10 = 2\pi r$

$\dfrac{5}{\pi} = r$

Then, apply the area formula, with $\dfrac{5}{\pi}$ as the value of r:

$$A = \pi\left(\frac{5}{\pi}\right)^2$$

$$= \pi\left(\frac{25}{\pi^2}\right)$$

$$= \frac{25}{\pi^2} \times \frac{\pi}{1}$$

$$= \frac{25}{\pi}$$

The correct answer is (1).

Arcs and Degree Measures of a Circle

An **arc** is a segment of a circle's circumference. A **minor arc** is the shortest arc connecting two points on a circle's circumference. For example, in the next figure, minor arc $\overset{\frown}{AB}$ is the one formed by the 60° angle from the circle's center (O).

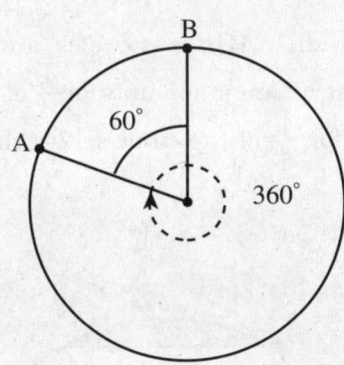

A circle, by definition, contains a total of 360°. The length of an arc relative to the circle's circumference is directly proportionate to the arc's degree measure as a fraction of the circle's total degree measure of 360°. For example, in the preceding figure, minor arc $\overset{\frown}{AB}$ accounts for $\frac{60}{360}$, or $\frac{1}{6}$, of the circle's circumference.

An arc of a circle can be defined either as a length (a portion of the circle's circumference) or as a degree measure. In the preceding figure, $\overset{\frown}{AB}$ =60°. If the circumference is 12π, then the length of minor arc $\overset{\frown}{AB}$ is $\frac{1}{6}$ of 12π, or 2π.

EXAMPLE 25 (EASIER):

Circle O has diameters $\overline{DB}$ and $\overline{AC}$, as shown in the figure below.

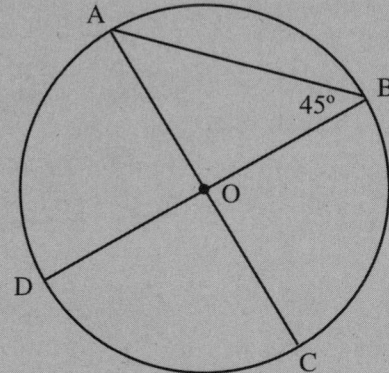

If the circumference of circle O is 12 inches, what is the length of minor arc $\overset{\frown}{BC}$?

(1) 3 inches

(2) $\frac{13}{4}$ inches

(3) $\frac{7}{2}$ inches

(4) $\frac{11}{3}$ inches

(5) 4 inches

Since $\overline{AO}$ and $\overline{BO}$ are both radii, $\triangle AOB$ is isosceles, and therefore $m\angle BAO = 45°$. It follows that $m\angle AOB = 90°$. That 90° angle accounts for $\frac{1}{4}$ of the circle's 360°. Accordingly, minor arc $\overparen{BC}$ must account for $\frac{1}{4}$ of the circle's 12-inch circumference, or 3 inches. **The correct answer is (1).**

EXAMPLE 26 (MORE CHALLENGING):

A hexagon is inscribed in a circle whose center is O, as shown below.

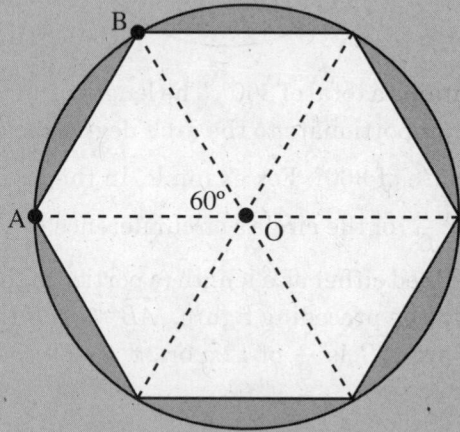

What is the unit length of $\overline{AB}$, expressed in terms of the diameter (d) of circle O?

(1) $\dfrac{d}{3}$

(2) $\dfrac{\pi}{d}$

(3) $\dfrac{d}{\pi}$

(4) $\dfrac{d}{2}$

(5) Not enough information is provided.

Since $\overline{AO}$ and $\overline{BO}$ are both radii, the 60° central angle tells you that $\triangle ABO$ is equilateral. Accordingly, the length of $\overline{AB}$ must equal the circle's radius, which is half its diameter, or $\dfrac{d}{2}$. **The correct answer is (4).**

Circles and Tangent Lines

A circle is **tangent** to a line (or line segment) if the two intersect at one and only one point (called the **point of tangency**). Here's the key rule to remember about tangents: A line that is tangent to a circle is *always* perpendicular to the line passing through the circle's center and the point of tangency.

The next figure shows a circle with center O inscribed by a square. Point P is one of four points of tangency. By definition, $\overline{OP} \perp \overline{AB}$.

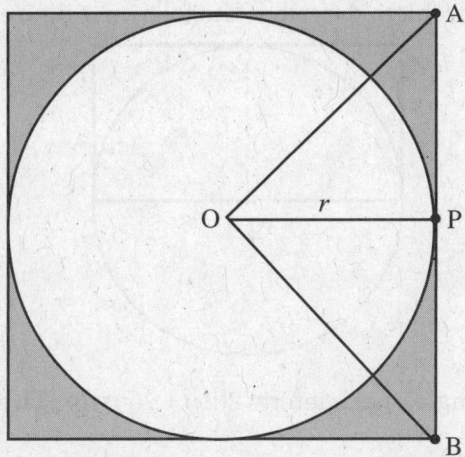

Also, notice the following relationships between the circle in the preceding figure and the inscribing square (r = radius):

Each side of the square is $2r$ in length.

The square's area is $(2r)^2$, or $4r^2$.

EXAMPLE 27 (EASIER):

Two parallel lines are tangent to the same circle. What is the shortest distance between the two lines?

(1) the circle's radius

(2) the circle's diameter

(3) the circle's circumference

(4) the product of the circle's radius and π

(5) π divided by the circle's radius

The two lines are both perpendicular to a chord that is the circle's diameter. Thus, the shortest distance between them is that diameter. **The correct answer is (2).**

EXAMPLE 28 (MORE CHALLENGING):

One side of a rectangle forms the diameter of a circle. The opposite side of the rectangle is tangent to the circle. In terms of the circle's radius (r), what is the perimeter of the rectangle?

(1) $2r$

(2) $3r$

(3) $4r$

(4) $6r$

(5) $8r$

The information in the problem describes the following figure:

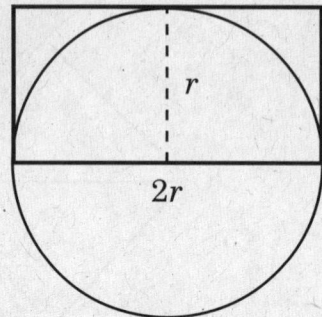

Given radius r, the rectangle's perimeter $= 2(2r) + 2(r) = 6r$. **The correct answer is (4).**

THREE-DIMENSIONAL (3-D) GEOMETRIC FIGURES

Three-dimensional (3-D) figures you might deal with on the GED® include cubes and other rectangular solids (box-shaped objects), cylinders, cones, and so-called "square" pyramids (pyramids that have a square base).

Rectangular Solids

Rectangular solids are box-shaped figures in which all corners are right angles. Any box-shaped figure has a total of six sides, or *faces*. The length of a side is generally referred to as an *edge*. A GED® question about a rectangular solid will involve one or both of two basic formulas (l = length, w = width, h = height):

Volume $= lwh$

Surface Area $= 2lw + 2wh + 2lw = 2(lw + wh + lh)$

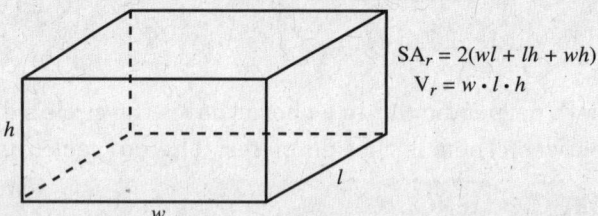

$$SA_r = 2(wl + lh + wh)$$
$$V_r = w \cdot l \cdot h$$

The volume formula is included on the Formula Sheet provided during the test.

To answer a GED® question involving a rectangular solid, plug what you know into the appropriate formula—surface area or volume—and then solve for the missing term. Depending on the question, you might need to apply both formulas.

EXAMPLE 29 (EASIER):

Which of the following does NOT describe the dimensions of a rectangular box whose capacity is 120 cubic inches?

(1) 6 inches, 6 inches, and $3\frac{1}{3}$ inches

(2) 4 inches, 8 inches, and $3\frac{3}{4}$ inches

(3) 8 inches, 2 inches, and $7\frac{1}{2}$ inches

(4) 5 inches, 10 inches, and $2\frac{2}{5}$ inches

(5) 9 inches, 5 inches, and $2\frac{1}{2}$ inches

For each answer choice, multiply the three numbers. The only product not equal to 120 is choice (5), $9 \times 5 \times 2\frac{1}{2}$, which equals $112\frac{1}{2}$. **The correct answer is (5).**

EXAMPLE 30 (MORE CHALLENGING):

A closed rectangular box with a square base is 5 inches in height. If the volume of the box is 45 square inches, what is the box's surface area?

(1) 45 square inches

(2) 66 square inches

(3) 78 square inches

(4) 81 square inches

(5) 90 square inches

First, determine the dimensions of the square base. The box's height is given as 5. Accordingly, the box's volume (45) = $5lw$, and $lw = 9$. Since the base is square, the base is 3 inches long on each side. Now you can calculate the total surface area:

$2lw + 2wh + 2lw = (2)(9) + (2)(15) + (2)(15) = 78$.

The correct answer is (3).

Cubes

A **cube** is a rectangular solid whose length, width, and height are all the same—in other words, all six faces are squares. The volume and surface-area formulas are even simpler than for other rectangular solids (let s = any edge):

volume $= s^3$, or $s = \sqrt[3]{\text{Volume}}$

surface area $= 6s^2$

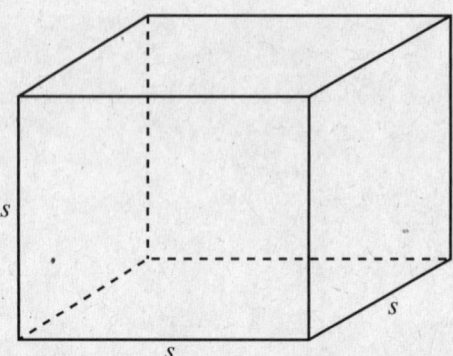

The volume formula is included on the Formula Sheet provided during the test.

GED® questions involving cubes (or other box shapes) are sometimes presented as "packing" problems. In this type of problem, your task is to determine how many small boxes fit into a larger, packing box. Another type of GED® cube question focuses on the *ratios* among the cube's linear, square, and cubic measurements.

EXAMPLE 31 (EASIER):

How many cube-shaped boxes, each box 18 inches on a side, can be packed into a storage unit measuring 6 feet long, 6 feet wide, and 5 feet high?

    (1) 32

    (2) 36

    (3) 42

    (4) 48

    (5) 64

First convert inches to feet: 18 inches $= 1\frac{1}{2}$ feet. You can pack 3 levels of 16 cube-shaped boxes, with a half-foot space left at the top of the storage unit. $3 \times 16 = 48$. **The correct answer is (4).**

EXAMPLE 32 (MORE CHALLENGING):

If the volume of one cube is 8 times greater than that of another, what is the ratio of any edge of the larger cube to any edge of the smaller cube?

    (1) 2 to 1

    (2) 4 to 1

    (3) 8 to 1

    (4) 12 to 1

    (5) 16 to 1

The ratio of the two volumes is 8:1. The edge ratio is the cube root of this ratio: $\sqrt[3]{8}$ to $\sqrt[3]{1}$, or 2:1. **The correct answer is (1).**

Cylinders

A **cylinder** is a three-dimensional figure with a circular base. The only type of cylinder a GED® question might involve is the *right* cylinder, in which the height and base are at 90° angles. The *surface area* of a right cylinder is the sum of three areas:

1 The circular base

2 The circular top

3 The rectangular surface around the cylinder's vertical face (visualize a rectangular label wrapped around a soup can)

The area of the vertical face is the product of the circular base's circumference (i.e., the rectangle's width) and the cylinder's height. The *volume* of a right cylinder is the product of the circular base's area and the cylinder's height. Given a radius r and height h of a cylinder:

Surface Area (SA) $= 2\pi r^2 + (2\pi r)(h)$

Volume $= \pi r^2 h$

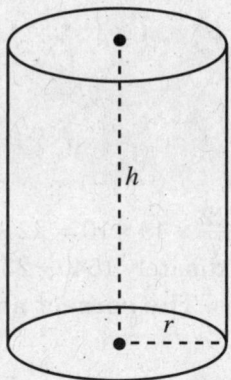

The volume formula is included on the Formula Sheet provided during the test.

A GED® cylinder problem might require little more than a straightforward application of either the surface-area or the volume formula. As with rectangular-solid questions, just plug what you know into the formula, then solve for what the question asks. A more complex cylinder problem might require you to apply other math concepts, or require you to convert one unit of measurement to another.

EXAMPLE 33 (EASIER):

What is the volume of a cylinder whose circular base has a radius of 3 centimeters and whose height is 7 centimeters?

    (1) 21π cm^3
    (2) 42π cm^3
    (3) 63π cm^3
    (4) 81π cm^3
    (5) Not enough information is provided.

The cylinder's volume = $\pi(3)^2(7) = 63\pi$ cm^3. **The correct answer is (3).**

EXAMPLE 34 (MORE CHALLENGING):

A cylindrical can with diameter 14 inches and height 10 inches is filled to one-fourth its capacity with water. Which of the following most closely approximates the volume of water in the pail? [231 cubic inches = 1 gallon]

    (1) 0.8 gallons
    (2) 1.7 gallons
    (3) 2.9 gallons
    (4) 4.2 gallons
    (5) 6.7 gallons

The volume of the pail = $\pi r^2 h \approx \frac{22}{7} \times 49 \times 10 = 22 \times 7 \times 10 = 1540$ cubic inches. The gallon capacity of the pail is approximately $1540 \div 231$, or about 6.7 gallons. One fourth of that amount is about 1.7 gallons. **The correct answer is (2).**

Cones and Pyramids

Two other three-dimensional figures you might encounter during the GED® Mathematics Test are the **cone** and the **square pyramid** (a four-sided pyramid with a square base). Both are shown below, along with their volume formulas:

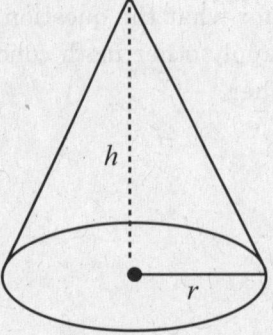 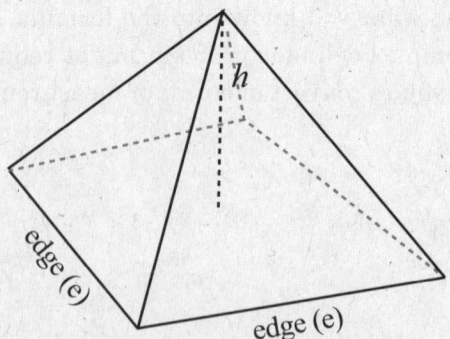

Volume of a cone: $\frac{1}{3} \times \pi \times$ radius^2 × height ($\pi \approx 3.14$)

Volume of a square pyramid: $\frac{1}{3} \times$ (base edge)^2 × height

The Formula Sheet provided during the exam includes both of these equations, so you do not need to memorize them. Notice that the volume of a cone is simply one-third that of a right cylinder, and that the volume of a square pyramid is simply one-third that of a rectangular solid.

EXAMPLE 35 (EASIER):

What is the volume of a pyramid whose height is 24 feet and whose square base measures 10 feet on each side?

   (1) 240 cubic feet

   (2) 480 cubic feet

   (3) 760 cubic feet

   (4) 800 cubic feet

   (5) 1200 cubic feet

The volume of the pyramid $= \frac{1}{3} \times \text{edge}^2 \times \text{height} = \frac{1}{3} \times 100 \times 24 = 800$ cubic feet. **The correct answer is (4).**

EXAMPLE 36 (MORE CHALLENGING):

Which of the following is nearest to the height of a cone with diameter 16 inches and volume 4480 cubic inches?

   (1) 22 inches

   (2) 36 inches

   (3) 44 inches

   (4) 56 inches

   (5) 70 inches

Given a diameter of 16, the radius is 8. Letting h = height, the cone's volume (4480) $= \frac{1}{3} \times \pi(8)^2(h) \approx \left(\frac{1}{3}\right)(3.14)(64)(h)$. Since the question asks for an approximation, try canceling out 3.14 and the denominator number 3. Solve for h:

$$4480 \approx 64h$$

$$\frac{4480}{64} \approx h$$

$$70 \approx h$$

The correct answer is (5).

RIGHT-TRIANGLE TRIGONOMETRY

Right-triangle trigonometry involves the ratios between sides of right triangles and the angle measures that correspond to these ratios. Refer to the following right triangle, in which the sides opposite angles A, B, and C are labeled a, b, and c, respectively (A and B are the two acute angles):

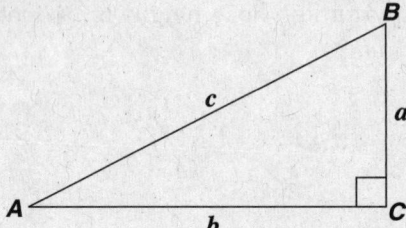

Referring to $\triangle ABC$, you express and define the six trigonometric functions sine, cosine, tangent, cotangent, secant, and cosecant for angle A as follows. Notice that each function in the right column is the *reciprocal*, or *multiplicative inverse*, of the function to the left of it.

$$\sin A = \frac{a}{c} \qquad \csc A = \frac{c}{a}$$

$$\cos A = \frac{b}{c} \qquad \sec A = \frac{c}{b}$$

$$\tan A = \frac{a}{b} \qquad \cot A = \frac{b}{a}$$

You would express and define the six functions for angle B similarly. The sine, cosine, and tangent functions are the most important ones. For the GED®, you should memorize the following three general definitions:

$$\text{sine} = \frac{\text{opposite}}{\text{hypotenuse}}$$

$$\text{cosine} = \frac{\text{adjacent}}{\text{hypotenuse}}$$

$$\text{tangent} = \frac{\text{opposite}}{\text{adjacent}}$$

These definitions will NOT be included on the Formula Sheet provided during the exam.

On the GED® you won't find any trigonometric tables, which list angle measures and their corresponding trigonometric function values. Though a question might provide specific angle measures, it's more likely that you'll express solutions to problems in terms of trigonometric functions. If the lengths of only two sides are given, you might need to use the Pythagorean theorem to find the length of the third side. For example, look at the next figure:

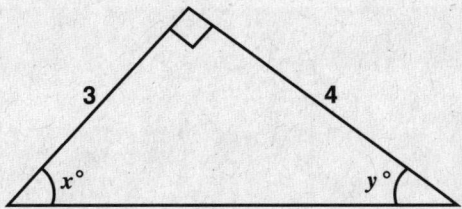

You should recognize the Pythagorean side triplet 3:4:5 in this figure ($3^2 + 4^2 = 5^2$). The length of the hypotenuse is 5. Applying the definitions of sine, cosine, and tangent to angles x and y, here are the results:

$$\sin x = \frac{4}{5} \qquad \sin y = \frac{3}{5}$$

$$\cos x = \frac{3}{5} \qquad \cos y = \frac{4}{5}$$

$$\tan x = \frac{4}{3} \qquad \tan y = \frac{3}{4}$$

For the GED®, you should also keep in mind the following trigonometric identity:

$$\text{tangent} = \frac{\text{sine}}{\text{cosine}}$$

The relationships among the sine, cosine, and tangent functions result in the following three additional observations for a triangle with acute angles A and B:

❶ By definition, $\tan A \times \tan B = 1$.

❷ For all right triangles, $\sin A = \cos B$ (and $\sin B = \cos A$). For all other triangles, $\sin A \neq \cos B$ (and $\sin B \neq \cos A$).

❸ In a right isosceles triangle (in which A and B each measures 45°), $\sin A = \sin B = \cos A = \cos B = \frac{\sqrt{2}}{2}$ (you can apply the Pythagorean theorem to show this fraction).

EXAMPLE 37 (EASIER):

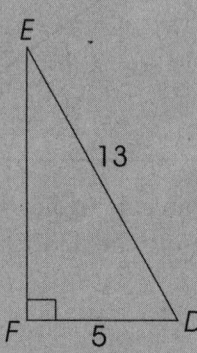

In △DEF, what is the value of tan$D$?

(1) $\frac{2}{5}$

(2) $\frac{3}{5}$

(3) $\frac{12}{13}$

(4) $\frac{12}{5}$

(5) $\frac{13}{5}$

You can find the length of $\overline{EF}$ by applying the Pythagorean theorem. Notice that the sides conform to the Pythagorean side ratio 5:12:13 ($5^2 + 12^2 = 13^2$). The length of $\overline{EF}$ = 12. In △DEF, tan $D = \dfrac{\text{opposite}}{\text{adjacent}} = \dfrac{12}{5}$. **The correct answer is (4).**

EXAMPLE 38 (MORE CHALLENGING):

A 50-foot wire is attached to the top of a vertical electric pole and is anchored on the ground. If the wire rises in a straight line at a 70° angle from the ground, what is the height of the pole, in linear feet?

(1) 50sin70°

(2) 50cos70°

(3) 50tan70°

(4) $\dfrac{\cos 70°}{50}$

(5) $\dfrac{50}{\cos 70°}$

As shown in the next figure, the height of the pole (x) is opposite the 70° angle, and the triangle's hypotenuse (length of the wire) is 50.

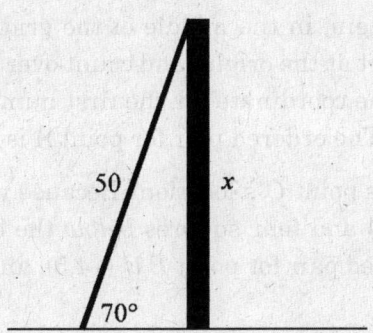

Apply the sine function: sine = opposite ÷ hypotenuse.

$\cos 70°$

$\dfrac{x}{50} = \sin 70°$

$x = 50\sin 70°$

The correct answer is (1).

COORDINATE GEOMETRY

http://bit.ly/hippo_alg30

Finding points on a plane is the study of **coordinate geometry**. A grid is commonly used to do this. The grid is divided into four sections. Each section is called a **quadrant**. The two number lines that divide the grid into quadrants are called the **x-axis** (the horizontal axis) and the **y-axis** (the vertical axis). The center of the grid, where the two axes meet, is called the **origin.** The points that are drawn on the grid are identified by **ordered pairs.** The x-coordinate is always written first. Look at the grid below.

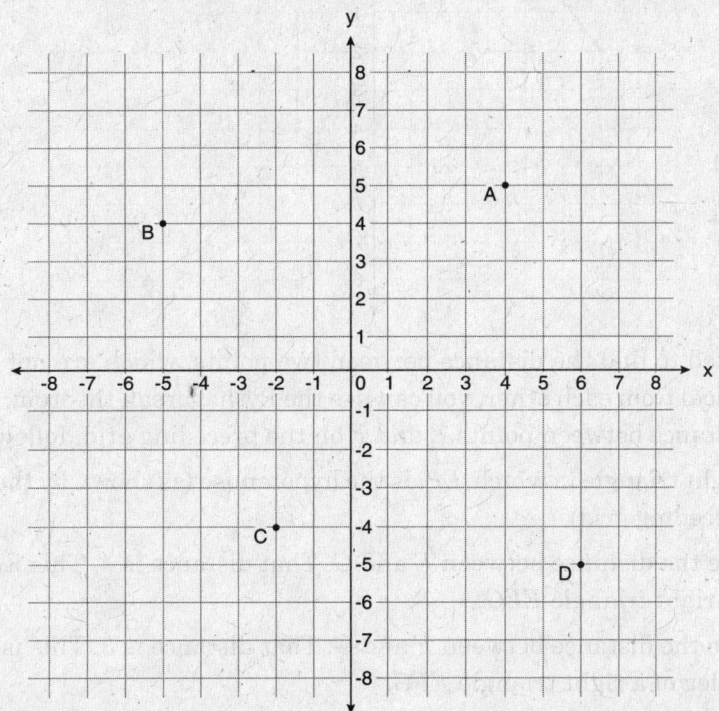

The ordered pair for the origin, in the middle of the grid, is (0,0). To determine the ordered pair for point *A*, start at the origin, and count over four squares to the right on the *x*-axis. This gives you the coordinate for the first number of the pair. Now, count up 5 squares on the *y*-axis. The ordered pair for point *A* is (4,5).

What ordered pair expresses point *C*'s location? Because you must count two squares to the *left* of the origin (0,0) and four squares *below* the origin, the ordered pair for point *C* is (–2,–4). The ordered pair for point *B* is (–4,5), and the ordered pair for point *D* is (6,–5).

Finding the Distance Between Two Points

Finding the distance between two points that are directly horizontal or vertical from each other is simply a matter of counting the number of squares that separate the points or subtracting the lesser number from the greater number. In the next grid, for example, the distance between points *A*(2,3) and *B*(7,3) is 5. The distance between points *C*(2,1) and *D*(2,–4) is also 5.

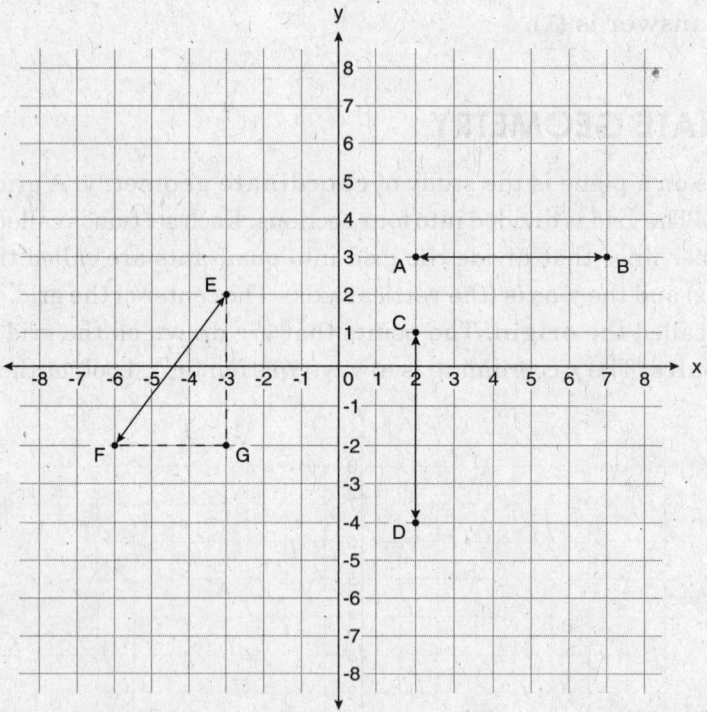

If you are asked to find the distance between two points, which are not directly horizontal or vertical from each other, you can use the Pythagorean theorem. For example, to find the distance between points *E* and *F* on the preceding grid, follow these steps:

❶ Draw a right triangle in which $\overline{EF}$ is the hypotenuse (as shown by the broken lines on the preceding grid).

❷ Determine the distance between *E* and *G*. That distance is 4. This is the length of one leg of right triangle *EFG*.

❸ Determine the distance between *F* and *G*. That distance is 3. This is the length of the other leg of a right triangle *EFG*.

❹ Apply the Pythagorean theorem to find the hypotenuse of $\triangle EFG$, which is the distance between E and F:

$$4^2 + 3^2 = c^2$$
$$16 + 9 = c^2$$
$$25 = c^2$$
$$5 = c$$

In applying the Pythagorean theorem to the coordinate grid, you may want to use the **distance formula,** which is a more specific way of expressing the theorem.

Distance between points = $\sqrt{\left(x_2 - x_1\right)^2 + \left(y_2 - y_1\right)^2}$, where the two points are (x_1, y_1) and (x_2, y_2)

The distance formula is included on the Formula Sheet provided during the exam. Apply this formula to the preceding example, and you obtain the same result:

$$\sqrt{\left(-6 - (-3)\right)^2 + \left(-2 - 2\right)^2} = \sqrt{-3^2 + (-4)^2} = \sqrt{9 + 16} = \sqrt{25} = 5$$

EXAMPLE 39 (EASIER):

On the coordinate plane, the distance between point A and point B is 8 units. If the coordinates of point A are (−4,5), which of the following CANNOT be the coordinates of point B?

   (1) (4,5)

   (2) (−4,−3)

   (3) (−12,5)

   (4) (−4,13)

   (5) (4,−3)

Points 1 and 3 are 8 units from point A, directly horizontal from point A. Points 2 and 4 are 8 units from point A, directly vertical from point A. Point 5 is diagonal to point 8 by more than 8 units. (Plotting the two points on the coordinate grid will show that the distance is greater than 8 units; there's no need to apply the distance formula.) **The correct answer is (5).**

EXAMPLE 40 (MORE CHALLENGING):

What is the distance between $(-3,1)$ and $(2,4)$ on the coordinate plane?

(1) $\sqrt{10}$

(2) 5

(3) $\sqrt{29}$

(4) $\sqrt{34}$

(5) 6

Apply the distance formula: $\sqrt{(-3-2)^2 + (1-4)^2} = \sqrt{25+9} = \sqrt{34}$. **The correct answer is (4).**

Finding the Midpoint of a Line Segment

To find the coordinates of the midpoint of a line segment, simply average the two end-points' x-values and y-values:

$$x_M = \frac{x_1 + x_2}{2} \text{ and } y_M = \frac{y_1 + y_2}{2}$$

These formulas are NOT included on the Formula Sheet provided during the test.

A GED® question might simply ask you to find the midpoint between two given points. Or, it might provide the midpoint and one endpoint, and then ask you to determine the other endpoint.

EXAMPLE 41 (EASIER):

What is the midpoint between $(-3,1)$ and $(-7,5)$ on the coordinate plane?

(1) $(5,3)$

(2) $(5,-3)$

(3) $(-5,3)$

(4) $(7,-3)$

(5) $(1,-3)$

First apply the formula to the two x-values: $\frac{-3 + (-7)}{2} = -\frac{10}{2} = -5$. Then apply the formula to the two y-values: $\frac{1+5}{2} = \frac{6}{2} = 3$. The midpoint is $(-5,3)$. **The correct answer is (3).**

EXAMPLE 42 (MORE CHALLENGING):

On the coordinate plane, the point $M(-1,3)$ is the midpoint of line segment whose endpoints are $A(2,-4)$ and B. What are the xy-coordinates of point B?

    (1) $(-1,-2)$

    (2) $(-3,8)$

    (3) $(8,-4)$

    (4) $(5,12)$

    (5) $(-4,10)$

Apply the midpoint formula to find the x-coordinate of point B:

$$-1 = \frac{x + 2}{2}$$
$$-2 = x + 2$$
$$-4 = x$$

Apply the midpoint formula to find the y-coordinate of point B:

$$3 = \frac{y + (-4)}{2}$$
$$6 = y - 4$$
$$10 = y$$

Thus, the xy-coordinates of point B are $(-4,10)$. **The correct answer is (5).**

Defining a Line on the Plane

http://bit.ly/hippo_alg26

You can define any line on the coordinate plane by the following general equation:

$$y = mx + b$$

In this equation:

    The variable m is the slope of the line.

    The variable b is the line's **y-intercept** (where the line crosses the y axis).

    The variables x and y are the coordinates of any point on the line. Any (x,y) pair defining a point on the line can substitute for the variables x and y.

http://bit.ly/hippo_alg28

Think of the **slope** of a line as a fraction in which the numerator indicates the vertical change from one point to another on the line (moving left to right) corresponding to a given horizontal change, which the fraction's denominator indicates. The common term used for this fraction is **rise-over-run**.

You can determine the slope of a line from any two pairs of (x,y) coordinates. In general, if (x_1,y_1) and (x_2,y_2) lie on the same line, calculate the line's slope according to the following formula:

$$\textbf{slope } (\boldsymbol{m}) = \frac{y_2 - y_1}{x_2 - x_1}$$

This formula is included on the Formula Sheet provided during the test.

In applying the formula, be sure to subtract corresponding values. For example, a careless test-taker calculating the slope might subtract y_1 from y_2 but subtract x_2 from x_1. Also, be sure to calculate rise-over-run, and not run-over-rise.

A GED® question might ask you to identify the slope of a line defined by a given equation, in which case you simply put the equation in the standard form $y = mx + b$, then identify the m-term. Or, it might ask you to determine the equation of a line, or just the line's slope (m) or y-intercept (b), given the coordinates of two points on the line.

EXAMPLE 43 (EASIER):

On the coordinate plane, what is the slope of the line defined by the two points $P(2,1)$ and $Q(-3,4)$?

(1) $-\dfrac{5}{3}$

(2) -1

(3) $-\dfrac{3}{5}$

(4) $\dfrac{1}{3}$

(5) Not enough information is provided.

Apply the slope formula:

slope $(m) = \dfrac{4-1}{-3-2} = \dfrac{3}{-5}$, or $-\dfrac{3}{5}$

The correct answer is (3).

EXAMPLE 44 (MORE CHALLENGING):

On the coordinate plane, at what point along the vertical axis (the y-axis) does the line passing through points $(5,-2)$ and $(3,4)$ intersect that axis?

(1) -8

(2) $-\dfrac{5}{2}$

(3) 3

(4) 7

(5) 13

The question asks for the line's y-intercept (the value of b in the general equation $y = mx + b$). First, determine the line's slope:

slope $(m) = \dfrac{y_2 - y_1}{x_2 - x_1} = \dfrac{4 - (-2)}{3 - 5} = \dfrac{6}{-2} = -3$

In the general equation ($y = mx + b$), $m = -3$. To find the value of b, substitute either (x, y) value pair for x and y, then solve for b. Substituting the (x,y) pair $(3,4)$:

$$y = -x + b$$
$$4 = -3(3) + b$$
$$4 = -9 + b$$
$$13 = b$$

The correct answer is (5).

Graphing a Line on the Plane

You can graph a line on the coordinate plane if you know the coordinates of any two points on the line. Just plot the two points, and then draw a line connecting them. You can also graph a line from one point on the line, if you also know either the line's slope or its y-intercept.

A GED® question might ask you to recognize the value of a line's slope (m) based on a graph of the line. If the graph identifies the precise coordinates of two points, you can determine the line's precise slope (and the entire equation of the line). Even without any precise coordinates, you can still estimate the line's slope based on its appearance.

Lines that slope *upward* from left to right:

- A line sloping *upward* from left to right has a positive slope (m).

- A line with a slope of 1 slopes upward from left to right at a 45° angle in relation to the x-axis.

- A line with a fractional slope between 0 and 1 slopes upward from left to right but at less than a 45° angle in relation to the x-axis.

- A line with a slope greater than 1 slopes upward from left to right at more than a 45° angle in relation to the x-axis.

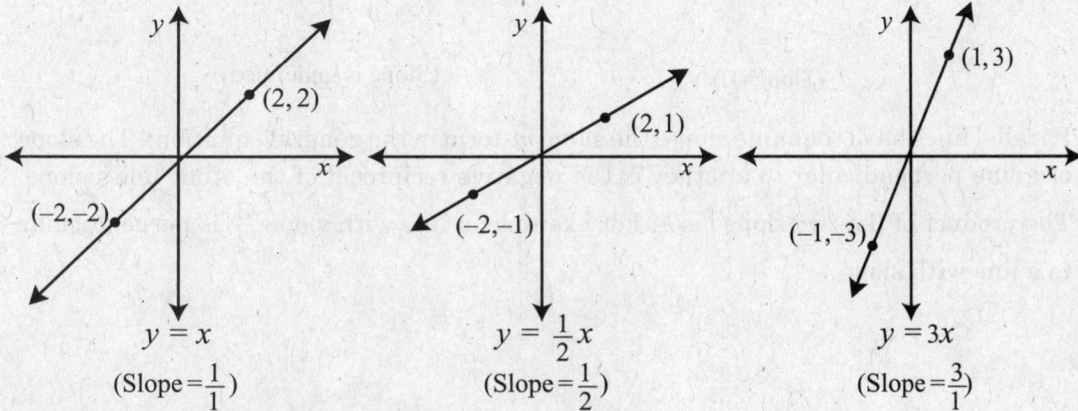

Lines that slope *downward* from left to right:

- A line sloping *downward* from left to right has a negative slope (m).

- A line with a slope of -1 slopes downward from left to right at a 45° angle in relation to the x-axis.

- A line with a fractional slope between 0 and –1 slopes downward from left to right but at less than a 45° angle in relation to the *x*-axis.

- A line with a slope less than –1 (for example, –2) slopes downward from left to right at more than a 45° angle in relation to the *x*-axis.

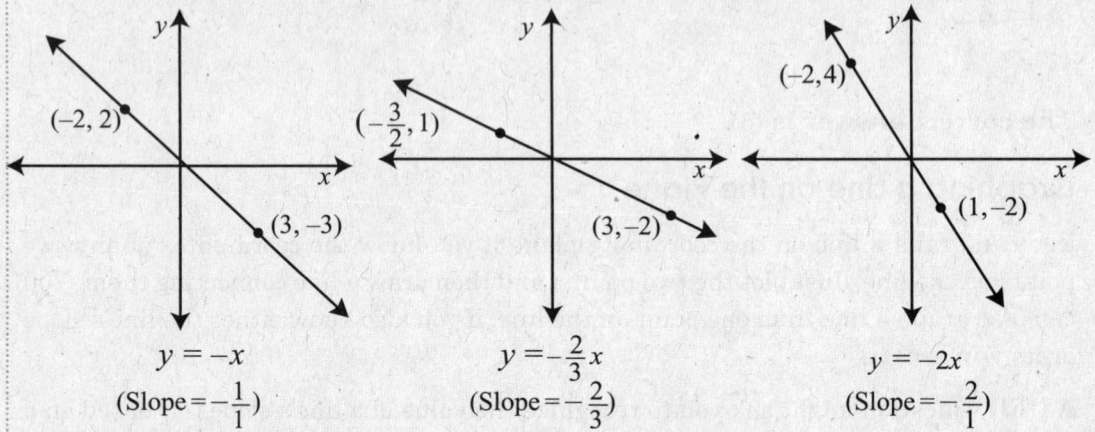

$$y = -x$$
$$\left(\text{Slope} = -\frac{1}{1}\right)$$

$$y = -\frac{2}{3}x$$
$$\left(\text{Slope} = -\frac{2}{3}\right)$$

$$y = -2x$$
$$\left(\text{Slope} = -\frac{2}{1}\right)$$

Horizontal and vertical lines:

- A *horizontal* line has a slope of zero ($m = 0$, and $mx = 0$).

- A *vertical* line has either an undefined or an indeterminate slope (the fraction's denominator is 0), so the *m*-term in the equation is ignored.

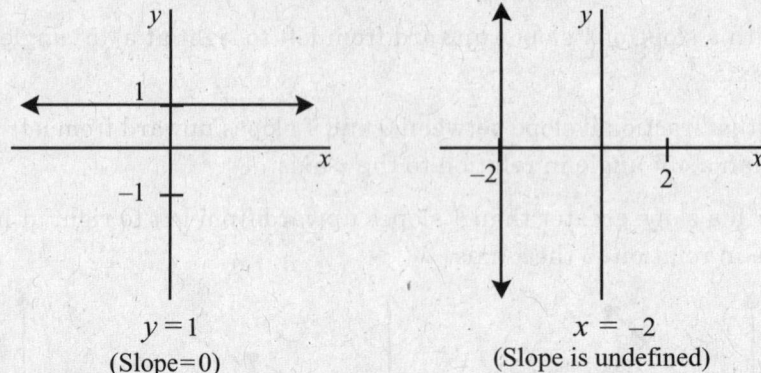

$$y = 1$$
$$(\text{Slope} = 0)$$

$$x = -2$$
$$(\text{Slope is undefined})$$

Parallel lines have the same slope (the same *m*-term in the general equation). The slope of a line perpendicular to another is the negative reciprocal of the other line's slope. The product of the two slopes is 1. For example, a line with slope $\frac{3}{2}$ is perpendicular to a line with slope $-\frac{2}{3}$.

 http://bit.ly/hippo_alg27

EXAMPLE 45 (EASIER):

Line P is shown on the coordinate plane below.

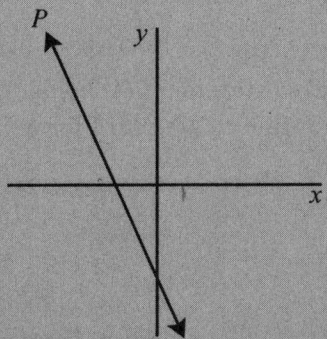

Which of the following could be the equation of line P ?

(1) $y = \dfrac{2}{5}x - \dfrac{5}{2}$

(2) $y = -\dfrac{5}{2}x + \dfrac{5}{2}$

(3) $y = \dfrac{5}{2}x - \dfrac{5}{2}$

(4) $y = \dfrac{2}{5}x + \dfrac{2}{5}$

(5) $y = -\dfrac{5}{2}x - \dfrac{5}{2}$

Notice that line P slopes downward from left to right at an angle greater than 45° in relation to the x-axis. Thus, the line's slope (m in the equation $y = mx + b$) < -1. Also notice that line P crosses the y-axis at a negative y-value (below the x-axis). The line's y-intercept (b in the equation $y = mx + b$) is negative. Only choice (5) provides an equation that meets both conditions. **The correct answer is (5).**

EXAMPLE 46 (MORE CHALLENGING):

If the equation $x = \dfrac{y + 5}{2}$ is graphed as a line on the coordinate plane, which statement about the line is accurate?

(1) The line has a slope of -2.

(2) The line crosses the y-axis at $(3,0)$.

(3) The line is vertical.

(4) The line crosses the x-axis at $(0,-5)$.

(5) The line is horizontal.

Before rewriting the equation to find the slope, quickly test the statements of choices (2) and (4) by plugging the *x*-value and *y*-value of each ordered pair into the equation. You'll see that the equation holds true for the ordered pair (0,–5):

$$0 = \frac{-5 + 5}{2}$$

(0,–5) is a point on the line, and so statement (4) holds true. If you want to test choices (1), (3), and (5), rewrite the equation in standard form:

$$x = \frac{y + 5}{2}$$
$$2x = y + 5$$
$$y = 2x - 5$$

The slope of the line is 2, and so choices (1), (3), and (5) are not accurate. **The correct answer is (4).**

SUMMING IT UP

- Geometry questions on the Mathematics Test cover the following areas: congruency and similarity; angles, parallel and perpendicular lines, and transversals; two-dimensional figures (triangles, quadrilaterals, polygons, and circles); three-dimensional figures (cubes and other rectangular solids, cylinders, cones, and square pyramids); basic right-triangle trigonometry; and coordinate geometry (points, lines, and other figures on the *xy*-coordinate plane).

- Lines and line segments are the fundamental elements for most GED® geometry problems, so it's important to be familiar with the basic rules of angles formed by intersecting lines.

- Most geometry formulas, such as the Pythagorean theorem, are included on the Formula Sheet that will be provided to you during the test. Other formulas, such as the definitions for the sine, cosine, and tangent functions, will NOT appear on the Formula Sheet, and you may want to memorize them before taking the test.

- Be sure you know the properties of all basic types of triangles. Not only will you encounter triangle problems on the GED®, you'll also need these skills for solving problems with four-sided figures, three-dimensional figures, and circles.

- For the GED®, know how to determine the perimeter and area of squares, rectangles, and parallelograms. GED® questions involving non-square rectangles may ask you to determine the area based on the perimeter, or vice versa.

- You won't need to work with a value of π any more precise than 3.14 or $\frac{22}{7}$. In fact, you might be able to answer a circle question using the symbol π itself, without approximating its value.

- Become familiar with the following basic terminology involving circles: circumference, radius, diameter, and chord. GED® circle problems typically involve other types of geometric figures as well, including triangles, squares, rectangles, and tangent lines. Learn the basics of circle problems, and you'll be a step ahead in solving the most advanced geometry problems.

- GED® questions involving cubes (or other box shapes) are sometimes presented as "packing" problems, where you need to determine how many small boxes fit into a larger, packing box. Another type of GED® cube question focuses on the *ratios* among the cube's linear, square, and cubic measurements.

- A GED® cylinder problem might require little more than a straightforward application of either the surface-area or the volume formula. As with rectangular-solid questions, just plug what you know into the formula, then solve for what the question asks.

- GED® coordinate questions involve the *xy*-plane defined by the horizontal *x*-axis and the vertical *y*-axis. You will need to know how to determine the slope of a line, so remember to calculate it as "rise over run" and not "run over rise."

PART VIII
TWO PRACTICE TESTS

Practice Test 2

DIRECTIONS FOR TAKING THE PRACTICE TEST

Directions: The GED® Practice Test has five separate subtests: Language Arts, Writing (Parts I and II); Social Studies; Science; Language Arts, Reading; and Mathematics.

- Read and follow the directions at the start of each test.

- Stick to the time limits.

- Enter your answers on the tear-out Answer Sheets provided.

- When you have completed the entire test, compare your answers with the correct answers given in the Answer Key and Explanations at the end of this Practice Test.

- Remember to check the "Are You Ready to Take the GED®?" section to gauge how close you are to mastering the GED® exam.

practice test 2

ANSWER SHEET PRACTICE TEST 2

Language Arts, Writing—Part I

1. ①②③④⑤	11. ①②③④⑤	21. ①②③④⑤	31. ①②③④⑤	41. ①②③④⑤
2. ①②③④⑤	12. ①②③④⑤	22. ①②③④⑤	32. ①②③④⑤	42. ①②③④⑤
3. ①②③④⑤	13. ①②③④⑤	23. ①②③④⑤	33. ①②③④⑤	43. ①②③④⑤
4. ①②③④⑤	14. ①②③④⑤	24. ①②③④⑤	34. ①②③④⑤	44. ①②③④⑤
5. ①②③④⑤	15. ①②③④⑤	25. ①②③④⑤	35. ①②③④⑤	45. ①②③④⑤
6. ①②③④⑤	16. ①②③④⑤	26. ①②③④⑤	36. ①②③④⑤	46. ①②③④⑤
7. ①②③④⑤	17. ①②③④⑤	27. ①②③④⑤	37. ①②③④⑤	47. ①②③④⑤
8. ①②③④⑤	18. ①②③④⑤	28. ①②③④⑤	38. ①②③④⑤	48. ①②③④⑤
9. ①②③④⑤	19. ①②③④⑤	29. ①②③④⑤	39. ①②③④⑤	49. ①②③④⑤
10. ①②③④⑤	20. ①②③④⑤	30. ①②③④⑤	40. ①②③④⑤	50. ①②③④⑤

Social Studies

1. ①②③④⑤	11. ①②③④⑤	21. ①②③④⑤	31. ①②③④⑤	41. ①②③④⑤
2. ①②③④⑤	12. ①②③④⑤	22. ①②③④⑤	32. ①②③④⑤	42. ①②③④⑤
3. ①②③④⑤	13. ①②③④⑤	23. ①②③④⑤	33. ①②③④⑤	43. ①②③④⑤
4. ①②③④⑤	14. ①②③④⑤	24. ①②③④⑤	34. ①②③④⑤	44. ①②③④⑤
5. ①②③④⑤	15. ①②③④⑤	25. ①②③④⑤	35. ①②③④⑤	45. ①②③④⑤
6. ①②③④⑤	16. ①②③④⑤	26. ①②③④⑤	36. ①②③④⑤	46. ①②③④⑤
7. ①②③④⑤	17. ①②③④⑤	27. ①②③④⑤	37. ①②③④⑤	47. ①②③④⑤
8. ①②③④⑤	18. ①②③④⑤	28. ①②③④⑤	38. ①②③④⑤	48. ①②③④⑤
9. ①②③④⑤	19. ①②③④⑤	29. ①②③④⑤	39. ①②③④⑤	49. ①②③④⑤
10. ①②③④⑤	20. ①②③④⑤	30. ①②③④⑤	40. ①②③④⑤	50. ①②③④⑤

Science

1. ①②③④⑤	11. ①②③④⑤	21. ①②③④⑤	31. ①②③④⑤	41. ①②③④⑤
2. ①②③④⑤	12. ①②③④⑤	22. ①②③④⑤	32. ①②③④⑤	42. ①②③④⑤
3. ①②③④⑤	13. ①②③④⑤	23. ①②③④⑤	33. ①②③④⑤	43. ①②③④⑤
4. ①②③④⑤	14. ①②③④⑤	24. ①②③④⑤	34. ①②③④⑤	44. ①②③④⑤
5. ①②③④⑤	15. ①②③④⑤	25. ①②③④⑤	35. ①②③④⑤	45. ①②③④⑤
6. ①②③④⑤	16. ①②③④⑤	26. ①②③④⑤	36. ①②③④⑤	46. ①②③④⑤
7. ①②③④⑤	17. ①②③④⑤	27. ①②③④⑤	37. ①②③④⑤	47. ①②③④⑤
8. ①②③④⑤	18. ①②③④⑤	28. ①②③④⑤	38. ①②③④⑤	48. ①②③④⑤
9. ①②③④⑤	19. ①②③④⑤	29. ①②③④⑤	39. ①②③④⑤	49. ①②③④⑤
10. ①②③④⑤	20. ①②③④⑤	30. ①②③④⑤	40. ①②③④⑤	50. ①②③④⑤

Language Arts, Reading

1. ① ② ③ ④ ⑤
2. ① ② ③ ④ ⑤
3. ① ② ③ ④ ⑤
4. ① ② ③ ④ ⑤
5. ① ② ③ ④ ⑤
6. ① ② ③ ④ ⑤
7. ① ② ③ ④ ⑤
8. ① ② ③ ④ ⑤
9. ① ② ③ ④ ⑤
10. ① ② ③ ④ ⑤

11. ① ② ③ ④ ⑤
12. ① ② ③ ④ ⑤
13. ① ② ③ ④ ⑤
14. ① ② ③ ④ ⑤
15. ① ② ③ ④ ⑤
16. ① ② ③ ④ ⑤
17. ① ② ③ ④ ⑤
18. ① ② ③ ④ ⑤
19. ① ② ③ ④ ⑤
20. ① ② ③ ④ ⑤

21. ① ② ③ ④ ⑤
22. ① ② ③ ④ ⑤
23. ① ② ③ ④ ⑤
24. ① ② ③ ④ ⑤
25. ① ② ③ ④ ⑤
26. ① ② ③ ④ ⑤
27. ① ② ③ ④ ⑤
28. ① ② ③ ④ ⑤
29. ① ② ③ ④ ⑤
30. ① ② ③ ④ ⑤

31. ① ② ③ ④ ⑤
32. ① ② ③ ④ ⑤
33. ① ② ③ ④ ⑤
34. ① ② ③ ④ ⑤
35. ① ② ③ ④ ⑤
36. ① ② ③ ④ ⑤
37. ① ② ③ ④ ⑤
38. ① ② ③ ④ ⑤
39. ① ② ③ ④ ⑤
40. ① ② ③ ④ ⑤

Mathematics—Part I

1. ① ② ③ ④ ⑤
2. [grid-in response]
3. ① ② ③ ④ ⑤
4. ① ② ③ ④ ⑤
5. ① ② ③ ④ ⑤
6. [grid-in response]
7. ① ② ③ ④ ⑤
8. ① ② ③ ④ ⑤

9. [grid-in response]
10. ① ② ③ ④ ⑤
11. ① ② ③ ④ ⑤
12. ① ② ③ ④ ⑤
13. ① ② ③ ④ ⑤
14. ① ② ③ ④ ⑤
15. ① ② ③ ④ ⑤
16. ① ② ③ ④ ⑤
17. ① ② ③ ④ ⑤
18. [grid-in response]

19. ① ② ③ ④ ⑤
20. ① ② ③ ④ ⑤
21. [grid-in response]
22. ① ② ③ ④ ⑤
23. ① ② ③ ④ ⑤
24. ① ② ③ ④ ⑤
25. [grid-in response]

 answer sheet

Mathematics—Part II

26. ①②③④⑤

27. ①②③④⑤

28.

29. ①②③④⑤

30. ①②③④⑤

31.

32. ①②③④⑤

33. ①②③④⑤

34.

35. ①②③④⑤

36. ①②③④⑤

37. ①②③④⑤

38. ①②③④⑤

39. ①②③④⑤

40. ①②③④⑤

41. ①②③④⑤

42. ①②③④⑤

43. ①②③④⑤

44. ①②③④⑤

45.

46. ①②③④⑤

47. ①②③④⑤

48. ①②③④⑤

49. ①②③④⑤

50. ①②③④⑤

ANSWER SHEET PRACTICE TEST 2

Language Arts, Writing—Part II Essay Test

_____

_____

_____

_____

_____

_____

_____

_____

_____

_____

_____

_____

_____

_____

_____

_____

_____

_____

_____

_____

_____

_____

answer sheet

Language Arts, Writing—Part II Essay Test (continued)

_____

_____

_____

_____

_____

_____

_____

_____

_____

_____

_____

_____

_____

_____

_____

_____

_____

_____

_____

_____

_____

_____

_____

_____

LANGUAGE ARTS, WRITING

The Language Arts, Writing Test consists of two parts. Part I is a multiple-choice section, and Part II is an essay section. You must begin with Part I.

You will have 75 minutes to work on Part I. If you finish Part I early, you can proceed to Part II right away. The total time allowed for both parts of the test is 2 hours (120 minutes).

LANGUAGE ARTS, WRITING, PART I

75 Minutes • 50 Questions

Directions: This part of the Language Arts, Writing Test consists of 50 multiple-choice questions based on documents that contain numbered sentences. After reading a document, answer the multiple-choice questions that follow it.

Some of the numbered sentences contain errors in usage, sentence structure, or mechanics (spelling, punctuation, and capitalization). Other sentences are correctly written. The best answer to a question referring to a correctly written sentence is the one that leaves the sentence unchanged. The best version of a sentence will be consistent with the rest of the document in verb tense and point of view.

The time allowed to answer all 50 questions is 75 minutes. If you finish Part I early, you may proceed immediately to Part II (the essay section).

Record your answers on the answer sheet provided.

QUESTIONS 1-8 REFER TO THE FOLLOWING PASSAGE OF TEXT.

(A)

(1) This state requires children under age 18 to wear a helmet when using a skateboard, inline or roller skates, or scooters. (2) Selecting a proper helmet is important in ensuring your child's safety when engaging in these activities.

(B)

(3) In choosing a helmet for your child, look for a helmet that are certified by the manufacturer to meet the CPSC bicycle helmet standard or the ASTM F1492 skateboard helmet standard. (4) A certified helmet will have inside it a CPSC or ASTM sticker. (5) For the safety certification to be valid, the sticker must be in the helmet.

(C)

(6) Loose helmets do not protect the head as well as securely fitting helmets. (7) The helmet should not shift in any direction when shaking your head. (8) The helmet should have a strap that forms a "Y" around each ear and a buckle that fastens securely but not too tightly. (9) Look for pads inside the helmet that you can remove and replace as needed for a secure fit. (10) When wearing the helmet, your child should be able to slide two fingers between the strap and chin.

(E)

(11) Be sure the helmet does not interfere with your child's vision, hearing, or head movement. (12) The helmet should sit low on the forehead, with the bottom edge parallel to the ground when wore flat on the head.

(F)

(13) Replace the helmet if it is damaged or whenever your child outgrows it. (14) Some manufacturers recommend replacing their helmets every five years or so.

1. Sentence 1: **This state requires children under age 18 to wear a helmet when using a skateboard, inline or roller skates, or scooters.**

   Which correction should be made to sentence 1?
   (1) replace <u>state</u> with <u>State</u>
   (2) change <u>children</u> to <u>child</u>
   (3) change <u>using</u> to <u>use</u>
   (4) insert a comma after <u>inline</u>
   (5) change <u>scooters</u> to <u>scooter</u>

2. Sentence 3: **In choosing a helmet for your child, look for <u>a helmet that are certified</u> by the manufacturer to meet the CPSC bicycle helmet standard or the ASTM F1492 skateboard helmet standard.**

   Which is the best way to write the underlined portion of sentence 3? If the original is the best way, select answer choice (1).
   (1) a helmet that are certified
   (2) a certified helmet
   (3) one that is certified
   (4) a helmet is certified
   (5) certified helmets

3. Sentence 4: **A certified helmet will have inside it a CPSC or ASTM sticker.**

   Which is the most effective version of sentence 4? If the original is the best version, select answer choice (1).
   (1) A certified helmet will have inside it a CPSC or ASTM sticker.
   (2) Inside a certified helmet will be a CPSC or ASTM sticker.
   (3) Inside it, a certified helmet have a CPSC or ASTM sticker.
   (4) A certified helmet will, inside it, have a CPSC or ASTM sticker.
   (5) A sticker will be inside a certified CPSC or ASTM helmet.

4. Which revision would improve the effectiveness of paragraph C?

   (1) move sentence 9 to follow sentence 7

   (2) move sentence 6 to follow sentence 10

   (3) move sentence 7 to follow sentence 9

   (4) remove sentence 10

   (5) move sentence 8 to follow sentence 6

5. Which sentence would be most effective if inserted at the beginning of paragraph C?

   (1) Most skateboard helmets are either CPSC or ASTM certified.

   (2) How a skateboard helmet fits is far more important than how it looks.

   (3) Price is only one factor to consider when choosing a skateboard helmet.

   (4) When choosing a helmet, you should also look for one that fits properly.

   (5) A strong strap is another feature to look for in a skateboard helmet.

6. Sentence 11: **Be sure the helmet does not interfere with your child's vision, hearing, or head movement.**

Which correction should be made to sentence 11?

   (1) change <u>does</u> to <u>will</u>

   (2) change <u>interfere</u> to <u>interfering</u>

   (3) insert the word <u>either</u> after <u>interfere</u>

   (4) insert the word <u>or</u> before <u>hearing</u>

   (5) no correction is necessary

7. Sentence 12: **The helmet should sit low on the forehead, with the bottom edge parallel to the ground <u>when wore flat</u> on the head.**

Which is the best way to write the underlined portion of sentence 12? If the original is the best way, select answer choice (1).

   (1) when wore flat

   (2) when the helmet is worn flat

   (3) wearing flat

   (4) if wearing a flat helmet

   (5) if you ware your helmet flat

8. Sentence 13: **Replace the helmet if it is damaged or whenever your child outgrows it.**

Which correction should be made to sentence 13?

   (1) change <u>is</u> to <u>was</u>

   (2) insert a comma after <u>damaged</u>

   (3) change <u>or</u> to <u>and</u>

   (4) change <u>whenever</u> to <u>when</u>

   (5) no correction is necessary

QUESTIONS 9–16 REFER TO THE FOLLOWING PASSAGE OF TEXT.

(A)

(1) Most vegetable gardeners replant their gardens every year because most such gardens consist of only annual plants. (2) But why replant your garden every year when you don't have to? (3) There are many perennials (plants that live more than two years) who produce just as much variety of nutritious and delicious produce. (4) Any vegetable gardener knows about annuals such as asparagus and rhubarb. (5) But what about perennials such as tree collards or the tree tomatoes, also known as the tamorillo?

(B)

(6) Perennials are ideal for gardeners whose time is limited for gardening. (7) Perennials are easier to mulch because they are long-term plants, and don't need weeding. (8) Perennial vines take up less space than most annuals. (9) Root crops, or tubers, is another approach to consider.

practice test

(10) Several tuber perennials are harvested in fall or winter, so your garden can provide fresh vegetables year-round.

(C)

(11) Adding perennials to a vegetable garden add beneficial vitamins and new flavors to one's diet. (12) Fewer nutrients are needed to grow them, because perennials (especially legumes) add nitrogen to the soil, whereas annuals generally don't. (14) Due to their deep root systems, many perennials are more drought tolerant than annuals. (15) Finally, killing many beneficial microbes in the soil is tilling, which perennials don't require.

9. Sentence 1: **Most vegetable gardeners replant their gardens every year because most such gardens consist of only annual plants.**

   Which is the best way to write the underlined portion of sentence 1? If the original is the best way, select answer choice (1).

   (1) because most such gardens consist of only
   (2) due to them consisting only of
   (3) because of the reason that they are strictly
   (4) for the reason that their garden consists of
   (5) since it consists of only

10. Sentence 3: **There are many perennials (plants that live more than two years) who produce just as much variety of nutritious and delicious produce.**

    Which correction should be made to sentence 3?

    (1) replace There with Their
    (2) insert a comma after perennials
    (3) insert the word will after that
    (4) change who to that
    (5) insert a comma after nutritious

11. Sentence 5: **But what about perennials such as tree collards or the tree tomatoes, also known as the tamorillo?**

    Which correction should be made to sentence 5?

    (1) insert a comma after such as
    (2) insert a comma after collards
    (3) remove the word the after or
    (4) change tomatoes to tomato
    (5) remove the word the after known as

12. Which sentence would be most effective if inserted at the beginning of paragraph B?

    (1) Legumes are an ideal example of a perennial that is both drought resistant and nutritious.
    (2) Any diet can be made more nutritious by adding perennial vegetables to it.
    (3) Perennials are perfect for people with only a small, dark patch available to garden.
    (4) A perennial garden will take up less of a gardener's time than an annual garden.
    (5) Growing perennial vegetables has several advantages over growing only annual vegetables.

13. Sentence 7: **Perennials are easier to mulch because they are long-term plants, and don't need weeding.**

    Which correction should be made to sentence 7?

    (1) change to to too
    (2) add a comma after mulch
    (3) insert the word they after and
    (4) change don't to doesn't
    (5) no correction is necessary

14. Sentence 9: **Root crops, or tubers, is another approach to consider.**

Which is the best way to write sentence 9? If the original is the best way, select answer choice (1).

(1) Root crops, or tubers, is another approach to consider.

(2) Considering root crops, or tubers, should be another approach.

(3) Root crops, or tubers, are two other approaches to consider.

(4) Planting root crops, or tubers, is another approach to consider.

(5) Root crops, or tubers, are considered to be another approach.

15. Sentence 11: **Adding perennials to a vegetable garden add beneficial vitamins and new flavors to one's diet.**

Which correction should be made to sentence 11?

(1) change <u>Adding</u> to <u>Add</u>

(2) insert a comma after <u>garden</u>

(3) insert the word <u>to</u> after <u>garden</u>

(4) change <u>add</u> to <u>adds</u>

(5) replace <u>one's</u> with <u>ones</u>

16. Sentence 15: **Finally, killing many beneficial microbes in the soil is tilling, which perennials don't require.**

The most effective revision of sentence 15 would include which group of words?

(1) finally kills many beneficial microbes

(2) don't require tilling, which kills many microbes

(3) not required by perennials if the soil is

(4) in the soil, which perennials don't require.

(5) many beneficial microbes, which kill

QUESTIONS 17–24 REFER TO THE FOLLOWING LETTER.

Mr. Jonathan Swanson
Human Resources Dept.
EnviroSafe Systems, Inc.
12270 Technology Parkway
Atlanta, GA 30301

Dear Mr. Swanson:

(A)

(1) About six months ago I met with you to discuss an employment opportunities at your company. (2) At the time, I was responding specifically to your advertised opening for Account Administrator. (3) I have not received a reply from you since our interview. (4) The resume I given you had included my relevant experience up to that time.

(B)

(5) Since our interview, I have been working part-time as a volunteer administrative assistant at Recycle the South. (6) We are a non-profit organization who's purpose is to provide recycling services, equipment, and education to businesses and consumers throughout the South (primarily Georgia, South Carolina, and Florida). (7) The enclosed resume updates my work experience to reflect this current position. (8) My function at Recycle the South is to help coordinate supporting services and supplies provided to us by a diverse group of private and public entities. (9) The specific duties and skills involved in my job at Recycle the South are described further in my current resume.

(C)

(10) With this new experience, I believe that what your organization is looking for in an administrative job candidate is exactly what I have to offer. (11) And I am free to leave my volunteer position at any time for any reason.

(D)

(12) Accordingly, if the position for which I interviewed back in June, or a similar position, become available, please contact me to arrange for another meeting. (13) As the enclosed resume indicates, I now

have a Facebook page. (14) My current contact and other information, along with my current resume, are always available at my Facebook page. (15) Note that my telephone number and email address have changed.

(E)

(16) Thank you for your time, and your consideration, I look forward to meeting with you again soon.

Sincerely,

Michael Tripp

17. Sentence 1: **About six months ago I met with you to discuss an employment opportunities at your company.**

Which correction should be made to sentence 1?

(1) remove the word with
(2) insert a comma after you
(3) remove the word an
(4) replace your with you're
(5) replace company with Company

18. Sentence 4: **The resume I given you had included my relevant experience up to that time.**

Which is the best way to write the underlined portion of sentence 4? If the original is the best way, select answer choice (1).

(1) given you had included
(2) provided you tells to you
(3) had given had provided to you
(4) provided to you included
(5) have provided was inclusive of

19. Sentence 6: **We are a non-profit organization who's purpose is to provide recycling services, equipment, and education to businesses and consumers throughout the South (primarily Georgia, South Carolina, and Florida).**

Which correction should be made to sentence 6?

(1) replace who's with whose
(2) change provide to provides
(3) insert a comma after consumers
(4) replace South with south
(5) no correction is necessary

20. Which revision would improve the effectiveness of paragraph B?

(1) move sentence 8 to follow sentence 5
(2) remove sentence 8
(3) move sentence 9 to the beginning of paragraph B
(4) remove sentence 7
(5) move sentence 7 to follow sentence 9

21. Sentence 10: **With this new experience, I believe that what your organization is looking for in an administrative job candidate is exactly what I have to offer.**

Which correction should be made to sentence 10?

(1) remove the word what
(2) remove the word in
(3) remove the word an
(4) change candidate to candidates
(5) no correction is necessary

22. Sentence 12: **Accordingly, if the position for which I interviewed back in June, or a similar position, become available, please contact me to arrange for another meeting.**

Which correction should be made to sentence 12?

(1) insert the word for after interviewed
(2) change position to positions
(3) change become to becomes
(4) change me to myself
(5) no correction is necessary

23. Sentence 16: **Thank you for your time, and your consideration, I look forward to meeting with you again soon.**

Which is the best way to write the underlined portion of sentence 16? If the original is the best way, select answer choice (1).

(1) time, and your consideration, I

(2) time and consideration, and I

(3) time and your consideration, I

(4) time and consideration, as I

(5) time, your consideration, and I

24. Which revision would improve the effectiveness of the letter?

(1) join paragraphs A and B

(2) move paragraph C to follow paragraph D

(3) join paragraphs D and E

(4) remove paragraph C

(5) join paragraphs C and D

QUESTIONS 25–34 REFER TO THE FOLLOWING DOCUMENT.

Registration Information

(A)

(1) The fastest and easiest way to register for all your classes each term through online registration. (2) Follow these four steps:

(B)

STEP 1: (3) Go to our Web site to access the online registration area of the site. (4) Click the "Register" tab.

(C)

STEP 2: (5) Click "Sign in" (see the menu on the screen's left side).

(D)

STEP 3: (6) If you have yet to created an online profile, you'll need to do that now. (7) Click the "Create profile" button and enter the information requested. (8) Be sure you wrote down the user name and password you create. (9) If you have already created a profile, type your name and password. (10) Once you sign in, click "Courses" to browse classes, or click "Search" for specific classes you wish to take.

(E)

STEP 4: (11) Add the courses you wish to take to your "Shopping Cart." (12) Complete your transaction and "Confirm" your registration. (13) Be sure to print a copy of your confirmation.

(F)

(13) You can also register in person. (14) Come to the main office before the first class meeting, where our staff will assist you in using the online registration system.

(G)

(15) Be sure to register before the first class meeting. (16) Walk-in registration is permitted only as available. (17) If you show up to class without registering beforehand, there is no guarantee you will be admitted.

(H)

(18) You can also select your classes in advance of in-person registration by consulting our printed class schedule. (19) Taking note of course names and numbers, and then fill out the "Application for Admission and Registration" form in the back of the schedule.

(I)

(20) Note that both online and in-person registration for the Spring term begins January 5th at 12:00 noon.

25. Sentence 1: **The fastest and easiest way to register for all your classes each term through online registration.**

Which correction should be made to sentence 1?

(1) insert a comma after <u>fastest</u>

(2) insert the word <u>yourself</u> after <u>register</u>

(3) insert the word <u>is</u> after <u>term</u>

(4) replace <u>through</u> with <u>threw</u>

(5) no correction is necessary

26. Sentence 3 and Sentence 4: **Go to our Web site to access the online registration area of the site. Click on the "Register" tab.**

The most effective combination of sentences 3 and 4 would begin with which group of words?

- **(1)** The registration area of our Web site
- **(2)** Click on the "Register for Classes"
- **(3)** Online registration at our Web site
- **(4)** Go to our Web site and click on
- **(5)** To access our Web site, click on

27. Sentence 6: **If you have yet to created an online profile, you'll need to do that now.**

Which correction should be made to sentence 6?

- **(1)** replace have yet to with have not yet
- **(2)** remove the comma after profile
- **(3)** insert the word so after the comma
- **(4)** replace you'll with you'd
- **(5)** remove the phrase do that

28. Sentence 8: **Be sure you wrote down the user name and password you create.**

Which is the best way to write the underlined portion of sentence 8? If the original is the best way, select answer choice (1).

- **(1)** you wrote down the user name
- **(2)** to write down the user name
- **(3)** the user name you wrote down
- **(4)** to have written your user name down
- **(5)** you had written down the user name

29. Which revision would improve the effectiveness of the Course Registration Information?

Begin a new paragraph with

- **(1)** sentence 8
- **(2)** sentence 9
- **(3)** sentence 10
- **(4)** sentence 12
- **(5)** sentence 13

30. Sentence 14: **Come to the main office before the first class meeting, where our staff will assist you in using the online registration system.**

Which is the best way to write the underlined portion of sentence 14? If the original is the best way, select answer choice (1).

- **(1)** meeting, where our staff will assist
- **(2)** meeting, our staff will assist
- **(3)** meeting. With our staff's assistance
- **(4)** meeting, where our staff assists
- **(5)** meeting. Our staff will assist

31. Sentence 17: **If you show up to class without registering beforehand, there is no guarantee you will be admitted.**

Which is the best way to write the underlined portion of sentence 17? If the original is the best way, select answer choice (1).

- **(1)** there is no guarantee you will be admitted
- **(2)** we would not guarantee to admit you
- **(3)** to admit you is no guarantee
- **(4)** admitting you is not to be guaranteed
- **(5)** there's no guaranteed admission of you

32. Sentence 19: **Taking note of course names and numbers, and then fill out the "Application for Admission and Registration" form in the back of the schedule.**

Which correction should be made to sentence 19?

(1) change <u>Taking</u> to <u>Take</u>

(2) change <u>course</u> to <u>courses</u>

(3) change <u>numbers</u> to <u>number</u>

(4) remove the <u>comma</u> after <u>numbers</u>

(5) insert a comma after <u>form</u>

33. Sentence 20: **Note that both online and in-person registration for the Spring term begins January 5th at 12:00 noon.**

Which correction should be made to sentence 20?

(1) insert a comma after <u>Note</u>

(2) remove the word <u>both</u>

(3) replace <u>Spring</u> with <u>spring</u>

(4) change <u>begins</u> to <u>begin</u>

(5) insert a comma after <u>5th</u>

34. Which revision would improve the effectiveness of the document?

(1) move paragraph F to follow paragraph G

(2) join paragraphs F and G

(3) move paragraph G to follow paragraph H

(4) move paragraph H to follow paragraph I

(5) remove paragraph I

QUESTIONS 35–42 REFER TO THE FOLLOWING PASSAGE OF TEXT.

(A)

(1) Someone once said that once you have a child your life changes forever. (2) It's true; parenthood has a way of making people grow up fast. (3) A person might have no cares one day and they are responsible for another human life the next day. (4) No one is fully prepared for the responsibility, even if they think they are.

(B)

(5) A parent is responsible for the life of another human being. (6) Parenting can be overwhelming at times. (7) Parents must feed, clothe and shelter their children as well as provide medical attention when necessary. (8) If a parent is careless, the results can be disastrous. (9) Who is there to take care of a child when a parent doesn't, maybe nobody?

(C)

(10) However, some people refuse to have children for the soul reason that they want to avoid the responsibility. (11) Just because a person doesn't have children doesn't mean that person is trying to avoid responsibility, of course. (12) Some people cannot either have children or cannot afford to. (13) Other people who have children but then shirk their responsibilities by neglecting or, even worse, abandoning them. (14) If you are truly unable to give a child proper care and attention, you should not have children in the first place. (15) But if you do, find a family member or someone else who can help take care of your child.

35. Sentence 3: **A person might have no cares one day and they are responsible for another human life the next day.**

The most effective revision of sentence 3 would include which group of words?

(1) one day. The next day they are

(2) one day but be responsible for

(3) one day might have no cares

(4) no cares one day. The next day

(5) for another human life one day

36. Sentence 4: **No one is fully prepared for the responsibility, even if they think they are.**

Which correction should be made to sentence 4?

(1) change <u>one</u> to <u>body</u>

(2) remove the comma after <u>responsibility</u>

(3) change <u>if</u> to <u>though</u>

(4) replace <u>they are</u> with <u>so</u>

(5) no correction is necessary

37. Sentence 5: **A parent is responsible for the life of another human being.**

Which revision should be made to the placement of sentence 5?

(1) move sentence 5 to follow sentence 2

(2) move sentence 5 to the end of paragraph B

(3) move sentence 5 to the end of paragraph A

(4) remove sentence 5

(5) no revision is necessary

38. Sentence 9: **Who is there to take care of a child when a parent doesn't, maybe nobody?**

If you rewrote sentence 9 beginning with

What if

the next words would probably be

(1) a child has got nobody

(2) the parent doesn't

(3) there is nobody to

(4) taking care of a child

(5) maybe nobody can

39. Which revision would improve the effectiveness of paragraph C?

(1) remove sentence 12

(2) move sentence 14 to the beginning of paragraph C

(3) move sentence 13 to flow sentence 12

(4) remove sentence 15

(5) move sentence 10 to follow sentence 12

40. Sentence 10: **However, some people refuse to have children for the soul reason that they want to avoid the responsibility.**

Which correction should be made to sentence 10?

(1) change <u>some</u> to <u>sometimes</u>

(2) change <u>to have</u> to <u>having</u>

(3) change <u>children</u> to <u>a child</u>

(4) replace <u>soul</u> with <u>sole</u>

(5) no correction is necessary

41. Sentence 12: **Some people cannot either have children or cannot afford to.**

Which is the best way to write sentence 12? If the original is the best way, select answer choice (1).

(1) Some people cannot either have children or cannot afford to.

(2) Some people cannot have children, or afford to have them.

(3) Some people either cannot have or cannot afford to have children.

(4) Having children are not possible or affordable for some people.

(5) For some people, children are not affordable, or can't have them.

42. Sentence 13: **Other people who have children but then shirk their responsibilities by neglecting or, even worse, abandoning them.**

Which correction should be made to sentence 13?

(1) remove the word <u>who</u>

(2) change <u>neglecting</u> to <u>neglect</u>

(3) remove the comma after <u>worse</u>

(4) change <u>abandoning</u> to <u>abandon</u>

(5) change <u>them</u> to <u>it</u>

QUESTIONS 43-50 REFER TO THE FOLLOWING DOCUMENT.

Planning Commission Report

(A)

(1) The Planning Commission has reviewed recommendations for improving pedestrian and motorist safety at the intersection of Regent and Madison Streets. (2) To recommend them was a citizen task force comprised of local engineers, residents and merchants.

(B)

(3) The Commission agrees that the recommendation to relocate the municipal bus stop from the south side of Regent Street to the street's opposite side. (4) A two-month study conducted by the task force provides convincing evidence that pedestrian traffic across the intersection could be reduced significantly by this change.

(C)

(5) The task force objected to a proposed redevelopment of the property at the intersection's northeast corner. (6) The task force based its objection on a concern over the safety of pedestrians walking past the garage entrance. (7) The proposal called for demolition of an existing structure and construction of a new two-story building. (8) The proposed building would consist of four lower-level retail units and five upper-level office units. (9) The structure would also include an underground parking garage for approximately 30 vehicles. (10) The task force made two alternative recommendations: a single-story retail building without parking or a municipal park.

(D)

(11) The Commission understands the safety issue concerning the proposed garage entrance. (12) However, an Environmental Impact Report on the proposed use of the property, not submitted yet, means that until then the Commission lacks the authority to issue an opinion about the proposed use.

(E)

(14) The Commission also agreed with the task force's additional recommendation, based on its two-month study, to construct a pedestrian sidewalk on the west side of Madison Street (along the east face of the building presently occupied by Smith Pharmacy). (15) We agree that the new sidewalk would further reduce pedestrian traffic across the intersection, thereby enhancing pubic safety.

(F)

(16) The Commission will submit this report to City Council for review.

43. Sentence 1: **The Planning Commission has reviewed recommendations for improving pedestrian and motorist's safety at the intersection of Regent and Madison Streets.**

    Which correction should be made to sentence 1?

    (1) change <u>has</u> to <u>having</u>
    (2) change <u>improving</u> to <u>improve</u>
    (3) change <u>motorist's</u> to <u>motorist</u>
    (4) change <u>intersection</u> to <u>intersections</u>
    (5) no correction is necessary

44. Sentence 2: <u>**To recommend them was a** citizen task force comprised of local engineers, residents and merchants.</u>

    Which is the best way to write the underlined portion of sentence 2? If the original is the best way, select answer choice (1).

    (1) Recommending them was a
    (2) The recommendation, being made by a
    (3) To make the recommendations, a
    (4) The recommendations were made by a
    (5) Having recommended them, a

45. Sentence 3: **The commission agrees that the recommendation to relocate the municipal bus stop from the south side of Regent Street to the street's opposite side.**

    Which correction should be made to sentence 3?
    (1) change <u>that</u> to <u>with</u>
    (2) change <u>from</u> to <u>on</u>
    (3) replace <u>south</u> with <u>South</u>
    (4) change <u>street's</u> to <u>streets'</u>
    (5) no correction is necessary

46. Sentence 10: **The task force made two alternative recommendations: a single-story retail building <u>without parking or</u> a municipal park.**

    Which is the best way to write the underlined portion of sentence 10? If the original is the best way, select answer choice (1).
    (1) without parking or
    (2) with no place to park
    (3) without parking, and
    (4) with no parking, also
    (5) no parking or

47. Which revision would improve the effectiveness of paragraph C?
    (1) remove sentence 5
    (2) move sentence 6 to follow sentence 9
    (3) move sentence 7 to the beginning of paragraph C
    (4) move sentence 8 to follow sentence 5
    (5) move sentence 9 to follow sentence 7

48. Sentence 12: **However, an Environmental Impact Report on the proposed use of the <u>property, not submitted yet, means that until then the</u> Commission lacks the authority to issue an opinion about the proposed use.**

    Which is the best way to write the underlined portion of sentence 12? If the original is the best way, select answer choice (1).
    (1) property, not submitted yet, means that until then the
    (2) property, which has not been submitted until the
    (3) property has not been submitted. Until it has, the
    (4) property is, so far, not submitted. Until the
    (5) property is not submitted. However, the

49. Sentence 14: **The Commission also agreed with the task force's additional recommendation, based on its two-month study, to construct a pedestrian sidewalk on the west side of Madison Street (along the east face of the building presently occupied by Smith Pharmacy).**

    Which correction should be made to sentence 14?
    (1) change <u>agreed</u> to <u>agrees</u>
    (2) replace <u>force's</u> with <u>forces</u>
    (3) remove the comma after <u>recommendation</u>
    (4) replace <u>based</u> with <u>baste</u>
    (5) remove the comma after <u>study</u>

50. Which revision would improve the effectiveness of the document?
    (1) join paragraphs A and B
    (2) move paragraph B to follow paragraph D
    (3) remove paragraph D
    (4) move paragraph D to follow paragraph E
    (5) join paragraphs D and E

LANGUAGE ARTS, WRITING, PART II

45 Minutes • 1 Essay

Directions: This part of the Language Arts, Writing Test assesses your ability to write an essay on a familiar topic. In the essay, you will present your opinion or explain your views about the assigned topic. Your essay will be evaluated based on the overall quality of your writing, including content, organization, and the clarity and correctness of your writing. You must write only about the topic provided. If you write on a different topic, your essay will not be scored, and you will have to retake both parts of the Language Arts, Writing Test.

You will have 45 minutes to plan, write, and revise your essay. You may use scratch paper for notes, outlines, or a rough draft. Write your essay on the two pages of lined paper provided. The notes you make on scratch paper will not be read or scored. Write legibly using a ballpoint pen, so that your writing can easily be read by the evaluators.

ESSAY TOPIC

Should fast-food chains provide lunches for students at high school campuses, or should only more healthful foods be offered at those campuses?

In your essay, explain your viewpoint, using your personal observations, experience, and knowledge to support your essay.

facebook.com/petersonspublishing

practice test

SOCIAL STUDIES

70 Minutes • 50 Questions

Directions: The Social Studies Test consists of multiple-choice questions involving general social studies concepts. The questions are based on brief passages of text and visual information (graphs, charts, maps, cartoons, and other figures). Some questions are based on both text and visual information. Study the information provided, and answer the question(s) that follow it, referring back to the information as needed. You will have 70 minutes to answer all 50 questions. Record your answers on the Social Studies section of the answer sheet provided.

QUESTION 1 REFERS TO THE FOLLOWING INFORMATION.

Following the conclusion of the French and Indian War in 1763, Great Britain and the American Colonies enjoyed a brief period of friendly relations. But soon Britain began to enforce restrictions on American trade, and taxes were levied on the colonists. After Americans protested, most taxes—with the exception of a few, including the tax on tea—were lifted. Tensions continued, however, and in 1770, British troops fired on a crowd in Boston, killing 5 people. On December 16, 1773, a group of colonists dressed as Indians boarded British ships and dumped chests of tea into the sea at Boston Harbor.

1. Colonists dumped chests of tea into Boston's harbor because

    (1) the British had put restrictions on American trade.

    (2) there was a tax on tea.

    (3) Britain had raised the tax on tea.

    (4) Britain had lifted the tax on tea.

    (5) British troops fired on a crowd of protesters in Boston three years earlier.

QUESTIONS 2 AND 3 REFER TO THE FOLLOWING TABLE.

IMPORTANT JOB FACTORS

Job Factor	Percentage Who Rated It "Very Important"
Open communication in company	65%
Effect of job on personal/family life	60%
Supervisor's management style	58%
Job security	54%
Job location	50%
Family-supportive policies	46%
Fringe benefits	43%
Salary/wages	35%
Management/ promotion opportunities	26%
Size of company	18%

2. Which of the following combinations might be most likely to make employees unhappy enough to consider leaving their jobs?

   (1) few management opportunities and few fringe benefits

   (2) a small number of total employees and an out-of-the-way office location

   (3) policies that are not family supportive and few fringe benefits

   (4) an uncommunicative supervisor and a company atmosphere of secrecy

   (5) lack of management opportunities and a large number of staff members

3. If you are the owner of a small business and are trying to hire a potentially valuable employee away from a large multinational competitor, what should you stress in interviews?

   (1) Salaries are competitive within the business or industry in which you operate.

   (2) The company is a growing one with ample opportunities for advancement.

   (3) No employee of the company has ever quit or been fired.

   (4) You cannot offer health coverage now, but you plan to in the near future.

   (5) You plan to move the business to a newer building with state-of-the-art features.

QUESTION 4 REFERS TO THE FOLLOWING INFORMATION.

The War Powers Act of 1973 placed the following limits on the president's use of the military:

- The president must report in writing to Congress within 48 hours after sending troops into any conflict.

- Congress then has sixty days to declare war or provide for the continued use of those troops.

- If Congress fails to provide such authorization, the president must remove the troops.

4. What is a result of the passage of the War Powers Act of 1973?

   (1) The president gained the power to declare war.

   (2) The president can commit troops to a long overseas war without the explicit approval of Congress.

   (3) The president cannot act quickly to send troops into combat in an emergency situation.

   (4) Congress can only approve combat operations lasting longer than sixty days if war is declared.

   (5) The president cannot send troops into combat overseas for more than sixty days without the approval of Congress.

QUESTIONS 5 AND 6 REFER TO THE FOLLOWING CARTOON.

5. Which statement best makes the cartoonist's point?

   (1) Poverty, drugs, and ignorance are root causes of gangs.

   (2) Gangs are the root cause of poverty, drugs, and ignorance.

   (3) Experts agree that poverty, drugs, and gangs are the major causes of ignorance.

   (4) Drugs are the major cause of gang violence.

   (5) Few people believe that poverty, drugs, and ignorance are root causes of gangs.

6. With which point of view would the cartoonist most clearly agree?

   (1) The only way to end gang violence is to eliminate poverty in our inner cities.

   (2) Gang violence can be ended only by implementing a law that puts repeat offenders in jail permanently.

   (3) Harsher criminal penalties for manufacturing illegal drugs are needed to reduce gang violence.

   (4) Only by eliminating poverty, drugs, and ignorance will we be able to end gangs and their violence.

   (5) The government has spent too much money trying to eliminate poverty and drugs.

7. When your dollar buys less in goods and services than it used to, you are experiencing the effects of monetary inflation. Among the following people, who would most immediately experience an adverse effect of inflation?

   (1) a government worker about to negotiate a new contract

   (2) an investor in enterprises involving real estate

   (3) an individual whose capital is mainly invested in common stock

   (4) a recent college graduate with little or no savings or assets

   (5) a retired individual living on a fixed pension

QUESTION 8 IS BASED ON THE FOLLOWING INFORMATION.

In the landmark Supreme Court case of *Marbury* v. *Madison* (1803), the Court held that an act of Congress in conflict with the Constitution was void and that it is the function of the Court to determine whether such a conflict exists.

8. What was the implication of *Marbury* v. *Madison*?

   (1) The Supreme Court could overrule the Constitution.

   (2) Congress had little real power.

   (3) The Constitution had to be amended.

   (4) The Constitution was no longer valid.

   (5) The Supreme Court could override acts of Congress.

QUESTIONS 9–11 REFER TO THE FOLLOWING PASSAGE AND MAP.

The world is split into 24 time zones. The four times zones for the 48 contiguous United States are shown below. Each new day begins at the International Date Line, which runs north-to-south through the Pacific Ocean—east of Asia, Australia, and New Zealand. A traveler "gains" a day by crossing the date line from east to west but "loses" a day by crossing the line from west to east. When a new day begins in the first time zone (just west of the date line), it is still the previous day in all 23 other time zones—for example, the local time would be 9:00 p.m. in Tokyo, Japan; 4:00 p.m. in Mumbai, India; 12 noon in London, England; and 7:00 a.m. in New York City.

Time Zones in the Continental United States

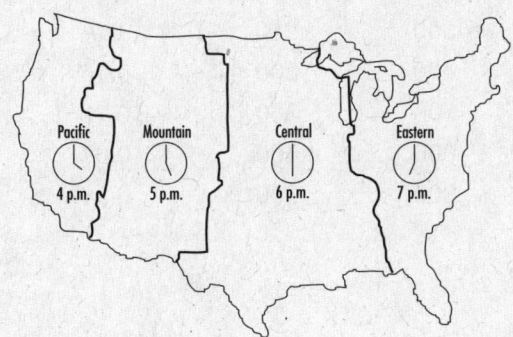

9. A government worker in Washington, D.C., has to make a phone call to a Portland, Oregon, business that opens at 9 a.m. What is the earliest time in Washington, D.C., that the government worker can reach the Portland business?

   (1) 8 a.m.

   (2) 9 a.m.

   (3) 10 a.m.

   (4) Noon

   (5) 9 p.m.

10. Each of the world's stock exchanges is open for trading during essentially the same daytime business hours, each according to its local time. Which statement CANNOT be true?

    (1) When the New York exchange opens, traders there can access all trading results from the same date at the Mumbai exchange.

    (2) The Tokyo exchange does not close until after the London exchange opens on the same date.

    (3) When the Tokyo exchange opens, traders there can access results of all trading from the previous date at the New York exchange.

    (4) The Mumbai exchange opens 17 hours before the New York exchange opens on the same date.

    (5) When the New York exchange opens, traders there know all of the previous day's activity at the Tokyo exchange.

11. Just before crossing the International Date Line traveling west to east, a sailor has set his watch to the local date as well as the local time, which is 12:30 a.m. Just after crossing the line, what date or time adjustment should the sailor make on his watch?

 (1) move the time back by one hour

 (2) move the date back by one day

 (3) move date forward by one day

 (4) make no adjustment to the time

 (5) make no adjustment to the date

QUESTION 12 REFERS TO THE FOLLOWING INFORMATION.

After World War I, President Wilson proposed the establishment of an international organization to help settle international disputes and prevent future wars. Wilson was successful in establishing the League of Nations as part of the peace treaty negotiated at the end of the war. Although the League of Nations was established in 1919, Wilson's dream was blocked when Congress refused to ratify the treaty and blocked U.S. involvement in the League. Without the United States, perhaps the world's most powerful nation at the time, the League of Nations proved ineffective and was unable to stop World War II from breaking out only 20 years later.

12. The author of the passage infers that

 (1) the Senate should not have the power to reject treaties.

 (2) the Senate should not be involved in foreign affairs.

 (3) the League of Nations would have been more successful had the United States joined.

 (4) Wilson was out of touch with the American people who did not want to become involved in European disputes.

 (5) the League of Nations was established in 1919.

QUESTIONS 13 AND 14 REFER TO THE FOLLOWING INFORMATION.

Farmers add fertilizer to improve their crops. But, if a farmer keeps increasing the amount of fertilizer, the improvement in yield will slow, and continuing to add more and more fertilizer doesn't help much. In fact, at some point, if too much fertilizer is used, the yield will decline because too much fertilizer will actually stunt growth or kill the crop. This pattern applies to all factors of production (the inputs that go into the production process). This relationship is called the Law of Diminishing Returns. The point at which the average output per unit of fertilizer starts to decline is the point of diminishing return on the investment in fertilizer.

The chart below shows how output is affected by changes in the number of workers hired at an automobile factory. Hiring more workers will increase output, but at some point simply hiring more and more workers, without expanding the factory, does not have much effect and may even cause output to fall.

XYZ AUTO FACTORY

Number of Workers	Autos Produced Weekly	Production per Worker
100	30	0.3
200	100	0.5
300	210	0.7
400	300	0.75
500	360	0.72
600	400	0.67
700	390	0.56

13. At what point does the XYZ Auto Factory begin to see diminishing returns in productivity for each new worker hired?

    (1) when more than 300 workers are hired

    (2) when more than 400 workers are hired

    (3) when more than 500 workers are hired

    (4) when more than 600 workers are hired

    (5) when more than 700 workers are hired

14. Which statement best explains the law of diminishing returns as applied to this factory?

    (1) Since the production capacity of the factory is limited by the equipment and space available, at some point simply hiring more workers doesn't do much to increase output.

    (2) Auto factories are more productive when robotic welding is used.

    (3) Hiring more workers will always increase automobile production.

    (4) Automobile companies maximize profits if they always keep workers at a minimum.

    (5) Automobile factories should never hire more than 600 workers.

QUESTION 15 REFERS TO THE FOLLOWING PASSAGE.

The men who wrote the U.S. Constitution divided the authority of the federal government into three independent branches of government: the legislative branch makes laws, the executive branch carries out the laws, and the judicial branch interprets the laws. This separation of powers prevents any one branch from gaining power over the entire federal government. Besides separating government into independent branches, the authors of the Constitution also established a system of checks and balances whereby each branch, under certain circumstances, can check the power of the other branches.

15. Which of the following is NOT an example of the system of checks and balances?

    (1) The president can veto a law passed by Congress.

    (2) State governments can overturn actions of the federal government in their states.

    (3) The Supreme Court can declare a law passed by Congress to be unconstitutional and invalidate it.

    (4) The Senate must approve top officials appointed by the president.

    (5) The Executive branch can only spend money if Congress has approved the federal budget.

practice test

QUESTION 16 REFERS TO THE FOLLOWING INFORMATION AND POLITICAL CARTOON.

Florida's ballot counts were critical in determining the outcome of the 2000 U.S. presidential election. Katherine Harris, Florida's Secretary of State at the time, halted the recounting of ballots in her state.

16. Which of the following best sums up the meaning of the cartoon?
   (1) Harris had convinced Bush to do whatever Harris wanted once he was elected.
   (2) Harris did not want more recounts because she feared Bush might lose.
   (3) Bush already knew who won the election and didn't care what Harris did.
   (4) Harris was a Democrat who wanted the election to end in defeat for Bush.
   (5) Bush had trained Harris well, and Harris was doing exactly what she was told to do.

QUESTIONS 17 AND 18 ARE BASED ON THE FOLLOWING CHARTS.

The Economy Before and After the New Deal, 1929-1941

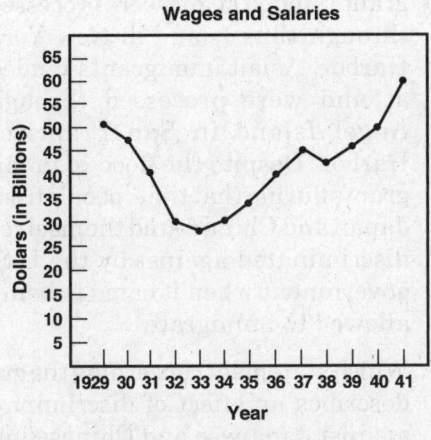

Wages and Salaries

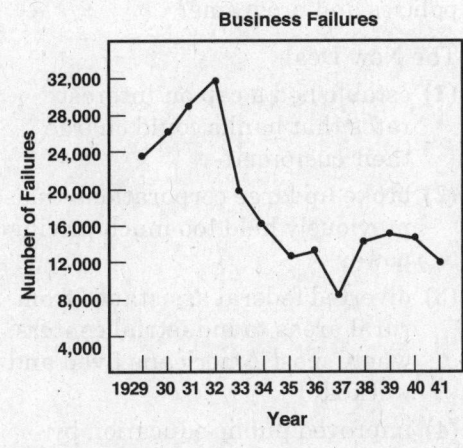

Business Failures

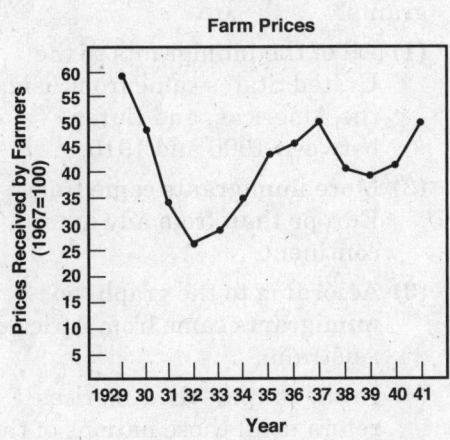

Farm Prices

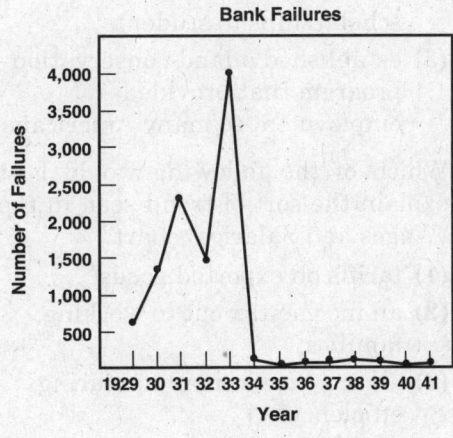

Bank Failures

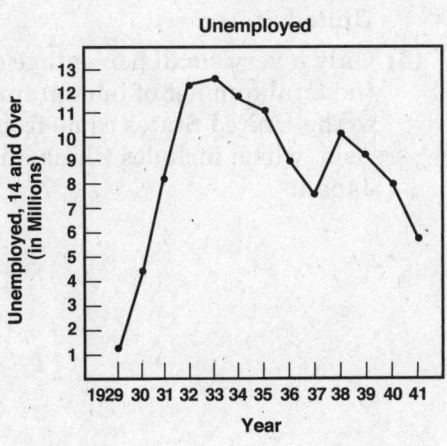

Unemployed

facebook.com/petersonspublishing

17. Based on the charts, which of the following was probably a feature of the Roosevelt Administration's New Deal policies and programs?

The New Deal

(1) established a cap on interest rates that banks could charge their customers

(2) broke up large corporations that previously held too much pricing power

(3) diverted federal assistance from rural areas to industrial centers, where most Americans lived and worked

(4) improved public education by providing need-based grants and scholarships to students

(5) established a land-conservation program that provided employment to many Americans

18. Which of the following would best explain the sort of trend seen in the "Wages and Salaries" chart?

(1) tariffs on exported goods

(2) an income-tax cut to working families

(3) an increase in manufacturing efficiency

(4) the growing labor-union movement

(5) federal insurance to protect bank deposits

QUESTIONS 19–21 ARE BASED ON THE FOLLOWING GRAPH AND TEXT.

Immigration to the United States, 1900–1910

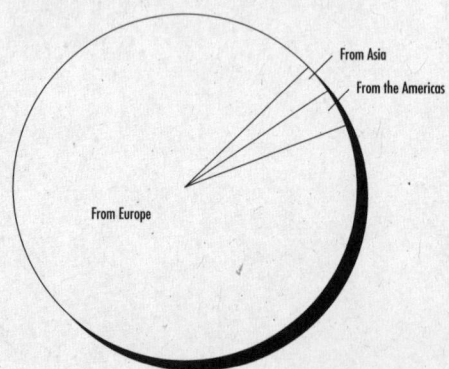

The early 1900s were a time when most immigrants traveled by boat to the United States. European immigrants landed at and were processed through Ellis Island in New York Harbor. Asian immigrants landed at and were processed through Angel Island in San Francisco Harbor. Despite the flood of immigrants during that time, people from Japan and China found themselves discriminated against by the U.S. government when it came to being allowed to immigrate.

19. Which statement concerning the graph describes an effect of discrimination against Japanese and Chinese immigrants?

(1) All of the immigrants to the United States came from Asia, the Americas, and Europe between 1900 and 1910.

(2) More immigrants came from Europe than from any other continent.

(3) According to the graph, no immigrants came from Africa or Australia.

(4) In the graph, "the Americas" refers to all those nations of the Western Hemisphere except the United States.

(5) Only a very small percentage of the total number of immigrants to the United States came from Asia, which includes China and Japan.

20. Based on the information in the graph and text, which of the following statements is true?

(1) Many more immigrants were processed through Ellis Island than through Angel Island in the early 1900s.

(2) Asian immigrants were often forced to live at Angel Island for several months when they first arrived.

(3) Ellis Island was the port of entry for passengers who did not travel first class.

(4) Immigrants at both Ellis Island and Angel Island had to pass brief medical examinations.

(5) Most immigrants from the rest of the Americas were refused entry to the United States between 1900 and 1910.

21. Racial tensions that characterized the aftermath of the Civil War in the United States probably had what effect on immigration to the United States between 1900 and 1910?

These tensions led to

(1) the United States' foreign policy of isolationism

(2) a near complete absence of immigration from Africa

(3) a reluctance by Asian immigrants to move to the United States

(4) more job opportunities for immigrants from the Americas

(5) more extensive immigration from Northern Europe

QUESTION 22 REFERS TO THE TABLE BELOW.

U.S. Federal Spending, Fiscal Year (FY) 2011
(in billions of dollars)

Category	Amount	Percentage of Total
Social Security	$ 725	20%
Medicare and Medicaid	$ 835	23%
Student Loans, Veteran's Benefits, and Other Mandatory Spending	$ 465	13%
Defense Spending	$ 700	19%
All Other Federal Programs	$ 646	18%
Interest on the Federal Debt	$ 227	6%
TOTAL	$3598	

[Note: Due to rounding to the nearest whole percentage point, breakdowns by percentage often don't add up to exactly 100%.]

practice test

22. Which one of the following categories accounted for the most spending by the federal government in FY 2011?

(1) Social Security

(2) Defense spending

(3) Interest on the Federal Debt

(4) Medicare and Medicaid

(5) Student Loans, Veteran's Benefits, and Other Mandatory Spending

QUESTIONS 23 AND 24 REFER TO THE FOLLOWING CARTOON.

23. Which statement best describes the idea that the artist who drew the cartoon was trying to convey?

(1) Repeat offenders are a problem in American society.

(2) Parole boards should carry malpractice insurance as doctors do.

(3) Only high wage earners such as doctors can afford to carry malpractice insurance.

(4) Parole boards should be held more accountable for those they release from prison.

(5) Parole boards should have more minority members.

24. If this cartoonist could speak to the parole board, what would he probably ask them to do?

(1) be less lenient with probable repeat offenders

(2) spend more time reviewing each case

(3) grant paroles to first-time offenders only

(4) convince lawmakers to make more funds available for new prisons

(5) grant parole more often to drug dealers

QUESTIONS 25 AND 26 REFER TO THE FOLLOWING ILLUSTRATION.

Latitude and Longitude

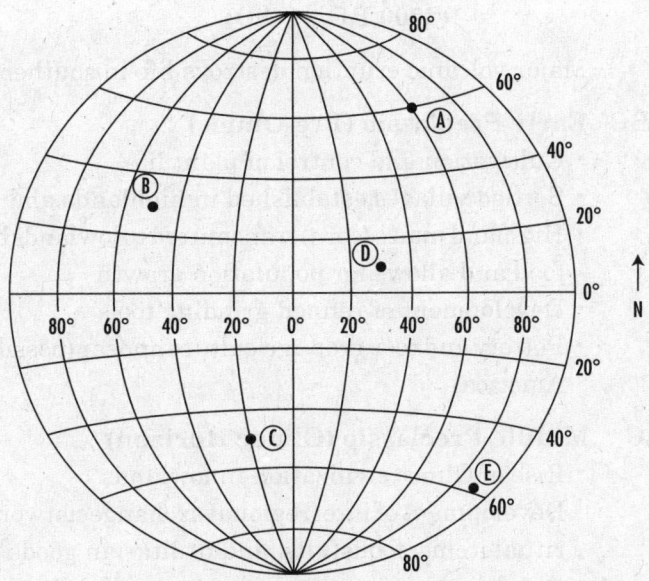

25. According to the illustration of the grid of Earth's latitude and longitude lines, which point lies at latitude 60° South and longitude 85° East?

    (1) Point A
    (2) Point B
    (3) Point C
    (4) Point D
    (5) Point E

26. What direction is point D from point A?

    (1) Southwest
    (2) Northeast
    (3) North
    (4) Southeast
    (5) West

27. A nation's power and influence in the world is a product of not only its tangible assets—for example, its mineral resources—but also its intangible assets, which cannot be quantified but which can nevertheless be of great value.

    Which of the following is an intangible component of a nation's power?

    (1) the number of troops in the army
    (2) national will and patriotism
    (3) economic productivity and growth rates
    (4) trade balance with other countries
    (5) Gross Domestic Product (GDP)

MESOAMERICA: PRECLASSIC (FORMATIVE) PERIOD

(2500 BC – 1 AD)

3000 BC — Major volcanic eruption destroys life in southern regions

2500 BC–1250 BC   Early Preclassic (Pre-Olmec)
- Cultivation and control of plant life
- Settled villages established in highlands and lowlands
- Highland maize (corn) transmitted to lowlands becomes staple food and allows for population growth
- Development of refined grinding tools
- Pottery and root-crop agriculture appear (possibly from South America)

1250 BC–400 BC   Middle Preclassic (Olmec Horizon)
- Rise of Olmec civilization in lowlands
- Development of interregional exchange networks to circulate ritual items, foodstuffs, and utilitarian goods
- Development of wealth, power, and well-defined class structure
- Development of craft specialization

400 BC–1 AD   Late Preclassic (Epi-Olmec)
- Collapse of Olmec civilization
- Rise of the two regional centers of Cuicuico and Teotihuacan
- Development of hydraulic irrigation, calendar system, and writing system
- Regional ceremonial centers become social and religious hubs
- Elaborate tombs, burial mounds, and pyramids suggest complex stratified society
- Widespread distribution of ceramic pottery (features of classic Mayan art style already identifiable)

---

28. Which activity would NOT have characterized life in Mesoamerican during the early Preclassic period?
- **(1)** grinding corn
- **(2)** making simple pottery
- **(3)** regional travel
- **(4)** building pyramids
- **(5)** growing crops

29. When did the rise of the Mayan civilization in Mesoamerica occur?
- **(1)** before the Preclassic period
- **(2)** during the Early Preclassic period
- **(3)** during the Middle Preclassic period
- **(4)** during the Late Preclassic period
- **(5)** following the Late Preclassic period

QUESTION 30 IS BASED ON THE FOLLOWING INFORMATION.

One role of the Federal Reserve Bank (called the "Fed") is to keep the banking system healthy. The Federal Reserve clears checks between banks, provides short-term loans to banks, and serves as a lender-of-last resort if a bank is in danger of collapse. Through the interest rates the Federal Reserve charges for its loans to banks (called the "discount rate"), it strongly influences the interest rates banks charge on loans to their customers.

30. What would be an immediate effect of the Fed lowering the discount rate?

   (1) More banks would fail.

   (2) Banks would increase the rates of interest they pay on savings accounts.

   (3) The interest rate the bank charges on loans to its customers would decrease.

   (4) Banks would make fewer loans to their customers.

   (5) The nations' economic growth would slow.

QUESTION 31 IS BASED ON THE FOLLOWING INFORMATION.

In American history, the majority of conflicts between Native Americans and European settlers and their descendents developed as a result of U.S. government attempts to move Native Americans to reservations. The battle at South Dakota's Wounded Knee (1890), during which nearly 200 Sioux Indians were killed, is generally considered the last major battle in this long series of conflicts.

For seventy days in 1973, 200 members of the American Indian Movement (AIM) occupied Wounded Knee, which is located near the Pine Ridge reservation, consistently one of the poorest counties in the nation. A standoff between U.S. marshals and the occupiers turned bloody. In support of the protesters, actor Marlon Brando famously refused to appear at the Academy Awards that year to accept his best-actor award. In his place, a Sioux Indian woman made a speech calling the world's attention to the protesters' cause.

31. Based on the information provided, what assumption can reasonably be made regarding the occupation at Wounded Knee?

   (1) The protestors wanted to return to the days before the Sioux were defeated in the Battle of Wounded Knee.

   (2) The protestors wanted to expand the Pine Ridge Reservation.

   (3) The protesters wanted to establish Wounded Knee as a national historic site in order to encourage tourism.

   (4) The protesters wanted to get media attention to draw attention to the unjust treatment of Native Americans.

   (5) The protesters wanted Native Americans to return to their reservations.

QUESTION 32 REFERS TO THE FOLLOWING INFORMATION.

The beginning of the twentieth century saw more reform in many areas of life in the United States. Under the administration of Teddy Roosevelt, trusts, or combinations of companies that reduced competition, came under increasing government scrutiny.

32. The scrutiny described in the previous paragraph was a response to which of the following?
   (1) an era of big business
   (2) a time of war and strife
   (3) a constitutional amendment
   (4) a series of natural disasters
   (5) a presidential scandal

QUESTIONS 33 AND 34 ARE BASED ON THE FOLLOWING MAP.

Major Events in North America and Southwest Asia, 1979-1990

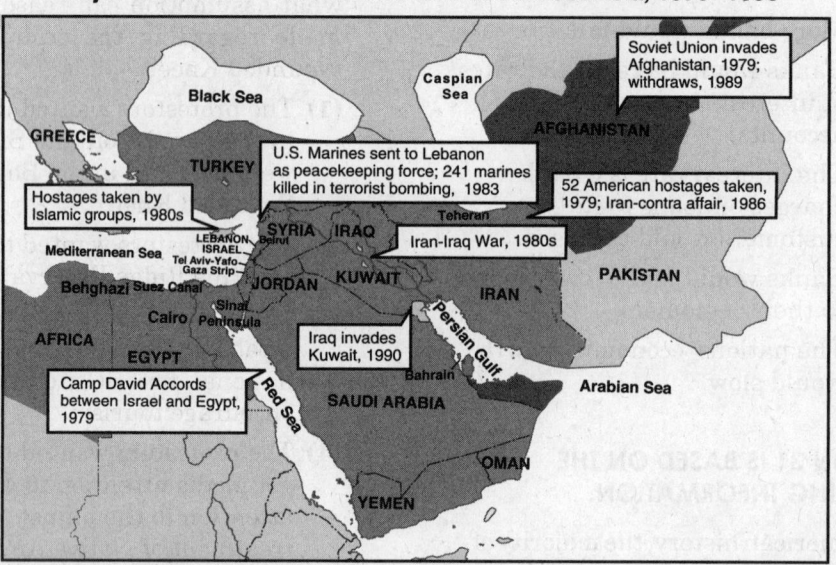

33. Based on the map, which of the following is most accurate?
   (1) Iran was the Middle Eastern country most hostile toward the United States during the 1980s.
   (2) Afghanistan was the only Middle Eastern nation to be invaded by an aggressor during the 1980s.
   (3) The Middle East was a relatively peaceful region during the 1980s.
   (4) There was no time during the 1980s when the entire Middle East region was without war or armed conflict.
   (5) The United States and Soviet Union managed to stay out of affairs in the Middle East during the 1980s.

34. During the 1990s and the 2000s, the Iranian government supported various Palestinian terrorist groups focused on the destruction of Israel and on replacing Israel with an Islamic Palestinian state.

   What does Iran's support of the terrorism described above suggest?

   (1) Religious doctrine plays a significant role in Iran's foreign policy.

   (2) Iran hopes to acquire all territory between its western border and Israel.

   (3) The Camp David accord of 1979 did not achieve an enduring peace.

   (4) Iran's enemies probably instigated the taking of hostages in Lebanon.

   (5) The war between Iran and Iraq never truly ended.

QUESTIONS 35–37 ARE BASED ON THE FOLLOWING PASSAGE.

   Although the American people cast their votes for the president, it is a special group of 538 people, called electors, who actually select the president. The Constitution gives each state the same number of electors as it has senators and representatives in Congress. The smallest states, with 2 senators and only one representative, get 3 electoral votes. The more populous states get more electoral votes; for example, California gets 55 electors.

   The candidate who gets the most votes in each state generally gets all of the state's electoral votes. Only Nebraska and Maine do not have this winner-take-all rule; they award some of their electoral votes on the basis of which candidate wins in each congressional district.

   A majority (270 electors) of electors is needed to select a president. If there is a tie or if there are 3 or more candidates and no one of them gets a majority, the president is selected by the House of Representatives with each state getting one vote.

35. When does the House of Representatives select the president?

   (1) anytime there are 3 or more candidates getting electoral votes

   (2) only when there is a tie in the electoral vote

   (3) when the electors can't agree on which candidate won in each state

   (4) when no candidate gets a majority of the popular vote nationwide

   (5) when no candidate gets a majority of the electoral votes

36. Which one of the following is NOT a result of the winner-take-all system for awarding electoral votes?

   (1) Electoral votes, not the popular vote, determine the president.

   (2) Candidates focus on the "swing" states where a small shift in voters could change the electoral vote.

   (3) Candidates ignore states where polls show they are almost certain to win or lose because shifting a few votes in these states will not make a difference in the electoral vote.

   (4) A candidate could be chosen president by the electors even though he/she lost the popular vote.

   (5) Third-party candidates are almost always shut out of the electoral college.

37. Which of the following is an argument for changing the current system of having the 538 electors choose the president?

 (1) The nation is a union of states, not individuals, so each state should decide which candidate it wants to support and then unite behind that choice.

 (2) The 538 presidential electors almost always choose the candidate who got the most popular votes.

 (3) Recounting ballots nationwide would be difficult in a close election; we need a system that won't require this.

 (4) The Constitution is a sacred document and should not be changed.

 (5) In a modern democracy, the president should be chosen by the people rather than by special electors who may or may not make the same choice as the people.

QUESTION 38 IS BASED ON THE FOLLOWING INFORMATION.

At the height of the civil rights movement in the 1960s, Dr. Martin Luther King, Jr., as head of the Southern Christian Leadership Conference, delivered a speech in which he stated:

"The whirlwind of revolt will continue to shake the foundation of our nation until the bright day of justice emerges. But that is something that I must say to my people who stand on the warm threshold which leads into the palace of justice. In the process of gaining our rightful place we must not be guilty of wrongful deeds. Let us not seek to satisfy our thirst for freedom by drinking from the cup of bitterness and hatred."

38. What did Dr. Martin Luther King, Jr. recommend as a means of attaining civil rights?

 (1) establishing black-only communities

 (2) relying on one's faith in God

 (3) passive resistance

 (4) forming an all-black militia

 (5) inciting social upheaval

QUESTION 39 REFERS TO THE FOLLOWING INFORMATION.

The Fourteenth Amendment to the U.S. Constitution states in part:

"All persons born or naturalized in the United States, and subject to the jurisdiction thereof, are citizens of the United States and of the State wherein they reside. No State shall make or enforce any law which shall abridge the privileges or immunities of citizens of the United States; nor shall any State deprive any person of life, liberty, or property, without due process of law; nor deny to any person within its jurisdiction the equal protection of the laws. . . ."

39. Which of the following would NOT be a violation of the Fourteenth Amendment?

 (1) A state restricts the right to vote to persons born in the United States.

 (2) A state passes a law that its state police do not need to obtain search warrants to search the homes of citizens not born in the United States.

 (3) A state passes a law allowing low-income African Americans and Hispanics—but not other poor people—to get reduced tuition at state universities.

 (4) A state outlaws casino gambling for all its citizens.

 (5) A state prohibits African American citizens from buying handguns.

QUESTION 40 REFERS TO THE FOLLOWING INFORMATION.

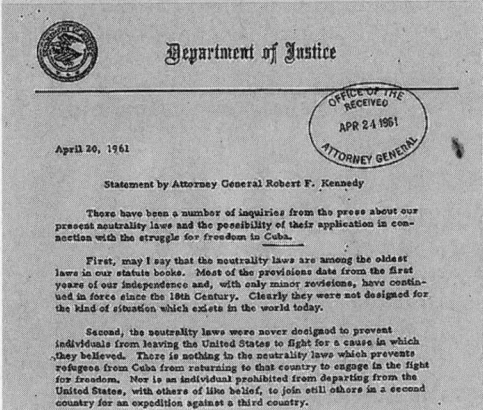

In April of 1961, with support from U.S. government's armed forces, a U.S.-trained force of Cuban exiles invaded Cuba to overthrow Fidel Castro's government but was quickly defeated by Soviet-bloc trained Cuban forces. Days after the failed "Bay of Pigs" invasion, U.S. Attorney General Robert Kennedy stated that longstanding U.S. neutrality laws "clearly . . . were not designed for the kind of situation which exists in the world today." As a result of the invasion, Castro sought protection against the Unites States from the Soviet Union, which suggested placing nuclear weapons in Cuba to ensure its security.

40. What did Kennedy's statement suggest about U.S. foreign policy?
    (1) The United States would never again support an invasion of Cuba.
    (2) The United States would use any means it could to overthrow dictatorships.
    (3) New weapons technology had necessitated a shift in U.S. foreign policy.
    (4) Any nation threatening the United States would be subject to U.S. nuclear attack.
    (5) Going forward, the United States would deal with its enemies diplomatically.

QUESTIONS 41–43 REFER TO THE FOLLOWING INFORMATION.

Aristocracy: government in which a small, privileged, hereditary group governs

Constitutional monarchy: government in which the real power is held by an elected parliament or congress but documents recognize a hereditary ceremonial king or queen

Dictatorship: government in which an individual and a small, trusted group of followers have all the power, usually to the detriment of the majority of citizens

Direct democracy: government in which all eligible citizens are entitled to participate in the process of making laws and setting policy

Representative democracy: government in which freely elected representatives of the great mass of citizens make laws and set policy

41. Why do people in the United States tend to oppose dictatorships?

    (1) The United States has never been governed by a dictatorship.

    (2) Most known dictatorships have operated to the detriment of the majority of their citizens.

    (3) Most people in the United States know little about forms of government other than democracy.

    (4) Dictatorships often deny equal trading rights in their nations to U.S. companies.

    (5) Most Americans have a basic belief in the rights of all people to have a say in their government.

42. What is the likely reason that the United States is a representative democracy and not a direct democracy?

    The nation's founders believed that

    (1) the country was too large for a direct democracy to function properly

    (2) aristocrats can make better decisions than common people

    (3) England's constitutional monarchy was oppressive

    (4) most people are not capable of understanding the lawmaking process

    (5) very few people are eligible to serve in Congress

43. Which of the following high school scenarios is most analogous to an aristocracy?

    An intramural sport in which

    (1) the team coach sets the practice schedule and appoints a captain to report absenteeism

    (2) co-captains for one round choose other team member as leaders for the next round

    (3) the only rule is that the last person left standing wins

    (4) all team members vote on their practice and tournament schedule, and what color uniforms they should wear

    (5) a team with a faculty advisor selects their own coach and practice schedule

QUESTION 44 REFERS TO THE FOLLOWING INFORMATION.

In June of 1991, Mount Pinatubo in the Philippines began one of the most violent volcanic eruptions of the twentieth century. The eruption created more than 60,000 refugees, many of them farmers and their families. The U.S. government sent $400 million in aid to help these people, but Philippine officials used much of the money to build four-lane highways and tall buildings in the capital city. This situation shows the needs to incorporate penalties into government grants to foreign countries so that the money is spent as it was intended.

44. Which statement best summarizes the position of the author of the paragraph?

    (1) The governments of poor countries should not be building four-lane highways and tall buildings.

    (2) The U.S. government needs to establish and enforce regulations on how foreign governments spend U.S. aid money.

    (3) Local officials can better select the projects that should be funded than foreign governments.

    (4) The U.S. government should not give money to foreign governments.

    (5) Penalties for spending U.S. aid money in a way that was not intended do not work.

QUESTION 45 REFERS TO THE FOLLOWING INFORMATION.

The 1930s saw the migration of hundreds of thousands from the U.S. prairie states such as Texas and Oklahoma westward, especially to California. Over-farming without taking adequate precautions against erosion had turned millions of acres to dust, and severe drought conditions transformed the entire prairie into a great "Dust Bowl" for much of the decade.

45. Why did so many prairie-state farming families migrate westward during the 1930s?

Their migration was mainly owing to

(1) insufficient demand for the crops they grew

(2) the promise of riches out west, especially in California

(3) the depletion of government farm subsidies

(4) inhospitable living conditions

(5) Native American efforts to reclaim their lands

QUESTIONS 46 AND 47 REFER TO THE FOLLOWING INFORMATION.

Deposits of Fertilizer Minerals

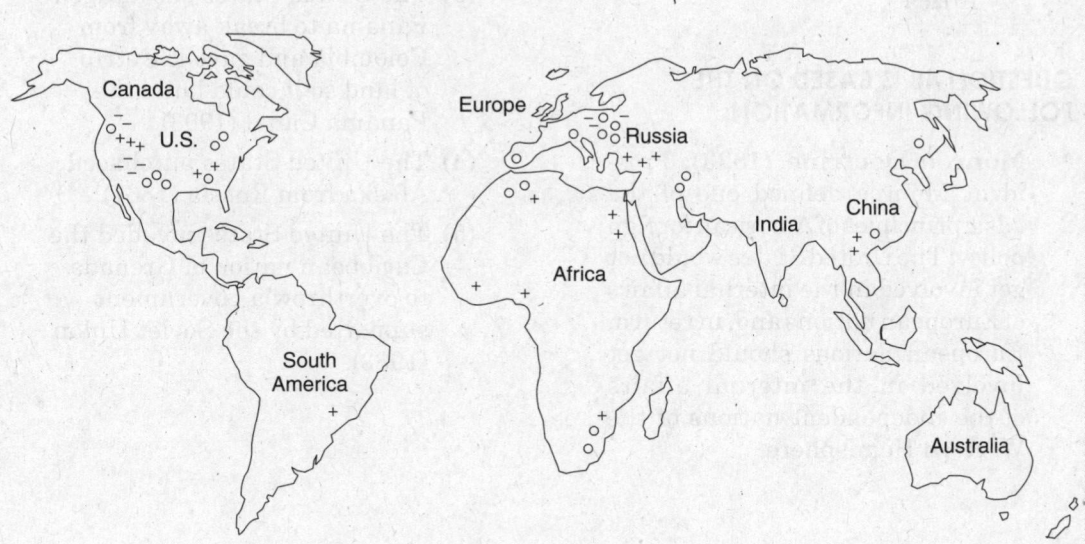

+ Phosphates

- Potash

○ Sulfer

practice test

46. Which area produces the least amount of fertilizer minerals?

  (1) South America

  (2) Australia

  (3) Africa

  (4) Russia

  (5) China

47. Based on the illustration, what can be inferred about potash?

Potash is

  (1) in greater supply worldwide than sulfur

  (2) the key ingredient of most fertilizers

  (3) found mainly near certain northern latitudes

  (4) important in providing the world's food supply

  (5) critical to the economy of South Africa

QUESTION 48 IS BASED ON THE FOLLOWING INFORMATION:

Monroe Doctrine (1823): President Monroe defined one of the basic principles of American foreign policy: The United States would not get involved in the internal affairs of European nations and, in return, European nations should not get involved in the internal affairs of the independent nations of the Western Hemisphere.

Roosevelt Corollary to the Monroe Doctrine (1904): President Theodore Roosevelt agreed with the Monroe Doctrine but went further, saying that the United States reserved the right to intervene in the internal affairs of other nations of the Western Hemisphere, especially when doing so would prevent European nations from intervening in the internal affairs of the nations of North and South America.

48. Which one of the events below was a violation of the Monroe Doctrine/Roosevelt Corollary?

  (1) France invaded Mexico and put in place a government favorable to France (1861).

  (2) Chile gained independence from Spain (1818).

  (3) The United States encouraged Panama to break away from Colombia and gave it a strip of land so it could build the Panama Canal (1903).

  (4) The United States purchased Alaska from Russia (1867).

  (5) The United States invaded the Caribbean nation of Grenada to overthrow a government supported by the Soviet Union (1983).

QUESTIONS 49 AND 50 REFER TO THE FOLLOWING GRAPH.

Federal Spending on Education, 1965 and 1971

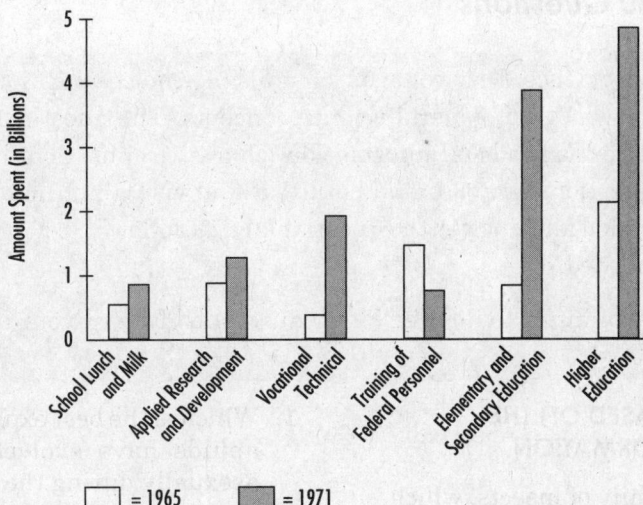

☐ = 1965   ▨ = 1971

49. According to the graph, for which category did spending decline between 1965 and 1971?

(1) school lunch and milk

(2) applied research and development

(3) vocational technical

(4) training of federal personnel

(5) elementary and secondary education

50. Which of the following statements does the information in the graph verify?

(1) Applied research and development accounted for a relatively small part of the overall education budget in both 1965 and 1971.

(2) The food served in most school lunch rooms did not adequately meet federal nutrition guidelines.

(3) The federal government spent a relatively small portion of its funds on education in both 1965 and 1971.

(4) In 1971, most Americans believed federal funds for education were not being wisely spent.

(5) The percent of American college students who were African-American was greater in 1971 than in 1965.

SCIENCE

80 Minutes • 50 Questions

Directions: The Science Test consists of multiple-choice questions designed to measure your knowledge of general science concepts. The questions are based on brief passages of text and visual information (charts, graphs, diagrams, and other figures). Some questions are based on both text and visual information. Study the information provided and answer the question(s) that follow it, referring back to the information as needed.

You will have 80 minutes to answer all 50 questions. Record your answers on the answer sheet provided.

QUESTION 1 IS BASED ON THE FOLLOWING INFORMATION.

The aphid family of insects, which is found throughout the world, spreads diseases to host plants and thus is widely considered to be destructive pests. During the autumn, when environmental conditions turn unfavorable to aphids, females produce eggs that hatch both male and female aphids, which then reproduce sexually. The genetic traits of this generation of aphids combine randomly, and with so many offspring the chances are very high that some will be hearty enough to survive the harsh fall and winter seasons. Eggs that are laid during the winter and that hatch in the spring, when environmental conditions turn favorable to the aphid population, produce only female offspring. In the absence of males, these female offspring then reproduce asexually. This form of reproduction occurs at a much quicker rate than sexual reproduction does.

1. Which is the best explanation for why aphids have evolved to reproduce asexually during the spring season?

   (1) During the spring, much of the male aphid population is lost due to the use of pesticides.

   (2) Most of the eggs produced during the winter season never hatch offspring.

   (3) Environmental conditions during the spring and summer support a large aphid population.

   (4) Male aphids typically survive a harsh winter season, whereas female aphids do not.

   (5) Spring is the only season of the year during which aphids can reproduce.

QUESTIONS 2 AND 3 REFER TO THE FOLLOWING CHART.

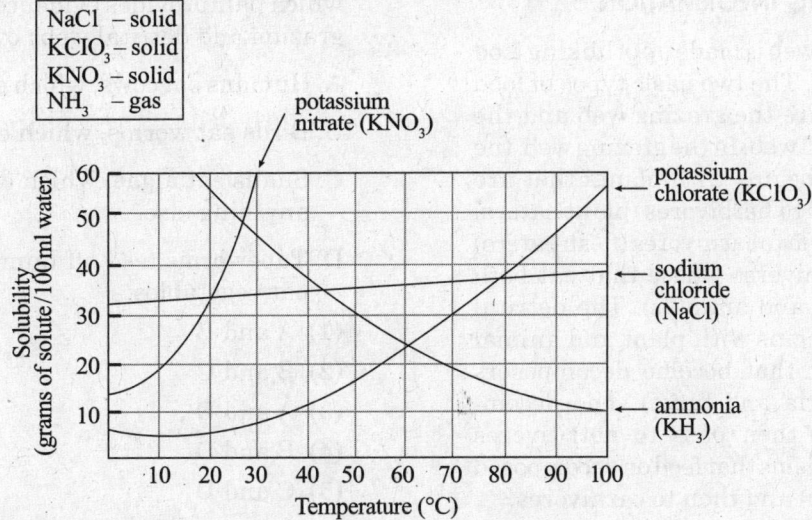

NaCl	– solid
KCIO$_3$	– solid
KNO$_3$	– solid
NH$_3$	– gas

2. A 20°C solution containing 100 ml of water and 15 grams of potassium nitrate (KNO$_3$) is heated to 25°C. Approximately how much more KNO$_3$ must be added to reach the saturation point—at which no more KNO$_3$ can be dissolved?

   (1) 0 grams
   (2) 15 grams
   (3) 30 grams
   (4) 45 grams
   (5) 55 grams

3. Which conclusion is best supported by the chart?

   (1) The solubility of ammonia is unpredictable.
   (2) The solubility of a solid increases as temperature decreases.
   (3) Ammonia is soluble at any temperature.
   (4) The solubility of a gas varies inversely with temperature.
   (5) Solids are soluble, but gases are not.

QUESTIONS 4 AND 5 REFER TO THE FOLLOWING INFORMATION.

A food web is made up of linking food chains. The two basic types of food webs are the grazing web and the detrital web. In the grazing web, the chain begins with plants that are passed to herbivores (plant eaters) and then to carnivores (flesh eaters) or omnivores (those that eat both plants and animals). The detrital web begins with plant and animal matter that become decomposers (bacteria and fungi). The decomposers then pass to detritivores (organisms that feed on decomposed matter) and then to carnivores.

4. Among the following statements, which pair provides evidence that the grazing and detrital webs overlap?

A. Humans eat cows, which eat grass.

B. Birds eat worms, which eat fungi.

C. Snails eat algae, which do not eat anything else.

D. Tapeworms feed off humans, who eat vegetables.

(1) A and B

(2) B and C

(3) A and D

(4) B and D

(5) C and D

5. What does the fact that tigers have no natural predators imply?

(1) Tigers are not part of any food chain.

(2) Tigers are at the top of a grazing food chain.

(3) Tigers are part of a food chain but not a food web.

(4) Tigers are at the top of a detrital food chain.

(5) Tigers are at the bottom of a grazing food chain.

QUESTION 6 REFERS TO THE FOLLOWING GRAPHIC.

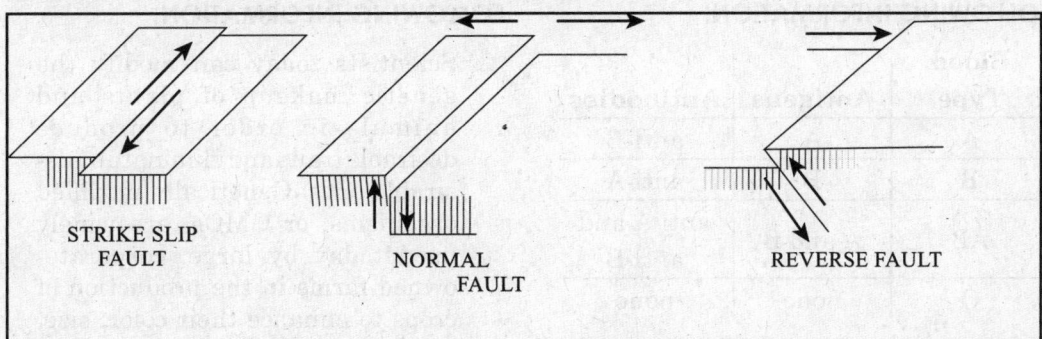

STRIKE SLIP FAULT

NORMAL FAULT

REVERSE FAULT

6. Which of the three types of faults can create a mountain range?

(1) only a normal fault

(2) either a normal or reverse fault

(3) only a reverse fault

(4) either a normal or strike-slip fault

(5) either a reverse or strike-slip fault

7. Energy can be stored or transferred, but it cannot be lost. Allison and Brian are holding the two ends of a rope. Allison then begins shaking her end of the rope up and down to create waves, which travel one after another toward Brian.

If Brian holds his end of the rope still, without allowing his arm to move, what will occur when the first wave reaches Brian?

(1) The wave's energy will be absorbed into Brian's body.

(2) Some wave energy will be reflected back toward Allison.

(3) Each successive wave will carry more energy.

(4) Allison will receive the same wave force that Brian received.

(5) All wave energy created by Allison will disappear.

practice test

QUESTION 8 IS BASED ON THE FOLLOWING INFORMATION.

Blood Type	Antigens	Antibodies
A	A	anti-B
B	B	anti-A
AB	A and B	anti-A and anti-B
O	none	none

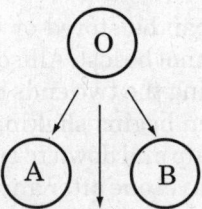

Blood types are differentiated according to which of two antigen types (A or B) the blood contains. When blood of one type is introduced into blood of a different type, antibodies (either anti-A anti-B) that are present in the one type but not the other will react with the foreign antigens, resulting in dangerous clumping of the blood.

8. Which would probably be a dangerous blood transfusion?

   (1) Blood type B introduced to blood type AB

   (2) Blood type A introduced to blood type AB

   (3) Blood type O introduced to blood type A

   (4) Blood type O introduced to blood type AB

   (5) Blood type AB introduced to blood type B

QUESTIONS 9 AND 10 REFER TO THE FOLLOWING INFORMATION.

Scientists today can modify the genetic makeup of plants and animals in order to produce desirable traits and eliminate undesirable ones. Genetically modified organisms, or GMOs, are widely used today by large, corporate-owned farms in the production of crops to enhance their color, size, and vitamin content, as well as to make crops more resistant to pests, disease, and severe weather conditions. Opponents of these so-called "Frankenfoods" point out that farm and migratory animals will often refuse to eat genetically altered feed, and they fear that GMO foods may cause cancer in humans. A large agribusiness company behind the development of many GMOs reports, however, that its own scientific studies show no incidence of cancer in humans or other animals resulting from the ingestion of genetically modified foods.

9. What is a possible criticism of the GMO studies conducted by the agribusiness corporations?

   (1) They started with a hypothesis that they were determined to show as true.

   (2) Their studies focused only on animals, and not plants.

   (3) They failed to account for other possible causes of cancer in humans.

   (4) They did not compare the health effects of genetically modified foods to those of organic foods.

   (5) They were not government-sponsored and therefore are not reliable.

10. GMO critics also worry that modified genes could spread to other plants, with potentially disastrous consequences for their ecosystems. In waging this criticism, what sort of scenario might these critics have in mind?

    (1) a genetically mutated "superweed" that comes to dominate an entire biome

    (2) small farmers in impoverished countries driven to ruin by agribusiness

    (3) the escalation of world hunger due to genetically modified famine rations

    (4) contamination of water supplies needed to support human communities

    (5) the spread of disease that a GMO was intentionally engineered to prevent

QUESTION 11 REFERS TO THE FOLLOWING INFORMATION.

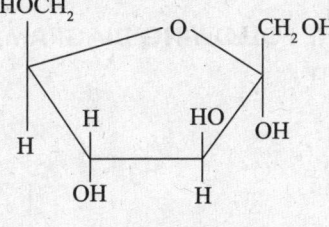

GLUCOSE

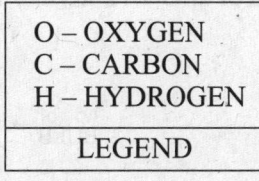

FRUCTOSE

O – OXYGEN
C – CARBON
H – HYDROGEN

LEGEND

11. What is the main difference between a glucose molecule and a fructose molecule?

    (1) The placement of the carbon atoms is different.

    (2) Glucose has fewer oxygen atoms.

    (3) Fructose has more carbon atoms.

    (4) They have a different total number of atoms.

    (5) Glucose has fewer hydrogen atoms.

QUESTION 12 REFERS TO THE FOLLOWING INFORMATION.

An individual human has about 35,000 genes, each of which occupies a certain position on a molecule of DNA, called a chromosome, inside the nucleus of every cell. Genes direct the production of proteins that result in all the specific physical traits of the individual. During sexual reproduction, the parent's chromosomes pair up and join to be passed on to the child, who inherits the DNA of both parents.

12. What theory best explains the wide variation in physical traits that you see among the thousands of people at a crowded festival or sporting event?

   (1) Each pair of corresponding genes from two parents blends together in the child.

   (2) The parents' genes combine randomly to form the child's DNA structure.

   (3) Children inherit only the traits of the parent whose genes are dominant.

   (4) Physical traits become less diverse with each passing generation.

   (5) Many physical traits disappear after the first generation of offspring.

QUESTION 13 REFERS TO THE FOLLOWING DIAGRAM.

CIRCUIT A

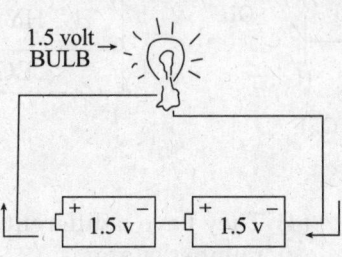

Effective voltage: 3.0 volts

CIRCUIT B

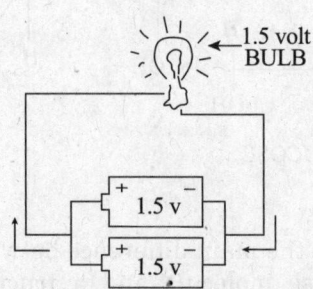

Effective voltage: 1.5 volts

13. Each light bulb represented above is part of a battery-charged electrical circuit. The light bulb acts as a resistor, which means that it uses up electricity that otherwise would be passed along the circuit toward the negative terminal of the battery pack. The end-to-end battery arrangement in circuit A combines battery voltages, whereas the parallel arrangement in circuit B does not.

If the hourly use of the light bulb is the same for both circuits, what can you infer from the two diagrams?

   (1) More electric current will return to the batteries in circuit B than in circuit A.

   (2) More electric current will return to the batteries in circuit A than in circuit B.

   (3) The batteries in circuit A will last longer than the batteries in circuit B.

   (4) The batteries in circuit B will last longer than the batteries in circuit A.

   (5) The light bulb is circuit A will last longer than the light bulb in circuit B.

QUESTION 14 REFERS TO THE FOLLOWING INFORMATION.

THE 5-KINGDOM CLASSIFICATION SYSTEM

Monera (bacteria): Single-celled prokaryotic organisms; reproduce by binary fission (simple cell division); found in every habitat

Protista (protists): Single-celled eukaryotic organism; include plantlike, animal-like, and fungi-like organisms; reproduce by binary fission

Fungi: Single-celled and multi-cellular eukaryotic organisms; cells reproduce by either budding (forming a string of cells) or binary fission

Plantae (plants): Multicellular eukaryotic organisms with cell walls; make their own food from the Sun's energy

Animalia (animals): Multicellular eukaryotic organisms without cell walls; ingest food and process it internally

The cells of eukaryotic organisms contain a distinct nucleus, and their DNA is organized into chromosomes. The cells of prokaryotic organisms lack these features.

14. In reproduction of yeast, a cell forms a "daughter" cell, and then the nucleus of the parent cell splits into a daughter nucleus, which migrates into the daughter cell. To which kingdom does yeast belong?

   (1) Monera
   (2) Protista
   (3) Fungi
   (4) Plantae
   (5) Animalia

15. When a source emits sound energy, sound waves spread out over an ever-enlarging sphere, decreasing in intensity as they travel. Also, some sound energy is absorbed by the air (or other medium) along the way.

   Which of the following do these phenomena best help to explain?

   (1) how a cheerleader's megaphone works
   (2) why people lose their hearing as they grow older
   (3) why acoustic tiling is used in opera houses
   (4) how an echo chamber works
   (5) why audio speakers should face the listener

practice test

QUESTION 16 REFERS TO THE FOLLOWING ILLUSTRATION.

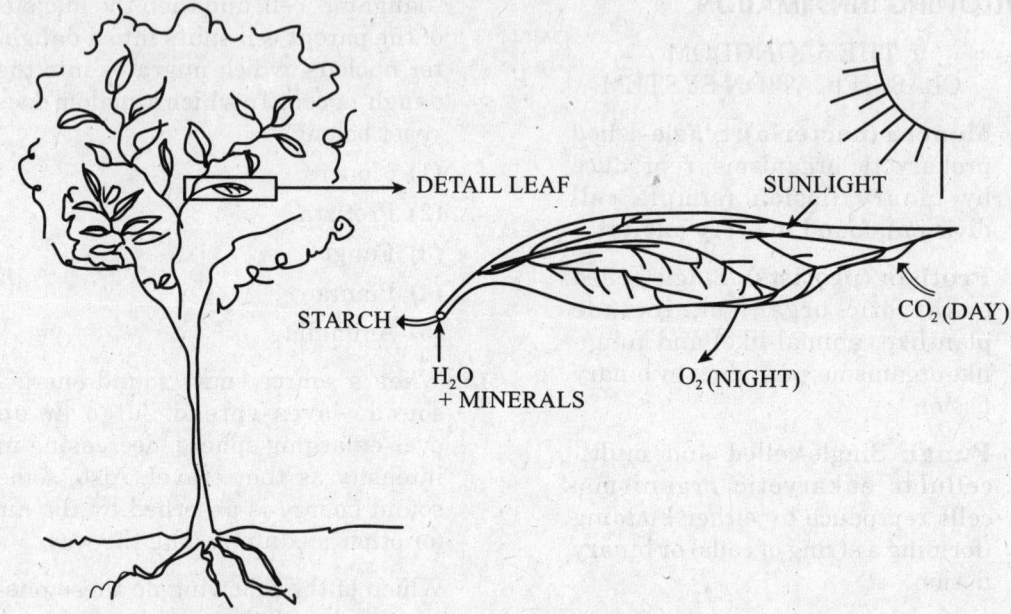

16. How does a green plant manufacture the carbohydrates it needs to grow and survive?

   (1) by combining hydrogen molecules and carbon-dioxide molecules

   (2) by isolating carbon-dioxide molecules and expelling them through leaves

   (3) by combining nitrogen molecules and oxygen molecules

   (4) by separating glucose molecules into hydrogen and carbon-dioxide molecules

   (5) by combining oxygen molecules and carbon-dioxide molecules

17. If you're careful in filling a glass with water, you can overfill the glass so that the water surface bulges a little without spilling. Which property does this phenomenon involve?

   (1) expansion

   (2) pressure

   (3) temperature

   (4) gravity

   (5) cohesion

QUESTION 18 REFERS TO THE FOLLOWING INFORMATION.

CLIMATE CHANGE PROJECTIONS
(issued by the U.S. Environmental Protection Agency in 2009)

Projected Change	Projected Impacts by Sector			
	Agriculture, forestry	Water resources	Human health/ mortality	Industry/settlement/ society
Warmer/fewer cold days/ nights; warmer/ more hot days/ nights over most land areas.	Increased yields in colder environments; decreased yields in warmer environments;	Effects on water resources relying on snow melt	Reduced human mortality from decreased cold exposure	Reduced energy demand for heating; increased demand for cooling; declining air quality in cities; reduced effects of snow, ice etc.
Warm spells/ heat waves: frequency increases over most land areas	Reduced yields in warmer regions due to heat stress at key devel. stages; fire danger increase	Increased water demand; water quality problems, e.g., algal blooms	Increased risk of heat-related mortality	Reduction in quality of life for people in warm areas without air conditioning; impacts on elderly and very young; reduced thermoelectric power production efficiency
Heavy precipitation events: frequency increases over most areas	Damage to crops; soil erosion, inability to cultivate land, water logging of soils	Adverse effects on quality of surface and groundwater; contamination of water supply	Deaths, injuries, infectious diseases, allergies and dermatitis from floods and landslides	Disruption of settlements, commerce, transport and societies due to flooding; pressures on urban and rural infrastructures
Area affected by drought: increases	Land degradation, lower yields/crop damage and failure; livestock deaths; land degradation	More widespread water stress	Increased risk of food and water shortage and wild fires; increased risk of water- and food-borne diseases	Water shortages for settlements, industry and societies; reduced hydropower generation potentials; potentials for population migration

18. What can you infer from the information in the table?

If current climate trends continue, then

(1) more humans will die from heat exposure than from exposure to cold temperatures

(2) the overall amount of precipitation across the world will increase

(3) snow runoff from mountains will reduce the need for fresh water supplies

(4) the incidence of human diseases will increase both in dry and in wet climates

(5) heat waves will begin to impact all humans equally, irrespective of age

QUESTION 19 REFERS TO THE FOLLOWING INFORMATION.

Most heart attacks occur as a result of coronary artery disease (CAD). CAD is the buildup over time of a material called plaque on the inner walls of the coronary arteries. Eventually, a section of plaque can break open, causing a blood clot to form at the site. A heart attack occurs if the clot becomes large enough to cut off most or all of the blood flow through the artery. The blocked blood flow prevents oxygen-rich blood from reaching the part of the heart muscle fed by the artery. The lack of oxygen damages the heart muscle. If the blockage isn't treated quickly, the damaged heart muscle begins to die. Common signs that a person is having a heart attack are chest pain and upper body discomfort in one or both arms, the back, neck, jaw, or stomach.

19. What can you infer about the coronary arteries?

They carry blood
(1) from the heart to the lungs
(2) from the lungs to the heart
(3) from the heart to the brain
(4) from the heart to the arms
(5) from the arms to the heart

QUESTION 20 REFERS TO THE FOLLOWING INFORMATION.

A telescope's large aperture (opening) enables it to collect more light than the human eye can. This feature is important to detect dim, distant stars as well as to distinguish a star's features, some of which appear lighter than others. Increasing a telescope's magnification by shortening the focal length of a lens makes a small, blurry image appear as a larger, blurry image.

20. What is the best way to detect specific features of a distant star?
(1) through a microscope, which shows smaller details
(2) with the naked eye from outer space
(3) through a lens with a long focal length
(4) by magnifying the image of the star
(5) through a telescope with a large aperture

QUESTIONS 21 AND 22 REFER TO THE FOLLOWING INFORMATION.

Most of the food humans consume is processed by our cells into useable energy through cell respiration, in which glucose and other molecules are broken down in the presence of oxygen into carbon dioxide and water to release chemical energy in the form of the compound ATP. One glucose molecule and six oxygen molecules are processed, or catabolized, to create 36 ATP molecules:

$$C_6H_{12}O_6 + 6\,O_2 \rightarrow 6\,CO_2 + 6\,H_2O + \text{energy}$$

If oxygen is absent, our cells can nevertheless produce some usable energy (2 ATP molecules) during a preliminary step of cell respiration, through the process of fermentation. The byproduct of fermentation in human cells is lactate, which stores energy for later retrieval should oxygen again become available. (The byproduct of fermentation in plants, fungi, and bacteria is alcohol.)

21. Which is required for our cells to produce useable energy?
(1) oxygen
(2) carbon dioxide
(3) water
(4) lactate
(5) glucose

22. When oxygen becomes available to retrieve stored lactate, a person can experience what is referred to as "oxygen debt." When is this likely to occur?

    (1) at the peak of vigorous aerobic exercise
    (2) during sleep
    (3) after a large meal
    (4) shortly after vigorous exercise
    (5) after drinking alcohol

QUESTION 23 IS BASED ON THE FOLLOWING ILLUSTRATION.

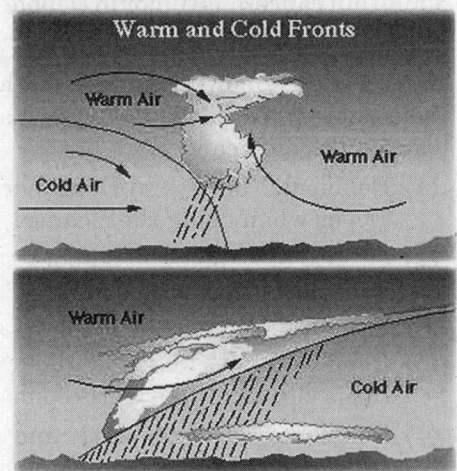

Warm and Cold Fronts

23. The border between two air masses is referred to as a *front*. An advancing front can be either warm or cold. What happens along a cold front?

    (1) The wind changes direction.
    (2) The skies clear.
    (3) The ground temperature increases.
    (4) The air condenses.
    (5) Wind velocity increases.

QUESTION 24 REFERS TO THE FOLLOWING INFORMATION.

It is a hostile environment of hydrochloric acid. Mucus is the first line of defense in protecting the lining, but when acidity increases it can erode the lining. If the acid breaks through the lining, the secretion of another protein is stimulated, which increases the production of hydrochloric acid, thereby establishing a destructive cycle. Until recently, a bland diet was recommended to prevent and reverse this disorder, but now physicians treat most forms of the disorder with antibiotics instead.

24. To what disorder is the information referring?

    (1) ear infections
    (2) stomach ulcers
    (3) sore throat
    (4) diarrhea
    (5) the common cold

25. The tendency of an object to rotate about an axis (a point of rotation) through the application of force is referred to as *torque*. Increasing the distance between the axis and the applied force increases the magnitude of the torque.

    Which of the following demonstrates the concept of torque LESS effectively than the others?

    (1) pedaling a bicycle up a hill
    (2) rolling a bowling ball down a lane
    (3) transporting a wheelbarrow full of rocks
    (4) riding a seesaw with a lighter person at the other end
    (5) turning a wrench to tighten a nut

QUESTION 26 REFERS TO THE FOLLOWING TABLE.

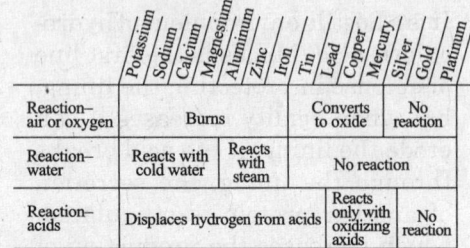

	Potassium	Sodium	Calcium	Magnesium	Aluminium	Zinc	Iron	Tin	Lead	Copper	Mercury	Silver	Gold	Platinum
Reaction–air or oxygen	Burns							Converts to oxide			No reaction			
Reaction–water	Reacts with cold water			Reacts with steam	No reaction									
Reaction–acids	Displaces hydrogen from acids								Reacts only with oxidizing acids		No reaction			

26. The more reactive a metal to oxygen, the more it tends to corrode. The table would be useful in the production of any of the following EXCEPT which one?

(1) oil rigs

(2) a boat hull

(3) fine jewelry

(4) pipes for plumbing

(5) cooking pans

QUESTIONS 27 AND 28 REFER TO THE FOLLOWING INFORMATION.

Nanotechnology involves scientific work with particles no greater than 100 nanometers in length, or about 1,000 times the length of a hydrogen atom. Nanotechnology is used today in the development of products ranging from cosmetics and household cleaning agents to composite fabrics and building materials that are strong yet light and pliable. Nanosized particles can easily permeate the skin's outer layer and the lining of blood vessels and nerve tissues, suggesting a variety of uses for nanotechnology in the field of medicine. However, the ease with which nanosized particles can permeate the body's protective barriers makes them toxic. This fact raises the concern that these tiny particles might contribute to various forms of cancer.

27. The information suggests all of the following possible applications of nanotechnology EXCEPT which one?

(1) finding cures for rare diseases

(2) enhancing personal appearance

(3) creating artificial limbs

(4) preventing skin cancer

(5) developing faster-acting medicines

28. For the past four years, Debbie has been using a strong-smelling bathroom cleanser advertised as containing nanosized cleaning agents. Debbie's physician recently discovered a small but cancerous tumor in Debbie's abdominal cavity.

Which of the following, if true, might help show that the cleanser is what caused Debbie's cancer?

(1) Debbie has always worn rubber gloves when using the cleaner.

(2) Several of Debbie's neighbors have developed cancerous tumors recently.

(3) Debbie and her husband take turns cleaning their bathroom.

(4) Debbie exercises regularly and tries to avoid stress.

(5) The cleanser is highly effective in killing mold on bathroom surfaces.

facebook.com/petersonspublishing

QUESTION 29 REFERS TO THE FOLLOWING DIAGRAM.

POPULATION AGE STRUCTURE – SPECIES X

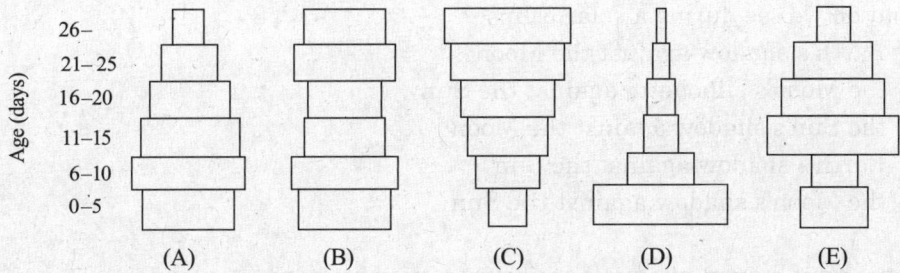

29. Which diagram represents a population whose members have been becoming increasingly infertile (unable to produce offspring) but are otherwise healthy?

    (1) population A
    (2) population B
    (3) population C
    (4) population D
    (5) population E

30. Each human gene can come in one or more varieties, called *alleles*. For each gene type, we inherit one allele from each parent. Each corresponding pair of alleles defines a unique physical or other trait. Either allele in a pair can be dominant or recessive. Two recessive alleles for one trait can actually mask the expression of alleles located at certain other sites on the chromosome and defining different but closely related traits.

    Which of the following groups of traits makes most sense as an example of this?

    (1) height, weight, and bone mass
    (2) hair color, eye color, and skin color
    (3) gender, sexual orientation, and body shape
    (4) intelligence, eyesight, and lung capacity
    (5) ear shape, foot size, and hairline

QUESTION 31 REFERS TO THE FOLLOWING ILLUSTRATION.

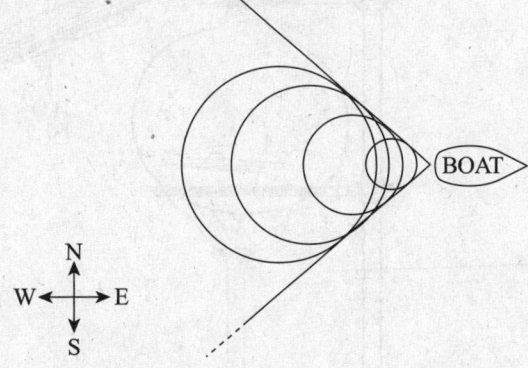

As a fast-moving boat skims along the water surface, it creates ring-shaped waves that extend away from the path of the boat. If the boat is moving faster than the waves it creates, the waves form a larger, *bow wave*, as shown in the illustration.

31. Referring to the illustration, why do the circles become smaller from west to east?

    (1) The western-most waves were created first.
    (2) The bow wave loses energy over time.
    (3) The speed of the boat is increasing.
    (4) The wind direction is east to west.
    (5) The bow wave is traveling east.

32. A solar eclipse depends on the alignment of the Sun, Moon, and Earth. During a solar eclipse, the Sun appears in the sky as a large dark circle surrounded by a bright ring.

What do we see during a solar eclipse?

(1) Earth's shadow against the Moon

(2) the Moon's silhouette against the Sun

(3) the Sun's shadow against the Moon

(4) Earth's shadow against the Sun

(5) the Moon's shadow against the Sun

QUESTION 33 IS BASED ON THE FOLLOWING ILLUSTRATION.

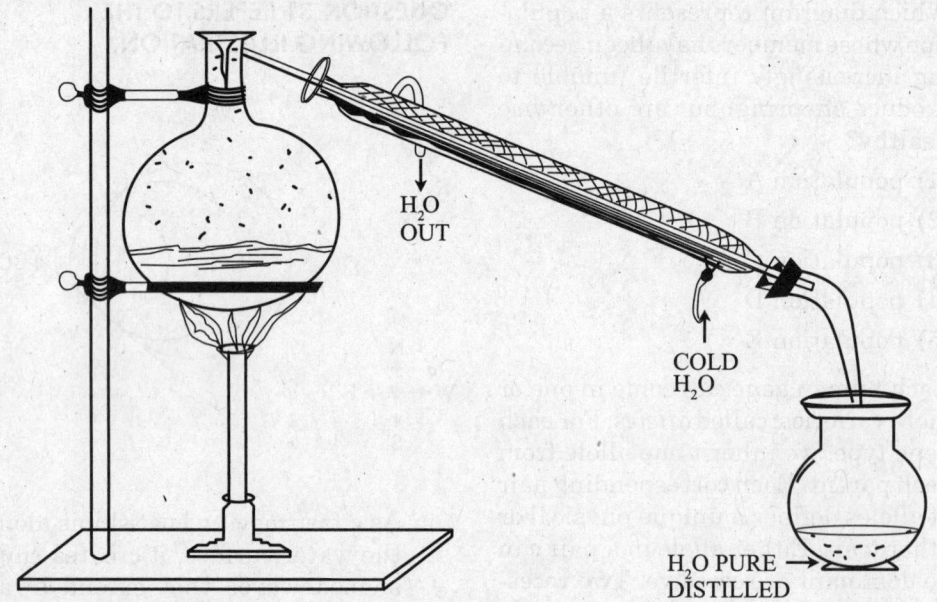

33. Referring to the lab setup shown above, how can water be distilled from other substances, thereby purifying it?

(1) by heating it up until the other substances decompose

(2) by filtering it through a series of sieves

(3) by mixing it with lighter liquids and then siphoning it off

(4) by separating it from the heavier substances through water pressure

(5) by boiling it and then condensing the water vapor

34. Electricity is produced whenever a magnet and a metal wire are moved relative to each other. Thus, an effective way to generate electricity is to spin a magnetic cylinder around a tightly coiled metal wire.

Which of the following sources of energy would be LEAST useful in driving the electric generator described above?

(1) sunlight

(2) wind

(3) water pressure

(4) steam

(5) human power

QUESTION 35 REFERS TO THE FOLLOWING INFORMATION.

Certain types of red-colored flowers produce nectar that is chemically ideal as food for a hummingbird. The hummingbird can easily locate these flowers because it can see the color red especially well. The recurved petals of these flowers remain out of the hummingbird's way while it extracts nectar with its long beak that is perfectly suited for the task. As it does so, the hummingbird's head feathers brush against the flowers, collecting pollen that it carries away and disperses.

35. Which chart depicts the evolutionary relationship between the hummingbirds and flowers described above?

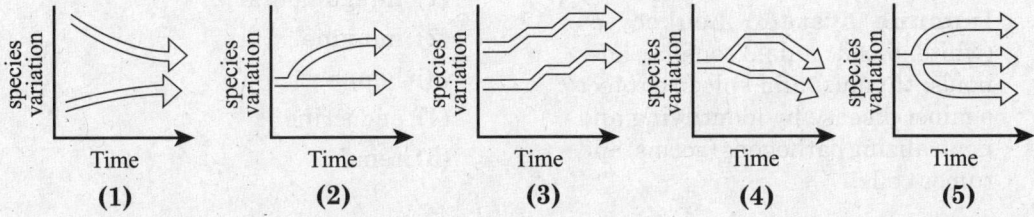

(1)　　　　(2)　　　　(3)　　　　(4)　　　　(5)

36. A botanist observes that the leaves of tomato plant A are beginning to wrinkle and mottle. Plant B, which sits directly next to plant A, appears healthy.

What experiment might help determine whether virus X is causing plant A's leaves to wrinkle and mottle?

(1) Move the two plants farther apart, and continue to observe their leaves.

(2) Examine a leaf from plant B under an electron microscope.

(3) Infect plant B with virus X and continue to observe plant B.

(4) Compare the number of healthy-looking tomatoes on the two plants.

(5) Continue to water plant A, but stop watering plant B.

QUESTION 37 REFERS TO THE FOLLOWING ILLUSTRATION.

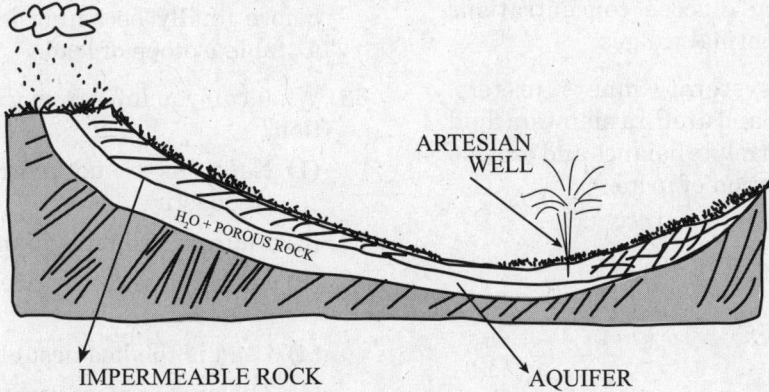

37. What allows water to be drawn through an artesian well without the aid of a pump?

(1) pressure on the aquifer from an impermeable rock layer just above it

(2) atmospheric pressure on the water table

(3) the downward pressure of water within the aquifer

(4) seismic (earthquake) activity occurring in the recharge area

(5) boiling temperatures of the water within an aquifer

QUESTION 38 REFERS TO THE FOLLOWING INFORMATION.

Following are brief descriptions of five organ systems found in vertebrate animals.

Integumentary system: Skin, hair and nails; sweat and oil glands provide physical, chemical, and biological barriers that protect the body.

Immune system: Leukocytes (white blood cells), tonsils, adenoids, thymus, and spleen protect against disease by identifying and neutralizing pathogens (germs) and tumor cells.

Lymphatic system: Lymph nodes (found in many organs), lymph tissue transfers lymph (a liquid) for the removal of interstitial fluid from tissues, absorbs and transports fatty acids and fats to the circulatory system, and transports immune cells to and from the lymph nodes.

Endocrine system: Endocrine glands (hypothalamus, pituitary, thyroid, adrenal, and others) secrete hormones that stimulate reactions throughout the body to maintain glucose concentrations within normal ranges.

Renal system: Kidneys, ureters, bladder, and urethra maintain fluid and electrolyte balance and provide for excretion of urine.

38. Patient X suffers from a disorder in which the glucose in his blood is not being taken up by the muscles to be processed into useable energy, and so fat cells are being used for this purpose instead. A reliable indicator of this disorder is an excessive amount of sugar (glucose) in the urine.

Which of the five systems does this disorder involve?

(1) integumentary
(2) immune
(3) lymphatic
(4) endocrine
(5) renal

QUESTION 39 REFERS TO THE FOLLOWING INFORMATION.

Each neutron and proton in an atom's nucleus has the same atomic mass: one dalton. If an atom loses neutrons due to radioactive decay, it may also lose protons, in which case, the atom becomes an atom of a different element. Uranium 238, a very unstable element, goes through many stages of radioactive decay. During this process, it becomes thorium, radium, and radon (among other elements), before finally becoming lead 206, a stable isotope of lead.

39. What can you infer from the information?

(1) Neutrons are not affected by radioactive decay.
(2) Radium is lighter than uranium.
(3) Lead 206 is the heaviest isotope of lead.
(4) Lead is the heaviest element.
(5) Thorium is more radioactive than uranium.

QUESTION 40 REFERS TO THE FOLLOWING DIAGRAM.

CROSS-SECTION OF A VASCULAR PLANT STEM AND ROOT

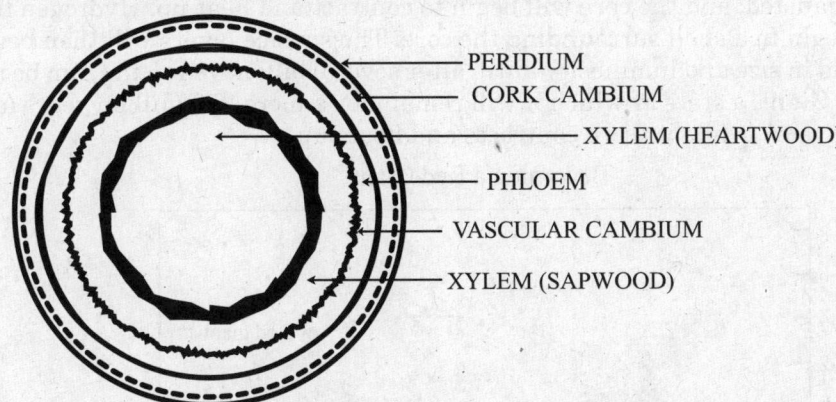

Xylem (heartwood): mature, dead tissue; provides support

Xylem (sapwood): live tissue; transports water to leaves

Vascular cambium: thin cylinder; divides to produce new xylem and phloem

Phloem: live tissue; conducts food from leaves to other plant parts

Cork cambium: inner layer of periderm that produces new bark as needed

40. As a tree grows, it increases in girth. Where does most of the increase occur?

(1) in the sap and vascular cambium

(2) in the heartwood and phloem

(3) in the heartwood and sapwood

(4) in the phloem and periderm

(5) in the cork cambium and periderm

41. As a light source emits light waves directly toward you, the waves vibrate at every angle: horizontally, vertically, and all angles in between. By placing a polarizing screen in front of your eyes, you can block horizontally oriented waves while allowing vertically oriented waves to pass. This is how polarized sunglasses work to block reflected light waves, which usually vibrate horizontally but not vertically.

What is a good way to demonstrate how a pair of polarized sunglasses works?

(1) Wear them while snow skiing, and then wear them indoors.

(2) Try squinting your eyes while looking through them.

(3) Place one pair over another to see how the second pair affects your vision.

(4) Look at yourself in a mirror while wearing them.

(5) Rotate them 90 degrees, and then look through them.

QUESTIONS 42 AND 43 REFER TO THE FOLLOWING INFORMATION.

About 10 billion years after the Sun's birth, the hydrogen fuel in the core will be exhausted, and the core will begin to contract and heat up. Hydrogen fusion will begin in a shell surrounding the core. The surface layers will then begin to expand in size and luminosity until, after several billion years, the Sun becomes a Red Giant, a state at which it will remain for a mere 250 million years (about 1 Sun-year), while its core contracts and heats up.

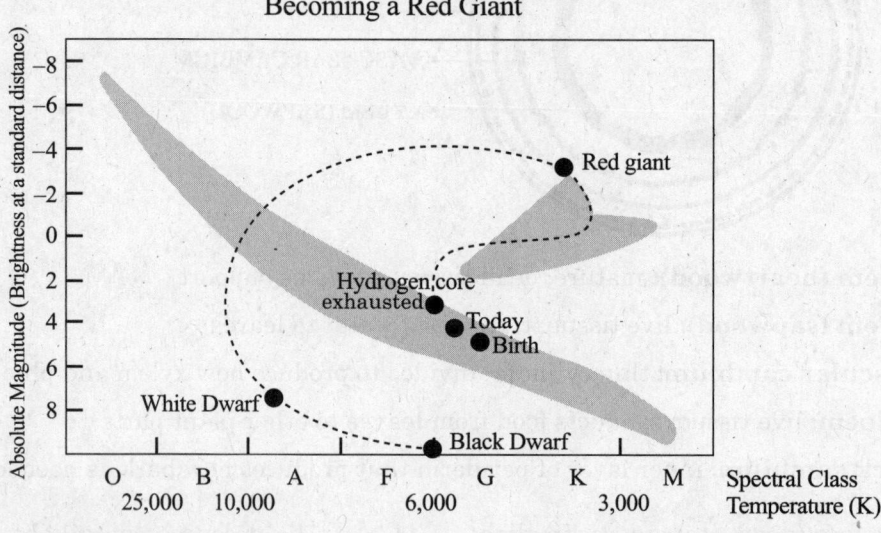

Becoming a Red Giant

NOTE: Absolute magnitude is a measure of luminosity (brightness) that uses an inverted scale. The shaded regions indicate the general distribution of all stars in terms of the variables measured.

42. What is the approximate age of the Sun?

   (1) 250 million Sun-years
   (2) 1 billion Sun-years
   (3) 5 billion Sun-years
   (4) 10 billion Sun-years
   (5) 20 billion Sun-years

43. What will happen to the Sun during its life ahead?

The Sun will

   (1) experience two more cooling cycles
   (2) darken as its surface continues to expand
   (3) expand and heat up, then contract and cool
   (4) travel farther away from most other stars
   (5) grow brighter even as it shrinks in size

QUESTION 44 REFERS TO THE FOLLOWING INFORMATION.

Within the phylum *chordata*, the sub-phylum *vertebrata* includes mammals, birds, reptiles, amphibians, and fish. All vertebrates share in common four characteristics during the embryonic stage of their life cycle:

- a hollow, dorsal (rear) nerve cord
- a notochord (backbone)
- gill slits (which develop into other structures in terrestrial vertebrates)
- a post-anal tail

44. Which part of the human anatomy shows that it belongs to the same sub-phylum as a lizard?
    - (1) outer skin
    - (2) spinal cord
    - (3) toes and fingers
    - (4) sex organs
    - (5) lungs

QUESTION 45 REFERS TO THE FOLLOWING INFORMATION.

Below are some terms associated with the functioning of *neurons*, which are the nerve cells that transmit information throughout the body.

Interneurons: Neurons of the peripheral nervous system; send signals back and forth between the brain or spinal cord and the limbs and sense organs

Sensory neurons: Neurons that transmit messages to the brain and the spinal cord from the sense organs

Motor neurons: Neurons that carry commands from the brain and spinal cord to the muscles and glands

Chemical exchange: the means by which neurons send and receive electrical signals associated with smell and taste

Mechanical stimulus: the means by which neurons send and receive electrical signals associated with sight, sound, and touch

45. What best explains why someone might feel no heat when poking a hot coal with an extended finger?
    - (1) A malfunctioning interneuron is preventing a chemical exchange.
    - (2) The person's motor neurons are functioning but certain sensory neurons are not.
    - (3) An electrical signal has failed to reach the person's spinal cord from the brain.
    - (4) All sensory neurons are functioning but certain interneurons are not.
    - (5) The peripheral nervous system has failed to make a mechanical exchange.

QUESTIONS 46 AND 47 REFER TO THE FOLLOWING CHART.

The pH Scale

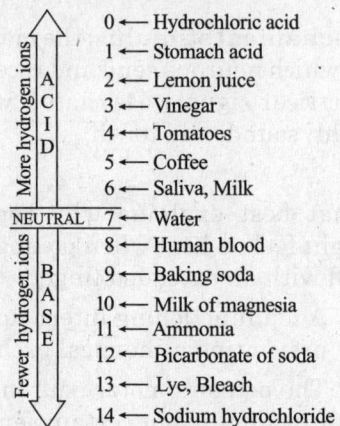

The pH scale is a compressed scale. Each level (0–14) represents a ten-fold change from the next level up or down.

46. Which statement does the information in the pH scale support?

- **(1)** Mixing human blood and saliva equally yields a mixture with a pH of about 7.
- **(2)** Bleach and lye burn your skin because they are highly acidic.
- **(3)** Milk is more effective than water in reducing the acidity of coffee.
- **(4)** It is easier to float in water high in hydrogen ions than in other water.
- **(5)** Drinking a carbonated beverage reduces the acidity inside your stomach.

47. Among the following, who would find pH measurements LEAST useful?

- **(1)** a dietician
- **(2)** a gardener
- **(3)** a physical therapist
- **(4)** a chef
- **(5)** a marine biologist

48. Humans normally maintain a constant internal body temperature of 98.6°F and are referred to as "warm-blooded." Except in hot weather, reptiles are normally cold to the touch and are often referred to as "cold-blooded." What does this mean?

Reptiles

- **(1)** produce a hormone that slows their blood flow
- **(2)** prey on their own young to replenish lost blood
- **(3)** prefer warmer air temperatures to colder ones
- **(4)** can reflect bright sunlight by altering their skin color
- **(5)** adjust their body temperature to the air temperature

QUESTION 49 REFERS TO THE FOLLOWING DIAGRAM.

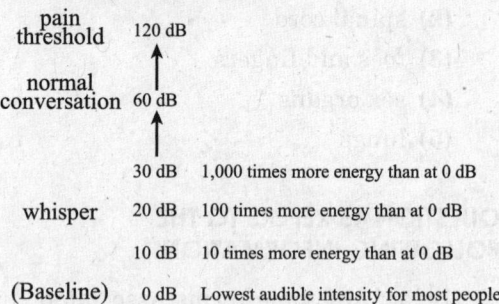

The decibel (dB) rating is a compressed measurement scale for sound intensity—i.e., the amount of sound energy (watts) passing through a square-meter area (m²) per second.

49. How much more sound energy is produced during normal conversation than while whispering?

- **(1)** 40 times as much
- **(2)** 100 times as much
- **(3)** 400 times as much
- **(4)** 1,000 times as much
- **(5)** 10,000 times as much

QUESTION 50 IS BASED ON THE FOLLOWING CHART.

Mineral	Calcium	Copper	Fluorine	Iodine	Iron	Magnesium	Phosphorus	Potassium	Sodium	Zinc
Area of Benefit	bones, teeth, muscles	blood	bones, teeth	thyroid hormone synthesis	blood	protein synthesis	bones, teeth	muscle contraction	pH balance	tissue growth
Dietary source	green vegetables, dairy products	seafood, legumes	fluoridated water	table salt, seafood	legumes, whole grains, eggs	green vegetables, whole grains	green vegetables, meat, dairy products	vegetables, fruits	table salt	meat, legumes, whole grains

50. What is a reason that older people are often advised to take multiple-mineral supplements?

(1) They begin to lose their hair.

(2) Their skin loses elasticity.

(3) They lose their appetite easily.

(4) They begin to lose bone mass.

(5) They begin losing their memory.

LANGUAGE ARTS, READING

65 Minutes • 40 Questions

Directions: The Language Arts, Reading Test consists of several passages of fiction and nonfiction reading material. Each passage is followed by several multiple-choice questions. After you read a passage, answer the questions that follow it, referring back to the passage as needed. Answer all questions based on what is stated and implied in the passage.

Immediately preceding each passage is a brief "purpose question" in bold type. These questions will help you focus your attention and to understand the purpose of each passage. You are not required to answer purpose questions.

Record your answers on the Language Arts, Reading section of the answer sheet provided.

QUESTIONS 1 TO 6 REFER TO THE FOLLOWING PASSAGE.

HOW DID THE BOYS PASS THE TIME
WHEN THEY HUNG OUT TOGETHER?

Just how I came to love her, timidly, and with secret blushes, I do not know. But that I did was brought home to me one night. Us fellers were seated on the curb before an apartment house where she had gone in. Some minutes passed. Then Avey, as unconcerned as if she had been paying an old-maid aunt a visit, came

5　out. I just stood there like the others, and something like a fuse burned up inside me. She never noticed us, but swung along lazy and easy as anything. Some one said she'd marry that feller on the top floor. Ned called that a lie because Avey was going to marry nobody but him. We had our doubts about that, but we did agree that she'd soon leave school and marry some one. The gang broke up, and

10　I went home, picturing myself as married.

Nothing I did seemed able to change Avey's indifference to me. I played basketball, and when I'd make a long clean shot she'd clap with the others, louder than they, I thought. I'd meet her on the street, and there'd be no difference in the way she said hello. She never took the trouble to call me by my name. It

15　was on a summer excursion down to Riverview that she first seemed to take me into account. The day had been spent riding merry-go-rounds, scenic-railways, and shoot-the-chutes. We had been in swimming, and we had danced. I was a crack swimmer then. She didn't know how. I held her up and showed her how to kick her legs and draw her arms. Of course she didn't learn in one day, but

20　she thanked me for bothering with her. I was also somewhat of a dancer. And I had already noticed that love can start on a dance floor. We danced. But though I held her tightly in my arms, she was way away. That college feller who lived on the top floor was somewhere making money for the next year. I imagined that she was thinking, wishing for him. Ned was along. He treated her until his

25　money gave out. She went with another feller. Ned got sore. One by one the boys' money gave out . She left them. Every one of them but me got sore.

—from *Cane*, by Jean Toomer

1. What word best describes Avey?

　(1) coy

　(2) affectionate

　(3) smart

　(4) honest

　(5) ambitious

2. What does the author mean by "take me into account" (lines 15–16)?

　(1) help me

　(2) forgive me

　(3) notice me

　(4) adopt me

　(5) bother me

3. What does the narrator probably believe about the person who lives on the top floor?

　(1) He is sore at Ned and the other gang members.

　(2) He is planning to see Avey again.

　(3) He taught Avey how to swim.

　(4) He was supposed to be at the dance but wasn't.

　(5) He is a member of a rival gang.

4. Which location is NOT mentioned in the passage as a place where the narrator saw Avey?

    (1) on the street
    (2) at a swimming hole or pool
    (3) on a dance floor
    (4) outside Avey's residence
    (5) at a basketball game

5. How can the passage's theme best be summed up?

    The passage tells a tale of

    (1) wounded pride
    (2) envy and regret
    (3) young love
    (4) sorrow and guilt
    (5) unfounded fears

6. Which of the following is most likely true, from the narrator's perspective?

    The events described in the passage

    (1) occurred quite some time ago
    (2) discouraged him from pursuing Avey
    (3) took place only in his imagination
    (4) were told to him by Ned
    (5) defined the course of his life

QUESTIONS 7 TO 12 REFER TO THE FOLLOWING POEM.

WHAT LIES AT THE BOTTOM OF THE WELL?

What mystery pervades a well!
The water lives so far—
A neighbor from another world
Residing in a jar

5 Whose limit none have ever seen,
But just his lid of glass—
Like looking every time you please
In an abyss's face!

The grass does not appear afraid,
10 I often wonder he
Can stand so close and look so bold
At what is awe to me.

Related somehow they may be,
The sedge stands next the sea—
15 Where he is floorless, and of fear
No evidence gives he.

But nature is a stranger yet;
The ones that cite her most
Have never passed her haunted house,
20 Nor simplified her ghost.

To pity those that know her not
Is helped by the regret
That those who know her, know her less
The nearer here they get.
    —"What Mystery Pervades a Well!"
        by Emily Dickinson

7. What does the poem suggest about people who claim to be the greatest nature lovers?

    (1) They are selfish in their appreciation of nature.
    (2) They show the least respect for nature.
    (3) They have not truly experienced nature.
    (4) They pity themselves when nature defeats them.
    (5) They do too little to preserve nature.

8. How does the poem derive its power?

   (1) by juxtaposing jarring, opposing ideas

   (2) by understating the mysteriousness of nature

   (3) by attributing human features to nature

   (4) by exploring deep human emotions

   (5) by repeating certain words and syllables

9. How does the speaker react when looking into a well?

   The speaker

   (1) marvels at what might lie under the surface

   (2) feels uneasy about a future that one cannot possibly know

   (3) worries about falling in or being pushed

   (4) regrets life's lost chances that cannot be regained

   (5) fears unseen dangers that might be lurking below

10. Which statement best summarizes the poem's third and fourth stanzas (lines 9–16)?

    (1) A deep well can be as mysterious as the sea.

    (2) Grass and sedge show us that we need not be afraid of deep water.

    (3) The well and the sea both appear bottomless but are not.

    (4) The sedge hides its fears better than the grass does.

    (5) Neither sedge nor grass seems afraid of deep water.

11. Which observation is LEAST similar to the one made in the poem's sixth stanza (lines 21–24)?

    (1) To best help others, let them help themselves.

    (2) The only constant in this world is change.

    (3) I regret that I have never done anything to regret.

    (4) Nothing succeeds like success itself.

    (5) To know yourself you must lose yourself in the service of others.

12. This poem was written by Emily Dickinson, who is universally admired for her masterful use of imagery. Which line of this poem best illustrates this skill?

    (1) line 2 ("The water lives so far")

    (2) line 4 ("Residing in a jar")

    (3) line 6 ("But just his lid of glass")

    (4) line 16 ("No evidence gives he")

    (5) line 17 ("But nature is a stranger yet")

QUESTIONS 13 TO 17 REFER TO THE FOLLOWING DOCUMENT.

IS IT RIGHT TO CONDUCT PERSONAL BUSINESS WHILE AT WORK?

County Policies for Use of the County Computer Network System (CCNS) and other Computerized Devices

A. Uses of the County Computer Network System (CCNS)

County employees should use the County's computer network system (CCNS) only to conduct official County business. However, brief and occasional use for personal reasons is permitted. Personal use of CCNS should not impede the conduct of County business; only incidental amounts of employee time, comparable to reasonable coffee breaks, should be used to attend to personal matters. Personal use of CCNS should not cause the County to incur a direct cost in addition to the costs of maintaining CCNS. Consequently, employees should not store or print personal material downloaded via CCNS.

B. Use of Personal Computer Devices

County employees shall not use their personal computer-hardware devices to conduct County business. Such devices include, but are not limited to, laptop, notebook and netbook computers, personal digital assistant (PDA) devices, and other handheld computing and communication devices. Connecting personal digital devices of any kind to the County's computer hardware is strictly prohibited. Employees who have been authorized to conduct County business from a remote location may do so only with equipment and software issued by the County.

C. Use of other Personal Digital Devices

Notwithstanding the rules set forth in paragraph B, employees may bring personal cellular phones and similar communication devices with them to work, provided that they use these devices only to monitor incoming messages and to communicate with others in the event of an emergency.

D. Sharing Network Computing Resources

Use of the computer workstation assigned to another employee, whether with or without consent of that employee, is prohibited. However, in the presence of a supervising staff member for purposes such as project collaboration, training, or troubleshooting, two or more employees may briefly work at the same computer workstation.

E. No Privacy Expectation

County employees should have no expectation of privacy regarding their use of CCNS. All records created by CCNS use, including but not limited to Internet browsing history and cached data, are subject to inspection and audit by County administration or its representatives at any time, with or without notice. Use of CCNS by an employee indicates that the employee understands that the County has a right to inspect and audit all Internet use; and consents to any inspections following proper procedures and protocols.

13. How is the document organized?

    (1) Guidelines for conduct are followed by warnings of consequences.

    (2) A statement of policy is supported by procedural rules.

    (3) Specific rules are illustrated by examples of violations.

    (4) Rules for behavior are supported by a notice of enforcement.

    (5) A code of conduct is compared to observed behavior.

14. What does the phrase "with or without notice" (paragraph E) suggest?

    (1) Employees need not notify anyone when accessing the Internet using CCNS.

    (2) Employees are deemed to have read and understood the County's privacy policy.

    (3) The County can inspect all e-mails sent and received by its employees.

    (4) Employee Web-browsing history is recorded and monitored by the County.

    (5) Employees need not be informed that their Internet use is being monitored.

15. If you were a County administrator and were hiring someone to ensure that you can enforce the policies and procedures discussed in the document, which characteristic would you look for in that person?

    (1) skill in interpersonal communications

    (2) knowledge of computer networking

    (3) ability to convince others through intimidation

    (4) skill in identifying suspicious behavior

    (5) expertise in Internet privacy and security

16. Based on the document, which of the following is an example of what County employees either should or should not do?

    County employees should

    (1) access the Internet from work only while on coffee or meal breaks

    (2) not conduct County business from home using their own computer

    (3) report any pain or injury resulting from computer use to a supervisor

    (4) print or save no more than a reasonable amount of data from the Internet

    (5) maximize work efficiency by sharing computing resources with coworkers

17. Which of the following additional provisions would best support the ones in the document?

    The best supporting provision would

    (1) require employees to wear badges identifying their assigned workstation

    (2) discourage employees from playing music while at work

    (3) encourage employees to log out when leaving their workstations unattended

    (4) discourage employees from troubleshooting computer problems on their own

    (5) encourage employees to report observed rule violations to their supervisor

QUESTIONS 18 TO 23 REFER TO THE FOLLOWING PASSAGE.

TO WHAT LENGTHS SHOULD A PERSON GO TO OBTAIN MONEY?

NORA. Father died on the 29th of September.

KROGSTAD. Quite correct. I have made inquiries. And here comes in the remarkable point—(Produces a paper.) which I cannot explain.

NORA. What remarkable point? I don't know—

5   KROGSTAD. The remarkable point, madam, that your father signed this paper three days after his death!

NORA. What! I don't understand—

KROGSTAD. Your father died on the 29th of September. But look here: he has dated his signature October 2nd! Is not that remarkable, Mrs. Helmer? (NORA
10   is silent.) It is noteworthy, too, that the words "October 2nd" and the year are not in your father's handwriting, but in one which I believe I know. Well, this may be explained; your father may have forgotten to date his signature, and somebody may have added the date at random, before the fact of your father's death was known. There is nothing wrong in that. Everything depends on
15   the signature. Of course it is genuine, Mrs. Helmer? It was really your father himself who wrote his name here?

NORA. (After a short silence, throws her head back and looks defiantly at him.) No, it was not. I wrote father's name.

KROGSTAD. Ah!—You are aware, madam, that that is a dangerous admission?

20   NORA. How so? You will soon get your money.

KROGSTAD. May I ask you one more question? Why did you not send the paper to your father?

NORA. It was impossible. Father was ill. If I had asked him for his signature, I should have had to tell him why I wanted the money; but he was so ill I really
25   could not tell him that my husband's life was in danger. It was impossible.

KROGSTAD. Then it would have been better to have given up your tour.

NORA. No, I couldn't do that; my husband's life depended on that journey. I couldn't give it up.

KROGSTAD. And did it never occur to you that you were playing me false?

30   NORA. That was nothing to me. I didn't care in the least about you. I couldn't endure you for all the cruel difficulties you made, although you know how ill my husband was.

KROGSTAD. Mrs. Helmer, you evidently do not realize what you have been guilty of. But I can assure you it was nothing more and nothing worse that made me
35   an outcast from society.

NORA. You! You want me to believe that you did a brave thing to save your wife's life?

KROGSTAD. The law takes no account of motives.

—from *A Doll's House*, by Henrik Ibsen

18. Of what has Nora been accused?

    (1) putting the wrong date on a document

    (2) lying to Krogstad

    (3) taking a journey when her father was ill

    (4) falsifying her father's signature

    (5) forgetting to have her father sign a document

19. Which conclusion can the reader draw from the dialogue?

    (1) Krogstad had lent Nora's father some money.

    (2) Krogstad and Nora had been plotting against Nora's husband.

    (3) Nora didn't want her husband to know that she had borrowed money from Krogstad.

    (4) Nora's husband and Krogstad were business partners.

    (5) Nora had intentionally signed the document with the wrong date.

20. Which of the following best describes the conversation between Nora and Krogstad?

    (1) intimate

    (2) superficial

    (3) warm

    (4) confidential

    (5) guarded

21. What does Krogstad most likely mean by the phrase "you were playing me false" (line 29)?

    (1) Nora never took her debt to Krogstad seriously.

    (2) Nora had been gambling with her father's money.

    (3) Krogstad had been deceived by Nora.

    (4) Nora was misinformed about her father's death.

    (5) Nora betrayed Krogstad by signing the paper herself.

22. Based on the dialogue, what is most likely correct about the relationship between Nora and Krogstad?

    (1) They met each other through Nora's father.

    (2) They have been acquaintances for quite a while.

    (3) They were once romantically involved with each other.

    (4) Krogstad is representing Nora as her lawyer.

    (5) They just met but have heard of each other before their meeting.

23. In lines 36–37 Nora asks, "You want me to believe that you did a brave thing to save your wife's life?" What is Nora's point?

    (1) Her motives justified her misdeed.

    (2) Krogstad's bravery did not save his wife's life.

    (3) Krogstad believes himself to be brave but is mistaken.

    (4) Her misdeed was no worse than Krogstad's.

    (5) Krogstad lied to Nora about saving his wife's life.

QUESTIONS 24 TO 29 REFER TO THE
FOLLOWING PASSAGE.

WILL THE GARDEN RETURN
IN SPRING?

The first frost wilted any remaining
green leaves, turning them to pulp.
The mums provided the only color.
"You need the winter as well as the
5 summer," Ralph could still hear
Arlene say. "Flowers need to sleep
before they bloom again."

Ralph couldn't make himself
pull up the spent plants, and their
10 bare stalks pierced the snow that
blanketed the garden. When the
wind blew in from the north, they
rustled like Arlene's rasping cough.

That first Christmas without
15 Arlene, Gloria brought over a
bunch of seed catalogs—*Select
Seeds, Burpee, Heirloom Flowers,
Ashdown Roses*.

"Hmm, I don't know. I think I'll
20 just throw some grass seed out there
come spring," Ralph said. He didn't
think he'd have the heart to start
over again.

"Suit yourself," Gloria said, but
25 she knew better.

It was a hard winter—a blizzard
on the first day of December. The
schools closed for the first time in
twenty-five years. In early January
30 it dropped to fifteen below zero, forty
below with the wind chill. The kind
of weather they used to have when
Ralph was a kid out in the country.
He hunkered down, watched the
35 Weather Channel, and peeked at
the seed catalogs.

But January advances on February, and February recedes to
March, with wet streets and snow
40 like dirty lace, the front yard
squishy with mud. One morning,
Ralph stood in the open doorway
sipping black coffee. I'm old, Ralph
thought, but he knew he wanted to
45 keep getting older. He tried to stop
the door from opening too much
to the cold and wind. The metal

pinwheel picked up speed—*flap,
flip, flap*. The wind rattled the
50 chains on the porch swing. Something caught Ralph's gaze. There in
the weak morning sun, the peace
lily had pushed up a slim stalk and
a shiny leaf. *First it sleeps*. Arlene
55 came flooding back. The wind raised
the hair on Ralph's arms and made
gooseflesh. *Then it creeps*. Ralph's
heart leapt. "Good golly. Would you
look at that," he said, the hot coffee
60 warming his hand, and he threw
wide the door in spite of the cold.

—from "The Widower's Garden,"
by Rikki Clark

24. Which best characterizes the theme
of the passage?
  (1) planning the year ahead
  (2) surviving a cold winter
  (3) remembering a loved one
  (4) weeding the garden
  (5) choosing plant seeds

25. The narrator indicates that Ralph
"didn't think he'd have the heart to
start over again" (lines 21–23). To
what activity is the narrator probably
referring?
  (1) moving to another city
  (2) growing new plants
  (3) planting grass seed
  (4) starting a new career
  (5) marrying again

26. If Gloria were an office manager, how
would she run her office?

As her character is revealed in the
passage, Gloria would most probably
  (1) demand that her staff strictly
      follow her every order
  (2) discipline any staff member who
      engages in misconduct
  (3) mismanage the office's day-to-
      day operations
  (4) be a supportive mentor for her
      subordinates
  (5) try to do everything herself
      instead of delegating tasks

27. What is the author's purpose in italicizing the words "*First it sleeps*" (line 54) and "*Then it creeps*" (line 57)?

The use of italics for these words probably signifies that

   (1) Gloria is saying these words to Ralph
   (2) the two sentences are also book titles
   (3) the words are not important to the story
   (4) Ralph is thinking of these words
   (5) the words are written on seed packages

28. What is the approximate time frame of the events in the passage?

The various events in the passage occur

   (1) over the Christmas season
   (2) on a cold morning in early Spring
   (3) during the month of February
   (4) during February and March
   (5) in early Winter and early Spring

29. Which word best conveys Ralph's feelings at the end of the passage?

   (1) joyful
   (2) sorrowful
   (3) regretful
   (4) anxious
   (5) grateful

QUESTIONS 30 TO 34 REFER TO THE FOLLOWING PASSAGE.

WHICH BETTER DEFINES A CITY: ITS PEOPLE OR ITS ARCHITECTURE?

An outsider approaches the subject gingerly, lest civic feelings be bruised. Los Angeles gives the impression of having erased much
5 of its history by allowing the city's development to run unchecked. As Los Angeles insider Dolores Hayden noted in the early 1980s, "It is . . . common for fond residents to quote
10 Gertrude Stein's sentence about Oakland when summing up urban design in Los Angeles: 'There's no there, there.'" Hayden has also acknowledged that Los Angeles is
15 generally "the first (American city) singled out as having a problem about sense of place."

In 1982, Hayden founded The Power of Place, a local nonprofit
20 group with a mission to retrieve some of the city's misplaced "there." The special emphasis of The Power of Place was on redressing an imbalance in memory—and
25 memorials. As Hayden pointed out, in 1987 less than half the population of Los Angeles was Anglo-American; yet almost 98 percent of the city's cultural and
30 historic landmarks were devoted to the history and accomplishments of Anglo-Americans. Even these personages came from a narrow spectrum of achievers: a small,
35 almost exclusively male, group of landholders, bankers, business leaders, and their architects.

The likeliest explanation for this under-representation may be
40 an urban variation on the great-man theory of history: History is what public figures do, and by their civic monuments shall ye know them—especially the struc-
45 tures they designed or built. In Hayden's view, however, "The task of choosing a past for Los Angeles is a political as well as an historic and cultural one." Hayden's goal
50 was to supplement the city's ample supply of monocultural landmarks and memorials with others representing its ethnic and gender-based diversity. Though much has been
55 accomplished toward this goal, more needs doing. Many historical sites no longer contain structures emblematic of their histories, or never did. Others are in blighted

60 neighborhoods, where preservation is especially challenging. But the effort is worthwhile to ensure that, once found, our sense of place as Los Angelinos is not lost.

30. What is the main idea of the passage?
   (1) Multicultural landmarks are better than monocultural ones.
   (2) Los Angeles should continue to correct cultural imbalances in its landmarks.
   (3) Due to its ethnic diversity, Los Angeles lacks a sense of place.
   (4) Urban planners should redesign Los Angeles to provide a sense of place for its residents.
   (5) Los Angeles residents do not care enough about their surroundings.

31. With which statement would Dolores Hayden LEAST likely agree?

   In Los Angeles, historical landmarks designated prior to the 1980s
   (1) do not adequately enhance a sense of place today
   (2) were chosen according to economic criteria
   (3) do not represent the history of all of the people of Los Angeles
   (4) celebrate the accomplishments of what is now a minority group
   (5) are not on a par with the historical landmarks of Oakland

32. What does the author mean by the phrase "civic feelings" (line 2)?
   (1) allegiance of a city's residents to their city
   (2) emotions that breed courtesy and good behavior
   (3) respect for others shown by people who behave in a civilized manner
   (4) defensiveness that city residents sometimes show toward outsiders
   (5) regularity with which citizens vote

33. Based on the passage, with which statement would Hayden MOST likely agree?
   (1) Politics should play no part in designating cultural and historic landmarks.
   (2) Only public buildings should be designated as cultural landmarks.
   (3) Some parts of history cannot be memorialized in surviving buildings and landmarks.
   (4) It is more important to preserve the homes and workplaces of working people than those of "great men."
   (5) A city's past cannot truly be memorialized, no matter how great the effort.

34. What is a current problem with carrying out Hayden's vision?
   (1) Some historical sites are difficult to preserve.
   (2) Much of the history of Los Angeles was never recorded.
   (3) Politicians typically oppose historic preservation.
   (4) Preservationists cannot agree on what sites to designate as historical.
   (5) Real-estate developers own most historical sites in Los Angeles.

QUESTIONS 35 TO 40 REFER TO THE FOLLOWING PASSAGE.

SHOULD MAY AND NEWLAND ELOPE?

Newland Archer was speaking with his fiancée, May Welland.

   "Sameness—sameness!" he muttered, the word running through his
5 head like a persecuting tune as he saw the familiar tall-hatted figures lounging behind the plate glass; and because he usually dropped in at the club at that hour, he had passed by
10 instead. And now he began to talk to

May of their own plans, their future, and Mrs. Welland's insistence on a long engagement.

"If you call it long!" May cried.
15 "Isabel Chivers and Reggie were engaged for two years, Grace and Thorley for nearly a year and a half. Why aren't we very well off as they are?"

20 "We might be much better off. We might be truly together—we might travel."

Her face lit up. "That would be lovely," she admitted; she would
25 love to travel. But her mother would not understand their wanting to do things so differently.

"As if the fact that it is different doesn't account for it!" Archer
30 insisted.

"Newland! You're so original!" she exulted.

His heart sank. He saw that he was saying all the things that
35 young men in the same situation were expected to say, and that she was making the answers that instinct and tradition taught her to make—even to the point of calling
40 him original.

"Original! We're all as like each other as those dolls cut out of the same folded paper. We're like patterns stenciled on a wall. Can't you
45 and I strike out for ourselves, May?"

"Goodness—shall we elope?" she laughed.

"If you would—"

"You do love me, Newland! I'm
50 so happy."

"But then—why not be happier?"

"We can't behave like people in novels, though, can we?"

"Why not—why not—why not?"

55 She looked a little bored by his insistence. She knew very well why they couldn't, but it was troublesome to have to produce a reason. "I'm not clever enough to
60 argue with you. But that kind of thing is rather—vulgar, isn't it?" she suggested, relieved to have hit on a word that would certainly extinguish the whole subject.

65 "Are you so much afraid, then, of being vulgar?"

She was evidently staggered by this. "Of course I should hate it— and so would you," she rejoined, a
70 trifle irritably.

Feeling that she had indeed found the right way of closing the discussion, she went on light-heartedly, "Oh, did I tell you
75 that I showed cousin Ellen my engagement ring?"

—from *The Age of Innocence*, by Edith Wharton

35. As revealed in the passage, what does Newland Archer most yearn for?

(1) personal wealth

(2) May Welland's respect

(3) a stable marriage

(4) variety in life

(5) Mrs. Welland's approval

36. What does May's reaction when Newland mentions Mrs. Welland's insistence on a long engagement suggest about her?

May's reaction suggests that she

(1) considers the engagement period planned by her mother to be brief

(2) feels that Newland Archer has insulted her mother

(3) disagrees with her mother about when she and Newland should marry

(4) believes that her friends' engagements periods were too long

(5) secretly hopes that Newland will call off their engagement

37. How does May Welland put an end to the discussion that Newland Archer starts?

(1) She asserts that what he has said during their discussion is pointless.

(2) She denounces elopement as too distasteful for her and Newland.

(3) She reminds him that their friends would disapprove of an elopement.

(4) She dismisses elopement as suitable only for romance novels.

(5) She accuses him of trying to go against her mother's wishes.

38. What would Newland probably conclude about May's responses to him?

He would conclude that they are influenced mainly by

(1) her educational background

(2) popular romance novels

(3) social customs and expectations

(4) her friends Isabel, Grace, and Ellen

(5) what her mother has told her to say

39. Edith Wharton wrote *The Age of Innocence* largely as a panorama of New York's upper middle-class society during the 1870s. What does the passage suggest about the prevailing attitude among that society toward leisure travel?

Leisure travel was considered to be

(1) irresponsible

(2) traditional

(3) a privilege

(4) dangerous

(5) uncommon

40. What does the passage suggest about women from the era and culture that are the setting for *The Age of Innocence*?

(1) They were discouraged from thinking for themselves.

(2) They were not so self-confident as women of the previous generation.

(3) They had too much power in decision making.

(4) They were overly argumentative and bossy.

(5) They expected that anything they wanted would be given to them.

MATHEMATICS

90 Minutes • 50 Questions

> **General Directions:** The Mathematics Test consists of 50 questions intended to measure your general mathematics skills, including your ability to solve math problems. The test consists of two parts:
> - Part I: 25 questions
> - Part II: 25 questions
>
> Part I and Part II are <u>not</u> separately timed. If you finish Part I early, you may begin working on Part II right away.
>
> The use of a calculator is allowed for Part I but <u>not</u> for Part II.

To answer some questions you will need to apply one or more mathematics formulas. The formulas provided on the next page will help you to answer those questions. Some questions refer to charts, graphs, and figures. Unless otherwise noted, charts, graphs, and figures are drawn to scale.

Answering Alternative-format Questions

To answer some questions you will be required to write a number instead of selecting among five choices. You will record your answers to these questions using the following alternative-format grid:

To record an answer in this grid, write your answer in the top row. Enter only one character—a number digit, decimal point, or fraction bar—in a box. You may start in any column that will allow you to enter your entire answer. Fill in the corresponding bubble below each character you have written. (GED® answer sheets are machine-read, so only filled-in bubbles will be read.) Leave blank all columns you did not use to record your answer. No answer to an alternative-format question can be a negative number.

Do <u>not</u> enter a mixed number in the grid. Instead, enter a fraction or a decimal number. To represent the mixed number $2\frac{1}{2}$, for example, enter either the fraction **5/2** or the decimal number **2.5.** Grid only one answer, even if there is more than one correct answer.

practice test

Formulas

AREA	**Triangle:** $\frac{1}{2}$ × base × height **Rectangle:** length × width **Parallelogram:** base × height **Circle:** π × radius^2 **Right cylinder:** area of circular base × height **Trapezoid:** $\frac{1}{2}$(base$_1$ + base$_2$) × height
PERIMETER	**Triangle:** side$_1$ + side$_2$ + side$_3$ **Rectangle:** (2 × length) + (2 × width) **Circle (circumference):** 2π × radius **or** π × diameter ($\pi \approx 3.14$)
VOLUME	**Right cylinder:** area of base × height **Rectangular solid:** length × width × height **Cube:** (side)^3 **Square pyramid:** $\frac{1}{3}$ × edge^2 × height **Cone:** $\frac{1}{3} \times \pi \times$ radius^2 × height ($\pi \approx 3.14$)
COORDINATE GEOMETRY	**Distance between points** = $\sqrt{(x_2 - x_1)^2 + (y_2 - y_1)^2}$, where the two points are (x_1, y_1) and (x_2, y_2) **Slope of a line** = $\frac{y_2 - y_1}{x_2 - x_1}$, where (x_1, y_1) and (x_2, y_2) are any two points on the line
MEASURES OF CENTRAL TENDENCY	**Mean (simple average)** = $\frac{x_1 + x_2 + x_3 \ldots x_n}{n}$, where each x is the value of a different term and n is the total number of terms **Median** = the middle term in value if the number of terms is an *odd* number **or** $\frac{x + y}{2}$ (where x and y are the two middle terms in value) if the number of terms is an *even* number
OTHER FORMULAS	**Pythagorean theorem:** (leg$_1$)^2 + (leg$_2$)^2 = (hypotenuse)^2 **Distance** = rate × time **Simple interest** = dollar amount × interest rate **Total cost** = cost per item × number of items

MATHEMATICS, PART I: QUESTIONS 1–25

The use of a calculator is allowed for questions 1–25.

1. Justin wants to telephone a friend who lives overseas. The rate is 48 cents for the first minute and 34 cents for each additional minute. If Justin is planning a 45-minute call to his friend, how much will the call cost?

    (1) $13.28

    (2) $14.96

    (3) $15.30

    (4) $15.44

    (5) $21.26

2. The number of attendees at a certain annual conference is 256 this year and has always doubled every five years. How many people attended the conference 20 years ago?

    Mark your answer in the grid on your answer sheet.

QUESTIONS 3 AND 4 REFER TO THE FOLLOWING GRAPH.

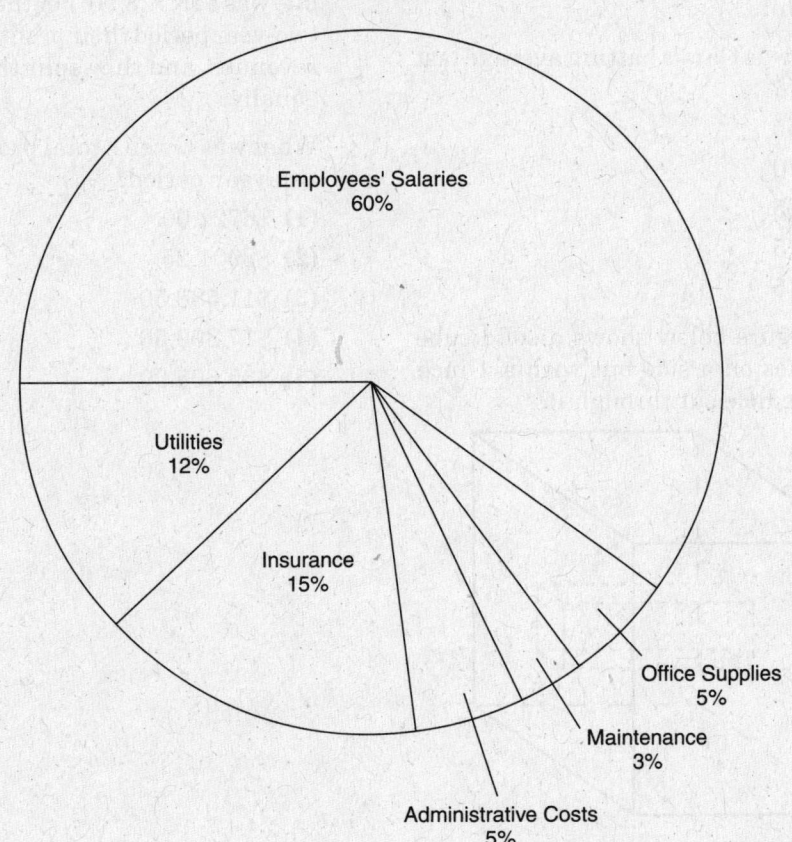

XY Lumber Co. Budget, 2011
$200,000

Employees' Salaries 60%

Utilities 12%

Insurance 15%

Office Supplies 5%

Maintenance 3%

Administrative Costs 5%

3. How much money was budgeted for administrative costs?
   (1) $1000
   (2) $10,000
   (3) $20,000
   (4) $100,000
   (5) Not enough information is provided.

4. By what fraction does the budget for insurance exceed the budget for utilities?
   (1) one fifth
   (2) one fourth
   (3) one third
   (4) one half
   (5) two thirds

5. A baseball player's "batting average" is the number of hits for every 1000 times the player is at bat. Last season Gary was at bat 248 times, resulting in 93 hits.

   What was Gary's batting average last season?
   (1) 155
   (2) 170
   (3) 285
   (4) 375
   (5) 415

6. The figure below shows a solid cube 3 inches on a side but with a 1-inch square hole cut through it.

   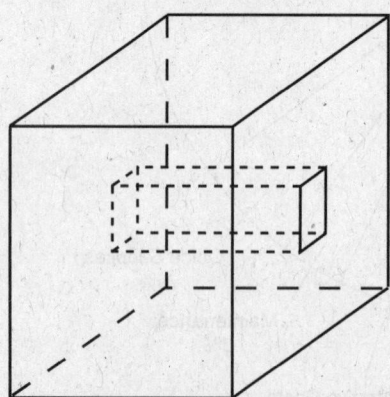

   How many square inches is the total surface area of the resulting solid figure?

   Mark your answer in the grid on your answer sheet.

7. A store clerk is preparing an advertisement for store items that are on sale. Items regularly priced at $175 will be sold for $105, and items regularly priced at $240 will be sold for $180.

   Which advertisement accurately describes this sale?
   (1) save 25–40%
   (2) prices slashed by 30%
   (3) all items half price
   (4) sale: 20–50% off
   (5) save more than a third

8. Gwen and Terri own a florist shop. In 2008, their total revenue was $16,876.10. In 2009, their total revenue was $18,728.90. For the combined, two-year period their profit was 50% of revenues, and they split those profits equally.

   What was Gwen's total profit over the two-year period?
   (1) $6722.00
   (2) $8901.25
   (3) $11,588.50
   (4) $17,802.50
   (5) $35,605.00

9. What is the result of the following operation?

$13 + 7 \times 17 \div 4$

Mark your answer in the grid on your answer sheet.

QUESTIONS 10 AND 11 REFER TO THE FOLLOWING GRAPH.

MARKETING, LEGAL, AND PRODUCTION EXPENSES
FOR XYZ COMPANY
(2006–2010)

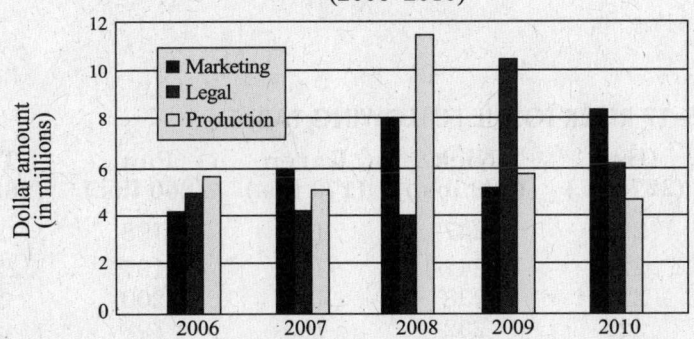

10. For which two years was the difference between marketing expenses and production expenses most nearly the same?

   (1) 2006 and 2007
   (2) 2008 and 2010
   (3) 2007 and 2009
   (4) 2006 and 2008
   (5) 2007 and 2010

11. During the greatest one-year increase in total marketing, legal, and production expenses, what was the approximate percent of the increase?

   (1) 22 percent
   (2) 40 percent
   (3) 55 percent
   (4) 70 percent
   (5) 75 percent

12. Jennifer is planning on making a new dress. She will need $3\frac{1}{2}$ yards of fabric, which is on sale for $2.50 a yard. She will also need a zipper that costs $1.99, two packs of buttons that cost $1.49 each, and a spool of thread that costs only 89 cents.

How much will the dress cost Jennifer to make?

   (1) $8.36
   (2) $13.12
   (3) $14.61
   (4) $24.85
   (5) $26.34

13. The degree sum of the interior angles of any polygon can be expressed as $(n-2)(180°)$, where n = the number of sides. If four of the five interior angles of a pentagon measure 110°, 60°, 120°, and 100°, what is the measure of the fifth interior angle?

    (1) 100°

    (2) 110°

    (3) 125°

    (4) 135°

    (5) 150°

14. If $\sqrt{ab} = 4$, then what is the value of a^2b^2 ?

    (1) −128

    (2) $\dfrac{1}{64}$

    (3) 64

    (4) 256

    (5) Not enough information is provided.

QUESTIONS 15–17 REFER TO THE FOLLOWING TABLE.

End of week:	Greg (227 lbs.)	Nick (249 lbs.)	Karen (173 lbs.)	Paul (200 lbs.)	Tony (268 lbs.)
1	226	247	172	198	266
2	224	242	168	197	260
3	224	238	165	200	255
4	225	232	163	198	254
5	223	232	163	199	259
6	219	231	161	196	258
7	216	233	160	191	261
8	218	230	163	190	256
9	214	231	162	190	253
10	215	232	164	188	252

The table shows the recorded weight of each of 5 dieters during a ten-week diet. Each dieter's starting weight is indicated in parentheses.

15. From the first day of the diet, which dieter experienced the LEAST variation in weight over the ten-week period?

    (1) Greg

    (2) Nick

    (3) Karen

    (4) Paul

    (5) Tony

16. At the end of each week, a nutritionist recorded the dieter's combined (net) gain or loss for the week. Which recorded figure is NOT accurate?

    (1) from end of week 1 to end of week 2: a net loss of more than 15 pounds

    (2) from end of week 4 to end of week 5: a net gain of less than 5 pounds

    (3) from end of week 5 to end of week 6: a net loss of more than 5 pounds

    (4) from end of week 7 to end of week 8: a net loss of more than 5 pounds

    (5) from end of week 9 to end of week 10: a net gain of less than 5 pounds

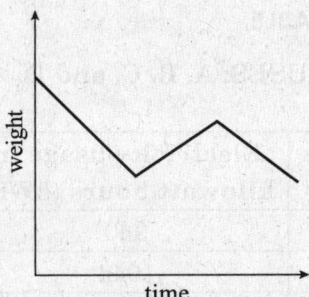

17. Which dieter's weight variation over the ten-week period is best represented by the above graph?

(1) Greg

(2) Nick

(3) Karen

(4) Paul

(5) Tony

18. In the below figure, $\overline{AB} \parallel \overline{DC}$ and $\overline{AD} \parallel \overline{BC}$.

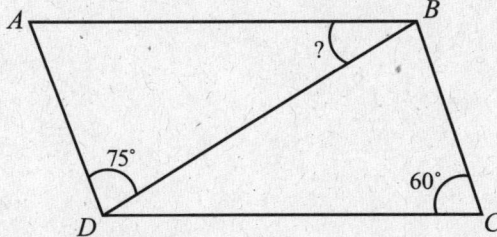

What is the degree measure of $\angle ABD$?

Express your answer in *degrees*. Mark your answer in the grid on your answer sheet.

19. One month ago, the balance in Melissa's checking account was $823.80. Since then, she has deposited a paycheck of $1645.38 and has written checks for $265.75 (credit card payment), $120.22 (phone bill), and $965.50 (for rent), as well as a fourth check (for car repair). The current balance in her account is $455.01.

What was the amount of the check Melissa wrote for car repair?

(1) $396.95

(2) $368.79

(3) $662.70

(4) $782.92

(5) $896.46

20. In an arithmetic series, the difference between one term and the next is the same for any two successive terms in the series. What is the sum of the first 50 terms of the arithmetic series −25, −24, −23, . . . ?

(1) −25

(2) −1

(3) 0

(4) 1

(5) 25

21. The average distance of three shot-put attempts was 12.9 meters. After another attempt, the average distance for all four attempts was 13.3 meters. What was the distance of the fourth shot-put attempt, in meters?

Mark your answer in the grid on your answer sheet.

22. The sailfish can swim through the water at speeds up to 72 miles per hour. Approximately how many kilometers (km) can the sailfish travel in 72 minutes? [1 km = 0.62 miles]

(1) 45 km

(2) 54 km

(3) 86 km

(4) 116 km

(5) 139 km

QUESTIONS 23 AND 24 REFER TO THE FOLLOWING TABLE.

ELECTRICITY USAGE AT FOUR HOUSES: A, B, C, and D
(Month of June)

House	Interior area (square area)	Interior volume (cubic feet)	Electricity usage in kilowatt hours (kWh)
A	1300	10,400	960
B	1500	12,000	1044
C	2000	16,200	1125
D	2300	18,400	1205

23. The month of June consists of 30 days. During June, how much more electricity was used at house C per day than at house A per day, on average?

   (1) 2.7 kWh

   (2) 2.8 kWh

   (3) 4.0 kWh

   (4) 4.8 kWh

   (5) 5.5 kWh

24. Assuming each house has a flat ceiling, which house has the greatest ceiling height?

   (1) House A

   (2) House B

   (3) House C

   (4) House D

   (5) All four houses have the same ceiling height.

25. A cone-shaped doll hat has a radius of 2 inches and the height of 5 inches. If the hat is turned upside down and filled with water, how much water will it hold?

Express your answer to the *nearest cubic inch*. Mark your answer in the grid on your answer sheet.

END OF PART I.

MATHEMATICS, PART II: QUESTIONS 26–50

The use of a calculator is NOT allowed for questions 26–50.

26. Which of the following simplifies to an integer?

(1) $\frac{5}{2} + \frac{3}{4}$

(2) $\frac{5}{3} + \frac{3}{4}$

(3) $\frac{5}{4} + \frac{3}{2}$

(4) $\frac{3}{5} + \frac{4}{3}$

(5) $\frac{3}{4} + \frac{5}{4}$

27. Which of the following expressions is a simplified form of $(-2x^2)^4$?

(1) $-16x^8$

(2) $-16x^6$

(3) $-8x^8$

(4) $8x^6$

(5) $16x^8$

28. The graph of the equation $y = 7x - 3$ is a straight line. The y-intercept of this line is at point P.

Show the location of point P by marking the coordinate grid on your answer sheet.

29. How many distinct (x, y) pairs satisfy the equation $6x - 4 = 3y$?

(1) 0

(2) 1

(3) 2

(4) 3

(5) infinitely many

30. If $p = (3)(5)(6)(9)(q)$, where q is a positive integer, then p must be divisible, with no remainder, by all the following integers—with the possible exception of which one?

(1) 27

(2) 36

(3) 45

(4) 54

(5) 90

31. What is the sum of $\sqrt{0.49}$, $\frac{3}{4}$, and 80%?

Mark you answer in the grid on your answer sheet.

32. If x is a real number, and if $x^3 = 100$, then x lies between which two consecutive integers?

(1) 1 and 2

(2) 2 and 3

(3) 3 and 4

(4) 4 and 5

(5) 5 and 6

33. The figure below shows the end of a packing box that holds six identical tubes.

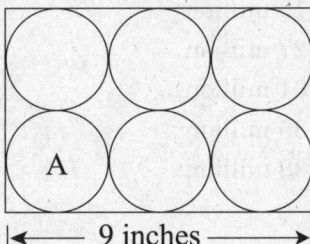

|← 9 inches →|

What is the circumference of tube A?

(1) 2π inches

(2) 3π inches

(3) 3.5π inches

(4) 4.5π inches

(5) Not enough information is provided.

34. A legislature passed a bill into law by a 5:3 margin. No legislator abstained. What fraction of the votes cast were in favor of the bill?

Mark your answer in the grid on your answer sheet.

35. A vending machine contains only dimes (d) and nickels (n). Which of the following represents the dollar value of all coins in the vending machine?

   (1) $0.05n \times 0.10d$

   (2) $0.15(n + d)$

   (3) $0.05d + 0.10n$

   (4) $0.10d + 0.05n$

   (5) $0.05n \times 0.10d$

QUESTIONS 36 AND 37 REFER TO THE FOLLOWING CHART.

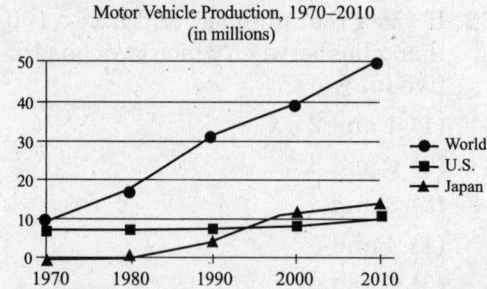

Motor Vehicle Production, 1970–2010
(in millions)

36. In 2000, world production of motor vehicles exceeded U.S. production by approximately how many units?

   (1) 19 million

   (2) 27 million

   (3) 31 million

   (4) 35 million

   (5) 38 million

37. Which statement about motor vehicle production from 1970 to 2010 is most accurate?

   (1) The increase in production was attributable mainly to countries other than the United States and Japan.

   (2) As a percentage of world production, U.S. production neither increased nor decreased.

   (3) World production increased steadily while U.S. production declined.

   (4) As a percentage of world production, Japan production neither increased nor decreased.

   (5) Japan production increased steadily while U.S. production declined.

38. A line is plotted on the (x,y) coordinate plane, as shown below.

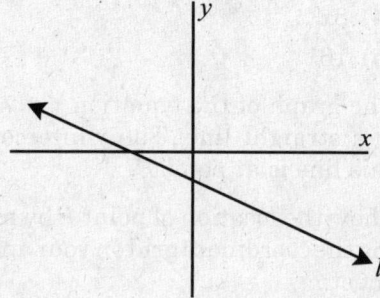

Assuming the scales on both axes are the same, which of the following could be the equation of l_1 ?

   (1) $y = \dfrac{2}{3}x - 3$

   (2) $y = -2x + 1$

   (3) $y = x + 3$

   (4) $y = -3x - \dfrac{2}{3}$

   (5) $y = -\dfrac{2}{3}x - 3$

39. If $f(a) = a^2$, then what is $f\left(a^4\right)$?

(1) a

(2) a^2

(3) a^4

(4) a^6

(5) a^8

40. In a deck of 52 cards, 4 are aces and 12 are face cards. Each of the remaining cards is a numbered card. If all aces are removed from the deck, which of the following describes a probability of $\frac{3}{4}$?

(1) the chances of drawing a card other than an ace

(2) the chances of drawing a Joker card

(3) the chances of drawing a card other than a face card

(4) the chances of drawing a face card

(5) none of the above

41. Which of the following is NOT equal to 4.23×10^{-2}?

(1) 4230×10^{-4}

(2) 0.00423×10^1

(3) 0.423×10^{-1}

(4) 42.3×10^{-3}

(5) 0.0423×10^0

42. Two square rugs, R and S, have a combined area of 20 square feet. If the area of rug R is four times the area of rug S, what is the perimeter of rug S?

(1) 4 feet

(2) 8 feet

(3) 10 feet

(4) 12 feet

(5) 16 feet

43. A total of N children are taking a field trip. The number of girls on the trip (G) exceeds the number of boys on the trip (B) by 17.

Which equation can you use to determine the number of girls taking the field trip?

(1) $B + (G - 17) = N$

(2) $N - G = B + 17$

(3) $G + (G - 17) = N$

(4) $N + G = 17 - G$

(5) $B + (B - 17) = N$

44. In which of the following forms can the quadratic expression $x^2 - 2x - 3$ be written?

(1) $(x - 3)(x + 1)$

(2) $(x - 3)(x - 2)$

(3) $(x + 3)(x - 1)$

(4) $(x - 2)(x + 1)$

(5) $(x - 1)(x - 2)$

45. David and Steven work together in the shipping-and-handling department of the same company. David can pack a total of 48 boxes in 5 hours. Steven can pack two-thirds the number of boxes each hour as David.

How many complete boxes can Steven pack in 3 hours?

Mark your answer using the grid on your answer sheet.

QUESTIONS 46 AND 47 REFER TO THE FOLLOWING INFORMATION AND FIGURE.

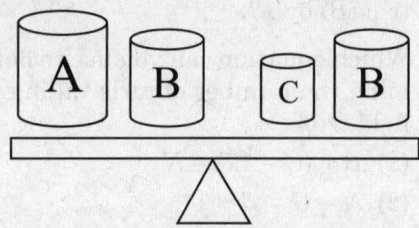

The balanced scale shows equal weights. Cylindrical canisters A, B, and C are proportionate to one another in shape. By volume, the capacity of canister A is 150% of canister B and 200% of canister C.

46. An object's *mass* is determined by the following equation:

$$mass = \frac{weight}{volume}$$

What does the figure suggest about the mass of one canister compared to the mass of another?

(1) The mass of canister B is $\frac{3}{4}$ that of canister C.

(2) The mass of canister C is twice that of canister A.

(3) The mass of canister A is $\frac{3}{2}$ that of canister B.

(4) The mass of canister C is $\frac{3}{4}$ that of canister B.

(5) The mass of canister A is twice that of canister B.

47. If the circular base of canister A is 900 cm², what is the area of canister B's base?

(1) 450 cm²

(2) 600 cm²

(3) 750 cm²

(4) 1200 cm²

(5) Not enough information is provided.

48. The figure below shows the order, but not precise values, of four points on the number line.

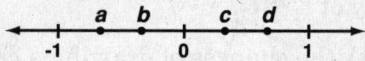

Which of the following represents the greatest value?

(1) $c - b$

(2) $a + b$

(3) $d - c$

(4) $b + c$

(5) Not enough information is provided.

Average (Mean) Gasoline Price Among 50 Stations	Number of Stations Charging More Than the Average Price	Number of Stations Charging Less Than the Average Price
January 1: $2.50	22	17
February 1: $2.65	15	28
March 1: $2.40	23	23

49. The table above shows the average price of gasoline among 50 gasoline-service stations on three different days, along with the number of stations charging more and less than the average on each day.

Based on the information in the table, which of the following statements about the price of gasoline among all 50 stations is NOT true?

(1) On March 1, the average price was equal to the median price.

(2) On February 1, the median price was less than the average price.

(3) The average price on March 1 price was less than the median price on January 1.

(4) The average price on February 1 was more than the average price on January 1.

(5) More stations charged the average daily price on February 1 than on January 1.

50. The figure below shows a wire (represented by the dashed line) connecting the outer edge of a porch roof to the base of the building's wall, creating angle of θ degrees at the base of the building. The height of the building is a feet, and the width of the porch roof is b feet.

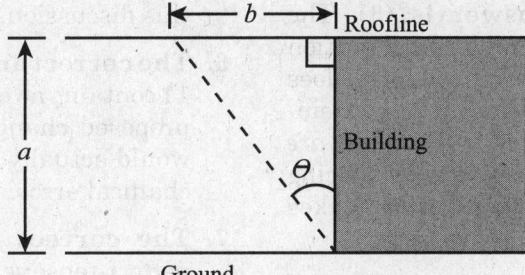

Which of the following represents the length of wire, in feet?

(1) $\dfrac{b}{\cos\theta}$

(2) $\dfrac{a}{\cos\theta}$

(3) $\dfrac{a}{\sin\theta}$

(4) $a\cos\theta$

(5) $b\sin\theta$

ANSWER KEY AND EXPLANATIONS

Language Arts Writing, Part I

1. (5)	11. (4)	21. (5)	31. (1)	41. (3)
2. (3)	12. (5)	22. (3)	32. (1)	42. (1)
3. (2)	13. (3)	23. (2)	33. (4)	43. (3)
4. (1)	14. (4)	24. (5)	34. (3)	44. (4)
5. (4)	15. (4)	25. (3)	35. (2)	45. (1)
6. (5)	16. (2)	26. (4)	36. (5)	46. (3)
7. (2)	17. (3)	27. (1)	37. (4)	47. (2)
8. (4)	18. (4)	28. (2)	38. (3)	48. (3)
9. (1)	19. (1)	29. (3)	39. (5)	49. (1)
10. (4)	20. (4)	30. (5)	40. (4)	50. (2)

1. **The correct answer is (5).** The list of items at the end of sentence 1 begins with *a skateboard*, which is singular. All list items should be grammatically parallel. Accordingly, *scooters* (plural) should be changed to *scooter* (singular).

2. **The correct answer is (3).** The problem with the underlined portion is that the verb *are* (plural form) does not agree in number with *helmet* (singular). One solution is to change *are* to *is*, as in choice (3). (Also, replacing *a helmet* with the pronoun *one* makes for a more concise sentence.)

3. **The correct answer is (2).** The problem with the original sentence is that the phrase *inside it* separates the verb *will have* from its object *a CPSC or ASTM sticker*. Among the four other alternatives, the sentence in choice (2) is the only one that fixes this problem without creating a new one.

4. **The correct answer is (1).** Sentence 8 tells us that the strap should be secure but not too tight, while sentence 10 tells us how to judge whether the strap is secure but not too tight. So it would make sense for sentence 10 to immediately follow sentence 8—which is what the revision proposed in choice (1) would accomplish.

5. **The correct answer is (4).** Paragraph C discusses in detail how to find a helmet that can fit properly. Choice (4) provides an ideal way to introduce this discussion.

6. **The correct answer is (5).** Sentence 11 contains no errors. Each of the four proposed changes is unnecessary or would actually create a usage or mechanical error.

7. **The correct answer is (2).** The perfect-tense verb form *worn* should be used here. Also, it is the *helmet*—not the edge—that is worn on the head.

8. **The correct answer is (4).** Using the word *whenever* together with *the helmet* implies that a child can outgrow a particular helmet more than once, which makes no sense. The word *when* makes much better sense.

9. **The correct answer is (1).** The original version, choice (1), is the best one. Choices (2) and (5) use incorrect pronouns (*them* and *it*). Choice (3) is wordy and illogical. (*They* should refer to gardens, not plants.) Choice (4) uses

the singular *garden* where the plural *gardens* should be used.

10. The correct answer is (4). The relative pronoun *who* should be used only to refer to people, but here it is used to refer to perennials, which are plants. Replacing *who* with *that* corrects the error.

11. The correct answer is (4). The singular *tree tomato* matches *the tamorillo* at the end of the sentence.

12. The correct answer is (5). Paragraph B is devoted entirely to discussing the merits of adding perennials to a vegetable garden (as is paragraph C). Choice (5) provides an ideal topic sentence for this discussion. The sentence is broad enough to embrace the entire discussion, and it flows nicely into the next sentence (6).

13. The correct answer is (3). What follows the comma and the conjunction *and* should be an independent clause (a clause that can stand alone as a complete sentence). Inserting the word *they* after *and* creates just such a clause: *they don't need weeding.*

14. The correct answer is (4). *Root crops* is not an *approach*. To fix this problem, the sentence in choice (4) adds *Planting* to the beginning of the sentence.

15. The correct answer is (4). The noun clause *Adding perennials to a vegetable garden* is considered singular, and so it takes the singular verb form *adds*, not the plural form *add*.

16. The correct answer is (2). Sentence 15 is awkward and confusing. Choice (2) is the only one that provides a group of words useful in constructing a clear, graceful version of the sentence: *Finally, perennials don't require tilling, which kills many beneficial microbes in the soil.*

17. The correct answer is (3). The word *opportunities* is plural and so should not be preceded by the article *an*. By simply removing the word *an*, you can correct the error.

18. The correct answer is (4). The underlined part uses the past-perfect tense, and *had given* (not *given*) could be the correct conjugation here. However, there's no reason why the simple past tense cannot be used instead, so choice (4) provides the grammatically correct version.

19. The correct answer is (1). The word *who's* is a contraction of *who is* and makes no sense here. The contraction should be replaced with the relative pronoun *whose*.

20. The correct answer is (4). Sentence 7 accomplishes nothing more than restating an idea expressed in sentence 9. Moreover, removing sentence 7 actually enhances the logical flow of the paragraph.

21. The correct answer is (5). Sentence 10 contains no errors. Choices (1) and (2) each proposes a change that would result in a confusing, run-on sentence. As for choice (3), removing the word *an* would also require changing *candidate* to *candidates*. As for choice (4), changing *candidate* to *candidates* would also require removing the word *an*.

22. The correct answer is (3). The first part of the sentence boils down to this: *if one position **or** another position **become** available.* The word *or* tells you that the plural verb form *become* is incorrect and should be replaced with *becomes*.

23. The correct answer is (2). The comma separating *consideration* from *I* splices together two main clauses. One way to correct this comma splice is to insert a logical conjunction, such as *and,* after the comma. Also, the comma after *time* serves only to interrupt the natural flow of ideas and should be removed. Choice (2) fixes both problems.

24. The correct answer is (5). Notice the natural flow from sentence 11 to sentence 12 and the close connection between their ideas. A paragraph break between the two sentences disrupts the flow and severs the connection. The letter would be more effective without the break.

25. The correct answer is (3). Sentence 1 is actually a sentence fragment (an incomplete sentence). A simple solution to this problem is the one suggested in choice (3), which transforms the prepositional phrase *through online registration* into the predicate *is through online registration*.

26. The correct answer is (4). The resulting single sentence should present ideas in their most logical sequence, which is to direct the reader first to the Web site, then to the site's online registration area, then to the tab. Choice (4) provides the ideal group of words with which to begin such a sentence: *Go to our Web site and click on the "Register for Classes" tab to access the online registration area of the site.*

27. The correct answer is (1). The first clause mixes the present and past tenses, confusing the time frame. To correct the problem, you can either replace *created* with *create* or make the change that choice (1) proposes: *If you have not yet created . . . .*

28. The correct answer is (2). The entire list of steps employs the present tense, as though the registrant is performing the steps while reading the registration information. There is no logical reason for the sudden shift to past tense in the underlined part of sentence 8. The past-tense form *wrote* should be replaced with the present-tense form *write*.

29. The correct answer is (3). Sentences 6 through 9 take you up to the point where you've successfully signed in at the Web site. Since sentences 10 and 11 are both part of the next sequential step—selecting your classes—step 4 should begin with sentence 10.

30. The correct answer is (5). Positioning the relative pronoun *where* immediately after *meeting* confuses the pronoun reference. (What does *where* refer to: *meeting* or *office*?) One solution is to completely reconstruct the sentence. Another solution is to separate *meeting* and *where* by splitting the sentence into two, as is done in choice (5).

31. The correct answer is (1). The original version is acceptable. Each other choice makes for an awkward or confusing sentence.

32. The correct answer is (1). *Taking note . . . , and then fill out* does not make grammatical sense. Changing *Taking* to *Take* fixes the problem by creating two independent clauses that are grammatically parallel.

33. The correct answer is (4). The compound subject *both online and in-person registration* takes the plural verb form *begin* rather than the singular form *begins*.

34. The correct answer is (3). Paragraphs F and H pertain to in-person registration, while paragraph G pertains to walk-in registration. Move paragraph G to follow paragraph H, and the ideas will flow more naturally and logically from one paragraph to the next.

35. The correct answer is (2). The conjunction *but* (instead of *and*) would more effectively convey the point of the sentence. Also, the plural pronoun *they* does not match its singular antecedent *a person*. Choice (2) solves both problems: *A person might have no cares one day but be responsible for another human life the next day.*

36. The correct answer is (5). Sentence 4 contains no errors. Each of the proposed corrections would either distort or obscure the sentence's meaning, which is quite clear as the sentence stands.

37. **The correct answer is (4).** Sentence 5 merely repeats an idea from sentence 3 and contributes very little to paragraph B. The passage would be more effective if sentence 5 were simply omitted.

38. **The correct answer is (3).** Of the five alternatives, choice (3) is the only one that follows naturally and logically after *What if*. Here's a good version of the revised sentence: *What if there is nobody to take care of a child when a parent doesn't?*

39. **The correct answer is (5).** The paragraph's ideas would flow much more logically from one to the next if sentence 10 were repositioned to follow sentence 12.

40. **The correct answer is (4).** The word *soul* should be replaced with its homonym *sole*, which means "only or singular."

41. **The correct answer is (3).** In the original sentence, the phrase following *either* is not grammatically parallel to the phrase following *or*. Choice (3) is the only one that corrects this problem with a sentence that is unambiguous and error-free.

42. **The correct answer is (1).** Sentence 13 is actually a sentence fragment (an incomplete sentence). Remove the word *who* to form a complete sentence that also makes sense.

43. **The correct answer is (3).** Use of the possessive *motorist's* implies that the recommendations are for the benefit of only one motorist, but in context the sentence clearly intends to refer to motorists generally. Replacing *motorist's* with *motorist* fixes the problem.

44. **The correct answer is (4).** The infinitive form *To recommend* is awkward and confusing here. Also, to what does the pronoun *them* refer: the two

roads or the recommendations? The reference is ambiguous. Choice (4) is the only one that solves both problems without creating another one.

45. **The correct answer is (1).** As it stands, sentence 3 is actually a sentence fragment (an incomplete sentence). Changing *that* to *with* completes the sentence, and the resulting sentence makes sense in the context of the paragraph as a whole.

46. **The correct answer is (3).** The sentence makes it clear that it is listing two recommendations, but what follows the colon reads like a single recommendation. Choice (3) inserts a comma in the appropriate position. Choice (3) also changes *or* to *and*, which helps distinguish one choice from the other.

47. **The correct answer is (2).** Sentence 6 mentions *the garage entrance,* but the report mentions nothing else about a garage until sentence 9. Moving sentence 6 so that it follows sentence 9 would clear up any possible confusion.

48. **The correct answer is (3).** Sentence 12 tries to convey too many ideas in a single sentence. The long string of modifying phrases makes the sentence especially confusing. The solution is to split the sentence into two sentences. The group of words in choice (3) is ideal for constructing a sentence pair that is easy to understand: *However, an Environmental Impact Report on the proposed use of the property has not been submitted. Until it has, the Commission lacks the authority to issue any opinion about the proposed use.* None of the other four groups of words works nearly so well as the group in choice (3).

49. **The correct answer is (1).** Except in sentence 14, the report consistently uses the present tense when referring to the Commission's opinions (*The Commission agrees*, in paragraph B; *The Commission understands*, in

answers practice test 2

paragraph D; *we agree*, in sentence 15). Nothing in the report provides any reason for the temporary shift to past tense in sentence 14. Accordingly, the past-tense verb *agreed* should be changed to the present-tense *agrees*.

50. The correct answer is (2). The recommendation discussed in paragraph B (relocating the bus stop) is closely related to the one discussed in paragraph E (installing a new sidewalk). Both recommendations cite the same two-month study, and they both cite the same concern over pedestrian traffic across the intersection. Accordingly, the report's ideas would flow more logically if paragraph B were positioned *immediately* before paragraph E.

Language Arts, Writing, Part II

Evaluating Your Practice Essay

Your actual GED® essay will be read and scored by 2 trained readers, who will evaluate it according to its *overall effectiveness*, considering how well you convey and support your main ideas, how well you organize those ideas, and how clearly and correctly you write throughout the essay.

It is difficult to be objective about one's own writing. So to help you evaluate your practice essay, you may wish to ask a mentor, teacher, or friend to read and evaluate it for you. In any case, use the following 4-point evaluation checklist. This list provides all of the elements of an effective, high-scoring GED® essay.

❶ Is the essay well-focused? (Does it clearly convey a central idea, and does it remain focused on that idea, as opposed to digressing from the topic or focusing too narrowly on certain minor points?)

❷ Does the essay develop its main ideas effectively, using persuasive reasons and relevant supporting examples?

❸ Is the essay well-organized? (Are the ideas presented in a logical sequence, so that the reader can easily follow them? Are transitions from one point to the next natural and logical? Does the essay have a clear ending, or did you appear to run out of time?)

❹ Does your essay demonstrate good control of grammar, sentence structure, word choice, punctuation, and spelling?

Each GED® reader will score your essay on a scale of 0–4 (the highest score is 4). If you can objectively answer "yes" to all four of the above questions, then your essay would earn a score of at least 3, and probably 4, from a trained GED® reader. Keep in mind, however, that the testing service will not award a separate score for the Writing Test, Part II (the essay). Instead, the service will combine your Part I and Part II scores according to its own formula, and then it will award a single overall Writing Test score.

Social Studies

1. (2)	11. (2)	21. (2)	31. (4)	41. (5)
2. (4)	12. (3)	22. (4)	32. (1)	42. (1)
3. (3)	13. (2)	23. (4)	33. (4)	43. (2)
4. (5)	14. (1)	24. (1)	34. (1)	44. (2)
5. (1)	15. (2)	25. (5)	35. (5)	45. (4)
6. (4)	16. (5)	26. (1)	36. (1)	46. (2)
7. (5)	17. (5)	27. (2)	37. (5)	47. (3)
8. (5)	18. (4)	28. (4)	38. (3)	48. (1)
9. (4)	19. (5)	29. (5)	39. (4)	49. (4)
10. (2)	20. (1)	30. (3)	40. (3)	50. (1)

1. **The correct answer is (2).** The Boston Tea Party protested the tax on tea. The tax had not been raised, choice (3), but neither had it been lifted (eliminated) choice (4). Choices (1) and (5) contributed to tensions between British and Americans but were not directly responsible for the protest against the tea tax.

2. **The correct answer is (4).** The flow of communication within the company and the management style of the supervisor are two of the three most highly rated qualities in their importance to workers.

3. **The correct answer is (3).** Choice (3) suggests a high degree of job security, which is higher on the list of qualities desired by employees than any of the qualities suggested in the other four choices.

4. **The correct answer is (5).** The purpose of the War Powers Act was to limit the power of the president to involve the country in wars without the approval of Congress. The Constitution gives Congress the power to declare war, but in today's world, formal declarations of war are no longer usually made. Korea, Vietnam, Iraq, Afghanistan, etc. were all "undeclared" wars.

5. **The correct answer is (1).** The drawing shows gangs growing out of (caused by) poverty, drugs, and ignorance.

6. **The correct answer is (4).** The cartoonist, who sees poverty, drugs, and ignorance as the causes of gangs, would probably agree that the only way to end gang violence is to eliminate these causes.

7. **The correct answer is (5).** A retired individual living on a fixed pension would see the value of his or her income depreciate in terms of what it can purchase. The other four choices would experience little or no immediate adverse effect from inflation.

8. **The correct answer is (5).** The *Marbury* v. *Madison* decision gave the Supreme Court the power to nullify an act of Congress if it violates the Constitution, as determined by the Court.

9. **The correct answer is (4).** Because Washington, D.C., is in the Eastern time zone and Portland, Oregon, is in the Pacific time zone, the time difference is 3 hours, so when it is 9 a.m. in Portland, it is noon in Washington, D.C.

10. **The correct answer is (2).** On any given date, the London exchange opens

after, not before, the Tokyo exchange. In fact, the London exchange does not open until after the Tokyo exchange has closed.

11. **The correct answer is (2).** By crossing from west to east, the sailor "loses" 23 hours. It is now the previous day. (The sailor should also set his watch's time *forward* one hour, to 1:30 a.m.)

12. **The correct answer is (3).** Inferring something is to strongly suggest something without actually stating it. The last sentence of the passage strongly suggests that the League of Nations would have been more successful had the United States joined. The passage does not provide clues as to the author's views on choices (1), (2), or (4), and choice (5) is not an inference since it is information directly stated by the author.

13. **The correct answer is (2).** When more than 400 workers are hired, the average production per worker begins to decline.

14. **The correct answer is (1).** The passage has no information about robot welding, choice (2). Hiring more workers will not always increase production, choice (3), which is shown by the last line in the table. Profits are not maximized by keeping labor at a minimum, choice (4); the level of workers needed to maximize profits depends on the size and equipment of the factory and the demand for the product. Although the table demonstrates this factory should not hire more than 600 workers, it's wrong to state that all auto factories should never hire more than 600 workers, choice (5), since factories vary in size and types of equipment.

15. **The correct answer is (2).** State governments do not have the power to check the federal government since, under the Constitution, federal law is supreme over state law. Of course, a federal law may be unconstitutional, but only the Supreme Court can make that determination, not a state government. All the other answer choices are examples of one branch of the federal government checking the power of another branch.

16. **The correct answer is (5).** The cartoon implies that Bush told Harris exactly what to say concerning recounts during the 2000 presidential election.

17. **The correct answer is (5).** The "Unemployment" chart shows that the unemployment rate declined in the years after the New Deal policies were initiated. This trend is consistent with the establishment of a federal program that employed many Americans.

18. **The correct answer is (4).** A strong labor union has the power to negotiate higher wages and salaries for its member-workers. (The first half of the twentieth century saw a growing labor-union movement in the United States.)

19. **The correct answer is (5).** Choice (5) is the only one that describes the situation regarding immigration from Japan and China to America.

20. **The correct answer is (1).** The large number of immigrants from Europe, who, it must be assumed, were processed through Ellis Island, would indicate that choice (1) is the correct answer.

21. **The correct answer is (2).** The great racial tensions between African Americans and whites of European descent were probably what caused immigration from Africa to be almost nonexistent.

22. **The correct answer is (4).** Of all the categories in the table, Medicare and Medicaid is the largest.

23. **The correct answer is (4).** The cartoon's message is that it is the parole boards themselves that are responsible when criminals who are

released early by parole become repeat offenders.

24. **The correct answer is (1).** The cartoonist would probably tell the parole board to be less lenient and more cautious about who they release, because this sort of leniency is the issue in the cartoon.

25. **The correct answer is (5).** Point E is located near latitude 60° S and longitude 85° E.

26. **The correct answer is (1).** North is labeled on the grid; as on most maps, north is towards the top of the map. Thus, point D is southwest of point A.

27. **The correct answer is (2).** National will and patriotism are an intangible component of a nation's power. All of the other choices are tangible assets that can be quantifiably measured.

28. **The correct answer is (4).** Building pyramids would have suggested that a small number of wealthy, powerful individuals could organize and exploit the labor of many lower-class workers. However, a stratified socioeconomic system did not appear in Mesoamerica until the Middle Preclassic period.

29. **The correct answer is (5).** In the Late Preclassic period, pottery had begun to show some features of classic Mayan art. This information suggests that the Mayan civilization was still to come. (Indeed, the Mayan civilization helps define the Classic Period of Mesoamerica.)

30. **The correct answer is (3).** If the Fed lowers the interest rate it charges banks (the discount rate), then banks will also begin to lower the rates they charge their loan customers. This would also generally cause the interest paid on savings accounts to go down, not up as in choice (2). It's likely that banks would make more loans, not fewer. as in choice (4); and the rate of growth in the nation's economy would likely increase, not decrease as

in choice (5). A change in the discount rate would not normally affect the number of banks that fail, choice (1).

31. **The correct answer is (4).** The occupation and the speech given at the Academy Awards showed that the protesters wanted to draw media attention to the unjust treatment of Native Americans. There is nothing to suggest they somehow wanted to return to the days before the Sioux were defeated, choice (1); to expand the Pine Ridge Indian Reservation, choice (2); to establish a national historic site, choice (3); or that they wanted Native Americans to return to their reservations, choice (5).

32. **The correct answer is (1).** As the paragraph implies, the preceding period was marked by the emergence of large companies that wielded too much power.

33. **The correct answer is (4).** As the map shows, the Middle East was a hotbed of military conflict throughout the entire decade of the 1980s.

34. **The correct answer is (1).** Modern-day Iran is a so-called "religious state," which means that religious doctrine (in this case, Islam) plays a significant role in both domestic and foreign policy.

35. **The correct answer is (5).** The House of Representatives selects the president when no candidate gets a majority of the electoral vote (270 or more votes). If there is a 269-269 tie, the House would select the president, but it would also have to select the president if there are 3 candidates with electoral votes and none has 270 or more votes, choice (2). However, just having 3 candidates doesn't mean one of them won't get 270 votes, so choice (1) is incorrect. State governments, not electors, determine which candidate wins in each state, choice (3), and which candidate wins the popular vote nationwide has nothing to do with the electoral vote, choice (4).

36. The correct answer is (1). The electoral vote determines who becomes president—a situation that is the result of the Constitution, not the winner-take-all rule. This would still be true without the winner-take-all rule. The candidates' tendency to focus on swing states, choice (2), and ignore the rest, choice (3), is a result of the winner-take-all rule, which also usually shuts out third-party candidates, choice (5). The winner-take-all rule also makes it more likely that the president could be a candidate who was not the winner in the popular vote, choice (4).

37. The correct answer is (5). This argument makes the case to change the electoral system for selecting the president. All the other arguments make the case to keep things as they are.

38. The correct answer is (3). King referred to the "whirlwind of revolt" that must continue until justice prevails. Yet, he urged his followers not to resort to aggression, as "we must not be guilty of wrongful deeds" or drink "from the cup of bitterness and hatred."

39. The correct answer is (4). The Fourteenth Amendment first defines citizenship and then states that all citizens must be treated equally. If a state prohibits casino gambling for all of its citizens, it is consistent with the Fourteenth Amendment. If a state singles out one ethnic group for different treatment, choices (3) and (5), it violates the Fourteenth Amendment. If a state treats naturalized citizens differently from citizens born in the United States, choice (1) and (2), it is also violating the Fourteenth Amendment.

40. The correct answer is (3). Although Kennedy's statement came before the Soviet Union placed nuclear missiles in Cuba, the threat of nuclear war already loomed. In a nuclear age, maintaining neutrality while an unfriendly nation with nuclear arms gains footholds in the Western world could too easily spell the demise of the United States. Kennedy saw a shift away from neutrality as necessary to the nation's survival.

41. The correct answer is (5). A belief in the right of people to have a say in their government is a traditional, strongly held American belief.

42. The correct answer is (1). In a direct democracy, all citizens participate in the lawmaking process and in setting policy. This form can be unwieldy in a large country with a vast population. It is more practical to elect individuals to represent the interests of particular geographically defined populations, or constituencies.

43. The correct answer is (2). Choice (2) describes an aristocracy: a small group of leaders determine who will follow them as leaders. Choice (1) describes a dictatorship. Choice (3) describes an absence of government. Choice (4) describes a direct democracy. Choice (5) describes a constitutional monarchy.

44. The correct answer is (2). In the last sentence, the author of the passage states her position, which is summarized in choice (2). The other statements do not accurately reflect the argument made by the author.

45. The correct answer is (4). During the 1930s, drought and dust storms made for difficult or, in some areas, intolerable living conditions in the prairie states.

46. The correct answer is (2). On the map, Australia has none of the symbols representing any fertilizer minerals.

47. The correct answer is (3). The only potash symbols on the map are in Europe and North America, at around the same latitude (an imaginary east-west line across the globe).

48. The correct answer is (1). When France invaded Mexico in 1861 and put in place a government favorable to its interests, this was a clear violation of the Monroe Doctrine. France was able to do this since the United States was in the midst of the Civil War. Answer choices (2) and (4) are events that reduced European power and influence in the Western Hemisphere; these are consistent with the Monroe Doctrine. Answer choices (3) and (5) are examples of U.S. intervention in Latin American nations and are consistent with the Roosevelt Corollary.

49. The correct answer is (4). Between 1965 and 1971, spending declined for only one category: training of federal personnel.

50. The correct answer is (1). Choices (2), (3), (4), and (5) may or may not be true statements; they cannot be verified by the information in the graph. Only choice (1) contains information that can be verified by the graph.

Science

1. (3)	11. (1)	21. (5)	31. (1)	41. (5)
2. (3)	12. (2)	22. (4)	32. (2)	42. (5)
3. (4)	13. (4)	23. (4)	33. (5)	43. (1)
4. (3)	14. (3)	24. (2)	34. (1)	44. (2)
5. (2)	15. (1)	25. (2)	35. (3)	45. (2)
6. (3)	16. (1)	26. (3)	36. (3)	46. (5)
7. (2)	17. (5)	27. (1)	37. (3)	47. (3)
8. (5)	18. (4)	28. (5)	38. (4)	48. (5)
9. (1)	19. (2)	29. (3)	39. (2)	49. (5)
10. (1)	20. (5)	30. (2)	40. (2)	50. (4)

1. The correct answer is (3). The fact that aphids rely on sexual reproduction during the harsh winter months is to ensure, through natural selection, that some of the population is hearty enough to survive. But during the gentler spring, when environmental conditions support a much larger population, their main goal is to generate as many offspring as possible, as quickly as possible. This goal is better achieved by asexual reproduction.

2. The correct answer is (3). At 20°C, all 15 grams are dissolved (the point lies below the KNO_3 solubility curve). From 25°C on the chart's horizontal axis, trace up to the solubility curve, and you'll find that about 45 grams of KNO_3 are soluble at that temperature. Thus, 30 more grams of KNO_3 must be added to saturate the water with KNO_3.

3. The correct answer is (4). Ammonia is the only gas among the four substances represented in the chart. For all three other substances, there is a direct relationship between temperature and solubility. In contrast, there is an inverse relationship for ammonia: as the temperature increases, solubility decreases. Choice (4) provides the only conclusion that is supported by the data in the chart.

4. **The correct answer is (3).** Statement A shows that humans are part of a grazing web, while statement D shows that humans are part of a detrital web. Since humans are a part of both web types, the two must overlap.

5. **The correct answer is (2).** All species of animals consume plants and/or animals, and so tigers must be part of a food chain. Since they prey on other animals but no other animals prey on them, they must be at the top of a grazing food chain. (Tigers are also part of a detrital chain, since their bodies are eventually consumed by decomposers and detritivores, such as vultures, that are farther up that chain.)

6. **The correct answer is (3).** Only the figure on the right (reverse fault) shows two bedrock masses compressing along a fault plane. This compression, or pushing together, forces one of the two masses upward (the right-hand rock in the figure), creating a mountain range.

7. **The correct answer is (2).** If Brian's arm were relaxed, the wave energy would work to move his arm up and down, thereby absorbing the energy. But since Brian is not allowing himself to absorb the wave energy, that energy will reflect back toward Allison.

8. **The correct answer is (5).** Blood type AB contains antibody A, which blood type B does not contain. As a result, antibody A will react against antigen B and will result in dangerous clumping of the blood.

9. **The correct answer is (1).** Although formulating a hypothesis is a proper initial step in a scientific experiment, in order for the results to be credible (believable), the experiment must be carried out objectively. In this case, the corporation clearly has a financial interest in showing that GMOs are safe to humans, and so the results of its studies are not credible.

10. **The correct answer is (1).** It is easy enough to imagine an out-of-control weed that can resist all of its natural survival threats because it has become genetically altered in the same way that crops are. Such a weed could easily overrun its ecosystem.

11. **The correct answer is (1).** Glucose and fructose both have the same chemical formula: $C_6H_{12}O_6$. The main difference is the placement of carbon in the molecular structure.

12. **The correct answer is (2).** If each pair of corresponding genes—for example, the one that determines hair color—"blended" together, as choice (1) suggests, every child of the same two parents would appear as a similar "blend" of the parent's physical traits; and so with each subsequent generation people would appear more and more the same. But what you see at a crowded festival is a broad diversity of physical traits. This suggests that the genes of two parents combine unpredictably, or randomly, to form the child's unique genetic structure, or DNA.

13. **The correct answer is (4).** In neither circuit is any current returned to the batteries to recharge them. Since the battery arrangement in circuit B generates only half the voltage as the arrangement in circuit A, the batteries in circuit B will last longer.

14. **The correct answer is (3).** Since a yeast cell contains a nucleus, it is a eukaryotic organism. The formation of a daughter cell describes budding, and so yeast matches the description of one sort of fungi.

15. **The correct answer is (1).** A megaphone funnels sound at its source, so instead of spreading spherically, the energy is all concentrated in one direction.

16. **The correct answer is (1).** As the illustration shows, carbon dioxide enters a plant's leaf through its underside, while water (hydrogen combined with oxygen) enters from the plant's roots. The plant then separates the hydrogen from the oxygen, expels the oxygen as waste, and combines the hydrogen and carbon-dioxide molecules to form glucose (carbohydrates).

17. **The correct answer is (5).** Water molecules form an especially strong bond with one another so that they resist breaking apart. In other words, water is very cohesive. This same property is at work when rainwater beads rather than spreading evenly.

18. **The correct answer is (4).** According to the table, floods and landslides in increasingly wet areas will serve to spread infectious diseases, while drought conditions in increasingly dry areas will serve to spread water and food-borne diseases.

19. **The correct answer is (2).** Blood in the coronary arteries is "oxygen-rich," which means it has just come from the lungs, and the clot blocks that blood from reaching the part of the heart muscle fed by the artery.

20. **The correct answer is (5).** A large aperture is needed to collect enough light to distinguish dark areas from lighter areas on the star.

21. **The correct answer is (5).** Glucose is the fuel that cells process into useable energy.

22. **The correct answer is (4).** If all available oxygen is depleted while exercising, your cells can continue to provide useable energy but will now produce and store lactate. When you stop exercising, oxygen will again become available and will retrieve the store of lactate. (Some will be converted into glucose, and some will be broken down into water and carbon dioxide.) Heavy breathing to "catch your breath" is the tell-tale sign that this is occurring.

23. **The correct answer is (4).** The bottom illustration shows a cold front. When air condenses, water vapor turns to liquid. (Both illustrations show condensation, in the form of rain where cold air meets warmer air.)

24. **The correct answer is (2).** The fact that dietary changes were once recommended as a treatment suggests that the disorder is one of the digestive system. The description of the acidic environment and the effect of the acid on the lining should tell you that the information is referring to a stomach disorder.

25. **The correct answer is (2).** Although a bowling ball rotates as it rolls, no torque is at play since the force is always applied at the same distance from the center.

26. **The correct answer is (3).** Gold and silver, which are used in fine jewelry, do not react with oxygen. In making this sort of jewelry, there would be no need to protect the metal from oxygen's corrosive effects.

27. **The correct answer is (1).** Nanotechnology is used today in the prevention, diagnosis, and treatment of diseases, but not to discover cures for rare diseases. Nanotechnology is used to make cosmetics, choice (2). It is also used to make strong yet light and pliable composite materials—which would be ideally suited for artificial limbs, choice (3). Since nanosized particles easily permeate the skin and blood vessels, nanotechnology is well suited for sun-blocks, which prevent skin cancer, choice (4), and for delivering medicines through the bloodstream, choice (5).

28. **The correct answer is (5).** If the cleanser works well, this fact shows that it contains nanosized particles, which are toxic and can enter Debbie's bloodstream—thereby suggesting that

facebook.com/petersonspublishing

the cleanser might have caused her cancer. Choice (1) provides evidence helping to show that these particles did *not* enter her bloodstream and hence that the cleanser is not what caused the cancer. Choice (2) suggests that something toxic in the environment rather than the cleanser caused Debbie's cancer. Choice (3) is incorrect because the less frequent the exposure to the cleanser, the less likely that the cleanser is what caused the cancer. Choice (4) provides no evidence useful in determining whether the cleanser caused Debbie's cancer.

29. **The correct answer is (3).** Increasing infertility results in a declining birth rate. Only diagram C suggests such a decline on a prolonged basis—through an inverted pyramid among all six age groups.

30. **The correct answer is (2).** Choice (2) makes the most sense. A pair of recessive alleles for skin color can mask the expression of alleles governing hair and eye color located at other sites on the chromosome. Albinos (animals with albinism) are characterized by a lack of pigment, which provides color, in the hair *and* eyes *and* skin, even though each of these three features is governed by alleles at different sites on the chromosome. A lack of pigment is the result of a congenital, or inherited, absence of melanin.

31. **The correct answer is (1).** The boat is moving from west to east. The waves farther west were created earlier than those that are farther east and have had more time to travel away from the boat's path.

32. **The correct answer is (2).** During a solar eclipse, the Moon is positioned directly between Earth and the Sun. The ring we see is the Moon's outline or silhouette.

33. **The correct answer is (5).** The illustrated lab setup shows undistilled water heated to its boiling point (left).

Substances whose boiling points are higher than that of the water remain in the flask. As more water vapor accumulates, it is forced down the cooling tube (condenser), where it cools back down to the boiling point, condenses to liquid, and collects in the beaker (right).

34. **The correct answer is (1).** The force of wind, water pressure, steam, or even human power (for example, pedaling a bicycle) can start a metal cylinder spinning enough to generate electricity. However, sunlight has no kinetic energy with which to accomplish this task.

35. **The correct answer is (3).** The figure in choice (3) illustrates the concept of co-evolution, in which two different species that interact with each other evolve in tandem as a result of that relationship.

36. **The correct answer is (3).** After infecting plant B with virus X, if its leaves also begin wrinkling and mottling, this evidence would support the hypothesis that it is virus X that is causing the wrinkling and mottling in plant A's leaves.

37. **The correct answer is (3).** The only explanation as to why the water in the aquifer would be forced up through the well is that there is pressure on the water toward the opening created when the well is drilled. The illustration shows an aquifer extending downward and at an angle from the surface (the recharge area). The volume of water above the aquifer's deeper waters can exert significant pressure on those deeper waters—pressure that a properly positioned artesian well can release.

38. **The correct answer is (4).** The disorder, diabetes, affects glucose levels and thus is a disorder of the endocrine system. (In diabetes, the islets of Langerhans, a gland located in the pancreas, fail in their production

of insulin, which is the hormone that directs the body's muscles to take up glucose for useable energy.)

39. The correct answer is (2). Each neutron and proton in a nucleus has the same mass. Thus, if an atom of one element loses protons through radioactive decay, it becomes lighter. Since uranium decays to become radon, it must be heavier than radium—and, conversely, radium must be lighter than uranium.

40. The correct answer is (2). As the sapwood matures and dies, the vascular cambium divides to replace it. The dead xylem adds to the girth of the heartwood at the tree's center. The vascular cambium also produces new phloem, and this layer increases in girth as well.

41. The correct answer is (5). In their normal wearing position, each lens blocks the horizontal waves coming from the reflective surface. Rotating a lens 90 degrees will eliminate most of its polarizing effect.

42. The correct answer is (5). The Sun is about midway to the time when its hydrogen core will be exhausted, at the age of 10 billion years, which is equivalent to about 40 Sun-years. Hence, the Sun is about 20 billion years old.

43. The correct answer is (1). Following the Sun's life path (the broken line), you can see that after its hydrogen core is exhausted, the Sun will go through a cooling period until it becomes a Red Giant, then a longer warming period, followed by a final cooling period.

44. The correct answer is (2). The hollow, dorsal (rear) nerve cord, which is common to all vertebrates, refers to the spinal cord.

45. The correct answer is (2). The ability to extend the finger indicates that the motor neurons reaching from the spinal cord to the finger are working properly. But the lack of any sensation of heat suggests that the sensory neurons that carry the "heat" information back to the brain via the spinal cord are malfunctioning.

46. The correct answer is (5). Bicarbonate of soda is a base with a pH of 12—at the opposite end of the pH scale as stomach acid. Thus drinking a soda (a carbonated beverage) serves to reduce the pH of your stomach acid. Choice (1) is incorrect because the pH scale is a compressed, or logarithmic, scale. The saliva-blood mixture must contain a far greater concentration of blood than saliva if it is to have a pH of 7, which is defined as neutral.

47. The correct answer is (3). A physical therapist would have no use for pH measurements. A dietician, choice (1), might alter a patient's diet to change acidity levels of stomach acid. A gardener, choice (2), would want to know that the soil's pH levels are appropriate for growing tomatoes. A chef, choice (4), would want the ingredients in a dish to be combined properly so the dish will not be too alkaline (salty) or too acidic (bitter). A marine biologist, choice (5), might study the effects of pH levels on fish or other aquatic life.

48. The correct answer is (5). Reptiles and other so-called "cold-blooded" animals adjust their internal body temperature up with rising air temperatures and down with falling air temperatures.

49. The correct answer is (5). Each additional 10-dB increase requires 10 times more energy than before. At an increase of four 10-dB intervals, the sound energy increases 10,000-fold ($10 \times 10 \times 10 \times 10$).

50. The correct answer is (4). Several of the minerals listed in the table are essential to developing and maintaining strong bones. In fact, minerals that are present in the body are found mainly in the bones.

Language Arts, Reading

1. (1)	9. (1)	17. (3)	25. (2)	33. (3)
2. (3)	10. (5)	18. (4)	26. (4)	34. (1)
3. (2)	11. (4)	19. (3)	27. (4)	35. (4)
4. (4)	12. (3)	20. (5)	28. (5)	36. (1)
5. (3)	13. (4)	21. (3)	29. (1)	37. (2)
6. (1)	14. (5)	22. (2)	30. (2)	38. (3)
7. (3)	15. (2)	23. (1)	31. (5)	39. (5)
8. (3)	16. (2)	24. (3)	32. (1)	40. (1)

1. **The correct answer is (1).** First, Avey seems not to notice the boys. Then, she seems to notice the narrator playing basketball, yet he's not sure. Later, she dances with him while acting a bit distant. She seems very aloof, perhaps pretending to be shy so that nobody can get to know her. This is a good example of *coy* ("affectedly shy or reticent") behavior.

2. **The correct answer is (3).** The narrator is desperate for Avey to notice him.

3. **The correct answer is (2).** The narrator mentions a rumor that Avey was going to marry the feller on the top floor, and later another rumor that the feller had gone away for a year to make money. As the narrator dances with Avey, her behavior suggests to him that she is thinking of that other feller, waiting for him to return so they can be together again.

4. **The correct answer is (4).** The narrator discusses waiting for Avey to come out of an apartment building, but the narrator does not tell us that it is her place of residence. To the contrary, he suggests that she is there to visit "that feller on the top floor."

5. **The correct answer is (3).** The characters in the story are all adolescents, and the passage centers around how the narrator came to fall in love with Avey.

6. **The correct answer is (1).** The narrator tells us that he "was a crack swimmer then," suggesting that he no longer is and, by implication, that the events described in the passage occurred some time ago.

7. **The correct answer is (3).** In the fifth stanza the speaker asserts, "The ones that cite [nature] most / Have never passed her haunted house, ..." In other words, they've never bothered to really get to know nature by wondering about or marveling at its mysteries.

8. **The correct answer is (3).** The poet uses *personification* (assigning human characteristics to nonhuman phenomena) throughout the poem in order to enliven the poem's ideas for the reader. In the first stanza, the well's water "lives" as a "neighbor" (and the second stanza refers to "his" lid). In the third stanza, the grass ("he") looks boldly at the well. In the fourth stanza, the sedge ("he") seems unafraid. In the fifth stanza, nature ("she") has a haunted house and a ghost.

9. **The correct answer is (1).** For the speaker, the deep abyss of a water-filled well inspires awe, or wonder (line 12).

10. **The correct answer is (5).** In the third stanza, the speaker remarks at how bold the grass is to grow right up to the well. Similarly, in the fourth

stanza the speaker notes how the sedge, by growing next to the sea, seems unafraid of its unknown depths.

11. **The correct answer is (4).** The poem's sixth stanza presents a *paradox*: an apparent contradiction or impossibility, which, in actuality, is entirely plausible. Here's the paradox: how can we know less about nature the nearer we get to it? Possibly by realizing how little we truly know about it. Each of the incorrect answer choices presents a similar statement—one that seems impossible or self-contradictory but actually makes sense once you understand it properly. Choice (4) is the only one that does not provide a paradox.

12. **The correct answer is (3).** *Imagery* refers to the use of language to convey a sense experience (sight, sound, etc.). Of the five lines listed, line 6 provides the best example: "lid of glass" effectively conveys an image of the circular surface of the water in a well.

13. **The correct answer is (4).** Paragraphs A through D provide specific rules, while paragraph E provides for a means of enforcing at least some of those rules.

14. **The correct answer is (5).** Reading paragraph E as a whole, its main point seems to be that employees should *not* expect to be notified if and when their Internet browsing is being monitored. In the context of the paragraph, choice (5) is the only one that provides a reasonable interpretation of the phrase "with or without notice."

15. **The correct answer is (2).** The person hired must know how to store and retrieve data processed through the County's computer network, and he or she must know how to identify the specific computer stations that are the source of that data. However, that person would probably not need expertise in monitoring employee behaviors that can be observed visually (for example, eavesdropping, print-ing, connecting personal-computing devices to County equipment, and so forth) or in protecting the privacy or security of employees who use CCNS.

16. **The correct answer is (2).** Paragraph B indicates that employees conducting County business from a remote location may do so "only with equipment and software issued by the County."

17. **The correct answer is (3).** Urging employees to logout when leaving their computer workstations unattended would help ensure compliance with the rule in Paragraph D prohibiting the use of another employee's workstation.

18. **The correct answer is (4).** Nora has been accused of signing her father's name to a document three days after her father's death.

19. **The correct answer is (3).** Nora implies that she didn't want to tell her husband she borrowed money because his life was in danger.

20. **The correct answer is (5).** From the beginning, neither party is being completely forthright with the other; in other words, both are guarding (or withholding) some of what they know.

21. **The correct answer is (3).** Krogstad obviously had figured out that Nora forged her father's signature, and his accusation that she had been "playing him false" strongly suggests that she had intentionally misled Krogstad into believing the signature was genuine.

22. **The correct answer is (2).** Nora's accusation that "I couldn't endure you for all the cruel difficulties you made" and the fact that Nora knows of Krogtad's wife suggest that they have been acquainted with each other for a while.

23. **The correct answer is (1).** Nora's question was in response to Krogstad's comparing her misdeed to a misdeed he had committed. Nora is outraged that Krogstad should draw the com-

parison. By her rhetorical question, she is implying that she was far more justified in her misdeed than he could possibly have been in his. (In the next line, Krogstad affirms this interpretation of Nora's question.)

24. **The correct answer is (3).** The passage's events—particularly Ralph's indecision about replanting the garden and, later, his observing new plants in the garden—are told in terms of how they remind Ralph of Arlene, who has recently died.

25. **The correct answer is (2).** The plants in the garden had died, and Ralph is not sure about replanting them for the next year—probably because they remind him too much of Arlene, whom he seems to miss.

26. **The correct answer is (4).** Gloria appears to be a friend (possibly a neighbor) who is trying to boost Ralph's spirits and encourage him to continue on with his life in the wake of his recent loss. Helping him replant a garden is one way of helping, so she would most likely support her staff members, as well.

27. **The correct answer is (4).** In the first paragraph, Ralph is remembering that Arlene once told him, "Flowers need to sleep before they bloom again." In the sentence after *First it sleeps* we are told that "Arlene came flooding back." Considering this in light of the first paragraph, it appears that Ralph is recalling Arlene saying these words to him. The use of italics signifies that he is thinking of these words.

28. **The correct answer is (5).** As the narration begins, the "first frost" is occurring, probably in early winter. Later in the passage, the narrator suggests the passing of months—from January through February and into March—but does not describe events occurring during that span. (The narration essentially "fast forwards" past those months.) As the narration ends,

Ralph is observing the first sign of spring in his garden.

29. **The correct answer is (1).** On the morning we're told of in the last paragraph, Ralph realizes that he is getting old but "knew he wanted to keep getting older." Then he sees new plant life in the garden and grows excited. ("Ralph's heart leapt."). He seems to have rekindled his sense of joy that morning.

30. **The correct answer is (2).** The passage argues for continuing the efforts of Dolores Hayden to achieve a cultural balance among Los Angeles' landmarks, in terms of whose accomplishments those landmarks celebrate.

31. **The correct answer is (5).** Hayden's purpose in quoting Stein was to point out that Los Angeles lacks a sense of place, not to compare Los Angeles to Oakland.

32. **The correct answer is (1).** In context, the word *civic* should be taken to mean "having to do with the city." That the city's feelings might be "bruised" by a criticism suggests that these feelings consist of a loyalty or allegiance to one's home city.

33. **The correct answer is (3).** Choice (3) restates the point in the third paragraph that many historical sites "no longer contain structures emblematic of their histories, or never did."

34. **The correct answer is (1).** In the final paragraph, the author points out that historical sites located in blighted neighborhoods can be especially difficult to preserve.

35. **The correct answer is (4).** The passage suggests that Newland is afraid his life is becoming too much of a routine. He repeatedly mutters the word "sameness," which he obviously dislikes. His longing for variety reveals itself in almost every aspect of his life, from the change in his daily

routine to his suggesting that he and May strike out on their own simply because it would be something different from what is expected of them.

36. **The correct answer is (1).** May's response ("If you call it long") strongly suggests that she considers her mother's proposed engagement period to be short, especially compared to the engagement periods of some of her acquaintances.

37. **The correct answer is (2).** May tells Newland's that his ideas are "rather vulgar." Then, speaking for both of them, she says, ". . . I should hate it—and so would you." May then changes the topic of discussion.

38. **The correct answer is (3).** Newland concludes that May was "making the answers that instinct and tradition taught her to." The context of this narrative suggests that what Newland means by "tradition" are the conventional behaviors, attitudes, and values of a culture.

39. **The correct answer is (5).** The passage tells us of May's belief that her mother—who, in context, symbolizes "society"—would consider May and Newland's desire to travel as different. In other words, leisure travel was not very common during this time.

40. **The correct answer is (1).** The passage reveals Newland's realization that his fiancée, who is typical of young women of the time, was spouting responses that simply parrot what she has been taught. The clear implication here is that she, like most young women of that time, had not been encouraged to think for herself or to speak her own mind.

Mathematics: Part I, Questions 1–25

1. (4)	7. (1)	11. (3)	16. (4)	21. 14.5 or 29/2
2. 16	8. (2)	12. (3)	17. (5)	22. (5)
3. (2)	9. 42.75 or 171/4	13. (5)	18. 45	23. (5)
4. (2)		14. (4)	19. (3)	24. (3)
5. (4)	10. (3)	15. (4)	20. (1)	25. 21
6. 64				

1. **The correct answer is (4).** The call would cost:

   $0.48 + ($0.34 × 44)
   $0.48 + 14.96 = $15.44

2. **The correct answer is 16.** Divide by 2 four times, as follows:

   5 years ago: 256 ÷ 2 = 128
   10 years ago: 128 ÷ 2 = 64
   15 years ago: 64 ÷ 2 = 32
   20 years ago: 32 ÷ 2 = 16

3. **The correct answer is (2).** Administrative costs were 5% of the total budget:

   0.05 × $200,000 = $10,000

4. **The correct answer is (2).** As a portion of the total budget, the budget for insurance (15%) exceeds the budget for utilities (12%) by 3%, which is 25% (or *one fourth*) of 12%.

5. **The correct answer is (4).** First calculate 93 as a portion of 248, expressed as a decimal number: $\frac{93}{248} = 0.375$. Express this portion in terms of 1000 by multiplying by 1000. Gary's batting average was 375.

6. **The correct answer is 64.** Without the square hole, each of the cube's six outer surfaces contains 9 square inches, for a total of 54 square inches of outer surface area. The square hole reduces that total by 2 square inches, to 52. Each of the four inner surfaces (inside the hole) accounts for an additional 3 square inches—for a total of 12 square inches of inner surface area. The solid's total surface area = 52 + 12 = 64 square inches.

7. **The correct answer is (1).** For each item, express the sale price as a percent of the regular price:

   $\frac{105}{175} = 0.6$ and $\frac{180}{240} = 0.75$

   The discount on the $175 item is 40% (100% − 60%), and the discount on the $240 item is 25% (100% − 75%).

8. **The correct answer is (2).** First, add the two figures:

   $16,876.10 + 18,728.90 = $35,605.00.

   Since their profit was 50% and they split that profit equally (50% each), divide the total by 4 to find each owner's profit:

   $35,605.00 ÷ 4 = $8901.25.

9. **The correct answer is 42.75 or 171/4.** Multiply and divide (in either order) before adding. Starting with division:

   13 + 7 × (17 ÷ 4) = 13 + (7 × 4.25)
   = 13 + 29.75
   = 42.75

10. **The correct answer is (3).** In 2007, the difference was about $1 million. In 2009, the difference was about $800,000.

11. **The correct answer is (3).** Visual observation tells you that the greatest overall increase occurred from 2007 to 2008. In 2007, combined expenses were about $15m ($6m + $4m + $5m). In

2008, combined expensed were about $23.5m ($8m + $4m + $11.5m). The increase was about $8.5m, which is a bit more than 55% of $15m.

12. **The correct answer is (3).** Rewrite $3\frac{1}{2}$ as the decimal number 3.5, and then multiply 3.5 by $2.50. Also multiply $1.49 by 2:

$3.5 \times \$2.50 = \$8.75$
$2 \times \$1.49 = \$2.98$

Add these two totals to the other two dollar figures:

$\$8.75 + \$2.98 + \$1.99 + \$0.89 = \$14.61$

13. **The correct answer is (5).** Since the figure has 5 sides, it contains 540°: $180(5-2)=540$. The sum of the measures of the five angles is 540°. To find the fifth angle (x), set up and solve an equation:

$$540 = x + 110 + 60 + 120 + 100$$
$$540 = x + 390$$
$$150 = x$$

14. **The correct answer is (4).** First, square both sides of the equation: $\sqrt{ab} = 4$; $ab = 16$. Although you do not know the individual values of a and b, $a^2b^2 = (ab)^2$. Accordingly, $(ab)^2 = (16)^2 = 256$.

15. **The correct answer is (4).** For each dieter, subtract the minimum recorded weight from the maximum:

Greg: $227 - 214 = 13$
Nick: $249 - 230 = 19$
Karen: $173 - 160 = 13$
Paul: $200 - 188 = 12$
Tony: $268 - 252 = 16$

16. **The correct answer is (4).** Tally up the gains and losses from the end of one week to the next. From the end of week 7 to the end of week 8:

Greg gained 2 pounds
Nick lost 3 pounds
Karen gained 3 pounds
Paul lost 1 pound
Tony lost 5 pounds

The losses for week 8 totaled 9 pounds, while the week's gains totaled 5 pounds, for a net loss of $9 - 5 = 4$ pounds.

17. **The correct answer is (5).** Tony generally lost weight through week 4, then gained weight through week 7, then lost weight through week 10.

18. **The correct answer is 45.** Quadrilateral $ABCD$ is a parallelogram. In any parallelogram, opposite vertices have the same angle measures. Thus, m$\angle DAB = 60°$. The sum of the measures of the three interior angles of $\triangle ABD = 180°$. Thus, m$\angle ABD = 45°$.

19. **The correct answer is (3).** First, add the deposit amount to the previous balance:

$\$823.80 + \$1645.38 = \$2469.18$

Next, add the three known check amounts:

$\$265.75 + \$120.22 + \$965.50 = \$1351.47$

Then subtract:

$\$2469.18 - \$1351.47 = \$1117.71$

To find the amount of the fourth check, subtract:

$\$1117.71 - \$455.01 = \$662.70$

20. **The correct answer is (1).** The 26th term is zero (0), and so the 50th term is 24 (not 25). Except for the first term, −25, each positive number "cancels out" a negative number, leaving a sum of −25.

21. **The correct answer is 14.5 or 29/2.** To find the distance for the fourth attempt, apply the arithmetic-mean formula:

$$13.3 = \frac{(3)(12.9) + x}{4}$$
$$53.2 = 38.7 + x$$
$$x = 14.5$$

22. **The correct answer is (5).** 72 minutes = 1 hr. 12 min., or 1.2 hrs. In this time, the sailfish can travel 72 × 1.2 = 86.4 miles. To convert to km, set up the following proportion and solve for x:

$$\frac{1}{0.62} = \frac{x}{86.4}$$
$$0.62x = 86.4$$
$$x = \frac{86.4}{0.62} \approx 139$$

23. **The correct answer is (5).** The June usage difference between houses C and A was 1125 − 960 = 165 kWh. Divide this monthly difference by 30 to find the average per-day difference:

$$165 \div 30 = 5.5 \text{ kWh.}$$

24. **The correct answer is (3).** The interior volume of each house is the product of its square-foot area and its ceiling height (volume = area × height). To determine a house's ceiling height, divide its volume by its square-foot area. For Houses A, B, and D, the quotient (ceiling height) is exactly 8.0 linear feet. For house C, however, the quotient is greater than 8.0 linear feet.

25. **The correct answer is 21.** The formula for the volume of a cone is $\frac{1}{3}\pi r^2 \times h$. Letting $r = 2$ and $h = 5$, first find the volume in terms of π:

$$\frac{1}{3}\pi 2^2 \times 5 = \frac{1}{3}\pi(4)(5) = \frac{20\pi}{3}$$

Then, using 3.14 as the approximate value of π, calculate the volume:

$$\frac{(20)(3.14)}{3} = \frac{62.8}{3} \approx 20.9 .$$

The nearest cubic inch is **21.**

Mathematics: Part II, Questions 26–50

26. (5)	32. (4)	36. (3)	41. (1)	46. (2)
27. (5)	33. (2)	37. (1)	42. (2)	47. (2)
28. (0,–3)	34. 5/8 or	38. (5)	43. (3)	48. (5)
29. (5)	.625	39. (5)	44. (1)	49. (1)
30. (2)	35. (4)	40. (3)	45. 19	50. (2)
31. 2.25 or				
9/4				

26. **The correct answer is (5).** Since the two fractions in choice (5) share the same denominator, you can simply add the numerator to find the sum:

$$\frac{3}{4} + \frac{5}{4} = \frac{8}{4} = 2$$

27. **The correct answer is (5).** Raise both the coefficient –2 and variable x^2 to the power of 4. When raising an exponent to a power, multiply:

$$(-2x^2)^4 = -2^4 x^{(2)(4)} = 16x^8$$

28. **The correct answer is (0,–3).** The y-intercept of the equation $y = 7x - 3$ is the point at which the line crosses the y-axis. At this point, the value of x is 0. Substitute 0 for x in the equation, and then solve:

$$y = 7(0) - 3; y = -3$$

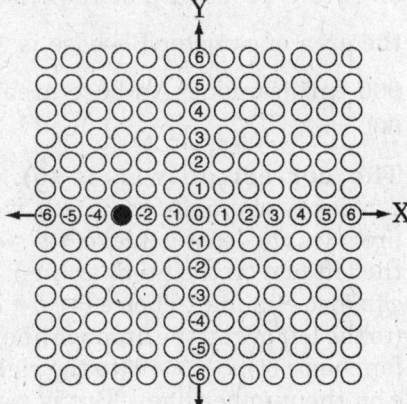

The y-intercept is at point (0,–3).

29. **The correct answer is (5).** A linear equation in two variables, regardless

of the number of terms or values of coefficients, allows an infinite number of combinations for the two variables.

30. **The correct answer is (2).** Multiplying together any combination of the factors of p will result in a product that is also a factor of p. The only number among the choices listed that is not a product of any of these combinations is 36.

31. **The correct answer is 2.25 or 9/4.** Since the answer choices are expressed in decimal terms, convert all three terms in the question to decimals, and then add:

$$\sqrt{0.49} = 0.7$$
$$\frac{3}{4} = 0.75$$
$$80\% = 0.8$$
$$0.7 + 0.75 + 0.8 = 2.25$$

32. **The correct answer is (4).** $4 \times 4 \times 4 = 64$, and $5 \times 5 \times 5 = 125$. Thus, x must lie between 4 and 5.

33. **The correct answer is (2).** Each tube has a diameter of 3. The circumference of any of the circles (including A) = πd (where d = diameter). Given a diameter of 3, the circumference of circle A = 3π.

34. **The correct answer is 5/8 or .625.** Think of the legislature as containing 8 voters divided into two parts: $\frac{5}{8} + \frac{3}{8} = \frac{8}{8}$. For every 5 votes in favor, 3 were cast against the bill. Thus, 5

out of every 8 votes, or $\frac{5}{8}$, were cast in favor of the motion.

35. The correct answer is (4). A dime = $0.10, and a nickel = $0.05. The total value of the dimes = ($0.10)($d$), and the total value of the nickels = ($0.05)($n$). Together, ($0.10)(d) + ($0.05)($n$) represents the dollar value of all coins in the vending machine.

36. The correct answer is (3). In 2000, world production was 39 million, while U.S. production was 8 million. The difference between the two numbers is 31 million.

37. The correct answer is (1). From 1970 to 2010, Japan and the United States together accounted for an increase of about 17 million motor vehicles per year. The increase in world production was far greater, about 40 million vehicles per year. Even accounting for the United States' and Japan's contributions to that 40-million figure, countries other than those two still accounted for most of the increase.

38. The correct answer is (5). The line shows a negative y-intercept (the point where the line crosses the vertical axis) and a negative slope less than −1 (that is, slightly more horizontal than a 45° angle). In equation 5, $-\frac{2}{3}$ is the slope and −3 is the y-intercept. Thus, equation 5 matches the graph of the line.

39. The correct answer is (5). Substitute a^4 for a in the expression a^2. When raising an exponential number to a power, multiply exponents:

$$\left(a^4\right)^2 = a^8$$

40. The correct answer is (3). Since the 4 aces were removed, the deck contains 48 cards. The chances of drawing a card other than one of the 12 face cards is $\frac{48-12}{48} = \frac{36}{48}$, or $\frac{3}{4}$

41. The correct answer is (1). $4230 \times 10^{-4} = 4.23 \times 10^{-1}$

42. The correct answer is (2). Rug R must be 4' × 4', and rug S must be 2' × 2'. The perimeter of Rug S is 8 feet.

43. The correct answer is (3). You can write the number of boys taking the trip as $G - 17$. The number of girls plus the number of boys totals N, and so $G + (G - 17) = N$. (You can find the number of girls taking the trip by solving for N.)

44. The correct answer is (1). Multiply each term of a binomial by each term of the other binomial, then add the four products: $(x - 3)(x + 1) = x^2 - 3x + x - 3 = x^2 - 2x - 3$.

45. The correct answer is 19. In 5 hours, Steven can pack $\frac{2}{3} \times 48 = 32$ boxes. Therefore, in 3 hours he can pack $0.6 \times 32 = 19.2$ boxes, or 19 *complete* boxes.

46. The correct answer is (2). The balanced scale shown in the figure demonstrates that canisters A and C are equal in weight. Given that the volume of canister A is twice that of canister C, the mass of canister C must be twice the mass of canister A.

47. The correct answer is (2). Given an A-to-C proportion of 150%, or $\frac{3}{2}$, the area of canister B's base is $\frac{2}{3}$ of 900 cm² (canister A's base area), or 600 cm².

48. The correct answer is (5). You can easily eliminate choice (2), which provides the least value: $a + b < a$ (to the left of a on the number line). You can also eliminate choice (4): $b + c < c$ (to the left of c on the number line). As for choice (1), $c - b > c$ (to the right of c on the number line). But is $c - b > d - c$, choice (3)? The answer depends on the specific values of the variables.

49. The correct answer is (1). The statement in choice (1) is not necessarily true. On March 1, the number of stations charging more than the average price was the same as the number of stations charging less than the average price; the median price is the average of the two middle prices, which may or may not be the same as the average of all 50 prices. The statement in choice (2) must be true. On February 1, more stations charged less than the average price than greater than the average price; in other words, the median price was less than the average price. The statement in choice (3) must be true. The median price on March 1 was the same as the average price: $2.40. The median price on January 1 was greater than the average price of $2.50. The statement in choice (4) must be true. The average price on February 1 was $2.65, more than an average price of $2.50 on January 1. The statement in choice (5) must be true. On January 1, 6 stations charged the average price for that day, whereas on February 1, the number was 8.

50. The correct answer is (2). Either the cosine or sine function can relate the length of wire to the angle of θ degrees. Applying the cosine function (let x = the length of the wire):

$$\cos\theta = \frac{a}{x}$$
$$x\cos\theta = a$$
$$x = \frac{a}{\cos\theta}$$

ARE YOU READY TO TAKE THE GED®?

Now that you have spent a great deal of time and effort studying for the GED® and taking this Practice Test, you may think you are well-prepared to take the GED® exam. But, don't rush to do so if you aren't completely certain that you are ready. One way to tell is by checking your scores from this Practice Test on the table below.

	All Set—Well-Prepared	Most Likely Ready	Possibly Ready	Need More Preparation
Language Arts, Writing, Part I	38–50	26–37	18–25	0–17
Language Arts, Writing, Part II	4	3	2	1
Social Studies	38–50	26–37	18–25	0–17
Science	38–50	26–37	18–25	0–17
Language Arts, Reading	30–40	21–29	14–20	0–13
Mathematics	38–50	26–37	18–25	0–17

If your scores are in the "All Set—Well-Prepared" column, you are probably ready to take the actual GED® exam, and you should apply to take the test soon. If some of your scores are in the "Most Likely Ready" column, you should focus your study on those areas where you need to improve most. "Most Likely Ready" means that you are probably ready enough to earn a GED® diploma, but it's not a bad idea to spend a little more time brushing up and improving your chances to pass the actual GED® exam.

If any of your scores fell in the lowest category, take a little more time to review the appropriate chapters in this book—and in any high school text books, if necessary. Study more, and then when you feel ready, try again with the next Practice Test.

Practice Test 3

DIRECTIONS FOR TAKING THE PRACTICE TEST

Directions: The GED® Practice Test has five separate subtests: Language Arts, Writing (Parts I and II); Social Studies; Science; Language Arts, Reading; and Mathematics.

- Read and follow the directions at the start of each test.
- Stick to the time limits.
- Enter your answers on the tear-out Answer Sheets provided.
- When you have completed the entire test, compare your answers with the correct answers given in the Answer Key and Explanations at the end of this Practice Test.
- Remember to check the "Are You Ready to Take the GED®?" section to gauge how close you are to mastering the GED® exam.

ANSWER SHEET PRACTICE TEST 3

Language Arts, Writing—Part 1

1. ①②③④⑤	11. ①②③④⑤	21. ①②③④⑤	31. ①②③④⑤	41. ①②③④⑤
2. ①②③④⑤	12. ①②③④⑤	22. ①②③④⑤	32. ①②③④⑤	42. ①②③④⑤
3. ①②③④⑤	13. ①②③④⑤	23. ①②③④⑤	33. ①②③④⑤	43. ①②③④⑤
4. ①②③④⑤	14. ①②③④⑤	24. ①②③④⑤	34. ①②③④⑤	44. ①②③④⑤
5. ①②③④⑤	15. ①②③④⑤	25. ①②③④⑤	35. ①②③④⑤	45. ①②③④⑤
6. ①②③④⑤	16. ①②③④⑤	26. ①②③④⑤	36. ①②③④⑤	46. ①②③④⑤
7. ①②③④⑤	17. ①②③④⑤	27. ①②③④⑤	37. ①②③④⑤	47. ①②③④⑤
8. ①②③④⑤	18. ①②③④⑤	28. ①②③④⑤	38. ①②③④⑤	48. ①②③④⑤
9. ①②③④⑤	19. ①②③④⑤	29. ①②③④⑤	39. ①②③④⑤	49. ①②③④⑤
10. ①②③④⑤	20. ①②③④⑤	30. ①②③④⑤	40. ①②③④⑤	50. ①②③④⑤

Social Studies

1. ①②③④⑤	11. ①②③④⑤	21. ①②③④⑤	31. ①②③④⑤	41. ①②③④⑤
2. ①②③④⑤	12. ①②③④⑤	22. ①②③④⑤	32. ①②③④⑤	42. ①②③④⑤
3. ①②③④⑤	13. ①②③④⑤	23. ①②③④⑤	33. ①②③④⑤	43. ①②③④⑤
4. ①②③④⑤	14. ①②③④⑤	24. ①②③④⑤	34. ①②③④⑤	44. ①②③④⑤
5. ①②③④⑤	15. ①②③④⑤	25. ①②③④⑤	35. ①②③④⑤	45. ①②③④⑤
6. ①②③④⑤	16. ①②③④⑤	26. ①②③④⑤	36. ①②③④⑤	46. ①②③④⑤
7. ①②③④⑤	17. ①②③④⑤	27. ①②③④⑤	37. ①②③④⑤	47. ①②③④⑤
8. ①②③④⑤	18. ①②③④⑤	28. ①②③④⑤	38. ①②③④⑤	48. ①②③④⑤
9. ①②③④⑤	19. ①②③④⑤	29. ①②③④⑤	39. ①②③④⑤	49. ①②③④⑤
10. ①②③④⑤	20. ①②③④⑤	30. ①②③④⑤	40. ①②③④⑤	50. ①②③④⑤

Science

1. ①②③④⑤	11. ①②③④⑤	21. ①②③④⑤	31. ①②③④⑤	41. ①②③④⑤
2. ①②③④⑤	12. ①②③④⑤	22. ①②③④⑤	32. ①②③④⑤	42. ①②③④⑤
3. ①②③④⑤	13. ①②③④⑤	23. ①②③④⑤	33. ①②③④⑤	43. ①②③④⑤
4. ①②③④⑤	14. ①②③④⑤	24. ①②③④⑤	34. ①②③④⑤	44. ①②③④⑤
5. ①②③④⑤	15. ①②③④⑤	25. ①②③④⑤	35. ①②③④⑤	45. ①②③④⑤
6. ①②③④⑤	16. ①②③④⑤	26. ①②③④⑤	36. ①②③④⑤	46. ①②③④⑤
7. ①②③④⑤	17. ①②③④⑤	27. ①②③④⑤	37. ①②③④⑤	47. ①②③④⑤
8. ①②③④⑤	18. ①②③④⑤	28. ①②③④⑤	38. ①②③④⑤	48. ①②③④⑤
9. ①②③④⑤	19. ①②③④⑤	29. ①②③④⑤	39. ①②③④⑤	49. ①②③④⑤
10. ①②③④⑤	20. ①②③④⑤	30. ①②③④⑤	40. ①②③④⑤	50. ①②③④⑤

Language Arts, Reading

1. ①②③④⑤   11. ①②③④⑤   21. ①②③④⑤   31. ①②③④⑤
2. ①②③④⑤   12. ①②③④⑤   22. ①②③④⑤   32. ①②③④⑤
3. ①②③④⑤   13. ①②③④⑤   23. ①②③④⑤   33. ①②③④⑤
4. ①②③④⑤   14. ①②③④⑤   24. ①②③④⑤   34. ①②③④⑤
5. ①②③④⑤   15. ①②③④⑤   25. ①②③④⑤   35. ①②③④⑤
6. ①②③④⑤   16. ①②③④⑤   26. ①②③④⑤   36. ①②③④⑤
7. ①②③④⑤   17. ①②③④⑤   27. ①②③④⑤   37. ①②③④⑤
8. ①②③④⑤   18. ①②③④⑤   28. ①②③④⑤   38. ①②③④⑤
9. ①②③④⑤   19. ①②③④⑤   29. ①②③④⑤   39. ①②③④⑤
10. ①②③④⑤   20. ①②③④⑤   30. ①②③④⑤   40. ①②③④⑤

Mathematics—Part I

1. ①②③④⑤   13. ①②③④⑤   19. ①②③④⑤
2. ①②③④⑤   14. [grid]   20. ①②③④⑤
3. ①②③④⑤   21. [grid]
4. ①②③④⑤
5. ①②③④⑤
6. ①②③④⑤
7. ①②③④⑤
8. ①②③④⑤
9. [grid]   15. ①②③④⑤
                 16. ①②③④⑤   22. ①②③④⑤
                 17. ①②③④⑤   23. ①②③④⑤
                 18. [grid]   24. ①②③④⑤
                                25. [grid]
10. ①②③④⑤
11. ①②③④⑤
12. [coordinate grid]

answer sheet

Mathematics—Part II

26. *(grid-in answer grid)*

27. ① ② ③ ④ ⑤
28. ① ② ③ ④ ⑤
29. ① ② ③ ④ ⑤

30. *(grid-in answer grid)*

31. ① ② ③ ④ ⑤
32. ① ② ③ ④ ⑤
33. ① ② ③ ④ ⑤

34. ① ② ③ ④ ⑤
35. ① ② ③ ④ ⑤
36. ① ② ③ ④ ⑤

37. *(grid-in answer grid)*

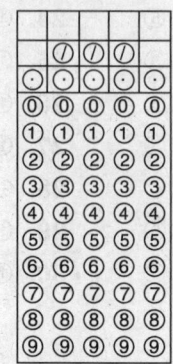

38. ① ② ③ ④ ⑤
39. ① ② ③ ④ ⑤
40. ① ② ③ ④ ⑤

41. *(grid-in answer grid)*

42. ① ② ③ ④ ⑤
43. ① ② ③ ④ ⑤
44. ① ② ③ ④ ⑤
45. ① ② ③ ④ ⑤
46. ① ② ③ ④ ⑤
47. ① ② ③ ④ ⑤
48. ① ② ③ ④ ⑤
49. ① ② ③ ④ ⑤
50. ① ② ③ ④ ⑤

ANSWER SHEET PRACTICE TEST 3

Language Arts, Writing—Part II Essay Test

_____

_____

_____

_____

_____

_____

_____

_____

_____

_____

_____

_____

_____

_____

_____

_____

_____

_____

answer sheet

Language Arts, Writing—Part II Essay Test (continued)

_____

_____

_____

_____

_____

_____

_____

_____

_____

_____

_____

_____

_____

_____

_____

_____

_____

_____

_____

_____

_____

LANGUAGE ARTS, WRITING

The Language Arts, Writing Test consists of two parts. Part I is a multiple-choice section, and Part II is an essay section. You must begin with Part I.

You will have 75 minutes to work on Part I. If you finish Part I early, you can proceed to Part II right away. The total time allowed for both parts of the test is 2 hours (120 minutes).

LANGUAGE ARTS, WRITING, PART I

75 Minutes • 50 Questions

Directions: This part of the Language Arts, Writing Test consists of 50 multiple-choice questions based on documents that contain numbered sentences. After reading a document, answer the multiple-choice questions that follow it.

Some of the numbered sentences contain errors in usage, sentence structure, or mechanics (spelling, punctuation, and capitalization). Other sentences are correctly written. The best answer to a question referring to a correctly written sentence is the one that leaves the sentence unchanged. The best version of a sentence will be consistent with the rest of the document in verb tense and point of view.

The time allowed to answer all 50 questions is 75 minutes. If you finish Part I early, you may proceed immediately to Part II (the essay section).

Record your answers on the answer sheet provided.

QUESTIONS 1–8 REFER TO THE FOLLOWING DOCUMENT.

(A)

(1) The Underwood Inn night manager is responsible for guest security and emergencies from 9 p.m. to 7 a.m. and is the representative of Management, and is expected to handle our guests in the same manner as the Innkeepers. (2) The night manager's duties include the ones listed below and any additional duties that maybe imposed by the Management.

(B)

- (3) The night Manager will answer the night phone from 9 p.m. (or closing) to 7 a.m. (or opening). (4) The evening Innkeeper will call just before leaving. (5) The morning Innkeeper will call when she arrived.

(C)

- (6) The night manager will walk around the premises at night to check security and lights. (7) Also check for any windows or doors left open. (8) So that it can be corrected promptly, the morning Innkeeper will be informed by the night manager of any security problem requiring further attention.

(D)

- (9) The night manager will be expected to handle guest complaints and requests in an expedient, courteous manner.

(E)

- (10) Any emergency should be written up in a report after the incident. (11) In case of emergency, call 911 immediately. (12) Then help the guest. (13) Do not offer any medical advice or make suggestions. (14) Leave that to the professional (that's why you call 911).

(F)

- (15) On nights that the night manager cannot answer the phone, he is expected to find a replacement who had been familiar with the Inn and was approved by management.

1. Sentence 1: **The Underwood Inn night manager is responsible for guest security and emergencies from 9 p.m. to <u>7 a.m. and is the representative of Management, and</u> is expected to handle our guests in the same manner as the Innkeepers.**

   Which is the best way to write the underlined portion of sentence 1? If the original is the best way, select answer choice (1).

   (1) 7 a.m. and is the representative of Management, and

   (2) 7 a.m., is the representative of Management, and

   (3) 7 a.m., and as the representative of Management

   (4) 7 a.m. and is representative of the Management, so

   (5) 7 a.m. is the representative of Management, and

2. Sentence 2: **The night manager's duties include the ones listed below and any additional duties that maybe imposed by the Management.**

   Which correction should be made to sentence 2?

   (1) change <u>manager's</u> to <u>manager</u>

   (2) change <u>include</u> to <u>includes</u>

   (3) replace <u>and</u> with <u>or</u>

   (4) replace <u>maybe</u> with <u>may be</u>

   (5) insert the word <u>on</u> after <u>imposed</u>

3. **Sentence 5: The morning Innkeeper will call <u>when she arrived</u>.**

   Which is the best way to write the underlined portion of sentence 5? If the original is the best way, select answer choice (1).

   (1) when she arrived

   (2) to say, I have arrived

   (3) having arrived

   (4) upon arrival

   (5) when arrived

4. **Sentence 6 and Sentence 7: The night manager will walk around the premises at night to check security and lights. Also check for any windows or doors left open.**

   The most effective combination of sentences 6 and 7 would include which group of words?

   (1) security and lights, and check

   (2) lights, checking especially for

   (3) security, lights, windows, doors

   (4) lights check, as well as for any

   (5) security and lights, also for

5. **Sentence 8: So that it can be corrected promptly, the morning Innkeeper will be informed by the night manager of any security problem requiring further attention.**

   The most effective revision of sentence 8 would begin with which group of words?

   (1) Any security problem requiring further attention, it will

   (2) The night manager will inform the morning Innkeeper

   (3) The morning Innkeeper will be informed of any security problem

   (4) Further attention to any security problem requiring correction

   (5) So that it can be corrected promptly, the night manager

6. **Sentence 9: The night manager will be expected to handle guest complaints and requests in an expedient, courteous manner.**

   Which correction should be made to sentence 9?

   (1) replace <u>night</u> with <u>knight</u>

   (2) change <u>guest</u> to <u>guest's</u>

   (3) change <u>and</u> to <u>or</u>

   (4) remove the comma after <u>expedient</u>

   (5) no correction is necessary

7. Which revision would improve the effectiveness of paragraph E?

   (1) move sentence 10 to follow sentence 14

   (2) move sentence 13 to the beginning of paragraph E

   (3) remove sentence 14

   (4) remove sentence 12

   (5) move sentence 11 to follow sentence 12

8. **Sentence 15: On nights that the night manager cannot answer the phone, he is expected to find a replacement who had been familiar with the Inn and was approved by management.**

   Which correction should be made to sentence 15?

   (1) remove the word <u>that</u>

   (2) change <u>replacement</u> to <u>replacements</u>

   (3) insert a comma after <u>replacement</u>

   (4) change <u>who</u> to <u>whoever</u>

   (5) change <u>had been</u> to <u>is</u>

QUESTIONS 9–17 REFER TO THE FOLLOWING PASSAGE OF TEXT.

(A)

(1) Movie critics who prefer films without special effects do not appreciate the role they play in the movie-going experience. (2) Movies are the only place outside your imagination where you can see things you might never seen in real life. (3) Flying ghosts, earthquakes that swallow entire metropolises, and battles in outer space are just a few of many.

(B)

(4) Such examples are the work of an elite group of skilled effects artists. (5) These artists have developed countless moviemaking tricks and techniques over the course of a century. (6) They are aided now, of course, by computer programs that transform digital bits and bites into images of worlds heretofore unimagined, let alone seen. (7) In numerous ways, effects artists and their techniques, and tools, make it both possible and practical for filmmakers to produce such imaginative movies.

(C)

(8) First, some movie scenes would cost too much to produce using ordinary methods, so they can be used to save money. (9) For example, to show an imaginary city, it would cost many millions of dollars to build real buildings, roads, and so on. (10) The clever use of special effects can cut those costs dramatically.

(D)

(11) Battle or disaster scenes involving explosions, floods, or avalanches can be very dangerous to film. (12) Effects artists can simulate disaster scenes in ways that gives audiences the thrill of witnessing a dangerous event without exposing actors to real hazards. (13) Special effects can also make movie-making safer. (14) Even in comedies, characters are sometimes placed in harm's way.

(E)

(15) Most important of all, special effects allow a movie maker to create a scene that would otherwise impossible to portray. (16) They allow moviegoers to experience non-existent, fantastic worlds. (17) In other words, special effects are a movie maker's means of communicating a unique imaginative vision.

9. Sentence 2: **Movies are the only place outside your imagination where you can see things you might never seen in real life.**

   Which correction should be made to this sentence?

   (1) change <u>are</u> to <u>is</u>

   (2) insert a comma after <u>imagination</u>

   (3) change <u>can</u> to <u>could</u>

   (4) insert the word <u>of</u> after <u>might</u>

   (5) change <u>seen</u> to <u>see</u>

10. Sentence 3: **Flying ghosts, earthquakes that swallow entire metropolises, and battles in <u>outer space are just a few of many</u>.**

    Which would be the best way to write the underlined part of the sentence? If the original is the best way, select answer choice (1).

    (1) outer space are just a few of many

    (2) outer space, to list just a few

    (3) outer space, for example

    (4) outer space is just one of many

    (5) outer space, just a few of many

11. Sentence 4 and Sentence 5: **Such examples are the work of an elite group of skilled effects artists. These artists have developed countless moviemaking tricks and techniques over the course of a century.**

    The most effective combination of sentences 4 and 5 would include which group of words?

    (1) effects artists, who over the course of a century

    (2) examples, such as developing countless

    (3) skilled effects artists have developed countless

    (4) moviemaking tricks and techniques, developing

    (5) elite group of skilled effects artists have developed

12. Sentence 7: **In numerous ways, effects artists and their techniques, and tools, make it both possible and practical for filmmakers to produce such imaginative movies.**

    Which is the best way to write the underlined portion of this sentence? If the original is the best way, select answer choice (1).

    (1) artists and their techniques, and tools, make

    (2) artists their techniques, and tools, make

    (3) artists, along with their techniques and tools, make

    (4) artists, and their techniques, and their tools, make

    (5) artists, their techniques and tools, make

13. Sentence 8: **First, some movie scenes cost too much to produce using ordinary methods, so they can be used to save money.**

    Which is the most effective revision of the underlined portion of sentence 8?

    (1) they used to

    (2) using these methods can

    (3) it can be used to

    (4) it can be useful to

    (5) using special effects can

14. Which revision would improve the effectiveness of paragraph D?

    (1) remove sentence 13

    (2) move sentence 12 to the beginning of paragraph D

    (3) remove sentence 14

    (4) move sentence 13 to the beginning of paragraph D

    (5) move sentence 11 to follow sentence 13

15. Sentence 12: **Effects artists can simulate disaster scenes in ways that gives audiences the thrill of witnessing a dangerous event without exposing actors to real hazards.**

    Which is the best way to write the underlined portion of sentence 12? If the original is the best way, select answer choice (1).

    (1) ways that gives

    (2) a way that gave

    (3) ways that give

    (4) a way giving

    (5) ways that gives to

16. Sentence 15: **Most important of all, special effects allow a movie maker to create a scene that would otherwise impossible to portray.**

Which correction should be made to sentence 15?

(1) remove the comma after <u>all</u>

(2) change <u>movie</u> to <u>movies</u>

(3) replace <u>scene</u> with <u>seen</u>

(4) change <u>would</u> to <u>is</u>

(5) insert the word <u>be</u> after <u>otherwise</u>

17. Sentence 17: **In other words, special effects are a movie maker's means of communicating a unique imaginative vision.**

Which correction should be made to sentence 17?

(1) remove the comma after <u>words</u>

(2) replace <u>effects</u> with <u>affects</u>

(3) replace <u>maker's</u> with <u>makers'</u>

(4) change <u>communicating</u> to <u>communicate</u>

(5) no correction is necessary

QUESTIONS 18–26 REFER TO THE FOLLOWING E-MAIL.

Subject: Beta version of our Web site
From: Shannon McDougal
To: Adrian Webster <adrian.webster@websterswebdesign.net>

Mr. Webster:

(A)

(1) I finally found time to try out the Web site beta version submitted to our company last week by you. (2) The navigation buttons, using the pull-down menus, and the product ordering page are all intuitive and user-friendly. (3) Overall, you've done a great job designing the site. (4) But I do have a few points of constructive criticism:

(B)

(5) Is it possible to use a three-column format instead of two columns? (6) That way, more information is visible "above the fold" on each page.

(C)

(7) The subheadings can be hard to distinguish from the text, at least for me. (8) Can you use a larger size or a contrasting color for these headings?

(D)

(9) Can you change the orientation of the menu buttons to horizontal, across the top of each page, instead of vertically (down the left side of the screen)? (10) I asked my boss, and me and her both like the horizontal design better.

(E)

(11) We have a new company logo that we wish to use on every page of the Web site. (12) We can e-mail an image of the logo to you. (13) Please let me know if you have any particular file format or size requirements.

(F)

(14) I'd like the site to include a site map. (15) I didn't see one in this beta version, but maybe that's something that will automatically be generated once the site design will be complete.

(G)

(16) We have not yet decided on a Web hosting service. (17) Do you have any recommendations, given our data and functionality requirements? (18) Of utmost importance is our customers' security and privacy, who will be entering credit card information at the site.

(H)

(19) Everyone here hopes to see the final product vary soon because we're anxious to "go live" with our new Web site by the end of this month.

Regards,
Shannon McDougal

18. Sentence 1: **I finally found time to try out the Web site beta version** <u>**submitted to our company last week by you.**</u>

   The most effective revision of sentence 1 would include which group of words? If the original is the best way, select answer choice (1).

   (1) submitted to our company last week by you

   (2) you submitted to our company last week

   (3) for our company. You submitted it last week

   (4) by you, submitted last week to our company

   (5) last week you submitted to our company

19. Sentence 2: **The navigation buttons, using the pull-down menus, and the product ordering page are all intuitive and user-friendly.**

   Which correction should be made to sentence 2?

   (1) remove the comma after <u>buttons</u>

   (2) remove the word <u>using</u>

   (3) remove the comma after <u>menus</u>

   (4) change <u>are all</u> to <u>is</u>

   (5) no correction is necessary

20. Sentence 5 and Sentence 6: **Is it possible to use a three-column format instead of two columns? That way, more information is visible "above the fold" on each page.**

   An effective combination of sentences 5 and 6 would include which of the following groups of words?

   (1) so that more information is visible

   (2) the more visible the information is

   (3) on each page, use a three-column format

   (4) Is it possible instead of two columns

   (5) format that is "above the fold"

21. Sentence 9: **Can you change the orientation of the menu buttons to horizontal, across the top of each page, instead of vertically (down the left side of the screen)?**

   Which correction should be made to sentence 9?

   (1) change <u>Can</u> to <u>Can't</u>

   (2) replace <u>to</u> with <u>from</u>

   (3) replace <u>across</u> to <u>a cross</u>

   (4) remove the comma after <u>page</u>

   (5) change <u>vertically</u> to <u>vertical</u>

22. Sentence 10: **I asked my boss, and me and her both** like the horizontal design better.

Which is the best way to write the underlined portion of sentence 10? If the original is the best way, select answer choice (1).

(1) and me and her both

(2) and her and I each

(3) she and I both

(4) and she and I both

(5) which she and myself both

23. Sentence 15: **I didn't see one in this beta version, but maybe that's something that will automatically be generated once the site design will be complete.**

Which correction should be made to sentence 15?

(1) change didn't to don't

(2) remove the comma after version

(3) change but to or

(4) change that's to its

(5) change will be to is

24. Sentence 18: **Of utmost importance is our customers' security and privacy, who will be entering credit card information at the site.**

The most effective revision of sentence 18 would begin with which group of words?

(1) Our customers, who will be entering

(2) Since our customers will be entering

(3) Credit-card information at the site

(4) Of utmost importance, entering

(5) Security and privacy when entering

25. Sentence 19: **Everyone here hopes to see the final product vary soon because we're anxious to "go live" with our new Web site by the end of this month.**

Which correction should be made to sentence 19?

(1) replace Everyone with Every one

(2) change hopes to hope

(3) replace vary with very

(4) replace we're with were

(5) replace month with Month

26. Which revision would improve the effectiveness of the e-mail?

(1) join paragraphs A and B

(2) join paragraphs B and C

(3) move paragraph E to follow paragraph G

(4) move paragraph B to follow paragraph D

(5) remove paragraph F

QUESTIONS 27-34 REFER TO THE FOLLOWING DOCUMENT.

Prepping a Room for Painting

(A)

(1) You should first remove all furniture from the room, including pictures and wall mirrors. (2) Or, if possible, you can put it all in the middle of the room, and then use a drop cloth to cover everything.

(B)

(3) Wash all surfaces you plan to paint using soapy water, and let dry. (4) If you forget to perform this important step, the paint won't stick and you'll might end up painting dust and dirt instead of walls.

(C)

(5) Patch all cracks and nail holes with putty. (6) Use a putty knife, not your fingers, and smooth out

the putty beyond the crack or hole. (7) When putty dries it shrinks. (8) Wait until it dries, and then apply more putty if needed. (9) Once it's dry, sand it down so it blends smoothly with the wall surface.

(D)

(10) Remove all nails, screws and other hardware with a screwdriver or other appropriate tool. (11) Remove all outlet and switch plates, and remove all door hardware if you plan to paint the doors.

(E)

(12) Spread drop cloths over the entire floor. (13) You can buy them at a paint store, but old sheets work just as well. (14) Use newspapers only if nothing else is available, since newspapers splattered with paint sticks to your feet.

(F)

(15) Before applying any paint, run tape around the borders of windows and other items that you don't want to paint. (16) Use masking tape or special painter's tape for this purpose.

27. Sentence 1: **You should first remove all furniture from the room, including pictures and wall mirrors.**

If you rewrote sentence 1 beginning with

Pictures, wall mirrors,

the next words should be

(1) and other furniture you should

(2) that are in the room with other

(3) and other furniture should

(4) should, along with all other

(5) should first be removed from

28. Sentence 2: **Or, if possible, you can put it all in the middle of the room, and then use a drop cloth to cover everything.**

Which correction should be made to sentence 2?

(1) remove the comma after <u>possible</u>

(2) change <u>can</u> to <u>could</u>

(3) remove the word <u>all</u>

(4) replace <u>everything</u> with <u>every thing</u>

(5) no correction is necessary

29. Sentence 3: **Wash all surfaces you plan to paint using soapy water, and let dry.**

The most effective revision of sentence 3 would begin with which group of words?

(1) All surfaces you plan

(2) Paint all surfaces using

(3) Let all surfaces dry

(4) Use soapy water

(5) Wash using soapy

30. Sentence 4: **If you forget to perform this important step, the paint won't stick and you'll might end up painting dust and dirt instead of walls.**

Which correction should be made to sentence 4?

(1) change <u>forget</u> to <u>forgot</u>

(2) change <u>you'll</u> to <u>you</u>

(3) insert the word <u>by</u> after <u>up</u>

(4) insert a comma after <u>dirt</u>

(5) no correction is necessary

31. Sentence 7 and Sentence 8: **When putty dries it shrinks. Wait until it dries, and then apply more putty if needed.**

The most effective combination of sentences 7 and 8 would include which group of words?

(1) Putty, which shrinks when

(2) until it dries, putty shrinks

(3) putty dries, so apply

(4) it shrinks, and wait

(5) it dries, so wait until

32. Sentence 12 and Sentence 13: **Spread drop cloths <u>over the entire floor. You can buy them at a paint store,</u> but old sheets work just as well.**

Which is the best way to write the underlined portion of sentences 12 and 13? If the original is the best way, select answer choice (1).

(1) over the entire floor. You can buy them at a paint store

(2) that you can buy at a paint store over the entire floor

(3) over the entire floor, which you can buy at a paint store

(4) you bought at a paint store over the entire floor

(5) over the entire floor, bought at a paint store

33. Sentence 14: **Use newspapers only if nothing else is available, since newspapers splattered with paint sticks to your feet.**

Which correction should be made to sentence 14?

(1) change <u>Use</u> to <u>Used</u>

(2) remove the word <u>since</u>

(3) change <u>splattered</u> with <u>splatter</u>

(4) change <u>sticks</u> to <u>stick</u>

(5) no correction is necessary

34. Which revision would improve the effectiveness of the document?

(1) join paragraphs A and B

(2) move paragraph C to follow paragraph D

(3) join paragraphs B and C

(4) join paragraphs D and E

(5) move paragraph F to follow paragraph A

QUESTIONS 35–43 REFER TO THE FOLLOWING PASSAGE OF TEXT.

(A)

(1) Constantly "plugged in" to the digital world, our society has become overloaded with stimuli. (2) We're constantly monitoring the Web and rushing to use all the high-tech devices and media outlets they've spawned. (3) We've become insatiable consumers of information, no matter what kind or how trivial. (4) We worry every moment that we will be "out of the loop" unless we are online all the time. (5) Continual interruptions and distractions from e-mails, cell-phone calls, and the latest news bite or viral video lowers our productivity at work or school. (6) In short, we've become addicted to random information, which we inject into our brains in small doses throughout each day. (7) We are constantly interrupted by this perpetual, distracting input.

(B)

(8) We rely on quick text messages to communicate with colleagues instead of face-to-face meetings. (9) When we do meet in person, our conversations are becoming more briefer and hurried. (10) Reducing all our communications to bullet points and 100-word text messages will shorten our attention span. (11) We can no longer concentrate or focus on one thing for any length of time. (12) Try reading a long article or a book chapter in one sitting. (13) It's

nearly impossible for most "plugged in" people now. (14) Will we ever be able to relax, cure our addiction, and learn to focus again? (15) Probably not, unless we unplug ourselves.

35. Sentence 2: **We're constantly monitoring the Web and rushing to use all the high-tech devices and media outlets they've spawned.**

Which correction should be made to sentence 2?

(1) replace <u>We're</u> with <u>We</u>

(2) change <u>monitoring</u> to <u>monitor</u>

(3) insert a comma after <u>Web</u>

(4) replace <u>they've</u> with <u>it's</u>

(5) change <u>spawned</u> to <u>spawn</u>

36. Sentence 4: **We worry every moment that we will be "out of the loop" unless we are online all the time.**

If you rewrote sentence 4 beginning with

Every moment

the next words should be

(1) we are out of the loop we are

(2) we worry that we will be

(3) that we will be "out of the loop"

(4) we are online all the time

(5) that we are online we were

37. Sentence 5: **Continual interruptions and distractions from e-mails, cell-phone calls, and the latest news bite or viral video lowers our productivity at work or school.**

Which correction should be made to sentence 5?

(1) insert a comma after <u>distractions</u>

(2) insert a comma after <u>bite</u>

(3) change <u>lowers</u> to <u>lower</u>

(4) insert the word <u>at</u> after <u>work or</u>

(5) no correction is necessary

38. Sentence 7: **We are constantly interrupted by this perpetual, distracting input.**

Which revision should be made to the placement of sentence 7?

(1) move sentence 7 to the beginning of paragraph B

(2) remove sentence 7

(3) move sentence 7 to follow sentence 4

(4) move sentence 7 to follow sentence 5

(5) no revision necessary

39. Sentence 8: **We rely on quick text messages to communicate with colleagues instead of face-to-face meetings.**

The most effective revision of sentence 8 would include which group of words?

(1) with colleagues, we rely on

(2) We rely on colleagues instead of

(3) to communicate with quick text

(4) text messages, face-to-face meetings

(5) face-to-face meetings and quick text

40. Sentence 9: **When we do meet in person, our conversations are becoming more briefer and hurried.**

Which correction should be made to sentence 9?

(1) change <u>we</u> to <u>you</u>

(2) replace <u>meet</u> with <u>meat</u>

(3) change <u>are</u> to <u>will</u>

(4) remove the word <u>more</u>

(5) insert the word <u>more</u> after <u>and</u>

41. Sentence 10: Reducing all our communications to bullet points and 100-word text messages will shorten our attention span.

Which is the best way to write the underlined portion of sentence 10? If the original is the best way, select answer choice (1).

(1) will shorten our attention span

(2) will shorten our attention spans

(3) has shortened our attention span

(4) shortened our attention span

(5) shortens your attention span

42. Sentence 14: Will we ever be able to relax, cure our addiction, and learn to focus again?

Which correction should be made to sentence 14?

(1) change Will to Can

(2) remove the word be

(3) insert the word to after the first comma

(4) remove the word and

(5) no correction is necessary

43. Which revision would improve the effectiveness of the passage?

Begin a new paragraph with

(1) sentence 10

(2) sentence 11

(3) sentence 12

(4) sentence 13

(5) sentence 14

QUESTIONS 44–50 REFER TO THE FOLLOWING LETTER.

Dear Community Member,

(A)

(1) Helping House is preparing for its sixth annual fundraising event to be held on Friday, August 27th, at 7 p.m. (2) Enclosed you'll find a brochure explaining what Helping House and the concept of transitional housing is all about.

(B)

(3) We offer our client-residents weekly group meetings, mentoring sessions, case management, advocacy, and crisis intervention. (4) Several past program residents have showed that they are ready for minimum supervision and are one step away from total independence.

(C)

(5) Our mission at Helping House is to provide transitional housing, eight men's beds, and six women's beds for chronically homeless and mentally ill adults in this County. (6) Clients referred to us from Mental Health United and Peer Road Outreach (PRO), two of our community partners.

(D)

(7) The main program focus is on rebuilding self-respect and self-confidence. (8) Talents and abilities are rekindled and cultivated through music, art, and writing workshops,

which induce their positive expressions. (9) Structure, discipline, and accountability foster the resumption of a productive daily life. (10) Transitioning clients to permanent support housing or living independently are what we try to accomplish in the end.

(E)

(11) Opening Helping House would have been impossible without generous contributions from community members. (12) Looking to the future, we are planning an affordable expansion of our facility. (13) Please consider making a financial donation to help our fundraising effort. (14) Our August 27th event will feature a silent auction that will allow bidders names to be seen by every one attending. (15) Your tax-deductible contribution will be greatly appreciated.

(F)

(16) Thank you for your continued support. (17) If you have any questions, please call me or Gail Westin at (303)555-7802.

Sincerely,

Leona Ruiz
Founder and CEO, Helping House, Inc.

44. Sentence 2: **Enclosed you'll find a brochure explaining what Helping House and the concept of transitional housing is all about.**

Which correction should be made to sentence 2?

(1) remove the word you'll
(2) insert the word for after brochure
(3) insert the word is after House
(4) change is to are
(5) no correction is necessary

45. Sentence 5: **Our mission at Helping House is to provide transitional housing, eight men's beds, and six women's beds for chronically homeless and mentally ill adults in this County.**

Which correction should be made to sentence 5?

(1) change to provide to providing
(2) replace women's with womens'
(3) insert a comma after adults
(4) replace County with county
(5) no correction is necessary

46. Sentence 6: **Clients referred to us from Mental Health United and Peer Road Outreach (PRO), two of our community partners.**

Which correction should be made to sentence 6?

(1) insert the word are after Clients
(2) change from to by
(3) replace Outreach with outreach
(4) replace two with to
(5) change partners to partner

47. Sentence 8: **Talents and abilities are rekindled and cultivated through music, art, and writing workshops, which induce their positive expressions.**

Which correction should be made to sentence 8?

(1) insert the word there after abilities
(2) insert a comma after rekindled
(3) change induce to induces
(4) remove the word their
(5) no correction is necessary

48. Sentence 10: **Transitioning clients to permanent support housing or <u>living independently are</u> what we try to accomplish in the end.**

Which correction should be made to sentence 10? If the original is the best way, select answer choice (1).

(1) living independently are

(2) to live independently, that is

(3) in living situations that are

(4) to a life independent of

(5) an independent life is

49. Sentence 14: **Our August 27th event will feature a silent auction that will allow <u>bidders names to be seen by every one attending.</u>**

Which is the best way to write the underlined portion of sentence 14? If the original is the best way, select answer choice (1).

(1) bidders names to be seen by every one attending

(2) everyone attending to see bidders' names

(3) every attendee to see every bidders names

(4) bidders names to all be seen by all attending

(5) bidders to attend by seeing their names

50. Which revision would improve the effectiveness of the letter?

(1) join paragraphs A and B

(2) move paragraph C to follow paragraph A

(3) move paragraph A to follow paragraph E

(4) join paragraphs D and E

(5) remove paragraph F

LANGUAGE ARTS, WRITING, PART II

45 Minutes • 1 Essay

Directions: This part of the Language Arts, Writing Test assesses your ability to write an essay on a familiar topic. In the essay, you will present your opinion or explain your views about the assigned topic. Your essay will be evaluated based on the overall quality of your writing, including content, organization, and the clarity and correctness of your writing. You must write only about the topic provided. If you write on a different topic, your essay will not be scored, and you will have to retake both parts of the Language Arts, Writing Test.

You will have 45 minutes to plan, write, and revise your essay. You may use scratch paper for notes, outlines, or a rough draft. Write your essay on the two pages of lined paper provided. The notes you make on scratch paper will not be read or scored. Write legibly using a ballpoint pen, so that your writing can easily be read by the evaluators.

ESSAY TOPIC

What are the three particular games or sports you most enjoy playing?

In your essay, identify those three games or sports and explain what it is about them that you enjoy so much. Use your personal observations, experience, and knowledge to support your essay.

SOCIAL STUDIES

70 Minutes • 50 Questions

Directions: The Social Studies Test consists of multiple-choice questions involving general social studies concepts. The questions are based on brief passages of text and visual information (graphs, charts, maps, cartoons, and other figures). Some questions are based on both text and visual information. Study the information provided, and answer the question(s) that follow it, referring back to the information as needed. You will have 70 minutes to answer all 50 questions. Record your answers on the Social Studies section of the answer sheet provided.

QUESTION 1 REFERS TO THE FOLLOWING INFORMATION.

A *bill of attainder* is a legislative act declaring a person or group of persons guilty of a crime and punishing them without benefit of a trial. During the eighteenth century, England applied bills of attainder to its colonies in America. Declaration of guilt usually meant, among other consequences, that the guilty party forfeited all of their property to the Crown. The U.S. Constitution forbids both the federal and state governments to enact bills of attainder.

1. The Fifth Amendment to the U.S. Constitution provides: "In all criminal prosecutions, the accused shall enjoy the right to a speedy and public trial, by an impartial jury. . . ." How does this amendment relate to the prohibition of bills of attainder as provided in the Constitution?

   The Fifth Amendment

   (1) extends that prohibition to the states
   (2) requires that bills of attainder be applied in a speedy manner
   (3) legalizes bills of attainder issued by the courts
   (4) reinforces that prohibition
   (5) extends that prohibition to U.S. colonies

QUESTIONS 2–4 ARE BASED ON THE FOLLOWING MAP AND INFORMATION.

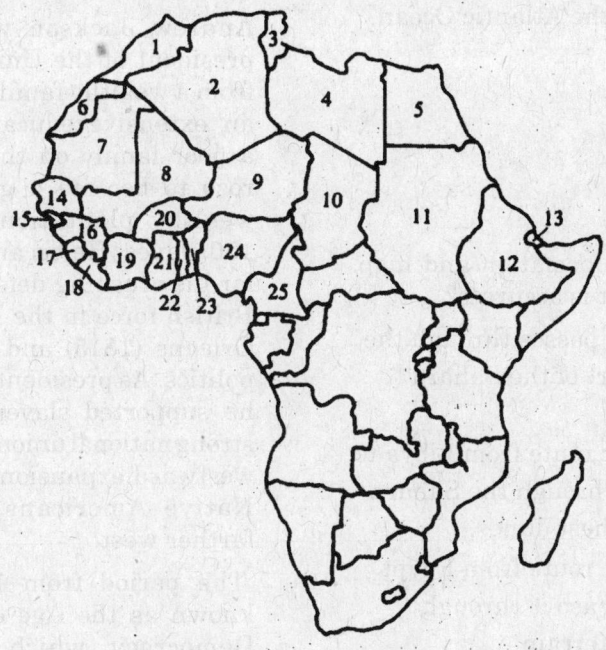

1. Morocco	10. Chad	18. Liberia
2. Algeria	11. Sudan	19. Cote d'lvoire
3. Tunisia	12. Ethiopia	20. Burkina Faso
4. Libya	13. Djibouti	21. Ghana
5. Egypt	14. Senegal	22. Togo
6. Western Sahara	15. Guinea-Bissau	23. Benin
7. Mauritania	16. Guinea	24. Nigeria
8. Mali	17. Sierra Leone	25. Cameroon
9. Niger		

Except where Egypt's northeast corner adjoins Saudi Arabia, the entire African continent is surrounded by seas and oceans: to the east are the Red Sea and, farther south, the Indian Ocean; to the west is the Atlantic Ocean; and to the north is the Mediterranean Sea. At Morocco's northern-most point is the Strait of Gibraltar, which separates Morocco from southern Europe and which marks the entrance to the Mediterranean Sea.

The Sahara Desert extends from the Atlantic Ocean to Egypt and the Red Sea. The Mediterranean Sea and the Atlas Mountains in central Algeria and Morocco mark the desert's northern boundary, while Sudan and the valley of the Niger River (in the country of Niger) mark its southern boundary. The desert's highest sand dunes are in southern Morocco, and its highest mountain peak—Emi Kousi (3,415 meters)—is in northern Chad.

practice test

2. How many of the *numbered* countries are situated at least partially along the coastline of the Atlantic Ocean?

   (1) four
   (2) five
   (3) nine
   (4) twelve
   (5) fourteen

3. Based on the information and map, which statement is accurate?

   (1) The equator passes through the southern part of the Sahara Desert.
   (2) The shortest route from Libya to Ethiopia is through the Sahara Desert's highest dunes.
   (3) The shortest route from Egypt to Burkina Faso is through high-desert terrain.
   (4) More than half the African continent consists of desert.
   (5) The shortest route from Liberia to Cameroon is through the Sahara Desert.

4. The 100-mile Suez Canal in northeastern Egypt was constructed in the mid-nineteenth century and links the Mediterranean Sea and the Gulf of Suez, which becomes the Red Sea.

   Which makes most sense as a reason for the canal's construction?

   (1) to allow water transportation from Europe to Asia without navigating around Africa
   (2) to provide water to the eastern Egyptian desert for agricultural purposes
   (3) to fortify African military defenses against European incursions
   (4) to symbolize Egyptian independence from Libyan rule
   (5) to provide jobs for West Africans who otherwise would be victims of famine

QUESTIONS 5–7 ARE BASED ON THE FOLLOWING INFORMATION.

Andrew Jackson was the first president of the United Sates not from a wealthy family and without an extensive education. Born to a poor family on the frontier, he rose to become a general and a wealthy plantation owner with 150 slaves. He became a war hero for his crushing defeat of a larger British force in the Battle of New Orleans (1815) and then entered politics. As president (1829–1837), he supported slavery but also a strong national union. He promoted westward expansion and removed Native Americans to territory farther west.

The period from 1830–1850 is known as the Age of Jacksonian Democracy, which was characterized by growing democracy in America. The right to vote was extended to all white males, rather than just property owners. Jackson even proposed the election of judges and the president by a popular vote. Jackson promoted himself as a "common man" and railed against the wealthy, well-educated elite that held economic and political power.

5. What fact about Andrew Jackson is inconsistent with the image of Jackson as a "common man"?

   (1) Jackson was not well educated.
   (2) Jackson supported the extension of the right to vote to white males who did not own property.
   (3) Jackson was a wealthy plantation owner who had many slaves.
   (4) Jackson criticized Eastern elites.
   (5) Jackson invited all supporters to his inauguration ball at the White House, not just the rich or well-connected.

6. From the previous passage, we can infer that, although Jackson supported the extension of democracy, he would NOT have supported the extension of the right to vote to:

   (1) Native Americans and slaves

   (2) women

   (3) white males under age 21

   (4) white males who were not landowners

   (5) white males who were not educated

7. Based on the passage, what value strongly influenced Jackson?

   (1) a belief in equal rights for all adult citizens

   (2) a belief in the importance of education

   (3) support of the established order

   (4) a hatred of special privilege based on class, education, or wealth

   (5) a revulsion to wealth

QUESTIONS 8 AND 9 REFER TO THE FOLLOWING CARTOON.

(Le Pelley; reprinted by permission from *The Christian Science Monitor*. © 1970 The Christian Science Publishing Society. All rights reserved.)

in order to form a more perfect Union, establish Justice, insure domestic Tranquility, provide for the common defence,

CONSTITUTION

The Congress shall have power...

To raise and support Armies ;...
To provide and maintain a Navy;
To make rules for the Government and Regulation of the land and naval Forces ; ...

'What it says isn't always what it means'

8. This cartoon refers to which principle of American government?

    (1) separation of church and state

    (2) equal voter representation

    (3) judicial review

    (4) equality before the law

    (5) individual state sovereignty

9. In 1970, the year that this cartoon was drawn, the United States was involved in the Vietnam War. Many young adults in this country sought to avoid being drafted to serve in the war. In light of this context, what is a possible message of the cartoon?

    (1) Members of Congress should read the Constitution more carefully.

    (2) The Supreme Court should rule that draft dodgers be put in jail.

    (3) Congress can justify a war by claiming that young men need a cause for which to fight.

    (4) The Constitutional powers of Congress are always open to interpretation.

    (5) Drafting citizens into military service should be unconstitutional.

QUESTION 10 REFERS TO THE FOLLOWING INFORMATION.

In order for a bill to become law in the United States, it must be passed in identical form by both the House of Representatives and the Senate and signed by the president. If the president vetoes the bill instead of signing it, the bill can still become law if two thirds of each house of Congress approves the bill in a new vote, overriding the president's veto. If the president neither signs nor vetoes a bill passed by Congress, the bill becomes law ten days later, unless Congress is no longer is session. If Congress has adjourned the unsigned bill does not become law; this is known as a pocket veto.

10. Which statement best summarizes the previous passage?

    (1) The president plays the key role in passing a new law.

    (2) The president has the power to block Congress from passing a law.

    (3) The president, by simply not signing a law, can keep it from taking effect.

    (4) The veto power gives the president the ability to rewrite bills passed by Congress before signing them.

    (5) The president can sometimes check the power of Congress to pass new laws.

QUESTION 11 REFERS TO THE FOLLOWING INFORMATION.

From the ninth through the eleventh centuries, the fearsome Germanic Scandinavian seafarers known as the Vikings, or Norse, raided and settled many regions of Northern Europe. Denmark and Scandinavia were well outside the borders of the Roman Empire, and by the end of the eighth century the region contained many small tribal kingdoms, where farming and fishing accounted for most of the economy. However, a growing Norse population found that its fertile land was in limited supply.

11. Why did the Norse probably develop their reputation as warriors and plunderers?

    (1) They were not organized under a centralized military command.

    (2) They were interested in trading their goods for spices and fabrics from Asia.

(3) They were forced to find places to settle outside their native land.

(4) They had successfully defended against invasion by the Roman Empire.

(5) Their religious zeal motivated them to force their beliefs on others.

QUESTION 12 REFERS TO THE FOLLOWING INFORMATION.

In the aftermath of the Civil War, the South struggled to rebuild destroyed cities, railroads, bridges, and farms. Perhaps even more difficult for the South was establishing a new economic system not based on slavery. Meanwhile, the North moved rapidly forward, undergoing rapid industrial development. Factories were expanding and modernizing, farms were becoming more mechanized, and new resources—coal, iron ore, copper, and petroleum—were being developed. It was also during this time that the telephone and electric lighting were invented and cross-country railroads completed.

12. Which statement best compares the North and the South during this time?

(1) The North and the South were facing the same challenges.

(2) The North was advancing much more rapidly than the South.

(3) The North and the South were both struggling to rebuild after the Civil War.

(4) The differences between North and South were diminishing.

(5) Both the North and the South were building new railroads.

QUESTIONS 13–17 ARE BASED ON THE FOLLOWING GRAPHS.

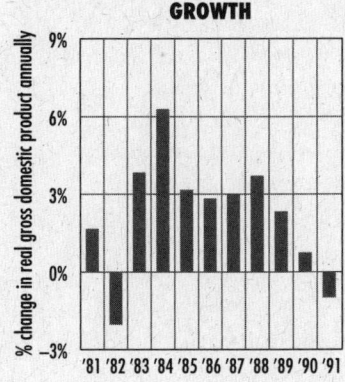

GROWTH

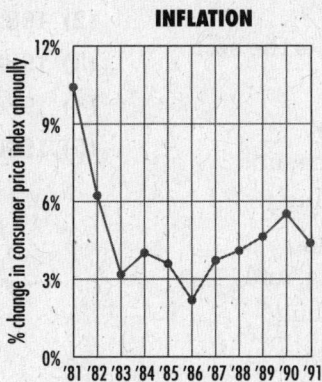

INFLATION

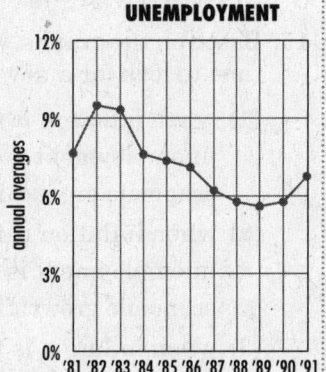

UNEMPLOYMENT

13. The greatest *decrease* in the growth of the gross domestic product was during which time period?

    (1) 1981–1982

    (2) 1984–1985

    (3) 1985–1987

    (4) 1988–1990

    (5) 1988–1991

14. Which statement best describes the relationship between the gross domestic product and the rate of unemployment?

    (1) A low rate of GDP growth is associated with high or rising unemployment.

    (2) A high rate of GDP growth often comes with high or rising unemployment.

    (3) A low or falling rate of unemployment is a sign of a low GDP growth rate.

    (4) A high or rising rate of unemployment is a sign of moderate GDP growth.

    (5) A negative GDP growth rate is associated with a falling rate of unemployment.

15. Based on the graphs, when is the best time to look for a new job?

    (1) when inflation is rising, unemployment is falling, and economic growth is rising

    (2) when inflation is falling, unemployment is rising, and economic growth is falling

    (3) when inflation is falling, unemployment is falling, and economic growth is rising

    (4) when inflation is falling, unemployment is falling, and economic growth is falling

    (5) when inflation is rising, unemployment is rising, and economic growth is rising

16. During the years shown in the graphs, the U.S. economy never achieved full employment, which economists define as an unemployment rate of 4 percent or lower among working-age adults.

Which statement best helps explain this definition of "full employment"?

    (1) The government is reluctant to acknowledge unemployment above the 4-percent rate.

    (2) Teenagers who are employed typically hold part-time rather than full-time jobs.

    (3) Older workers often refuse to accept low-wage employment.

    (4) At any given time, many people are in transition between jobs.

    (5) Many people who would like to work are unable to find jobs.

17. In 2009, the Obama administration attempted to end a nationwide economic recession through spending programs aimed at creating new jobs across the nation. Based solely on these facts, which year shown on the graph does 2009 resemble?

    (1) 1981

    (2) 1982

    (3) 1983

    (4) 1988

    (5) 1990

18. After Franklin D. Roosevelt had served four terms as president, the Twenty-second Amendment to the Constitution was enacted, limiting future presidents to two 4-year terms. U.S. senators are elected for six-year terms, and they can be reelected to that office indefinitely.

What was the effect of the Twenty-second Amendment?

(1) to nullify certain actions taken by Roosevelt during his final two terms

(2) to ensure that any Senator serves longer than any president

(3) to discourage a vice president from later running for president

(4) to destabilize the federal government by upsetting the status quo

(5) to put more power in the hands of Congress, especially the Senate

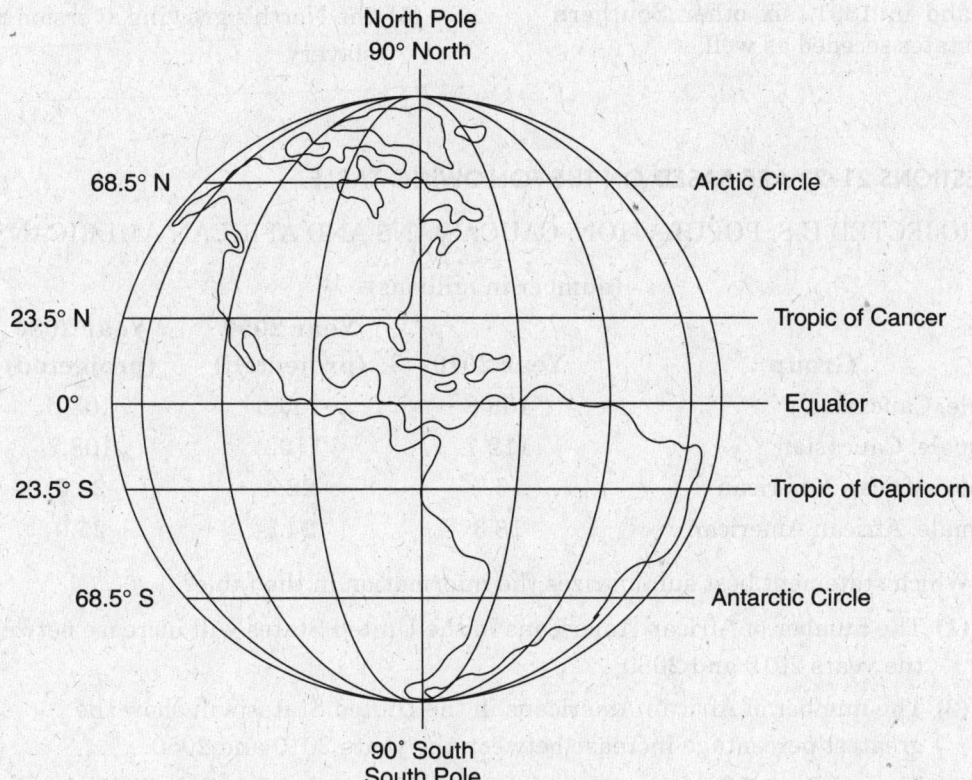

19. Referring to the above figure, which of the following accurately describes the location of ALL of the 48 contiguous U.S. states, which exclude Hawaii and Alaska?

(1) between the Tropic of Capricorn and the equator

(2) between the Tropic of Cancer and the equator

(3) between the Tropic of Cancer and the Arctic Circle

(4) between the equator and the Arctic Circle

(5) between the Tropic of Capricorn and the Antarctic Circle

practice test

QUESTION 20 REFERS TO THE FOLLOWING INFORMATION.

In the United States, by the mid-nineteenth century, the North was becoming industrialized while the South remained a mainly agricultural region of large cotton and tobacco plantations and had a comparatively sparse population. Northerners were growing increasingly critical of the use of slaves by Southern plantation owners, and many Northerners began to talk about abolishing the institution of slavery. In 1860, South Carolina seceded (withdrew) from the Union, and in 1861, six other Southern states seceded as well.

20. Based on this passage, what would most likely be the source of friction between the North and the South that would have caused southern states to secede?

(1) the North's efforts to industrialize the South

(2) the dominance of the North in population

(3) the North's success in industrialization

(4) the South wanting to base its economy on industrialization like the North

(5) the North's growing aversion to slavery

QUESTIONS 21–23 ARE BASED ON THE FOLLOWING TABLE.

PROJECTED U.S. POPULATION: CAUCASIANS AND AFRICAN AMERICANS

(number in millions)

Group	Year 2010	Year 2050 (projected)	Year 2080 (projected)
Male, Caucasian	108.8	105.6	103.6
Female, Caucasian	112.7	116.2	108.7
Male, African American	16.7	22.4	22.6
Female, African American	18.3	24.7	25.0

21. Which statement best summarizes the information in the table?

(1) The number of African Americans in the United States will increase between the years 2010 and 2080.

(2) The number of African Americans in the United States will show the greatest percentage increase between the years 2010 and 2050.

(3) The number of Caucasian females in the United States will increase between the years 2010 and 2050.

(4) The number of Caucasians in the United States will be greater than the number of African Americans in the years between 2010 and 2080.

(5) The total number of African Americans in the United States will increase between the years 2010 and 2080, both in actual numbers and in relation to the total number of Caucasians.

22. In the United States, the combined Hispanic and African American population is expected to surpass the Caucasian population by the year 2050. If that projection turns out to be accurate, what would this development suggest about the projections in the table?

(1) This development would have no effect on the projections in the table.

(2) The African American population will be higher than projected in the table.

(3) The Hispanic population will be higher than projected in the table.

(4) The Caucasian population will be lower than projected in the table.

(5) The Caucasian population will be higher than projected in the table.

23. Which expectation best supports the projections in the table?

(1) Average life expectancies in the United States are anticipated to increase steadily.

(2) An increasing number of African Americans are expected to obtain college degrees.

(3) The birthrate among U.S. Caucasians is expected to continue declining.

(4) More women than men are expected to immigrate to the United States during the twenty-first century.

(5) More Africans and Asians than Europeans are expected to immigrate to the United States during the twenty-first century.

24. The 9 justices of the U.S. Supreme Court all receive lifetime appointments from the president. What would be LEAST likely to occur if the Supreme Court Justices were elected (and re-eletcted) by the people for four-year terms rather than appointed for life terms?

(1) The Justices would be more likely to consider public opinion when deciding a case.

(2) The Justices would be more likely to consider the views of major donors to their re-election campaigns when deciding cases.

(3) The Justices would spend less time on legal decisions and more time campaigning and raising money.

(4) Justices would be more likely to air their disagreements publicly.

(5) There would be little change— the Justices would continue to decide cases using their own judgement and legal precedent.

25. The consumer price index (CPI) is used as a measure of inflation, or a general rise in prices in terms of a specific currency, such as the U.S. dollar. The index measures the prices of a "typical consumer's market basket" of goods and services. Which of the following items would NOT be included in this market basket?

(1) rent

(2) meat

(3) automobiles

(4) electricity

(5) wages

QUESTIONS 26 AND 27 REFER TO THE FOLLOWING MAP.

Expansion of the Continental United States

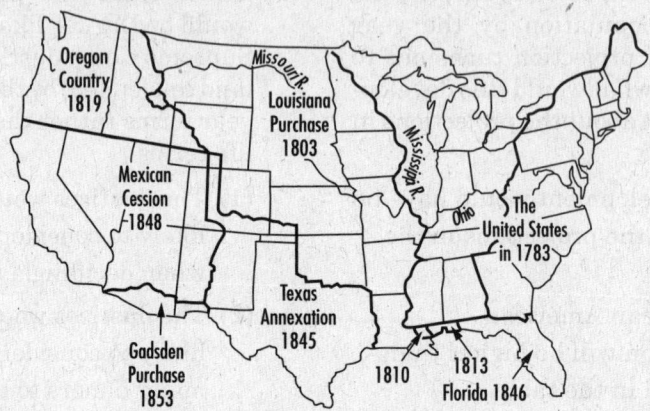

26. The Mexican War of 1846–1848 was ended by the Treaty of Guadalupe Hidalgo, which gave what large area of land to the United States?

    (1) The Louisiana Purchase

    (2) The Mexican Cession

    (3) Oregon Country

    (4) The Gadsden Purchase

    (5) Florida

27. Based on the map, which statement is LEAST accurate?

    (1) Texas was annexed before the Gadsden Purchase was made.

    (2) The Louisiana Purchase extended from the Gulf of Mexico to the Canadian border.

    (3) Initially, all territory of the United States was located east of the Mississippi River.

    (4) The expansion of the continental United States occurred entirely during the nineteenth century.

    (5) The entire region east of the Mississippi River was annexed before the areas west of that river.

QUESTION 28 REFERS TO THE FOLLOWING INFORMATION.

Under the U.S. Constitution, the president's job includes the task of enforcing all federal laws as the chief executive of all federal departments and agencies. In addition, the president determines U.S. foreign policy, negotiates treaties (which must get Senate approval for ratification) and is the commander in chief of the nation's armed forces. The president appoints federal judges (to life terms), subject to Senate approval. The president also has the power to grant reprieves and pardons to those who have been convicted of committing federal crimes.

28. Which presidential action below is within the scope of the presidential powers described in this passage?

    (1) The president pardons a person a state court has convicted of murder.

    (2) The president pardons a person who has been accused, but not yet convicted, of passing top-secret documents to another country.

    (3) The president begins secret negotiations between the United States and Russia.

(4) The president fires a justice of the Supreme Court.

(5) The president repeals a law passed by Congress.

QUESTIONS 29 AND 30 REFER TO THE FOLLOWING INFORMATION.

In 1985, Mikhail Gorbachev became the Soviet Union's leader. He introduced a policy of economic reform known as *Perestroika* as well as *Glasnost,* a policy of openness between the Soviet government and its people. These policies were intended to spur economic growth and revitalize the government of the Soviet Union. Although Gorbachev considered himself a Communist, the policies he introduced opened the door to free expression, economic reform, and nationalism that ended with the fall of Communism and the breakup of the Soviet Union into 15 separate nations (Russia is the largest).

29. Which statement best summarizes *Glasnost*?

(1) *Glasnost* was a policy of economic reform that failed to end economic stagnation.

(2) *Glasnost* was a policy of openness that brought greater freedom of expression in the Soviet Union, which ultimately helped to bring about the fall of the Communist Party and the breakup of the Soviet Union.

(3) *Glasnost* refers to the growth of nationalistic identities within the Soviet Union that led to its breakup into 15 separate nations.

(4) *Glasnost* refers to the general lack of government transparency and openness in Russian government.

(5) *Glasnost* refers to Gorbachev's political platform, which successfully revitalized communism and the Soviet Union.

30. Which of the following is a statement of fact rather than an opinion or value judgment?

(1) Gorbachev failed in his goal of reforming communism and revitalizing the Soviet Union.

(2) Gorbachev would have been more successful had he tried more gradual reform rather than introducing far-reading political and economic reforms all at once.

(3) To accomplish his reform goals, Gorbachev should have only introduced *Glasnost* or *Perestroika* one at a time, rather than together.

(4) Gorbachev followed the right policies, but it was too late to save communism or the Soviet Union.

(5) Gorbachev should be regarded as a hero because, although his policies didn't have the result he intended, they brought an end to what Ronald Reagan called the "Evil Empire."

QUESTION 31 REFERS TO THE FOLLOWING INFORMATION.

Businesses generally try to provide just enough supply of goods and services to meet the demand for them. If too high a price is set, businesses won't be able to sell their entire supply. On the other hand, setting too low a price leaves businesses without enough supply to meet demand.

31. If the demand for automobiles increases, but the supply does not change, what will most likely happen to the price and the quantity exchanged?

(1) The price and the quantity will both stay the same.

(2) The price and the quantity exchanged will increase.

(3) The price will increase and the quantity exchanged will decrease.

(4) The price will decrease and the quantity exchanged will increase.

(5) The price will stay the same and the quantity exchanged will increase.

QUESTIONS 32 AND 33 REFER TO THE FOLLOWING INFORMATION.

Listed below are several policies and programs established by various Democratic U.S. presidents.

New Deal: The social and economic programs under President Franklin D. Roosevelt in the 1930s that reformed the U.S. banking system and created the Agricultural Adjustment Administration, the Civilian Conservation Corps, the Public Works agency, the Tennessee Valley Authority, the Social Security system, and the National Labor Relations Board, as well as establishing minimum wage and hours laws.

Fair Deal: A continuation of the New Deal. Under President Harry Truman, the Fair Deal brought a public housing bill.

New Frontier: Under President John F. Kennedy, the program included government aid for education, housing, mass transportation, equal-opportunity employment, Medicare, tax reform, and the Peace Corps.

Great Society: President Johnson's program that concentrated on antipoverty, health, education, conservation, and urban-planning measures.

Recovery and Reinvestment Act: President Obama's program focused on creating jobs in infrastructure development and new technologies, providing funding for education and health care, and providing tax credits, subsidies, and other aid to middle-class families and small businesses.

32. Which of the following would LEAST likely be an outgrowth of the listed policies and programs?

   (1) a rental housing subsidy

   (2) a reduction in capital gains taxes

   (3) a college loan or scholarship

   (4) a food bank for the homeless

   (5) a highway construction project

33. Mr. and Mrs. Welsh have retired and are living on a small pension. The pension, however, does not completely cover the cost of their medical bills. Under which program listed above can they expect help with their medical expenses?

   (1) the New Frontier

   (2) the Fair Deal

   (3) the New Deal

   (4) the Great Society

   (5) the Recovery and Reinvestment Act

QUESTION 34 IS BASED ON THE FOLLOWING INFORMATION.

In the Supreme Court's landmark case, *Brown* v. *The Board of Education of Topeka* (1954), an earlier decision was overturned. In the earlier case, *Plessy* v. *Ferguson* (1896), the doctrine of "separate but equal" was established with regard to education. In the *Brown* case, the Court decided that public school segregation, which had been a state-prescribed issue, was a violation of the equal-protection clause of the Fourteenth Amendment to the Constitution.

34. Which was most likely a result of the Court's decision in the *Brown* case?

   (1) imposing quotas on prestigious private colleges to ensure admission of racial minorities

   (2) redrawing voting districts to include racial minority groups in as many districts as possible

   (3) opening private country-club memberships to racial minorities

   (4) mandatory bussing of schoolchildren to public schools in other districts

   (5) ensuring racial minorities the right to vote in all federal presidential primary elections

practice test

QUESTIONS 35 AND 36 REFER TO THE FOLLOWING INFORMATION.

CHINESE DYNASTIES: EARLY IMPERIAL THROUGH LATE IMPERIAL

Early Imperial China

	Dynasty
221–207 BCE	Qin
206 BCE–9 AD	Western Han
9–25 AD	Hsing (Wang Mang interregnum)
25–220 AD	Eastern Han
220–265 AD	Three Kingdoms
265–316 AD	Western Chin
317–420 AD	Eastern Chin

Classical Imperial China

581–618 AD	Sui
618–907 AD	T'ang
907–979 AD	10 Kingdoms
960–1279 AD	Song

- Liao (916–1125 AD)
- Western Xia (1038–1227 AD)
- Jin (1115–1234 AD)

Later Imperial China

1279–1368 AD	Yuan
1368–1644 AD	Ming
1644–1911 AD	Qing

Modern China

1912	Xinhai Revolution
1912–present	People's Republic of China

The Silk Road was a loose network of travel routes first established in ancient times in Asia for the purpose of exchanging goods—from fabrics to spices to art and other objects—among the people of different regions. Over the centuries, the Silk Road reached throughout Central Asia, branched south into India, and eventually extended west to the Mediterranean Sea and even northern Europe. The reach and use of the many routes that constituted the Silk Road reached their zenith during China's T'ang Dynasty, which set the world's standard for taste in luxury goods, especially silk and porcelain.

35. The history of the Silk Road provides insight into all of the following aspects of human nature with the possible EXCEPTION of which one?

- **(1)** curiosity about other lands and cultures
- **(2)** interest in free trade and commerce
- **(3)** desire to acquire territory and dominate others
- **(4)** ingenuity in getting from place to place
- **(5)** interest in bettering one's living standard

36. During which period of time in history was the Silk Road used most extensively?

(1) the fifth century

(2) the ninth century

(3) the eleventh century

(4) the fourteenth century

(5) the sixteenth century

QUESTION 37 REFERS TO THE FOLLOWING INFORMATION.

Congress is made up of the House of Representatives and the Senate. Most of the work of Congress in passing laws and determining the federal budget is carried out in the 16 standing committees of the Senate and the 22 standing committees of the House. However, ultimately all legislation is voted on by all members of both the House and the Senate. There are 2 senators from every state, but the number of representatives from a state currently varies from 1 to 53, based on the state's population. Senators serve staggered six-year terms, while members of the House are elected every two years. Only the Senate has the power to approve treaties and Presidential appointments of federal judges and key government officials.

37. Which statement correctly identifies a similarity between the House and the Senate?

(1) The length of the term of office for senators and representatives is the same.

(2) There is the same number of Senators from each state.

(3) The Senate and the House have the same powers.

(4) In both the Senate and the House of Representatives, most of the work of producing legislation is done by a limited number of standing committees.

(5) There is the same number of Senators as Representatives in Congress.

QUESTIONS 38 AND 39 REFER TO THE FOLLOWING TEXT AND GRAPH.

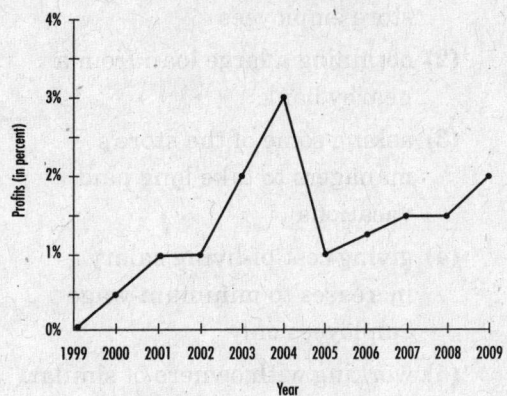

Profits for Garcia's Goodies

Mr. Garcia owns Garcia's Goodies, a gourmet grocery store he started in 1999. The line graph above shows the after-tax profits the store generated in each year of the first decade the store was in business.

38. Which would best explain the spike in profitability in 2004?

In 2004

(1) a new movie theater opened across the street from Garcia's Goodies

(2) a bountiful sugar-cane harvest resulted in lower sugar price worldwide

(3) all taxpayers in Garcia's state received a one-time state-tax rebate

(4) the fast-food restaurant next-door to Garcia's Goodies closed down

(5) Garcia won several thousand dollars in the state lottery

39. When profits fell in 2005, which strategy would most likely have helped Mr. Garcia reverse that decline?

(1) reducing the number of full-time store employees

(2) obtaining a large loan from a nearby bank

(3) asking some of the store's managers to take long paid vacations

(4) giving cost-of-living salary increases to minimum-wage employees only

(5) working with owners of similar, nearby stores to raise prices on most items

QUESTIONS 40 AND 41 REFER TO THE FOLLOWING PASSAGE.

The railroad changed the way Americans viewed time. Before, most people used the sun to set their clocks. Because the sun appears to move across the sky from east to west, a city a little to the east of a neighboring town marked noon a few minutes earlier. In the early days of the railroad, each city and each railroad had its own time. The main terminal in Buffalo, New York, had four clocks—one for each railroad using the train station and one on "Buffalo time." In 1883, an association of railroad managers ended the confusion with Standard Railway Time. They divided the nation into time zones, and every community within a time zone was on the same time. An Indianapolis newspaper noted, "The sun is no longer [the boss]. People—55 million people—must now eat, sleep, and work, as well as travel by railroad time." In 1918, Standard Railway Time became federal law.

40. Which of the following was NOT an effect of the establishment of Standard Railway Time?

(1) Trains began to run on time.

(2) Four time zones were created in the United States.

(3) All railroad companies in the same cities used the same time.

(4) The sun no longer determined the time.

(5) Towns and cities in the same time zone all hit noon at exactly the same instant.

41. On what assumption was the establishment of standard time zones based?

(1) The government regulates too many aspects of people's lives.

(2) The public interest is best served if each city uses the real time as determined by the sun.

(3) The public interest is best served if everyone in a city and all its public transport carriers use the same time.

(4) Imposing an artificial system of time with time zone boundaries is wrong because it violates the laws of nature.

(5) The public interest is best served if trains run on time.

QUESTIONS 42 AND 43 REFER TO THE FOLLOWING INFORMATION AND TABLE.

U.S. National Parks and Their Visitors

Year	No. of Parks	No. of Visitors (in thousands)
1970	35	45,879
1960	29	26,630
1950	28	13,919
1940	26	7,358
1930	22	2,775
1920	19	920
1910	13	119

When Theodore Roosevelt became U.S. President in 1900, the U.S. National Park system consisted of just five parks: Yellowstone, Yosemite, Sequoia, General Grant, and Mount Rainier. As president, Roosevelt doubled that number to ten. He also added land to Yosemite and convinced Congress to appropriate funds to purchase buffalo for Yellowstone and to care for these buffalo.

42. Which of the following does NOT help explain the increase in the number of parks compared to park visitors over the sixty-year period shown?

(1) a significant increase in the U.S. population

(2) improved transportation systems throughout the country

(3) an increase in leisure time among U.S. and non-U.S. households

(4) an increasing commitment to conservation on the part of the federal government

(5) a dramatic rise in disposable income among U.S. households

43. To this day, Yellowstone and Yosemite each attract more visitors per year than any of the system's other parks.

Which of the following is a fact, rather than an opinion, that helps explain the enduring popularity of both Yellowstone and Yosemite?

(1) Both parks are far away from any major metropolitan area.

(2) In the United States, wild buffalo can be found in few places outside Yellowstone.

(3) Yosemite is located in California, the most populous state in the United States.

(4) They are among the National Park system's most beautiful parks.

(5) Both parks were among the earliest included in the park system.

QUESTION 44 REFERS TO THE FOLLOWING MAP.

The First 13 Colonies

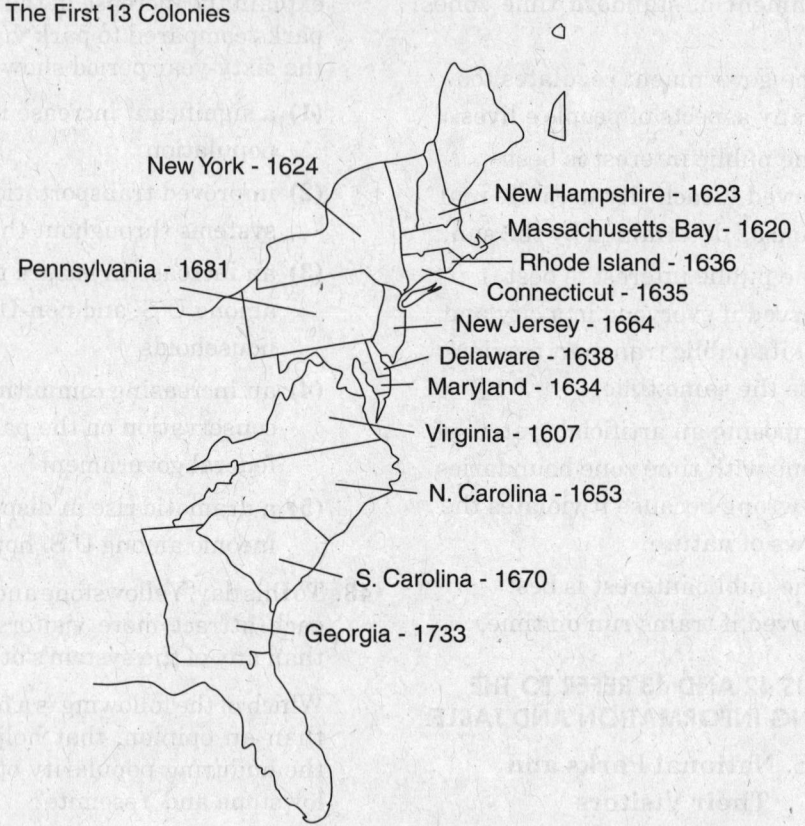

New York - 1624

New Hampshire - 1623

Massachusetts Bay - 1620

Rhode Island - 1636

Connecticut - 1635

Pennsylvania - 1681

New Jersey - 1664

Delaware - 1638

Maryland - 1634

Virginia - 1607

N. Carolina - 1653

S. Carolina - 1670

Georgia - 1733

Washington, D.C., was established as the nation's capital in 1791 and is located between Virginia and Maryland at the confluence of two rivers, about 60 miles upriver from the Chesapeake Bay.

44. Which is the LEAST plausible reason for this choice of location?

   (1) From this spot the settlers could more easily acquire land to the south.

   (2) Some of the area's neighborhoods were already well established.

   (3) Its location was not far from major ports and provided an economic base for the city.

   (4) Locating the capital near coastal waterways allowed for boat traffic.

   (5) The location was not far from lands to the west that the United States hoped to acquire.

45. Under the Constitution, only the U.S. president or his appointees can negotiate treaties with other countries, though the Senate must ratify all such treaties.

Which is the best reason that it would be unconstitutional for California to negotiate with the Mexican government to share the costs of border security?

(1) Foreign governments have little incentive to abide by the terms of treaties with just one state.

(2) Providing adequate border security is too expensive for any one state, even California.

(3) California's governor is a U.S. citizen, not a citizen of Mexico.

(4) Ratification of this sort of agreement by the U.S. Senate would be highly unlikely.

(5) The two governments cannot agree as to the best method of securing the border.

QUESTIONS 46–48 REFER TO THE FOLLOWING TEXT AND CARTOON.

In 1949, the North Atlantic Treaty Organization (NATO) was formed by several Western nations as a military alliance to defend against attacks by nonmember states. Though initially a political association, NATO built up a formidable military structure in response to the Korean War (1950), which raised suspicions that Communist countries were allying themselves against the West.

In response to the NATO's formation, the Soviet "bloc" formed a similar alliance under the Warsaw Pact to defend against the Western allies. Mainly due to the weakening of the Soviet Union throughout the 1980s, members of the Warsaw Pact gradually withdrew their membership, and the Soviet Union itself ultimately collapsed and formally dissolved the Warsaw Pact in 1991. NATO's member nations, which had remained more or less galvanized in opposition to the Soviet bloc for four decades, suddenly found themselves without a mutual adversary.

The **NORTH ATLANTIC TEA & ORIGAMI** Society

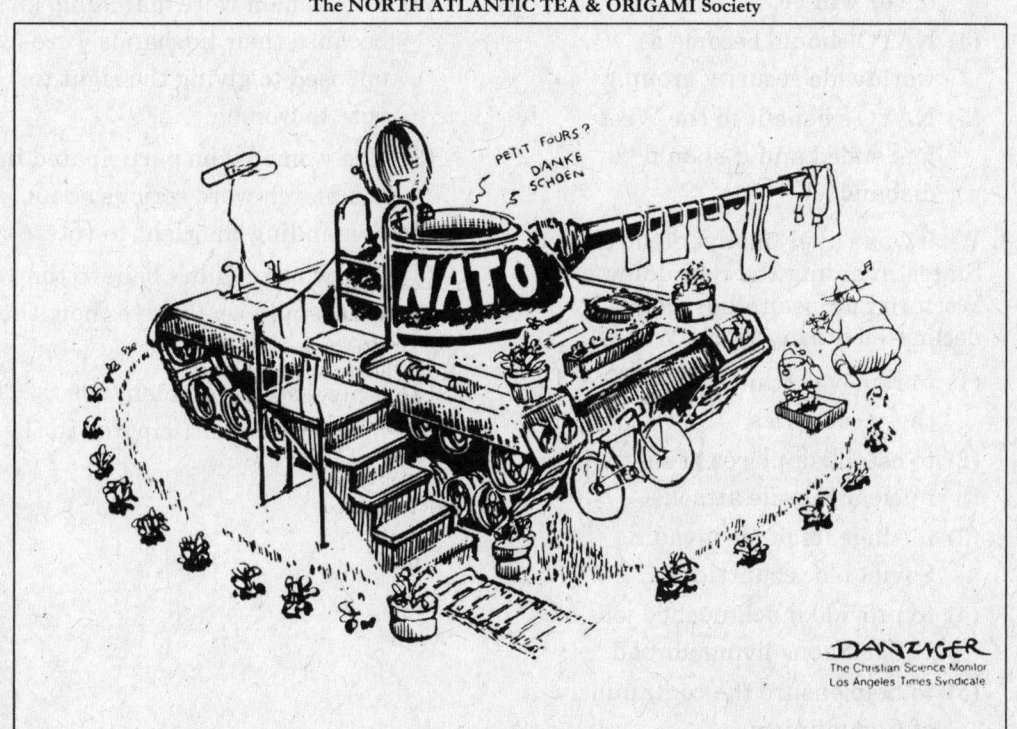

46. Which statement BEST expresses the message of this 1990 cartoon?

    (1) NATO has become too involved in Japanese affairs.

    (2) NATO is not a well-managed organization.

    (3) NATO has become unnecessary since the fall of communism.

    (4) NATO should undertake joint training exercises with Eastern European countries.

    (5) NATO was a better organization before World War I.

47. With which of the following statements would the cartoonist most probably agree?

    (1) NATO needs a powerful enemy to be strong itself.

    (2) France needs to rejoin NATO before the organization can become strong again.

    (3) NATO has never been a useful organization for the United States to be a part of and it never will be.

    (4) NATO should become a worldwide security group.

    (5) NATO's benefit to the West has ended and it should be disbanded.

48. What was a likely motive of the United States in aiding the rebuilding of its Western European allies that had been decimated during World War II?

    (1) to remove tyrants from power in these countries

    (2) to establish places of safety from nuclear missile attacks

    (3) to stage itself for invading Soviet bloc countries

    (4) to provide much-needed jobs for U.S. citizens living abroad

    (5) to help ensure the containment of Communism

QUESTIONS 49 AND 50 REFER TO THE FOLLOWING PASSAGE.

From 1848 to 1919, American women fought for a constitutional amendment giving them suffrage, or the right to vote. Year after year, more and more women attended rallies and marched in the streets. In one parade, a reporter noted that "women doctors, women lawyers, women architects, women artists, actresses and sculptors; women waitresses, domestics; a huge division of industrial workers . . . all marched with an intensity and purpose that astonished the crowds that lined the streets." In 1919, Congress passed the Nineteenth Amendment, giving women the right to vote. A year later, the states ratified it, and female suffrage became the law of the land.

49. Which statement is supported by the evidence provided by the reporter who witnessed the march?

    (1) Men did not participate in the march.

    (2) The women were marching because their husbands were opposed to giving the right to vote to women.

    (3) The women who participated in the march were serious about demanding the right to vote.

    (4) The women didn't believe that men would really give them the right to vote.

    (5) Only working women, not housewives, participated in the march.

50. Which statement correctly compares the women's suffrage movement and the civil rights movement of the 1950s and 1960s?

(1) Only the women's suffrage movement relied on protest marches to draw attention to their cause and show determination and strength.

(2) Both movements used voter registration drives as an important part of their movement.

(3) Both movements quickly achieved their goals.

(4) While the women's suffrage movement focused only on the right to vote, the civil rights movement sought a broader range of rights.

(5) Nonviolence was an important part of the women's suffrage movement but not the civil rights movement.

SCIENCE

80 Minutes • 50 Questions

Directions: The Science Test consists of multiple-choice questions designed to measure your knowledge of general science concepts. The questions are based on brief passages of text and visual information (charts, graphs, diagrams, and other figures). Some questions are based on both text and visual information. Study the information provided and answer the question(s) that follow it, referring back to the information as needed.

You will have 80 minutes to answer all 50 questions. Record your answers on the answer sheet provided.

QUESTION 1 REFERS TO THE FOLLOWING INFORMATION.

The amount of bone in the elderly skeleton—a key determinant in its susceptibility to fractures—is believed to be a function of two major factors. The first is the peak amount of bone mass attained, which is determined by a variety of variables. One of the variables is genetic inheritance. Another is gender, as elderly men experience only half as many hip fractures as elderly women. Race may be another variable: African American women have a lower incidence of osteoporosis fractures than Caucasian women. Still other variables include diet, exposure to sunlight, and physical activity.

The second major factor is the rate of bone loss after peak bone mass has been attained. While many of the variables that affect peak bone mass also affect rates of bone loss, additional factors influencing bone loss include physiological stresses such as pregnancy and lactation. Hormonal status, reflected primarily by estrogen and progesterone levels, exerts the greatest effect on rates of decline in skeletal mass.

1. Among the following, who is likely to achieve the lowest peak bone mass?

   (1) an elderly Caucasian woman

   (2) a pregnant Caucasian woman

   (3) an elderly African American man

   (4) a pregnant African American woman

   (5) an elderly African American woman

QUESTION 2 REFERS TO THE FOLLOWING ILLUSTRATION.

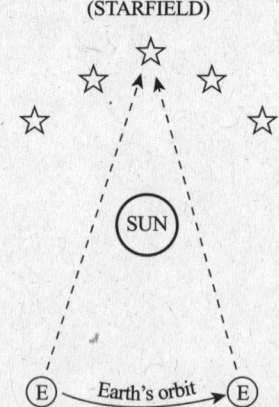

2. What does the above illustration show?

   (1) the Earth at Summer solstice

   (2) the phases of the Moon

   (3) the apparent motion of the Sun

   (4) the first phase of a solar eclipse

   (5) the distance of stars from Earth

QUESTIONS 3 AND 4 REFER TO THE FOLLOWING INFORMATION AND CHART.

Cell metabolism, the creation of energy by the processing of glucose and other sugars at the cellular level, can be accomplished either (1) in the presence of oxygen, through the process of aerobic respiration, or (2) without oxygen, through the process of anaerobic respiration.

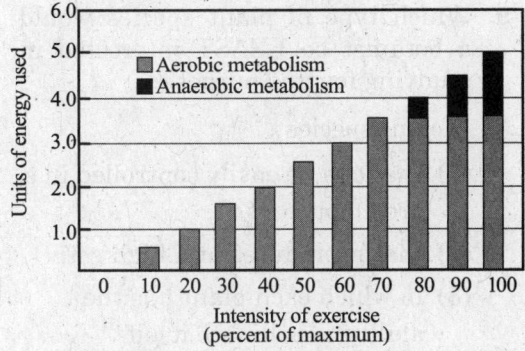

3. What can you infer from the information presented above?

   (1) Intense exercise uses more anaerobically metabolized energy than light exercise.

   (2) Most of the energy you spend is through some form of exercise.

   (3) The longer you exercise, the more fuel you metabolize anaerobically.

   (4) Non-athletes have a higher metabolic rate then athletes.

   (5) Intense exercise requires less oxygen than moderate exercise.

4. Referring to the chart, which activity is most likely to require 4.0 arbitrary units of energy?

   (1) swimming four laps of a full-length pool

   (2) lifting a very heavy weight once

   (3) practicing yoga during your lunch break

   (4) running two laps around the high-school track

   (5) cycling up a short but steep hill

QUESTIONS 5 AND 6 REFER TO THE FOLLOWING INFORMATION.

Except for the element hydrogen (a gas), all elements in their normal form have the same number of protons (which carry a positive charge) as neutrons (which carry no charge). Atoms can gain or lose neutrons, creating other isotopes (forms) of the same element. When the number of protons and neutrons do not match, an atom can become unstable and give off particles of energy (radiation), and its nucleus begins to decay and lose protons.

5. What can you infer from the information?

   (1) Hydrogen is an unstable element.

   (2) Gases are less stable than other elements.

   (3) Neutrons provide stability to atoms.

   (4) Electrons are more stable than protons.

   (5) Isotopes are less stable than non-isotopes.

6. In its normal form, carbon has an atomic mass of 12 units (the unit of measure is the *dalton*) and is referred to as carbon 12. What is true of the isotope carbon 14?

   Carbon 14

   (1) contains more protons than neutrons

   (2) carries a negative charge

   (3) contains two more neutrons than protons

   (4) carries a positive charge

   (5) is stable because it is even-numbered

7. Many species of small animals have learned to exploit all resources available around them to grow in population as quickly as possible. If environmental conditions change, these so-called "strategists" can quickly run out of resources needed to grow, or even sustain, their population.

   What is a good example of a strategist?

   (1) fungi
   (2) termites
   (3) weeds
   (4) rabbits
   (5) algae

QUESTION 8 REFERS TO THE FOLLOWING DIAGRAM.

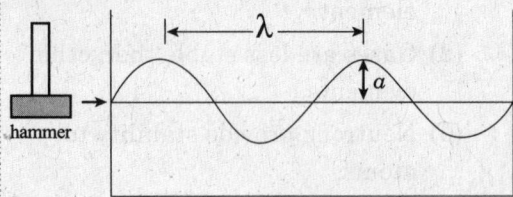

a = amplitude
λ = wavelength
velocity (v) = wavelength (λ) × frequency

8. A hammer strikes the side of a tank every 5 seconds. If the hammer were to begin striking every 4 seconds instead, but with the same force, what would be the result?

   (1) a decrease in wavelength
   (2) a decrease in amplitude
   (3) an increase in wavelength
   (4) an increase in amplitude
   (5) no change in amplitude or wavelength

QUESTION 9 REFERS TO THE FOLLOWING INFORMATION.

The hereditary patterns of a plant species can be seen by observing the physical traits of two individual "parent" plants and then noting the traits of the "daughter" plants. Though many plants can be studied in this way, some are more useful than others in drawing predictive conclusions.

9. Which type of plant species would a botanist be LEAST interested in studying for this purpose?

   A plant species

   (1) that can be easily controlled in a greenhouse
   (2) that reproduces at a high rate
   (3) in which each plant has the ability to pollinate itself
   (4) that exhibits many different kinds of traits
   (5) that exhibits many subtle variations of just one trait

10. Erosion is the movement of rock and soil on the surface of the Earth, generally by a natural process. Which activity is most likely to create a condition conducive to erosion?

    (1) constructing a paved road along a valley floor
    (2) covering a soggy hillside with a waterproof tarp
    (3) tilling, or churning, the soil after a crop harvest
    (4) racing dirt bikes around remote meadowlands
    (5) dredging sand from the bottom of a harbor

QUESTION 11 REFERS TO THE FOLLOWING INFORMATION.

The human retina is composed of cells called rods, which register black and white, and cells called cones, which register color. Electrical signals from the rods and the cones are sent to the front of the retina to capture light-wave information entering through the eye's pupil. This information is then sent to the brain where it is interpreted and perceived as visual images.

11. What is the most likely explanation as to why dogs see the world only in black, white, and shades of gray?

    (1) The cones of a dog's retina are located behind the retina, blocked from light.

    (2) In a dog, the eye's retina is not connected to the optic nerve.

    (3) A dog's retina consists entirely of rods.

    (4) Humans are more sensitive to bright light than dogs are.

    (5) The retinas of dogs contain more cones than rods.

QUESTION 12 REFERS TO THE FOLLOWING ILLUSTRATION.

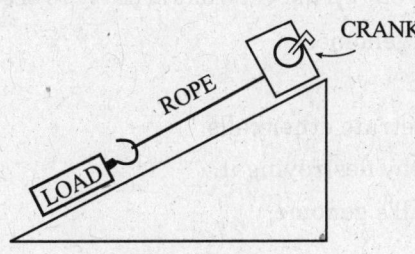

Incline Plane

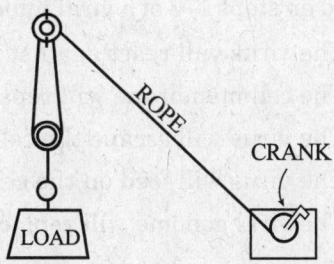

Simple Pulley

12. What purpose do the two machines illustrated above both serve?

    (1) to distribute the weight of the load more evenly

    (2) to increase the distance the load must be moved

    (3) to reduce the distance the load must be moved

    (4) to decrease the time it takes to move the load a given distance

    (5) to decrease the magnitude of force needed to move the load

QUESTION 13 REFERS TO THE FOLLOWING DIAGRAM AND INFORMATION.

VIRAL INFECTION

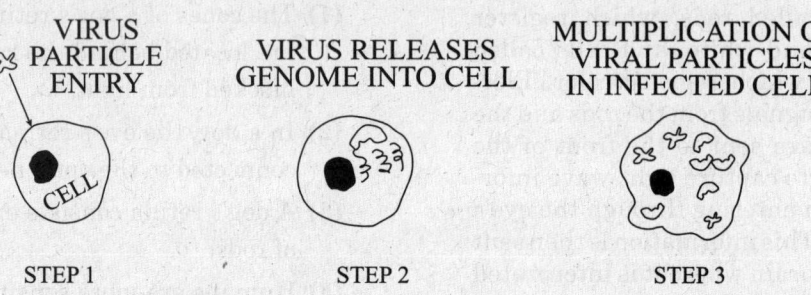

Step 1: A virus particle attaches to a receptor site on the cell wall, from where it penetrates the cell wall.

Step 2: The virus particle sheds its protein shell and releases its genome into the cell.

Step 3: The viral genome creates new virus particles within the cell, causing the cell to swell in size.

13. Based on steps 1–3 of a viral infection, as shown above, what is likely to occur next?

   (1) The virus will react against the cell genome.

   (2) The cell membrane will repair itself.

   (3) The virus will escape the cell to penetrate other cells.

   (4) The virus will feed on the cell, thereby destroying it.

   (5) The viral genome will replace the cell's genome.

QUESTION 14 REFERS TO THE FOLLOWING INFORMATION.

When atoms share one or more electrons in their outer electron shells in order for each to complete its own shell, a covalent bond is formed between the atoms. The more electrons shared, the stronger the bond. The atoms of some elements always have a complete outer shell of electrons. These elements are said to be inert, meaning that they do not react with other elements to form compounds. Most covalent compounds are gases or liquids at room temperature. Oxygen, hydrogen, and nitrogen are examples of elements usually found in a covalent compound.

14. What can you infer from the information?

   (1) Covalent compounds are usually created in laboratories.

   (2) The most commonly found elements in nature are reactive.

   (3) Most covalent compounds are metals rather than liquids or gases.

   (4) Gases form covalent bonds only with other gases.

   (5) Hydrogen atoms always have complete outer electron shells.

QUESTIONS 15 AND 16 REFER TO THE FOLLOWING INFORMATION.

Sometimes when two or more atoms or molecules come in contact they react chemically with each other, resulting in the formation of one or more new substances (products). If the formation of the products requires <u>more</u> energy than is available from the original substances (the reactants), external energy, usually heat or light, must be absorbed for this purpose. This type of reaction is referred to as *endothermic*. On the other hand, if the formation of the products requires <u>less</u> than all of the energy available from the reactants, energy is released in an *exothermic* reaction. In order to start either type of reaction in the first place, however, the energy of the reactants must be raised by some external energy source. For example, you need to heat paper before it will react by burning, which is what releases heat in an exothermic reaction.

The following two charts represent an endothermic reaction and an exothermic reaction—in one or the other order.

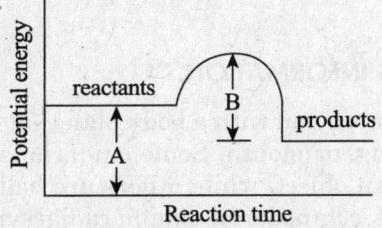 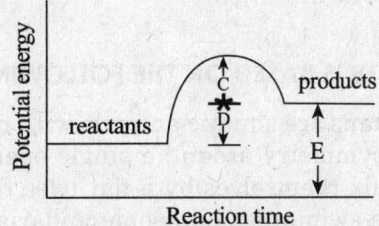

15. Which letter identifies the amount of energy absorbed in an endothermic reaction?

   (1) A

   (2) B

   (3) C

   (4) D

   (5) E

16. Wood burns when oxygen atoms in the air contact and react with carbon atoms in the wood. Why does fanning the flames of a bonfire cause more flames to appear?

   Fanning a fire

   (1) separates air's two primary elements: nitrogen from oxygen

   (2) helps more oxygen atoms contact and react with more carbon atoms

   (3) cools the wood, thereby allowing its carbon atoms to absorb more energy

   (4) extinguishes small flames, which are replaced by larger flames

   (5) increases air pressure, which in turn increases temperature

QUESTION 17 REFERS TO THE FOLLOWING INFORMATION.

Urodeles, a class of small, lizard-like creatures, have the ability to replace their limbs and organs. Specialized bone, skin, and blood cells at the site of a wound revert to cells as unspecialized as those in the embryonic limb through *dedifferentiation*. The resulting mass of unspecialized cells proliferates rapidly. Then when the new limb takes shape, the cells take on the specialized roles they had previously cast off.

17. Which is the best term for the process described above?

   (1) cloning

   (2) selective mating

   (3) random reproduction

   (4) cell regeneration

   (5) genetic mutation

QUESTION 18 IS BASED ON THE FOLLOWING INFORMATION.

Cnidarians are aquatic animals with no eyes and with a body plan that exhibits radial symmetry around a single opening, or mouth. Some cnidarians permanently fix themselves by a flat base to an object, while others are bell-shaped and free-swimming. Like some cnidarians, echinoderms exhibit radial symmetry, but almost always in a five-pointed star configuration. Also, unlike cnidarians, echinoderms have a spiny outer skin.

18. Which pictured animal is a cnidarian?

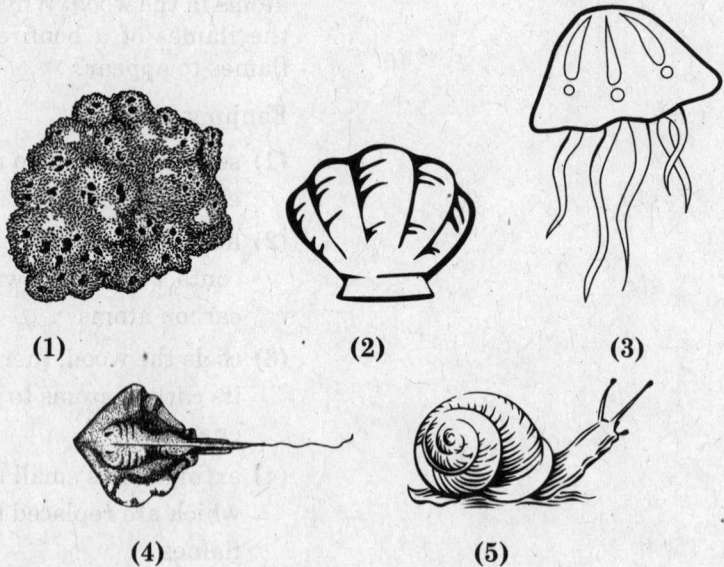

   (1)   (2)   (3)

   (4)   (5)

19. A transverse wave is one in which the oscillating (cyclical) motion of particles is perpendicular to the direction of the wave's motion. A longitudinal wave is one in which oscillation occurs along the same axis, or in the same direction, as the wave's motion.

Which of the following creates transverse waves?

(1) snapping the string of a bow to shoot an arrow

(2) bouncing on a coiled spring mattress

(3) riding a surfboard toward a shoreline

(4) wiggling your fingers while waving your hand

(5) vigorously shaking out a dusty blanket

QUESTION 20 REFERS TO THE FOLLOWING DIAGRAM.

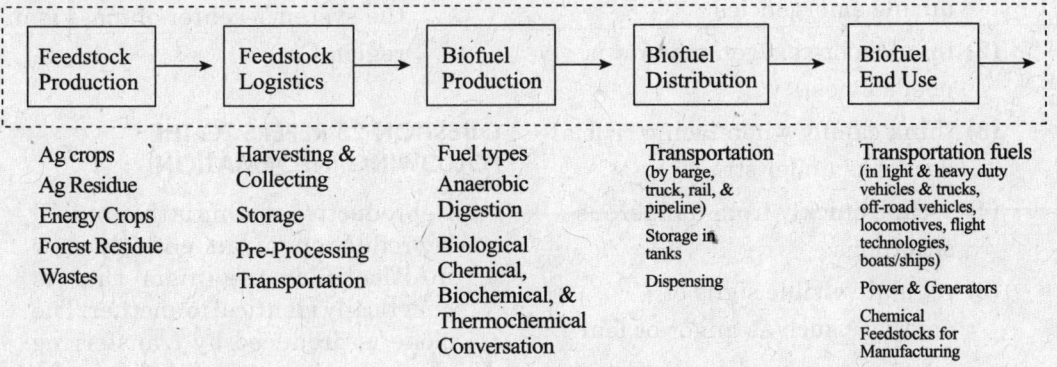

Feedstock Production	Feedstock Logistics	Biofuel Production	Biofuel Distribution	Biofuel End Use
Ag crops Ag Residue Energy Crops Forest Residue Wastes	Harvesting & Collecting Storage Pre-Processing Transportation	Fuel types Anaerobic Digestion Biological Chemical, Biochemical, & Thermochemical Conversation	Transportation (by barge, truck, rail, & pipeline) Storage in tanks Dispensing	Transportation fuels (in light & heavy duty vehicles & trucks, off-road vehicles, locomotives, flight technologies, boats/ships) Power & Generators Chemical Feedstocks for Manufacturing

20. Any change in pesticide application rates would affect which part of the biofuel supply chain?

(1) feedstock production

(2) feedstock logistics

(3) biofuel production

(4) biofuel distribution

(5) biofuel end use

QUESTION 21 REFERS TO THE FOLLOWING INFORMATION.

When a person faces sudden stress, he or she may experience an "adrenaline rush," during which the adrenal glands secrete hormones that work to increase blood-sugar levels and increase oxygen consumption and blood flow in skeletal muscles, while decreasing oxygen consumption and blood flow in smooth muscles.

21. Why do these internal bodily responses make sense?

They help a person to

(1) maintain steady blood pressure during emergencies

(2) inhale more oxygen when it is needed most

(3) think calmly when facing crucial decisions under stress

(4) escape quickly from dangerous situations

(5) regulate visible signs of emotions such as anger or fear

QUESTION 22 REFERS TO THE ILLUSTRATION BELOW.

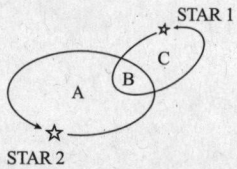

In a simple two-star system, in which the two stars are bound by mutual gravitation, each star orbits around a mutual center of mass. The star with the lower mass receives greater acceleration and hence has a larger orbit.

22. What does this information tell you about the illustration's features?

(1) Star 1 has the greater mass; the system's center of mass is in region B.

(2) Star 2 has the greater mass; the system's center of mass is in region B.

(3) Star 1 has the greater mass; the system's center of mass is in region A.

(4) Star 2 has the greater mass; the system's center of mass is in region A.

(5) Star 1 has the greater mass; the system's center of mass is in region C.

QUESTION 23 REFERS TO THE FOLLOWING INFORMATION.

Reproductive cloning is the asexual reproduction of an entirely new multicellular organism that is genetically identical to another. The clone is produced by transferring the genetic material from the nucleus of a diploid cell into an egg whose nucleus, and thus its genetic material, has been removed. The new organism is identical to another because it carries the DNA of only a single fertilized cell. In other words, it has just one parent. Cloning has been used for thousands of years in cultivating plants. Recently developed technologies have made the cloning of animals not just a possibility but a reality.

23. Recently developed cloning technologies might be applied toward achieving any of the following objectives EXCEPT which one?

(1) preventing the extinction of an endangered animal species

(2) increasing the supply of food in developing countries

(3) producing new foods that enhance variety in our diet

(4) producing desirable characteristics in offspring

(5) reducing the incidence of birth defects and other undesirable genetic traits

QUESTION 24 REFERS TO THE FOLLOWING ILLUSTRATION.

In the laboratory setup shown below, an upside-down beaker has been partially filled with the gaseous form of hydrogen (H_2), which is the lightest element.

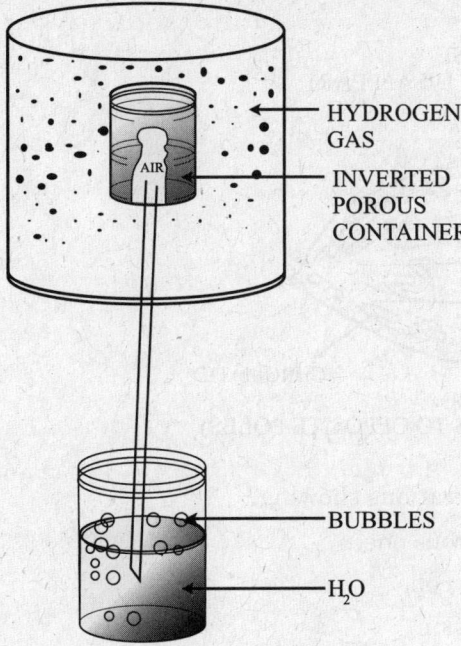

24. What is occurring in the illustration?

(1) Hydrogen bubbles are escaping through the water in the glass.

(2) Hydrogen is applying pressure on the air inside the porous cup.

(3) The water is boiling and releasing water vapor in the form of bubbles.

(4) Water is passing through the tube and mixing with the hydrogen.

(5) Air pressure in the porous cup is raising the water level in the glass.

QUESTION 25 REFERS TO THE FOLLOWING INFORMATION.

Like ocean waves, light waves travel in a succession of wave fronts. When light from above a calm lake travels straight down into the water, perpendicular to the water's surface, each wave front will continue straight toward the lake bottom. But if the light hits the water's surface at an angle, it will bend toward the bottom of the lake when it reaches the surface.

25. Which of the following best explains why light bends in this way?

(1) Water absorbs light, which is why a deep ocean bottom is very dark.

(2) Water magnetizes light, which is then drawn toward the North Pole.

(3) Water molecules are heavier than air molecules.

(4) Light travels slower through water than through air.

(5) Water divides a light wave into different color waves.

QUESTION 26 REFERS TO THE FOLLOWING ILLUSTRATIONS.

MITOSIS

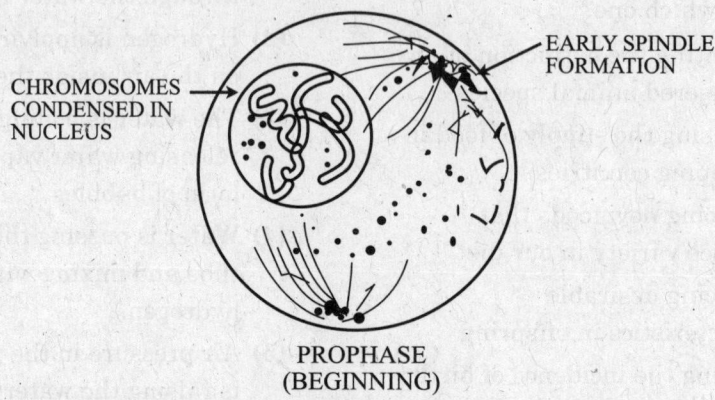

CHROMOSOMES
CONDENSED IN
NUCLEUS

EARLY SPINDLE
FORMATION

PROPHASE
(BEGINNING)

CHROMOSOMES

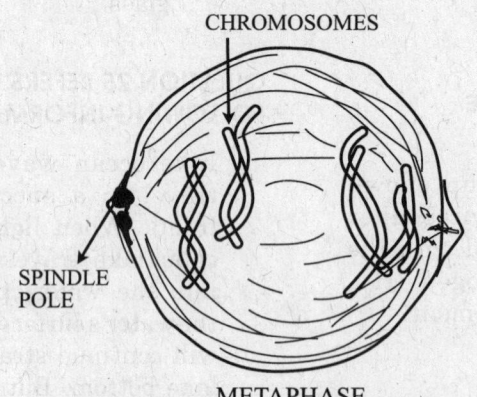

SPINDLE
POLE

METAPHASE
(WALLS OF NUCLEUS DISAPPEAR)

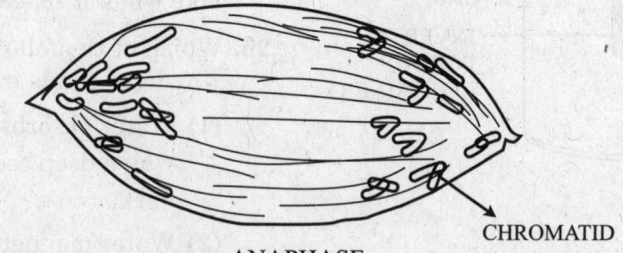

CHROMATID

ANAPHASE
(ALIGNMENT OF CHROMATIDS TO OPPOSITE POLES)

26. What process is the sequence of three illustrations showing?

(1) A healthy cell is mutating into a cancerous one.

(2) A cell is creating an identical matching cell.

(3) A nuclear reaction is creating an explosion.

(4) A virus created inside a cell is destroying the cell.

(5) A cell's damaged nucleus is repairing itself.

27. Advocates of a "no-regrets" attitude toward climate change and increased levels of air and water pollution recommend adapting to such developments rather than attempting to halt or reverse them.

Which of the following policies might an advocate of a strict "no-regrets" approach recommend?

(1) Move away from coal-burning to solar and other renewable fuel sources.

(2) Cultivate trees, which emit oxygen into the atmosphere.

(3) Cultivate organic crops, which are less likely to cause health problems.

(4) Look for inexpensive ways to desalinize salt water for drinking.

(5) Exploit the availability of water on the Moon.

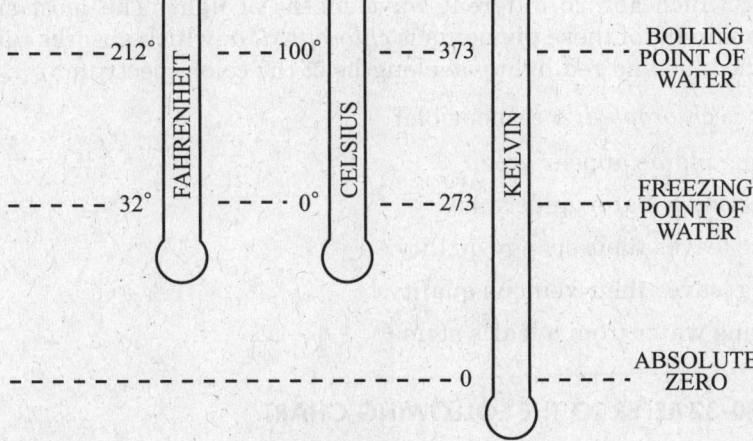

28. Three different systems for measuring temperature are shown above. The Kelvin scale was developed more recently than the other two, mainly for use in science laboratories. Why was the Kelvin scale probably adopted?

The Kelvin scale was probably adopted because the Celsius and Fahrenheit scales

(1) were not precise enough for science

(2) did not measure barometric pressure

(3) were inconvenient for gauging low temperatures

(4) were not commonly used anymore

(5) required that numbers be converted from one scale to the other

QUESTION 29 REFERS TO THE FOLLOWING DIAGRAM.

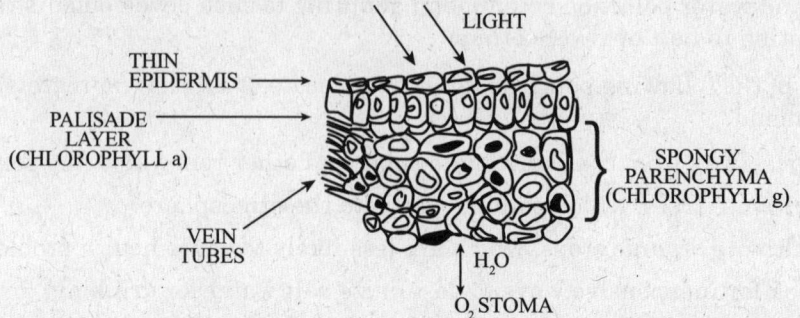

Through photosynthesis, a plant captures light energy from the Sun with various pigments, which absorb different wavelengths of light. The most significant and predominant of these pigments is *chlorophyll a*, which absorbs rather than reflects the blue and red light wavelengths of the color spectrum.

29. For what is *chlorophyll a* responsible?

    (1) making plants appear green

    (2) protecting a leaf's epidermis

    (3) giving leaves their spongy quality

    (4) giving leaves their veinous quality

    (5) drawing water from a leaf's stoma

QUESTIONS 30-32 REFER TO THE FOLLOWING CHART.

TEMPERATURES AND SNOW ACCUMULATION—NORTHERN GREENLAND

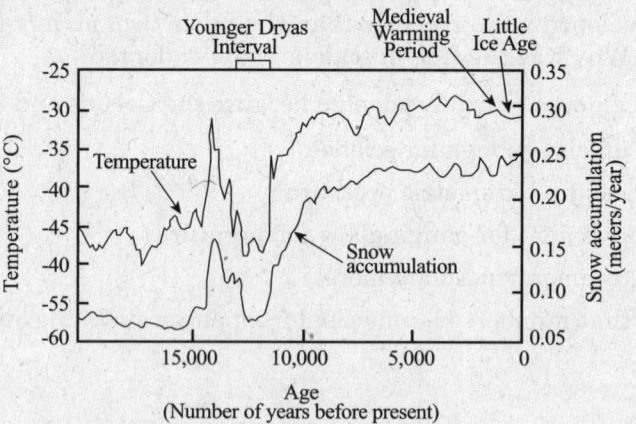

30. Which is an accurate description of Northern Greenland's climate from the Medieval Warming Period through the Little Ice Age?

    (1) Snow accumulation varied by about 0.2 meters.

    (2) Temperature remained relatively constant.

    (3) Snow accumulation remained relatively constant.

    (4) Temperature varied by about two degrees (C).

    (5) The amount of accumulated snow decreased.

31. The Younger Dryas Interval began about 12,800 years ago and ended about 11,000 years ago. What can you infer from the chart about Greenland during this time interval?

The Younger Dryas time interval was generally characterized by

   (1) gradually cooling temperatures
   (2) wet and hot weather
   (3) glacial accumulation
   (4) cold and dry weather
   (5) a rising sea level

32. Scientists gleaned the chart data from tree rings, ice cores, and rock sediments in Greenland. Based on the chart information, how do these sorts of geologic records help scientists?

These geologic records help scientists

   (1) prove the theory that human activities contribute to global warming
   (2) trace the migration of sea animals as global temperatures shift
   (3) identify long-term cyclical patterns in the Earth's climate
   (4) predict the amount of snowfall during the next century
   (5) show how temperature extremes affect the rate of tree growth

33. The visible light spectrum contains varying wavelengths, each appearing as a distinct color. White light contains the entire color spectrum. Objects around us exhibit their particular colors because they reflect the wavelengths of only those colors while absorbing all other wavelengths.

Why is a ripe banana yellow in color?

   (1) Sunlight is primarily yellow.
   (2) Banana skin contains yellow pigment.
   (3) Banana skin absorbs yellow light.
   (4) White light emits short wavelengths.
   (5) Banana skin absorbs blue light.

QUESTION 34 REFERS TO THE FOLLOWING INFORMATION.

Definitions of different types of mixtures:

Solution: Molecules of one or more substances are distributed uniformly among molecules of another substance.

Suspension: Small particles of a substance are dispersed throughout a gas or liquid; the particles settle to the bottom if left undisturbed.

Colloid: Very small particles of one substance are distributed evenly throughout another substance; particles are smaller than those of a suspension and do not settle.

34. Which of the following is an example of a suspension?

   (1) gasoline
   (2) paint
   (3) fog
   (4) muddy water
   (5) milk

practice test

QUESTIONS 35 AND 36 REFER TO THE FOLLOWING DIAGRAM.

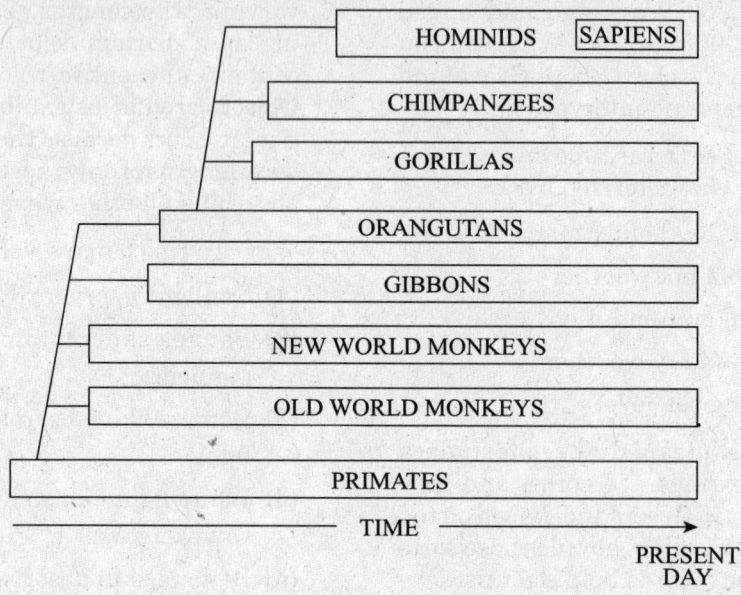

35. Which is the best title for the chart?

(1) "Early Anthropoids by Category"

(2) "The Missing Evolutionary Link"

(3) "The Evolution of Hominids"

(4) "What All Apes Have in Common"

(5) "Our Branch on the Primate Tree"

36. Based on the chart, which statement is accurate?

(1) Gorillas descended from orangutans.

(2) Gibbons descended from old world monkeys.

(3) Chimpanzees descended from gorillas.

(4) Early hominids descended from new world monkeys.

(5) Hominids descended from gorillas.

QUESTIONS 37 AND 38 REFER TO THE FOLLOWING INFORMATION.

In a plant, water tends to move toward areas with the lowest water and water-vapor concentration. When water reaches a leaf from the root system and xylem, it moves through the spongy mesophyll to the stomata, which are small openings in the leaf's surface that open and close to allow the exchange of gases.

37. What might reduce the amount of water reaching a leaf's surface?

    An increase in the

    (1) temperature of the water moving up through the xylem

    (2) humidity of the surrounding air

    (3) air movement (wind) around the leaf

    (4) intensity of sunlight on the plant

    (5) amount of water collecting around the root system

38. The process by which oxygen is exchanged for carbon dioxide through the stomata is referred to as transpiration. What does this process explain?

    (1) why a cactus doesn't need much water to survive

    (2) why plants close their stomata at night

    (3) why pine trees grow in high-altitude climates

    (4) why a rain forest has so many different plant species

    (5) why many plants go through a yearly growth cycle

QUESTION 39 REFERS TO THE FOLLOWING CHART.

Rates of Radioactive Decay in a Nucleus
(to 10 grams in weight)

	Carbon 14	Radium 229
10 grams	present time	present time
20 grams	5,780 years ago	4 minutes ago
40 grams	11,560 years ago	8 minutes ago
80 grams	23,120 years ago	12 minutes ago

39. Which conclusion CANNOT be drawn from the table?

    (1) The rate of radioactive decay in radium 229 is constant.

    (2) It takes 5,780 years for half of a carbon 14 nucleus to decay.

    (3) Radioactive decay occurs in both carbon 14 and radium 229.

    (4) It takes 6 minutes for half of a radium 229 nucleus to decay.

    (5) The rate of radioactive decay in carbon 14 is constant.

An electrical current sent through a coil of insulated wire creates a strong magnetic field within the coil. Wrapping the coil around an iron core enhances the magnetic field because iron is not only attracted to magnetic fields but is also easily magnetized. Certain other metals, such as nickel and cobalt, also have these two properties. Some such metals can be permanently magnetized. Others, including iron, lose their magnetism when the magnetic field is removed.

40. If the electric current described above can be started and stopped by a switch, what would happen if the switch is turned off?

The core will

(1) no longer be a magnet

(2) become nickel

(3) begin to corrode

(4) repel the coil

(5) recharge the coil

41. When you throw an object in either a northerly or southerly direction, when the object bounces off the Earth's surface it will change path very slightly, rather than continuing in straight path. The direction of this path change will always be east.

What is responsible for the path change described above?

(1) lines of longitude

(2) the Earth's rotation

(3) opposing magnetic forces

(4) the Earth's gravitational pull

(5) orbital velocity

In an ecological food chain, tertiary consumers eat secondary consumers, which in turn eat primary consumers, which in turn eat producers. In this chain, the producers are plants that generate their own food through photosynthesis: a process of using light energy and carbon to create glucose.

Although lichens are fungi and corals are animals, both use the energy that photosynthesizing algae produce for their sustenance and growth. Lichens rely solely on algae for their energy. As for corals, while some species can exist solely by capturing food, most receive energy by hosting millions of single-celled algae organisms known as *zooxanthellae*. The *zooxanthellae* are provided safety from predation as well as certain by-products of the coral's metabolism, such as ammonia, which *zooxanthellae* require to grow and reproduce. In return, the coral use a portion of the energy *zooxanthellae* produce through photosynthesis for its own sustenance, growth, and reproduction.

42. How can the organisms described above be categorized?

(1) Lichens are secondary consumers, corals are primary consumers, and *zooxanthellae* are producers.

(2) Lichens and *zooxanthellae* are primary consumers, and corals are producers.

(3) Algae are secondary consumers, and *zooxanthellae* and fungi are primary consumers.

(4) Lichens are primary consumers, corals are primary and secondary consumers, and algae are producers.

(5) *Zooxanthellae* are primary consumers, coral are secondary consumers, and lichens are tertiary consumers.

QUESTION 43 REFERS TO THE FOLLOWING DIAGRAM.

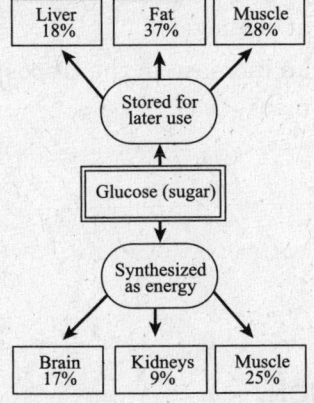

43. Which conclusion does the diagram best support?

(1) Eating the right foods can improve your intelligence.

(2) Athletes typically must eat a lot to be competitive.

(3) Eating foods high in sugar can damage the liver.

(4) People should not exercise immediately after eating.

(5) It is common to feel sleepy after eating a large meal.

QUESTIONS 44 AND 45 REFER TO THE FOLLOWING INFORMATION.

Humans can hear sound-wave frequencies ranging from about 20 Hz (20,000 kHz) to about 20,000 Hz. We experience a wave's frequency as "pitch."

Animal	Range of Hearing (Hertz = 1 cycle/sec.)
dog	30 Hz – 30,000 Hz
cat	15 Hz – 40,000 Hz
bat	2000 Hz – 100,000 Hz
porpoise	30 Hz – 150,000 Hz
elephant	3 Hz – 10,000 Hz
human	20 Hz – 20,000 Hz

44. Many species of animals rely heavily on their sense of hearing for survival and communication. What might this fact, along with the data in the table, help explain?

(1) why dogs respond to a high-pitched whistle

(2) why elephants have large ears

(3) how blind bats can navigate dark caves

(4) why porpoises are so easily trained

(5) why cats don't respond to human commands

45. To monitor activities beneath the ocean surface, sonar devices used on navy ships emit sound waves with frequencies ranging from about 1000 kHz to 100,000 kHz that are intense enough to interfere with the ability of porpoises to communicate and navigate. What refinement in the frequency range on these devices might remedy this problem?

(1) Reduce the upper range limit to 20,000 kHz.

(2) Raise the lower range limit to 50,000 kHz.

(3) Limit the range size to 10,000 kHz.

(4) Extend the range size to 200,000 kHz.

(5) None of the refinements listed above would help.

46. The column of air between you and the outer edge of the atmosphere has weight and applies pressure against you. As air cools, it becomes denser, it sinks, and it will not condense (will not become liquid). What can you expect when atmospheric pressure is low?

(1) an increase in the atmosphere's oxygen content

(2) a greater chance of rain

(3) expansion of the exosphere

(4) reduced oxygen concentrations at sea level

(5) an increase in the troposphere's mass

QUESTION 47 REFERS TO THE FOLLOWING ILLUSTRATION.

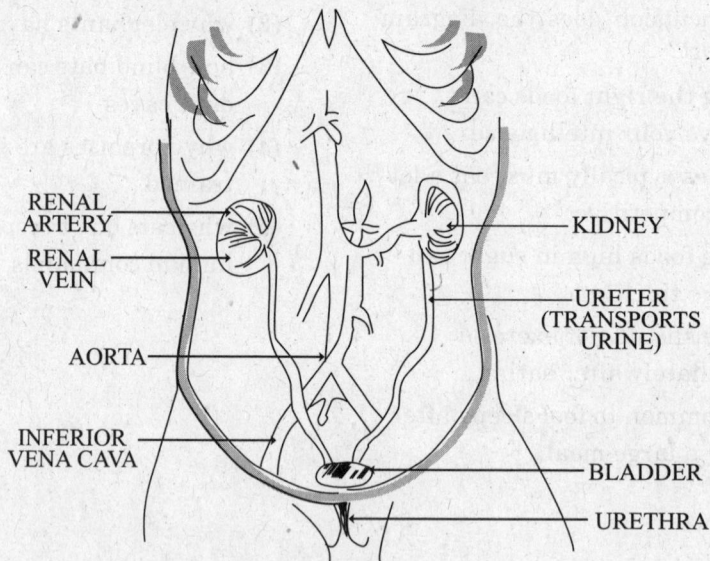

47. Which is a function of the renal system?

(1) to prevent dehydration (thirst)

(2) to supply energy that pumps the heart

(3) to regulate sexual reproduction

(4) to remove waste from bodily fluids

(5) to filter fat cells out of the blood

Positively charged particles and negatively charged particles attract each other. An oxygen atom is highly electromagnetic, which means that it attracts electrons from atoms with which it has bonded—for example, hydrogen atoms—toward its nucleus. The result is a polar bond in which the oxygen atom takes a slightly negative charge, while the other atoms take a slightly positive charge, reinforcing the bond.

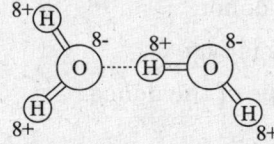

48. Water (H_2O) consists of two hydrogen atoms bonded with one oxygen atom. Which of the following explains the process described and illustrated above?

    (1) why we breathe air instead of water

    (2) why ice cracks but water doesn't

    (3) why some water feels "softer" than other water

    (4) why water freezes at a temperature of 32°F

    (5) why snowflakes have their unique patterns

A certain strain of bacteria called *lyngbya majuscula,* an ancient ancestor of modern-day algae, is making a comeback in ocean waters just off the world's most industrialized coastal regions. This primitive strain of bacteria has survived for nearly 3 billion years due to a variety of survival mechanisms. It can produce its own fertilizer by pulling nitrogen out of the air; it relies on a different spectrum of light than algae do, allowing it to thrive even in deep, murky waters; and when it dies and decays, it releases its own nitrogen and phosphorous, on which the next generation of *lyngbya* feeds.

49. What is one way that *lyngbya majuscula* has survived for billions of years?

    (1) It is threatened by few, if any, natural predators.

    (2) As a species, it is self-sustaining.

    (3) It does not depend on light for its existence.

    (4) It emits harmful toxins that ward off predators.

    (5) It adapts easily to changes in water temperature.

QUESTION 50 REFERS TO THE FOLLOWING DIAGRAM.

Safe Blood Transfusions (Donor→Donee) by Blood Type (A, B, AB, O)

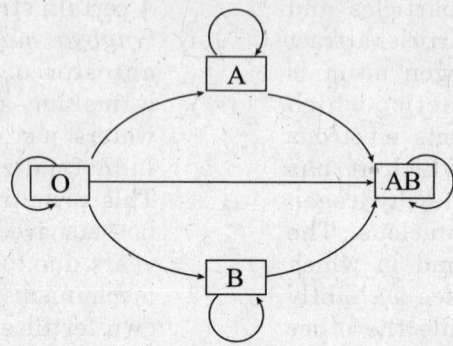

50. Which conclusion can best be drawn from the diagram?

(1) A blood donee should be a blood relative of the donor.

(2) The blood type in greatest demand at hospitals is type O.

(3) The blood type of the donor must match the type of the donee.

(4) Blood type AB is the rarest of the four types.

(5) It is unsafe to use blood-type AB for transfusions.

LANGUAGE ARTS, READING

65 Minutes • 40 Questions

Directions: The Language Arts, Reading Test consists of several passages of fiction and nonfiction reading material. Each passage is followed by several multiple-choice questions. After you read a passage, answer the questions that follow it, referring back to the passage as needed. Answer all questions based on what is stated and implied in the passage.

Immediately preceding each passage is a brief "purpose question" in bold type. These questions will help you focus your attention and to understand the purpose of each passage. You are not required to answer purpose questions.

Record your answers on the Language Arts, Reading section of the answer sheet provided.

QUESTIONS 1 TO 6 REFER TO THE FOLLOWING PASSAGE.

WHAT DO THE THINGS PEOPLE OWN SAY ABOUT THEM?

The light fell on the inner surface of the tub in a pattern of delicate wrinkled lines which slipped with a green sparkle over the curving
5 porcelain as the clear water trembled. Babbitt lazily watched it; noted that along the silhouette of his legs against the radiance on the bottom of the tub, the shadows
10 of the air-bubbles clinging to the hairs were reproduced as strange jungle mosses. He patted the water, and the reflected light capsized and leaped and volleyed. He was
15 content and childish. He played. He shaved a swatch down the calf of one plump leg.

The drain-pipe was dripping, a dulcet and lively song: drippety drip
20 drip dribble, drippety drip drip drip. He was enchanted by it. He looked at the solid tub, the beautiful nickel taps, the tiled walls of the room, and felt virtuous in the possession
25 of this splendor.

He roused himself and spoke gruffly to his bath-things. "Come here! You've done enough fooling!" he reproved the treacherous soap,
30 and defied the scratchy nail-brush with "Oh, you would, would you!" He stopped himself, and rinsed himself, and austerely rubbed himself; he noted a hole in the Turkish towel,
35 and meditatively thrust a finger through it, and marched back to the bedroom, a grave and unbending citizen.

There was a moment of gorgeous
40 abandon, a flash of melodrama such as he found in traffic-driving, when he laid out a clean collar, discovered that it was frayed in front, and tore it up with a magnificent yeeeeeing
45 sound.

Most important of all was the preparation of his bed and the sleeping-porch.

It is not known whether he
50 enjoyed his sleeping-porch because of the fresh air or because it was the standard thing to have a sleeping-porch.

Just as he was an Elk, a Booster,
55 and a member of the Chamber of Commerce, just as the priests of the Presbyterian Church determined his every religious belief and the senators who controlled the Repub-
60 lican Party decided in little smoky rooms in Washington what he should think about disarmament, tariff, and Germany, so did the large national advertisers fix the surface
65 of his life, fix what he believed to be his individuality. These standard advertised wares—toothpastes, socks, tires, cameras, instantaneous hot-water heaters—were his
70 symbols and proofs of excellence; at first the signs, then the substitutes, for joy and passion and wisdom.

—from *Babbitt*, by Sinclair Lewis

1. Which is most likely correct about Babbitt's daily routine?

   (1) He eats shortly after bathing.

   (2) He shaves every morning.

   (3) He wears a suit and tie to work.

   (4) He bathes shortly before sleeping.

   (5) He washes his hair in the bathtub.

2. As revealed in the passage, what is Babbitt's primary character trait?

   (1) Cowardice

   (2) Hypocrisy

   (3) Mindlessness

   (4) Idealism

   (5) Virtue

3. Based on the passage, which statement about Babbitt is most likely accurate?

   (1) He is a heedless driver.

   (2) He has difficulty sleeping.

   (3) He rarely attends church.

   (4) He is full of joy.

   (5) He has no interest in politics.

4. Based on how the first word in each pair is used in the passage, which word-pair association is incorrect?

   (1) dulcet—sweet (line 19)

   (2) reproved—corrected (line 29)

   (3) austerely—harshly (line 33)

   (4) meditatively—thoughtfully (line 35)

   (5) grave—dignified (line 37)

5. In referring to Babbitt's sleeping-porch as "the standard thing to have" (line 52) and to his other things as "standard advertised wares" (lines 66–67), what does the narrator mean?

   (1) Having these things shows poor taste.

   (2) These things meet the highest standard of quality.

   (3) These things were issued by the military.

   (4) Nearly everyone has these kinds of things.

   (5) These things are considered symbols of a good life.

6. Which activity would a person like Babbitt probably enjoy the most?

   (1) Watching a romantic movie

   (2) Engaging in a debate at a town-hall meeting

   (3) Swimming naked in a lake

   (4) Playing golf at a country club

   (5) Shopping at a flea market or thrift store

practice test

QUESTIONS 7 TO 11 REFER TO THE FOLLOWING DOCUMENT.

WHY IS IT IMPORTANT TO BE ON TIME FOR WORK?

FROM: J. R. Smith, Personnel Manager, SnapRite Service Company

TO: SnapRite Company employees

SUBJECT: Time-card policies and procedures

In light of recent time-card punching practices of some SnapRite Company employees, management has instituted a new time-card punching procedure for all employees. This new procedure will take effect on March 1 for all non-salaried employees. The new procedure is as follows:

1. Each employee should arrive at the SnapRite premises no sooner than 15 minutes before and no later than 5 minutes before shift begins. Upon arrival, each employee should avoid loitering. Each employee should report to the floor manager's office as soon as possible after arriving at the SnapRite premises.

2. Each employee must punch his or her time card no more than 5 minutes before shift begins and no later than 2 minutes after shift begins.

3. Each employee must punch his or her time card no more than 2 minutes before or 5 minutes after shift ends.

4. If an employee is discovered punching another employee's time card, both employees may be subject to suspension.

5. If an employee punches in before the permitted punch-in time or punches out after the permitted punch-out time more than twice in a 30-day period or more than four times in a 90-day period, the employee may be subject to suspension.

6. An employee's failure to punch a time card for a shift may result in a punitive reduction of wages for that shift.

7. Any time-card related behavior that management considers fraudulent or malicious may be grounds for termination of employment.

---

7. What is management's purpose in issuing the memo?

    (1) to identify which employees have been reporting their hours improperly

    (2) to curb fraudulent behavior on the part of SnapRite employees

    (3) to guide SnapRite employees toward appropriate reporting of their work hours

    (4) to warn SnapRite employees about the consequences of deceiving management

    (5) to eliminate bias against SnapRite employees who are not paid by the hour

8. Which of the following best describes the tone of the memo?

    (1) matter-of-fact

    (2) emotionally charged

    (3) stern and intimidating

    (4) accusatory and suspicious

    (5) condescending

9. Based on the information in the memo, which of the following statements is most likely true?

    (1) In the past, SnapRite has used an honor system for its workers to report their work hours.

    (2) Some SnapRite employees have exercised poor judgment regarding time-card procedures.

    (3) SnapRite employees consider the company's policies to be overly strict and burdensome.

    (4) SnapRite employees are notorious for breaking company rules and regulations.

    (5) SnapRite employees will be able to punch their time-cards whatever time they report for work.

10. To which of the following employees is the memo LEAST likely to apply?

    (1) assembly-line workers

    (2) janitorial staff

    (3) maintenance staff

    (4) receptionists

    (5) sales representatives

11. Under the new policy, what would happen to a long-time employee who punches in 2 minutes late every day and punches out 3 minutes early every day?

    The employee would

    (1) not be subject to suspension.

    (2) be subject to suspension for working at least 3 minutes less than required.

    (3) be subject to suspension for reporting late to work.

    (4) be subject to suspension for punching out more than 2 minutes early.

    (5) automatically be suspended because the behavior is habitual.

QUESTIONS 12 TO 17 REFER TO THE FOLLOWING PASSAGE.

DOES HIGGINS REALIZE THAT ELIZA IS IN THE ROOM?

(ELIZA returns with a pair of down-at-heel slippers. She places them on the carpet before HIGGINS, and sits as before without a word.)

5   HIGGINS *(yawning again)*: Oh Lord! What an evening! What a crew! What a silly tomfoolery! *(He raises his shoe to unlace it, and catches sight of his slippers. He*

10   *stops unlacing and looks at them as if they had appeared there of their own accord).* Oh! they're there, aren't they? . . .

PICKERING: Were you nervous at

15   the garden party? *I* was. Eliza didn't seem a bit nervous. . . .

HIGGINS: Yes, for the first three minutes. But when I saw we were going to win hands down, I felt like a

20   bear in a cage, hanging about doing nothing. The dinner was worse: sitting gorging there for over an hour, with nobody but a damned fool of a fashionable woman to talk

25   to! I tell you, Pickering, never again for me. No more artificial duchesses. The whole thing has been simply purgatory.

PICKERING: You've never been

30   broken in properly to the social routine. *(Strolling over to the piano)* I rather enjoy dipping into it occasionally myself: it makes me feel young again. Anyhow, it was a

35   great success: an immense success. I was quite frightened once or twice because Eliza was doing it so well. You see, lots of the real people can't do it at all: they're such fools that

40   they think style comes by nature to people in their position; and so they never learn. There's always something professional about doing something superlatively well.

45   HIGGINS: Yes, that's what drives me mad: the silly people don't know their own silly business. *(Rising)* However, it's over and done with; and now I can go to bed at last

50   without dreading tomorrow . . . . What the devil have I done with my slippers?

LIZA *(snatching up the slippers and hurling them at him one after the*

55   *other with all her force)*: There are your slippers. And there. Take your slippers, and may you never have a day's luck with them!

HIGGINS *(astounded)*: What on

60   earth—! *(He comes to her)* What's the matter? Get up. *(He pulls her up).* Anything wrong?

LIZA *(breathless)* Nothing wrong—with you. I've won your bet for you,

65   haven't I? That's enough for you. *I* don't matter, I suppose.

—from *Pygmalion*,
by George Bernard Shaw

12. Which best describes the garden party, from Higgins's point of view?

(1) A waste of time

(2) A nerve-wracking experience

(3) A welcome distraction

(4) A tedious ordeal

(5) A joyous event

13. What does the playwright's use of a pair of slippers serve to emphasize?

(1) Eliza's yearning for a better life

(2) Higgins's exquisite style and taste

(3) Eliza's refusal to take orders from Higgins

(4) Higgins's status as an upper-class man of leisure

(5) Eliza's resentment toward Higgins

14. What was Eliza probably doing just before the scene presented in the passage?

    (1) Behaving in a manner expected of her

    (2) Eavesdropping on a conversation between Higgins and Pickering

    (3) Having a conversation with Pickering

    (4) Waiting for Higgins to return from the party

    (5) Changing out of the clothes she wore to the party

15. Which words from the dialogue best reveal how Pickering and Higgins both feel about socialites of their day?

    (1) "What an evening! What a crew! What a silly tomfoolery!" (lines 6–7)

    (2) "...nobody but a damned fool of a fashionable woman to talk to!" (lines 23–25)

    (3) "No more artificial duchesses." (line 26)

    (4) "You've never been broken in properly to the social routine." (lines 29–31)

    (5) "... lots of the real people can't do it at all ..." (lines 38–39)

16. Which would be the most accurate characterization of Eliza, from Pickering's point of view?

    (1) professional

    (2) artificial

    (3) a fool

    (4) caged like a bear

    (5) fashionable

17. The author ends *Pygmalion* in prose narrative, where he first warns that the story does not end how readers of romance literature would prefer. Which of the following endings is MOST likely?

    (1) Eliza grows to love Higgins and eventually marries him, and the marriage turns out happy.

    (2) Eliza considers marrying Higgins for his money, but decides against it because they are incompatible.

    (3) Eliza and Higgins continue the same sort of relationship that is revealed in the passage.

    (4) Eliza becomes romantically involved with a man she met at the garden party.

    (5) Higgins wants Eliza to marry him, but she declines because she loves another man.

QUESTIONS 18-23 REFER TO THE FOLLOWING POEM.

WHERE IS A GOOD PLACE TO SPEND THE NOON HOUR?

"Silent Noon"

Your hands lie open in the long fresh grass,—
The finger-points look through like rosy blooms:
Your eyes smile peace. The pasture gleams and glooms
'Neath billowing skies that scatter and amass.
5 All round our nest, far as the eye can pass,
Are golden kingcup-fields with silver edge
Where the cow-parsley skirts the hawthorne-hedge.
'Tis visible silence, still as the hour-glass.

Deep in the sun-searched growths the dragon-fly
10 Hangs like a blue thread loosened from the sky:—
So this winged hour is dropped to us from above.
Oh! clasp we to our hearts, for deathless dower,
This close-companioned inarticulate hour
When twofold silence was the song of love.

—*Dante Gabriel Rossetti*

18. Which comparison does the speaker draw in the poem?

The poem's speaker compares

(1) Romantic love to a billowing sky

(2) The sand in an hourglass to the passing of time

(3) A time of the day to a stage in one's life

(4) A dragonfly's fluttering wings to a beating heart

(5) Blossoming flowers to a human hand

19. Who is the speaker most likely addressing in the poem?

(1) A person whom the speaker loves

(2) The poem's reader

(3) Anyone who appreciates natural beauty

(4) The speaker himself or herself

(5) A personified Nature

20. Read as a whole, the poem expresses the speaker's appreciation for which of the following?

(1) A place of retreat from noisy city life

(2) A relatively quiet time of the day

(3) Certain sights and sounds of a pasture

(4) The relaxing warmth of the midday sun

(5) The flora and fauna of the countryside

21. One meaning of *dower* is "a gift brought by a bride to her husband." With this meaning in mind, what might the poet mean in the use of the words "deathless dower" (line 12)?

The poet's use of these words might mean that the speaker

(1) is about to be married.

(2) will die long before the pasture disappears.

(3) considers the noon hour a gift.

(4) has experienced an unexpected surprise.

(5) hopes to live a long life.

22. What does the speaker imply about the hawthorne-hedge (line 7)?

(1) It gleams in the sunlight.

(2) It borders the pasture.

(3) It makes a good nest.

(4) It blossoms like a rose.

(5) It is home to a dragon-fly.

23. Which of the following groups of words from the poem provides an example of the same poetic device as the one illustrated in line 8 ("'Tis visible silence, still as the hour-glass.")?

(1) "the cow-parsley skirts" (line 7)

(2) "the sun-searched growths" (line 9)

(3) "like a blue thread loosened" (line 10)

(4) "This . . . inarticulate hour" (line 13)

(5) "When twofold silence" (line 14)

QUESTIONS 24 TO 29 REFER TO THE FOLLOWING PASSAGE.

WHAT IS EDEL THINKING ABOUT?

She is lying at the top of the stairs, her back arched by the steps, her hands clawed. Her hair is fanned about her. It is too long; she would

5 never have let it grow this much, though Norah—or is it the nurse?—keeps it clean. The shampoo they use smells of nettles; she gets whiffs of it now as if she were lying in a

10 field. She cannot remember the last time she had color in her hair, though once she would have been particular about such things. Was it weeks ago, or months? Time has

15 bloated and clogged. These days, oddly, it is only when she has fallen that she comes to her senses. It brings her to know mostly the unpalatable. Just now, for example,

20 a flight below—down to the return, then down again—sitting at the kitchen table is her daughter, watching a small portable TV while she lies here, stricken.

25 A microwave with pictures is how Norah has described it. It is one of the new things that has been added to the house.

"So you can have the big TV

30 upstairs," Norah had said, "all to yourself."

The ground floor of her own house is a mystery to her now, like upstairs might be to a child

35 frightened of the dark. It is so long since she's been in the kitchen that she has to work to imagine it. In her mind's eye she sees it flooded with a gauzy early morning light coming in

40 through the French window Victor had installed forty years ago when the walls smelled of lime and the house had a bald, ripening air, as did their lives.

45 Norah is at the table, a pale full moon of melamine on a tubular pod—unless it has been changed too—eating a meal she had prepared for both of them. She can hear

50 the lonely scrape of cutlery. Norah had brought dinner upstairs to her on a tray earlier and had fed her, spoon by spoon, though she hadn't much interest. Appetite evades her

55 these days. In the end Norah had whipped the dish away fiercely. Or was that the nurse?

She may be confused about some things, but just now, Edel

60 Elworthy—for that is her name, she is sure of that—knows that as she lies here, her daughter has turned up the volume on the TV. She can hear the unctuous urgency of a hair

65 advertisement—gloss and sheen and self-worth all rolled into one voice of honey—and she knows that Norah is deliberately ignoring her.

—from "The Scream," by Mary Morrissy

24. What happened just before the events described in the passage?

    (1) Edel lost consciousness.

    (2) The nurse gave Edel a bath.

    (3) Edel fell near the stairs.

    (4) Norah arrived home with groceries.

    (5) Edel asked Norah for dinner.

25. As used in the passage, what does the word *unpalatable* (line 19) mean?

    (1) Unpleasant

    (2) Rude

    (3) Untrue

    (4) Unbelievable

    (5) Hidden

26. What does the passage suggest about Norah?

    (1) She won't let Edel come downstairs.

    (2) She is paid to care for Edel.

    (3) She has difficulty hearing.

    (4) She eats the same foods as Edel.

    (5) She refuses to color Edel's hair.

27. What does the narration reveal about Edel's state of mind?

    (1) She is confused about where she is.

    (2) She is alert as to what is going on around her.

    (3) She is imagining things that are not real.

    (4) She is angry that she cannot care for herself.

    (5) She is distrustful of the people around her.

28. Considering the context in which it is used, which figure of speech from the passage best conveys a sense of longing on Edel's part?

    (1) "time has bloated and clogged" (lines 14–15)

    (2) "the house had a bald, ripening air" (lines 42–43)

    (3) "a pale full moon of melamine" (lines 45–46)

    (4) "the lonely scrape of cutlery" (line 50)

    (5) "rolled into one voice of honey" (lines 66–67)

29. Which phrase best characterizes the scenario described in the passage?

    (1) A day in a life

    (2) A tense situation

    (3) A life-altering event

    (4) A comedy of errors

    (5) A moment in time

QUESTIONS 30 TO 34 REFER TO THE FOLLOWING PASSAGE FROM A LETTER.

WHY IS THE AUTHOR WRITING A NEW BOOK?

I had two little curly-headed twin daughters to begin with, and my stock in this line was gradually increased, till I have been the
5 mother of seven children, the most beautiful and the most loved of whom lies buried near my Cincinnati residence. It was at his dying bed and at his grave that I
10 learned what a poor slave mother may feel when her child is torn away from her. In those depths of sorrow which seemed to me immeasurable, it was my only prayer to God that
15 such anguish might not be suffered in vain. There were circumstances about his death of such peculiar bitterness, of what seemed almost cruel suffering, that I felt that I

20 could never be consoled for it unless
this crushing of my own heart might
enable me to work out some great
good to others.

I allude to this here because I
25 have often felt that much that is
in that book ("Uncle Tom's Cabin")
had its root in the awful scenes and
bitter sorrows of that summer. It
has left now, I trust, no trace on
30 my mind except a deep compassion
for the sorrowful, especially for
mothers who are separated from
their children.

I am now writing a work which
35 will contain, perhaps, an equal
amount of matter with "Uncle Tom's
Cabin." It will contain all the facts
and documents upon which that
story was founded, and an immense
40 body of facts, reports of trial, legal
documents, and testimony of people
now living South, which will more
than confirm every statement in
"Uncle Tom's Cabin."

45 I must confess that till I began
the examination of facts in order to
write this book, much as I thought
I knew before, I had not begun to
measure the depth of the abyss. The
50 law records of courts and judicial
proceedings are so incredible as to
fill me with amazement whenever
I think of them. It seems to me that
the book cannot but be felt, and,
55 coming upon the sensibility awaked
by the other, do something.

I suffer exquisitely in writing
these things. It may be truly said
that I suffer with my heart's blood.
60 Many times in writing "Uncle
Tom's Cabin" I thought my heart
would fail utterly, but I prayed
earnestly that God would help me
till I got through, and still I am
65 pressed beyond measure and above
strength.

—Harriet Beacher Stowe

30. To what does the author trace her
compassion for slave mothers?

(1) Her writing of "Uncle Tom's
Cabin"

(2) Her hatred of injustice

(3) The loss of her own son

(4) Her meeting a young woman in
Cincinnati

(5) Her reading of legal documents
and testimony

31. What does the author disclose about
the new book she is writing?

The new book will be

(1) at least as long as "Uncle Tom's
Cabin."

(2) based on the lives of her
parents.

(3) more successful than "Uncle
Tom's Cabin."

(4) a call to abolish slavery.

(5) fictional, like "Uncle Tom's
Cabin."

32. To what does the author refer by
her words "the depth of the abyss"
(line 49)?

(1) The endless array of
documentation

(2) The cruelty of the judicial
process

(3) The suffering of young mothers

(4) The horrors of slavery

(5) The immeasurable intensity of
grief

33. What effect does the author believe her new book will have on its readers?

(1) It will prompt readers to read her last book.

(2) It will arouse empathy in its readers.

(3) It will cause readers intense suffering.

(4) It will console readers of "Uncle Tom's Cabin."

(5) It will infuriate readers of "Uncle Tom's Cabin."

34. What does the passage reveal about its author?

(1) She did not understand the demands of writing.

(2) She conducted little research for her writing.

(3) She had difficulty earning a living as a writer.

(4) She wrote with little effort.

(5) She was deeply and emotionally involved in her work.

QUESTIONS 35-40 REFER TO THE FOLLOWING PASSAGE.

DO THE MEN IN THE BOAT KNOW WHERE THEY ARE?

Slowly the land arose from the sea. From a black line it became a line of black and a line of white, trees and sand. Finally, the captain said
5 that he could make out a house on the shore.

"That's the house of refuge, sure," said the cook. "They'll see us before long, and come out after us."
10   The distant lighthouse reared high. "The keeper ought to be able to make us out now, if he's looking through a spyglass," said the captain. "He'll notify the life-
15 saving people."

"None of those other boats could have got ashore to give word of the wreck," said the oiler, in a low voice. "Else the life-boat would be
20 out hunting us."

Finally, a new sound struck the ears of the men in the boat. It was the low thunder of the surf on the shore. All but the oarsman watched
25 the shore grow. Under the influence of this expansion, doubt and direful apprehension was leaving the minds of the men. The management of the boat was still most absorbing,
30 but it could not prevent a quiet cheerfulness. In an hour, perhaps, they would be ashore.

But then: "Cook," remarked the captain, "there don't seem to be
35 any signs of life about your house of refuge."

"No," replied the cook. "Funny they don't see us!"

The surf's roar was dulled, but its
40 tone was, nevertheless, thunderous and mighty. As the boat swam over the great rollers, the men sat listening to this roar. "We'll swamp sure," said everybody.
45   It is fair to say here that there was not a life-saving station within twenty miles in either direction, but the men did not know this fact, and in consequence they made dark and
50 opprobrious remarks concerning the eyesight of the nation's life-savers. Four scowling men sat in the dinghy and surpassed records in the invention of epithets.
55   "Funny they don't see us."

The lightheartedness of a former time had completely faded. To their sharpened minds it was easy to conjure pictures of all kinds of
60 incompetency and blindness and, indeed, cowardice. There was the shore of the populous land, and it was bitter and bitter to them that from it came no sign.

65   "Well," said the captain, ultimately. "I suppose we'll have to make a try for ourselves. If we stay out here too long, we'll none of us have strength left to swim after the
70   boat swamps."

—from "The Open Boat,"
by Stephen Crane

35. What poses the greatest danger to the men in the dinghy?

(1) depletion of food rations

(2) their inability to steer toward shore

(3) their sheer exhaustion

(4) the size of the waves

(5) freezing water temperatures

36. In stating that the men "made dark and opprobrious remarks" (lines 49–50) regarding life savers, what does the narrator probably mean?

The men's remarks were

(1) unfair considering the facts.

(2) impossible to hear from the shore.

(3) meant to be scornful and abusive.

(4) intended as good-natured fun.

(5) a waste of time considering their situation.

37. At the end of the passage, what is the situation in the boat?

(1) The men are contemplating swimming to shore.

(2) The captain is convinced that the boat can be saved.

(3) The men are convinced that they will all perish.

(4) The men are confident that they will soon be rescued.

(5) The men plan to stay in the boat until they are sighted.

38. The men in the boat experience a variety of emotions, including all EXCEPT which of the following?

(1) hopefulness

(2) sadness

(3) anxiousness

(4) lightheartedness

(5) disappointment

39. Which basic conflict best expresses the story's theme, as revealed in the passage?

The basic conflict is between

(1) nature's beauty and its terror

(2) fate and free will

(3) nature's power and human will

(4) individual survival and the common good

(5) the forces of evil and those of good

40. In Stephen Crane's seven-part short story "The Open Boat," the point of view shifts from part to part. Which is correct about this excerpt from the story?

It is presented from the point of view of

(1) an observer first, then the boat's captain.

(2) one of the men in the boat.

(3) the lighthouse keeper on the shore.

(4) the cook and the captain.

(5) an observer who is not part of the story.

practice test

MATHEMATICS

90 Minutes • 50 Questions

General Directions: The Mathematics Test consists of 50 questions intended to measure your general mathematics skills, including your ability to solve math problems. The test consists of two parts:

- Part I: 25 questions
- Part II: 25 questions

Part I and Part II are <u>not</u> separately timed. If you finish Part I early, you may begin working on Part II right away.

The use of a calculator is allowed for Part I but <u>not</u> for Part II.

To answer some questions you will need to apply one or more mathematics formulas. The formulas provided on the next page will help you to answer those questions. Some questions refer to charts, graphs, and figures. Unless otherwise noted, charts, graphs, and figures are drawn to scale.

Answering Alternative-format Questions

To answer some questions you will be required to write a number instead of selecting among five choices. You will record your answers to these questions using the following alternative-format grid:

To record an answer in this grid, write your answer in the top row. Enter only one character—a number digit, decimal point, or fraction bar—in a box. You may start in any column that will allow you to enter your entire answer. Fill in the corresponding bubble below each character you have written. (GED® answer sheets are machine-read, so only filled-in bubbles will be read.) Leave blank all columns you did not use to record your answer. No answer to an alternative-format question can be a negative number.

Do <u>not</u> enter a mixed number in the grid. Instead, enter a fraction or a decimal number. To represent the mixed number $2\frac{1}{2}$, for example, enter either the fraction **5/2** or the decimal number **2.5.** Grid only one answer, even if there is more than one correct answer.

Formulas

AREA	**Triangle:** $\frac{1}{2} \times$ base $\times$ height **Rectangle:** length $\times$ width **Parallelogram:** base $\times$ height **Circle:** $\pi \times$ radius^2 **Right cylinder:** area of circular base $\times$ height **Trapezoid:** $\frac{1}{2}$ (base$_1$ + base$_2$) $\times$ height
PERIMETER	**Triangle:** side$_1$ + side$_2$ + side$_3$ **Rectangle:** (2 $\times$ length) + (2 $\times$ width) **Circle (circumference):** $2\pi \times$ radius **or** $\pi \times$ diameter ($\pi \approx 3.14$)
VOLUME	**Right cylinder:** area of base $\times$ height **Rectangular solid:** length $\times$ width $\times$ height **Cube:** (side)^3 **Square pyramid:** $\frac{1}{3} \times$ edge$^2 \times$ height **Cone:** $\frac{1}{3} \times \pi \times$ radius$^2 \times$ height ($\pi \approx 3.14$)
COORDINATE GEOMETRY	**Distance between points** = $\sqrt{(x_2 - x_1)^2 + (y_2 - y_1)^2}$, where the two points are (x_1, y_1) and (x_2, y_2) **Slope of a line** = $\frac{y_2 - y_1}{x_2 - x_1}$, where (x_1, y_1) and (x_2, y_2) are any two points on the line
MEASURES OF CENTRAL TENDENCY	**Mean (simple average)** = $\frac{x_1 + x_2 + x_3 \ldots x_n}{n}$, where each x is the value of a different term and n is the total number of terms **Median** = the middle term in value if the number of terms is an *odd* number *or* $\frac{x + y}{2}$ (where x and y are the two middle terms in value) if the number of terms is an *even* number
OTHER FORMULAS	**Pythagorean theorem:** (leg$_1$)^2 + (leg$_2$)^2 = (hypotenuse)^2 **Distance** = rate $\times$ time **Simple interest** = dollar amount $\times$ interest rate **Total cost** = cost per item $\times$ number of items

practice test

MATHEMATICS, PART I: QUESTIONS 1–25

The use of a calculator is allowed for questions 1–25.

1. A compact disc player priced originally at $75 is sold for $65. What is the approximate rate of the discount?

    (1) 10 percent

    (2) 13.3 percent

    (3) 15.4 percent

    (4) 18.5 percent

    (5) 20.2 percent

2. When Felicia checked out at the grocery store, she gave the clerk $20.00 and received $3.80 as the correct amount of change. Which of the following could Felicia have bought?

    (1) eight cans of olives at $2.15 each

    (2) four frozen dinners at $3.95 each

    (3) six bags of apples at $2.70 each

    (4) five dozen organic eggs at $3.20 per dozen

    (5) seven cans of dog food at $2.30 each

3. If $a = 3$, $b = -3$, and $c = \frac{1}{3}$, then what is the value of ab^2c^2 ?

    (1) −27

    (2) −1

    (3) 3

    (4) 9

    (5) 27

4. Uniformly sized 2-inch sugar cubes are to be packed into boxes, each one measuring $10 \times 12 \times 15$ inches. Packaging "pellets" are to be used to fill any empty space in the box.

    What is the minimum volume of pellets needed for one box of sugar cubes?

    (1) 0 cubic inches

    (2) 120 cubic inches

    (3) 150 cubic inches

    (4) 250 cubic inches

    (5) 320 cubic inches

QUESTIONS 5 AND 6 REFER TO THE FOLLOWING TABLE.

Worldwide Sales of Three XYZ Motor Company Models
(2009–2010 Model Year)

		Automobile Model	
Purchaser Category		Basic	Standard	Deluxe
	U.S. institutions	3.6	8.5	1.9
	U.S. consumers	7.5	11.4	2.0
	Foreign institutions	1.7	4.9	2.2
	Foreign consumers	1.0	5.1	0.8

Note: All numbers are in thousands.

The table shows worldwide sales of three XYZ Motor Company models during the 2009–10 model year.

5. Based on the table, which of the following does NOT describe sales of at least 10,000 automobiles?

   (1) all U.S. institution sales of the standard and deluxe models

   (2) all foreign institution sales

   (3) all consumer sales of the basic and deluxe model

   (4) all foreign sales of the standard model

   (5) all institution sales of the standard model

6. During the 2009–10 period, how many more standard models than basic models were sold?

   (1) 6900

   (2) 9200

   (3) 16,100

   (4) 23,000

   (5) Not enough information is provided.

7. $52x(31x + 27x)$ has the same value as which of the following?

   (1) $31x(52x + 27x)$

   (2) $31x + 52x + 27x$

   (3) $(52x)(27x) + (31x)(27x)$

   (4) $(31x)(52x) + (31x)(27x)$

   (5) $(52x)(31x) + (52x)(27x)$

8. If $\sqrt[3]{p + q} + 4 = 0$, what is the sum of p and q?

   (1) −64

   (2) −16

   (3) 4

   (4) 8

   (5) 64

9. The small squares that form part of a quilt shown below are 10 inches on each side.

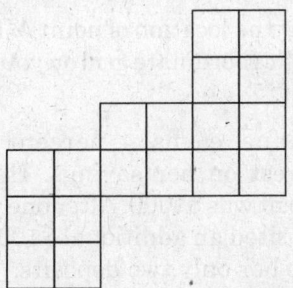

Katie plans to disassemble this part of the quilt and rearrange the squares to form a long, rectangular section consisting of two rows of the small squares. After the squares are rearranged, what will be the perimeter of this new part of the quilt, expressed in inches?

Mark your answer in the grid on your answer sheet

10. Joe earns $13.50 an hour when he works on weekdays and time-and-a-half per hour when he works on the weekend. Last week, he worked 40 hours Monday through Friday and 6 hours on Saturday. How much did he earn for the week?

   (1) $540.00

   (2) $621.00

   (3) $661.50

   (4) $785.50

   (5) $977.50

11. Of 60 pairs of socks in a drawer, 40% are blue, and the remaining pairs of socks are all gray. If 4 pairs of blue socks are removed from the drawer, what is the ratio of gray pairs of socks to blue pairs of socks?

   (1) 1 to 2

   (2) 5 to 9

   (3) 3 to 5

   (4) 9 to 5

   (5) 2 to 1

12. What is the midpoint *M* of a line segment connecting points (5,2) and (−11,6) on the *xy*-coordinate plane?

Show the location of point *M* by marking the coordinate grid on your answer sheet.

13. Brianna earns 4 percent **simple** interest on her savings. Her initial deposit was $1000. After one year, she deposited an additional $1000. These were her only two deposits.

Which of the following is nearest to Brianna's account balance after two years?

(1) $2040

(2) $2080

(3) $2120

(4) $2160

(5) $2240

14. Of all the horses stabled at the Circle-Y ranch, $\frac{1}{4}$ are black and $\frac{2}{5}$ are white.

What portion of the horses are neither black nor white?

Mark your answer in the grid on your answer sheet.

QUESTIONS 15 AND 16 REFER TO THE FOLLOWING CHART.

**SHARE PRICES OF COMMON STOCK
(ARDENT, BIOFIRM, AND COMPUWIN CORPORATIONS)**

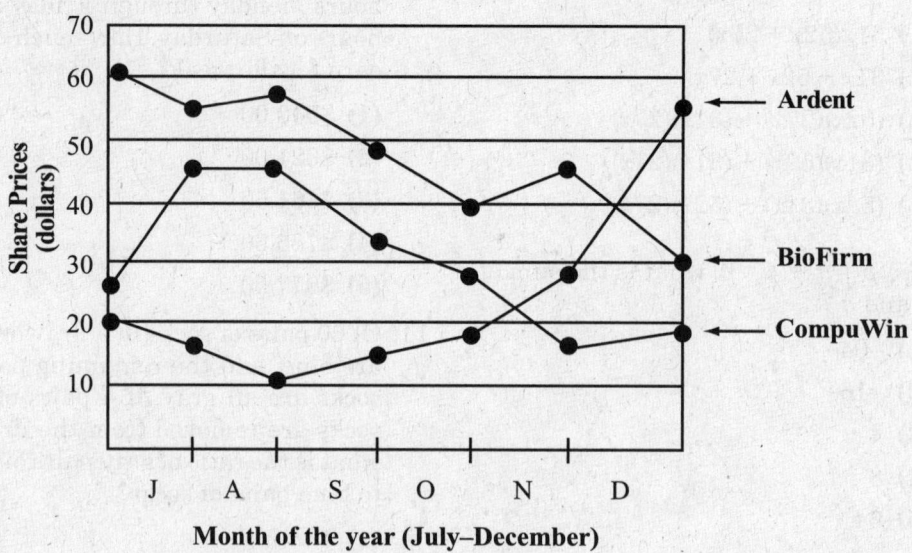

Month of the year (July–December)

15. What was the approximate median among the seven end-of-month prices shown for CompuWin stock?

(1) $18

(2) $26

(3) $28

(4) $33

(5) $49

16. At the beginning of July, an investor bought 40 shares of Ardent stock and then held all 40 shares until the end of December, at which time she sold all 40 shares. The investor's profit upon the sale of these 40 shares amounted to approximately what amount?

(1) $850

(2) $980

(3) $1100

(4) $1300

(5) $1400

17. A pyramid with a square base has a volume of 125 cubic feet and a height (h) of 15 feet, as shown in the below figure.

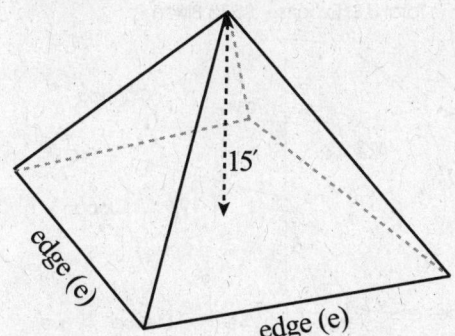

What is the area of the pyramid's square base?

(1) 5 square feet

(2) 15 square feet

(3) 25 square feet

(4) 36 square feet

(5) Not enough information is provided.

18. In the below figure, l_1 is parallel to l_2.

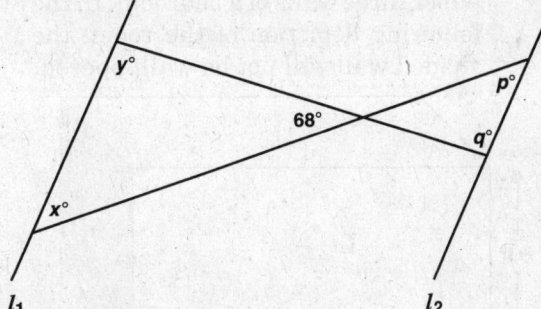

What is the value of $p + y$? [Note: angle sizes are not drawn to scale in the figure.]

Mark your answer in the grid on your answer sheet.

19. Kyle wants to buy a truck with a fuel capacity of at least 80 liters. Which of the following is the smallest tank capacity that will suit Kyle's needs? [One gallon = 3.785 liters]

(1) 21.5 gallons

(2) 24.0 gallons

(3) 26.5 gallons

(4) 30.5 gallons

(5) 38.0 gallons

20. An interior decorator plans to wallpaper three walls of a bedroom. In the following depiction of the room, the shaded wall will not be wallpapered.

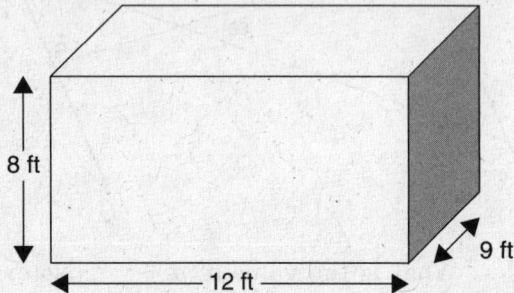

Wallpaper is measured by the square yard. Each single roll of wallpaper contains 4 square yards of wallpaper. What is the LEAST number of wallpaper rolls that must be purchased to cover the three walls?

(1) 7

(2) 8

(3) 10

(4) 66

(5) 84

21. In a geometric series, each term is a constant multiple of the preceding one. In geometric series *Q*, the first term is 0.9 and the second term is 0.81.

What is the third term in series *Q*?

Mark your answer in the grid on your answer sheet.

QUESTIONS 22–24 REFER TO THE FOLLOWING GRAPH.

Top Purchasers of U.S. Exports

1999
Total U.S. Exports – $510 Billion

- Canada 23%
- Japan 11%
- Mexico 10%
- UK 6%
- Germany 4%
- South Korea 3.5%
- Taiwan 3%
- France 3%
- Other 36.5%

2000
Total U.S. Exports – $575 Billion

- Canada 23%
- Japan 10%
- Mexico 9%
- UK 5%
- Germany 4%
- South Korea 4%
- Taiwan 3%
- France 3%
- Other 39%

22. In the year 2000, how much more was spent on U.S. exports by the United Kingdom (UK) than by Taiwan?

(1) $2.3 billion

(2) $5.1 billion

(3) $5.75 billion

(4) $11.5 billion

(5) $17.25 billion

23. Excluding "Other" purchasers, how many purchasers spent more than $20 billion for U.S. exports in the year 1999?

(1) two

(2) three

(3) four

(4) five

(5) six

facebook.com/petersonspublishing

24. Which country increased its U.S.-dollar purchases of U.S. exports the LEAST from 1999 to 2000?

(1) Taiwan

(2) Mexico

(3) Canada

(4) UK

(5) Germany

25. A faucet is dripping at a constant rate. By noon on Sunday, 3 ounces of water have dripped from the faucet into a bucket. If a *total* of 7 ounces have dripped into the bucket by 5 p.m. the same day, how many ounces altogether will have dripped into the bucket by 2:00 a.m. the following day?

Mark your answer in the grid on your answer sheet.

END OF PART I.

practice test

MATHEMATICS, PART II: QUESTIONS 26–50

The use of a calculator is NOT allowed for questions 26–50.

26. Jason ate one third of a pizza for dinner, and his brother ate one sixth of the same pizza. What portion of the pizza was left over?

Mark your answer in the grid on your answer sheet.

QUESTION 27 REFERS TO THE FOLLOWING GRAPH.

Disease X Medication Sales

27. Which is accurate about annual sales of oral medication for disease X?

Sales of oral medication did NOT increase

(1) from 2003 to 2004

(2) from 2005 to 2006

(3) from 2006 to 2007

(4) from 2007 to 2008

(5) from 2008 to 2009

28. A certain line on the xy-plane contains the (x,y) points $(-2,1)$ and $(3,5)$. What is the slope of the line?

(1) $-\dfrac{5}{4}$

(2) $-\dfrac{2}{3}$

(3) $\dfrac{4}{5}$

(4) $\dfrac{5}{4}$

(5) $\dfrac{3}{2}$

29. 4.62×10^8 can be written as which of the following numbers?

(1) 46,200

(2) 462,000

(3) 4,620,000

(4) 46,200,000

(5) 462,000,000

30. In an upcoming election, Jenkins, Ramirez, and 3 other candidates are competing for two city council seats. Polls show that all candidates have an equal chance of victory.

What is the probability that either Jenkins or Ramirez will be elected?

Mark your answer in the grid on your answer sheet.

31. Which expression has the greatest value?

(1) 250×4

(2) $400 \times \dfrac{2}{5}$

(3) 4000×0.04

(4) $\dfrac{1}{4} \times 4000$

(5) 40×40

32. What is the value of m in the following system of two equations?

$$4m = 12 - 3n$$

$$\frac{3n}{4} = 3 - m$$

(1) −6

(2) −3

(3) 2

(4) 8

(5) any real number

33. Referring to distributions D and E (below), which of the following measurements has the greatest value?

Distribution D : {2, 5, 9, 9}
Distribution E : {3, 6, 9, 10}

(1) the range of distribution D

(2) the median of distribution E

(3) the median of distribution D

(4) the range of distribution E

(5) the arithmetic mean of distribution E

34. If $x < -1$, which of the following is greatest in value?

(1) x^3

(2) $x + 1$

(3) x^2

(4) $| x |$

(5) $x - 1$

35. Cynthia drove for seven hours at an average rate of 50 miles per hour (mph) and for one hour at an average rate of 60 mph. Which of the following represents her average rate for the entire trip?

(1) $\dfrac{7(50) + 60}{8}$

(2) $\dfrac{2(50 + 60)}{7}$

(3) $\dfrac{7(50 + 60)}{8}$

(4) $\dfrac{50 + 60}{2}$

(5) $\dfrac{7(60) + 50}{8}$

36. The ratio of Jennifer's weekly salary to Carl's weekly salary is 2:3. If Jennifer's salary were to double, it would be $1000. What is Carl's current weekly salary?

(1) $750

(2) $1000

(3) $1200

(4) $1500

(5) Not enough information is provided.

37. If $\frac{x}{3}$, $\frac{x}{7}$, and $\frac{x}{9}$ are all positive integers, what is the least possible value of x?

Mark your answer in the grid on your answer sheet.

38. M college students agree to rent an apartment for D dollars per month, sharing the rent equally. If the rent is increased by $100, what amount must each student contribute?

(1) $\dfrac{M + 100}{D}$

(2) $\dfrac{D}{M} + 100$

(3) $\dfrac{D}{M}$

(4) $\dfrac{M}{D + 100}$

(5) $\dfrac{D + 100}{M}$

QUESTIONS 39 AND 40 REFER TO THE FOLLOWING GRAPH.

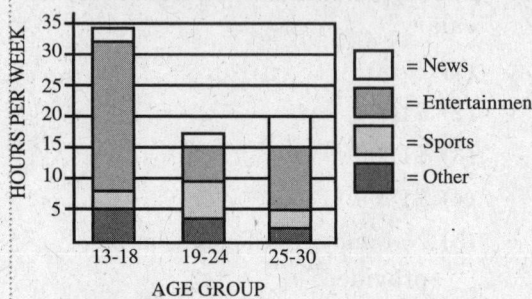

AVERAGE NUMBER OF HOURS PER WEEK
SPENT WATCHING TELEVISION

39. Assume that 27-year-olds are representative of the 25–30 age group. Approximately how many hours per week does the average 27-year-old spend watching news on television?

(1) 2

(2) 5

(3) 8

(4) 10

(5) 20

40. The 19–24 age group spends approximately 55 percent of its television-viewing time watching which of the following groups of program types?

(1) entertainment, news, and sports programs

(2) programs other than entertainment

(3) news and educational programs

(4) programs other than news and sports

(5) sports and entertainment programs

41. The two parallel sides of trapezoid T have a combined length of 14 centimeters. If the height of trapezoid T is 14 centimeters, what is the area of trapezoid T?

Express your answer in square centimeters. Mark your answer in the grid on your answer sheet.

42. In which of the following forms can the algebraic expression $x^3 + 3x^2 + 2x$ be written?

(1) $x(x + 1)(x + 1)$

(2) $x^2(2x + 1)$

(3) $x(x + 3)(x - 1)$

(4) $x^2(3x - 1)$

(5) $x(x + 2)(x + 1)$

43. If $x > 0$, and if $x + 3$ is a multiple of 3, which of the following is NOT a multiple of 3?

(1) x

(2) $x + 6$

(3) $2x + 6$

(4) $3x + 5$

(5) $6x + 18$

44. In the below figure, $\triangle RST$ has angle measures 90, θ, and β degrees.

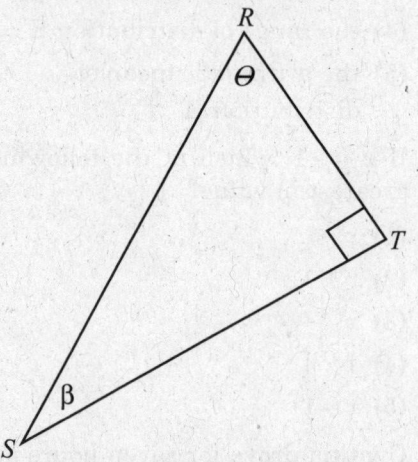

Which of the following is true for all possible values of θ and β?

(1) $\tan\theta = \tan\beta$

(2) $\sin\beta = \cos\beta$

(3) $\sin\theta \times \cos\beta = 1$

(4) $\tan\theta \times \tan\beta = 1$

(5) $\sin\theta = \cos\theta$

45. Eight years from now, Carrie's age will be twice Ben's age. If Carrie's current age is C and Ben's current age is B, which of the following represents Carrie's current age?

(1) B

(2) B + 4

(3) B + 8

(4) 2B + 8

(5) 3B

46. As shown in the below figure, from runway 1 airplanes must turn 120° to the right onto runway 2 or 135° to the left onto runway 3.

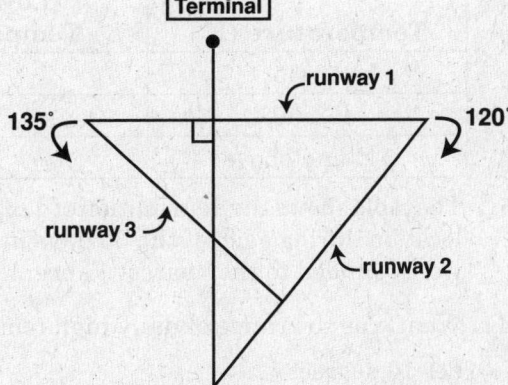

Note: Figure is not drawn to scale.

Which of the following does NOT indicate a complete turn from one runway to another?

(1) 30°

(2) 55°

(3) 60°

(4) 75°

(5) 105°

QUESTIONS 47 AND 48 REFER TO THE FOLLOWING TABLE.

Temperature (F°)	Number of Days in April (Low Daily Temperature)	Number of Days in April (High Daily Temperature)
41°–45°	14	3
46°–50°	12	9
51° and above	4	18

The table shows the distribution of daily low and daily high temperatures in a certain location during each of the 30 days in April. Recorded low and high temperatures were rounded to the nearest Fahrenheit degree (F°).

47. What was the range of daily high temperatures during the month of April?

   (1) 10 degrees

   (2) 14 degrees

   (3) 15 degrees

   (4) 51 degrees

   (5) Not enough information is provided.

48. Based solely on the information in the table, which statement CANNOT be true about April's temperatures?

   (1) On four of the days, the low temperature was 41° and the high temperature was 51°.

   (2) On four of the days, the low temperature was 46° and the high temperature was 51°.

   (3) On four of the days, both the low and the high temperatures were between 41° and 45°.

   (4) On four of the days, both the low and the high temperatures exceeded 50°.

   (5) On four of the days, both the low and the high temperatures were between 46° and 50°.

49. A certain function is defined as $f(x) = \dfrac{a}{x^2}$, where a and x are both positive numbers. Which of the following graphs best depicts this function?

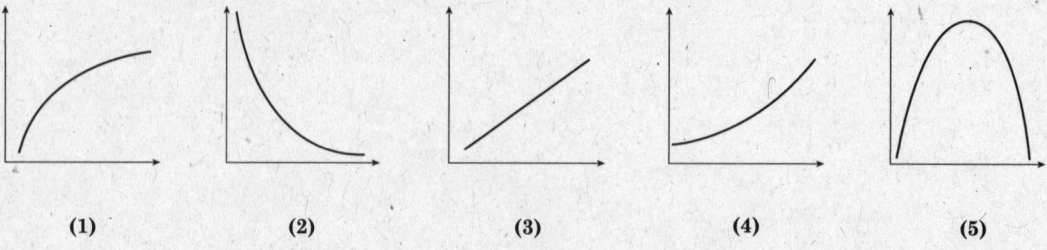

  (1)   **(2)**   **(3)**   **(4)**   **(5)**

50. In the below figure, *O* lies at the center of the larger circle.

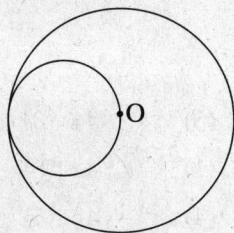

What is the ratio of the smaller circle's area to the larger circle's area?

(1) π:12

(2) π:15

(3) 2:3π

(4) 1:4

(5) 1:5

ANSWER KEY AND EXPLANATIONS

Language Arts, Writing, Part I

1. (3)	11. (1)	21. (5)	31. (5)	41. (3)
2. (4)	12. (3)	22. (4)	32. (1)	42. (5)
3. (4)	13. (5)	23. (5)	33. (4)	43. (5)
4. (2)	14. (4)	24. (2)	34. (2)	44. (4)
5. (2)	15. (3)	25. (3)	35. (4)	45. (4)
6. (5)	16. (5)	26. (3)	36. (2)	46. (1)
7. (1)	17. (5)	27. (3)	37. (3)	47. (4)
8. (5)	18. (2)	28. (5)	38. (2)	48. (5)
9. (5)	19. (2)	29. (4)	39. (1)	49. (2)
10. (1)	20. (1)	30. (2)	40. (4)	50. (2)

1. **The correct answer is (3).** Using the conjunction *and* both before and after the underlined part implies that the sentence lists three distinct ideas. But the underlined part and what follows it are really part of the same idea. Choice (3) clarifies the sentence's meaning by moving the comma to follow *7 a.m.* and removing *and* before *is*.

2. **The correct answer is (4).** The word *maybe* means "possibly" and makes no sense in context. It should be replaced with its homonym *may be* (which means "might be").

3. **The correct answer is (4).** The tense shift from future (*will call*) to past (*arrived*) is illogical. Also, sentences 4 and 5 leave it unclear whether *she* refers to the evening Innkeeper or the morning Innkeeper. Choice (4) is the only one that fixes both problems without creating another one.

4. **The correct answer is (2).** Checking for open windows and doors is part of checking for security, so creating a subordinate clause using the group of words in choice (2) makes sense in context. Here's a good version of the entire sentence: *The night manager will walk around the premises at night to check security and lights, checking especially for any window or door left open.*

5. **The correct answer is (2).** The main problem with the original sentence is that the pronoun *it* precedes its antecedent *problem* and is separated from *problem* by intervening phrases. Choice (2) reconstructs the sentence in a way that makes the reference clear. Here's a good version of the entire revised sentence: *The night manager will inform the morning Innkeeper of any security problem requiring further attention so that it can be corrected promptly.*

6. **The correct answer is (5).** Sentence 9 contains no errors. Choices (1), (2), (3), and (4) propose either an unnecessary change or a change that actually creates a usage or mechanical error.

7. **The correct answer is (1).** The most logical order to present the ideas in this paragraph is chronologically. The action described in sentence 10 should be performed after all others described in the paragraph. Accord-

ingly, sentence 10 should be positioned as the last sentence in paragraph E.

8. **The correct answer is (5).** The shift from present tense (*is expected*) to past-perfect tense (*had been familiar*) is confusing and illogical. By changing it to the present tense (*is familiar*) you can fix the problem.

9. **The correct answer is (5).** The word *seen* is the perfect-tense form of *see*. The word should either be preceded by *have* (present perfect) or be changed to *see* (present tense), as in choice (5).

10. **The correct answer is (1).** The original ending words are clear and grammatically correct. Revising with choice (2), (3), or (5) would result in a sentence fragment. Revising with choice (4) would result in a subject-verb agreement error.

11. **The correct answer is (1).** An effective way to combine sentences 4 and 5 is to transform sentence 5 into a subordinate clause that begins with the relative pronoun *who*. Here's the resulting sentence: *These examples are the work of an elite group of skilled effects artists, who over the course of a century have developed countless moviemaking tricks and techniques.*

12. **The correct answer is (3).** Setting off the phrase *and tools* as an appositive obscures the intended meaning of the sentence. (What tools? Whose tools?) One solution is to simply remove both commas. Another solution is the one presented in choice (3), which makes it clear whose tools the sentence is referring to.

13. **The correct answer is (5).** In the original sentence, the intended antecedent of *they* is *special effects* (see the previous sentence). However, the reference is unclear. Choice (5) fixes this problem by replacing the pronoun with its antecedent.

14. **The correct answer is (4).** Sentence 13 states a general idea that the other three sentences all support with detail, so it makes sense to begin the paragraph with this sentence. Notice that sentence 14 begins with *Even in comedies*, which suggests that sentence 14 should follow sentences 12 and 13, both of which discuss another movie genre.

15. **The correct answer is (3).** The verb form *give* agrees in number with the plural noun *ways*. In other words, "it" gives, but "they" give. Choice (3) is the only one that corrects this error.

16. **The correct answer is (5).** The verb form *would be* makes sense in context because it conveys a contrary-to-fact idea (something that could have been true but in reality is not).

17. **The correct answer is (5).** Sentence 17 contains no errors. Each proposed change would result in either a usage or a mechanical error.

18. **The correct answer is (2).** To make the sentence clearer, either *submitted* and *by you* should be positioned together (*submitted by you*) or the active phrase *you submitted* should be used—as in choice (2). Choices (3) and (5) also fix the problem. However, choice (3) proposes an unbalanced, awkward sentence pair, while choice (5) confuses the sentence's meaning. (Which event happened last week?)

19. **The correct answer is (2).** The three list items should be grammatically parallel, but they're not. Removing the word *using* from the second item corrects the problem. The sentence would then read: *The navigation buttons, the pull-down menus, and the product ordering page are all intuitive and user-friendly.*

20. **The correct answer is (1).** Choice (1) provides a good way to transform the second sentence into a dependent clause beginning with *so that*. Here's a complete revised version: *Is it possible to use a three-column format instead of two columns so that more informa-*

tion is visible "above the fold" on each page?

21. The correct answer is (5). This sentence should ask about changing button orientation from horizontal to *vertical*, not to *vertically*.

22. The correct answer is (4). This sentence contains two independent clauses, each of which can stand alone as a complete sentence. The second clause contains the compound subject *me and her*, which incorrectly employs object pronoun cases. Choice (4) supplies the correct cases for a sentence's subject: *she and I*.

23. The correct answer is (5). The future-tense *will be* is improper here, even though the writer is referring to a future time, because the completion of the site design precedes another future event: the automatic generation of a site map. The present-tense verb form *is* should be used instead of the future tense *will be*.

24. The correct answer is (2). The main structural problem with original sentence is that it separates *who* from its intended antecedent *customers*. Choice (2) solves this problem, and it is the only choice that provides the beginning of an effective revision: *Since our customers will be entering credit card information at the site, security and privacy are of utmost importance.*

25. The correct answer is (3). The word *vary* (differ or fluctuate) doesn't make sense here. The writer no doubt intended to use the word *very* (extremely).

26. The correct answer is (3). Paragraph E does not provide "constructive criticism," and so it should not be included among the other items in the list. A better position for paragraph E is immediately following paragraph G.

27. The correct answer is (3). The revised beginning of the sentence lists items to remove from the room. The next words should complete the list: *Pictures, wall mirrors, and other furniture should be removed from the room first.*

28. The correct answer is (5). Sentence 2 contains no errors. Any of the proposed changes would create a problem either in sentence sense, usage, or grammar.

29. The correct answer is (4). Starting the sentence with *Use soapy water* makes for the clearest, most concise version of sentence 3: *Use soapy water to wash all surfaces you plan to paint, and let dry.*

30. The correct answer is (2). The phrase *you'll might* (*you will might*) is incorrect and should be changed to *you might*.

31. The correct answer is (5). Notice that sentence 7 states the reason for the step that sentence 8 suggests. Connecting the two sentences using the conjunction *so* is an effective way to convey the relationship between the two sentences: *Putty shrinks when it dries, so wait until it dries, and then apply more putty if needed.*

32. The correct answer is (1). The original underlined portion is the best version. Choices (2) and (4) create run-on sentences. Choices (3) and (5) create pronoun-reference problems. Also, each incorrect version obscures the idea that old sheets work better.

33. The correct answer is (4). The plural noun *newspapers* takes the plural verb form *stick* instead of the singular form *sticks*.

34. The correct answer is (2). Paragraph C instructs the reader to fill cracks and holes (including nail holes) with putty, while paragraph D instructs the reader to remove nails (and other hardware). The sequence of these two steps should be reversed.

35. The correct answer is (4). The two-word noun *the Web* is singular and takes the singular contraction *it's* (it has) rather than the plural contraction *they've* (they have).

36. **The correct answer is (2).** According to the sentence, what we do every moment is worry. This idea is clearest if the phrases *every moment* and *we worry* are positioned one after the other (in either order).

37. **The correct answer is (3).** The plural noun *distractions* takes the plural verb form *lower* rather than the singular form *lowers*.

38. **The correct answer is (2).** Sentence 7 essentially repeats an idea expressed in sentence 5 and should simply be removed.

39. **The correct answer is (1).** Sentence 8 intends to make the point that we rely on one thing instead of another. But positioning *instead of . . .* after *colleagues* implies that we might communicate with face-to-face meetings, which makes no sense. The group of words in choice (1) provides for a more coherent sentence: *To communicate with colleagues, we rely on quick text messages instead of face-to-face meetings.*

40. **The correct answer is (4).** The comparative adjective *more briefer* is incorrect and should be replaced with the single word *briefer*.

41. **The correct answer is (3).** The present tense, used throughout the passage, should be used in sentence 10 as well. The future-tense form *will shorten* should be replaced with the present-perfect form *has shortened*.

42. **The correct answer is (5).** Sentence 14 contains no errors. Each of the proposed changes would result in an error in either usage or grammar.

43. **The correct answer is (5).** Sentences 14 and 15 refer to ideas not only in paragraph B but also in paragraph A. What's more, these two sentences together provide an effective recap and conclusion to the passage as a whole.

Accordingly, they are best set off as a distinct, final paragraph.

44. **The correct answer is (4).** The compound object *House* and *concept* should take the plural verb *are* rather than the singular form *is*.

45. **The correct answer is (4).** Use the capitalized form of the word *county* only when referring to a specific county by name (for example, Orange County).

46. **The correct answer is (1).** As it stands, sentence 6 is actually a sentence fragment (an incomplete sentence) consisting of two dependent clauses. Inserting *are* after *Clients* transforms the first clause into an independent clause and clarifies the sentence's meaning.

47. **The correct answer is (4).** The pronoun *their* has no antecedent. (Who are they?) Since the question does not allow for rewriting either sentence 7 or sentence 8, the appropriate correction is to simply remove the word *their*—especially considering that the resulting sentence blends gracefully in style and structure with sentences 7 and 9.

48. **The correct answer is (5).** The underlined part should be grammatically parallel to the noun *housing*, but it's not. Also, the plural verb form *are* is incorrect because the subject *Transitioning* is considered singular. Choice (5) fixes both errors.

49. **The correct answer is (2).** The word *bidders* is incorrect in context and should be changed to either the plural possessive *bidders'* or the singular form *bidder*. Also, *every one* should be replaced with *everyone*. Choice (4) corrects both errors. (It also inverts the structure of the sentence to make it more graceful.)

50. **The correct answer is (2).** Paragraphs B, C, and D provide information about the Helping House transi-

tional housing program. Notice that paragraph C provides comparatively general information about Helping House's mission and the people it seeks to help, while paragraphs B and D provide details about how Helping House carries out that mission and helps those people. The most effective way to present these ideas is by starting with generalities, *then* delving into details.

Language Arts, Writing, Part II

Evaluating Your Practice Essay

Your actual GED® essay will be read and scored by 2 trained readers, who will evaluate it according to its *overall effectiveness*, considering how well you convey and support your main ideas, how well you organize those ideas, and how clearly and correctly you write throughout the essay.

It is difficult to be objective about one's own writing. So to help you evaluate your practice essay, you may wish to ask a mentor, teacher, or friend to read and evaluate it for you. In any case, use the following 4-point evaluation checklist. This list provides all of the elements of an effective, high-scoring GED® essay.

1. Is the essay well-focused? (Does it clearly convey a central idea, and does it remain focused on that idea, as opposed to digressing from the topic or focusing too narrowly on certain minor points?)

2. Does the essay develop its main ideas effectively, using persuasive reasons and relevant supporting examples?

3. Is the essay well-organized? (Are the ideas presented in a logical sequence, so that the reader can easily follow them? Are transitions from one point to the next natural and logical? Does the essay have a clear ending, or did you appear to run out of time?)

4. Does your essay demonstrate good control of grammar, sentence structure, word choice, punctuation, and spelling?

Each GED® reader will score your essay on a scale of 0–4 (the highest score is 4). If you can objectively answer "yes" to all four of the above questions, then your essay would earn a score of at least 3, and probably 4, from a trained GED® reader. Keep in mind, however, that the testing service will not award a separate score for the Writing Test, Part II (the essay). Instead, the service will combine your Part I and Part II scores according to its own formula, and then it will award a single overall Writing Test score.

Social Studies

1. (4)	11. (3)	21. (5)	31. (2)	41. (3)
2. (5)	12. (2)	22. (1)	32. (2)	42. (4)
3. (3)	13. (5)	23. (3)	33. (1)	43. (5)
4. (1)	14. (1)	24. (5)	34. (4)	44. (1)
5. (3)	15. (3)	25. (5)	35. (3)	45. (1)
6. (1)	16. (4)	26. (2)	36. (2)	46. (3)
7. (4)	17. (2)	27. (5)	37. (4)	47. (1)
8. (3)	18. (5)	28. (3)	38. (3)	48. (5)
9. (4)	19. (4)	29. (2)	39. (1)	49. (3)
10. (5)	20. (5)	30. (1)	40. (1)	50. (4)

1. **The correct answer is (4).** The Fifth Amendment protects citizens from being convicted in a criminal court without trial. This protection is similar to, and hence reinforces, the protection provided in the Constitution against a legislature doing the same thing.

2. **The correct answer is (5).** Western Morocco (identified on the map by the number 1) lies along the Pacific coastline, as do either the western or southern boundaries of the countries numbered 6, 7, 14, 15, 16, 17 18, 19, 21, 22, 23, 24, and 25.

3. **The correct answer is (3).** The desert's highest mountain peak is in northern Chad (country 10 on the map). The shortest route from Egypt (country 5) to Burkina Faso (country 20) passes through Northern Chad, and so the route must pass through high-desert terrain.

4. **The correct answer is (1).** Europe is to the north of Africa, across the Mediterranean Sea. A waterway connecting that sea to the Red Sea (east of Egypt, Sudan, and Ethiopia) facilitated global trade by allowing water transport between Europe and Asia (to the east) without going around the African continent.

5. **The correct answer is (3).** The fact that Jackson was a wealthy plantation owner is inconsistent with his image as a "common man" rather than a member of the wealthy elite. The others facts all helped Jackson promote the image of himself as a "common man" and friend of ordinary citizens.

6. **The correct answer is (1).** We can infer that Jackson would not have supported the extension of the right to vote to Native Americans and slaves since he ordered the removal of Indians and supported slavery. From the reading, we know he supported extending the right to all adult, white males, choices (4) and (5). However, the passage doesn't provide enough information to make inferences regarding his position on voting rights for women, choice (2), or his position on what age males become adults, choice (3).

7. **The correct answer is (4).** A value is a deep-seated belief that helps determine a person's ideas and outlook on life. Jackson hated the fact that many wealthy, better educated people looked down on him and often were able to advance ahead of him due to special privilege. Much of his

political life is defined by criticism of the political and economic elite and the positions he took in support of ordinary citizens (the "common man"). Since the right to vote was extended to only white males, we know he did not value equal rights for all, choice (1). In addition, formal education, choice (2), and the established order, choice (3), were not values that strongly influenced him. Since Jackson himself became wealthy, we can assume that a revulsion to wealth, choice (5), was not among his deep-seated beliefs and values.

8. **The correct answer is (3).** The power of the judicial system (which includes the U.S. Supreme Court) to review the constitutionality of laws—or to interpret laws—is the principle of American government to which the cartoon refers.

9. **The correct answer is (4).** In the cartoon, the Congressman is reading that Congress has the Constitutional authority to raise and support Armies and a Navy, while the Supreme Court judge explains, "What it says isn't always what it means." The judge is holding a paper that says "draft exemption for ethical views." In the context of the times, the likely message is that, despite what the Constitution plainly says, the Supreme Court has decided that Congress cannot force citizens to serve in a war to which they object on ethical grounds.

10. **The correct answer is (5).** Congress, not the president, choice (1), plays the key role in debating, writing, and passing a new law. The president cannot always block Congress, choice (2), which can override his veto,. Not signing a law, choice (3), will not keep it from taking effect, unless Congress has adjourned. The veto power, choice (4), does not give the president the power to do any rewriting of bills.

11. **The correct answer is (3).** The fact that their fertile land was limited was

probably the reason for the Norse movement to find new homes across the seas. Wherever they were not welcome, they saw little practical choice but to seize land by force.

12. **The correct answer is (2).** The statement in choice (2) captures the main difference between North and South. Choice (1) is incorrect since the North and South faced different challenges: the South had to rebuild and reform, and the North did not. The North, unlike the South, was not destroyed during the Civil War and did not have to rebuild, choice (3). The passage explained that regional differences between the North and South were continuing, not diminishing, choice (4). It's true that both the North and South were building new railroads, choice (5), but this statement misses the main point of the passage and the differences that characterized the North and South during this period.

13. **The correct answer is (5).** The greatest decrease—from about 4% growth to about a 1% contraction (negative growth)—occurred from 1988–1991.

14. **The correct answer is (1).** The left-hand and right-hand charts show an inverse relationship overall between GDP and unemployment: when the economy is growing, unemployment declines. Conversely, when economic growth slows, unemployment increases. This observation makes sense. A low rate of economic growth typically means that employers are not expanding their businesses and therefore not hiring additional employees, and employers may actually be laying off workers in response to sluggish business.

15. **The correct answer is (3).** The best time to look for a job would be when the economy is growing (which is when businesses are more likely to need additional workers), unemployment is falling (which means fewer available workers for employers to choose from),

and inflation is falling (which is when businesses are more confident about investing for their future).

16. **The correct answer is (4).** Common sense tells you that, at any given time, some portion of the working-age population will be experiencing a brief lapse in employment while transitioning from one job to another. It makes sense to take such factors into account when defining *full employment*.

17. **The correct answer is (2).** 1982 saw the unemployment rate rise dramatically from the previous year, while the growth rate turned from positive to negative. That recessionary scenario is similar to the one in 2008–09, which prompted Obama's spending programs designed to reduce the unemployment rate and to stimulate economic growth.

18. **The correct answer is (5).** The two-term limit is part of the system of checks and balances, which prevents any individual (for example, the president) or group of individuals from gaining too much power in the nation. Conversely, the two-term limit gives Congress more power.

19. **The correct answer is (4).** The 48 contiguous states are located entirely south of the Arctic Circle. Though most of these states are north of the Tropic of Cancer, portions of the southern United States are located just south of that latitude line.

20. **The correct answer is (5).** The information in the passage supports the view that the North's growing aversion to slavery caused the South, where the ruling elite depended on slavery, to secede. Nothing in the passage suggests that the North was trying to industrialize the South, choice (1); that the South saw the North's growing industrialization as a threat, choice (3); or that the South wanted to become more like the North, choice (4). The growing dominance of the North in population caused fears that the North could eventually force the South to free its slaves through a constitutional amendment, but the North's larger population itself, choice (2), was not a threat.

21. **The correct answer is (5).** Choice (5) gives the most complete description of the relationship between the African American population and the Caucasian population. Each of the other choices describes only one portion of the facts presented in the table.

22. **The correct answer is (1).** Proportionate changes among the three demographic groups would have no effect on the number of people in each group.

23. **The correct answer is (3).** The table shows a declining Caucasian population from 2010 to 2080. An expected decline in the birthrate among Caucasians would lead to this projection. Choice (1) runs contrary to the projected decline in the Caucasian population. Choice (2) is not directly related to the information in the table. Choice (4) runs contrary to the projected decline in the Caucasian female population. Choice (5) supports the projected increase in the African American population but not the projected decline in the Caucasian population.

24. **The correct answer is (5).** Requiring Supreme Court Justices to face popular elections would certainly produce major changes in how the Justices would behave, making the statement in choice (5) the least likely occurrence. To be re-elected, justices would have to give a higher priority to public opinion, choice (1); fundraising, choice (2); campaigning, choice (3); and the news media, choice (4).

25. **The correct answer is (5).** Rent, food, transportation (automobiles), and electricity are all goods or services purchased by typical consumers.

answers practice test 3

Wages represent income, not spending.

26. The correct answer is (2). The Mexican Cession was added to the United States in 1848 as a result of the Mexican War, which ended that year.

27. The correct answer is (5). No part of Florida, which lies east of the Mississippi River, was annexed by the United States until after the Louisiana Purchase (west of the river).

28. The correct answer is (3). The president's power to conduct foreign affairs and negotiate treaties means opening talks with a foreign power, such as Russia, clearly falls within the scope of presidential powers. The president can only pardon people convicted of federal crimes, choice (1), and can only issue a pardon if the person is convicted, choice (2). The president cannot fire Supreme Court justices, choice (4), who are appointed for life, nor can the president repeal a law passed by Congress, choice (5).

29. The correct answer is (2). Only this statement defines *Glasnost* and correctly states the results of the policy. *Perestroika,* not *Glasnost,* was a policy of economic reform, choice (1). The term does not refer to the breakup of the Soviet Union into 15 separate nations, choice (3), although the policy may have helped cause this. *Glasnost* means "openness," not the lack thereof, choice (4). *Glasnost* was part of Gorbachev's political platform, but it was not successful in revitalizing communism or the Soviet Union, choice (5).

30. The correct answer is (1). Since communism and the Soviet Union itself came to an end, it is an undisputed fact that Gorbachev failed in his goal to revitalize them. Statements of what "should" have happened are statements of opinion, choices (3) and (5). Statements of right or wrong, choice

(4), are value judgments rather than facts. Statements of what "would have happened if…," choice (2), are opinions rather than statements of fact since they can never be proven or disproven.

31. The correct answer is (2). An increase in demand means that more automobiles will be purchased at any given price. So the number of automobiles exchanged will increase. Also, since demand exceeds supply, sellers will be able to set higher prices for their automobiles—at least until excess demand has been met.

32. The correct answer is (2). An income-tax reduction for the middle and lower classes might further the sorts of goals of these programs, a capital gains tax cut mainly helps wealthier investors, who are not the people that these policies and programs are aimed at helping.

33. The correct answer is (1). The Kennedy Administration's New Frontier program was responsible for the advent of Medicare, a program designed to financially help the elderly with medical-care costs.

34. The correct answer is (4). Though the *Brown* decision may have led to integration with respect to other aspects of American society as well, the most direct result of the decision was to impose integration requirements on public schools. One common way to meet the requirements was to transport white school students to predominantly African-American schools, and vice versa.

35. The correct answer is (3). The Silk Road was neither established nor used for military conquest or invasion. It was established and used to trade art and craft works and other cultural artifacts, choice (1), as well as other goods, choice (2). Its enduring and widespread use shows a universal desire to possess things that make life richer and more pleasurable, choice

(5). The fact that the network of routes was not planned out reflects the ingenuity of all the people who established and used the network, choice (4).

36. **The correct answer is (2).** The use of the Silk Road peaked during the T'ang dynasty, which the timeline indicates ruled from 618–917. The ninth century refers to the time period from 800–899.

37. **The correct answer is (4).** Standing committees wield most of the power in producing new legislation. The term of office of a senator is six years while that of a representative is two years, so choice (1) is incorrect. Each state gets two senators, but representatives are apportioned based on a state's population, so rarely does a state have the same number of each, choice (2). The Senate—not the House—has the power to ratify treaties and approve presidential appointments, choice (3). Choice (5) is wrong because there are 100 senators but 435 representatives in Congress.

38. **The correct answer is (3).** A one-time tax rebate would provide additional "pocket money" to consumers, who typically spend these sorts of windfalls on items they wouldn't otherwise buy. For many people, specialty foods at gourmet stores fall into this category. Once the money is spent, these consumers return to their prior spending habits, which would explain a temporary spike in profits.

39. **The correct answer is (1).** Reducing costs (such as salaries paid to employees) would likely have helped increase profits. The strategies presented in choices (2) and (4) clearly would have added to Garcia's costs, thereby serving to decrease profitability. Choice (3) provides a strategy that would not affect Garcia's costs either way but might hurt his business if it is less efficient without his managers. The strategy outlined in choice (5) might very well hurt Garcia's profits

if customer demand declines due to higher prices.

40. **The correct answer is (1).** The establishment of standard time did not make the trains run any differently. All of the other choices correctly state an effect of the establishment of standard time.

41. **The correct answer is (3).** The establishment of standard time was based on the assumption that it would be in the public interest to have everyone in a city, including all the railroads, running on the same standard time. The establishment of standard time goes against the view that there is too much government regulation, choice (1). The establishment of standard time zones also goes against the view that time should be determined by the sun, choice (2), and that doing otherwise violates the laws of nature, choice (4). The establishment of standard time had nothing to do with making the trains run on time, choice (5).

42. **The correct answer is (4).** Though the number of national parks nearly tripled from 1910 to 1970, the number of park visitors increased by a much higher percent. Any of the other answer choices would help to explain the disproportionate increase in the number of visitors. Choice (4) only helps explain the increase in the number of parks.

43. **The correct answer is (5).** Choice (5) provides accurate factual information about both parks. This information helps explain why both parks are so well-known, which no doubt contributes to their popularity. The statement in choice (1) applies to most national parks. The statements in choices (2) and (3) refer only to one park or the other, and the statement in choice (4) is an opinion.

44. **The correct answer is (1).** The map shows that most of the lands to the south had been settled long before

1791. All of the other answer choices make sense as reasons for the choice of location.

45. The correct answer is (1). Only the federal government has the military needed to ensure that another country abides by the terms of a treaty.

46. The correct answer is (3). The key word is *unnecessary*, because the drawing shows that the tank and its occupants have little to do except decorate a garden.

47. The correct answer is (1). The cartoon implies that NATO's reason for existence (the Soviet Union) has disappeared. Therefore, the cartoonist would probably agree that a powerful enemy once again would lead to a stronger NATO.

48. The correct answer is (5). In the interest of defending against Soviet aggression and expansion, it would make sense for the United States to help strengthen its allies, especially the ones bordering the Soviet bloc countries.

49. The correct answer is (3). The statement by the reporter that the women "all marched with an intensity and purpose that astonished the crowds" supports the conclusion that the marchers were serious about demanding the right to vote. It would be likely that some men, choice (1), and some housewives, choice (5), partici-

pated in the march, but the reporter doesn't provide evidence one way or the other in this passage. There is also no information about the views of the women's husbands, choice (2). The seriousness of the women indicates a determination that would not likely be based on the view that they could not accomplish their goal, choice (4)..

50. The correct answer is (4). The women's suffrage movement focused entirely on getting the right to vote while the civil rights movement involved a struggle or a broader range of rights including the right to vote, the right to be served at whites-only public facilities, and the right to be free from racial discrimination in obtaining employment, education, and housing. Protest marches and a general endorsement of nonviolent protest characterized both the women's suffrage movement and the civil rights movement, so choices (1) and (5) are incorrect. Choice (2) is wrong because only the civil rights movement could effectively use voter registration drives as a tactic to obtain rights. Neither movement quickly achieved its goals; both struggles continued for decades, so choice (3) is also incorrect.

Science

1. (1)	11. (3)	21. (4)	31. (4)	41. (2)
2. (3)	12. (5)	22. (1)	32. (3)	42. (4)
3. (1)	13. (3)	23. (3)	33. (5)	43. (2)
4. (5)	14. (2)	24. (2)	34. (4)	44. (3)
5. (5)	15. (4)	25. (4)	35. (5)	45. (1)
6. (3)	16. (2)	26. (2)	36. (1)	46. (2)
7. (2)	17. (4)	27. (5)	37. (2)	47. (4)
8. (1)	18. (3)	28. (3)	38. (1)	48. (5)
9. (5)	19. (5)	29. (1)	39. (4)	49. (2)
10. (4)	20. (1)	30. (4)	40. (1)	50. (2)

1. **The correct answer is (1).** The peak bone mass is lower in women than in men, and apparently it is lower in Caucasian women than in African American women. Pregnancy affects bone loss but not peak bone mass.

2. **The correct answer is (3).** The figure shows the Earth moving from one position to another relative to the Sun. Since the specific stars (and other celestial bodies visible in the early morning sky) appearing behind the Sun have changed, it appears from Earth that the Sun has moved from a position in front of one group of stars to a position in front of another group of stars.

3. **The correct answer is (1).** High-intensity exercise involves a combination of aerobic and anaerobic metabolism, whereas lighter exercise requires energy produced only through aerobic metabolism.

4. **The correct answer is (5).** 4.0 arbitrary units of energy are used when exercise intensity is at 80 percent. Cycling up a short but steep hill involves strenuous, intense exertion (mainly involving your leg muscles), which does not require oxygen. Even so, your cells will probably process quite a bit of oxygen, which is why you might be short of breath by the time you reach the top.

5. **The correct answer is (5).** In its normal form, an atom has the same number of protons and neutrons. It becomes less stable when it becomes an isotope by gaining or losing neutrons.

6. **The correct answer is (3).** An atom of an element becomes an isotope by either gaining or losing neutrons. The isotope carbon 14 has gained two neutrons from its normal form carbon 12, which contains an equal number of protons and neutrons—six of each.

7. **The correct answer is (2).** It is common knowledge that a termite population can grow dramatically to consume all available wood in its immediate environment (for example, in a house's frame). If the wood disappears, the termite population will decline very quickly.

8. **The correct answer is (1).** There is an inverse relationship between wavelength and frequency. The force of the hammer has not changed, so the wave velocity (v) remains constant in the formula $v = \lambda f$. Since the wave frequency (f) has increased, the wavelength (λ) must decrease.

9. **The correct answer is (5).** If the flowers of a particular species are always either one color (for example, red) or another (for example, white), then through a sufficient number of experiments, you can draw clear conclusions about the probability of a daughter plant's flowers being one color as opposed to the other. But drawing such conclusions is difficult when there are many subtle variations of one physical trait. (There may be too many combinations to track, and the variations may be too subtle to classify.)

10. **The correct answer is (4).** Racing dirt bikes around remote meadowlands clears away vegetation from the paths the bikers take. This leaves bare earth, which can erode more easily than earth that is covered with rooted vegetation.

11. **The correct answer is (3).** Cones are the only cell types in a retina that recognize color, and so the fact that dogs don't see color is explained by the absence of any cones in their retinas.

12. **The correct answer is (5).** Both the incline plane (left) and the pulley (right) reduce the magnitude, or intensity, of effort required to move the load from one level up to another. The total force required is still the same, but that force is spread out over a greater distance. (In the case of the incline plane, the increase in distance is the length of the ramp in excess of the vertical distance; in the case of the pulley, the increase in distance is the extra length of the rope that the pulley requires.)

13. **The correct answer is (3).** The cell has swollen due to the reproduction of the virus within the cell. At some point, the virus particles are likely to breach (break through) the cell wall, releasing themselves to spread to other cells, where the process will repeat itself.

14. **The correct answer is (2).** It is common knowledge that oxygen, hydrogen, and nitrogen are among the most abundant elements in nature. These elements are usually found bonded with elements by covalence, which means that they have reacted with other elements to form covalent bonds.

15. **The correct answer is (4).** In the right-hand graph, some energy in addition to what was available from the reactants has been absorbed during the formation of the products. The amount is the difference between the energy of the reactants and the energy of the products. Letter C, choice (3), identifies the amount of activation energy. The left-hand graph with letters A and B, choices (1) and (2), represents an exothermic reaction. Letter E, choice (5), identifies the energy available from the original substances *plus* the external energy absorbed in the endothermic reaction.

16. **The correct answer is (2).** Fanning a fire simply blows more oxygen atoms toward it, so that more will come in contact and react with the wood's carbon atoms in an exothermic reaction.

17. **The correct answer is (4).** The term "cell regeneration" aptly describes the development of a new limb consisting of the same types of specialized cells that were lost. Choice (1) is incorrect because to clone is to create a duplicate of a cell or group of cells, but not to regenerate the original cells(s) that were lost.

18. **The correct answer is (3).** The animal shown in choice (3) is the only one that exhibits radial, or circular, symmetry around a center. (The picture shows a jellyfish.)

19. **The correct answer is (5).** Each shake of a blanket creates a wave of energy emanating from where you are gripping the blanket. The wave travels outward, toward the far end

of the blanket, while the oscillation is up and down—perpendicular to the outward direction of the wave.

20. **The correct answer is (1).** Pesticides are applied to crops while they are growing in the fields. This activity occurs during the initial link of the supply chain: feedstock production.

21. **The correct answer is (4).** An increase in blood flow and oxygen consumption in skeletal muscles facilitates the sort of muscle activity needed for bursts of strength, agility, and energy. The adrenal glands' response is an evolutionary survival mechanism—for fighting or fleeing from predators and other dangers.

22. **The correct answer is (1).** The star with the greater mass must have the smaller orbit, which means that Star 1 has the greater mass. Both stars must orbit around the center of mass, and so that center must be within region B.

23. **The correct answer is (3).** Cloning *reduces* variety, and so choice (3) is not an objective that cloning would seek to achieve.

24. **The correct answer is (2).** Hydrogen diffuses (moves to mix with other gases) more quickly than any other element. Thus, in the illustration, it is moving through the porous cup wall to mix with the air in the cup. This forces the air in the tube down into the water, from which that air escapes in the form of bubbles.

25. **The correct answer is (4).** The theory provided in choice (4) makes sense. When a wave front reaches the water surface at an angle, one end reaches the water first, and the other end reaches the water last. Water slows the speed of light, so the leading edge of the wave front slows first as the trailing end "catches up" to it. This is why light appears to bend when it enters water at an angle to the surface.

26. **The correct answer is (2).** The first illustration shows poles forming in the cell, connected by spindles. The next illustration shows the cell's nucleus broken down, allowing the chromosomes to line up across the center of the spindle. The third illustration shows each chromosome splitting apart into two identical chromatids, as one half of the cell pulls the matching sets of chromosomes apart. It appears that the cell is attempting to reproduce itself.

27. **The correct answer is (5).** Exploiting resources on the Moon is probably the ultimate adaptation strategy, since it does not depend at all on what occurs here on Earth in terms of climate change. Each of the other four policies seeks to slow or halt pollution or climate change.

28. **The correct answer is (3).** The Kelvin scale starts at "absolute zero," which is −273° on the Celsius scale. Starting with the lowest possible temperature avoided the need to use negative numbers.

29. **The correct answer is (1).** Since *chlorophyll a* absorbs mainly blue and red wavelengths, it must reflect green light. Green, red, and blue are the three additive primaries in the color spectrum, and it is this property of *chlorophyll a* that gives green plants their color.

30. **The correct answer is (4).** To determine temperature for a particular time, refer to the numbers in the chart's left-hand scale. During the Medieval Warming Period, temperatures peaked at about 31 degrees (C). During the Little Ice Age, they hit a low of about 29 degrees (C).

31. **The correct answer is (4).** The chart shows the Younger Dryas Interval as a period of comparatively low temperatures (cold weather) and low amounts of snow accumulation. Common sense tells you that snow accumulation can

decrease due to either a decrease in precipitation (specifically, snow) or a sufficient rise in temperature that melts snow (or both). Since the chart tells us that temperatures were low during the Younger Dryas Interval, the best explanation for the low snow accumulation is that precipitation was low—in other words, the weather was relatively dry.

32. The correct answer is (3). The chart shows a continual series—going back 20,000 years—of warming-cooling cycles, accompanied by cycles in the amount of snow accumulation.

33. The correct answer is (5). The skin of a banana reflects the wavelengths for yellow while absorbing all other wavelengths, including blue.

34. The correct answer is (4). Dirt particles are large and dense, and they will settle to the bottom (of a lake, for example) if left undisturbed. Paint, fog, and milk are colloids. Gasoline is a solution.

35. The correct answer is (5). The chart shows all hominids, including *Homo sapiens* (humans), branching from "Primates" (the trunk at the bottom of the chart).

36. The correct answer is (1). The chart shows the "Gorilla" branch as an offshoot of the "Orangutan" branch, which means that gorillas are direct descendants of orangutans.

37. The correct answer is (2). Humid air contains more water vapor than dry air. The moister air will attract less water to the leaf's surface, which is where transpiration occurs.

38. The correct answer is (1). A plant's oxygen is released into the air in the form of water and water vapor. Cacti have little leaf surface compared to most other plants. Thus they lose very little water through evaporation.

39. The correct answer is (4). The half-life of radium 229 is 4 minutes.

In other words, it takes four minutes for half its current mass to decay.

40. The correct answer is (1). The core described in the paragraph is iron. Iron loses its magnetism when a magnetic field is removed, which in this case would occur when the switch is turned off.

41. The correct answer is (2). When an object is bounced off the Earth's surface, the rotational movement alters the object's path in the direction of the Earth's rotation (though the degree of the deflection is very slight).

42. The correct answer is (4). The first sentence of the second paragraph tells us that corals and lichen both maintain a mutually beneficial relationship with photosynthesizing algae. So we know that both corals and lichen are primary consumers, while algae are producers. But the paragraph also tells us that some corals eat other animals, while other corals rely on algae for their food. So some corals are secondary consumers, while others are primary consumers.

43. The correct answer is (2). As the illustration shows, nearly half of the glucose manufactured by eating food is directed to the muscles, either for immediate use as energy or for storage to be converted to energy later. Competitive athletes burn more fuel for energy than most people, and therefore they must produce more glucose by eating more.

44. The correct answer is (3). A bat can make high-frequency sounds (some of which humans can't hear) that it listens to as it echoes off the walls of a dark cave. By processing this information, the bat is able to map the logistics of the cave and fly around its interior without colliding into the cave walls.

45. The correct answer is (1). The table shows that the lowest frequency that a porpoise can hear is *higher* than the lowest frequency that humans can hear, which is given as 20 Hz, or 20,000 kHz. (1 Hz = 1000 kHz.) So, by eliminating all sonar frequencies above 20,000 kHz, the sonar would no longer interfere with the ability of porpoises to hear other sounds.

46. **The correct answer is (2).** Low atmospheric pressure means lighter air that exerts less downward pressure on the Earth. Light air suggests that it is warming, and hence expanding and rising. Warm water vapor is more likely to condense, resulting in rain or other forms of precipitation.

47. **The correct answer is (4).** As your cells metabolize glucose for energy, they leave by-products (waste) in the fluids in and around your body's cells. These by-products must be filtered out of this "interstitial" fluid and removed from the body. As the diagram shows, this is the function of the renal system.

48. **The correct answer is (5).** Positively charged particles and negatively charged particles are attracted to each other. Hence the positively charged hydrogen atoms in a water molecule and the negatively charged oxygen atoms in other water molecules will

form a magnetic (but not a chemical) bond, as the illustration shows. The process repeats and builds upon itself, as water molecules link together in lattice patterns that characterize snowflakes.

49. **The correct answer is (2).** Among the explanations given for *lyngbya*'s survival is that, when it dies and decays, the decaying matter, which is rich in the nutrients the strain needs to grow, sinks to the sea floor where it nourishes the next generation of *lyngbya*. In this sense, the strain has survived partly by its ability to sustain itself rather than relying on external nutrient sources.

50. **The correct answer is (2).** It is safe to donate blood type O for transfusions with any of the four types. Since it is the most useful type, it is probably in higher demand at facilities performing transfusions than any of the other three types.

Language Arts, Reading

1. (4)	9. (2)	17. (2)	25. (1)	33. (2)
2. (3)	10. (5)	18. (5)	26. (4)	34. (5)
3. (1)	11. (4)	19. (1)	27. (2)	35. (4)
4. (2)	12. (4)	20. (2)	28. (2)	36. (3)
5. (5)	13. (5)	21. (3)	29. (5)	37. (1)
6. (4)	14. (1)	22. (2)	30. (3)	38. (2)
7. (3)	15. (5)	23. (4)	31. (1)	39. (3)
8. (1)	16. (1)	24. (3)	32. (4)	40. (5)

1. **The correct answer is (4).** After finishing his bath, Babbitt prepares his bed and sleeping-porch. It seems that he is about to go to bed, and there is nothing in the passage that suggests otherwise or that this behavior is not routine for him.

2. **The correct answer is (3).** The second paragraph points out that Babbitt considers himself "virtuous" in the possession of all the nice things that surround him. However, the final paragraph makes clear that Babbitt has been led to think about himself this way by advertisers. In short, Babbitt is a person who does not think independently about what he wants, or should want, out of life. One word that characterizes an unwillingness to think for oneself about such things is *mindless*.

3. **The correct answer is (1).** In the passage, Babbitt tears up a frayed collar with abandon, a moment that the author describes as "a flash of melodrama such as he found in traffic-driving." The clear suggestion here is that Babbitt enjoys driving somewhat heedlessly (carelessly).

4. **The correct answer is (2).** The soap seems to be evading Babbitt, and by his words he seems to be scolding the soap. The word *corrected* does not make

sense in this context. (To *reprove* is to rebuke.)

5. **The correct answer is (5).** The final sentence of the passage makes it clear that people like Babbitt (wrongly) consider having these "standard" things symbols of a life lived with excellence, joy, passion, and wisdom.

6. **The correct answer is (4).** Babbitt seems concerned about appearances—how his possessions, surroundings, and even his opinions reflect on his socio-economic status in this community. Active membership in a country club is a common means of enhancing that status.

7. **The correct answer is (3).** The memo introduces new policies and procedures designed as a guideline for employees to follow regarding the time cards. It is the goal of the management that all employees act appropriately.

8. **The correct answer is (1).** Management has carefully written the document in a very matter-of-fact, unemotional tone so employees are not offended or made uneasy by the memo.

9. **The correct answer is (2).** Based on the information in the memo, especially the opening sentence, the most likely scenario is that at least some SnapRite employees have been

careless or even deceptive in recording their work hours.

10. **The correct answer is (5).** Sales representatives are generally paid either on a commission or salary basis, and therefore would not need to record hours worked. All other types of employees listed are typically paid by the hour.

11. **The correct answer is (4).** Since the employee is not late by *more than* 2 minutes, the employee could not be suspended on this basis. However, punching out 3 minutes early violates the policy against punching out more than 2 minutes early. The employee is subject to suspension because in committing the violation *every day,* the employee clearly has broken the rule at least three times during a 30-day period.

12. **The correct answer is (4).** Higgins suggests that he became bored with the party after a few minutes of nervousness. In his opinion, dinner carried on far too long, and he had nobody to talk to except a "damned fool of a fashionable woman." He goes on to characterize the entire event as "purgatory."

13. **The correct answer is (5).** Higgins does not seem to notice that Eliza has brought him his slippers, and he fails to acknowledge Pickering's compliments toward her. By throwing Higgins's slippers at him, Eliza vents her resentment for his failing to acknowledge her or her role in helping him win a bet that day.

14. **The correct answer is (1).** The passage's initial stage direction suggests that Eliza had been behaving in a way that Higgins expects of her—fetching his slippers, then sitting quietly nearby, probably awaiting his next request.

15. **The correct answer is (5).** Pickering observes that socialites like those attending the party never learn how to behave with true style because they mistakenly assume it will come to them naturally due to their social position. Higgins agrees with Pickering, remarking that "the silly people don't know their own silly business."

16. **The correct answer is (1).** Pickering indicates that "Eliza was doing it so well," (line 37) and adds in lines 42–44 that "[t]here's always something *professional* about doing something superlatively well."

17. **The correct answer is (2).** The action described in choice (2) reveals Eliza to be a practical, calculating person who makes decisions based on "head" rather than "heart."

18. **The correct answer is (5).** In lines 1 and 2, the speaker observes the points of "your" open-handed fingers poking through blades of grass like "rosy blooms."

19. **The correct answer is (1).** In the poem, the speaker begins by addressing someone else (notice "your" in lines 1 and 3), and then refers to himself or herself as well (notice "our" in lines 5 and 12, and "us" in line 11). References to a "close-companioned inarticulate hour" and to "two-fold silence" in lines 13 and 14 both suggest that the speaker is accompanied by one other person: a close companion whom the speaker loves (see line 14). In all likelihood, then, it is that person whom the speaker is addressing throughout the poem.

20. **The correct answer is (2).** Notice that the octet (lines 1–8) and the sestet (lines 9–14) close by noting the silence of the hour in which the speaker finds himself or herself. Moreover, in line 14, the speaker characterizes this experience as a "song of love," clearly showing an appreciation for the quiet of the noon hour.

21. **The correct answer is (3).** When the speaker exclaims, "clasp we to our hearts"... this ... hour" (lines 12–13),

facebook.com/petersonspublishing

the speaker probably means that "we" (the speaker and a companion) cherish the noon hour as a valuable gift (perhaps from Nature or from God).

22. **The correct answer is (2).** In lines 5–7, the speaker describes the surrounding fields with "silver edge," which most likely refers to a hedge that establishes the pasture's perimeter, or border.

23. **The correct answer is (4).** In both lines 8 and 13, the poet uses a word in a way that goes beyond its basic definition. (This device is called *connotation*.) To express a quality of *silence* (line 8), the poet uses the adjective *visible* in a more figurative, broader sense—to mean "conspicuous or obvious"—than that which the word ordinarily suggests: able to be seen. Similarly, in line 13, the poet uses the adjective *inarticulate* in a broader, more imaginative sense—to mean "peaceful or quiet"—than that which the word ordinarily suggests: unable to speak fluently or clearly.

24. **The correct answer is (3).** As the passage begins, Edel is lying at the top of the stairs. We know that Edel had fallen because the narrator reveals that "it is only when she has fallen that she comes to her senses" (lines 16–17).

25. **The correct answer is (1).** Through the narrator, Edel is using the word *unpalatable* (line 19) to describe the situation in which Norah is in the kitchen watching television while Edel is lying stricken on the floor upstairs. This situation is most certainly an unpleasant one for Edel.

26. **The correct answer is (4).** The narrator tells us that Norah is "eating a meal she had prepared for both of them" (lines 48–49).

27. **The correct answer is (2).** According to the narrator, Edel knows Norah is eating a meal at the table because she "can hear the lonely scrape of cutlery"

(lines 49–50). Edel also knows her daughter has turned up the volume on the TV and can hear exactly what type of advertisement is playing.

28. **The correct answer is (2).** Edel is remembering how the house, particularly the kitchen, smelled and felt (its "air") forty years ago. She longs (deeply desires) to experience life in the house the way she once experienced it.

29. **The correct answer is (5).** The passage describes all that is going through Edel's mind and what she is aware of just after she "comes to her senses" at the top of the stairs. The passage's sole concern is with describing a particular moment in time from Edel's perspective.

30. **The correct answer is (3).** In the first paragraph, the author indicates that through her son's death she learned "what a poor slave mother may feel when her child is torn away from her," and in the second paragraph she writes that this sorrowful event instilled in her "deep compassion for . . . mothers who are separated from their children."

31. **The correct answer is (1).** The book will "contain, perhaps, an equal amount of matter" as the previous book; in other words, it may be as long. (The book will "contain facts and documents," so it will not be fictional.)

32. **The correct answer is (4).** A careful reading of the third and fourth paragraphs makes it clear that the author is referring to the horrors of slavery, which she thought she knew, but now finds she "had not begun to measure."

33. **The correct answer is (2).** In the third paragraph, the author writes, "It seems to me that the book cannot but be felt," suggesting that her readers will feel the pain she documents.

34. **The correct answer is (5).** The passage vividly conveys the sense of

emotion with which the author approaches her writing.

35. The correct answer is (4). We know that the boat is a dinghy (a tiny boat) and that the men all know from the sound of the surf that "we'll swamp sure," no doubt because of the waves. (A small boat can swamp when waves crash over its sides.)

36. The correct answer is (3). The words "Four scowling men . . ." in the next sentence (lines 52–54) strongly suggest that the remarks were intended in an angry, scornful way. Also, the narrator goes on to relate the men's attitude toward the people on shore (the life savers) by using words such as *incompetence, blindness,* and *cowardice.* The narrator's use of the words "bitter and bitter" (line 63) further suggests that the men's remarks were meant to be scornful and abusive.

37. The correct answer is (1). The captain's words in the final paragraph suggest that the boat will probably capsize or sink, after which the men will no doubt swim toward shore to save their own lives.

38. The correct answer is (2). The men express *hope* that they will soon be ashore, and they share some *lighthearted* moments before their *disappointment* that nobody on shore sees them. Underlying these other emotions is their continual *anxiety* about their situation. On the other hand, nowhere in the passage does the narrator suggest that any of the men experience *sadness* while in the boat together.

39. The correct answer is (3). The passage's most pervasive theme involves the men's common struggle against a particular force of nature: the sea.

40. The correct answer is (5). The narrator is an outside observer—someone who is not part of the story. (Dialogue between characters does *not* serve to shift the point of view away from the outside observer.)

answers practice test 3

Mathematics, Part I: Questions 1–25

1. (2)	7. (5)	12. (–3,4)	16. (5)	21. .729
2. (3)	8. (1)	13. (3)	17. (3)	22. (4)
3. (3)	9. 220	14. 7/20 or 0.35	18. 112	23. (4)
4. (2)	10. (3)		19. (1)	24. (2)
5. (2)	11. (4)	15. (3)	20. (2)	25. 71/5 or 14.2
6. (3)				

1. **The correct answer is (2).** Calculate the discount rate using the original price: $\frac{10}{75} = 13\frac{1}{3}\%$ or, rounding to the nearest tenth of a percent, 13.3.

2. **The correct answer is (3).** Felicia paid $16.20 for the items she bought ($20.00 – $3.80). At $2.70 each, six bags of apples cost $16.20.

3. **The correct answer is (3).** $ab^2c^2 =$ $3 \times 9 \times \frac{1}{9} = \frac{27}{9} = 3$.

4. **The correct answer is (2).** The cubes will leave a 1-inch gap at one end of the box's 15-inch side. The rectangular face at that end measures 10 × 12 inches, and so 120 cubic inches of pellets are required to fill the void.

5. **The correct answer is (2).** The question asks you to select the choice that does NOT describe sales totaling *at least* 10,000. Choice (2) describes 1.7K + 4.9K + 2.2K = 9.8K sales, which is less than $10,000. Choice (1) describes 8.5K + 1.9K = 10.4K sales. Choice (3) describes 7.5K + 1.0K + 2.0 + 0.8 = 11.3K sales. Choice (4) describes 4.9K + 5.1K = 10.0K sales. Choice (5) describes 8.5K + 4.9K = 13.4K sales.

6. **The correct answer is (3).** The number of basic models sold was 13,800 (the sum of all numbers in the "Basic" column, multiplied by 1000 as indicated in the note below the chart). The number of standard models sold was 29,900 (the sum of all numbers in

the "Standard" column, also multiplied by 1000). The difference is 16,100.

7. **The correct answer is (5).** There's no need to perform any calculations. This problem illustrates the distributive law: $a(b + c) = ab + ac$. Choice (5) correctly applies this property (you can ignore the variable x):

   $52(31 + 27) = (52)(31) + (52)(27)$.

8. **The correct answer is (1).** Isolate $\sqrt[3]{p + q}$ on one side of the equation, then "cube" both sides:

$$\sqrt[3]{p + q} = -4$$
$$\left(\sqrt[3]{p + q}\right)^3 = (-4)^3$$
$$p + q = -64$$

9. **The correct answer is 220.** The quilt consists of 18 squares, each measuring 10 inches per side. After rearranging the squares, the resulting rectangle will consist of 2 rows of 9 squares. Each side of 2 rows is 10 × 2 = 20 inches in length, and each side of 9 rows is 10 × 9 = 90 inches in length. The perimeter = 2(20) + 2(90) = 220 inches.

10. **The correct answer is (3).** To determine Joe's time-and-a-half pay rate, divide $13.50 by 2 ($6.75) and add to the $13.50 he usually makes per hour. His time-and-a-half rate is $20.25. Multiply $13.50 by 40, and then multiply $20.25 by 6. Finally, add these two figures together:

    $13.50 × 40 = $540
    $20.25 × 6 = $121.50
    $540 + $121.50 = $661.50

11. **The correct answer is (4).** Before 4 pairs of socks were removed, the drawer contained 24 pairs of blue socks ($60 \times 40\% = 24$) and 36 pairs of gray socks. ($24 + 36 = 60$). After removing 4 pairs of blue socks, the drawer contains 20 pairs of blue socks and 36 gray socks. Therefore, the ratio of gray pairs to blue pairs is 36 to 20, or 9 to 5.

12. **The correct answer is (–3,4).** You can express the midpoint's coordinates using the midpoint formula:

$$M = \left(\frac{x_1 + x_2}{2}, \frac{y_1 + y_2}{2} \right)$$
$$= \left(\frac{5 + (-11)}{2}, \frac{2 + 6}{2} \right)$$
$$= \left(\frac{-6}{2}, \frac{8}{2} \right)$$
$$= (-3, 4)$$

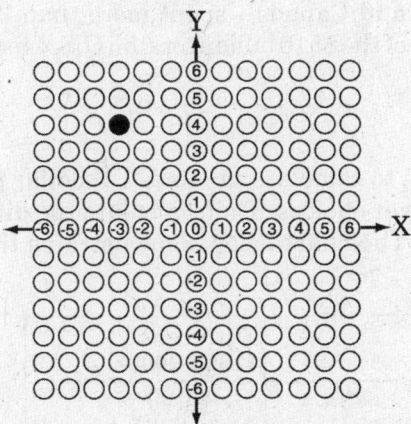

13. **The correct answer is (3).** After one year, Brianna's initial $1000 deposit grows to $1040 ($1000 \times 1.04$). Upon her second deposit, her balance is $1040 + $1000 = $2040. That sum then earns 4% interest, and the balance after the second year = $2040 \times 1.04 = $2121.60.

14. **The correct answer is 7/20 or .35.** First find the LCD and add the two fractions: $\frac{5}{20} + \frac{8}{20} = \frac{13}{20}$. The remaining horses account for $1 - \frac{13}{20} = \frac{7}{20}$, or 35%, of the horses.

15. **The correct answer is (3).** From beginning to end, the seven end-of-month share prices for CompuWin stock were approximately: $26, $45, $46, $33, $28, $17, and $19. Of these seven values, the middle one (the median) is $28.

16. **The correct answer is (5).** The investor paid about $800 for 40 shares of Ardent stock (priced at about $20 per share), and then sold those 40 shares for about $2200 (priced at about $55 per share). Accordingly, the investor's profit amounted to approximately $1400.

17. **The correct answer is (3).** The volume of a pyramid with a square base = $\frac{1}{3}$ edge^2 × height. Given a volume of 125 and height of 15, here is how you can solve for e^2:

$$125 = \frac{1}{3}e^2 \times 15$$
$$375 = 15e^2$$
$$25 = e^2$$

18. **The correct answer is 112.** Since the two lines are parallel, the two triangles are similar (the same shape), and their corresponding angles are congruent ($x = p$ and $y = q$). For any triangle, the three interior angle measures total 180°. Therefore, $x + y = 112$. Substituting p for x gives you the answer to the question: $p + y = 112$.

19. **The correct answer is (1).** Set up and solve an equation that expresses the gallons-to-liters proportion. Letting x equal the gallon equivalent of 80 liters:

$$\frac{1}{3.785} = \frac{x}{80}$$
$$3.785x = 80$$
$$x = \frac{80}{3.785} \approx 21.14$$

Among the five alternatives, choice (1) provides the smallest tank size that will accommodate 21.14 gallons (80 liters).

20. The correct answer is (2). Two of the walls are 12 feet by 8 feet, and one wall is 9 feet by 8 feet. Find the area of the three walls:

2×12 feet $\times 8$ feet $= 192$ square feet
1×9 feet $\times 8$ feet $= 72$ square feet

The total area of the three walls is 192 square feet $+ 72$ square feet $= 264$ square feet. Since wallpaper is sold by the square yard, it is necessary to convert from square feet to square yards.

Since 9 square feet $= 1$ square yard,

264 square feet / 9 square feet $= 29\frac{1}{3}$ square yards.

From the information provided, you know that each wallpaper roll contains 4 square yards of wallpaper. So $29\frac{1}{3}$

square yards divided by $4 = 7\frac{1}{3}$ rolls.

Since wallpaper is only sold by the full roll, you will need to purchase 8 rolls, choice (2).

21. The correct answer is .729. You can determine the constant multiple by dividing 0.81 by 0.9. The quotient is 0.9. To find the third term, multiply the second term (0.81) by the same multiple: $0.81 \times 0.9 = .729$.

22. The correct answer is (4). In 2000, the UK accounted for 5% of U.S. export dollars, while Taiwan accounted for 3%. The difference was 2% of the $575 billion total. Compute the dollar difference: $575b \times 0.02 = \$11.5$ billion.

23. The correct answer is (4). First, express $20 billion as a percentage of $510 billion: $\frac{20}{510} \approx 3.9\%$. In the year 1999, each of five individual purchasers—Germany, UK, Mexico, Japan, and Canada—spent more than 3.9% of the $510 billion total on U.S. exports.

24. The correct answer is (2). The first step is to calculate the total US-dollar purchases for 1999 and 2000 for each of the answer choices. Then calculate the difference in those purchases from 1999 to 2000. The chart below demonstrates these calculations.

Country	1999	2000	Difference (1999-2000)
Taiwan	$510 billion × 3% = $15.3 billion	$575 billion × 3% = $17.25 billion	Increased $1.95 billion
Mexico	$510 billion × 10% = $51 billion	$575 billion × 9% = $51.75 billion	Increased $750,000 thousand
Canada	$510 billion × 23% = $117.3 billion	$575 billion × 23% = $132.25 billion	Increased $14.95 billion
UK	$510 billion × 6% = $30.6 billion	$575 billion × 5% = $28.75 billion	Decreased $1.85 billion
Germany	$510 billion × 4% = $20.4 billion	$575 billion × 4% = $23 billion	Increased $2.6 billion

All of the countries increased their US-dollar purchases except the UK, so answer choice (4) can be eliminated. Taiwan, Canada, and Germany all had increases in the billions of dollars, but Mexico only increased by $750,000. The question asks for the LEAST increase, so the correct answer is Mexico, choice (2).

25. The correct answer is 71/5 or 14.2. Between noon and 5 p.m. on Sunday, 4 ounces dripped into the bucket. The drip rate is 4 ounces in 5 hours, or $\frac{4}{5}$ ounce per hour. 9 hours later, at 2 a.m. on Monday, an additional $\frac{4}{5} \times 9 = \frac{36}{5}$ ounces will have dripped into the bucket. The total accumulation of water is $7 + \frac{36}{5} = \frac{71}{5}$, or 14.2 ounces.

Mathematics, Part II: Questions 26–50

26. 1/2 or 0.5	31. (5)	36. (1)	41. 98	46. (2)
27. (1)	32. (5)	37. 63	42. (5)	47. (5)
28. (3)	33. (2)	38. (5)	43. (4)	48. (3)
29. (5)	34. (3)	39. (2)	44. (4)	49. (2)
30. 2/5 or .4	35. (1)	40. (4)	45. (4)	50. (4)

26. The correct answer is 1/2 or 0.5. First, add the fractions:
$$\frac{1}{3} + \frac{1}{6} = \frac{2+1}{6} = \frac{3}{6}, \text{ or } \frac{1}{2}.$$
Subtracting the total from 1 (the whole pizza) leaves one half of the pizza.

27. The correct answer is (1). For each year, the gray portion of the bar indicates sales of oral medication. In 2003, those sales totaled a bit more than $1 million, but in 2004, they totaled no more than $1 million.

28. The correct answer is (3). The line has a slope of $m = \frac{5-1}{3-(-2)} = \frac{4}{5}$.

29. The correct answer is (5). Because the number you are writing is to the 8th power, shift the decimal point 8 places to the right.

30. The correct answer is 2/5 or .4. There are 5 candidates, and so the possibility that one of two specific candidates being elected is 2 in 5, or
$$\frac{2}{5} \cdot \frac{2}{5} = \frac{4}{10} = 0.4$$

31. The correct answer is (5). For each expression, combine by multiplication:

choice (1): $250 \times 4 = 1000$

choice (2): $400 \times \frac{2}{5} = 400 \times 0.4 = 160$

choice (3): $4000 \times 0.04 = 160$

choice (4): $\frac{1}{4} \times 4000 = 0.25 \times 4000$
$$= 1000$$

choice (5): $40 \times 40 = 1600$

32. The correct answer is (5). If you multiply the second equation by 4, and then isolate the m-term, it reveals that the two equations are the same:
$$4 \times \frac{3n}{4} = 4(3 - m)$$
$$3n = 12 - 4m$$
$$4m = 12 - 3n$$

Given one linear equation in two variables, there are an infinite number of possible values for each variable.

33. **The correct answer is (2).** The median of distribution E = the average of 6 and 9 (the two middle terms) = 7.5. Each of the other four measurements has a value of 7.

34. **The correct answer is (3).** The quantities described in choices (1), (2), and (5) are all negative (less than 0). Choices (3) and (4) describe positive values greater than 1, but x^2 is the square of $|x|$ and therefore must be greater in value.

35. **The correct answer is (1).** Think of Cynthia's average rate as the average of eight equally weighted one-hour trips. Seven of those trips receive a weight of 50, and one of the trips receives a weight of 60. You can express this as follows: $\dfrac{7(50) + 60}{8}$.

36. **The correct answer is (1).** Jennifer's weekly salary is $500. Given a 2:3 ratio, Carl's salary must be $750.

37. **The correct answer is 63.** The answer to the question is the least value of x that is a multiple of all three denominators—in other words, the question asks for the least common denominator. Work your way up in multiples of the largest denominator, 9, you'll find that 63 is the lowest multiple that is also a multiple of both 7 and 3. Thus, $x = 63$.

38. **The correct answer is (5).** The total rent is $D + 100$, which must be divided by the number of students (M).

39. **The correct answer is (2).** To answer the question, determine the height of the News (white) portion of the graph's right-hand bar.

40. **The correct answer is (4).** Together, the "Entertainment" and "Other" portions of the middle bar (19–24) account for about 9 of the 17 total hours. Since

$17 \times 6 = 102$ (just over 100), you can multiply 9 by 6 to estimate the percent.

41. **The correct answer is 98.** Apply the formula for the area of a trapezoid:

$\dfrac{1}{2}$ (base$_1$ + base$_2$) × height = $\dfrac{1}{2}$ (14) × 14 = 7 × 14 = 98 square centimeters.

42. **The correct answer is (5).** First, factor out x from the trinomial: $x(x^2 + 3x + 2)$. The trinomial can now be factored into the two binomials provided in choice (5).

43. **The correct answer is (4).** $3x$ is a multiple of 3; thus, adding 5 to that number yields a number that is not a multiple of 3. Choice (1) is incorrect because $x > 0$ and therefore must equal 3 or some multiple of 3. Choices (2), (3), and (5) are incorrect because any integer multiplied by 3 is a multiple of 3, and any multiple of 3 (such as 6 or 18) added to a multiple of 3 is also a multiple of 3.

44. **The correct answer is (4).** For any right triangle, the tangent of one acute angle is the reciprocal of the tangent of the other acute angle. Thus, their product is 1.

45. **The correct answer is (4).** Equate Carrie's age in 8 years ($C + 8$) to twice Ben's age in 8 years ($B + 8$), and then solve for C:

$$C + 8 = 2(B + 8)$$
$$C = 2(B + 8) - 8$$
$$C = 2B + 16 - 8$$
$$C = 2B + 8$$

46. **The correct answer is (2).** The key to this problem is in determining the interior angles of the various triangles formed by the runways. The interior angle formed by the 120° turn from runway 1 to 2 is 60° (a 180° turn would reverse the airplane's direction). Similarly, the interior angle formed by the 135° turn from runway 1 to 3 is 45° (180° − 135°). Two right-triangle

"angle triplets" emerge: a 45°-45°-90° triplet and a 30°-60°-90° triplet, as shown in the figure below. Since the sum of any triangle's interior angles is 180°, the remaining angles can also be determined:

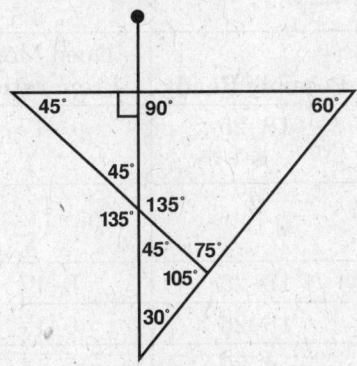

The only angle measure listed among the answer choices that does not appear in the above figure is 55°.

47. **The correct answer is (5).** The table does not indicate the highest temperature recorded during April, and so it is not possible to determine the range of temperatures for April.

48. **The correct answer is (3).** According to the table, high temperatures of 41°–45° were recorded only on *three* days in April.

49. **The correct answer is (2).** *f*(*x*) varies inversely with *x*. In other words, as the value of *x* increases, the value of *y* decreases. Since *x* is squared, the relationship is exponential, and the graph must be curved (not a straight line). Only choice (2) provides a graph that fits this functional relationship.

50. **The correct answer is (4).** The area of a circle = πr^2. Letting the radius of the smaller circle = *r*, the radius of the larger circle = 2*r*, and its area = $\pi(2r)^2$, or $4\pi r^2$. The ratio of the smaller circle's area to the larger circle's area is $\pi r^2 : 4\pi r^2$, or 1:4.

answers

practice test 3

ARE YOU READY TO TAKE THE GED®?

Now that you have spent a great deal of time and effort studying for the GED® and taking this Practice Test, hopefully you are well-prepared to take the GED® exam. But, it's best to make sure that you are completely ready. Check your scores from this Practice Test on the table below to see where you stand.

	All Set—Well-Prepared	Most Likely Ready	Possibly Ready	Need More Preparation
Language Arts, Writing, Part I	38–50	26–37	18–25	0–17
Language Arts, Writing, Part II	4	3	2	1
Social Studies	38–50	26–37	18–25	0–17
Science	38–50	26–37	18–25	0–17
Language Arts, Reading	30–40	21–29	14–20	0–13
Mathematics	38–50	26–37	18–25	0–17

If your scores are in the "All Set—Well-Prepared" column, you are probably ready to take the actual GED® exam, and you should apply to take the test soon. If some of your scores are in the "Most Likely Ready" column, you should focus your study on those areas where you need to improve most. "Most Likely Ready" means that you are probably ready enough to earn a GED® diploma, but it's not a bad idea to spend a little more time brushing up and improving your chances to pass the actual GED® exam.

If any of your scores fell in the lowest category, take more time to review the pertinent chapters in this book—and in any high school text books, if necessary. Good luck!

Word List

A

abbreviate (verb) to make briefer, to shorten. *Because time was running out, the speaker had to abbreviate his remarks.* **abbreviation** (noun).

abrasive (adjective) irritating, grinding, rough. *The manager's rude, abrasive way of criticizing the workers was bad for morale.* **abrasion** (noun).

abridge (verb) to shorten, to reduce. *The Bill of Rights is designed to prevent Congress from abridging the rights of Americans.* **abridgment** (noun).

absolve (verb) to free from guilt, to exonerate. *The criminal jury absolved Mr. Callahan of the murder of his neighbor.* **absolution** (noun).

abstain (verb) to refrain, to hold back. *After his heart attack, William was warned by his doctor to abstain from smoking, drinking, and overeating.* **abstinence** (noun), **abstemious** (adjective).

accentuate (verb) to emphasize, to stress. *The overcast skies and chill winds only accentuate our gloomy mood.* **accentuation** (noun).

acrimonious (adjective) biting, harsh, caustic. *The election campaign became acrimonious, as the candidates traded insults and accusations.* **acrimony** (noun).

adaptable (adjective) able to be changed to be suitable for a new purpose. *Some scientists say that the mammals outlived the dinosaurs because they were more adaptable to a changing climate.* **adapt** (verb), **adaptation** (noun).

adulation (noun) extreme admiration. *Few young actors have received greater adulation than did Marlon Brando after his performance in* A Streetcar Named Desire. **adulate** (verb), **adulatory** (adjective).

adversary (noun) an enemy or opponent. *When the former Soviet Union became an American ally, the United States lost a major adversary.* **adversarial** (adjective).

adversity (noun) misfortune. *It's easy to be patient and generous when things are going well; a person's true character is revealed under adversity.* **adverse** (adjective).

aesthetic (adjective) relating to art or beauty. *Mapplethorpe's photos may be attacked on moral grounds, but no one questions their aesthetic value—they are beautiful.* **aestheticism** (noun).

affected (adjective) false, artificial. *At one time, Japanese women were taught to speak in an affected high-pitched voice, which was thought girlishly attractive.* **affect** (verb), **affectation** (noun).

aggressive (adjective) forceful, energetic, and attacking. *Some believe that a football player needs a more aggressive style of play than a soccer player.* **aggression** (noun).

alacrity (noun) promptness, speed. *Thrilled with the job offer, he accepted with alacrity— "Before they can change their minds!" he thought.* **alacritous** (adjective).

allege (verb) to state without proof. *Some have alleged that Foster was murdered, but all the evidence points to suicide.* **allegation** (noun).

alleviate (verb) to make lighter or more bearable. *Although no cure for AIDS has been found, doctors are able to alleviate the suffering of those with the disease.* **alleviation** (noun).

ambiguous (adjective) having two or more possible meanings. *The phrase, "Let's table that discussion" is ambiguous; some think it means, "Let's discuss it now," while others think it means, "Let's save it for later."* **ambiguity** (noun).

ambivalent (adjective) having two or more contradictory feelings or attitudes; uncertain. *She was ambivalent toward her impending marriage; at times she was eager to go ahead, while at other times she wanted to call it off.* **ambivalence** (noun).

amiable (adjective) likable, agreeable, friendly. *He was an amiable lab partner, always smiling, on time, and ready to work.* **amiability** (noun).

amicable (adjective) friendly, peaceable. *Although they agreed to divorce, their settlement was amicable and they remained friends afterward.*

amplify (verb) to enlarge, expand, or increase. *Uncertain as to whether they understood, the students asked the teacher to amplify his explanation.* **amplification** (noun).

anachronistic (adjective) out of the proper time. *The reference, in Shakespeare's* Julius Caesar *to "the clock striking twelve" is anachronistic, since there were no striking timepieces in ancient Rome.* **anachronism** (noun).

anarchy (noun) absence of law or order. *For several months after the Nazi government was destroyed, there was no effective government in parts of Germany, and anarchy ruled.* **anarchic** (adjective).

anomaly (noun) something different or irregular. *The tiny planet Pluto, orbiting next to the giants Jupiter, Saturn, and Neptune, has long appeared to be an anomaly.* **anomalous** (adjective).

antagonism (noun) hostility, conflict, opposition. *As more and more reporters investigated the Watergate scandal, antagonism between Nixon and the press increased.* **antagonistic** (adjective), **antagonize** (verb).

antiseptic (adjective) fighting infection; extremely clean. *A wound should be washed with an antiseptic solution. The all-white offices were bare and almost antiseptic in their starkness.*

apathy (noun) lack of interest, concern, or emotion. *Tom's apathy toward his job could be seen in his lateness, his sloppy work, and his overall poor attitude.* **apathetic** (adjective).

arable (adjective) able to be cultivated for growing crops. *Rocky New England has relatively little arable farmland.*

arbiter (noun) someone able to settle disputes; a judge or referee. *The public is the ultimate arbiter of commercial value; it decides what sells and what doesn't.*

arbitrary (adjective) based on random or merely personal preference. *Both computers cost the same and had the same features, so in the end I made an arbitrary decision about which one to buy.*

arcane (adjective) little-known, mysterious, obscure. *Eliot's* Waste Land *is filled with arcane lore, including quotations in Latin, Greek, French, German, and Sanskrit.* **arcana** (noun, plural).

ardor (noun) a strong feeling of passion, energy, or zeal. *The young revolutionary proclaimed his convictions with an ardor that excited the crowd.* **ardent** (adjective).

arid (adjective) very dry; boring and meaningless. *The arid climate of Arizona makes farming difficult. Some find the law a fascinating topic, but for me it is an arid discipline.* **aridity** (noun).

ascetic (adjective) practicing strict self-discipline for moral or spiritual reasons. *The so-called Desert Fathers were hermits who lived an ascetic life of fasting, study, and prayer.* **asceticism** (verb).

assiduous (adjective) working with care, attention, and diligence. *Although Karen is not a naturally gifted math student, by assiduous study she managed to earn an A in trigonometry.* **assiduity** (noun).

astute (adjective) observant, intelligent, and shrewd. *Safire's years of experience in Washington and his personal acquaintance with many political insiders made him an astute commentator on politics.*

atypical (adjective) not typical; unusual. *In* The Razor's Edge, *Bill Murray, best known as a comic actor, gave an atypical dramatic performance.*

audacious (adjective) bold, daring, adventurous. *Her plan to cross the Atlantic single-handed in a 12-foot sailboat was audacious, if not reckless.* **audacity** (noun).

audible (adjective) able to be heard. *Although she whispered, her voice was picked up by the microphone, and her words were audible throughout the theater.* **audibility** (noun).

auspicious (adjective) promising good fortune; propitious. *The news that a team of British climbers had reached the summit of Everest seemed an auspicious sign for the reign of newly crowned Queen Elizabeth II.*

authoritarian (adjective) favoring or demanding blind obedience to leaders. *Despite Americans' belief in democracy, the American government has supported authoritarian regimes in other countries.* **authoritarianism** (noun)

B

belated (adjective) delayed past the proper time. *She called her mother on January 5th to offer her a belated "Happy New Year."*

belie (verb) to present a false or contradictory appearance. *Lena Horne's youthful appearance belied her long, distinguished career in show business.*

benevolent (adjective) wishing or doing good. *In old age, Carnegie used his wealth for benevolent purposes, donating large sums to found libraries and schools.* **benevolence** (noun).

berate (verb) to scold or criticize harshly. *The judge angrily berated the two lawyers for their unprofessional behavior.*

bereft (adjective) lacking or deprived of something. *Bereft of parental love, orphans sometimes grow up to be insecure.*

bombastic (adjective) inflated or pompous in style. *Old-fashioned bombastic political speeches don't work on television, which demands a more intimate style of communication.* **bombast** (noun).

bourgeois (adjective) middle class or reflecting middle-class values. *The Dadaists of the 1920s produced art deliberately designed to offend bourgeois art collectors, with their taste for respectable, refined, uncontroversial pictures.* **bourgeois** (noun).

buttress (noun) something that supports or strengthens; a projecting structure of masronry or wood. *The endorsement of the American Medical Association is a powerful buttress for the claims made about this new medicine. The buttress on the south wall of the Medieval castle was beginning to crumble.* **buttress** (verb).

camaraderie (noun) a spirit of friendship. *Spending long days and nights together on the road, the members of a traveling theater group develop a strong sense of camaraderie.*

candor (noun) openness, honesty, frankness. *In his memoir about the Vietnam War, former defense secretary McNamara described his mistakes with remarkable candor.* **eandid** (adjective).

capricious (adjective) unpredictable, whimsical. *The pop star Madonna has changed her image so many times that each new transformation now appears capricious rather than purposeful.* **caprice** (noun).

carnivorous (adjective) meat-eating. *The long, dagger-like teeth of the Tyrannosaurus make it obvious that this was a carnivorous dinosaur.* **carnivore** (noun).

carping (adjective) unfairly or excessively critical; querulous. *New York is famous for its demanding critics, but none is harder to please than the carping John Simon, said to have single-handedly destroyed many acting careers.* **carp** (verb).

catalytic (adjective) bringing about, causing, or producing some result. *The conditions for revolution existed in America by 1765; the disputes about taxation that arose later were the catalytic events that sparked the rebellion.* **catalyze** (verb).

caustic (adjective) burning, corrosive. *No one was safe when the satirist H. L. Mencken unleashed his caustic wit.*

censure (noun) blame, condemnation. *The news that the senator had harassed several women brought censure from many feminists.* **censure** (verb).

chaos (noun) disorder, confusion, chance. *The first few moments after the explosion were pure chaos: no one was sure what had happened, and the area was filled with people running and yelling.* **chaotic** (adjective).

circuitous (adjective) winding or indirect. *We drove to the cottage by a circuitous route so we could see as much of the surrounding countryside as possible.*

circumlocution (noun) speaking in a roundabout way; wordiness. *Legal documents often contain circumlocutions that make them difficult to understand.*

circumscribe (verb) to define by a limit or boundary. *Originally, the role of the executive branch of government was clearly circumscribed, but that role has greatly expanded over time.* **circumscription** (noun).

circumvent (verb) to get around. *When James was caught speeding, he tried to circumvent the law by offering the police officer a bribe.*

clandestine (adjective) secret, surreptitious. *As a member of the underground, Balas took part in clandestine meetings to discuss ways of sabotaging the Nazi forces.*

cloying (adjective) overly sweet or sentimental. *The deathbed scenes in the novels of Dickens are famously cloying: as Oscar Wilde said, "One would need a heart of stone to read the death of Little Nell without dissolving into tears . . . of laughter."*

cogent (adjective) forceful and convincing. *The committee members were won over to the project by the cogent arguments of the chairman.* **cogency** (noun).

cognizant (adjective) aware, mindful. *Cognizant of the fact that it was getting late, the master of ceremonies cut short the last speech.* **cognizance** (noun).

cohesive (adjective) sticking together, unified. *An effective military unit must be a cohesive team, all its members working together for a common goal.* **cohere** (verb), **cohesion** (noun).

collaborate (verb) to work together. *To create a truly successful movie, the director, writers, actors, and many others must collaborate closely.* **collaboration** (noun), **collaborative** (adjective).

colloquial (adjective) informal in language; conversational. *Some expressions from Shakespeare, such as the use of thou and thee, sound formal today but were colloquial English in Shakespeare's time.*

competent (adjective) having the skill and knowledge needed for a particular task; capable. *Any competent lawyer can draw up a will.* **competence** (noun).

complacent (adjective) smug, self-satisfied. *Until recently, American auto makers were complacent, believing that they would continue to be successful with little effort.* **complacency** (noun).

composure (noun) calm, self-assurance. *The company's president managed to keep his composure during his speech even when the teleprompter broke down, leaving him without a script.* **composed** (adjective).

conciliatory (adjective) seeking agreement, compromise, or reconciliation. *As a conciliatory gesture, the union leaders agreed to postpone a strike and to continue negotiations with management.* **conciliate** (verb), **conciliation** (noun).

concise (adjective) expressed briefly and simply; succinct. *Less than a page long, the Bill of Rights is a concise statement of the freedoms enjoyed by all Americans.* **concision** (noun).

condescending (adjective) having an attitude of superiority toward another; patronizing. *"What a cute little car!" she remarked in a condescending style. "I suppose it's the nicest one someone like you could afford!"* **condescension** (noun).

condolence (noun) pity for someone else's sorrow or loss; sympathy. *After the sudden death of Princess Diana, thousands of messages of condolence were sent to her family.* **condole** (verb).

confidant (noun) someone entrusted with another's secrets. *No one knew about Jane's engagement except Sarah, her confidant.* **confide** (verb), **confidential** (adjective).

conformity (noun) agreement with or adherence to custom or rule. *In my high school, conformity was the rule: everyone dressed the same, talked the same, and listened to the same music.* **conform** (verb), **conformist** (noun, adjective).

consensus (noun) general agreement among a group. *Among Quakers, voting traditionally is not used; instead, discussion continues until the entire group forms a consensus.*

consolation (noun) relief or comfort in sorrow or suffering. *Although we miss our dog very much, it is a consolation to know that she died quickly, without suffering.* **console** (verb).

consternation (noun) shock, amazement, dismay. *When a voice in the back of the church shouted out, "I know why they should not be married!" the entire gathering was thrown into consternation.*

consummate (verb) to complete, finish, or perfect. *The deal was consummated with a handshake and the payment of the agreed-upon fee.* **consummate** (adjective), **consummation** (noun).

contaminate (verb) to make impure. *Chemicals dumped in a nearby forest had seeped into the soil and contaminated the local water supply.* **contamination** (noun).

contemporary (adjective) modern, current; from the same time. *I prefer old-fashioned furniture rather than contemporary styles. The composer Vivaldi was roughly contemporary with Bach.* **contemporary** (noun).

contrite (adjective) sorry for past misdeeds. *The public is often willing to forgive celebrities who are involved in some scandal, as long as they appear contrite.* **contrition** (noun).

conundrum (noun) a riddle, puzzle, or problem. *The question of why an all-powerful, all-loving God allows evil to exist is a conundrum many philosophers have pondered.*

convergence (noun) the act of coming together in unity or similarity. *A remarkable example of evolutionary convergence can be seen in the shark and the dolphin, two sea creatures that developed from different origins to become very similar in form.* **converge** (verb).

convoluted (adjective) twisting, complicated, intricate. *Tax law has become so convoluted that it's easy for people to accidentally violate it.* **convolute** (verb), **convolution** (noun).

corroborating (adjective) supporting with evidence; confirming. *A passerby who had witnessed the crime gave corroborating testimony about the presence of the accused person.* **corroborate** (verb), **corroboration** (noun).

corrosive (adjective) eating away, gnawing, or destroying. *Years of poverty and hard work had a corrosive effect on her beauty.* **corrode** (verb), **corrosion** (noun).

credulity (noun) willingness to believe, even with little evidence. *Con artists fool people by taking advantage of their credulity.* **credulous** (adjective).

criterion (noun) a standard of measurement or judgment. *In choosing a design for the new taxicabs, reliability will be our main criterion.* **criteria** (plural).

critique (noun) a critical evaluation. *The editor gave a detailed critique of the manuscript, explaining its strengths and its weaknesses.* **critique** (verb).

culpable (adjective) deserving blame, guilty. *Although he committed the crime, because he was mentally ill he should not be considered culpable for his actions.* **culpability** (noun).

cumulative (adjective) made up of successive additions. *Smallpox was eliminated only through the cumulative efforts of several generations of doctors and scientists.* **accumulation** (noun), **accumulate** (verb).

curtail (verb) to shorten. *The opening round of the golf tournament was curtailed by the severe thunderstorm.*

D

debased (adjective) lowered in quality, character, or esteem. *The quality of TV journalism has been debased by the many new tabloid-style talk shows.* **debase** (verb).

debunk (verb) to expose as false or worthless. *Magician James Randi loves to debunk psychics, mediums, clairvoyants, and others who claim supernatural powers.*

decorous (adjective) having good taste; proper, appropriate. *Prior to her visit to Buckingham Palace, the young woman was instructed to demonstrate the most decorous behavior.* **decorum** (noun).

decry (verb) to criticize or condemn. *The workers continued to decry the lack of safety in their factory.*

deduction (noun) a logical conclusion, especially a specific conclusion based on general principles. *Based on what is known about the effects of greenhouse gases on atmospheric temperature, scientists have made several deductions about the likelihood of global warming.* **deduce** (verb).

delegate (verb) to give authority or responsibility. *The president delegated the vice president to represent the administration at the peace talks.* **delegate** (noun).

deleterious (adjective) harmful. *About thirty years ago, scientists proved that working with asbestos could be deleterious to one's health, producing cancer and other diseases.*

delineate (verb) to outline or describe. *Naturalists had long suspected the fact of evolution, but Darwin was the first to delineate a process—natural selection—through which evolution could occur.* **delineation** (noun)

demagogue (noun) a leader who plays dishonestly on the prejudices and emotions of his followers. *Senator Joseph McCarthy was a demagogue who used the paranoia of the anti-Communist 1950s as a way of seizing fame and power in Washington.* **demagoguery** (noun).

demure (adjective) modest or shy. *The demure heroines of Victorian fiction have given way to today's stronger, more opinionated, and more independent female characters.*

denigrate (verb) to criticize or belittle. *The firm's new president tried to· explain his plans for improving the company without appearing to denigrate the work of his predecessor.* **denigration** (noun).

depose (verb) to remove from office, especially from a throne. *Iran was once ruled by a monarch called the Shah, who was deposed in 1979.*

derelict (adjective) neglecting one's duty. *The train crash was blamed on a switchman who was derelict, having fallen asleep while on duty.* **dereliction** (noun).

derivative (adjective) taken from a particular source. *When a person first writes poetry, her poems are apt to be derivative of whatever poetry she most enjoys reading.* **derivation** (noun), **derive** (verb).

desolate (adjective) empty, lifeless, and deserted; hopeless, gloomy. *Robinson Crusoe was shipwrecked and had to learn to survive alone on a desolate island. The murder of her husband left Mary Lincoln desolate.* **desolation** (noun).

destitute (adjective) very poor. *Years of rule by a dictator who stole the wealth of the country had left the people of the Philippines destitute.* **destitution** (noun).

deter (verb) to discourage from acting. *The best way to deter crime is to ensure that criminals will receive swift and certain punishment.* **deterrence** (noun), **deterrent** (adjective).

detractor (noun) someone who belittles or disparages. *Neil Diamond has many detractors who consider his music boring, inane, and sentimental.* **detract** (verb).

deviate (verb) to depart from a standard or norm. *Having agreed upon a spending budget for the company, we mustn't deviate from it; if we do, we may run out of money soon.* **deviation** (noun).

devious (adjective) tricky, deceptive. *The CEO's devious financial tactics were designed to enrich his firm while confusing or misleading government regulators.*

didactic (adjective) intended to teach, instructive. *The children's TV show* Sesame Street *is designed to be both entertaining and didactic.*

diffident (adjective) hesitant, reserved, shy. *Someone with a diffident personality should pursue a career that involves little public contact.* **diffidence** (noun).

diffuse (verb) to spread out, to scatter. *The red dye quickly became diffused through the water, turning it a very pale pink.* **diffusion** (noun).

digress (verb) to wander from the main path or the main topic. *My high school biology teacher loved to digress from science into personal anecdotes about his college adventures.* **digression** (noun), **digressive** (adjective).

dilatory (adjective) delaying, procrastinating. *The lawyer used various dilatory tactics, hoping that his opponent would get tired of waiting for a trial and drop the case.*

diligent (adjective) working hard and steadily. *Through diligent efforts, the townspeople were able to clear away the debris from the flood in a matter of days.* **diligence** (noun).

diminutive (adjective) unusually small, tiny. *Children are fond of Shetland ponies because their diminutive size makes them easy to ride.* **diminution** (noun).

discern (verb) to detect, notice, or observe. *I could discern the shape of a whale off the starboard bow, but it was too far away to determine its size or species.* **discernment** (noun).

facebook.com/petersonspublishing

disclose (verb) to make known; to reveal. *Election laws require candidates to disclose the names of those who contribute large sums of money to their campaigns.* **disclosure** (noun).

discomfit (verb) to frustrate, thwart, or embarrass. *Discomfited by the interviewer's unexpected question, Peter could only stammer in reply.* **discomfiture** (noun).

disconcert (verb) to confuse or embarrass. *When the hallway bells began to ring halfway through her lecture, the speaker was disconcerted and didn't know what to do.*

discredit (verb) to cause disbelief in the accuracy of some statement or the reliability of a person. *Although many people still believe in UFOs, among scientists the reports of "alien encounters" have been thoroughly discredited.*

discreet (adjective) showing good judgment in speech and behavior. *Be discreet when discussing confidential business matters— don't talk among strangers on the elevator, for example.* **discretion** (noun).

discrepancy (noun) a difference or variance between two or more things. *The discrepancies between the two witnesses' stories show that one of them must be lying.* **discrepant** (adjective).

disdain (noun) contempt, scorn. *The professor could not hide his disdain for those students who were perpetually late to his class.* **disdain** (verb), **disdainful** (adjective).

disingenuous (adjective) pretending to be candid, simple, and frank. *When Texas billionaire H. Ross Perot ran for president, many considered his "jest plain folks" style disingenuous.*

disparage (verb) to speak disrespectfully about, to belittle. *Many political ads today both praise their own candidate and disparage his or her opponent.* **disparagement** (noun), **disparaging** (adjective).

disparity (noun) difference in quality or kind. *There is often a disparity between the kind of high-quality television people say they want and the low-brow programs they actually watch.* **disparate** (adjective).

disregard (verb) to ignore, to neglect. *If you don't write a will, when you die, your survivors may disregard your wishes about how your property should be handled.* **disregard** (noun).

disruptive (adjective) causing disorder, interrupting. *When the senator spoke at our college, angry demonstrators picketed, heckled, and engaged in other disruptive activities.* **disrupt** (verb), **disruption** (noun).

dissemble (verb) to pretend, to simulate. *When the police questioned her about the crime, she dissembled innocence.*

dissipate (verb) to spread out or scatter. *The windows and doors were opened, allowing the smoke that had filled the room to dissipate.* **dissipation** (noun).

dissonance (noun) lack of music harmony; lack of agreement between ideas. *Most modern music is characterized by dissonance, which many listeners find hard to enjoy. There is a noticeable dissonance between two common beliefs of most conservatives: their faith in unfettered free markets and their preference for traditional social values.* **dissonant** (adjective).

diverge (verb) to move in different directions. *Frost's poem* The Road Less Traveled *tells of the choice he made when "Two roads diverged in a yellow wood."* **divergence** (noun), **divergent** (adjective).

diversion (noun) a distraction or pastime. *During the two hours he spent in the doctor's waiting room, the game on his cell phone was a welcome diversion.* **divert** (verb).

divination (noun) the art of predicting the future. *In ancient Greece, people wanting to know their fate would visit the priests at Delphi, supposedly skilled at divination.* **divine** (verb).

divisive (adjective) causing disagreement or disunity. *Throughout history, race has been the most divisive issue in American society.*

divulge (verb) to reveal. *The people who count the votes for the Oscar awards are under strict orders not to divulge the names of the winners.*

dogmatic (adjective) holding firmly to a particular set of beliefs with little or no basis. *Believers in Marxist doctrine tend to be dogmatic, ignoring evidence that contradicts their beliefs.* **dogmatism** (noun).

dominant (adjective) greatest in importance or power. *Turner's* Frontier Thesis *suggests that the existence of the frontier had a dominant influence on American culture.* **dominate** (verb), **domination** (noun).

dubious (adjective) doubtful, uncertain. *Despite the chairman's attempts to convince the committee members that his plan would succeed, most of them remained dubious.* **dubiety** (noun).

durable (adjective) long lasting. *Denim is a popular material for work clothes because it is strong and durable.*

duress (noun) compulsion or restraint. *Fearing that the police might beat him, he confessed to the crime, not willingly but under duress.*

E

eclectic (adjective) drawn from many sources; varied, heterogeneous. *The Mellon family art collection is an eclectic one, including works ranging from ancient Greek sculptures to modern paintings.* **eclecticism** (noun).

efficacious (adjective) able to produce a desired effect. *Though thousands of people today are taking herbal supplements to treat depression, researchers have not yet proved them efficacious.* **efficacy** (noun).

effrontery (noun) shameless boldness. *The sports world was shocked when a professional basketball player had the effrontery to choke his head coach during a practice session.*

effusive (adjective) pouring forth one's emotions very freely. *Having won the Oscar for Best Actress, Sally Field gave an effusive acceptance speech in which she marveled, "You like me! You really like me!"* **effusion** (noun).

egotism (noun) excessive concern with oneself; conceit. *Robert's egotism was so great that all he could talk about was the importance—and the brilliance—of his own opinions.* **egotistic** (adjective).

egregious (adjective) obvious, conspicuous, flagrant. *It's hard to imagine how the editor could allow such an egregious error to appear.*

elated (adjective) excited and happy; exultant. *When the New England Patriots' last, desperate pass was dropped, the elated fans of the New York Giants began to celebrate.* **elate** (verb), **elation** (noun).

elliptical (adjective) very terse or concise in writing or speech; difficult to understand. *Rather than speak plainly, she hinted at her meaning through a series of nods, gestures, and elliptical half sentences.*

elusive (adjective) hard to capture, grasp, or understand. *Though everyone thinks they know what "justice" is, when you try to define the concept precisely, it proves to be quite elusive.*

embezzle (verb) to steal money or property that has been entrusted to your care. *The church treasurer was found to have embezzled thousands of dollars by writing phony checks on the church bank account.* **embezzlement** (noun).

emend (verb) to correct. *Before the letter is mailed, please emend the two spelling errors.* **emendation** (noun).

emigrate (verb) to leave one place or country to settle elsewhere. *Millions of Irish emigrated to the New World in the wake of the great Irish famines of the 1840s.* **emigrant** (noun), **emigration** (noun).

eminent (adjective) noteworthy, famous. *Vaclav Havel was an eminent author before he was elected president of the Czech Republic.* **eminence** (noun).

emissary (noun) someone who represents another. *In an effort to avoid a military showdown, former President Jimmy Carter was sent as an emissary to Korea to negotiate a settlement.*

emollient (noun) something that softens or soothes. *She used a hand cream as an emollient on her dry, work-roughened hands.* **emollient** (adjective).

empathy (noun) imaginative sharing of the feelings, thoughts, or experiences of another. *It's easy for a parent to have empathy for the sorrow of another parent whose child has died.* **empathetic** (adjective).

empirical (adjective) based on experience or personal observation. *Although many people believe in ESP, scientists have found no empirical evidence of its existence.* **empiricism** (noun).

emulate (verb) to imitate or copy. *The British band Oasis admitted their desire to emulate their idols, the Beatles.* **emulation** (noun).

encroach (verb) to go beyond acceptable limits; to trespass. *By quietly seizing more and more authority, Robert Moses continually encroached on the powers of other government leaders.* **encroachment** (noun).

enervate (verb) to reduce the energy or strength of someone or something. *The extended exposure to the sun along with dehydration enervated the shipwrecked crew, leaving them almost too weak to spot the passing vessel.*

engender (verb) to produce, to cause. *Countless disagreements over the proper use of national forests have engendered feelings of hostility between ranchers and environmentalists.*

enhance (verb) to improve in value or quality. *New kitchen appliances will enhance your house and increase the amount of money you'll make when you sell it.* **enhancement** (noun).

enmity (noun) hatred, hostility, ill will. *Long-standing enmity, like that between the Protestants and Catholics in Northern Ireland, is difficult to overcome.*

enthrall (verb) to enchant or charm. *The Swedish singer Jenny Lind enthralled American audiences in the nineteenth century with her beauty and talent.*

ephemeral (adjective) quickly disappearing; transient. *Stardom in pop music is ephemeral; many of the top acts of ten years ago are forgotten today.*

equanimity (noun) calmness of mind, especially under stress. *FDR had the gift of facing the great crises of his presidency—the Depression and the Second World War—with equanimity and even humor.*

eradicate (verb) to destroy completely. *American society has failed to eradicate racism, although some of its worst effects have been reduced.*

espouse (verb) to take up as a cause; to adopt. *No politician in America today will openly espouse racism, although some behave and speak in racially prejudiced ways.*

euphoric (adjective) a feeling of extreme happiness and well-being; elation. *One often feels euphoric during the earliest days of a new love affair.* **euphoria** (noun).

evanescent (adjective) vanishing like a vapor; fragile and transient. *As she walked by, the evanescent fragrance of her perfume reached me for just an instant.*

exacerbate (verb) to make worse or more severe. *The roads in our town already have too much traffic; building a new shopping mall will exacerbate the problem.*

exasperate (verb) to irritate or annoy. *Because she was trying to study, Sharon was exasperated by the yelling of her neighbors' children.*

exculpate (verb) to free from blame or guilt. *When someone else confessed to the crime, the previous suspect was exculpated.* **exculpation** (noun), **exculpatory** (adjective).

exemplary (adjective) worthy to serve as a model. *The Baldrige Award is given to a company with exemplary standards of excellence in products and service.* **exemplar** (noun), **exemplify** (verb).

exonerate (verb) to free from blame. *Although the truck driver was suspected at first of being involved in the bombing, later evidence exonerated him.* **exoneration** (noun), **exonerative** (adjective).

expansive (adjective) broad and large; speaking openly and freely. *The LBJ Ranch is located on an expansive tract of land in Texas. Over dinner, she became expansive in describing her dreams for the future.*

expedite (verb) to carry out promptly. *As the flood waters rose, the governor ordered state agencies to expedite their rescue efforts.*

expertise (noun) skill, mastery. *The software company was eager to hire new graduates with programming expertise.*

expiate (verb) to atone for. *The president's apology to the survivors of the notorious Tuskegee experiments was his attempt to expiate the nation's guilt over their mistreatment.* **expiation** (noun).

expropriate (verb) to seize ownership of. *When the Communists came to power in China, they expropriated most businesses and turned them over to government-appointed managers.* **expropriation** (noun).

extant (adjective) currently in existence. *Of the seven ancient Wonders of the World, only the pyramids of Egypt are still extant.*

extenuate (verb) to make less serious. *Jeanine's guilt is extenuated by the fact that she was only twelve when she committed the theft.* **extenuating** (adjective), **extenuation** (noun).

extol (verb) to greatly praise. *At the party convention, speaker after speaker rose to extol their candidate for the presidency.*

extricate (verb) to free from a difficult or complicated situation. *Much of the humor in the TV show* I Love Lucy *comes in watching Lucy try to extricate herself from the problems she creates by fibbing or trickery.* **extricable** (adjective).

extrinsic (adjective) not an innate part or aspect of something; external. *The high price of old baseball cards is due to extrinsic factors, such as the nostalgia felt by baseball fans for the stars of their youth, rather than the inherent beauty or value of the cards themselves.*

exuberant (adjective) wildly joyous and enthusiastic. *As the final seconds of the game ticked away, the fans of the winning team began an exuberant celebration.* **exuberance** (noun).

F

facile (adjective) easy; shallow or superficial. *The one-minute political commercial favors a candidate with facile opinions rather than serious, thoughtful solutions.* **facilitate** (verb), **facility** (noun).

fallacy (noun) an error in fact or logic. *It's a fallacy to think that "natural" means "healthful"; after all, the deadly poison arsenic is completely natural.* **fallacious** (adjective).

felicitous (adjective) pleasing, fortunate, apt. *The sudden blossoming of the dogwood trees on the morning of Matt's wedding seemed a felicitous sign of good luck.* **felicity** (noun).

feral (adjective) wild. *The garbage dump was inhabited by a pack of feral dogs that had escaped from their owners and become completely wild.*

fervent (adjective) full of intense feeling; ardent, zealous. *In the days just after his religious conversion, his piety was at its most fervent.* **fervid** (adjective), **fervor** (noun).

flagrant (adjective) obviously wrong; offensive. *Nixon was forced to resign the presidency after a series of flagrant crimes against the U.S. Constitution.* **flagrancy** (noun).

flamboyant (adjective) very colorful, showy, or elaborate. *At Mardi Gras, partygoers compete to show off the most wild and flamboyant outfits.*

florid (adjective) flowery, fancy; reddish. *The grand ballroom was decorated in a florid style. Years of heavy drinking had given him a florid complexion.*

foppish (adjective) describing a man who is foolishly vain about his dress or appearance. *The foppish character of the 1890s wore bright-colored spats and a top hat; in the 1980s, he wore fancy suspenders and a shirt with a contrasting collar.* **fop** (noun).

formidable (adjective) awesome, impressive, or frightening. *According to his plaque in the Baseball Hall of Fame, pitcher Tom Seaver turned the New York Mets "from lovable losers into formidable foes."*

fortuitous (adjective) lucky, fortunate. *Although the mayor claimed credit for the falling crime rate, it was really caused by several fortuitous trends.*

fractious (adjective) troublesome, unruly. *Members of the British Parliament are often fractious, shouting insults and sarcastic questions during debates.*

fragility (noun) the quality of being easy to break; delicacy, weakness. *Because of their fragility, few stained-glass windows from the early Middle Ages have survived.* **fragile** (adjective).

fraternize (verb) to associate with on friendly terms. *Although baseball players aren't supposed to fraternize with their opponents, players from opposing teams often chat before games.* **fraternization** (noun).

frenetic (adjective) chaotic, frantic. *The floor of the stock exchange, filled with traders shouting and gesturing, is a scene of frenetic activity.*

frivolity (noun) lack of seriousness; levity. *The frivolity of the Mardi Gras carnival is in contrast to the seriousness of the religious season of Lent that follows.* **frivolous** (adjective).

frugal (adjective) spending little. *With our last few dollars, we bought a frugal dinner: a loaf of bread and a piece of cheese.* **frugality** (noun).

fugitive (noun) someone trying to escape. *When two prisoners broke out of the local jail, police were warned to keep an eye out for the fugitives.* **fugitive** (adjective).

G

gargantuan (adjective) huge, colossal. *The building of the Great Wall of China was one of the most gargantuan projects ever undertaken.*

genial (adjective) friendly, gracious. *A good host welcomes all visitors in a warm and genial fashion.*

grandiose (adjective) overly large, pretentious, or showy. *Among Hitler's grandiose plans for Berlin was a gigantic building with a dome several times larger than any ever built.* **grandiosity** (noun).

gratuitous (adjective) given freely or without cause. *Since her opinion was not requested, her harsh criticism of his singing seemed a gratuitous insult.*

gregarious (adjective) enjoying the company of others; sociable. *Naturally gregarious, Emily is a popular member of several clubs and a sought-after lunch companion.*

guileless (adjective) without cunning; innocent. *Deborah's guileless personality and complete honesty make it hard for her to survive in the harsh world of politics.*

gullible (adjective) easily fooled. *When the sweepstakes entry form arrived bearing the message, "You may be a winner!" my gullible neighbor tried to claim a prize.* **gullibility** (noun).

H

hackneyed (adjective) without originality, trite. *When someone invented the phrase, "No pain, no gain," it was clever, but now it is so commonly heard that it seems hackneyed.*

haughty (adjective) overly proud. *The fashion model strode down the runway, her hips thrust forward and a haughty expression, like a sneer, on her face.* **haughtiness** (noun).

hedonist (noun) someone who lives mainly to pursue pleasure. *Having inherited great wealth, he chose to live the life of a hedonist, traveling the world in luxury.* **hedonism** (noun), **hedonistic** (adjective).

heinous (adjective) very evil, hateful. *The massacre by Pol Pot of more than a million Cambodians is one of the twentieth century's most heinous crimes.*

hierarchy (noun) a ranking of people, things, or ideas from highest to lowest. *A cabinet secretary ranks just below the president and vice president in the hierarchy of the executive branch.* **hierarchical** (adjective).

hypocrisy (noun) a false pretense of virtue. *When the sexual misconduct of the television preacher was exposed, his followers were shocked at his hypocrisy.* **hypocritical** (adjective).

I

iconoclast (noun) someone who attacks traditional beliefs or institutions. *Comedian Stephen Colbert enjoys his reputation as an iconoclast, though people in power often resent his satirical jabs.* **iconoclasm** (noun), **iconoclastic** (adjective).

idiosyncratic (adjective) peculiar to an individual; eccentric. *Cyndi Lauper sings pop music in an idiosyncratic style, mingling high-pitched whoops and squeals with throaty gurgles.* **idiosyncrasy** (noun).

idolatry (noun) the worship of a person, thing, or institution as a god. *In Communist China, Chairman Mao was the subject of idolatry; his picture was displayed everywhere, and millions of Chinese memorized his sayings.* **idolatrous** (adjective).

impartial (adjective) fair, equal, unbiased. *If a judge is not impartial, then all of her rulings are questionable.* **impartiality** (noun).

impeccable (adjective) flawless. *The crooks printed impeccable copies of the Super Bowl tickets, making it impossible to distinguish them from the real ones.*

impetuous (adjective) acting hastily or impulsively. *Stuart's resignation was an impetuous act; he did it without thinking, and he soon regretted it.* **impetuosity** (noun).

impinge (verb) to encroach upon, touch, or affect. *You have a right to do whatever you want, so long as your actions don't impinge on the rights of others.*

implicit (adjective) understood without being openly expressed; implied. *Although most clubs had no rules excluding minorities, many had an implicit understanding that no member of a minority group would be allowed to join.*

impute (verb) to credit or give responsibility to; to attribute. *Although Helena's comments embarrassed me, I don't impute any ill will to her; I think she didn't realize what she was saying.* **imputation** (noun).

inarticulate (adjective) unable to speak or express oneself clearly and understandably. *A skilled athlete may be an inarticulate public speaker, as demonstrated by many post-game interviews.*

incisive (adjective) clear and direct expression. *Franklin settled the debate with a few incisive remarks that summed up the issue perfectly.*

incompatible (adjective) unable to exist together; conflicting. *Many people hold seemingly incompatible beliefs: for example, supporting the death penalty while believing in the sacredness of human life.* **incompatibility** (noun).

inconsequential (adjective) of little importance. *When the flat screen TV was delivered, it was a different shade of gray than I expected, but the difference was inconsequential.*

incontrovertible (adjective) impossible to question. *The fact that Alexandra's fingerprints were the only ones on the murder weapon made her guilt seem incontrovertible.*

incorrigible (adjective) impossible to manage or reform. *Lou is an incorrigible trickster, constantly playing practical jokes no matter how much his friends complain.*

incremental (adjective) increasing gradually by small amounts. *Although the initial cost of the Medicare program was small, the incremental expenses have grown to be very large.* **increment** (noun).

incriminate (verb) to give evidence of guilt. *The fifth amendment to the Constitution says that no one is required to reveal information that would incriminate him or her in a crime.* **incriminating** (adjective).

incumbent (noun) someone who occupies an office or position. *It is often difficult for a challenger to win a seat in Congress from the incumbent.* **incumbency** (noun), **incumbent** (adjective).

indeterminate (adjective) not definitely known. *The college plans to enroll an indeterminate number of students; the size of the class will depend on the number of applicants and how many accept offers of admission.* **determine** (verb).

indifferent (adjective) unconcerned, apathetic. *The mayor's small proposed budget for education suggests that he is indifferent to the needs of our schools.* **indifference** (noun).

indistinct (adjective) unclear, uncertain. *We could see boats on the water, but in the thick morning fog their shapes were indistinct.*

indomitable (adjective) unable to be conquered or controlled. *The world admired the indomitable spirit of Nelson Mandela; he remained courageous despite years of imprisonment.*

induce (verb) to cause. *The doctor prescribed a medicine that was supposed to induce a lowering of the blood pressure.* **induction** (noun).

ineffable (adjective) difficult to describe or express. *He gazed in silence at the sunrise over the Taj Mahal, his eyes reflecting an ineffable sense of wonder.*

inevitable (adjective) unable to be avoided. *Once the Japanese attacked Pearl Harbor, American involvement in World War II was inevitable.* **inevitability** (noun).

inexorable (adjective) unable to be deterred; relentless. *It's difficult to imagine how the mythic character of Oedipus could have avoided his evil destiny; his fate appears inexorable.*

ingenious (adjective) showing cleverness and originality. *The Post-it note is an ingenious solution to a common problem—how to mark papers without spoiling them.* **ingenuity** (noun).

inherent (adjective) naturally part of something. *Compromise is inherent in democracy, since everyone cannot get his or her way.* **inhere** (verb), **inherence** (noun).

innate (adjective) inborn, native. *Not everyone who takes piano lessons becomes a fine musician, which shows that music requires innate talent as well as training.*

innocuous (adjective) harmless, inoffensive. *I was surprised that Melissa took offense at such an innocuous joke.*

inoculate (verb) to prevent a disease by infusing with a disease-causing organism. *Pasteur found he could prevent rabies by inoculating patients with the virus that causes the disease.* **inoculation** (noun).

insipid (adjective) flavorless, uninteresting. *Some TV shows are so insipid that you can watch them while reading without missing a thing.* **insipidity** (noun).

insolence (noun) an attitude or behavior that is bold and disrespectful. *Some feel that news reporters who shout questions at the president are behaving with insolence.* **insolent** (adjective).

insular (adjective) narrow or isolated in attitude or viewpoint. *Americans are famous for their insular attitudes; they seem to think that nothing important has ever happened outside of their country.* **insularity** (noun).

insurgency (noun) uprising, rebellion. *The angry townspeople had begun an insurgency bordering on downright revolution; they were collecting arms, holding secret meetings, and refusing to pay certain taxes.* **insurgent** (adjective).

integrity (noun) honesty, uprightness; soundness, completeness. *"Honest Abe" Lincoln is considered a model of political integrity. Inspectors examined the building's support beams and foundation and found no reason to doubt its structural integrity.*

interlocutor (noun) someone taking part in a dialogue or conversation. *Annoyed by the constant questions from someone in the crowd, the speaker challenged his interlocutor to offer a better plan.* **interlocutory** (adjective).

interlude (noun) an interrupting period or performance. *The two most dramatic scenes in King Lear are separated, strangely, by a comic interlude starring the king's jester.*

interminable (adjective) endless or seemingly endless. *Addressing the United Nations, Castro announced, "We will be brief"—then delivered an interminable 4-hour speech.*

intransigent (adjective) unwilling to compromise. *Despite the mediator's attempts to suggest a fair solution, the two parties were intransigent, forcing a showdown.* **intransigence** (noun).

intrepid (adjective) fearless and resolute. *Only an intrepid adventurer is willing to undertake the long and dangerous trip by sled to the South Pole.* **intrepidity** (noun).

intrusive (adjective) forcing a way in without being welcome. *The legal requirement of a search warrant is supposed to protect Americans from intrusive searches by the police.* **intrude** (verb), **intrusion** (noun).

intuitive (adjective) known directly, without apparent thought or effort. *An experienced chess player sometimes has an intuitive sense of the best move to make, even if she can't explain it.* **intuit** (verb), **intuition** (noun).

inundate (verb) to flood; to overwhelm. *As soon as the playoff tickets went on sale, eager fans inundated the box office with orders.*

invariable (adjective) unchanging, constant. *When writing a book, it was her invariable habit to rise at 6 a.m. and work at her desk from 7 to 12.* **invariability** (noun).

inversion (noun) a turning backwards, inside-out, or upside-down; a reversal. *Latin poetry often features inversion of word order; for example, the first line of Virgil's* Aeneid: *"Arms and the man I sing."* **invert** (verb), **inverted** (adjective).

inveterate (adjective) persistent, habitual. *It's very difficult for an inveterate gambler to give up the pastime.* **inveteracy** (noun).

invigorate (verb) to give energy to, to stimulate. *As her car climbed the mountain road, Lucinda felt invigorated by the clear air and the cool breezes.*

invincible (adjective) impossible to conquer or overcome. *For three years at the height of his career, boxer Mike Tyson seemed invincible.*

inviolable (adjective) impossible to attack or trespass upon. *In the president's remote hideaway at Camp David, guarded by the Secret Service, his privacy is, for once, inviolable.*

irrational (adjective) unreasonable. *Richard knew that his fear of insects was irrational, but he was unable to overcome it.* **irrationality** (noun).

irresolute (adjective) uncertain how to act, indecisive. *The line in the ice cream shop grew as the irresolute child wavered between her two favorite ice cream flavors before finally choosing one.* **irresolution** (noun).

J

jeopardize (verb) to put in danger. *Terrorist attacks jeopardize the fragile peace in the Middle East.* **jeopardy** (noun).

juxtapose (verb) to put side by side. *Juxtaposing the two editorials revealed the enormous differences in the writers' opinions.* **juxtaposition** (noun).

L

languid (adjective) without energy; slow, sluggish, listless. *The hot, humid weather of late August can make anyone feel languid.* **languish** (verb), **languor** (noun).

latent (adjective) not currently obvious or active; hidden. *Although he had committed only a single act of violence, the examining psychiatrist said it's likely he always had a latent tendency toward violence.* **latency** (noun).

laudatory (adjective) giving praise. *The ads for the movie are filled with laudatory comments from critics.*

lenient (adjective) mild, soothing, or forgiving. *The judge was known for his lenient disposition; he rarely imposed long jail sentences on criminals.* **leniency** (noun).

lethargic (adjective) lacking energy; sluggish. *Visitors to the zoo are surprised that the lions appear so lethargic, but, in the wild, lions sleep up to 18 hours a day.* **lethargy** (noun).

liability (noun) an obligation or debt; a weakness or drawback. *The insurance company had a liability of millions of dollars after the town was destroyed by a tornado. Slowness afoot is a serious liability in an aspiring basketball player.* **liable** (adjective).

lithe (adjective) flexible and graceful. *The ballet dancer was almost as lithe as a cat.*

longevity (noun) length of life; durability. *The reduction in early deaths from infectious diseases is responsible for most of the increase in human longevity over the past two centuries.*

lucid (adjective) clear and understandable. *Hawking's* A Short History of the Universe *is a lucid explanation of modern scientific theories about the origin of the universe.* **lucidity** (noun).

lurid (adjective) shocking, gruesome. *While the serial killer was on the loose, the newspapers were filled with lurid stories about his crimes.*

M

malediction (noun) curse. *In the fairy tale "Sleeping Beauty," the princess is trapped in a death-like sleep because of the malediction uttered by an angry witch.*

malevolence (noun) hatred, ill will. *Critics say that Iago, the villain in Shakespeare's* Othello, *seems to exhibit malevolence with no real cause.* **malevolent** (adjective).

malinger (verb) to pretend incapacity or illness to avoid a duty or work. *During the labor dispute, hundreds of employees malingered, forcing the company to slow production and costing it millions in profits.*

malleable (adjective) able to be changed, shaped, or formed by outside pressures. *Gold is a very useful metal because it is so malleable. A child's personality is malleable and deeply influenced by the things his or her parents say and do.* **malleability** (noun).

mandate (noun) order, command. *The new policy of using only organic produce in the restaurant went into effect as soon as the manager issued his mandate about it.* **mandate** (verb), **mandatory** (adjective).

maturation (noun) the process of becoming fully grown or developed. *Free markets in the former Communist nations are likely to operate smoothly only after a long period of maturation.* **mature** (adjective and verb), **maturity** (noun).

mediate (verb) to act to reconcile differences between two parties. *During the baseball strike, both the players and the club owners were willing to have the president mediate the dispute.* **mediation** (noun).

mediocrity (noun) the state of being middling or poor in quality. *The New York Mets finished in ninth place in 1968 but won the world's championship in 1969, going from horrible to great in a single year and skipping mediocrity.* **mediocre** (adjective).

mercurial (adjective) changing quickly and unpredictably. *The mercurial personality of Robin Williams, with his many voices and styles, made him perfect for the role of the ever-changing genie in* Aladdin.

meticulous (adjective) very careful with details. *Repairing watches calls for a craftsperson who is patient and meticulous.*

mimicry (noun) imitation, aping. *The continued popularity of Elvis Presley has given rise to a class of entertainers who make a living through mimicry of "The King."* **mimic** (noun and verb).

misconception (noun) a mistaken idea. *Columbus sailed west with the misconception that he would reach the shores of Asia.* **misconceive** (verb).

mitigate (verb) to make less severe; to relieve. *Wallace certainly committed the assault, but the verbal abuse he'd received helps to explain his behavior and somewhat mitigates his guilt.* **mitigation** (noun).

modicum (noun) a small amount. *The plan for your new business is well designed; with a modicum of luck, you should be successful.*

mollify (verb) to soothe or calm; to appease. *Samantha tried to mollify the angry customer by promising him a full refund.*

morose (adjective) gloomy, sullen. *After Chuck's girlfriend dumped him, he lay around the house for a couple of days, feeling morose.*

mundane (adjective) everyday, ordinary, commonplace. *Moviegoers in the 1930s liked the glamorous films of Fred Astaire because they provided an escape from the mundane problems of life during the Great Depression.*

munificent (adjective) very generous; lavish. *Ted Turner's billion-dollar donation to the United Nations was one of the most munificent acts of charity in history.* **munificence** (noun).

mutable (adjective) likely to change. *A politician's reputation can be highly mutable, as seen in the case of Harry Truman—mocked during his lifetime, revered afterward.*

N

narcissistic (adjective) showing excessive love for oneself; egoistic. *Andre's room, decorated with photos of himself and the sports trophies he has won, suggests a narcissistic personality.* **narcissism** (noun).

nocturnal (adjective) of the night; active at night. *Travelers on the Underground Railroad escaped from slavery to the North by a series of nocturnal flights. The eyes of nocturnal animals must be sensitive in dim light.*

nonchalant (adjective) appearing to be unconcerned. *Unlike the other players on the football team who pumped their fists when their names were announced, John ran on the field with a nonchalant wave.* **nonchalance** (noun).

nondescript (adjective) without distinctive qualities; drab. *The bank robber's clothes were nondescript; none of the witnesses could remember their color or style.*

notorious (adjective) famous, especially for evil actions or qualities. *Warner Brothers produced a series of movies about notorious gangsters such as John Dillinger and Al Capone.* **notoriety** (noun).

novice (noun) beginner. *Lifting your head before you finish your swing is a typical mistake committed by the novice at golf.*

nuance (noun) a subtle difference or quality. *At first glance, Monet's paintings of water lilies all look much alike, but the more you study them, the more you appreciate the nuances of color and shading that distinguish them.*

nurture (verb) to nourish or help to grow. *The money given by the National Endowment for the Arts helps nurture local arts organizations throughout the country.* **nurture** (noun).

O

obdurate (adjective) unwilling to change; stubborn, inflexible. *Despite the many pleas he received, the governor was obdurate in his refusal to grant clemency to the convicted murderer.*

objective (adjective) dealing with observable facts rather than opinions or interpretations. *When a legal case involves a shocking crime, it may be hard for a judge to remain objective in his rulings.*

oblivious (adjective) unaware, unconscious. *Karen practiced her oboe with complete concentration, oblivious to the noise and activity around her.* **oblivion** (noun), **obliviousness** (noun).

obscure (adjective) little known; hard to understand. *Mendel was an obscure monk until decades after his death when his scientific work was finally discovered. Most people find the writings of James Joyce obscure; hence the popularity of books that explain his books.* **obscure** (verb), **obscurity** (noun).

obsessive (adjective) haunted or preoccupied by an idea or feeling. *His concern with cleanliness became so obsessive that he washed his hands twenty times every day.* **obsess** (verb), **obsession** (noun).

obsolete (adjective) no longer current; old-fashioned. *W. H. Auden said that his ideal landscape would include water wheels, wooden grain mills, and other forms of obsolete machinery.* **obsolescence** (noun).

obstinate (adjective) stubborn, unyielding. *Despite years of effort, the problem of drug abuse remains obstinate.* **obstinacy** (noun).

obtrusive (adjective) overly prominent. *Philip should sing more softly; his bass is so obtrusive that the other singers can barely be heard.* **obtrude** (verb), **obtrusion** (noun).

ominous (adjective) foretelling evil. *Ominous black clouds gathered on the horizon, for a violent storm was fast approaching.* **omen** (noun).

onerous (adjective) heavy, burdensome. *The hero Hercules was ordered to clean the Augean Stables, one of several onerous tasks known as "the labors of Hercules."* **onus** (noun).

opportunistic (adjective) eagerly seizing chances as they arise. *When Princess Diana died suddenly, opportunistic publishers quickly released books about her life and death.* **opportunism** (noun).

opulent (adjective) rich, lavish. *The mansion of newspaper tycoon Hearst is famous for its opulent decor.* **opulence** (noun).

ornate (adjective) highly decorated, elaborate. *Baroque architecture is often highly ornate, featuring surfaces covered with carving, sinuous curves, and painted scenes.*

ostentatious (adjective) overly showy, pretentious. *To show off his wealth, the millionaire threw an ostentatious party featuring a full orchestra, a famous singer, and tens of thousands of dollars' worth of food.*

ostracize (verb) to exclude from a group. *In Biblical times, those who suffered from the disease of leprosy were ostracized and forced to live alone.* **ostracism** (noun).

P

pallid (adjective) pale; dull. *Working all day in the coal mine had given him a pallid complexion. The new musical offers only pallid entertainment: the music is lifeless, the acting dull, the story absurd.*

parched (adjective) very dry; thirsty. *After two months without rain, the crops were shriveled and parched by the sun.* **parch** (verb).

pariah (noun) outcast. *Accused of robbery, he became a pariah; his neighbors stopped talking to him, and people he'd considered friends no longer called.*

partisan (adjective) reflecting strong allegiance to a particular party or cause. *The vote on the president's budget was strictly partisan: every member of the president's party voted yes, and all others voted no.* **partisan** (noun).

pathology (noun) disease or the study of disease; extreme abnormality. *Some people believe that high rates of crime are symptoms of an underlying social pathology.* **pathological** (adjective).

pellucid (adjective) very clear; transparent; easy to understand. *The water in the mountain stream was cold and pellucid. Thanks to the professor's pellucid explanation, I finally understand relativity theory.*

penitent (adjective) feeling sorry for past crimes or sins. *Having grown penitent, he wrote a long letter of apology, asking forgiveness.*

penurious (adjective) extremely frugal; stingy. *Haunted by memories of poverty, he lived in penurious fashion, driving a twelve-year-old car and wearing only the cheapest clothes.* **penury** (noun).

perceptive (adjective) quick to notice, observant. *With his perceptive intelligence, Holmes was the first to notice the importance of this clue.* **perceptible** (adjective), **perception** (noun).

perfidious (adjective) disloyal, treacherous. *Although he was one of the most talented generals of the American Revolution, Benedict Arnold is remembered today as a perfidious betrayer of his country.* **perfidy** (noun).

perfunctory (adjective) unenthusiastic, routine, or mechanical. *When the play opened, the actors sparkled, but by the thousandth night their performance had become perfunctory.*

permeate (verb) to spread through or penetrate. *Little by little, the smell of gas from the broken pipe permeated the house.*

persevere (adjective) to continue despite difficulties. *Although several of her teammates dropped out of the marathon, Gail persevered.* **perseverance** (noun).

perspicacity (noun) keenness of observation or understanding. *Journalist Murray Kempton was famous for the perspicacity of his comments on social and political issues.* **perspicacious** (adjective).

peruse (verb) to examine or study. *Caroline perused the contract carefully before she signed it.* **perusal** (noun).

pervasive (adjective) spreading throughout. *As news of the disaster reached the town, a pervasive sense of gloom could be felt.* **pervade** (verb).

phlegmatic (adjective) sluggish and unemotional in temperament. *It was surprising to see Tom, who is normally so phlegmatic, acting excited.*

placate (verb) to soothe or appease. *The waiter tried to placate the angry customer with the offer of a free dessert.* **placatory** (adjective).

plastic (adjective) able to be molded or reshaped. *Because it is highly plastic, clay is an easy material for beginning sculptors to use.*

plausible (adjective) apparently believable. *According to the judge, the defense attorney's argument was both powerful and plausible.* **plausibility** (noun).

polarize (verb) to separate into opposing groups or forces. *For years, the abortion debate has polarized the American people, with many people voicing extreme views and few trying to find a middle ground.* **polarization** (noun).

portend (verb) to indicate a future event; to forebode. *According to folklore, a red sky at dawn portends a day of stormy weather.*

potentate (noun) a powerful ruler. *The Tsar of Russia was one of the last hereditary potentates of Europe.*

pragmatism (noun) a belief in approaching problems through practical rather than theoretical means. *Roosevelt's approach to the Great Depression was based on pragmatism: "Try something," he said. "If it doesn't work, try something else."* **pragmatic** (adjective).

preamble (noun) an introductory statement. *The preamble to the Constitution begins with the famous words, "We the people of the United States of America..."*

precocious (adjective) mature at an unusually early age. *Picasso was so precocious as an artist that, at nine, he is said to have painted far better pictures than his teacher.* **precocity** (noun).

predatory (adjective) living by killing and eating other animals; exploiting others for personal gain. *The tiger is the largest predatory animal native to Asia. Microsoft has been accused of predatory business practices that prevent other software companies from competing with it.* **predation** (noun), **predator** (noun).

predilection (noun) a liking or preference. *To relax from his presidential duties, Kennedy had a predilection for spy novels featuring James Bond.*

predominant (adjective) greatest in numbers or influence. *Although hundreds of religions are practiced in India, the predominant faith is Hinduism.* **predominance** (noun), **predominate** (verb).

prepossessing (adjective) attractive. *Smart, lovely, and talented, she has all the prepossessing qualities that mark a potential movie star.*

presumptuous (adjective) going beyond the limits of courtesy or appropriateness. *The senator winced when the presumptuous young staffer addressed him as "Chuck."* **presume** (verb), **presumption** (noun).

pretentious (adjective) claiming excessive value or importance. *For a shoe salesman to call himself a "Personal Foot Apparel Consultant" seems awfully pretentious.* **pretension** (noun).

procrastinate (verb) to put off, to delay. *If you habitually procrastinate, try this technique: never touch a piece of paper without either filing it, responding to it, or throwing it out.* **procrastination** (noun).

profane (adjective) impure, unholy. *It is inappropriate and rude to use profane language in a church.* **profane** (verb), **profanity** (noun).

proficient (adjective) skillful, adept. *A proficient artist, Louise quickly and accurately sketched the scene.* **proficiency** (noun).

proliferate (verb) to increase or multiply. *Over the past twenty-five years, high-tech companies have proliferated in northern California, Massachusetts, and Seattle.* **proliferation** (noun).

prolific (adjective) producing many offspring or creations. *With more than 300 books to his credit, Isaac Asimov was one of the most prolific writers of all time.*

prominence (noun) the quality of standing out; fame. *Barack Obama rose to political prominence after his keynote address to the 2004 Democratic National Convention.* **prominent** (adjective).

promulgate (verb) to make public, to declare. *Lincoln signed the proclamation that freed the slaves in 1862, but he waited several months to promulgate it.*

propagate (verb) to cause to grow; to foster. *John Smithson's will left his fortune for the founding of an institution to propagate knowledge, without saying whether that meant a university, a library, or a museum.* **propagation** (noun).

propriety (noun) appropriateness. *The principal questioned the propriety of the discussion the teacher had with her students about another instructor's gambling addiction.*

prosaic (adjective) everyday, ordinary, dull. *"Paul's Case" tells the story of a boy who longs to escape from the prosaic life of a clerk into a world of wealth, glamour, and beauty.*

protagonist (noun) the main character in a story or play; the main supporter of an idea. *Leopold Bloom is the protagonist of James Joyce's great novel* Ulysses.

provocative (adjective) likely to stimulate emotions, ideas, or controversy. *The demonstrators began chanting obscenities, a provocative act that they hoped would cause the police to lose control.* **provoke** (verb), **provocation** (noun).

proximity (noun) closeness, nearness. *Neighborhood residents were angry over the proximity of the sewage plant to the local school.* **proximate** (adjective).

prudent (adjective) wise, cautious, and practical. *A prudent investor will avoid putting all of her money into any single investment.* **prudence** (noun), **prudential** (adjective).

pugnacious (adjective) combative, bellicose, truculent; ready to fight. *Ty Cobb, the pugnacious outfielder for the Detroit Tigers, got into more than his fair share of brawls, both on and off the field.* **pugnacity** (noun).

punctilious (adjective) very concerned about proper forms of behavior and manners. *A punctilious dresser like James would rather skip the party altogether than wear the wrong color tie.* **punctilio** (noun).

pundit (noun) someone who offers opinions in an authoritative style. *The Sunday morning talk shows are filled with pundits, each with his or her own theory about the week's political news.*

punitive (adjective) inflicting punishment. *The jury awarded the plaintiff one million dollars in punitive damages, hoping to teach the defendant a lesson.*

purify (verb) to make pure, clean, or perfect. *The new plant is supposed to purify the drinking water provided to everyone in the nearby towns.* **purification** (noun).

Q

quell (verb) to quiet, to suppress. *It took a huge number of police officers to quell the rioting.*

querulous (adjective) complaining, whining. *The nursing home attendant needed a lot of patience to care for the three querulous, unpleasant residents on his floor.*

R

rancorous (adjective) expressing bitter hostility. *Many Americans are disgusted by recent political campaigns, which seem more rancorous than ever before.* **rancor** (noun).

rationale (noun) an underlying reason or explanation. *Looking at the sad faces of his employees, it was hard for the company president to explain the rationale for closing the business.*

raze (verb) to completely destroy; demolish. *The old Coliseum building will soon be razed to make room for a new hotel.*

reciprocate (verb) to give and take mutually. *If you'll watch my children tonight, I'll reciprocate by taking care of yours tomorrow.* **reciprocity** (noun).

reclusive (adjective) withdrawn from society. *During the last years of her life, actress Greta Garbo led a reclusive existence, rarely appearing in public.* **recluse** (noun).

reconcile (verb) to make consistent or harmonious. *FDR's greatness as a leader can be seen in his ability to reconcile the demands and values of the varied groups that supported him.* **reconciliation** (noun).

recrimination (noun) a retaliatory accusation. *After the governor called his opponent unethical, his opponent angrily replied with recriminations that the governor was a hypocrite.* **recriminate** (verb), **recriminatory** (adjective).

recuperate (verb) to regain health after an illness. *Although Marie left the hospital two days after her operation, it took her a few weeks to fully recuperate.* **recuperation** (noun), **recuperative** (adjective).

redoubtable (adjective) inspiring respect, awe, or fear. *Johnson's knowledge, experience, and personal clout made him a redoubtable political opponent.*

refurbish (verb) to fix up; renovate. *It took three days' work by a team of carpenters, painters, and decorators to completely refurbish the apartment.*

refute (verb) to prove false. *The company invited reporters to visit their plant in an effort to refute the charges of unsafe working conditions.* **refutation** (noun).

relevance (noun) connection to the matter at hand; pertinence. *Testimony in a criminal trial may be admitted only if it has clear relevance to the question of guilt or innocence.* **relevant** (adjective).

remedial (adjective) serving to remedy, cure, or correct some condition. *Affirmative action can be justified as a remedial step to help minority members overcome the effects of past discrimination.* **remediation** (noun), **remedy** (verb).

remorse (noun) a painful sense of guilt over wrongdoing. *In Poe's story* The Tell-Tale Heart, *a murderer is driven insane by remorse over his crime.* **remorseful** (adjective).

remuneration (noun) pay. *In a civil lawsuit, the attorney often receives part of the financial settlement as his or her remuneration.* **remunerate** (verb), **remunerative** (adjective).

renovate (verb) to renew by repairing or rebuilding. *The television program* This Old House *shows how skilled craftspeople renovate houses.* **renovation** (noun).

renunciation (noun) the act of rejecting or refusing something. *King Edward VII's renunciation of the British throne was caused by his desire to marry an American divorcee, something he couldn't do as king.* **renounce** (verb).

replete (adjective) filled abundantly. *Graham's book is replete with wonderful stories about the famous people she has known.*

reprehensible (adjective) deserving criticism or censure. *Although Pete Rose's misdeeds were reprehensible, not all fans agree that he deserves to be excluded from the Baseball Hall of Fame.* **reprehend** (verb), **reprehension** (noun).

repudiate (verb) to reject, to renounce. *After it became known that Duke had been a leader of the Ku Klux Klan, most Republican leaders repudiated him.* **repudiation** (noun).

reputable (adjective) having a good reputation; respected. *Find a reputable auto mechanic by asking your friends for recommendations based on their own experiences.* **reputation** (noun), **repute** (noun).

resilient (adjective) able to recover from difficulty. *A professional athlete must be resilient, able to lose a game one day and come back the next with confidence and enthusiasm.* **resilience** (noun).

resplendent (adjective) glowing, shining. *In late December, midtown New York is resplendent with holiday lights and decorations.* **resplendence** (noun).

responsive (adjective) reacting quickly and appropriately. *The new director of the Internal Revenue Service has promised to make the agency more responsive to public complaints.* **respond** (verb), **response** (noun).

restitution (noun) return of something to its original owner; repayment. *Some Native American leaders are demanding that the U.S. government make restitution for the lands taken from them.*

revere (verb) to admire deeply, to honor. *Millions of people around the world revered Mother Teresa for her saintly generosity.* **reverence** (noun), **reverent** (adjective).

rhapsodize (verb) to praise in a wildly emotional way. *That critic is such a huge fan of Toni Morrison that she will surely rhapsodize over the writer's next novel.* **rhapsodic** (adjective).

S

sagacious (adjective) discerning, wise. *Only a leader as sagacious as Nelson Mandela could have united South Africa so successfully and peacefully.* **sagacity** (noun).

salvage (verb) to save from wreck or ruin. *After the hurricane destroyed her home, she was able to salvage only a few of her belongings.* **salvage** (noun), **salvageable** (adjective).

sanctimonious (adjective) showing false or excessive piety. *The sanctimonious prayers of the TV preacher were interspersed with requests that the viewers send him money.* **sanctimony** (noun).

scapegoat (noun) someone who bears the blame for others' acts; someone hated for no apparent reason. *Although Buckner's error was only one reason the Red Sox lost, many fans made him the scapegoat, booing him mercilessly.*

scrupulous (adjective) acting with extreme care; painstaking. *Disney theme parks are famous for their scrupulous attention to small details.* **scruple** (noun).

scrutinize (verb) to study closely. *The lawyer scrutinized the contract, searching for any sentence that could pose a risk for her client.* **scrutiny** (noun).

secrete (verb) to emit; to hide. *Glands in the mouth secrete saliva, a liquid that helps in digestion. The jewel thieves secreted the necklace in a tin box buried underground.*

sedentary (adjective) requiring much sitting. *When Officer Samson was given a desk job, she had trouble getting used to sedentary work after years on the street.*

sequential (adjective) arranged in an order or series. *The courses for the chemistry major are sequential; you must take them in order, since each course builds on the previous ones.* **sequence** (noun).

serendipity (noun) the act of lucky, accidental discoveries. *Great inventions sometimes come about through deliberate research and hard work, sometimes through pure serendipity.* **serendipitous** (adjective).

servile (adjective) like a slave or servant; submissive. *The tycoon demanded that his underlings behave in a servile manner, agreeing quickly with everything he said.* **servility** (noun).

simulated (adjective) imitating something else; artificial. *High-quality simulated gems must be examined under a magnifying glass to be distinguished from real ones.* **simulate** (verb), **simulation** (noun).

solace (verb) to comfort or console. *There was little the rabbi could say to solace the husband after his wife's death.* **solace** (noun).

spontaneous (adjective) happening without plan. *When the news of Kennedy's assassination broke, people everywhere gathered in a spontaneous effort to share their shock and grief.* **spontaneity** (noun).

spurious (adjective) false, fake. *The so-called Piltdown Man, supposed to be the fossil of a primitive human, turned out to be spurious, although who created the hoax is still uncertain.*

squander (verb) to use up carelessly, to waste. *Those who had made donations to the charity were outraged to learn that its director had squandered millions on fancy dinners and first-class travel.*

stagnate (verb) to become stale through lack of movement or change. *Having had no contact with the outside world for generations, Japan's culture gradually stagnated.* **stagnant** (adjective), **stagnation** (noun).

staid (adjective) sedate, serious, and grave. *This college is definitely not a "party school"; the students all work hard, and the campus has a reputation for being staid.*

stimulus (noun) something that excites a response or provokes an action. *The arrival of merchants and missionaries from the West provided a stimulus for change in Japanese society.* **stimulate** (verb).

stoic (adjective) showing little feeling, even in response to pain or sorrow. *A soldier must respond to the death of his comrades in stoic fashion, since the fighting will not stop for his grief.* **stoicism** (noun).

strenuous (adjective) requiring energy and strength. *Hiking in the foothills of the Rockies is fairly easy, but climbing the higher peaks can be strenuous.*

submissive (adjective) accepting the will of others; humble, compliant. *At the end of Ibsen's play* A Doll's House, *Nora leaves her husband and abandons the role of submissive housewife.*

substantiate (verb) verified or supported by evidence. *The charge that Nixon had helped to cover up crimes was substantiated by his comments about it on a series of audio tapes.* **substantiated** (adjective), **substantiation** (noun).

sully (verb) to soil, stain, or defile. *Nixon's misdeeds as president did much to sully the reputation of the American government.*

superficial (adjective) on the surface only; without depth or substance. *Her wound was superficial and required only a light bandage. His superficial attractiveness hides the fact that his personality is lifeless and his mind is dull.* **superficiality** (noun).

superfluous (adjective) more than is needed, excessive. *Once you've won the debate, don't keep talking; superfluous arguments will only bore and annoy the audience.*

suppress (verb) to put down or restrain. *As soon as the unrest began, thousands of helmeted police were sent into the streets to suppress the riots.* **suppression** (noun).

surfeit (noun) an excess. *Most American families have a surfeit of food and drink on Thanksgiving Day.* **surfeit** (verb).

surreptitious (adjective) done in secret. *Because Iraq avoided weapons inspections, many believed it had a surreptitious weapons development program.*

surrogate (noun) a substitute. *When the congressman died in office, his wife was named to serve the rest of his term as a surrogate.* **surrogate** (adjective).

sustain (verb) to keep up, to continue; to support. *Because of fatigue, he was unable to sustain the effort needed to finish the marathon.*

T

tactile (adjective) relating to the sense of touch. *The thick brush strokes and gobs of color give the paintings of van Gogh a strongly tactile quality.* **tactility** (noun).

talisman (noun) an object supposed to have magical effects or qualities. *Superstitious people sometimes carry a rabbit's foot, a lucky coin, or some other talisman.*

tangential (adjective) touching lightly; only slightly connected or related. *Having enrolled in a class on African-American history, the students found the teacher's stories about his travels in South America of only tangential interest.* **tangent** (noun).

tedium (noun) boredom. *For most people, watching the Weather Channel for 24 hours would be sheer tedium.* **tedious** (adjective).

temerity (noun) boldness, rashness, excessive daring. *Only someone who didn't understand the danger would have the temerity to try to climb Everest without a guide.* **temerarious** (adjective).

temperance (noun) moderation or restraint in feelings and behavior. *Most professional athletes practice temperance in their personal habits; too much eating or drinking, they know, can harm their performance.* **temperate** (adjective).

tenacious (adjective) clinging, sticky, or persistent. *Tenacious in pursuit of her goal, she applied for the grant unsuccessfully four times before it was finally approved.* **tenacity** (noun).

tentative (adjective) subject to change; uncertain. *A firm schedule has not been established, but the Super Bowl in 2015 has been given the tentative date of February 1.*

terminate (verb) to end, to close. *The Olympic Games terminate with a grand ceremony attended by athletes from every participating country.* **terminal** (noun), **termination** (noun).

terrestrial (adjective) of the Earth. *The movie* Close Encounters of the Third Kind *tells the story of the first contact between beings from outer space and terrestrial humans.*

therapeutic (adjective) curing or helping to cure. *Hot-water spas were popular in the nineteenth century among the sickly, who believed that soaking in the water had therapeutic effects.* **therapy** (noun).

timorous (adjective) fearful, timid. *The cowardly lion approached the throne of the wizard with a timorous look on his face.*

toady (noun) someone who flatters a superior in hopes of gaining favor; a sycophant. *"I can't stand a toady!" declared the movie mogul. "Give me someone who'll tell me the truth—even if it costs him his job!"* **toady** (verb).

tolerant (adjective) accepting, enduring. *San Franciscans have a tolerant attitude about lifestyles: "Live and let live" seems to be their motto.* **tolerate** (verb), **toleration** (noun).

toxin (noun) poison. *DDT is a powerful toxin once used to kill insects but now banned in the United States because of the risk it poses to human life.* **toxic** (adjective).

tranquillity (noun) freedom from disturbance or turmoil; calm. *She moved from New York City to rural Vermont seeking the tranquillity of country life.* **tranquil** (adjective).

transgress (verb) to go past limits; to violate. *No one could fathom why the honor student transgressed by shoplifting hundreds of dollars of merchandise from his favorite clothing store.* **transgression** (noun).

transient (adjective) passing quickly. *Long-term visitors to this hotel pay a different rate than transient guests who stay for just a day or two.* **transience** (noun).

transitory (adjective) quickly passing. *Public moods tend to be transitory; people may be anxious and angry one month but relatively content and optimistic the next.* **transition** (noun).

translucent (adjective) letting some light pass through. *Panels of translucent glass let daylight into the room while maintaining privacy.*

transmute (verb) to change in form or substance. *In the Middle Ages, the alchemists tried to discover ways to transmute metals such as iron into gold.* **transmutation** (noun).

treacherous (adjective) untrustworthy or disloyal; dangerous or unreliable. *Nazi Germany proved to be a treacherous ally, first signing a peace pact with the Soviet Union, then invading. Be careful crossing the rope bridge; parts are badly frayed and treacherous.* **treachery** (noun).

tremulous (adjective) trembling or shaking; timid or fearful. *Never having spoken in public before, he began his speech in a tremulous, hesitant voice.*

trite (adjective) boring because of over-familiarity; hackneyed. *Her letters were filled with trite expressions, like "All's well that ends well" and "So far so good."*

truculent (adjective) aggressive, hostile, belligerent. *Hitler's truculent behavior in demanding more territory for Germany made it clear that war was inevitable.* **truculence** (noun).

truncate (verb) to cut off. *The poor copying job truncated the playwright's manuscript: the last page ended in the middle of a scene, halfway through the first act.*

turbulent (adjective) agitated or disturbed. *The night before the championship match, Martina was unable to sleep, her mind turbulent with fears and hopes.* **turbulence** (noun).

U

unheralded (adjective) little known, unexpected. *In a year of big-budget, much-hyped, mega-movies, this unheralded foreign film has surprised everyone with its popularity.*

unpalatable (adjective) distasteful, unpleasant. *Although I agree with the candidate on many issues, I can't vote for her because I find her position on capital punishment unpalatable.*

unparalleled (adjective) with no equal; unique. *Tiger Woods's victory in the Masters golf tournament by a full twelve strokes was an unparalleled accomplishment.*

unstinting (adjective) giving freely and generously. *Eleanor Roosevelt was much admired for her unstinting efforts on behalf of the poor.*

untenable (adjective) impossible to defend. *The theory that this painting is a genuine van Gogh became untenable when the artist who actually painted it came forth.*

untimely (adjective) out of the natural or proper time. *The untimely death of a youthful Princess Diana seemed far more tragic than Mother Teresa's death of old age.*

unyielding (adjective) firm, resolute, obdurate. *Despite criticism, Cuomo was unyielding in his opposition to capital punishment; he vetoed several death penalty bills as governor.*

usurper (noun) someone who takes a place or possession without the right to do so. *Kennedy's most devoted followers tended to regard later presidents as usurpers, holding the office they felt he or his brothers should have held.* **usurp** (verb), **usurpation** (noun).

utilitarian (adjective) purely of practical benefit. *The design of the Model T car was simple and utilitarian, lacking the luxuries found in later models.*

utopia (noun) an imaginary, perfect society. *Those who founded the Oneida community dreamed that it could be a kind of utopia—a prosperous state with complete freedom and harmony.* **utopian** (adjective).

V

validate (verb) to officially approve or confirm. *The election of the president is validated when the members of the Electoral College meet to confirm the choice of the voters.* **valid** (adjective), **validity** (noun).

variegated (adjective) spotted with different colors. *The brilliant, variegated appearance of butterflies makes them popular among collectors.* **variegation** (noun).

venerate (verb) to admire or honor. *In Communist China, Chairman Mao Zedong was venerated as an almost god-like figure.* **venerable** (adjective), **veneration** (noun).

verdant (adjective) green with plant life. *Southern England is famous for its verdant countryside filled with gardens and small farms.* **verdancy** (noun).

vestige (noun) a trace or remainder. *Today's tiny Sherwood Forest is the last vestige of a woodland that once covered most of England.* **vestigial** (adjective).

vex (verb) to irritate, annoy, or trouble. *It vexes me that she never helps with any chores around the house.* **vexation** (noun).

vicarious (adjective) experienced through someone else's actions by way of the imagination. *Great literature broadens our minds by giving us vicarious participation in the lives of other people.*

vindicate (verb) to confirm, justify, or defend. *Lincoln's Gettysburg Address was intended to vindicate the objectives of the Union in the Civil War.*

virtuoso (noun) someone very skilled, especially in an art. *Vladimir Horowitz was one of the great piano virtuosos of the twentieth century.* **virtuosity** (noun).

vivacious (adjective) lively, sprightly. *The role of Maria in* The Sound of Music *is usually played by a charming, vivacious young actress.* **vivacity** (noun).

volatile (adjective) quickly changing; fleeting, transitory; prone to violence. *Public opinion is notoriously volatile; a politician who is very popular one month may be voted out of office the next.* **volatility** (noun).

W

whimsical (adjective) based on a capricious, carefree, or sudden impulse or idea; fanciful, playful. *Dave Barry's* Book of Bad Songs *is filled with the kind of goofy jokes that are typical of his whimsical sense of humor.* **whim** (noun).

Z

zealous (adjective) filled with eagerness, fervor, or passion. *A crowd of the candidate's most zealous supporters greeted her at the airport with banners, signs, and a marching band.* **zeal** (noun), **zealot** (noun), **zealotry** (noun).

College Portraits
No rankings, no spin... just the facts!

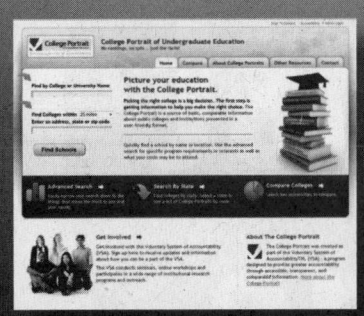

Free access and use—no fees, no log in required!

Visit a website with reliable and user-friendly information on more than 300 public colleges and universities:

>> Learn about the student experience on campus

>> Compare admissions, majors, campus life, class size, and more

>> Calculate your cost to attend a participating university

>> Search by state, distance from home, size, and more

>> Find links and contact information for each campus

 **College Portrait** of Undergraduate Education — Voluntary System of Accountability

Sponsored by the Association of Public and Land-grant Universities and the American Association of State Colleges and Universities

www.collegeportraits.org

Save 10% on the cost of college

Visit
simpletuition.com/smarterstudent
to find out how!

simpletuition
plan · pay less · pay back

NOT GETTING NOTICED?

10% OFF
your order with coupon
code **GMAT10P**
at checkout

Get a job-winning resume in as little as 48 hours from the industry experts at ResumeEdge.

RESULTS-GENERATING RESUME SERVICES INCLUDE:

✔ Resume Writing | ✔ Social Media Profile Development | ✔ Resume Builder Tool | ✔ Job Interview Coaching

The ResumeEdge Difference

- Certified Professional Resume Writers
- One-on-one contact with your writer
- 98% customer satisfaction rating
- Experts in more than 40 industries
- As little as 48-hour turnaround for most orders
- An established business since 2001
- Resume writing partner to leading sites such as **Dice.com**

*"I received calls from every potential employer that I sent my resume to. **I was offered a fantastic position** and feel that it was due, in no small part, to the great resume that [my editor] put together for me!"* —N.G.

LEARN MORE—visit ResumeEdge.com or call 888.438.2633

ResumeEdge
A **nelnet** SERVICE

NOTES

NOTES

WITHDRAWN
from St. Joseph County Public Library

WITHDRAWN

from St. Joseph County Public Library
Excess X   Damaged
Date 8-13-14   Initials SMP